Florida

POSTCARDS FROM

One of the playful residents of SeaWorld in Orlando. See chapter 12.
© James Lemass/SeaWorld Florida.

"Houston, we have a problem . . . " a U.S. Apollo astronaut suit on display at the Kennedy Space Center. See chapter 13. © M. Timothy O'Keefe Photography.

Every year, eager baseball fans from across the country flock to Florida for spring training. See chapter 2. © M. Timothy O'Keefe Photography.

Playing out of a sand trap in Tarpon Springs. See chapter 11. © M. Timothy O'Keefe Photography.

Braving the rapids at Islands of Adventure theme park. See chapter 12. © Universal Orlando.

Visit the house where "Papa" Hemingway wrote some of his most famous works and check out other Hemingway haunts while in Key West. See chapter 6. © *Michael Ventura Photography.*

Sloppy Joe's Bar, the quintessential Key West watering hole. See chapter 6 for more on Key West nightlife. © *Kelly/Mooney Photography.*

As many as 40,000 pairs of birds nest in Tampa Bay every year, including the brown pelican. See chapter 11. © Richard Cummins.

Every winter, millions of sunbathers head for the warm, pristine beaches of South Florida. See chapter 1 for a list of the best beaches in the region. © Trevor Wood/Tony Stone Worldwide.

Warm weather and an abundance of marine life make Florida a year-round destination for anglers from throughout the world. © *Mark Barrett/Silver Image Photography.*

The oldest hotel in Coral Gables, the stately Biltmore is a National Historic Landmark—one of only two operating hotels in Florida so designated. See chapter 4. © *Tom Salyer/Silver Image Photography.*

Most everything in Miami's South Beach has an Art Deco feel, such as this trendy cafe. See chapter 5. © *Michael Ventura Photography.*

Miami Beach—home to a multitude of hotels, clubs, and crowded beaches—offers a great nightlife, but if you're looking for peace and quiet, look elsewhere. See chapter 4 for information on accommodations in Miami. © Alan Schein/The Stock Market.

When should I travel to get the best airfare?
Where do I go for answers to my travel questions?
What's the best and easiest way to plan and book my trip?

frommers.travelocity.com

Frommer's, the travel guide leader, has teamed up with **Travelocity.com**, the leader in online travel, to bring you an in-depth, easy-to-use resource designed to help you plan and book your trip online.

At **frommers.travelocity.com**, you'll find free online updates about your destination from the experts at Frommer's plus the outstanding travel planning and purchasing features of Travelocity.com. Travelocity.com provides reservations capabilities for 95 percent of all airline seats sold, more than 47,000 hotels, and over 50 car rental companies. In addition, Travelocity.com offers more than 2,000 exciting vacation and cruise packages. Travelocity.com puts you in complete control of your travel planning with these and other great features:

Expert travel guidance from Frommer's - over 150 writers reporting from around the world!

Best Fare Finder - an interactive calendar tells you when to travel to get the best airfare

Fare Watcher - we'll track airfare changes to your favorite destinations

Dream Maps - a mapping feature that suggests travel opportunities based on your budget

Shop Safe Guarantee - 24 hours a day / 7 days a week live customer service, and more!

Whether traveling on a tight budget, looking for a quick weekend getaway, or planning the trip of a lifetime, Frommer's guides and Travelocity.com will make your travel dreams a reality. You've bought the book, now book the trip!

A New Star-Rating System & Other Exciting News from Frommer's!

In our continuing effort to publish the savviest, most up-to-date, and most appealing travel guides available, we've added some great new features.

Frommer's guides now include a new **star-rating system**. Every hotel, restaurant, and attraction is rated from 0 to 3 stars to help you set priorities and organize your time.

We've also added **seven brand-new features** that point you to the great deals, in-the-know advice, and unique experiences that separate travelers from tourists. Throughout the guide look for:

Finds	Special finds—those places only insiders know about
Fun Fact	Fun facts—details that make travelers more informed and their trips more fun
Kids	Best bets for kids—advice for the whole family
Moments	Special moments—those experiences that memories are made of
Overrated	Places or experiences not worth your time or money
Tips	Insider tips—some great ways to save time and money
Value	Great values—where to get the best deals

We've also added a **"What's New"** section in every guide—a timely crash course in what's hot and what's not in every destination we cover.

Other Great Guides for Your Trip:

Frommer's Florida from $70 a Day

Frommer's South Florida

Frommer's Walt Disney World & Orlando

Frommer's Portable Tampa Bay

Frommer's®

Florida

2002

by Bill Goodwin, Lesley Abravanel & Jim and Cynthia Tunstall

Here's what the critics say about Frommer's:

"Amazingly easy to use. Very portable, very complete."

—*Booklist*

"The only mainstream guide to list specific prices. The Walter Cronkite of guidebooks—with all that implies."

—*Travel & Leisure*

"Complete, concise, and filled with useful information."

—*New York Daily News*

"Hotel information is close to encyclopedic."

—*Des Moines Sunday Register*

Hungry Minds™

Best-Selling Books • Digital Downloads • e-Books • Answer Networks •
e-Newsletters • Branded Web Sites • e-Learning
New York, NY • Cleveland, OH • Indianapolis, IN

About the Authors

Bill Goodwin began his career as an award-winning newspaper reporter before serving as speechwriter and legal counsel for two U.S. senators. These days he spends as much time as possible exploring the ins and outs of other places with naturally hot air; he's also the author of *Frommer's South Pacific*.

Lesley Abravanel is a freelance journalist and a graduate of the University of Miami School of Communication. When she isn't combing South Florida for the latest hotels, restaurants, and attractions, she is on the lookout for vacationing celebrities, about whom she writes in her weekly columns, "Nocturnal Admissions," for miami.citysearch.com and "Velvet Underground," for the *Miami Herald*'s weekly entertainment newspaper, *The Street*. She is the Miami correspondent for *Black Book Magazine* and is also the author of *Frommer's South Florida*.

Jim and Cynthia Tunstall have been waiting impatiently in Walt Disney World lines since the Magic Kingdom's opening bell in 1971. In the 3 decades since, they've sampled just about every element of a great Orlando vacation. Those experiences are the credentials that allow these Florida insiders to separate the good from the bad and the ugly. Based close to the Disney epicenter, they have written three other Orlando-related books including *Frommer's Walt Disney World & Orlando*.

Published by:

Hungry Minds, Inc.

909 Third Ave.
New York, NY 10022

ISBN 0-7645-6460-9
ISSN 1044-2391

Editor: Lorraine Festa
Production Editor: Donna Wright
Cartographer: John Decamillis
Photo Editor: Richard Fox
Production by Hungry Minds Indianapolis Production Services

Front cover photo: Kayaking at Little Palm Island, Lower Keys
Back cover photo: The Incredible Hulk coaster at Universal Orlando

Special Sales

For general information on Hungry Minds' products and services, please contact our Customer Care department; within the U.S. at 800/762-2974, outside the U.S. at 317/572-3993 or fax 317/572-4002. For sales inquiries and reseller information, including discounts, bulk sales, customized editions, and premium sales, please contact our Customer Care department at 800/434-3422.

Manufactured in the United States of America

5   4   3

Contents

4   Getting to Know Miami   77

by Lesley Abravanel

5   What to See & Do in Miami   147

by Lesley Abravanel

6   The Keys   193

by Lesley Abravanel

7   South Florida Side Trips: The Everglades & Biscayne National Park   246

by Lesley Abravanel

List of Maps

An Invitation to the Reader

In researching this book, we discovered many wonderful places—hotels, restaurants, shops, and more. We're sure you'll find others. Please tell us about them, so we can share the information with your fellow travelers in upcoming editions. If you were disappointed with a recommendation, we'd love to know that, too. Please write to:

Frommer's Florida 2002
Hungry Minds, Inc. • 909 Third Avenue • New York, NY 10022

An Additional Note

Please be advised that travel information is subject to change at any time—and this is especially true of prices. We therefore suggest that you write or call ahead for confirmation when making your travel plans. The authors, editors, and publisher cannot be held responsible for the experiences of readers while traveling. Your safety is important to us, however, so we encourage you to stay alert and be aware of your surroundings. Keep a close eye on cameras, purses, and wallets, all favorite targets of thieves and pickpockets.

What the Symbols Mean

New! Frommer's Star Ratings & Icons

Every hotel, restaurant, and attraction listing in this guide has been ranked for quality, value, service, amenities, and special features using a star-rating scale. In country, state, and regional guides, we also rate towns and regions to help you narrow down your choices and budget your time accordingly. Hotels and restaurants in the Very Expensive and Expensive categories are rated on a scale of one (highly recommended) to three stars (exceptional). Those in the Moderate and Inexpensive categories rate from zero (recommended) to two stars (very highly recommended). Attractions, towns, and regions are rated according to the following scale: zero stars (recommended), one star (highly recommended), two stars (very highly recommended), and three stars (must-see).

In addition to the rating system, we also use seven icons to highlight insider information, useful tips, special bargains, hidden gems, memorable experiences, kid-friendly venues, places to avoid, and other useful information:

| Finds | Fun Fact | Kids | Moments | Overrated | Tips | Value |

The following abbreviations are used for credit cards:

| AE | American Express | DISC | Discover | V | Visa |
| DC | Diners Club | MC | MasterCard | | |

FROMMERS.COM

Now that you have the guidebook to a great trip, visit our website at **www.frommers.com** for travel information on nearly 2,000 destinations. With features updated regularly, we give you instant access to the most current trip-planning information available. At Frommers.com, you'll also find the best prices on airfares, accommodations, and car rentals—and you can even book travel online through our travel booking partners. At Frommers.com you'll also find the following:

- Daily Newsletter highlighting the best travel deals
- Hot Spot of the Month/Vacation Sweepstakes & Travel Photo Contest
- More than 200 Travel Message Boards
- Outspoken Newsletters and Feature Articles on travel bargains, vacation ideas, tips and resources, and more!

What's New in Florida

The economic boom of the 1990s brought a host of new hotels, restaurants, and other facilities to Florida. Here's a brief rundown of what's new in the Sunshine State.

PLANNING YOUR TRIP TO FLORIDA Several no-frills airlines have beefed up service to Florida, including **AirTran, America West, JetBlue Airways, MetroJet,** and **Southwest Airlines. Tower Air,** another cut-rate carrier, has gone out of business. **Amtrak** still plans to add rail service to St. Augustine, Titusville (Cape Canaveral), and Fort Pierce but hadn't done so at press time. See chapter 2.

The Active Vacation Planner Plans are underway to hike the entrance and camping fees and possibly make some other changes at Florida's outstanding state parks. Check with the state Division of Recreation and Parks or with the individual parks to find out what's up. See chapter 2.

MIAMI For complete information on Miami, see chapter 4, "Settling into Miami," and chapter 5, "What to See & Do in Miami."

Accommodations Two **Ritz-Carlton** hotels (© **800/241-3333**) have opened—on South Beach (1 Lincoln Rd.), Key Biscayne (415 Grand Bay Drive)—and a third is scheduled to open in Coconut Grove (2700 Tigertail Ave.) in October 2001. To compete with the *hauter*-than-thou Delano Hotel on South Beach, the **Shore Club,** 1901 Collins Ave. (© **305/695-3100**), was scheduled to open at press time. To fill the void of a luxury hotel near downtown Miami, The **Mandarin Oriental** (© **305/913-8288**) has opened at 500 Brickell Key Drive. For the shabby chic set, the **Townhouse,** 159 20th St. (© **877/534-3800**), opened on South Beach and is making a splash with its rooftop waterbeds and hallway exercise equipment.

Dining Soon, Miami will have three new sushi options. **Nobu,** a hot New York sushi import, will be opening in 2001 at Shore Club, 1901 Collins Ave., South Beach (© **305/695-3100**), as will **Sushi Samba** (at the corner of Pennsylvania Avenue and Lincoln Road; no phone at press time); and **Bond St. Lounge,** located at Townhouse Hotel, 150 20th St., in South Beach © **305/534-3800** opened in December 2000. South Beach's **Rumi** (© **305/672-4353**), schedule to open summer 2001, will be a high-style, high-concept supper club featuring haute, Floribbean cuisine. **Azul** (© **305/913-8258**), at the new Mandarin Oriental, 500 Brickell Key Dr., is a superb global fusion restaurant that's worth busting the bank account for.

Sightseeing South Beach's **Bass Museum of Art,** 2121 Park Ave. (© **305/673-7530**), has expanded and received a dramatically new look designed by world-renowned Japanese architect Arata Isozaki. Additions include triple the amount of exhibition space, an outdoor sculpture terrace, and museum cafe.

Shopping **Merrick Park,** an upscale shopping center located between

Ponce de León Boulevard and Le Jeune Road, has opened in Coral Gables and features the city's first Dean & DeLuca gourmet grocery. It's also home to Armani, Yves St. Laurent, and a host of other pricey stores. In South Beach, the area between Fifth and Eighth streets on Collins Avenue features a slew of high-end stores; new additions include Intermix and Club Monaco. Lincoln Road continues to become an outdoor mall, recently adding Bebe to the mix with Victoria's Secret on the horizon.

After Dark At press time, the hottest nightspots are located on the still sizzling South Beach. However, over the causeway, a burgeoning nocturnal buzz is emanating from the once desolate area of **downtown Miami,** off of Biscayne Boulevard and into the newly hip **Design District** (NE 36th St. to 41st St. and NE Second Ave. to N. Miami Ave.) in which after-hours clubs and a few funky nightspots have cropped up. South Beach's **Rumi,** 330 Lincoln Rd., (✆ **305/672-4353**), scheduled to open summer 2001, will be a high-style, high-concept supper club featuring haute, Floribbean cuisine.

THE GOLD COAST For complete information on this region, see chapter 8.

Accommodations The $600 million **Diplomat Resort Country Club and Spa,** 3555 South Ocean Drive (✆ **800/327-1212**), has been thoroughly revamped into a 1,060-unit full-service beach resort and convention center with a 155-acre golf course. The **Marriott Harbour Beach Resort,** 3030 Holiday Drive (✆ **800/222-6543**), has undergone over $20 million in renovations, adding a 24,000-square-foot European spa. Las Olas Boulevard's quaint **Riverside Hotel,** 620 E. Las Olas Blvd. (✆ **800/325-3280**), intends to expand its capacity to 221 rooms by February 2002. Palm Beach's stately **Breakers Hotel,** 1 S. County Rd. (✆ **800/833-3141**), received a $100 million renovation, which added the Oceanfront Spa and Beach Club and expanded the Breakers Ocean Course to a 6,200-yard, par-70 championship golf course.

Dining The Boca Raton Resort and Club, 501 E. Camino Real (✆ **800/327-0101**), has added two new restaurants—**Lucca,** a Tuscan-style waterfront restaurant designed by David Rockwell and run by Drew Nieporent's Myriad Restaurant Group; and **27 Ocean Blue,** an eclectic restaurant fusing Pacific Rim, Caribbean, southern, Hawaiian, and New World cuisines.

Shopping West Palm Beach's **City Place,** 222 Lakeview Ave. (✆ **561/835-0862**), is not unlike Coconut Grove's CocoWalk or Fort Lauderdale's Beach Place shopping, dining, and entertainment complexes. The $550 million outdoor, Mediterranean-style complex features 78 stores, including Macy's and FAO Schwarz; a multiplex movie theater; and several restaurants such as Legal Seafoods and the Cheesecake Factory.

SOUTHWEST FLORIDA For complete information on this region, see chapter 10.

Fort Myers Beach The **Edison Beach House,** 830 Eastero Blvd. (✆ **800/399-2511**), sporting kitchen-equipped suites, has brought a touch of class to Fort Myers Beach's busy Times Square district. Several new luxury condominium complexes have opened here, too.

Sanibel and Captiva Islands On Sanibel, the **Buttonwood Cottages,** 1234 Buttonwood (✆ **887/395-COTTAGE**), have been spiffed up and offer an affordable alternative to the island's high-priced resorts. On

Captiva, **'Tween Waters Inn,** 15951 Capitva Rd. (© **800/223-5865**), is upgrading its historic cottages.

Naples   The boom has brought several new hotels to Naples, including the intimate **Hotel Escalante,** 290 5th Ave S. (© **877/GULF-INN**), on the edge of the trendy 5th Avenue South shopping-and-dining district; and the **Hilton Naples & Towers** (© **800/HILTONS**), north of the historic district. Also, the **Ritz-Carlton Naples Golf Resort** (© **800/241-3333**) was expected to open in late 2001. Guests at this high-luxe hotel will have golf privileges at the Greg Norman–designed Tiburon Golf Club. The venerable **Naples Beach Hotel & Golf Club,** 851 Gulf Shore Blvd. (© **800/237-7600**), has opened its new full-service spa, adding another dimension to this relaxed beachside resort. **The Ritz-Carlton Naples,** 280 Vanderbilt Beach Rd. (© **800/241-3333**), opened its new $50-million spa complex in April 2001. On the dining front, the new **Yabba Island Grill,** 711 5th Ave. S. (© **941/262-5787**), provides an affordable alternative in the town's hottest area.

THE TAMPA BAY AREA   For complete information on this region, see chapter 11.

Tampa   **Busch Gardens Tampa Bay,** 3000 E. Busch Blvd. (© **813/987-5283**), has added "Rhino Rally," a safari-like ride in which you travel via Land Rovers through the park's game preserve. The 717-room **Tampa Waterside Marriott,** 400 N. Florida Ave. (© **800/228-9290**), now sits across the street from the Tampa-Hillsborough Convention Center and a few blocks from the **Channelside at Garrison Seaport,** Channelside Drive, a new promenade with shops, restaurants, and a multiscreen cinema. **Centro Ybor,** located between 7th and

8th Avenues and 16th and 17th streets, has brought movies and more dining and shopping to the heart of Ybor City, Tampa's nightlife district.

St. Petersburg   The **Florida International Museum,** 100 2nd St. N. (© **877/535-7469**), has added a permanent exhibit about the Cuban Missile Crisis. After being closed for several years, **Sunken Gardens,** 1825 4th St. N. (© **813/896-3186**), has been reopened as the city's botanical gardens. **BayWalk,** a block-size mall bordered by 1st and 2nd streets and 2nd and 3rd avenues, has added shopping-and-entertainment options to downtown. Dubbed the **Friendship Trail Bridge,** the 2.6-mile-long old span of the Gandy Bridge across Tampa Bay is now the nation's longest over-water hiking and biking trail.

Sarasota & Bradenton   Now operated by Florida State University, the **Ringling Museums,** 5401 Bay Shore Road (© **941/359-5700**), have undergone extensive renovation. The 270-room **Ritz-Carlton Sarasota** (© **800/241-3333**) is scheduled to open in mid-2001 on the downtown waterfront just north of the Ringling Causeway. At the heart of trendy Southside Village, the new **Fred's,** 1917 S. Osprey Ave. (© **941/364-5811**), is Sarasota's most popular meet-and-eat restaurant.

WALT DISNEY WORLD & ORLANDO   For complete information on Walt Disney World & Orlando, see chapter 12.

Accommodations   Disney lost a resort (but not rooms) when it consolidated Dixie Landings Resort into the adjoining Port Orleans Resort. Disney's **Animal Kingdom Lodge** added 1,293 rooms in April 2001. WDW started construction on its fourth All-Star hotel, the **Pop Century Resort,** which will add 5,760 rooms in 2002. Universal Orlando in January 2001 opened its second Loews resort, a 654-room **Hard Rock Hotel,** and hopes to add a third, the 1,000-room **Royal Pacific,** in the second half of 2002. At press time, Westin's **Grand Bohemian,** a 250-suite hotel located downtown across from city hall, opened in April 2001.

Walt Disney World Theme Parks & Attractions Disney's **Main Street Electrical Parade** said good-bye in spring 2001 and was replaced by another nighttime extravaganza, **SpectroMagic.** The **Magic Carpets of Aladdin** in summer 2001 became the first new big-league ride added to Adventureland in the Magic Kingdom since the park opened in 1971. Disney–MGM Studios added **Who Wants to Be a Millionaire—Play It!** based on the Disney-ABC TV hit game show. Over at Animal Kingdom, Countdown to Extinction was renamed **Dinosaur** in honor of the 2000 movie and the ride lowered its minimum height requirement.

Disney also bumped its adult single-day ticket prices by $2 to $48, the third such increase in 2 years (adult admission was $28 in 1989). Prices for a child's ticket (age 3 to 9) increased $1 to $38. (SeaWorld started the price-hike war, but Disney raised the bet with increases for most of its parks and ticket categories.)

Universal & SeaWorld Men in Black: Alien Attack is the most high-profile, kick-your-keister ride added to either of the Universal parks since last year. We won't spoil the fun, but you get to cruise the streets and blast mega-ugly aliens, much like Tommy Lee Jones and Will Smith did in the same-named movie.

At Islands of Adventure, **Flying Unicorn** is a small roller coaster that travels through a mythical forest on the Lost Continent and lets kids discover wizardry with the help of elves

that show how to board a Unicorn that heads to the clouds.

SeaWorld opened its second park, **Discovery Cove,** where for $200 a head you can swim with a dolphin.

Universal increased its 1-day, one-park admission in line with Disney's—going up to $48 for adults and $38 for kids ages 3 to 9. SeaWorld and its sister park, Busch Gardens in Tampa, raised single-day prices $2 to $47.95 for adults and $38.95 for kids 3 to 9, the third such increase in 2 years.

Other Attractions & Shopping In November 2000, developers of **The Holy Land Experience,** 4655 Vineland Rd. (© **866/872-4659**) set out to prove that the Bible can compete with Disney. The $20 million park opened near Universal, letting visitors explore Noah's Ark, see rare manuscripts, and hear storytellers.

In fall 2000, **Orlando Premium Outlets** opened on the south end of International Drive with 110 tenants, including Coach, Cole-Haan, and Polo/Ralph Lauren.

NORTHEAST FLORIDA For complete information on this region, see chapter 13.

Cocoa Beach, Cape Canaveral & the Kennedy Space Center As part of a $130 million expansion, the **Kennedy Space Center,** NASA Parkway (Fla. 405) (© **321/452-2121**), has upgraded its regular bus tours and has added "NASA Up Close" tours that are narrated by space program experts and go to places the regular tours don't. You can now check space shuttle launch schedules and buy launch tickets online at **www.ksctickets.com**.

Daytona Beach Daytona Beach's telephone area code has changed to **386,** which spells FUN. With six oceanside holes, the new **Ocean Hammock Golf Club** (© **904/477-4653**), on Fla. A1A in Palm Coast, about halfway between St. Augustine and Daytona Beach, has been described as the "Pebble Beach of Florida." **The Plaza Resort & Spa,** 600 N. Atlantic Ave (© 800/767-4471), has been completely renovated and now has rooms with Jacuzzi tubs and this area's only full-service spa.

St. Augustine Modeled on Colonial Williamsburg, Virginia, the new **Old St. Augustine Village Museum,** 250 St. George St. (© **904/823-9722**), is one of the city's top attractions and the only one that explains the complete history of America's oldest town.

Jacksonville The reconstructed **Ritz Theatre & LaVilla Museum,** 829 N. Davis St. (© **904/632-5555**), celebrates the LaVilla neighborhood, once known as The Harlem of the South. The huge, 966-unit **Adam's Mark Jacksonville,** 100 N. Atlantic Ave. (© **800/444-ADAM**), opened in February 2001, downtown on the north side of the St. Johns River. The chic but affordable **B.B.'s,** 1019 Hendricks Ave. (© **904/306-0100**), is leading a dining explosion on the city's Southbank Riverwalk.

Amelia Island The new 18-hole **Royal Amelia Golf Links,** 4477 Amelia Rd. (© **904/491-8500**), offers an alternative to the pricey courses at Amelia Island Plantation and the Ritz-Carlton Amelia Island. Blending in with Fernandina Beach's historic buildings, the **Hampton Inn & Suites,** 19 S. 2nd St. (© 800/ HAMPTON), brings Victorian ambience and modern Jacuzzi rooms to the old town.

NORTHWEST FLORIDA: THE PANHANDLE For complete information on this region, see chapter 14.

Pensacola The Coast Guard Auxiliary is now offering guided tours of the **Pensacola Lighthouse,** Radford Boulevard (© 850/492-0310), opposite the National Museum of Naval Aviation.

Destin & Fort Walton Beach The Resort at Sandestin, 9300 Hwy. 98 W. (© **800/277-0800**), has opened the **Raven,** its fourth golf course, bringing its total to 81 championship holes.

1

The Best of Florida

Every year millions of visitors escape bleak northern winters to bask in Florida's warmth, lured to the Sunshine State by the promise of clear skies and 800 miles of spectacular sandy beaches. A host of kid-pleasers, from Busch Gardens to Walt Disney World, makes this the country's most popular year-round family vacation destination.

Here you can choose from a wide array of accommodations, from deluxe resorts to mom-and-pop motels. You can visit remote little towns like Apalachicola or a megalopolis like Miami. Devour fresh seafood, from amberjack to oysters—and then work off those calories in such outdoor pursuits as bicycling, golfing, or kayaking. Despite overdevelopment in many parts of the state, Floridians have maintained thousands of acres of wilderness areas, from the little respite of Clam Pass County Park in downtown Naples to the magnificent Everglades National Park, which stretches across the state's southern tip.

Choosing the "best" of all this is a daunting task, and the selections in this chapter are only a rundown on some of the highlights. You'll find numerous other outstanding resorts, hotels, destinations, activities, and attractions—all described in the pages of this book. With a bit of serendipity you'll come up with some bests of your own.

1 The Best Beaches

- **Virginia Key** (Key Biscayne): The producers of "Survivor" could feasibly shoot their show on this ultra-secluded, picturesque, and deserted key, where people go purposely not to be found. See chapter 5.
- **Matheson Hammock Park Beach** (South Miami): This beach features an enclosed, man-made lagoon that is flushed naturally by the tidal action of the adjacent Biscayne Bay. The serene beach is surrounded by the bay's warm, calm waters; its backdrop is a tropical hardwood forest. See chapter 5.
- **Bahia Honda State Park** (Bahia Honda Key): One of the nicest and most peaceful beaches in Florida, located amidst 635-acres of nature trails and even a portion

- of Henry Flagler's railroad. See chapter 6.
- **John U. Lloyd Beach State Park** (Dania Beach): Unfettered by high-rise condominiums, T-shirt shops, and hotels, this wonderful beach boasts an untouched shoreline surrounded by a canopy of Australian pine to ensure complete seclusion. See chapter 8.
- **Lover's Key State Park** (Fort Myers Beach): You'll have to walk or take a tram through a bird-filled forest of mangroves to this gorgeous, unspoiled beach just a few miles south of busy Fort Myers Beach. Although Sanibel Island gets all the accolades, the shelling here is just as good if not better. See chapter 10.

- **Cayo Costa State Park** (off Captiva Island): These days, deserted tropical islands with great beaches are scarce in Florida, but this 2,132-acre barrier strip of sand, pine forests, mangrove swamps, oak hammocks, and grasslands provides a genuine get-away-from-it-all experience. Access is only by boat from nearby Gasparilla, Pine, and Captiva Islands. See chapter 10.

- **Naples Beach** (Naples): Many Florida cities and towns have beaches, but few are as lovely as the gorgeous strip that runs in front of Naples's famous Millionaires' Row. You don't have to be rich to wander its length, peer at the mansions, and stroll on historic Naples Pier to catch a sunset over the gulf. See chapter 10.

- **Caladesi Island State Park** (Clearwater Beach): Even though 3½-mile-long Caladesi Island is in the heavily developed Tampa Bay area, it has a lovely, relatively secluded beach with soft sand edged in sea grass and palmettos. Dolphins cavort in offshore waters. In the park itself, there's a nature trail, and you might see one of the rattlesnakes, black racers, raccoons, armadillos, or rabbits that live here. The park is accessible only by ferry from Honeymoon Island State Recreation Area off Dunedin. See chapter 11.

- **Canaveral National Seashore** (Cape Canaveral): Midway between the crowded attractions at Daytona Beach and the Kennedy Space Center is a protected stretch of coastline 24 miles long, backed by cabbage palms, sea grapes, and palmettos. Its neighbor is the 140,000-acre Merritt Island National Wildlife Refuge, home to hundreds of Florida birds, reptiles, alligators, and mammals. Wooden boardwalks lead from a free parking lot to the huge expanse of soft brown sand and a few well-spaced picnic tables. See chapter 13.

- **Gulf Islands National Seashore** (Pensacola): You could argue that all of Northwest Florida's gulf shore is one of America's great beaches—an almost-uninterrupted stretch of pure white sand that runs the entire length of the Panhandle, from Perdido Key to St. George Island. The Gulf Islands National Seashore preserves much of this natural wonder in its undeveloped state. Countless terns, snowy plover, black skimmers, and other birds nest along the dunes topped with sea oats. East of the national seashore and equally beautiful are Grayton Beach State Park near Destin and St. George Island State Park off Apalachicola. See chapter 14.

- **St. Andrews State Park** (Panama City Beach): With more than 1,000 acres of dazzling white sand and dunes, this preserved wilderness demonstrates what Panama City Beach looked like before motels and condominiums lined its shore. Lacy, golden sea oats sway in gulf breezes, and fragrant rosemary grows wild. The area is home to foxes, coyotes, and a herd of deer. See chapter 14.

2 The Best Snorkeling

- **John Pennekamp Coral Reef State Park** (Key Largo): This is the country's first undersea preserve, with 188 square miles of protected coral reefs. The water throughout much of the park is shallow, so it's an especially great place for snorkelers to see an incredibly

Florida

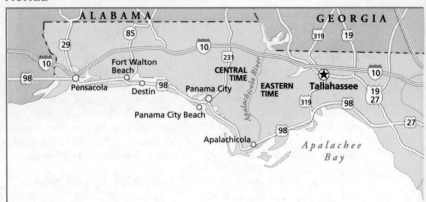

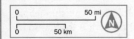

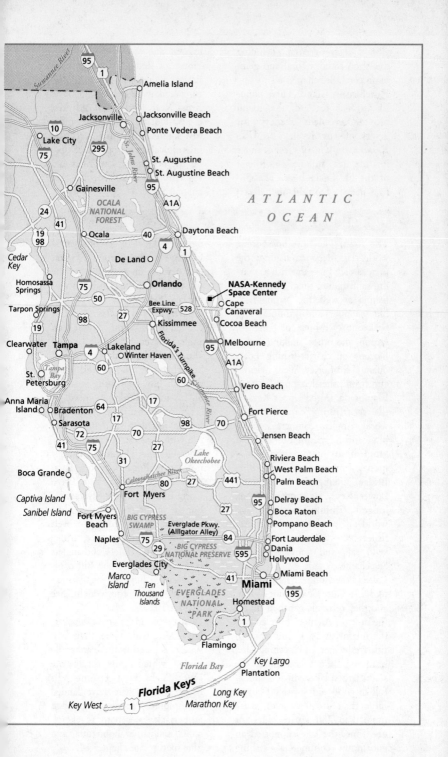

vibrant array of coral, including tree-sized elkhorn coral and giant brain coral. See chapter 6.

- **Hutchinson Island:** Three popular artificial reefs off this island provide excellent scenery for divers of any level. The **USS Rankin,** sunk in 120 feet of water in 1988, lies 7 miles east-northeast of the St. Lucie Inlet. The 58-foot-deep **Donaldson Reef,** located due east of the Gilbert's House of Refuge Museum, consists of a cluster of plumbing fixtures sunk in 58 feet of water. The **Ernst Reef,** made from old tires, is a 60-foot dive located 4½ miles east-southeast of the St. Lucie inlet. Local dive shops have "tips" on the best spots, and rules and regulations for safe diving. See chapter 9.

3 The Best Fishing

- **The Keys:** The Keys boast some world-class deep-sea fishing; the prize is such big-game fish as marlin, sailfish, and tuna. There's reef fishing as well, for "eating fish" like snapper and grouper, and backcountry fishing for bonefish, tarpon, and other "stalking" fish. Dozens of charter-fishing boats operate from Key West marinas and from other less-popular keys. Islamorada, in the Upper Keys, is the sportfishing capital of the world. Anglers compete for trophy sailfish, marlin, wahoo, and kingfish at many annual big-money tournaments. Seven-Mile Bridge, linking the Middle and Lower Keys, is known as "the longest fishing bridge in the world"; it's a favorite spot for local fishers who wait for barracuda, yellowtail, and dolphin to bite. See chapter 6.

- **Lake Okeechobee:** Many visitors to the Treasure Coast come to fish, and they certainly get their fill off the miles of Atlantic shore and on the inland rivers. If you want to fish freshwater and nothing else, head for Lake Okeechobee, the state's largest lake, which is chock-full of good eating fish. It covers more than 467,000 acres; that's more than 730 square miles. At one time, the lake supported an enormous commercial fishing industry. Due to a commercial fishing-net ban, much of that industry has died off, leaving the sportfishers all the rich bounty of the lake. See chapter 9.

- **Stuart:** Known as the "Sailfish Capital of the World," Stuart is an angler's haven. The fish bite all year, but peak months are December through March and June through July. Sailfishing is an art of its own—beginners need to learn to feel that exact moment to let the reel drag so that the fish run with the lure. See chapter 9.

- **Boca Grande:** The deep, shadowy holes of Boca Grande Pass, between Gasparilla and Cayo Costa Islands off Fort Myers, harbor the mighty tarpon, the "silver king of the seas." Teddy Roosevelt and his rich buddies used to bag tarpon in these waters, and anglers from around the globe still compete every July in the World's Richest Tarpon Tournament. See chapter 10.

- **Destin:** Florida's largest charterboat fleet, with more than 140 vessels, is based in this Panhandle town, which calls itself the "World's Luckiest Fishing Village." Anglers here have landed championship catches of grouper, amberjack, snapper, mackerel, cobia, sailfish, wahoo, tuna, and blue marlin. See chapter 14.

4 The Best Golf Courses

- **Biltmore Hotel** (Miami): The beautiful, rolling 18-hole golf course designed by Donald Ross and located at the majestic Biltmore Hotel in Coral Gables is open to the public and a favorite of Bill Clinton. See chapter 4.
- **Doral Golf Resort and Spa** (Miami): Four championship courses make the Doral one of Miami's best golf destinations, featuring the legendary Blue Monster course, which is the site of the annual Doral-Ryder Open. See chapter 4.
- **Turnberry Isle Resort and Club** (Aventura, North Miami Beach): These two courses by Robert Trent Jones are open only to guests but are among the city's best. See chapter 4.
- **The Inn at Boca Teeca** (Boca Raton): For over three decades, this inn has been attracting golf fanatics who could care less about the small, but comfortable, rooms because they're too busy out on the superb 27-hole golf course at the Inn's Boca Teeca Country Club, open only to members and guests of the inn. See chapter 8.
- **PGA National Resort & Spa** (Palm Beach): This rambling resort, the national headquarters of the PGA, is a premier golf destination, with five 18-hole courses on more than 2,300 acres. See chapter 8.
- **Emerald Dunes Golf Course** (West Palm Beach): The gorgeous Tom Fazio–designed course featuring 60 acres of water and stunning views of the ocean is pricey but one of the few in the area open to the public. See chapter 8.
- **Indian River Plantation Beach Resort** (Stuart): This is a terrific destination for golfers, but unless you're a guest at the resort or are

playing with a member, you cannot play these courses. See chapter 9.
- **Champions Club at Summerfield** (Stuart): The best in the area, this rural, somewhat-challenging championship course was designed by Tom Fazio and built in 1994. It offers great glimpses of wildlife amid the wetlands. See chapter 9.
- **Lely Flamingo Island Club** (Naples): Designed by Robert Trent Jones Sr., Lely Flamingo's hourglass fairways and fingerlike bunkers present many challenges. It's part of a development that includes the Lely Mustang, a Lee Trevino–course that is more forgiving but still fun. See chapter 10.
- **Tiburon Golf Club** (Naples): Greg Norman designed the 27 championship holes at this new course to play like a British Open—but without the thick thatch rough. See chapter 10.
- **Naples Beach Hotel & Golf Club** (Naples): One of the state's oldest, this resort course is relatively flat, but small greens and masterful bunkers will test your skills. And one of Florida's most charming resort hotels is across the street. See chapter 10.
- **Mangrove Bay Golf Course** (St. Petersburg): One of the nation's top 50 municipal courses, the Mangrove Bay course hugs the inlets of Old Tampa Bay and offers 18-hole, par-72 play. Facilities include a driving range; lessons and golf-club rental are also available. See chapter 11.
- **The Westin Innisbrook Resort** (Tarpon Springs): *Golfweek* has called Innisbrook's Copperhead Course, former home of the annual JCPenney Classic, number one in Florida. One thousand students a year go through Innisbrook's

Golf Institute, and golfers from around the world come to play the 600 acres of courses. See chapter 11.

- **Walt Disney World** (Orlando): The resorts surrounding the theme parks have 99 regulation holes that let you walk in the footsteps (and share the frustrations) of some of the game's greatest players. Those with a shorter stroke can play through the miniature courses, Fantasia Gardens and Winter Summerland. See chapter 12.

- **Ladies Professional Golf Association/LPGA International** (Daytona Beach): This "women-friendly" course has multiple tee settings, unrestricted tee times, a great pro shop, and state-of-the-art facilities. Designed by Rees-Jones, the older of the two courses here was chosen as one of the "Top Ten You Can Play" by *Golf Magazine*. See chapter 13.

- **TPC at Sawgrass** (Ponte Vedra Beach, near Jacksonville): With 99 holes, Pete Dye's Tournament Players Club (TPC) at Sawgrass makes top-10 lists everywhere. The 17th hole, on a tricky island,

is one of the most photographed holes in the world. See chapter 13.

- **Ocean Hammock Golf Club** (Palm Coast, between Daytona Beach and St. Augustine): Opened in late 2000 with six of its holes actually skirting the Atlantic Ocean, this Jack Nicklaus–designed course is the first authentic seaside links built in Florida since the 1920s. See chapter 13.

- **Amelia Island Plantation** (Amelia Island): This exclusive resort has three of the state's best courses. Long Point Club, designed by Tom Fazio, is the most beautiful and challenging. Pete Dye's Amelia Links is another oceanfront course. Both are open only to resort guests. See chapter 13.

- **Marriott's Bay Point Resort** (Panama City Beach): Thirty-six holes of championship golf at this Marriott include the Lagoon Legends course, one of the country's most difficult. Nearby is The Hombre, an 18-holer where O. J. Simpson played a round right after his acquittal. See chapter 14.

5 The Best Family Attractions

- **Parrot Jungle and Gardens** (Miami): Watch your head because flying above are hundreds of parrots, macaws, peacocks, cockatoos, and flamingos. Continuous, suitable but cheesy shows star roller-skating cockatoos, card-playing macaws, and numerous stunt-happy parrots. There are also tortoises, iguanas, and a rare albino alligator on exhibit. See chapter 5.

- **Sea Grass Adventures** (Miami): This is not your typical nature tour. With Sea Grass Adventures, you will be able to wade in the

water on Key Biscayne with your guide and catch an assortment of sea life in nets provided by the guides. At the end of the program, participants gather on the beach while the guide explains what everyone's just caught, passing the creatures around in miniature viewing tanks. See chapter 5.

- **Miami Museum of Science and Space Transit Planetarium** (Miami): The Museum of Science features more than 140 hands-on exhibits that explore the mysteries of the universe. Live demonstrations and collections of rare natural history specimens make a visit here fun and informative. Many of the demos involve audience participation, which can be lots of fun for willing and able kids and adults alike. See chapter 5.

- **Busch Gardens Tampa Bay** (Tampa): Although the thrill rides, live entertainment, shops, restaurants, and games get most of the ink at this 335-acre family theme park, Busch Gardens ranks among the top zoos in the country, with several thousand animals living in naturalistic environments. If you can get them off the roller coasters, the kids can find out what all those wild beasts they've seen on the Discovery Channel look like in person. See chapter 11.

- **Museum of Science and Industry (MOSI)** (Tampa): One of the largest educational science centers in the Southeast, MOSI has more than 450 interactive exhibits in which the kids can experience hurricane-force winds, defy the laws of gravity, cruise the mysterious world of microbes, explore the human body, and more. They can also watch stunning movies in MOSIMAX, Florida's first IMAX dome theater. See chapter 11.

- **Universal Studios Florida** (Orlando): The "other" Orlando heavyweight delivers two parks— Universal Studios Florida and Islands of Adventure. Their rides in many cases are based on Hollywood blockbusters or cartoon heroes. Kids can get slimed at Nickelodeon studios or spun silly

in the world of Dr. Seuss while their parents scream on the Incredible Hulk Coaster and take the plunge at Dudley Do-Right's Ripsaw Falls. See chapter 12.

- **Walt Disney World** (Orlando): Introduce your wee ones to many of the Disney characters at **Mickey's Toontown Fair** in the Magic Kingdom. See and savor the latest technology at **Innoventions** or explore Chinese history in the World Showcase at Epcot. Hold on for the ride of your life at **Disney– MGM Studios' Rock 'n' Roller Coaster**. And get close to Bengal tigers and giant fruit bats at Animal Kingdom. See chapter 12.

- **Kennedy Space Center** (Cape Canaveral): Especially since the multimillion-dollar renovation and expansion, this family destination is a must-see. There is plenty to keep kids and parents busy for at least a full day, including interactive computer games, IMAX films, and dozens of informative displays on the space program. Try to schedule a trip during a real launch; there are more than a dozen each year. See chapter 13.

- **Daytona USA** (Daytona Beach): Opened in late 1996 on Daytona International Speedway grounds, this huge state-of-the-art interactive attraction is an exciting and fast-paced stop even for nonrace fans. Kids can see real stock cars, go-karts, and motorcycles, and even participate in a pit stop on a NASCAR Winston Cup race car. See chapter 13.

6 The Best Offbeat Travel Experiences

- **Jimbo's on Key Biscayne** (Miami): Located at the very end of Key Biscayne on the lagoon where they shot *Flipper,* Jimbo's has become the quintessential, albeit

hard-to-find, South Florida watering hole, snack bar, and hangout for a wacky assortment of colorful characters from shrimpers and yachters to politicos. Dollar beers and excellent smoked fish are sold from a cooler, vacant shacks serve as backdrops for films, and visitors are able to test their skills in a game of bocce ball. See chapter 4.

- **Columbus Day Regatta** (Miami): This unique observation of Columbus Day revolves around a so-called regatta in Biscayne Bay but always ends with participants stripping down to their bare necessities and partying at the sandbar in the middle of the bay. There is a boat race at some point of the day, but most people are too preoccupied to notice. See chapter 5.

- **People-Watching on South Beach and Worth Avenue** (Miami and Palm Beach): As cliché as the notion of people-watching may seem, it's never the same old scenario on Miami's neon-hued Riviera, where equally colorful locals and luminaries proudly prance as if every day was the Easter parade. In Palm Beach, titled nobility, bejeweled socialites, and an assortment of upper crusties put on the ritz on the city's version of Rodeo Drive. See chapters 5 and 8.

- **Swimming with the Dolphins at the Dolphin Research Center** (Marathon): Of the four such centers on the continental United States, the Dolphin Research Center is the most impressive. With advanced reservations, you can splash around with dolphins in their natural lagoon homes. It's an amazing experience. See chapter 6.

- **Underwater Stay at Jules' Undersea Lodge** (Key Largo): Submerge yourself in this single-room Atlantis-like hotel that offers a surprisingly comfortable suite 30 feet underwater. Don't worry, there's plenty of breathing room. See chapter 6.

- **Fantasy Fest** (Key West): Mardi Gras takes a Floridian vacation as

the streets of Key West are overtaken by wildly costumed revelers who have no shame and no parental guidance. This week-long, hedonistic, X-rated Halloween party is *not* for children under 18. See chapter 6.

- **Babcock Wilderness Adventures** (Fort Myers): Experienced naturalists lead "swamp buggy" tours through the Babcock Ranch, including the mysterious Telegraph Swamp, where alligators lounge in the sun. Although the Babcock Ranch is the largest cattle operation east of the Mississippi (with bison and quarter horses too), it is a major wildlife preserve inhabited by countless birds and other creatures. See chapter 10.

- **Swimming with the Manatees** (Crystal River, north of Clearwater): Some 300 manatees spend the winter in the Crystal River, and you can swim, snorkel, or scuba with them in the warm-water natural spring of Kings Bay, about 7 miles north of Homosassa Springs. It's not uncommon to be surrounded in the 72°F (21°C) water by 30 to 40 "sea cows," who nudge and caress you as you swim with them. See chapter 11.

- **SeaWorld** (Orlando): Spend a big chunk of your day and budget at Discovery Cove, an all-inclusive theme park where visitors can take a 45-minute swim with a bunch of dolphins, snorkel alongside a tank of sharks, and dive near a coral reef. See chapter 12.

- **Learning to Surf the Big Curls at Cocoa Beach Surfing School** (Cocoa Beach): Even if you don't know how to hang ten, this school will get you riding the waves with the best of them. It offers equipment and lessons for beginners or pros at these world-famous surf beaches. See chapter 13.

7 The Best Small Towns

- **Sebastian:** Known as one of the last remaining fishing villages, Sebastian is located at the northern tip of the Treasure Coast region in Indian River County. The area's small-town feel and laid-back, relaxed atmosphere is one of its biggest draws. See chapter 9.

- **Boca Grande** (Southwest Florida): Founded in the 1880s, this little village on Gasparilla Island retains the flavor of those Victorian times. Luxurious mansions coexist with simple homes of fishermen who guide rich folks in search of tarpon, just as their ancestors did a century ago. The du Ponts, Mellons, and Astors once arrived, for the wintertime "social season," at the town's railway depot, which has been restored and now houses shops and the Loose Caboose Restaurant and Ice Cream Parlor. See chapter 10.

- **Olde Naples** (Naples): Started in 1886 as a real-estate development, the original part of Naples retains much of Old Florida's charm, with tree-lined streets dividing many of the original clapboard homes. With the houses on Millionaires' Row virtually hidden by dense foliage and with no high-rises in sight, Naples Beach seems far removed from today's modern city. See chapter 10.

- **Tarpon Springs** (Tampa Bay Area): Tarpon Springs calls itself the "Sponge Capital of the World" because immigrants from Greece settled here in the late 1800s to harvest the sponges that grew in abundance offshore. Their descendants make Tarpon Springs a fascinating center of transplanted Greek culture. Sponges still arrive at the historic Sponge Docks, where a lively, carnival-like atmosphere and Greek cuisine prevail. Restored Victorian homes facing Spring Bayou also make this one of the most picturesque towns in the state. See chapter 11.

- **Fernandina Beach** (Amelia Island): You can stay at two of Florida's ritziest resorts on Amelia Island, but the real charm here is in the quaint town of Fernandina Beach, where a 50-block area of Victorian and Queen Anne homes is listed on the National Register of Historic Places. See chapter 13.

- **Apalachicola** (Northwest Florida): Located at the mouth of the Apalachicola River, this gulf-shore town was a major cotton port before the Civil War, and a later timber boom resulted in the fine Victorian homes that still grace Apalachicola's uncurbed streets. It was here that Dr. John Gorrie invented the forerunner of the air conditioner, which revolutionized Florida's tourism industry. Today, the major industry is seafood, with famous Apalachicola oysters eaten fresh off the boats. See chapter 14.

- **Pensacola** (Northwest Florida): One of America's oldest communities, Pensacola has preserved its Spanish, French, and English heritages in the Seville Historic District and Historic Pensacola Village. Spanish-named streets are bordered by both French-style wrought-iron balconies reminiscent of New Orleans and English colonial churches like those in Williamsburg, Virginia. See chapter 14.

8 The Best Spas

- **Agua at the Delano Hotel** (Miami; ☎ **800/555-5001** or 305/672-2000): One trip to this sublime, celebrity-saturated, and rooftop spa overlooking the Atlantic in a haute hotel and you'll feel like you're in heaven. Try the milk-and-honey massage and you'll understand. See chapter 4.

- **The Spa at Turnberry Isle Resort and Club** (Miami; ☎ **800/327-7028** or 305/936-2929): The Turnberry Spa, which has been renovated to the tune of $10 million, consists of three levels of deluxe pampering and includes aerobics and fitness classes, stress reductions, massage therapy, and a juice bar designed for complete rejuvenation. See chapter 4.

- **The Spa of Eden, Eden Roc** (Miami; ☎ **800/327-8337** or 305/531-0000): The modern, 55,000-square-foot Spa of Eden has excellent facilities and exercise classes, including yoga, plus a tempting array of treatments from shiatsu and Swedish massages to salt-glow applications and mud baths.

- **Marriott's Harbor Beach** (Fort Lauderdale; ☎ **800/996-3426** or 954/389-3300): This new $8-million, 24,000-square-foot European spa is the first full-service seaside facility of its kind in Fort Lauderdale. See chapter 8.

- **PGA National Resort & Spa** (Palm Beach Gardens; ☎ **800/633-9150** or 561/627-2000): This lauded golf resort provides the perfect pampering for sore golfers and bored nongolfers with its Mediterranean Spa featuring just about every treatment imaginable, including special ones for pregnant women. See chapter 8.

- **Sanibel Harbour Resort & Spa** (Fort Myers; ☎ **800/767-7777** or 941/466-2166): Many call this high-rise resort overlooking Sanibel Island the best spa value in the country. The spa obliges your every whim. Try the amazing Betar Bed, a suspended "bed of music" that floats you to a level where stresses disappear. There are also mud, algae, seaweed, and mineral wraps; Swiss showers; paraffin facials; and more. Day packages, makeovers, and men's sports packages are popular. The fitness center is state-of-the-art. See chapter 10.

- **Naples Beach Hotel & Golf Club** (Naples; ☎ **800/237-7600** or 941/261-2222): A new spa adds complete relaxation to a stay at this venerable hotel, already one of Florida's most relaxing resorts. A deep-body massage followed by a milk-and-honey wrap will leave you on cloud nine, and a special wedding package will have you primed for the big day. See chapter 10.

- **Safety Harbor Resort and Spa** (Tampa Bay Area; ☎ **800/237-0155** or 813/726-1161): Tucked away off the beaten track amid moss-draped oaks and cobblestone streets, Safety Harbor is the oldest continually running spa in the United States, and Florida's only spa built around natural healing springs. The feeling is very European. The Phil Green tennis school is also on the grounds, and many tennis programs are available. See chapter 11.

- **The Plaza Resort & Spa** (Daytona Beach; ☎ **800/767-4471** or 386/255-4471): Women can pamper themselves at The Plaza's Ocean Waters Spa while their testosterone-driven males are off watching the Daytona 500 stock car races. He may come home reeking of exhaust fumes, but you'll smell of roses after a floral wrap. The spa offers intimate rooms where couples can be massaged together, and the recently refurbished hotel has romantic rooms with Jacuzzi tubs. See chapter 13.

9 The Best Luxury Resorts

- **Mandarin Oriental** (Brickell Key, Miami; ✆ 305/373-0141): The swank and stunning Mandarin Oriental features a waterfront location, residential-style rooms (most with balconies), superb service, and several upscale dining and bar facilities previously unknown to its nearby downtown Miami locale. See chapter 4.

- **Ritz-Carlton** (South Beach, Key Biscayne, and Palm Beach locations; ✆ 800/241-3333): Consistently superior service, amenities, and scrupulous attention to all things luxurious make these Ritz-Carlton properties among South Florida's most desirable upscale accommodations. See chapters 4 and 8.

- **The Breakers** (Palm Beach; ✆ 800/833-3141 or 561/655-6611): This stately, historic hotel epitomizes la dolce vita, Palm Beach–style, featuring expansive manicured lawns, an elegant lobby, the state's oldest and very scenic golf course, and impeccable service. See chapter 8.

- **Naples Beach Hotel & Golf Club** (Naples; ✆ 800/237-7600 or 941/261-2222): A beachside setting on Millionaires' Row couldn't be better for carrying on the hallowed-but-relaxed Old Florida traditions at this family-operated hotel. A championship 18-hole golf course, a tennis club, and a full-service spa are all on the premises. The beachside chickee hut bar is one of Florida's best sunset venues, and the dining room serves an exceptional, reasonably priced breakfast buffet. See chapter 10.

- **The Ritz-Carlton Naples** (Naples; ✆ 800/241-3333 or 941/598-3300): This opulent 14-story Mediterranean-style hotel at Vanderbilt Beach is a favorite of affluent guests, who like standard Ritz-Carlton amenities such as imported marble floors, antique art, Oriental rugs, Waterford crystal chandeliers, and afternoon British-style high tea. Guests relax in high-backed rockers on the verandahs or unwind by the heated swimming pool set in a landscaped terrace, but they must walk through a narrow mangrove forest to reach the beach. See chapter 10.

- **South Seas Resort** (Captiva Island; ✆ 800/237-3102 or 941/472-5111): Built on what was once a 330-acre copra plantation, this exclusive spot is one of the best choices in Southern Florida for serious tennis buffs (22 courts with pro). Its gulf-side golf course is one of the most picturesque nine-holers anywhere. There are no high-rise buildings, just an assortment of luxury homes and condominiums, some with private pools and their own tennis courts. With three bedrooms or more, some units are ideal for families or couples who want to share the cost of a vacation. See chapter 10.

- **Don CeSar Beach Resort and Spa** (St. Pete Beach; ✆ 800/637-7200, 800/282-1116, or 813/360-1881): Dating back to 1928 and listed on the National Register of Historic Places, this "Pink Palace" tropical getaway is so romantic you may bump into six or seven honeymooning couples in one weekend. The lobby has classic high windows and archways, crystal chandeliers, marble floors, and original artworks. Most rooms have high ceilings and offer views of the gulf or Boca Ciega Bay. See chapter 11.

- **Disney's Grand Floridian Resort & Spa** (Orlando; ✆ **407/934-7639**): This magnificent Victorian inn has an opulent five-story lobby complete with a Chinese Chippendale aviary. An orchestra plays big-band music every evening near **Victoria & Albert's,** the Grand Floridian's five-star restaurant. See chapter 12.
- **Hyatt Regency Grand Cypress Resort** (Orlando; ✆ **800/835-7377**): This standout has some impressive treats, including a half-acre pool with a dozen waterfalls and three spas, 12 tennis courts, a 45-hole Jack Nicklaus–designed golf course, and a 45-acre nature walk. They all add up to luxury. See chapter 12.

- **Amelia Island Plantation** (Amelia Island; ✆ **800/874-6878** or 904/261-6161): Set amidst magnolias, oak trees, and the Atlantic Ocean, this gracious resort is straight out of the Deep South. It's more rustic than the nearby Ritz, but it has excellent hiking and biking paths, tennis, swimming, horseback riding, and boating. Golfers especially enjoy exclusive use of two of the top courses in Florida. See chapter 13 and "The Best Golf Courses," in section 4, earlier in this chapter.
- **The Ritz-Carlton Amelia Island** (✆ **800/241-3333** or 904/277-1100): Set on 13 acres of stunning beachfront, this Ritz-Carlton is more glitzy than its older neighbor, the Amelia Island Plantation, but it's also more relaxed than some of its siblings. You'll find all the first-class amenities, as well as remarkable service. The Grill, the hotel's finest restaurant, is one of the island's best. See chapter 13.

10 The Best Romantic Hideaways

- **Hotel Place St. Michel** (Coral Gables; ✆ **800/848-HOTEL** or 305/444-1666): This European-style hotel in the heart of Coral Gables is one of the city's most romantic options. The accommodations and hospitality are very Old World European, complete with dark wood-paneled walls, cozy beds, beautiful antiques, and a quiet elegance that seems startlingly out of place in trendy Miami. See chapter 4.
- **Hotel Impala** (Miami Beach; ✆ **800/646-7252** or 305/673-2021): During the heyday of 1990s excess, the Miami Beach was known for the fabulous parties thrown by the eclectic designer Gianni Versace. The late Versace desired an intimate European-styled guest house that

would please well-seasoned travelers, and the Impala is the result. His personal touch on this renovated Mediterranean inn is still evident, from the Greco-Roman frescos and friezes to an intimate garden that is perfumed with the scents from carefully hanging lilies and gardenias. See chapter 4.
- **Little Palm Island** (Little Torch Key; ✆ **800/343-8567**): Accessible only by boat, this private 5-acre island is not only remote, it's romantic, featuring no TVs, telephones, or faxes in the luxurious thatched cottages. See chapter 6.
- **Marquesa Hotel** (Key West; ✆ **800/ 869-4631** or 305/292-1919): Don't be fooled by the Marquesa's location in the heavily populated Key West: This charming B&B is in a wonderful world

of its own, far enough from the tumult, yet close enough if you want it. See chapter 6.

- **Island's End Resort** (St. Pete Beach; © 727/360-5023). Sitting right on Pass-a-Grille where the Gulf of Mexico meets Tampa Bay, this little all-cottage retreat is a great hideaway from the maddening crowds of St. Pete Beach. You won't have an on-site restaurant, a bar, and other such amenities, but you can step from your cottage right onto the beach. And if you get the unit with two living rooms, you'll have a whirlpool tub and your own private gulf-side swimming pool. See chapter 11.

- **Turtle Beach Resort** (Siesta Key, off Sarasota; © 941/349-4554): Sitting beside the bay, this intimate little charmer began life years ago as a traditional Old Florida fishing camp, but today it's one of the state's most romantic retreats. It's a tightly-packed little place, but high wooden fences surround each unit's private outdoor hot tub, and one-way mirror walls let you lounge in bed while passersby see only reflections of themselves. See chapter 11.

- **Disney's Wilderness Lodge** (Lake Buena Vista): This Disney property is reminiscent of a lodge at Yosemite. The geyser out back, the mammoth stone hearth in the lobby, the dining room's 340° view of Bay Lake, and the nightly electric water pageants are just a few of the reasons to stay here. Guest rooms have patios or balconies overlooking the lake, woodlands, or a meadow. See chapter 12.

- **Peabody Orlando** (Orlando; © 800/732-3639 or 407/352-4000): This is the home of the famous mallards that trek through the lobby each morning accompanied by the music of John Philip Sousa. Even standard rooms are lavishly furnished. See chapter 12.

- **The Lodge & Club at Ponte Vedra Beach** (Jacksonville; © 800/243-4304 or 904/273-9500): Every unit at this intimate hotel in upscale Ponte Vedra Beach has a romantic seat built in front of its ocean-view window, plus there's a big bathroom with a two-person tub and a separate shower. Gas fireplaces in most units add even more charm. One of the three swimming pools and whirlpools here is reserved exclusively for couples. You can get married in the semicircular meeting room overlooking the Atlantic. See chapter 13.

- **Henderson Park Inn** (Destin; © 800/336-4853 or 850/837-4853): Nestled against the eastern edge of lovely Henderson Beach State Recreation Area, this Cape Hatteras–style bed-and-breakfast offers romantic escapes without screaming kids. The individually decorated rooms ooze Victorian charm, with high ceilings, fireplaces, Queen Anne furniture, and gulf views from private balconies. Some even have canopy beds. See chapter 14.

- **Seaside** (near Destin; © 800/277-8696 or 904/231-1320): If residents of Northwest Florida don't stay at the Henderson Park Inn for their getaways, they head for the romantic gulf-front cottages at Seaside. Built in the 1980s but evoking the 1880s, the Victorian-style village of Seaside (a short drive east of Destin) has several of the cozy cottages designed especially for honeymooners. See chapter 14.

11 The Best Moderately Priced Accommodations

- **Hotel Leon** (South Beach, ✆ **305/ 673-3767**): A true value, this charismatic and hip sliver of a property has won the loyalty of fashion industrialists and romantics alike. Built in 1929 and restored in 1996, the hotel still retains many original details such as facades, woodwork, and even fireplaces. See chapter 4.

- **The Pelican** (South Beach; ✆ **800/7-PELICAN** or 305/673-3373): Owned by the creative owners of the Diesel Jeans company, The Pelican is South Beach's only self-professed "toy-hotel," in which each of its 30 rooms and suites is decorated as outrageously as some of the area's more colorful drag queens. See chapter 4.

- **Indian Creek Hotel** (Miami Beach; ✆ **800/207-2727** or 305/ 531-2727): A charming, Key West–style hotel that's full of character, the Indian Creek Hotel takes you back in time, with period furnishings, attitude-free service, and a quaint pool and garden, completely lacking waterslides, tiki huts, or calypso bands. See chapter 4.

- **Townhouse** (South Beach; ✆ **877/534-3800** or 305/534-3800): New York hipster Jonathan Morr decided to take matters into his own hands when he realized that Miami Beach had lost touch with the young bohemian bon vivants who gave the city its original cache. His solution: this 67-room, five-story hotel, in which standard rooms started at just $99 during its opening in the fall of 2000. As with anything, the $99 rate proved too good to be true, elevating to a still-reasonable starting rate of $125. See chapter 4.

- **Whitelaw Hotel** (South Beach; ✆ **05/398-7000**): With a slogan that reads "clean sheets, hot water, and stiff drinks," the Whitelaw Hotel stands apart from the other boutique hotels with its fierce sense of humor, but it never compromises on the fabulous amenities found at some of the areas more serious properties. See chapter 4.

- **Conch Key Cottages** (Marathon; ✆ **800/330-1577** or 305/289-1377): This oceanfront hideaway offers rustic but immaculate and well-outfitted cottages that are especially popular with families. Each has a hammock, barbecue grill, and kitchen. See chapter 6.

- **Banyan Marina Apartments** (Fort Lauderdale; ✆ **954/524-4430**): These fabulous waterfront apartments located on a beautifully landscaped residential island may have you vowing never to stay in a hotel again. See chapter 8.

- **Harborfront Inn Bed & Breakfast** (Stuart; ✆ **800/294-1703** or 561/288-7829): Located on the riverfront and within walking distance of the shops and restaurants of downtown, the Harborfront Inn Bed & Breakfast offers Old Floridian hospitality. See chapter 9.

- **Best Western Pink Shell Beach Resort** (Fort Myers Beach; ✆ **800/237-5786** or 941/463-6161): This popular, family-oriented spot fronting both the gulf and the bay has hotel rooms, suites, one- and two-bedroom apartments, and beach cottages. The pink-sided cottages make up for a lack of luxury with lots of 1950s-style charm. Units in two mid-rise, gulf-front buildings have lovely views of Sanibel Island from their screened balconies. See chapter 10.

- **Island's End Resort** (St. Pete Beach; ✆ **813/360-5023**): A wonderful respite from the madding crowd, and a great bargain to boot, this little all-cottage hideaway sits right on the southern tip of St. Pete Beach, smack-dab on Pass-a-Grille, where the Gulf of Mexico meets Tampa Bay. You can step from the six contemporary cottages right onto the beach. One unit even has its own private swimming pool. See chapter 11.

- **DoubleTree Guest Suites** (Lake Buena Vista; ✆ **800/222-8733** or 407/934-1000): Children have their own check-in desk here, and all units are two-room with beds for six. It's also next to WDW. See chapter 12.

- **Disney's Port Orleans Resort** (Lake Buena Vista; ✆ **407/934-7639** or 407/934-5000): Recently merged with the neighboring Dixie Landings Resort, it has the best location, landscaping, and, perhaps, the coziest atmosphere of the resorts in this class. See chapter 12.

- **Best Western Lake Buena Vista Hotel** (Lake Buena Vista; ✆ **800/348-3765** or 407/828-2424): This 12-acre, 18-story lakefront hotel is well kept and immaculate, with more-upscale rooms and public areas than you might expect at a Best Western. And it has a great location next to WDW. See chapter 12.

- **Disney's Caribbean Beach Resort** (Lake Buena Vista; ✆ **407/934-7639**): Here's good value by Disney standards. Units on the 200-acre resort are grouped in five villages around a duck-filled lake. The welcoming rooms feature oak furniture and chintz bedspreads. There are seven swimming pools, a 1.4-mile promenade, and a festive food court. See chapter 12.

- **Casa Monica Hotel** (St. Augustine; ✆ **800/648-1888** or 904/827-1888): Built in 1888 as a luxury hotel, this Spanish-style building was gutted and restored to its previous elegance in 1998. Most interesting of the guest quarters are suites installed in two tile-topped towers and a fortresslike central turret. One suite in the turret has a half-round living room with gunport windows overlooking St. Augustine's historic district. See chapter 13.

- **Gibson Inn** (Apalachicola; ✆ **904/653-2191**): Built in 1907 as a seaman's hotel and gorgeously restored in 1985, this cupola-topped inn is such a brilliant example of Victorian architecture that it's listed on the National Register of Historic Inns. No two guest rooms are alike (some still have the original sinks in the sleeping area), but all are richly furnished with period reproductions. Grab a drink from the bar and relax in one of the high-back rockers on the old-fashioned verandah. See chapter 14.

12 The Best Seafood Restaurants

- **Joe's Stone Crab** (South Beach; ✆ **305/673-0365**): Open only during stone-crab season (October through May), this always packed Miami institution knows how to reel in the crowds with the freshest, meatiest stone crabs and the essential accoutrements that go with them, from creamed spinach to excellent sweet potato French fries. See chapter 4.

- **Fishbone Grille** (downtown Miami; ✆ **305/530-1915**): Fish are flying in the open kitchen of this extremely popular, reasonably priced seafood joint. Whether you take yours grilled, blackened, or sautéed, the chefs here work wonders with fish in every size, shape, and color. Snapper, grouper, dolphin, tuna, sea bass, shrimp— you name it, they've got it. See chapter 4.

- **Grillfish** (South Beach and Coral Gables; ☎ **305/538-9908**): From the beautiful Byzantine-style mural and the gleaming oak bar, you'd think you were eating in a much more expensive restaurant. Grillfish manages to pay the exorbitant South Beach rent because the restaurant has a loyal following of locals who come for fresh, simple seafood in a relaxed but upscale atmosphere. See chapter 4.

- **Big Fish** (downtown Miami; ☎ **305/373-1770**): This hard-to-find, charismatic seafood shack on the Miami River is definitely a big fish in the little pond of downtown restaurants. With a spectacular riverfront setting, Big Fish has a terrific view of the Miami skyline and some of the freshest catch around. See chapter 4.

- **Atlantic's Edge** (Islamorada; ☎ **305/664-4651**): Of the many seafood restaurants in the Keys, this one is tops, with an innovative menu that includes some of the freshest and tastiest fish around. It's also the most elegant offering in the Keys. See chapter 6.

- **Marker 88** (Islamorada; ☎ **305/ 852-9315**): Bahamian conch, stone crabs from the Florida Bay, and shrimp from the West Coast are just some of the fresh items, innovatively prepared, at this Upper Keys institution. See chapter 6.

- **Hobo's Fish Joint** (Coral Springs; ☎ **954/346-5484**): Huge portions of extremely fresh fish are prepared in well over a dozen ways at this steakhouse-style restaurant with wood floors and white tablecloths. Despite the fact that it's located away from the ocean in the

utterly suburban enclave of Coral Springs, this joint is definitely worth a jaunt. See chapter 8.

- **Conchy Joe's Seafood** (Jensen Beach; ☎ **561/334-1130**): Known for fresh seafood and Old Florida hospitality, Conchy Joe's enjoys an excellent reputation that's far bigger than the restaurant itself. Dining is either indoors or on a covered patio overlooking the St. Lucie River. See chapter 9.

- **Channel Mark** (Fort Myers Beach; ☎ **941/463-9127**): Every table looks out on a maze of channel markers on Hurricane Bay, and a dock with palms growing through it makes the Channel Mark a relaxing place for a waterside lunch. The atmosphere changes dramatically at night, when the relaxed tropical ambience is ideal for kindling romance. Congenial owners Mike McGuigan and Andy Welsh put a creative spin on their seafood dishes, and their delicately seasoned crab cakes are tops. See chapter 10.

- **Mad Hatter** (Sanibel Island; ☎ **941/472-0033**): Brian and Jayne Baker's little gulf-front restaurant has only 12 tables, but each has a glorious water view that's best at sunset. They offer a fantasy of New American cuisines with some exotic accents. The menu changes frequently, with no dish repeated (so as not to bore their loyal local following). Whatever they serve, you'll enjoy. See chapter 10.

- **Lobster Pot** (Redington Shores, near St. Pete Beach; ☎ **813/391-8592**): Owner Eugen Fuhrmann supplies the finest seafood dishes on the St. Pete and Clearwater Beaches. Among his amazing variety of lobster dishes is one flambéed in brandy with garlic, and the bouillabaisse is as authentic as any you'll find in the south of France. See chapter 11.

- **Fulton's Crab House** (Lake Buena Vista; ☎ **407/934-2628**): Located in a riverboat replica, Fulton's has a nostalgic mood and an array of good seafood, though meals can get a bit pricey if you opt for stone or king crab. There's an excellent wine list. See chapter 12.
- **Back Porch** (Destin; ☎ **904/837-2022**): The food isn't gourmet at this cedar-shingled shack, whose long porch offers glorious beach and gulf views, but this is where charcoal-grilled amberjack originated. Today, you'll see it on menus throughout Florida. Other fish and seafood, as well as chicken and juicy hamburgers, also come from the coals. See chapter 14.
- **Chef Eddie's Magnolia Grill** (Apalachicola; ☎ **904/653-8000**): Chef Eddie Cass's pleasant restaurant occupies a small bungalow built in the 1880s that is still in possession of the original black cypress paneling in its central hallway. Nightly specials emphasize fresh local seafood and New Orleans–style sauces. Chef Eddie received more than 2,000 orders for his spicy seafood gumbo at a recent Florida Seafood Festival. See chapter 14.

13 The Best Local Dining Experiences

- **Tantra** (South Beach; ☎ **305/672-4765**): Edible nirvana is found in this culinary temple inspired by the Kama Sutra and entirely devoted to the senses with a grass floor, hookah pipes, and a sensual cuisine that's said to be an aphrodisiac. See chapter 4.
- **BED** (South Beach; ☎ **305/532-9070**): Eating in bed will never be the same once you've experienced this restaurant cum nightclub whose name stands for Beverage, Entertainment, and Dining; and food is indeed served in beds and not on tables. See chapter 4.
- **Big Fish** (downtown Miami; ☎ **305/373-1770**): Located on the Miami River across from the spectacular Miami skyline, Big Fish is indeed just that, in a little pond—or river—whose scenic value is priceless. See chapter 4.
- **Versailles** (Little Havana; ☎ **305/444-0240**): This iconoclastic Cuban diner isn't as swanky as its palatial French namesake, but it is full of mirrors, through which you can view the colorful—and audible—Cuban clientele that congregates here for down-home cuisine and hearty conversation. See chapter 4.
- **The Green Turtle Inn** (Islamorada; ☎ **305/664-9031**): Turtle chowder, campy pianist Tina Martin, and a handful of colorful locals contribute to this quintessential Keys landmark. See chapter 6.
- **Islamorada Fish Company** (Islamorada; ☎ **800/258-2559** or 305/664-9271): We're not sure which is better—the view or the seafood—but whatever it is, it's a winning combination. See chapter 6.
- **Blue Heaven** (Key West; ☎ **305/296-8666**): What was once a well-kept secret in Key West's Bahama Village is now a popular eatery known for fresh food and a motley, bohemian crowd. See chapter 6.
- **Mai Kai** (Fort Lauderdale; ☎ **954/563-3272**): At this fabulous vestige of Polynesian kitsch, you're expected to forget you're in the middle of a tacky stretch of Fort Lauderdale and pretend you're somewhere in Hawaii or Tahiti as hula dancers and

fire-eaters entertain, and potent and sickly sweet cocktails are served in coconuts. See chapter 8.

- **Taverna Opa** (Hollywood; ☎ 954/929-4010): Don't get nervous if you hear plates breaking when you enter this raucous, authentic Greek taverna situated directly on the Intracoastal Waterway—it's just the restaurant's lively waitstaff making sure your experience here is 100% Greek. See chapter 8.

- **Farmers Market Restaurant** (Fort Myers; ☎ 941/334-1687): The retail Farmers Market next door may be tiny, but the best of the cabbage, okra, green beans, and tomatoes ends up here at this simple eatery, frequented by everyone from business executives to truck drivers. The specialties of the house are Southern favorites like smoked ham hocks with a bowl of black-eyed peas. See chapter 10.

- **Fourth Street Shrimp Store** (St. Petersburg; ☎ 813/822-0325): The outside of this place looks like it's covered with graffiti, but it's actually a gigantic drawing of people eating. Inside, murals on two walls seem to look out on an early 19th-century seaport (one painted sailor permanently peers in to see what you're eating). This is the best and certainly the most interesting bargain in St. Petersburg. See chapter 11.

- **Moore's Stone Crab** (Longboat Key, off Sarasota; ☎ 941/383-1748): Located in Longbeach, the old fishing village on the north end of Longboat Key, this popular bayfront restaurant still looks a little like a packing house (it's an offshoot of a family seafood

business), but the view of the bay dotted with mangrove islands makes a fine complement to stone crabs fresh from the family's own traps. See chapter 11.

- **Singleton's Seafood Shack** (Mayport/Jacksonville; ☎ 904/246-9440): This rustic Old Florida fish camp has kept up with the times by offering fresh fish in more ways than just battered and fried. Yet it has retained the charming casualness of a riverside fish camp. Even if you don't want seafood, this spot is worth stopping in just for a feel of Old Florida. See chapter 13.

- **Hopkins' Boarding House** (Pensacola; ☎ 904/438-3979): There's a delicious peek into the past at this Victorian boardinghouse, surrounded by ancient trees and a wraparound porch with old-fashioned rocking chairs. Everyone eats family-style—at your elbow could be the mayor or a mechanic, for everyone in town dines here. Platters are piled high with seasonal Southern-style vegetables from nearby farms. In true boardinghouse fashion, guests bus their own dishes. See chapter 14.

- **The Boss Oyster** (Apalachicola; ☎ 904/653-9364): This rustic, dockside eatery is a good place to see if what they say about the aphrodisiac properties of Apalachicola oysters is true. The bivalves are served raw, steamed, or under a dozen toppings ranging from capers to crabmeat. They'll even steam three dozen of them and let you do the shucking. Dine inside or at picnic tables on a screened dockside porch. See chapter 14.

14 The Best Bars & Nightspots

- **Mac's Club Deuce** (South Beach; ☎ 305/673-9537): Standing on

its own amidst an oasis of trendiness, Mac's Club Deuce is the quintessential dive bar, with cheap drinks and a cast of characters ranging from your typical barfly to your atypical drag queen. See chapter 5.

- **Tobacco Road** (downtown Miami; ✆ **305/374-1198**): Al Capone used to hang out here when it was a speakeasy. Now, locals flock to this Road-well-traveled to hear live, local bands perform, as well as national acts such as George Clinton and the P-Funk All-Stars, Koko Taylor, and the Radiators. It's small, it's gritty, and it's meant to be that way, here at the proud owner of Miami's very first liquor license. See chapter 5.

- **Upstairs at the Van Dyke Cafe** (South Beach; ✆ 305/534-3600): Even though this jazz bar isn't located in a basement, but rather on the second floor of the Van Dyke Cafe, it resembles a classy speakeasy in which local jazz performers play to an intimate, enthusiastic crowd of mostly adults and sophisticated young things, who huddle at the small tables often until the wee hours. See chapter 5.

- **Cafe Nostalgia** (Little Havana; ✆ **305/541-2631**): As the name implies, Cafe Nostalgia is dedicated to reminiscing about old Cuba. After watching a Celia Cruz film, you can dance to the hot sounds of Afro-Cuban jazz. This place gets packed after midnight, and dance space is mostly between the tables. See chapter 5.

- **La Covacha** (West Miami; ✆ **305/ 594-3717**): This hut, located virtually in the middle of nowhere, is the hottest Latin joint in the entire city. Do not wear silk here, as you *will* sweat. Friday is *the* night, so much so that the owners had to place a red velvet rope out front to maintain some semblance of order. See chapter 5.

- **Rose Bar at the Delano** (South Beach; ✆ **305/672-2000**): If every rose has its thorn, the thorn at this painfully chic hotel bar is the excruciatingly high priced cocktails. Otherwise, the crowd here is full of the so-called glitterati, fabulati, and other assorted poseurs who view life through (Italian-made) rose-colored sunglasses. See chapter 5.

- **crobar** (South Beach; ✆ **305/531-8225**): With its intense, dance-heavy sound system, an industrially chic ambience, and huge crowds, this Chicago import has raised the bar on South Beach nightlife with crazy theme nights (the monthly Sex night is particularly, uh, stimulating), top name DJs, and the occasional celebrity appearance. See chapter 5.

- **Level** (South Beach; ✆ **305/532-1525**): The megastore of nightclubs, Level is a 40,000-square-foot space featuring four dance floors, three levels, five rooms, and nine bars. It's like a nocturnal video game, in which your status is determined by which level you can land on. See chapter 5.

- **Nikki Beach Club** (South Beach; ✆ **305/538-1111**): What the Playboy Mansion is to Hollywood, the Nikki Beach Club is to South Beach. It's here where "Survivor" meets "The Brady Bunch in Hawaii," with a bit of St. Tropez thrown in for taste. See chapter 5.

- **Fox's Sherron Inn** (South Miami; ✆ **305/661-9201**): The spirit of Frank Sinatra is alive and well at this dark and smoky watering hole, which dates back to 1946. Everything down to the vinyl booths and the red lights makes Fox's a retro fabulous dive bar. See chapter 5.

- **Lola** (South Beach; ✆ **305/695-8697**): Lola redefines the neighborhood bar, striking the perfect balance between chill and chic. This bar, located away from the South Beach mayhem, is a show-girl in her own right—a swank, sultry lounge where people are encouraged to come as they are, leaving the attitude at home. See chapter 5.

- **Duval Street** (Key West): South Florida's own version of Bourbon Street, Duval Street is party central with bars galore. See chapter 6.

- **Clematis Street** (West Palm Beach): Until recently, nightlife in Palm Beach County was either an oxymoron or reserved for haughty private clubs on the island of Palm Beach. Thanks to a downtown revitalization, downtown West Palm now boasts a strip of its own with trendy restaurants, clubs, and bars. See chapter 8.

- **Las Olas Boulevard/Riverwalk** (Fort Lauderdale): Moving off the beachfront strip and onto the more quaint (but no less calm) riverside, Fort Lauderdale now boasts its very own downtown nightlife scene with restaurants, bars, and clubs. See chapter 8.

- **Shooters Waterfront Cafe USA** (Fort Myers; © **941/334-2727**): A setting right on the river makes this Fort Myers's most popular watering hole. There's music every night, and the place is absolutely packed after work on Friday and Saturday. See chapter 10.

- **The Dock at Crayton Cove** (Naples; © **941/263-9940**): Right on the City Dock, this lively pub is a perfect place for an open-air meal or a libation while watching the action on Naples Bay. See chapter 10.

- **Frankie's Patio Bar & Grill** (Tampa; © **813/249-3337**): All you have to do is stroll along 7th Avenue East, between 15th and 20th streets, in Tampa's Ybor City

to find a club or bar to your liking. Frankie's stands out for its exposed industrial pipes—a stark contrast to the Spanish-style architecture prevalent here. There's seating indoors, on a large outdoor patio, or on an open-air balcony over-looking the action on the street. Pick up a calendar at the reception desk: There's that much live jazz, blues, reggae, and rock here. See chapter 11.

- **Church Street Station** (down-town Orlando): This renovated train depot, between Garland and Orange avenues, is an architec-tural treat and a genuine good time. There are 20 shows nightly in this collection of bars, restau-rants, and shops. Enjoy live music and bustling dance floors, or sip a cocktail while sitting along cob-blestone streets. See chapter 12.

- **CityWalk** (Orlando): This 12-acre entertainment complex is a collection of eateries and night-time entertainment spots. It's a haven for theme restaurant afi-cionados, and it features a Hard Rock Cafe, a NASCAR Café, a Motown Café, and a NBA-themed restaurant. You'll also find plenty of places to dance the night away to the sounds of jazz, reggae, hip-hop, and pop. See chapter 12.

- **Pleasure Island** (Orlando): This 16-acre, all-in-one complex of clubs, restaurants, and shops runs the entertainment gamut from country to jazz to modern rock to dance music. Catch an improvisa-tional comedy show or hustle along on the disco floor—there's something here for everyone. Big-name artists occasionally make special appearances on two out-door stages, but a nightly fire-works display ensures that every night here ends with a bang. See chapter 12.

- **Ocean Deck Restaurant & Beach Club** (Daytona Beach; ✆ 904/257-3200): Reggae rules at this hot, noisy, packed, and always-fun beach bar near Daytona Beach's municipal pier, the town's "happening" district. By contrast, the upstairs restaurant is suitable for children, and it has great ocean views to accompany its fine and inexpensive fare. See chapter 13.

- **Seville Quarter** (Pensacola; ✆ 904/434-6211): In Pensacola's Seville Historic District, this restored antique brick complex with New Orleans–style wrought-iron balconies contains pubs and restaurants whose names capture the ambience: Rosie O'Grady's Goodtime Emporium, Lili Marlene's Aviator's Pub, Apple Annie's Courtyard, End o' the Alley Bar, Phineas Phogg's Balloon Works (a dance hall, not a balloon shop), and Fast Eddie's Billiard Parlor (which has electronic games for kids too). Live entertainment ranges from Dixieland jazz to country and western. See chapter 14.

- **Flora-Bama Lounge** (Perdido Key, near Pensacola; ✆ 904/492-0611): This slapped-together gulf-side pub is almost a shrine to country music, with jam sessions from noon until way past midnight on Saturday and Sunday. Flora-Bama is the prime sponsor and a key venue for the Frank Brown International Songwriters' Festival during the first week of November. Take in the great gulf views from the Deck Bar. See chapter 14.

- **Shuckums Oyster Pub & Seafood Grill** (Panama City Beach; ✆ 904/235-3214): "We shuck 'em, you suck 'em" is the motto of this extremely informal pub, which became famous when comedian Martin Short tried unsuccessfully to shuck oysters here during the making of an MTV Spring-Break special. The original bar is virtually papered over with dollar bills signed by old and young patrons who have been flocking here since 1967. See chapter 14.

2

Planning Your Trip to Florida

by Bill Goodwin

Whether you plan to spend a day, a week, 2 weeks, or longer in Florida, you'll need to make many "where," "when," and "how" choices *before* you leave home. This chapter explains how best to plan your trip.

1 The Regions in Brief

The first decision you'll have to make is where to go in Florida. You'll find ample sun, sea, and sand all along the 800 miles of shoreline here, but not every place in the Sunshine State is warm all the time. Many Florida beaches are lined with towering hotels and condominiums, whereas others are pristinely preserved in their natural states. You can spend your days in busy cosmopolitan cities or while them away in picturesque small towns steeped in history. You can take the kids to see Mickey Mouse, or you can find a romantic retreat far from the madding crowds.

Here is a brief rundown of the state's regions to help get you started.

MIAMI & MIAMI BEACH Sprawling across the southeastern corner of the state, metropolitan Miami is a city with many distinct personalities and a vibrant, international flair. Here you will hear Spanish and many other languages, not to mention accents, spoken all around you, for this cosmopolitan area is a melting pot of immigrants from Latin America, the Caribbean, and, undeniably, the northeastern United States in particular. Cross the causeways and you'll come to the sands of Miami Beach, long a resort mecca and home to the hypertrendy South Beach,

famous for its art deco architecture, electric nightlife, and celebrity sightings. See chapters 4 and 5.

THE KEYS From the southern tip of Florida, U.S. 1 travels through a 100-mile-long string of islands stretching from Key Largo to the famous, laid-back "Conch Republic" of Key West, only 90 miles from Cuba and the southernmost point in the United States (it's always warm down here). While some of the islands are crammed with strip malls and tourist traps, most are dense with unusual species of tropical flora and fauna. The Keys don't have the best beaches in Florida, but the waters here—all in a vast marine preserve—offer the state's best scuba diving and snorkeling and some of its best deep-sea fishing. See chapter 6.

THE EVERGLADES Encompassing more than 2,000 square miles and 1.5 million acres, Everglades National Park covers the entire southern tip of Florida. The park, along with nearby Big Cypress National Preserve, protects a unique and fragile "River of Grass" ecosystem teeming with wildlife that is best seen by canoe, by boat, or on long or short hikes. To the east of the Everglades is Biscayne National Park, preserving the northernmost living-coral reefs in the continental United States. See chapter 7.

THE GOLD COAST North of Miami, the Gold Coast is aptly named, for here are booming Hollywood and Fort Lauderdale and ritzy Boca Raton and Palm Beach—sun-kissed, sandy playgrounds of the rich and famous. Beyond its dozens of gorgeous beaches, the area offers fantastic shopping, entertainment, dining, boating, golfing, tennis, and just plain relaxing. With some of the country's most famous golf courses and even more tennis courts, this area attracts big-name tournaments. See chapter 8.

THE TREASURE COAST Despite gaining unprecedented numbers of new residents in recent years, the beach communities running from Hobe Sound north to Sebastian Inlet retain their small-town feel. In addition to a vast array of wildlife, the area has a rich and colorful history. Its name stems from a violent 1715 hurricane that sank an entire fleet of treasure-laden Spanish ships. Excavators turned up hundreds of ancient coins in the 1950s and 1960s, and you'll still see treasure hunters prowling the beaches with metal detectors. The sea around Sebastian Inlet draws surfers to the largest swells in the state. See chapter 9.

SOUTHWEST FLORIDA Ever since inventor Thomas Alva Edison built a home here in 1885, some of America's wealthiest families have spent their winters along Florida's southwest coast. They are attracted by the area's subtropical climate, shell-strewn beaches, and intricate waterways winding among 10,000-plus islands. Many charming remnants of old Florida coexist with modern resorts in the sophisticated riverfront towns of Fort Myers and Naples and on islands like Gasparilla, Useppa, Sanibel, Captiva, and Marco. And thanks to some timely preservation, the area has many wildlife refuges, including the "backdoor" entrance to Everglades National Park. See chapter 10.

THE TAMPA BAY AREA Halfway down the west coast of Florida lies Tampa Bay, one of the state's most densely populated areas. A busy seaport and commercial center, the city of Tampa is home to Busch Gardens Tampa Bay, which is both a major theme park and one of the country's largest zoos. Boasting a unique pier and fine museums, St. Petersburg's waterfront downtown is one of Florida's most pleasant. Most visitors elect to stay near the beaches skirting the narrow barrier islands running some 25 miles between St. Pete Beach and Clearwater Beach. Across the soaring Sunshine Skyway lies Sarasota, one of Florida's prime performing-arts venues, the riverfront town of Bradenton, and another string of barrier islands with great beaches and resorts spanning every price range. See chapter 11.

WALT DISNEY WORLD & ORLANDO Walt Disney announced plans to build the Magic Kingdom in 1965, a year before his death and 6 years before the theme park opened, changing forever what was then a sleepy Southern town. In fact, Walt created a whole new world—if not universe—in central Florida. Today, at the dawn of the millennium, it seems that at least one full-scale theme park opens every year. Walt Disney World claims four distinct parks, two entertainment districts, enough hotels and restaurants to fill a small city, and several smaller attractions including water parks and miniature-golf courses. And then there are the rapidly expanding Universal Orlando, Sea-World, and many more non-Disney attractions. Orlando is Florida's most popular tourist destination, and its visitors have never had more options. See chapter 12.

NORTHEAST FLORIDA The northeast section of the state contains the oldest permanent settlement in

America—St. Augustine, where Spanish colonists arrived and settled more than 4 centuries ago. Today, its history comes to life in a quaint historic district. St. Augustine is bordered to the north by Jacksonville, an up-and-coming sunbelt metropolis with miles of oceanfront beach and beautiful marine views along the St. Johns River. Up on the Georgia border, Amelia Island has two of Florida's finest resorts and its own historic town of Fernandina Beach. To the south of St. Augustine, Daytona Beach is home of the Daytona International Speedway and is a spring-break mecca for the college crowd. Another brand of excitement is offered down at Cape Canaveral, where the Kennedy Space Center launches all manned U.S. space missions. See chapter 13.

NORTHWEST FLORIDA: THE PANHANDLE Historical roots run deep in Florida's narrow northwest extremity; and Pensacola's historic district, which blends Spanish, French, and British cultures, is a highlight of any visit to today's Panhandle. So, too, are the powdery, dazzlingly white beaches that stretch for more than 80 miles past the resorts of Pensacola Beach, Fort Walton Beach, Destin, and Panama City Beach. The Gulf Islands National Seashore has preserved much of this beach and its wildlife, and inland are state parks that offer some of the state's best canoeing adventures. All this makes the area a favorite summertime vacation destination for residents of neighboring Georgia and Alabama, with whom Northwest Floridians share many Deep South traditions. Sitting in a pine and oak forest just 30 miles from the Georgia line, the state capital of Tallahassee has a moss-draped, football-loving charm all its own. See chapter 14.

2 Visitor Information & Money

VISITOR INFORMATION
Your best sources for detailed information about a specific destination in Florida are the **local visitor information offices.** They're listed under "Orientation" or "Essentials" in the following chapters.

Contact **Visit Florida,** P.O. Box 1100, Tallahassee, FL 32302-1100 (✆ **888/7-FLA-USA;** www.flausa.com), the state's official tourism marketing agent, for a free comprehensive guide to the state. Visit Florida also operates **welcome centers** 16 miles west of Pensacola on I-10, 4 miles north of Jennings on I-75, 7 miles north of Yulee on I-95, and 3 miles north of Campbellton on U.S. 231. There's also a walk-in information office in the west foyer of the New Capitol Building in Tallahassee (see chapter 14).

Once you're here, you can call Visit Florida's 24-hour **tourist assistance** hotline (✆ **800/656-8777**) if you need help with lost travel documents, directions, emergencies, or references to attractions, restaurants, and shopping anywhere in the state. Hotline operators speak several languages, including Spanish, French, German, Portuguese, Japanese, and Korean.

MONEY
The easiest way to get cash while you're traveling in Florida is to use your debit or credit cards at **ATMs.** Of the big national banks, **First Union Bank** and **Bank of America** have offices with ATMs throughout Florida.

Most ATMs are linked to a national network that most likely includes your bank at home. **Cirrus** (✆ **800/424-7787;** www.mastercard.com/atm/) and **Plus** (✆ **800/843-7587;** www.visa.com/atms) are the two most popular networks; check the back of your

ATM card to see which network your bank belongs to. Use the toll-free numbers to locate ATMs in your destination. Be sure to check your bank's daily withdrawal limit and your credit limits before leaving home.

THEFT Almost every credit-card company has an emergency toll-free number you can call if your wallet or purse is stolen. Your own bank's customer service number is on the back of your credit card; write it down and put it someplace where it isn't likely to be lost or stolen. If you do lose it, the toll-free information directory (© **800/555-1212**) will provide the number. Citicorp Visa's U.S. emergency number is © **800/336-8472.** American Express cardholders and traveler's check holders should call © **800/221-7282** for all money emergencies. MasterCard holders should call © **800/307-7309.**

The credit-card companies may be able to wire you a cash advance off your credit card immediately; in many places, they can deliver an emergency credit card in a day or two.

Odds are that if your wallet is gone, the police won't be able to recover it for you. However, after you realize that it's gone and you cancel your credit cards, it is still worth informing the police. Your credit-card company or insurer may require a police report number.

3 When to Go

To a large extent, the timing of your visit will determine how much you'll spend—and how much company you'll have—once you get here. That's because room rates can more than double during the high seasons, when countless visitors migrate to Florida.

The weather determines the high seasons (see "Climate," below). In subtropical Southern Florida, it's during the winter, from mid-December to mid-April. On the other hand, you'll be rewarded with incredible bargains if you can stand the heat and humidity of a South Florida summer between June and early September. In North Florida, the reverse is true: Tourists flock here during the summer, from Memorial Day to Labor Day.

Presidents' Day weekend in February, Easter week, Memorial Day weekend at the end of May, the Fourth of July, Labor Day weekend at the start of September, Thanksgiving, Christmas, and New Year's are busy throughout the state, and especially at Walt Disney World and the other Orlando area attractions, which can be packed anytime school's out (see chapter 12).

Northern and Southern Florida share the same "shoulder seasons": April and May and from September to November, when the weather is pleasant throughout Florida and hotel rates are considerably less than during the high seasons. If price is a consideration, then these months of pleasant temperatures and fewer tourists are the best times to visit.

See the accommodations sections in the chapters that follow for specifics about the local high, shoulder, and off-seasons.

CLIMATE Northern Florida has a temperate climate, and even in the warmer southern third of the state, it's subtropical, not tropical. Accordingly, Florida sees more extremes of temperatures than, say, the Caribbean islands.

Spring sees warm temperatures throughout Florida, but it also brings tropical showers.

Summer runs from May to September in Florida, when it's hot and very humid throughout the state. If you're in an inland city during these months, you may not want to do anything too taxing when the sun is at its peak. Coastal areas, however, reap the benefits of sea breezes. Severe afternoon thunderstorms are prevalent during the summer heat (there aren't professional sports teams here named *Lightning* and *Thunder* for nothing), so schedule your activities for earlier in the day, and take precautions to avoid being hit by lightning during the storms.

Fall is a great time to visit—the really hottest days are gone, and the crowds have thinned out. Unless a hurricane blows through, November usually is Florida's driest month. August through November is hurricane season here, but even if one threatens, the National Weather Service closely tracks the storms and gives ample warning if there's need to evacuate coastal areas.

Winter can get a bit nippy throughout the state, and sometimes downright cold in Northern Florida. Although snow is rare, a flake or two has been known to fall as far south as Miami. The "cold snaps" usually last only a few days in the southern half of the state, however, and daytime temperatures quickly return to the 70s.

For up-to-the-minute weather info, tune in to cable TV's Weather Channel, or click on its website: www. weather.com.

Average Temperatures in Selected Florida Cities (°F)

	Jan	Feb	Mar	Apr	May	June	July	Aug	Sept	Oct	Nov	Dec
Key West	69	72	74	77	80	82	85	85	84	80	74	72
Miami	69	70	71	74	78	81	82	84	81	78	73	70
Tampa	60	61	66	72	77	81	82	82	81	75	67	62
Orlando	60	63	66	71	78	82	82	82	81	75	67	61
Tallahassee	53	56	63	68	72	78	81	81	77	74	66	59

FLORIDA CALENDAR OF EVENTS

January

Toyota Gator Bowl, Jacksonville. Yet two more of the country's better college football teams battle it out in Alltel Stadium. © **904/798-1700.** Usually January 1.

Outback Bowl, Tampa. Two top college teams kick off at Houlihan's Stadium, preceded by weeklong series events. Call © **813/874-2695.** Usually January 1.

Epiphany Celebration, Tarpon Springs. After morning services at St. Nicholas Cathedral, young folks dive for the Epiphany cross in Spring Bayou. © **727/937-3540.** First Saturday in January.

Key West Literary Seminar. This 3-day festival attracts the biggest names in literature. Some past participants include Frank McCourt, Joyce Carol Oates, Amy Tan, and Jamaica Kincaid. This event sells out months in advance. Call © **888/293-9291** for details or check out the website at www. Keywestliteraryseminar.org. Early to mid-January.

Art Miami, Miami. This annual fine-arts fair attracts more than a hundred galleries from all over the world. International, modern, and contemporary works are featured here, attracting thousands of visitors and buyers. For information call © **312/553-8924** or visit www.art-miami.com. Early January.

Art Deco Weekend, South Beach, Miami. Gain a newfound appreciation for the Necco-wafered art deco buildings, deco furniture, history,

The Boys of Spring

Major-league baseball fans can watch the Florida Marlins in Miami and the Tampa Bay Devil Rays in St. Petersburg throughout their seasons from April through September, but the entire state is a baseball hotbed from late February through March, when many other teams tune up for the regular season with "Grapefruit League" exhibition games.

Most of Florida's spring-training stadiums are relatively small, so fans can see their favorite players up close, maybe even get a handshake or an autograph. Also, tickets are priced from $5 to $12, a bargain when compared with admission for regular-season games. Many games sell out by early March, so don't wait until you're in Florida to buy tickets.

The teams can move from year to year, so contact the **Florida Sports Foundation,** 2964 Wellington Circle N., Tallahassee, FL 32308 (© **850/ 488-8347;** fax 850/922-0482; www.flasports.com), or the main office of **Major League Baseball,** 350 Park Ave., New York, NY 10022 (© **212/ 339-7800;** www.majorleaguebaseball.com), to find out where your favorite teams will be playing. The schedules usually are available in January prior to the beginning of the Grapefruit League season in February.

Here's where they played in 2001. See the outdoor activities sections in subsequent chapters for specifics.

Atlanta Braves, Lake Buena Vista, near Orlando (© **407/939-1500** or 407/939-2200; www.atlantabraves.com); **Baltimore Orioles,** Fort Lauderdale (© **800/236-8908** or 954/776-1921; www.theorioles.com); **Boston Red Sox,** Fort Myers (© **877/733-7699** or 941/334-4799; www.redsox.com); **Cincinnati Reds,** Sarasota (© **941/954-4464** or 941/955-6501; www.cincinnatireds.com); **Cleveland Indians,** Winter Haven (© **941/293-3900** or 813/291-5803; www.indians.com); **Detroit Tigers,** Lakeland (© **941/603-6278** or 941/686-8075; www.detroittigers. com); **Florida Marlins,** Melbourne (© **321/633-4487** or 321/633-9200; www.flamarlins.com); **Houston Astros,** Kissimmee, near Orlando (© **407/839-3900** or 407/933-6500; www.astros.com); **Kansas City Royals,** Davenport (© **941/424-2500** or 941/424-7211; www.kcroyals.com); **Los Angeles Dodgers,** Vero Beach (© **561/569-6858** or 561/569-4900; www.dodgers.com); **Minnesota Twins,** Fort Myers (© **800/338-9467** or 941/768-4200; www.mntwins.com); **Montreal Expos,** Jupiter (© **561/ 775-1818,** ext. 6; www.montrealexpos.com); **New York Mets,** Port St. Lucie (© **561/871-2115** or 561/871-2100; www.nymets.com); **New York Yankees,** Tampa (© **813/879-2244** or 813/875-7753; www.yankees. com); **Philadelphia Phillies,** Clearwater (© **727/442-8496** or 215/436-1000; www.phillies.com); **Pittsburgh Pirates,** Bradenton (© **941/ 748-4610;** www.pirateball.com); **St. Louis Cardinals,** Jupiter (© **561/775-1818,** ext. 7; www.stlcardinals.com); **Tampa Bay Devil Rays,** St. Petersburg (© **727/825-3250** or 727/825-3137; www.devilray.com); **Texas Rangers,** Port Charlotte (© **941/625-9500;** www.texasrangers.com); **Toronto Blue Jays,** Dunedin (© **800/707-8269** or 813/733-0429; www.bluejays.com).

and fashion at this weekend-long festival of street fairs, films, lectures, and other events. Held along the Beach between 5th and 15th streets. Call ℂ **305/672-2014** for details. Usually held Martin Luther King Jr. weekend.

Royal Caribbean Golf Classic, Key Biscayne, Miami. Watch as pro golfers such as Lee Trevino tee off for over $1 million at this tournament played on the scenic Crandon Park Golf Course. Call ℂ 305/374-6180. Late January.

Goodland Mullet Festival, Marco Island. Stan Gober's Idle Hour Seafood Restaurant in Goodland is mobbed during a massive party featuring the Buzzard Lope dance and the Best Men's Legs Contest. ℂ **941/394-3041;** www.stansidlehour.com. Sunday before Super Bowl.

Zora Neale Hurston Festival of the Arts and Humanities, Eatonville. A 4-day celebration of the author's life and works, held in the nation's first African-American municipality. Call ℂ **800/352-3865** or 407/647-3307 for details. Usually last week in January.

February

Edison Pageant of Light, Fort Myers. The spectacular Parade of Lights tops off arts-and-crafts shows, pageants, and a 5K race. ℂ **800/237-6444** or 941/338-3500; www.leeislandcoast.com. First 2 weeks in February.

Gasparilla Pirate Fest, Tampa. Hundreds of boats and rowdy "pirates" invade the city, then parade along Bayshore Boulevard, showering crowds with beads and coins. ℂ **813/273-6495** or 813/251-4500; www.visittampabay.com. Early February.

Everglades Seafood Festival, Florida City. Fish lovers flock to

Florida City for a 2-day feeding frenzy, in which delicacies from stone crabs to gator tails are served from shacks and booths on the outskirts of this quaint old Florida town. ℂ **941/695-4100.** First full weekend in February.

Miami Film Festival. Not exactly Cannes, but the Miami Film Festival sponsored by the Film Society of America is an impressive 10-day celluloid celebration, featuring world premieres of Latin American, domestic, and other foreign and independent films. Actors, producers, and directors plug their films and participate in Q & A sessions with the audiences. ℂ **305/377-FILM.** Early to mid-February.

Speedweeks, Daytona. Nineteen days of events with a series of races that draw the top names in NASCAR stock-car racing, all culminating in the Daytona 500. All events take place at the Daytona International Speedway. Especially for the **Daytona 500,** tickets must be purchased even a year in advance. They go on sale January 1 of the prior year. ℂ **904/253-7223;** www.daytonaintlspeedway.com. First 3 weeks of February.

Miami International Boat Show. This show draws almost a quarter of a million boat enthusiasts to the Miami Beach Convention Center and the surrounding locations to see the megayachts, sailboats, dinghies, and accessories. It's the biggest anywhere. Call ℂ **305/531-8410** for more information and ticket prices. Mid-February.

Florida State Fair, Tampa. Despite all its development, Florida still is a major agricultural state, which status it celebrates at this huge annual exposition. Judged competitions, botanical gardens, crafts building, carny rides, nationally known entertainers. © **800/345-FAIR;** www.floridastatefair.com. Mid-February.

Mardi Gras at Universal Studios, Orlando. Authentic parade floats from New Orleans, stilt walkers, and traditional doubloons and beads thrown to the crowd add to the fun of this event, and all are included in the regular park admission. © **800/837-2273** or 407/363-8000; www.universalorlando.com. Mid-February.

Coconut Grove Arts Festival, Coconut Grove, Miami. Florida's largest art festival features over 300 artists who are selected from thousands of entries to exhibit their work. Possibly one of the most crowded street fairs in South Florida, the festival attracts art lovers, artists, and lots of college students who seem to think this event is the Mardi Gras of art fairs. Call © **305/447-0401.** Presidents' Day weekend.

March

Bike Week, Daytona Beach. An international gathering of motorcycle enthusiasts draws a crowd of more than 200,000. In addition to major races held at Daytona International Speedway (featuring the world's best road racers, motocrossers, and dirt trackers), there are motorcycle shows, beach parties, and the Annual Motorcycle Parade, with thousands of riders. © **800/854-1234** or 904/255-0981; www.officialbikeweek.com. First week in March.

Sanibel Shell Fair, Sanibel and Captiva Islands. A show of shells from around the world and the sale of unusual shell art. © **941/472-2155;** www.sanibel-captiva.org. Begins first Thursday in March.

Spring Break, Daytona Beach, Miami Beach, Panama City Beach,

Key West, and other beaches. College students from all over the United States and Canada flock to Florida for endless partying, wet T-shirt and bikini contests, free concerts, volleyball tournaments, and more. Tune into MTV if you can't be here. Call the local visitor information offices. Three weeks in March.

Calle Ocho Festival, Miami. What Carnivale is to Rio, the Calle Ocho Festival is to Miami—a 10-day extravaganza, also known as Carnival Miami, featuring a lengthy block party spanning 23 blocks, live salsa music, parades and, of course, tons of savory Cuban delicacies. Those afraid of mob scenes should avoid this party at all costs. Southwest 8th Street between 4th and 27th avenues. © **305/644-8888.** Early to mid-March.

Grand Prix of Miami, Homestead. A little bit of Daytona in Miami, the Grand Prix is a premier racing event, attracting celebrities, Indy car drivers, and curious spectators who get a buzz from the smell of gasoline. Get tickets early; this event sells out quickly. © **305/250-5200.** Sometime in March.

Winter Party, Miami Beach. Gays and lesbians from around the world book trips to Miami as far as a year in advance to attend this weekend-long series of parties and events benefiting the Dade Human Rights Foundation. Travel arrangements can be made through Different Roads Travel, the event's official travel company, by calling © **888/ROADS-55, ext. 510.** For information on specific events and prices, call © **305/538-5908** or visit www.winterparty.com. Early March.

April

Bay Hill Invitational, Orlando. Hosted by Arnold Palmer and featuring Orlando-based golfers like

Tiger Woods, this PGA Tour event is held at the Bay Hill Club, 9000 Bay Hill Blvd. Call ✆ **407/876-2429** or 407/876-2888 for details. Mid-March.

Springtime Tallahassee, Tallahassee. The state capital welcomes abundant azaleas, camellias, and other blossoms. A don't-miss event for garden lovers. ✆ **800/628-2866** or 850/413-9200; www. seetallahassee.com. Runs 4 weeks from late March.

Festival of States, St. Petersburg. Since 1921, one of the South's largest civic celebrations offers national band competition, three parades, concerts, sports, and more. ✆ **727/898-365;** festivalofstates@ aol.com. First full week in April.

Black College Reunion, Daytona Beach. Some 75,000 students from 115 predominantly African-American universities bring a sometimes-rowdy end to the spring-break season. ✆ **800/854-1234** or 904/255-0415; www.daytonabeach.com. Mid-April.

PGA Seniors Golf Championship, Palm Beach Gardens. Held at the PGA National Resort & Spa, it's the oldest and most prestigious of the senior tournaments. Call ✆ **561/624-8400** for the lineup. Mid-April.

Epcot International Flower & Garden Festival, Orlando. This event showcases gardens, topiary characters, floral displays, speakers, and seminars. Call ✆ **407/824-4321** or visit www.disneyworld.com. Six weeks, beginning mid-April.

Sunfest, West Palm Beach. A huge party happens on Flagler Drive in the downtown area with four stages of continuous music, a crafts marketplace, a juried art show, a youth park, and fireworks. Call

✆ **561/659-5992** for details. Late April to early May.

Orlando International Fringe Festival. From sword swallowing to a 7-minute version of Hamlet, this 10-day festival presents over 100 acts. See drama, comedy, political satire, and experimental theater at various outdoor stages in downtown Orlando. Call ✆ **407-648-0077** for ticket information. Late April to early May.

May

Isle of Eight Flags Shrimp Festival, Amelia Island. Blessing of the fleet, best-decorated shrimp boat contest, and tons of shrimp to eat. ✆ **800/2-AMELIA;** www.ameliaisland.org. First weekend in May.

The Shell Air & Sea Show, Fort Lauderdale. It's a tough call as far as what's more crowded—the air, the sea, or the ground, which attracts over two million onlookers craning their necks for a view of big-name airwolves such as the Blue Angels and the Thunderbirds. ✆ **954/467-3555.** Early May.

Florida Springfest, Pensacola. National rock, country, jazz, reggae, and pop musicians perform over 4 days, plus children's activities and more. ✆ **850/469-1069;** www.visitpensacola.com. Mid-May.

Mayfest, Destin. Upscale arts-and-crafts festival attracts more than 20,000 people to look, buy, and sample fine cuisine at the Panhandle's ritziest resort. ✆ **850/837-6241;** www.destinchamber.com. Third full weekend in May.

Coconuts Dolphin Tournament, Key Largo. This is the largest fishing tournament in the Keys, offering $5,000 and a Dodge Ram pickup truck to the person who breaks the record for the largest fish caught. The competition is fierce! Call ✆ **305/451-4107** for details.

Mid-May, usually the weekend before Memorial Day.

June

Fiesta of Five Flags, Pensacola. Extravaganza commemorates the Spanish conquistador Tristan de Luna's arrival in 1559. ✆ **850/433-6512;** www.visitpensacola.com. First week in June.

Gay Weekend, Orlando. This weekend, grown out of the "Gay Day" that has been unofficially held at Walt Disney World since the early 1990s, attracts tens of thousands of gay and lesbian travelers to central Florida. Special events at other attractions, including Universal and SeaWorld, also cater to gay and lesbian travelers. You can get information at **www.gayday.com**. First weekend in June.

Billy Bowlegs Festival, Fort Walton Beach. A fleet of modern-day pirates captures the Emerald Coast in a rollicking, weeklong bash honoring notorious buccaneer William Augustus Bowles. A treasure hunt, parade, and carnival, too. ✆ **800/322-3319;** www.destin-fwb.com. First week of June.

Coconut Grove Goombay Festival, Miami. They may say it's better in the Bahamas, but you may disagree after attending Miami's own Bahamian bash, featuring lots of dancing in the streets, marching bands, scorching Caribbean temperatures, and the ever buzz-worthy and refreshing Goombay punch. Call ✆ **305/372-9966** for festival details. Early June.

Spanish Night Watch Ceremony, St. Augustine. Actors in period dress lead a torchlight procession through historic St. Augustine and reenact the closing of the city gates with music and pageantry. ✆ **800/OLD-CITY;** www.visitoldcity.com. Third Saturday in June.

July

Pepsi 400, Daytona. A race marking the halfway point in the NASCAR Winston Cup Series for stock cars. Held at the Daytona International Speedway at 11am. ✆ **904/253-7223;** www.daytonaintlspeedway. com. July 4.

World's Richest Tarpon Tournament, Boca Grande. Some $175,000 is at stake in the great tarpon waters off Southwest Florida. ✆ **800/237-6444** or 941/964-2995; www.charlotte-online.com/bocagrande. Second Wednesday and Thursday in July.

Lower Keys Underwater Music Fest, Looe Key. At this outrageous celebration, boaters go out to the underwater reef of Looe Key Marine Sanctuary off Big Pine Key, drop speakers into the water, and pipe in music. A snorkeling Elvis can usually be spotted at this entertaining event. Call ✆ **800/872-3722** for details. Usually second Saturday of July.

Blue Angels Air Show, Pensacola. World-famous navy pilots do their aerial acrobatics just 100 yards off Pensacola Beach. ✆ **800/874-1234** or 850/434-1234; www. visitpensacola.com. Early July.

Space Week Celebration, Cape Canaveral. Kennedy Space Center celebrates humans landing on the moon. Science fairs, space art, and a space-station design competition are featured. ✆ **407/452-2121;** www.kennedyspacecenter.com. Mid-July.

August

Miami Reggae Festival, Miami. Jamaica's best dance-hall and reggae artists turn out for this 2-day festival. Burning Spear, Steel Pulse, Spragga Benz, and Jigsy King have participated recently. Call Jamaica Awareness at ✆ **305/891-2944** for more details. Early August.

September

Labor Day Pro-Am Surfing Festival, Cocoa Beach. One of the largest surfing events on the East Coast draws pros and amateurs from around the country. Rock-and-roll bands, swimsuit contests. ☎ **800/ 927-9659;** www.space-coast.com. Labor Day weekend.

October

Destin Seafood Festival, Destin. The "World's Luckiest Fishing Village" cooks its bountiful catch in every style of cuisine imaginable. Also offered are arts, crafts, and music. Comes right after Destin Fishing Rodeo, with 450 angler awards, giant dock parties. ☎ **850/ 837-6241;** www.destinchamber. com. First full weekend in October.

Biketoberfest, Daytona. Road-racing stars compete at the CCS Motorcycle Championship at Daytona International Speedway, plus parties, parades, concerts, and more. ☎ **904/253-7223** for ticket information, ☎ **800/854-1235** for other activities; www.daytonabeach. com. Mid-October.

Clearwater Jazz Holiday, Clearwater. Top jazz musicians play for 4 days and nights at bayfront Coachman Park in this free musical extravaganza. ☎ **727/461-0011.** Mid-October.

Columbus Day Regatta, Miami. Find anything that can float—from an inner tube to a 100-foot yacht— and you'll fit right in. Yes, there actually is a race, but how can you keep track when you're partying with a bunch of seminaked psychos in the middle of Biscayne Bay? It's free and it's wild. Rent a boat, jet ski, or sailboard to get up close. Be sure to secure a vessel early, though—everyone wants to be there. Check local newspapers for exact date and time. Columbus Day weekend.

Halloween Horror Nights, Orlando. Universal Studios transforms its grounds for 19 nights into haunted attractions with live bands, a psychopath's maze, special shows, and hundreds of ghouls and goblins roaming the streets. The studio closes at dusk, reopening in a new macabre form at 7pm. Full admission is charged for the event, which is geared toward adults. ☎ **800/ 837-2273** or 407/363-8000; www. universalorlando.com. Mid-October through Halloween.

Mickey's Not-So-Scary Halloween Party, Orlando. At Walt Disney World, guests are invited to trick or treat in the Magic Kingdom, starting at 7pm. The party includes parades, storytelling, live music, and a bewitching fireworks display. Call ☎ 407/934-7639 for information;www.disneyworld. com. End of October.

Guavaween, Tampa. Ybor City's Latin-style Halloween celebration begins with the "Mama Guava Stumble," a wacky costume parade. All-night concerts from rock to reggae. ☎ 813/248-3712; www. visittampabay.com. October 31.

John's Pass Seafood Festival, Madeira Beach. Tons of fish, shrimp, crab, and other seafood go down the hatch at one of Florida's largest seafood festivals. ☎ 727/391-7373; www.gulfbeaches-tampabay.com. Last weekend in October.

Fantasy Fest, Key West. Mardi Gras takes a Florida holiday as the streets of Key West are overtaken by wildly costumed revelers who have no shame and no parental guidance. Definitely leave the kids at home and join the parade! Call ☎ 305/296-1817. Last week of October.

Jacksonville Jazz Festival. This free weeklong, nonstop music event in Metropolitan Park features major artists. 𝒞 **904/353-7770**; www. jaxcvb.com. Late October or early November.

November

Frank Brown International Song-writers' Festival, Pensacola. Composers gather at the infamous Flora-Bama Lounge and other beach venues to perform their country-music hits. 𝒞 **850/492-7664.** First week in November.

Florida Seafood Festival, Apalachicola. Book a room at the Gibson Inn 5 years in advance of this huge chow-down in Florida's oystering capital. 𝒞 **850/653-9419;** www.baynavigator.com. First Saturday in November.

The Walt Disney World Festival of the Masters, Orlando. One of the largest art shows in the South takes place at Downtown Disney Market-place over 3 days. The exhibition features top artists, photographers, and craftspeople, all winners of juried shows throughout the country. Free admission. 𝒞 **407/824-4321;** www.disneyworld.com. Second weekend in November.

Miami Bookfair International, downtown Miami. Bibliophiles, literati, and some of the world's most prolific authors descend upon downtown Miami for a weeklong homage to the written word in what happens to be the largest book fair in the U.S. The weekend street fair draws the biggest crowds: Regular folk mix with wordsmiths such as Tom Wolfe and Jane Smiley while indulging in snacks, antique books, and literary gossip. All lectures are free, but fill up quickly, so get there early. Call 𝒞**305/237-3258** for lecture schedules. Mid-November.

Daytona Beach Fall Speedway Spectacular. Featuring the Annual Turkey Rod Run, this is the Southeast's largest combined car show and swap meet, with thousands of street rods and classic vehicles on display and for sale. It takes place at the International Speedway. 𝒞 **904/255-7355;** www. daytonabeach.com. Thanksgiving weekend.

Blue Angels Homecoming Air Show, Pensacola. World-famous navy pilots do their aerial acrobatics just 100 yards off the beach. 𝒞 **850/452-2311;** www.visitpensacola.com. Second weekend in November.

Fort Myers Beach Sand Sculpting Contest, Fort Myers Beach. Some 50,000 gather to sculpt or see the world's finest sand castles. 𝒞 **800/782-9283** or 941/463-6451; www. fmbchamber.com. First weekend in November.

White Party Week, Miami. This weeklong series of parties to benefit AIDS research is built around the main event, the White Party, which takes place at Villa Vizcaya and sells out as early as a year in advance. Philanthropists and celebrities such as Calvin Klein and David Geffen join thousands of white-clad, mainly gay men (and some women) in what has become one of the world's hottest (and hardest-to-score) tickets. Call 𝒞 **305/667-9296** or visit www.whitepartyweek. com for a schedule of parties and events. Thanksgiving week.

Epcot International Food & Wine Festival, Orlando. Sip and savor the food and wines of 30 cultures. Events include wine tastings, seminars, and celebrity-chef cooking demonstrations. Call 𝒞 **407/827-7200** or 407/824-4321 for ticket information.

December

Edison/Ford Winter Homes Holiday House, Fort Myers. Christmas music and thousands of lights hail the holiday season. At the same time, candles create a spectacular Luminary Trail along the full length of Sanibel Island's Periwinkle Way. ☎ **800/237-6444** or 941/338-3500; www.leeislandcoast.com. First week of December.

Captiva Sea Kayak Classic, Captiva Island. Sea kayaker and surf skiers from around the nation depart from the beach in front of 'Tween Waters Inn for a series of races. ☎ **941/472-5161;** www.sanibel-captiva.org. First weekend in December.

Christmas at Walt Disney World, Orlando. As you would imagine, all of the Disney properties get into the holiday spirit. In the Magic Kingdom, Main Street is lavishly decked out with lights and holly and an 80-foot glistening tree. Attend Mickey's Very Merry Christmas Party in the Magic Kingdom, and Holidays Around the World and the Candlelight Procession at Epcot. Call ☎ **407/824-4321** for holiday events, ☎ **407/934-7639** for special travel packages, or visit www.disney.com. Throughout December.

British Night Watch & Grand Illumination Ceremony, St. Augustine. Torchlight procession through the Spanish Quarter kicks off a month of Christmas festivities and the "Nights of Lights," in which 1.25 million twinkling bulbs bathe the Old City. ☎ **800/OLD-CITY;** www.visitoldcity.com. First Saturday in December; Nights of Lights to January 31.

The Citrus Bowl Parade, Orlando. This parade features lavish floats and high school bands in a nationally televised event. Reserved seats are $12, but you can watch along the route in downtown Orlando free. ☎ **800/297-2695** or 407/423-2476. Late December.

Winterfest Boat Parade, Ft. Lauderdale. People who complain that the holiday season isn't as festive in South Florida as it is in colder parts of the world haven't been to this spectacular boat parade along the Intracoastal Waterways. Boats decked out in magnificent holiday regalia gracefully—and boastfully—glide up and down the water as if it were a sheet of ice. If you're not on a boat, the best views are from waterfront restaurants or anywhere you can squeeze in along the water. ☎ **954/767-0686.** Late December.

4 Health & Insurance

STAYING HEALTHY

Florida doesn't present any unusual health hazards for most people. Folks with certain medical conditions such as liver disease, diabetes, and stomach ailments, however, should avoid eating raw **oysters,** which can carry a natural bacterium linked to severe diarrhea, vomiting, and even fatal blood poisoning. Cooking kills the bacteria, so, if in doubt, order your oysters steamed, broiled, or fried.

Florida has millions of **mosquitoes** and invisible biting **sand flies** (known as "no-see-ums"), especially in the coastal and marshy areas. Fortunately, neither insect carries malaria or other diseases. Keep these pests at bay with a good insect repellent.

It's especially important to protect yourself against **sunburn.** Don't underestimate the strength of the sun's rays down here, even in the middle of winter. Limit your exposure to the sun, especially during the first few days of your trip and, thereafter, from 11am to 2pm. Use a sunscreen with a high protection factor and apply it liberally. Remember that children need more protection than adults do.

Pack in your carry-on luggage any **prescription medications** you need to take. Also bring along copies of your prescriptions in case you lose your pills or run out.

If you suffer from a chronic illness, consult your doctor before your departure. For conditions like epilepsy, diabetes, or heart problems, wear a **Medic Alert Identification Tag** (✆ **800/825-3785;** www.medicalert.org), which will immediately alert doctors to your condition and give them access to your records through Medic Alert's 24-hour hotline. Membership is $35, plus a $15 annual fee. If you have dental problems, a nationwide referral service known as **1-800-DENTIST** (✆ **800/336-8478**) will provide the name of a nearby dentist or clinic.

If you do get sick, you may want to ask the concierge at your hotel to recommend a local doctor—perhaps his or her own. This will probably yield a better recommendation than any 800-number would. If you can't find a doctor who can help you right away, try the emergency room at the local hospital. Many emergency rooms have walk-in clinics for emergency cases that are not life threatening. You may not get immediate attention, but you won't pay the high price of an emergency-room visit, which is usually a minimum of $300 just for signing your name, on top of whatever treatment you receive.

INSURANCE

Many travelers buy insurance policies providing health and accident, trip-cancellation and -interruption, and lost-luggage protection. The coverage you should consider will depend on how you're getting to Florida and how much protection is already contained in your existing health insurance or other policies. Some credit- and charge-card companies may insure you against travel accidents if you buy plane, train, or bus tickets with their cards. Before purchasing additional insurance, read your policies and agreements carefully. Call your insurers or credit/charge-card companies if you have any questions.

Among the reputable issuers of travel insurance are **Access America** (✆ **800/284-8300;** www.worldaccess. com); **Travel Guard International** (✆ **800/826-1300;** www.travelguard. com); **Travel Insured International, Inc.** (✆ **800/243-3174;** www. travelinsured.com); **Travelex Insurance Services** (✆ **888/457-4602;** www.travelex-insurance.com); and **Worldwide Assistance** (✆ **800/ 821-2828;** www.worldwideassistance. com or www.europ-assistance.com). Scuba divers can sign up with **Divers Alert Network** (DAN) (✆ **800/ 446-2671** or 919/684-2948; www. diversalertnetwork.org).

5 Tips for Travelers with Special Needs

FOR TRAVELERS WITH DIS-ABILITIES A disability shouldn't stop anyone from traveling. There are more resources out there than ever before. Here in Florida, for example, **Walt Disney World** and **Universal Studios** both assist guests with disabilities. Disney's many services are detailed in their *Guidebook for Guests with Disabilities.* Disney no longer mails copies prior to visits, but you can pick one up at Guest Services near the front entrance to the parks. Also, you can call ✆ **407/824-4321** if you have any questions. For information about Universal Studios, CityWalk, and Islands of Adventure, contact Universal Studios Escape, 1000 Universal Studios Dr., Orlando, FL 32816 (✆ **407/393-8080**).

Nationwide, *A World of Options,* a 658-page book of resources for disabled travelers, covers everything from biking trips to scuba outfitters. It costs

$35 ($30 for members) and is available from **Mobility International USA,** P.O. Box 10767, Eugene, OR 97440 (© **541/343-1284,** voice and TDD; www.miusa.org). Annual membership for Mobility International is $35, which includes their quarterly newsletter, *Over the Rainbow.* **The Moss Rehab Hospital** (© **215/456-9600**) has been providing friendly and helpful phone advice and referrals to disabled travelers for years through its **Travel Information Service** (© **215/456-9603;** www.mossresourcenet.org).

You can join **The Society for the Advancement of Travel for the Handicapped** (SATH), 347 Fifth Ave., Suite 610, New York, NY 10016 (© **212/447-7284;** fax 212-725-8253; www.sath.org), for $45 annually, $30 for seniors and students, to gain access to their vast network of connections in the travel industry. They provide information sheets on travel destinations, and referrals to tour operators that specialize in traveling with disabilities. Their quarterly magazine, *Open World for Disability and Mature Travel,* is full of good information and resources.

Many of the major car-rental companies now offer hand-controlled cars for drivers with disabilities. In more than 100 cities across the U.S., **Wheelchair Getaways** (© **800/873-4973;** www.blvd.com/wg.htm) rents specialized vans with wheelchair lifts and other features.

Travelers with disabilities may also want to consider joining a tour that caters specifically to them. One of the best operators is **Flying Wheels Travel,** 143 W. Bridge (P.O. Box 382), Owatonna, MN 55060 (© **800/535-6790;** www.flyingwheelstravel.com). They offer various escorted tours and cruises, with an emphasis on sports, as well as private tours in minivans with lifts. Other reputable specialized tour operators include **Access Adventures**

(© **716/889-9096;** www.melwood.com/camp/accessadv.htm), which offers sports-related vacations; **Accessible Journeys** (© **800/TINGLES** or 610/521-0339), for slow walkers and wheelchair travelers; **The Guided Tour, Inc.** (© **215/782-1370**); **Wilderness Inquiry** (© **800/728-0719** or 612/379-3858); and **Directions Unlimited** (© **800/533-5343**).

You can obtain a copy of *Air Transportation of Handicapped Persons* by writing to Free Advisory Circular No. AC12032, Distribution Unit, U.S. Department of Transportation, Publications Division, M-4332, Washington, DC 20590. You can download a copy at www.dot.gov (search the site for "handicapped persons").

In addition, both **Amtrak** (© **800/USA-RAIL;** www.amtrak.com) and **Greyhound** (© **800/752-4841;** www.greyhound.com) offer special fares and services for those with disabilities. Call at least a week in advance of your trip for details.

The National Park Service issues free "Golden Access Passports," which entitle people with disabilities and a guest of their choice to free admission into national parks, forests, and wildlife refuges. Get the passports at park entrances.

Vision-impaired travelers should contact the **American Foundation for the Blind,** 11 Penn Plaza, Suite 300, New York, NY 10001 (© **800/232-5463;** www.afb.org), for information on traveling with Seeing Eye dogs.

FOR SENIORS   With one of the largest retired populations of any state, Florida offers a wide array of activities and benefits for senior citizens. Don't be shy about asking for discounts, but always carry some kind of identification, such as a driver's license, that shows your date of birth.

Also, mention the fact that you're a senior citizen when you first make your travel reservations. For example, both **Amtrak** (© **800/USA-RAIL;** www.amtrak.com) and **Greyhound** (© **800/752-4841;** www.greyhound. com) offer discounts to persons over 62. And many hotels offer seniors discounts, including the **Choice Hotels** (www.hotelchoice.com), which operates the Clarion Hotels, Quality Inns, Comfort Inns, Sleep Inns, Econo Lodges, Friendship Inns, and Rodeway Inns. They give 30% off their published rates to anyone over 50, provided you book your room through their nationwide toll-free reservations numbers (that is, not directly with the hotels or through a travel agent).

Members of the **AARP,** 601 E St. NW, Washington, DC 22049 (© **800/ 424-3410** or 202/434-2277; www. aarp.com), formerly the American Association of Retired Persons, get discounts not only on hotels but also on airfares and car rentals too.

Other helpful organizations include the not-for-profit **National Council of Senior Citizens,** 8403 Colesville Rd., Suite 1200, Silver Spring, MD 20910 (© **301/578-8800;** www. ncscinc.org), which offers a newsletter six times a year (partly devoted to travel tips) and discounts on hotel and auto rentals. **Golden Companions,** P.O. Box 5249, Reno, NV 89513 (© **775/324-2227**), helps travelers 45-plus find compatible companions through a personal voice-mail service. Contact them for more information.

Companies specializing in seniors' travel include **Grand Circle Travel,** 347 Congress St., Suite 3A, Boston, MA 02210 (© **800/221-2610** or 617/350-7500; www.gct.com), and **SAGA International Holidays,** 222 Berkeley St., Boston, MA 02115 (© **800/343-0273;** www.sagaholidays. com).

If you want something more than the average vacation or guided tour, try **Elderhostel,** 75 Federal St., Boston, MA 02110-1941 (© **877/426-8056;** www.elderhostel.org). On Elderhostel's escorted tours, the days are packed with seminars, lectures, and field trips; sightseeing tours are led by academic experts. They're not luxury vacations, but they're fun and fulfilling.

FOR FAMILIES   Florida is a great family destination, with most of its hotels and restaurants willing and eager to cater to families traveling with children. Many hotels and motels let children 17 and under stay free in their parents' room (be sure to ask when you reserve).

At the beaches, it's the exception rather than the rule for a resort not to have a children's activities program (some will even mind the youngsters while the parents enjoy a night off!). Even if they don't have a children's program of their own, most will arrange baby-sitting services.

If you call ahead before dining out, you'll see that most restaurants have some facilities for children, such as booster chairs and low-priced kids' menus.

Family Travel Times is published six times a year by **TWYCH** (Travel With Your Children; © **888/822- 4388** or 212/477-5524; www.familytraveltimes.com) and includes a weekly call-in service for subscribers. Subscriptions are $40 a year for quarterly editions. Ask for a free publication list and a sample issue when you call.

FOR GAY & LESBIAN TRAVELERS Florida is not without its intolerant contingent, but there are active gay and lesbian groups in most cities here. In fact, the editors of *Out and About,* a gay and lesbian newsletter, have described Miami's **South Beach** as the "hippest, hottest, most happening gay travel destination in the world." For many years that could also be said of **Key West,** which still is one of the country's most popular destinations for gays. **Fort Lauderdale**—where gays own more than 20 motels, 40 bars, and numerous other businesses—is definitely on the gay-friendly map.

The popularity of **Orlando** with gay and lesbian travelers is highlighted with Gay Weekend in early June, which draws as many as 40,000 participants and includes events at Disney World, Universal Studios, and SeaWorld. You can get information on the event at **www.gayday.com. Universal City Travel** (© **800/224-3838**) offers a "Gay Weekend" tour package including tickets to Universal Studios, SeaWorld, and Church Street Station. For information about events for that weekend, or throughout the year, contact the **Gay, Lesbian & Bisexual Community Services of Central Florida,** 934 N. Mills Ave., Orlando, FL 32803 (© **407/425-4527** or 407/843-4297; www.glbcc. org). Welcome packets usually include the latest issue of the *Triangle,* a quarterly newsletter (© **407/849-0099**) dedicated to gay and lesbian issues, and a calendar of events pertaining to the gay and lesbian community. Although not a tourist-specific packet, it includes information and ads for the area's gay and lesbian clubs.

Watermark, P.O. Box 533655, Orlando, FL 32853 (© **407/481-2243;** fax 407/481-2246; www. watermarkonline.com), is a biweekly tabloid newspaper covering the gay and lesbian scene, including dining and entertainment options, in Orlando, the Tampa Bay area, and Daytona Beach.

In addition to its editor's choices, *Out and About,* 8 W. 19th St., #401, New York, NY 10011 (© **800/929-2268** or 212/645-6922; www. outandabout.com), offers guidebooks and a monthly newsletter packed with good information on the global gay and lesbian scene. *Our World,* 1104 N. Nova Rd., Suite 251, Daytona Beach, FL 32117 (© **904/441-5367;** www.ourworldmag.com), is a slicker monthly magazine promoting and highlighting travel bargains and opportunities.

There are also two good biannual English-language gay guidebooks, both focused on gay men but including information for lesbians as well. You can get the *Spartacus International Gay Guide* and *Odysseus* on www. amazon.com and from most gay and lesbian bookstores, including Philadelphia's Giovanni's Room (© **215/923-2960;** www.giovannisroom.com) and A Different Light Bookstore (© **800/343-4002,** 415/431-0891, or 310/854-6601; www.adlbooks.com) with stores in San Francisco and West Hollywood, California. Both lesbians and gays might want to pick up a copy of *Gay Travel A to Z* ($16). **The Ferrari Guides** (www.q-net.com) is yet another very good series of gay and lesbian guidebooks.

The **International Gay & Lesbian Travel Association** (IGLTA) (© **800/448-8550** or 954/776-2626; fax 954/776-3303; www.iglta.org) connects travelers with the appropriate gay-friendly service organization or tour specialist. With around 1,200 members, it offers quarterly newsletters, marketing mailings, and a membership directory that's updated quarterly. Membership often includes gay or lesbian businesses, but it's open to individuals for $150 yearly, plus a $100 administration fee for new members. Members are kept informed of gay and gay-friendly hoteliers, tour operators, and airline and cruise-line representatives. Contact the IGLTA for a list of member agencies, who will be tied into IGLTA's information resources.

General gay and lesbian travel agencies include **Family Abroad** (© **800/999-5500** or 212/459-1800; gay and lesbian); **Above and Beyond Tours** (© **800/397-2681;** mainly gay men); and **Yellowbrick Road** (© **800/642-2488;** gay and lesbian).

6 Getting There

BY PLANE

Most major domestic airlines fly to and from many Florida cities. Choose from **American** (© **800/433-7300;** www.im.aa.com), **Continental** (© **800/525-0280;** www. continental. com), **Delta** (© **800/221-1212;** www.delta.com), **Northwest/KLM** (© **800/225-2525;** www.nwa.com), **TWA** (© **800/221-2000;** www.twa. com), **United** (© **800/241-6522;** www.united.com), and **US Airways** (© **800/428-4322;** www.usairways. com).

Of these, Delta and US Airways have the most extensive network of commuter connections within Florida (see "Getting Around," later in this chapter).

Several so-called no-frills airlines— low fares but few if any amenities—fly to Florida. The biggest and best is **Southwest Airlines** (© **800/435-9792;** www.southwest.com), which has flights from many U.S. cities to Fort Lauderdale, Jacksonville, Orlando, and Tampa.

Others flying to Florida include **AirTran** (© **800/AIR-TRAN;** www. airtran); **American Trans Air** (© **800/435-9282;** www.ata.com); **Carnival Air** (© **800/824-7386**), an arm of the popular cruise line; **Delta Express,** a branch of Delta Airlines (© **800/325-5205;** www.delta. com); **Eastwind** (© **800/644-3592;** www.eastwindairlines.com); **JetBlue**

(© **800/538-2583;** www.jetblue. com); **MetroJet,** an arm of US Airways (© **800/888-638-7653;** www. flymetrojet.com); **Midway** (© **800/ 44-MIDWAY;** www.midwayair.com); **Midwest Express** (© **800/452-2022;** www.midwestexpress.com); **PanAm** (© **800/FLY-PANAM;** www.flypanam. com); **Pro Air** (© **800/477-6247;** www.proair.com); **Spirit** (© **800/722-7117;** www.spiritair.com); **SunJet** (© **800/478-6538;** www.sunjet.com); and **Vanguard** (© **800/826-4827;** www.flyvanguard.com).

Internet resources such as **Travelocity** (www.travelocity.com) and **Microsoft Expedia** (www.expedia. com) make it relatively easy to compare prices, and even purchase tickets. See "Planning Your Trip Online," later in this chapter.

FINDING THE BEST AIRFARE
There's no shortage of **discounted and promotional fares** to Florida. November, December, and January often see fare wars that can result in savings of 50% or more. Watch for advertisements in your local newspaper and on TV, call the airlines, or check out their websites (see "Planning Your Trip Online," later in this chapter).

If you call the airlines or a travel agent, ask for the lowest fares, and ask whether it's cheaper to book in advance, fly in midweek, or stay over a Saturday night. Don't stop at the 7-day advance purchase; ask how much

---

Tips Merger Mania

At press time, the U.S. Federal Aviation Administration was considering the merger of United Airlines and US Airways. Under the proposal, the two airlines would operate as one under the United Airlines banner, but some US Airways operations were to be spun off into DC Air, a new cut-rate carrier to be based in Washington, D.C. The FAA recently approved American Airlines' purchases of TWA. In other words, please don't blame us if the airlines mentioned in this book no longer exist when you're ready to fly to Florida.

the 14- and 30-day plans cost. Decide when you want to go before you call, since many of the best deals are nonrefundable.

No-frills airlines have reduced the attractiveness of **charter flights** to Florida, but some still go, especially during the winter season and particularly from Canada, such as **Air Transat** (✆ **800/470-1011**; www.airtransat.com) and **Canada 3000** (✆ **800/993-4378**; www.canada3000.com). They can cost less than regularly scheduled flights, but they are very complicated. It's best to ask a good travel agent to find one for you and to explain the disadvantages as well as the advantages.

Also known as bucket shops, **consolidators** are a good place to find low fares. Consolidators buy seats in bulk from the airlines and then sell them back to the public at prices below even the airlines' discounted rates. Their small boxed ads usually run in the Sunday travel section at the bottom of the page. Before you pay, however, ask for a confirmation number from the consolidator and then call the airline itself to confirm your seat. Be prepared to book your ticket with a different consolidator—there are many to choose from—if the airline can't confirm your reservation. Also be aware that bucket-shop tickets are usually nonrefundable or rigged with stiff change or cancellation penalties, often as high as 50% to 75% of the ticket price.

Among the consolidators, **Council Travel** (✆ **800/226-8624**; www.counciltravel.com) and **STA Travel** (✆ **800/781-4040**; www.statravel.com) cater especially to young travelers, but their bargain-basement prices are available to people of all ages. **Travel Bargains** (✆ **800/AIR-FARE**; www.1800airfare.com) was formerly owned by TWA but now offers the deepest discounts on many other airlines, with a 4-day advance purchase.

Other reliable consolidators include **MyTravelCo.com** (✆ **800/FLY-CHEAP** for airfares or **888/CRUISES** for cruises; www.mytravelco.com); **TFI Tours International** (✆ **800/745-8000** or 212/736-1140), which serves as a clearinghouse for unused seats; or "rebaters" such as **Travel Avenue** (✆ **800/333-3335** or 312/876-1116; www.travelavenue.com) and the **Smart Traveller** (✆ **800/448-3338** in the U.S. or 305/448-3338), which rebate part of their commissions to you.

Another possibility is a travel club such as **Moment's Notice** (✆ **718/234-6295**; www.moments-notice.com) or **Sears Discount Travel Club** (✆ **800/433-9383,** or 800/255-1487 to join), both of which supply unsold tickets at discounted prices. You pay an annual membership fee to get the club's hotline number. Of course, you're limited to what's available, so you have to be flexible. You may not even have to join these clubs to get the deals, however, since some airlines now unload unsold seats directly through their websites.

If you live overseas, see "Getting to & Around the U.S.," in chapter 3.

BY CAR

Florida is reached by **I-95** along the east coast, **I-75** from the Central states, and **I-10** from the west. **The Florida Turnpike,** a toll road, links Orlando, West Palm Beach, Fort Lauderdale, and Miami (it's a shortcut from Wildwood on I-75 north of Orlando to Miami). **I-4** cuts across the state from Cape Canaveral through Orlando to Tampa.

See "Getting Around," later in this chapter, for more information about driving in Florida and the car-rental firms operating here.

If you're a member, your local branch of the **American Automobile Association (AAA)** will provide a free trip-routing plan. AAA also has nationwide emergency road service for its members (© **800/AAA-HELP;** www.aaa.com).

BY TRAIN

Amtrak (© **800/USA-RAIL;** www. amtrak.com) offers train service to Florida from both the East and West Coasts. It takes some 26 hours from New York to Miami, 68 hours from Los Angeles to Miami, and Amtrak's fares aren't much less—if not more—than many of the airlines' lowest fares.

Amtrak's *Silver Meteor* and *Silver Star* both run twice daily between New York and either Miami or Tampa, with intermediate stops along the East Coast and in Florida. Amtrak has announced plans to begin stopping at St. Augustine, Daytona Beach, Titusville (Cape Canaveral), and Fort Pierce, but these stops had not been implemented at press time. Meantime, Amtrak's Thruway Bus Connections are available from the Fort Lauderdale Amtrak station and Miami International Airport to Key West; from Tampa to St. Petersburg, Treasure Island, Clearwater, Sarasota, Bradenton, and Fort Myers; and from Deland to Daytona Beach. From the West Coast, the *Sunset Limited* runs three times weekly between Los Angeles and Orlando. It stops in Pensacola, Crestview (north of Fort Walton Beach and Destin), Chipley (north of Panama City Beach), and Tallahassee. Sleeping accommodations are available for an extra charge.

If you intend to stop off along the way, you can save money with Amtrak's **Explore America** (or All Aboard America) fares, which are based on three regions of the country.

Amtrak's **Auto Train** runs daily from Lorton, Virginia (12 miles south of Washington, D.C.), to Sanford, Florida (just northeast of Orlando). You ride in a coach while your car is secured in an enclosed vehicle carrier. You should make your train reservations as far in advance as possible.

7 Escorted & Package Tours

More than 120 travel companies offer hundreds of package tour options to the Sunshine State. Quite often these deals will result in savings not just on airfares but on hotels and other activities as well. You pay one price for a package that varies from one tour operator to the next. Airfare, transfers, and accommodations are always covered, and sometimes meals and specific activities are thrown in.

Before you start your search for the lowest airfare, therefore, you may want to consider booking your flight as part of a travel package, such as an escorted tour or a package tour. What you lose in adventure, you could gain in time and money saved when you book accommodations, and maybe even food and entertainment, along with your flight—but not necessarily (see "Package Tours," below).

ESCORTED TOURS

Some people love escorted tours. They let you relax and take in the sights while a bus driver fights traffic for you and a guide explains what you're seeing. They spell out your costs up front, and they take you to the maximum number of sights in the minimum amount of time with the least amount of hassle.

In 1999, for example, the very reputable **Tauck Tours** (© **800/468-2825;** fax 203/221-6828; www.tauck.com) offered a 10-day, 9-night escorted tour beginning in Tampa and ending at Walt Disney World in Orlando. It included accommodations, most meals, bus transportation between the cities, most activities, and a guide, but not your airfare to join the tour in Tampa or to return home from Orlando. These "land" costs were about $2,500 to $2,665 per person, double occupancy ($3,500 if you traveled alone). The hotels were all top-end, so this was a good deal, especially during the high winter season in South Florida.

If you do choose an escorted tour, you should ask a lot of questions before you buy:

What is the **cancellation policy?** Is a deposit required? Can the tour company cancel the trip if they don't get enough people? Do you get a refund if they cancel? If you cancel? How late can you cancel if you are unable to go? When do you pay in full?

How busy is the **schedule?** How much sightseeing is planned for each day? Is ample time allowed for relaxing by the pool, shopping, or wandering?

What is the **size** of the group? The smaller the group, the more flexible the itinerary, and the less time you'll spend waiting for people to get on and off the bus. Tour operators may be evasive about this, because they may not know the exact size of the group until everybody has made reservations; but they should be able to give you a rough estimate. Some tours have a minimum group size and may cancel the tour if they don't book enough people.

What is included in the **price?** Don't assume anything. You may have to pay for transportation to and from the airport. A box lunch may be included in an excursion, but drinks might cost extra. Beer might be included, but wine might not. Can you opt out of certain activities, or does the bus leave once a day, with no exceptions? Are all your meals planned in advance? Can you choose your entree at dinner, or does everybody get the same chicken cutlet?

If you choose an escorted tour, think strongly about purchasing **travel insurance** from an independent agency, especially if the tour operator asks you to pay up front. (See "Health & Insurance," earlier in this chapter.)

One final caveat: Since escorted tour prices are based on double occupancy, the single traveler is usually penalized (see the Tauck Tours example cited above).

PACKAGE TOURS

Package tours are not the same thing as escorted tours. They are simply a way to buy airfare and accommodations at the same time. If you plan to spend your time at one destination, such as Walt Disney World and Orlando, they are a smart way to go. In many cases, a package that includes airfare, hotel, and transportation to and from the airport will cost you less than just the hotel alone would have, had you booked it yourself. That's because packages are sold in bulk to tour operators who resell them to the public at a cost that drastically undercuts standard rates.

In addition to these all-inclusive tours, many Florida hotels and resorts and even some motels offer **golf and tennis packages,** which bundle the cost of room, greens and court fees, and sometimes equipment into one price. These deals usually don't include airfare, but they do represent savings over paying for the room and golf or tennis separately. Saddlebrook Resort-Tampa (see section 1 in chapter 11) recently offered a 3-night wintertime spa-golf package for $486 per couple, including room, breakfast, two dinners, and 3 days of golf (with a cart) or 2 days of spa treatments. The resort regularly charges from $185 to $197 during winter just for a double room. See the accommodations sections in the following chapters for hostelries offering special packages to their guests.

Summer, early fall, and the first 3 weeks of December are good times to search for discounted deals in Southern Florida. For example, the Naples Beach Hotel & Golf Club in Naples (see section 5 in chapter 10) recently offered a bed-and-breakfast special for $99 to $124 a night per room, including a full breakfast buffet, during September and December. Regular autumn room rates range up to $235 double, without breakfast.

A few words of **caution** are in order.

First, given the propensity of discounted airfares to Florida, and the number of hotels here offering various room-and-activities packages, especially during the off-seasons, you could save just as much by making your own arrangements. This is particularly true if you're renting a car and don't need transportation from and to the airport, a cost often included in package plans.

Second, think twice before buying a package that includes meals. Many hotels include breakfasts in their rates anyway, as indicated at the top of the listings in this book. Florida has a multitude of good restaurants in all price ranges, and prepaying for a dinner package could mean shelling out twice if you decide to dine out.

Third, the least-expensive tours may put you up at a bottom-end hotel. And since the lower costs depend on volume, some more-expensive tours could send you to a large, impersonal property. And since the tour prices are based on double occupancy, the single traveler is almost invariably penalized.

Fourth, ask the same questions you would of an escorted tour operator (see above).

FINDING A PACKAGE OR ESCORTED TOUR

There are more package tours to Orlando than to the rest of Florida combined—so many that it can be a little confusing finding the one that's best for you, partly because each package seems to offer a different combination of services. Start by looking at the ads in your Sunday newspaper's travel section. See chapter 12, "Walt Disney World & Orlando" for specific tours to those destinations.

The major airlines package their flights to Florida together with accommodations. These include **America West Vacations** (© **800/356-6611;** www.americawest.com), **American Airlines Vacations** (© **800/321-2121;** fax 800/472-2987; www.aavacations.com), **Continental Airlines Vacations** (© **800/634-5555;** fax 954/357-4661; www.continental.com), **Delta Vacations** (© **800/367-9112;** fax 954/468-4765; www.deltavacations.com), **Midwest Express Vacations** (© **800/444-4479;** fax 414/351-5256; www.midwestexpressvac.com), **Northwest World Vacations** (© **800/727-1111;** fax 800/655-7890; www.nwaworldvacations.com), **Southwest Airlines Vacations** (© **800/524-6442;** fax 407/857-0232; www.southwest.com), and **US Airways Vacations** (© **800/455-0123;** www.usairwaysvacations.com).

Another option is the old, reliable **American Express Vacations** (© **800/241-1700;** fax 954/357-4682; www.americanexpress.com). Check out AmEx's Web travel page (http://travel.americanexpress.com) for last-minute travel bargains, deeply discounted vacation packages, and reduced airline fares. **Northwest Airlines** (www.nwa.com) posts "Cyber Saver Bargain Alerts" on its website weekly, offering special hotel rates, package deals, and discounted airline fares. See "Planning Your Trip Online" below, for more tips.

Liberty Travel (© **888/271-1584;** www.libertytravel.com) is one of the biggest packagers in the Northeastern states. It usually boasts a full-page ad in Sunday papers.

As noted above, many Florida hotels offer packages of their own, as do many of the national chains. If you already know where you want to stay, call the resort itself and ask about any land-and-air or other packages.

8 Planning Your Trip Online

It's possible to get some great deals on airfare, hotels, and car rentals via the Internet. Grab your mouse and surf before you take off—you could save a bundle on your trip. The websites highlighted below are worth checking out, especially since all services are free. Always check the lowest published fare, however, before you shop for flights online.

Arthur Frommer's Budget Travel (www.frommers.com) Home of the Encyclopedia of Travel and *Arthur Frommer's Budget Travel* magazine and daily newsletter, this site offers detailed information on 200 cities and islands around the world, and up-to-the-minute ways to save dramatically on flights, hotels, car reservations, and cruises.

Microsoft Expedia (www.expedia. com) The best part of this multi-purpose travel site is the "Fare Tracker." You fill out a form on the screen indicating that you're interested in cheap flights from your hometown, and, once a week, they'll e-mail you the best airfare deals on up to three destinations. The site's "Travel Agent" will steer you to bargains on hotels and car rentals, and with the help of hotel and airline seat pinpointers, you can book everything right on line. This site is even useful once you're booked. Before you depart, log on to Expedia for maps and up-to-date travel information, including weather reports and foreign exchange rates.

Travelocity (www.travelocity.com) This is one of the best travel sites out there, especially for finding cheap airfare. In addition to its "Personal Fare Watcher," which notifies you via e-mail of the lowest airfares for up to five different destinations, Travelocity will track the three lowest fares for any routes on any dates in minutes. You can book a flight right then and there, and if you need a rental car or hotel,

Travelocity will find you the best deal via the SABRE computer reservations system (another huge travel agent database). Click on "Last Minute Deals" for the latest travel bargains, including a link to "H.O.T. Coupons" (www.hotcoupons.com), where you can print out electronic coupons for travel in the U.S. and Canada.

The Trip (www.thetrip.com) This site is really geared toward the business traveler, but vacationers-to-be can also use The Trip's exceptionally powerful fare-finding engine, which will e-mail you every week with the best city-to-city airfare deals for as many as 10 routes. The Trip uses the Internet Travel Network, another reputable travel agent database, to book hotels and restaurants.

E-Savers Programs Several major airlines offer a free e-mail service known as E-Savers, via which they'll send you their best bargain airfares on a regular basis. Here's how it works: Once a week (usually Wednesday), or whenever a sale fare comes up, subscribers receive a list of discounted flights to and from various destinations, both international and domestic. Here's the catch: These fares are usually only available if you leave the very next Saturday (or sometimes Friday night) and return on the following Monday or Tuesday. It's really a service for the spontaneously inclined and travelers looking for a quick getaway. But the fares are cheap, so it's worth taking a look. If you have a preference for certain airlines (in other words, the ones you fly most frequently), sign up with them first.

Here's a partial list of airlines and their websites, where you can not only get on the e-mailing lists, but also book flights directly:

- **American Airlines:** www.im. aa.com
- **British Airways:** www.british-airways.com

- **Canadian Airlines International:** www.cdnair.ca
- **Continental Airlines:** www.continental.com
- **NorthwestAirlines:** www.nwa.com
- **TWA:** www.twa.com
- **United Airlines:** www.ual.com
- **US Airways:** www.usairways.com
- **Virgin Airways:** www.virgin-atlantic. com

One caveat: You'll get frequent-flier miles if you purchase one of these fares, but you can't use miles to buy the ticket.

Smarter Living (www.smarterliving. com) If the thought of all that surfing and comparison shopping gives you a headache, then head right for Smarter Living. Sign up for their newsletter service, and every week you'll get a customized e-mail summarizing the discount fares available from your departure city. Smarter Living tracks more than 15 different airlines, so it's a worthwhile time-saver.

TOP GENERAL SITES FOR FLORIDA

Following are some of the best websites for Florida and its major metropolitan regions. For specific attractions, you will find Web addresses throughout this book.

Beach Directory
www.beachdirectory.com
This guide to beaches along Florida's Gulf Coast includes a virtual tour, maps, recommendations from "Dr. Beach," and a guide to restaurants and lodgings.

FLA USA
www.flausa.com
A product of Florida's official tourism bureau, this extensive website includes information on attractions, beaches, golfing, and water sports, as well as airport information, weather, and maps. The beach guide is nicely organized by region, and there's advice

on Florida's natural attractions in the Activities section.

Florida Association of Convention and Visitors Bureaus
www.facvb.org
Links to more than a dozen bureaus throughout the state. Most of the sites include information on attractions, dining, lodging, and shopping.

Florida State Parks
www8.myflorida.com/communities/learn/st ateparks
Though the home page is awkwardly designed (this is a government site, after all), you can find parks by clicking on Parks Map or Park Index. From there you can learn about camping at each park, including information on fees, nearby attractions, and facilities.

See Florida
www.see-florida.com
A nicely organized guide to theme parks, marine attractions, museums, boating, fishing, and much more. See Florida includes guides to dozens of Florida cities and has advice for first-time visitors to the Sunshine State.

MIAMI
CitySearch: Miami
miami.citysearch.com
Reviews and listings for Miami arts and entertainment, restaurants, shopping, and attractions. Click on the calendar link for events recommended by the editors.

For AOL Members: Digital City South Florida
Keyword: South Florida
Entertainment, dining, sports, and festival listings produced in cooperation with the *Sun-Sentinel*.

Just Go: South Florida
www.justgo.com/southflorida
This site includes listings and reviews for dining, music, theater, and movies. Just Go does a nice job in spotlighting upcoming concerts and makes it easy to find restaurants by cuisine and neighborhood.

Miami Herald

www.herald.com

Miami's leading news source can give you a sense of what's going on in the city, but don't expect extensive entertainment listings.

Miami New Times

www.miaminewtimes.com

Miami's leading alternative weekly includes features and listings for music, theater, film, and more.

Sun-Sentinel: Showtime

www.sun-sentinel.com/showtime

A nice roundup of music, theater, sports, and dining choices for South Florida with coverage of local festivals and events. For hard news and weather, see **www.sun-sentinel.com**.

Time Out: Miami

www.timeout.com/miami

This site features reviews and listings for attractions, entertainment, restaurants, hotels, and shopping throughout the city. It also includes categories for kids and for gay/lesbian activities. Time Out is a lively guide with a youthful approach but has features for everyone.

Tropicool Miami (Miami Convention & Visitors Bureau)

www.miamiandbeaches.com

A nice site to get an overview of Miami and its beckoning beaches. The content is boosterish, but it's still informative.

WALT DISNEY WORLD & GREATER ORLANDO

For AOL Members: Digital City Orlando

Keyword: Orlando

Entertainment, dining, sports, and weather, produced in cooperation with the Orlando Sentinel.

Go2Orlando

www.go2orlando.com

Detailed practical information on attractions, dining, lodging, shopping, beaches, and recreation. Produced in conjunction with the Orlando Sentinel, Go2Orlando is a clean, well-organized place to browse. Planning tools include restaurant and hotel searches by area and price.

Orlando.com Vacation Guide

www.orlando.com/vacation

A well-organized roundup of attractions, events, and tips for planning your Orlando vacation. You'll also find dining, shopping, and lodging guides and can book a room through the site. Other sections cover nightlife, kids' activities, and outdoor recreation.

Orlando Sentinel

www.orlandosentinel.com

Everything you'd expect from a big-city newspaper—the online calendar, which includes listings for the arts, dining, attractions, and sports, is especially useful for visitors.

Orlando Weekly

www.orlandoweekly.com

Cutting-edge reviews and recommendations for arts, movies, music, and much more from Orlando's alternative weekly newspaper.

TAMPA & ST. PETERSBURG

City of St. Petersburg

www.stpete.org

A city roundup of what's going on in St. Pete. Though it's intended primarily for locals, the site has a nice calendar of events.

St. Petersburg Times

www.sptimes.com

Click on the A-Z Index, which lists arts, entertainment, and local activities, such as a guide to baseball spring training.

Tampa Bay CitySearch

www.tampabay.citysearch.com

Reviews and listings for arts and entertainment, restaurants, shopping, and attractions. Click on the calendar for events recommended by the editors.

Tampa Bay Online: Dining

tampabayonline.net/dining

Honest reviews from the *Tampa Bay Tribune* and suggestions for budget dining, defined as restaurants where two people can eat for under $20. There's also a search box that helps you find restaurants near your hotel.

Tampa Bay Online: Entertainment
http://tampabayonline.net/getalife

Peruse critics' picks for music, movies, and the arts. Search music listings based on type of club or type of music.

Tampa Tribune
www.tampatrib.com

Get up-to-date on happenings around town—entertainment links are at the bottom of the page.

KEY WEST
Discover: Key West
http://key-west.com

A well rounded guide to Key West, including an events calendar and extensive listings for attractions, sight-seeing and eco-tours, theater, and art galleries. You'll also find a dining guide, lodging options, and sections on fishing and shopping.

Gay Key West Travel Guide
www.gaykeywestfl.com

A guide to gay-friendly lodgings, restaurants, and clubs.

9 Getting Around

Having a car is the best and easiest way to see Florida's sights, or just to get to and from the beach. Public transportation is available only in the cities and larger towns, and even there it may provide infrequent or even inadequate service. When it comes to getting from one city to another, cars and planes are the ways to go.

BY PLANE

The commuter arms of **Continental** (© 800/525-0280; www.continental.com), **Delta** (© 800/221-1212; www.delta.com), and **US Airways** (© 800/428-4322; www.usair.com) provide extensive service between Florida's major cities and towns. Fares for these short hops tend to be reasonable.

Cape Air (© 800/352-0714; www.flycapeair.com) flies between Key West, Fort Myers, and Naples, which means you can avoid backtracking to Miami from Key West if you're touring the state. (You can also take a boat between Key West and Fort Myers Beach, Naples, or Marco Island during the winter months; see the introduction to chapter 10.)

BY CAR

Jacksonville is about 350 miles north of Miami and 500 miles north of Key West, so don't underestimate how long it will take you to drive all the way down the state. The speed limit is either 65 miles per hour or 70 miles per hour on the rural interstate highways, so you can make good time between cities. Not so on U.S. 1, U.S. 17, U.S. 19, U.S. 41, and U.S. 301; although most have four lanes, these older highways tend to be heavily congested, especially in built-up areas.

Every major car-rental company is represented here, including **Alamo** (© 800/327-9633; www.goalamo.com), **Avis** (© 800/331-1212; www.avis.com), **Budget** (© 800/527-0700; www.budgetrentacar.com), **Dollar** (© 800/800-4000; www.dollarcar.com), **Enterprise** (© 800/325-8007; pickenterprise.com), **Hertz** (© 800/654-3131; www.hertz.com), **National** (© 800/227-7368; www.nationalcar.com), and **Thrifty** (© 800/367-2277; www.thrifty.com).

If you decide to rent a car, shop around and ask a lot of questions. Reservations clerks are used to being asked for the lowest rate available, and most will find it in order to get your business. You may have to try different dates, different pickup and drop-off points, and different discount offers to find the best deal. It changes constantly. Also, if you're a member of any organization (AARP or AAA, for

Florida Driving Times & Distances

Boldface numbers *indicate distances in miles*
Lightface numbers *indicate driving times*

example), be sure to ask if you're entitled to discounts. It's not widely known, but members of **Costco Wholesale** stores get hefty discounts at Alamo (use ID number 472074 or A1 for weekends), Avis (ID number A108300), and Dollar (ID number PC5005).

Check the rental firms' websites. Most will automatically bring up the lowest available rate, and there are boxes to click if you are an association member or have a discount coupon or ID number. You can comparison shop on Internet sites such as **Travelocity** (www.travelocity.com) and **Microsoft Expedia** (www.expedia.com), which will make reservations for you once you've found the best deal.

State and local **taxes** will add as much as 20% to your final bill. You'll pay an additional $2.05 per day in statewide use tax, and local sales taxes will tack on at least 6% to the total, including the statewide use tax (the state is being sued over this tax-on-a-tax practice). Some airports add another 35¢ per day and as much as 10% in "recovery" fees. You can avoid the recovery fee by picking up your car in town rather than at the airport. Budget and Enterprise both have numerous rental locations away from the airports. But be sure to weigh the cost of transportation to and from your hotel against the amount of the fee.

Most of the companies pad their profits by selling **Loss/Damage Waiver** (LDW) insurance at $15 or more per day. Your automobile insurance carrier and credit-card companies may already provide coverage, so check with them before wasting your money on something you don't need.

Also, the rental companies will offer to refill your **gas** tank at "competitive" prices per gallon when you return. Regular gas is always less expensive in town, so fill up your vehicle on the way back to the airport.

Competition is so fierce among Florida rental firms that most have now stopped charging **drop-off fees** if you pick up a car at one place and leave it at another. For example, I recently picked up a car at Tampa and dropped it off at Fort Myers for the same price I would have paid had I returned it to Tampa. Be sure to ask if there's a drop-off fee.

You must have a **valid credit card** (not a debit or check card) in your name, and most companies require you to be at least 25 years old to rent a car. Some also set maximum ages and may deny cars to anyone with a bad driving record. Ask about rental requirements and restrictions when you book in order to avoid problems later.

Some packages are available that include airfare, accommodations, and a rental car with unlimited mileage. Compare these prices with the cost of booking airline tickets and renting a car separately to see if these offers are good deals.

BY TRAIN

You'll find that train travel isn't terribly feasible within Florida, and it's not much less expensive than flying, if at all. See "Getting There," earlier in this chapter, for Florida towns served by **Amtrak** (© **800/USA-RAIL;** www.amtrak.com).

10 The Active Vacation Planner

Bird watching, boating and sailing, camping, canoeing and kayaking, fishing, golfing, tennis—you name it, the Sunshine State has it. In fact, you'll find these activities almost everywhere you go. Of course, beach lovers and water-sports enthusiasts can indulge their passions almost anywhere along the state's lengthy coastlines. Merely head east or west, and you'll easily find plenty to do—or viewed another way, Florida's multitudinous water-sports operators will find you.

These and other activities are described in the outdoor activities sections of the following chapters, but here's a brief overview of some of the best places to move your muscles, with tips on how to get more detailed information.

The **Florida Sports Foundation,** 2964 Wellington Circle N., Tallahassee, FL 32308 (© **850/488-8347;** fax 850/922-0482; www.flasports.com),

publishes free brochures, calendars, schedules, and guides to outdoor pursuits and spectator sports throughout Florida. I've noted some of its specific publications in the sections below.

For excellent color maps of state parks, campgrounds, canoe trails, aquatic preserves, caverns, and more, contact the **Florida Department of Environmental Protection,** Office of Communications, 3900 Commonwealth Blvd., Tallahassee, FL 32399 (© **850/488-2960;** www.dep.state.fl.us). Some of the department's publications are mentioned below.

ACTIVITIES A TO Z
BIKING & IN-LINE SKATING

Florida's relatively flat terrain makes it ideal for riding bikes and in-line skating. You can bike right into the **Everglades National Park** along the 38-mile-long Main Park Road, for example, and bike or skate from St. Petersburg to Tarpon Springs on the

47-mile-long converted railroad bed known as the **Pinellas Trail.** Many towns and cities have designated routes for cyclists, skaters, joggers, and walkers, such as the paved pathways running the length of Sanibel Island, the lovely Bayshore Boulevard in **Tampa,** and the bike lanes from downtown **Sarasota** out to St. Armands, Lido, and Longboat Keys. We've detailed all the many options in the following chapters.

BIRD WATCHING With hundreds of both land- and sea-based species, Florida is one of America's best places for bird watching-if you're not careful, pelicans will even steal your picnic lunch on the historic **Naples Pier.** The **J. N. "Ding" Darling National Wildlife Refuge** is great for watching, and it shares Sanibel Island with luxury resorts and fine restaurants.

With its northeast Florida section now open, the **Great Florida Birding Trail** will eventually cover some 2,000 miles throughout the state. Fort Clinch State Park on Amelia Island and Merritt Island National Wildlife Refuge in Cape Canaveral are gateways to the northeast trail. Information is available from the Birding Trail Coordinator, Florida Fish & Wildlife Conservation Commission, 620 S. Meridian St., Tallahassee, FL 32399-1600 (© **850/922-0664**; fax 850/488-1961; www.floridabirdingtrail.com). You can download trail maps from the website.

The Florida Audubon Society manages four exceptional sites: Corkscrew Swamp Sanctuary near Naples, Madalyn Baldwin Center for Birds of Prey in Maitland, Turkey Creek Wildlife Sanctuary in Palm Bay, and Sabal Point Wildlife Sanctuary on the Wekiva River in Central Florida.

Many of the state's wildlife preserves have gift shops that carry books about Florida's birds, including the *Florida Wildlife Viewing Guide,* in which authors Susan Cerulean and Ann Morrow profile 96 great parks, refuges, and preserves throughout the state. The guide is also available directly from the publisher, Falcon Press, at © **800/582-2665.**

BOATING & SAILING With some 1,350 miles of shoreline, it's not surprising that Florida is a boating and sailing mecca. In fact, you won't be anyplace near the water very long before you see flyers and other advertisements for rental boats and for cruises on sailboats. Many of them are mentioned in the following chapters.

The Moorings, the worldwide sailboat charter company, has its headquarters in Clearwater and its Florida yacht base nearby in St. Petersburg (© **800/437-7880** or 813/530-5424; www.moorings.com). From St. Pete, experienced sailors can take its bareboats as far as the Keys and the Dry Tortugas, out in the Gulf of Mexico.

Key West keeps gaining prominence as a world sailing capital. *Yachting* magazine sponsors the largest winter regatta in America here each January, and smaller events take place regularly.

Even if you've never hauled on a halyard, you can learn the art of sailing at **Steve and Doris Colgate's Offshore Sailing School,** headquartered at the South Seas Plantation Resort & Yacht Harbour on Captiva Island, with an outpost in St. Petersburg. The prestigious **Annapolis Sailing** has bases in St. Petersburg and on Marathon in the Keys.

The free *Florida Boating & Fishing* has tips about safe boating in the state, available from the **Florida Sports Foundation** (see the introduction to this section, above), is a treasure trove of regulations; locations of marinas, hotels, and resorts; marine products and services; and more, in magazine format.

CAMPING   Florida is literally dotted with RV parks (if you own such a vehicle, it's the least-expensive way to spend your winters here). But for the best tent camping, look to Florida's national preserves and 110 state parks and recreation areas. Options range from luxury sites with hot-water showers and cable TV hookups to primitive island and beach camping with no facilities whatsoever.

Regular and primitive camping in **St. George Island State Park** near Apalachicola, in fact, is a birdwatcher's dream, and you'll be on one of the nation's most magnificent beaches. Equally great are the sands at **St. Andrews State Park** in Panama City Beach (with sites right beside the bay). Other top spots are **Fort DeSoto Park** in St. Pete Beach (more gorgeous bay-side sites), the remarkably preserved **Cayo Costa Island State Park** between Boca Grande and Captiva Island in Southwest Florida, **Canaveral National Seashore** near the Kennedy Space Center, **Anastasia State Park** in St. Augustine, **Fort Clinch State Park** on Amelia Island, and **Bill Baggs Cape Florida Recreation Area** on Key Biscayne in Miami. Down in the Keys, the ocean-side sites in **Long Key State Recreation Area** are about as nice it gets.

Many sites are accessible only by boat, such as the "chickee" huts (round, square, or rectangular thatch or tin roofs supported by poles, with open sides) on stilts in Everglades National Park and the backcountry sites in **Collier Seminole State Park** near Marco Island.

These are all popular campgrounds, so reservations are essential, especially in the high seasons. All of Florida's state parks take bookings up to 11 months in advance.

The **Florida Department of Environmental Protection,** Division of Recreation and Parks, Mail Station 535, 3900 Commonwealth Blvd., Tallahassee, FL 32399-3000 (© **850/ 488-2960;** www.dep.state.fl.us), publishes an annual guide of tent and RV sites in Florida's state parks and recreation areas.

Pet owners note: Pets are permitted at some—but not all—state park beaches, campgrounds, and food service areas. Before bringing your animal, check with the department or with the individual parks to see if your pet will be allowed. And bring your rabies certificate, which is required.

For private campgrounds, the **Florida Association of RV Parks & Campgrounds,** 1340 Vickers Dr., Tallahassee, FL 32303 (© **850/562- 7151;** fax 850/562-7179; www. floridacamping.com), issues an annual *Camp Florida* directory with locator maps and details about its member establishments throughout the state.

CANOEING   &   KAYAKING
Canoers and kayakers have almost limitless options here: picturesque rivers,

---

Tips **Changes Afoot**

At press time, Governor Jeb Bush was pushing to raise the entrance and camping fees at Florida's state parks and recreation areas. Accordingly, it's a good idea to contact the department, or each park directly, to find out what you'll have to pay to use these magnificent facilities. On the Web, you can try clicking onto www8.myflorida.com/communities/learn/ stateparks/information/fees.html for statewide admission and camping fees. Also at press time, the Division of Recreation and Parks' website was being incorporated into www.myflorida.com, the state's general information site.

sandy coastlines, marshes, mangroves, and gigantic Lake Okeechobee. Exceptional trails run through several parks and wildlife preserves, including **Everglades National Park,** the **J. N. "Ding" Darling National Wildlife Refuge** on Sanibel Island, and **Collier Seminole State Park** and the **Briggs Nature Center,** both on the edge of the Everglades near Marco Island.

Another local favorite is **Myakka River State Park** near Sarasota, Florida's largest state park with approximately 28,000 acres of pure backcountry.

According to the Florida state legislature, however, the state's official "Canoe Capital" is the Panhandle town of **Milton,** on U.S. 90 near Pensacola. Up there, Blackwater River, Coldwater River, Sweetwater Creek, and Juniper Creek are perfect for tubing, rafting, and paddleboating, as well as canoeing and kayaking.

Another good venue: the waterways winding through the marshes between **Amelia Island** and the mainland.

Many conservation groups throughout the state offer half-day, full-day, and overnight canoe trips. For example, **The Conservancy of Naples** (© **941/262-0304;** www. conservancy.org) has a popular series of moonlight canoe trips through the mangroves, among other programs.

Based during the winter at Everglades City, on the park's western border, **North American Canoe Tours, Inc.** (© **941/695-4666** November through April, or 860/739-0791 May through October; www.evergladesadventures.com) offers weeklong guided canoe expeditions through the Everglades.

Thirty-six creek and river trails, covering 950 miles altogether, are itemized in the excellent free *Canoe Trails* booklet published by the **Florida Department of Environmental Protection,** Office of Communications, 3900 Commonwealth Blvd., Tallahassee, FL 32399 (© **850/ 488-2960;** www.dep.state.fl.us).

Specialized guidebooks include *A Canoeing and Kayaking Guide to the Streams of Florida:* Volume 1, *North Central Florida and Panhandle,* by Elizabeth F. Carter and John L. Eearch, and Volume 2, *Central and Southern Peninsula,* by Lou Glaros and Dough Sphar. Both are published by Menasha Ridge Press.

ECO-ADVENTURES If you don't want to do it yourself, you can observe Florida's flora and fauna on guided field expeditions—and contribute to conservation efforts while you're at it.

The **Sierra Club,** America's oldest and largest grassroots environmental organization, offers eco-adventures through its Florida chapters. Recent outings have included canoeing or kayaking through the Everglades, hiking the Florida Trail in America's southernmost national forest, camping on a barrier island, and exploring the sinkhole phenomenon in North Central Florida. You do have to be a Sierra Club member, but you can join at the time of the trip. Contact the club's national outings office at 85 Second St., Second Floor, San Francisco, CA 94105-3441 (© **415-977-5630;** www.sierraclub.org).

The Florida chapter of **The Nature Conservancy** has protected 578,000 acres of natural lands in Florida and presently owns and manages 36 preserves. For a small fee, you can join one of its field trips or work parties that take place periodically throughout the year; fees vary from year to year, event to event, so call for more information. Participants get a chance to learn about and even participate in the preservation of the ecosystem. For details of all the preserves and adventures, contact The Nature Conservancy, Florida Chapter, 222 S. Westmonte Dr., Suite 300, Altamonte Springs, FL 32714 (© **407/682-3664;** fax 407/682-3077; www.tnc.org).

A nonprofit organization dedicated to environmental research, the **Earthwatch Institute,** 3 Clocktower Place, Suite 100 (P.O. Box 75), Maynard, MA 01754 (© **800/776-0188** or 617/926-8200; fax 617/926-8532; www.earthwatch.org), has excursions to survey dolphins and manatees around Sarasota and to monitor the well-being of the captive-raised whooping cranes that have been released in the wilds of Central Florida. Another research group, the **Oceanic Society,** Fort Mason Center, Building E, San Francisco, CA 94123 (© **800/326-7491** or 415/441-1106; fax 415/474-3395; www.oceanicsociety.org), also has Florida trips among its expeditions, including manatee monitoring in the Crystal River area north of Tampa.

FISHING In addition to the amberjack, bonito, grouper, mackerel, mahi-mahi, marlin, pompano, redfish, sailfish, snapper, snook, tarpon, tuna, and wahoo running offshore and in its inlets, Florida has countless miles of rivers and streams, plus about 30,000 lakes and springs stocked with more than 100 species of freshwater fish. Indeed, Floridians seem to fish everywhere: off canal banks and old bridges, from fishing piers and fishing fleets. You'll even see them standing alongside the Tamiami Trail (U.S. 41) that cuts across the Everglades—one eye on their line, the other watching for alligators.

We listed our favorite places to fish in chapter 1, but nearly every marina in Florida harbors charter boats. You don't have to pay them a small fortune to try your luck, for most ports also have party boats that take groups out to sea. You'll have lots of company, but their rates are reasonable, they provide the gear and bait, and you won't need a fishing license.

Anglers age 16 and older need fishing licenses for any other kind of saltwater or freshwater fishing, including lobstering and spearfishing. Licenses are sold at bait and tackle shops.

The **Florida Department of Environmental Protection,** 3900 Commonwealth Blvd., Tallahassee, FL 32399-3000 (© **850/488-2960;** www.dep.state.fl.us), publishes the annual *Fishing Lines,* a free magazine with a wealth of information about fishing in Florida, including regulations and licensing requirements. It also distributes free brochures with annual freshwater and saltwater limits. And the **Florida Sports Foundation** (see the introduction to this section, above) publishes *Florida Fishing & Boating,* another treasure trove of information.

HIKING Although you won't be climbing any mountains in this relatively flat state, there are thousands of beautiful hiking trails in Florida. The ideal hiking months are October through April, when the weather is cool and dry and mosquitoes are less prominent. Like anywhere else, you'll find trails that are gentle and short and others that are challenging—some trails in the Everglades require you to wade waist-deep in water!

If you're venturing into the backcountry, watch out for gators, and don't ever try to feed them (or any wild animal). You risk getting bitten (they can't tell the difference between the food and your hand). You're also upsetting the balance of nature, since animals fed by humans lose their ability to find their own food. Most Florida snakes are harmless, but a few have deadly bites, so it's a good idea to avoid them all.

The **Florida Trail Association,** P.O. Box 13708, Gainesville, FL 32604 (© **800/343-1882** or 352/378-8823; www.florida-trail.org), maintains a large percentage of the public trails in the state and puts out an excellent book packed with maps, details, and color photos.

For a copy of *Florida Trails,* which outlines the many options, contact

Visit Florida (see "Visitor Information," earlier in this chapter). Another resource is *A Guide to Your National Scenic Trails,* Office of Greenways and Trails, Department of Environmental Protection, 3900 Commonwealth Blvd., Tallahassee, FL 32399 (© **850/488-2960**). You can also contact the office of **National Forests in Florida,** Woodcrest Office Park, 325 John Knox Rd., Suite F-100, Tallahassee, FL 32303 (© **850/942-9300**). And *Hiking Florida,* by M. Timothy O'Keefe (Falcon Press), details 132 hikes throughout the state, with maps and photos.

The **Florida Conservation Foundation, Inc.,** 1191 Orange Ave., Winter Park, FL 32789 (© **407/644-5377;** http://sundial.sundial.net/~florida/), publishes information about the state's ecology, including *Common Florida Natural Areas,* an illustrated brochure explaining what you'll find in each ecosystem.

GOLF   Florida is the unofficial golf capital of the United States-some would say the world-since the **World Golf Hall of Fame** has moved into its new home near St. Augustine. This state-of-the-art museum and shrine is worth a brief visit even if you're not in love with the game.

One thing's for certain: Florida has more golf courses than any other state—more than 1,150 at last count and growing. We picked the best in chapter 1, but suffice it to say that you can tee off almost anytime there's daylight. The highest concentrations of excellent courses are in Southwest Florida around Naples and Fort Myers (more than 1,000 holes!), in the Orlando area (Disney alone has 99 holes open to the public), and in the Panhandle around Destin and Panama City Beach. And it's a rare town in Florida that doesn't have a municipal golf course—even Key West has 18 great holes.

Greens fees are usually much lower at the municipal courses than at privately owned clubs. Whether public or private, greens fees tend to vary greatly depending on the time of year. You could pay $150 or more at a private course during the high season, but less than half that when the tourists are gone. The fee structures vary so much that it's best to call ahead and ask, and always reserve a tee time as far in advance as possible.

You can learn the game or hone your strokes at one of several excellent golf schools in the state. David Ledbetter has teaching facilities in Orlando and Naples, Fred Griffin is in charge of the Grand Cypress Academy of Golf at Grand Cypress Resort in Orlando, and you'll find Jimmy Ballard's school at the Ocean Reef Club on Key Largo. The Westin Innisbrook Resort at Tarpon Springs has its Innisbrook Golf Institute. Amelia Island (near Jacksonville) is home to Amelia Island Plantation Golf School, and Saddlebrook Resort north of Tampa hosts the Arnold Palmer Golf Academy.

You can get information about most Florida courses, including current greens fees, and reserve tee times through **Tee Times USA,** P.O. Box 641, Flagler Beach, FL 32136 (© **800/374-8633,** 888/465-3567, or 904/439-0001; fax 904/439-0099; www.golfflorida.net). This company also publishes a vacation guide that includes many stay-and-play golf packages.

Florida Golf, published by the **Florida Sports Foundation** (see the introduction to this section), lists every course in Florida. It's the state's official golf guide and is available from Visit Florida (see "Visitor Information & Money," earlier in this chapter).

Golfer's Guide magazine publishes monthly editions covering most regions of Florida; it is available free at all the local visitors centers and hotel lobbies, or you can contact the magazine at P.O. Box 5926, Hilton Head, SC 29938 (© **800/864-6101** or 843/842-7878; fax 843/842-5743; www.golfersguide.com). Northwest Florida is covered by *Gulf Coast Tee Time,* published by Tee Time LLC, 3 W. Garden St., Pensacola, FL 32501 (© **888/520-4300** or 850/435-4858; fax 850/435-7383; www.teetimeweb. com).

You also can get more information from the **Professional Golfers' Association (PGA),** 100 Avenue of the Champions, Palm Beach Gardens, FL 33418 (© **561/624-8400;** www.pga. com), or the **Ladies Professional Golf Association (LPGA),** 2570 Volusia Ave., Suite B, Daytona Beach, FL 32114 (© **904/254-6200;** www. lpga.com).

More than 700 courses are profiled in *Florida Golf Guide* by Jimmy Shacky (Open Roads Publishing; $19.95), available at bookstores.

SCUBA DIVING & SNORKELING Divers love the Keys, where you can see magnificent formations of tree-sized elkhorn coral and giant brain coral, as well as colorful sea fans and dozens of other varieties, sharing space with 300 or more species of rainbow-hued fish. Reef diving is good all the way from Key Largo to Key West, with plenty of tour operators, outfitters, and dive shops along the way. Particularly worthy are **John Pennekamp Coral Reef State Park** in Key Largo and **Looe Key National Marine Sanctuary** off Big Pine Key. *Skin Diver* magazine picked Looe Key as the number-one dive spot in North America. Also, the clearest waters in which to view some of the 4,000 sunken ships along Florida's coast are in the Middle Keys and the waters between Key West and the Dry Tortugas. Snorkeling in the Keys is particularly fine between Islamorada and Marathon.

In Northwest Florida, the 100-fathom curve draws closer to the white, sandy Panhandle beaches than

---

 The Cave Diving Capital of the World

The "cave diving capital of the world" can be found between High Springs and Branford, about 25 miles northwest of Gainesville.

The two most renowned spots are in crystal-clear Ginnie Springs, on the Santa Fe River, and in **Ichetucknee Springs State Park,** Route 2, Box 108, Fort White, FL 32038 (© **904/497-2511;** www8.myflorida.com/ communities/learn/stateparks/district2/ichetucknee), a few miles farther north. Underwater explorers have found artifacts from the native tribes that once inhabited the region around Ichetucknee, and topside explorers often sight limpkin, wood duck, otter, and beaver. This 2,241-acre state park also offers camping, nature trails, canoeing, and tubing.

The **Ginnie Springs Resort,** 7300 NE Ginnie Springs Rd., High Springs (© **800/874-8571** or 904/454-2202; www.ginniesprings.com), is a 200-acre campsite park along the Santa Fe River with dive packages and canoe rentals.

The **Steamboat Dive Inn,** U.S. 27 at U.S. 129, Branford, FL 32008 (© **904/935-DIVE;** www.steamboatdiveinn.com), on the Suwannee River, has its own on-site, full-service diving center with certified instructors for every level. Also in Branford, the **Branford Dive Center,** U.S. 27 and the Suwannee River, Branford, FL 32008 (© **904/935-1141**), offers guides, air, rentals, accessories, and instruction.

to any other spot on the Gulf of Mexico. It's too far north here for coral, but you can see brilliantly colored sponges and fish and, in Timber Hole, discover an undersea "petrified forest" of sunken planes, ships, and even a railroad car. And the battleship USS *Massachusetts* lies in 30 feet of water just 3 miles off Pensacola. Every beach town in Northwest Florida has dive shops to outfit, tour, or certify visitors.

In the Crystal River area, north of the St. Petersburg and Clearwater beaches, you can snorkel with the manatees as they bask in the warm spring waters of Kings Bay.

If you want to keep up with what's going on statewide, you can subscribe to *Florida Scuba News,* a monthly magazine published in Jacksonville (© **904/783-1610;** www.scubanews. com). You might also want to pick up a specialized guidebook. Some good ones include *Coral Reefs of Florida,* by Gilbert L. Voss (Pineapple Press), and *The Diver's Guide to Florida and the Florida Keys,* by Jim Stachowicz (Windward Publishing).

TENNIS Year-round sunshine makes Florida great for tennis. There are some 7,700 places to play, from municipal courts to exclusive resorts. Even some of the municipal facilities—Cambier Park Tennis Center in Naples leaps to mind—are equal to those at expensive resorts, and they're either free or close to it.

If you can afford it, you can learn from the best in Florida. **Nick Bollettieri** has sports academies in Bradenton. The Saddlebrook Resort in Wesley Chapel north of Tampa is home to the **Hopman Tennis Program,** while Safety Harbor Resort and Spa near St. Petersburg hosts the **Phil Green Tennis Program.** Amateurs can hobnob with the superstars at **ATP Tour International Headquarters** in Ponte Vedra Beach, near Jacksonville. **Mary Jo Fernandez** is affiliated with the **Arthur Ashe Tennis Center** at the Doral Golf Resort & Spa in Miami. And **Chris Evert, Robert Seguso,** and **Carling Basset** have their own center in Boca Raton.

Other top places to learn and play are **Amelia Island Plantation** on Amelia Island; **Colony Beach and Tennis Resort** on Longboat Key off Sarasota (which *Tennis* magazine picked as the number-two tennis resort in the nation); **Sanibel Harbour Resort & Spa** in Fort Myers, whose 5,500-seat stadium has hosted Davis Cup matches; **South Seas Plantation Resort & Yacht Harbour** on Captiva Island; **The Registry Resort** in Naples; and **World Tennis Center Resort & Club** in Naples, where the World Tennis Academy is headed by renowned tennis psychologist and coach Roland Carlstedt.

11 Tips on Accommodations

Florida has such a vast array of accommodations—from rock-bottom roadside motels to some of the nation's finest resorts—that we can cover only the tip of the iceberg in this book. Whether you'll spend a pittance or a bundle depends on your budget and your tastes. But, to repeat a well-worn phrase, you can enjoy "champagne on a beer budget"—if you plan carefully.

The annual trip-planning guide published by the state's tourism promotion agency, *Visit Florida* (see "Visitor Information," earlier in this chapter), lists most hotels and motels in the state. It's particularly handy if you're taking your animal along, since it tells whether they accept pets.

Another excellent source is **Superior Small Lodgings** ⚘, a national organization of quality hotels, motels, and inns. None of these properties has more than 75 rooms, and all have been inspected for cleanliness, quality, comfort, privacy, and safety. Contact the local tourist information offices for lists of members in their areas, or the **Florida Superior Small Lodging Association,** 926 Elysium Blvd., Mount Dora, FL 32757 (© **352/ 735-4635;** fax 352/735-3944; www.SuperiorSmallLodging.com). Many hotels and motels recommended in this book are members.

Inn Route, P.O. Box 6187, Palm Harbor, FL 34684 (© **800/524-1880;** fax 281/403-9335; www.florida-inns.com; innroute@worldnet.att.net), publishes the *Inns of Florida,* which lists inns and bed-and-breakfasts throughout the state. Inn Route also inspects each property, thus ensuring the quality and cleanliness of its members.

At the inexpensive end, **Hostelling International/American Youth Hostels,** 735 15th St. NW, Suite 840, Washington, DC 20005 (© **202/ 783-6161**; www.hiayh.org), offers low-cost accommodations in Miami Beach, Key West, Florida City, Orlando, St. Augustine, and Clearwater Beach.

MONEY-SAVING TIPS

The rates quoted in this book are "rack" or "published" rates; that is, the highest regular rates charged by a hotel or motel. Not long ago the rack rate was what you paid, unless you were part of a tour group or had purchased a vacation package. Today most hotels give discounts to corporate travelers, government employees, senior citizens, automobile club members, active duty military personnel, and others.

Most hotels don't advertise these discounted rates or even volunteer them at the front desk, but you can take advantage of them by asking politely if there is a special rate that might apply to you. One company that does advertise a major discount is **Choice Hotels** (see "For Seniors" under "Tips for Travelers with Special Needs," earlier in this chapter).

Computerized reservations systems also have permitted many larger properties to adjust their rates on an almost daily—if not hourly—basis, depending on how much business they anticipate having. Even if they don't officially reduce their rates, they may drop them rather than having beds go empty. Don't hesitate to ask if a less-expensive rate is available on the days you plan on being there.

Most rack rates include commissions for travel agents, which many hotels will knock off if you make your own reservations and bargain a little.

Downtown hotels catering to business travelers during the week usually have big discounts on Friday and Saturday nights. If you're staying over a weekend in an off-beach city such as Tampa, always ask about a special rate or package deal. Weekend rates don't apply in the resort areas, nor in college towns like Tallahassee, but you should ask about weekday or weeklong vacation packages.

Many Florida hotels and motels offer weekly rates, which, as a general rule, will knock off the price of one night if you stay for seven.

Most also have free self-parking, but fees can run up the cost at some downtown and beachfront hotels. We've indicated in the listings if a hotel or resort charges for parking; if no charge is given, parking is free. And many hotels jack up the price of long-distance phone calls made from your room. Accordingly, always inquire about the costs of parking, and use a pay phone if the hotel tacks a hefty surcharge on calls.

You're probably better off dealing directly with a hotel, but if you don't like bargaining, check out one of the national **reservation services.** They usually work as consolidators, buying up or reserving rooms in bulk and then dealing them out to customers at a profit. Most of them offer online reservation services as well. The more reputable providers include **Accommodations Express** (© 800/950-4685; www.accommodationsxpress.com); **Hotel Reservations Network** (© 800/96HOTEL; www.180096HOTEL.com); **Quikbook** (© 800/789-9887, includes fax-on-demand service; www.quikbook.com); and **Room Exchange** (© 800/846-7000 in the U.S., 800/486-7000 in Canada; www.hotelrooms.com).

Online, try booking your hotel through **Arthur Frommer's Budget Travel** (www.frommers.com), and save up to 50% off the rack rate. **Microsoft Expedia** (www.expedia.com) features a "Travel Agent" that will also direct you to affordable lodgings.

CONDOMINIUMS, HOMES & COTTAGES

It may seem at first impression that many Florida beaches are lined with great walls of high-rise condominium buildings. That's not much of an overstatement, for the state literally has thousands upon thousands of condominium units. People actually live in many of them year-round, but others are for rent on a daily, weekly, or monthly basis. In addition, many private homes and cottages are for rent throughout Florida.

Be aware, however, that in Florida real estate and resort parlance, the word *villa* does not mean a luxurious house standing all by itself. Down here, "villa" means an apartment.

Some of the resorts listed in this book actually are condominium complexes operated as full-service hotels, but usually you'll have to do without such hotel amenities as on-site restaurants, room service, and even daily maid service. On the other hand, almost every condominium, home, and cottage has a fully equipped kitchen, and many have washers, dryers, and other such niceties of home, which means they can represent significant savings, especially if you're traveling with children or are sharing with another couple or family.

We have pointed out a few of the best condominium complexes in the "Where to Stay" sections of the following chapters, and we have named some of the **reputable real estate agencies** that have inventories of condominiums, private homes, and cottages to rent.

If you think a condominium will meet your needs, your best bet is to contact the rental agencies well in advance and request a brochure describing all the properties they represent, and their rates.

 FAST FACTS: Florida

American Express There are a number of American Express offices in Florida. Call Cardmember Services (© 800/528-4800; www.americanexpress.com) for the location nearest you.

Banks Banks are usually open Monday to Friday from 9am to 3 or 4pm, and most have automated teller machines (ATMs) for 24-hour banking. You won't have a problem finding a Cirrus or PLUS machine. See "Money," earlier in this chapter.

Car Rentals See "Getting Around," earlier in this chapter.

Climate See "When to Go," earlier in this chapter.

Currency Exchange See "Money," in "Preparing for Your Trip," in chapter 3.

Emergencies Call ✆ **911** anywhere in the state to summon the police, the fire department, or an ambulance.

Liquor Laws You must be 21 to purchase or consume alcohol in Florida. This law is strictly enforced, so if you look young, carry some photo identification that gives your date of birth. Minors can usually enter bars where food is served.

Newspapers/Magazines Most cities of any size have a local daily paper. The well-respected *Miami Herald* is generally available all over the state, with regional editions available in many areas. In the major cities, you can also find coin-operated boxes for *USA Today,* the *Wall Street Journal,* and the *New York Times.*

Safety Whenever you're traveling in an unfamiliar city, stay alert. Be aware of your immediate surroundings. Always lock your car doors and the trunk when your vehicle is unattended, and don't leave any valuables in sight. See "Safety," in "Preparing for Your Trip," in chapter 3, for more information.

Taxes The Florida state sales tax is 6%. Many municipalities add 1% or more to that, and most levy a special tax on hotel and restaurant bills. In general, expect at least 10% to be added to your final hotel bill. There also are hefty taxes on rental cars here (see "Getting Around," earlier in this chapter).

Time The Florida peninsula observes eastern standard time, but most of the Panhandle west of the Apalachicola River is on central standard time, 1 hour behind the rest of the state.

3

For Foreign Visitors

by Bill Goodwin

The pervasiveness of American culture around the world may make you feel that you already know a lot about the United States, but leaving your own country still requires a degree of planning. This chapter will help prepare you for the more common problems that visitors sometimes encounter.

1 Preparing for Your Trip

ENTRY REQUIREMENTS

Immigration laws have been a hot political issue in the United States in recent years, so it's wise to check at any U.S. embassy or consulate for current information and requirements. You can also plug into the U.S. State Department's Internet site at **www. state.gov**.

VISAS Canadians may enter the United States without passports or visas; you need only proof of residence. Citizens of Andorra, Argentina, Australia, Austria, Belgium, Brunei, Denmark, Finland, France, Germany, Iceland, Ireland, Italy, Japan, Liechtenstein, Luxembourg, Monaco, the Netherlands, New Zealand, Norway, San Marino, Slovenia, Spain, Sweden, Switzerland, and the United Kingdom need only a valid passport and a round-trip air or cruise ticket in their possession upon arrival in order to enter the United States for stays of up to 90 days. Once here, you may then visit Mexico, Canada, Bermuda, and/or the Caribbean islands and return to the United States without needing a visa. Further information is available from any U.S. embassy or consulate.

If you're from any other country, you must have (1) a valid **passport** with an expiration date at least 6 months later than the scheduled end of your visit to the United States and (2) a **tourist visa,** which may be obtained without charge from the nearest U.S. consulate.

Obtaining a Visa To obtain a tourist visa, submit a completed application form with a 1½-inch-square photo and demonstrate binding ties to your residence abroad. If you cannot go in person, contact the nearest U.S. embassy or consulate for directions on applying by mail. Your travel agent or airline office may also be able to provide you with the visa application forms and instructions. The U.S. embassy or consulate where you apply will determine whether you receive a multiple- or single-entry visa and any restrictions regarding the length of your stay. This may take a few days or even weeks, so apply well in advance.

British subjects can obtain up-to-date visa information by calling the **U.S. Embassy Visa Information Line** (© 0891/200-290) or the **London Passport Office** (© 0990/210-410) for recorded information.

DRIVER'S LICENSES Foreign driver's licenses are generally recognized in the U.S., although you may want to get an international driver's license if your home license is not written in English.

MEDICAL REQUIREMENTS

Unless you're arriving from an area known to be suffering from an epidemic (particularly cholera or yellow fever), inoculations or vaccinations are not required for entry into the United States. If you have a disease that requires treatment with narcotics or syringe-administered medications, carry a valid signed prescription from your physician to allay any suspicions that you may be smuggling narcotics (a serious offense that carries severe penalties in the U.S.).

For HIV-positive visitors, requirements for entering the United States are somewhat vague and change frequently. For up-to-the-minute information concerning HIV-positive travelers, contact the Centers for Disease Control's **National Center for HIV** (© **404/332-4559**; www.hivatis.org) or the **Gay Men's Health Crisis** (© **212/367-1000**; www.gmhc.org).

CUSTOMS REQUIREMENTS

Every visitor over 21 years of age may bring in, free of duty, 1 liter (about 1 qt.) of wine or hard liquor, 200 cigarettes or 100 cigars (but no cigars made in Cuba) or 3 pounds of smoking tobacco, and $100 worth of gifts. You must spend at least 72 hours in the United States and must not have claimed the exemptions within the preceding 6 months. It is altogether forbidden to bring in foodstuffs (particularly cheese, fruit, cooked meats, and canned goods) and plants (vegetables, seeds, tropical plants, and so on). Foreign tourists may bring in or take out up to $10,000 in U.S. or foreign currency with no formalities; larger sums must be declared to Customs upon entering or leaving.

Penalties are severe for smuggling illegal narcotics into the United States, so if you have a disease requiring treatment with medications containing narcotics or drugs (especially those administered by syringe), carry a valid signed prescription from your physician to allay any suspicions that you are smuggling drugs.

For more specific information regarding U.S. Customs, call your nearest U.S. embassy or consulate, or the **U.S. Customs** office at © **202/927-1770**; www.customs.ustreas.gov.

What You Can Bring Home Check with your country's Customs or Foreign Affairs department for the latest guidelines(including information on items that are not allowed to be brought into your home country(just before you leave home.

U.K. citizens should contact **HM Customs & Excise,** Passenger Enquiry Point, 2nd Floor Wayfarer House, Great South West Road, Feltham, Middlesex, TW14 8NP (© **0181/910-3744;** from outside the U.K. 44/181-910-3744), or consult their website at www.open.gov.uk.

For a clear summary of **Canadian** rules, write for the booklet *I Declare,* issued by **Canada Customs and Revenue Agency,** 2265 St. Laurent Blvd., Ottawa K1G 4KE (© **800/461-9999** from within Canada or 204/983-3500) or visit the agency's comprehensive website at www.ccra-adrc.gc.ca.

Australian visitors should contact **Australian Customs Services,** GPO Box 8, Sydney NSW 2001 (© **02/9213-2000;** www.customs.gov.au).

New Zealand visitors may obtain a free pamphlet from New Zealand consulates and Customs offices: *New Zealand Customs Guide for Travellers, Notice no. 4.* For more information, contact **New Zealand Customs,** 50 Anzac Ave., P.O. Box 29, Auckland (© **09/359-6655;** www.customs.govt.nz).

INSURANCE

Unlike many European countries, the United States does not usually offer free or low-cost medical care to its citizens or visitors. Doctors and hospitals are expensive, and in most cases they will require advance payment or proof of coverage before they render their services. Policies can cover everything from the loss or theft of your baggage and trip cancellation to the guarantee of bail in case you're arrested. Good policies will also cover the costs of an accident, repatriation, or death. See "Health & Insurance," in chapter 2, for more information. Packages such as **Europ Assistance** (www.europ-assistance.com) in Europe are sold by automobile clubs and travel agencies at attractive rates. **Worldwide Assistance Services, Inc.** (© 800/821-2828; www.worldwideassistance.com) is the agent for Europ Assistance in the United States.

Although lack of health insurance may prevent you from being admitted to a hospital in nonemergencies, don't worry about being left on a street corner to die: the American way is to fix you now and bill the living daylights out of you later.

Canadians should check with their provincial health-plan offices or call **HealthCanada** (© 613/957-3025; www.hc-sc.gc.ca) to find out the extent of their coverage and what documentation and receipts they must take home in case they are treated in the United States.

In Great Britain, most big travel agents offer their own insurance, and they will probably try to sell you their package when you book a holiday. Think before you sign. **Britain's Consumers' Association** recommends that you insist on seeing the policy and reading the fine print before buying travel insurance. The **Association of British Insurers** (© 0171/600-3333; www.abi.org.uk) gives advice by phone and publishes the free *Holiday Insurance,* a guide to policy provisions and prices. You might also shop around for better deals: Try **Columbus Travel Insurance Ltd.** (© 0171/375-0011) or, for students, **Campus Travel** (© 0171/730-2101).

MONEY

The U.S. monetary system has a decimal base: one American dollar ($1) = 100 cents (100¢). Notes come in $1 (sometimes called a "buck"), $5, $10, $20, $50, and $100 denominations (the last two are not welcome when paying for small purchases and are not accepted in taxis or at subway ticket booths). There are also $2 bills, but you are unlikely to see any because they are no longer made. There are six denominations of coins: 1¢ (one cent, known here as "a penny"), 5¢ (five cents, or "a nickel"), 10¢ (ten cents, or "a dime"), 25¢ (twenty-five cents, or "a quarter"), 50¢ (fifty cents, or "a half dollar"), and the rare $1 piece.

Changing foreign currency in the United States is a hassle, so leave any currency other than U.S. dollars at home—it will prove more of a nuisance than it's worth. Even banks here may not want to change your home currency into U.S. dollars. The exceptions are the currency exchange desks in the Miami, Orlando, Tampa, and Fort Myers airports, and **Thomas Cook Foreign Exchange,** which changes foreign currency and sells commission-free foreign and U.S. traveler's checks, drafts, and wire transfers. Thomas Cook's Florida office is in Fort Lauderdale (© 800/287-7362; www.us.thomascook.com).

Traveler's checks denominated in U.S. dollars are readily accepted at most hotels, motels, restaurants, and large stores. Do not bring traveler's checks denominated in other currencies. Sometimes a passport or other photo identification is necessary. The three types of traveler's checks that are most widely recognized—and least likely to be denied—are **Visa, American Express,** and **Thomas Cook.** Be

Speaking Your Language

You can call Visit Florida's 24-hour **tourist assistance hotline** (✆ 800/ 656-8777) if you need help with lost travel documents, directions, emergencies, or information about attractions, restaurants, and shopping anywhere in the state. Hotline operators speak several languages, including Spanish, French, German, and Portuguese. The phone call is free.

In Orlando, **Walt Disney World** (✆ 407/2-DISNEY) has numerous services designed to meet the needs of foreign visitors, including personal translators and a special phone number (✆ 407/824-7900) to speak to someone in French, Spanish, German, and other languages.

sure to record the numbers of the checks, and keep that information in a safe place (not in your wallet or purse) in case they get lost or stolen.

American Express, Diners Club, Discover, MasterCard (EuroCard in Europe, Access in Britain, Chargex in Canada), and Visa (BarclayCard in Britain) **credit and charge cards** are the most widely used form of payment in the United States. You should bring at least one with you—if for no other reason than to rent a car, since all rental companies require them.

Some **automated teller machines (ATMs)**, located throughout Florida, will allow you to draw U.S. currency against your bank and credit cards. When available, this is the easiest way to get U.S. dollars, and you get the bank's rate of exchange, normally better than you will receive at hotels and other businesses. Check with your bank before leaving home, and remember that you will need your personal identification number (PIN) to do so. See "Money," in chapter 2, for more information.

SAFETY

GENERAL   While tourist areas are generally safe, and crime rates have been decreasing in the U.S., urban areas here tend to be less safe than those in Europe or Japan. You should always stay alert. This is particularly true of large U.S. cities. It is wise to ask your hotel's front-desk staff or the

city's or area's tourist office if you're in doubt about which neighborhoods are safe.

Remember also that hotels are open to the public, and in a large hotel, security may not be able to screen everyone entering. Always lock your room door. Don't assume that once inside your hotel you are automatically safe and no longer need to be aware of your surroundings.

DRIVING   Recently more and more crime has involved vehicles, so safety while driving is particularly important. Question your rental agency about personal safety, or ask for a brochure of traveler safety tips when you pick up your car. Obtain written directions from the agency, or a map with the route clearly marked, showing how to get to your destination.

Make sure that you have enough gasoline in your tank to reach your intended destination so that you're not forced to look for a service station in an unfamiliar and possibly unsafe neighborhood, especially at night. If you do drive off a highway into a doubtful neighborhood, leave the area as quickly as possible. If you have an accident in such a neighborhood, even on the highway, stay in your car with the doors locked until you assess the situation or until the police arrive. If you are bumped from behind on the street or are involved in a minor accident with no injuries and the situation appears to be suspicious, motion to the other driver to follow you. *Never* get out of your car in such situations. If you see someone on the road who indicates a need for help, do *not* stop. Take note of the location, drive on to a well-lighted area, and telephone the police by dialing ℭ **911** from any telephone.

Park in well-lighted, well-traveled areas if possible. Always keep your car doors locked, whether attended or unattended. Look around you before you get out of your car, and never leave any packages or valuables in sight. If someone attempts to rob you or steal your car, do *not* try to resist the thief or carjacker—report the incident to the police department immediately.

2 Getting to & Around the U.S.

A number of U.S. airlines offer service from Europe and Latin America to Florida, including American, Delta, Northwest, and United (see "Getting There," in chapter 2). Many of the major international airlines, such as **British Airways** (www.british-airways.com), **KLM Royal Dutch Airlines** (www.klm.com), and **Lufthansa** (www.lufthansa.com), also have direct flights from Europe to various Florida cities, either in their own planes or in conjunction with an American "partner" airline (Northwest-KLM, to name one such partnership). You can get here from Australia and New Zealand via **Air New Zealand** (www.airnz.com), **Qantas** (www.qantas.com), **American** (www.aa.com), and **United** (www.ual.com), with a change of planes in Los Angeles. Call the airlines' local offices or contact your travel agent, and be sure to ask about promotional fares and discounts.

From Great Britain, **Virgin Atlantic Airways** (ℭ **800/662-8621** in the U.S., or 01/293-74-77-47 in the U.K.; www.virgin-atlantic.com) has attractive deals on its flights from London and Manchester to Miami and Orlando. From Germany, **LTU International Airways** (ℭ **800/888-0200** in the U.S., 11/948-8466 in Germany; www.ltu.com) frequently has reduced fares to Miami, Orlando, and Fort Myers from Frankfurt, Munich, and Düsseldorf. From Johannesburg and Cape Town, **South**

African Airways and **Delta Airlines** (www.delta.com) fly to Fort Lauderdale.

Canadians should check with **Air Canada** (ℭ **800/776-3000;** www.aircanada.ca), which offers service from Toronto and Montréal to Miami, Tampa, West Palm Beach, Fort Lauderdale, and Fort Myers. Also ask your travel agent about **Air Transat** (ℭ **800/470-1011;** www.airtransat.com) and **Canada 3000** (ℭ **800/993-4378;** www.canada3000.com), which have wintertime charter flights to several Florida destinations.

AIRFARES Whichever airline you choose, always ask about **advance purchase excursion (APEX)** fares, which represent substantial savings over regular fares. Most require tickets to be bought 21 days prior to departure.

On the World Wide Web, the European Travel Network (ETN) operates a site at **www.discount-tickets.com**, which offers cut-rate prices on international airfares to the United States, accommodations, car rentals, and tours. Another site to click for current discount fares worldwide is **www.etn.nl/discount.htm#disco**.

IMMIGRATION & CUSTOMS CLEARANCE When you arrive in the U.S., getting through immigration control may take as long as 2 hours on some days, especially summer weekends. Accordingly, you should make very generous allowances for delay in

Travel Tip

Be sure to keep a copy of all your travel papers separate from your wallet or purse, and leave a copy with someone at home should you need it faxed in an emergency.

planning connections between international and domestic flights.

In contrast, travelers arriving by car or by rail from Canada will find border-crossing formalities streamlined to the vanishing point. And air travelers from Canada, Bermuda, and some places in the Caribbean can sometimes go through Customs and Immigration at the point of departure, which is much quicker.

For further information, see "Getting There" in chapter 2.

GETTING AROUND THE U.S.

BY AIR   The United States is one of the world's largest countries, with vast distances separating many of its key sights. From New York to Miami, for example, is more than 1,350 miles (2,173km) by road or train. Accordingly, flying is the quickest and most comfortable way to get around the country.

Some large airlines (for example, Northwest and Delta) offer travelers on their transatlantic or transpacific flights special discount tickets under the name **Visit USA,** allowing mostly one-way travel from one U.S. destination to another at very low prices. These discount tickets are not on sale in the United States and must be purchased abroad in conjunction with your international ticket. This system is the best, easiest, and fastest way to see the United States at low cost.

BY TRAIN   Long-distance trains in the United States are operated by **Amtrak** (© **800/USA-RAIL;** www. amtrak.com), the national passenger rail corporation. See "Getting There," in chapter 2, for information about Amtrak's services to and within Florida.

Be aware that with a few notable exceptions (for instance, the Northeast Corridor line between Boston and Washington, D.C.), intercity service is not up to European standards. Delays are common, routes are limited and often infrequently served, and fares are seldom significantly lower than discount airfares. Thus, cross-country train travel should be approached with caution.

International visitors can buy a **USA Railpass,** good for 15 or 30 days of unlimited travel on Amtrak. The pass is available through many foreign travel agents (see Amtrak's website for a complete list), and with a foreign passport, you can also buy them at some Amtrak offices in the United States, including Boston, Chicago, Los Angeles, Miami, New York, San Francisco, and Washington, D.C. The prices are based on a zone system—eastern, central, and western United States—and are highest in the peak summer months and at holidays. Reservations are generally required and should be made for each part of your trip as early as possible.

BY BUS   Although it's the least-expensive way to get around the country, long-distance bus service here can be both slow and uncomfortable—certainly not an option for everyone. **Greyhound** (© **800/231-2222;** www.greyhound.com), the sole nationwide bus line, offers an **International Ameripass** for unlimited travel, ranging from $155 for 7 days to $449 for 60 days. Passes must be purchased online or at a Greyhound terminal at least 21 days before beginning travel. Special rates are available for senior citizens and students.

Important Note

In the United States we drive on the **right side of the road** as in Europe, not on the left side as in the United Kingdom, Australia, New Zealand, and South Africa.

BY CAR   Traveling by car gives you the freedom to make (and alter) your itinerary to suit your own needs and interests. And especially in Florida, it offers the possibility of visiting some of the off-the-beaten-path locations, places that cannot be reached easily by public transportation. For information on renting cars in the United States, see "Getting Around," in chapter 2, and "Automobile Organizations" and "Automobile Rentals," in "Fast Facts: For the Foreign Traveler," below.

3 Shopping Tips

The U.S. government charges very low duties when compared with the rest of the world, so you could get some excellent deals here on imported electronic goods, cameras, and clothing. Of course, it all depends on the value of your home currency versus the dollar, and how much duty you'll have to pay on your purchases when you get home.

Many computers and most other electronic equipment sold here use only 110- to 120-volt AC (60-cycle) electricity. You will need a transformer to use them at home if your power is 220 to 240 volts AC (50 cycles). Be sure to ask the salesperson if an item has a universal power adapter.

The national "discount" chain stores consistently offer some of our best shopping deals. For televisions, VCRs, radios, camcorders, computers, and other electronic goods, go to **Best Buy, Circuit City,** and **Radio Shack.** Best Buy also has a wide selection of music. **CompUSA, Computer City,** and **Micro Center** specialize in computer hardware, accessories, and software.

Our major department store chains are **Sears, Macy's, Saks Fifth Avenue, Lord & Taylor, Bloomingdale's,** and **JCPenney.** In Florida, you'll also find **Burdines, Jordan Marsh,** and **Dillard's** anchoring many shopping malls. You get real deals in department stores only during sales, when selected merchandise is marked down 25% or more. The **Marshall's** and **TJ Maxx** chains carry name-brand clothing at department-store sale prices, but their stock tends to vary greatly from store to store.

Another popular source are **outlet malls,** in which manufacturers operate their own shops, selling directly to the consumer. Sometimes you can get very good buys at the outlets, especially when sales are going on. Most lingerie and china outlets have good prices when compared with those at department stores, but that's not necessarily the case with designer clothing. In addition, some manufacturers produce items of lesser quality so that they can charge less at their outlets, so inspect the quality of all merchandise carefully. The main advantage to outlet malls is that if you are looking for a specific brand—Levi's jeans, for example—the company's outlet will have it.

You'll find national chain stores, department stores, and outlet malls throughout Florida. Many are listed under "Shopping" in the following chapters. You will also find listings for them in the local telephone directory.

FAST FACTS: **For the Foreign Traveler**

Automobile Organizations Auto clubs will supply maps, suggested routes, guidebooks, accident and bail-bond insurance, and emergency road service. The **American Automobile Association (AAA)** is the major auto club in the United States. If you belong to an auto club in your home country, inquire about AAA reciprocity before you leave. You may be able to join AAA even if you're not a member of a reciprocal club; to inquire, call AAA (*C* **800/222-4357;** www.aaa.com). AAA is actually an organization of regional auto clubs; in Florida, look under "AAA Automobile Club South" in the White Pages of the telephone directory. AAA has a nationwide emergency road-service telephone number (*C* **800/AAA-HELP**).

Automobile Rentals See "Getting Around," in chapter 2.

Currency & Currency Exchange See "Money," under "Preparing for Your Trip," above.

Electricity Like Canada, the United States uses 110 to 120 volts AC (60 cycles), compared with 220 to 240 volts AC (50 cycles) in most of Europe, Australia, and New Zealand. If your small appliances use 220 to 240 volts, you'll need a 110-volt transformer and a plug adapter with two flat parallel pins to operate them here. Downward converters that change 220 to 240 volts to 110 to 120 volts are difficult to find in the United States, so bring one with you.

Embassies & Consulates All embassies are located in the national capital, Washington, D.C. Some consulates are located in major U.S. cities, and most nations have a mission to the United Nations in New York City. Some key embassies are listed here:

Australia: 1601 Massachusetts Ave. NW, Washington, DC 20036 (*C* **202/797-3000;** www.austemb.org). There are Australian consulates in New York City, Honolulu, Houston, Los Angeles, and San Francisco.

Canada: 501 Pennsylvania Ave. NW, Washington, DC 20001 (*C* **202/ 682-1740;** www.canadianembassy.org). In Florida, there's a Canadian consulate at 200 S. Biscayne Blvd., Suite 1600, Miami, FL 33131 (*C* **305/ 579-1600**). Other Canadian consulates are in Buffalo (NY), Chicago, Detroit, Los Angeles, New York, and Seattle.

Republic of Ireland: 2234 Massachusetts Ave. NW, Washington, DC 20008 (*C* **202/462-3939**). Irish consulates are in Boston, Chicago, New York City, and San Francisco.

New Zealand: 37 Observatory Circle NW, Washington, DC 20008 (*C* **202/328-4800;** www.emb.com/nzemb). New Zealand consulates are in Los Angeles, Salt Lake City, San Francisco, and Seattle.

United Kingdom: 3100 Massachusetts Ave. NW, Washington, DC 20008 (*C* **202/462-1340**). In Florida, there's a full-service British consulate in Miami at Suite 2800, Brickell Bay Dr. (*C* **305/374-1522**), and a vice consulate for emergency situations in Orlando at the Sun Bank Tower, Suite 2110, 200 S. Orange Ave. (*C* **407/426-7855**). Other British consulates are in Atlanta, Boston, Chicago, Cleveland, Dallas, Houston, Los Angeles, and New York City.

Emergencies Call ✆ **911** to report a fire, contact the police, or get an ambulance anywhere in the United States. This is a toll-free call (no coins are required at public telephones).

Visit Florida, the state's tourist information agency, operates a 24-hour, multilanguage **tourist assistance hotline** (✆ **800/656-8777**), which will give advice and information in case of an emergency.

If you encounter traveler's problems, check the local telephone directory to find an office of the **Traveler's Aid Society** (www.travelersaid.org), a nationwide, not-for-profit social-service organization geared to helping travelers in difficult straits. Their services might include reuniting families separated while traveling, providing food and/or shelter to people stranded without cash, or even offering emotional counseling. If you're in trouble, seek them out.

Gasoline (Petrol) Petrol is known as gasoline (or simply "gas") in the United States, and petrol stations are known as both gas stations and service stations. Gasoline costs about half as much (about $1.70 per gallon or more) here as it does in Europe. One U.S. gallon equals 3.8 liters, or .85 Imperial gallon. A majority of gas stations in Florida are now actually convenience grocery stores with gas pumps outside. They do not service your automobile for you; all but a very few stations have self-service gas pumps.

Holidays Banks, government offices, post offices, and many stores, restaurants, and museums are closed on the following legal national holidays: January 1 (New Year's Day), the third Monday in January (Martin Luther King Jr. Day), the third Monday in February (Presidents' Day, Washington's Birthday), the last Monday in May (Memorial Day), July 4 (Independence Day), the first Monday in September (Labor Day), the second Monday in October (Columbus Day), November 11 (Veterans' Day/Armistice Day), the last Thursday in November (Thanksgiving Day), and December 25 (Christmas). The Tuesday following the first Monday in November is Election Day and is a federal government holiday in presidential-election years (the next is in 2004).

Legal Aid The foreign tourist will probably never become involved with the American legal system. If you are "pulled over" for a minor driving infraction (for example, of the highway code, such as speeding), never attempt to pay the fine directly to a police officer; this could be construed as attempted bribery, a much more serious crime. Pay fines by mail, or directly into the hands of the clerk of the court. If accused of a more serious offense, say and do nothing before consulting a lawyer or your embassy or consulate. Here the government must prove a person's guilt beyond a reasonable doubt, and everyone has the right to remain silent, whether he or she is suspected of a crime or actually arrested. If arrested, a person can make one telephone call to a party of his or her choice, and foreigners have a right to call their embassies or consulates.

Mail If you aren't sure what your address will be in the United States, mail can be sent to you, in your name, **c/o General Delivery** at the main post office of the city or region where you expect to be. You must pick up your mail in person and must produce proof of identity (driver's license, passport, and so on).

Generally to be found at intersections, **mailboxes** are blue with a red-and-white stripe and carry the inscription U.S. MAIL. If your mail is addressed to a U.S. destination, don't forget to add the five-digit postal code, or ZIP code, after the two-letter abbreviation of the state to which the mail is addressed (FL for Florida).

Domestic postage rates are 21¢ for a postcard and 34¢ for a letter. Airmail postcards to Canada cost 50¢, while letters are 60¢. Airmail postcards to other countries are 70¢.

Newspapers/Magazines All over Florida, you'll be able to purchase *USA Today,* our national daily, and the *Miami Herald,* one of the most highly respected dailies in the country. Every city has its own daily paper.

Taxes In the United States there is no value-added tax (VAT) or other indirect tax at the national level. However, every state, county, and city has the right to levy its own local tax on all purchases, including hotel and restaurant checks, airline tickets, and so on. For Florida's sales taxes, see "Fast Facts: Florida" in chapter 2.

Telephone, Telegraph, & Fax The telephone system in the United States is run by private corporations, so rates, especially for long-distance service and operator-assisted calls, can vary widely. Generally, hotel surcharges on long-distance and local calls are astronomical, so you're usually better off using a **public pay telephone,** which you'll find clearly marked in most public buildings and private establishments as well as on the street. Convenience grocery stores and gas stations always have them. Many convenience groceries and packaging services sell **prepaid calling cards** in denominations up to $50; these can be the least-expensive way to call home. Many public phones at airports now accept American Express, MasterCard, and Visa credit cards. Local calls made from public pay phones in Florida cost 35¢.

Most **long-distance and international calls** can be dialed directly from any phone. For calls within the United States and to Canada, dial 1 followed by the area code and the seven-digit number. For other international calls, dial **011** followed by the country code, city code, and telephone number of the person you are calling.

Calls to area codes 800, 888, and 877 are toll-free. However, calls to numbers in area codes 700 and 900 (chat lines, bulletin boards, "dating" services, and so on) can be very expensive-usually a charge of 95¢ to $3 or more per minute, and they sometimes have minimum charges that can run as high as $15 or more.

For **collect (reversed-charge) calls** and for **person-to-person calls,** dial 0 (zero, *not* the letter O) followed by the area code and number you want; an operator will then come on the line, and you should specify that you are calling collect, or person-to-person, or both. If your operator-assisted call is international, ask for the overseas operator.

For local **directory assistance** ("information"), dial 411; for long-distance information, dial 1, then the appropriate area code and 555-1212.

Telegraph and telex services are provided primarily by Western Union (www.westernunion.com). You can bring your telegram into the nearest Western Union office (there are hundreds across the country) or dictate it over the phone (© **800/325-6000**). You can also telegraph money, or have it telegraphed to you, very quickly over the Western Union system, but this service can cost as much as 15% to 25% of the amount sent.

Most hotels have **fax** machines available for guest use (be sure to ask about the charge to use it), and many hotel rooms are even wired for guests' fax machines. A less expensive way to send and receive faxes may be at stores such as **Mail Boxes Etc.** (© 800/789-4MBE; www.mbe.com), a national chain of packing service shops (look in the Yellow Pages directory under "Packing Services"). Some Mail Boxes Etc. stores also have computers with Internet access for sending and receiving e-mail.

There are two kinds of telephone directories in the United States. The so-called **White Pages** list private and business subscribers in alphabetical order. The inside front cover lists emergency numbers for police, fire, ambulance, the Coast Guard, poison-control center, crime-victims hotline, and so on. The first few pages will tell you how to make long-distance and international calls, complete with country codes and area codes. Government numbers are usually found on pages printed on blue paper. Printed on yellow paper, the so-called **Yellow Pages** list all local services, businesses, industries, and churches and synagogues by type of activity, with an index at the front or back. The Yellow Pages also include city plans or detailed area maps, often showing postal ZIP codes and public transportation routes.

Time   The continental United States is divided into four **time zones:** eastern standard time (EST), central standard time (CST), mountain standard time (MST), and Pacific standard time (PST). Alaska and Hawaii have their own zones. For example, noon in New York City (EST) is 11am in Chicago (CST), 10am in Denver (MST), 9am in Los Angeles (PST), 8am in Anchorage (AST), and 7am in Honolulu (HST). Most of Florida observes eastern standard time, though the Panhandle west of the Apalachicola River is on central standard time (1 hour earlier than Tallahassee, Orlando, and Miami).

Daylight saving time is in effect from 2am on the first Sunday in April through 2am on the last Sunday in October. Daylight saving time moves the clock 1 hour ahead of standard time.

Tipping   Tipping is so ingrained in the American way of life that the annual income tax of tip-earning service personnel is based on how much they should have received in light of their employers' gross revenues. Accordingly, they may have to pay tax on a tip you didn't actually give them.

Here are some rules of thumb: bartenders, 10% to 15% of the check; bellhops, at least 50¢ per bag, or $2 to $3 for a lot of luggage; cab drivers, 10% of the fare; chambermaids, $1 per day; checkroom attendants, $1 per garment; hairdressers and barbers, 15% to 20% of the bill; waiters and waitresses, 15% to 20% of the check; valet parking attendants, $1 per vehicle; rest-room attendants, 25¢. We do not tip theater ushers, gas station attendants, or the staff at cafeterias and fast-food restaurants.

Toilets   You won't find public toilets (euphemistically referred to here as "restrooms") on the streets in most U.S. cities, but they can be found in hotel lobbies, bars, restaurants, museums, libraries, department stores, railway and bus stations, and service stations. Note, however, that restaurants and bars in resorts or heavily visited areas may reserve their restrooms for the use of their patrons.

4

Getting to Know Miami

by Lesley Abravanel

There's much more to South Florida than the neon-hued nostalgia of *Miami Vice* and pink flamingos. In fact, what used to be a relatively sleepy, beachy keen vacation destination has awoken from its humid slumber, upped its tempo, and finally earned its place in the Palm Pilots of cutting edge jet-setters worldwide. But don't be fooled by the hipper than thou, celebrity-drenched playground commonly known as South Beach. While the chic elite do, indeed, flock to Miami's hippest enclave, it is surprisingly accessible to the average Joe, Jane, or José. For every Phillippe Starck–designed, bank-account-busting boutique hotel on South Beach, there's a kitschy, candy-coated Art Decorated one that's much less taxing on the pocket book. For each Pan-MediterAsian haute cuisinerie, there's always the down-home, no-nonsense Cuban bodega offering hearty food at ridiculously cheap prices.

Beyond the whole "scene," Miami has an endless number of sporting, cultural, and recreational activities to keep you entertained. Did I mention our sparkling beaches that are beyond compare? Crystal clear waters span a turquoise horizon and sandy beaches are filled with palm fronds and seashells. Plus there's excellent shopping and other nightlife activities that include ballet, theater, and opera.

Cross over the bridge onto the mainland, be it the Keys, the Gold Coast, or the Treasure Coast, and you've just exposed yourself not only to more UV rays, but to a world of cultural, historical, and sybaritic surprises. In these spots you can take in a spring baseball game, walk in the footsteps of Papa Hemingway, get up close and personal with the area's sea life, or just soak up the serenity of unspoiled landscapes.

Forget what you've heard about South Florida being Heaven's Waiting Room. That slogan is as passé as the concept of Early Bird dinners (which you can still get, they just no longer define the region). In fact, according to some people, South Florida *is* heaven. So what are you waiting for?

1 Orientation

ARRIVING

Originally carved out of scrubland in 1928 by Pan American Airlines, **Miami International Airport (MIA)** has become second in the United States for international passenger traffic and tenth in the world for total passengers. Despite the heavy traffic, the airport is quite user-friendly and not as much of a hassle as you'd think. And, unlike most airports, you'll even find signs printed in both Spanish and English. You can change money or use your Honor or Plus System ATM card at Nation's Bank of South Florida, located near the exit. Visitor information is available 24 hours a day at the **Miami International Airport Main**

Visitor Counter, Concourse E, second level (© **305/876-7000**). Information is also available at **www.miami-airport.com**. Because MIA is the busiest airport in South Florida, travelers may want to consider flying into the less crowded **Fort Lauderdale–Hollywood International Airport (FLL)** (© **954/ 359-1200**), which is closer to north Miami than MIA, or the **Palm Beach International Airport (PBI)** (© **561/471-7420**), which is about an hour and a half from Miami.

GETTING INTO TOWN
The airport is located about 6 miles west of downtown and about 10 miles from the beaches, so it's likely you can get from the plane to your hotel room in less than half an hour. Of course, if you're arriving from an international destination, it will take more time to go through Customs and Immigration.

BY CAR   All the major car-rental firms operate off-site branches reached via shuttle from the terminals. See "Getting Around," later in this chapter, for a list of major rental companies. Signs at the airport's exit clearly point the way to various parts of the city. If you're arriving late at night, you might want to take a taxi to your hotel and have the car-rental firm deliver a car to your hotel the next day.

BY TAXI   Taxis line up in front of a dispatcher's desk outside the airport's arrivals terminals. Most cabs are metered, though some have flat rates to popular destinations. The fare should be about $20 to Coral Gables, $18 to downtown, and $24 to South Beach, plus tip, which should be at least 10% and more for each bag the driver handles. Depending on traffic, the ride to Coral Gables or downtown takes about 15 to 20 minutes, and to South Beach, 20 to 25 minutes. One of the more reliable companies in the city (with an easy-to-remember number) is **Yellow Cab** (© **305/444-4444**).

BY LIMO OR VAN   Group limousines (multipassenger vans) circle the arrivals area looking for fares. Destinations are posted on the front of each van, and a flat rate is charged for door-to-door service to the area marked.

   SuperShuttle (© **305/871-2000;** www.supershuttle.com/mia.htm) is one of the largest airport operators, charging between $10 and $20 per person for a ride within the county. Its vans operate 24 hours a day and accept American Express, MasterCard, and Visa. This is a cheaper alternative to a cab, but be prepared to be in the van for quite a while, as you may have to make several stops to drop all passengers off before you reach your own destination.

   Private limousine arrangements can be made in advance through your local travel agent. A one-way meet-and-greet service should cost about $50.

BY PUBLIC TRANSPORTATION   Public transportation in South Florida is a major hassle bordering on a nightmare. Painfully slow and unreliable, buses heading downtown leave the airport only once per hour (from the arrivals level), and connections are spotty at best. It could take about an hour and a half to get to South Beach. Journeys to downtown and Coral Gables are more direct. The fare is $1.25, plus an additional 25¢ for a transfer.

VISITOR INFORMATION
The best up-to-date information is provided by the **Greater Miami Convention and Visitor's Bureau,** 701 Brickell Ave., Suite 700, Miami, FL 33131 (© **800/ 933-8448** or **305/539-3000**; fax **305/530-3113**; www.tropicoolmiami.com).

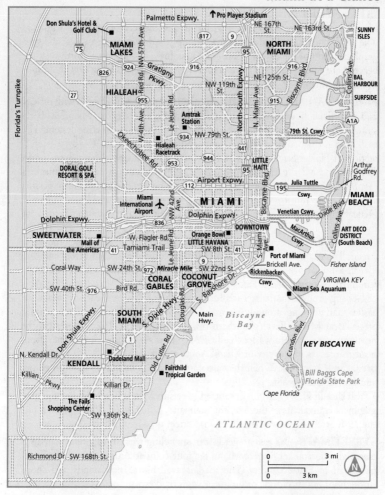

Several chambers of commerce in Greater Miami will send out information on their particular neighborhoods; for addresses and numbers, please see "Visitor Information & Money," in chapter 2.

When you arrive at the Miami International Airport, you can pick up visitor information at the airport's main visitor counter on the second floor of Concourse E. It's open 24 hours a day.

Always check local newspapers for special things to do during your visit. The city's only daily, the *Miami Herald,* is a good source for current events listings, particularly the "Weekend" section in Friday's edition and the paper's entertainment weekly offshoot, *The Street,* available free every Friday in freestanding boxes anchored to city streets. Even better is the free weekly alternative paper, the *Miami New Times,* available in bright red boxes throughout the city.

Information on everything from dining to entertainment in Miami is available on the Internet at **www.miami.citysearch.com**.

CITY LAYOUT

Miami may seem confusing at first, but it quickly becomes easy to negotiate. The small cluster of buildings that make up the downtown area is at the geographical heart of the city. In relation to downtown, the airport is northwest, the beaches are east, Coconut Grove is south, Coral Gables is west, and the rest of the city is north.

FINDING AN ADDRESS   Miami is divided into dozens of areas with official and unofficial boundaries. Street numbering in the city of Miami is fairly straightforward, but you must first be familiar with the numbering system. The mainland is divided into four sections—NE, NW, SE, and SW—by the intersection of Flagler Street and Miami Avenue. Flagler divides Miami from north to south and Miami Avenue divides the city from east to west. Street numbers (1st Street, 2nd Street, and so forth) start from here and increase as you go further out, as do numbers of avenues, places, courts, terraces, and lanes. Streets in Hialeah are the exceptions to this pattern; they are listed separately in map indexes.

Numerical addresses are descriptive, with the first digits giving the cross streets. For example, 12301 Biscayne Blvd. is located at 123rd Street and 501 Ocean Dr. is at 5th Street. It's also helpful to remember that avenues generally run north–south, while streets go east–west.

Getting around the barrier islands that make up Miami Beach is somewhat easier than moving around the mainland. Street numbering starts with 1st Street, near Miami Beach's southern tip, and increases to 192nd Street, in the northern part of Sunny Isles. Collins Avenue makes the entire journey from head to toe. As in the city of Miami, some streets in Miami Beach have numbers as well as names. When they are part of listings in this book, both names and numbers are given.

You should know that the numbered streets in Miami Beach are not the geographical equivalents of those on the mainland, but they are close. For example, the 79th Street Causeway runs into 71st Street on Miami Beach.

STREET MAPS   It's easy to get lost in sprawling Miami, so a reliable map is essential. The Trakker Map of Miami is a four-color accordion map that encompasses all of Dade County. The map is available at newsstands and shops throughout South Florida or online at www.trakkermaps.com.

Some maps of Miami list streets according to area, so you'll have to know which part of the city you are looking for before the street can be found. All the listings in this book include area information for just this reason.

THE NEIGHBORHOODS IN BRIEF

South Beach—The Art Deco District   South Beach's 15 blocks and 10 miles of beach are alive with a frenetic, circus-like atmosphere and are center stage for a motley crew of characters, from eccentric locals, senior citizens, snowbirds, and college students to gender benders, celebrities, club kids, and curiosity-seekers. Individuality is as widely accepted on South Beach as Visa or MasterCard. Bolstered by a Caribbean-chic cafe society and a sexually charged, tragically hip nightlife, people-watching on South Beach is almost as good as a front row seat at a Milan fashion show. Sure, the beautiful people do flock to South Beach, but the models aren't the only sights worth drooling over. The thriving Art Deco District within South Beach contains the largest concentration of Art Deco architecture in the world. In 1979, much of South Beach was listed in the National Register of Historic Places. The pastel-hued structures are super-models in their own right—only these models improve with age.

Miami Beach Before South Beach's late '80s renaissance, during the fabulous '50s, Miami Beach was America's true Riviera. The stomping ground of choice for the Rat Pack and notorious mobsters such as Al Capone, its huge self-contained resort hotels were vacations unto themselves. Then, in the 1960s and 1970s, people who fell in love with Miami began to buy apartments rather than rent hotel rooms. Tourism declined, the Rat Pack fled to Vegas, Capone disappeared, and many area hotels fell into disrepair.

However, since the late 1980s, Miami Beach has experienced a tide of revitalization. Huge beach hotels are finding their niche with new international tourist markets and are attracting large convention crowds. The **Miami Beach Convention Center,** 1901 Convention Center Dr., Miami Beach, FL 33139 (© **305/673-7311**), has more than 1 million square feet of exhibition space.

Surfside, Bal Harbour, and **Sunny Isles** make up the north part of the beach. Hotels, motels, restaurants, and beaches line Collins Avenue. For visitors, it seems that, with some outstanding exceptions, the farther north one goes, the cheaper lodging becomes. All told, excellent prices, location, and facilities make Surfside and Sunny Isles attractive places to stay, although a little rough around the edges.

In exclusive Bal Harbour, where well-paid police officers are instructed to ticket drivers who go above the 30 mph speed limit, the Rodeo Drive of Miami known as the Bal Harbour Shops attracts shoppers who don't flinch at four-, five-, and six-figure price tags. Few hotels remain amid the many beachfront condominium towers. Fancy homes, tucked away on the bay, hide behind gated communities.

Note that **North Miami Beach,** a residential area near the Dade–Broward County line, is a misnomer. It is actually northwest of Miami Beach on the mainland and has no beaches. North Miami Beach is part of North Dade County and has some of Miami's better restaurants and shops. Located within North Miami Beach is the posh residential community of **Aventura,** best known for its high-priced condos, Turnberry Isle Resort, and the Aventura Mall. Also, South Beach, the historic Art Deco District, is treated as a separate neighborhood.

Key Biscayne Miami's forested and secluded Key Biscayne is technically one of the first islands in the Florida Keys. However, this island is nothing like its southern neighbors. Located south of Miami Beach, off the shores of Coconut Grove, Key Biscayne is protected from the troubles of the mainland by the long Rickenbacker Causeway and a $1 toll. Key Biscayne is largely an exclusive residential community, with million-dollar homes and sweeping water views, although it also offers visitors great public beaches, some top resort hotels, and several good restaurants.

Downtown Miami's downtown boasts one of the world's most beautiful cityscapes. Unfortunately, that's about all it offers. During the day, a vibrant community of students, businesspeople, and merchants make their way through the bustling streets. Vendors sell fresh-cut pineapples and mangos while young Latin American consumers on shopping sprees lug bags and boxes. At night, downtown is desolate and not a place in which you'd want to get lost. A downtown revitalization project is in the works, in which a cultural arts center, among other things, is expected to bring downtown back to life.

Design District With restaurants springing up between galleries and furniture stores galore, the Design District is, as locals say, the new South Beach, adding a touch of New York's SoHo to an area formerly known as downtown Miami's "Don't Go." The district, which is a hotbed for furniture import companies, interior designers, architects, and more, has also become a player in Miami's ever-changing nightlife, with a cavernous nightclub–restaurant–production/recording studio–live music venue that has become hipster central for South Beach expatriates and artsy bohemian types. The district is loosely defined as the area bounded by NE 2nd Avenue, NE 5th Avenue East and West, and NW 36th Street to the South.

Biscayne Corridor From downtown near Bayside to the '70s, where trendy curio shops and upscale restaurants are slowly opening, Biscayne Boulevard is aspiring to reclaim itself as a safe thoroughfare where tourists can wine, dine, and shop. Previously known for sketchy, dilapidated 1950s- and '60s-era hotels that had fallen on hard times, residents fleeing the high prices of the beaches in search of affordable housing are renovating Biscayne block by block, making this once again famous boulevard worthy of a Sunday drive. With the trendy Design District immediately west of 36th and Biscayne by 2 blocks, there is hope for the area.

Little Haiti During a brief period in the late 1970s and early '80s, almost 35,000 Haitians arrived in Miami. Most of the new refugees settled in a 200-square-block area north of downtown. Extending from 41st to 83rd streets and bordered by I-95 and Biscayne Boulevard, Little Haiti is a neighborhood with at least 60,000 residents, more than half of whom were born in Haiti. Tourists are not recommended to venture into this neighborhood.

Little Havana If you've never been to Cuba, just visit this small section of Miami and you'll come pretty close. The sounds, tastes, and rhythms all remind you of Cuba's capital city. Some even jokingly say you don't have to speak a word of English to live an independent life here. Street signs are in Spanish and English. Cuban coffee shops, tailor and furniture stores, and inexpensive restaurants line "Calle Ocho" (pronounced *Ka*-yey O-choh), SW 8th Street, the region's main thoroughfare. Salsa and merengue beats ring loudly from old record stores while old men in *guayaberas* smoke cigars over their daily game of dominoes.

Coral Gables "The City Beautiful," created by George Merrick in the early 1920s, is one of Miami's first planned developments. But this is not Levittown. The houses here were built in a Mediterranean style along lush tree-lined streets that open onto beautifully carved plazas, many with centerpiece fountains. The best architectural examples of the era have Spanish-style tiled roofs and are built from Miami oolite, native limestone commonly called "coral rock." The Gables's European-flared shopping and commerce center is home to many thriving corporations. Some of the city's best restaurants, headed by world-renowned chefs, are located here. You'll also find landmark hotels, great golfing, and upscale shopping.

Coconut Grove There was a time when Coconut Grove was inhabited by artists, intellectuals, hippies, and radicals, but gentrification has pushed most alternative types out, leaving in their place a multitude of commercialized cafes, boutiques, and nightspots. The intersection of Grand Avenue, Main Highway, and McFarlane Road pierces the area's heart. Right in the center of it all is CocoWalk and the Shops at Mayfair, filled with lovely boutiques, eateries, and bars. Sidewalks here are often crowded, especially at night, when University of Miami students who frequent this adopted college town come out to play.

Southern Miami–Dade County   To locals, South Miami is both a specific area, southwest of Coral Gables, and a general region that encompasses all of southern Dade County and includes Kendall, Perrine, Cutler Ridge, and Homestead. For the purposes of clarity, this book has grouped all these southern suburbs under the rubric "Southern Miami–Dade County." Similar attributes unite the communities: They are heavily residential, and all are packed with shopping malls amidst a few remaining plots of farmland. Tourists don't usually stay in these parts, unless they are on their way to the Everglades or the Keys. However, this area contains many of the city's top attractions, making it likely you'll spend some time during the day here.

2 Getting Around

Officially, Dade County has opted for a "unified, multimodal transportation network," which basically means you can get around the city by train, bus, and taxi. However, in practice, the network doesn't work too well. Things may improve when the city completes its transportation center in 2005, but until then, unless you are going from downtown Miami to a not-too-distant spot, you are better off in a rented car or a taxi.

With the exception of downtown Coconut Grove and South Beach, Miami is not a walker's city. Because it is so spread out, most attractions are too far apart to make walking between them feasible. In fact, most Miamians are so used to driving that they do so even when going just a few blocks.

BY PUBLIC TRANSPORTATION

BY RAIL   Two rail lines, operated by the **Metro-Dade Transit Agency** (© **305/770-3131** for information; www.co.miami-dade.fl.us/mdta/), run in concert with each other.

Metrorail, the city's modern high-speed commuter train, is a 21-mile elevated line that travels north–south, between downtown Miami and the southern suburbs. Locals like to refer to this semi-useless rail system as Metro*fail.* If you are staying in Coral Gables or Coconut Grove, you can park your car at a nearby station and ride the rails downtown. However, that's about it. Unfortunately for visitors, the line's usefulness is limited. The first addition to the system, scheduled for completion in mid-2001, will only extend the rail from the Okeechobee station to

Joy Ride
Metromover offers a fun, futuristic ride that you might want to take to complement your downtown tour.

just west of the Palmetto Expressway. There are plans to extend the system to service Miami International Airport, but until those tracks are built, these trains don't go most places tourists go, with the exception of Vizcaya in Coconut Grove. Metrorail operates daily from about 6am to midnight. The fare is $1.25.

Metromover, a 4.4-mile elevated line, connects with Metrorail at the Government Center stop and circles downtown. This is a good way to get to Bayside if you don't have a car. Riding on rubber tires, the single-car train winds past many of the area's most important attractions and shopping and business districts. You may not go very far, but you will get a beautiful perspective from the towering height of the suspended rails. System hours are daily from about 6am to midnight. The fare is 25¢.

BY BUS   Miami's suburban layout is not conducive to getting around by bus. Lines operate and maps are available, but instead of getting to know the city, you'll find that relying on bus transportation will acquaint you only with how it feels to wait at bus stops. In short, a bus ride in Miami is grueling. You can get a bus map by mail, either from the Greater Miami Convention and Visitor's Bureau (see above) or by writing the Metro-Dade Transit System, 3300 NW 32nd Ave., Miami, FL 33142. In Miami, call ℂ **305/770-3131** for public-transit information. The fare is $1.25.

BY CAR

Tales circulate about vacationers who have visited Miami without a car, but they are very few indeed. If you are counting on exploring the city, even to a modest degree, a car is essential. Miami's restaurants, attractions, and sights are far from one another, so any other form of transportation is impractical. You won't need a car, however, if you are spending your entire vacation at a resort, are traveling directly to the Port of Miami for a cruise, or are here for a short stay centered in one area of the city, such as South Beach, where everything is within walking distance and parking is a costly nightmare.

When driving across a causeway or through downtown, allow extra time to reach your destination because of frequent drawbridge openings. Some bridges open about every half hour for large sailing vessels to make their way through the wide bays and canals that crisscross the city, stalling traffic for several minutes.

RENTALS   It seems as though every car-rental company, big and small, has at least one office in Miami. Consequently, the city is one of the cheapest places in the world to rent a car. Many firms regularly advertise prices in the neighborhood of $140 per week for their economy car. You should also check first with the airline you have chosen. There are often special discounts when you book a flight and reserve your rental car simultaneously. A minimum age, generally 25, is usually required of renters. Some rental agencies have also set maximum ages. A national car-rental broker, **A Car Rental Referral Service (ℂ 800/404-4482)**, can often find companies willing to rent to drivers over the age of 21 and can also get discounts from major companies as well as some regional ones.

National car-rental companies with toll-free numbers include **Alamo** (ℂ **800/327-9633**), **Avis** (ℂ **800/331-1212**), **Budget** (ℂ **800/527-0700**), **Dollar** (ℂ **800/800-4000** or 800/327-7607), **Hertz** (ℂ **800/654-3131**), **National** (ℂ **800/328-4567**), and **Thrifty** (ℂ **800/367-2277**). One excellent company that has offices in every conceivable part of town and offers extremely competitive rates is **Enterprise (ℂ 800/325-8007)**. Just make sure that you call several companies and comparison shop. Car-rental prices can fluctuate more than airfares. For information on car-rental insurance, see "Getting There," in chapter 2.

Many companies offer cellular phones or electronic map rental. It might be wise to opt for these additional safety features, although the cost can be exorbitant; the phone especially can come in handy if you get lost.

Finally, think about splurging on a convertible. Not only is it one of the best ways to see the beautiful surroundings, but it's an ideal way to perfect a tan! At most companies, the price for convertibles is approximately 20% more.

PARKING   Always keep plenty of quarters on hand to feed hungry meters. Or, on Miami Beach, stop by the chamber of commerce at 1920 Meridian Ave. or any Publix grocery store to buy a magnetic **parking card** in denominations of $10, $20, or $25. Parking is usually plentiful (except on South Beach and Coconut Grove), but when it's not, be careful: Fines for illegal parking can be stiff.

In addition to parking garages, valet services are commonplace and often used. Expect to pay from $5 to $15 for parking in Coconut Grove and on South Beach's busy weekend nights.

LOCAL DRIVING RULES   Florida law allows drivers to make a right turn on a red light after a complete stop, unless otherwise indicated. In addition, all passengers are required to wear seat belts, and children under 3 must be securely fastened in government-approved car seats.

BY TAXI

If you're not planning on traveling much within the city, an occasional taxi is a good alternative to renting a car. If you plan on spending your vacation within the confines of South Beach's Art Deco District, you might also want to avoid the parking hassles that come with renting your own car. Taxi meters start at $1.50 for the first quarter-mile and 25¢ for each one-eighth mile. There are standard flat-rate charges for frequently traveled routes—for example, Miami Beach's Convention Center to Coconut Grove would cost about $16.

Major cab companies include **Metro** (© **305/888-8888**), **Yellow** (© **305/444-4444**), and, on Miami Beach, **Central** (© **305/532-5555**).

BY BIKE

Miami is a biker's paradise, with several scenic places in which to spin your wheels, including most of Miami Beach, where the hard-packed sand and boardwalks make it an easy and scenic route. However, unless you are a former New York City bike messenger, you won't want to use a bicycle as your main means of transportation.

For more information on bicycles, including where to rent the best ones, see chapter 5, "What to See & Do in Miami."

 FAST FACTS: Miami

Airport   See "Orientation," earlier in this chapter.

American Express   You'll find American Express offices in downtown Miami at 330 Biscayne Blvd. (© **305/358-7350**); 9700 Collins Ave., Bal Harbour (© **305/865-5959**); and 32 Miracle Mile, Coral Gables (© **305/446-3381**). Offices are open weekdays from 9am to 5pm and Saturday from 10am to 4pm. The Bal Harbour office is also open on Sunday from noon to 6pm. To report lost or stolen traveler's checks, call © **800/221-7282**.

Area Code   The original area code for Miami and all of Dade County was 305. That is still the code for older phone numbers, but all phone numbers assigned since July 1998 have the area code 786 (SUN). For all local calls, even if you're calling across the street, you must dial the area code 305 or 786 first. Even though the Keys still share the Dade County area code of

305, calls to there from Miami are considered long distance and must be preceded by 1-305. (Within the Keys, simply dial the seven-digit number.) The area code for Fort Lauderdale is 954; for Palm Beach, Boca Raton, Vero Beach, and Port St. Lucie, it's 561.

Business Hours Banking hours vary, but most banks are open weekdays from 9am to 3pm. Several stay open until 5pm or so at least 1 day during the week, and many banks feature automated teller machines (ATMs) for 24-hour banking. Most stores are open daily from 10am to 6pm; however, there are many exceptions (noted in "Shopping," chapter 5. As far as business offices are concerned, Miami is generally a 9-to-5 town.

Car Rentals See "Getting Around," above.

Climate See "When to Go" in chapter 2.

Curfew Although not strictly enforced, there is an alleged curfew in effect for minors after 11pm on weeknights and midnight on weekends in all of Miami–Dade County. After those hours, children under 17 cannot be out on the streets or driving unless accompanied by a parent or on their way to work. Somehow, however, they still manage to sneak out and congregate in popular areas such as Coconut Grove and South Beach.

Dentists **A&E Dental,** 11400 N. Kendall Dr., Mega Bank Building (② 305/271-7777), offers round-the-clock care and accepts MasterCard and Visa.

Doctors In an emergency, call an ambulance by dialing ② 911 from any phone. The Dade County Medical Association sponsors a **Physician Referral Service** (② 305/324-8717) weekdays from 9am to 5pm. **Health South Doctors' Hospital,** 5000 University Dr., Coral Gables (② 305/666-2111), is a 285-bed acute-care hospital with a 24-hour physician-staffed emergency department.

Drugstores See "Pharmacies," below.

Embassies/Consulates See chapter 3.

Emergencies To reach the police, ambulance, or fire department, dial ② 911 from any phone. No coins are needed. Emergency hotlines include **Crisis Intervention** (② 305/358-HELP or 305/358-4357) and the **Poison Information Center** (② 800/282-3171).

Eyeglasses **Pearle Vision Center,** 7901 Biscayne Blvd. (② 305/754-5144), in Miami, can usually fill prescriptions in about an hour.

Hospitals See "Doctors," above.

Information See "Visitor Information," earlier in this chapter.

Laundry/Dry Cleaning For dry-cleaning self-service machines and a wash-and-fold service by the pound, call **All Laundry Service,** 5701 NW 7th St. (② 305/261-8175); it's open daily from 7am to 10pm. **Clean Machine Laundry,** 226 12th St., South Beach (② 305/534-9429), is convenient to South Beach's Art Deco hotels; it's open 24 hours. **Coral Gables Laundry & Dry Cleaning,** 250 Minorca Ave., Coral Gables (② 305/446-6458), has been dry cleaning, altering, and laundering since 1930. It offers a lifesaving same-day service and is open weekdays from 7am to 7pm and Saturday from 8am to 3pm.

Liquor Laws Only adults 21 or older may legally purchase or consume alcohol in the state of Florida. Minors are usually permitted in bars that serve food. Liquor laws are strictly enforced; if you look young, carry identification. Beer and wine are sold in most supermarkets and convenience stores. The city of Miami's liquor stores are closed on Sunday. Liquor stores in the city of Miami Beach are open all week.

Lost Property If you lost it at the airport, call the **Airport Lost and Found** office (℡ 305/876-7377). If you lost it on the bus, Metrorail, or Metromover, call **Metro-Dade Transit Agency** (℡ 305/770-3131). If you lost it somewhere else, phone the **Dade County Police Lost and Found** (℡ 305/375-3366). You may also want to fill out a police report for insurance purposes.

Luggage Storage/Lockers In addition to the baggage check at Miami International Airport, most hotels offer luggage storage facilities. If you are taking a cruise from the Port of Miami (see "Cruises & Other Caribbean Getaways" in chapter 5), bags can be stored in your ship's departure terminal.

Newspapers/Magazines The *Miami Herald* is the city's only English-language daily. It is especially known for its Latin American coverage and has a decent Friday "Weekend" entertainment guide. The most respected alternative weekly is the give-away tabloid called *New Times,* which contains up-to-date listings and reviews of food, films, theater, music, and whatever else is happening in town. Also free, if you can find it, is *Ocean Drive,* an oversized glossy magazine that's limited on text and heavy on ads and society photos; it's available at a number of chic South Beach boutiques and restaurants. It is also available on newsstands.

For a large selection of foreign-language newspapers and magazines, check with any of the large bookstores (see chapter 5) or try **News Café** at 800 Ocean Dr., South Beach (℡ 305/538-6397), or in Coconut Grove at 2901 Florida Ave. (℡ 305/774-6397). Adjacent to the **Van Dyke Café,** 846 Lincoln Rd., South Beach (℡ 305/534-3600) is a fantastic newsstand with magazines and newspapers from all over the world. Also check out **Eddie's Normandy,** 1096 Normandy Dr., Miami Beach (℡ 305/866-2026), and **Worldwide News,** 1629 NE 163rd St., North Miami Beach (℡ 305/940-4090).

Pharmacies **Walgreens Pharmacy** has dozens of locations all over town, including 8550 Coral Way (℡ 305/221-9271), in Coral Gables; 1845 Alton Rd. (℡ 305/531-8868), in South Beach; and 6700 Collins Ave. (℡ 305/861-6742), in Miami Beach. The branch at 5731 Bird Rd. at SW 40th Street (℡ 305/666-0757) is open 24 hours, as is **Eckerd Drugs,** 1825 Miami Gardens Dr. NE, at 185th Street, North Miami Beach (℡ 305/932-5740).

Photographic Needs One of the more expensive places to have your film developed is **One Hour Photo** in the Bayside Marketplace (℡ 305/377-FOTO). **Coconut Grove Camera,** 3317 Virginia St. (℡ 305/445-0521), features 30-minute color processing and maintains a huge selection of cameras and equipment. It rents, too. Walgreens or Eckerd's will develop film for the next day for about $6 or $7.

Police For emergencies, dial ℡ 911 from any phone. No coins are needed. For other matters, call ℡ 305/595-6263.

Post Office The **Main Post Office**, 2200 Milam Dairy Rd., Miami, FL 33152 (© 305/639-4280), is located west of Miami International Airport. Letters addressed to you and marked "c/o General Delivery" can be picked up at 500 NW 2nd Ave. Conveniently located post offices include 1300 Washington Ave. in South Beach, and 3191 Grand Ave. in Coconut Grove. There is one central number for all post offices: © 800/275-8777.

Radio About five dozen radio stations can be heard in the Greater Miami area. On the AM dial, 610 (WIOD), 790 (WNWS), 1230 (WJNO), and 1340 (WPBR) are all talk. There is no all-news station in town, although 940 (WINZ) gives traffic updates and headline news in between its talk shows. WDBF (1420) is a good big-band station and WPBG (1290) features golden oldies. The two most popular R&B stations are WEDR or 99 Jams (99.1) and Hot 105 (105.1). The best rock stations on the FM dial are WZTA (94.9) and the progressive college station WVUM (90.5). WKIS (99.9) is the top country station. Top-40 music can be heard on WHYI (100.3) and classic disco on Mega 103 (103.5). Public radio can be heard either on WXEL (90.7) or WLRN (91.3). WGTR (97.3) plays easy listening. WDNA (88.9) has the best Latin jazz and multiethnic sounds.

Religious Services Miami houses of worship are as varied as the city's population and include St. Patrick Catholic Church, 3716 Garden Ave., Miami Beach (© 305/531-1124); Coral Gables Baptist Church, 5501 Granada Blvd. (© 305/665-4072); Temple Judea, 5500 Granada Blvd., Coral Gables (© 305/667-5657); Coconut Grove United Methodist, 2850 SW 27th Ave. (© 305/443-0880); Christ Episcopal Church, 3481 Hibiscus St. (© 305/442-8542); and Plymouth Congregational Church, 3400 Devon Rd., at Main Highway (© 305/444-6521).

Restrooms Stores rarely let customers use the restrooms, and many restaurants offer their facilities for customers only. Most malls have bathrooms, as do many fast-food restaurants. Many public beaches and large parks provide toilets, though in some places you have to pay or tip an attendant. Most large hotels have clean restrooms in their lobbies.

Safety As always, use your common sense and be aware of your surroundings at all times. Don't walk alone at night, and be extra wary when walking or driving though downtown Miami and surrounding areas.

Reacting to several highly publicized crimes against tourists several years ago, both local and state governments have taken steps to help protect visitors. These measures include special highly visible police units patrolling the airport and surrounding neighborhoods and better signs on the state's most tourist-traveled routes.

When driving around Miami, always keep a good map handy, keep the doors locked, and stay alert. Never stop on a highway—if you get a flat tire, drive to the nearest well-lighted, populated place. If you are renting a car, you may consider additional safety features in the car, such as cellular telephones or electronic maps.

Spas & Massage There are some great spa packages at some ritzier hotels, but those without spas often have relationships with on-call massage therapists. Ask the concierge to make an appointment for an in-room session. Popular day spas include the **Russian Turkish Baths**, 5445

Collins Ave. at the Castle Hotel (© **305/867-8316**), otherwise known as "The Schvitz," where the old guard meets the new in eucalyptus-scented Turkish steam rooms and aroma baths bolstered by marble columns. **Il Paradiso Day Spa,** 345 Alton Rd., Miami Beach (© **305/672-2600**), is the city's best-kept secret, tucked away in a house, offering massages, reflexology, facials, manicures, and the ever-popular Peppermint Twist, in which a blend of seaweed and essential oil of peppermint has been known to reduce cellulite.

Taxes A 6% state sales tax (plus 0.5% local tax, for a total of 6.5% in Miami) is added on at the register for all goods and services purchased in Florida. In addition, most municipalities levy special taxes on restaurants and hotels. In Surfside, hotel taxes total 10.5%; in Bal Harbour, 9.5%; in Miami Beach (including South Beach), 11.5%; and in the rest of Dade County, a whopping 12.5%. In Miami Beach, Surfside, and Bal Harbour, the resort (hotel) tax also applies to hotel restaurants and restaurants with liquor licenses.

Taxis See "Getting Around," earlier in this chapter.

Television The local stations are Channel 6, WTVJ (NBC); Channel 4, WCIX (CBS); Channel 7, WSVN (Fox); Channel 10, WPLG (ABC); Channel 17, WLRN (PBS); Channel 23, WLTV (independent); and Channel 33, WBFS (independent).

Time Zone Miami, like New York, is in the Eastern Standard Time zone. Between April and October, daylight saving time is adopted, and clocks are set 1 hour ahead. America's eastern seaboard is 5 hours behind Greenwich Mean Time. To find out what time it is, call © **305/324-8811**.

Transit Information For Metrorail or Metromover schedule information, phone © **305/770-3131** or surf over to **www.co.miami-dade.fl.us/mdta/**.

Weather Hurricane season runs from August through November. For an up-to-date recording of current weather conditions and forecast reports, call © **305/229-4522**.

3 Accommodations

As much a part of the landscape as the palm trees, many of Miami's hotels are on display as if they were contestants in a beauty pageant. The city's long-lasting status on the destination hot list has given rise to an ever-increasing number of upscale hotels. And no place in Miami has seen a greater increase in construction than Miami Beach. Since the renaissance that began in the late 1980s, the beach has turned what used to be a beachfront retirement home into a sand-swept haute spot for the Gucci and Prada set. Contrary to popular belief, however, the beach does not discriminate, and it's the juxtaposition of the chic elite and the hoi polloi that contributes to its allure.

While the increasing demand for rooms on South Beach means increasing costs, you can still get a decent room at a fair price. In fact, most hotels in the Art Deco District are less Ritz-Carlton than they are Holiday Inn, unless, of course, they've been renovated. Keep in mind that most hotels in this area were built in the 1930s for the middle class. Unless you plan to center your vacation entirely in and around your hotel, most of the cheaper Deco hotels are adequate and a wise choice for those who plan to use the room only to sleep. The smart vacationer can almost name his price if he's willing to live without a few luxuries, such as an oceanfront view. Always remember to ask about packages, since it's often possible to get a better deal than the published rates.

Many of the old hotels from the 1930s, 1940s, and 1950s have been totally renovated, giving way to dozens of "boutique" hotels. Keep in mind that when a hotel claims that it was just renovated, that can mean they've completely gutted the building—or just added a few coats of fresh paint. Always ask what specific changes were made during a renovation, and be sure to ask if a hotel will be undergoing construction while you're there. You should also find out how near your room will be to the center of the nightlife crowd; trying to sleep directly on Ocean Drive, especially during the weekend, is next to impossible, unless your lullaby of choice happens to include throbbing salsa and bass beats.

Also, keep in mind that along South Beach's Collins Avenue are dozens of hotels and motels—in all price categories—so there's bound to be a vacancy. If you do try the walk-in routine, don't forget to ask to see one of the rooms first. A few dollars could mean all the difference.

SEASONS & RATES   South Florida's tourist season is well defined, beginning in mid-November and lasting until Easter. Hotel prices escalate until about March, after which they begin to decline. During the off-season, hotel rates are typically 30% to 50% lower than their winter highs.

But timing isn't everything. In many cases, rates also depend on your hotel's proximity to the beach and how much ocean you can see from your window. Small motels a block or two from the water can be up to 40% cheaper than similar properties right on the sand.

Rates below have been broken down into two broad categories: winter (generally, Thanksgiving through Easter) and off-season (about mid-May through August). The months in between, the shoulder season, should fall somewhere in between the highs and lows. Rates always go up on holidays. Remember, too, that state and city taxes can add as much as 12.5% to your bill in some parts of Miami. Some hotels, especially those in South Beach, also tack on additional service charges. And parking is pricey.

PRICE CATEGORIES   The hotels below are divided first by area, then by price, using the following guidelines: **very expensive,** over $250; **expensive,** $180 to $250; **moderate,** $90 to $180; and **inexpensive,** below $90. Prices are based on published rates (or rack rates) for a standard double room during the high season. Check with the reservations agent, since many rooms are also available above and below the category ranges listed. And always ask about packages, since it's often possible to get a better deal than these "official" rates. Most important, always call the hotel to confirm rates, which may be subject to change without notice because of special events, holidays, or blackout dates.

LONG-TERM STAYS   If you plan to visit Miami for a month, a season, or more, think about renting a room in a long-term hotel or condominium apartment. Long-term accommodations exist in every price category, from budget to deluxe, and in general are extremely reasonable, especially during the off-season. Check with the reservation services below, or write a short note to the chamber of commerce in the area where you plan to stay. In addition, many local real estate agents also handle short-term rentals (meaning less than a year).

RESERVATION SERVICES **Central Reservations** (© 800/950-0232 or 305/274-6832; www.reservation-services.com) works with many of Miami's hotels and can often secure discounts of up to 40%. It also gives advice on specific locales, especially in Miami Beach and downtown.

The **South Florida Hotel Network** (© 800/538-3616 or 305/538-3616) lists more than 300 hotels throughout the area, from Palm Beach to Miami and down to the Keys.

For bed-and-breakfasts throughout the state, contact **Florida Bed and Breakfast Inns** (© 800/524-1880).

SOUTH BEACH

Choosing a hotel on South Beach is similar to deciding whether you'd rather pay a $1.50 for french fries at Denny's or $8.50 for the same fries—but let's call them *pomme frites*—in a pricey haute cuisinerie. Fortunately, for every chichi hotel in South Beach—and there are many—there are just as many moderately priced, more casual options.

Prices mentioned here are rack rates—that is, the price you would be quoted if you walked up to the front desk and inquired about rates. The actual price you will end up paying will usually be less than this—especially if a travel agent makes the reservations for you. Many hotels on South Beach have stopped quoting seasonal and off-season rates and have, instead, chosen to go with a low-to-high rate representing the hotel's complete pricing range.

VERY EXPENSIVE

The Delano ☆ *Overrated* Unless your name's Madonna, Gwyneth, or the equivalent, you will definitely feel like you are paying for the privilege of staying here. The hipper-than-thou hotel is known for its extravagant decor and deco architecture in which Alice in Wonderland meets South Beach. Dolled up in the whimsically minimalist style of designer Philippe Starck, the Delano may not be the friendliest place in which to stay, but it certainly is amusing to look at, with 40-foot sheer white curtains hanging outside, mirrors everywhere, white billowing curtains, Adirondack chairs, and faux-fur-covered beds. The rooms are done up sanitarium style: sterile, yet toxically trendy, in pure white save for a perfectly crisp green Granny Smith apple in each room—the only freebie you're going to get here. A bathroom renovation is taking place in all the rooms—but they will remain small and spartan. Bathrooms in the suites and bungalows have been done up in Italian marble with oversized monolithic bathtubs. An attractive, white-clad staff look as if they were hand-picked from last month's *Vogue*. While they may sigh if you ask for something, eventually they'll get it for you. The gym here is great, but is costs $15 a day, even if you are a guest. The fantastic wading pool, thankfully, is free, but get out early to snag a chair. The Blue Door restaurant, formerly part-owned by Madonna, serves lots of attitude with its pricey cuisine; the lobby's Rose Bar is command central for the chic elite who don't flinch at paying in excess of $10 for a martini. The hotel's major saving grace is Agua, the rooftop spa, where, if you can afford it, an hour massage while overlooking the ocean is blissful.

1685 Collins Ave., South Beach, FL 33139. © 800/555-5001 or 305/672-2000. Fax 305/532-0099. 209 units, 1 penthouse. Winter $325–$810 standard; $750–$2,000 suite; $2,000–$3,000 bungalow or 2-bedroom; $2,800–$3,000 penthouse. Off-season $245–$660 standard; $600–$2,000 suite; $940–$3,000 bungalow or 2-bedroom; $2,400–$3,000 penthouse. Additional person $35. AE, DC, DISC, MC, V. Valet parking $20. **Amenities:** 3 restaurants; bar; large outdoor pool; 24-hour state-of-the-art David Barton gym; extensive water-sports equipment; children's programs; concierge; business center; room service; in-room massage; same-day laundry and dry-cleaning service. *In room:* A/C, TV/VCR, CD player, minibar, hair dryer.

Ritz-Carlton ★★★   The luxe life comes to a congested and somewhat seedy corner of South Beach in the form of this beachfront, lushly landscaped Ritz-Carlton, which has restored a landmark 1950s building to its original Art Moderne style and filled it with the hotel's signature five-star service. Far from ostentatious, the Ritz-Carlton's South Beach property moves away from gilded opulence in favor of the more soothing pastel-washed touches of Deco. Though South Beach is better known for its trendy boutique hotels, the Ritz-Carlton offers comfort to those who might prefer 100% cotton sheets and goose-down pillows to high-style minimalism.

With impeccable service, an impressive stretch of sand, and a world-class 13,000-square-foot spa and wellness center, the Ritz-Carlton kicks sand in the faces of some of the smaller hotels that think they're doing *you* a favor by allowing you to sleep there.

1 Lincoln Rd., South Beach, FL 33139. (*C*) **800/241-3333** or 305/648-5900. Fax 305/648-1448. www. ritzcarlton.com. 375 units. Winter $450–$750 double. Off-season $275–$625 double. AE, DISC, MC, V. Valet parking $30. **Amenities:** 3 restaurants; outdoor heated pool; health club; spa; extensive water-sports rentals; children's program; 24-hour business center; salon; 24-hour room service; baby-sitting; overnight laundry service. *In room:* A/C, TV, dataport, minibar, hair dryer, coffeemaker, iron, safe.

The Tides ★★★   This 12-story Art Deco masterpiece is reminiscent of a gleaming ocean liner, with porthole windows and lots of stainless steel and frosted glass. Rooms are starkly white but much more luxurious and comfortable than those at the Delano. Also, all rooms are at least twice the size of a typical South Beach hotel room and have a view of the ocean. They feature king beds, spacious closets, large bathrooms, and even a telescope from which to view the vast ocean. The penthouses on the 9th and 10th floors are situated at the highest point on Ocean Drive, allowing for a priceless panoramic view of the ocean, the skyline, and the beach. Although small, the freshwater pool is a welcome plus, but it really doesn't fit with the rest of the hotel, lacking in ambience and view (it overlooks an alley). The hotel's restaurant, Twelve Twenty, is an elegant, excellent, and pricey eatery with seating in the lobby. The Terrace is a less expensive outdoor cafe.

1220 Ocean Dr., South Beach, FL 33139. (*C*) **800/OUTPOST** or 305/604-5000. Fax 305/672-6288. www. islandoutpost.com. 45 units. Winter $475 suite; $2,500 penthouse. Off-season $350 suite; $2,000 penthouse. Additional person $15. AE, DC, DISC, MC, V. Valet parking $18. **Amenities:** 2 restaurants; lounge; bar; outdoor heated pool; small health club and discount at large nearby health club; concierge; secretarial services; 24-hour room service; in-room massage; baby-sitting; laundry and dry-cleaning service. *In room:* A/C, TV/VCR, stereo/CD player w/selection of music, video rentals, minibar, hair dryer.

Villas at Caffé Milano ★★   With prices like these, you could've actually gone to Milan, but nonetheless, this 11-room boutique hotel boasts enormous, luxurious oceanfront rooms with state-of-the-art industrial-style kitchen appliances, flat- or big-screen televisions, and DVD players. In addition to the fantastic in-room amenities, the service here is particularly attentive, as it should be. The one drawback, for some, is its location on a busy stretch of Ocean Drive— noise level is rather high here and there's nothing the hotel can do about it. But they will try to fulfill any other requests you might have.

850 Ocean Dr., South Beach, FL 33139. (*C*) **888/535-5135** or 305/ 535-8879. Fax: 305/695-2942. 11 units. Year-round $600–$750 double. AE, DC, DISC, MC, V. Valet parking $18. **Amenities:** Restaurant; lounge; dry-cleaning service. *In room:* A/C, TV/VCR, DVD, kitchen, coffeemaker, hair dryer, washer and dryer, Jacuzzi in one unit.

South Beach Accommodations

Hotel Dining

While travelers don't necessarily choose a hotel by their dining options, some of Miami's best restaurants can be found inside hotels. Some of the city's most hailed cuisine can be had at Hotel Astor's **Astor Place Bar and Grill,** the Delano's **Blue Door,** The Hotel's **Wish,** and the Mandarin Oriental's **Azul. Nobu,** a New York import scheduled to open at the Shore Club, will surely join the list. *Warning:* In some cases, your tab at these restaurants may be almost as high as the price of a room.

EXPENSIVE

The Hotel ★★★   Kitschy fashion designer Todd Oldham whimsically restored this 1939 gem (formerly the Tiffany Hotel) as he would have a vintage piece of couture. He laced it with lush, cool colors, hand-cut mirror, and glass mosaics from his ready-to-wear factory, then added artisan detailing, terrazzo floors, and porthole windows. The small, soundproof rooms are very comfortable and incredibly stylish, though the bathrooms are a bit cramped. There's no need to pay more for an oceanfront view—go up to the rooftop, where the pool is located, and you'll see the most amazing view of the Atlantic. The hotel's restaurant, Wish, is one of South Beach's best.

801 Collins Ave., South Beach, FL 33139. ✆ **877/843-4683** or 305/531-2222. Fax 305/531-2222. www. thehotelofsouthbeach.com. 52 units. Year-round $195–$345 double. AE, DC, DISC, MC, V. Valet parking $18. **Amenities:** Restaurant; bar; pool bar; small pool; health club; concierge; business center; room service. *In room:* A/C, TV/VCR, stereo system with CD and cassette players, Kiehl's bath products, video library, dataport, minibar, coffeemaker, hair dryer.

Hotel Astor ★★★   Cozy-chic best describes this diminutive Deco hotel built in 1936. A 1995 renovation greatly improved on the original design of this simple three-story property which has hosted the likes of Cameron Diaz and Madonna and continues to attract a lively local crowd to the small but sleek lobby bar. There is a small lap pool and a beautiful waterfall outside the bar area, but if you're looking to catch some sun, you may want to consider walking the 2 blocks to the beach because there are very few lounge chairs at the pool. The rooms are small but soothing in beige tones, featuring plush and luxurious details—swivel stands for the large-screen TVs, Belgian linens and towels, and funky custom mood lighting with dimmer switches. The mattresses are incredibly plush and difficult to leave. Views are probably the worst thing about this hotel, as most rooms face the street or a neighboring seedy hotel. The hotel staff is known for its extreme attentiveness—especially Arturo, the hotel's "Cheers"-y bartender who actually knows everybody's names and their drinks of choice. Astor Place Bar and Grill in the hotel's basement is one of the city's best and most expensive. Two disabled-accessible rooms are available.

956 Washington Ave., South Beach, FL 33139. ✆ **800/270-4981** or 305/531-8081. Fax 305/531-3193. www. hotelastor.com. 40 units. Winter $150–$800 double. Off-season $110–$500 double. Additional person $30. AE, DC, MC, V. Valet parking $20. **Amenities:** Restaurant; 2 bars; small outdoor pool; access to nearby health club; 24-hour concierge service; secretarial services; limited room service; in-room massage; baby-sitting; laundry and dry-cleaning service. *In room:* A/C, TV, dataport, minibar, fridge, hair dryer.

Hotel Impala ★★★   This renovated Mediterranean inn is one of the areas best, and it's just beautiful, from the Greco-Roman frescos and friezes to an intimate garden that is perfumed with the scents from hanging lilies and gardenias.

Rooms are extremely comfortable, with super-cushy sleigh beds, sisal floors, wrought iron fixtures, imported Belgian cotton linens, wood furniture, and fabulous roomy bathrooms done up in stainless steel and coral rock. Adjacent to the hotel is Spiga, an intimate, excellent Italian restaurant that is reasonably priced. Enclaves like this one are rare on South Beach.

1228 Collins Ave., South Beach, FL 33139. (C) **800/646-7252** or 305/673-2021. Fax 305/673-5984. hotelimpala1@aol.com. 17 units. Winter $200–$400 double. Off-season $169–$279 double. AE, DC, MC, V. Valet parking $18. No children under 16 permitted. **Amenities:** Restaurant; concierge; room service. *In room:* A/C, TV/VCR, stereo, CD player, complimentary videos, dataport, hair dryer.

Raleigh Hotel ★★   Upon entering the lobby of this oceanfront Art Deco hotel, you will feel like you've stepped back into the 1940s. Polished wood, original terrazzo floors, and an intimate martini bar add to the fabulous atmosphere that's favored by fashion photographers and production crews, for whom the hotel's fleur-de-lis pool is the favorite subject. In fact, one look at the pool and you'll expect Esther Williams to splash up in a dramatic, aquatic plié. Should you glance quickly inside the dimly lit lobby restaurant, the constantly changing Tiger Oak Room (last we checked, it was Pan-Asian), you could swear Dorothy Parker and her fellow round-tablers took a detour from New York's Algonquin Hotel and landed here. Rooms are tidy and efficient, nothing too elaborate, but that's not why people stay here. It's the Raleigh's romantic Deco lure that has people skipping over from the chilly, antiseptic Delano a few blocks up for much needed warmth.

1775 Collins Ave., Miami Beach, FL 33139. (C) **800/848-1775** or 305/534-6300. Fax 305/538-8140. www.raleighhotel.com. 107 units. Winter $299–$749 double. Off-season $199–$599 double. Rates are cheaper if booked on the hotel's website. AE, DC, DISC, MV, V. Valet parking $20. **Amenities:** Restaurant; bar; coffee bar; fantastic large outdoor pool; small open-air fitness center; concierge; business services; room service (24-hr. in winter, limited off-season); massage; overnight laundry service. *In room:* A/C, TV/VCR, CD player, dataport, minibar.

MODERATE

Abbey Hotel ★★ (Finds   This charming, off-the-beaten-path '40s revival boutique hotel is possibly the best deal on the entire beach. A haven for artists looking for quiet inspiration, the Abbey has recently undergone a $2.5 million renovation that restored its original Deco glory. Soft white-covered chairs and candles grace the lobby, and the rooftop sundeck has been restored to its 1940s glamour as a bar and grill. Rooms are furnished with oversized earth-toned chairs and chrome beds that are surprisingly comfortable. The lobby also doubles as a chic Mediterranean-style restaurant. It's extremely quiet at this hotel, as it is located in the midst of a sleepy residential neighborhood, but it's only 1 block from the beach and within walking distance of the Jackie Gleason Theater, the Convention Center, the Bass Museum of Art, and the Miami City Ballet.

300 21st St., Miami Beach, FL 33139. (C) **305/531-0031.** Fax 305/672-1663. www.abbeyhotel.com. 50 units. Winter $165–$210 double; $225 studio. Off-season $145–$190 double; $205 studio. AE, DC, DISC, MC, V. Offsite parking $15. **Amenities:** Restaurant; bar; exercise room; spa within a solarium; concierge; business center; room service; laundry and dry-cleaning service. *In room:* A/C, TV/VCR, dataport, hair dryer, iron. Studios also have stereo with CD player, minibar, safe.

Crest Hotel Suites ★★   One of South Beach's best-kept secrets, the Crest Hotel is located next to the pricier, trendier Albion Hotel and features a quietly fashionable, contemporary, relaxed atmosphere with fantastic service. Built in 1939, the Crest was restored to preserve its Art Deco architecture, but inside the hotel is thoroughly modern with rooms resembling cosmopolitan apartments.

All suites have a living room/dining room area, kitchenette, and executive work-space. An indoor/outdoor cafe with terrace and poolside dining isn't besieged with trendy locals, but does attract a younger crowd. Crest Hotel Suites is conveniently located in the heart of the Art Deco Historic District near all the major attractions. Around the corner from the hotel is Lincoln Road, with its sidewalk cafes, gourmet restaurants, theaters, and galleries.

1670 James Ave., Miami Beach, FL 33139. © **800/531-3880** or 305/531-0321. Fax 305/531-8180. www.
cresthotel.com. Winter $155–$235 double. Off-season $115–$175 double. Packages available and 10% discount offered if booked on website. AE, MC, V. **Amenities:** Restaurant; cafe; pool; laundry and dry-cleaning service. *In room:* A/C, TV, dataport, kitchenette, fridge, coffeemaker.

Hotel Leon ⭐ *Finds*   The Hotel Leon is like a reasonably priced high-fashion garment found hidden on a rack full of overpriced threads. This charismatic sliver of a property has won the loyalty of fashion industrialists and romantics alike. Built in 1929 and restored in 1996, the hotel still retains many original details such as facades, woodwork, and even fireplaces (every room has one, not that you'll need to use it). The very central location 1 block from the ocean is a plus, especially since the Leon lacks a pool. Most of the spacious and stylish rooms are immaculate and reminiscent of a loft apartment; spacious bathrooms with large, deep tubs are especially enticing. Gleaming wood floors and simple pale furnishings are appreciated in a neighborhood where many others overdo the Art Deco motif. However, some rooms have not seen such upgrades and are to be avoided; do not hesitate to ask to change rooms. In the standard rooms, there are no minibars or fridges, but you can order room service. Service is warm, friendly, and accommodating. In 2000, proprietors opened Hotel Aqua, a modern and moderately priced 50-room hotel located at 1530 Collins Ave., Miami Beach (© **305/538-4361**).

841 Collins Ave., South Beach, FL 33139. © **305/673-3767.** Fax 305/673-5866. www.hotelleon.com. 18 units. Winter $145–$245 suite; $395 penthouse. Off-season $100–$195 suite; $335 penthouse. Additional person $10. AE, DC, MC, V. Valet parking $18. "Well-behaved" pets accepted for $20 per night. **Amenities:** Restaurant and lobby bar; reduced rates at local gym; concierge; business services; room service (breakfast); massage; baby-sitting; laundry and dry-cleaning service. *In Room:* A/C, TV, CD players w/CDs, hair dryer.

Pelican Hotel ⭐⭐   Owned by the same creative folks behind the Diesel Jeans company, the Pelican is South Beach's only self-professed "toy-hotel," in which each of its 30 rooms and suites is decorated as outrageously as some of the area's more colorful drag queens. Each room has been designed daringly and rather wittily by Swedish interior decorator Magnus Ehrland, whose countless trips to antiques markets combined with his wild imagination have turned Room 309, for instance, into the "Psychedelic(ate) Girl," Room 201 into the "Executive Fifties" suite, and Room 313 into the "Jesus Christ Megastar" room. But the most popular room is the tough-to-score Room 215, or the "Best Whorehouse," which is said to have made even former Hollywood madam Heidi Fleiss red with envy. As South Beach is known for poseurs of all types, this hotel fits right in.

826 Ocean Dr., Miami Beach, FL 33139. © **800/7-PELICAN** or 305/673-3373. Fax 305/673-3255. www.
Pelicanhotel.com. Winter $170–$220 double; $240 oceanfront suite. Off-season $135–$155 double; $225 oceanfront suite. AE, DC, MC, V. Valet parking $16. **Amenities:** Restaurant; bar; access to area gyms; concierge; business services; same-day laundry and dry cleaning. *In room:* A/C, TV/VCR, stereo/CD player, dataport, fridge, hair dryer, iron, safe.

Townhouse ⭐⭐   New York hipster Jonathan Morr felt that Miami Beach had lost touch with the bon vivants who gave the city its original cachet, so he decided to take matters into his own hands. His solution: this 67-room, five-story hotel in which standard rooms started at just $99 during its opening in the fall of 2000. The $99 rate proved too good to be true, but even the revised starting rate of $125 is still a great deal. The charm of this hotel is found in its clean and simple yet chic design with quirky details: exercise equipment that stands alone in the hallways, free laundry machines in the lobby, a water bed–lined rooftop. Comfortable, shabby chic rooms boast L-shaped couches for extra guests (for whom you aren't charged), and the hotel's basement features the hot New York import, Bond St. Lounge.

150 20th St., South Beach, FL 33139. © **877/534-3800** or 305/534-3800. Fax 305/534-3811. www. townhousehotel.com. Winter $195–$225 double; $395 penthouse. Off-season $125–$155 double; $395 penthouse. Rates include Parisian-style breakfast. AE, MC, V. Valet parking $17–$18. **Amenities:** Restaurant; bar; workout stations; bike rental; free laundry. *In room:* A/C, TV/VCR, CD player, dataport, fridge, hair dryer (upon request), safe.

Whitelaw Hotel ★★ With a slogan that reads "clean sheets, hot water and stiff drinks," the Whitelaw Hotel stands apart from the other boutique hotels with a fierce sense of humor, but never compromising on its fabulous amenities. Only half a block from Ocean Drive, this hotel, like its clientele, is full of distinct personalities, pairing such disparate elements as luxurious Belgian sheets with shag carpeting to create a completely innovative setting. All-white rooms manage to be homey and plush and not antiseptic. Bathrooms are large and well stocked with just about everything you may have forgotten at home. Complimentary cocktails in the lobby every night from 8 to 10pm contribute to a very social atmosphere.

808 Collins Ave., Miami Beach, FL 33139. © **305/398-7000.** Fax 305/398-7010. www.whitelawhotel.com. Winter $175 double; $195 suite. Off-season $125 double; $145 suite. Rates include breakfast. AE, MC, V. Parking $12. **Amenities:** Bar. *In room:* A/C, TV/VCR, stereo, dataport, minibar, hair dryer, safe.

INEXPENSIVE

Banana Bungalow This hostel-like hotel is cheap, campy, and quintessentially Miami Beach. Popular with the MTV set, the Banana Bungalow is a redone 1950s two-story motel where it's always Spring Break. The hotel surrounds a pool and deck complete with shuffleboard, a small alfresco cafe serving cheap meals, and a tiki bar where young European travelers hang out. The best rooms face a narrow canal where motorboats and kayaks are available for a small charge. In general, rooms are clean and well kept, despite a few rusty faucets and chipped Formica furnishings. This is one of the only hotels in this price range with a private pool.

2360 Collins Ave., Miami Beach, FL 33139. © **800/7-HOSTEL** or 305/538-1951. Fax 305/531-3217. www.bananabungalow.com. 90 units. Winter $13–$16 per person in shared units; $95–$104 double. Off-season $12–$14 per person in shared units; $50–$60 double. MC, V. Free parking. **Amenities:** Cafe; bar; large pool; access to nearby health club; game room; coin-op laundry. *In room:* A/C, TV, fridge.

Beachcomber Hotel ★ The Beachcomber Hotel was built in 1937 and renovated in 1997. The rooms are decorated in a colorful Art Deco style, and all have a private bathroom and shower. A Deco terrace on Collins Avenue provides the perfect place for sipping a cocktail. The hotel's restaurant serves breakfast, lunch, and dinner, but dine there only as a last resort. Check before arrival if a continental breakfast is included in your rate. The property's location couldn't be better, since it's away from the noise but near the action.

1340 Collins Ave., South Beach, FL 33139. © **888/305-4683** or 305/531-3755. Fax 305/673-8609. www.beachcombermiami.com. 29 units. Winter $90–$145 double. Off-season $70–$125 double. Continental breakfast included. AE, DC, DISC, MC, V. Municipal parking $7. **Amenities:** Restaurant; bar. *In room:* A/C, TV, fridge, hair dryer.

Brigham Gardens ⋆⋆ This funky place, consisting of two buildings—Art Deco and Mediterranean—is a homey and affordable oasis run by a mother-daughter team that will make sure you feel like a member of the family. Also, the location is prime. Because most rooms have full kitchens—you can also barbecue in the garden—you'll find many people staying for longer than a weekend. When you enter the tropically landscaped garden, you'll hear macaws and parrots chirping and see cats and lizards running through the bougainvillea. The tiny but lush grounds are framed by quaint Mediterranean buildings—they're pleasant, although in need of some sprucing up. A rooftop sundeck with a view of the ocean is the hotel's newest attraction.

1411 Collins Ave., South Beach, FL 33139. © **305/531-1331.** Fax 305/538-9898. www.brighamgardens. com. 23 units. Winter $100–$145 1-bedroom. Off-season $70–$110 1-bedroom. Additional person $5. 10% discount on stays of 7 days or longer. Pets accepted for $6 a night. AE, MC, V. **Amenities:** Coin-op washers and dryers. *In room:* A/C, TV, kitchen, microwave, coffeemaker.

Clevelander A South Beach institution favored by the beer-swilling set, the Clevelander is best known for its neon- and glass-blocked poolside and bar used in countless photo shoots and Budweiser commercials. As far as its reputation as a hotel, well, it's conveniently located on Ocean Drive and it's dirt cheap considering its location. Unfortunately, the dirt doesn't stop there. It seems that the hotel is more concerned with polishing its poolside glass than its rooms. And the noise level can be deafening—but the party animals don't seem to mind.

1020 Ocean Dr., Miami Beach, FL 33139. © **305/531-3485.** Fax 305/534-4707. 57 units. Winter $140–$170 double. Off-season $99–$135 double. AE, DC, MC, V. Valet parking $6. **Amenities:** Outdoor cafe; bar; outdoor pool; health club. *In room:* A/C, TV.

Park Washington Hotel ⋆⋆ The Park Washington, designed in the 1930s by Henry Hohauser, is a large refurbished hotel just 2 blocks from the ocean that offers some of the best values in South Beach. Most of the rooms have original furnishings and well-kept interiors, and some have kitchenettes. Bathrooms are small and clean. Guests also enjoy a decent-sized outdoor heated pool with a sundeck, bikes for rent, and access to a nearby health club. The hotel attracts a large gay clientele. It offers privacy, lush landscaping, a great pool and sundeck, consistent quality, and a value-oriented philosophy.

1020 Washington Ave., South Beach, FL 33139. © **305/532-1930.** Fax 305/672-6706. www. parkwashingtonresort.com. 36 units. Winter $129–$159 double. Off-season $79–$109 double. Rates include self-serve coffee and Danish. Additional person $20. AE, MC, V. Off-site parking $6. **Amenities:** Pool. *In room:* A/C, TV, kitchenettes in some rooms, fridge.

Villa Paradiso ⋆⋆ This guesthouse, like Brigham Gardens, is more like a cozy apartment house than a hotel. There's no elegant lobby or restaurant, but the amicable hosts are happy to give you advice on what to do. The recently renovated, spacious apartments are simple but elegant—hardwood floors, French doors, and stylish wrought-iron furniture—and are remarkably quiet considering their location, a few blocks from Lincoln Road and all of South Beach's best clubs. Most have full kitchens or at least a fridge, and Murphy beds or foldout couches for extra friends. Bathrooms have recently been renovated with marble tile. All rooms overlook the hotel's pretty courtyard garden.

1415 Collins Ave., Miami Beach, FL 33139. ℂ 305/532-0616. Fax 305/673-5874. www.villaparadiso.com. 17 units. Winter $100–$145 apartment. Off-season $69–$105 apartment. Weekly rates are 10% cheaper. Additional person $5–$10. AE, DC, MC, V. Parking nearby $12. Pets (including small "nonbarking" dogs) accepted for $10 with a $100 deposit. **Amenities:** Coin-op washers and dryers. *In room:* A/C, TV, kitchen, fridge, coffeemaker.

MIAMI BEACH: SURFSIDE, BAL HARBOUR & SUNNY ISLES

The area just north of South Beach encompasses Surfside, Bal Harbour, and Sunny Isles. Unrestricted by zoning codes throughout the 1950s, 1960s, and especially the 1970s, area developers went crazy, building ever bigger and more brazen structures, especially north of 41st Street, which is now known as "Condo Canyon." Consequently, there's now a glut of medium-quality condos, with a few scattered holdouts of older hotels and motels casting shadows over the beach by afternoon.

VERY EXPENSIVE

Alexander All-Suite Luxury Hotel ✦✦✦   This luxury hotel is a place you'd expect to see Robin Leach shouting "champagne wishes and caviar dreams" from the balcony. Just a few miles from either happening South Beach or ritzy Bal Harbour, the Alexander is pricey, but worth it for the size of the suites and the doting attention. The Alexander features spacious one- and two-bedroom miniapartments with private balconies overlooking the Atlantic Ocean and Miami's Intracoastal Waterway. Each contains a living room, a fully equipped kitchen, *two* bathrooms—one with just a shower and the other with an extremely inviting shower/tub combo—and a balcony. The rooms are elegant without being pretentious and have every convenience you could want. The hotel itself is well decorated, with sculptures, paintings, antiques, and tapestries, most of which were garnered from the Cornelius Vanderbilt mansion. An ongoing renovation to upgrade the suites promises to keep the Alexander on the forefront of modern luxury. Two oceanfront pools are surrounded by lush vegetation; one of these "lagoons" is fed by a cascading waterfall. Shula's Steakhouse, owned by former Dolphins football coach Don Shula, is open for lunch and dinner daily, and is a favorite of both meat eaters and Dolphins fans.

5225 Collins Ave., Miami Beach, FL 33140. ℂ 800/327-6121 or 305/865-6500. Fax 305/341-6553. www. alexanderhotel.com. 150 units. Winter $325 1-bedroom suite; $470 2-bedroom suite. Off-season $250 1-bedroom suite; $370 2-bedroom suite. Additional person $35. Packages available. AE, MC, V. Valet parking $18. Very small pets accepted for a $250 nonrefundable deposit for cleaning the suite. **Amenities:** 2 restaurants; 2 bars; 2 large outdoor pools; small fitness center; Jacuzzis; sauna; water-sports equipment; concierge; car rental through concierge; business center and secretarial services; salon; limited room service; in-room massage; laundry and dry-cleaning service. *In room:* A/C, TV, VCR upon request, fax, dataport, kitchen, coffeemaker, hair dryer, radio.

Beach House Bal Harbour ✦✦✦   The Beach House Bal Harbour is the closest thing the city has to a summer beach home—comfortable, unpretentious, and luxurious, yet decidedly low-key. In place of an elaborate hotel lobby, the public spaces of the Rubell-owned Beach House are divided into a series of intimate homey environments, from the wicker-furnished screened-in porch to the Asian-inspired Bamboo Room, with overstuffed Ralph Lauren leather couches and Japanese bric-a-brac. The 24-hour Pantry, inspired by Long Island's Sagaponack General Store, is packed with all the needs of the hotel's "unplugged" urban clientele. The ultraspacious rooms are literally brimming with the comforts of home, including whitewashed wood wainscoting and plush furnishings, also by Ralph Lauren. The Atlantic Restaurant offers a little of Nantucket right here in Miami. Sheila Lukins, author of the best-selling Silver Palate cookbooks, creates some delicious feasts, such as buttermilk fried chicken with Austin baked beans and homemade cornbread. The 200-foot private beach, hammock grove, and topiary garden are so lush they're said to have caused several New York hipsters to renege on their summer shares in the Hamptons in favor of this Beach House.

9449 Collins Ave., Surfside, FL 33154. © 877/782-3557 or 305/865-3551. Fax 305/861-6596. www. rubellhotels.com. 170 units. Winter $215–$315 double; $245–$305 junior suite. Off-season $180–$210 double; $230–$270 junior suite. Year-round $800 1-bedroom suite. AE, DC, DISC, MC, V. Valet parking $15. **Amenities:** Restaurant; 24-hour pantry; bar; heated pool; health club & spa; water-sports equipment; children's playground; business center. *In room:* A/C, TV, stereo/CD player, dataport, fridge, hair dryer, iron.

Eden Roc Renaissance Resort and Spa ★★ Just next door to the mammoth Fontainebleau, this large Morris Lapidus–designed flamboyant hotel, opened in 1956, seems almost intimate by comparison. The hotel completed a top-to-bottom $24 million renovation in late 1999 and an $11 million renovation of the beachfront in 2001. The nautical Deco decor is a bit gaudy, but nonetheless reminiscent of Miami Beach's Rat-Packed glory days of the '50s. The 55,000-square-foot modern Spa of Eden has excellent facilities and exercise classes, including yoga. The big, open, and airy lobby is often full of name-tagged conventioneers and tourists looking for a taste of Miami Beach kitsch. The rooms, uniformly outfitted with purple and aquatic-colored interiors and retouched 1930s furnishings, are unusually spacious, and the bathrooms boast Italian marble baths. Because of the hotel's size, you should be able to negotiate a good rate unless there's a big event going on. Harry's Grille specializes in seafood and steaks. From Jimmy Johnson's, the poolside sports bar, patrons can watch swimmers through an underwater "porthole" window.

4525 Collins Ave., Miami Beach, FL 33140. © 800/327-8337 or 305/531-0000. Fax 305/674-5568. www.edenrocresort.com. 349 units. Winter $299–$359 double; $369 suite; $2,500 penthouse. Off-season $159–$224 double; $310 suite; $1,500 penthouse. Additional person $15. Packages available. AE, DC, DISC, MC, V. Valet parking $20–$25. Pets under 20 lb. accepted for a $75 fee. **Amenities:.** 2 restaurants; lounge; bar; 2 outdoor pools; squash courts; racquetball courts; basketball courts; rock-climbing arena; health club & spa; water-sports equipment; concierge; tour desk; car-rental desk; business center; salon; limited room service; in-room massage; baby-sitting; laundry and dry-cleaning service. *In room:* A/C, TV, VCRs for rent, dataport, kitchenettes in suites and penthouses, minibar, hair dryer.

Fontainebleau Hilton ★★ *Kids* In many ways, this is the quintessential Miami Beach hotel. Also designed by Morris Lapidus, who oversaw an expansion in 2000, this grand monolith has symbolized Miami decadence. Since its opening in 1954, the Fontainebleau has hosted presidents, pageants, and movie productions, including the James Bond thriller *Goldfinger*. Club Tropigala is reminiscent of Ricky Ricardo's Tropicana and features a Las Vegas–style floor show with dozens of performers and two orchestras. Rooms are newly luxurious and decorated in various styles from 1950s to ultramodern; bathrooms are done up in Italian marble a la Caesar's Palace. Adding to the Fontainebleau's opulence is the 7,000-square-foot Octopus pool; the water slide and river raft ride bring a bit of Disney to Deco-land.

4441 Collins Ave., Miami Beach, FL 33140. © 800/HILTONS or 305/538-2000. Fax 305/674-4607. www. fontainebleau.hilton.com. 1,206 units. Winter $289–$459 double. Off-season $209–$329 double. Year-round $525–$1300 suite. Additional person $30. Packages available. AE, DC, DISC, MC, V. Overnight valet parking $13. Pets accepted at no extra cost. **Amenities:** 7 restaurants (including 2 by the pool); 5 cocktail lounges; 2 large outdoor pools; 7 lighted tennis courts; state-of-the-art health club; 3 whirlpool baths; water-sports

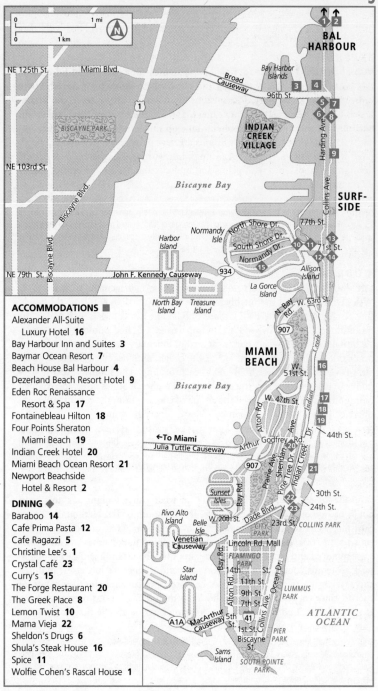

0 1 mi
0 1 km

BAL HARBOUR

NE 125th St.
Miami Blvd.
Bay Harbor Islands
Broad Causeway
96th St.

BISCAYNE PARK

NE 103rd St.

INDIAN CREEK VILLAGE

Harding Ave.

Biscayne Bay

Collins Ave.

SURF-SIDE

77th St.
Normandy Isle
North Shore Dr.
South Shore Dr.
Harbor Island
Normandy Dr.
71st St.
Allison Island
La Gorce Island

NE 79th St.
John F. Kennedy Causeway
934
North Bay Island
Treasure Island

N. Bay Rd.
W. 63rd St.
907

MIAMI BEACH

Biscayne Bay

Indian Creek

W. 51st St.

W. 47th St.

Alton Rd.
Arthur Godfrey Rd.
44th St.

←To Miami
Julia Tuttle Causeway

Collins Ave.
Indian Creek Dr.

Sheridan Ave.
Prairie Ave.
Pine Tree Dr.
907

30th St.

Sunset Isles

22
23
24th St.

Rivo Alto Island
Belle Isle
W. 20th St.
23rd St. COLLINS PARK

Venetian Causeway
Lincoln Rd. Mall

CITY PARK

FLAMINGO PARK

Star Island
14th St.

Dade Blvd.
Bay Rd.

Ocean Dr.

9th St.
7th St.

LUMMUS PARK

A1A
MacArthur Causeway
5th St.
41
1st St.
Biscayne St.

Alton Rd.
Collins Ave.

PIER PARK

ATLANTIC OCEAN

Sams Island
SOUTH POINTE PARK

ACCOMMODATIONS ■

Alexander All-Suite
    Luxury Hotel **16**
Bay Harbour Inn and Suites **3**
Baymar Ocean Resort **7**
Beach House Bal Harbour **4**
Dezerland Beach Resort Hotel **9**
Eden Roc Renaissance
    Resort & Spa **17**
Fontainebleau Hilton **18**
Four Points Sheraton
    Miami Beach **19**
Indian Creek Hotel **20**
Miami Beach Ocean Resort **21**
Newport Beachside
    Hotel & Resort **2**

DINING ◆

Baraboo **14**
Cafe Prima Pasta **12**
Cafe Ragazzi **5**
Christine Lee's **1**
Crystal Café **23**
Curry's **15**
The Forge Restaurant **20**
The Greek Place **8**
Lemon Twist **10**
Mama Vieja **22**
Sheldon's Drugs **6**
Shula's Steak House **16**
Spice **11**
Wolfie Cohen's Rascal House **1**

rentals; children's programs; game rooms; concierge; tour desk; car-rental desk; business center; shopping arcade; salon; room service; in-room massage; baby-sitting; laundry and dry-cleaning service. *In room:* A/C, TV, fax, dataport, minibar, coffeemaker, hair dryer, iron, safe.

EXPENSIVE

Miami Beach Ocean Resort ✿ Popular with tour groups and Europeans, this oceanfront resort is overpriced and not the best choice for those who have some extra bucks to spare. Reminiscent of an insipid chain hotel, the Miami Beach Ocean Resort *is* quiet, very quiet, and located on the ocean, which can be a plus for some. The vast lobby is done up in Mexican tile, wood fretwork, and Pier One–type furnishings. Rooms are very basic and unremarkably decorated with wicker and rattan furnishings, but with new carpeting. A huge outdoor area is landscaped with palms and hibiscus and has a large heated pool as its centerpiece.

3025 Collins Ave., Miami Beach, FL 33140. ✆ **800/550-0505** or 305/534-0505. Fax 305/534-0515. www. mbo.com. 243 units. Winter $220–$265 double. Off-season $180–$195 double. AE, DC, MC, V. Valet parking $8. **Amenities:** Restaurant; garden cafe; poolside bar; lounge; outdoor heated pool; bike rental; game room; concierge; tour desk; car-rental desk; salon; room service; baby-sitting; coin-op washers and dryers; laundry and dry-cleaning service. *In room:* A/C, TV, coffeemaker, hair dryer.

MODERATE

Bay Harbor Inn and Suites ✿✿ Under the management of Johnson & Wales University, this thoroughly renovated inn is just moments from the beach, fine restaurants, and the Bal Harbour Shops. The inn comes in two parts. The more modern section overlooks a swampy river, a heated outdoor pool, and a yacht named *Celeste* where guests eat a complimentary breakfast buffet. On the other side of the street, "townside" is the cozier, antiques-filled portion, where glass-covered bookshelves hold good beach reading. The rooms have a hodgepodge of wood furnishings (mostly Victorian replicas). Suites boast an extra half bathroom. You can often smell the aroma of cooking from the restaurant below, operated by students at Johnson & Wales Culinary Institute.

9660 E. Bay Harbor Dr., Bay Harbor Island, FL 33154. ✆ **305/868-4141.** Fax 305/867-9094. www. bayharborinn.com. 45 units. Winter $149–$239 double; $159–$279 suite. Off-season $80–$159 double; $95–$179 suite. Additional person $35. Rates include continental breakfast. AE, MC, V. Free parking and dockage space. **Amenities:** Restaurant; brunch room; bar; exercise room; concierge; business center; limited room service. *In room:* A/C, TV, dataport, minibar, hair dryer.

Baymar Ocean Resort Depending on what you're looking for, this hotel could be one of the beach's best buys. It's just south of Bal Harbour, in sleepy Surfside, right on the ocean, with a low-key beach that attracts few other tourists. In 2001, efficiencies were transformed into junior suites and all carpets were removed and replaced with terra-cotta tile. The location is close enough to walk to tennis courts, and some shopping and dining; it's just a few minutes' drive to larger attractions. It may not be worth it to pay more for the oceanfront rooms, since they tend to be smaller than the others. Rooms overlooking the large pool and sundeck area can get loud on busy days. The first-floor ocean-view rooms have a nice shared balcony space.

9401 Collins Ave., Miami Beach, FL 33154. ✆ **800/8-BAYMAR** or 305/866-5446. Fax 305/866-8053. www. baymar.com. 96 units. Winter $115–$125 double; $125–$235 suite. Off-season $75–$95 double; $95–$185 suite. Additional person $10. AE, DC, DISC, MC, V. Parking $5. **Amenities:** Restaurant; lounge; tiki bar; Olympic-size pool. *In room:* A/C, TV, kitchen.

Dezerland Beach Resort Hotel Designed by car enthusiast Michael Dezer, the Dezerland is where "Happy Days" meets Miami Beach, with its visible homage to hot rods and antique cars. Visitors, many of them German tourists, are welcomed by a 1959 Cadillac stationed by the front door, one of a dozen mint-condition classics around the grounds and lobby. This kitschy beachfront hotel recently underwent a $2 million renovation of its guest rooms, lobby, and public areas. The rooms are still somewhat lackluster despite the fact that the renovation added new drapes, bedspreads, furniture, and wall coverings. Though named for various fabulous cars, these, alas, are the Pintos of hotel rooms—nothing more than a typical motel room. The lovely pool, however, has its requisite Cadillac—a mosaic pink one, located at the bottom of the pool. For '50s kitsch and car fanatics, this is a fun play to stay; otherwise, you may think you were taken for a ride.

8701 Collins Ave., Miami Beach, FL 33154. © 800/331-9346 in the U.S., 800/331-9347 in Canada, or 305/865-6661. Fax 305/866-2630. www.dezerhotels.com. 227 units. Winter $99–$139 double. Off-season $69–$99 double. Additional person $10. Special packages and group rates available. AE, DC, DISC, MC, V. **Amenities:** Restaurant; pool; nearby tennis courts; small spa; Jacuzzi; water-sports rentals; game room; car-rental desk; tour desk; shuttle service to Aventura Mall and nearby antiques shop; coin-op washers and dryers. *In room:* A/C, TV, kitchen in some rooms, fridge on request, hair dryer, iron, safe.

Four Points Sheraton Miami Beach ⭐
Right on the Miami Beach boardwalk, this chain hotel aspires to elegance with gaudy interiors inspired by the grandeur of ancient Greece. *Yikes!* A lobby of marble and rich mahogany goes against the grain of a typical South Beach hotel and only adds to this contrived, out-of-place decor. However, it's not all an eyesore. Its location right on the beach is obviously a perk, as are its spacious rooms and good service. It's not luxury, but it's a decent choice near the trendier side of town.

4343 Collins Ave., Miami Beach, FL 33140. © 800/525-6994 or 305/531-7494. Fax 305/532-2490. 216 units. Winter $199–$299 double. Off-season $119–$199 double. AE, DC, DISC, MC, V. Valet parking $12.50. **Amenities:** Restaurant; bar; pool; exercise room; Jacuzzi; concierge; car-rental desk; business center; room service; same-day dry cleaning. *In room:* A/C, TV, dataport, coffeemaker.

Indian Creek Hotel ⭐⭐
Located off the beaten path, the Indian Creek Hotel is a meticulously restored 1936 building featuring one of the beach's first operating elevators. This is the most charming hotel in the area, with impeccable service. Because of its location facing the Indian Creek waterway and its lush landscaping, this place feels more like an old-fashioned Key West bed-and-breakfast than your typical Miami Beach Art Deco hotel. The rooms are outfitted in Art Deco furnishings, such as an antique writing desk, with pretty tropical prints and small but spotless bathrooms. As of March 2001, half the rooms were completely renovated. Just 1 short block from a good stretch of sand, the hotel is also within walking distance of shops and restaurants. A landscaped pool area is a great place to lounge in the sun.

2727 Indian Creek Dr. (1 block west of Collins Ave.), Miami Beach, FL 33140. © 800/491-2772 or 305/531-2727. Fax 305/531-5651. www.indiancreekhotelmb.com. 61 units. Winter $140–$240 double. Off-season $90–$150 double. Additional person $10. Group packages and summer specials available. AE, DC, DISC, MC, V. Limited street parking. **Amenities:** Restaurant; bar; pool; concierge; car-rental desk; limited room service; laundry and dry-cleaning service. *In room:* A/C, TV/VCR, CD player, dataport, fridge in suites, hair dryer.

Newport Beachside Hotel & Resort
This hotel is a great budget option, especially for young families who don't mind being away from the hustle and bustle of South Beach. The continental Newport Pub restaurant is very good and reasonably priced. The pool area is massive, which makes it great for kids. The hotel is situated directly on the beach, and for the aspiring angler, there is also a fishing pier out back. At night, by their poolside bar, a calypso band plays.

Another plus is its location directly across the street from the R. K. Centres, a destination for both tourists and residents with ample shopping and numerous restaurants from fine dining to fast food. Guest rooms are comfortable and spacious, and most have ocean views and balconies.

16701 Collins Ave., Miami, FL 33160. ℂ **800/327-5476** or 305/949-1300. Fax 305/947-5873. 300 units. Winter $129–$299 double. Off-season $95–$250 double. AE, DC, MC, V. Valet parking $5. **Amenities:** Restaurant; sports bar; massive outdoor pool; concierge; business center; baby-sitting. *In room:* A/C, TV, minibar, fridge, coffeemaker, hair dryer, iron, safe, microwave.

KEY BISCAYNE

The island is far enough from the mainland to make it feel semiprivate, yet close enough to downtown for guests to take advantage of everything Miami has to offer.

VERY EXPENSIVE

Ritz-Carlton Key Biscayne ★★★   Described by some as an oceanfront mansion, the Ritz Carlton takes Key Biscayne to the height of luxury with 44 acres of tropical gardens, a 20,000-square-foot European-style spa, and a world-class tennis center under the direction of tennis pro Cliff Drysdale. Decorated in British colonial style, the Ritz-Carlton looks as if it was straight out of Bermuda with its impressive flower-laden landscaping. The Ritz Kids programs provide children ages 5 to 12 with fantastic activities, and the 1,200-foot beachfront offers everything from pure relaxation to fishing, boating, or windsurfing. Spacious and luxuriously appointed rooms are elegantly Floridian, featuring large balconies overlooking the ocean or the lush gardens.

415 Grand Bay Dr., Key Biscayne, FL 33149. ℂ **800/241-3333** or 305/648-5900. Fax 305/648-1448. www. ritzcarlton.com. 352 units. Winter $270–$850 suite. Off-season $225–$800 suite. AE, DC, DISC, MC, V. Valet parking (call for fees). **Amenities:** 3 restaurants; 3 bars; 2 outdoor heated pools; tennis center w/lessons available; health club & spa; water-sports equipment; children's programs; 24-hour room service; overnight laundry service. *In room:* A/C, TV, dataport, minibar, hair dryer, safe.

Silver Sands Beach Resort   If Key Biscayne is where you want to be and you don't want to pay the prices of the Sonesta next door, consider this quaint one-story motel. Everything is crisp and clean, and the pleasant staff will help with anything you may need, including baby-sitting. But despite the name, it's certainly no resort. Except for the beach and pool, you'll have to leave the premises for almost everything else, including food. The well-appointed rooms are very beachy, sporting a tropical motif and simple furnishings. Oceanfront suites have the added convenience of full kitchens with stoves and pantries. You'll sit poolside with an unpretentious set of Latin-American families and Europeans who have come for a long and simple vacation—and get it.

301 Ocean Dr., Key Biscayne, FL 33149. ℂ **305/361-5441.** Fax 305/361-5477. 56 units. Winter $149–$349 double. Off-season $129–$309 double. Additional person $30. Weekly rates available. AE, DC, MC, V. Free parking. **Amenities:** Medium-sized pool; secretarial services; coin-op washers and dryers. *In room:* A/C, TV, VCRs in some rooms, kitchenette, fridge, coffeemaker, microwave.

Sonesta Beach Resort Key Biscayne ★★ *Kids*   The Sonesta is an idyllic, secluded resort in the middle of Miami—like a souped-up summer camp. Families and couples alike love this place for its oceanfront location and its many high-caliber amenities, which make it almost impossible to venture off the property. An $8 million renovation of the lobby and expansion of the spa has kept the Sonesta sparkling and at the top of the list of vacationers looking for a relaxing resort vacation. Each of the plush 292 rooms, also recently upgraded, has a

Accommodations in Coral Gables, Coconut Grove, Downtown & Key Biscayne

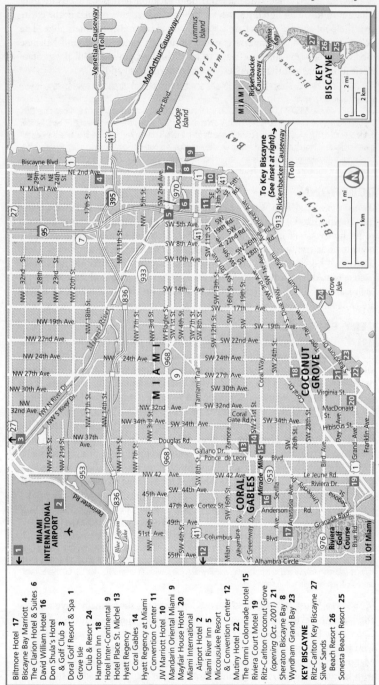

Biltmore Hotel **17**
Biscayne Bay Marriott **4**
The Clarion Hotel & Suites **6**
David William Hotel **16**
Don Shula's Hotel
& Golf Club **3**
Doral Golf Resort & Spa **1**
Grove Isle
Club & Resort **24**
Hampton Inn **18**
Hotel Inter-Continental **9**
Hotel Place St. Michel **13**
Hyatt Regency
Coral Gables **14**
Hyatt Regency at Miami
Convention Center **11**
JW Marriott Hotel **10**
Mandarin Oriental Miami **9**
Mayfair House Hotel **20**
Miami International
Airport Hotel **2**
Miami River Inn **5**
Miccousukee Resort
& Convention Center **12**
Mutiny Hotel **22**
The Omni Colonnade Hotel **15**
Riviera Court Motel **19**
Ritz-Carlton Coconut Grove
(opening Oct. 2001) **21**
Sheraton Biscayne Bay **8**
Wyndham Grand Bay **23**

KEY BISCAYNE
Ritz-Carlton Key Biscayne **27**
Silver Sands
Beach Resort **26**
Sonesta Beach Resort **25**

private balcony or terrace. There are also 12 one- and two-bedroom suites as well as fully furnished three- and four-bedroom vacation homes with private pool adjacent to the main hotel. Known for having the best piña coladas in the entire city, the pool and beach bars are popular with locals and vacationers alike. The hotel's Two Dragons restaurant is good, featuring Chinese, Thai, and Japanese food. Although you may not want to leave the lush grounds, Bill Baggs State Recreation Area and the area's best beaches are right at hand.

350 Ocean Dr., Key Biscayne, FL 33149. ℂ **800/SONESTA** or 305/361-2021. Fax 305/361-3096. www. sonesta.com. 292 units. Winter $295–$465 double; $875–1,475 suite; $1,750 penthouse. Off-season $195–$285 double; $650–$1,000 suite; $1,250 penthouse. 15% gratuity added to food and beverage bills. Special packages available. AE, DC, DISC, MC, V. Valet parking $12. **Amenities:** 4 restaurants; 2 bars; lounge; outdoor heated Olympic-style pool; access to nearby golf; 9 tennis courts; health club & spa; extensive watersports equipment rental; bike/moped rental; excellent children's programs; sports court; sailing lessons; shuttle service to shopping; business center; salon; limited room service; laundry and dry-cleaning service. *In room:* A/C, TV, dataport, minibar, coffeemaker, hair dryer.

DOWNTOWN

If you've ever read Tom Wolfe's *Bonfire of the Vanities,* you may understand what downtown Miami is all about. If not, it's this simple: Take a wrong turn and you could find yourself in some serious trouble. Desolate and dangerous at night, downtown is trying to change its image, but it's a long, tedious process. Most downtown hotels cater primarily to business travelers and pre- and postcruise passengers. Although business hotels are expensive, quality and service are of a high standard. Look for discounts and packages for the weekend, when offices are closed and rooms often go empty.

VERY EXPENSIVE

Hotel Inter-Continental Miami ✨   This hotel presents a serious catch-22: It's got a front-row view of all of Miami Beach, Biscayne Bay, the Miami River, and the Atlantic Ocean, but it is also located in downtown Miami. It depends on what you're looking for. If it's the view, then you will want to stay here. If it's location, you may want to reconsider. A $34 million renovation has brought it up to speed, rendering it downtown proper's swankiest hotel. It boasts more marble than the Liberace Museum (both inside and out), but it's warmed by bold colors and a fancified Florida flavor. The five-story lobby features a marble centerpiece sculpture by Henry Moore and is topped by a pleasing skylight. Plenty of plants, palm trees, and eclectic furnishings also add charm and enliven the otherwise stark space. Perfectly designed for business travelers, each room is outfitted with a desk and Internet-ready telephone lines.

100 Chopin Plaza, Miami, FL 33131. ℂ **800/327-3005** or 305/577-1000. Fax 305/577-0384. www. interconti.com. 640 units. Winter $255–$335 double. Off-season $150–$245 double. Year-round $550–$3,000 suite. Additional person $20. Weekend and other packages available. AE, DC, DISC, MC, V. Valet parking $17. **Amenities:** 3 restaurants; 2 lounges; Olympic-size outdoor heated pool; access to nearby golf course; spa; concierge; tour desk; car-rental desk; large business center; shopping arcade; salon and barbershop; room service; coin-op washers and dryers; laundry and dry-cleaning service. *In room:* A/C, TV/VCR, CD player, minibar, hair dryer; kitchenettes in some suites.

Mandarin Oriental Miami ✨✨✨   Corporate big shots finally have a high-end luxury hotel to stay in while wheeling and dealing their way through Miami. Catering to business travelers, conventioneers, and the occasional leisure traveler who doesn't mind spending in excess of $500 a night for a room, the swank Mandarin Oriental features a waterfront location, residential-style rooms, most with balconies, and several upscale dining and bar facilities. Much of the hotel's staff was flown in from Bangkok and Hong Kong to demonstrate the hotel's unique brand of superattentive Asian-inspired service. The hotel's two restaurants, the high-end Azul and the more casual Café Sambal, are up to Mandarin standards and are both wonderful.

500 Brickell Key Dr., Miami, FL 33131. © 305/913-8288. Fax 305/913-8300. www.mandarinoriental.com. 329 units. $550–$740 double; $1,200–$4,000 suite. AE, DC, DISC, MC, V. Valet parking $24. **Amenities:** 2 restaurants; bar; outdoor pool; state-of-the-art health club; full-service spa; outdoor Jacuzzi; concierge; 24-hour business center. *In room:* A/C, TV, dataport, minibar, hair dryer, iron, safe.

MODERATE

Biscayne Bay Marriott ✿   Just 7 miles east of the airport, the Biscayne Bay Marriott Hotel and Marina is on the sketchy outskirts of downtown Miami, yet it manages to create its own world of tranquility and entertainment. The 603-room hotel is equipped with a 220-slip full-service marina. Water-sports rentals are available nearby. There's also 24-hour on-site security and valet parking. Some rooms face the bay, and some have balconies. The views are fantastic. If you want to stay in a Marriott, however, you may want to consider the newer J W Marriott (see below) on the less-desolate Brickell Avenue a few miles south.

1633 N. Bayshore Dr., Miami, FL 33132. © **305/374-3900.** Fax 305/375-0597. www.marriott.com. 600 units. Winter $194–$250 double. Off-season $124–$204 double. AE, DC, DISC, MC, V. Valet parking $15. **Amenities:** 3 restaurants; 2 lounges; pool; health club; Jacuzzi; concierge; business center; limited room service; coin-op washers and dryers; laundry and dry-cleaning service. *In room:* A/C, TV, dataport, minibar, coffeemaker, hair dryer.

JW Marriott Hotel ✿✿   Located smack in the middle of the business-oriented Brickell Avenue near downtown Miami, the JW Marriott is a *really* nice Marriott catering mostly to business travelers, but located conveniently enough between Coconut Grove and South Beach that it isn't a bad choice for vacationers, either. A small but elegant lobby features the classy, appropriately named Drake's Power Bar. The buzz of business deals being sealed amidst clouds of cigar smoke contributes to the smoky, but not staid, atmosphere here. Rooms are equipped with every amenity you might need. A lovely outdoor pool, fitness center, sauna, and hot tub should become everybody's business at this hotel. Next door is the area's bustling brewery, Gordon Biersch, which attracts well-heeled, young professional types who gather for postwork revelry.

1111 Brickell Ave., Miami, FL 33131. © **800/228-9290** or 305/374-1224. Fax 305/374-4211. www. marriott.com. Winter $219 deluxe room; $319 concierge room; $450 junior suite. Off-season $189 deluxe room; $229 concierge room; $350 junior suite. AE, DC, DISC, MC, V. Valet parking $18; self-parking $16. **Amenities:** 3 restaurants; bar; outdoor pool; health club; sauna; concierge; tour desk; business center; laundry service. *In room:* A/C, TV, dataport, minibar, coffeemaker, hair dryer, iron, safe.

Miami River Inn ✿✿✿   The Miami River Inn, listed on the National Register of Historic Places, is a quaint country-style hideaway consisting of four cottages smack in the middle of downtown Miami. In fact, it's so hidden that most locals don't even know it exists. It's also Miami's *only* bed-and-breakfast. Every room has hardwood floors and is uniquely furnished with antiques dating from 1908. In one room, you might find a hand-painted bathtub or an armoire from the turn of the 20th century restored to perfection. Thirty-eight rooms have private baths—4 have a shower only, 6 have a tub only, and 28 have a splendid shower and tub combo. One-and two-bedroom apartments are available as well. In the foyer you can peruse a library filled with books about old Miami.

118 SW South River Dr., Miami, FL 33130. © **800/468-3589** or 305/325-0045. Fax 305/325-9227. www.miamiriverinn.com. 40 units. Winter $99–$229 double. Off-season $69–$109 double. Rates include

continental breakfast. Additional person $15. AE, DC, DISC, MC, V. Free parking. Pets accepted for $25 per night. **Amenities:** Small, lushly landscaped swimming pool; access to nearby YMCA facilities; Jacuzzi; baby-sitting; coin-op washers and dryers; laundry and dry-cleaning service. *In room:* A/C, TV, dataport, hair dryer, iron, safe.

INEXPENSIVE

Clarion Hotel & Suites ✴ This hotel is especially designed for the seasoned business traveler. Its location in downtown Miami (right on the river) provides excellent access to the commercial world of nearby Brickell Avenue and the legal precincts in downtown. Due to its position adjoining the Hyatt, a Metromover station, and some major parking lots, this hotel does, however, lack a room with a view, which may be disheartening for some guests. The spacious and elegantly appointed guest rooms and suites offer many amenities, and the two-room apartment suites are ideal for extended stays.

100 SE 4th St., Miami, FL 33131. ✆ **800/838-6501** or 305/374-5100. Fax 305/381-9826. www.clarionmiaconctr. com. 149 units. Year-round $99–$169 double. AE, DC, DISC, MC, V. Valet parking $15. **Amenities:** Restaurant; lounge; outdoor heated pool; exercise room; room service (7am–11:30pm), laundry service. *In room:* A/C, TV, dataport, coffeemaker, hair dryer.

WEST MIAMI/AIRPORT AREA

As Miami continues to grow at a rapid pace, expansion has begun westward, where land is plentiful. Several resorts have taken advantage of the space to build world-class tennis and golf courses. While there's no sea to swim in, a plethora of facilities makes up for the lack of an ocean view.

EXPENSIVE

Doral Golf Resort and Spa ✴ This 650-acre golf and tennis resort is in the middle of nowhere, but with all it's got, it's really a destination in itself. While the pamperings in the spa are nothing to sneer at, the next-door golf resort hosts world-class tournaments and boasts the Great White Course—the Southeast's first desert-scape course, designed by The Shark himself, Greg Norman. The season is usually booked well in advance, often by repeat guests. The Blue Lagoon water park features two 80,000-gallon pools with cascading waterfalls, a rock facade, and the 125-foot Blue Monster water slide. Rooms here, like the hotel itself, are spacious, all with private balconies, many overlooking a golf course or garden. The hotel itself shines in a polished marble and gold decor. The spa's restaurant serves tasty, healthy fare—so good you won't realize it's health food, actually. The hotel is just moments from the Miami airport. For a spa or golf vacation, the Doral is an ideal choice. Otherwise, consider investing your money in a hotel that's better located. Disabled-accessible rooms are available.

4400 NW 87th Ave., Miami, FL 33178. ✆ **800/71-DORAL** or 305/592-2000. Fax 305/594-4682. www. doralresort.com. 693 units. Winter $339 double; $425 suite; $545 1-bedroom suite; $879 2-bedroom suite. Off-season $155 double; $225 suite; $305 1-bedroom suite; $405 2-bedroom suite. Additional person $35. Golf and spa packages available. AE, DC, DISC, MC, V. Valet parking $15. **Amenities:** Restaurant; sports bar; 4 pools and a 125-ft. water slide; 5 golf courses and driving range; 10 tennis courts; health club & world-class spa; bike rental; concierge; business center; room service; baby-sitting; laundry and dry-cleaning service. *In room:* A/C, TV, fax, dataport, minibar, coffeemaker, hair dryer, iron, safe.

Miccosukee Resort and Convention Center ✴ Located on the edge of the Everglades, about 30 to 40 minutes west of the airport, the Miccosukee Resort is the closest thing South Florida's got to Las Vegas, but accommodations really are just a step above a Holiday Inn. The Miccosukee tribe was originally part of the lower Creek Nation and lived in areas now known as Alabama and

Georgia. Following the final Seminole War in 1858, the last of the Miccosukees settled in the Everglades. Following the lead set recently by many other Native American tribes, they built the resort to accumulate gambling revenue. Although many tourists go out to the resort solely to gamble, it also has expansive meeting and banquet facilities, spa services, great children's programs, entertainment (I saw Isaac Hayes here), and excursions to the Florida Everglades. Guest rooms are standard, furnished with custom pieces made exclusively for the resort, but if you're here, you're not likely to spend that much time in your room.

500 SW 177th Ave. (at intersection with SW 8th St.), Miami, FL 33194. ✆ **877/242-6464** or 305/221-8623. Fax 305/221-8309. www.miccosukee.com. 302 units. Winter $99 double; $135 suite. Year-round $325 presidential. All rooms sleep up to 4 people. AE, DC, DISC, MC, V. Free parking. **Amenities:** 3 restaurants; 24-hour deli; indoor heated pool; state-of-the-art health club & spa; game room; 24-hour room service; laundry and dry-cleaning service. In room: A/C, TV, in-room movies, dataport, minibar, coffeemaker, hair dryer; some suites have whirlpool and wet bars.

MODERATE

Don Shula's Hotel and Golf Club   Guests come to Shula's mostly for the golf, but there's plenty here to keep nongolfers busy, too. Opened in 1992 to much fanfare from the sports and business community, Shula's resort is an all-encompassing oasis in the middle of the planned residential neighborhood of Miami Lakes, complete with a Main Street and nearby shopping facilities—a good thing, since the site is more than a 20-minute drive on the highways from anything. The guest rooms, located in the main building or surrounding the golf course, are plain but pretty in typical, uninspiring Florida decor—pastels, wicker, and light wood. As expected, the hotel's Athletic Club features state-of-the-art equipment and classes, but costs hotel guests $10 per day or $35 per week. The award-winning Shula's Steak House and the more casual Steak House Two get high rankings nationwide.

Main St., Miami Lakes, FL 33014. ✆ **800/24-SHULA** or 305/821-1150. Fax 305/820-8190. 330 units. Winter $129–$289 suite. Off-season $99–$209 suite. Additional person $10. Business packages available. AE, DC, MC, V. **Amenities:** 6 restaurants; 2 bars; 2 pools; 2 golf courses and a driving range; 9 tennis courts; health club; saunas; sporting courts. In room: A/C, TV/VCR.

Miami International Airport Hotel ⭐   I don't know of a nicer airport hotel, and you can't beat the convenience—it's actually in the airport at Concourse E. You'll find every amenity of a first-class tourist hotel. The rooms are modern, clean, and spacious, with newly renovated furnishings, mattresses, fixtures, and carpeting. You might think you'd be deafened by the roar of the planes, but all of the rooms have been soundproofed and actually allow very little noise. In addition, the hotel has modern security systems and is extremely safe.

Airport Terminal Concourse E (at the intersection of NW 20th St. and LeJeune Rd.; P.O. Box 997510), Miami, FL 33299-7510. ✆ **800/327-1276** or 305/871-4100. Fax 305/871-0800. www.miahotel.com. 260 units. Winter $179–]$650 double. Off-season $130–$270 double. Additional person $10. AE, DC, MC, V. Parking $10. **Amenities:** Restaurant; cocktail lounge; large rooftop pool; racquetball courts; well-equipped health club; Jacuzzi; sauna; concierge; tour desk; business center; limited room service; salon; laundry and dry-cleaning service. In room: A/C, TV, dataport, hair dryer, iron.

BARGAIN CHAINS

If you must stay near the airport, consider any of the dozens of moderately priced chain hotels. You'll find one of the cheapest and most recommendable options at either of the **Days Inn** locations at 7250 NW 11th St. or 4767 NW 36th St. (✆ **800/329-7466** or 305/888-3661), each about 2 miles from the airport. Rates range from $47 to $69.

The larger property on 36th Street offers slightly cheaper rates with singles starting as low as $49. The 11th Street locale may charge more for weekends, but prices usually start at $70. Prices include free transportation from the airport.

A more luxurious option is the **Wyndham** at 3900 NW 21st St. (© **800/ 933-1100**), with rates from $100 to $225. There's also another location in downtown Miami at 1601 Biscayne Blvd. (© **800/WYNDHAM** or 305/ 374-0000). Rates there run from a high of $238 in season to $158 during the summer.

NORTH DADE

Turnberry Isle Resort and Club ★★★ One of Miami's classiest (if not *the* classiest) resorts, this gorgeous 300-acre compound has every possible facility for active guests, particularly golfers. You'll pay a lot to stay here—but it's worth it. The main attractions are two Trent Jones courses, available only to members and guests of the hotel. A new seven-story Jasmine wing looks like a Mediterranean village surrounded by tropical gardens that are joined by covered marble walkways to the other wings. Treat yourself to a "Turnberry Retreat" at the Turnberry Spa, which has been renovated to the tune of $10 million. Impeccable service from check-in to checkout brings loyal fans back to this resort for more. Its location in the well-manicured residential and shopping area of North Miami Beach known as Aventura means you'll find excellent shopping and some of the best dining in Miami right in the neighborhood. Unless you're into boating, the higher-priced resort rooms are where you'll want to stay; you'll be steps from the spa facilities and the renowned Veranda restaurant. The well-proportioned rooms are gorgeously tiled to match the Mediterranean-style architecture. The huge bathrooms even have a color TV mounted within reach of the whirlpool bathtubs and glass-walled showers. The only drawback to this hotel is that you'll need to take a shuttle to the beach.

19999 W. Country Club Dr., Aventura, FL 33180. © **800/327-7028** or 305/936-2929. Fax 305/933-6560. www.turnberryisle.com. 395 units. Winter $395–$495 double; $605–$1,200 suite; $3,000–$4,200 penthouse. Off-season $175–$275 double; $375–$730 suite; $$2,500–$3,500 penthouse. AE, DC, DISC, MC, V. Valet parking $12; free self-parking. **Amenities:** 6 restaurants; numerous bars and lounges; 2 outdoor pools; 2 golf courses; 2 tennis complexes; state-of-the-art spa; extensive water-sports equipment rental; concierge; secretarial services; 24-hour room service; baby-sitting. *In room:* A/C, TV/VCR, CD player, fax, dataport, minibar, fridge and coffeemaker on request, hair dryer.

CORAL GABLES

If you're looking for luxury, Coral Gables has a number of wonderful hotels, but if you're on a tight budget, you may be better off elsewhere. Coconut Grove eases into Coral Gables, which extends north toward Miami International Airport and offers a few less expensive hotels. Two popular and well-priced chain hotels in the area are a **Holiday Inn** (© **800/327-5476** or 305/667-5611) at 1350 S. Dixie Hwy., with rates between $75 and $125, and a **Howard Johnson** (© **800/446-4656** or 305/665-7501) at 1430 S. Dixie Hwy., with rates ranging from $65 to $95. Both are located directly across the street from the University of Miami and are popular with families and friends of students.

VERY EXPENSIVE

Biltmore Hotel ★★★ A romantic sense of old world glamour combined with a rich history permeate the Biltmore as much as the pricey perfume of the guests who stay here. Built in 1926, it's the oldest Coral Gables hotel and a

National Historical Landmark—one of only two operating hotels in Florida to receive the designation. Rising above the Spanish-style estate is a majestic 300-foot copper-clad tower, modeled after the Giralda bell tower in Seville and visible throughout the city. Over the years, the Biltmore has passed through many incarnations (including a post–World War II stint as a VA hospital), but is now back to its original 1926 splendor. More intriguing than scary is the rumor that ghosts of wounded soldiers and even Al Capone, for whom the Everglades Suite is nicknamed, roam the halls here. But don't worry. The hotel is far from a haunted house. It is warm, welcoming, and extremely charming. Now under the management of the Westin Hotel group, the hotel boasts large Moorish-style rooms decorated with tasteful period reproductions and some high-tech amenities. The enormous lobby, with its 45-foot vaulted ceilings, makes a bold statement of elegance. Always a popular destination for golfers, including former President Clinton (who stays in the Al Capone suite), the Biltmore is situated on a lush, rolling 18-hole course that is as challenging as it is beautiful. The spa is fantastic and the enormous winding pool is legendary—it's where a pre-*Tarzan* Johnny Weismuller broke the world's swimming record.

1200 Anastasia Ave., Coral Gables, FL 33134. ✆ **800/727-1926** or 305/445-1926; Westin 800/228-3000. Fax 305/442-9496. www.biltmorehotel.com. 275 units. Winter $339–$509. Off-season $259–$479. Additional person $20. Special packages available. AE, DC, DISC, MC, V. Valet parking $14; free self-parking. **Amenities:** 5 restaurants; 2 bars; 21,000-sq.-ft. swimming pool; 18-hole golf course; 10 lighted tennis courts; state-of-the-art health club; spa; sauna; concierge; car rental; business center; salon; 24-hour room service; baby-sitting; laundry and dry-cleaning service. *In room:* A/C, TV, VCR on request, fax, dataport, minibar, hair dryer, iron, safe; kitchenette in tower suite.

Hyatt Regency Coral Gables ★★ High on style, comfort, and price, this Hyatt is part of Coral Gables's Alhambra, an office-hotel complex with a Mediterranean motif. The building itself is gorgeous, designed with pink stone, arched entrances, grand courtyards, and tile roofs. Most recently, the pool and lobby were beautifully renovated. Inside you'll find overstuffed chairs on marble floors surrounded by opulent antiques and chandeliers. The large guest rooms are comfortable, if uninspired. A few rooms have balconies. Though the hotel fails to authentically mimic something much older and much farther away, it is attractive in its newness and an excellent place from which to admire the more historic properties in the neighborhood. Disabled-accessible rooms are available.

50 Alhambra Plaza, Coral Gables, FL 33134. ✆ **800/233-1234** or 305/441-1234. Fax 305/441-0520. www.hyatt.com. 242 units. Winter $340 double. Off-season $254 double. Year-round $375–$1,800 1-bed-room suite; $575–$2,050 2-bedroom suite. Additional person $25. Packages and senior discounts available. AE, MC, V. Valet parking $14; self-parking $11. **Amenities:** Restaurant; bar; large outdoor heated pool; nearby golf course; health club; Jacuzzi; 2 saunas; concierge; business center; limited room service; in-room massage; baby-sitting; same-day laundry and dry-cleaning service. *In room:* A/C, TV, fax in some rooms, dataport, mini-bar, coffeemaker, hair dryer, iron, safe.

EXPENSIVE

David William Hotel ★★ This sister hotel to the Biltmore shares many of the same amenities without the Biltmore's price. You can even take a shuttle to the Biltmore to play a round of golf, enjoy the health club and spa, play tennis, or take a dip in the pool. The luxurious one- and two-bedroom suites are extremely spacious and have eat-in kitchens for extended stays. For a spectacular view of Miami, go up to the roof and have a drink by the pool. The hotel, which has undergone a recent external renovation, is directly across the street from the Granada Golf Course, less than 5 miles from the airport and only 20 minutes from Miami Beach. Donna's Bistro, a fusion restaurant with a homey feel, is spectacular. Executive chef Donna Wynter was the Chef de Cuisine at the Biltmore Hotel and has worked as a chef at New York's Tavern on the Green and Toscana Ristorante. If you want luxury without the price, this is your best alternative in the Gables.

700 Biltmore Way, Coral Gables, FL 33134. © **800/757-8073** or 305/445-7821. Fax 305/913-1943. www.davidwilliamhotel.com. 116 units. Winter $249–$489 double. Off-season $209–$269 double. AE, DISC, MC, V. Valet parking $9. **Amenities:** Restaurant; coffee shop; lounge; gourmet market; rooftop pool; limited room service. *In room:* A/C, TV, fax, kitchenette, minibar, coffeemaker, hair dryer, iron, safe.

Hotel Place St. Michel ✦✦✦ This European-style hotel in the heart of Coral Gables is one of the city's most romantic options. The accommodations and hospitality are straight out of Old World Europe, complete with dark wood–paneled walls, cozy beds, beautiful antiques, and a quiet elegance that seems startlingly out of place in trendy Miami. Everything here is charming— from the brass elevator and parquet floors to the paddle fans. One-of-a-kind furnishings make each room special. All bathrooms, with the exception of two rooms, have a shower and tub and are on the smaller side but hardly cramped. Guests are treated to fresh fruit baskets upon arrival and enjoy perfect service throughout their stay. The exceptional Restaurant St. Michel is a very romantic dining choice.

162 Alcazar Ave., Coral Gables, FL 33134. © **800/848-HOTEL** or 305/444-1666. Fax 305/529-0074. www. hotelplacestmichel.com. 27 units. Winter $165 double; $200 suite. Off-season $125 double; $160 suite. Additional person $10. Rates include continental breakfast. AE, DC, MC, V. Self-parking $7. **Amenities:** Restaurant; lounge; deli; access to nearby health club; concierge; room service; in-room massage; laundry and dry-cleaning service. *In room:* A/C, TV, dataport, hair dryer, iron.

INEXPENSIVE
Riviera Court Motel Besides the Holiday Inn down the road, this family-owned motel is the best discount option in the area. The comfortable and clean two-story property, dating from 1954, has a small pool and is set back from the road, so the rooms are all relatively quiet. Vending machines are the only choice for refreshments, but guests are near many great dining spots. You can also choose to stay in one of the efficiencies, which all have fully stocked kitchens.

5100 Riviera Dr. (on U.S. 1), Coral Gables, FL 33146. © **800/368-8602** or 305/665-3528. 30 units. Winter $75–$88 double. Off-season $68–$80 double. 10% discount for seniors and AAA members. AE, DC, DISC, MC, V. **Amenities:** Pool. *In room:* A/C, TV.

COCONUT GROVE
This waterfront village hugs the shores of Biscayne Bay, just south of U.S. 1 and about 10 minutes from the beaches. Once a haven for hippies, head shops, and arty bohemian characters, the Grove succumbed to the inevitable temptations of commercialism and has become a Gap nation, featuring a host of fun, themed restaurants, bars, a megaplex, and lots of stores. Outside of the main shopping area, however, you will find the beautiful remnants of old Miami in the form of flora, fauna, and, of course, water.

VERY EXPENSIVE
Grove Isle Club and Resort ✦✦✦ Hidden away in the bougainvillea and lushness of the Grove, the Grove Isle Resort is off the beaten path on its own lushly landscaped 20-acre island just outside the heart of Coconut Grove. The isolated exclusivity of this resort contributes to a country club vibe, though, for the most part, the people here aren't snooty; they just value their privacy and precious relaxation time. Everyone dresses in white and pastels, and if they're not

on their way to a set of tennis, they're not in a rush to get anywhere. You'll step into rooms that are elegantly furnished with mosquito-netted canopy beds and a patio overlooking the bay. You'll need to reserve early here—rooms go very fast. Baleen, a fantastic yet pricey haute cuisinerie, serves fresh seafood and other regional specialties in a spectacular, elegant dining room, or, better yet, outside on the water.

4 Grove Isle Dr., Coconut Grove, FL 33133. Ⓒ **800/88-GROVE** or 305/858-8300. Fax 305/854-6702. 49 units. Winter $350–$495 suite. Off-season $295–$475 suite. Rates include breakfast. Additional person $20. AE, DC, MC, V. Valet parking $15. **Amenities:** Large outdoor heated pool; 12 outdoor tennis courts; deluxe health club; water-sports rentals; concierge; secretarial services; salon; room service; in-room massage; baby-sitting; laundry and dry-cleaning service. *In room:* A/C, TV/VCR, video rental delivered to room for $5, dataport, mini-bar, hair dryer, iron, safe.

Ritz-Carlton Coconut Grove   The third and smallest of Miami's Ritz-Carlton hotels, scheduled to open in October 2001, promises to be the most intimate of its properties, surrounded by 2 acres of tropical gardens and over-looking Biscayne Bay and the Miami skyline. Decorated as if it were a turn-of-the-19th-century mansion, the hotel's understated luxury will be a welcome addition to an area known for its gaudiness. Expect the Ritz-Carlton standard of service and comfort.

2700 Tigertail Ave., Coconut Grove, FL 33133. Ⓒ **800/241-3333** or 305/648-5900. Fax 305/648-1448. www. ritzcarlton.com. 115 units. Winter $475–$750 double. Off-season $285–$550 double. AE, DC, DISC, MC, V. Valet parking. **Amenities:** 2 restaurants; cigar bar; outdoor pool; health club; concierge; business center; 24-hour room service. *In room:* A/C, TV, dataport, minibar, hair dryer.

Wyndham Grand Bay Hotel 🏵🏵🏵   Grand in size and stature, the Grand Bay Hotel looks like it belongs in Acapulco with its ziggurat structure and trop-ical landscaping, but once you see the massive bright red structure done by late Condé Nast editorial director Alexander Lieberman in the driveway, you know you're not in Mexico. Ultraluxurious, the Grand Bay is quietly elegant, and, as a result, has hosted the likes of privacy fanatics such as Michael Jackson. British singer George Michael filmed his "Careless Whisper" video here because of its sweeping views of Biscayne Bay. Rooms are superb, with views of the bay and the Coconut Grove Marina, and they're decorated in soft peach tones with a country French theme. Bathrooms are equally luxurious. Service is outstanding, and the clientele ranges from families to jet-setters. Bice, a sublime Northern Italian restaurant, is the hotel's most popular dining option.

2669 S. Bayshore Dr. (at 27th Ave.), Coconut Grove, FL 33133. Ⓒ **800/327-2788** or 305/858-9600. Fax 305/ 858-1532. www.wyndham.com. 181 units. Winter $359–$400 suite. Off-season $279–$349 suite. Additional person $20. AE, DC, MC, V. Valet parking $16. **Amenities:** 4 restaurants; lounge serving afternoon tea; indoor heated pool and outdoor pool; 24-hour health club; Jacuzzi; sauna; concierge; business center; baby-sitting. *In room:* A/C, TV, CD player, fax, dataport, minibar, coffeemaker, hair dryer, iron, safe.

MODERATE

Hampton Inn   This very standard chain hotel is a welcome reprieve in an area otherwise known for very pricey accommodations. The rooms are nothing excit-ing, but the freebies, like local phone calls, parking, in-room movies, breakfast buffet, and hot drinks around the clock make this a real steal. Although there is no restaurant or bar, it is close to lots of both—only about half a mile to the heart of the Grove's shopping and retail area and about as far from Coral Gables. Rooms are brand new, sparkling clean, and larger than that of a typical motel. Located at the residential end of Brickell Avenue, it's a quiet, convenient loca-tion 15 minutes from South Beach and 5 minutes from Coconut Grove. If you'd rather save your money for dining and entertainment, this is a good bet.

2800 SW 28th Terrace (at U.S. 1 and SW 27th Ave.), Coconut Grove, FL 33133. ✆ **888/287-3390** or
305/448-2800. Fax 305/442-8655. www.Hampton-inn.com. 137 units. Winter $134–$154 double. Off-season
$104–$124 double. Rates include continental breakfast buffet and local calls. AE, DC, DISC, MC, V. Free parking. **Amenities:** Large outdoor pool; Jacuzzi; exercise room. *In room:* A/C, TV, microwave on request.

4 Dining

Don't be fooled by the plethora of superlean model types you're likely to see posing throughout Miami. Contrary to popular belief, dining in this city is as much
a sport as in-line skating on Ocean Drive. With over 6,000 restaurants to choose
from, dining out in Miami has become a passionate pastime for locals and visitors alike. In fact, we excel when it comes to food; our star chefs have fused
Californian-Asian with Caribbean and Latin elements to create a world-class flavor all its own: *Floribbean.* Think mango chutney splashed over fresh swordfish
or a spicy sushi sauce served alongside Peruvian ceviche.

Formerly synonymous with early-bird specials, Miami's new-wave cuisine, 10
years in the making, now rivals that of San Francisco or even New York. It's
pricey, but if you can manage to splurge at least once, it's worth it.

Thanks to a thriving cafe society in both South Beach and Coconut Grove,
you can also enjoy a moderately priced meal and linger for hours without having a waiter hover over you, waiting to "turn" your table. In Little Havana, you
can chow down on a meal that serves about six for less than $10. And since
seafood is plentiful, it doesn't have to cost you an arm and a leg to enjoy the
appendages of a crab or lobster. Don't be put off by the looks of our recommended seafood shacks in places such as Key Biscayne—oftentimes these spots
get the best and freshest catches.

Whatever you're craving, Miami's got it—with the exception of decent Chinese food and a New York–style slice of pizza. Like many cities in Europe, it is
fashionable to dine late in South Beach, preferably after 9, sometimes as late as
midnight. Service on South Beach is notoriously slow and arrogant, but it comes
with the turf. On the mainland—especially in Coral Gables, and, more recently,
downtown and on Brickell Avenue—you can also experience fine, creative dining without the pretense.

The biggest complaint when it comes to Miami dining isn't the haughtiness,
but rather the dearth of truly moderately priced restaurants, especially in South
Beach and Coral Gables. I've tried to cover a range of cuisines in a range of
prices. But with new restaurants opening on a weekly basis, you're bound to find
a savory array of dining choices in every budget.

Many restaurants keep extended hours in season (roughly December to
April), and may close for lunch and/or dinner on Monday, when the traffic is
slower. Always call ahead, since schedules do change. Also, always look carefully
at your bill—many Miami restaurants add a 15% gratuity to your total. Feel free
to adjust it if you feel your server deserves more or less. If you want to picnic on
the beach or pick up some dessert, check out the gourmet food shops, green
markets, and bakeries listed in "Shopping" in chapter 5.

SOUTH BEACH

The renaissance of South Beach has spawned dozens of first-rate restaurants. In
fact, big-name restaurants from across the country have capitalized on South
Beach's international appeal and opened, and continue to open, branches here
with great success. A few old standbys remain from the *Miami Vice* days, but the
flock of newcomers dominates the scene, with places going in and out of style
as quickly as the tides.

To Central Miami Beach ↑

The Bass Museum of Art

COLLINS PARK

22nd St.

20th St.

19th St.

18th St.

Miami Beach Convention Center

Jackie Gleason Theater of Performing Arts

17th St.

Venetian Causeway

BELLE ISLAND

Lincoln Rd.

Lincoln Road Mall

16th St.

15th St.

Española Way

14th St.

Miami Beach Post Office

13th St.

12th St.

FLAMINGO PARK

11th St.

10th St.

Beach Patrol Station

Art Deco Welcome Center

9th St.

8th St.

7th St.

6th St.

5th St.

4th St.

3rd St.

2nd St.

1st St.

Commerce St.

Biscayne St.

SOUTH POINTE PARK

Government Cut

ATLANTIC OCEAN

LUMMUS PARK

Dade Boulevard

Purdy Ave.

West Ave.

Bay Rd.

Alton Rd.

Lenox Ave.

Michigan Ave.

Jefferson Ave.

Meridian Ave.

Pennsylvania Ave.

Washington Ave.

Collins Ave.

Ocean Dr.

James Ave.

The Lincoln Road area is packed with places offering good food and great atmosphere; I recommend strolling and browsing. With very few exceptions, the places on Ocean Drive are crowded with tourists and priced accordingly. You'll do better to venture a little farther into the pedestrian-friendly streets just west of Ocean Drive.

VERY EXPENSIVE

Astor Place ★★★ NEW WORLD CUISINE Caribbean cowboy chef Johnny Vinczenz has returned Astor Place to its original chic-chuck-wagon glory, whipping his chef's lasso into an epicurean frenzy with signature dishes straight from the American-Caribbean heartland: wild mushroom pancake short stack with balsamic syrup, sautéed local yellowtail snapper, and wasabi skillet-seared tuna steak. Portions are huge and often enough for two to share. Appetizers are also generous in size, popular among the many lightweight model types who frequent the place. Desserts are glorious; chocoholics will be in heaven with the Cuarto de Chocolates featuring flourless chocolate cake, a chocolate dome, and peanut-butter chocolate bars. Sunday's Gospel Brunch is the ideal way to pay penance for your sins of the night before, but beware: The live gospel music is LOUD! Comfortable booths and soothing lighting give way to a scene that's reminiscent of a Hollywood movie premiere. Beware of whiplash-inducing situations (that is, celebrity sightings) especially on weekend nights.

In the Hotel Astor, 956 Washington Ave., South Beach. ✆ 305/672-7217. Reservations recommended. Main courses $27–$36. AE, MC, V. Mon–Sat 7:30–11am and 11:30am–2:30pm; Sun–Thurs 7–11pm, Fri–Sat 7pm–midnight; Sunday Gospel Brunch noon–2:30pm.

BED ★★ ECLECTIC BED—that's Beverage. Entertainment. Dining—is one of the most innovative dining lounges to land in South Beach in a very long time. When you walk inside, you'll feel as if you've entered a Buddhist temple. An array of inviting mosquito-netted beds awaits diners. You'll rest your head against soft cushiony pillows. A deejay spins Euro mood music and some techno. You'll have no problem appreciating the taste and aroma of the exquisite (and exquisitely priced) cuisine, featuring dishes such as Asian spice–crusted yellowtail snapper with scallop noodles and shiitake sauce. For dessert, try a little Pillow Talk—Grand Marnier crème anglaise with meringue pillows—or take a Roll in the Hay—a tropical fruit crêpe with coconut haystacks. Beware of crumbs in the sheets, as they aren't always changed between customers, and for the agoraphobic, do not go to BED on a weekend night—it's a nightmare.

929 Washington Ave., South Beach. ✆ 305/532-9070. Reservations required. Main courses $29–$37. AE, DC, MC, V. Wed–Sun: first lay (no actual seats) 8:30pm; second lay 10:30pm. Reservations only accepted on the day you plan to dine there. Lounge 11pm–3am.

China Grill ★★★ PAN-ASIAN Unless your surname is Pacino, DeNiro, or Winfrey (you get the idea), you might find yourself digging a hungry hole to China Grill at the gauche hour of 6pm or the ungodly, indigestion-inducing hour of midnight. But with an incomparable, albeit dizzying, array of amply portioned dishes such as the outrageous crispy spinach, wasabi mashed potatoes, seared rare tuna in spicy Japanese pepper, broccoli rabe dumplings, lobster pancakes, and a sinfully delicious dessert sampler complete with sparklers, this hub of South Beach flash is well worth the wait. Keep in mind that China Grill is a family-style restaurant and that dishes are meant to be shared.

404 Washington Ave., South Beach. ✆ 305/534-2211. Reservations strongly recommended. Main courses $15–$25. AE, DC, M, V. Mon–Thurs 11:45am–midnight, Fri 11:45am–1am, Sat 6pm–1am, Sun 6pm–midnight.

Escopazzo ✿✿✿ ITALIAN   Escopazzo means "crazy" in Italian, but the only sign of insanity in this primo Northern Italian eatery is the fact that it only seats 70. The wine bottles have it better—the restaurant's cellar holds 1,000 bottles of various vintages. Should you be so lucky to score a table at this romantic local favorite, you'll have trouble deciding between dishes such as pappardelle with wild game and mushroom ragout, swordfish carpaccio, and braised leg of lamb with juniper berries, rosemary, and fennel. Eating here is like dining with a big Italian family—service is excellent and nobody's happy until you are blissfully full.

1311 Washington Ave., South Beach. ✆ **305/674-9450**. Reservations required. Main courses $18–$28. AE, MC, V. Mon, Tues, and Thurs 6pm–midnight, Fri–Sat 6pm–1am, Sun 6–11pm.

Gaucho Room ✿✿✿ STEAK   This restaurant will set you back *mucho dinero*, but it is one of the best steak houses in the city. The Gaucho Room is a hip Argentinean dining room that serves prime aged meats with unparalleled service. Argentine rib eye is marinated in garlic, herbs, and olive oil before being grilled and served on butcher blocks. *Warning:* Those with gentler palates should probably request light seasoning on their food.

In the Loews Hotel, 1601 Collins Ave. (St. Moritz Bldg.), South Beach. ✆ **305/604-5290**. Reservations recommended. Main courses $22–$52. AE, MC, V. Daily 7pm–1am.

Joe's Stone Crab Restaurant ✿✿ SEAFOOD   Unless you grease the palms of one of the stone-faced maitre d's with some stone-cold cash, you'll be waiting for those famous claws for up to 2 hours—if not more. As much a Miami landmark as the beaches themselves, Joe's is a microcosm of the city, attracting everyone from T-shirted locals to a bejeweled Ivana Trump. Whatever you wear, however, will be eclipsed by a kitschy, unglamorous plastic bib that your waiter will tie on you unless you say otherwise. Open only during stone-crab season (October through May), Joe's reels in the crowds with the freshest, meatiest stone crabs and their essential accoutrements: creamed spinach and excellent sweet potato fries. Not feeling crabby? The fried chicken and liver and onions on the regular menu are actually considered by many as far superior—they're definitely far cheaper—to the crabs. Oh yeah, and save room for dessert. The Key lime pie here is the best in town. If you don't feel like waiting, try Joe's Take Away, which is located next door to the restaurant—it's a lot quicker and just as tasty.

11 Washington Ave. (at Biscayne St., just south of 1st St.), South Beach. ✆ **305/673-0365**, or 305/673-4611 for takeout. www.joesstonecrab.com. Reservations not accepted. Market price varies but averages $62.95 for a serving of jumbo crab claws, $38.95 for large claws. AE, DC, DISC, MC, V. Daily 11:30am–2:30pm; Mon–Thurs 5–10pm, Fri–Sat 5–11pm, Sun 4:45–10pm. Open mid-Oct to mid-May.

Mark's South Beach ✿✿✿ NEW WORLD/MEDITERRANEAN   Named after owner and chef Mark Militello, this is one of the best restaurants in all of Miami. A cozy, contemporary restaurant nestled in the basement of the quietly chic Hotel Nash, Mark's New World and Mediterranean-influenced menu changes nightly. What doesn't change is the consistency and freshness of the restaurant's exquisite cuisine. The roast garlic stuffed tenderloin of beef with polenta and a ragout of root vegetables is exceptional and worth every bit of cholesterol it may have. Cornmeal-dusted black grouper wrapped in Serrano ham and zucchini is in a school of its own. Desserts, including an impressive cheese cart, are outrageous, especially the pistachio cake with chocolate sorbet. Unlike many South Beach eating establishments, the knowledgeable servers are here because of their experience in the restaurant—not modeling—business.

In the Hotel Nash, 1120 Collins Ave., South Beach. ✆ **305/604-9050**. Reservations recommended. Main courses $18–$38. AE, DC, DISC, MC, V. Daily 6–11pm.

Nobu SUSHI   Despite the fact that at press time Nobu wasn't even open yet, the sushi palace, owned by star chef Nobuyuki Matsuhisa, was already taking reservations. The raw facts: Nobu has been hailed as one of the best sushi restaurants in the world, with always packed eateries in New York, London, and Los Angeles. The Omakase, or Chef's Choice—a multicourse menu entirely up to the chef for $70 per person and up—gets consistent raves.

At the Shore Club Hotel, 1901 Collins Ave., South Beach. ✆ **305/695-3100**. Reservations required. Main courses $10–$70. AE, MC, V. Daily 6pm–1am.

Pacific Time ★★★ PAN-ASIAN   Chef and co-owner (and former model) Jonathan Eismann was awarded the Robert Mondavi Award for Culinary Excellence in June 1994, and his restaurant, Pacific Time, has been recognized by *Bon Appétit* and *Esquire* magazines as one of America's "Best New Restaurants." Eismann's dishes are stunning hybrids of Chinese, Japanese, Korean, Vietnamese, Korean, Mongolian, and Indonesian flavors. One of the best dishes is the Mongolian lamb salad, which has a lightly sweet, earthy taste with a crunchy kick of onion. For a main course, the ever-changing menu offers many locally caught fish specialties such as Szechuan grilled local grouper served on a bed of shredded shallots and ginger with a sweet sake-infused sauce and tempura-dunked sweet potato slivers on the side. The famous chocolate bombe is every bit as decadent as they say, with hot bittersweet chocolate bursting from the cupcake-like center. The wine list is quite wonderful and extensive.

915 Lincoln Rd. (between Jefferson and Michigan Aves.), South Beach. ✆ **305/534-5979**. Reservations recommended. Main courses $20–$32. AE, DC, MC, V. Sun–Thurs 6–11pm, Fri–Sat 6pm–midnight.

Tantra ★★★ ECLECTIC   Marrakesh meets Miami Beach in this truly original, outrageously priced exotic outpost devoted to the ancient Indian tantric philosophy of tempting the senses with all things pleasurable. Begin with your surroundings: a sultry interior of soft grass (yes, it's real; they resod weekly) and starry lights overhead. In the front room by the bar, there are low-lying couches and pillow-lined booths bolstered by drapes that can be closed for privacy. Belly dancers mix with cocktail waitresses singing the praises of Tantra's special aphrodisiac cocktails and offering you a puff of Turkish tobacco from the communal hookah pipe (they insist it's clean, but I'd be wary). A private VIP room off to the side features a hammock and a peaceful spiritual soundtrack.

Tantra serves a combination of Middle Eastern, Mediterranean, and Indian dishes that really are divine. Consider the Tantra Love Apple: a ripe tomato layered with Laura Chenel goat cheese and basil oil, garnished with pomegranate seeds; or perhaps Nine Jewel Indian Spiced Rack of Lamb. The $52 filet mignon is delicious, but its price tag borders on obscene.

Don't come to Tantra looking for a serene vibe to match the setting and menu. Tantra practically turns into a nightclub after dinner, attracting a crowd of celebrities and scenesters.

1445 Pennsylvania Ave. (at Española Way), South Beach. ✆ **305/672-4765**. Reservations required. Main courses $26–$46. AE, DC, DISC, MC, V. Daily 7pm–1am. Late-night menu available.

Tuscan Steak ★★★ ITALIAN/STEAK   This excellent Northern Italian restaurant, a member of the China Grill scion, is all about meat served Italian style, in large family-style portions. With a rich wood interior, the atmosphere

Jugglers, dancers and an assortment of acrobats fill the street.

She shoots you a wide-eyed look as a seven-foot cartoon character approaches.

What brought you here was wanting the kids

to see something magical while they still believed in magic.

With 700 airlines, 50,000 hotels and over 5,000 cruise and vaca-

on getaways, you can now go places you've always dreamed of.

Travelocity.com
A Sabre Company
Go Virtually Anywhere.

"WORLD'S LEADING TRAVEL WEB SITE, 5 YEARS IN A ROW" WORLD TRAVEL AWARDS

I HAVE TO CALL THE TRAVEL AGENCY
AGAIN. DARN, OUT TO LUNCH. NOW I
HAVE TO CALL THE AIRLINE. I HATE
CALLING THE AIRLINES. I GOT PUT ON
HOLD AGAIN. "INSTRUMENTAL TOP-
40" ... LOVELY. I HATE GETTING PUT ON
HOLD. TICKET PRICES ARE ALL OVER
THE MAP. HOW DO I DIAL INTERNA-
TIONALLY? OH SHOOT, FORGOT THE
RENTAL CAR. I'M STILL ON HOLD. THIS
MUSIC IS GIVING ME A HEADACHE. I
WONDER IF SOMEONE ELSE HAS
CHEAPER FLIGHTS. FORGET IT, CAN'T
TAKE IT ANYMORE ... I'M HANGING UP.

YAHOO! TRAVEL
100% MUZAK-FREE

Booking your trip online at Yahoo! Travel is simple. You
compare the best prices. You click. You go have fun.
Tickets, hotels, rental cars, cruises & more. Sorry, no muzak.

is reminiscent of the dining room of a well-connected *family*—ornate and very loud. The house salad is a massive undertaking of the classic antipasto, filled with shredded slices of salami and pepperoni, chunks of mozzarella, and a delicate vinaigrette. Everything here is a la carte, so be sure to order the sautéed spinach with garlic and the onion mashed potatoes with whichever steak you choose. All steaks are big enough for at least three people to share. The house specialty is a delicious T-bone steak served with pungent garlic puree. On any given weekend night, reservations are secondary to being friends with the ultra-tanned host, so expect a long wait for a table. The background music is straight out of Studio 54 and so is the flashy crowd.

433 Washington Ave., South Beach. ✆ 305/534-2233. Reservations strongly recommended on weekends. Main courses $20–$65. Family-style meals are $50 per person, including appetizer and main course. AE, DISC, MC, V. Sun–Thurs 6pm–midnight, Fri–Sat 6pm–1am.

Wish ★★★ ECLECTIC   Wish got its start as a haute vegetarian restaurant, located in the stylish Todd Oldham–designed The Hotel. It was, and still is, a terrific setting (request an outside table in the serene, umbrellaed courtyard), but the foodies couldn't bear a meal without meat. Culinary whiz Andrea Curto came on board and redirected the menu, which now features an international fusion of ingredients including imported meats, poultry, and seafood. Two of Wish's finest are pan-seared scallops with blackened corn, pecans, purple Thai sticky rice, and adzuki-bean puree; and orange beurre blanc and spicy-seared yellowfin tuna with chive potato napoleon, roasted Japanese eggplant, Chinese long bean, and soy wasabi vinaigrette.

In The Hotel, 801 Collins Ave., South Beach. ✆ 305/531-2222. Reservations recommended. Main courses $16–$32. AE, DC, DISC, MC, V. Daily 6–10:30pm.

EXPENSIVE

Joia Restaurant and Bar ★★ ITALIAN   Owned by Miami nightlife diva Ingrid Casares, famous for her friendship with Madonna, Joia exudes a cozy atmosphere of self-conscious camaraderie, with a few tables indoors and several outdoors in a large courtyard. On any given night you're bound to see celebrities such as Ben Stiller, Donald Trump, Rupert Everett, and, yes, Madonna. Without harping on the service too much (it's leisurely), the pasta here is among the freshest anywhere on the beach. There is a laundry list of appetizers, salads, and pastas in every conceivable shape, from penne to farfalle. Recommended dishes include the *rigatoni al funghi,* a mushroom-lover's delight, with large tube pasta filled with shiitake and porcini mushrooms; the *gnocchi di zucca,* homemade potato and pumpkin dumplings in a tomato or cheese sauce; and the *bauletti di pollo al funghi,* a folded chicken breast stuffed with Fontina cheese, mushrooms, and sage. The wine list is exquisite. If you're not up for a lengthy meal here, grab a seat at the bar and witness what could only be described as a taste of la dolce vita, South Beach style. As in any club of the moment, Joia also has a private VIP room in the back, where we hear the service is a bit quicker.

140 Ocean Dr., South Beach. ✆ 305/674-8855. Reservations recommended. Main courses $12–$30. AE, DC, DISC, MC, V. Daily noon–4pm; Sun–Thurs 6pm–midnight, Fri–Sat 6pm–1am.

Nemo ★★★ PAN-ASIAN   What Wolfgang Puck is to foodies on the West Coast, Nemo's chef, Michael Schwartz, is to Miami. Hailing from Puck's lauded Chinois in L.A., Schwartz's Pan-Asian cuisine is masterful. Located on the quickly developing South Beach area known as SoFi (for "south of Fifth Street"),

Nemo is a funky, high-style eatery with an open kitchen and an outdoor court-yard canopied by trees and lined with an eclectic mix of model types, foodies, and Schwartz groupies. Among the reasons to eat in this restaurant whose name is actually "omen" spelled backward: wok-charred salmon with roasted pumpkin seeds, crispy prawns with salsa, and an inspired dessert menu by Hedy Gold-smith that's not for the faint of calories. Seating inside is comfy cozy, but bor-ders on cramped. On Sunday mornings, the open kitchen is converted into a buffet counter for the restaurant's unparalleled brunch. Coveted tables outside surround the serene courtyard, and, most recently, the pool at the adjacent Mer-cury Hotel. Be prepared for a wait, which tends to spill out onto the street.

100 Collins Ave., South Beach. ⓒ 305/532-4550. Reservations recommended. Main courses $22–$36; Sun brunch $26. AE, MC, V. Mon–Fri noon–3pm and 7pm–midnight, Sun 11am–3pm and 6–11pm. Valet park-ing $10.

MODERATE

Balan's ⭐⭐ MEDITERRANEAN   Balan's provides undeniable evidence that the Brits actually do know a thing or two about cuisine. A direct import from London's hip Soho area, Balan's draws inspiration from various Mediterranean and Asian influences, labeling its cuisine "Mediterrasian." With a brightly colored interior straight out of a mod '60s flick, Balan's is a local favorite among the gay and arty crowds. The moderately priced food is rather good here—especially the sweet-potato soufflé with leeks and roasted garlic, fried goat cheese, and porto-bello mushrooms, and the Chilean sea bass with roasted tomato. Adding to the ambience is the restaurant's people-watching vantage point on Lincoln Road.

1022 Lincoln Rd. (between Lenox and Michigan), South Beach. ⓒ 305/534-9191. Reservations not accepted. Main courses $6–$16. AE, DISC, MC, V. Daily 8am–midnight.

Bond St. Lounge ⭐⭐ SUSHI   A New York City import, the sceney Bond St. Lounge is located in the basement of the shabby chic Townhouse Hotel and is packing in hipsters as tightly as the crab meat in a California Roll. Despite its tiny size, Bond St. Lounge's superfresh nigiri and sashimi, and funky sushi rolls such as the sun-dried tomato and avocado or the arugula crispy potato, are worth cramming in for. As the evening progresses, however, Bond St. becomes more of a bar scene than a restaurant, but sushi is always available at the bar to accompany your sake Bloody Mary.

Townhouse Hotel, 150 20th St., South Beach. ⓒ 305/534-3800. Reservations not accepted. Sushi $6–$12. AE, MC, V. Daily 6pm–2am.

Grillfish ⭐⭐ SEAFOOD   From the beautiful Byzantine–style mural and the gleaming oak bar, you'd think you were eating in a much more expensive restau-rant, but Grillfish manages to pay the exorbitant South Beach rent with the help of a loyal local following who come for fresh, simple seafood in a relaxed but upscale atmosphere.

The servers are friendly and know the menu well. The barroom seafood chowder is full of chunks of shellfish, as well as some fresh white fish fillets in a tomato broth. The small ear of corn, included with each entree, is about as close as you'll get to any type of vegetable offering besides the pedestrian salad. Still, at these prices, it's worth a visit to try some local fare including mako shark, swordfish, tuna, marlin, and wahoo. At press time, Grillfish was prepar-ing to dive into a meaty venture right next door, at Grillsteak (1438 Collins Ave., same hours, credit cards, price range, and reservation policy). The early buzz has Grillsteak getting along with Grillfish swimmingly. A second Grillfish location is at 2325 Galliano St., Coral Gables (℘305/445-6411).

1444 Collins Ave. (corner of Española Way), South Beach. ℘ 305/538-9908. Reservations for 6 or more only. Main courses $9–$16. AE, DC, DISC, MC, V. Daily 6pm–midnight.

Jeffrey's ★★ *Finds* CONTINENTAL/BISTRO   Some say this is the most romantic restaurant on the beach; South Beach's gay crowd certainly seems to agree. Old-fashioned lace curtains and candlelight are a welcome respite from the glitz and chrome of the rest of the island. Most people don't even realize this restaurant exists. But don't think that means there are empty tables. Jeffrey's certainly has its fair share of regulars.

You can choose a succulent three-quarter-pound burger or try a hearty chicken breast marinated in balsamic sauce and served with freshly mashed sweet potatoes over spinach, on white lace tablecloths. Some of the better seafood options include the conch fritters and the meaty crab cakes. Most desserts are tasty, but the homemade *tarte tatin*, a caramelly deep-dish apple tart, is delicious.

1629 Michigan Ave. (half block south of Lincoln Rd.), South Beach. ℘ 305/673-0690. Reservations highly recommended. Main courses $12–$24. AE, DC, MC, V. Tues–Sat 6–11pm, Sun 5–10pm. Closed Sept.

Joe Allen ★★ *Finds* AMERICAN   It's hard to compete in a city with haute spots everywhere you look, but Joe Allen, a restaurant that has proven itself in both New York and London, has stood up to the challenge by establishing itself off the beaten path in possibly the only area of South Beach that has managed to remain impervious to trendiness and overdevelopment. Located on the bay side of the beach, Joe Allen is nestled in an unassuming building conspicuously devoid of excess neon lights, valet parkers, and fashionable pedestrians. Inside, however, one discovers a hidden jewel: a stark yet elegant interior and no-nonsense, fairly priced, ample-portioned dishes such as meat loaf, pizza, fresh fish, and salads. The scene has a homey feel flavored by locals looking to escape the hype without compromising quality.

1787 Purdy Ave. (3 blocks west of Alton Rd.), South Beach. ℘ 305/531-7007. Reservations recommended, especially on weekends. Main courses $13–$24. MC, V. Mon–Fri 11:30am–11:45pm.

Larios on the Beach ★ CUBAN   If you're a fan of singer Gloria Estefan, you will definitely want to check out this restaurant, which she and her husband Emilio co-own; if not, you may want to reconsider, as the place is an absolute mob scene, especially on weekends. The classic Cuban dishes get a so-so rating from the Cubans, but a better one from those who aren't as well versed in the cuisine. The portions here are larger than life, as are some of the restaurant's patrons, who come here for the sidewalk scenery and the well-prepared black beans and rice. Inside, the restaurant turns into a makeshift salsa club, with music blaring over the animated conversations and the sounds of English clashing with Spanish. Because of its locale on Ocean Drive, Larios is a great place to bring someone who's never experienced the Cuban culture or tasted its cuisine.

820 Ocean Dr., South Beach. ℘ 305/532-9577. Reservations recommended. Main courses $8–$24. AE, MC, V. Sun–Thurs 11:30am–midnight, Fri–Sat 11:30am–2am.

L'Entrecote de Paris ★★ FRENCH   New York's got the Statue of Liberty and Miami's got L'Entrecote de Paris. We don't complain. Everything in this little piece of Paris, a classy little bistro, is simple. For dinner, you choose between salmon or steak, and beyond a few salads, that's it—but both are great. The salmon looks like spa cuisine, served with a pile of bald steamed potatoes and a salad with simple greens and an unmatchable vinaigrette. The steak, on the other hand, is the stuff cravings are made of, even if you're not a die-hard carnivore. Its salty sharp sauce is rich but not thick, and full of the beef's natural flavor. The slices are served on top of your own little hibachi, which also keeps the accompanying fries warm.

Most diners are very Euro and pack a petit attitude. Servers, however, are superquick and professional, and almost friendly in a French kind of way, making up for the close quarters. The short and very French wine list includes several well-priced bottles for under $20. I loved the *profiteroles au chocolat*, a perfect puff pastry filled with vanilla ice cream and topped with a dark bittersweet chocolate sauce.

413 Washington Ave., South Beach. ℂ 305/673-1002. Reservations recommended on weekends. Fixed-price dinner $14–$21. DC, MC, V. Tues–Sat 6pm–1am.

Macarena ★★ SPANISH/MEDITERRANEAN   This Macarena has long outlived its passé line-dance namesake and is rather hip, actually, looked after by a young crew of Spanish imports whose families own several popular restaurants in Madrid. Show up before 10pm and you're sure to get a table. After that time, especially on weekends, it's standing room only. The gorgeous Euro crowd shows up for foot-stomping flamenco (every Wednesday, Friday, and Saturday—call for show times) and an outrageous selection of tapas, as well as Miami's very best paella (order a large portion and share it among at least four people). The garlic shrimp are tasty and aromatic, and the yellow squash stuffed with seafood and cheese is especially delicious. Really, all the seafood, such as mussels in marinara sauce and clams in green sauce, is worth sampling. With such reasonable prices, you can taste lots of dishes and leave satisfied. Try some of the terrific sangria made with slices of fresh fruit and a subtle tinge of sweet soda. Sidewalk seating is available on busy Washington Avenue, but the action is more entertaining inside.

1334 Washington Ave., South Beach. ℂ 305/531-3440. Reservations recommended on weekends. Main courses $12–$20; tapas $5–$9. AE, DC, MC, V. Daily 7pm–midnight.

Spiga ★★ ITALIAN   This intimate Italian restaurant is cool without being pretentious, concentrating on the food rather than the fanfare that has become central to so many South Beach eateries. Like the hotel in which it resides, Spiga's atmosphere is wonderfully low-key, making it a quiet favorite with locals and some luminaries. The complimentary bruschetta with grilled eggplant, served to you at one of the few tables inside or out, is the first of many culinary treats. The garlicky gnocchi with tomato and basil is an incredible illustration of how simple doesn't have to mean bland. The pungent Gorgonzola polenta appetizer is a meal in itself, and the risotto with bay scallops is a rousing display of culinary precision. The place is vaguely reminiscent of a Florentine trattoria, and if you stop to listen, you'll notice the prevailing language here is, in fact, Italian.

Hotel Impala, 1228 Collins Ave., South Beach. ℂ 305/534-0079. $7–$15. AE, DC, MC, V. Daily 6pm–midnight.

Van Dyke Cafe ★ AMERICAN   The younger, jazzier sibling of Ocean Drive's News Café, the Van Dyke is similar in spirit and cuisine but different in attitude. Unlike the much scenier and much more touristy News Café, Van Dyke is a locals' favorite, at which people-watching is also premium, but attitude is practically nonexistent. Both cafes have nearly the same menu, with decent salads, sandwiches, and omelets, but the Van Dyke's warm wood-floored interior, upstairs jazz bar, accessible parking, and intense chocolate soufflé make it a less taxing alternative. Also, unlike News, Van Dyke turns into a sizzling nightspot, featuring live jazz nearly every night of the week (a $5 cover charge is added to your bill if you sit at a table; the bar's free). Outside there's a vast tree-lined seating area.

846 Lincoln Rd., South Beach. ℂ 305/534-3600. Reservations recommended for evenings. Main courses $8–$17. AE, DC, MC, V. Sun–Thurs 8am–1am, Fri–Sat 8am–3am.

MODERATE/INEXPENSIVE

Big Pink ✿ AMERICAN   Real Food for Real People is the motto to which this restaurant strictly adheres. Located on what used to be a gritty corner of Collins Avenue, Big Pink—owned by the folks at the higher-end Nemo—is quickly identified by a whimsical Pippi Longstocking–type mascot, whose picture is largely displayed on a sign outside. Scooters and motorcycles line the streets surrounding the place, which is a favorite among beach bums, club kids, and those craving Big Pink's comforting and hugely portioned pizzas, sandwiches, salads, and hamburgers. The fare is above average at best, and the menu is massive, but it comes with a good dose of kitsch, such as their "gourmet" spin on the classic TV dinner, which is done perfectly, right down to the compartmentalized dessert. Televisions line the bar area and family-style table arrangement (there are several booths, too) promotes camaraderie among diners. Outdoor tables are also available.

157 Collins Ave., Miami Beach. ℂ 305/532-4700. Main courses $7–$12. AE, DC, MC, V. Sun–Thurs 9am–1am, Fri–Sat 9am–2am.

11th Street Diner AMERICAN   Like many of Miami's residents, this retro-diner is a transplant from the Northeast. Uprooted from its 1948 Wilkes Barre, Pennsylvania, foundation, the actual structure was dismantled and rebuilt on a bustling corner of Washington Avenue. It's a popular round-the-clock spot that attracts a friendly yet motley crew of locals, club kids, and curious tourists and is well known for its slow service and greasy diner fare. Come in for breakfast and you'll find bleary-eyed patrons chowing down after a night of partying.

1065 Washington Ave., South Beach. ℂ 305/534-6373. Items $5–$7. AE, MC, V. Tues 8am–1am; Wed–Mon 24 hours.

El Rancho Grande ✿✿ MEXICAN   Hidden just off Lincoln Road, El Rancho Grande was once a well-kept secret among devout Mexican food fanatics. It's not such a secret anymore. With a relatively restrained decor (clay pots, sponge-painted yellow walls), El Rancho Grande doesn't hold anything back when it comes to the cuisine. The Aztec Soup, a hot and spicy blend of chicken and tortilla strips, is some of the best I've had. Fresh, spicy salsa and expertly prepared, hugely portioned enchiladas, burritos, and fajitas are sensational. The scene is young and lively without being too rowdy. Margaritas are a little weak when frozen, and better ordered on the rocks. Expect a wait at the small bar for your table, especially on weekends.

1626 Pennsylvania Ave., Miami Beach. ℂ 305/673-0480. Items $8–$12. AE, DC, MC, V. Daily 11am–11pm.

Front Porch Café ✿ AMERICAN   Located in an unassuming, rather dreary-looking Art Deco hotel, the Front Porch Café is a relaxed local hangout known for cheap breakfasts. While some of the wait staff might be a bit sluggish (many are bartenders or club kids by night), it seems that nobody here is in a rush. If you are, this is *not* the place for you. Enjoy home-style French toast with bananas and walnuts, omelets, fresh fruit salads, pizzas, and classic breakfast pancakes that put IHOP to shame. Front Porch Café is also known for its daily dose of local gossip, which flows as freely as the syrup.

In the Penguin Hotel, 1418 Ocean Dr., South Beach. ℭ **305/531-8300.** Main courses $5–$11. Daily 8:30am–10:30pm. AE, DC, DISC, MC, V.

INEXPENSIVE

Le Sandwicherie SANDWICHES   You can get mustard, mayo, or oil and vinegar on sandwiches elsewhere in town, but you'd be missing out on all the local flavor. This gourmet sandwich bar, open until the crack of dawn, caters to ravenous club kids, biker-types, and the body artists who work in the tattoo parlor next door. For many people, in fact, no night of clubbing is complete without capping it off with a turkey sub from Le Sandwicherie.

229 14th St. (behind the Amoco station), South Beach. ℭ **305/532-8934.** Sandwiches and salads $5–$10. No credit cards. Daily 9:30am–5am. Delivery 9:30am–10pm.

Lincoln Road Café ⍟ *Value* CUBAN   A local favorite, this down-to-earth Cuban-accented cafe is very popular for its cheap breakfasts. For $5, you can indulge in a hearty portion of eggs any style, with bacon, ham, sausage, Cuban toast, and coffee. Lunch and dinner specials are delicious and very cheap as well; try the ubiquitous black beans and rice or a chicken fricassee with plantains. The few tables inside are usually passed up in favor of the several outdoors, but in the evenings the house is full inside and out, as talented Latin musicians perform.

941 Lincoln Rd., South Beach. ℭ **305/538-8066.** Items $5–$10. AE, DC, MC, V. Daily 8am–midnight.

News Café ⍟ AMERICAN   In the late '80s, South Beach pioneer Mark Soyka opened this cafe on a depressed, decrepit Ocean Drive, sparking what some now call the South Beach renaissance. The thriving News has become part of Miami history and it still draws locals onto what has become the most tourist-ridden street in the area. Whether you come by foot, blade, Harley, or Ferrari, you should wait for an outside table, which is where you need to be to fully appreciate the experience. Service is notoriously slow and often arrogant (perhaps because the tip is included), but the menu, while not newsworthy, has some fairly good items, such as the Middle Eastern platter of hummus, tahini, tabouli, and grape leaves; hamburgers; and omelets. If it's not too busy, you can enjoy a leisurely cappuccino outside; creative types like to bring their laptops and sit here all day. There's also an extensive collection of national and international newspapers and magazines at the in-house newsstand.

800 Ocean Dr., South Beach. ℭ **305/538-6397.** Items $5–$10. AE, DC, MC, V. Open 24 hours.

Pizza Rustica ⍟ PIZZA   Italians often scoff at the way Americans have mangled their recipe for pizza. But at Pizza Rustica, even the Italians marvel at these thin-crusted gourmet meals. This is the real deal—no thick, doughy, greasy concoctions here. Instead, Rustica features several delicious, huge slices of gourmet, authentically Tuscan-style pizza. Spinach and Gorgonzola cheese blend harmoniously with a brush of olive oil and garlic on a slate of the delicious, crispy dough. There's also a four-cheese, arugula, and rosemary potato slice, among others.

863 Washington Ave., South Beach. ℭ **305/674-8244.** Slice $4. No credit cards. Daily 11am–4am.

Puerto Sagua ⍟ CUBAN/SPANISH   This brown-walled diner is one of the only old holdouts on South Beach. Its steady stream of regulars ranges from *abuelitos* (little old grandfathers) to hipsters who stop in after clubbing. It has endured because the food is good, if a little greasy. Some of the less heavy dishes are a superchunky fish soup with pieces of whole flaky grouper, chicken and seafood paella, or marinated kingfish. Also good are most of the shrimp dishes, especially the shrimp in garlic sauce, which is served with white rice and salad.

This is one of the most reasonably priced places left on the beach for simple, hearty fare. Don't be intimidated by the hunched, older waiters in their white button shirts and black pants. Even if you don't speak Spanish, they're usually willing to do charades. Anyway, the extensive menu, which ranges from BLTs to grilled lobsters to yummy fried plantains, is translated into English. Hurry, before another boutique goes up in its place.

700 Collins Ave., South Beach. ✆ 305/673-1115. Main courses $8–$24; sandwiches and salads $5–$10. AE, DC, MC, V. Daily 7:30am–2am.

Sport Café ✪ ITALIAN   When Sport Café first opened, way back when South Beach was still a fledgling in the trendoid business, it had a plain interior, wooden chairs, and a view of the parking lot. Televisions inside were tuned to soccer matches at all times—hence the name. The key to Sport's success was, and still is, its good, cheap, homemade Italian food—nothing fancy. Only now the cafe has moved up the block to a large corner space complete with private outdoor garden. The restaurant might have moved on to better digs, but one thing remains the same: The food is still great and the soccer matches continue to kick the crowd into a European-style frenzy. Try the nightly specials, especially when the owners' mother is cooking her secret lasagna.

560 Washington Ave., South Beach. ✆ 305/674-9700. Reservations accepted for 4 or more. Main courses $8–$14; sandwiches and pizzas $6–$9. AE, MC, V. Daily noon–1am.

Sushi Rock Café ✪ SUSHI   Perhaps it has something to do with its campy name, but for some reason almost every rock star that comes to town makes a requisite stop here for a sushi fix. Aerosmith's Joe Perry and Steven Tyler ate here almost every night during their Miami-based recording sessions, and David Lee Roth has been spotted here more than once. Sushi Rock is known for a sporadically fresh assortment of sushi, hand rolls, and traditional Japanese cuisine, funky atmosphere, and hip late-night crowds.

1351 Collins Ave. (at 14th St.), South Beach. ✆ 305/532-2133. Items $5–$15. AE, DC, MC, V. Mon–Thurs noon–midnight, Fri–Sat noon–1am, Sun noon–11pm.

MIAMI BEACH: SURFSIDE, BAL HARBOUR & SUNNY ISLES

The area north of the Art Deco District—from about 21st Street to 163rd Street—had its heyday in the 1950s when huge hotels and gambling halls blocked the view of the ocean. Now, many of the old hotels have been converted into condos or budget lodgings and the bayfront mansions have been renovated by and for wealthy entrepreneurs, families, and speculators. The area has many more residents, albeit seasonal, than visitors. On the culinary front, the result is a handful of superexpensive, traditional restaurants and a number of value-oriented spots.

VERY EXPENSIVE

Forge Restaurant ✪✪✪ STEAK/AMERICAN   English oak paneling and Tiffany glass suggest high prices and haute cuisine, and that's exactly what you get at the Forge. Each elegant dining room possesses its own character and features high ceilings, ornate chandeliers, and European artwork. The atmosphere is elegant but not too stuffy. On Wednesday night, however, it's pandemonium as the who's who of Miami society gather for dinner, dancing, and schmoozing.

Like the rest of the menu, appetizers are mostly classics, from Beluga caviar to baked onion soup to shrimp cocktail and escargot. When they're in season, order the stone crabs. For the main course, any of the seafood, chicken, or veal dishes are recommendable, but the Forge is especially known for its award-winning steaks. Its wine selection is equally lauded—ask for a tour of the cellar.

432 Arthur Godfrey Rd. (41st St.), Miami Beach. (✆ **305/538-8533.** Reservations required. Main courses $21–$55. AE, DC, MC, V. Sun–Thurs 6pm–midnight, Fri–Sat 6pm–1am.

EXPENSIVE

Baraboo ★★ MEDITERRANEAN Baraboo, a crowded eatery in up-and-coming North Beach, is named for the small Wisconsin town that served as the original winter quarters of the Ringling Brothers Circus. Strolling mimes and magicians work the room, entertaining—or harassing, at times—diners who are indulging in the Mediterranean fare. Though not necessarily a theme restaurant, if they took away the clowning around, Baraboo could be a serious restaurant, featuring excellent ravioli with spinach, ricotta, and egg yolk; potato-crusted sea bass with saffron-sage sauce; and roasted muscovy duck breast. If you prefer to remain outside the big top, there are several outdoor tables that will protect you from a wayward mime or magician.

7300 Ocean Terrace (at 73rd St. and Collins Ave.), North Beach. (✆ **305/867-4242.** Reservations recommended, required on weekends. Main courses $9.50–$22. AE, MC, V. Tues–Sun 11:30am–1am.

Christine Lee's ★★ CHINESE This Cantonese restaurant is a 35-year-old Miami staple that serves excellent but overpriced Chinese steak, shrimp and lobster sauce, and steak kew. Considering the dearth of good Chinese restaurants in Miami, this is a good choice if you absolutely *must* satisfy your cravings for Chinese, but it will definitely cost you more than it should.

17082 Collins Ave. (✆ **305/947-1717.** Reservations recommended. Main courses $6.95–$29. AE, DISC, MC, V. Daily 4–11pm; winter lunch 11am–3pm.

Crystal Café ★★★ CONTINENTAL/NEW WORLD The setting is sparse, with a bottle of wine and Lucite salt and pepper grinders and as the only centerpiece on each of the 15 or so tables. I promise you won't need the seasoning. Chef Klime has done it all with the help of his affable wife and a superb wait staff. Enjoy his unique sparkle at this little-known hideaway, which attracts stars like Julio Iglesias and other in-the-know gourmands.

With approximately 30 entrees, including a few nightly specials, each is beautifully presented and perfectly prepared. The shrimp cake appetizer, for example, is the size of a bread plate and rests on top of a small mound of lightly sautéed watercress and mushrooms. Surrounding the delicately breaded disc are concentric circles of beautiful sauces. The veal Marsala is served in a luscious brown sauce thickened not with heavy cream or flour but with delicate vegetable broth and a hearty mix of mushrooms. The osso buco is a masterpiece.

726 41st St., Miami Beach. (✆ **305/673-8266.** Reservations recommended on weekends. Main courses $11–$25. AE, DC, DISC, MC, V. Tues–Thurs 5–10pm, Fri–Sat 5–11pm.

Shula's Steak House ★★ AMERICAN/STEAK Climb a sweeping staircase in the Alexander All-Suite Luxury Hotel and go through the glass hallway—designed like an atrium, so exotic flora and fauna beckon both within and without—and you'll find yourself in this magnificent restaurant that has been acclaimed as one of the greatest steak houses in all of North America. If you're feeling adventurous, try the 48-ounce club (you can get your name engraved on a gold plaque if you can finish this absolutely *huge* piece of meat) or settle for the 20-ounce Kansas City strip or the 12-ounce filet mignon. Fresh seafood abounds when in season, and the oysters Rockefeller are a particularly good choice. The entertaining staff is very knowledgeable, and there's a sizable and reasonably priced wine list. The restaurant also has the "No Name Lounge," where live piano music, premium spirits, and cigar smoking are available.

There's another branch of Shula's at 7601 NW 154th St. (in Don Shula's Golf Club off the Palmetto Expressway; **☏ 305/820-8102**) in West Dade.

In the Alexander Hotel, 5225 Collins Ave., Miami Beach. **☏ 305/341-6565.** Reservations recommended. Main courses $18–$58. AE, DISC, MC, V. Daily 11am–3:30pm and 6–11pm. Free valet parking.

MODERATE

Cafe Prima Pasta ★★ ITALIAN   Proving that good things do come in small packages, this tiny corner cafe's home cooking draws nightly hordes of carbo-craving diners who don't seem to mind waiting for a table for upward of an hour, maybe more on weekends. The scent of garlic wafting into the street is guaranteed to kill any vampire, and it makes the wait for a table a bit more torturous. Other choice ingredients include the ripest, freshest tomatoes, the finest olive oil, mozzarella that melts in your mouth, and fish that puts some seafood restaurants to shame. The spicy garlic and oil dip that comes with the bread is hard to resist and will likely linger with you for days, like the memory of this fine meal. Though tables are packed in a bit, the atmosphere still manages to be romantic.

414 71st St. (half a block east of the Byron movie theater), Miami Beach. **☏ 305/867-0106.** Reservations not accepted. Main courses $9–$17; pastas $7–$9. No credit cards. Mon–Thurs noon–midnight, Fri noon–1am, Sat 1pm–1am, Sun 5pm–midnight.

Cafe Ragazzi ★★ ITALIAN   This diminutive Italian cafe, with its rustic decor and a swift, knowledgeable wait staff, enjoys great success for its tasty simple pastas. The spicy *puttanesca* sauce with a subtle hint of fish is perfectly prepared. Also recommended is the salmon with radicchio. You can choose from many decent salads and carpaccio, too. Lunch specials are a real steal at $7, including soup, salad, and daily pasta. Unlike Café Prima Pasta, Café Ragazzi is light on sceniness—people come here for the food only. Expect to wait on weekend nights.

9500 Harding Ave. (on corner of 95th St.), Surfside. **☏ 305/866-4495.** Reservations accepted for 4 or more. Main courses $9–$18. MC, V. Mon–Fri 11:30am–3pm and 5:30–11pm, Sat–Sun 5:30–11pm.

Lemon Twist ★★ MEDITERRANEAN   In addition to great Mediterranean fare, there is a twist to this place in the form of a complimentary shot of the eponymous house spirit (a lemon vodka shot). But that comes after your meal. To start, you will receive a bowl of perfectly marinated olives, which can endanger your appetite, so go easy on them. A soothing, mellow interior makes for a romantic dining experience, or, if you prefer, outdoor tables are available (though the street is hardly as scenic). Specialties such as spinach lasagna with smoked salmon and shank of lamb caramelized with whole garlic are savored by a savvy crowd that has likely escaped South Beach for this refreshing change of scenery that's also graced with fine, friendly service.

908 71st St. (on 79th St. Causeway), Miami Beach/Normandy Isle. **☏ 305/868-2075.** Reservations recommended on weekends. Main courses $9–$18. AE, MC, V ($25 minimum). Tues–Sun 5:30pm–midnight. Closed July 4 weekend.

Mama Vieja ⋐ COLOMBIAN   This funky Colombian hangout looks like a total dive from the outside, but once inside you will want to dive right in to the supremely fresh national specialties such as *pargo rojo estofado a la mama vieja* (red snapper stuffed with a supercreamy and delicate seafood sauce in a rice base). Brightly painted walls and elevated porches look out onto a large-screen TV showing music videos from the old country. The walls and ceilings are decorated with hundreds of hats that have been donated by customers and signed in exchange for a free meal. Bring in an interesting hat and mention it to the server before placing your order so that he or she can bring you to the attention of the owner. All the dishes here are worth trying and are so reasonably priced that it's easy to order a lot. Try to save room for the milky sweet desserts and a good strong coffee—you'll need it if you want to dance it off after at Lola, the very popular, unpretentious hot spot next door.

235 23rd St. (just west of Collins Ave.), South Beach. ℭ **305/538-2400.** Main courses $4.95–$14.95. AE, DC, DISC, MC, V. Daily noon–midnight.

Spice ⋐⋐ ITALIAN/ASIAN   The owners of Café Prima Pasta decided that their excellent Italian fare needed a little Asian spice, so they opened this interesting restaurant to prove that the Italian-Asian combination does not have to be washed down with a Pepto-Bismol cocktail. (Actually, the menu's split down the middle, so you won't find mu shu lasagna or anything like that.) Though the Italian dishes on the menu are better—the seafood linguine is top-notch—the Asian items such as the duck with soba noodles aren't too shabby, either. And while the food here is quite good, even better is the restaurant's loungy atmosphere, which often features live music.

928 71st St., North Beach. ℭ **305/861-6707.** Reservations recommended. Main courses $8–$15. AE, DC, MC, V. Fri–Sat 7pm–5am, Sun–Thurs. 7pm–2am.

Wolfie Cohen's Rascal House ⋐ DELI   Open since 1954 and still going strong, this historic, nostalgic culinary extravaganza is one of Miami Beach's greatest traditions. Scooch into one of the ancient vinyl booths—which have hosted many a notorious bottom, from Frank Sinatra to mob boss Sam Giancana—and review the huge menu that's loaded with authentic Jewish staples. Consider the classic corned beef sandwich, stuffed cabbage, brisket, or potato pancakes. If you're lucky, the waitress will give you a wax-paper doggy bag to wrap up the leftover rolls and danish from your breadbasket.

17190 Collins Ave., Sunny Isles. ℭ **305/947-4581.** Main courses $8–$30. AE, MC, V. Daily 24 hours.

INEXPENSIVE

Curry's AMERICAN   Established in 1937, this large dining room on the ocean side of Collins Avenue is one of Miami Beach's oldest, and kitschiest, restaurants. Neither the restaurant's name nor the tacky Polynesian wall decorations are indicative of its offerings, which are straightforwardly American and reminiscent of the area's heyday. Broiled and fried fish dishes are available, but the best selections, including steak, chicken, and ribs, come off the open charcoal grill perched by the front window. Prices are incredibly reasonable here, and

---

You Should Have Such Luck

Since 1954, over 6.7 million stuffed cabbages, 750,000 chickens, and 26.5 million pickles have been consumed by over 100 million diners at the Rascal House.

include an appetizer, soup, or salad, as well as a potato or vegetable, dessert, and coffee or tea.

7433 Collins Ave., Miami Beach. ✆ 305/866-1571. Main courses (including appetizer and dessert) $9–$20. MC, V. Daily 4–10pm.

Greek Place GREEK   This little hole-in-the-wall diner with sparkling white walls and about 10 wooden stools serves fantastic Greek and American diner-style food. Daily specials like *pastitsio,* chicken *alcyone,* and roast turkey with all the fixings are big lunchtime draws for locals working in the area. Typical Greek dishes like shish kebab, souvlaki, and gyro are cooked to perfection as you wait. Even the hamburger, prime ground beef delicately spiced and freshly grilled, is wonderful.

233 95th St. (between Collins and Harding Aves.), Surfside. ✆ 305/866-9628. Main courses $6–$7. No credit cards. Mon–Fri 10am–5:30pm, Sat 11am–3pm.

Sheldon's Drugs ⋆ AMERICAN   This typical old-fashioned drugstore counter was a favorite breakfast spot of Isaac Bashevis Singer. Consider stopping into this historic site for a good piece of pie and a side of history. According to legend, the author was sitting at Sheldon's eating a bagel and eggs when his wife got the call in 1978 that he had won the Nobel Prize for Literature. The menu hasn't changed much since then. You can get eggs and oatmeal and a good tuna melt. A blue-plate special might be generic spaghetti and meatballs or grilled frankfurters. The food is pretty basic, but you can't beat the prices.

9501 Harding Ave., Surfside. ✆ 305/866-6251. Main courses $4–$8; soups and sandwiches $2–$5. AE, DISC, MC, V. Mon–Sat 7am–9pm, Sun 7am–4pm.

KEY BISCAYNE

Key Biscayne has some of the world's nicest beaches, hotels, and parks, yet it's not known for great food. Locals, or "Key rats" as they're known, tend to go off-island for meals or take-out, but here are some of the best on-the-island choices.

EXPENSIVE

Rusty Pelican ⋆ CONTINENTAL   The Pelican's private tropical walkway leads over a lush waterfall into one of the most romantic dining rooms in the city, located right on beautiful blue-green Biscayne Bay. The restaurant's windows look out over the water onto the sparkling stalagmites of Miami's magnificent downtown. Inside, quiet wicker paddle fans whirl overhead and saltwater fish swim in pretty tableside aquariums.

The restaurant's surf-and-turf menu features conservatively prepared prime steaks, veal, shrimp, and lobster. The food is good, but the atmosphere—the reason why you're here—is even better, especially at sunset, when the view over the city is magical.

3201 Rickenbacker Causeway, Key Biscayne. ✆ 305/361-3818. Reservations recommended. Main courses $16–$20. AE, DC, MC, V. Daily 11:30am–4pm; Sun–Thurs 5–11pm, Fri–Sat 5pm–midnight.

Stefano's ⋆ ITALIAN   For its cheesy mid-80s ambience, Stefano's has no match. Its restaurant and disco share the same strobe-lit atmosphere. Food is traditional and reliable, if a little pricey. You'll find an older country club crowd here in the evenings, enjoying steaks, pastas, and seafood. Among the best entrees are the flavorful *risotto frutti di mare* (saffron risotto with shrimp, clams, mussels, and calamari) and the very cheesy lasagna. The best dish with meat is the surf and turf, or *mare e terra,* in which you get an Angus filet mignon and a meaty lobster tail.

After 7:30pm, the band starts playing American pop and Latin favorites. Some nights you feel as if you've accidentally happened upon your long-lost cousin's wedding, as you watch the parade of taffeta dresses and tipsy uncles.

24 Crandon Blvd., Key Biscayne. ℂ 305/361-7007. Reservations recommended on weekends. Main courses $11–$29; appetizers $8–$12. AE, DC, MC, V. Sun–Thurs 5–11pm, Fri–Sat 5pm–5am. Disco open later Sun–Thurs.

Sundays on the Bay ✷ AMERICAN Although its food is fine, Sundays is really a fun tropical bar that features an unbeatable view of downtown, Coconut Grove, and the Sunday's marina. The menu features local favorites—grouper, tuna, snapper, and good shellfish in season. Competent renditions of such classic dishes as oysters Rockefeller, shrimp scampi, and *lobster fra diablo* are recommendable. Particularly popular is the Sunday brunch, when a buffet the size of Bimini attracts a lively, hungry crowd.

5420 Crandon Blvd., Key Biscayne. ℂ 305/361-6777. Reservations recommended for Sun brunch. Main courses $15–$24; Sun brunch $18.95. AE, DC, MC, V. Daily 11:30am–11:45pm; Sun brunch 11am–4pm.

INEXPENSIVE

Bayside Seafood Restaurant and Hidden Cove Bar ✷ SEAFOOD Known by locals as "the Hut," this ramshackle restaurant and bar is a laid-back outdoor tiki hut and terrace that serves pretty good sandwiches and fish platters on paper plates. A blackboard lists the latest catches, which can be prepared blackened, fried, broiled, or in a garlic sauce. The fish dip is wonderfully smoky and moist, if a little heavy on mayonnaise. Local fishers and yachties share this rustic outpost with equal enthusiasm and loyalty. A completely new air-conditioned area for those who can't stand the heat is a welcome addition, as are the new deck and spruced-up decor. But behind it all, it's nothing fancier than a hut—if it was anything else, it wouldn't be nearly as appealing.

3501 Rickenbacker Causeway, Key Biscayne. ℂ 305/361-0808. Reservations accepted for 15 or more. Appetizers, salads, and sandwiches $4.50–$8; platters $7–$13. AE, MC, V. Daily 11:30am until closing (which varies).

Jimbo's *Finds* SEAFOOD Locals like to keep quiet about Jimbo's, an unassuming seafood shack that started as a gathering spot for fishermen and has since become the quintessential South Florida watering hole, snack bar, and hangout for those in the know. Grab yourself a dollar can of beer from the cooler and take in the view of the tropical lagoon where they shot *Flipper*. You may even see a manatee or two. Vacant shacks that served as backdrops for films such as *True Lies* surround this hidden enclave, which attracts everyone from shrimpers and politicians to well-oiled beach bums. Oddly enough, there's even a bocce court here, and the owner, Jimbo, may challenge you to a game. Play if you must, but word has it he never loses. The smoked fish here is the best in town.

Off the Rickenbacker Causeway at Sewerline Rd., Virginia Key. ℂ 305/361-7026. No credit cards. Daily 6am–6.30pm.

Oasis CUBAN Everyone, from the city's mayor to the local handymen, meet for delicious paella and Cuban sandwiches at this little shack. They gather outside, around the little take-out window, or inside at the few tables for superpowerful *cafesitos* and rich *croquetas*. It's slightly dingy, but the food is good and cheap.

19 Harbor Dr. (on corner of Crandon), Key Biscayne. ℂ 305/361-5709. No credit cards. Main courses $4–$12; sandwiches $3–$4. Daily 6am–9pm.

Dining in Coral Gables, Coconut Grove, Downtown & Key Biscayne

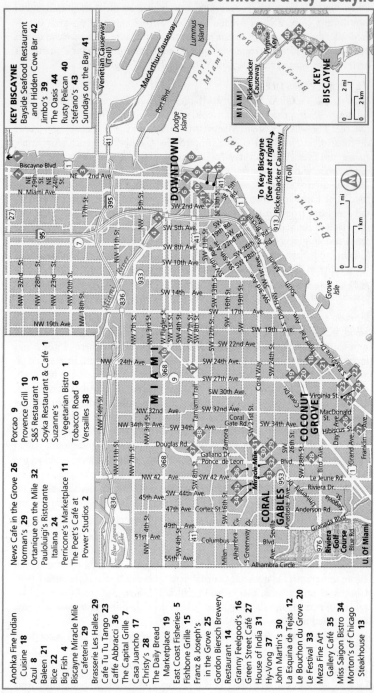

KEY BISCAYNE
Bayside Seafood Restaurant
and Hidden Cove Bar **42**
Jimbo's **39**
The Oasis **44**
Rusty Pelican **40**
Stefano's **43**
Sundays on the Bay **41**

Anohka Fine Indian
Cuisine **18**
Azul **8**
Baleen **21**
Bice **22**
Big Fish **4**
Biscayne Miracle Mile
Cafeteria **29**
Brasserie Les Halles **29**
Cafe Tu Tu Tango **23**
Caffe Abbracci **36**
The Capital Grille **7**
Casa Juancho **17**
Christy's **28**
The Daily Bread
Marketplace **19**
East Coast Fisheries **5**
Fishbone Grille **15**
Franz & Joseph's
in the Grove **25**
Gordon Biersch Brewery
Restaurant **14**
Granny Feelgood's **16**
Green Street Café **27**
House of India **31**
Hy-Vong **37**
John Martin's **30**
La Esquina de Tejas **12**
Le Bouchon du Grove **20**
Le Festival **33**
Meza Fine Art
Gallery Café **35**
Miss Saigon Bistro **34**
Morton's of Chicago
Steakhouse **13**

News Café in the Grove **26**
Norman's **29**
Ortanique on the Mile **32**
Pauloluigi's Ristorante
Italiana **24**
Perricone's Marketplace **11**
The Poet's Café at
Power Studios **2**
Porcao **9**
Provence Grill **10**
S&S Restaurant **3**
Soyka Restaurant & Café **1**
Suzanne's
Vegetarian Bistro **1**
Tobacco Road **38**
Versailles **38**

KEY BISCAYNE

131

DOWNTOWN

Downtown Miami is a large sprawling area divided by the Brickell bridge into two distinct areas: Brickell Avenue and the bayfront area near Biscayne Boulevard. You shouldn't walk from one to the other—it's quite a distance and unsafe at night. Convenient Metromover stops do adjoin the areas, so for a quarter it's better to hop on the scenic sky tram (closed after midnight).

VERY EXPENSIVE

Azul ★★★ GLOBAL FUSION   If there was an Epicurean version of the Academy Awards, this restaurant would win Best Director, hands down. Executive chef Michelle Bernstein, Miami's wunderkind in the kitchen, creates a tour de force of international cuisine, inspired by Caribbean, French, Argentine, Asian, and even American flavors. Like a stunning designer gown, the restaurant's decor, with its waterfront view, high ceilings, walls burnished in copper, and silk-covered chairs, is complemented by sparkling jewels—in this case, the food. The hamachi carpaccio appetizer is a sumptuous arrangement of yellowtail (imported from Japan), shaved fennel, mixed greens, and cucumber. Entrees, or "Plates of Resistance" as they're called here, include braised langoustine openfaced ravioli; ginger-lemongrass glazed Chilean sea bass served with black rice, kimchi, and Napa cabbage; and chicken with red Thai curry. Desserts range from fruity to chocolatey and shouldn't be skipped.

At the Mandarin Oriental Hotel, 500 Brickell Key Dr., Miami. ✆ **305/913-8258.** Reservations strongly recommended. Main courses $24–$38. AE, DC, DISC, MC, V. Mon–Fri noon–3pm; Mon–Sat 7–11pm.

Morton's of Chicago ★ STEAK   A private club-like ambience, with dark wood, leather booths, and tablecloths, makes Morton's of Chicago the preferred spot for major business transactions and quiet, romantic dinners. A vast menu includes a wide variety of excellent steaks, namely the New York Prime, and an award-winning menu consisting of shrimp Alexander, oysters on the half shell, sea scallops with apricot chutney, swordfish medallions with béarnaise sauce, and a dense, hot Godiva chocolate cake that's out of this world. Private dining rooms are perfect in which to carry on clandestine conversations and romantic liaisons. The open kitchen is probably the only thing here that's not private. At lunchtime, the power is tangible as business deals are sliced and diced as often as the steak is. At night, the scene is more elegant, attracting older sophisticates and pre- and posttheater crowds.

1200 Brickell Ave., Miami ✆ **305/400-9990.** Reservations recommended. Main courses $20–$30. AE, DC, MC, V. Mon–Fri 11:30am–11pm, Sat 2:30–11pm, Sun 2:30–10pm.

Porcao ★★ BRAZILIAN   The name sounds eerily like "pork out," which is what you'll be doing at this exceptional Brazilian *churrascaria*. For about $30, you can feast on salads and meats *after* you sample the unlimited gourmet buffet, which includes such fillers as pickled quail eggs, marinated onions, and an entire prosciutto. Do not stuff yourself here, as the next step is the meaty part: Choose as much lamb, filet mignon, chicken hearts, and steaks as you like, grilled, skewered, and sliced right at your table. Side dishes also come with the meal, including beans and rice and fried yucca.

801 Brickell Bay Dr., Miami. ✆ **305/373-2777.** Prix fixe $31.50 per person, all you can eat. AE, DC, MC, V. Daily noon–midnight.

EXPENSIVE

Capital Grille ★★ STEAK   This place reeks of power. Seated among wine cellars filled with high-end classics, the dark wood paneling, pristine white tablecloths, chandeliers, and marble floors all contribute to the clubby atmosphere. For an appetizer, start with the lobster and crab cakes. If you're not in the mood for beef or lobster, try the pan-seared red snapper and asparagus covered with Hollandaise. The wine cellars you're surrounded by are filled with about 5,000 bottles of wine—too extensive and rare to list. There are private dining rooms for large parties and smaller ones for more intimate settings. While some people prefer the more stalwart style and service of Morton's up the block, others find Capital to be a bit livelier. The food's pretty much the same between the two, though I personally find the steaks at Morton's to be a notch better; however, the atmosphere at the Capital Grille is *much* more inviting.

444 Brickell Ave., Miami. © 305/374-4500. Reservations recommended. Main courses $17–$32. AE, DC, DISC, MC, V. Mon–Fri 11:30am–3pm; Mon–Thurs 5–10:30pm, Fri 5–11pm, Sat 6–11pm, Sun 5–10 pm.

East Coast Fisheries SEAFOOD   East Coast Fisheries is a no-nonsense retail market and restaurant offering a terrific variety of the freshest fish available. The dozen or so plain wood tables are surrounded by refrigerated glass cases filled with snapper, salmon, mahi-mahi, trout, tuna, crabs, oysters, lobsters, and the like. The absolutely huge menu features every fish imaginable, cooked the way you want it—grilled, fried, stuffed, Cajun style, Florentine, hollandaise, or blackened. However, the smell of frying grease detracts from the otherwise quaint old Miami feel right on the riverfront. Service is fast, but good prices and good food can mean long lines on weekends.

360 W. Flagler St., Miami. © 305/372-1300. Reservations recommended. Main courses $17–$24. AE, MC, V. Daily 11am–10pm. From I-95 south, exit at NW 8th St. (exit 5A). Follow to NW 3rd St. and turn right. The next block is North River Dr. Turn left. The restaurant is 3 blocks down on the right.

MODERATE

Big Fish ★★ *Finds* SEAFOOD/ITALIAN   This scenic seafood shack on the Miami River is a real catch—if you can find it. Hard to locate, but well worth the search, Big Fish's remote location keeps many people biting. In fact, Big Fish added some Italian options to its all-seafood menu in the hopes of luring more people, and that worked, too. With a spectacular riverfront setting, Big Fish has a sweeping view of the Miami skyline and some of the freshest catch around; the pasta served with it is only a starchy diversion. But the setting may be the real draw, right there on the sketchy Miami River where freighters, fishing boats, dinghies, and sometimes yachts slink by to the amusement of the faithful diners who no longer have to fish around for a charming, serene seafood restaurant.

55 SW Miami Avenue Rd. © 305/373-1770. Main courses $8–$28. AE, DC, MC, V. Daily 11am–11pm. Cross the Brickell Ave. Bridge heading south and take the first right on SW 5th St. The road narrows under a bridge. The restaurant is just on the other side.

Fishbone Grille ★★ SEAFOOD   Fish are flying in the open kitchen of this extremely popular, reasonably priced seafood joint. Whether you take yours grilled, blackened, or sautéed, the chefs here work wonders with superfresh snapper, grouper, dolphin, tuna, sea bass, and shrimp, to name just a few. For nonfish eaters, there are delicious pizzas and an excellent New York strip steak. All meals come with salad and a fantastic slab of jalapeño cornbread. The interior is plain and simple; the only thing elaborate is the long list of daily specials.

650 S. Miami Ave. (SW 7th Ave., next to Tobacco Rd.), Miami. © 305/530-1915. Reservations recommended for 6 or more. Main courses $9–$20. AE, DC, DISC, MC, V. Mon–Thurs 11:30am–10pm, Fri 11:30am–11pm, Sat 5–11pm, Sun 5:30–9 pm.

Gordon Biersch Brewery Restaurant CONTINENTAL   Best known for its home-brewed lager beers and strict adherence to the 1516 German Purity Law (which mandates the use of only malt, hops, water, and yeast in the brewing process), Gordon Biersch is always buzzing with locals who cram into every bit of the restaurant's sprawling 10,800 square feet. The food, for a beer hall, is particularly good, but sometimes too exotic. There are the usual suspects—burgers and pizza—offset by heavier dishes such as chicken and andouille sausage gumbo and cashew chicken stir-fry. A popular lunch place for local businesspeople, Gordon Biersch is absolutely packed and oppressive on Friday night, when happy hour turns into harassment hour.

1201 Brickell Ave. (next to the JW Marriott), Miami. © **786/425-1130.** Main courses $7.25–$19.95. AE, DC, MC, V. Sun–Thurs 11:30am–midnight, Fri–Sat 11:30am–2am.

Provence Grill ★★ FRENCH   This restaurant serves some of the best French meals this side of Toulouse. The brothers Cormouls-Houles use their prodigious culinary skills to assemble an affordable menu that allows the rest of us to know just how the French really live—and they do it, dare we say, with incredible panache. The grilled specialties, from chicken to salmon, are imbued with only the best seasonings and sauces. Sautéed mussels with garlic and chives are fabulous as a meal and as a dipping sauce for the crusty bread. Canard lovers will enjoy the grilled duck filet in a red port sauce. Real culinary adventurers should try the dessert menu—crème brûlée spiced with lavender (a local French favorite) is just one selection—which is truly a delight. A full bar outside brings you back from your French delusions of grandeur and returns you to a delightful downtown Miami state of mind with beautiful views of the downtown skyline.

1001 South Miami Ave., Miami. © **305/373-1940.** Main courses $13.95–$21.95; appetizers $4.95–$6.95. AE, MC, V. Mon–Fri 11am–3pm, Sun–Thurs 5:30–10:30pm, Fri–Sat 5:30–11pm.

Soyka Restaurant & Café ★ AMERICAN   Brought to us by the same man who owns the News and Van Dyke cafes in South Beach, Soyka is a much-needed addition to the seedy area known as the Biscayne Corridor. The motif inside is industrial chic, reminiscent of a souped-up warehouse you might find in New York. Lunches focus on burgers, sandwiches, and wood-fired oven pizzas. Dinners include simple fare such as an excellent, massive Cobb salad, or more elaborate dishes such as the delicious turkey Salisbury steak. The bar area offers a few comfy couches and bar stools and tables on which to dine, if you prefer not to sit in the open dining room. A children's menu is available for both lunch and dinner. A lively crowd of bohemian Design District types, professionals, and singles gather here for a taste of urban life. On weekends, the place is packed and very loud. Do not expect an after-dinner stroll around the neighborhood—it's still too dangerous for pedestrian traffic. Head over the causeway to South Beach and stroll there.

5556 NE 4th Court (Design District), Miami. © **305/759-3117.** Reservations recommended. Main courses $10.75–$24. AE, MC, V. Daily 11am–11pm (bar open until midnight), Fri–Sat 11am–midnight (bar open until 1am). Happy hour Mon–Fri 4–7pm.

Suzanne's Vegetarian Bistro ★★ HEALTH FOOD   If you're in the mood to detox without compromising taste, Suzanne's Vegetarian Bistro can help you with delicious organic vegetarian fare from salads and sandwiches to a massive lotus bowl of miso soup with soba noodles and vegetables. Located in a charming house situated on a seedy stretch of Biscayne Boulevard, Suzanne's is a haven of healthy eating with excellent service and a wait staff that appears to really care about you. There's also a great selection of organic wines.

7251 Biscayne Blvd. Ⓒ **305/758-5859.** Main courses $6.75–$12.95. AE, MC, V. Tues–Sat noon–10 pm, Sun noon–9pm.

INEXPENSIVE

Granny Feelgood's AMERICAN/HEALTH FOOD   Owner Irving Fields has been in the business of serving healthful food for more than 28 years, and his flagship store's offerings are priced right. Due to its proximity to the courthouse, there's a lot of legal eagle traffic and networking going on here. Locals love Granny's for the fresh fish and poultry specials, a line of salads that define greenery and good health, and the always-impeccable service by a family-oriented staff who likes to get to know its clientele. Tourists swinging through downtown on the Metromover or just spinning by can munch healthily on anything from a brown rice and steamed vegetable plate to Granny's famous tuna salad platter. The chef's identity is a secret, but I happen to know he was trained under local chef extraordinaire Allen Susser, and also did a stint on nearby Fisher Island's swanky members-only restaurant.

25 W. Flagler St., Miami. ⒸⒸ **305/377-9600.** Reservations not accepted. Main courses $9–$12. AE, MC, V. Mon–Fri 7am–5pm.

Perricone's Marketplace ⭐ ITALIAN   A large selection of groceries and wine, plus an outdoor porch and patio for dining, makes this one of the most welcoming spots downtown. Its rustic setting in the midst of downtown is a fantastic respite from city life. Sundays offer buffet brunches and all-you-can-eat dinners, too. But it's most popular weekdays at noon, when the suits show up for delectable sandwiches, quick and delicious pastas, and hearty salads.

15 SE 10th St. (corner of S. Miami Ave.), Miami. ⒸⒸ **305/374-9693.** Sandwiches $6.95–$8.25; pastas $11.50–$16.95. AE, MC, V. Sun–Mon 7:30am–10:30pm, Tues–Sat 7:30am–midnight.

Poet's Café at Power Studios ⭐⭐ *Finds* ECLECTIC   Everything flows here in a rhythmic motion, from the tasty reasonably priced food to the sublime atmosphere. With a chef hailing from the Wolfgang Puck school of cuisine, the Poet's Café, located in the multimedia nightlife, entertainment, and production complex known as Power Studios, features delicious Puckian pizzas as well as an assortment of excellent sandwiches—peanut butter and banana is a treat, though the chicken sandwich on focaccia is best if you're looking for something substantial—appetizers (have the crab cakes), salads, and entrees. Seating is your choice—either downstairs in the main bar and restaurant area, or preferably upstairs in the rooftop garden/cinema, which overlooks the funky Design District. Weekends pack in a powerful crowd of scenesters, arty types, and even foodies.

3701 NE 2nd Ave., Miami. ⒸⒸ **305/576-1336.** $5–$15. AE, DC, MC, V. Tues–Sun 11am–3am.

S&S Restaurant AMERICAN/DINER FARE   This tiny chrome-and-linoleum-counter restaurant in the middle of downtown looks like a truck stop. But locals have been coming back since it opened in 1938. Expect a wait at lunchtime while the mostly male clientele, from lawyers to linemen, wait patiently for huge quantities of old-fashioned fast food. You'll get a slice of Miami history along with your pie at S&S. Although the neighborhood has become pretty undesirable, the food—basic, comforting diner fare with some excellent stews and soups—hasn't changed in years.

1757 NE 2nd Ave., Miami. (✆ **305/373-4291.** Main courses $5–$11. No credit cards. Mon–Fri 6am–4pm, Sat–Sun 6am–2 or 2:30pm (later on Heat game nights).

Tobacco Road AMERICAN   Miami's oldest bar is a bluesy Route 66–inspired institution favored by barflies, professionals, and anyone else who wishes to indulge in good and greasy bar fare—chicken wings, nachos, and so on—for a reasonable price in a down-home, gritty-but-charming atmosphere. The burgers are also good—particularly the Death Burger, a deliciously unhealthy combo of choice sirloin topped with grilled onions, jalapeños, and pepper jack cheese—bring on the Tums! Also a live music venue, the Road, as it is known by locals, is well traveled, especially during Friday's happy hour and Tuesday's lobster night, when 100 1¼-pound lobsters go for only $10.99 a piece.

626 S. Miami Ave. (✆ **305/374-1198.** Main courses $7–$10. AE, DC, MC, V. Mon–Sat 11:30am–5am, Sun noon–midnight. Cover charge $5 Fri–Sat night.

LITTLE HAVANA

The main artery of Little Havana is a busy commercial strip called Southwest 8th Street, or Calle Ocho. Auto body shops, cigar factories, and furniture stores line this street, and on every corner there seems to be a pass-through window serving superstrong Cuban coffee and snacks. In addition, many of the Cuban, Dominican, Nicaraguan, Peruvian, and other Latin American immigrants have opened full-scale restaurants ranging from intimate candlelit establishments to bustling stand-up lunch counters.

MODERATE

Casa Juancho ★★ SPANISH   A generous taste of Spain comes to Miami in the form of the cavernous Casa Juancho, which looks like it escaped from a production of *Don Quixote*. The numerous dining rooms are decorated with traditional Spanish furnishings and enlivened nightly by strolling Spanish musicians who tend to be annoying and expect tips—do not encourage them to play at your table; you'll hear them loud and clear from other tables, trust me. Try not to be frustrated with the older staff that doesn't speak English or respond quickly to your subtle glance—the food's worth the frustration. Your best bet is to order lots of *tapas,* small dishes of Spanish finger food. Some of the best include mixed seafood vinaigrette, fresh shrimp in hot garlic sauce, and fried calamari rings. A few entrees stand out, like roast suckling pig, baby eels in garlic and olive oil, and Iberian-style snapper.

2436 SW 8th St. (just east of SW 27th Ave.), Little Havana. (✆ **305/642-2452.** Reservations recommended, but not accepted Fri–Sat after 8pm. Main courses $15–$34; tapas $6–$8. AE, DC, DISC, MC, V. Sun–Thurs noon–midnight, Fri–Sat noon–1am.

INEXPENSIVE

Hy-Vong ★★ VIETNAMESE   Expect to wait hours for a table, and don't even think of mumbling a complaint. Despite the poor service, it's worth it. Vietnamese cuisine combines the best of Asian and French cooking with spectacular results. Food at Hy-Vong is elegantly simple and superspicy. Appetizers include small, tightly packed Vietnamese spring rolls and kimchi, a spicy, fermented cabbage. Star entrees include pastry-enclosed chicken with watercress cream-cheese sauce and fish in tangy mango sauce.

Enjoy the wait with a traditional Vietnamese beer and lots of company. Outside this tiny storefront restaurant, you'll meet interesting students, musicians, and foodies who come for the large delicious portions.

3458 SW 8th St. (between 34th and 35th aves.), Little Havana. ℂ **305/446-3674.** Reservations not accepted. Main courses $8–$15. No credit cards. Wed–Sun 6–11pm. Closed 2 weeks in Aug

La Esquina de Tejas ✸✸ CUBAN   Best known as the diner where Ronald Reagan ate during his 1983 campaign in Miami, La Esquina de Tejas has gained a national reputation for its great food and low prices. There's a shrine dedicated to the former president in the "Presidential Quarters," and the menu even has his signed autograph and the presidential seal of approval. This is Cuban food at its best. You must try the *arroz a la marinera,* the Cuban version of Spanish paella. It's filled with clams, oysters, mussels, lobster, shrimp, squid, snapper, stone crab, and scallops cooked in fresh seafood broth. If you're not in the mood for seafood (after all, this is a Cuban joint), try the *vaca frita,* a grilled, shredded flank steak served with moro rice (black beans cooked with white rice) and *maduros* (sweet, fried plantains). Another specialty is the *masas de puerco fritas,* a pork tenderloin cut in chunks, roasted, and then quickly deep-fried and served with mojo marinade, grilled onions, garlic, olive oil, and bitter orange. You won't regret a trip here.

101 SW 12th Ave., Little Havana. ℂ **305/545-0337.** Daily specials $4–$12; appetizers 75¢–$5.50. AE, MC, V. Daily 8am–9pm.

Versailles ✸✸ CUBAN   Versailles is the meeting place of Miami's Cuban power brokers, who meet daily over *cafe con leche* to discuss the future of the exiles' fate. A glorified diner, the place sparkles with glass, chandeliers, murals, and mirrors meant to evoke the French palace. There's nothing fancy here— nothing French, either—just straightforward food from the home country. The menu is a veritable survey of Cuban cooking and includes specialties such as *Moors and Christians* (flavorful black beans with white rice), *ropa vieja,* and fried whole fish.

3555 SW 8th St., Little Havana. ℂ **305/444-0240.** Soup and salad $2–$10; main courses $5–$8. DC, DISC, MC, V. Mon–Thurs 8am–2am, Fri 8am–3:30am, Sat 8am–4:30am, Sun 9am–2am.

NORTH DADE

Although there aren't many hotels in North Dade, the population in the winter months explodes due to the onslaught of seasonal residents from the Northeast. A number of exclusive condominiums and country clubs, including William's Island, Turnberry, and the Jockey Club, breed a demanding clientele, many of whom dine out nightly. That's good news for visitors, who can find superior service and cuisine at value prices.

VERY EXPENSIVE

Chef Allen's ✸✸✸ NEW WORLD CUISINE   If anyone deserves to have a restaurant named after him, it's chef Allen Susser, winner of the esteemed James Beard Award for Best American Chef in the Southeast—the Academy Award of cuisine—and practically every other form of praise and honor awarded by the most discriminating palates. Chef Allen, the man, is royalty around here. Chef Allen, the restaurant, is his province, and foodies are his disciples. His platform? New World Cuisine and the harmony of exotic tropical fruits, spices, and vegetables. It is under Chef Allen's magic that ordinary Key limes and mangos reappear in the form of succulent salsas and sauces. A traditional antipasto is transformed into a Caribbean one, with papaya-pineapple barbeque shrimp, jerk calamari, and charred rare tuna. Whole yellowtail in coconut milk and curry sauce is a particularly spectacular entree. Unlike other restaurants where location is key, Chef Allen's, located in the rear of a strip mall, could be in the desert, and hordes of people would still make the trek.

19088 NE 29th Ave. (at Biscayne Blvd.), North Miami Beach. ✆ **305/935-2900.** Reservations recommended. Main courses $26–$35. AE, DC, MC, V. Sun–Thurs 6–10:30pm, Fri–Sat 6–11pm.

MODERATE

Lagoon 🍴 SEAFOOD/CONTINENTAL   This old bayfront fish house has been around since 1936. Major road construction nearby should have guaranteed its doom years ago, but the excellent view and incredible specials make it a worthwhile stop. If you can disregard the somewhat dirty bathrooms and nonchalant service, you'll find the best-priced juicy Maine lobsters around.

Yes, it's true! Lobster lovers can get two 1½ pounders for $22.95. Try them broiled with a light buttery seasoned coating. This dish is not only inexpensive but incredibly succulent, too. Side dishes include fresh vegetables, like broccoli or asparagus, as well as a huge baked potato, stuffed or plain.

488 Sunny Isles Blvd. (163rd St.), North Miami Beach. ✆ **305/947-6661.** Main courses $12–$40; appetizers $6–$14. AE, MC, V. Daily 4:30–11pm. Happy hour daily 4:30–6pm.

INEXPENSIVE

Laurenzo's Café 🍴🍴 ITALIAN   This recently expanded lunch counter in the middle of a chaotic grocery store has been serving delicious buffet lunches to the *paesanos* for years. New additions include an open kitchen and wood-burning pizza oven. A meeting place for the growing Italian population in Miami, the store has been open for more than 40 years. Daily specials usually include lasagna or eggplant parmigiana and two or three salad options. Also good are the rustic pizzas. Choose a wine from the vast selection and take your meal to go, or sit in the trellis-covered area amid busy shoppers.

16385 W. Dixie Hwy. (at the corner of 164th St. and W. Dixie Hwy.), North Miami Beach. ✆ **305/945-6381.** MC, V. Main courses $4–$12; salads $2–$5. Mon–Fri 11am–7:30pm, Sat 11am–7pm, Sun 11am–4pm.

CORAL GABLES & ENVIRONS
VERY EXPENSIVE

Christy's 🍴🍴 STEAK/AMERICAN   Power is palpable at this elegant English-style restaurant where an ex-president could be sitting at one table and a rock star at another. But Christy's is the kind of place where conversations are at a hush and no one seems to care who they're sitting next to. The selling point here, rather, is the corn-fed beef and calf's liver, not to mention the broiled lamb chops, prime rib of beef with horseradish sauce, teriyaki marinated filet mignon, and perfectly tossed Caesar salad. Baked sweet potatoes and a sublime blackout cake are also yours for the taking. Just like a fine wine or the typical Christy's customer, the meat here is aged a long time. A landmark since 1978, Christy's has thrived amid the comings and goings of neighboring nouveau spots.

3101 Ponce de León Blvd., Coral Gables. ✆ **305/446-1400.** Reservations recommended. Main courses $19.50–$35. AE, DC, MC, V. Mon–Thurs 11:30am–4pm, Fri 4–11pm, Sat 5–11pm, Sun 5–10pm.

Norman's 🍴🍴🍴 NEW WORLD CUISINE   *Gourmet* magazine called Norman's the best restaurant in South Florida, but many disagree. They think it's the best restaurant in the entire United States. Gifted chef and cookbook author Norman van Aken takes New World Cuisine (which, along with chef Allen Susser, he helped create) to another plateau with dishes that have landed him on such shows as the Discovery Channel's "Great Chefs of the South" and on the wish lists of gourmands everywhere. The open kitchen invites you to marvel at

Kids Family-Friendly Restaurants

Baraboo (see p. 126) While the cuisine may be a bit funky for kids' palates, the wandering magicians and mimes are guaranteed to entertain the little ones, who will likely eat anything after the magician says "abracadabra."

Big Pink (see p. 123) One of South Beach's only family-friendly sit-down restaurants, Big Pink is a fun, noisy restaurant with a comprehensive menu consisting of macaroni and cheese, hamburgers, and other comfort foods guaranteed to satisfy the pickiest kids.

Bubba Gump Shrimp Co. Named after the character from the motion picture *Forrest Gump,* this is a great place to bring the entire family on a lazy Sunday afternoon. You get to eat some good moderately priced seafood, watch ships sail by on the bay, and shop at the Bayside Marketplace afterward. In Bayside Marketplace, 401 Biscayne Blvd, Miami. © **305/379-8866.**

Wilderness Grill Let the kids run wild in this noisy theme restaurant that serves as many sound effects as it does hamburgers. Shops at Sunset (57th and U.S. 1), 5701 Sunset Dr., #114, South Miami. © **305/ 740-3033.**

the mastery that lands on your plate in the form of pan-roasted swordfish with black-bean *muneta;* stuffed baby bell pepper in cumin-scented tomato broth with avocado *crema;* char-grilled New York strip steak with *chimichurri* sabayon, pommes frites, and Créole mustard–spiced caramelized red onions; plantain-crusted dolphin; or chicken and tiny shrimp paella with garbanzo beans and chorizo mojo, to name a few. Save room for the funky, fantastic desserts.

21 Almeria Ave. (between Douglas and Ponce de León), Coral Gables. © **305/446-6767.** Reservations highly recommended. Main courses $26–$38. AE, DC, MC, V. Mon–Thurs 6–10:30pm, Fri–Sat 6–11pm.

EXPENSIVE

Caffe Abbracci ✰✰ ITALIAN You'll understand why this restaurant's name means "hugs" in Italian the moment you enter the dark romantic enclave: Your appetite will be embraced by the savory scents of fantastic Italian cuisine wafting through the restaurant. The homemade black and red ravioli filled with lobster in pink sauce, risotto with porcini and portobello mushrooms, and the house specialty—grilled veal chop topped with tricolor salad—are irresistible and perhaps the culinary equivalent of a warm, embracing hug. A cozy bar and lounge was added recently to further encourage the warm and fuzzy feelings.

318 Aragon Ave. (between LeJeune Rd. and Miracle Mile), Coral Gables. © **305/441-0700.** Reservations recommended for dinner. Main courses $16–$25; pastas $15–$20. AE, DC, MC, V. Mon–Fri 11:30am–3pm; Sun–Thurs 6–11pm, Fri–Sat 6pm–midnight.

Le Festival ✰✰ FRENCH Le Festival's contemporary pink awning hangs over one of Miami's most traditional Spanish-style buildings, hinting at the unusual combination of cuisine and decor that awaits inside. The modern dining rooms, enlivened with New French features and furnishings, belie the traditional highlights of a well-planned menu.

Shrimp and crab cocktails, fresh patés, and an unusual cheese soufflé are star starters. Both meat and fish are either simply seared with herbs and spices or doused in wine and cream sauces. Dessert can be a delight if you plan ahead: Grand Marnier and chocolate soufflés are individually prepared and must be ordered at the same time as the entrees. There's also a wide selection of other homemade sweets.

2120 Salzedo St. (5 blocks north of Miracle Mile), Coral Gables. ℂ 305/442-8545. Reservations required for dinner. Main courses $16–$25. AE, DC, DISC, MC, V. Mon–Fri 11:45am–2:30pm; Mon–Thurs 6–10:30pm, Fri–Sat 6–11pm.

MODERATE

Brasserie Les Halles ✦✦ FRENCH   Known especially for its fine steaks and delicious salads, this very welcome addition to the Coral Gables dining scene became popular as soon as it opened in 1997 and has since continued to do a brisk business. The modest and moderately priced menu is particularly welcome in an area of overpriced, stuffy restaurants. For starters, try the mussels in white wine sauce and the escargot. For a main course, the duck confit is an unusual and rich choice. Pieces of duck meat wrapped in duck fat are slow-cooked and served on salad frissé with baby potatoes with garlic. Service by the young French staff is polite but a bit slow. The tables tend to be a little too close, although there is a lovely private balcony space overlooking the long, thin dining room where large groups can gather.

2415 Ponce de León Blvd. (at Miracle Mile), Coral Gables. ℂ 305/461-1099. Reservations recommended on weekends. Main courses $12.50–$22.50. AE, DC, DISC, MC, V. Daily 11:30am–midnight.

John Martin's ✦ IRISH PUB   Forest green and dark wood give way to a very intimate pub-like atmosphere in which local businesspeople and barflies alike come to hoist a pint or two. The menu offers some tasty British specialties, such as bangers and mash and shepherd's pie, as well as Irish lamb stew and corned beef and cabbage.

Of course, to wash it down, you'll want to try one of the ales on tap or one of the more than 20 single-malt scotches. The crowd is upscale and chatty, as is the young wait staff. Check out happy hour on weeknights, plus the Sunday brunch with loads of hand-carved meats and seafood.

253 Miracle Mile, Coral Gables. ℂ 305/445-3777. Reservations recommended on weekends. Main courses $9–$20; sandwiches and salads $5–$16. AE, DC, DISC, MC, V. Mon–Thurs 11:30am–midnight, Fri–Sat 11:30am–1am, Sun noon–10pm.

Meza Fine Art Gallery Café ✦✦ ECLECTIC   This unique restaurant is located in a sleek, arty atmosphere featuring paintings, performance artists, and a multimedia array of talent—very Warhol. As eclectic as the art and artists who convene here, the menu is varied, featuring well-priced, well-prepared dishes such as pan-seared tuna with sesame crust and balsamic vinegar reduction and a delicious grilled *churrasco* skirt steak with *chimichurri*. Live music nightly from jazz and Latin to electronica brings out a motley crew of youngsters who look as if they stepped out of a Gap ad. A lively bar scene attracts a 30s-and-under crowd on late weekend nights. Earlier in the evenings, Meza caters to an older, more sophisticated dining crowd.

275 Giralda Ave., Coral Gables. ℂ 305/461-2723. Main courses $6.95–$13.95. Three-course twilight dinner served Mon–Sat 6–8pm for $15.95 per person, including glass of wine. AE, DC, DISC, MC, V. Daily noon–3pm; Mon–Thurs 6–10:30pm, Fri–Sun 6pm–2am.

Ortanique on the Mile ★★ NEW WORLD CARIBBEAN Ortanique is as unique to the Gables as the orange-like fruit is to Jamaica. You'll be greeted as you walk in by soft spider-like lights and canopied mosquito netting that will make you wonder whether you're on a secluded island or inside one of King Tut's temples. A friendly host greets you at the door and glides you past simple canvas oils hanging from papaya- and mango-colored walls, and hand-painted columns laced with ortaniques.

Chef Cindy Hutson has truly perfected her tantalizing New World Caribbean menu. For starters, an absolute must is the pumpkin bisque with a hint of pepper sherry. Afterward, move on to the tropical mango salad with fresh marinated Sable hearts of palm, julienne mango, baby field greens, toasted Caribbean candied pecans, and passion fruit vinaigrette. For an entree, I recommend the pan-sautéed Bahamian black grouper marinated in teriyaki and sesame oil. It's served with an ortanique orange liqueur sauce and topped with steamed seasoned chayote, zucchini, and carrots on a lemon-orange *boniato*–sweet plantain mash. For dessert, try the chocolate mango tower—layers of brownie, chocolate mango mousse, meringue, and sponge cake, accompanied by mango sorbet and tropical fruit salsa. Entrees may not be cheap, but they're a lot less than airfare to the islands, from where most, if not all, the ingredients used here hail.

278 Miracle Mile (next to Actor's Playhouse), Coral Gables. ℂ 305/446-7710. Reservations requested. Main courses $11–$29. AE, DC, MC, V. Mon–Tues 6–10pm, Wed–Sat 6–11pm, Sun 5:30–9:30pm.

INEXPENSIVE

Biscayne Miracle Mile Cafeteria ★ AMERICAN Here you'll find no bar, no music, and no flowers on the tables—just great Southern-style cooking at unbelievably low prices. The menu changes, but roast beef, baked fish, and barbecued ribs are typical entrees, few of which exceed $5.

Food is picked up cafeteria style and brought to one of the many unadorned Formica tables. The restaurant is always busy. The kitschy 1950s decor is an asset in this last of the old-fashioned cafeterias, where the gold-clad staff is proud and attentive. Enjoy it while it lasts.

147 Miracle Mile, Coral Gables. ℂ 305/444-9005. Main courses $3.50–$4.50. MC, V. Daily 11am–8:30pm.

Daily Bread Marketplace GREEK This place is great for take-out food and homemade breads. The falafel and gyro sandwiches are large, fresh, and filling. The spinach pie for less than $1 is also recommended, though it's short on spinach and heavy on pastry. Salads, including luscious tabouli, hummus, and eggplant, are also worth a go. To take in or eat out, the Middle Eastern fare here is a real treat, especially in an area so filled with fancy French and Cuban fare. Plus, you can pick up hard-to-find groceries such as grape leaves, fresh olives, couscous, fresh nuts, and pita bread.

2400 SW 27th St. (off U.S. 1 under the monorail), Coral Gables. ℂ 305/856-0363 or 305/856-0366. Sandwiches and salads $3–$6. MC, V. Mon–Sat 8am–8pm, Sun 11am–5pm.

House of India ★ INDIAN House of India's curries, *kormas*, and kabobs are very good, but the restaurant's well-priced all-you-can-eat lunch buffet is unsurpassed. All the favorites are on display, including tandoori chicken, naan, various meat and vegetarian curries, as well as rice and dal (lentils). This place isn't fancy and could use a good scrub-down (in fact, I've heard it described as a "greasy spoon"), but the service is excellent and the food is good enough to keep you from staring at your surroundings.

22 Merrick Way (near Douglas and Coral Way, a block north of Miracle Mile), Coral Gables. © **305/ 444-2348.** Reservations recommended. Main courses $8–$17. AE, DC, DISC, MC, V. Daily 11:30am–3pm; Sun–Thurs 5–10pm, Fri–Sat 5–11pm.

Miss Saigon Bistro ⭐⭐ VIETNAMESE   Unlike Andrew Lloyd Webber's bombastic Broadway show, this Miss Saigon is small, quiet, and not at all flashy. Servers at this family-run restaurant—among them, the owners' son—will graciously offer to recommend dishes or even to custom-make something for you. The menu is varied and reasonably priced and the portions are huge—large enough to share. Noodle dishes and soup bowls are hearty and flavorful; caramelized prawns are fantastic, as is the whole snapper with lemongrass and ginger sauce. Despite the fact that there are few tables inside and a hungry crowd usually gathers outside in the street, they will not at all rush you through your meal, which is worth savoring.

146 Giralda Ave., Coral Gables. © **305/446-8006.** Main courses $10–$16.95. AE, DC, DISC, MC, V. Mon–Thurs 11am–3pm and 5:30–10pm, Fri–Sat 5:30–11pm, Sun 5:30–10pm.

COCONUT GROVE

Coconut Grove was long known as the artists' haven of Miami, but the rush of developers trying to cash in on the laid-back charm of this old settlement has turned it into something of an overgrown mall. Still, there are several great dining spots both in and out of the confines of Mayfair or CocoWalk.

EXPENSIVE

Anokha Fine Indian Cuisine ⭐⭐⭐ INDIAN   This is the best Indian restaurant in Miami. Anokha's motto is "a guest is equal to God and should be treated as such," and they do stick to it. The food here is from the gods, with fantastic tandooris, curries, and stews. The restaurant's location at the end of a quiet stretch of Coconut Grove is especially enticing because it prevents the throngs of pedestrians from overtaking what some people consider a diamond in the rough.

3195 Commodore Plaza, Coconut Grove. © **786/552-1030.** AE, DC, MC, V. Main courses $13–$21. Tues–Sun 11:30am–10:30pm.

Baleen ⭐⭐⭐ SEAFOOD/MEDITERRANEAN   While the prices aren't lean, the cuisine here is worth every pricey, precious penny. Oversized crab cakes, oak-smoked diver scallops, and steak house–quality meats are among Baleen's excellent offerings. The lobster bisque is the best on Biscayne Bay. Everything here is a la carte, so order wisely, as it tends to add up quicker than you can put your fork down. The restaurant's spectacular waterfront setting makes Baleen a true knockout. Brunch is particularly noteworthy as well.

4 Grove Isle Dr. (in the Grove Isle Hotel), Coconut Grove. © **305/858-8300.** Reservations recommended. Main courses $17–$36. AE, DC, MC, V. Daily 7am–11pm.

Bice ⭐⭐⭐ ITALIAN   Located in the ritzy Grand Bay Hotel, it is not surprising that Bice is a first-class establishment. As you exit the elevator on the hotel's mezzanine level, an ornate glass chandelier lights the way into the beautiful, expansive bar area with dim lighting and a sleek, rich wood floor. To the left of the maitre d' stand is the restaurant's private wine room, with an impressive collection encased in wall-to-wall glass, and a banquet table that comfortably seats six. Upon entering the dining room, you feel as if you're sailing on a grand ocean liner, with several cozy tables and booths, high ceilings, and a glorious view of the hotel's sprawling waterfall and pool area. Knowledgeable and friendly servers rush a fresh basket of warm assorted breads—focaccia, breadsticks—to the table as you begin to peruse the comprehensive Italian menu. Every appetizer sounds so good that it's almost impossible to decide. Beef carpaccio is a delight on the palate with hearts of palm and Reggiano cheese; a colorful grilled vegetable pyramid consists of gargantuan portions of meaty portobello mushrooms, fresh asparagus, and peppers with bursts of mouthwatering goat cheese lying within; Maryland crab cakes with the perfect hint of lemon are exceptional. For main courses, the pastas, homemade and extremely fresh, are eclipsed by a heavenly slab of Nebraska filet mignon with peppercorn sauce and a tower of french fries and onion rings. The veal chop is also sublime. For dessert, the crème brûlée and coffee gelato are delicious. Unlike many chichi restaurants, especially those found within swanky hotels, all dishes at Bice are generous in portion—huge actually—and the only thing stuffy about dining here is how you'll feel after indulging.

2669 S. Bayshore Dr. (in the Grand Bay Hotel), Coconut Grove. ✆ **305/860-0960.** Reservations recommended. Main courses $13–$34. AE, MC, V. Daily 7–11am, 11:30am–3pm, and 6–11pm.

Le Bouchon du Grove ✪✪ FRENCH   Planet Hollywood came and went in Coconut Grove, but the marks of commercialism still remain. Thankfully, there's a haven from the Disneyfied madness of the Grove in the form of this very authentic, exceptional French bistro. An excellent starter is the wonderful *gratinée Lyonnaise* (traditional French onion soup). Fish is brought in fresh daily; try the Chilean sea bass when in season *(filet de loup poele)*. Though it is slightly heavy on the oil, it is delivered with succulent artichokes, tomato confit, and seasoned roasted garlic that is a gastronomic triumph. The *carre d'agneau roti* (roasted rack of lamb with Provence herbs) is served warm and tender, with an excellent amount of seasoning. There is an excellent selection of pricey but doable French and American red and white wines. Try the St. Emilion 1996 Baron Rothschild ($34, or $7 per glass), which compliments nearly the entire menu.

3430 Main Highway, Coconut Grove. ✆ **305/448-6060.** Reservations recommended. Main courses $16–$24. AE, MC, V. Mon–Thurs 9:30am–11pm, Fri–Sun 8am–midnight.

MODERATE

Franz & Joseph's in the Grove ✪✪ CONTINENTAL/ITALIAN   This is a favorite restaurant of theatergoers and actors—Kathleen Turner and Jean Stapleton to name two—alike. Franz or Joseph, the gracious owners of this romantic restaurant that is chock full of Old-World charm, will personally greet you at the door. Before you sit down to dine, enjoy a glass of wine at the intimate, atmospheric bar and begin to give in to the European ambience here. A few starters are recommended: the escargot in Roquefort butter with grilled herb bread is wonderful as is the stuffed avocado with marinated sea scallops, mussels, and shrimp—a local favorite and absolutely fresh. I also recommend the soup du jour, whatever it is. Don't be afraid to order pasta, either. The penne with spicy grilled chicken, plum tomatoes, spinach, and feta cheese is wonderful. But if you've come to Florida for the seafood, you can't go wrong with the restaurant's filet of snapper, pan-seared with mango chutney and glazed banana over rice. Well-prepared steaks and exotic chicken dishes are a specialty here, too. Their delicious desserts are made on premises. The kitchen is small, so the food is consistently fresh and cooked to order. The last thing the chef does each night before going home, is order for the next day's menu.

3145 Commodore Plaza, Coconut Grove. © **305/448-2282**. Reservations highly recommended. Main courses $15–$20. AE, MC, V. Tues–Sun 11:30am–2:30pm and 6–10:30pm.

Green Street Café ⭐ CONTINENTAL   The location and the loads of outdoor seating (great for people-watching) relieve Green Street of the pressure to turn out fine meals, but the food is still well above average. Continental-style breakfasts include fresh croissants and rolls, cinnamon toast, and cereal. Heartier American-style offerings include eggs and omelets, pancakes, waffles, and French toast. Soup, salad, and sandwich lunches are overstuffed chicken-, turkey-, and tuna-based meals. Dinners are more elaborate, with several decent pasta entrees as well as fresh fish, chicken, and burgers, including one made of lamb.

3110 Commodore Plaza, Coconut Grove. © **305/567-0662**. Reservations not accepted. Main courses $10–$15. AE, MC, V. Sun–Thurs 7am–11:30pm, Fri–Sat 7am–1am.

Pauloluigi's Ristorante Italiana ⭐ ITALIAN   Pauloluigi's serves rich dishes that include cold and hot appetizers, homemade soups and salads, pastas, and pizzas. Owners Paul and Lola Shalaj, restaurant entrepreneurs for the past 27 years, have gained and kept a large devoted clientele with their tasty light Italian cuisine, generous portions, and friendly environment that has served as the perfect fine-dining hideaway for both local and national customers alike.

A favorite is the *jumbo rigatti rubino*, a chicken dish with a side of sausages, asparagus, and portobello mushrooms in light marinara sauce. There's also *chicken Marsala, linguine al fruitti di mare* (for poultry and seafood lovers), and a special children's menu. Sample a wine from their excellent list.

3324 Virginia St., Coconut Grove. © **305/445-9000**. Reservations recommended. Main courses $9–$17. AE, MC, V. Daily noon–4pm and 5–11pm, Fri–Sat 5pm–1am.

INEXPENSIVE

Cafe Tu Tu Tango ⭐ SPANISH/INTERNATIONAL   This second-floor restaurant in the bustling CocoWalk is designed to look like a disheveled artist's loft. Dozens of original paintings—some only half-finished—hang on the walls and on studio easels. Flamenco and other Latin-inspired tunes complement a menu with a decidedly Spanish flare. Hummus spread on rosemary flat bread and baked goat cheese in marinara sauce are two good starters. Entrees include roast duck with dried cranberries, toasted pine nuts, and goat cheese, plus Cajun chicken egg rolls filled with corn, cheddar cheese, and tomato salsa. Pastas, ribs, fish, and pizzas round out the eclectic offerings, and several visits have proved each consistently good. Try the sweet, potent sangria and enjoy the warm, lively atmosphere from a seat with a view.

3015 Grand Ave. (on the second floor of CocoWalk), Coconut Grove. © **305/529-2222**. Reservations not accepted. Main courses $4–$10. AE, MC, V. Sun–Wed 11:30am–midnight, Thurs 11:30am–1am, Fri–Sat 11:30am–2am.

News Café in the Grove ⭐ AMERICAN   Like its predecessor in South Beach, this big modern diner offers everything from Caesar salads to hummus to burgers to omelets to ice cream sundaes. The food is predictably good and the service lively and pleasant. The best part is that it's open around the clock to serve the after-movie crowd from CocoWalk and Mayfair, as well as the real late-night club-goers.

2901 Florida Ave. (behind Mayfair), Coconut Grove. © **305/774-6397**. Main courses $12–$19. AE, DC, MC, V. Daily 24 hours.

SOUTH MIAMI & WEST MIAMI

Mostly residential, these areas have several eating establishments worth the drive.

MODERATE

Coco Pazzo ★★ ITALIAN   The atmosphere here depends on where you choose to sit: the outside cafe, with a full view of all the shopping frenzy and active children, or the more serene, airy lushness of the Tuscan dining room inside. The hand-painted murals of the ocean and the wide-open kitchen invite you into the dining area. Owner Pino Luongo, who owns 14 other Coco Pazzos nationwide, strives to combine the best of Tuscan cuisine with accents of Latin and Caribbean favorites. One of the restaurant's signature dishes is the *focaccia alla robiola,* a thin-crusted focaccia stuffed with robiola cheese and drizzled with white truffle oil. Another great choice is the *calamari alla griglia,* or grilled calamari stuffed with oxtails in red wine sauce. My favorite is the *salmone con insalata estiva,* which is grilled salmon with mesclun lettuce, asparagus, mango, and balsamic reduction. For dessert try the tiramisù with mascarpone cream and ladyfingers soaked in espresso. While service here isn't up to par with the Coco Pazzo in New York, it'll do. Remember, you are in a shopping mall—would you rather be in the food court?

Inside the Shops at Sunset, 5701 Sunset Dr., South Miami. ⓒ **305/665-6055.** Reservations accepted weekdays only. Main courses $14–$25; lunch menu $4.50–$14. AE, DC, MC, V. Sun–Thurs 11:30am–10pm, Fri–Sat 11:30am–midnight.

Tropical Chinese ★★ CHINESE   This strip mall restaurant way out there in West Miami Dade is hailed as the best Chinese restaurant in the city. While the food is indeed very good—certainly more interesting than at your typical beef-and-broccoli shop—it still seems somewhat overpriced. Garlic spinach and prawns in a clay pot is delicious with the perfect mix of garlic cloves, mushrooms, and fresh spinach, but it's not cheap at $16.99. And unlike most Chinese restaurants, the dishes here are not large enough to share. Sunday afternoon dim sum is extremely popular and lines often snake around the shopping center.

7991 Bird Rd., West Miami. ⓒ **305/262-7576.** Reservations highly recommended. Main courses $10–$25. AE, DC, MC, V. Mon–Fri 11:30am–10:30pm, Sat 11am–10:30pm, Sun 10:30am–10pm.

INEXPENSIVE

Crepe Maker Café ★ CREPES/FRENCH   Create your own delicious crepes at this little French cafe. You can choose from ham, tuna, black olives, red peppers, capers, artichoke hearts, and pine nuts. Some of the best combinations include a Philly cheese steak with mushrooms and a classic cordon bleu. Delicious dessert crepes have ice cream, strawberries, peaches, walnuts, and pineapples. Enjoy your crepe fresh off the griddle at the counter or on a bar stool. The soups are also delicious. Kids can run around in a small play area, too.

8269 SW 124th St., South Miami. ⓒ **305/233-4458** or 305/233-1113. Crepes $3–$7.50. No credit cards. Sun and Tues–Thurs 10:30am–8:30pm, Fri–Sat 10:30am–10:30pm. Crepe cart in CocoWalk Tues–Wed 4–10pm, Thurs 11am–11pm, Fri–Sat 11am–1am, Sun 11am–11pm.

El Toro Taco Family Restaurant ★★ *Finds* MEXICAN   Until I discovered this Mexican oasis in the midst of South Florida farmland, I'd never had good enough reason to leave my quasi-cosmopolitan confines in Miami for rural Homestead way down south. This 96-seat family-run restaurant has put major miles on my car since I first stumbled upon it a few years ago when I was lost and very hungry. Fabulous, and I mean fabulous, Mexican fare, from the usual tacos, enchiladas, and burritos drenched with the freshest and zestiest salsa this side of Baja, is what you'll find here in abundance. It may sound odd to travel from a big city with tons of restaurants to farm country for Mexican food, but trust me, it's so cheap and delicious, it's worth the trip.

1 S. Krome Ave., Homestead ℂ 305/245-8182. Main courses $1.39–$8.75. DISC, MC, V. Tues–Sun 11am–9pm.

Kon Chau ✪ CHINESE/DIM SUM   Don't be put off by the rather unappealing shopping center in which this cheap dim sum palace is located. If you want fancy plastic chopsticks and fancy prices, go up the block to Tropical Chinese. If you want delicious dim sum at ridiculously low prices, Kon Chau is where you'll find it. A simple checklist allows you to choose as much of whatever you want, from savory steamed shrimp dumplings to airy pork buns, for as little as $1 a piece.

8376 Bird Rd., West Miami. ℂ 305/553-7799. Items $1 and up. MC, V. Mon–Sat 11am–10pm, Sun 10am–10pm.

Shorty's ✪ BARBECUE   A Miami tradition since 1951, this honky-tonk of a log cabin is still serving some of the best ribs and chicken in South Florida. People line up for the smoke-flavored, slow-cooked meat that's so tender it seems to fall off the bone. The secret, however, is to ask for your order with sweet sauce. The regular stuff tastes bland and bottled. A second Shorty's is located in Davie at 5989 S. University Dr. (ℂ **305/944-0348**).

9200 S. Dixie Hwy. (between U.S. 1 and Dadeland Blvd.), South Miami. ℂ **305/670-7732**. Main courses $5–$9. DISC, MC, V. Mon–Thurs 11am–10pm, Fri–Sat 11am–11pm.

Tea Room ✪ ENGLISH TEA   Do stop in for a spot of tea at this recently rebuilt tearoom in historic Cauley Square off U.S. 1. The little lace-curtained room is an unusual site in this heavily industrial area better known for its warehouses than its doilies.

Try one of the simple sandwiches, such as the turkey club with potato salad and a small lettuce garnish or onion soup full of rich brown broth and stringy cheese. Daily specials, such as spinach and mushroom quiche, and delectable desserts are a must before beginning your explorations of the old antiques and art shops in this little enclave of civility down south.

12310 SW 224th St. (at Cauley Square), South Miami. ℂ **305/258-0044**. Sandwiches and salads $7–$12; soups $3–$4. AE, DISC, MC, V. Mon–Sat 11am–4pm.

5

What to See & Do in Miami

by Lesley Abravanel

If there's one thing Miami doesn't have, it's an identity crisis. In fact, it's the city's vibrant, multifaceted personality that attracts millions each year, from all over the world. South Beach may be on the top of many Miami to-do lists, but the rest of the city, a fascinating assemblage of multicultural neighborhoods, should not be neglected. Once considered "God's Waiting Room," the Magic City now attracts an eclectic mix of old and young, celebs and plebes, American and international, and geek and chic with an equally varied roster of activities.

For starters, Miami boasts some of the most natural beauty there is, with blinding blue waters, fine, sandy beaches, and lush tropical parks. The city's human-made brilliance, in the form of Crayola-colored architecture, never seems to fade in Miami's unique Art Deco District. For cultural variation, you can experience the taste, sounds, and rhythms of Cuba in Little Havana. Lose yourself in the city's nature and its neighborhoods, and, best of all, its people—a sassy collection of artists and intellectuals, beach bums and international transplants, dolled-up drag queens and bodies beautiful. No wonder celebrities love to vacation here—the spotlight is on the city and its residents. And unlike most stars, Miami is always ready for its close-up. With so much to do and see, Miami is a virtual amusement park that's bound to entertain all those who pass through its palm-lined gates.

1 Miami's Beaches

Perhaps Miami's most popular attraction is its incredible 35-mile stretch of beachfront, which runs from the tip of South Beach north to Sunny Isles and circles Key Biscayne and the numerous other pristine islands dotting the Atlantic. The characteristics of Miami's many beaches are as varied as the city's population: There are beaches for swimming, socializing, or serenity; for family, seniors, or gay singles; some to make you forget you're in the city, others darkened by huge condominiums. But for whatever beach vacation you're looking for, you'll find it in one of Miami's two distinct beach areas: Miami Beach and Key Biscayne.

MIAMI BEACH'S BEACHES Collins Avenue fronts more than a dozen miles of white-sand beach and blue-green waters from 1st to 192nd streets. Although most of this stretch is lined with a solid wall of hotels and condos, beach access is plentiful. There are lots of public beaches here, wide and well maintained, complete with lifeguards, toilet facilities, concession stands, and metered parking (bring lots of quarters). Except for a thin strip close to the water, most of the sand is hard-packed—the result of a $10 million Army Corps of Engineers Beach Rebuilding Project meant to protect buildings from the effects of eroding sand.

In general, the beaches on this barrier island become less crowded the farther north you go. A wooden boardwalk runs along the hotel side of the beach from 21st to 46th streets—about 1½ miles—offering a terrific sun-and-surf experience without getting sand in your shoes. Aside from "The Best Beaches," listed below, Miami's lifeguard-protected public beaches include 21st Street, at the beginning of the boardwalk; 35th Street, popular with an older crowd; 46th Street, next to the Fontainebleau Hilton; 53rd Street, a narrower, more sedate beach; 64th Street, one of the quietest strips around; and 72nd Street, a local old-timers' spot.

KEY BISCAYNE'S BEACHES   If Miami Beach doesn't provide the privacy you're looking for, try Virginia Key and Key Biscayne. Crossing the Rickenbacker Causeway ($1 toll), however, can be a lengthy process, especially on weekends, when beach bums and tan-o-rexics flock to the Key. The 5 miles of public beach here are blessed with softer sand and are less developed and more laid-back than the hotel-laden strips to the north.

THE BEST BEACHES

Here are my picks:

- **Best Party Beach:** In Key Biscayne, **Crandon Park Beach,** on Crandon Boulevard, is National Lampoon's *Vacation* on the sand. It's got a diverse crowd consisting of dedicated beach bums and lots of leisure-seeking families, set to a soundtrack of salsa, disco, and reggae music blaring from a number of competing stereos. With 3 miles of oceanfront beach, 493 acres of park, 75 grills, three parking lots, several soccer and softball fields, and a public 18-hole championship golf course, Crandon is like a theme park on the sand. Admission is $2 per vehicle. It's open daily from 8am to sunset.

- **Best Beach for People-Watching: Lummus Park Beach,** aka Glitter Beach, runs along Ocean Drive from about 6th to 14th streets on South Beach. It's the best place to go if you're seeking entertainment as well as a great tan. On any day of the week, you might spy models primping for a photo shoot, nearly naked (topless is legal here) sun-worshippers avoiding tan lines, and an assembly line of washboard abs off of which you could (but shouldn't) bounce your bottle of sunscreen. Pop star Sisquo's "The Thong Song" was inspired by this beach.

- **Best Swimming Beach:** The **85th Street Beach,** along Collins Avenue, is the best place to swim away from the maddening crowds. It's one of Miami's only stretches of sand with no condos or hotels looming over sunbathers. Lifeguards patrol the area throughout the day.

- **Best Windsurfing Beach: Hobie Beach,** on the right side of the causeway leading to Key Biscayne, is not really a beach, but an inlet with predictable winds and a number of places where you can rent Windsurfers.

- **Best Shell-Hunting Beach:** You'll find plenty of colorful shells at **Bal Harbour Beach,** Collins Avenue at 96th Street, just a few yards north of Surfside Beach. There's also an exercise course and good shade—but no lifeguards.

- **Best (Ahem) All-Around Tanning Beach:** For that all-over tan, head to **Haulover Beach,** just north of the Bal Harbour border, and join nudists from around the world in a top-to-bottom tanning session.

- **Best Surfing Beach: Haulover Beach/Harbor House,** just north of Miami Beach, seems to get Miami's biggest swells. Go early to avoid getting mauled by the aggressive young locals prepping for Maui.

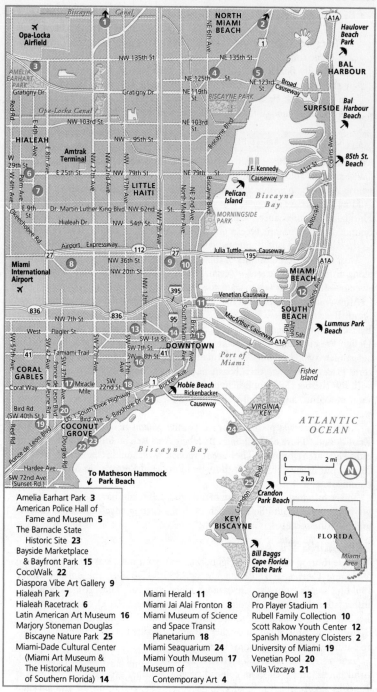

Biscayne Canal

NORTH MIAMI BEACH

A1A

Haulover Beach Park

Opa-Locka Airfield

NW 135th St.

NE 135th St.

BAL HARBOUR

AMELIA EARHART PARK

NE 125th St.

NE 123rd St.

Broad Causeway

Gratigny Dr.

Gratigny Dr.

NE 119th St.

BISCAYNE PARK

SURFSIDE

Bal Harbour Beach

Opa-Locka Canal

NW 103rd St.

NE 103rd St.

NW 95th St.

85th St. Beach

HIALEAH

Amtrak Terminal

E 25th St.

NW 79th St.

NE 79th St.

J.F. Kennedy Causeway

Pelican Island

Biscayne Bay

LITTLE HAITI

Dr. Martin Luther King Blvd.

NW 62nd St.

MORNINGSIDE PARK

Hialeah Dr.

NW 54th St.

Airport Expressway

112

27

Julia Tuttle Causeway

195

Miami International Airport

NW 36th St.

NW 20th St.

MIAMI BEACH

Venetian Causeway

A1A

836

NW 7th St.

836

395

SOUTH BEACH

MacArthur Causeway

Lummus Park Beach

West Flagler St.

95

SW 1st St.

DOWNTOWN

5th St.

A1A

CORAL GABLES

Tamiami Trail

SW 7th St.

SW 8th St.

41

Port of Miami

Fisher Island

Coral Way

Miracle Mile

SW 22nd St.

Hobie Beach

Rickenbacker Causeway

VIRGINIA KEY

ATLANTIC OCEAN

Bird Rd. (SW 40th St.)

Bird Ave.

COCONUT GROVE

US-1 South Dixie Highway

Hardee Ave.

SW 72nd Ave. (Sunset Rd.)

To Matheson Hammock Park Beach

Biscayne Bay

Crandon Park Beach

0   2 mi
0   2 km

KEY BISCAYNE

FLORIDA

Miami Area

Bill Baggs Cape Florida State Park

Amelia Earhart Park **3**
American Police Hall of
  Fame and Museum **5**
The Barnacle State
  Historic Site **23**
Bayside Marketplace
  & Bayfront Park **15**
CocoWalk **22**
Diaspora Vibe Art Gallery **9**
Hialeah Park **7**
Hialeah Racetrack **6**
Latin American Art Museum **16**
Marjory Stoneman Douglas
  Biscayne Nature Park **25**
Miami-Dade Cultural Center
  (Miami Art Museum &
  The Historical Museum
  of Southern Florida) **14**

Miami Herald **11**
Miami Jai Alai Fronton **8**
Miami Museum of Science
  and Space Transit
  Planetarium **18**
Miami Seaquarium **24**
Miami Youth Museum **17**
Museum of
  Contemporary Art **4**

Orange Bowl **13**
Pro Player Stadium **1**
Rubell Family Collection **10**
Scott Rakow Youth Center **12**
Spanish Monastery Cloisters **2**
University of Miami **19**
Venetian Pool **20**
Villa Vizcaya **21**

- **Best Scenic Beach: Matheson Hammock Park Beach** is the epitome of tranquility, tucked away off of scenic Old Cutler Road in South Miami. And while it's scenic, it's not too much of a scene. It's a great beach for those seeking "alone time."
- **Best Family Beach:** Because of its man-made lagoon, which is fed naturally by the tidal movement of the adjacent Biscayne Bay, the waters at **Matheson Hammock Park Beach** are extremely calm here, not to mention safe and secluded enough for families to keep an eye on the kids.

2 The Art Deco District

"You know what they used to say?" recalls Art Deco revivalist Dona Zemo, "Who's Art?" "You'd say, 'This is an Art Deco building,' and they'd say, 'Really, who is Art?' These people thought 'Art Deco' was some guy's name."

How things have changed. This guy Art has become one of the most popular Florida attractions since, well, that mouse Mickey. The district is roughly bounded by the Atlantic Ocean on the east, Alton Road on the west, 6th Street to the south, and Dade Boulevard (along the Collins Canal) to the north.

Most of the finest examples of the whimsical Art Deco style are concentrated along three parallel streets—Ocean Drive, Collins Avenue, and Washington Avenue—from about 6th to 23rd streets.

After years of neglect and calls for the wholesale demolition of its buildings, South Beach got a new lease on life in 1979. Under the leadership of Barbara Baer Capitman, a dedicated crusader for the Art Deco region, and the Miami Design Preservation League (founded by Baer Capitman), an area made up of an estimated 800 buildings was granted a listing on the National Register of Historic Places. Designers then began highlighting long-lost architectural details with soft sherbet shades of peach, periwinkle, turquoise, and purple. Developers soon moved in, and the full-scale refurbishment of the area's hotels was under way.

Not everyone was pleased, though. Former Miami Beach commissioner Abe Resnick said, "I love old buildings. But these Art Deco buildings are 40, 50 years old. They aren't historic. They aren't special. We shouldn't be forced to keep them." But Miami Beach kept those buildings, and Resnick lost his seat on the commission.

Today, hundreds of hotels, restaurants, and nightclubs have been renovated or are in the process, and South Beach is on the cutting edge of Miami's cultural and nightlife scene.

EXPLORING THE AREA

If you're touring this unique neighborhood on your own, start at the **Art Deco Welcome Center,** 1001 Ocean Dr. (© **305/531-3484**), the only beachside building across from the Clevelander Hotel and bar. They give away lots of informational material including maps and pamphlets. Art Deco books (including *The Art Deco Guide,* an informative compendium of all the buildings here), T-shirts, postcards, mugs, and other paraphernalia are for sale. It's open Monday to Saturday from 9am to 6pm, sometimes later.

Take a stroll along **Ocean Drive** for the best view of sidewalk cafes, bars, colorful hotels, and even more colorful people. Another great place for a walk is **Lincoln Road,** which is lined with galleries, cafes, and funky art and antiques stores. The Community Church, at the corner of Lincoln Road and Drexel

Avenue, is the neighborhood's first church and one of its oldest surviving buildings, dating from 1921.

For details on guided tours, see "Sightseeing Cruises & Organized Tours," later in this chapter.

3 Animal Parks

For a tropical climate, Miami's got a lot of nontropical animals to see, and we're not talking about the motorists on I-95. Everything from dolphins and alligators to lions, tigers, and bears call Miami home (most in parks, some in nature). Call to inquire about discount packages or coupons, which may be offered at area retail stores or in local papers.

Miami Metrozoo ★★ *Kids* This 290-acre complex is quite a distance from Miami proper and the beaches—about 45 minutes—but worth the trip. Isolated and never really crowded, it's also completely cageless—animals are kept at bay by cleverly designed moats. This is a fantastic spot to take the kids; there's a wonderful petting zoo and play area, and the zoo offers several daily programs designed to educate and entertain. Mufasa and Simba (of Disney fame) were modeled on a couple of Metrozoo's lions. Other residents include two rare white Bengal tigers, a Komodo dragon, rare koala bears, a number of kangaroos, and an African meerkat. The air-conditioned Zoofari Monorail tour offers visitors a nice overview of the park. An Andean Condor exhibit opened in 2000, and the zoo is always upgrading its facilities, including the impressive aviary. *Note:* The distance between animal habitats can be great, so you'll be doing a lot of walking here. Young children and the elderly, especially in summer, should take several rest breaks during the day (there are benches and shaded gazebos strategically positioned throughout the zoo). Also, because the zoo can be miserably hot during summer months, plan these visits in the early morning or late afternoon.

12400 SW 152nd St., South Miami. © 305/251-0400. www.miamimetrozoo.org. Admission $8 adults, $4 children 3–12. Daily 9:30am–5:30pm (ticket booth closes at 4pm). Free self-parking. From U.S. 1 south, turn right on SW 152nd St. and follow signs about 3 miles to the entrance.

Miami Seaquarium ★★ *Kids* If you've been to Orlando's SeaWorld, you may be disappointed with Miami's version, which is considerably smaller and not as well maintained, but kids love it. It's hardly a sprawling seaquarium, but you will want to arrive early to enjoy the effects of its mild splash. You'll need at least 3 hours to tour the 35-acre oceanarium and see all four daily shows starring a number of showy ocean mammals. You can cut your visit to 2 hours if you limit your shows to the better, albeit corny, Flipper Show and Killer Whale Show. The highly regarded Water and Dolphin Exploration Program (WADE) allows visitors to touch and swim with dolphins in the Flipper Lagoon for $125 per person. Reservations are necessary for this program; call © **305/365-2501**.

4400 Rickenbacker Causeway (south side), en route to Key Biscayne. © **305/361-5705**. www. miamiseaquarium.com. Admission $23 adults, $18 children 3–9, free for children under 3. Daily 9:30am–6pm (ticket booth closes at 4:30pm).

Monkey Jungle ★ *Overrated* Personally, I think this place is disgusting. It reeks, the monkeys are either sleeping or in heat, and it's really far from the city, even farther than the zoo. But if primates are your thing and you'd rather pass on the zoo, you'll be in paradise. You'll see rare Brazilian golden lion tamarins and Asian macaques. There are no cages to restrain the antics of the monkeys as they swing, chatter, and play their way into your heart. Screened-in trails wind through acres of "jungle," and daily shows feature the talents of the park's most progressive pupils. New exhibits in 2001 included the Cameroon Jungle and the Lemurs of Madagascar.

14805 SW 216th St., South Miami. (℃ 305/235-1611. www.monkeyjungle.com. Admission $13.50 adults, $10.50 seniors and active-duty military, $8 children 4–12. Daily 9:30am–5pm (tickets sold until 4pm). Take U.S. 1 south to SW 216th St., or from Florida Turnpike, take exit 11 and follow the signs.

Parrot Jungle and Gardens ★★ (Kids) This Miami institution will take flight from its current location in South Miami and head north in 2003 to a new $46 million home on Watson Island, along the McArthur Causeway near Miami Beach. While the island will double as a protected bird sanctuary, the jungle's soon-to-be former digs in the heart of South Miami in a circa 1900 coral rock structure are a lot more charming and kitschier. Continuous cheesy shows star roller-skating cockatoos, card-playing macaws, and numerous stunt-happy parrots. There are also tortoises, iguanas, and a rare albino alligator on exhibit. The park's website sometimes offers downloadable discount coupons. In its current locale, a suggested 4 hours is enough to make sure you see all the sites and shows.

11000 SW 57th Ave., Southern Miami–Dade County. (℃ 305/666-7834. www.parrotjungle.com. Admission $15.95 adults, $13.95 seniors, $10.95 children 3–10. Daily 9:30am–6pm. Cafe opens at 8am. Take U.S. 1 south and turn left at SW 57th Ave., or exit Kendall Dr. from the Florida Turnpike and turn right on SW 57th Ave.

Sea Grass Adventures ★ (Value) Even better than the Seaquarium is Sea Grass Adventures, in which a naturalist from the Marjory Stoneman Douglas Biscayne Nature Center will introduce kids and adults to an amazing variety of creatures that live in the sea grass beds of the Bear Cut Nature Preserve near Crandon Beach on Key Biscayne. Not just a walking tour, you will be able to wade in the water with your guide and catch an assortment of sea life in nets provided by the guides. At the end of the program, participants gather on the beach while the guide explains what everyone's just caught, passing the creatures around in miniature viewing tanks. A real bargain at just $10 per person. Call for available dates and reservations.

Marjory Stoneman Biscayne Nature Center, 6767 Crandon Blvd., Key Biscayne. (℃ 305/361-6767.

4 Miami's Museum & Art Scene

Miami has never been known as a cultural mecca as far as museums are concerned. Though several exhibition spaces have made forays into collecting nationally acclaimed work, limited support and political infighting have made it a difficult proposition. Recently, with the reinvention of the Wolfsonian, the reincarnation of MOCA, and the increased daring of the Miami Art Museum, the scene has improved dramatically. It's now safe to say that world-class exhibitions start here. Listed below is a cross-section of the valuable treasures that have become a part of the city's cultural heritage, and as such, are as diverse as the city itself.

For gallery lovers, see "Specialized Tours," below, for scheduled gallery walks.

IN SOUTH BEACH

Work continues to proceed on the **Miami Beach Cultural Park,** which comprises a trio of arts buildings on Collins Park and Park Avenue (off Collins Avenue), bounded by 21st to 23rd streets—the newly expanded Bass Museum of Art (see below), the new Arquitectonica-designed home of the Miami City Ballet, and the Miami Beach Regional Library, which broke ground in January

2001 and will have a special focus on the arts. Collins Park, the former site of the Miami Beach Library, will return to its original incarnation as an open space extending to the Atlantic, but it will also be the site of large sculpture installations and cultural activities planned jointly by the organizations that share the space.

Bass Museum of Art ✹✹✹   The Bass Museum of Art has expanded and received a dramatically new look. World-renowned Japanese architect Arata Isozaki designed the magnificent new facility, which has triple the former exhibition space, and added an outdoor sculpture terrace, a museum cafe and courtyard, and a museum shop, among other improvements. In addition to providing space in which to show the permanent collection, exhibitions of a scale and quality not presently seen in Miami will now be featured at the Bass. The museum's permanent collection includes European paintings from the 15th through the early 20th centuries with special emphasis on Northern European art of the Renaissance and Baroque periods, including Dutch and Flemish masters such as Bol, Flinck, Rubens, and Jordaens.

2121 Park Ave. (1 block west of Collins Ave.), South Beach. ✆ 305/673-7530. www.bassmuseum.org. Admission $5 adults, $3 students and seniors, free for children 6 and under; second and fourth Wed of the month by donation from 5–9pm. Tues–Sat 10am–5pm, Sun 1–5pm (every second and fourth Wed open 1–9pm). Closed major holidays.

Holocaust Memorial ✹✹✹   This heart-wrenching memorial is hard to miss and would be a shame to overlook. The powerful centerpiece, Kenneth Triester's *Sculpture of Love & Anguish,* depicts victims of the concentration camps crawling up a giant, yearning hand, stretching up to the sky, marked with an Auschwitz number tattoo. Along the reflecting pool is the story of the Holocaust, told in cut marble slabs. Inside the center of the memorial is a tableau that is one of the most solemn and moving tributes to the millions of Jews who lost their lives in the Holocaust I've seen. You can walk through an open hallway lined with photographs and the names of concentration camps and their victims. From the street, you'll see the outstretched arm, but do stop and tour the sculpture at ground level.

1933 Meridian Ave. (at Dade Blvd.), South Beach. ✆ 305/538-1663. Free admission. Daily 9am–9pm.

Sanford L. Ziff Jewish Museum ✹   Chronicling over 230 years of Jewish heritage and experiences in Florida, the Jewish Museum presents a fascinating look at religion and culture through films, lectures, and exhibits such as "Passages: An Immigrant's Journey," featuring memorabilia, photos, and documents tracing the immigration to the United States of 24 families of various ethnic and religious backgrounds. The museum is housed in a former synagogue.

301 Washington Ave., South Beach. ✆ 305/672-5044. www.jewishmuseum.com. $5 adults, $4 seniors and students, $10 families. Free admission Sat. Tues–Sun 10am–5pm.

Wolfsonian ✹✹✹ *Finds*   Mitchell Wolfson Jr., heir to a family fortune built on movie theaters, was known as an eccentric, but I'd call him a pack rat. A premier collector of propaganda and advertising art, Wolfson was spending so much money storing his booty that he decided to buy the warehouse that was housing it. It ultimately held more than 70,000 of his items from Nazi propaganda to King Farouk of Egypt's match collection. Thrown in the eclectic mix are also zany works from great modernists such as Charles Eames and Marcel Duchamp. He then gave this incredibly diverse and controversial collection to Florida International University. The former storage facility has been retrofitted with such painstaking detail that it's the envy of curators around the world. The museum also hosts lectures and swinging events surrounding particular exhibits.

1001 Washington Ave., South Beach. ℂ **305/531-1001**. Admission $5 adults; $3.50 seniors, students, and children 6–12; $5 tour-group members. Free admission Thurs evenings. Free admission for members, children under 6, and students or faculty of Florida universities. Mon–Tues.

IN & NEAR DOWNTOWN

American Police Hall of Fame and Museum   This strange museum appeals mostly to those fascinated by police and their gadgetry. Once inside, you'll find a combination of reality and fantasy that's part thoughtful tribute, part Hollywood-style drama. Just past the car featured in the motion picture *Blade Runner* is a mock prison cell, in which visitors can take pictures of themselves pretending they're doing 5 to 10. Also on hand are execution devices, including a guillotine and an electric chair (whose controversial use was recently abolished in Florida). Even if you don't go inside, you can't miss the museum, which has a real police car attached to its facade. Try not to speed by—you never know what sort of radar the car's got.

3801 Biscayne Blvd., Miami. ℂ 305/573-0070. www.aphf.org. Admission $6 adults, $4 seniors over 61, $3 children 11 and under, $1 police officers. 50% off coupons often available from hotel racks. Daily 10am–5:30pm. Go north on U.S. 1 from downtown; it's the building with a police car affixed to its side.

Diaspora Vibe Art Gallery ✷✷   This art complex housed in an old bakery is a funky artist hangout and home to some of the greatest artworks of Miami's diverse Caribbean, Latin American, and African-American cultures. The gallery has two seasons of shows, often focusing on emerging artists. During the winter, three artists are selected by the gallery to travel to and exhibit their work in Paris.

On the last Friday of every month from May through October is the gallery's fabulous "Final Fridays," during which a new artist's work is spotlighted inside, while outside in the courtyard are live music performances and delicious Caribbean cuisine. It's a real scene.

561 NW 32nd St., Studio 48 (Bakehouse Art Complex), Miami. ℂ **305/759-1110**. www.diasporavibe.com. "Final Fridays" admission $15; other times, free admission. Mon–Fri by appointment; Sat–Sun 1–6pm; May–Oct last Fri of the month 7–11pm.

Latin American Art Museum   In addition to the permanent collection of contemporary artists from Spain and Latin America, this 3,500-square-foot museum hosts monthly exhibitions of works from Latin America and the Caribbean Basin. Usually, the exhibitions focus on a theme, such as international women or surrealism. It's not a major attraction, but worth a stop if you're interested in Latin American art. On the same block, you'll find great design stores and a few other galleries.

2206 SW 8th St., Little Havana. ℂ **305/644-1127**. hispmuseum@aol.com. Free admission. Tues–Fri 11am–5pm, Sat 11am–4pm. Closed Aug and major holidays.

Miami Art Museum at the Miami–Dade Cultural Center ✷✷✷   The Miami Art Museum (MAM) features an eclectic mix of modern and contemporary works by such artists as Eric Fischl, Max Beckmann, Jim Dine, and Stuart Davis. Rotating exhibitions span the ages and styles, and often focus on Latin American or Caribbean artists. There are also fantastic themed exhibits such as the Andy Warhol exhibit, which featured all-night films by the artist, make-your-own pop art, cocktail hours, and parties with local deejays. JAM at MAM is the museum's popular happy hour, which takes place the second Thursday of

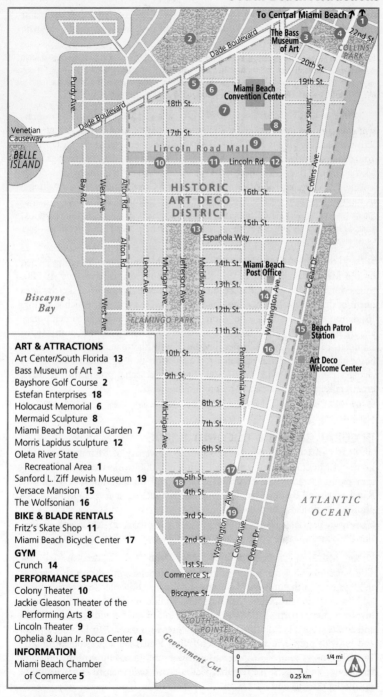

South Beach Attractions

To Central Miami Beach

The Bass Museum of Art

22nd St.

COLLINS PARK

20th St.

19th St.

Dade Boulevard

Miami Beach Convention Center

18th St.

17th St.

James Ave.

Purdy Ave.

Venetian Causeway

Dade Boulevard

BELLE ISLAND

Lincoln Road Mall

Lincoln Rd.

Collins Ave.

HISTORIC ART DECO DISTRICT

16th St.

15th St.

Bay Rd.

West Ave.

Alton Rd.

Alton Rd.

Española Way

14th St.

Miami Beach Post Office

13th St.

Lenox Ave.

Michigan Ave.

Jefferson Ave.

Meridian Ave.

12th St.

11th St.

Washington Ave.

Ocean Dr.

Biscayne Bay

FLAMINGO PARK

West Ave.

Beach Patrol Station

Art Deco Welcome Center

10th St.

9th St.

Pennsylvania Ave.

8th St.

Michigan Ave.

7th St.

6th St.

5th St.

4th St.

3rd St.

2nd St.

1st St.

Commerce St.

Biscayne St.

Washington Ave.

Collins Ave.

Ocean Dr.

ATLANTIC OCEAN

LUMMUS PARK

SOUTH POINTE PARK

Government Cut

ART & ATTRACTIONS
Art Center/South Florida **13**
Bass Museum of Art **3**
Bayshore Golf Course **2**
Estefan Enterprises **18**
Holocaust Memorial **6**
Mermaid Sculpture **8**
Miami Beach Botanical Garden **7**
Morris Lapidus sculpture **12**
Oleta River State
    Recreational Area **1**
Sanford L. Ziff Jewish Museum **19**
Versace Mansion **15**
The Wolfsonian **16**

BIKE & BLADE RENTALS
Fritz's Skate Shop **11**
Miami Beach Bicycle Center **17**

GYM
Crunch **14**

PERFORMANCE SPACES
Colony Theater **10**
Jackie Gleason Theater of the
    Performing Arts **8**
Lincoln Theater **9**
Ophelia & Juan Jr. Roca Center **4**

INFORMATION
Miami Beach Chamber
    of Commerce **5**

0   1/4 mi
0   0.25 km

N

the month and is tied in to a particular exhibit. Almost as artistic as the works inside the museum is the composite sketch of the people—young and old—who attend these events.

101 W. Flagler St., Miami. © 305/375-3000. Admission $5 adults, $2.50 seniors and students, free for children under 12; by contribution on Tues. Tues–Fri 10am–5pm; third Thurs of each month 10am–9pm; Sat–Sun noon–5pm. Closed major holidays. From I-95 south, exit at Orange Bowl–NW 8th St. and continue south to NW 2nd St.; turn left at NW 2nd St. and go 1½ blocks to NW 2nd Ave.; turn right.

Museum of Contemporary Art (MOCA) ★★★   MOCA boasts an impressive collection of internationally acclaimed art with a local flavor. A high-tech screening facility allows for film presentations to complement the exhibitions. You can see works by Jasper Johns, Roy Lichtenstein, Larry Rivers, Duane Michaels, and Claes Oldenberg, plus there are special exhibitions by such artists as Yoko Ono, Sigmar Polke, John Baldessari, and Goya. Guided tours are offered in English, Spanish, French, Creole, Portuguese, German, and Italian.

770 NE 125th St., North Miami. © 305/893-6211. Fax 305/891-1472. www.mocanomi.org. Admission $5 adults, $3 seniors and students with ID, free for children 12 and under. Tues–Sat 11am–5pm, Sun noon–5pm. Closed major holidays.

Rubell Family Art Collection ★★★ *Finds*   This impressive collection owned by the Miami hotelier family, the Rubells, is housed in a two-story 40,000-square-foot former Drug Enforcement Agency warehouse in a sketchy area north of downtown Miami. The building looks like a fortress, which is fitting: Inside is a priceless collection of more than a thousand works of contemporary art, by the likes of Keith Haring, Damien Hirst, Julian Schnabel, Jean-Michel Basquiat, Paul McCarthy, Charles Ray, and Cindy Sherman. But be forewarned: Some of the art is extremely graphic and may be off-putting to some. The gallery changes exhibitions twice yearly and there is a seasonal program of lectures, artists' talks, and performances by prominent artists.

95 NW 29th St. (on the corner of NW 1st Ave. near the Design District), Miami. © 305/573-6090. Free admission. Thurs–Sat 11am–4pm and by appointment.

IN CORAL GABLES & COCONUT GROVE

Lowe Art Museum ★★   Located on the University of Miami campus, the Lowe Art Museum has a dazzling collection of 8,000 works that include American paintings, Latin American art, Navajo and Pueblo Indian textiles, and Renaissance and Baroque art. Traveling exhibits such as *Rolling Stone* magazine's photo collection also stop here.

University of Miami, 1301 Stanford Dr. (at Ponce de León Blvd.), Coral Gables. © 305/284-3603. Admission $5 adults, $3 seniors, $2 students with ID. Tues, Wed, Fri, and Sat 10am–5pm, Thurs noon–7pm.

Miami Museum of Science and Space Transit Planetarium ★★ *Kids* The Museum of Science features more than 140 hands-on exhibits that explore the mysteries of the universe. Live demonstrations and collections of rare natural history specimens make a visit here fun and informative. Many of the demos involve audience participation, which can be lots of fun for willing and able kids and adults alike. There is also a Wildlife Center with more than 175 live reptiles and birds of prey. The adjacent Space Transit Planetarium projects astronomy and laser shows as well as interactive demonstrations of upcoming computer technology and cyberspace features. Call, or visit their website, for a listing of upcoming exhibits and laser shows.

3280 S. Miami Ave. (just south of the Rickenbacker Causeway), Coconut Grove. © 305/646-4200 for general information, or 305/854-2222 for planetarium show times. www.miamisci.org. $10 adults, $8 seniors and students, $6 children 3–12, free for children 2 and under; laser shows $6 adults, $3 seniors and children 3–12. Half price 4:30–6pm weekdays; 25% discount for AAA members. Museum of Science, daily 10am–6pm; call for planetarium show times (last show is at 4pm).

5 Historic Homes & Sites

South Beach's well-touted Art Deco District is but one of many colorful neighborhoods that can boast dazzling architecture. The rediscovery of the entire Biscayne Corridor (from downtown to the 80s) has given light to a host of ancillary neighborhoods on either side that are filled with Mediterranean-style homes and Frank Lloyd Wright gems. Coral Gables is home to many large and beautiful homes, mansions, and churches that reflect architecture from the 1920s, '30s, and '40s. Some of the homes, or portions of their structure, have been created from coral rock and shells. Even if you don't stay at the Biltmore Hotel, definitely take a tour of it. Call ✆ **305/445-1926** for more information.

Barnacle State Historic Site ★★   The former home of naval architect and early settler Ralph Middleton Munroe is now a museum in the heart of Coconut Grove. It's the oldest house in Miami and rests on its original foundation, which sits on 5 acres of hardwood and landscaped lawns. The house's quiet surroundings, wide porches, and period furnishings illustrate how Miami's first snowbird lived in the days before condo-mania and luxury hotels. Enthusiastic and knowledgeable state park employees offer a wealth of historical information to those interested in quiet, low-tech attractions like this one. Call for details on the fabulous monthly moonlight concerts during which folk, blues, or classical music is presented and picnicking is encouraged.

3485 Main Hwy. (1 block south of Commodore Plaza), Coconut Grove. ✆ **305/448-9445.** Fax 305/448-7484. Admission $1. Concerts $5, free for children under 10. Fri–Mon 9am–4pm. Tours Fri–Sun at 10am, 11:30am, 1pm, and 2:30pm. Group tours Mon–Thurs with 2-week advance reservations. From downtown Miami, take U.S. 1 south to 27th Ave., make a left, and continue to S. Bayshore Dr.; then make a right, follow to the intersection of Main Hwy., and turn left.

Coral Castle ★★ (Finds)   There's plenty of competition, but Coral Castle is probably the strangest attraction in Florida. In 1923, the story goes, a 26-year-old crazed Latvian, suffering from unrequited love of a 16-year old who left him at the altar, immigrated to South Miami and spent the next 25 years of his life carving huge boulders into a prehistoric-looking roofless "castle." It seems impossible that one rather short man could have done all this, but there are scores of affidavits on display from neighbors who swear it happened. Apparently, experts have studied this phenomenon to help figure out how the Great Pyramids and Stonehenge were built. Rocker Billy Idol was said to have been inspired by this place to write his song "Sweet Sixteen." An interesting 25-minute audio tour guides you through the spot, now in the National Register of Historic Places. Although Coral Castle is overpriced and undermaintained, it's worth a visit when in the area.

28655 S. Dixie Hwy., Homestead. ✆ **305/248-6345.** www.coralcastle.com. Admission $7.75 adults, $6.50 seniors, $5 children 7–12. Mon–Sat 9am–7pm, Sun 9am–6pm. Take U.S. 1 south to SW 286th St.

Spanish Monastery Cloisters ★★★ (Finds)   Did you know that the alleged oldest building in the Western Hemisphere dates from 1133 and is located in Miami? The Spanish Monastery Cloisters were first erected in Segovia, Spain. Centuries later, newspaper magnate William Randolph Hearst purchased and brought them to America in pieces. The carefully numbered stones were quarantined for years until they were finally reassembled on the present site in 1954.

It has often been used as a backdrop for movies and commercials and is a very popular tourist attraction.

16711 W. Dixie Hwy. (at NE 167th St.), North Miami Beach. ℂ 305/945-1461. monastery@earthlink.net. Admission $5 adults, $2.50 seniors, $2 children 3–12. Mon–Sat 10am–4pm, Sun 1–5pm.

Venetian Pool ⭐⭐⭐ (Kids)   Miami's most beautiful and unusual swimming pool, dating from 1924, is hidden behind pastel stucco walls and is honored with a listing in the National Register of Historic Places. Underground artesian wells feed the free-form lagoon, which is shaded by three-story Spanish porticos and features both fountains and waterfalls. It can be cold in the winter months. During summer, the pool's 800,000 gallons of water are drained and refilled nightly, ensuring a cool, *clean* swim. Visitors are free to swim and sunbathe here, just as Esther Williams and Johnny Weissmuller did decades ago. For a modest fee, you or your children can learn to swim during special summer programs.

2701 DeSoto Blvd. (at Toledo St.), Coral Gables. ℂ 305/460-5356. www.venetianpool.com. Admission and hours vary seasonally. Nov–Mar, $5 for those 13 and older, $2 children under 13; April–Oct, $8 for those 13 and older, $4 children under 13. Children must be 3 years old or 38 inches tall to enter or provide proof of 3 years of age with birth certificate.

Villa Vizcaya ⭐⭐⭐   Sometimes referred to as the "Hearst Castle of the East," this magnificent villa is more Gatsby-esque than anything elseyou'll find in Miami. It was built in 1916 as a winter retreat for James Deering, cofounder and former vice-president of International Harvester. The industrialist was fascinated by 16th-century art and architecture, and his ornate mansion, which took 1,000 artisans 5 years to build, became a celebration of that period. Most of the original furnishings, including dishes and paintings, are still intact. A free guided tour of the 34 furnished rooms takes about 45 minutes. The spectacularly opulent villa wraps itself around a central courtyard. Outside, lush formal gardens, accented with statuary, balustrades, and decorative urns, front an enormous swath of Biscayne Bay. While Vizcaya is a premier venue for society events and weddings, there are several events that are open to the public such as the Renaissance Fair; definitely take the tour of the rooms, but immediately thereafter, you will want to wander and get lost in the resplendent gardens.

3251 S. Miami Ave. (just south of Rickenbacker Causeway), North Coconut Grove. ℂ 305/250-9133. Admission $10 adults, $5 children 6–12, free for children 5 and under. Villa daily 9:30am–5pm (ticket booth closes at 4:30pm); gardens daily 9:30am–5:30pm.

6 Nature Preserves, Parks & Gardens

The Miami area is a great place for outdoors types, with beaches, parks, and gardens galore. Plus, South Florida has two national parks; see chapter 7, for coverage of the Everglades and Biscayne National Park.

BOTANICAL GARDENS & A SPICE PARK

Fairchild Tropical Garden ⭐⭐⭐   This garden at 10901 Old Cutler Rd. (ℂ 305/667-1651; www.ftg.org), is the largest of its kind in the continental United States. A veritable rain forest of both rare and exotic plants, as well as 11 lakes and countless meadows, are spread across 83 acres. Palmettos, vine pergola, palm glades, and other unique species create a scenic, lush environment. More than 100 species of bird have been spotted at the garden (ask for a checklist at the front gate), and it's home to a variety of animals. You should not miss the 30-minute narrated tram tour (tours leave on the hour from 10am to 3pm weekdays and 10am to 4pm on weekends) to learn about the various flowers and trees on the grounds. There is also a museum, a cafe, a picnic area, and a gift shop with fantastic books on gardening and cooking and edible gifts. A new 2-acre rain-forest exhibit will save you a trip to the Amazon.

Admission is $8 for adults, and free for children 12 and under accompanied by an adult. Open daily, except December 25, from 9:30am to 4:30pm. Take I-95 south to U.S. 1, turn left onto Le Jeune Road, and follow it straight to the traffic circle; from there, take Old Cutler Road 2 miles to the park.

Although an ocean and a continent apart, Hawaii and Florida share similar climates because both lie near the Tropic of Cancer. As a result, the organization known as the National Tropical Botanical Gardens has four gardens and three preserves in Hawaii and one in South Florida—**The Kampong** ⋆. Located on Biscayne Bay in Coconut Grove (4013 Douglas Rd.), the Kampong contains a stunning array of flowering trees and tropical fruit trees including mango, avocado, and pomelos. In the early 1900s, noted plant explorer David Fairchild (for whom the Fairchild Tropical Gardens are named) traveled the world seeking rare plants of economic and aesthetic value that might be cultivated in the United States. In 1928, he and his wife, Marian (daughter of Alexander Graham Bell), built a two-story residence here (listed on the National Register of Historic Places) amid some of his collections, borrowing the Malaysian word *kampong* for his home in a garden. In the 1960s, the Fairchilds sold the Kampong to Catherine Hauberg Sweeney, who donated the property to the National Tropical Botanical Garden to promote and preserve this South Florida treasure. It's a must-see. Tours are by appointment only, from Monday to Friday. For tour information, call ℭ **305/442-7169.**

A testament to Miami's unusual climate, the **Preston B. Bird and Mary Heinlein Fruit and Spice Park** ⋆, 24801 SW 187th Ave., Homestead (ℭ **305/ 247-5727**), harbors rare fruit trees that cannot survive elsewhere in the country. If a volunteer is available, you'll learn some fascinating things about this 30-acre living plant museum, where the most exotic varieties of fruits and spices—ackee, mango, Ugli fruits, carambola, and breadfruit—grow on strange-looking trees with unpronounceable names.

The best part? You're free to take anything that *naturally* falls to the ground. You'll also find samples of interesting fruits and jellies made from the park's bounty in the gift store. Cooks who like to experiment should visit the park store, which carries a number of exotic ingredients and cookbooks.

Admission to the spice park is $3.50 for adults and $1 for children under 12. It's open daily from 10am to 5pm; closed major holidays. Tours are included in the price of admission and are offered 11am, 1pm, and 2:30pm. Take U.S. 1 south, turn right on SW 248th Street, and go straight for 5 miles to SW 187th Avenue. Hours are 10am to 5pm daily.

MORE MIAMI PARKS

Because so many people are so focused on the beach itself, the **Miami Beach Botanical Garden,** 2000 Convention Center Dr., Miami Beach (ℭ **305/ 673-7256**), remains, for the most part, a secret garden. The lush, tropical 4½-acre garden is a fabulous, all-natural retreat from the hustle and bustle of the silicone-enhanced city. Open Monday through Friday from 8:30am to 5pm, Saturday and Sunday from 9:30am to 5pm. Free admission.

The **Amelia Earhart Park,** 401 E. 65th St., Hialeah (ℭ **305/685-8389**), is the only real reason to travel to industrial, traffic-riddled Hialeah—but your kids will love it. There are five lakes stocked with bass and bream for fishing; playgrounds; picnic facilities; and a big red barn that houses cows, sheep, and goats for petting, and ponies for riding. There's also a country store and dozens of old-time farm activities like horseshoeing, sugarcane processing, and more. Parking is free on weekdays and $3.50 per car on weekends. Open daily from 9am to sunset. To drive here, take I-95 north to the NW 103rd Street exit, go west to East 4th Avenue, and then turn right. Parking is 1½ miles down the street.

At the historic **Bill Baggs Cape Florida State Recreation Area,** 1200 Crandon Blvd. (© **305/361-5811**), at the southern tip of Key Biscayne, you can explore the unfettered wilds and enjoy some of the most secluded beaches in Miami. There's also a recently reopened lighthouse. A rental shack rents bikes, hydrobikes, kayaks, and many more water toys. It's a great place to picnic, and a newly constructed restaurant serves homemade Latin food, including great fish soups and sandwiches. Just be careful that the raccoons don't get your lunch—the furry black-eyed beasts are everywhere. Admission is $4 per car with up to eight people. Open daily from 8am to sunset. Tours of the lighthouse are available every Thursday through Monday at 10am and 1pm. Arrive at least half an hour early to sign up—there is only room for 10 people on each.

Tropical Park, 7900 SW 40th St. (© **305/226-8315**), has it all. Enjoy a game of tennis and racquetball for a minimal fee, or swim and sun yourself on the secluded little lake. You can use the fishing pond for free, and they'll even supply you with the rods and bait. If you catch anything, however, you're on your own. Open daily from sunrise to sunset.

Named after the late champion of the Everglades, the **Marjory Stoneman Douglas Biscayne Nature Center,** 6767 Crandon Blvd., Key Biscayne (© **305/361-6767**), has just moved into a brand-new $4 million facility and offers hands-on marine exploration, hikes through coastal hammocks, bike trips, and beach walks. Local environmentalists and historians lead intriguing trips through the local habitat. Be sure to wear comfortable closed-toe shoes for hikes through wet or rocky terrain. Open daily 10am–7pm Memorial Day–Labor Day; 10am–4pm rest of year. $4 park admission.

The **Oleta River State Recreation Area,** 3400 NE 163rd St., North Miami (© **305/919-1846**), consists of 993 acres—the largest urban park in the state—on Biscayne Bay. The beauty of the Oleta River combined with the fact that you're essentially in the middle of a city makes this park especially worth visiting. With miles of bicycle and canoe trails, a sandy swimming beach, shaded picnic pavilions, and a fishing pier, Oleta River State Recreation Area offers visitors an outstanding outdoor recreational experience cloistered from the confines of the big city. Open daily 8am–sunset. Admission for pedestrians and cyclists is $1 per person. By car: driver plus car $2; driver plus 1 to 7 passengers and car $4.

7 Sightseeing Cruises & Organized Tours

BOAT & CRUISE-SHIP TOURS

Celebration ⚐ This 1-hour air-conditioned cruise will take you past Millionaires' Row and the Venetian Islands for just $10. There's also a food stand and cash bar. The tours are bilingual.

Bayside Marketplace Marina, 401 Biscayne Blvd., Downtown. © 305/373-7001. Tickets $10 adults, children sail free. Millionaire's Row tour daily 1, 3, 5, and 7pm. Evening party cruise Fri–Sat 9–11pm.

Heritage Miami II Topsail Schooner   This relaxing ride aboard Miami's only tall ship is a fun way to see the city. The 2-hour cruise passes by Villa Vizcaya, Coconut Grove, and Key Biscayne and puts you in sight of Miami's spectacular skyline and island homes. Call to make sure the ship is running on schedule. On Friday, Saturday, and Sunday evenings, there are 1-hour tours to see the lights of the city, leaving at 6:30pm, for $10 per person.

Bayside Marketplace Marina, 401 Biscayne Blvd., Downtown. ℂ 305/442-9697. Fax 305/442-0119. Tickets $15 adults, $10 children 12 and under. Sept–May only. Tours leave daily at 1:30, 4, and 6:30pm, and Fri–Sun also at 9, 10, and 11pm.

Water Taxi ★★★ *Value*   Not exactly a tour, per se, the Water Taxi is a cheap and fantastic way to see the city via local waterways. The two major routes run between Bayside Marketplace and the 5th Street Marina on South Beach; the second is basically a downtown water shuttle service between the various hotels in downtown as well as the Port of Miami, the Hard Rock Cafe at Bayside, East Coast Fisheries, and Fisher Island. Cost is $7 one-way, $12 round-trip, and $15 for an all-day pass. The Bayside/South Beach trip is the best one to take because there aren't as many stops.

ℂ 305/467-6677. www.watertaxi.com.

A SIGHTSEEING TOUR

While there are several sightseeing tour operators in Miami, most unfortunately either don't speak English or are just plain shoddy. The following is the one we'd recommend:

Miami Nice Excursion Travel and Service ★   Pick your destination. The Miami Nice tours will take you to the Everglades, Fort Lauderdale, South Beach, the Seaquarium, Key West, Cape Canaveral, or wherever you desire. The best trip for first-timers is the City Tour, a comprehensive tour of the entire city and its various neighborhoods. If you've got the time, you will definitely want to add on a side trip to the Everglades and/or Key West. Included in most Miami trips is a fairly comprehensive city tour narrated by a knowledgeable guide. The company is one of the oldest in town.

18430 Collins Ave., Miami Beach. ℂ 305/949-9180. Tours $29–$55 adults, $25 children. Daily 7am–10pm. Call ahead for directions to various pickup areas.

SPECIALIZED TOURS

A great option for seeing the city is to take a tour led by **Dr. Paul George.** Dr. George is a history teacher at Miami–Dade Community College and a historian at the Historical Museum of Southern Florida. He also happens to be "Mr. Miami." There's a set calendar of tours, but all of them are fascinating to South Florida buffs. Tours focus on neighborhoods, such as Little Havana, Brickell Avenue, or Key Biscayne, and on themes, such as Miami cemeteries and the Miami River. The often long-winded discussions can be a bit much for those who just want a quick look around, but Dr. George certainly knows his stuff. The cost is $15 to $25; reservations are required (ℂ **305/375-1621**). Tours leave from the Historical Museum at 101 W. Flagler St., Downtown. Here are my picks for other terrific tours. Call for details and reservations:

Art Deco Biking Tour ★★   If you'd rather bike than walk, catch this fun and interesting morning tour on the third Sunday of every month.

601 5th St., South Beach. ℂ 305/674-0150. mbbicycle@aol.com. $10 per person, plus $10 for bike rental. Tours depart from the Miami Beach Bicycle Center.

Biltmore Hotel Tour ★★★ (Value) Learn about the history and mysteries of this wonderful spot. Ask about free weekly fireside sessions presented by Miami Storytellers.

1200 Anastasia Ave., Coral Gables. © 305/445-1926. www.biltmorehotel.com. Free admission. Tours depart on Sunday at 1:30, 2:30, and 3:30pm.

Coral Gables Art and Gallery Tour ★★★ (Value) This is a fabulous and *free* event that draws art aficionados and the generally curious to sip wine and analyze the various works of art displayed in the many galleries in Coral Gables. Art lovers are shuttled to more than 20 participating galleries.

Various locations in Coral Gables. For information, call Elite Fine Art (© 305/448-3800). Free. First Friday of the month, 7–10pm.

Miami Design Preservation League ★★ These walking tours offer a fascinating inside look at the city's historic Art Deco District.

Art Deco Welcome Center, 1001 Ocean Dr., South Beach. © 305/672-2014. www.mdpl.org. Walking tours $10 per person. Tours leave Saturday at 10:30am and Thursday at 6:30pm. Self-guided audio tours also available daily for $10. No reservations necessary.

Murder, Mystery and Mayhem Bus Tour ★★★ Visit the past by video and bus to Miami–Dade's most celebrated crimes and criminals from the 1800s to the present.

Leaves Sat at 10pm from the Dade Cultural Center, 101 W. Flagler St., Miami. Advance reservations required; call © 305/375-1621. Tickets $35.

Second Thursdays: Miami Beach Arts Night ★★★ (Value) The artistic equivalent of a triathlon, this free cultural open house in Miami Beach takes place monthly at various venues throughout the city.

Call © 305/673-7600. www.2ndthursdays.com. Free. Second Thursday of every month 6–9pm.

8 Water Sports

BOATING

Private rental outfits include **Boat Rental Plus,** 2400 Collins Ave., Miami Beach (© **305/534-4307**), where 50-horsepower 18-foot powerboats rent for some of the best prices on the beach. There's a 2-hour minimum and rates go from $99 to $449. There are great specials on Sunday. All rates include taxes and gas. A $250 cash or credit-card deposit is required. Cruising is permitted only in and around Biscayne Bay. Ocean access is prohibited. Renters must be over 21. The rental office is at 23rd Street, on the inland waterway in Miami Beach. It's open daily from 10am to sunset.

Club Nautico of Coconut Grove, 2560 S. Bayshore Dr. (© **305/858-6258**), rents high-quality powerboats for fishing, water-skiing, diving, and cruising in the bay or ocean. All boats are Coast Guard equipped, with VHF radios and safety gear. Rates range from $199 for 4 hours and $299 for 8 hours, to as much as $419 on weekends. Club Nautico is open daily from 9am to 5pm (weather permitting). Other locations include the Crandon Park Marina, 4000 Crandon Blvd., Key Biscayne (© **305/361-9217**), with the same rates and hours as the Coconut Grove location; and the Miami Beach Marina, Pier E, 300 Alton Rd., South Beach (© **305/673-2502**), where rates are $229 for 4 hours and $299 for 8 hours for a 20-foot boat, and $259 for 4 hours and $359 for 8 hours for a 24-footer. Nautico on Miami Beach is open daily from 9am to 5pm.

JET SKIS/WAVERUNNERS

Don't miss a chance to tour the islands on the back of your own powerful watercraft. Bravery is, however, a prerequisite, as Miami's waterways are full of speeding jet skiers and boaters who think they're in the Indy 500. Many beachfront concessionaires rent a variety of these popular (and loud) water scooters. The latest models are fast and smooth. Try **Tony's Jet Ski Rentals,** 3601 Rickenbacker Causeway, Key Biscayne (② **305/361-8280**), one of the city's largest rental shops, located on a private beach in the Miami Marine Stadium lagoon. There are three models available accommodating up to three people. Rates range from $45 for a half-hour to $80 for a full hour, depending on the number of riders. Open daily from 10:30am to 6:30pm.

KAYAKING

The laid-back **Urban Trails Kayak Company** rents boats at 10800 Collins Ave. (② **305/947-1302**). It offers scenic routes through rivers with mangroves and islands as your destination. Most of the kayaks are sit-on-tops, and most are plastic, although there are some fiberglass models available. Rates are $8 an hour, $20 for up to 4 hours, and $25 for over 4 hours. Tandems are $12 an hour, $30 for up to 4 hours, and $35 for the day. Open daily from 9am to 5pm.

The outfitters here give interested explorers a map to take with them and quick instructions on how to work the paddles and boats. If you have at least four people, you can get a guided half day tour for $35 per person. This is a fun way to experience some of Miami's unspoiled wildlife, and it's good exercise, too.

SAILING

You can rent sailboats and catamarans through the beachfront concessions desk of several top resorts, such as the Doral Golf Resort and Dezerland Beach Resort Hotel (see chapter 4), and the Sheraton Bal Harbour Beach Resort (9701 Collins Ave., Bal Harbour; ② **800/999-9898** or 305/865-7511).

Sailboats of Key Biscayne Rentals and Sailing School, in the Crandon Marina (next to Sundays on the Bay), 4000 Crandon Blvd., Key Biscayne (② **305/361-0328** days, 305/279-7424 evenings), can also get you out on the water. A 22-foot sailboat rents for $27 an hour, or $81 for a half day. A Cat-25 or J24 is available for $35 an hour or $110 for a half day. If you've always had a dream to win the America's Cup but can't sail, the able teachers at Sailboats will get you started. It offers a 10-hour course over 5 days for $300 for one person or $400 for you and a buddy.

Shake-a-Leg, 2600 Bayshore Dr., Coconut Grove (② **305/858-5550**), is a unique sailing program for disabled and able-bodied people alike. The program pairs up sailors for day and evening cruises and offers sailing lessons as well. Consider a moonlight cruise (offered monthly) or a race clinic. Shake-a-Leg members also welcome able-bodied volunteers for activities on and off the water. It costs $60 for nonmembers to rent a boat for 3 hours; free for volunteers. Open Wednesday through Sunday from 9am to 5pm.

SCUBA DIVING

In 1981, the government began a wide-scale project designed to increase the number of habitats available to marine organisms. One of the program's major accomplishments has been the creation of nearby artificial reefs, which have attracted all kinds of tropical plants, fish, and animals. In addition, Biscayne National Park (see "Biscayne National Park," in chapter 7) offers a protected marine environment just south of downtown.

Several dive shops around the city offer organized weekend outings, either to the reefs or to one of over a dozen old shipwrecks around Miami's shores. Check "Divers" in the Yellow Pages for rental equipment and for a full list of undersea tour operators.

Divers Paradise of Key Biscayne, 4000 Crandon Blvd. (© **305/361-3483**), offers two dive expeditions daily to the more than 30 wrecks and artificial reefs off the coast of Miami Beach and Key Biscayne. You can take a 3-day certification course for $399, which includes all the dives and gear. If you already have your C-card, a dive trip costs about $90 if you need equipment and only $35 if you bring your own gear. It's open Monday to Friday from 10am to 6pm and Saturday and Sunday from 8am to 6pm. Call ahead for times and locations of dives.

WINDSURFING

Many hotels rent Windsurfers to their guests, but if yours doesn't have a watersports concession stand, head for Key Biscayne.

Sailboards Miami, Rickenbacker Causeway, Key Biscayne (© **305/361-SAIL**), operates out of big yellow trucks on Hobie Beach, the most popular windsurfing spot in the city. For those who've never ridden a board but want to try it, they offer a 2-hour lesson for $69 that's guaranteed to turn you into a wave warrior or you get your money back. After that, you can rent a board for $20 an hour or $38 for 2 hours. If you want to make a day of it, a 10-hour card costs $150. Open daily from 10am to 5:30pm. Make your first right after the tollbooth to find the outfitters.

9 More Ways to Play, Indoors & Out

BIKING

The cement promenade on the southern tip of the island is a great place to ride. Biking up the beach is great for surf, sun, sand, exercise, and people-watching— just be sure to keep your eyes on the road as the scenery can be most distracting. Most of the big beach hotels rent bicycles, as does the **Miami Beach Bicycle Center,** 601 5th St., South Beach (© **305/674-0150**), which charges $5 per hour or $14 per day. It's open Monday to Saturday from 10am to 7pm, Sunday from 10am to 5pm.

Bikers can also enjoy more than 130 miles of paved paths throughout Miami. The beautiful and quiet streets of Coral Gables and Coconut Grove are great for bicyclists. Old trees form canopies over wide, flat roads lined with grand homes and quaint street markers. Several bike trails are spread throughout these neighborhoods, including one that begins at the doorstep of **Grove Cycle,** 3216 Grand Ave., Coconut Grove (© **305/444-5415**). Open Tuesday to Saturday from 11am to 5:30pm, Sunday from 11am to 6pm.

The terrain in Key Biscayne is perfect for biking, especially along the park and beach roads. If you don't mind the sound of cars whooshing by, **Rickenbacker Causeway** is also fantastic, since it is one of the only bikeable inclines in Miami from which you get fantastic elevated views of the city and waterways. **Key Biking,** 61 Harbor Dr., Key Biscayne (© **305/361-0061**), rents mountain bikes for $5 an hour or $15 a day. It's open Monday through Friday from 10am to 7pm, Saturday from 10am to 6pm, and Sunday from 11am to 4pm.

If you want to avoid the traffic altogether, head out to **Shark Valley** in the Everglades National Park—one of South Florida's most scenic bicycle trails and a favorite haunt of city-weary locals. For more information, see chapter 7.

A Berry Good Time

South Florida's farming region has been steadily shrinking in the face of industrial expansion, but you'll still find several spots where you can get back to nature while indulging in a local gastronomic delight—picking your own produce at the "U-Pic-'Em" Farms that dot South Dade's landscape. Depending on what's in season, you can get everything from fresh herbs and vegetables to a mélange of citrus and berries. During berry season—January to April—it's not uncommon to see hardy pickers leaving the groves with hands and faces that are stained a tale-telling crimson and garnished with happy smiles. On your way through South Dade, keep an eye out for the bright red "U-Pic" signs. There are also a number of fantastic fruit stands in the region.

Burr's Berry Farms, 12741 SW 216th St. (© **305/251-0145**), located in the township of Goulds, has created a sensation with their fabulous fruit milk shakes. To get there, go south on U.S. 1 and turn right on SW 216th Street. The fruit stand is about 1 mile west and on the same road as Monkey Jungle. Open daily from 9am to 5:30pm.

For fresh fruit in a yummy pastry or tart, head over to **Knaus Berry Farm** at 15980 SW 248th St. (© **305/247-0668**), in an area known as the Redlands. Some people erroneously call this farm an Amish farm, but in actuality it's run by a sect of German Baptists. The stand offers items ranging from fresh flowers to ice cream, but be sure to indulge in one of their famous homemade cinnamon buns. Be prepared to wait on a long line to stock up—people flock here from as far away as Palm Beach. Head south on U.S. 1 and turn right on 248th Street. The stand is 2½ miles farther on the left-hand side. Open Monday through Saturday from 8am to 5:30pm.

Biking note: Children under the age of 16 are required by Florida law to wear a helmet, which can be purchased at any bike store or retail outlet selling biking supplies.

FISHING

Some of the best surf casting in the city can be had at **Haulover Beach Park** at Collins Avenue and 105th Street, where there's a bait-and-tackle shop right on the pier. **South Pointe Park,** at the southern tip of Miami Beach, is another popular fishing spot and features a long pier, comfortable benches, and a great view of the ships passing through Government Cut.

You can also do some deep-sea fishing. One bargain outfitter, the **Kelley Fishing Fleet,** at the Haulover Marina, 10800 Collins Ave. (at 108th Street), Miami Beach (© **305/945-3801**), has half day, full day, and night fishing aboard diesel-powered "party boats." The fleet's emphasis on drifting is geared toward trolling and bottom fishing for snapper, sailfish, and mackerel, but it also schedules 2- and 3-day trips to the Bahamas. Half day and night fishing trips are $29 for adults and $20 for children; full day trips are $36 for adults and $18 for children; rod and reel rental is $5. Daily departures are scheduled at 9am, 1:45pm, and 8pm; reservations are recommended.

Tips **A Fisherman's Friend**

The Biscayne Bay area is prime tarpon fishing country and a pretty good spot for a lot of other trophy sportfish: snook, bonefish, dolphin, and sailfish. For a fee, local guides are happy to show you the hot spots and make sure you hook up. One such guide is **Capt. David Parsons (© 305/ 968-9603)**, who owns a 28-foot boat, *Hakuna Matada*. He will take you from Biscayne Bay to the Atlantic Ocean in search of the best catch of the day.

Also at the Haulover Marina is the charter boat *Helen C* (10800 Collins Ave.; © 305/947-4081). Although there's no shortage of private charter boats here, Capt. Dawn Mergelsberg is a good pick, since she puts individuals together to get a full boat. Her *Helen* is a twin-engine 55-footer, equipped for big-game "monster" fish like marlin, tuna, dolphin, shark, and sailfish. The cost is $85 per person. Full-day trips are available and cost $800. Group rates and specials are also available. Sailings are scheduled for 8am to noon and 1 to 5pm daily; call for reservations. Private charters and transportation are also available. Children are welcome.

Key Biscayne offers deep-sea fishing to those willing to get their hands dirty and pay a bundle. The competition among the boats is fierce, but the prices are basically the same no matter which you choose. The going rate is about $400 to $450 for a half day and $600 to $700 for a full day of fishing. These rates are usually for a party of up to six, and the boats supply you with rods and bait as well as instruction for first-timers. Some will take you out to Key Biscayne and even out to the Upper Keys if the fish aren't biting in Miami.

You might consider the following boats, all of which sail out of the Key Biscayne marina: *Sunny Boy III* (© 305/361-2217), *Queen B* (© 305/ 361-2528), and *L & H* (© 305/361-9318). Call for reservations.

Bridge fishing is also popular in Miami; you'll see people with poles over almost every waterway. But look carefully for signs telling you whether it's legal to do so wherever you are. Some bridges forbid fishing. The prime catches here are tarpon, snook, bonefish, dolphin, and sailfish.

GAMBLING

Although gambling is technically illegal in Miami, there are plenty of loopholes that allow all kinds of wagering. Gamblers can try their luck at offshore casinos, bingo, jai alai, card rooms, horse tracks, and dog races.

Especially popular is **Miccosukee Indian Gaming,** 500 SW 177th Ave. (off S.R. 41; © 800/741-4600 or 305/222-4600), where a touch of Vegas meets west Miami. This tacky casino isn't Caesar's Palace, but you can play tab slots, high-speed bingo (watch out for the serious blue-haired players who will scoff if you make too much noise or if you win before they do), and even poker (with a $10 maximum pot). With more than 85,000 square feet of playing space, the complex even offers overnight accommodations for those who can't get enough of the thrill.

One of the most popular gambling "cruises to nowhere" is the **Europa Sea Kruz.** It departs every afternoon and evening from Dock A at 1280 5th St., South Beach (© 800/688-PLAY or 305/538-8300). Tickets cost $10 to $15. A reasonably priced a la carte menu offers basic American fare, from hamburgers to grilled chicken and salads. Most evenings, you'll hear live music on board. You and a few hundred other passengers can play blackjack or the slots. The biggest drawback—if you're losing big or just get bored, you're stuck at sea for 4½ hours.

A newer and more elegant option is the *Casino Princesa,* which docks behind the Hard Rock Cafe in Bayside Marketplace. This 200-foot $15 million yacht has more than 200 slot machines, 32 tables, a restaurant, and four lounges in 10,000 square feet of gaming space on two decks. A major bargain (unless, of course, you lose) at $5.95 per person. Ships sail for 4½ hours from 12:30 to 5pm on weekdays and weekends and also from 7:30pm to midnight on weekend nights. Call ✆ **305/379-5825** for updated schedules.

GOLF

There are more than 50 private and public golf courses in the greater Miami area. Contact the **Greater Miami Convention and Visitors Bureau (✆ 800/ 283-2707** or 305/539-3063) for a list of more courses and costs.

The best hotel courses in Miami are found at the **Doral Golf Resort and Spa** (see chapter 4), home of the legendary Blue Monster course as well as the Gold Course designed by Raymond Floyd, the Great White Shark Course and the Silver Course, refinished by Jerry Pate.

Other hotels with excellent golf courses include the **Biltmore Hotel,** with modest greens fees and an 18-hole par-71 course located on the hotel's spectacular grounds, and the **Turnberry Isle Resort and Spa,** with two Robert Trent Jones–designed courses for guests and members. For more information, see chapter 4, "Accommodations."

Otherwise, the following represent some of the area's best public courses. **Crandon Park Golf Course,** formerly known as the Links, 6700 Crandon Blvd., Key Biscayne (✆ **305/361-9129**), is the no. 1 ranked municipal course in the state and one of the top five in the country. The park is situated on 200 bayfront acres and offers a pro shop, rentals, lessons, carts, and a lighted driving range. The course is open daily from dawn to dusk; greens fees (including cart) are $86 per person during the winter and $45 per person during the summer. Special twilight rates are available.

One of the most popular courses among real enthusiasts is the **Doral Park Golf and Country Club,** 5001 NW 104th Ave., West Miami (✆ **305/ 591-8800**); it's not related to the Doral Hotel or spa. Call to book in advance, since this challenging 18-holer is popular with locals. The course is open from 6:30am to 6pm during the winter and until 7pm during the summer. Cart and greens fees vary, so call ✆ **305/594-0954** for information.

Known as one of the best in the city, the **Golf Club of Miami,** 6801 Miami Gardens Dr., at NW 68th Avenue (✆ **305/829-8456**), has three 18-hole

---

⌐Tips Par for the Course

You can get information about most Florida courses, including current greens fees, and reserve tee times through **Tee Times USA,** P.O. Box 641, Flagler Beach, FL 32136 (✆ **800/374-8633,** 888/465-3567, or 904/439-0001; fax 904/439-0099). This company also publishes a vacation guide that includes many stay-and-play golf packages.

courses of varying degrees of difficulty. You'll encounter lush fairways, rolling greens, and some history to boot. The west course, designed in 1961 by Robert Trent Jones and updated in the 1990s by the PGA, was where Jack Nicklaus played his first professional tournament and Lee Trevino won his first professional championship. The course is open daily from 6:30am to sunset. Cart and greens fees are $45 to $75 per person during the winter, and $20 to $34 per person during the summer. Special twilight rates are available.

Golfers looking for some cheap practice time will appreciate **Haulover Park,** 10800 Collins Ave., Miami Beach (© **305/940-6719**), in a pretty bayside location. The longest hole on this par-27 course is 125 yards. It's open daily from 7:30am to 5:30pm during the winter, and until 7:30pm during the summer. Greens fees are $5 per person during the winter and $4 per person during the summer. Handcarts cost $1.40.

IN-LINE SKATING

Miami's consistently flat terrain makes in-line skating easy. Lincoln Road, for example, is a virtual skating rink as bladers compete with bikers and walkers for a slab of slate. But the city's heavy traffic and construction make it tough to find long routes. Remember to keep a pair of sandals or sneakers with you, since many area shops won't allow you inside with skates on.

Because of the popularity of blading and skateboarding, the city has passed a law prohibiting skating on the west side (the cafe-lined strip) of Ocean Drive in the evenings. In addition, the city has passed a law that all bladers must skate slowly and safely. You wouldn't want to mow down an elderly stroller.

You can still have fun, though, and the following rental outfit can help chart an interesting course for you and supply you with all the necessary gear. In South Beach, **Fritz's Skate Shop,** 726 Lincoln Rd. Mall (© **305/532-1954**), rents top-quality skates, including safety pads, for $8 per hour, $24 per day, and $34 overnight. If you're an in-line skater newbie, an instructor will hold your hand for $25 an hour. The shop also stocks lots of gear and clothing.

JUST FOR KIDS

The **Scott Rakow Youth Center,** 2700 Sheridan Ave. (© **305/673-7767**), is a hidden treasure on Miami Beach. This two-story facility boasts an ice-skating rink, bowling alleys, a basketball court, gymnasium equipment, and full-time supervision for kids. Call for a schedule of organized events. The only drag is that it's not open to adults (except on Sunday, which is family day). Admission is $1.50 per day for visiting children 9 to 17. Open daily from 2 to 8:30pm.

SWIMMING

There is no shortage of water here. See "The Best Beaches," and also the Venetian Pool under "Historic Homes & Sites," earlier in this chapter, for descriptions of good swimming options.

TENNIS

Hundreds of tennis courts in South Florida are open to the public for a minimal fee. Most courts operate on a first-come, first-served basis, and are open from sunrise to sunset. For information and directions, call the **City of Miami Beach Recreation, Culture, and Parks Department** (© **305/673-7730**), or the **City of Miami Parks and Recreation Department** (© **305/575-5256**).

The three hard courts and seven clay courts at the **Key Biscayne Tennis Association,** 6702 Crandon Blvd. (© **305/361-5263**), get crowded on weekends, since they're some of Miami's most beautiful. You'll play on the same courts as Lendl, Graf, Evert, McEnroe, and other greats; this is the venue for one of the world's biggest annual tennis events, the Ericsson Open (see "Florida Calendar of Events" in chapter 2). There's a pleasant, if limited, pro shop, plus many good pros. Only four courts are lit at night, but if you reserve at least 48 hours in advance, you can usually take your pick. They cost $6 per person per hour. The courts are open daily from 8am to 9pm.

Hotels with the best tennis facilities are the Biltmore, Turnberry Isle Resort and Spa, the Doral Golf Resort and Spa, and the Inn and Spa at Fisher Island. See chapter 4 for information about these accommodations.

10 Spectator Sports

Check the *Miami Herald*'s sports section for a daily listing of local events and the paper's Friday "Weekend" section for comprehensive coverage and in-depth reports. For last-minute tickets, call the venue directly, since many season ticket holders sell singles and return unused tickets. Expensive tickets are available from brokers or individuals, listed in the classified sections of the local papers. Some tickets are also available through **Ticketmaster** (✆ **305/358-5885**).

BASEBALL

The **Florida Marlins** shocked the sports world in 1997 when they became the youngest expansion team to win a World Series, but then floundered as their star players were sold off by former owner Wayne Huizenga. If you're interested in catching a game, be warned: The summer heat in Miami can be unbearable, even in the evenings. As long as the rebuilding process continues and the Marlins continue to struggle, tickets are easy to come by.

Home games are held at the **Pro Player Stadium,** 2267 NW 199th St., North Miami Beach (✆ **305/626-7426**). Tickets are $4 to $30. Box office hours are Monday to Friday from 8:30am to 6pm, Saturday from 8:30am to 4pm, and before games; tickets are also available through Ticketmaster. The team currently holds spring training in Melbourne, Florida.

BASKETBALL

The **Miami Heat** (✆ **305/577-HEAT** or 305/835-7000), now led by celebrity coach Pat Riley, made its NBA debut in November 1988 and their games remain one of Miami's hottest tickets. Courtside seats are full of visiting celebrities from Puff Daddy to Madonna. The season lasts from October to April, with most games beginning at 7:30pm. They'll now play in the brand-new waterfront **American Airlines Arena** located downtown on Biscayne Boulevard. Tickets are $14 to $50. Box office hours are Monday to Friday from 10am to 4pm (until 8pm on game nights); tickets are also available through Ticketmaster.

FOOTBALL

Miami's golden boys are the **Miami Dolphins,** the city's most recognizable team, followed by thousands of "dolfans." The team plays at least eight home games during the season, between September and December, at **Pro Player Stadium,** 2267 NW 199th St., North Miami Beach (✆ **305/620-2578**). Tickets cost between $20 and $40. The box office is open Monday to Friday from 8:30am to 5:30pm; tickets are also available through **Ticketmaster** (✆ **305/350-5050**).

HORSE RACING

Wrapped around an artificial lake, **Gulfstream Park,** at U.S. 1 and Hallandale Beach Boulevard, Hallandale (© **305/931-7223**), is both pretty and popular. Large purses and important races are commonplace at this suburban course, and the track is often crowded. Call for schedules. Admission is $3 to the grandstand and $3 to the clubhouse; free parking. From January through March, post times are Wednesday to Monday at 1pm. Many weekends feature live concerts by musicians well past their heyday, from Peter Frampton to Air Supply.

You might remember the pink flamingos at **Hialeah Park,** 2200 E. 4th Ave., Hialeah (© **305/885-8000**), from *Miami Vice*. This famous colony is the largest of its kind. The track, listed on the National Register of Historic Places, is one of the most beautiful in the world, featuring old-fashioned stands and acres of immaculately manicured grounds. Admission is $1 to the grandstand and $2 to the clubhouse on weekdays, and $2 and $4, respectively, on weekends. Children 17 and under enter free with an adult. Parking starts at $2. Races are held mid-March to mid-May, but the course is open year-round for sightseeing Monday to Saturday from 9am to 5pm. Call for post times.

ICE HOCKEY

The young **Florida Panthers** (© **954/835-7000**) have already made history. In the 1994–95 season, they played in the Stanley Cup finals, and they have amassed a legion of fans who love them. Much to the disappointment of Miamians, they moved to a new venue in Sunrise, the next county north of Miami–Dade. Call for directions and ticket information.

JAI ALAI

Jai alai, sort of a Spanish-style indoor lacrosse, was introduced to Miami in 1924 and is regularly played in two Miami-area frontons. Although the sport has roots stemming from ancient Egypt, the game as it's now played was invented by Basque peasants in the Pyrenees Mountains during the 17th century.

Players use woven baskets, called cestas, to hurl balls, called pelotas, at speeds that sometimes exceed 170 miles per hour. Spectators, who are protected behind a wall of glass, place bets on the evening's players.

The **Miami Jai Alai Fronton,** 3500 NW 37th Ave., at NW 35th Street (© **305/633-6400**), is America's oldest fronton, dating from 1926. It schedules 13 games per night. Admission is $1 to the grandstand, $5 to the clubhouse. It's open year-round. There are games Monday and Wednesday to Saturday at 7pm and matinees on Monday, Wednesday, and Saturday at noon.

11 Cruises & Other Caribbean Getaways

Cruising has come a long way since the days of bingo, shuffleboard, and even the delusional *Love Boat*. Whether you prefer megaships with rock-climbing walls or a smaller, less elaborate ship that just sails you to your destination, a floating vacation can be a very enticing option for people traveling to South Florida. The proximity to the Caribbean makes a 3-, 4- or 7-day cruise an excellent diversion from the hustle and bustle of the big city.

If you want to catch a weekend in the Caribbean while you're in South Florida but aren't enthralled with the idea of boat travel, there are a number of air packages available as well. Travel to Cuba is strictly prohibited from Miami (or anywhere in the United States) for all but those who have obtained licenses from the U.S. State Department, although many people choose to go there from Mexico, Jamaica, or the Bahamas.

The following sections aren't intended to be detailed descriptions of the cruising and package options available out of Miami and the Keys—that would fill up an entire book on its own—but they will give you a good overview of the cruising and package picture.

CRUISES

The Port of Miami is the world's busiest cruise-ship port, with a passenger load of close to 3 million annually. The popularity of these cruises shows no sign of tapering off, and the trend in ships is toward bigger, more luxurious liners. Usually all-inclusive, cruises offer value and simplicity compared to other vacation options. Most of the Caribbean-bound cruise ships sail weekly out of the Port of Miami. They are relatively inexpensive, can be booked without advance notice, and make for an excellent excursion.

All the shorter cruises are well equipped for gambling. Their casinos open as soon as the ship clears U.S. waters—typically 45 minutes after leaving port. Usually, four full-size meals are served daily, with portions so huge they're impossible to finish. Games, movies, and other onboard activities ensure you're always busy. Passengers can board up to 2 hours before departure for meals, games, and cocktails.

There are dozens of cruises from which to choose—from a 1-day excursion to a trip around the world. You can get a full list of options from the **Metro–Dade Seaport Department,** 1015 North America Way, Miami, FL 33132 (© **305/371-7678**). It's open Monday through Friday from 8am to 5pm.

The cruise lines and ships listed below offer 2- and 3-day excursions to the Caribbean, Key West, and other longer itineraries that change often. If you want more information, contact the individual line, or, for Bahamas cruises, call the **Bahamas Tourist Office,** 19495 Biscayne Blvd., Suite 809, Aventura, FL 33180 (© **305/932-0051**). All passengers must travel with a passport or proof of citizenship for reentry into the United States.

For detailed information on Caribbean cruises, pick up copies of *Frommer's Caribbean Cruises* and *Frommer's Caribbean Ports of Call.*

Carnival Cruise Lines (© **800/327-9501** or 305/599-2200; www.carnival. com) has 3- and 4-day cruises to Key West and the Caribbean as well as 7-day excursions that include stops in Mexico, Jamaica, and the Cayman Islands. Carnival's ships are appropriately known as Fun Ships, catering to a young party-hearty crowd. There's also a smoke-free ship called the *Paradise.* Cruises usually depart from Miami Friday through Monday. Prices range from $400 to $3,000, not including port charges, which can be as high as $100 per person.

Cunard (© **800/528-6273** or 305/463-3000; www.cunardline.com), which moved here in late 1997, is known for its old-world elegance. If you're looking for Internet cafes and ice-skating rinks, Cunard isn't for you. It caters to an older, sophisticated crowd. Its Miami ships include the legendary throwback from the halcyon days of the mighty luxe ocean liner, *Queen Elizabeth 2,* as well as the *Caronia* and the *Queen Mary 2.* Itineraries are usually at least 10 days long, though there are some that last 6 days, such as the jazz, fine arts, and big-band cruises. Prices start at $3,300 per person.

Norwegian Cruise Line (© **800/327-7030** or 305/436-0866; www.ncl. com) has four ships based in Miami during the winter months and usually one in the summer. NCL is known for its excellent theme cruises—mostly sports oriented. A mixture of young and old can be found on their ships. Ships go to Key West, the Bahamas, and the Western Caribbean. Its shortest cruises are 3 days; the longest—from Miami to France—is 15 days. Rates range from $349 per person for an inside cabin on the shortest cruises to $4,500 per person for the very best cabin on the transcontinental journey.

Royal Caribbean International (© **800/327-6700** or 305/539-6000; www.rccl.com), one of the premier lines in Miami, has about half a dozen ships departing Miami at any given time. The Port of Miami actually had to renovate three cruise terminals in 1999—at a price of $60 million—to accommodate Royal Caribbean's 142,000-ton ship *Voyager of the Seas,* which boasts an ice-skating rink and a rock-climbing wall, among other theme-park-like diversions. *Explorer of the Seas* is the line's second, newer, theme park at sea, also featuring extreme sports and an assortment of high-tech activities. As a result, RCI caters to a young, active crowd as well as families with children. The line mostly offers Caribbean cruises and some Bahamas destinations. The *Legend of the Seas* and the *Splendor of the Seas* offer 3- and 4-night Bahamas trips starting at $400. Longer trips can range from $1,600 per person to $7,500 for an 11-night cruise through the Caribbean.

FLIGHTS & WEEKEND PACKAGES

For those who want a quick getaway to the Caribbean without the experience of cruising, many airlines and hotels team up to offer extremely affordable weekend packages.

For example, the Bahamas' most entertaining and family-friendly resort, the **Atlantis** on Paradise Island (© **888-528-7155;** www.atlantis.com), is a tropical theme park offering extensive water sports plus an active casino. Reasonably priced 3-day packages start at about $390, depending on departure date. It's generally cheaper to fly midweek. Flights on **Continental Airlines** (© **800/ 786-7202**) or **Paradise Airlines** (© **800/231-0856**) depart at least twice daily from Miami International. You can also choose to stay in the company's other luxurious resorts: the Paradise Beach Resort or the Ocean Club. Book package deals through **Paradise Island Vacations** (© **800/722-7466**).

Other groups that arrange competitively priced packages include **American Flyaway Vacations,** operated by American Airlines (© **800/321-2121**); **Bahamas Air** (© **800/222-4262** or 305/593-1910); **Chalks Ocean Airways** (© **305/371-8628**); and the slightly run-down **Princess Casino** in Freeport (© **305/359-9898**). Call for rates, since they vary dramatically throughout the year and also depend on what type of accommodations you choose.

12 Shopping

There is no question that Miami is one of the world's premier shopping cities; more than 10 million visitors came here last year and they spent in excess of $13 billion. Visitors come to Miami from all over—from Latin America to Hong Kong—in search of something all-American. So if you're not into sunbathing and outdoor activities, or you just can't take the heat, you'll be in good company in one of Miami's many malls—and you are not likely to emerge empty-handed.

THE SHOPPING SCENE

Below, you'll find descriptions of some of the more popular retail areas, where many stores are conveniently clustered together to make browsing easier.

As a general rule, shop hours are Monday through Saturday from 10am to 6pm and Sunday from noon to 5pm. Many stores stay open late (until 9pm or so) one night of the week (usually Thursday). Shops in Coconut Grove are open until 9pm Sunday through Thursday, and even later on Friday and Saturday nights. South Beach's stores stay open later—as late as midnight. Department stores and shopping malls also keep longer hours, with most staying open from 10am to 9 or 10pm Monday through Saturday, and noon to 6pm on Sunday.

The 6.5% state and local sales tax is added to the price of all nonfood purchases.

Most Miami stores can wrap your purchase and ship it anywhere in the world via United Parcel Service (UPS). If they can't, you can send it yourself, either through UPS (© 800/742-5877) or through the U.S. Mail (see "Fast Facts: Miami" in chapter 4).

SHOPPING AREAS

AVENTURA   On Biscayne Boulevard between Miami Gardens Drive and the county line is a 2-mile stretch of major retail stores including Best Buy, Borders, Circuit City, Linens N' Things, Marshall's, Sports Authority, and more. Also here is the mammoth Aventura Mall, housing a fabulous collection of shops and restaurants; and Loehmann's Plaza, a small shopping village anchored around Loehmann's, the discount clothing store (see "Fashion," below).

CALLE OCHO   For a taste of "Little Havana," take a walk down 8th Street between SW 27th Avenue and 12th Avenue, where you'll find some lively street life and many shops selling cigars, baked goods, shoes, furniture, and record stores specializing in Latin music. Be sure to take your Spanish dictionary if you need it.

COCONUT GROVE   Downtown Coconut Grove, centered on Main Highway and Grand Avenue and branching onto the adjoining streets, is one of Miami's most pedestrian-friendly zones. The Grove's wide sidewalks, lined with cafes and boutiques, provide hours of browsing pleasure. Coconut Grove is best known for its chain stores (Gap, Banana Republic) and some funky holdovers from the days when the Grove was a bit more bohemian, plus excellent sidewalk cafes centered around CocoWalk and the Streets of Mayfair.

CORAL GABLES—MIRACLE MILE   Actually only a half-mile long, this central shopping street was an integral part of George Merrick's original city plan. Today, the strip still enjoys popularity, especially for its bridal stores, ladies' shops, haberdashers, and gift shops. Recently, newer chain stores, like Barnes and Noble, Old Navy, and Starbucks, have been appearing on the Mile. At press time, **Merrick Park,** a mammoth upscale shopping center between Ponce de León Boulevard and Le Jeune Road, and slated to feature Armani, Yves St. Laurent, Dean & DeLuca, the Palm, and the Greenhouse Spa, among others, was in construction, set to open September 2002. The Gables also features several excellent restaurants before it terminates at the City Hall rotunda.

DOWNTOWN MIAMI   If you're looking for discounts on all types of goods—especially watches, fabric, buttons, lace, shoes, luggage, and leather—Flagler Street just west of Biscayne Boulevard is the best place to start. I wouldn't necessarily recommend buying expensive items here as many stores are on the shady side. They do not understand the word *warranty.* Be prepared for some hustling and haggling. Most signs are printed in English, Spanish, and Portuguese; however, many shopkeepers may not be entirely fluent in English.

SOUTH BEACH—LINCOLN ROAD ⭐   This luxurious pedestrian mall, originally designed in 1957 by Morris Lapidus, recently underwent a multimillion-
dollar renovation restoring it to its former glory. Here, shoppers find an array
of clothing and art and a menagerie of South Beach's finest sidewalk cafes
flanked on one end by a multiplex movie theater, and at the other, the Atlantic
Ocean.

COLLINS & WASHINGTON AVENUES (between 6th & 9th Streets)
This is the Madison Avenue of Miami. For the hippest clothing boutiques
including Armani, Versace, Benetton, Agnes B, Guess?, Club Monaco, Kenneth
Cole, and Nicole Miller, among others, stroll along this pretty strip of the Deco
District.

SHOPPING A TO Z
ANTIQUES/COLLECTIBLES
Miami's antiques shops are scattered in small pockets around the city. Many that
feature lower-priced furniture can be found in North Miami, in the 1600 block
of Northeast 123rd Street near West Dixie Highway. About a dozen shops sell
china, silver, glass, furniture, and paintings. But you'll find the bulk of the better antiques in Coral Gables and in Southwest Miami along Bird Road between
64th and 66th avenues and between 72nd and 74th avenues. There are dozens
of shops with eclectic offerings; be sure to check out **Dietel's Antiques** (6572
Bird Rd., South Miami; ✆ 305/666-0724). For international collections from
Bali to France, check out the burgeoning scene in the Design District centered
on Northeast 40th Street west of 1st Avenue. Of note in this district is **Fine
Antiques William Limited** (91 NE 40th St., Design District; ✆ **305/
868-8889**). Miami also hosts several large antiques shows each year. In October
and November, the most prestigious one—the **Antique Show**—hits the Miami
Beach Convention Center (✆ **305/754-4931**). Exhibitors from all over come
to display their wares, including jewelry. There's also a decent monthly show at
the **Coconut Grove Convention Center** (✆ **305/444-8454**). Miami's huge
concentration of Deco buildings from the '20s and '30s makes this the place to
find the best selections of Deco furnishings and decorations. Following are some
more of my favorites:

Architectural Antiques   A great place to browse—if you don't mind a little
dust—this huge warehouse has an impressive stash of ironwork, bronzes, paintings, lamps, furniture, and sculptures, which have been salvaged from estates
worldwide. Don't be surprised to find odd items too, like an old British phone
booth or a pair of gargoyles off an ancient church. 2500 SW 28th Lane (just west of
U.S. 1), Miami. ✆ 305/285-1330. archantique@earthlink.net.

Modernism Gallery   Specializing in 20th-century furnishings from Gilbert
Rohde, Noguchi, and Heywood Wakefield, this shop has some of the most
beautiful examples of Deco goods from France and the United States. If they
don't have what you're looking for, ask. They possess the amazing ability to find
the rarest items. 1622 Ponce de León Blvd., Coral Gables. ✆ 305/442-8743.

Senzatempo *Finds*   If the names Charles Eames, George Nelso, or Gio Ponti
mean anything to you, then this is where you'll want to visit. There's retro, Euro
fabulous designer furniture and decorative arts from 1930 to 1960, as well as
collectible watches, timepieces, and clocks. 1655 Meridian Ave. (at Lincoln Rd.), South
Beach. ✆ 305/534-5588.

ART GALLERIES

Miami's finest art galleries are located within walking distance of one another in Coral Gables along Ponce de León Boulevard, extending from U.S. 1 to Bird Road. Check out **Elite Fine Art** (3140 Ponce de León Blvd.; ✆ 305/448-3800) when you're there. Still others are clustered in Bal Harbour's ritzy shopping district. South Beach's Lincoln Road, which once had dozens of galleries, now has only a few—a result of soaring rents. Stop by **Britto Central** at 818 Lincoln Rd (✆ 305/531-8821). Also, check out the burgeoning art scene in the Design District north of downtown just west of Biscayne Boulevard around 40th Street. A highlight here is **Evelyn S. Poole Ltd.** on Decorator's Row at 3925 N. Miami Ave (✆ 305/573-7463; www.evelynpoolettd.com).

If you happen to be in town on the first Friday of the month, you should take the free trolley tour of the Coral Gables Art District (call ✆ **305/448-3800**).

Listed below are more galleries of note.

Ambrosino Gallery   This well-respected gallery shows works by contemporary artists and stages performance art and installations. Closed for Christmas holidays. 769 NE 125th St. North Miami (across from the Museum of Contemporary Art). ✆ **305/891-5577**. www.ambrosinogallery.com.

Barbara Gillman Gallery   This gallery's ongoing exhibit of jazz photographer Herman Leonard's fantastic black and white photographs of legends such as Billie Holiday and Frank Sinatra has been so popular it hasn't changed in years. In addition to the works of Leonard and other renowned artists such as Andres Serrano, Andy Warhol, and James Rosenquist, the gallery displays the work of new local talent. 5582 NE 4th Court #5, Miami. ✆ **305/759-9155**.

Meza Fine Art Gallery Café *(Finds*   Dine amidst fine works of art in this funky gallery and cafe that specializes in Latin American artists, including Carlos Betancourt, Javier Marin, and Gloria Lorenzo (see also chapter 4). 275 Giralda Ave., Coral Gables. ✆ **305/461-2723**.

Wallflower Gallery *(Finds*   Funky, eclectic, and reminiscent of Andy Warhol's Factory, the Wallflower Gallery features an assortment of exhibits from local artists from erotica to exotica and everything in between. Performance art and live music are also featured here. 10 NE 3rd St., Miami. ✆ **305/579-0069**.

BOOKS

Barnes and Noble Booksellers   With half a dozen outlets in the area and more on the way, this huge chain offers anything readers could ask for, including a comfortable cafe, a large children's section, and tons of magazines. Plus, you'll get a 10% discount on all best-sellers and incredible close-out specials. 152 Miracle Mile, Coral Gables. ✆ **305/446-4152**. www.bn.com.

Books & Books   A dedicated following turns out to browse at this warm and wonderful little independent shop. Enjoy the upstairs antiquarian room, which specializes in art books and first editions. If that's not enough intellectual stimulation for you, the shop hosts free lectures from noted authors and experts almost nightly, from Monica Lewinsky to Martin Amis.

At the South Beach location (933 Lincoln Rd.; ✆ **305/532-3222**), you'll rub elbows with tanned and buffed South Beach bookworms sipping cappuccinos at the Russian Bear Cafe inside the store. They stock a large selection of gay literature and also feature lectures. 265 Aragon Ave., Coral Gables. ✆ **305/442-4408**. www.booksandbooks.com.

Kafka's Cyberkafe Check your e-mail and surf the Web while you sip a latte or snack on a sandwich or pastry with friendly neighborhood regulars. This popular used bookstore also stocks a wide range of foreign and domestic magazines and caters to an international youth hostel–type crowd. 1464 Washington Ave., South Beach. ℭ **305/673-9669.**

CIGARS

Although it is illegal to bring Cuban cigars into this country, somehow forbidden Cohibas show up at every dinner party and nightclub in town. Not that I condone it, but if you hang around the cigar smokers in town, no doubt one will be able to tell you where you can get some of the highly prized contraband. Be careful, however, of counterfeits.

The stores listed below sell excellent hand-rolled cigars made with domestic and foreign-grown tobacco. Many of the *viejos* (old men) got their training in Cuba working for the government-owned factories in the heyday of Cuban cigars.

La Gloria Cubana This tiny storefront shop employs about 45 veteran Cuban rollers who sit all day rolling the very popular torpedoes and other critically acclaimed blends. They've got backorders until next Christmas, but it's worth stopping in. They will sell you a box and show you around. 1106 SW 8th St., Little Havana. ℭ **305/858-4162.**

Mike's Cigars *Finds* Mike's recently moved to this location, but it's one of the oldest and best smoke shops in town. Since 1950, Mike's has been selling the best from Honduras, the Dominican Republic, and Jamaica, as well as the very hot local brand, La Gloria Cubana. Many say it has the best prices, too. 1030 Kane Concourse (at 96th St.), Bay Harbor Island. ℭ **305/866-2277.** www.mikescigars.com.

COSMETICS, FRAGRANCES & BEAUTY PRODUCTS

Brownes & Co. *Finds* Designed to look like an old-fashioned apothecary, this beauty emporium combines the best selection of makeup and hair products— MAC, Shu Uemura, Kiehl's, Stila, and Dr. Hauschka, just to name a few—with lots of delicious-smelling bath and body stuff, plus a full-service beauty salon. Feel free to browse and sample here, as you won't be bothered by perfume-spritzing salespeople. If you do need help, the staff is a collection of experts when it comes to beauty and hair products. Upstairs is the store's renowned salon, Some Like It Hot. 841 Lincoln Rd., South Beach. ℭ **305-532-8703.** www.brownesbeauty.com.

FASHION

Miami didn't become a fashion capital until, believe it or not, the pastel-hued, Armani-clad cops on *Miami Vice* had their close-ups. Before that, Miami was all about old men in white patent leather shoes and well-tanned women in bikinis. How things have changed. Miami is now a fashion mecca in its own right, with the some of the same high-end stores you'd find on Rue de Fauborg St. Honore in Paris or Bond Street in London. You'll find all of it, including Prada and Gucci, right here at the posh Bal Harbour Shops. For funkier frocks, South Beach is the place, where designers such as Cynthia Rowley, Betsey Johnson, and Giorgio Armani compete for window shoppers with local up-and-coming designers and those who design for drag queens and club kids only. The strip on Collins Avenue between 7th and 10th streets has become quite upscale, including such shops as Armani Exchange, Laundry Industry, Agnes B., and Nicole Miller, along with the inescapable Gap and Banana Republic. Of course, there's also more mainstream shopping in the plethora of malls and outdoor shopping and entertainment complexes.

UNISEX

Base A beautiful store featuring one-of-a-kind clothing made in St. Vincent that's light, breezy, fashionable, and, of course, pricey. Keep your eyes out for excellent sales. 939 Lincoln Rd., South Beach. © 305/531-4982.

Glitzy Tartz This outlandish boutique features everything you'd want if you were a go-go boy or girl, in vinyl, mesh, and lamé—all in several sizes way too tight to accentuate the, uh, positive. 1251 Washington Ave., South Beach. © 305/535-0068.

Island Trading One more part of music mogul Chris Blackwell's empire, Island sells everything you'll need to wear in a tropical resort town: batik sarongs, sandals, sundresses, bathing suits, cropped tops, and more. Many of the unique styles are created on the premises by a team of young, innovative designers. 1332 Ocean Dr., South Beach. © 305/673-6300.

Women's

Alice's Day Off For beachwear, Alice's is the place. Season after season, you'll find pretty and flattering floral patterns and many flashy bikinis. If an itsy-bitsy bikini is not your style, Alice's also has a range of more modest cuts. Three locations: Miami International Mall, 1455 NW 107th Ave, Miami. © 305/477-0393; Dadeland Mall, 7223 SW 88th St. Miami. © 305/663-7299; 5900 SW 72nd St., South Miami. © 305/284-0301. www.alicesdayoff.com.

Place Vendome For cheap and funky club clothes from zebra print pants to bright, shiny tops. Two locations: 934 Lincoln Rd., South Beach. © 305/673-4005; Aventura Mall, North Miami Beach. © 305/932-8931.

Therapy Opened by Ellen Lansburgh, who ran successful shops in Aspen and New York that catered to a famous clientele, including Cher and Goldie Hawn, this intimate boutique offers one-of-a-kind pieces. The clothes, made of luxurious fabrics such as silk, taffeta, and tulle, are elegant and comfortable. 1065 Kane Concourse, Bay Harbor Islands. © 305/861-6900.

Men's

Giorgio's One of the finest custom men's stores, Giorgio's features an extensive line of Italian suits and all the latest by Canelli. 208 Miracle Mile, Coral Gables. © 305/448-4302.

La Casa de las Guayaberas *(Finds* Miami's premier purveyor of the traditional yet retro-hip Cuban shirt known as the *guayabera*—a loose-fitting, pleated, button-down shirt—was founded by Ramon Puig, who emigrated to Miami over 40 years ago. He still uses the same scissors he did back then, only now he's joined by a team of seamstresses who hand-sew 20 shirts a day in all colors and styles. Prices range from $15 to $375. 5840 SW 8th St., Little Havana. © 305/266-9683.

Wilke Rodriguez Miami designer Eddie Rodriguez is a Latin Hugo Boss, with high-fashion suits in linens and light wool blends made especially for warmer climates. Cool T-shirts, shorts, and jackets are also part of this line, which is a local status symbol for many of Miami's fashion-conscious males. Prices range from the high $50s for T-shirts to $275 and up for jackets. 801 Washington Ave., South Beach. © 305/534-4030.

Accessories

SEE This fantastic eyewear store featuring an enormous selection of stylish specs—all priced at $169, including your prescription. The staff is patient and knowledgeable. 921 Lincoln Rd., South Beach. © 305/672-6622.

Simons and Green Fantastic sterling silver jewelry, leather goods, and other assorted high-end tchotchkes and gift items are what you'll find in this quaint mainstay on South Miami's Sunset Drive. 5842 Sunset Dr., South Miami. © 305/667-1692.

Children's

Most department stores have extensive children's sections. But if you can't find what you are looking for, consider one of the many Baby Gaps or Gap Kids outlets around town or try one of the specialty boutiques listed here.

French Kids Inc. This fashionable boutique imports beautiful (and expensive) clothes for newborns to teenagers. 5829 Sunset Dr., South Miami. © 305/667-5880.

Roland Children's Wear You'll find a unique assortment of kid's clothes for dress-up or playtime. They specialize in cute, funky stuff. 450 41st St., Miami Beach. © 305/531-0130.

Lingerie

Belinda's This German designer makes some of the most beautiful and intricate teddies, nightgowns, and wedding dresses. The styles are a little too Stevie Nicks for me, but the creations are absolutely worth admiring. The prices are appropriately up there. 827 Washington Ave., South Beach. © 305/532-0068.

Corset Corner As the name suggests, this little old store on Miracle Mile sells the basic, good old-fashioned gear. 300 Miracle Mile, Coral Gables. © 305/444-6643.

La Perla The only store in Florida that specializes in this superluxurious Italian intimate apparel. Of course, you could fly to Milan for the price of a few bras and a nightgown, but you can't find better quality. Also in Bal Harbour, see Flash Lingerie (© **305/868-7732**), which carries a diverse selection of imports. 9700 Collins Ave. (in the Bal Harbour Shops), Bal Harbour. © 305/864-2070.

FOOD

There are dozens of ethnic markets in Miami, from Cuban bodegas to Jamaican import shops and Guyanese produce stands. Check the phone book under grocers for listings. I've listed a few of the biggest and best markets in town that sell prepared foods as well as staple items. On Saturday mornings, vendors set up stands loaded with papayas, melons, tomatoes, and citrus, as well as cookies, ice creams, and sandwiches on South Beach's Lincoln Road.

Biga Bakery You'll be happy to pay upward of $6 a loaf when you sink your teeth into these inimitable Old-World–style breads. Also, most of the locations have a to-die-for prepared food counter serving up everything from chicken curry salad to hummus and pot pies. Pastries and cakes are as gorgeous as they are delicious. Several locations include 1080 Alton Rd., South Beach. © **305/535-1008;** 305 Alcazar, Coral Gables. © **305/446-2111.** Check directory for other locations.

Epicure This is the closest thing Miami Beach has got to the famed Balducci's or Dean & DeLuca. Here, you'll find not only fine wines, cheeses, meats, fish, and juices, but some of the best produce, such as portobello mushrooms the size of a yarmulke. This neighborhood landmark is best known for supplying the

Jewish residents of the beach with all the Jewish favorites, such as matzo ball soup, gefilte fish, and deli items. Prices are steep, but generally worth it. The cakes in particular are rich and decadent, and a rather large one doesn't cost more than $10. 1656 Alton Rd., Miami Beach. (✆ 305/672-1861.

JEWELRY

For name designers like Gucci and Tiffany & Co., go to the Bal Harbour Shops (see "Malls," below).

International Jeweler's Exchange   At least 50 jewelers hustle their wares from individual counters at one of the city's most active jewelry centers. Haggle your brains out for excellent prices on timeless antiques from Tiffany's, Cartier, or Bulgari, or on unique designs you can create yourself. 18861 Biscayne Blvd. (in the Fashion Island), North Miami Beach. (✆ 305/931-7032.

Seybold Building   Jewelers of every assortment gather here daily to sell diamonds and gold. With 300 jewelry stores located inside this independently owned and operated multilevel treasure chest, the glare is blinding as you enter. You'll see handsome and up-to-date designs, but note that there aren't too many bargains to be had here. 36 NE 1st St., Downtown. (✆ 305/374-7922. www. seyboldbldg.com.

MALLS

There are so many malls in Miami and more being built that it would be impossible to mention them all. What follows is a list of the biggest and most popular.

You can find any number of nationally known department stores including Saks Fifth Avenue, Macy's, Lord & Taylor, Sears, and JCPenney in the Miami malls listed below, but Miami's own is **Burdines,** at 22 E. Flagler St., Downtown ((✆ 305/835-5151), and 1675 Meridian Ave. (just off Lincoln Rd.) in South Beach ((✆ 305/674-6311). One of the oldest and largest department stores in Florida, Burdines specializes in good-quality home furnishings and fashions.

Aventura Mall   A multimillion-dollar makeover has made this spot one of the premier places to shop in South Florida. With more than 2.3 million square feet of space, this airy, Mediterranean-style mall has a 24-screen movie theater and more than 250 stores. The mall offers moderate to high-priced merchandise and is extremely popular with families. A large indoor playground, Adventurer's Cove, is a great spot for kids. There are numerous theme restaurants and a food court that eschews the usual suspects in favor of local operations. The mall provides free shuttle service to and from the top downtown and Miami Beach hotels. 19501 Biscayne Blvd. (at 197th St. near the Dade–Broward County line), Aventura. (✆ 305/935-1110. www.shopaventuramall.com.

Bal Harbour Shops   One of the most prestigious fashion meccas in the country, Bal Harbour offers the best-quality goods from the finest names. Giorgio Armani, Dolce & Gabbana, Christian Dior, Fendi, Joan & David, Krizia, Rodier, Gucci, Brooks Brothers, Waterford, Cartier, H. Stern, Tourneau, and many others are sandwiched between Neiman-Marcus and a newly expanded Saks Fifth Avenue. Well-dressed shoppers stroll in a pleasant open-air emporium, featuring several good cafes, covered walkways, and lush greenery. 9700 Collins Ave. (on 97th St., opposite the Sheraton Bal Harbour Hotel), Bal Harbour. (✆ 305/866-0311. www.balharbourshops.com.

Bayside Marketplace   A popular stop for cruise-ship passengers, this touristy waterfront marketplace is filled with the usual suspects of chain stores as well as a slew of tacky gift shops and carts hawking assorted junk in the heart of downtown Miami. The second-floor food court is stocked with dozens of fast-food choices and bars. Most of the restaurants and bars stay open later than the stores. In June you can watch the Opsail show, and in February, the Miami Sailboat Show. Beware of the adjacent amphitheater known as Bayfront Park, which usually hosts large-scale concerts and festivals, causing major pedestrian and vehicle traffic jams. 401 Biscayne Blvd., Downtown. ✆ 305/577-3344. www. baysidemarketplace.com.

Dadeland Mall   One of the county's first malls, Dadeland features more than 175 specialty shops but if you're not in the area, however, the mall is not worth the trek. Additionally, many non-Spanish-speaking people are put off by Dadeland because of the predominance of Spanish-speaking store employees. 7535 N. Kendall Dr. (intersection of U.S. 1 and SW 88th St., 15 minutes south of Downtown), Kendall. ✆ 305/665-6226.

Dolphin Mall   As if Miami needed another mall, this $250 million megamall and amusement park rivals Broward County's monstrous Sawgrass Mills outlet. The 1.4-million-square-foot mall features outlets such as Off Saks Fifth Avenue, plus shops, a 28-screen movie theater, and, not to be outdone by the Mall of the Americas, a roller coaster. Florida Turnpike at S.R. 836, West Miami. ✆ 305/365-7446.

Falls Shopping Center   Traffic to this mall borders on brutal, but once you get there, you'll feel a slight sense of serenity. Tropical waterfalls are the setting for this outdoor shopping center with dozens of moderately priced and slightly upscale shops. Miami's first Bloomingdale's is here, as are Polo, Ralph Lauren, Caswell-Massey, and more than 60 other specialty shops. If you are planning to visit any of the nearby attractions, which include Metro Zoo and Monkey Jungle, check with customer service for information on discount packages. 8888 Howard Dr. (at the intersection of U.S. 1 and 136th St., about 3 miles south of Dadeland Mall), Kendall. ✆ 305/255-4570. www.shopthefalls.com.

Sawgrass Mills   Just as some people need to take a tranquilizer to fly, others need one to traipse through this mammoth mall—the largest outlet mall in the country. Depending on what type of shopper you are, this experience can either be blissful or overwhelming. If you've got the patience, it is worth setting aside a day to do the entire place. Though it's located in Broward County, it is a phenomenon that attracts thousands of tourists and locals sniffing out bargains. (See chapter 9, "The Treasure Coast," for more details.)

From Miami, buses run three times daily; the trip takes just under an hour and costs $10 round-trip. Call **Coach USA** (✆ 305/887-6223) for exact pickup points at major hotels. If you are driving, take I-95 north to 595 west to Flamingo Road. Exit and turn right, driving 2 miles to Sunrise Boulevard. You can't miss this monster on the left. Parking is free, but don't forget where you parked your car or you might spend a day looking for it. 12801 W. Sunrise Blvd., Sunrise. ✆ 800/ FL-MILLS.

Shops at Sunset Place   Completed in early 1999 at a cost of over $140 million, this sprawling outdoor shopping complex offers more than just shopping. Visitors experience high-tech special effects, such as daily tropical storms (minus the rain) and the electronic chatter of birds and crickets. In addition to a 24-screen movie complex and an IMAX theater, there's a GameWorks—Steven Spielberg's Disney-esque playground for adults—a Virgin Records store, and a NikeTown. 5701 Sunset Dr. (at 57th Ave. and U.S. 1, near Red Rd.), South Miami. ✆ 305/ 663-0482.

MUSIC

Blue Note Records *(Finds)*   Here for more than 15 years, Blue Note is music to the ears of music fanatics with hard-to-find progressive and underground music. There are new, used, and discounted CDs and old vinyl, too. Call to find out about performances. Some great names show up occasionally. A second location features jazz and LPs only. 16401 NE 15th Ave., North Miami Beach. © 305/940-3394. Fax 305/948-3583. For jazz/LPs: 2299 NE 164th St., North Miami Beach © 305/354-4563. www. bluenoterecords.com.

Casino Records Inc.   The young, hip salespeople here speak English and tend to be music buffs. You'll find the largest selection of Latin music in Miami, including pop icons such as Willy Chirino, Gloria Estefan, Albita, and local boy Nil Lara. Their slogan translates to "If we don't have it, forget it." Believe me, they've got it. 1208 SW 8th St., Little Havana. © 305/856-6888.

Esperanto Music *(Finds)*   According to the experts, this independently owned record store boasts the city's best collection of Cuban and Latin music. 513 Lincoln Rd, Miami Beach. © 305/ 534-2003.

Revolution Records and CDs   Here you'll find a quaint and fairly well-organized collection of CDs, from hard-to-find jazz to original recordings of Buddy Rich. They'll search for anything and let you hear whatever you like. 1620 Alton Rd., Miami Beach. © 305/673-6464.

Yesterday and Today Records *(Finds)*   This is Miami's most unique and well-stocked store for vinyl—you know, the audio dinosaur that went out with the Victrola? Y & T, as it's known, is a collector's heaven, featuring every genre of music imaginable on every format. Chances are, you could find some eight-track tapes, too. 7902 NW 36th St., Miami. © 305/468-0311.

SPORTS EQUIPMENT

People-watching seems to be the number-one sport in South Florida, but for the more athletic pursuits consider these shops. One of the area's largest chains is the **Sports Authority,** with at least six locations throughout the county. Check the white pages for details.

Alf's Golf Shop   This is the best pro shop around. The knowledgeable staff can help you with equipment for golfers of every level, and the neighboring golf course offers discounts to Alf's clients. 524 Arthur Godfrey Rd., Miami Beach. © 305/ 673-6568; 15369 S. Dixie Hwy., Miami. © 305/378-6086.

Bird's Surf Shop   If you're a hard-core surfer or just want to look like one, head to Bird's Surf Shop. Although Miami doesn't regularly get huge swells, if you're here during the winter and one should happen to hit, you'll be ready. The shop carries more than 150 boards. Call its surf line (© 305/947-7170) to find the best waves from South Beach to Cape Hatteras and even the Bahamas and Florida's West Coast. 250 Sunny Isles Blvd., North Miami Beach. © 305/940-0929. www. birdsurfshop.com.

Island Water Sports   You'll find everything from booties to gloves to baggies and tanks. Check in here before you rent that WaveRunner or Windsurfer. 16231 Biscayne Blvd., North Miami. © 305/944-0104.

Golf Headquarters *(Finds)*   This chain store guarantees the lowest prices on golf equipment and accessories. There's more than 6,000 square feet of store here; you can even practice your swing at an indoor driving range, where a radar gun will clock your speed. 7930 NW 36th Ave. (near the airport), Miami. © 305/593-2999.

X-Isle Surf Shop   Prices are slightly higher at this beach location, but you'll find the hottest styles and equipment. They also offer surfboard rental. Free surf report at ☎ **305/534-7873.** 437 Washington Ave., South Beach. ☎ **305/673-5900.**

THRIFT STORES/RESALE SHOPS

Children's Exchange   Selling everything from layettes to overalls, this pleasant little shop is chock-full of good Florida-style stuff for kids to wear to the beach and in the heat. 1415 Sunset Dr., Coral Gables. ☎ **305/666-6235.**

Red White & Blue   Miami's best-kept secret is this mammoth thrift store that is meticulously organized and well stocked. You've got to search for great stuff, but it is there. There are especially good deals on children's clothes and housewares. 12640 NE 6th Ave., North Miami. ☎ **305/893-1104.**

WINES & SPIRITS

Most gourmet stores carry wines and beers. See "Food," above.

Estate Wines & Gourmet Foods   This exceedingly friendly storefront in the middle of Coral Gables' main shopping street offers a small but well-chosen selection of vintages from around the world. It also sells a great array of gourmet cheeses, pâtés, salads, and sandwiches. 92 Miracle Mile (at Douglas and Galiano), Coral Gables. ☎ **305/442-9915.**

13 Miami After Dark

With all the hype, you'd have expected Miami to have long outlived its 15 minutes of fame by now. But you'd be wrong. Miami's nightlife, especially in South Beach, is hotter than ever. Practically every club has installed closely guarded velvet ropes to create an air of exclusivity. Don't be fooled or intimidated by them—you can go clubbing in the magic city, I've provided tips below to ensure entry. South Beach is certainly Miami's uncontested nocturnal nucleus, but more and more suburban areas, such as the Design District, South Miami, and even Little Havana, are providing fun alternatives without the ludicrous cover charges and drink prices. And while South Beach dances to a more electronic beat, other parts of Miami dance to a Latin beat—from salsa and merengue to tango and cha cha. However, if you're looking for a less frenetic good time, Miami's bar scene offers something for everyone, from haute hotel bars to sleek, loungey watering holes.

If the possibility of a celebrity sighting doesn't fulfill your cultural needs, Miami also offers a variety of first-rate diversions in theater, music, and dance, including a world-class ballet under the aegis of Edward Villella, a recognized symphony, and a talented opera company.

For up-to-date listing information, and to make sure time hasn't elapsed for the club of the moment, check the *Miami Herald*'s "Weekend" section, which runs on Friday, or the more comprehensive listings in *New Times*, Miami's free alternative weekly, available each Wednesday, or visit www.miamicitysearch.com online.

BARS & LOUNGES

There are countless bars in and around Miami with the highest concentration on trendy South Beach. The selection listed below is a mere sample. Keep in mind that many of the popular bars—and the easiest to get into—are in hotels. For a clubbier scene, if you don't mind making your way through hordes of inebriated club kids, a stroll on Washington Avenue will provide you with ample

Ground Rules: Stepping Out in Miami

First things first: Nightlife on South Beach doesn't really get going until after 11pm. As a result, you may want to consider taking what is known as a disco nap so that you'll be fully charged until the wee hours. Second: If you're unsure of what to wear out on South Beach, your safest bet will be anything black. Third: Do *not* try to tip the doormen manning the velvet ropes. That will only make you look desperate and you'll find yourself standing outside for what will seem like an ungodly amount of time. Instead, try to land your name on the ever-present guest lists by calling the club early in the day yourself, or, better yet, having the concierge at your hotel do it for you. Concierges have connections. If you don't have connections and you find yourself without a concierge, then act assertive, not surly, at the velvet rope, and your patience will usually be rewarded with admittance. If all else fails—for men, especially—surround yourself with a few leggy model types and you'll be noticed quicker. Finally, have fun. It may look like serious business when you're on the outside, but once you're in, it's another story. Attacking clubland with a sense of humor is the best approach to a successful, memorable evening out.

insight into what's hot and what's not. Just hold onto your bags. It's not dangerous, but occasionally a few shady types manage to slip into the crowd. Another very important tip when in a club: Never put your drink down out of your sight—there have been unfortunate incidents in which drinks have been spiked with illegal chemical substances. For a less hard-core, collegiate nightlife, head to Coconut Grove. Unless mentioned, the bars listed below generally don't charge a cover. Most require proof that you are over 21 to enter.

Blue A very laid-back, very locals scene set to a sultry soundtrack of deep soul and deep house music has Miami's hipsters feeling the blues on a nightly basis from 10pm to 5am. Before you whip out the St. John's Wort, reconsider your mood and dive into this so-not-trendy-it's-trendy lounge, in which the pervasive color blue will actually heighten your spirits as an eclectic haze of models, locals, and lounge lizards gather to commiserate in their dreaded trendy status. 222 Española Way (between Washington and Collins Aves.), South Beach. ✆ **305/534-1009.** No cover.

Clevelander If wet T-shirt contests and a fraternity party atmosphere are your thing, then this Ocean Drive mainstay is your kind of place. Popular with tourists and locals who like to pretend they're tourists, the Clevelander attracts a lively, sporty, adults-only crowd. A great time to check the Clevelander out is on a weekend afternoon. 1020 Ocean Dr., South Beach. ✆ **305/531-3485.** www.clevelanderhotel.com. No cover.

Fox's Sherron Inn *Finds* The spirit of Frank Sinatra is alive and well at this dark and smoky watering hole that dates back to 1946. Everything down to the vinyl booths and the red lights make Fox's a retro fabulous dive bar. 6030 S. Dixie Hwy. (at 62nd Ave.), South Miami. ✆ **305/661-9201.** No cover.

Laundry Bar   The only place in Miami where it's okay to let friends drink and dry. Laundry Bar features working washers, dryers, a fully stocked bar, and several other distractions to help make doing your laundry a fun rather than a dreaded chore. It's also one of the only bars on South Beach open from 7am to 5am daily. 721 Lincoln Lane (behind Burdines off Lincoln Rd.), South Beach. ✆ **305/531-7700.** www.laundrybar.com. No cover.

Lola *(Finds)*   Lola redefines the neighborhood bar, striking the perfect balance between chill and chic. This bar, located away from the South Beach mayhem, is a showgirl in her own right—a swank, sultry lounge where people are encouraged to come as they are, leaving the attitude at home. Attracting a mixed crowd of gay, straight, young, and old(er), Lola reinvents itself each night with deejays spinning everything from retro '80s music to hard rock and classic oldies. 247 23rd St., South Beach. ✆ **305/695-8697.** No cover.

Mac's Club Deuce   Standing on its own amidst an oasis of trendiness, Mac's Club Deuce is the quintessential dive bar, with cheap drinks and a cast of characters ranging from your typical barfly to your atypical drag queen. For no-nonsense imbibing, this is the place to be, with a well-stocked juke box, friendly bartenders, a pool table, and best of all, it's an insomniac's dream, open daily from 8am to 5am. 222 14th St., South Beach. ✆ **305/673-9537.** No cover.

Purdy Lounge   With the exception of a wall of lava lamps, Purdy is not unlike your best friend's basement, featuring a pool table and a slew of board games such as Operation to keep the attention deficit disordered from getting bored. With no cover and no attitude, a line is inevitable, so be prepared to wait. 1811 Purdy Ave., Miami Beach. ✆ **305/531-4622.** No cover.

Wet Willie's   With such telling drinks as "Call a Cab," this beachfront oasis is not the place to go if you have a long drive ahead of you. A popular pre-and post-beach hangout, Wet Willie's inspires serious drinking. Popular with the Harley Davidson set, tourists, and beachcombers, this bar is best known for its rooftop patio (get there early if you plan to get a seat) and its half-nude bikini beauties. 760 Ocean Dr., South Beach. ✆ **305/532-5650.** No cover. There's another Wet Willie's in Coconut Grove at 3390 Mary St., but it's not as fun (✆ **305/443-5060**), on the third level of Mayfair.

THE CLUB & MUSIC SCENE
LIVE MUSIC
Surprisingly, Miami's live music scene is not thriving. More thriving than local bands are local deejays who skyrocket to fame thanks to the city's lauded dance club scene. However, there are several places that strive to bring Miami up to speed as far as live music is concerned. You just have to look—and listen—for it a bit more carefully.

Churchill's Hideaway *(Finds)*   British expatriate Dave Daniels couldn't live in Miami without a true English-style pub, so he opened Churchill's Hideaway, the city's premier space for live, loud rock music. Filthy and located in a rather unsavory neighborhood, Churchill's is committed to promoting and extending the lifeline of the lagging local music scene. 5501 NE 2nd Ave., Miami. ✆ **305/757-1807.** Cover $0–$5.

Jazid *(Finds)*   Smoky, sultry, and illuminated by flickering candelabras, Jazid is the kind of place where you'd expect to hear Sade's "Smooth Operator" on constant rotation. Instead, however, you'll hear live jazz—sometimes on acid—soul and funk. 1342 Washington Ave., South Beach. ✆ **305/673-9372.** No cover.

Checking into Hotel Bars

While South Beach is known for its trendy club scene, hotel bars are very much a part of the nightlife. Among the hottest hotel bars are the **Rose Bar** at the Delano (1685 Collins Ave., South Beach; ✆ **305/ 672-2000**), the **lobby bar at the Hotel Astor** (956 Washington Ave., South Beach; ✆ **305/ 672-1402**), the **Bond St. Lounge** at the Townhouse (150 20th St., South Beach; ✆ **305/534-3800**), the **Tower Bar** at the Shore Club (1901 Collins Ave., Miami Beach; ✆ **305/695-3222**), the **lobby bar at the Whitelaw Hotel** (808 Collins Ave., Miami Beach; ✆ **305/398-7000**), and the **Marlin Bar** at the Marlin Hotel (1200 Collins Ave., Miami Beach; ✆ **305/604-5063**).

Power Studios *Finds*   A nocturnal funhouse for the Ritalin generation, Power Studios takes the concept of multimedia to new heights with several performance spaces, an art gallery, a disco, an outdoor Latin-Caribbean patio, and a rooftop restaurant and cinema. Local bands—good ones, at that—clamor for a spot in the limelight, as many as four or five performing on a nightly basis. 3701 NE 2nd Ave., Miami. ✆ **305/573-8042**. Cover $0–$10.

Satchmo Blues   This is a very popular happy-hour hangout. In fact, it's a restaurant, club, and bar all rolled into one. Every Friday night it's packed by locals and curious visitors—spilling over the sidewalks and into the streets—looking for an exciting night out. If you're lucky enough to get inside, you can listen to a live jazz, blues, or rock band playing everything from Chuck Berry to Miles Davis. 60 Merrick Way, Coral Gables (1 block from Coral Way and Douglas Rd). ✆ **305/ 774-1883**. www.miamiblues. Cover $5–$10 Fri–Sat.

Tobacco Road   Al Capone used to hang out here when it was a speakeasy. Now, locals flock here to see local bands perform, as well as national acts such as George Clinton and the P-Funk All-Stars, Koko Taylor, and the Radiators. It's small, it's gritty, and it's meant to be that way. 626 S. Miami Ave. (over the Miami Ave. Bridge near Brickell Ave.), Downtown. ✆ **305/374-1198**. Cover $5 Fri–Sat.

Upstairs at the Van Dyke Café *Finds*   The cafe's jazz bar, located on the second floor, resembles a classy speakeasy in which local jazz performers play to an intimate, enthusiastic crowd of mostly adults and sophisticated young things, who huddle at the small tables often until the wee hours. 846 Lincoln Rd., Miami Beach. ✆ **305/534-3600**. Cover $3–$6 for a seat; no cover at the bar.

DANCE CLUBS

Anyone who's ever salvaged a disastrous party knows the rescue effort usually boils down to one thing: good music. Fortunately, the club music found on Miami's ever-evolving social circuit is good enough to get even the most rhythmically challenged wallflowers dancing. *Note:* As with anything on Miami's nocturnal circuit, call in advance to make sure that the dance club you're planning to go to hasn't become a video arcade.

To keep things fresh in clubland, local promoters throw one-nighters, which are essentially parties with various themes or motifs, from funk to fashion. Because these change so often, we can't possibly list them here. Word of mouth, local advertising, and listings in the free weekly *New Times,* miami. citysearch.com, or the Weekend section of the *Miami Herald* are the best ways to find out about these ever-changing events.

320   The second coming of the haute spot formerly known as Bar Room (which closed abruptly after its twentysomething owner was thrown in prison for dealing in "family" business), 320 imitates its predecessor in that it aims to create itself in the likeness of Studio 54. Unfortunately, it falls flat because it tries too hard. 320 Lincoln Rd., South Beach. ✆ **305/672-2882.** Cover $15 and up, unless you're on the guest list (see "Ground Rules: Stepping Out in Miami," above).

Bongos Cuban Café   Gloria Estefan's latest hit in the restaurant business pays homage to the sites, sounds, and cuisine of pre-Castro Cuba, Bongo's is a mammoth restaurant attached to the American Airlines Arena in downtown Miami. At the American Airlines Arena, 601 Biscayne Blvd. ✆ **786/777-2100.** Cover $20.

Club Space   Clubland hits the mainland with this cavernous downtown warehouse of a club. With over 30,000 square feet of dance space, you can spin around a la Stevie Nicks (albeit to a techno beat) without having to worry about banging into someone. However, after hours, Club Space packs them in. While Saturday caters to a more homogeneous crowd, Friday is a free-for-all. Conveniently, the club often runs shuttles from the beach. 142 NE 11th St., Miami. ✆ 305/ **577-1007.** Cover $0–$20.

crobar *(Finds*   Still haunted by the ghost of clubs past, the space formerly known as the Cameo Theatre is now possessed by a mod industrial spirit. With its intense, dance-heavy sound system, an industrially chic ambience, and crowds big enough to scare away any memories of a sadly abandoned Cameo, this Chicago import has raised the bar on South Beach nightlife with crazy theme nights, top-name deejays, and the occasional celebrity appearance. On Sunday, the club hosts an extremely popular gay night. 1445 Washington Ave., South Beach. ✆ **305/531-8225.** www.crobarmiami.com. Cover $25.

Level   Overdone and some say overhyped, Level takes the notion of South Beach excess even further with its outlet mall–sized, 40,000-square-foot space featuring four dance floors, three levels, five rooms, and nine bars. Like a video game, your status here is determined by which level you can land on. If you call in advance, the accommodating staff will usually put you on the guest list. Friday night is a very popular gay night, while the rest of the week attracts a mixed crowd of straight, gay, and somewhere in between. Celebs love Level because it has so many VIP rooms. 1235 Washington Ave., South Beach. ✆ **305/532-1525.** www. levelnightclub.com. Cover $20–$30.

Living Room at the Strand   What you'll find in this model-decorated Living Room is a blanket of beautiful people lazing about, sipping the finest champagne, and waxing philosophical on the ways of the fabulous world. Beware of the often nasty, so-called Door Nazis, who get their thrills from rejecting the sea of people that only parts for six-foot Amazonian model types or Eurotrash who wouldn't be caught dead anywhere else. 671 Washington Ave., South Beach. ✆ 305/ **532-2340.** www.livingroom2000.com. Cover $15–$20.

Nikki Beach Club *(Finds*   What the Playboy Mansion is to Hollywood, the Nikki Beach Club is to South Beach. It's the product of local nightlife royalty— Tommy Pooch and Eric Omores. Bare-naked ladies and men actually venture into the daylight (around 4pm) to see, be seen, and, at times, be obscene. At night, it's very sexy in a tiki hut sort of way. The Sunday afternoon beach party is almost legendary and worth a glimpse—that is, if you can get in. Also located within this bastion of hedonism is the superhot **Pearl,** a mod-ish, 380-seat, orange hued restaurant and lounge that features a Continental menu created by Nikki chef Brian Rutherford. Forget the food and go for the eye candy. 101 Ocean Dr., South Beach. ⓒ 305/538-1111. Cover $10–$20.

Rumi   Named after a 13th-century Sufi mystic, South Beach's first upscale supper club was, at press time, scheduled to open summer 2001. Designed by hot NYC designers Nancy Mah and Scott Kester, Rumi will be an urbane oasis of reds, tans, and chocolates, reminiscent of the golden age of supper clubs of the '30s and '40s. This massive space features intimate lounge areas as well as private and public dining rooms, in which haute Florida-Caribbean cuisine will be served until the tables conspicuously disappear and give way to a neo-Zen-like stomping ground for South Beach's chic elite. 330 Lincoln Rd., South Beach. ⓒ 305/672-4353. www.rumimiami.com. No cover.

THE GAY & LESBIAN SCENE

Miami and the beaches have long been host to what is called a "first-tier" gay community. Similar to the Big Apple, the Bay Area, or LaLa land, Miami has had a large alternative community since the days when Anita Bryant used her citrus power to boycott the rise in political activism in the early '70s. Well, things have changed and Miami–Dade now has a gay rights ordinance.

Newcomers intending to party in any bar, whether downtown or certainly on the beach, will want to check ahead for the schedule, as all clubs must have a gay or lesbian night to pay their rent. Best bets are Sundays at crobar and Fridays at Level. Miami Beach, in fact, is the capital of the gay circuit party scene, rivaling San Francisco, Palm Springs, and even the mighty Sydney, Australia, for tourist dollars.

Cactus Bar & Grill   Somewhere, over the causeway, there is life beyond South Beach for Miami's gay society. Housed in a large two-story space, Cactus attracts a mix of unpretentious, professional, and also very attractive men and women. There's something for everyone here, whether it's the indoor pool tables, the outdoor swimming pool, or drinks that are considerably cheaper than on South Beach. Friday evening happy hours and Sunday afternoon Tea Dances are a virtual cattle call, attracting hordes of folks looking to quench their thirst for fun at Miami's sprawling urban oasis. 2401 Biscayne Blvd., Downtown. ⓒ 305/438-0662. No cover.

Federation 1235   Hordes of gay men (and some women) join the Federation at Level every Friday, when the dance floor is packed with wall-to-wall hard bodies. 1235 Washington Ave., South Beach. ⓒ 305/532-1525. Cover $20–$30.

Loading Zone   A leather and Levi bar known for its cruisability, pool tables, movies, and pitchers of beer. There's an in-house leather store for the kinky shopper. 1426 Alton Rd., South Beach. ⓒ 305/531-5623. Cover $15–$20.

Salvation   For those seeking liberation from the cookie-cutter mold of run-of-the-mill Saturday night dance clubs, Salvation is where you'll find it. Housed in an old warehouse, Salvation is spacious but always filled to capacity with shirtless, sweaty circuit boys dancing themselves into oblivion. Major deejays spin here, and, at times, divas sing here, such as Bette Midler, who did a rare and ribald cabaret performance to an SRO audience. 1771 West Ave., Miami Beach. ⓒ 305/673-6508. Cover $20.

Score   There's a reason this Lincoln Road hotbed of gay social activity is called Score. In addition to the huge pick-up scene, Score offers a multitude of bars, dance floors, lounge-like areas, and outdoor tables in case you need to come up for air. Sunday afternoon Tea Dances are legendary here. 727 Lincoln Rd., South Beach. ℂ 305/535-1111. No cover.

Twist   One of the of the most popular bars (and hideaways) on South Beach (and literally across the street from the police station), this recently expanded bar has a casual yet lively local atmosphere. It's open from 1pm to 5am. 1057 Washington Ave., South Beach. ℂ 305/538-9478. No cover.

LATIN CLUBS

Considering that Hispanics make up a large part of Miami's population and that there's a huge influx of Spanish-speaking visitors, it's no surprise that there are some great Latin nightclubs in the city.

Plus, with the meteoric rise of the international music scene based in Miami, many international stars come through the offices of MTV Latino, SONY International, and a multitude of Latin TV studios based in Miami—and they're all looking for a good club scene on weekends. Most of the Anglo clubs reserve at least 1 night a week for Latin rhythms.

Cafe Nostalgia   As the name implies, Cafe Nostalgia is dedicated to reminiscing about old Cuba. After watching a Celia Cruz film, you can dance to the hot sounds of Afro-Cuban jazz. With pictures of old and young Cuban stars smiling down on you and a live band celebrating Cuban heritage, Cafe Nostalgia sounds like a bit much, and it is. Be prepared—it's packed after midnight and dance space is mostly between the tables. Open Thursday to Sunday from 9pm to 4am. Films are shown from 10pm to midnight, followed by live music. Another location is on Miami Beach next to the Forge restaurant. 2212 SW 8th St. (Calle Ocho), Miami. ℂ 305/541-2631. Cover $10 Thurs–Sun.

Casa Panza *(Finds*   This *casa* is one of Little Havana's liveliest and most popular nightspots. Every Tuesday, Thursday, and Saturday night, Casa Panza, in the heart of Little Havana, becomes the House of Flamenco, with shows at 8 and 11pm. You can either enjoy a flamenco show or strap on your own dancing shoes and participate in the celebration. Enjoy a fantastic Spanish meal before the show, or just a glass of sangria before you start stomping. 1620 SW 8th St. (Calle Ocho), Miami. ℂ 305/643-5343. No cover.

La Covacha *(Finds*   Forget about the love shack and get thee to the Latin shack that is La Covacha. This hut, located virtually in the middle of nowhere (West Miami), is the hottest Latin joint in the entire city. Sunday features the best in Latin rock, with local and international acts. Friday is *the* night here, so much that the owners had to place a red velvet rope out front to maintain some semblance of order. 10730 NW 25th St. (at NW 107th Ave.), Miami. ℂ 305/594-3717. Cover $0–$10.

Mango's Tropical Café   Claustrophobic types do not want to go near Mango's. Ever. One of the most popular spots on Ocean Drive, this outdoor enclave of Latin liveliness shakes with the intensity of a Richter-busting earthquake. Welcome and *bienvenido,* Mango's is *Cabaret,* Latin style. Nightly live Brazilian and other Latin music, not to mention scantily clad male and female dancers, draw huge gawking crowds in from the sidewalk from 11am to 5am. But pay attention to the music if you can: Incognito international musicians often lose their anonymity and jam with the house band on stage. 900 Ocean Dr., South Beach. ℂ 305/673-4422. Cover $5–$15; varies by performer.

THE PERFORMING ARTS
THEATER

Highbrows and culture vultures complain that there is a dearth of decent cultural offerings in Miami. What do locals tell them? Go back to New York! In all seriousness, however, the performing arts scene has improved greatly in recent years. The city's Broadway Series features Tony Award–winning shows (the touring version, of course). The performances aren't always Broadway caliber, but they are usually pretty good and not nearly as pricey! Local arts groups such as the Miami Light Project, a not-for-profit cultural organization that presents live performances by innovative dance, music, and theater artists, have had huge success in attracting big-name artists such as Nina Simone and Philip Glass to Miami. In addition, a burgeoning bohemian movement in Little Havana has given way to performance spaces that have become nightclubs in their own right.

The **Actors' Playhouse,** at the newly restored Miracle Theater at 280 Miracle Mile, Coral Gables (ℂ **305/444-9293**), is a grand 1948 Art Deco movie palace with a 600-seat main theater and a smaller theater/rehearsal hall that hosts a number of excellent musicals for children throughout the year. In addition to these two rooms, the Playhouse recently added a 300-seat children's balcony theater. Tickets run from $26 to $50.

The **Coconut Grove Playhouse,** 3500 Main Hwy., Coconut Grove (ℂ **305/442-4000**), was also a former movie house, built in 1927 in an ornate Spanish rococo style. Today, this respected venue is known for its original and innovative staging of both international and local dramas and musicals. The house's second, more intimate Encore Room is well suited to alternative and experimental productions. Tickets run from $37 to $42.

The **Gables Stage** at the Biltmore Hotel, Anastasia Avenue, Coral Gables (ℂ **305/445-1119**), stages at least one Shakespearean play, one classic, and one contemporary piece a year. This well-regarded theater usually tries to secure the rights to a national or local premiere as well. Tickets cost $22 and $28; $10 and $17 for students and seniors.

The **Jerry Herman Ring Theatre** is on the main campus of the University of Miami in Coral Gables (ℂ **305/284-3355**). The University's Department of Theater Arts uses this stage for advanced-student productions of comedies, dramas, and musicals. Faculty and guest actors are regularly featured, as are contemporary works by local playwrights. Performances are usually scheduled Tuesday through Saturday during the academic year. In the summer, don't miss "Summer Shorts," a selection of superb one-acts. Tickets sell for $5 to $20.

The **New Theater,** 65 Almeria Ave., Coral Gables (ℂ **305/443-5909**), prides itself on showing world-renowned works from America and Europe. As the name implies, you'll find mostly contemporary plays, with a few classics thrown in for variety. Performances are staged Thursday to Sunday year-round. Tickets are $20 on weekdays, $25 weekends. If tickets are available on the day of the performance, and they usually are, students pay half price.

CLASSICAL MUSIC

In addition to a number of local orchestras and operas, which regularly offer quality music and world-renowned guest artists, each year brings a slew of special events and touring artists. One of the most important and longest-running series is produced by the **Concert Association of Florida (CAF),** 555 17th St., South Beach (© **305/532-3491**). Known for more than a quarter of a century for its high-caliber, star-packed schedules, CAF regularly arranges the best "serious" music concerts for the city. Season after season, the schedules are punctuated by world-renowned dance companies and seasoned virtuosi like Itzhak Perlman, Andre Watts, and Kathleen Battle. Since CAF does not have its own space, performances are usually scheduled in the Dade County Auditorium or the Jackie Gleason Theater of the Performing Arts (see below). The season lasts from October through April, and ticket prices range from $20 to $70.

Florida Philharmonic Orchestra   South Florida's premier symphony orchestra, under the direction of James Judd, presents a full season of classical and pops programs interspersed with several children's and contemporary popular music performances. The Philharmonic performs downtown in the Gusman Center for the Performing Arts and at the Dade County Auditorium. 1243 University Dr., Miami. © **800/226-1812** or 305/476-1234. Tickets $15–$60. When extra tickets are available, students are admitted free on day of performance.

Miami Chamber Symphony   This professional orchestra is an inexpensive alternative to the high-priced classical venues. Renowned international soloists perform regularly. The season runs October to May, and most concerts are held in the Gusman Concert Hall, on the University of Miami campus. 5690 N. Kendall Dr., Kendall. © **305/858-3500**. Tickets $12–$30.

New World Symphony   This organization, led by artistic director Michael Tilson Thomas, is a stepping stone for gifted young musicians seeking professional careers. The orchestra specializes in ambitious, innovative, energetic performances and often features renowned guest soloists and conductors. The symphony's season lasts from October to May during which time there are many free concerts. 541 Lincoln Rd., South Beach. © **305/673-3331**. www.nws.org. Tickets free–$58. Rush tickets (remaining tickets sold 1 hour before performance) $20. Students $10 (1 hour before concerts limited seating).

OPERA

Florida Grand Opera   Around for over 60 years, this company regularly features singers from top houses in both America and Europe. All productions are sung in their original language and staged with projected English supertitles. Tickets become scarce when Placido Domingo or Luciano Pavarotti (who made his American debut here in 1965) comes to town. The opera's season runs roughly from November to April, with five performances each week. A new multimillion-dollar headquarters for the opera is scheduled to open in late 2002; until then, performances take place at the Miami–Dade Auditorium and the Broward Center for the Performing Arts. Box office: 1200 Coral Way, Miami. © **800/ 741-1010** or 305/854-1643; 305/854-7890 for box office. www.fgo.org. Tickets $19–$145. Student discounts available.

DANCE

Several local dance companies train and perform in the Greater Miami area. In addition, top traveling troupes regularly stop at the venues listed above. Keep your eyes open for special events and guest artists.

Ballet Flamenco La Rosa   For a taste of local Latin flavor, see this lively troupe perform impressive flamenco and other styles of dance on Miami stages. © **305/672-0552** or 305/757-8475. Tickets $25 at door, $20 in advance, $18 for students and seniors.

Miami City Ballet This artistically acclaimed and innovative company, directed by Edward Villella, features a repertoire of more than 60 ballets, many by George Balanchine, and more than 20 world premieres. The company moved into a new $7.5 million headquarters in January 2000—the Ophelia and Juan Jr. Roca Center at the Collins Park Cultural Center in Miami Beach. The three-story center features eight rehearsal rooms, a ballet school, a boutique, and ticket offices. The City Ballet season runs from September to April. Ophelia and Juan Jr. Roca Center, Collins Ave. and 22nd St., Miami Beach. (C) **305/532-4880** or 305/532-7713 for box office. Tickets $17–$50.

MAJOR VENUES

After a much-needed $1 million face-lift, the **Colony Theater,** on Lincoln Road in South Beach ((C) **305/674-1026**), has become an architectural showpiece of the Art Deco District. This multipurpose 465-seat theater stages performances by the Miami City Ballet and the Ballet Flamenco La Rosa, as well as off-Broadway shows and other special events.

At the **Miami–Dade Auditorium,** West Flagler Street at 29th Avenue, Miami ((C) **305/547-5414**), performers gripe about the lack of space, but for patrons, this 2,430-seat auditorium is the only Miami space in which you can hear the opera—for now. A multimillion-dollar performing arts center downtown has been in the works for years. For now, the Dade County Auditorium is home to the city's Florida Grand Opera, and it also stages productions by the Concert Association of Florida, many Spanish programs, and a variety of other shows.

At the 1,700-seat **Gusman Center for the Performing Arts,** 174 E. Flagler St., Downtown Miami ((C) **305/372-0925**), seating is tight, and so is funding, but the sound is superb. In addition to producing a regular stage for the Phil-harmonic Orchestra of Florida and the Miami Film Festival, the elegant Gus-man Center features pop concerts, plays, film festival screenings, and special events. The auditorium was built as the Olympia Theater in 1926, and its ornate palace interior is typical of that era, complete with fancy columns, a huge pipe organ, and twinkling "stars" on the ceiling.

Not to be confused with the Gusman Center (above), the **Gusman Concert Hall,** 1314 Miller Dr., at 14th Street, Coral Gables ((C) **305/284-6477**), is a roomy 600-seat hall that gives a stage to the Miami Chamber Symphony and a varied program of university recitals.

The elegant **Jackie Gleason Theater of the Performing Arts (TOPA),** located at Washington Avenue at 17th Street, South Beach ((C) **305/673-7300**), is the home of the Miami Beach Broadway Series, which recently presented *Rent, Phantom of the Opera,* and *Les Misérables.* This 2,705-seat hall also hosts other big-budget Broadway shows, classical concerts, opera, and dance performances.

At press time, the city granted a budget in excess of $200 million for its official performing arts center. Planned are a 2,400-seat ballet/opera house and a 2,000-seat concert hall for the Florida Philharmonic, Florida Grand Opera, New World Symphony, and Miami City Ballet, and a major concert series. Designed by world-renowned architect Cesar Pelli, the center will be the focal point of a planned Arts, Media and Entertainment District in mid-Miami. The complex will be wrapped in limestone, slate, decorative stone, stainless steel, glass curtain walls, and tropical landscaping. A major new destination point for the community, more than 500,000 people, including 100,000 schoolchildren, will attend the center's year-round schedule of performances and activities. Millions more will participate in related events and will visit the site annually.

MOVIES & MORE
CINEMAS

In addition to the annual Miami Film Festival in February and other, smaller film events (See " Florida Calendar of Events" in chapter 2), Miami is lucky to have some wonderful art cinemas showing a range of films from *Fresa y Chocolate* to *Crumb*.

Absinthe Cinemateque, 235 Alcazar Ave., Coral Gables (© **305/446-7144**), is a small one-screen theater that shows good movies, often Spanish-language films, without the hustle and bustle of the crowded multiplexes. Tickets are $6.

Astor Art Cinema, 4120 Laguna St. (© **305/443-6777**), is an oasis in the midst of a desert of Cineplex Odeons and AMCs in Coral Gables. This quaint double theater hosts foreign, classic, independent, and art films and serves decent popcorn, too. Tickets are $5, $3 for seniors.

The **Bill Cosford Cinema** at the University of Miami (© **305/284-4861**) is named after the deceased *Herald* film critic. This well-endowed little theater was recently revamped and boasts high-tech projectors, new air-conditioning, and new decor. It sponsors independent films, lectures by visiting filmmakers, and festivals. Admission is $5.

The **Mercury Theatre,** Biscayne Boulevard at 55th Street, Miami (© **305/ 759-8809**), is the city's newest art house cinema, showing classic and contemporary films from all over the world.

Miami's **Artemis Performance Network,** a group of performing artists, visual artists, musicians, presenters, educators, and administrators, is turning Little Havana into a bohemian hangout. Backed by the support of the Miami–Dade County Cultural Affairs Council and others, the network sponsors events at a loft-like performance space known as PS 742. Events such as Surreal Saturdays (first Saturday of every month) feature a funky roster of spoken word, multimedia, and musical artists. It's at 742 SW 16th Ave., Little Havana (© **305/ 643-6611**).

6

The Keys

by Lesley Abravanel

The drive from Miami to the Keys is a slow descent into an unusual but breathtaking American ecosystem: On either side of you, for miles ahead, lies nothing but emerald waters. (On weekends, however, also for miles ahead on a narrow highway, is plenty of traffic.) Strung out across the Atlantic Ocean like loose strands of cultured pearls are more than 400 islands that make up this 150-mile-long chain of the Keys. Of course you want to go for the peaceful waters and the year-round warmth, but don't forget to explore the amazing sea life. Countless species of brilliantly colored fish can be found swimming above the ocean's floor. You'll also discover a stunning abundance of tropical and exotic plants, birds, and reptiles.

Despite the usually calm landscape, these rocky islands can be treacherous, as a series of tropical storms, hurricanes, and tornadoes reminded residents in the summer and fall of 1998 when millions of dollars of damage was inflicted. The exposed coast has always posed dangers to those on land as well as at sea.

When Spanish explorers Juan Ponce de León and Antonio de Herrera sailed amid these craggy, dangerous rocks in 1513, they and their men dubbed the string of islands "Los Martires" (The Martyrs) because they thought the rocks looked like men suffering in the surf. It wasn't until the early 1800s that the larger islands were settled by rugged and ambitious pioneers, who amassed great wealth by salvaging cargo from ships sunk nearby. Actually, legend has it that these shipwrecks were sometimes caused by the "wreckers," who occasionally removed navigational markers from the shallows to lure unwitting captains aground. At the height of the salvaging mania (in the 1830s), Key West boasted the highest per capita income in the country.

However, wars, fires, hurricanes, mosquitoes, and the Depression took their toll on these resilient islands in the early part of this century, causing wild swings between fortune and poverty. In 1938, the spectacular Overseas Highway (U.S. 1) was finally completed atop the ruins of Henry Flagler's railroad, opening the region to tourists, who had never before been able to drive to this seabound destination. These days, the highway connects more than 30 of the populated islands in the Keys. The hundreds of small, undeveloped islands that surround these "mainline" keys are known locally as the "backcountry" and are home to dozens of exotic animals and plants. Therein lie some of the most renowned outdoor sporting opportunities, from bone fishing to spear fishing and—at appropriate times of the year—diving for lobsters. To get to the backcountry, you must take to the water—a vital part of any trip to the Keys. Whether you fish, snorkel, dive, or just cruise, include some time on a boat in your itinerary; otherwise, you haven't truly seen the Keys.

The sea and the teeming life beneath it are the main attractions here. Warm, shallow waters nurture living coral that supports a complex delicate ecosystem of plants and animals—sponges, anemones, jellyfish, crabs, rays, sharks, turtles, snails, lobsters, and thousands of types of fish. This vibrant underwater habitat thrives on one of only two living tropical reefs in the entire North American continent (the other is off the coast of Belize). As a result, anglers, divers, snorkelers, and water-sports enthusiasts of all kinds come to explore. Keen observers and sportsmen have begun to differentiate between the shallow waters of the western (Gulf) side of the island chain and the deeper and rougher waters of the eastern (Atlantic) side.

Heavy traffic has taken its toll on this fragile ecoscape, but conservation efforts are underway. In fact, environmental efforts in the Keys exceed those in many high-traffic visitor destinations.

Although the atmosphere throughout the Keys is that of a laid-back beach town, don't expect to find many impressive beaches here, especially after the damaging effects of the tropical storms and hurricanes in 1998. Beaches are mostly found in a few private resorts and some small, sandy beaches in John Pennekamp State Park, Bahia Honda State Park, and in Key West. One great exception is Sombrero Beach in Marathon.

The Keys are divided into three sections, both geographically and in this chapter. The Upper and Middle Keys are closest to the Florida mainland, so they are popular with weekend warriors who come by boat or car to fish, drink, or relax in towns like Key Largo, Islamorada, and Marathon. Further on, just beyond the impressive 7-mile bridge (which actually measures only 6.4 miles), are the Lower Keys, a small, unspoiled swath of islands teeming with wildlife. Here, in the protected regions of the Lower Keys is where you're most likely to catch sight of the area's many endangered animals. With patience, you may spot the rare eagle, egret, or Key deer. Also, keep an eye out for alligators, turtles, rabbits, and a huge variety of birds.

The last section of this chapter is devoted to the renowned island called Key West, literally at the end of the road. Made famous by the Nobel Prize–winning rogue Ernest Hemingway, this tiny island is the most popular destination in the Florida Keys, overrun with cruise-ship passengers and day-trippers, as well as franchises and T-shirt shops. More than 1.6 million visitors pass through each year. Still, you'll find in this "Conch Republic" a tightly knit community of permanent residents who cling fiercely to their live-and-let-live attitude—an atmosphere that has made Key West famously popular with painters, writers, and free spirits.

EXPLORING THE KEYS BY CAR

After you have gotten off the Florida Turnpike and landed on U.S. 1, which is also known as the Overseas Highway (see "Getting There," under "Essentials," below), you'll have no trouble negotiating these narrow islands.

The Overseas Highway is the only main road connecting the Keys. The scenic, lazy drive from Miami to Key West can be very enjoyable if you have the patience to linger and explore the diverse towns and islands along the way. If you have the time, I recommend allowing at least 2 days to work your way down to Key West and 3 or more days once there.

Most of U.S. 1 is a narrow, two-lane highway, with some wider passing zones along the way. The speed limit is usually 55 miles per hour (35 to 45 mph on

The Florida Keys

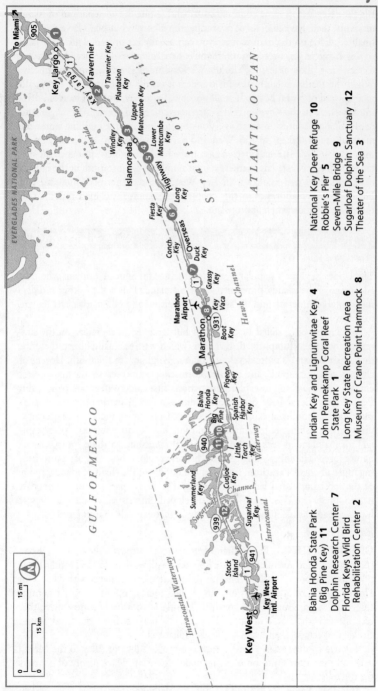

National Key Deer Refuge **10**
Robbie's Pier **5**
Seven-Mile Bridge **9**
Sugarloaf Dolphin Sanctuary **12**
Theater of the Sea **3**

Indian Key and Lignumvitae Key **4**
John Pennekamp Coral Reef
State Park **1**
Long Key State Recreation Area **6**
Museum of Crane Point Hammock **8**

Bahia Honda State Park
(Big Pine Key) **11**
Dolphin Research Center **7**
Florida Keys Wild Bird
Rehabilitation Center **2**

Big Pine Key and in some commercial areas). Despite the protestations of island residents, there has been talk of expanding the highway, but plans have not been finalized. Even on the narrow road, you can usually get from downtown Miami to Key Largo in just over an hour. If you're determined to drive straight through to Key West, allow at least 3½ hours. Weekend travel is another matter entirely: When the roads are jammed with travelers from the mainland, the trip could take upward of 5 to 6 hours. If at all possible, I strongly urge you to avoid driving anywhere in the Keys on Friday afternoons or Sunday evenings.

To find an address in the Keys, don't bother looking for building numbers; most addresses (except in Key West and parts of Marathon) are delineated by mile markers (MM), small green signs on the roadside, which announce the distance from Key West. The markers start at number 127, just south of the Florida mainland. The zero marker is in Key West, at the corner of Whitehead and Fleming streets. Addresses in this chapter are accompanied by a mile marker (MM) designation when appropriate.

1 The Upper & Middle Keys: Key Largo ⍟⍟ to Marathon ⍟

58 miles SW of Miami

The Upper Keys are a popular, year-round refuge for South Floridians who take advantage of the islands' proximity to the mainland. This is the fishing and diving capital of America, and the swarms of outfitters and billboards never let you forget it.

Key Largo, once called Rock Harbor but renamed to capitalize on the success of the 1948 Humphrey Bogart film (which wasn't actually filmed there), is the largest key and is more developed than its neighbors to the south. Dozens of chain hotels, restaurants, and tourist information centers service the many water enthusiasts who come to explore the nation's first underwater state park, **John Pennekamp Coral Reef State Park,** and its adjacent marine sanctuary. **Islamorada,** the unofficial capital of the Upper Keys, offers the area's best atmosphere, food, fishing, entertainment, and lodging. It's an unofficial "party capital" for mainlanders seeking a quick tropical excursion. In these "purple isles," nature lovers can enjoy walking trails, historic explorations, and big-purse fishing tournaments. **Marathon,** smack in the middle of the chain of islands, is one of the most populated keys. It is part fishing village, part tourist center, part nature preserve. This area's highly developed infrastructure includes resort hotels, a commercial airport, and a highway that expands to four lanes.

ESSENTIALS

GETTING THERE   From Miami International Airport, take Le Jeune Road (Northwest 42nd Avenue) to Route 836 west. Follow signs to the Florida Turnpike South (about 7 miles). The turnpike extension connects with U.S. 1 in Florida City. Continue south on U.S. 1. For a scenic option, weather permitting, take Card Sound Road south of Florida City, a backcountry drive that reconnects with U.S. 1 in upper Key Largo. The view from the Card Sound Bridge is spectacular and well worth the dollar toll.

If you're coming from Florida's west coast, take Alligator Alley to the Miami exit and then turn south onto the turnpike extension. Have plenty of quarters for the tolls.

American Eagle (© 800/433-7300) has daily nonstop flights from Miami to Marathon, which is near the midpoint of the chain of keys and at the very

---

Moments No Place like Homestead

On its own, there's not much to the waterfront shack that is Alabama Jack's. The bar serves beer and wine only, and the restaurant specializes in greasy bar fare. But this quintessential Old Floridian dive, located between Homestead and Key Largo, is a colorful must on the drive south. Hordes of Harley Davidson bikers, local Miamians, barflies, and anglers flock here with much devotion, and the views of the mangroves are spectacular. Pull up a barstool, order a cold one, and take in the sights—at the bar and in the bay. To get there, pick up Card Sound Road (the old Route 1) a few miles after you pass Homestead, heading toward Key Largo. Alabama Jack's is on the right-hand side and can't be missed. 5800 Card Sound Rd., Homestead. © **305/248-8741.**

---

southern end of the area referred to here as the Upper and Middle Keys. Fares range from $88 to $336 round-trip, depending on the season.

Greyhound (© **800/231-2222;** www.greyhound.com) has buses leaving Miami for Key Largo every day. Prices range up to $20. Seats fill quickly in season, so come early. It's first come, first served.

VISITOR INFORMATION   Avoid the many "Tourist Information Centers" that dot the main highway. Most are private companies hired to lure visitors to specific lodgings or outfitters. You're better off sticking with the official, not-for-profit centers that are extremely well located and staffed. In particular, the **Key Largo Chamber of Commerce,** U.S. 1 at MM 106, Key Largo, FL 33037 (© **800/822-1088** or 305/451-1414; fax 305/451-4726; www.keylargo.org) runs an excellent facility, with free direct-dial phones and plenty of brochures. Headquartered in a handsome clapboard house, the chamber operates as an information clearinghouse for all of the Keys and is open daily from 9am to 6pm.

The **Islamorada Chamber of Commerce,** in the Little Red Caboose, U.S. 1 at MM 82.5, P.O. Box 915, Islamorada, FL 33036 (© **800/322-5397** or 305/ 664-4503; fax 305/664-4289; www.islamoradachamber.com), also offers maps and literature on the Upper Keys.

You can't miss the big blue Visitors Center at MM 53.5, the **Greater Marathon Chamber of Commerce,** 12222 Overseas Hwy., Marathon, FL 33050 (© **800/842-9580** or 305/743-5417; fax 305/289-0183; www. floridakeysmarathon.com).

OUTDOOR SIGHTS & ACTIVITIES

Anne's Beach (at MM 73.5) is really more of a picnic spot than a full-fledged beach, but die-hard suntanners still congregate on this tiny strip of coarse sand that was damaged beyond recognition during the series of storms in 1998. Plans are in place to reconstruct the boardwalk and huts, but at press time, work had not yet started.

A better choice for real beaching is **Sombrero Beach** 🌟🌟 in Marathon at the end of Sombrero Beach Road (near MM 50). This wide swath of uncluttered beachfront actually benefited from Hurricane George in September 1998 with generous deposits of extra sand and a facelift courtesy of the Monroe County Tourist Development Council. More than 90 feet of sand is dotted with stands of palms, Australian Pines, and Royal Poincianas. There are barbecue grills, clean bathrooms, and some brand new tiki huts. Admission and parking at this little-known spot is free.

If you are interested in seeing the Keys in their natural state, before modern development, you must venture off the highway and take to the water. Two backcountry islands that offer a glimpse of the "real" Keys are **Indian Key and Lignumvitae Key** ⭐⭐. Visitors come here to relax and enjoy the islands' colorful birds and lush hammocks (elevated pieces of land above a marsh).

Named for the lignum vitae ("wood of life") trees found there, **Lignumvitae Key** supports a virgin tropical forest, the kind that once thrived on most of the Upper Keys. Over the years, human settlers imported "exotic" plants and animals to the Keys, irrevocably changing the botanical makeup of many backcountry islands and threatening much of the indigenous wildlife. Over the past 25 years, the Florida Department of Natural Resources has successfully removed most of the exotic vegetation, leaving this 280-acre site much as it existed in the 18th century. The island also holds a historic house built in 1919 that has survived numerous hurricanes. **Indian Key,** a much smaller island on the Atlantic side of Islamorada, was occupied by Native Americans for thousands of years before European settlers arrived. The 10-acre historic site was also the original seat of Dade County before the Civil War. You can see the ruins of the previous settlement and tour the lush grounds on well-marked trails. Off Indian Key Fill, Overseas Hwy., MM 79. ✆ **305/664-4815.**

If you want to see both islands, plan to spend at least half a day. To get there, you can rent your own power boat at **Robbie's Rent-A-Boat** (U.S. 1 at MM 77.5 on the bay side). Rates range from $70 for a 15-foot boat for half a day to $175 for an 18-foot boat for a full day. It's then a $1 admission fee to each island, which includes an informative hour-long guided tour by park rangers. This is a good option if you are a confident boater.

However, I also recommend taking Robbie's **ferry service.** A visit to one island costs $15, $10 for kids 12 and under, which includes the $1 park admission; trips to both islands cost $25 per person. (If you have time for only one island, make it Lignumvitae.) Not only is the ferry more economical, but it's easier to enjoy the natural beauty of the islands when you aren't negotiating the shallow reefs along the way. The runabouts, which carry up to six people, depart from Robbie's Pier Thursday to Monday at 9am and 1pm for Indian Key, and at 10am and 2pm for Lignumvitae Key. In the busy season, you may need to book as early as 2 days before departure. Call ✆ **305/664-4815** for information from the park service or ✆ **305/664-9814** for Robbie's.

Pigeon Key ⭐⭐   At the curve of the old bridge on Pigeon Key is an intriguing historical site that has been under renovation since late 1993. This 5-mile-long island was once the camp for the crew that built the old railway in the early part of the century and later served as housing for the bridge builders. From here, your vista includes both bridges, many old wooden cottages, and a truly tranquil stretch of lush foliage and sea. If you miss the shuttle tour or would rather walk or bike to the key, it's about 2.5 miles. Either way, you may want to bring a picnic to enjoy after a brief self-guided walking tour and museum visit. There is also an informative 28-minute video of the island's history offered every hour starting at 10am. Parking is available at the Knight's Key end of the bridge, at MM 48, or at the Visitors Center at the old train car across the highway on the ocean side.

East end of the 7-Mile Bridge near MM 47, Marathon. ✆ 305/743-5999. Open 9am–5pm; shuttle tours run every hour 10am–3pm. Admission $7.50, $5 for children under 13. Price includes shuttle transportation from the Visitors Center.

Seven-Mile Bridge ★★★   A stop at the Seven-Mile Bridge is a rewarding and relaxing break from the drive south. Built alongside the ruins of oil magnate Henry Flagler's incredible Overseas Railroad, the "new" bridge (between MM 40 and 47) is still considered an architectural feat. The wide arched span, completed in 1982 at a cost of more than $45 million, is impressive, its apex being the highest point in the Keys. The new bridge and its now-defunct neighbor provide an excellent vantage point from which to view the stunning waters of the Keys. In the daytime, you may want to walk, jog, or bike along the scenic 4-mile stretch of old bridge, or join local anglers, who catch barracuda, yellowtail, and dolphin (the fish, not the mammal) on what is known as "the longest fishing pier in the world."

Between MM 40 and 47 on U.S. 1. *℃* **305/289-0025.**

Tropical Crane Point Hammock ★★   Crane Point Hammock is a little-known but worthwhile stop, especially for those interested in the rich botanical and archaeological history of the Keys. This privately owned 64-acre nature area is considered one of the most important historical sites in the Keys. It contains what is probably the last virgin thatch palm hammock in North America. It also has an archaeological dig site with pre-Columbian and prehistoric Bahamian artifacts.

Also headquarters for the Florida Keys Land and Sea Trust, the hammock's impressive nature museum has simple, informative displays of the Keys' wildlife, including a walk-through replica of a coral-reef cave and life-size dioramas with tropical birds and Key deer. Kids can participate in art projects, see 6-foot-long iguanas, climb through a scaled-down pirate ship, and touch a variety of indigenous aquatic and landlubbing creatures.

5550 Overseas Hwy. (MM 50), Marathon. *℃* **305/743-9100.** Admission $7.50 for adults, $6 for seniors over 64, $4 for students, and free for children under 6. Mon–Sat 9am–5pm; Sun noon–5pm.

VISITING WITH THE ANIMALS

Dolphin Research Center ★★★ *Kids*   If you've always wanted to touch, swim, or play with dolphins, this is the place to do it. Of the three such centers in the continental United States (all located in the Keys), the Dolphin Research Center is the most organized and informative. Although some people argue that training dolphins is cruel and selfish, this is one of the most respected institutions that study and protect the mammals. Knowledgeable trainers at the Dolphin Research Center will also tell you that the dolphins need stimulation and enjoy human contact. They certainly seem to. They nuzzle and seem to smile and kiss the lucky few that get to swim with them in the daily program. The "family" of 15 dolphins swims in a 90,000-square-foot natural saltwater pool carved out of the shoreline.

If you can't get into the swim program, you can still take the interesting hour-long walking tour of the facilities or sign up for a class in hand signals or feed the dolphins from docks. Because the Dolphin Encounter swimming program is the most popular, reservations must be made at least one month in advance. The cost is $125 per person. If you're not brave enough to swim with the dolphins or you have a child under 12 (not permitted to swim with dolphins), try the Dolphin Splash program, in which participants stand on an elevated platform from which to "meet and greet" the dolphins. A height requirement of 44 inches is enforced, and children under the required height must be held up by an adult. Cost for this program is $70 per person; free for children under 3.

The 10 "Keymandments"

The Keys have always attracted independent spirits, from Ernest Hemingway and Tennessee Williams to Jimmy Buffett, Zane Grey, and local hero Mel Fisher. Writers, artists, and free thinkers have long drifted down here to escape.

Although you'll generally find a very laid-back and tolerant code of behavior in the Keys, some rules do exist. Be sure to respect the 10 "Keymandments" while you're here, or suffer the consequences.

- Don't anchor on a reef. (Reefs are alive.)
- Don't feed the animals. (They'll want to follow you home, and you can't keep them.)
- Don't trash our place (or we'll send Bubba to trash yours).
- Don't touch the coral. (After all, you don't even know them. Some pose a mild risk of injury as well.)
- Don't speed (especially on Big Pine Key, where deer reside and tar-and-feathering is still practiced).
- Don't catch more fish than you can eat. (Better yet, let them go. Some of them support schools.)
- Don't collect conch. (This species is protected by Bubba.)
- Don't disturb the bird nests. (They find it very annoying.)
- Don't damage the sea grass. (And don't even think about making a skirt out of it.)
- Don't drink and drive on land or sea. (There's absolutely nothing funny about it.)

U.S. 1 at MM 59 (on the bay side), Marathon. © 305/289-1121. Swim with the Dolphins, $125 per person. Call on the first day of the month to book for the following month. Educational walking tours five times daily: 10am, 11am, 12:30pm, 2pm, and 3:30pm. Admission $12.50 adults, $10 seniors, $7.50 children 4–12, free for children 3 and under. Daily 9:30am–4pm.

Florida Keys Wild Bird Center ⭐ Wander through lush canopies of mangroves on narrow wooden walkways to see some of the Keys' most famous residents—the large variety of native birds, including broad-wing hawks, great blue and white herons, roseate spoonbills, white ibis, cattle egrets, and a number of pelicans. This not-for-profit center operates as a hospital for the many birds that have been injured. Visit at feeding time, usually about 2pm, when you can watch the dedicated staff feed the hundreds of hungry beaks.

U.S. 1 at MM 93.6 Bayside, Tavernier. © 305/852-4486. fkwbc@reefnet.com. Donations suggested. Daily 8:30am–6pm.

Robbie's Pier ⭐⭐⭐ (Value) One of the best and definitely one of the cheapest attractions in the Upper Keys is the famed Robbie's Pier. Here, the fierce steely tarpons, a prized catch for backcountry anglers, have been gathering for the past 20 years. You may recognize these prehistoric-looking giants that grow up to 200 pounds; many are displayed as trophies and mounted on local restaurant walls. To see them live, head to Robbie's Pier, where tens and sometimes hundreds of these behemoths circle the shallow waters waiting for you to feed them. Kayak tours promise an even closer glimpse.

U.S. 1 at MM 77.5, Islamorada. ✆ **305/664-9814**. Admission $1. Bucket of fish $2. Daily 8am–5pm. Look for the Hungry Tarpon restaurant sign on the right after the Indian Key channel.

Theater of the Sea ★   Established in 1946, the Theater of the Sea is one of the world's oldest marine zoos. Although the facilities could use some sprucing up, the dolphin and sea lion shows are entertaining and informative, especially for children who can also see sharks, sea turtles, and tropical fish. If you want to swim with dolphins and you haven't booked well in advance, this is the place you may be able to get into with just a few hours, or days, notice as opposed to the more rigid Dolphin Research Center in Marathon (see above). A 30-minute orientation will prepare you for your swim. Children under 5 are not permitted to participate. Other programs allow visitors to swim with sea lions or stingrays. The facility also serves as a haven for dozens of stray cats that have free run of the grounds and gift shop.

U.S. 1 at MM 84.5, Islamorada. ✆ **305/664-2431**. www.theaterofthesea.com. Admission $17.25 adults, $10.75 children 3–12. Dolphin swim $110; sea lion swim $75; stingray swim $35 per person. Reservations required. Daily 9:30am–5:45pm (ticket office closes at 4pm).

TWO EXCEPTIONAL STATE PARKS

One of the best places to discover the diverse ecosystem of the Upper Keys is in its most famous park, **John Pennekamp Coral Reef State Park** ★★★, located on U.S. 1 at MM 102.5, in Key Largo (✆ **305/451-1202**). Named for a former *Miami Herald* editor and conservationist, the 188-square-mile park is the nation's first undersea preserve. It's a sanctuary for part of the only living coral reef in the continental United States. The original plans for Everglades National Park included this part of the reef within its boundaries, but opposition from local homeowners made its inclusion politically impossible.

Because the water is extremely shallow, the 40 species of coral and more than 650 species of fish here are particularly accessible to divers, snorkelers, and glass-bottomed-boat passengers. To experience this park, visitors must get in the water—you can't see the reef from the shore. Your first stop should be the Visitors Center, which is full of educational fish tanks and a mammoth 30,000-gallon saltwater aquarium that re-creates a reef ecosystem. At the adjacent dive shop, you can rent snorkeling and diving equipment and join one of the boat trips that depart for the reef throughout the day. Visitors can also rent motorboats, sailboats, Windsurfers, and canoes. The 2-hour glass-bottomed-boat tour is the best way to see the coral reefs if you refuse to get wet. Inexperienced but certified scuba divers can rent gear here, too, and an off-the-shore dive excursion is nonthreatening and educational. Watch for the lobsters and other sea life residing in the fairly shallow ridge walls beneath the coastal waters. But remember: These are protected waters.

Canoeing around the park's narrow mangrove channels and tidal creeks is also popular. You can go on your own in a rented canoe or, in winter, sign up for a tour led by a local naturalist. Hikers have two short trails from which to choose: a boardwalk through the mangroves and a dirt trail through a tropical hardwood hammock. Ranger-led walks are usually scheduled daily from the end of November to April. Phone for schedule information and reservations.

Park admission is $2.50 per vehicle for one occupant; for two or more, it is $4 per vehicle, plus 50¢ per passenger; $1.50 per pedestrian or bicyclist. On busy weekend days, there's often a line of cars to get into the park. Call ✆ **305/451-1621** for information. On your way into the park, ask the ranger for a map.

Glass-bottomed-boat tours cost $18 for adults and $10 for children 11 and under. Snorkeling tours are $25.95 for adults and $19.95 for children 17 and under, including equipment. Sailing and snorkeling tours are $31.95 for adults, $26.95 for children 17 and under, including equipment but not tax. Canoes rent for $10 per hour. For experienced boaters only, four different-sized Reef boats (powerboats) rent for $27.50 to $50 per hour; cheaper half-day and full-day rates available, call © **305/451-6325.** A $300 deposit (and up depending on boat size) is required. Open daily from 8am to 5pm; phone for tour and dive times. Reservations are recommended for all of the above. Also, see below for more options on diving, fishing, and snorkeling these reefs.

Long Key State Recreation Area ⭐⭐⭐, U.S. 1 at MM 68, Long Key (© **305/664-4815**), is one of the best places in the Middle Keys for hiking, camping, snorkeling, and canoeing. This 965-acre site is situated atop the remains of an ancient coral reef. At the entrance gate, ask for a free flyer describing the local trails and wildlife.

There are two nature trails here perfect for hiking. The Golden Orb Trail is a 1-mile loop around a lagoon that attracts a large variety of birds. Rich in West Indian vegetation, this trail leads to an observation tower that offers good views of the mangroves. Layton Trail, the only part of the park that doesn't require an admission fee, is a quarter-mile shaded loop that goes through tropical hammocks before opening onto Florida Bay. The trail is well marked with interpretive signs; you can easily walk it in about 20 minutes.

The park's excellent 1½-mile canoe trail is also short and sweet, allowing visitors to loop around the mangroves in about an hour. You can rent canoes at the trailhead for about $4 per hour. Long Key is also a great spot to stop for a picnic if you get hungry on your way to Key West.

Railroad builder Henry Flagler created the Long Key Fishing Club here in 1906, and the waters surrounding the park are still popular with game fishers. In summer, sea turtles lumber onto the protected coast to lay their eggs.

Admission is $3.25 per car plus 50¢ per person (except for the Layton Trail, which is free). Open daily from 8am to sunset.

WATER SPORTS FROM A TO Z

There are literally hundreds of outfitters in the Keys who will arrange all kinds of water activities, from cave dives to parasailing. If those recommended below are booked up or unreachable, ask the local chamber of commerce for a list of qualified members.

BOATING In addition to the rental shops in the state parks, you will find dozens of outfitters along U.S. 1 offering a range of runabouts and skiffs for boaters of any experience level. **Captain Pip's,** U.S. 1 at MM 47.5, Marathon (© **800/707-1692** or 305/743-4403), rents 18- to 24-foot motorboats with 90- to 225-horsepower engines for $130 to $225 per day. Overnight accommodations are available and include a free boat rental; 2-night minimum $220 to $255; weekly $1190 to $1890.

Robbie's Rent-a-Boat, U.S. 1 at MM 77.5, Islamorada (© **305/664-9814**), rents 14- to 27-foot motorboats with engines ranging from 15 to 200 horsepower. Boat rentals are $70 to $205 for a half day and $90 to $295 for a full day.

CANOEING & KAYAKING I can think of no better way to explore the uninhabited, shallow backcountry on the Gulf side than by kayak or canoe. You can reach places big boats just can't get to because of their large draft. Sometimes manatees will cuddle up to the boats, thinking them another friendly species.

For a more enjoyable time, ask for a sit-inside boat—you'll stay drier. Also, a fiberglass (as opposed to plastic) boat with a rudder is generally more stable and easier to maneuver. Many area hotels rent kayaks and canoes to guests, as do the outfitters listed here. **Florida Bay Outfitters,** U.S. 1 at MM 104, Key Largo (✆ **305/451-3018**), rents canoes and sea kayaks for use in and around John Pennekamp Coral Reef State Park for $25 to $30 for a half day and $35 to $50 for a whole day. Canoes cost $25 for a half day and $35 for a whole day. At **Coral Reef Park Co.,** on U.S. 1 at MM 102.5, Key Largo (✆ **305/451-1621**), you can rent canoes and kayaks for $8 per hour, $28 for a half day; most canoes are sit-on-tops.

DIVING & SNORKELING   The **Florida Keys Dive Center,** on U.S. 1 at MM 90.5, Tavernier (✆ **305/852-4599**), takes snorkelers and divers to the reefs of John Pennekamp Coral Reef State Park and environs every day. PADI (Professional Association of Diving Instructors) training courses are also available for the uninitiated. Tours leave at 8am and 12:30pm and cost $25 per person to snorkel (plus $8 rental fee for mask, snorkel, and fins) and $59 per person to dive (plus an extra $20 if you need to rent all the gear).

At **Hall's Dive Center & Career Institute,** U.S. 1 at MM 48.5, Marathon (✆ **305/743-5929**), snorkelers and divers can choose to dive at Looe Key, Sombrero Reef, Delta Shoal, Content Key, and Coffins Patch. Tours are scheduled daily at 9am and 1pm. You will spend 1 hour at each of two sites per tour. If you mention this book, you will get a special discounted rate of $30 per person to snorkel (additional gear is $11) and $40 per person to dive (tanks are $8.50 each). Choose from an impressive array of equipment.

With **SNUBA Tours of Key Largo** (✆ **305/451-6391;** www.pennekamp. com/sw/snuba.htm), you can dive down to 20 feet attached to a comfortable breathing apparatus that really gives you the feeling of scuba diving without having to be certified. You can tour shallow coral reefs teeming with hundreds of colorful fish and plant life, from sea turtles to moray eels. Reservations are required; call to find out where and when to meet. A 2- to 3-hour underwater tour (typically 1pm to 4pm) costs $75, including all equipment. If you have never dived before, you may require a 1-hour lesson in the pool, which costs an additional $45.

FISHING   **Robbie's Partyboats & Charters,** on U.S. 1 at MM 84.5, Islamorada (✆ **305/664-8070** or 305/664-4196), located at the south end of the Holiday Isle Docks (see the Holiday Isle Resort in "Where to Stay," below), offers day and night deep-sea and reef fishing trips aboard a 65-foot party boat. Big-game fishing charters are also available, and "splits" are arranged for solo fishers. Party-boat fishing costs $25 for a half-day morning tour (rod and reel rental $3); it's $15 extra if you want to go back out on an afternoon tour. Charters run $400 for a half day, $600 for a full day; splits begin at $65 per person. Phone for information and reservations.

Bud n' Mary's Fishing Marina, on U.S. 1 at MM 79.8, Islamorada (✆ **800/ 742-7945** or 305/664-2461), one of the largest marinas between Miami and Key West, is packed with sailors offering guided backcountry fishing charters. This is the place to go if you want to stalk tarpon, bonefish, and snapper. If the seas are not too rough, deep-sea and coral fishing trips can be arranged. Charters cost $500 to $550 for a half day, $750 to $800 for a full day, and splits begin at $125 per person.

The Bounty Hunter, 15th Street, Marathon (✆ **305/743-2446**), offers full- and half-day outings. For years, Captain Brock Hook's huge sign has boasted no fish, no pay. You're guaranteed to catch something. Choose your prey from shark, barracuda, sailfish, or whatever else is running. Prices are $350 for a half day, $375 for three-fourths day, and $450 for a full day. Rates are for groups of no more than six people.

SHOPPING

On your way to the Keys, you'll find an outlet center, the **Prime Outlets at Florida City** (© 305/248-4727), at 250 E. Palm Dr. (where the Florida Turnpike meets U.S. Hwy. 1), in Florida City. The center holds more than 60 stores, including Nike Factory Store, Bass Co. Store, Levi's, OshKosh, and Izod. Travelers can pick up a free discount coupon booklet called the Come Back Pack from the Customer Service Center. The outlet is open Monday to Saturday, from 10am to 9pm, Sunday from 11am to 6pm.

The Upper and Middle Keys have no shortage of tacky tourist shops selling shells and T-shirts (the ubiquitous "beads and trinkets") and other hokey souvenirs, but for real Keys-style shopping, check out the **weekend flea markets.** One of the best is held every Saturday and Sunday bay side at MM 103.5 (© 305/451-0677). Dozens of vendors open their stalls from 9am until 4 or 5pm, selling every imaginable sort of antiques, T-shirts, plants, shoes, books, toys, and games, as well as a hearty dose of good old-fashioned junk.

A mecca for fishing and sports enthusiasts, **The World Wide Sportsman** (© 305/664-4615) at MM 81.5, is not only the largest fishing store in the Keys, but also a meeting place for anglers from all over the world. Every possible gizmo and gadget, plus hundreds of T-shirts, hats, books, and gift items are displayed in its more than 25,000 square feet. The salespeople are knowledgeable and eager to help. Travel specialists can even arrange for charter trips and backcountry tours. The store is open daily from 7am until 8:30pm.

WHERE TO STAY

U.S. 1 is lined with chain hotels in all price ranges. In the Upper Keys, the best moderately priced options are the **Holiday Inn Key Largo Resort & Marina,** U.S. 1 at MM 99.7 (© 800/THE-KEYS or 305/451-2121), and right next door, at MM 100, the **Ramada Limited Resort & Casino** (© 800/THE-KEYS or 305/451-3939). Both hotels share three pools and a casino boat; however, the Ramada is cozier and offers slightly cheaper rates. Also, the **Best Western Suites at Key Largo,** 201 Ocean Dr., MM 100 (© 800/462-6079 or 305/451-5081), is just 3 miles from John Pennekamp Coral Reef State Park. Another good option in the Upper Keys is **Islamorada Days Inn,** U.S. 1 at MM 82.5 (© 800/ DAYS-INN or 305/664-3681). In the Middle Keys, the **Howard Johnson** at 13351 Overseas Hwy., MM 54 in Marathon (© 800/321-3496 or 305/ 743-8550), also offers reasonably priced ocean-side rooms.

Since the real beauty of the Keys lies mostly beyond the highways, there is no better way to see this area than by boat. Why not stay in a floating hotel? Especially if traveling with a group, houseboats can be economical. To rent a houseboat, call Ruth and Michael Sullivan at **Smilin' Island Houseboat Rentals** (MM 99.5), Key Largo (© 305/451-1930). Rates are from $750 to $1,350 for 3 nights. Boats accommodate up to six people.

For land options, consider these recommendations, grouped first by price and then geographically from north to south.

VERY EXPENSIVE

Cheeca Lodge ★★★   One of the better places to stay in the Upper Keys, Cheeca has been hosting celebrities, royalty, and politicians since its opening in

1949. Guests now enjoy the luxury of the Cheeca's freshly renovated and remodeled rooms. All of the 203 units offer all the amenities of a world-class resort in a very laid-back setting. You may not feel compelled to leave the sprawling grounds, but it's good to know the hotel is conveniently situated near the best restaurants and nightlife. Located on 27 acres of beachfront property, this rambling resort is known for its excellent sports facilities, including one of the only golf courses in the Upper Keys. All rooms are spacious and have small balconies. The nicer ones overlook the ocean and have large marble bathrooms. The Atlantic's Edge restaurant is one of the best in the Upper Keys (see "Where to Dine," later in this chapter).

U.S. 1 at MM 82 (P.O. Box 527), Islamorada, FL 33036. © **800/327-2888** or 305/664-4651. Fax 305/664-2893. www.cheeca.com. 203 units. Winter $295–$650 double; $400 suite. Off-season $195–$430 double; $285 suite. AE, DC, DISC, MC, V. **Amenities:** 2 restaurants; 2 lounges (1 pool side); 3 outdoor heated pools; kids' pool; 9-hole, par-3 golf course; 6 lighted tennis courts; access to nearby health club; Jacuzzi; 5 hot tubs; water-sports equipment rental; bike rental; children's nature programs; concierge; tour desk; car-rental desk; room service; in-room massage; baby-sitting; laundry and dry-cleaning services. *In room:* A/C, TV/VCR, CD player, dataport, kitchenette (in suites), minibar, coffeemaker, hairdryer.

Hawk's Cay Resort ★★★ *Kids*   Located on its own 60-acre island in the Middle Keys, this resort has a relaxed and casual island atmosphere and is also great for kids. If it's recreation you're looking for, Hawk's Cay is far superior to the more luxurious Cheeca Lodge. It offers an impressive array of activities—sailing, fishing, snorkeling, and water-skiing to name a few—and the unique opportunity to have your own dolphin encounter in a special pool. (You'll need to reserve a spot well in advance for the dolphins—there's a waiting list.) The rooms are large and newly renovated with island-style furniture and bright tropical bedspreads and curtains. Every room opens onto a private balcony with ocean or tropical views (pricing varies depending on the view). The large bathrooms are well appointed and have granite countertops. The clubhouse has an exercise room, whirlpool, and steam room. In addition to a lagoon and several pools for families, the resort boasts a secluded pool for adults only. Organized children's activities, including special marine- and ecologically inspired programs, will keep your little ones busy while you relax.

61 Hawk's Cay Blvd. at MM 61, Duck Key, Fl 33050. © **888/814-9104** or 305/743-7000. Fax 305/743-5215. www.hawkscay.com. 176 units. Winter $230–$385 double, $435–$875 suite; off-season $190–$260 double, $335–$775 suite. Packages available. AE, DC, DISC, MC, V. **Amenities:** 3 restaurants; lounge; outdoor heated pool; adults-only private pool; nearby golf course (transportation available); 8 tennis courts (2 lighted); small exercise room; Jacuzzi; water-sports equipment; bike rental; children's programs ($25–$35 per child); game room; concierge; limited room service; in-room massage. *In room:* A/C, TV, fridge, coffeemaker.

Westin Beach Resort ★★   In addition to a $3 million overhaul, the resort distinguishes itself by its secluded yet convenient location—it's set back on 12 private acres of gumbo-limbo and hardwood trees, making it invisible from the busy highway. Despite its hideaway location, the sprawling pink-and-blue four-story complex is surprisingly large. A three-story atrium lobby is flanked by two wings that face 1,200 feet of the Florida Bay. The large guest rooms have tasteful tropical decor and private balconies. The suites are twice the size of standard rooms with double-size balconies and better-quality wicker furnishings. Ten suites feature private spa tubs and particularly luxurious bathrooms with adjustable showerheads, bidets, and lots of room for toiletries. The Fun Factory offers fantastic activities for the kids.

U.S. 1 at MM 97, Key Largo, FL 33037. © **800/728-2738**, 800/539-5274, or 305/852-5553. Fax 305/852-8669. www.keylargoresort.com. 200 units. Winter $189–$389; Jacuzzi suites start at $299. Off-season $109–$369; Jacuzzi suites start at $279. AE, DC, DISC, MC, V. **Amenities:** 2 restaurants; snack bar; 2 outdoor heated swimming pools; 2 lighted tennis courts; exercise room; Jacuzzi; water-sports equipment/rentals; bike rental; children's programs; concierge; secretarial services; 24-hour room service; in-room massage; baby-sitting; laundry and dry-cleaning service. *In room:* A/C, TV, dataport, minibar, coffeemaker, hairdryer, iron.

EXPENSIVE

Jules' Undersea Lodge ⭐⭐⭐ Staying here is certainly an experience of a lifetime—if you're brave enough to take the plunge. Originally built as a research lab in the 1970s, this small underwater compartment now operates as a single-room hotel. As expensive as it is unusual, Jules' is most popular with diving honeymooners. The lodge rests on pillars on the ocean floor. To get inside, guests swim 21 feet under the structure and pop up into the unit through a 4-by-6-foot "moon pool" that gurgles soothingly all night long. The 30-foot-deep underwater suite consists of a bedroom and galley and sleeps up to six. Room service will deliver your meals, daily newspapers, even a late-night pizza in waterproof containers at no extra charge.

51 Shoreland Dr., Key Largo, FL 33037. ⓒ 305/451-2353. Fax 305/451-4789. www.jul.com. 2 units. $250–$350 per person. Rates include breakfast and dinner as well as all equipment and unlimited scuba diving in the lagoon for certified divers. Packages available. AE, DISC, MC, V. From U.S. 1 S., at MM 103.2, turn left onto Transylvania Ave., across from the Central Plaza shopping mall. **Amenities:** Entertainment center; dining area. *In room:* A/C, telephone, kitchenette.

Marriott Key Largo Bay Beach Resort ⭐⭐ While hardly quaint, this amenities-laden 17-acre complex has everything an active or resting traveler could want, including a private beach. Guests enjoy the new European health spa, a nine-hole minigolf course, and tennis courts. All guests are welcome to sail for free on a gambling cruise ship that anchors in international waters from 2pm until 2am daily. Rooms are decorated in a pleasant, if generic, tropical style, and most have balconies overlooking the stunning Florida Bay. For real pampering, consider the enormous suites, which can easily sleep a family of five. All have large wraparound terraces and large sitting areas. With its rates being slightly cheaper than the nearby Westin and Cheeca Lodge, you'll find it a good value.

103800 Overseas Hwy. at MM 103, Key Largo, FL 33037. ⓒ 800/932-9332 or 305/453-0000. Fax 305/453-0093. www.marriottkeylargo.com. 153 units. Winter $289–$649; off-season $209–$449. AE, DC, MC, V. **Amenities:** Restaurant; snack bar; large outdoor pool; access to nearby tennis and racquetball courts; health center & spa; Jacuzzi; water-sports equipment/rentals; bike rental; children's programs; game room; concierge; business center; limited room service; in-room massage; baby-sitting; laundry and dry-cleaning services. *In room:* A/C, TV, VCR on request, dataport, minibar, coffeemaker, hairdryer, iron, safe.

The Moorings ⭐⭐⭐ Staying at The Moorings is more like staying at a secluded beach house than at a hotel. You'll never see another soul on this 18-acre resort if you choose not to. There isn't even maid service unless you request it. The romantic whitewashed units, from cozy cottages to three-bedroom houses, are spacious and modestly decorated with funky island prints, bamboo, and tropical motifs. All have full kitchens, and most have washers and dryers. Some have CD players and VCRs; ask when you book. The real reason to come to this cool resort is to relax on the more than 1,000-foot beach (one of the only real beaches around). There is a hard tennis court, a few kayaks and windsurfers, but absolutely no motorized water vehicles. There is no room service or restaurant (although Morada Bay across the street is excellent). This is a place for people who like each other a lot. Leave the kids at home unless they are extremely well behaved and not easily bored.

123 Beach Rd. near MM 81.5 on the ocean side, Islamorada, FL 33036. ⓒ 305/664-4708. Fax 305/664-4242. www.themooringsvillage.com. 18 cottages. Winter daily $200–$250 small cottages; $475 1-bedroom house; $3,325–$7,875 weekly oceanfront house. Off-season $150–$275, $1,900–$4,500 weekly.

2-night minimum for smaller cottages; 1-week minimum for larger cottages. MC, V. **Amenities:** 3 restaurants; large outdoor heated pool; tennis court; water-sports equipment rental. *In room:* A/C, TV, kitchen, coffeemaker, hairdryer.

MODERATE

Banana Bay Resort & Marina ⊛   It doesn't look like much from the sign-cluttered Overseas Highway, but when you enter the lush grounds of Banana Bay, you will realize you're in one of the most bucolic and best-run properties in the Upper Keys. Built in the early 1950s as a fishing camp, the resort is a beach-front maze of pink-and-white two-story buildings hidden among banyans and palms. Guest rooms are very similar, but those with better views are more expensive. The rooms are moderately sized, and many have private balconies where you can enjoy your complimentary coffee and newspaper every morning. The hotel's kitschy restaurant serves three meals a day, indoors or poolside. Two accessible units for disabled travelers are available.

U.S. 1 at MM 49.5, Marathon, FL 33050. © **800/BANANA-1** or 305/743-3500. Fax 305/743-2670. www. bananabay.com. 60 units. Winter $115–$210 double; off-season $85–$160 double. Rates include continental breakfast. Weekend and 3- and 7-night packages available. AE, DC, DISC, MC, V. **Amenities:** Restaurant; bar; pool; fitness center; Jacuzzi; water-sports equipment rental; free use of bikes; game room; self-service laundromat. *In room:* A/C, TV, fax, dataport, fridge, hairdryer.

Conch Key Cottages ⊛⊛   Here's your chance to play castaway in the Keys. Occupying its own private microisland just off U.S. 1, Conch Key Cottages is a unique and comfortable hideaway run by live-in owners Ron Wilson and Wayne Byrnes, who are constantly fixing and adding to their unique property. This is a place to get away from it all; the cottages aren't located close to much else, except maybe one or two interesting eateries. The cabins, which were built at different times over the past 40 years, overlook their own stretch of natural, but very small, private beach and have screened-in porches, cozy bedrooms, and bathrooms. Each has a hammock, a barbecue grill, and a two-person kayak. Request one of the two-bedroom cottages—especially if you are traveling with the family. They are the most spacious and well designed, practically tailor-made for couples or families. On the other side of the pool are a handful of efficiency apartments that are similarly outfitted, but enjoy no beach frontage. All have fully equipped kitchens. There's also a small heated freshwater pool.

Near U.S. 1 at MM 62.3, Marathon, FL 33050. © **800/330-1577** or 305/289-1377. Fax 305/743-8207. www.conchkeycottages.com. 12 cottages. Dec 15–Sept 8 $110–$274; Sept 9–Dec 14 $74–$215. DISC, MC, V. **Amenities:** 2 pools. *In room:* A/C, TV, no phone.

Faro Blanco Marine Resort ⊛   Spanning both sides of the Overseas High-way and all on waterfront property, this huge, two-shore marina and hotel com-plex offers something for every taste. Free-standing, camp-style cottages with a small bedroom are the resort's least-expensive accommodations, but they are in dire need of rehabilitation. Old appliances and a musty odor also make them the least-desirable units on the property. The houseboats are the best choice and value. Permanently tethered in a tranquil marina, these white rectangular boats look like floating mobile homes and are uniformly clean, fresh, and recom-mendable. They have colonial American-style furnishings, fully equipped kitch-enettes, front and back porches, and water, water everywhere. The boats are so tightly moored, you hardly move at all, even in the roughest weather. Finally, there are two unusual rental units located in a lighthouse on the pier. Circular staircases, unusually shaped rooms and showers, and nautical decor make it a unique place to stay, but some guests might find it claustrophobic.

1996 Overseas Hwy., U.S. 1 at MM 48.5, Marathon, FL 33050. ℭ **800/759-3276** or 305/743-9018. Fax 305/866-5235. www.usahotelguide.com/states/florida/floridakeys/middlekeys/faroblanco.html. 123 units. 31 houseboats with 4 units each. Winter $89–$150 cottage; $109–$200 houseboat; $185 lighthouse; $267–$327 condo. Off-season $79–$119 cottage; $99–$178 houseboat; $145 lighthouse; $215–$263 condo. AE, DISC, MC, V. **Amenities:** 4 restaurants; 2 lounges; Olympic-size pool; fully equipped dive shop; barbecue and picnic areas; playground. *In room:* A/C, TV.

Holiday Isle Resort ⟨★⟩   A huge resort complex encompassing five restaurants, several lounges, tiki huts, a large marina, many retail shops, and four distinct (if not distinctive) hotels, the Holiday Isle is one of the biggest resorts in the Keys. It attracts a spring-break kind of crowd year-round. Its Tiki Bar claims to have invented the rum runner drink (151-proof rum, blackberry brandy, banana liqueur, grenadine, and lime juice), and there's no reason to doubt it. Hordes of partyers are attracted to the resort's nonstop merrymaking, live music, and beachfront bars. As a result, some of the accommodations can be noisy. Rooms can be bare-bones budget to oceanfront luxury, as the broad range of prices reflects. Even the nicest rooms could use a good cleaning. El Capitan and Harbor Lights, two of the least-expensive hotels on the property, are both austere. Like the other hotels here, rooms could use a thorough rehab. Howard Johnson's, another Holiday Isle property, is a little farther from the action and a tad more civilized. If you plan to be here for a few days, choose an efficiency or a suite; both have kitchenettes.

U.S. 1 at MM 84, Islamorada, FL 33036. ℭ **800/327-7070** or 305/664-2321. Fax 305/664-2703. www. holidayisle.com. 199 units. Winter $85–$425 double. Off-season $65–$350 double. AE, DISC, MC, V. **Amenities:** 8 restaurants; 12 bars; 2 outdoor heated pools; kids' pool; water-sports equipment/rentals. *In room:* A/C, TV.

Kona Kai Resort & Gallery ⟨★★⟩   Unique to the Upper Keys, this little haven, with just 11 units, is both casual and elegant. Quaint rooms dot the lushly landscaped 2-acre property, which boasts a large variety of native vegetation like palms, bougainvillea, and ferns, plus an impressive collection of fruit-bearing trees, such as carambola, passion fruit, banana, Key lime, guava, and coconut. An orchid house has over 250 beautiful plants. Lounge chairs, hammocks, a Jacuzzi, and compact artificial beach are available for those who just want to relax, while a slew of activities are available for the more active set. For the adventurous, owners Ronnie and Joe Harris will organize excursions to the Everglades, the backcountry, or wherever. No phones in the rooms and a 3-night minimum stay requirement in the winter make relaxing imperative. All the rooms are very private and simply furnished; bathroom amenities are fabulous, with lotions, soaps, and shampoos made from tropical fruits. CDs from local musicians are there for your in-room listening pleasure. Home-grown tropical fruits from the hotel's garden are there for guests to sample. For more substantial meals, you'll need to visit a nearby restaurant—there are three within walking distance and several more a short drive away. Smoking is not permitted in the rooms. An art gallery featuring work by American and international painters, photographers, and sculptors doubles as the property's office and lobby. Even if you are not staying here, stop in to see the artwork.

97802 Overseas Hwy. (U.S. 1 at MM 97.8), Key Largo, FL 33037. ℭ **800/365-7829** or 305/852-7200. Fax 305/852-4629. www.konakairesort.com. 11 units. Winter $196–233 double, $257–$658 1- to 2-bedroom suite. Off-season $108–$129 double, $143–$433 1- to 2-bedroom suite, 3-night minimum stay in winter; 2-night minimum off-season. AE, DISC, MC, V. Children under 16 not permitted. Closed September. **Amenities:** Heated pool; tennis court; spa; Jacuzzi; water-sports equipment/rentals; boat ramp/dockage; concierge; in-room massage and facials. *In room:* A/C, TV, VCR, CD player (suites only), kitchen, fridge, hairdryer.

Lime Tree Bay Resort Motel   The Lime Tree Bay Resort is the only hotel in the tiny town of Layton (population 183). Midway between Islamorada and Marathon, the hotel is only steps from Long Key State Recreation Area. It's situated on a very pretty piece of waterfront graced with hundreds of mature palm trees and lots of other tropical foliage. Motel rooms and efficiencies have tiny bathrooms with standing showers but are clean and well maintained. The best deal is the two-bedroom bay-view cottage. The large living area with new fixtures and furnishings leads out to a large private deck where you can enjoy a view of the Gulf from your hammock. A full kitchen and two full bathrooms make it a comfortable space for six people. Fifteen efficiencies and suites have kitchenettes.

U.S. 1 at MM 68.5 in Layton, Long Key, FL 33001. ℂ 800/723-4519 or 305/664-4740. Fax 305/664-0750. www.limetreebayresort.com. 30 units. Winter $107–$247 double; off-season $84–$189 double. AE, DC, DISC, MC, V. **Amenities:** Restaurant; small outdoor pool; tennis court; Jacuzzi; water-sports equipment/rental. *In room:* A/C, TV, dataport.

INEXPENSIVE

Bay Harbor Lodge ⭐   A small, simple retreat that's big on charm, the Bay Harbor Lodge is an extraordinarily welcoming place. The lodge is far from fancy, though it features new windows and paint, and the widely ranging accommodations are not created equal. The motel rooms are small and ordinary in decor, but even the least expensive is recommendable. The efficiencies are larger motel rooms with fully equipped kitchenettes. The oceanfront cottages are larger still, have full kitchens, and represent one of the best values in the Keys. The vinyl-covered furnishings and old-fashioned wallpapers won't win any design awards, but elegance isn't what the "real" Keys are about. The 1½ lush acres of grounds are planted with banana trees and have an outdoor heated pool and several small barbecue grills. A small beach is ideal for some quiet sunning and relaxation. Guests are free to use the rowboats, paddleboats, canoes, kayaks, and snorkeling equipment. Bring your own beach towels.

97702 Overseas Hwy., U.S. 1 at MM 97.7 (off the southbound lane of U.S. 1), Key Largo, FL 33037. ℂ 800/ 385-0986 or 305/852-5695. www.thefloridakeys.com/bayharborlodge. 16 units. Winter $75–$165 double. Off-season $65–$95 efficiency; $85–$125 double. MC, V. **Amenities:** Freshwater pool; water-sports equipment/rental. *In room:* A/C, TV, fridge, microwave, coffeemaker, hairdryer.

Ragged Edge Resort ⭐⭐   This small oceanfront property's 11 units are spread out along more than half a dozen gorgeous, grassy waterfront acres. All are immaculately clean and comfortable, and most are outfitted with full kitchens and tasteful furnishings. There's no bar, restaurant, or staff to speak of, but the retreat's affable owner, Jackie Barnes, is happy to lend you bicycles or good advice on the area's offerings. A large dock attracts boaters and a good variety of local and migratory birds.

243 Treasure Harbor Rd. (near MM 86.5), Islamorada, FL 33036. ℂ 800/436-2023 or 305/852-5389. www. ragged-edge.com. 11 units. Winter $69–$189; off-season $48–$125. AE, MC, V. **Amenities:** Outdoor pool; free use of bikes; laundromat. *In room:* A/C, kitchen (most units), fridge, coffeemaker.

CAMPING

John Pennekamp Coral Reef State Park ⭐⭐   One of Florida's best parks (see earlier in this chapter), Pennekamp offers 47 well-separated campsites, half of which are available by advance reservation, the rest distributed on a first-come, first-served basis. The car-camping sites are small but well equipped with bathrooms and showers. Note that the local environment provides fertile breeding grounds for insects, particularly in the late summer. Two man-made beaches and a small lagoon nearby attract many large wading birds. Reservations are held until 5pm, and the park must be notified of late arrival by phone on the check-in date. Pennekamp opens at 8am and closes around sundown.

U.S. 1 at MM 102.5 (P.O. Box 487), Key Largo, FL 33037. ℭ 305/451-1202. 47 campsites. Reservations can be made in advance. $24–$26 per site for camping. Park entry $4 per vehicle (50¢ for each additional person). Yearly permits and passes available. AE, DISC, MC, V. No pets.

Long Key State Park ⚶ The Upper Keys' other main state park is more secluded than its northern neighbor—and more popular. All sites are located oceanside and surrounded by narrow rows of trees and nearby toilet and bathroom facilities. Reserve well in advance, especially in winter. If you prefer not to stay overnight, the park is available for daytime picnicking for $3.25 per vehicle plus 50¢ per person.

U.S. 1 at MM 67.5 (P.O. Box 776), Long Key, FL 33001. ℭ **305/664-4815.** 60 oceanfront sites. $24–$26 per site for 1–4 people. $3.25 per vehicle. Special permits and passes available. AE, DISC, MC, V. No pets.

WHERE TO DINE

Although not known as a culinary hot spot, the Upper and Middle Keys do offer some excellent restaurants, most of which specialize in seafood. And dining opportunities are always improving. Often, visitors (especially those who fish) take advantage of accommodations that have kitchen facilities and cook their own meals. Some restaurants will even clean and cook your catch, for a fee.

VERY EXPENSIVE

Atlantic's Edge ⭐⭐⭐ SEAFOOD/REGIONAL Ask for a table by the oceanfront window to feel really privileged at this restaurant, the most elegant in the Keys. Although the service and food are generally first rate, don't get dressed up—a sports coat for men will be fine but isn't necessary. You can choose from an innovative, varied menu, which offers several choices of fresh fish, steak, chicken, and pastas. The crab cakes, made with stone crab when in season, are the very best in the Keys; served on a warm salad of baby greens with a mild sauce of red peppers, they're the stuff cravings are made of. Other excellent dishes include a Thai-spiced fresh baby snapper and the vegetarian angel-hair pasta with mushrooms, asparagus, and peppers in a rich broth. Service can sometimes be less than efficient but is always courteous and professional.

In the Cheeca Lodge, U.S. 1 at MM 82, Islamorada. ℭ **305/664-4651.** Reservations recommended. Main courses $20–$36. AE, DC, DISC, MC, V. Daily 6–10pm.

EXPENSIVE

Barracuda Grill ⭐⭐ SEAFOOD Owned by Lance Hill and his wife, Jan (a former sous chef at Little Palm Island), this small, casual spot serves excellent seafood, steaks, and chops. It's too bad it's open only for dinner. Some of the favorite dishes are the Caicos Gold Conch and Mangrove Snapper and Mango. Try the Tipsy Olives appetizer, marinated in gin or vodka, to kick-start your meal. Decorated with barracuda-themed art, the restaurant also features a well-priced American wine list with lots of California vintages.

U.S. 1 at MM 49.5 (bay side), Marathon. ℭ **305/743-3314.** Main courses $10–$32. AE, MC, V. Mon–Sat 6–10pm.

Marker 88 ⭐⭐⭐ SEAFOOD/REGIONAL An institution in the Upper Keys, Marker 88 has been pleasing locals and visitors since it opened in the early 1970s. Chef-owner Andre Mueller fuses tropical fruit and fish with such items as crabmeat stuffing, asparagus, tomatoes, lemons, olives, capers, and mushrooms to make the most delectable and innovative seafood dishes around. Taking full advantage of his island location, Andre offers dozens of seafood selections, including Keys lobster, Bahamas conch, Florida Bay stone crabs, Gulf Coast shrimp, and an impressive variety of fish from around the country. After you've figured out what kind of seafood to have, you can choose from a dozen styles of preparation. The Keys' standard is meunière, which is a subtle, tasty sauce of lemon and parsley. Although everything looks tempting, don't overorder—portions are huge. The waitresses, who are pleasant enough, require a bit of patience, but the food is worth it.

U.S. 1 at MM 88 (bay side), Islamorada. ✆ 305/852-9315. Reservations recommended. Main courses $14–$33. AE, DC, DISC, MC, V. Tues–Sun 5–11pm. Closed in September.

Morada Bay ★★ CARIBBEAN/AMERICAN This lovely bay-side bistro offers superfresh, innovative seafood as well as more basic offerings, such as chicken fajitas, hamburgers, and salads. Salads such as the Sunshine Salad are large and lavished with slices of avocado, mango, and tomato. When in season, delicious raw oysters are imported from Long Island. Fish dishes are always fresh and served in a number of styles; I like mine jerked with a peppery coating and nearly black finish. If you can't decide, share a few items from the tapas menu: jumbo shrimp cocktails, fried calamari, conch fritters, smoked fish dip, or a charcuterie of sausage and ham on country bread.

U.S. 1 at MM 81.6, Islamorada. ✆ 305/664-0604. Reservations recommended for large groups. Main courses $17–$28. AE, MC, V. Daily 11:30am–10pm.

MODERATE

Green Turtle Inn ★★ SEAFOOD The Green Turtle Inn was established in 1947 as a place where anglers and travelers to and from Key West could stop for local delicacies made from sea turtles harvested in local waters. It has become the quintessential Keys eatery, with a friendly, local flavor and delicious and *different* fare, such as turtle steaks, soups, and chowders. Alligator steak is also popular and, yes, it does taste like chicken. Campy house pianist Tina Martin has become somewhat of a local celebrity, but it's really the Turtle Chowder for which the Inn has become best known. The restaurant also has a cannery so you can take some of the chowder to your friends who won't believe how good it is until they taste it for themselves.

U.S. 1 at MM 81.5, Islamorada. ✆ 305/664-9031. Main courses $13.50–$21.95. AE, DISC, MC, V. Tues–Sun Noon–10pm.

Lazy Days Oceanfront Bar and Seafood Grill ★ SEAFOOD/AMERICAN Opened in 1992, the Lazy Days quickly became one of the most popular restaurants around, mostly because of its large portions and lively atmosphere. Dining on the oceanfront outdoor veranda is highly recommended. Meals are pricier than the casual dining room would suggest, but the food is good enough and the menu varied. Steamed clams with garlic and bell peppers make a tempting appetizer. The menu focuses on—what else?—seafood, but you can also find good pasta dishes such as linguine with littleneck clams. Most main courses come with baked potato, vegetables, a tossed salad, and French bread, making appetizers redundant.

U.S. 1 at MM 79.9, Islamorada. ✆ 305/664-5256. Main courses $11–$24. AE, DISC, MC, V. Wed–Sun 11:30am–10pm.

Lorelei Restaurant and Cabana Bar ★★ SEAFOOD/BAR FOOD   Don't resist the siren call of the enormous, sparkling roadside mermaid—you won't be dashed onto the rocks. This big old fish house and bar is a great place for a snack, a meal, or a beer. Inside, a good-value menu focuses mainly on seafood. When in season, lobsters are the way to go. For $20, you can get a good-sized tail—at least a 1 pounder—prepared any way you like. Other fare includes the standard clam chowder, fried shrimp, and doughy conch fritters. Salads and soups are hearty and satisfying. For those tired of fish, the menu also offers a few beef selections. The outside bar has live music every evening, and you can order snacks and light meals from a limited menu that is satisfying and well priced.

U.S. 1 at MM 82, Islamorada. © 305/664-4656. Main courses $12–$24. AE, DC, DISC, MC, V. Daily 7am–10:30pm. Outside bar serves breakfast 7–11am; lunch/appetizer menu 11am–9pm. Bar closes at midnight.

INEXPENSIVE

Calypso's ★ SEAFOOD/PASTA   The awning still bears the name of the former restaurant, Demar's, but the food here is all Todd Lollis's. Even though he looks like he might be more comfortable at a Grateful Dead concert than in a kitchen, this inspired young chef turns out inventive seafood dishes in a casual and rustic waterside setting. If it's available, try the butter pecan sauce over whatever fish is freshest. Don't miss the white wine sangria, full of tangy oranges and limes and topped with a dash of cinnamon. The prices are surprisingly reasonable, but the service can be a little more laid-back than you're used to. The toughest part is finding the place. From the south, turn right at the blinking yellow lights near MM 99.5 to Ocean Bay Drive; turn right. Look for the blue vinyl-sided building on the left.

1 Seagate Blvd. (near MM 99.5), Key Largo. © 305/451-0600. Main courses $8–$16. MC, V. Wed–Mon 11:30am–10pm; Fri until 11pm.

Islamorada Fish Company ★★ SEAFOOD   The original Islamorada Fish Company has been selling seafood out of its roadside shack since 1948. It's still the best place to pick up a cooler of stone crab claws in season (mid-October through April). Also great are the fried-fish sandwiches, served with melted American cheese, fried onions, and coleslaw. A few hundred yards up the road (at MM 81.6) is Islamorada Fish Company Restaurant & Bakery, the newer establishment, which looks like an average diner, but has a selection of fantastic seafood and pastas. It's also the place for breakfast. Locals gather for politics and gossip as well as delicious grits, oatmeal, omelets, and homemade pastries. © 305/664-8363; open Thursday to Tuesday 6am to 9pm, Wednesday 6am to 2pm. Discover, MasterCard, and Visa are accepted.

U.S. 1 at MM 81.5 (up the street from Cheeca Lodge), Islamorada. © 800/258-2559 or 305/664-9271. www.islamoradafishco.com. Reservations not accepted. Main courses $8–$27; appetizers $4–$7. DISC, MC, V. Sun–Thurs, 11am–9pm; Fri–Sat, 11am–10pm.

Key Largo's Crack'd Conch SEAFOOD   This colorful little shack looks appealing from the road and isn't a bad place to stop for a beer—more than 100 imported and domestic flavors to choose from—and a decent basket of fried clams, shrimp, chicken, and, of course, conch. Prices are higher than they ought to be, considering the quality and atmosphere, but they won't bust your budget.

U.S. 1 at MM 105.5 (ocean side). © 305/451-0732. Reservations not accepted. Main courses $9–$15; sandwiches $3.25–$7. AE, DC, DISC, MC, V. Thurs–Tues noon–10pm.

Time Out Barbecue ★★ BARBECUE   This barbecue joint serves up hot and hearty old-fashioned barbecue that is among the best around. According to management, the secret is in the slow-cooking—more than 10 hours for the melt-in-your-mouth soft pork sandwich. Topped off with delicious, not-too-creamy coleslaw and sweet baked beans, any of the many offerings are worth a stop. You can grab a seat at the picnic table on the grassy lawn next to the Trading Post.

U.S. 1 at MM 81.5 (ocean side). (C) 305/664-8911. Sandwiches $4.25–$6; rib and chicken platters to share $7–$15. MC, V. Daily 11am–10pm.

THE UPPER & MIDDLE KEYS AFTER DARK

Nightlife in the Upper Keys tends to start before the sun goes down, often at noon, since most people—visitors and locals alike—are on vacation. Also, many anglers and sports-minded folk go to bed early.

Hog Heaven opened in the early 1990s, the joint venture of some young locals tired of tourist traps. Located at MM 85.3 just off the main road on the ocean side in Islamorada ((C) **305/664-9669**), it's a welcome respite from the neon-colored cocktail circuit. This whitewashed biker bar offers a waterside view and diversions that include big-screen TVs and video games. The food isn't bad, either. The atmosphere is cliquish since most patrons are regulars, so start up a game of pool or skeet to break the ice.

No trip is complete without a stop at the **Tiki Bar at the Holiday Isle Resort,** U.S. 1 at MM 84, Islamorada ((C) **800/327-7070** or 305/664-2321). Hundreds of revelers visit this ocean-side spot for drinks and dancing at any time of day, but the live rock music starts at 8:30pm. (See "Where to Stay," earlier in this chapter.) The thatched-roof Tiki Bar draws a high-energy but laid-back mix of thirsty people, all in pursuit of a good time. In the afternoon and early evening (when everyone is either sunburned, drunk, or just happy to be dancing to live reggae), head for **Kokomo's,** just next door. Kokomo's often closes at 7:30pm on weekends, so get there early. For information, call the Holiday Isle Resort.

Locals and tourists mingle at the outdoor cabana bar at **Lorelei** (see "Where to Dine," above). Most evenings after 5pm, you'll find local bands playing on a thatched-roof stage—mainly rock and roll, reggae and sometimes blues.

Woody's Saloon and Restaurant, on U.S. 1 at MM 82, Islamorada ((C) **305/664-4335**), is a lively, wacky, raunchy place serving up mediocre pizzas and live bands almost every night. The house band, Big Dick and the Extenders, showcases a 300-pound Native American who does a lewd, rude, and crude routine of jokes and songs starting at 9pm, Tuesday through Sunday. He is a legend. By the way, don't think you're lucky if you are offered the front table: It's the target seat for Big Dick's haranguing. Avoid the lame karaoke performance on Sunday and Monday evenings. There's a small cover charge most nights. Drink specials, contests, and the legendary Big Dick keep this place packed until 4am almost every night.

For a more subdued atmosphere, try the handsome wood bar at **Zane Grey's** (on the second floor of World Wide Sportsman at MM 81.5). Outside, enjoy a view of the calm waters of the bay; inside, soak up the history of some real old anglers. You'll feel like a real swell in this stained-glass, mahogany-decked club. It is open from 11am to 11pm, and later on weekends. Call to find out who is playing on weekends ((C) **305/664-4244**), when there is live entertainment and no cover charge.

2 The Lower Keys: Big Pine Key to Coppitt Key

128 miles SW of Miami

Unlike their neighbors to the north and south, the Lower Keys (including Big Pine, Sugarloaf, and Summerland) are devoid of rowdy spring-break crowds, boast few T-shirt and trinket shops, and have almost no late-night bars. What they do offer are the very best opportunities to enjoy the vast natural resources on land and water that make the area so rich. Stay overnight in the Lower Keys, rent a boat, and explore the reefs—it might be the most memorable part of your trip.

ESSENTIALS

GETTING THERE   See "Essentials" for the Upper and Middle Keys, earlier in this chapter. Continue south on U.S. 1. The Lower Keys start at the end of the Seven-Mile Bridge.

VISITOR INFORMATION   The **Big Pine and Lower Keys Chamber of Commerce,** ocean side of U.S. 1 at MM 31 (P.O. Box 430511), Big Pine Key, FL 33043 (© **800/872-3722** or 305/872-2411; fax 305/872-0752; www. lowerkeyschamber.com), is open Monday through Friday from 9am to 5pm and Saturday from 9am to 3pm. The pleasant staff will help with anything a traveler may need. Call, write, or stop in for a comprehensive, detailed information packet.

WHAT TO SEE & DO

Once the centerpiece of the Lower Keys and still a great asset is **Bahia Honda State Park**⟨★, U.S. 1 at MM 37.5, Big Pine Key (© **305/872-2353**), which, even after the violent storms of 1998, has one of the most beautiful coastlines in South Florida. Bahia Honda (pronounced *Bah*-ya) is a great place for hiking, bird watching, swimming, snorkeling, and fishing. The 524-acre park encompasses a wide variety of ecosystems, including coastal mangroves, beach dunes, and tropical hammocks. There are miles of trails packed with unusual plants and animals and a small white beach. Shaded seaside picnic areas are fitted with tables and grills. Although the beach is never wider than 5 feet even at low tide, this is the Lower Keys' best beach area.

True to its name (Spanish for "deep bay"), the park has relatively deep waters close to shore, and they are perfect for snorkeling and diving. Easy offshore snorkeling here gives even novices a chance to lie suspended in warm water and simply observe diverse marine life passing by. Or else head to the stunning reefs at Looe Key, where the coral and fish are more vibrant than anywhere else in the United States. Snorkeling trips depart daily from March through September and cost $25.95 for adults, $20.95 for youths 6 to 14, and free for children 5 and under. Call © **305/872-3210** for a schedule.

Admission to the park is $4 per vehicle (plus 50¢ per person), $1.50 per pedestrian or bicyclist, free for children 5 and under. If you are alone in a car, you'll pay only $2.50. Open daily from 8am to sunset.

The most famous residents of the Lower Keys are the tiny Key deer. Of the estimated 300 existing in the world, two-thirds live on Big Pine Key's **National Key Deer Refuge** ⟨★. To get your bearings, stop by the rangers' office at the Winn-Dixie Shopping Plaza near MM 30.5 off U.S. 1. They'll give you an informative brochure and map of the area. The refuge is open Monday through Friday from 8am to 5pm.

If the office is closed, head out to the Blue Hole, a former rock quarry now filled with the fresh water that's vital to the deer's survival. To get there, turn right at Big Pine Key's only traffic light onto Key Deer Boulevard (take the left fork immediately after the turn) and continue 1½ miles to the observation-site parking lot, on your left. The half-mile **Watson Hammock Trail,** about a third of a mile past the Blue Hole, is the refuge's only marked footpath. Try coming out here in the early morning or late evening to catch a glimpse of these gentle, dog-sized deer. They are more active in cool hours and in cooler times of the year. Refuge lands are open daily from half an hour before sunrise to half an hour after sunset. Don't be surprised to see a lazy alligator warming itself in the sun, particularly in outlying areas around the Blue Hole. Whatever you do, do not feed the deer—it will threaten their survival. Call the **park office** (© **305/ 872-2239**) to find out about the infrequent free tours of the refuge, scheduled throughout the year.

The only man-made attraction in the Lower Keys is the **Sugarloaf Bat Tower,** off U.S. 1 at MM 17 (next to Sugarloaf Airport on the bay side). In a vain effort to battle the ubiquitous troublesome mosquitoes in the Lower Keys, developer Clyde Perkey built this odd structure to lure bug-eating bats. Despite his alluring design and a pungent bat aphrodisiac, his guests never showed. Since 1929, this wooden, flat-topped, 45-foot-high pyramid has stood empty and deserted, except for the occasional tourist who stops to wonder what it is. There is no sign or marker to commemorate this odd remnant of ingenuity. It's worth a 5-minute detour to see it. To get there, turn right at the Sugarloaf Airport sign and then right again onto the dirt road that begins just before the airport gate; the tower is about 100 yards ahead.

OUTDOOR PURSUITS

BICYCLING   If you have your own bike, or your lodging offers a rental (many do), the Lower Keys is a great place to get off busy U.S. 1 to explore the beautiful back roads. On Big Pine Key, cruise along Key Deer Boulevard (at MM 30). Those with fat tires can ride into the National Key Deer Refuge.

BIRD WATCHING   Bring your birding books. A stopping point for migratory birds on the Eastern Flyway, the Lower Keys are populated with many West Indian bird species, especially during spring and fall. The small vegetated islands of the Keys are the only nesting sites in the United States for the great white heron and the white-crowned pigeon. They're also some of the very few breeding places for the reddish egret, the roseate spoonbill, the mangrove cuckoo, and the black-whiskered vireo. Look for them on Bahia Honda and the many uninhabited islands nearby.

BOATING   Dozens of shops rent powerboats for fishing and reef exploring. Most also rent tackle, sell bait, and have charter captains available. **Bud Boats,** at the Old Wooden Bride Fishing Camp and Marina, MM 30 in Big Pine Key (© **305/872-9165**), has a wide selection of well-maintained boats. Depending on the size, rentals cost between $70 and $250 for a day, between $50 and $130 for a half day. Another good option is **Jaybird's Powerboats,** U.S. 1 at MM 33, Big Pine Key (© **305/872-8500**). They rent for full days only. Prices start at $155 for a 19-footer.

CANOEING & KAYAKING   The Overseas Highway (U.S. 1) touches on only a few dozen of the many hundreds of islands that make up the Keys. To really see the Lower Keys, rent a kayak or canoe—perfect for these shallow waters. **Reflections Kayak Nature Tours,** operating out of Parmer's Resort, on U.S. 1 at MM 28.5, Little Torch Key (© **305/872-2896**), offers fully outfitted backcountry wildlife tours, either on your own or with an expert. A former U.S. Forest Service guide, Mike Wedeking, keeps up an engaging discussion describing the area's fish, sponges, coral, osprey, hawks, eagles, alligators, raccoons, and deer. The 3-hour tours cost $49 per person and include spring water, fresh fruit, granola bars, and use of binoculars. Bring a towel and sea sandals or sneakers.

DIVING & FISHING   A day spent fishing, either in the shallow backcountry or in the deep sea, is a great way to ensure yourself a fresh fish dinner, or you can release your catch and just appreciate the challenge. Whichever you choose, **Larry Threlkeld's Strike Zone Charters,** U.S. 1 at MM 29.5, Big Pine Key (© **305/872-9863**), is the charter service to call. Prices for fishing boats start at $450 for a half day and $595 for a full day. If you have enough anglers to share the price, it isn't too steep. They may be able to match you with other interested visitors.

Especially since the *Adolphus Busch Sr.* was sunk off Looe Key in 100 feet of water, the lower Keys also offers some prime diving. To get to the 210-foot island freighter on your own boat, head to coordinates 24.31.819N, 81.27.643W, between Looe Key and American Shoals. Strike Zone will take you for $50 without equipment.

HIKING   You can hike throughout the flat marshy Keys, on both marked trails and meandering coastlines. The best places to trek through nature are **Bahia Honda State Park** at MM 29.5 and **National Key Deer Refuge** at MM 30 (for more information on both, see "What to See & Do," above). Bahia Honda Park has a free brochure describing an excellent self-guided tour along the Silver Palm Nature Trail. You'll traverse hammocks, mangroves, and sand dunes and cross a lagoon. You can do the walk (which is less than a mile) in under half an hour and explore a great cross-section of the natural habitat in the Lower Keys.

SNORKELING & DIVING   Snorkelers and divers should not miss the Keys' most dramatic reefs at the **Looe Key National Marine Sanctuary.** Here, you'll see more than 150 varieties of hard and soft coral—some, centuries old—as well as every type of tropical fish, including the gold and blue parrot fish, moray eels, barracudas, French angels, and tarpon. **Looe Key Dive Center,** U.S. 1 at MM 27.5, Ramrod Key (© **305/872-2215**), offers a mind-blowing 5-hour tour aboard a 45-foot catamaran with two shallow 1-hour dives for snorkelers and scuba divers. Snorkelers pay $25, and divers with their own equipment pay $40; on Wednesdays and Saturdays you can do a fascinating dive to a wreck for $45. Good-quality rentals are available. (See "What to See & Do," above, for other diving options.)

SHOPPING

Certainly not known for great shopping, the Lower Keys do happen to be home to many talented visual artists, particularly those who specialize in depicting their natural surroundings. The **Artists in Paradise Gallery,** on Big Pine Key in the Winn-Dixie Shopping Plaza, near MM 30.5, 1 block north of U.S. 1 at the traffic light (© **305/872-1828**), displays a changing selection of watercolors, oils, photos, and sculptures. This cooperative gallery displays the work of more than a dozen artists who share the task of watching the store. Hours are usually daily from 10am to 6pm.

WHERE TO STAY

There are a number of cheap, fairly gross fish shacks along the highway for those who want bare-bones accommodations. So far, there are no national hotel chains in the Lower Keys. For information on lodging in cabins or trailers at local campgrounds, see "Camping," below.

VERY EXPENSIVE

Little Palm Island ✦✦✦   This exclusive island escape—host to presidents and royalty—is not just a place to stay while in the Lower Keys; it is a destination all its own. Built on a private 5-acre island, it's accessible only by boat. Guests stay in thatched-roof duplexes amid lush foliage and flowering tropical plants. Many villas have ocean views and private sun decks with rope hammocks. Inside, the romantic suites have all the comforts and conveniences of a luxurious contemporary beach cottage, but without telephones, TVs, or alarm clocks. As if its location weren't idyllic enough, a new full-service spa opened on the island. Note that on the breezeless south side of the island, you may get invaded by mosquitoes, even in the winter. (So bring spray and lightweight long-sleeved clothing.) Known for its innovative and pricey food, Little Palm also hosts visitors just for dinner or lunch. If you are staying on the island, opt for the full American plan, which includes three meals a day for about $140 per person. If you pay a la carte, you could spend that much just on dinner. At these prices, Little Palm appeals to those who aren't keeping track. One accessible unit available for the traveler with disabilities.

Launch is at the ocean side of U.S. 1 at MM 28.5, Little Torch Key, FL 33042. ✆ 800/343-8567 or 305/872-2524. Fax 305/872-4843. www.littlepalmisland.com. 28 bungalows, 2 deluxe suites. Winter $795–$1,695 per couple. Off-season $695–$1,595. Rates include transportation to and from the island and unlimited (nonmotorized) water sports. Meal plans include 2 meals daily for $125 per person per day, 3 meals at $140 per person. AE, DC, DISC, MC, V. No children under 16. **Amenities:** Restaurant; bar; 2 pools (1 outdoor with small waterfall; 1 indoor); health club and spa; extensive water-sports equipment/rental; concierge; courtesy van from Key West or Marathon airport; ferry service to and from the mainland; limited room service; in-room massage; laundry and dry-cleaning services. *In room:* A/C, dataport, minibar, coffeemaker, hairdryer, Jacuzzi.

MODERATE

Deer Run Bed and Breakfast ✦✦ *(Finds)*   Located directly on the beach, this small, homey, smoke-free B&B is a real find. One upstairs and two downstairs guest rooms are comfortably furnished with queen-size beds and good closets. Rattan and 1970s-style chairs and couches furnish the living room, along with 13 birds and three cats. Breakfast, which is served on a pretty, fenced-in porch, is cooked to order. The wooded area around the property is full of deer, which are often spotted on the beach as well. Ask to use one of the bikes to explore nearby nature trails. The owner prefers adults and mature children only.

Long Beach Dr. (P.O. Box 431), Big Pine Key, FL 33043. ✆ 305/872-2015. Fax 305/872-2842. deerrunbb@ aol.com. 3 units. Winter from $165 double; off-season from $95 double. Rates include full breakfast. No credit cards. From U.S. 1, turn left at the Big Pine Fishing Lodge (MM 33); continue for about 2 miles. No children under 16. **Amenities:** Jacuzzi; free use of bikes. *In room:* A/C, TV.

INEXPENSIVE

Parmer's Resort ✦✦   Parmer's, a fixture here for more than 20 years, is well known for its charming hospitality and helpful staff. This downscale resort offers modest but comfortable cottages, each one of them unique. Some are waterfront, many have kitchenettes, and others are just a bedroom. Room 26, a one-bedroom efficiency, is especially nice, with a small sitting area that faces the water. Room 6, a small efficiency, has a kitchenette and an especially large bathroom. The rooms all have linoleum floors, dated painted rattan furnishings, fake flowers, and thrift-store art—but they're very clean. Many can be combined to accommodate large families. The hotel's waterfront location almost makes up for the fact that you must pay extra for maid service.

Barry Ave. (P.O. Box 430665), near MM 28.5, Little Torch Key, FL 33043. ℂ **305/872-2157.** Fax 305/872-2014. www.parmersresort.com. 45 units. Winter and summer, from $69 double; from $95 efficiency. Fall $55–$65 double; from $75 efficiency. Rates include continental breakfast. AE, DISC, MC, V. Turn right onto Barry Ave. Resort is a half-mile down on the right. **Amenities:** Heated pool; boat ramp; bike rental; laundromat. *In room:* A/C, TV.

CAMPING

Bahia Honda State Park ★★★ (ℂ **305/872-2353;** www8.myflorida.com/communities/learn/stateparks/district5) offers some of the best camping in the Keys, even after the devastating storms of 1998. It is as loaded with facilities and activities as it is with campers. However, don't be discouraged by its popularity—this park encompasses more than 500 acres of land. There are 80 campsites and six spacious and comfortable cabin units that were reconstructed between 2000 and 2001. Cabins hold up to eight guests and come complete with linens, kitchenettes, and utensils. You'll enjoy the wraparound terrace, barbecue pit, and rocking chairs.

For one to four people, camping here costs about $25 per site without electricity and $26 with electricity. Depending on the season, cabin prices change: Prices range from $50 to $110. Additional people (over four) cost $6 each. MasterCard and Visa are accepted.

Another excellent value can be found at the **KOA Sugarloaf Key Resort** ★★, near MM 20. This ocean-side facility has 200 fully equipped sites, with water, electricity, and sewer, that rent for about $70 a night (no-hook-up sites cost about $38). Or pitch a tent on the 5 acres of lush waterfront property. The resort also rents travel trailers. The 22-foot Dutchman sleeps six and is equipped with eating and cooking utensils. It costs about $100 a day. More luxurious trailers go for $160 a day. All major credit cards are accepted. For details, write them at P.O. Box 420469, Summerland Key, FL 33042 (ℂ **800/562-7731** or 305/745-3549; fax 305/745-9889; sugarloaf@koa.net).

WHERE TO DINE

There aren't many fine dining options in the Lower Keys, but the following are worth a stop for those passing through.

MODERATE

Mangrove Mama's Restaurant SEAFOOD/CARIBBEAN   As the dedicated locals who come daily for happy hour will tell you, this is a true Lower Keys institution and a dive in the best sense of the word. The restaurant is a shack that used to have a gas pump as well as a grill. Now, guests share the property with some miniature horses (out back) and stray cats. A handful of simple tables, inside and out, are shaded by banana trees and palm fronds. Fish is the menu's mainstay, although soups, salads, sandwiches, and omelets are also good. Grilled teriyaki chicken and club sandwiches are tasty alternatives to fish, as are meatless chef's salads and spicy barbecued baby back ribs.

U.S. 1 at MM 20, Sugarloaf Key. ℂ **305/745-3030.** Main courses $10–$20; lunch $6–$9; brunch $5–$7. MC, V. Daily 11:30am–10pm (11am in season).

The Truth About Keys Cuisine

There are few world-class chefs in the Florida Keys, but that's not to say the food isn't great. Restaurants here serve very fresh fish and a few local specialties—most notably conch fritters and chowder, Key lime pie, and stone crab claws and lobster when they're in season.

Although a commercial net-fishing ban has diminished the stock of once-abundant fish in these parts, even the humblest of restaurants can be counted on to take full advantage of the gastronomic treasures of their own backyard. The Keys have everything a cook could want: the Atlantic and the Gulf of Mexico for impeccably fresh seafood; a tropical climate for year-round farm stand produce, including great tomatoes, beans, berries, and citrus fruit; and a freshwater swamp for rustic delicacies such as alligator, frog legs, and hearts of palm.

Conch fritters and chowder are mainstays on most tourist-oriented menus. Because the queen conch was listed as an endangered species by the U.S. government in 1985, however, the conch in your dish was most likely shipped fresh-frozen from the Bahamas or the Caribbean.

Key lime pie consists of the juice of tiny yellow Key limes (a fruit unique to South Florida), along with condensed milk, all in a graham cracker crust. Experts debate whether the true Key lime pie should have a whipped cream or a meringue topping, but all agree that the filling should be yellow, *never* green.

Another unique offering, the **Florida lobster** is an entirely different species from the more common Maine variety and has a sweeter meat. It's also known as the "Spiny" lobster because of all the bumps on its shell. You'll see only the tails on the menu because the Florida lobster has no claws.

Stone crabs are even better—succulent, sweet, tender, and very meaty. They've been written about and talked about by kings, presidents, and poets. Although you'll find them on nearly every menu in season (from October until May), consider buying a few pounds of jumbos at the fish store to take to the beach in a cooler. Don't forget to ask to have them cracked for you, and get a cup of creamy mustard sauce. Topped off with a cold bottle of champagne, there is no better meal. You'll be glad to know that after their claws are harvested, the crabs grow new ones, thus ensuring a long-lasting supply of these unique delicacies.

Monte's SEAFOOD   Monte's has survived for more than 20 years because the food is very good and incredibly fresh. Certainly nobody goes to this restaurant/ fish market for its atmosphere: Plastic place settings rest on plastic-covered pic-nic-style tables in a screen-enclosed dining patio. The day's catch may include shark, tuna, lobsters, stone crabs, or shrimp.

U.S. 1 at MM 25, Summerland Key. ℂ **305/745-3731.** Main courses $13–$17; lunch $6–$10. No credit cards. Mon–Sat 9am–10pm; Sun 10am–9pm.

INEXPENSIVE

Coco's Kitchen ⭐ CUBAN/AMERICAN   This tiny storefront has been dishing out black beans, rice, and shredded beef to fans of Cuban cuisine for more than 10 years. The owners, who are actually from Nicaragua, cook not only superior Cuban food but also some local specialties, Italian food, and Caribbean food. Specialties include fried shrimp, whole fried yellowtail, and Cuban-style roast pork (available only on Saturdays). The best bet is the daily special, which may be roasted pork or fresh grouper, served with rice and beans or salad and crispy fries. Top off the huge, cheap meal with a rich caramel-soaked flan.

283 Key Deer Blvd. (in the Winn-Dixie Shopping Center), Big Pine Key. ☎ 305/872-4495. Main courses $4.79–$11.95; breakfast $2–$4.50. No credit cards. Mon–Sat 7am–7:30pm. Turn right at the traffic light near MM 30.5. Stay in the left lane.

No Name Pub PUB FOOD/PIZZA   This funky old bar out in the boonies serves snacks and sandwiches until 11pm on most nights, and drinks until midnight. Pizzas are tasty—thick-crusted and supercheesy. Try one topped with local shrimps, or consider a bowl of chili with all the fixings—hearty and cheap. Also decent is the smoked fish dip. Everything is served on paper plates. Locals hang out at the rustic bar, one of the Florida Keys' oldest, drinking beer and listening to a jukebox heavy with 1980s selections. The decor, if you can call it that, is basic—the walls and ceilings are plastered with thousands of autographed dollar bills.

¼ mile south of No Name Bridge on N. Watson Blvd., Big Pine Key. ☎ 305/872-9115. Pizzas $6–$18; subs $5. MC, V. 11am–11pm. Turn right at Big Pine's only traffic light (near MM 30.5) onto Key Deer Blvd. Turn right on Watson Blvd. At stop sign, turn left. Look for a small wooden sign on the left marking the spot.

THE LOWER KEYS AFTER DARK

Although the mellow islands of the lower Keys aren't exactly known for wild nightlife, there are some friendly bars and restaurants where locals and tourists gather to hang out and drink.

One of the most scenic is **Sandbar** (☎ 305/872-9989), a wide-open breezy wooden house built on slender stilts and overlooking a wide channel on Barry Avenue (near MM 28.5). It attracts an odd mix of bikers and blue-hairs daily from 11am until 10pm and is a great place to overhear local gossip and colorful metaphors. Pool tables are the main attraction, but there's also live music some nights. The drinks are reasonably priced, and the food isn't too bad, either. For another fun bar scene, see **No Name Pub,** listed above in "Where to Dine."

3 Key West ⭐⭐⭐

159 miles SW of Miami

The locals, or "conchs" (pronounced *conks*), and the developers here have been at odds for years. This once low-key island has been thoroughly commercialized—there's a Hard Rock Cafe smack in the middle of Duval Street and thousands of cruise ship passengers descending on Mallory Square each day. It's definitely not the seedy town Hemingway and his cronies once called their own.

Laid-back Key West still exists, but it's now found in different places: the backyard of a popular guest house, for example, or an art gallery, or a secret garden, or the hip hangouts of Bahama Village. Fortunately there are plenty of these, and Key West's greatest historic charm is found just off the beaten path. Don't be afraid to explore these residential areas, as conchs are notoriously friendly. Of course, there's always the calm waters of the Atlantic and the Gulf of Mexico all around.

ACCOMMODATIONS ■

Abaco Inn **30**
Angelina Guest House **27**
The Brass Key **3**
Chelsea House **10**
The Grand **4**
Island City House Hotel **6**
Key West Hilton Resort & Marina **21**
Key West International Hostel **11**
La Pensione **9**
Marquesa Hotel **14**
Oasis **7**
Ocean Key Resort **18**
Pier House Resort & Caribbean Spa **17**
Rainbow House **15**
South Beach Oceanfront Motel **32**
Southernmost Point Guest House **31**
Weatherstation Inn **12**
Wyndam Beach Resort **16**

ATTRACTIONS ●

Aquarium **19**
Audubon House & Tropical Gardens **26**
Cemetery **8**
Chamber of Commerce **22**
East Martello Museum and Gallery **1**
Ernest Hemingway Home and Museum **28**
Fort Zachary Beach **33**
Harry S. Truman
   Little White House Museum **13**
Higgs Beach **5**
Lighthouse Museum **29**
Mallory Square **20**
Mel Fisher Maritime Heritage Museum **24**
Memorial Sculpture Garden **23**
Oldest House/Wrecker's Museum **25**
Smathers Beach **2**

The heart of town offers party people a good time. Here, you'll find good restaurants, fun bars, live music, rickshaw rides, and lots of shopping. Don't bother with a watch or tie—this is the home of the perennial vacation.

ESSENTIALS

GETTING THERE   For directions by car, see "Essentials" for the Upper and Middle Keys, earlier in this chapter. Continue south on U.S. 1. When entering Key West, stay in the far-right lane onto North Roosevelt Boulevard, which becomes Truman Avenue in Old Town. Continue for a few blocks, and you will find yourself on Duval Street, in the heart of the city. If you stay to the left, you'll also reach the city center after passing the airport and the remnants of historic houseboat row, where a motley collection of boats once made up one of Key West's most interesting neighborhoods.

Several regional airlines fly nonstop from Miami to Key West; fares are about $120 to $300 round-trip. **American Eagle** (© **800/443-7300;** www.aa.com)

and **US Airways Express** (© 800/428-4322; www.usairways.com) land at **Key West International Airport,** South Roosevelt Boulevard (© 305/296-5439), on the southeastern corner of the island.

Greyhound (© 800/231-2222; www.greyhound.com) has buses leaving Miami for Key West every day for about $30 to $32 one-way and $57 to $60 round-trip. Seats fill up in season, so come early. The ride takes about 4½ hours.

GETTING AROUND With limited parking, narrow streets, and congested traffic, driving in Old Town Key West is more of a pain than a convenience. Unless you're staying in one of the more remote accommodations, consider trading in the car for a bicycle. The island is small and as flat as a board, which makes it easy to negotiate, especially away from the crowded downtown. Many tourists also choose to cruise by moped, an option that can make navigating the streets risky, especially since there are no helmet laws in Key West. So be careful and spend the extra few bucks to rent a helmet; hundreds of visitors are seriously injured each year.

Rates for simple one-speed cruisers start at about $8 per day (from $40 per week). Mopeds start at about $12 for 2 hours, $25 per day, and $100 per week. The best shops include **The Bicycle Center** at 523 Truman Ave. (© 305/294-4556); the **Moped Hospital,** 601 Truman Ave. (© 305/296-3344); and **Tropical Bicycles & Scooter Rentals** at 1300 Duval St. (© 305/294-8136). **The Bike Shop,** 1110 Truman Ave. (© 305/294-1073), rents mountain bikes for $12 per day ($60 per week). Cruisers go for $8 per day and $40 per week. A $150 deposit is required for cruisers, $250 for mountain bikes.

PARKING Parking in Key West's Old Town is particularly limited. There is a well-placed **municipal parking lot** at Simonton and Angela streets just behind the firehouse and police station. If you have brought a car, you may want to stash it here while you enjoy the very walkable downtown section of Key West.

VISITOR INFORMATION The **Florida Keys and Key West Visitors Bureau,** P.O. Box 1147, Key West, FL 33041 (© 800/FLA-KEYS; www. keywest.com), offers a free vacation kit packed with visitor information. The **Key West Chamber of Commerce,** 402 Wall St., Key West, FL 33040 (© 800/527-8539 or 305/294-2587; www.keywestchamber.com), also offers both general and specialized information. The lobby is open daily from 8:30am to 6pm; phones are answered from 8am to 8pm. The **Key West Visitors Center** also provides information on accommodations, goings-on, and restaurants; the number is © 800/LAST-KEY. It's open weekdays from 8am to 5:30pm and weekends from 8:30am to 5pm. Gay travelers will want to call the **Key West Business Guild** (© 305/294-4603), which represents more than 50 guest houses and B&Bs in town, as well as many other gay-owned businesses. Ask for its color brochure. Or try **Good Times Travel** (© 305/294-0980), which will set up lodging and package tours on the island.

ORIENTATION A mere 2-by-4-mile island, Key West is simple to navigate, even though there is no real order to the arrangement of streets and avenues. As you enter town on U.S. 1 (also called Roosevelt Boulevard), you will see most of the moderately priced chain hotels and fast-food restaurants. The better restaurants, shops, and outfitters are crammed onto Duval Street, the main thoroughfare of Key West's Old Town. On surrounding streets are the many inns and lodges in picturesque Victorian/Bahamian homes. On the southern side of the island is the coral beach area and some of the larger resort hotels.

The area called Bahama Village has only recently become known to tourists. With several cool restaurants and guest houses opened over the years, this hippie-ish neighborhood, complete with street-roaming chickens and cats, is the most urban and rough you'll find in the Keys. You might see a few seedy drug dealings on street corners, but it's nothing to be overly concerned with. Resident business owners tend to keep a vigilant eye on the neighborhood. It looks worse than it is. It's actually quite funky and a welcome diversion from the Duvalian mainstream.

SEEING THE SIGHTS

Before shelling out big bucks for any of the dozens of worthwhile attractions in Key West, I recommend getting an overview on either of the two comprehensive island tours, **The Conch Tour Train** or the **Old Town Trolley** (see "Organized Tours," below). There are simply too many attractions to list (including a Ripley's Believe It or Not! on Duval Street) and a number of historic houses. I've highlighted my favorites below but encourage you to seek out others.

Audubon House & Tropical Gardens ★★   This well-preserved home, dating from the early 19th century, stands as a prime example of early Key West architecture. Named after renowned painter and bird expert John James Audubon, who was said to have visited the house in 1832, the graceful two-story home is a peaceful retreat from the bustle of Old Town. Included in the price of admission is a self-guided audio tour that lasts about half an hour. With voices of several characters from the house's past, the tour never gets boring—although it is at times a bit hokey. See rare Audubon prints, gorgeous antiques, historical photos, and lush tropical gardens. Even if you don't want to spend the time and money to explore the grounds and home, check out the impressive gift shop, which sells a variety of fine mementos at reasonable prices.

205 Whitehead St. (between Greene and Caroline Sts.) ℂ 305/294-2116. Admission $8.50 adults, $3.50 children 6–12. Daily 9:30am–5pm (last admission at 4:45pm). Discounts for students and AAA and AARP members.

Ernest Hemingway Home and Museum ★★★   Hemingway's particularly handsome stone Spanish Colonial house, built in 1851, was one of the first on the island to be fitted with indoor plumbing and a built-in fireplace, and it contains the first swimming pool built on Key West. The author owned the home from 1931 until his death in 1961, and he lived there with about 50 cats, whose descendants, including the famed six-toed cats, still roam the premises. It was during those years that the Nobel Prize winner wrote some of his most famous works, including *For Whom the Bell Tolls, A Farewell to Arms,* and *The Snows of Kilimanjaro.* Fans may want to take the optional half-hour tour. It's interesting and included in the price of admission. If you're feline phobic, however, beware: There are cats everywhere.

907 Whitehead St. (between Truman Ave. and Olivia St.) ℂ 305/294-1575 or 305/294-1136. Fax 305/294-2755. www.hemingwayhome.com. Admission $9 adults, $5 children. Daily 9am–5pm. Limited parking.

Harry S. Truman Little White House Museum ★★   President Harry Truman used to refer to the White House as the "Great White Jail." On temporary leave from the big house, Truman discovered the serenity of Key West and made

---

Impressions

I've a notion to move the Capitol to Key West and just stay.

—President Harry S. Truman

his escape to what became known as the Little White House, which is open to the public for touring. The house is fully restored, and the exhibits document Truman's time in the Keys. Tours are every 20 minutes.

111 Front St., Key West ℂ305/294-9911. www.trumanlittlewhitehouse.com. Admission $8 adults, $4 children under 12. Daily 9am–5pm.

Key West Cemetery ★★★ *Finds* This funky, picturesque cemetery is the epitome of the quirky Key West image, as irreverent as it is humorous. Many tombs are stacked several high, condominium style—the rocky soil made digging 6 feet under nearly impossible for early settlers. Headstones reflect residents' lighthearted attitudes toward life and death. I TOLD YOU I WAS SICK is one of the more famous epitaphs, as is the tongue-in-cheek widow's inscription AT LEAST I KNOW WHERE HE'S SLEEPING TONIGHT.

Entrance at Margaret and Angela Sts. ℂ 305/294-WALK for tour reservations. Free admission. Daily dawn to dusk.

East Martello Museum and Gallery Adjacent to the airport, the East Martello Museum is located in a Civil War–era brick fort that itself is worth a visit. The museum contains a bizarre variety of exhibits that collectively do a thorough job of interpreting the city's intriguing past. Historical artifacts include model ships, a deep-sea diver's wooden air pump, a crude raft from a Cuban "boat lift," a supposedly haunted doll, a Key West–style children's playhouse from 1918, and a horse-drawn hearse. Exhibits illustrate the Keys' history of salvaging, sponging, and cigar making. After seeing the galleries, climb a steep spiral staircase to the top of a lookout tower for good views over the island and ocean.

3501 S. Roosevelt Blvd. ℂ 305/296-3913. Admission $6 adults, $4 seniors, $3 children 8–12, free for children 7 and under. Daily 9:30am–5pm (last admission is at 4pm).

Key West Aquarium ★★ *Kids* The oldest attraction on the island, the Key West Aquarium is a modest but fascinating exhibit. A long hallway of eye-level displays showcase dozens of varieties of fish and crustaceans. See delicate sea horses swaying in the backlit tanks. Kids can touch sea cucumbers and sea anemones in a shallow tank in the entryway. If you can, catch one of the free guided tours where you can witness the dramatic feeding frenzy of the sharks, tarpon, barracudas, stingrays, and turtles.

1 Whitehead St. (at Mallory Sq.). ℂ 305/296-2051. www.keywestaquarium.com. Admission $8 adults, $4 children 4–12, free for children under 4. Tickets are good for 2 consecutive days. Look for discount coupons at local hotels, at Duval St. kiosks, and from trolley and train tours. Daily 10am–6pm; tours at 11am, 1pm, 3pm, and 4pm.

Key West Lighthouse Museum ★ When the Key West Lighthouse opened in 1848, many locals mourned. Its bright warning to ships signaled the end of a profitable era for wreckers, the pirate salvagers who looted reef-stricken ships. The story of this and other Keys lighthouses is illustrated in a small museum that was formerly the keeper's quarters. When radar and sonar made the lighthouse obsolete, it was opened to visitors as a tourist attraction. It's worth mustering the energy to climb the 88 claustrophobic steps to the top, where you'll be rewarded with magnificent panoramic views of Key West and the ocean.

938 Whitehead St. ℂ 305/294-0012. Admission $6 adults, $2 children 7–12, free for children 6 and under. Daily 9:30am–5pm (last admission at 4:30pm).

Key West's Shipwreck Historeum   You'll see more-impressive artifacts at nearby Mel Fisher's museum, but the dramatic reenactments of the old ship-wrecking days at this place are unique and entertaining. The interactive show is best for teens and adults and includes scenes starring Key West's wealthiest wrecker Asa Tift, plus lots of intriguing video clips and stories of the area's heyday.

1 Whitehead St. (at Mallory Sq.). (C) **305/292-8990**. Fax 305/292-5536. Admission $8 adults, $4 children 4–12. Shows daily every half-hour 9:45am–4:45pm.

Mel Fisher Maritime Heritage Museum ★★★   This museum honors local hero Mel Fisher, whose death in 1998 was mourned throughout South Florida, and who, along with a crew of other salvagers, found a multimillion-dollar treasure trove in 1985 aboard the wreck of the Spanish galleon *Nuestra Señora de Atocha*. The admission price is somewhat steep, but if you're into diving, pirates, and sunken treasures, check out this small informative museum, full of doubloons, pieces of eight, emeralds, and solid-gold bars. A 1700 English merchant slave ship, the only tangible evidence of the transatlantic slave trade, is on view on the museum's second floor. A dated but informative film provides a good background for Fisher's incredible story.

200 Greene St. (C) **305/294-2633**. Admission $6.50 adults, $2 children 6–12, free for children 5 and under. Daily 9:30am–5pm. Take U.S. 1 to Whitehead St. and turn left on Greene.

Memorial Sculpture Garden ★   Installed in 1997, this impressive sculpture garden contains a large monument to the wreckers who made Key West rich more than a century ago. Also on display are 36 bronze busts of the island's most colorful leaders and characters. There's Harry Truman, Henry Flagler, and, of course, Ernest Hemingway, all mounted on elegant coral columns.

Mallory Sq. between Whitehead and Wall Sts. Free admission.

Oldest House/Wrecker's Museum ★   Dating from 1829, this old New England Bahama House has survived pirates, hurricanes, fires, warfare, and economic ups and downs—it gives witness to a slower, easier time in the island's life. The 1½-story home was designed by a ship's carpenter and incorporates many features from maritime architecture, including portholes and a ship's hatch designed for ventilation before the advent of air-conditioning. Especially interesting is the detached kitchen building outfitted with a brick "beehive"

Moments **A Great Escape**

Many people complain that Key West's quirky, quaint panache has been lost to the vulture of capitalism, evidenced in the glut of T-shirt shops and tacky bars. But that's not entirely so. For a quiet respite, visit the Key West Botanical Gardens, a little-known slice of serenity tucked between the Aqueduct Authority plant and the Key West Golf Course. The 11-acre gardens—maintained by volunteers and funded by donations—contain the last hardwood hammock in Key West, plus a colorful representation of wildflowers, butterflies, and birds. Although the gardens received a terrible blow from the storms of 1998, the calm remains within them. Botanical Garden Way and College Rd., Stock Island. Free admission. Daily 8am–sunset. Follow College Rd.; then turn right just past Bayshore Manor.

Going, Going, Gone: Where to Catch the Famous Key West Sunset

A tradition in Key West, the Sunset Celebration can be relaxing or overwhelming, depending on your vantage point. If you're in town, you must check out this ritual at least once. Every evening, locals and visitors gather at the docks behind Mallory Square (at the westernmost end of Whitehead Street) to celebrate the day gone by. Secure a spot on the docks early to experience the carnival of portrait artists, acrobats, food vendors, animal acts, and other performers trading on the island's Bohemian image. But the carnival atmosphere isn't for everyone: Hold onto your bags and wallets as the tight crowds make Mallory Square at sunset prime pick-pocketing territory. In season, the crowd can be overwhelming, especially when the cruise ships are in port.

A better choice is the Hilton's **Sunset Deck** (© 305/294-4000), a luxurious bar on top of its restaurant at the intersection of Front and Greene streets. From the civilized calm of a casual bar, you can look down on the mayhem with a drink in hand.

Also near the Mallory madness is the **Ocean Key House's** bar. This long open-air pier serves up drinks and decent bar food against a dramatic pink- and yellow-streaked sky. It's located at the very tip of Duval Street (© 800/328-9815 or 305/296-7701).

For the very best potent cocktails and great bar food on an outside patio or enclosed lounge, try **Pier House's Havana Docks** at 1 Duval St. (© 305/296-4600). There's usually live music and a lively gathering of visitors enjoying this island's bounty.

oven and vintage cooking utensils. Although not a must-see on the Key West tour, history and architecture buffs will appreciate the finely preserved details.

322 Duval St. © 305/294-9502. Admission $5 adults; $1 children 6–12; free for children 5 and under. Daily 10am–4pm.

ORGANIZED TOURS

BY TROLLEY-BUS & TRAM Yes, it's more than a bit hokey to sit on this 60-foot tram of yellow cars, but it's worth it—at least once. The city's whole story is packed into a neat, 90-minute package on the **Conch Tour Train,** which covers the island and all its rich, raunchy history. Operating since 1958, the trains are open-air, which can make the ride uncomfortable in bad weather. The "train's" engine is a propane-powered Jeep disguised as a locomotive. Tours depart from both Mallory Square and the Welcome Center, near where U.S. 1 becomes North Roosevelt Boulevard, on the other side of the island. For more information, contact the **Conch** at (© 305/294-5161). The cost is $18 for adults, $9 for children 4 to 12, and free for children 3 and under. Daily departures are every half-hour from 9am to 4:30pm.

The **Old Town Trolley** is the choice in bad weather or if you are staying at one of the many hotels on its route. Humorous drivers maintain a running commentary as the enclosed tram loops around the island's streets past all the major sights. Trolleys depart from Mallory Square and other points around the island, including many area hotels. For details, call © **305/296-6688.** Tours are $18 for adults, $9 for children 4 to 12, and free for children 3 and under. Departures are daily every half-hour (though not always on the half-hour) from 9am to 4:45pm. Whichever you choose, these historic trivia-packed tours are well worth the price of admission.

BY AIR Proclaimed by the mayor as "the official air force of the Conch Republic," **Island Airplane Tours,** at Key West Airport, 3469 S. Roosevelt Blvd. (© **305/294-8687**), offers windy rides in its open-cockpit 1940 Waco biplanes that take you over the reefs and around the islands. Thrill seekers—and only they—will also enjoy a spin in the company's S2-B aerobatics airplane, which does loops, rolls, and sideways figure-eights. Company owner Fred Cabanas was "decorated" in 1991, after he spotted a Cuban airman defecting to the United States in a Russian-built MIG fighter. Sightseeing flights cost $50 to $200, depending on the duration.

BY BOAT The Pride of Key West, *Fireball,* at Zero Duval St. (© **305/296-6293;** fax 305/294-8704), is a 58-foot glass-bottomed catamaran that goes on both day and evening coral-reef tours and sunset cruises. Reef trips cost $20 per person; sunset cruises (4:30pm) are $25 per person and include snacks, sodas, and a glass of champagne. Kids sail for half-price.

The Wolf, at Schooner Wharf, Key West Seaport (© **305/296-9653;** fax 305/294-8388), is a 44-passenger topsail schooner, equipped with a cannon, that sets sail daily for daytime and sunset cruises around the Keys. Key West Seaport is located at the end of Greene Street. Day tours cost $35 per person (six people or more only); sunset sails cost $40 per person and include free champagne, wine, beer, soda, and live music.

Schooner Western Union (© **305/292-9830**) was built in 1939 and served as a cable-repair vessel until it was designated the flagship of the city of Key West and began day, sunset, and charter sailings. Sunset sailings are especially memorable and include entertainment, cocktails, and a cannon fire. Prices vary.

OTHER TOURS For a lively look at Key West, try a 2-hour tour of the island's five **most famous pubs.** It starts daily at 2:30pm, lasts 1½ hours, costs $21, and includes four drinks. Another fun tour is the 1-mile, 90-minute **nightly ghost tour,** leaving at 8pm from the Holiday Inn La Concha, 430 Duval St. Cost is $18 for adults and $10 for children under 12. This spooky and interesting tour gives participants insight into the many old island legends. Both tours are offered by the Key West Tour Association. Finally, there's a cemetery tour, which leaves daily at 10:30am (© **305/294-WALK**).

OUTDOOR PURSUITS

BICYCLING & MOPEDING A popular mode of transportation for locals and visitors, bikes and mopeds are available at many rental outlets in the city (see "Getting Around," earlier in this chapter). Escape the hectic downtown scene and explore the island's scenic side streets. Head away from Duval Street to South Roosevelt Boulevard and the beachside enclaves along the way.

BEACHES Unlike the rest of the Keys, you'll actually find a few small beaches here, although they don't compare with the state's wide natural wonders up the coast. A narrow rocky beach is typical of the Key's beaches. Here are your options: **Smathers Beach,** off South Roosevelt Boulevard west of the airport; **Higgs Beach,** along Atlantic Boulevard between White Street and

Reynolds Road; and **Fort Zachary Beach,** located off the western end of Southard Boulevard.

A magnet for partying teenagers, Smathers Beach is Key West's largest and most overpopulated beach. It was renovated in the spring of 2000 due to erosion and hurricane damage. It looks lovely. Despite the number of rowdy teens, the beach is actually quite clean. If you go early enough in the morning, you may notice some people sleeping on the beach from the night before.

Higgs Beach is a favorite among Key West's gay crowds, but what many people don't know is that beneath the sand is an unmarked cemetery of African slaves who died while waiting for freedom. Higgs has a playground and tennis courts and is near the minute Rest Beach, which is actually hidden by the White Street Pier.

Although there is an entrance fee ($3.75 per car, plus more for each passenger), I recommend Fort Zachary, since it also includes a great historical fort, a Civil War museum, and a large picnic area with tables, barbecue grills, bathrooms, and showers. Plus, large trees scattered across 87 acres provide shade for those who are reluctant to bake in the sun. The vulnerable point was damaged by Hurricane George in 1998, but replanting of native vegetation has made it better than before.

DIVING   One of the area's largest scuba schools, **Dive Key West Inc.,** 3128 N. Roosevelt Blvd. (✆ **800/426-0707** or 305/296-3823; fax 305/296-0609; www.divekeywest.com), offers instruction on all levels. Its dive boats take participants to scuba and snorkel sites on nearby reefs.

Wreck dives and night dives are two of the special offerings of **Lost Reef Adventures,** 261 Margaret St. (✆ **800/952-2749** or 305/296-9737). Regularly scheduled runs and private charters can be arranged. Phone for departure information.

FISHING   As any angler will tell you, there's no fishing like Keys fishing. Key West has it all: bonefish, tarpon, dolphin, tuna, grouper, cobia, and more. Sharks, too.

Step aboard a small exposed skiff for an incredibly diverse day of fishing. In the morning, you can head offshore for sailfish or dolphin (the fish, not the mammal), and then by afternoon, get closer to land for a shot at tarpon, permit, grouper, or snapper. Here in Key West, you can probably pick up more cobia—one of the best fighting and eating fish around—than anywhere else in the world. For a real fight, ask your skipper to go for the tarpon—the greatest fighting fish there is, famous for its dramatic "tail walk" on the water after it's hooked. Shark fishing is also popular.

You'll find plenty of competition among the charter fishing boats in and around Mallory Square. You can negotiate a good deal at **Charter Boat Row,** 1801 N. Roosevelt Ave. (across from the Shell station), home to more than 30 charter fishing and party boats. Just show up to arrange your outing, or call **Garrison Bite Marina** (✆ **305/292-8167**) for details.

⌒Tips Reel Deals

When looking for the best deals on fishing excursions, know that the bookers from the kiosks in town generally take 20% of a captain's fee in addition to an extra monthly fee. You can usually save yourself money by booking directly with a captain or going straight to one of the docks.

The advantage of the smaller, more expensive charter boats is that you can call the shots. They'll take you where you want to go, to fish for what you want to catch. These "light tackles" are also easier to maneuver, which means you can go to backcountry spots for tarpon and bonefish, as well as out to the open ocean for tuna and dolphin. You'll really be able to feel the fish, and you'll get some good fights. Larger boats, for up to six or seven people, are cheaper and best for kingfish, billfish, and sailfish. Consider Captain Vinnie Argiro's **Heavy Hitters Charters** (© 305/745-6665) if you want a light-tackle experience. For a larger boat, try Captain Henry Otto's 44-foot *Sunday,* docked at the Hyatt in Key West (© **305/294-7052**).

The huge commercial party boats are more for sightseeing than serious angling, though you can get lucky and get a few bites at one of the fishing holes. One especially good deal is the *Gulfstream III* (© **305/296-8494**), an all-day charter that goes out daily from 9:30am until 4pm. You'll pay $35, plus $3 for a rod and reel. This 65-foot party boat usually has at least 30 other anglers. Bring your own cooler or buy snacks on the boat. Beer and wine are allowed.

For serious anglers, nothing compares to the light-tackle boats that leave from **Oceanside Marina** (© 305/294-4676) on Stock Island, at 5950 Peninsula Ave., 1½ miles off U.S. 1. It's a 20-minute drive from Old Town on the Atlantic side. There are more than 30 light-tackle guides, which range from flatbed, backcountry skiffs to 28-foot open boats. There are also a few larger charters and a head or party boat that goes to the Dry Tortugas. Call the dockmaster for details.

For the light-tackle experience of your life, call **Captain Bruce Cronin** at © 305/294-4929 or **Captain Kenny Harris** at © 305/294-8843, two of the more famous (and pricey) captains still working these docks for over 20 years. You'll pay from $550 for a full day, usually about 8am until 4pm, and from $400 for half a day.

GOLF   A relative newcomer in terms of local recreation, golf is gaining in popularity here as it is in many visitor destinations. One of the area's only courses is **Key West Golf Club** (© 305/294-5232), an 18-hole course located just north of the island of Key West at MM 4.5 (turn onto College Road to the course entrance). Designed by Rees Jones, the course has plenty of mangroves and water hazards on its 6,526 yards. It's open to the public and has a new pro shop. Call ahead for tee-time reservations. $125 per player, including cart.

KAYAKING   **Mosquito Coast Outfitters,** housed in a woodsy wine bar at 1017 Duval St. (© 305/294-7178), operates a first-rate kayaking and snorkeling tour every day as long as the weather is mild. The tours depart at 9am sharp and cost $45 per person. Included in the price are snacks, soft drinks, and a guided tour of the mangrove-studded islands of Sugar Key or Geiger Key just north of Key West. You'll be back by about 3pm.

SHOPPING

You'll find all kinds of unique gifts and souvenirs in Key West, from coconut postcards to Key lime pies. On Duval Street, T-shirt shops outnumber almost any other business. If you must get a wearable memento, be careful of unscrupulous salespeople. Despite efforts to curtail the practice, many shops have been known to rip off unwitting shoppers. It pays to check the prices and the exchange rate before signing any sales slips. You are entitled to a written estimate of any T-shirt work before you pay for it.

At Mallory Square is the **Clinton Street Market,** an overly air-conditioned mall of kiosks and stalls designed for the many cruise-ship passengers who never venture beyond this supercommercial zone. Amid the dreck are some delicious coffee and candy shops and some high-priced hats and shoes. There's also a free and clean restroom.

Once the main industry of Key West, cigar making is enjoying renewed success at the handful of factories that survived the slow years. Stroll through **"Cigar Alley,"** between Front and Greene streets, where you will find *viejitos* (little old men) rolling fat stogies just as they used to do in their homeland across the Florida Straits. Stop at the **Key West Cigar Factory,** at 308 Front St. (© **305/294-3470**), for an excellent selection of imported and locally rolled smokes, including the famous El Hemingway. Remember, buying or selling Cuban-made cigars is illegal. Shops advertising "Cuban Cigars" are usually referring to domestic cigars made from tobacco grown from seeds that were brought from Cuba decades ago. To be fair, though, many premium cigars today are grown from Cuban seed tobacco—only it is grown in Latin America and the Caribbean, not Cuba.

If you are looking for local or Caribbean art, you will find nearly a dozen galleries and shops clustered on Duval Street between Catherine and Fleming streets. You'll also find some excellent shops scattered on the side streets. One worth seeking out is the **Haitian Art Co.,** 600 Frances St. (© **305/296-8932**), where you can browse through room upon room of original paintings from well-known and obscure Haitian artists in a range of prices from a few dollars to a few thousand. Also, check out **Cuba, Cuba!** at 814 Duval St. (© **305/295-9442**). Here, you will find paintings, sculpture, and photos by Cuban artists, and books and art from the island.

A favorite stop in the Keys is the deliciously fragrant **Key West Aloe** at 524 Front St., between Simonton and Duval streets (© **305/294-5592**). Since 1971, this shop has been selling a simple line of bath products, including lotions, shampoos, and soothing balms for those who want a reminder of the tropical breezes once they're back home. At the main shop (open until 8pm), you can find great gift baskets, tropical perfumes, and candies and cookies, too. In addition to frangipani, vanilla, and hibiscus scents, sample Key West for Men, a unique and alluringly musky bestseller.

Literature and music buffs will appreciate the many bookshops and record stores on the island. **Key West Island Bookstore** (© **305/294-2904**) at 513 Fleming St. carries new, used, and rare books and specializes in fiction by residents of the Keys, including Hemingway, Tennessee Williams, Shel Silverstein, Ann Beattie, Richard Wilbur, and John Hersey. **Flaming Maggie's** (© **305/294-3931**) at 830 Fleming St. carries a wide selection of gay books. Both shops are open daily.

One of the area's newer and funkier shops is the combination museum and gift shop called **Reworx** just behind the quirky gift gallery **Pandemonium** and the mosaic car at 825 Duval St. (© **305/294-0351.** Actually, this is Pandemonium's number, but the owners are friends. For Reworx, ask for Valerie.) Mammoth functional art made from salvaged metal parts is on display, and smaller works from recycled material are on sale. Admission to the adjacent museum of industrial art from recycled items is $7 for adults, $5 for children aged 5 to 12, and well worth it.

Also worth checking out in the newly revitalized Bahama Village section of town are the shops along Petronia Street between Thomas and Whitehead streets. Especially interesting is **Maskerville** (© **305/293-6937**), which sells a variety of feather-laden artwork from masks to lampshades. Just next door is **Hello Gorgeous,** at 315 Petronia (© **305/294-1770**), which carries unique clothing, shoes, and jewelry for women and impersonators (the name comes from one of Barbra Streisand's more memorable lines).

Off the beaten track at 814 Fleming St. (© **305/294-7901**) is the **Helio Gallery Store,** featuring locally made crafts and fine art.

For anything else, from bed linens to candlesticks to clothing, go to downtown's oldest and most renowned department store, **Fast Buck Freddie's,** at 500 Duval St. (© **305/294-2007**). For the same merchandise at reduced prices, try **Half Buck Freddie's** ⭐, 726 Caroline St. (© **305/294-6799**). Here you can shop for out-of-season bargains and "rejects" from the main store.

WHERE TO STAY

You'll find a wide variety of places to stay in Key West, from resorts with all the amenities to seaside motels, quaint bed-and-breakfasts, and clothing-optional guest houses. Unless you're in town during Key West's most popular holidays—Fantasy Fest (around Halloween) where Mardi Gras meets South Florida for the NC-17 set, Hemingway Days (in July) where Papa is seemingly and eerily alive and well, and Christmas and New Year's—or for a big fishing tournament (many are held from October to December) or boat-racing tourney, you can almost always find a place to stay at the last minute. However, you may want to book early, especially in the winter, when prime properties fill up and many require 2- or 3-night minimums. Prices at these times are also extremely high. Finding a decent room for under $100 a night is a real trick.

Another suggestion is to call **Vacation Key West** (© **800/595-5397** or 305/295-9500; www.flakeysol.com/vkw). The phones are answered weekdays from 9am to 6pm and Saturday from 11am to 2pm. This wholesaler offers discounts of 20% to 30% and can usually find last-minute deals. They represent mostly larger hotels and motels but also can place visitors in guest houses. The **Key West Innkeepers Association,** P.O. Box 6172, Key West, FL 33041 (© **800/492-1911** or 305/292-3600), can also help find lodging in any price range from its dozens of members and affiliates.

Most major hotel chains have at least one location in Key West; most are clustered on North Roosevelt Boulevard (U.S. 1). Moderately priced options include **Howard Johnson,** 3031 N. Roosevelt Blvd. (© **800/942-0913** or 305/296-6595); the **Ramada Inn,** 3420 N. Roosevelt Blvd. (© **800/330-5541** or 305/294-5541); the **Econo Lodge,** 3820 N. Roosevelt Blvd. (© **800/553-2666** or 305294-5511); the **Holiday Inn Beachside,** 3841 N. Roosevelt Blvd. (© **800/292-7706** or 305/294-2571); and the **Quality Inn,** 3850 N. Roosevelt Blvd. (© **800/228-5151** or 305/294-6681). The Howard Johnson and the Holiday Inn are the only hotels with gulf-view rooms; the other hotels listed are just across the street. Duval Street is less than 5 minutes away by car or taxi.

A last resort should be the **Holiday Inn La Concha Hotel** at 430 Duval St. (© **800/745-2191**). It is centrally located but has few amenities for the price.

Gay travelers will want to call the **Key West Business Guild** (© **305/294-4603**), which represents more than 50 guest houses and B&Bs in town, as well as many other gay-owned businesses. Be advised that most gay guest houses have a clothing-optional policy. One of the most elegant and popular ones is **Big Ruby's** (© **800/477-7829** or 305/296-2323) at 409 Applerouth Lane (a little alley just off Duval Street). A low cluster of buildings surrounds a lushly land-scaped courtyard where a hearty breakfast is served each morning and wine is poured at dusk. The mostly male guests hang out by a good-sized pool, tanning in the buff. Also popular is **Oasis** at 823 Fleming St. (© **305/296-2131**), which is superclean and friendly; enjoy the central location and a 14-seat hot tub.

Another luxurious property is **The Brass Key** at 412 Frances St. (© **305/ 296-4719**), which is more romantic and traditionally decorated and welcomes many lesbian travelers as well. *Out and About* gave it a five-star rating. For women only, the **Rainbow House,** 525 United St. (© **800/74-WOMYN** or 305/292-1450) is a large, fairly well maintained guest house with lots of privacy and amenities, including two pools and two hot tubs. Rates in season range from $109 to $229.

VERY EXPENSIVE

Hilton Key West Resort and Marina ★★   Completed in fall 1996, this Hilton, which saw a light room renovation in 2001, is a truly luxurious addition to downtown's hotel scene, situated at the very end of Duval Street in the middle of all of Old Town's action. The sparkling rooms are large and well appointed, with tropical decor and all the modern conveniences. Choose a suite in the main building if you want a large Jacuzzi in your living room. Otherwise, the marina building has great views. The secluded beach is great for an escape from the Duval Street frenzy. This giant is very popular with corporate and convention visitors. Flagler's, the elegant indoor dining room, offers ample breakfasts and a huge Sunday brunch.

Hilton's gorgeous **Sunset Key Guest Cottages** ★★★—whitewashed interiors, picture windows, fabulous views—are located 100 yards offshore on Sunset Key and are accessible only by private launch. Check in at the Hilton and take a 10-minute cruise to the island, where there are no cars, only a gourmet grocery, restaurant, bar, and free-form tropical pool with whirlpool jets. Sunset guests also have access to all water sports at the Hilton marina. Cottages are equipped with full kitchens, high-tech entertainment centers, and one, two, or three massive bedrooms. For true luxe, consider hiring a private chef for a meal or two.

245 Front St. (at the end of Duval St.), Key West, FL 33040. © **800/221-2424** or 305/294-4000. Fax 305/294-4086. www.keywestresort.hilton.com. 215 units. Winter $299–$525 double; $375–$800 suite. Off-season $195–$425 double; $300–$800 suite. 37 Sunset Key Cottages, up to 5 people: winter $575–$1,825; off-season $325–$1,095. Private chef: $75 per person plus add'l chef/hotel fees, tax, and gratuities. AE, DC, DISC, MC, V. Self parking $7, valet parking $10. **Amenities:** 2 restaurants; pool bar; outdoor heated pool; health club; Jacuzzi; water-sports equipment/rental; full-service marina; bike rental; game room; concierge; business center; limited room service; in-room massage; self-service laundry; dry-cleaning service. *In room:* A/C, TV, dataport, minibar, coffeemaker, hairdryer, iron.

Pier House Resort and Caribbean Spa ★★★   Pier House is one of the area's best resort choices, offering luxurious rooms, top-notch service, and a full-service spa. If you're looking for something a bit more intimate than the Wyndham Reach, Pier House is an ideal choice. Its location—at the foot of Duval Street and just steps from Mallory Docks—is the envy of every hotel on the island. Set back from the busy street, on a short strip of beach, this hotel is a welcome oasis of calm. The accommodations here vary tremendously, from relatively simple business-style rooms to romantic guest quarters complete with integrated stereo systems and whirlpool tubs. Their best waterfront suites and rooms have recently been renovated. Although every accommodation has either a balcony or a patio, not all overlook the water. My favorites, in the two-story spa building, don't have any view at all. But what they lack in scenery, they make up for in opulence; each well-appointed spa room has a sitting area and a huge Jacuzzi bathroom.

1 Duval St. (near Mallory Docks), Key West, FL 33040. © 800/327-8340 or 305/296-4600. Fax 305/ 296-9085. www.pierhouse.com. 142 units. Winter $290–$460 double; off-season $200–$355 double. AE, DC, DISC, MC, V. **Amenities:** 3 restaurants, 4 bars; heated swimming pool; health club ($10 per day) and spa treatments; 2 Jacuzzis; sauna; water-sports equipment/rentals; bike rental; concierge; limited room service; in-room massage; baby-sitting; laundry services. *In room:* A/C, TV, dataport, minibar, coffeemaker, hairdryer.

Wyndham Casa Marina Resort ☆☆ *(Kids)*
Located on Kokomo Beach, Key West's largest private beach, the Casa Marina Resort is one of the island's most desirable. La Casa Marina (as it was called before it became a Wyndham property) was built in 1921 at the very end of the now defunct Florida East Coast Railway Line by the heirs of railroad tycoon Henry Flagler. The setting couldn't be more idyllic, and to further complement its surroundings, the hotel itself is luxurious with beamed ceilings, polished pine floors, and French Provincial furniture. Rooms are comfortable and soothing in Caribbean decor; the best ones are those with oceanfront balconies or French doors overlooking the oceanfront lawn. The pools are gorgeous with stunning views of the Atlantic. Families love the Casa Marina for its Kid's Retreat, which runs Thursday through Sunday and offers full- and half-day programs ($35 full day; $25 half-day). Evening activities are available for the whole family.

1500 Reynolds St., Key West, FL 33040 ©800/626-0777 or 305/296-3535. www.casamarinakeywest.com. 311 units. Winter $199–$749; off-season $169–$669. AE, DC, DISC, MC, V. From Key West International Airport, go west on Roosevelt Blvd. 1 mile to Atlantic Blvd. and turn left. Go 1 mile to Reynolds St. and turn right. Hotel is on left. **Amenities:** 2 restaurants; 2 outdoor pools; lighted tennis court; exercise room; sauna; water-sports equipment/rental; bike/moped rental; children's programs; concierge; tour desk; courtesy airport transportation; massage; baby-sitting. *In room:* A/C, TV, coffeemaker, hairdryer.

Wyndham Reach Resort ☆☆
Unlike Wyndham's Casa Marina resort, the Reach is better suited to adults only and not families. The location here can be either a highlight or a drawback; it's a 5-minute walk away from the center of the Duval Street action. Supported by stilts that leave the entire ground floor for car parking, the hotel offers four floors of rooms designed around atriums. The wonderful guest rooms are large and feature tile floors, sturdy wicker furnishings, and tropical colors. Each has a vanity area separate from the bathroom. The rooms are so nice you can easily forgive the small closets and diminutive dressers. All have sliding glass doors that open onto balconies, and some have ocean views. The grounds are amply planted with palms and surround a small pool area. There's also a private pier for fishing and tanning. The protected waters are tame and shallow.

1435 Simonton St., Key West, FL 33040. © 800/626-0777. For reservations © 800/996-3426. Fax 305/ 296-4633. www.wyndham.com/reachresort. 150 units. Winter $259–$709 single or double. Off-season $149–$589 single or double. AE, DC, DISC, MC, V. Valet parking: $9.50. **Amenities:** 2 restaurants; bar; outdoor heated swimming pool; nearby tennis and golf; health club and spa; water-sports equipment/rental; bike rental; concierge; tour desk; business center; salon; room service; in-room massage; baby-sitting; dry cleaning. *In room:* A/C, TV, minibar, fridge, coffeemaker.

EXPENSIVE

Island City House Hotel ☆☆
A small resort unto itself, the Island City House consists of three separate and unique buildings that share a common junglelike patio and pool. The first building, unimaginatively called the Island City

House building, is a historic three-story wooden structure with wraparound verandas that allow guests to walk around the entire edifice on any floor. The warmly dressed old-fashioned interiors here include wood floors and many antique furnishings. Many rooms have full-size kitchens, queen-size beds, and sumptuous floral window treatments. The tile bathrooms could use more counter space, and the room lighting isn't always perfect, but eccentricities are part of this hotel's charm.

The unpainted wooden Cigar House has particularly large bedrooms, similar in ambience to those in the Island City House. Most rooms are furnished with wicker chairs and king-size beds and have big bathrooms (although lacking in counter space). The Arch House is the least appealing of the three buildings, but still recommended. Built of Dade County pine, the Arch House's cozy bedrooms are furnished in wicker and rattan and come with small kitchens and bathrooms.

411 William St., Key West, FL 33040. ℂ **800/634-8230** or 305/294-5702. Fax 305/294-1289. www. islandcityhouse.com. 24 units. Winter $175–$315; off-season $115–$210. Rates include breakfast. AE, DC, DISC, MC, V. **Amenities:** Outdoor heated pool; access to nearby health club; Jacuzzi; bike rental; concierge; in-room massage; baby-sitting; self-service laundromat; laundry and dry-cleaning services. *In room:* A/C, TV, coffeemaker, hairdryer.

Marquesa Hotel ★★★ *(Finds* The Marquesa offers the charm of a small historic hotel coupled with the amenities of a large resort. It encompasses four buildings, two swimming pools, and a three-stage waterfall that cascades into a lily pond. Two of the hotel's houses are luxuriously restored Victorian homes whose rooms are outfitted with extraplush antiques and oversize contemporary furniture. The rooms in the two other, newly constructed, buildings are even richer; many have four-poster wrought-iron beds with bright floral spreads. The green marble bathrooms are lush and spacious. The decor is simple, elegant, and spotless. These are the only hotel rooms I have ever seen that I would love to have in my own home. The hotel also boasts one of Key West's most elegant restaurants, The Cafe Marquesa. One accessible room for disabled travelers is available.

600 Fleming St. (at Simonton St.), Key West, FL 33040. ℂ **800/869-4631** or 305/292-1919. Fax 305/ 294-2121. www.marquesa.com. 27 units. Winter $260–$395 double; off-season $170–$285 double. No children under 12. AE, DC, MC, V. **Amenities:** Restaurant; 2 outdoor swimming pools (1 is heated); access to nearby health club; bike rental; concierge; limited room service. *In room:* A/C, TV, dataport, minibar, hairdryer.

Ocean Key Resort ★ You can't get much more central than this modern hotel, located across from the Pier House at the foot of Duval Street. Beyond its location, however, it's rather lackluster. Most of the guest rooms here are suites, ample-sized accommodations fitted with built-in couches. However, some of the rooms are closetlike, so ask to see your accommodations first. Many rooms have sliding glass doors that open onto small balconies, some of which enjoy unobstructed water views. All suites have Jacuzzi tubs in either the master bedroom or living room.

Zero Duval St., Key West, FL 33040. ℂ **800/328-9815** or 305/296-7701. Fax 305/292-7685. www. oceankeyhouse.com. 99 units. Winter from $289–$549 2-bedroom suite; off-season $199–$449 2-bedroom suite. AE, DC, DISC, MC, V. **Amenities:** 2 restaurants; outdoor heated pool; access to nearby health club; water-sports equipment/rental; concierge; tour desk; room service; laundry and dry-cleaning services. *In room:* A/C, TV, VCRs and video rentals available upon request, minibar.

Weatherstation Inn ★ Originally built in 1912 as a weather station, this beautifully restored and meticulously maintained two-story, Renaissance-style inn is located just 2 blocks from Duval Street. It's situated on the tropical grounds of the former Old Navy Yard, now an exclusive and very private gated community. Harry Truman, Eisenhower, and JFK have all visited the station. Spacious and uncluttered, each room is uniquely furnished to complement the interior architecture: hardwood floors, tall sash windows, and high ceilings. The large modern bathrooms are especially appealing. Continental breakfast is served poolside. The staff is friendly and accommodating.

57 Front St., Key West, FL 33040. ⓒ **800/815-2707** or 305/294-7277. Fax 305/294-0544. www. weatherstationinn.com. 8 units. Winter $195–$315 double; off-season $150–$215 double. Rates include continental breakfast. AE, MC, V. **Amenities:** Outdoor pool; concierge. *In room:* A/C, TV, dataport, hairdryer.

MODERATE

Chelsea House ⓐ Despite its decidedly English name, the Chelsea House is "all-American," a term that in Key West isn't code for "conservative." Chelsea House caters to a mixed gay/straight clientele and displays its liberal philosophy most prominently on the clothing-optional sundeck. One of only a few guest houses in Key West that offer TVs, VCRs, private bathrooms, and kitchenettes in each guest room, Chelsea House has a large number of repeat visitors. The apartments come with full kitchens and separate living areas, as well as palm-shaded balconies in back. The bathrooms and closets could be bigger, but both are adequate and serviceable. When weather permits, which is almost always, breakfast is served outside by the pool.

707 Truman Ave., Key West, FL 33040. ⓒ **800/845-8859** or 305/296-2211. Fax 305/296-4822. www. chelseahousekw.com. 20 units. Winter $130–$229 double; off-season $85–$135 double. Rates include breakfast. AE, DC, DISC, MC, V. Private parking. Children 14 and under not accepted. Pets accepted; $15 per night. **Amenities:** Outdoor pool; access to nearby health club; bike rental; concierge. *In room:* A/C, TV/VCR, fax, kitchenette, coffeemaker, hairdryer.

La Pensione ⓐⓐ This classic bed-and-breakfast, located in the 1891 home of a former cigar executive, distinguishes itself from other similar inns by its extreme attention to details. The friendly and knowledgeable staff treats the stunning home and its guests with extraordinary care. The comfortable rooms all have air-conditioning, ceiling fans, king-size beds, and private bathrooms. Many have French doors opening onto spacious verandas. Although the rooms have no phones or televisions, the distractions of Duval Street, only steps away, should keep you adequately occupied during your visit. Breakfast, which includes made-to-order Belgian waffles, fresh fruit, and a variety of breads or muffins, can be taken on the wraparound porch or at the communal dining table.

809 Truman Ave. (between Windsor and Margaret Sts.), Key West, FL 33040. ⓒ **800/893-1193** or 305/ 292-9923. Fax 305/296-6509. www.lapensione.com. 9 units. Winter from $168 double; off-season from $98 double. Rates include breakfast. No children accepted. There's a 10% discount for readers who mention this book. AE, DC, DISC, MC, V. **Amenities:** Outdoor pool; access to nearby health club; bike rental. *In room:* A/C.

South Beach Oceanfront Motel This standard two-story motel is located directly on the ocean, with a private pier and within walking distance of Duval Street. It underwent a multimillion-dollar renovation in which rooms were gutted and completely redone. Because the structure is perpendicular to the water, most of the rooms overlook a pretty Olympic-size swimming pool rather than a wide swath of beach. The best, and by far most expensive, are the lucky pair of beachfront rooms on the end (nos. 115 and 215). Three rooms have kitchenettes and private balconies that overlook the pool and ocean. When making reservations, ask for a room that's as close to the beach (and as far from the road) as possible. Accessible rooms are available for disabled travelers.

508 South St. (at the Atlantic Ocean), Key West, FL 33040. ✆ **800/354-4455** or 305/296-5611. Fax 305/294-8272. www.oldtownresorts.com. 47 units. Winter $230–$300; off-season $155–$200. AE, MC, V. **Amenities:** Outdoor pool; Jacuzzi; bike rental; concierge; self-service laundry. *In room:* A/C, TV, coffeemaker, hairdryer.

Southernmost Point Guest House ★★ *Finds* One of the few inns that actually welcome children and pets, this romantic and historic guest house is a real find. The antiseptically clean rooms are not as fancy as the house's ornate 1885 exterior, but each is unique and includes some combination of basic beds and couches and a hodgepodge of furnishings, including futon couches, high-back wicker chairs, and plenty of mismatched throw rugs. Each room is different. Room 5 is best; situated upstairs, it has a private porch, an ocean view, and windows that let in lots of light. Every room has a refrigerator and a full decanter of sherry. Mona Santiago, the hotel's kind, laid-back owner, provides chairs and towels that can be brought to the beach, which is just a block away. Plus, guests can help themselves to wine as they soak in the new 14-seat hot tub. Kids will enjoy the swings in the backyard and the pet rabbits.

1327 Duval St., Key West, FL 33040. ✆ **305/294-0715**. Fax 305/296-0641. www.southernmostpoint.com. 6 units. Winter $105–$250; off-season $65–$$95. Rates include breakfast. AE, MC, V. **Amenities:** Hot tub. *In room:* A/C, fridge.

INEXPENSIVE

Abaco Inn ★ This tidy little guest house is situated on a secluded lane just off Duval Street. Although there is no pool or view, the three simple but comfortable rooms are well stocked, immaculate, and charming. Each room has a sizeable private bath, queen bed, and a twin-size Murphy bed. Once the home of a cigar maker, the house dates from the early 1900s. Now, it is owned and operated by George Fontana, a friendly and knowledgeable tour guide and writer. Look for his column on local characters in the *Key West Citizen*. You can't beat the price in this superconvenient location. No smoking is allowed on the property.

415 Julia St. (between Truman Ave. and Virginia St.), Key West, FL 33040. ✆ **800/358-6307** or 305/296-2212. Fax 305/295-0349. www.abaco-inn.com. 3 units. Winter from $99 double; off-season from $69 double. 3-day minimum stay in season. Additional person $15 extra. AE, DISC, MC, V. **Amenities:** Bike rental; concierge. *In room:* A/C, TV, microwave, fridge, coffeemaker, hairdryer.

Angelina Guest House ★★ This youth hostel–type guest house is about the cheapest in town and conveniently located near a hot, hippie restaurant called Blue Heaven (see "Where to Dine," below). It is generally safe and full of character. The rooms are all furnished differently in a modest style, recently upgraded with new decor. Only three rooms do not have private baths. Two rooms have full kitchens, and one has a microwave and small refrigerator; there are no televisions or telephones. A new pool with waterfall and tropical landscaping was an excellent addition. Even though the Angelina is sparse, it's a good place to crash if you are on the cheap. Many repeat guests consider "this old house" their home away from home. One accessible unit is available for the disabled traveler.

302 Angela St. (at the corner of Thomas St.), Key West, FL 33040. ✆ **305/294-4480**. Fax 305/272-0681. www.angelinaguesthouse.com. 13 units. Winter $75–$195; off-season $49–$125. Rates include continental breakfast. DISC, MC, V. **Amenities:** Outdoor pool; concierge. *In room:* A/C.

Blue Lagoon Motel More than half of the rooms at this funky ocean-side resort rent for less than $100 year-round—an all-too-unusual occurrence in Key

West, especially for full-service resorts. The rooms, furnished in heavy cedar wood, are basic and a bit run-down but still decent—along the lines of a Howard Johnson or other budget accommodation. Second-floor rooms are generally quieter. The pricier waterfront rooms aren't really worth the extra money (although some include a jet-ski ride). Guests tend to be young college-aged kids out for a wild time. Although pretty far from Old Town, the resort is convenient by scooter and car, and it is literally surrounded by WaveRunners, boats, parasailing, and diving fun.

3101 N. Roosevelt Blvd., Key West, FL 33040-4118. © **305/296-1043.** Fax 305/296-6499. 72 units. Winter $80–$240 double; off-season $50–$110 double. MC, V. *In-room:* A/C, TV.

The Grand ★★ *Finds*   Don't expect cabbies or locals to know about this well-kept secret, located in a modest residential section of Old Town, about 5 blocks from Duval Street. It's got almost everything you could want, including a very moderate price tag. Proprietor Elizabeth Rose goes out of her way to provide any and all services for her appreciative guests. All rooms have private bathrooms, air-conditioning, telephones, and private entrances. The four two-room efficiencies have new bathrooms. The floors are painted in bright colors, and beds are dressed in light tropical prints. Room no. 2 on the back side of the house is the best deal; it's small, but it has a porch and the most privacy. Suites are a real steal, too. The large two-room units come with a complete kitchen. This place is undoubtedly the best bargain in town.

1116 Grinnell St. (between Virginia and Catherine Sts.), Key West, FL 33040. © **888/947-2630** or 305/294-0590. Fax 305/294-0477. www.keywest.com/thegrand.html. 10 units. Winter $98–$158; off-season $88–$128. Rates include continental breakfast. AE, DISC, MC, V. **Amenities:** Concierge. *In room:* A/C, TV, fridge.

Key West International Hostel   This well-run affordable hostel is a 3-minute walk to the beach and to Old Town. Very busy with European backpackers, this is a great place to meet people. The dorm rooms are dark and sparse, but clean enough. The higher-priced motel rooms are a good deal, especially those equipped with full kitchens. The common area room has been upgraded, and a two-bedroom suite has been added for those looking to upgrade a bit. Amenities include a pool table under a tiki roof, and bicycle rentals for $8 per day. There's also cheap food available for breakfast, lunch, and dinner. They also have discounted prices for snorkeling, diving, and sunset cruises.

718 South St., Key West, FL 33040. © **800/51-HOSTEL** or 305/296-5719. Fax 305/296-0672. keywesthostel@aol.com. 100 units. Year-round members $18.50, nonmembers $21.50. Motel units $75–$105 in season; $55–$85 off-season. MC, V. **Amenities:** Kitchen; bike rental. *In room:* A/C, TV, fridge, coffeemaker, hairdryer.

WHERE TO DINE

You'll find many cuisines represented in Key West: Thai, Cuban, Bahamian, Japanese, and barbecue. Like many cities with sizable visitor populations year-round, there is plenty of poor dining to be found here. There are the usual drive-through fast-food franchises (mostly up on Roosevelt Boulevard) and Duval Street even succumbed to the lure of a Hard Rock Cafe. But over the years, an upscale and high-quality dining scene has begun to thrive. Wander Old Town or the newly spruced up Bahama Village and browse menus after you have exhausted the list of my picks below.

If you don't feel like venturing out, call **We Deliver** (© **305/293-0078**), a service that will bring you anything you want from any of the area's restaurants or stores for a small fee (between $3 and $6). We Deliver operates between 3 and

11pm. If you are staying in a condominium or efficiency, you may want to stock your refrigerator with groceries, beer, wine, and snacks from the area's oldest grocer, **Fausto's Food Palace.** Open since 1926, there are now two locations: 1105 White St. and 522 Fleming St. The Fleming Street location will deliver (**$\textcircled{C}$ 305/ 294-5221** or 305/296-5663). Fausto's has a $25 minimum.

VERY EXPENSIVE

Cafe des Artistes ★★★ FRENCH Open for nearly 2 decades, the Cafe des Artistes' impressive longevity is the result of its winning combination of food and atmosphere. The fact that it was once part of a hotel built in 1935 by Al Capone's bookkeeper adds to its allure, but it's really the food that people come for. Traditional French meals benefit from a subtle tropical twist. The food is served by uniformed waiters well versed in the virtues of fine food. Start with the duck-liver pâté made with fresh truffles and old cognac, or Maryland crabmeat served with an artichoke heart and herbed tomato confit. And ask about the escargot du jour. Nouvelle and traditional French entrees include lobster flambé with mango and basil and wine-basted lamb chops rubbed with rosemary and ginger.

1007 Simonton St. (near Truman Ave.). $\textcircled{C}$ **305/294-7100.** Reservations recommended. Main courses $25–$38. AE, MC, V. Daily 6–11pm.

Café Marquesa ★★★ CONTEMPORARY AMERICAN This superb restaurant is one of Key West's best. The intimate 50-seat restaurant has a theater-kitchen set cleverly behind a *trompe l'oeil* of a kitchen, with large mahogany-framed mirrors, giving diners a view of the entire restaurant. But it's the food you'll really want to admire. Specialties include peppercorn-dusted, seared yellowfin tuna with saffron risotto; grilled Florida lobster tail and diver sea scallops with Thai basil sauce, black Thai rice, and Asian vegetables; and an almost perfect feta and pine nut-crusted rack of lamb with rosemary demi-glacé, creamy polenta, and eggplant caponata. If you're looking to splurge, financially and gastronomically, this is the place.

The Marquesa Hotel, 600 Fleming St. $\textcircled{C}$ **305/292-1919.** Reservations highly recommended. Main courses $20–$36. AE, DC, MC, V. No smoking. Daily 7–11pm summer; 6–11pm winter.

Louie's Backyard ★★ CARIBBEAN Nestled amid blooming bougainvillea on a lush slice of the Gulf, Louie's remains one of the most romantic restaurants on earth. Famed chef Norman Van Aiken of Norman's in Miami brought his talents farther south and started what has become one of the finest dining spots in the Keys. After dinner, sit at the dockside bar and watch the waves crash, almost touching your feet, while enjoying a cocktail at sunset. You can't go wrong with the fresh catch of the day or any seafood dish for that matter. The weekend brunches are also great. Even if you can't stay for dinner, go for lunch; this is one dining experience you won't want to miss.

700 Waddell Ave. $\textcircled{C}$ **305/294-1061.** Reservations highly recommended. Main courses $25–$30; lunch $8–$15. AE, DC, MC, V. Daily 11:30am–3pm and 6–10:30pm.

EXPENSIVE

Antonia's ★★ REGIONAL ITALIAN The food is great, but the atmosphere is a bit fussy for Key West. If you don't have a reservation in season, don't bother. Still, if you are organized and don't mind paying high prices for dishes that go for much less elsewhere, try this old favorite. From the perfectly seasoned homemade focaccia to an exemplary crème brûlée, this elegant little standout is amazingly consistent. The menu includes a small selection of classics, such as *zuppa* *di pesce,* rack of lamb in a rosemary sauce, and veal Marsala. However, the way to go is with the nightly specials. You can't go wrong with any of the handmade pastas.

615 Duval St. (C) **305/294-6565.** Fax 305/294-2743. Reservations suggested. Main courses $18–$26; pastas $12–$15. AE, DC, MC, V. Daily 6–11pm.

Bagatelle ✪✪✪ SEAFOOD/TROPICAL   Reserve a seat at the elegant second-floor veranda overlooking Duval Street's mayhem. From the calm above, you may want to start your meal with the excellent herb-and-garlic stuffed whole artichoke or the sashimi-like seared tuna rolled in black peppercorns. Also recommended is a lightly creamy garlic-herb pasta topped with Gulf shrimp, Florida lobster, and mushrooms. The best chicken and beef dishes are given a tropical treatment: grilled with papaya, ginger, and soy.

115 Duval St. (C) **305/296-6609.** Reservations recommended. Main courses $14–$21; lunch $5–$10. AE, DISC, MC, V. Sun–Thurs 11:30am–10pm; Fri–Sat 11:30am–11pm.

La Trattoria ✪ ITALIAN   Have a true Italian feast in a relaxed atmosphere. Each dish here is prepared and presented according to old, Italian tradition and is cooked to order. The antipasti are scrumptious. Try the delicious baked bread crumb–stuffed mushroom caps; they're firm yet tender. The stuffed eggplant with ricotta and roasted peppers is light and flavorful. Or have the seafood salad of shrimp, calamari, and mussels, fish-market fresh and tasty. The pasta dishes here are also great. Try the *penne Venezia,* with mushrooms, sun-dried tomatoes, and crabmeat, or the cannelloni stuffed with veal and spinach. For dessert, don't skip the homemade tiramisu; it's light yet full-flavored. The dining room is spacious but still intimate, and the waiters are friendly and informative. Before you leave, be sure to visit Virgilio's, the restaurant's very own cocktail lounge with live jazz until 2am.

524 Duval St. (C) **305/296-1075.** Pasta $10–$17; main courses $17–$22. AE, DC, DISC, MC, V. Daily 5:30–11pm.

Mangoes ✪✪✪ FLORIBBEAN   This restaurant's large brick patio, shaded by overgrown banyan trees, is so alluring to passersby that it's packed almost every night of the week. Many people don't realize how pricey the meals can be here because, upon first glance, it looks like a casual Duval Street cafe. Both prices and cuisine are a notch above casual. Appetizers include conch chowder laced with sherry, lobster dumplings with tangy Key lime sauce, and grilled shrimp cocktail with spicy mango chutney. Spicy sausage with black beans and rice, crispy curried chicken, and local snapper with passion fruit sauce are typical among the entrees, but Mangoes' outstanding individual-size designer pizzas are the best menu items by far. They're baked in a Neapolitan-style oven fired by buttonwood. Even though it is right on tourist-laden Duval Street, Mangoes enjoys a good reputation among locals.

700 Duval St. (at Angela St.) (C) **305/292-4606.** Reservations recommended for 6 or more. Main courses $12–$24; pizzas $10–$12; lunch $7–$14. AE, DC, DISC, MC, V. Daily 11am–midnight; pizza until 1am.

MODERATE
Alonzo's Oyster Bar ✪ SEAFOOD   Alonzo's Oyster Bar offers good seafood in a Key West casual setting. It's located on the ground floor of the A&B Lobster House at the end of Front Street in the marina. To start off your meal, try the steamed beer shrimp—tantalizingly fresh jumbo shrimp in a garlic, Old Bay, beer, and cayenne pepper sauce. Don't forget to dunk your bread.

A house specialty is white clam chili, a delicious mix of tender clams, white beans, and potatoes served with a dollop of sour cream. An excellent entree is the pan-fried lobster cakes, served with sweet corn mashed potatoes, chipotle gravy, and roasted corn salsa. Alonzo's is the casual section of the A&B Lobster House; if you want to dress up, go upstairs for their "fine dining." The staff is cheerful and informative, and the service is very good.

231 Margaret St. ⊘ **305/294-7496.** Appetizers $5–$8; main courses $11–$17. MC, V. Daily 11am–11pm.

Blue Heaven 🎯🎯 *Finds* SEAFOOD/AMERICAN/NATURAL This little hippie-run gallery and restaurant has become the place to be in Key West—and with good reason. Be prepared to wait in line. The food here is some of the best in town, especially for breakfast. You can enjoy homemade granola, huge tropical fruit pancakes, and seafood Benedict. Dinners are just as good and run the gamut from fresh-caught fish dishes to Jamaican-style jerk chicken, curried soups, and vegetarian stews. But if you're a neat freak, don't bother. Some people are put off by the dirt floors and roaming cats and birds. The building used to be a bordello, where Hemingway was said to hang out watching cockfights.

729 Thomas St. (at the corner of Petronia St.). ⊘ **305/296-8666.** Main courses $9–$24; lunch $5–$13; breakfast $3–$8.50. DISC, MC, V. Mon–Tues 6–10:30pm; Wed–Sat 8am–3pm and 6–10:30pm; Sun brunch 8am–1pm and 6–10:30pm.

Mangia, Mangia 🎯 *Value* ITALIAN/AMERICAN Mangia, Mangia is one of Key West's best values. Locals appreciate that they can get good, inexpensive food here in a town filled with many tourist traps. Off the beaten track, in a little corner storefront, this great Chicago-style pasta place serves some of the best Italian food in the Keys. The family-run restaurant offers superb homemade pastas of every description, including one of the tastiest marinaras around. The simple grilled chicken breast brushed with olive oil and sprinkled with pepper is another good choice. You wouldn't know it from the glossy glass front room, but there's a fantastic little outdoor patio dotted with twinkling pepper lights and lots of plants. You can relax out back with a glass of one of their excellent wines—they're said to have the largest selection in the Keys—or homemade beer while you wait for your table.

900 Southard St. (at Margaret St.) ⊘ **305/294-2469.** Reservations not accepted. Main courses $9–$15. AE, MC, V. Daily 5:30–10pm.

Pepe's *Finds* AMERICAN This old dive has been serving good, basic food for nearly a century. Steaks and Apalachicola Bay oysters are the big draw for regulars who appreciate the rustic barroom setting and historic photos on the walls. Look for original scenes of Key West in 1909, when Pepe's first opened. If the weather is nice, choose a seat on the patio under a stunning mahogany tree. Burgers, fish sandwiches, and standard chili satisfy hearty eaters. Buttery sautéed mushrooms and rich mashed potatoes are the best comfort food in Key West. Stop by early for breakfast when you can get old-fashioned chipped beef on toast and all the usual egg dishes. In the evening, there are reasonably priced cocktails on the deck.

806 Caroline St. (between Margaret and Williams Sts.) ⊘ **305/294-7192.** Main courses $13–$22; breakfast $2–$9; lunch $5–$9. DISC, MC, V. Daily 6:30am–10:30pm.

Turtle Kraals Wildlife Grill 🎯 *Finds* SOUTHWESTERN/SEAFOOD You'll join lots of locals in this out-of-the-way converted warehouse with indoor and dockside seating that serves innovative seafood at great prices. Try the twin lobster tails stuffed with mango and crabmeat or any of the big quesadillas or fajitas. Kids will like the wildlife exhibits and the very cheesy menu. Blues bands play most nights.

213 Margaret St. (corner of Caroline St.) ⓒ **305/294-2640**. Main courses $10–$20. DISC, MC, V. Mon–Thurs 11am–10:30pm; Fri–Sat 11am–11pm. Sun noon–10:30pm. Bar closes at midnight.

INEXPENSIVE

Anthony's Cafe ⭐ ITALIAN DELI/ROTISSERIE   Although owned and operated by a Greek import, this rustic Italian-style trattoria is a welcome addition to an area crowded with more expensive and less delicious options. Fragrant roasted chicken and overstuffed sandwiches on fresh baked bread are the best choices. Also good are the many salads and daily specials.

1111 Duval St. (at Amelia St.). ⓒ **305/296-8899**. Breakfast $2–$5; sandwiches and salads $5.50–$7 with a side; hot plates $8–$13. Cash only. Daily 8am–10pm.

Bahama Mama's Kitchen ⭐⭐ BAHAMIAN   Sit outside under an umbrella and enjoy the authentic Bahamian dishes made from recipes that have been handed down through owner Corey's family for the past 150 years. Prepared fresh daily, all dishes are created with their special "Bahamian" seasonings. Try the coconut shrimp butterflied, soaked in coconut oil, battered with egg, and then rolled in fresh shredded coconut and deep-fried. The fresh catch of the day comes blackened, broiled, or fried and is served with island plantains, shrimp hash cakes, and crab rice. The service is good and the staff is friendly.

In the Bahama Village Market, 324 Petronia St. ⓒ **305/294-3355**. Appetizers $4–$7; main courses $9–$13. MC, V. Daily 11am–10pm.

The Deli DINER/AMERICAN   In operation since 1950, this family-owned corner eatery has kept up with the times. It's really more of a diner than a deli and has a vast menu with all kinds of hearty options, from meatloaf to yellowtail snapper. The seafood options are pretty good. A daily selection of more than a dozen vegetables includes the usual diner choices of beets, corn, and coleslaw with some distinctly Caribbean additions, such as rice and beans and fried plantains. Most dinners include a choice of two vegetables and homemade biscuits or corn bread. Breakfasts are made to order and attract a loyal following of locals. The Deli also offers ice cream sundaes and gourmet coffees.

531 Truman Ave. (corner of Truman Ave. and Simonton St.). ⓒ **305/294-1464**. Full meals $7–$23; sandwiches $3–$8. DISC, MC, V. Daily 7:30am–10pm.

El Siboney Restaurant ⭐ *Value* CUBAN   For good, cheap Cuban food, stop at this corner dive that looks more like a gas station than a diner. Be prepared, however, to wait like the locals for succulent roast pork, Cuban sandwiches, grilled chicken, and *ropa vieja* (a stew-like dish of beef, onion, garlic, and tomatoes), all served with heaps of rice and beans.

900 Catherine St. (at Margaret St.). ⓒ **305/296-4184**. Main courses $5–$13. No credit cards. Mon–Sat 11am–9:30pm.

PT's Late Night ⭐ *Finds* AMERICAN   This place is worth knowing about not only because it's one of the only places in town serving food past 10pm, but also because it happens to serve good food at extremely reasonable prices. Enjoy heaping plates of nachos, sizzling fajitas served with all the trimmings, and superfresh salads—so big they can be a meal in themselves. PT's is more like a sports bar than a restaurant, and service can be a bit slow and brusque.

920 Caroline St. (at the corner of Margaret St.). ⓒ **305/296-4245**. Main courses $5–$14; DISC, MC, V. Daily 11am–4am.

KEY WEST AFTER DARK

Duval Street is the Bourbon Street of Florida. Amid the T-shirt shops and clothing boutiques, you'll find bar after bar serving neon-colored frozen drinks to revelers who bounce from one to the next from noon till dawn. Bands and crowds vary from night to night and season to season. Your best bet is to start at Truman Avenue and head up Duval to check them out for yourself. Cover charges are rare, except in gay clubs (see below), so stop into a dozen and see which you like.

Captain Tony's Saloon   Just around the corner from Duval's beaten path, this smoky old wooden bar is about as authentic as you'll find. It comes complete with old-time regulars who remember the island before cruise ships docked here; they say Hemingway drank, caroused, and even wrote here. The owner, Captain Tony Tarracino, a former controversial Key West mayor—"immortalized" in Jimmy Buffett's "Last Mango in Paradise"—has recently capitalized on the success of this once-quaint tavern by franchising the place. 428 Greene St. ☏ **305/294-1838.**

Durty Harry's   This large entertainment complex features live rock bands almost every night. You can wander to one of the many outdoor bars or head up to Upstairs at Rick's, an indoor/outdoor dance club that gets going late. For the more racy singles or couples, there is the Red Garter, a pocket-sized strip club popular with bachelor and divorce parties. The hawker outside reminds couples, in case they've forgotten, that "the family that strips together sticks together." 208 Duval St. ☏ **305/296-4890.**

Epoch   Until an arsonist put an end to the former legend in 1995, this former gay club was the place to dance to everything from techno to house and disco to reggae. Now expanded to include seven bars, an even bigger dance floor, a huge outside deck overlooking Duval Street, and a new state-of-the-art sound system, this is a better-than-ever choice for people of any orientation who can appreciate a good time. 623 Duval St. ☏ **305/296-8521.**

Jimmy Buffett's Margaritaville Cafe   This cafe, named after another Key West legend, is a worthwhile stop. Although Mr. Buffett moved to glitzy Palm Beach years ago, his name is still attracting large crowds. This kitschy restaurant/bar/gift shop features live bands every night—from rock to blues to reggae and everything in between. The touristy cafe is furnished with plenty of Buffett memorabilia, including gold records, photos, and drawings. The margaritas are high priced but tasty. The cheeseburgers aren't worth singing about. 500 Duval St. ☏ **305/292-1435.**

Sloppy Joe's   You'll have to stop in here just to say you did. Scholars and drunks debate whether this is the same Sloppy Joe's that Hemingway wrote about, but there's no argument that this classic bar's turn-of-the-century wooden ceiling and cracked tile floors are Key West originals. There's live music nightly as well as a cigar room and martini bar. 201 Duval St. ☏ **305/294-5717,** ext. 10.

THE GAY SCENE

Key West's Bohemian live-and-let live atmosphere extends to its thriving and quirky gay community. Since Tennessee Williams and before, Key West has provided the perfect backdrop to a gay scene unlike that of many large urban areas. Seamlessly blended with the prevailing culture, there is no "gay ghetto" in Key West, where alternative lifestyles are embraced and even celebrated.

Although restaurants and businesses welcome visitors without discrimination, nightlife *is* inevitably nightlife. In Key West, the best music and dancing can be found at the predominantly gay clubs. While many of the area's other hot spots

Literary Key West

Counting Ernest Hemingway and Tennessee Williams among your denizens would give any city the right to call itself a literary mecca. But over the years, tiny Key West has been home—or at least home away from home—to dozens of literary types who are drawn to some combination of its gentle pace, tropical atmosphere, and lighthearted mood (not to mention its lingering reputation for an oft-ribald lifestyle). Writers have long known that more than a few muses prowl the tree-laden streets of Key West.

Robert Frost first visited Key West in 1934 and stayed here for the remainder of his life. In the early 20th century, writers like John Dewey, Archibald MacLeish, John Dos Passos, Wallace Stevens, and S. J. Perelman were drawn to the island. Later, Ernest Hemingway's affection for Key West attracted even more writers.

Even as Key West boomed and busted and boomed again, and despite the island's growing popularity with world travelers, writers continued to move to Key West or visit with such regularity that they were deemed honorary "conchs." Novelists Phil Caputo, Tom McGuane, Jim Harrison, John Hershey, Alison Lurie, and Robert Stone were among these.

Of course, one of Key West's favorite sons also earned a spot in the annals of local literary history. Famous for his good-time, tropical-laced music, Jimmy Buffett was also a surprisingly well-received novelist in the 1990s. Although Buffett now makes the infinitely ritzier Palm Beach his Florida home, his presence is still felt in virtually every corner of Key West.

But it is Nobel Prize–winner and avid outdoorsman Ernest Hemingway who is most identified with Key West. Much of the island has changed since he lived here from 1931 to 1961. Even the famous Sloppy Joe's bar, which Hemingway frequented mostly from 1933 to 1937, changed locations. Fortunately, the Ernest Hemingway House & Museum on Whitehead Street has been lovingly preserved. But perhaps to get the best feel for what Hemingway loved most about Key West, visit the docks at Garrison Bight. It is from there that Hemingway and his many famous (and infamous) friends and contemporaries departed for Caribbean ports of call and for sport upon the sea.

Key West pays homage to its literary legacy with the annual January Key West Literary Seminar. For information, call ℂ **888/293-9291** or visit www.keywestliteraryseminar.org.

are geared toward tourists who like to imbibe, the gay clubs are for those who want to rave, gay or not. Cover varies, but is rarely more than $10.

Two adjacent popular late-night spots are the **801 Bourbon Bar/Number One Saloon** (801 Duval St. and 514 Petronia St. ℂ 305/294-9349 for both), featuring great drag and lots more disco. A mostly male clientele frequents this hot spot from 9pm until 4am. Another Duval Street favorite is **Diva's** at 711 Duval St. (ℂ **305/292-8500**), where you might catch drag queens belting out torch songs or judges voting on the best package in the wet jockey shorts contest.

Sunday nights are fun at two local spots. **Tea by the Sea,** on the pier at the Atlantic Shores Motel (510 South St.; © **800/520-3559**), attracts a faithful following of regulars and visitors alike. The clothing-optional pool is always an attraction. Show up after 7:30pm. Better known around town as La-Te-Da, **La Terraza de Marti,** the former Key West home of Cuban exile Jose Marti, at 1125 Duval St. (© **305/296-6706**), is a great spot to gather poolside for the best martini in town—but don't bother with the food. Just upstairs from there is **The Crystal Room** (© **305/296-6706**), with a high-caliber cabaret performance featuring the popular Randy Roberts in the winter.

4 The Dry Tortugas ★★

70 miles W. of Key West

Few people realize that the Florida Keys don't end at Key West. About 70 miles west is a chain of seven small islands known as the Dry Tortugas. As long as you have come this far, you might wish to visit them, especially if you're into bird watching, which is their primary draw.

Ponce de León, who discovered this far-flung cluster of coral keys in 1513, named them "Las Tortugas" because of the many sea turtles, which still flock to the area during the nesting season in the warm summer months. Oceanic charts later carried the preface "dry" to warn mariners that fresh water was unavailable here. Modern intervention has made drinking water available, but little else.

These undeveloped islands make a great day trip for travelers interested in seeing the truly natural anomalies of the Florida Keys—especially the birds. The Dry Tortugas are nesting grounds and roosting sites for thousands of tropical and subtropical oceanic birds. Visitors will also find a historical fort, good fishing, and terrific snorkeling around shallow reefs.

GETTING THERE

BY BOAT The **Yankee Fleet,** based in Key West (© **800/634-0939** or 305/294-7009), offers day trips from Key West for sightseeing, snorkeling, or both. Cruises leave daily at 7:30am from the Land's End Marina at Margaret Street. Breakfast is served on board. The journey takes 3 hours. Once on the island, called Garden Key, you can join a guided tour or explore it on your own. Boats return to Key West by 7pm. Tours cost $98 per person, including breakfast; $63 for children 16 and under; $75 for seniors, students, and military personnel. Snorkeling equipment rental is free. Phone for reservations.

The **Sunny Days Catamaran's "Fast Cat"** (© **800/ 236-7937;** 305/292-6100) is faster than the loud Yankee fleet and a better value. Included in the $85 round-trip adult fare and $55 for children is a continental breakfast and a buffet lunch with cold cuts, fresh veggies, fruits, and salads, plus a snorkeling excursion to a wreck in 5 to 20 feet of water. The high-speed power cat leaves Key West at 8am and returns by 6pm.

BY PLANE **Seaplanes of Key West,** based at Key West Airport (© **800/950-2-FLY** or 305/294-0709), offers daily excursions. Weather permitting, flights depart at 8am, 10am, noon, and 2pm. The 40-minute trip at about 500 feet offers a great introduction to these little-known islets. Fares, which include snorkeling equipment and a cooler for use on the island, start at $179 for adults, $129 for kids 12 and under, $99 for kids 6 and under for a half-day; and $305 for adults, $225 for kids 12 and under, and $170 for kids 6 and under for a full day. Bring a bathing suit, snorkeling equipment, and some snacks to enjoy on these remote and beautiful islands. Overnight camping at Fort Jefferson costs $329 for adults, $235 for kids 12 and under, and $179 for kids 6 and under.

EXPLORING THE DRY TORTUGAS

Fort Jefferson, a huge six-sided 19th-century fortress, is built almost at the water's edge of Garden Key, giving the appearance that it floats in the middle of the sea. The monumental structure is surrounded by formidable 8-foot-thick walls that rise up from the sand to a height of nearly 50 feet. Impressive archways, stonework, and parapets make this 150-year-old monument a grand sight. With the invention of the rifled cannon, the fort's masonry construction became obsolete, and the building was never completed. For 10 years, from 1863 to 1873, Fort Jefferson served as a prison, a kind of "Alcatraz East." Among its prisoners were four of the "Lincoln Conspirators," including Samuel A. Mudd, the doctor who set the broken leg of fugitive assassin John Wilkes Booth. In 1935, Fort Jefferson became a national monument administered by the National Park Service. For more information about Fort Jefferson and the Dry Tortugas, call the **Everglades National Park Service** at © **305/242-7700.**

OUTDOOR PURSUITS

BIRD WATCHING   Bring your binoculars and your bird books. Bird watching is *the* reason to visit this little cluster of tropical islands. The islands, uniquely situated in the middle of the migration flyway between North and South America, serve as an important rest stop for the more than 200 winged varieties that pass through here annually. The season peaks from mid-March to mid-May, when thousands of birds—including thrushes, orioles, boobies, swallows, black noddies, and snooty terns—show up. Many other species from the West Indies can be found year-round.

DIVING & SNORKELING   The warm, clear, shallow waters of the Dry Tortugas combine to produce optimum conditions for snorkeling and scuba diving. Four endangered species of sea turtles—the green, leatherback, Atlantic ridley, and hawksbill—can be found here, along with a myriad of marine species. The region just outside the seawall of Garden Key's Fort Jefferson is excellent for underwater touring; an abundant variety of fish, coral, and more live in just 3 or 4 feet of water.

FISHING   Fishing for snapper, tarpon, grouper, and other fish is popular. The mandatory saltwater fishing permit costs $7 for 3 days and $17 for 7 days. No bait or boating services are available in the Tortugas, but there are day docks on Garden Key as well as a cleaning table. The water is roughest in winter, but the fishing is excellent year-round. Outfitters from Key West can arrange day charters (see "Outdoor Pursuits," earlier in this chapter).

CAMPING

The rustic beauty of tiny Garden Key is a camper's dream. Don't worry about sharing your site with noisy RVs or motor homes; they can't get here. The abundance of birds doesn't make it quiet, but camping here—a stone's throw from the water—is as picturesque as it gets. Campers are allowed to pitch tents only on Garden Key. Picnic tables, cooking grills, and toilets are provided, but there are no showers. All supplies must be packed in and out. Sites are $3 per person per night and are available on a first-come, first-served basis. With only 10 sites, they book up fast. For more information, call the **National Park Service** (© **305/242-7700**).

7

South Florida Side Trips: The Everglades & Biscayne National Park

by Lesley Abravanel

Miami has been called the "gateway to the world," because its port leads the pack in passengers heading to the Caribbean and to Latin America. But many tourists also take some time out to see the wild plant and animal life in the swampy Everglades, and the underwater treasures of Biscayne National Park.

1 A Glimpse of Everglades National Park— The Southeast Portion

35 miles SW of Miami

Marjory Stoneman Douglas, who fought tirelessly to save this fragile resource until her death in 1998 at the age of 108, might well be called the Mother of the Everglades. This vast and unusual ecosystem is actually a shallow, 40-mile-wide, slow-moving river. Rarely more than knee-deep, the water is the lifeblood of this wilderness. Subtle shifts in water level dictate the life cycle of the native plants and animals. Most folks viewed it as a worthless swamp until Douglas focused attention on the area with her moving and insightful book *The Everglades: River of Grass,* published in 1947.

In that same year, 1.5 million acres—less than 20% of Everglades wilderness—were established as Everglades National Park. At that time, few lawmakers understood how neighboring ecosystems relate to each other: You can't just chop off a chunk of a much larger wilderness and expect it to survive. The park is heavily affected by surrounding territories and is at the butt end of every environmental insult that occurs upstream in Miami.

Recently, environmental activists have succeeded in persuading politicians to enact legislation to clean up the pollution that has threatened this unusual ecosystem ever since the days when heavy industry—most notably the sugar industry—first moved into the area. There has been a marked decrease in the indigenous wildlife here, but Everglades National Park nevertheless remains one of the few places where you can see dozens of endangered species in their natural habitat, including the swallowtail butterfly, American crocodile, leatherback turtle, southern bald eagle, West Indian manatee, and Florida panther.

Take your time on the trails, and a hypnotic beauty begins to unfold. Follow the rustling of a bush, and you might see a small green tree frog or tiny brown anole lizard, with its bright-red spotted throat. Crane your neck to see around a bend and discover a delicate, brightly painted mule-ear orchid.

The slow and subtle splendor of this exotic land may not be immediately appealing to kids raised on video games and rapid-fire commercials, but they'll certainly remember the experience and thank you for it later. Meanwhile, you'll find plenty of dramatic fun around the park, such as airboat rides, alligator wrestling, and biking to keep the kids satisfied for at least a day.

In the 1800s, before the southern Everglades were designated a national park, the only inhabited piece of this wilderness was a quiet fishing village called Flamingo. Accessible only by boat and leveled every few years by hurricanes, the mosquito-infested town never grew very popular. When the 38-mile-long road from Florida City was completed in 1922, many of those who did live here fled to someplace either more or less remote. Today, Flamingo is a

Lazy River
It takes a month for 1 gallon of water to move through Everglades National Park.

center for visitor activities and the main jumping-off point for backcountry camping and exploration. Flamingo is now home to National Park Service and concessionaire employees and their families.

Some 1,400 residents still live in the small enclave in the eastern section of the park, though the local agency governing the area has recently begun a buy-out program to remove them so that the area can be returned to its original state.

Everglades National Park's northern Shark Valley entrance and the eastern approaches described below are the most accessible from Miami and the rest of Florida's east coast. You'll stumble upon interesting and entertaining diversions along the way, like Indian villages, alligator farms, and boat rides. An excellent tram tour goes deep into the park along a trail that's also terrific for biking. This is also the best way to reach the park's only accommodation (and full-service outfitters), the Flamingo Lodge.

JUST THE FACTS
GETTING THERE & ACCESS POINTS   Everglades National Park has four entrances. If you want to take the more scenic route, then skip the speedier turnpike and head west on the Tamiami Trail, on which you may actually see alligators tanning on the roadside. The following three are the most popular entrances and the ones most convenient to visitors from Florida's east coast, including Miami. No matter which part of Miami you are starting from, the drive should take no longer than an hour (unless of course you are traveling during rush hour: between 8 and 9:30am or from 4 until 6pm. Then, the roads, especially State Route 836, will be backed up, and your driving time could be doubled).

The main entrance, in Homestead on the park's east side, is located 10 miles southwest of Florida City. From Miami, take State Route 836 west to the Florida Turnpike south until it ends in Florida City. Signs will point you southwest onto the road that leads into the park, State Route 9336. The Park Ranger Station at the main entrance is open 24 hours.

The Shark Valley entrance, on the park's north side, is located on the Tamiami Trail (U.S. 41), about 35 miles west of downtown Miami. From Miami, take State Route 836 west to the Florida Turnpike south; exit on Tamiami Trail (U.S. 41) and go west for approximately 30 miles. The park will be on the left. Shark Valley is known for its 15-mile trail loop that's used for bicycling and walking and for an excellent interpretive tram tour. This entrance is open daily from 8:30am to 5:30pm, with some seasonal variation. Call ahead.

Chekika, popular with day visitors, picnickers, and campers, is located halfway between the two entrances mentioned above, in the northeast section of

Everglades National Park

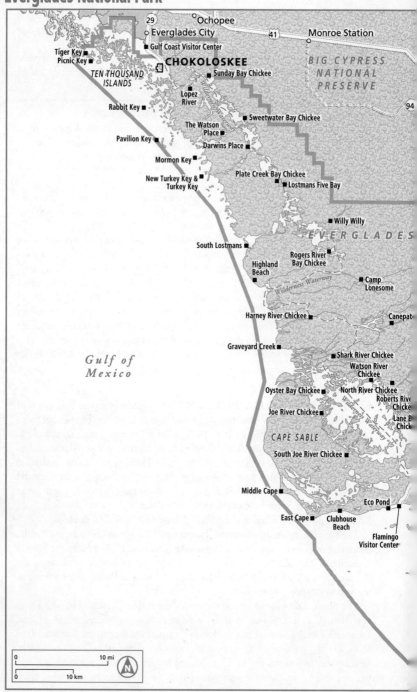

Ochopee
29
Everglades City
Gulf Coast Visitor Center
41
Monroe Station

Tíger Key
Picnic Key
TEN THOUSAND ISLANDS
CHOKOLOSKEE
Sunday Bay Chickee

BIG CYPRESS NATIONAL PRESERVE

94

Lopez River
Rabbit Key
Sweetwater Bay Chickee
The Watson Place
Pavilion Key
Darwins Place
Mormon Key
Plate Creek Bay Chickee
New Turkey Key & Turkey Key
Lostmans Five Bay

Willy Willy
EVERGLADES

South Lostmans
Rogers River Bay Chickee
Highland Beach
Wilderness Waterway
Camp Lonesome

Harney River Chickee
Canepat

Graveyard Creek

Gulf of Mexico

Shark River Chickee
Watson River Chickee
Oyster Bay Chickee
North River Chickee
Roberts River Chickee
Joe River Chickee
Lane B Chick
CAPE SABLE
South Joe River Chickee
Wilderness Waterway

Middle Cape
Eco Pond
East Cape
Clubhouse Beach
Flamingo Visitor Center

0   10 mi
0   10 km

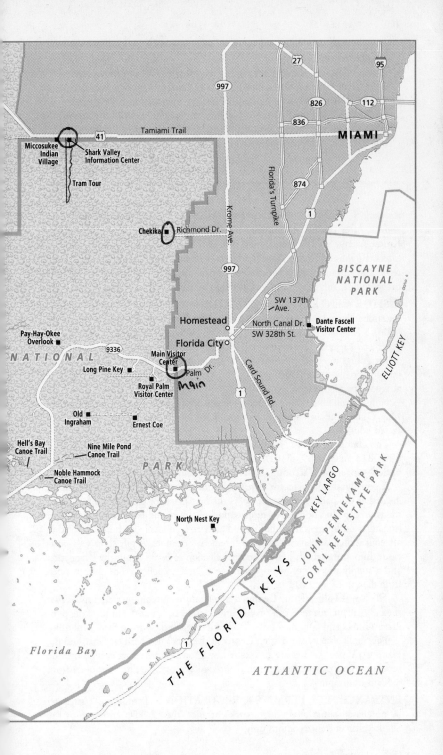

Tamiami Trail

MIAMI

Miccosukee Indian Village

Shark Valley Information Center

Tram Tour

Chekika • Richmond Dr.

BISCAYNE NATIONAL PARK

SW 137th Ave.

Homestead

North Canal Dr. SW 328th St.

Dante Fascell Visitor Center

Florida City

Pay-Hay-Okee Overlook

NATIONAL

Main Visitor Center

Long Pine Key

Palm Dr.

Main

Royal Palm Visitor Center

Old Ingraham

Ernest Coe

Hell's Bay Canoe Trail

Nine Mile Pond Canoe Trail

PARK

Noble Hammock Canoe Trail

Card Sound Rd.

KEY LARGO

JOHN PENNEKAMP CORAL REEF STATE PARK

ELLIOTT KEY

North Nest Key

THE FLORIDA KEYS

Florida Bay

ATLANTIC OCEAN

Krome Ave.

Florida's Turnpike

Impressions

There are no other Everglades in the world. They are, they have always been, one of the unique regions of the earth, remote, never wholly known. Nothing anywhere else is like them: their vast glittering open-ness, wider than the enormous visible round of the horizon, the racing free saltiness and sweetness of their massive winds, under the dazzling blue heights of space.

—Marjory Stoneman Douglas,
The Everglades: River of Grass, 1947

---

the park. Chekika can be reached from Miami as if going to Shark Valley (see above). After exiting on Tamiami Trail (Highway 41), head west 5 miles to Krome Avenue (177th Avenue) and turn left. Then proceed to Southwest 168th Street (Richmond Avenue) and head west (left) until you reach a stop sign. Turn right; the entrance will be on the left. There are picnic facilities and a 20-site campground. You can enter Chekika from 8:30am until sundown.

VISITOR CENTERS & INFORMATION   General inquiries and specific questions should be directed to **Everglades National Park Headquarters,** 40001 S.R. 9336, Homestead, FL 33034 (© **305/242-7700**). Ask for a copy of *Parks and Preserves,* a free newspaper that's filled with up-to-date information about goings-on in the Everglades. Headquarters is staffed by helpful phone operators daily from 8:30am until 4:30pm. You can also try the park's website at **www.nps.gov/ever/**.

Note that all hours listed are for the high season, generally November through May. During the slow summer months, many offices and outfitters keep abbreviated hours.

The **Flamingo Lodge, Marina and Outpost Resort,** in Flamingo (© **800/ 600-3813** or 941/695-3101), is the one-stop clearinghouse—and the only option—for in-park accommodations, equipment rentals, and tours.

Especially since its recent expansion, the **Ernest F. Coe Visitor Center,** located at the park's main entrance, is the best place for gathering information for your trip. In addition to information on tours and boat rentals, and free brochures outlining trails, wildlife, and activities, you will also find state-of-the-art educational displays, films, and interactive exhibits. A gift shop sells postcards, film, unusual gift items, the best selection of books about the Everglades, and a supply of your most important gear: insect repellent. The shop is open from 8am until 5pm daily.

The **Royal Palm Visitor Center,** a small nature museum located 3 miles past the park's main entrance, is a smaller information center at the head of the popular Anhinga and Gumbo-Limbo Trails and is open daily from 8am until 4pm.

The Shark Valley Information Center at the park's northern entrance and the Flamingo Visitor Center are also staffed by knowledgeable rangers who provide brochures and personal insight into the park's activities. They are open from 8:30am until 5pm.

ENTRANCE FEES, PERMITS & REGULATIONS   Permits and passes can be purchased either at the main park entrance, the Chekika entrance, or the Shark Valley entrance stations only.

Even if you are just visiting the park for an afternoon, you'll need to buy a 7-day permit, which costs $10 per vehicle. Pedestrians and cyclists are charged $5 each and $4 at Shark Valley.

An Everglades Park Pass, valid for a year's worth of unlimited admissions, is available for $20. U.S. citizens may purchase a 12-month Golden Eagle Passport for $65, which is valid for entrance into any U.S. national park. U.S. citizens aged 62 and older pay only $10 for a Golden Age Passport—that's valid for life. A Golden Access Passport is available free to U.S. citizens with disabilities.

Permits are required for campers to stay overnight either in the backcountry or in primitive campsites. See Camping, in "Where to Stay," later in this chapter.

Those who want to fish without a charter captain must obtain a standard State of Florida saltwater fishing license. These are available in the park at Flamingo Lodge or any tackle shop or sporting goods store nearby. Nonresidents will pay $17 for a 7-day license or $7 for 3 days. Florida residents can get a fishing license good for the whole year for $14. Snook and crawfish licenses must be purchased separately at a cost of $2.

Charter captains carry vessel licenses that cover all paying passengers, but ask to be sure. Freshwater fishing licenses are available at various bait and tackle shops outside the park at the same rates. A good one nearby is **Don's Bait & Tackle** located at 30710 S. Federal Hwy., in Homestead right on U.S. 1 (✆ **305/247-6616**). Most of the area's freshwater fishing, limited to murky canals and artificial lakes near housing developments, is hardly worth the trouble when so much good saltwater fishing is available.

Firearms are not allowed anywhere in the park.

SEASONS   There are two distinct seasons in the Everglades: high season and mosquito season. High season is also dry season and lasts from late November to May. Despite the bizarre cold and wet weather patterns that El Niño brought in 1998, most winters here are warm, sunny, and breezy—a good combination for keeping the bugs away. This is the best time to visit because low water levels attract the largest variety of wading birds and their predators. As the dry season wanes, wildlife follows the receding water; and by the end of May, the only living things you are sure to spot will cause you to itch. The worst, called "no-see-ums," are not even swattable. If you choose to visit during the buggy season, be vigilant in applying bug spray.

Also, realize that many establishments and operators either close or curtail offerings in the summer, so always call ahead to check schedules.

RANGER PROGRAMS   More than 50 ranger programs, free with admission, are offered each month during high season and give visitors an opportunity to gain an expert's perspective. Ranger-led walks and talks are offered year-round from the Royal Palm Visitor Center west of the main entrance, and at Flamingo, Shark Valley, and Gulf Coast during the winter months. Some programs occur regularly, such as Glade Glimpses, a walking tour during which rangers point out flora and fauna and discuss issues affecting the Everglade's survival. These tours are scheduled at 10:15am, noon, and 3:30pm daily. The Anhinga Ambles, a similar program that takes place on the Anhinga Trail, starts at 10:30am, 1:30pm, and 4pm.

Park rangers tend to be helpful, well informed, and good-humored. Since times, programs, and locations vary from month to month, check a schedule, available at any of the visitor centers (see above).

SAFETY There are dangers inherent in this vast wilderness area. Always let someone know your itinerary before you set out on an extended hike. It's mandatory that you file an itinerary when camping overnight in the backcountry. When you're on the water, watch for weather changes; severe thunderstorms and high winds often develop rapidly. Swimming is not recommended because of the presence of alligators, sharks, and barracudas. Watch out for the region's four indigenous poisonous snakes: diamondback and pygmy rattlesnakes, coral snakes (identifiable by their colorful rings), and water moccasins (which swim on the surface of the water). Again, bring insect repellent to ward off mosquitoes and biting flies.

First aid is available from park rangers. The nearest hospital is in Homestead, 10 miles from the park's main entrance.

SEEING THE HIGHLIGHTS

Shark Valley provides a fine introduction to the wonder of the Everglades, but don't plan on spending more than a few hours here. Bicycling or taking a guided tram tour are fantastic ways to see the park's highlights.

If you want to see a greater array of plant and animal life, make sure that you venture into the park through the main entrance, pick up a trail map, and dedicate at least a day to exploring from there.

Stop first along the Anhinga and Gumbo-Limbo Trails, which start right next to one another, 3 miles from the park's main entrance. These trails provide a thorough introduction to Everglades flora and fauna and are highly recommended to first-time visitors. Each of them is 0.5 mile round-trip. **Anhinga Trail** is one of the most popular trails in the park because of its abundance of wildlife. **Gumbo-Limbo Trail** meanders through a shaded, junglelike hammock of gumbo limbo trees, royal palms, ferns, and air plants. Both trails are wheelchair accessible. There's more water and wildlife here than in most parts of the Everglades, especially during dry season. Alligators, turtles, river otters, herons, egrets, and other animals abound, making this one of the best trails for seeing wildlife. Arrive early to spot the widest selection of exotic birds; like the Anhinga Trail's namesake, a large black fishing bird so used to humans that many of these birds build their nests in plain view. Others travel deeper into the park during daylight hours. Take your time—at least an hour is recommended. If you treat the trails and modern boardwalk as pathways to get through quickly, rather than destinations to experience and savor slowly, you'll miss out on the still beauty and hidden treasures that await.

Also, it's worth climbing the **observation tower** at the end of the quarter-mile-long Pa-hay-okee Trail for sweeping vistas of the river of grass. The panoramic view of undulating grass and seemingly endless expanses gives the impression of a semiaquatic Serengeti. Flocks of tropical and semitropical birds traverse the landscape, alligators and fish stir the surface of the water, small grottoes of trees thrust up from the sea of grass marking higher ground, and the vastness of the hidden world you've entered seems unparalleled.

If you want to get closer to nature, a few hours in a canoe along any of the trails allows paddlers the chance to sense the park's fluid motion and to become a part of the ecosphere. Visitors who choose this option end up feeling more like explorers than merely observers. (See "Sports & Outdoor Activities," below.)

No matter which option you choose (and there are many), I strongly recommend staying for the 7pm program, available during high season at the Long Pine Key Amphitheater. This talk and slide show given by one of the park's

Island Hopping

Beginning at Marco Island and heading south into the Everglades, there are a whopping 10,000 islands, whose primary residents are the same red mangrove trees that can be found throughout the Everglades. Often called "walking trees" because of their roots, mangrove trees arch above the ground like crouched legs.

rangers will give you a detailed overview of the park's history, natural resources, wildlife, and threats to its survival.

SPORTS & OUTDOOR ACTIVITIES

BIKING   The relatively flat 38-mile-long paved Main Park Road is great for biking because of the multitude of hardwood hammocks and a dwarf cypress forest, but Shark Valley is the best biking trail by far. Expect to spend 2 to 3 hours along either.

If the park isn't flooded from excess rain (which it often is, especially in spring), Shark Valley in Everglades National Park is South Florida's most scenic bicycle trail. Many locals haul their bikes out to the Glades for a relaxing day of wilderness-trail riding. You can ride the 15-mile loop with no other traffic in sight. Instead, you'll share the flat paved road only with other bikers and a menagerie of wildlife. Don't be surprised to see a gator lounging in the sun or a deer munching on some grass. Otters, turtles, alligators, and snakes are common companions in the Shark Valley area. There are no shortcuts, so if you become tired or are unable to complete the entire 15-mile trip, turn around and return on the same road.

Those who love to mountain bike, and who prefer solitude, might check out the **Southern Glades Trail,** a 14-mile-long unpaved trail opened in late 1998 that is lined with native trees and teeming with wildlife such as deer, alligators, and the occasional snake. The remote trail runs along the C-111 canal, off State Route 9336 and Southwest 217th Street.

You can rent bikes at the Flamingo Lodge, Marina and Outpost Resort (see "Where to Stay," below) for $17 per 24 hours, $14 per full day, $8.50 per half day (any 4-hr. period), and $3 per hour. A $50 deposit is required for each rental. **Bicycles are also available from Shark Valley Tram Tours,** at the park's Shark Valley entrance (© **305/221-8455**), for $3.25 per hour; rentals can be picked up anytime after 8:30am and must be returned by 4pm.

BIRD WATCHING   More than 350 species of birds make their homes in the Everglades. Tropical birds from the Caribbean and temperate species from North America can be found here, along with exotics that have blown in from more distant regions. Eco and Mrazek Ponds, located near Flamingo, are two of the best places for birding, especially in early morning or late afternoon in the dry winter months. Pick up a free birding checklist from a visitor center (see "Just the Facts," above), and ask a park ranger what's been spotted in recent days.

BOATING   Motorboating around the Everglades seems like a great way to see plants and animals in remote habitats. However, environmentalists are taking stock of the damage motorboats (especially airboats) inflict on the delicate ecosystem. If you choose to motor, remember that most of the areas near land are "no wake" zones and that, for the protection of nesting birds, landing is prohibited on most of the little mangrove islands. There's a long list of restrictions and restricted areas, so get a copy of the park's boating rules from National Park Headquarters before setting out (see "Just the Facts," above).

The Everglades' only marina—accommodating about 50 boats with electric and water hookups—is the Flamingo Lodge Marina and Outpost Resort, located in Flamingo. The well-marked channel to the Flamingo is accessible to boats with a maximum 4-foot draft and is open year-round. Reservations can be made through the marina store (℃ **941/695-3101, ext. 304**). Skiffs with 15-horsepower motors are available for rent. These low-power boats cost $90 per day, $65 per half day (any 5-hr. period), and $22 per hour. A $125 deposit is required.

CANOEING   Canoeing through the Everglades may be one of the most serene, surprisingly diverse adventures you'll have. From a canoe, your vantage point is priceless—it's the one place in the state where you realize just how flat and close to the water level you are. Canoers in the Glades can co-exist with the gators and birds there in a way no one else can; they behave as if you are part of the ecosystem—something that can't happen on an airboat.

Everglades National Park's longest "trails" are designed for boat and canoe travel, and many are marked as clearly as walking trails. The Noble Hammock Trail, a 2-mile loop, takes 1 to 2 hours and is recommended for beginning canoers. The Hell's Bay Trail, a 3- to 6-mile course for hardier paddlers, takes 2 to 6 hours, depending on how far you choose to go. Park rangers can recommend other trails that best suit your abilities, time limitations, and interests.

You can rent a canoe at the Flamingo Lodge, Marina and Outpost Resort (see "Where to Stay," below) for $40 for 24 hours, $32 per full day, $22 per half day (any 4-hr. period), and $8 per hour. They also have family canoes that rent for $12, $30, $40, and $50, respectively. A deposit is required. Skiffs, kayaks, and tandem kayaks are also available. The concessionaire will shuttle your party to the trailhead of your choice and pick you up afterward. Rental facilities are open daily from 6am to 8pm.

You can also take a canoe tour from the Parks Docks on Chokoloskee Causeway on Route 29, a half-mile south of the traffic circle at the ranger station in Everglades City. Call Everglades National Park Boat Tours at ℃ **800/445-7724.**

FISHING   About one-third of Everglades National Park is open water. Freshwater fishing is popular in brackish Nine-Mile Pond (25 miles from the main entrance) and other spots along the Main Park Road, but because of the high

---

At Home in the Everglades

The Everglades offers a protective area in which an eclectic mix of mammals and reptiles flourishes. One such mammal is the endangered sea cow, or manatee, which typically inhabits saltwater except during winter months when they migrate to the rivers and springs for warmth. It is an amorphous-looking, gray-toned creature with no distinct shape; it can grow to 13 feet in length and 1,300 pounds. Although their size is intimidating, they are extremely timid mammals.

Also sharing space among the mangroves, and found in most bodies of water in the Everglades, are the ubiquitous alligators, reminiscent of a half-submerged log. The alligator is a protected species in the state, but a designated alligator hunting season done on a lottery system exists to control the population.

mercury levels found in the Everglades, freshwater fishers are warned not to eat their catch. Before casting, check in at a visitor center, as many of the park's lakes are preserved for observation only. Fishing licenses are required. See "Just the Facts," earlier in this chapter.

Saltwater anglers will find snapper and sea trout plentiful. Charter boats and guides are available at Flamingo Lodge, Marina and Outpost Resort (see "Where to Stay," below). Phone for information and reservations.

ORGANIZED TOURS

AIRBOAT TOURS   Shallow-draft, fan-powered airboats were invented in the Everglades by frog hunters who were tired of poling through the brushes. And even though airboats are the most efficient way to get around, they are not permitted in the park. Just outside the boundaries, however, you'll find a number of outfitters offering rides. These shallow-bottom runabouts tend to inflict severe damage on the animals and plants there. If you choose to ride on one, you should consider bringing earplugs; these high-speed boats are loud. Airboat rides are offered at the **Miccosukee Indian Village,** just west of the Shark Valley entrance on U.S. 41, on the Tamiami Trail (✆ **305/223-8380**). Native American guides will take you through the reserve's rushes at high speed and stop along the way to point out alligators, native plants, and exotic birds. The price is $7.

The **Everglades Alligator Farm,** 4 miles south of Palm Drive/State Route 9336 and on Southwest 192nd Avenue (✆ **305/247-2628**), offers half-hour guided airboat tours from 9am until 6pm daily. The price, which includes admission to the park, is $12 for adults, $6 for children.

MOTORBOAT TOURS   Both Florida Bay and backcountry tours are offered at the **Flamingo Lodge, Marina and Outpost Resort** (see "Where to Stay," below). Both are available in 1½- and 2-hour versions that cost an average of $16 for adults, $8 for children, under 6 free. There are also charter-fishing and sightseeing boats that can be booked through the main reservation number (✆ **941/695-3101**). Florida Bay tours cruise nearby estuaries and sandbars, while six-passenger backcountry boats visit smaller sloughs. Tours depart throughout the day, and reservations are recommended.

TRAM TOURS   At the park's Shark Valley entrance, open-air tram buses take visitors on 2-hour naturalist-led tours that delve 7½ miles into the wilderness. At the trail's midsection, passengers can disembark and climb a 65-foot observation tower that offers good views of the Glades. Visitors will see plenty of wildlife and endless acres of sawgrass. Tours run November to April only, daily from 9am to 4pm, and are sometimes stalled by flooding or particularly heavy mosquito infestation. Reservations are recommended from December to March. The cost is $9.30 for adults, $5.15 for children 12 and under, and $8.25 for seniors. For further information, contact the **Shark Valley Tram Tours** at ✆ **305/ 221-8455.**

SHOPPING

You won't find big malls or lots of boutiques in this area, although there is an outlet center nearby, the **Keys Factory Shops** (✆ **305/248-4727**), at 250 E. Palm Drive (where the Florida Turnpike meets U.S. 1), in Florida City, with more than 60 stores, including Nike Factory Store, Bass Co. Store, Levi's, OshKosh, and Izod. You can pick up a free coupon booklet from the Customer Service Center called the Come Back Pack, which includes coupons good for discounts at the outlet center. It's open Monday to Saturday until 9pm, Sunday until 6pm.

A necessary stop and good place for a refreshment is one of Florida's best-known fruit stands, **Robert Is Here** (© 305/246-1592). Robert has been selling home-grown treats for nearly 40 years at the corner of Southwest 344th Street (Palm Drive) and Southwest 192nd Avenue. You'll find the freshest pineapples, bananas, papayas, mangos, and melons anywhere, as well as his famous shakes in unusual flavors like Key lime, coconut, orange, and cantaloupe. Exotic fruits, bottled jellies, hot sauces, and salad dressings are also available. This is a great place to pick up culinary souvenirs and sample otherwise unavailable goodies. Open daily 8am until 7pm.

Along Tamiami Trail, there are several roadside shops hawking Native American handicrafts, including one at the **Miccosukee Indian Village** (© 305/223-8380), just west of the Shark Valley entrance. At nearly every one of these shops, you'll find the same stock of feathered dreamcatchers, stuffed alligator heads and claws, turquoise jewelry, and other trinkets. Be sure to take note of the unique, colorful, handmade cloth Miccosukee dolls.

WHERE TO STAY

The only lodging in the park proper is the Flamingo Lodge, a fairly priced and very recommendable option. However, there are a few hotels just outside the park that are even cheaper. A $45 million casino hotel was recently built adjacent to the Miccosukee bingo and gaming hall on the northern edge of the park.

Although bugs can be a major nuisance, especially in the warm months, camping is really the way to go in this very primitive environment. Tenters have dozens of campsites and chickee platforms (see below for details) from which to choose. The best places for camping are found within the Everglades National Park, which consists of three campgrounds for tenters and RVs; Long Pine Key offers 108 drive-up sites; Flamingo has 234 drive-up sites and 64 walk-in-sites; and Cheeka has 20 sites. For campsite reservations in any of the aforementioned, call © 800/365-2267.

IN & AROUND EVERGLADES NATIONAL PARK

Flamingo Lodge, Marina and Outpost Resort ★★ The Flamingo Lodge is the only lodging actually located within the boundaries of Everglades National Park. This woodsy, sprawling complex offers rooms overlooking the Florida Bay in either a two-story simple motel or the lodge. Either option feels very much like being at summer camp, with a few more amenities. More interesting than the actual motel, however, are the visitors who crop up on the lawn—alligators, raccoons, and other nomadic creatures. The hotel is open year-round although the restaurant closes in the summer.

1 Flamingo Lodge Hwy., Flamingo, FL 33034. © 800/600-3813 or 941/695-3101. Fax 941/695-3921. www.flamingolodge.com. 127 units. Winter from $95 double, from $135 cottage, $135–$150 suite. Off-season $65–$80 double, $89–$100 cottage, $99–$110 suite. Rates for cottages or suites are for 1 to 4 people. Children under 18 stay free. Continental breakfast included in rates from May to October. AE, DC, DISC, MC. Take Florida Tpk. south to Florida City; exit on U.S. 1. At 4-way intersection, turn right onto Palm Drive; continue for 3 miles and turn left at Robert Is Here fruit stand. Turn right at the 3-way intersection. The park entrance is 3 miles ahead. Continue for about 38 more miles to reach lodge. **Amenities:** Waterside restaurant and bar; freshwater swimming pool; bike, canoe, and kayak rentals; marina with boat tours; boat rentals; houseboat and fishing charters; convenience store; coin-op washers and dryers. *In room:* A/C, TV/VCR in standard rooms or suites but not in cottages, kitchen in cottages only.

LODGING IN EVERGLADES CITY

Since Everglades City is 35 miles southeast of Naples and 83 miles west of Miami, many people choose to explore this western entrance to Everglades

National Park, located right off the Tamiami Trail. An annual seafood festival held the first weekend in February is a major event that draws hordes of people.

Ivey House B&B ★★ *Finds*   Housed in what used to be a recreational center for the men who built the Tamiami Trail, the Ivey House is named after Earl W. Ivey, who was in charge of creating the trail's roadbed. Today, the Ivey House offers three types of accommodations. In the original house are 10 small rooms that share communal bathrooms (one each for women and men). The Ivey's new inn (opened in 2001) adds 17 rooms (with private bathrooms) that face a courtyard with a beautifully landscaped shallow "conversation" pool. One private cottage consists of two bedrooms, a full kitchen, private bath, and a screened-in porch.

Owners Sandee and David are extremely knowledgeable about the Everglades, and usually the guests are as well. A living room area offers guests the opportunity to mingle. A typical continental breakfast is available from 7 to 9am only. Boxed lunches, stored in a cooler so you can bring it along for your Everglades excursions, are offered for $9.50 each. Dinners weren't available at press time but will be available in 2002. The Ivey House is closed in September. No smoking in any of the buildings.

107 Camellia St., Everglades City, Florida 34139 © **941/695-3299.** Fax 941/695-4155. www.iveyhouse.com. 27 units. Winter $60–$85 main house (older units); $125–$155 (cottage, 2-night minimum); $100 and up for one of the newer units. Off-season $50–$70 main house; $90–$105 cottage; $90 and up for newer rooms. MC, V. **Amenities:** Restaurant; small pool; free use of bikes; Everglades excursions available. *In room:* AC (all rooms), TV, kitchen (cottage only), fridge (inn and cottage).

CAMPING & HOUSEBOATING IN THE EVERGLADES

Campgrounds are available in Flamingo and Long Pine Key, where there are more than 300 sites designed for tents and RVs. They have level parking pads, tables, and charcoal grills. There are no electrical hookups, and showers are cold water. Private ground fires are not permitted, but supervised campfire programs are conducted during winter months. Reservations may be made in advance through The National Park Reservations Service at © **800/365-CAMP.** Campsites are $14 per night with a 14-day consecutive stay limit, 30 days a year maximum.

Camping is also available in the backcountry year-round on a first-come, first-served basis and is only accessible by boat, on foot, or by bicycle. Campers must register in person or by telephone no more than 24 hours before the start of their trip. Permits must be obtained at ranger stations in either Flamingo or Everglades City. Campers can use only designated campsites, which are plentiful and well marked on visitor maps.

Many backcountry sites are *chickee huts*—covered wooden platforms on stilts. They're accessible only by canoe and can accommodate free-standing tents (without stakes). Ground sites are located along interior bays and rivers, and beach camping is also popular. In summer especially, mosquito repellent is necessary gear.

Houseboat rentals are one of the park's best-kept secrets. Available through the Flamingo Lodge, Marina and Outpost Resort, motorized houseboats make it possible to explore some of the park's more remote regions without having to worry about being back by nightfall. You can choose from two different types of houseboats. The first, a 40-foot pontoon boat, sleeps six to eight people in a single large room that's separated by a central head (bathroom) and shower. There's a small galley (kitchen) that contains a stove, oven, and charcoal grill. Prices aren't cheap unless you are with a good-sized group. It rents for between $340 and $475 for 2 nights (with a 2-night minimum in high season).

The newer, sleeker Gibson fiberglass boats sleep six, have toilets and showers, air-conditioning, and electric stoves. There's also a full rooftop sundeck. These rent for $575 for 2 nights (with a 2-night minimum). With either boat, the seventh night is free when renting for a full week.

Boating experience is helpful but not mandatory, as the boats only cruise up to 6 miles per hour and are surprisingly easy to use. In-season, reservations should be made months in advance; call © **800/600-3813** or 941/695-3101.

NEARBY IN HOMESTEAD & FLORIDA CITY

Homestead and Florida City, two adjacent towns that were almost blown off the map by Hurricane Andrew in 1992, have come back better than before. Located about 10 miles from the park's main entrance, along U.S. 1, 35 miles south of Miami, these somewhat rural towns offer several budget lodging options, including a handful of chain hotels. There is a very recommendable **Days Inn** (© **305/245-1260**) in Homestead and a **Hampton Inn** (© **800/426-7866** or 305/247-8833) right off the turnpike in Florida City. The best option is the Best Western Gateway to the Keys.

Best Western Gateway to the Keys   This two-story, pink-and-white standard motel offers contemporary style and comfort about 10 miles from the park's main entrance. A decent-sized pool and a small spa are especially attractive. Each identical standard room has bright, tropical bedspreads and oversized picture windows. The suites offer convenient extras like a microwave, coffeemaker, an extra sink, and a small fridge. Clean and conveniently located if you're en route to the Keys, the only drawback is that in season there is often a 3-day minimum stay requirement. You'd do best to call the local reservation line (© **305/246-5100**) instead of the toll-free number—on several occasions, the hotel made an exception to the rule while the central reservation line was not able to.

411 S. Krome Ave. (U.S. 1), Florida City, FL 33034. © **800/528-1234** or 305/246-5100. Fax 305/242-0056. www.bestwestern.com. 114 units. Winter from $91–$109; off-season from $71–$89. Rates include continental breakfast. During races and very high season, there may be a 3-night minimum. AE, DC, DISC, MC, V. **Amenities:** Pool; laundry and dry-cleaning. *In room:* A/C, TV, dataport, fridge, coffeemaker, hair dryer.

WHERE TO DINE IN & AROUND THE PARK

You won't find fancy nouvelle cuisine in this suburbanized farm country, but there are plenty of fast-food chains along U.S. 1 and a few old favorites worth a taste.

Here for nearly a quarter of a century, **El Toro Taco** (see chapter 4, "Settling into Miami") at 1 S. Krome Ave. (near Mowry Drive and Campbell Drive; © **305/245-8182**) opens daily at 9:30am and stays crowded until at least 9pm most days. The fresh grilled meats, tacos, burritos, salsas, guacamole, and stews are mild and delicious. No matter how big your appetite, it's hard to spend more than $12 per person at this Mexican outpost. Bring your own beer or wine.

Housed in a squat, one-story, windowless stone building that looks something like a medieval fort, the **Capri Restaurant,** 935 N. Krome Ave., Florida City (© **305/247-1542**), has been serving hearty Italian American fare since 1958. Great pastas and salads complement a full menu of meat and fish dishes. Portions are big. They serve lunch and dinner every day (except Sunday) until 11pm.

The **Miccosukee Restaurant** (© **305/223-8380**), just west of the Shark Valley entrance on the Tamiami Trail (U.S. 41), serves authentic pumpkin bread, fry bread, fish, and not-so-authentic Native American interpretations of tacos and fried chicken. This interesting spot is worth a stop for brunch, lunch, or dinner.

In Everglades City, **The Oyster House** (© 941/695-2073) on Chokoloskee Causeway, Highway 29 South, is a large, but homey, seafood restaurant with modest prices, excellent service, and a fantastic view of the 10,000 islands. Try the hush puppies.

Once inside the Everglades, you'll want to eat at the only restaurant within the boundaries of this huge park, **The Flamingo Restaurant** (© 941/695-3101). Located in the Flamingo Lodge (see "Where to Stay," above), this is a very civilized and affordable restaurant. Besides the spectacular view of Florida Bay and numerous Keys from the large, airy dining room, you'll also find fresh fish, including my very favorite, mahimahi. Fish are grilled, blackened, or deep-fried; and dinner entrees come with salad or conch chowder, and steamed vegetables, black beans, and rice or baked potato. The large menu has something for everyone, including basic and very tasty sandwiches, pastas, burgers, and salads. A kids' menu offers standard choices like hot dogs, grilled cheese, or fried shrimp for less than $6. Prices are surprisingly moderate, with full meals starting at about $11 and going no higher than $22. You may need reservations for dinner, especially in season.

2 Biscayne National Park

35 miles S. of Miami, 21 miles E. of Everglades National Park

With only about 500,000 visitors each year (mostly boaters and divers), the unusual Biscayne National Park is one of the least-crowded parks in the country. Perhaps that's because the park is a little more difficult than most to access—more than 95% of its 182,00 acres are underwater.

The park's significance was first formally acknowledged in 1968 when, in an unprecedented move and against intense pressure from developers, President Lyndon Johnson signed a bill to conserve the barrier islands off South Florida's east coast as a national monument, a protected status that's a rung below national park. After being twice enlarged, once in 1974 and again in 1980, the waters and land surrounding the northernmost coral reef in North America became a full-fledged national park—the largest of its kind in the country.

To be fully appreciated, Biscayne National Park should be thought of more as a preserve than a destination. I suggest using your time here to explore underwater life—but most of all, to relax.

The park consists of 44 islands, but you can visit only a few of them. The most popular one is **Elliott Key,** which has campsites and a visitor center plus freshwater showers (cold water only), and restrooms. It's located about 9 miles from Convoy Point. There are trails and a buoyed swim area. During Columbus Day weekend, there is a very popular regatta in which a lively crowd of party people gather—sometimes in the nude—to celebrate a long weekend. If you'd prefer to rough it a little more, the 29-acre island known as **Boca Chita Key,** once an exclusive haven for yachters, has now become a popular spot for all manner of boaters. Visitors can tour the island's restored historic buildings, including the county's second-largest lighthouse and a tiny chapel. Facilities include showers, solar-powered restrooms, and drinking fountains, as well as barbecue grills, and picnic tables.

The park's small mainland mangrove shoreline and keys are best explored by boat. Its extensive reef system is renowned by divers and snorkelers worldwide.

JUST THE FACTS

GETTING THERE & ACCESS POINTS   The park's mainland entrance is Convoy Point, located 9 miles east of Homestead. To reach the park from Miami, take the Florida Turnpike to the Speedway Boulevard (Exit 6). Turn left, heading south 4½ miles. Then turn left again at North Canal Drive (Southwest 328th Street), and follow signs to the park. If you're coming from U.S. 1, whether you're heading north or south, turn east at North Canal Drive (Southwest 328th Street).

As I mentioned earlier, most of Biscayne National Park is accessible only to boaters. Mooring buoys abound, since it's illegal to anchor on coral. When no buoys are available, boaters must anchor on sand or on the new docks surrounding the small harbor off Boca Chita. Boats can dock overnight for $15. Even the most experienced boaters should carry updated nautical charts of the area, which are available at Convoy Point. The waters are often murky, making the abundant reefs and sandbars difficult to detect—and there are more interesting ways to spend a day than waiting for the tide to rise. There's a boat launch at adjacent Homestead Bayfront Park, and 66 slips on Elliott Key, available free on a first-come, first-served basis.

Transportation to and from the visitor center to the island costs $21 per person. Call for seasonal schedule (© **305/230-1100**).

VISITOR CENTERS & INFORMATION   The **Convoy Point Visitor Center,** 9700 SW 328th St., at the park's main entrance (© **305/230-7275;** fax 305/230-1190), is the natural starting point for any venture into the park without a boat. In addition to providing comprehensive information about the park, rangers will show you a short video on request. Open Monday to Friday from 8:30am to 4:30pm and Saturday and Sunday from 8:30am to 5pm.

For information on transportation, glass-bottom boat tours, and snorkeling and scuba diving expeditions, contact the park concessionaire, **Biscayne National Underwater Park, Inc.,** P.O. Box 1270, Homestead, FL 33030 (© **305/230-1100;** fax 305/230-1120; captsaw@bellsouth.net). The company is open daily from 8:30am to 5pm and later in winter.

For more information contact **Biscayne National Park,** 9700 SW 328th St., Homestead, FL 33033-5634 (© **305/230-7275;** www.nps.gov/bisc/).

ENTRANCE FEES & PERMITS   Entering Biscayne National Park is free. There is a $15 per night overnight docking fee at Boca Chita Key Harbor and Elliott Key Harbor ($7.50 per night for holders of Golden Age or Golden Access Passports).

SEEING THE HIGHLIGHTS

Since Biscayne National Park is primarily underwater, the only way to truly experience it is with snorkel or scuba gear. You can rent a speedboat in Miami and cruise south for about an hour and a half, but a better idea would be to take one of the organized tours offered every day from the main visitor center). Beneath the surface, the aquatic universe pulses with multicolored life: Bright parrot fish and angelfish, gently rocking sea fans, and coral labyrinths abound. Before entering the water, be sure to apply waterproof sunblock—once you begin to explore, it's easy to lose track of time, and the Florida sun is brutal, even during winter.

Afterward, take a picnic out to Elliott Key and taste the crisp salt air blowing off the Atlantic. Or, head to Boca Chita, an intriguing island that was once the private playground of wealthy yachters.

SPORTS & OUTDOOR ACTIVITIES

CANOEING & KAYAKING   Biscayne National Park offers excellent canoeing, both along the coast and across open water to nearby mangroves and artificial islands that dot the longest uninterrupted shoreline in the state of Florida. Since tides can be strong, only experienced canoeists should attempt to paddle far from shore. If you plan to go far, first obtain a tide table from the visitor center (see "Just the Facts," above) and paddle with the current. Free ranger-led canoe tours are scheduled for most weekend mornings; phone for information. You can rent a canoe at the park; rates are $8 an hour or $22 for 4 hours. Kayakers will have to bring their own boats but are welcome to explore the same quiet routes.

FISHING   Ocean fishing is excellent year-round; many people cast their lines right from the breakwater jetty at Convoy Point. A fishing license is required (see "Entrance Fees, Permits & Regulations," under "Just the Facts," in section 1, for complete information). Bait is not available in Biscayne but is sold in adjacent Homestead Bayfront Park. Stone crabs and Florida lobsters can be found here, but you're allowed to catch these only on the ocean side when they're in season. There are strict limitations on size, season, number, and method of take (including spear fishing) for both fresh- and saltwater fishing. The latest regulations are available at most marinas, bait and tackle shops, and at the park's visitor centers. Or you can contact the **Florida Game and Fresh Water Fish Commission,** Bryant Building, 620 S. Meridian St., Tallahassee, FL 32399-1600 (© **904/488-1960**).

HIKING & EXPLORING   Since the majority of this park is underwater, hiking is not the main attraction here, but there are some interesting sights and trails. At Convoy Point you can walk along the 370-foot boardwalk, and along the half-mile jetty that serves as a breakwater for the park's harbor. From there you can usually see brown pelicans, little blue herons, snowy egrets, and a few exotic fish.

Elliott Key is accessible only by boat, but once you're there, you have two good trail options. True to its name, the Loop Trail makes a 1½-mile circle from the bay-side visitor center, through a hardwood hammock and mangroves, to an elevated ocean-side boardwalk. It's likely that you'll see purple and orange land crabs scurrying around the mangrove roots.

Reopened in 1998, Boca Chita Key was once the playground for wealthy tycoons; it still offers the peaceful beauty that attracted elite anglers from cold climates. Many of the historical buildings are still intact, including an ornamental lighthouse, which was thankfully never put into use. Since it was built on the western side of the island in the path of shallow reefs, boaters would have followed the beacon only to go aground.

Take advantage of the tours, usually led by an interpretative park ranger and available every Sunday at 1pm. The tour, including the boat trip, takes about 3 hours. The price for adults is $19.95 and $9.95 for children. However, call in advance to see if the sea is calm enough for the boat trip—the boats won't run in rough seas.

SNORKELING & SCUBA DIVING   The clear, warm waters of Biscayne National Park are packed with colorful tropical fish that swim in the offshore reefs. If you don't have your own gear, or don't want to lug it the park, you can rent or buy snorkeling and scuba gear at the full-service dive shop at Convoy Point. Rates are in line with dive shops on the mainland.

The best way to see the park from underwater is to take a snorkeling or scuba diving tour operated by **Biscayne National Underwater Park, Inc. (© 305/ 230-1100).** Tours depart at 1:30pm daily, last about 4 hours, and cost $27.95 per person including equipment. They also run two-tank dives for certified divers and provide instruction for beginners. The price is $35.50 per person. Dives depart at 9am Monday to Friday, at 8:30am weekends. Make your reservations in advance. The shop is open daily from 9am to 5pm.

SWIMMING You can swim at the protected beaches of Elliott Key, Boca Chita Key, and adjacent Homestead Bayfront Park, but none of these beaches matches the width or softness of other South Florida beaches. Check the water conditions before heading into the sea. The strong currents that make this a popular destination for windsurfers and sailors can be dangerous even for strong swimmers.

WINDSURFING & SURFING Strong and steady winds provide an excellent venue for windsurfers. Feel free to bring your own board and take on some of South Florida's most beautiful surf.

GLASS-BOTTOM BOAT TOURS

If you prefer not to dive, the best way to see the sites without getting wet is on the glass-bottom boat tour. **Biscayne National Underwater Park, Inc. (© 305/ 230-1100)** offers daily trips to view some of the country's most beautiful coral reefs and tropical fish. Boats depart year-round from Convoy Point at 10am and stay out for about 3 hours. At $19.95 for adults, $17.95 for seniors, and $9.95 for children 12 and under, the scenic and informative tours are well worth the price. Boats carry fewer than 50 passengers; therefore, reservations are almost always necessary. The company also offers guided canoe, scuba, and snorkeling reef trips led by underwater naturalists.

WHERE TO STAY

There are no facilities available for overnight guests to this watery park. Most noncamping visitors come for an afternoon on their way to the Keys and stay overnight in nearby Homestead, where there are many national chain hotels and other affordable lodgings. See "Where to Stay" in section 1 of this chapter.

CAMPING

Although you won't find hotels or lodges in Biscayne National Park, it does have some of the state's most pristine campsites. Since they are inaccessible by motor vehicle, you'll be sure to avoid the mass of RVs so prevalent in many of the state's other campgrounds. Sites are on Elliott Key and Boca Chita, and can be reached only by boat. If you don't have your own, call © 305/230-1100 to arrange a drop-off. Transportation to and from the visitor center costs $21 per person. The best facilities are on the northeast side of newly reopened Boca Chita, where there are brand-new showers, solar-powered restrooms, and drinking fountains, as well as barbecue grills and picnic tables. With a backcountry permit, available from the ranger station, you can pitch your tent somewhere even more private. Ask for a map at the visitor center, and be sure to bring plenty of bug spray. Sites cost $10 a night for up to six persons staying in one or two tents. Reservations are not accepted.

8

The Gold Coast: Hallandale to the Palm Beaches

by Lesley Abravanel

Named not for the sun-kissed skin of the area's residents but for the gold salvaged from shipwrecks off its coastline, the Gold Coast embraces more than 60 miles of beautiful Atlantic shoreline—from the pristine sands of Jupiter in northern Palm Beach County to the legendary strip in Fort Lauderdale.

If you haven't visited the cities along Florida's southeastern coast in the last few years, you'll be amazed at how much has changed. Miles of sprawling grassland and empty lots have been replaced with luxurious resorts and high-rise condominiums. Taking advantage of their close proximity to Miami, the cities that make up the Gold Coast have attracted millions looking to escape crowded sidewalks, traffic jams, and the everyday routines of life.

Fortunately, amid all the building, much of the natural treasure of the Gold Coast remains. There are 300 miles of Intracoastal Waterway, not to mention Fort Lauderdale's Venetian-inspired canals. And, just a few miles inland, is the unspoiled splendor of the Everglades.

The most popular areas in the Gold Coast are Fort Lauderdale, Boca Raton, and Palm Beach. While Fort Lauderdale is a favored beachfront destination, Boca Raton and Palm Beach are better known for their country-club lifestyles and excellent shopping. Further north is the quietly popular Jupiter, best known for spring training at the Roger Dean Stadium and for its former resident Burt Reynolds. In between these better-traveled destinations are a few things worth stopping for, but not much. The drive north along the coastline is one of the best ways to fully appreciate what the Gold Coast is all about—it's a perspective you won't find in a shopping mall.

But tourists aren't the only people coming here; thousands of transplants, fleeing the increasing population influx in Miami and the frigid winters up North, have made this area their home. As a result, there has been a construction boom in the existing cities and westward into the swampy areas of the Everglades. More than 20 homes per day are being built in Broward County alone. There has also been a great revitalization of several downtown areas, including Hollywood, Fort Lauderdale, and West Palm Beach. These once-desolate urban centers have been spruced up and now attract more young travelers and families than ever before.

Unfortunately, like its neighbors to the south, the Gold Coast can be prohibitively hot and buggy in the summer. The good news is that bargains are plentiful in the summer months (between May and October), when many locals take advantage of package deals and uncrowded resorts.

For the purposes of this chapter, the Gold Coast will consist of the towns of Hallandale, Hollywood, Pompano Beach, Fort Lauderdale, Dania, Deerfield, Boca Raton, Delray Beach, Boynton Beach, and the Palm Beaches.

EXPLORING THE GOLD COAST BY CAR

Like most of South Florida, the Gold Coast consists of a mainland and an adjacent strip of barrier islands. You'll have to check the maps to keep track of the many bridges that allow access to the islands where most of the tourist activity is centered. Interstate 95, which runs north–south, is the area's main highway. Farther west is the Florida Turnpike, a toll road that can be worth the expense since the speed limit is higher and it is often less congested than I-95. Also on the mainland is U.S. 1, which generally runs parallel to I-95 (to the east) and is a narrower thoroughfare mostly crowded with strip malls and seedy hotels.

I recommend taking Fla. A1A, a slow ocean-side road that connects the long, thin islands of Florida's whole east coast. Although the road is narrow, it is the most scenic and forces you into the relaxed atmosphere of these resort towns.

1 Broward County: Hallandale & Hollywood to Fort Lauderdale

23 miles N. of Miami

Until the 2000 election fiasco, most people had never heard of Broward County. Less exposed than the highly hyped Miami, Broward County is a lot calmer and, according to some, a lot friendlier than the magic city. In fact, a friendly rivalry exists between residents of Miami-Dade County and Broward County. Miamians consider themselves more sophisticated and cosmopolitan than their northern neighbors who, in turn, dismiss the alleged sophistication as snobbery and actually prefer their own county's gentler pace.

With more than 23 miles of beachfront and 300 miles of navigable waterways, Broward County is also a great outdoor destination. Scattered amid the shopping malls, condominiums, and tourist traps is a beautiful landscape lined with hundreds of parks, golf courses, tennis courts, and, of course, beaches.

Like many other small American towns, South Florida's city of Hollywood has been working on redeveloping its downtown area for years. Once a sleepy community wedged between Fort Lauderdale and Miami, Hollywood is now a bustling area of 1.5 million people belonging to an array of ethnic and racial identities: from white and African American, to people of Jamaican, Chinese, and Dominican descent. *Money* magazine trumpeted the self-described "City of the Future" as having an ethnic makeup that mirrors what America will look like by the year 2022. A spate of redevelopment has made the pedestrian-friendly center along Hollywood Boulevard and Harrison Street east of Dixie Highway a popular destination for travelers and locals alike. Some predict Hollywood will be South Florida's next big destination—South Beach without the attitude, traffic jams, and parking nightmares. While the prediction is a dubious one, Hollywood is definitely awakening from its long slumber. Prices are a fraction of other tourist areas, and a quasi-bohemian vibe is apparent in the galleries, clubs, and restaurants that dot the new "strip." Its gritty undercurrent, however, prevents it from becoming too trendy.

Fort Lauderdale and its well-known strip of beaches, restaurants, bars, and souvenir shops has also undergone a major transformation. Once famous (or

Fort Lauderdale Attractions & Accommodations

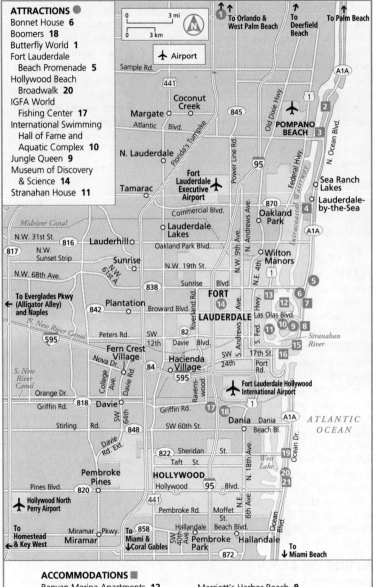

ATTRACTIONS ●

Bonnet House **6**
Boomers **18**
Butterfly World **1**
Fort Lauderdale
  Beach Promenade **5**
Hollywood Beach
  Broadwalk **20**
IGFA World
  Fishing Center **17**
International Swimming
  Hall of Fame and
  Aquatic Complex **10**
Jungle Queen **9**
Museum of Discovery
  & Science **14**
Stranahan House **11**

ACCOMMODATIONS ■

Banyan Marina Apartments **12**
Blue Seas Courtyard **4**
The Diplomat Resort
  Country Club & Spa **21**
Hyatt Regency Pier Sixty-Six **16**
La Casa Del Mar **7**
Lago Mar Resort and Club **15**
Marriott's Harbor Beach **8**
Riverside Hotel **13**
Ronny Dee Resort Motel **3**
Sea Downs (and the Bougainvillea) **19**
Traders Ocean Resort **2**

infamous) for the annual mayhem it hosted during Spring Break, this area is now attracting a more affluent, better-behaved yachting crowd.

In addition to beautiful wide beaches, the city, also known as the Venice of America, has more than 300 miles of navigable waterways and innumerable canals, which permit thousands of residents to anchor boats in their backyards. Boating is not just a hobby here; it's a lifestyle. Visitors can easily get on the water, too, by renting a boat or simply by hailing a moderately priced water taxi.

Huge cruise ships also take advantage of Florida's deepest harbor, Port Everglades. It is the second-busiest cruise-ship base in Florida after Miami and one of the top five in the world. For further information on cruises, see chapter 5, "What to See & Do In Miami" and consult *Frommer's Caribbean Cruises* or *Frommer's Caribbean Ports of Call.*

ESSENTIALS

GETTING THERE   If you're driving north from Miami, it's a straight shot to Hollywood or Fort Lauderdale. Visitors on their way to or from Orlando should take the Florida Turnpike to Exit 53, 54, 58, or 62, depending on the location of your accommodations.

The **Fort Lauderdale/Hollywood International Airport** (© 954/359-6100; www.fll.net) is small, easy to negotiate, and located just 15 minutes from both of the downtown areas it services.

Amtrak (© 800/USA-RAIL) stations are at 200 SW 21st Terrace (Broward Boulevard and I-95), Fort Lauderdale (© 954/587-6692), and 3001 Hollywood Blvd., Hollywood (© 954/921-4517).

VISITOR INFORMATION   The **Greater Fort Lauderdale Convention & Visitors Bureau,** 1850 Eller Dr., Suite 303 (off I-95 and I-595 east), Fort Lauderdale, FL 33316 (© 954/765-4466; fax 954/765-4467; www.sunny.org), is an excellent resource in English, Spanish, and French. I highly recommend calling them in advance to request a free comprehensive guide covering events, accommodations, and sightseeing in Broward County. In addition, once you are in town, you can call an **information line** (© 954/527-5600) to get easy-to-follow directions, travel advice, and assistance from multilingual operators who staff a round-the-clock help line. Also available 24 hours a day are operators who can book discount scuba, cruise, or cultural packages. Call © 800/22-SUNNY for information.

The **Greater Hollywood Chamber of Commerce,** 330 N. Federal Hwy. (on the corner of U.S. 1 and Taylor Street), Hollywood, FL 33020 (© 954/923-4000; fax 954/923-8737), is open Monday through Friday from 8:30am to 5pm.

HITTING THE BEACH

The southern part of the Gold Coast, Broward County, has the region's most popular and amenities-laden beaches, which stretch for more than 23 miles. Most do not charge for access, though all are well maintained. Here's a selection of some of the county's best from south to north.

Hollywood Beach, stretching from Sheridan Street to Georgia Street, is a major attraction in the city of Hollywood, a virtual carnival with a motley assortment of young hipsters, big families, and sunburned French Canadians who dodge bicyclists and skaters along the rows of tacky souvenir shops, T-shirt shops, game rooms, snack bars, beer stands, hotels, and even miniature golf courses. The 3-mile-long Hollywood Beach **Broadwalk** is notable as one of the area's only beach paths where diversions are right on the beach separated from the sand and sea by only a thin paved strip instead of a busy highway and tall buildings. Popular with runners, skaters, and cruisers, the broadwalk is also renowned as a hangout for thousands of retirement-age snowbirds who get together for frequent dances and shows at a faded outdoor amphitheater. Despite efforts to clear out a seedy element, the area remains a haven for drunks and scammers, so keep alert.

If you tire of the hectic diversity that defines Hollywood's broadwalk, enjoy the natural beauty of the beach itself, which is wide and clean. There are lifeguards, showers, bathroom facilities, and public areas for picnics and parties.

The **Fort Lauderdale Beach Promenade** underwent a $26 million renovation, and it looks fantastic. It's especially peaceful in the mornings when there's just a smattering of joggers and walkers, but even at its most crowded on the weekend, the expansive promenade provides room for everyone. Note, however, that the beach is hardly pristine; it is across the street from an uninterrupted stretch of hotels, bars, and retail outlets. Also nearby is a mega-retail and dining complex, Beach Place, on Fla. A1A, midway between Las Olas Boulevard and Sunrise Boulevard (see "Shopping & Browsing," later in this chapter).

Just across the road, on the sand, most days you will find hard-core volleyballers, who always welcome anyone with a good spike, and an inviting ocean welcoming swimmers of any level. The unusually clear waters are under the careful watch of some of Florida's best-looking lifeguards. Freshen up afterward in any of the clean showers and restrooms conveniently located along the strip. Pets have been banned from most of the beach in order to maintain the impressive cleanliness not commonly associated with such highly trafficked public beaches; a designated area for pets exists away from the main sunbathing areas.

Especially on weekends, parking along the ocean-side meters is nearly impossible to find. Try biking, skating, or hitching a ride on the water taxi instead. The strip is located on Fla. A1A, between SE 17th Street and Sunrise Boulevard.

Dania Beach's **John U. Lloyd Beach State Park** 🔆, 6503 N. Ocean Dr., Dania (© **954/923-2833**) is 251 acres of barrier island between the Atlantic Ocean and the Intracoastal Waterway, from Port Everglades on the north to Dania on the south. Its natural setting contrasts sharply with the urban development of Fort Lauderdale. Lloyd Beach, one of Broward County's most important nesting beaches for sea turtles, produces some 10,000 hatchlings a year. The park's broad, flat beach is popular for swimming and sunning. Self-guided nature trails are great for those who are too restless to sunbathe. The park's summertime Sea Turtle Awareness Program is wonderful. Call for details.

ACTIVE PURSUITS

BOATING   Often called the "yachting capital of the world," Fort Lauderdale provides ample opportunity for visitors to get out on the water, either along the Intracoastal Waterway or out on the open ocean. If your hotel doesn't rent boats, try **Bill's Sunrise Watersports,** 2025 E. Sunrise Blvd., Fort Lauderdale (© **954/ 462-8962**). They will outfit you with a variety of craft, including jet skis, WaveRunners, 13-foot Cigarette boats, 15-foot jet boats, and 8-foot powerboats, year-round. Bill's is open daily from 9am to 6pm. Rates start at $50 per half-hour for WaveRunners, $75 to $85 for boats (2-hr. minimum), and $60 for parasailing.

CRUISES   The **Jungle Queen,** 801 Sea Breeze Blvd. (3 blocks south of Las Olas Boulevard on Fla. A1A), in the Bahia Mar Yacht Center, Fort Lauderdale

(© **954/462-5596**), a Mississippi River–style steamer, is one of Fort Lauderdale's best-known attractions, cruising up and down the New River. All-you-can-eat dinner cruises and 3-hour sightseeing tours take visitors past Millionaires' Row, Old Fort Lauderdale, and the new downtown. Cruises depart nightly at 7pm and cost $29 for adults and $15 for children 12 and under. Sightseeing tours are scheduled daily at 10am and 2pm and cost $13.25 for adults and $8.75 for children 10 and under.

If you're interested in gambling, several casino boat companies operate day cruises out of Port Everglades and offer blackjack, slots, and poker. **Discovery Cruise Lines** (© **800/937-4477**) has daily cruises to the Bahamas, where you can gamble, eat, and party for 5 to 6 hours for about $120. The price includes breakfast, lunch, and dinner, but drinks cost extra.

Sea Escape (© **800/327-2005** or 954/453-3333) also launches daily casino cruises. But theirs don't travel more than a few miles offshore. These trips "to nowhere" depart from Monday to Thursday from 11am to 4:30pm and 7:30pm to 12:30am. The party cruises offer buffet meals and full casinos for $33 to $38 a person. I'd recommend spending an additional $20 for a cabin (do not expect *Love Boat* luxe here) so you can stretch out and relax in between hands. Even though the cruises don't go far from the coast, 5 or 6 hours is a long time to spend at sea, especially if the weather is rough. Evening cruises, which return at 1:30am on weekends, cost $48 and offer full buffet dinners and a Las Vegas–style show. Port charges are included, although you must pay a $3 departure tax and $2.65 passenger charge. This is one of the best deals you'll find. Sea Escape also has a new 2- and 3-night cruise option, where visitors can go to Nassau, the Bahamas, for as little as $199 per person with all meals included.

FISHING   Completed in 1999 at a cost of more than $32 million, the **IGFA World Fishing Center** at 300 Gulf Stream Way (© **954/922-4212**) in Dania Beach is an angler's paradise. One of the highlights of this museum, library, and park is the virtual reality fishing simulator, which allows visitors to actually reel in their own computer-generated catch. Also included in the 3-acre park are displays of antique fishing gear, record catches, famous anglers, various vessels, and a wetlands lab. To get a list of local captains and guides, call **IGFA headquarters** (© **954/927-2628**) and ask for the librarian. Admission is $5 for adults, $4 for children between 3 and 12, and free for children under 3. On the grounds is also **Bass Pro Outdoor World Store,** a huge multifloor retail complex situated on a 3-acre lake.

GAME PARKS   **Boomers,** at 1801 NW 1st St., east of I-95 between Griffin and Sterling road exits, in Dania, is good for kids during the day—at night the park attracts a rowdy bunch of teenagers. The newest addition to the park is a 100-foot high, 3,200-foot long wooden roller coaster (the thrills are high, but the lines are long). With a massive 24-hour video arcade, five challenging miniature-golf greens, go-carts and NASCAR racing, batting cages, and a huge sky coaster, this place provides exhaustive entertainment. Plan to spend all day or night. Call for prices and hours (© **954/921-1411**). Rides average $6.

For adults who love video games but can't deal with hordes of kids, there's **Dave & Busters** at 3000 Oakwood Blvd. in Hollywood, just off the Sheridan Street exit of I-95 (© **954/923-5505**). This 50,000-square-foot complex features a full bar and sit-down restaurant, as well as a more casual spot with table service. On weekends this place is packed with young adults on dates and rowdy

---

Kids Wild Things

Deerfield Island Park, surrounded by the Intracoastal Waterway and two canals, is an urban wilderness area that is accessible only by boat. The heavily wooded 56-acre site includes an 8½-acre mangrove swamp and is home to the gopher tortoise. The park also serves as a nesting place for squirrels, raccoons, and armadillos. Visitors can hike the park's two main trails. The half-mile Coquina Trail runs through a coastal hardwood hammock and includes an observation platform overlooking the Intracoastal. The ¾-mile Mangrove Trail includes a 1,600-foot boardwalk through a mangrove wetland. Picnic areas with grills and tables are available on a first-come, first-serve basis, and there is also a small playground. A free boat shuttle transports visitors to the island hourly, but book early as the shuttle fills up quickly. Call for times and reservations. Open Wednesday to Sunday from 9am to 5pm. 1720 Deerfield Island Park, Deerfield Beach, ⒸⒸ 954/360-1320.

---

groups of guys of all ages. An admission of $3 is charged only on Friday and Saturday after 10pm. D&B's opens weekdays at 11am and weekends at 11:30am and usually closes by 1am.

GameWorks, the mega-arcade of Hollywood movie mogul Steven Spielberg is located in the Sawgrass Mills outlet center (See "Shopping & Browsing," below) and features high-tech interactive games, plus a restaurant and bar.

GOLF More than 50 golf courses in all price ranges compete for players. Some of the best include **Emerald Hills** at 4100 North Hills Dr., Hollywood, just west of I-95 between Sterling Road and Sheridan Street. This beauty consistently lands on the "best of" lists of golf writers throughout the country. The 18th hole on a two-tier green is the challenging course's signature; it's surrounded by water and is more than a bit rough. It's also pricey. Greens fees start at $125. Call Ⓒ **954/961-4000** for tee times. For one of Broward's best municipal challenges, try the 18-holer at the **Orangebrook Golf Course** at 400 Entrada Dr. in Hollywood (Ⓒ **954/967-GOLF**). Built in 1937, this is one of the state's oldest courses and one of the area's best bargains. Morning and noon rates range from $27 to $33. After 2pm, you can play for less than $20, including a cart. Men must wear collared shirts to play here, and no spikes are allowed.

SCUBA DIVING In Broward County, the best wreck dive is the *Mercedes I,* a 197-foot freighter that washed up in the backyard of a Palm Beach socialite in 1984 and was sunk for divers the following year off Pompano Beach. The artificial reef, filled with colorful sponges, spiny lobsters, and barracudas, is located 97 feet below the surface, a mile offshore between Oakland Park Boulevard and Sunrise Boulevard. Dozens of reputable dive shops line the beach. Ask at your hotel for a nearby recommendation or contact **Lauderdale Undersea Adventures,** 1525 S. Andrews Ave., Fort Lauderdale (Ⓒ **954/462-3400**).

SPECTATOR SPORTS Baseball fans can get their fix at the **Fort Lauderdale Stadium,** 5301 NW 12th Ave. (Ⓒ **954/938-4980**), where the Baltimore Orioles play Spring Training exhibition games starting in early March; call Ⓒ **954/776-1921** for tickets. General admission is $6, a spot in the grandstand $9, kids 14 and under $3, and box seats $12. During the season, the Florida Marlins play just south of Hallandale at the Pro Player Stadium near the Dade–Broward County line. Call Ticketmaster for tickets (© **305/358-5885**), which range from $2 to $40. Tickets go on sale in January.

Pompano Park Racing, 1800 SW 3rd St., Pompano Beach (© **954/ 972-2000**), features parimutuel harness racing from October to early August. Grandstand admission is free; clubhouse admission is $2.

A sort of Spanish-style indoor lacrosse, jai alai was introduced to Florida in 1924 and still draws big crowds, who bet on the fast-paced action. Broward's only fronton, **Dania Jai Alai,** 301 E. Dania Beach Blvd. at the intersection of

 One If by Land, Taxi If by Sea

Plan to spend at least an afternoon or evening cruising Fort Lauderdale's 300 miles of waterways in the only way you can: by boat. The **Water Taxi of Fort Lauderdale** (© **954/467-6677**) is one of the greatest innovations for water lovers since those cool Velcro sandals. A trusty fleet of older port boats serves the dual purpose of transporting and entertaining visitors as they cruise through "The Venice of America."

Taxis operate on demand and also along a fairly regular route, carrying up to 48 passengers. If you stay at a hotel on the route, you can be picked up at your hotel, usually within 15 minutes of calling, and then be shuttled to any of the dozens of restaurants, bars, and attractions on or near the waterfront. If you aren't sure where you want to go, ask one of the personable captains who can point out historic and fun spots along the way.

For a day cruise with the kids, make a stop at the Museum of Discovery & Science, where you can catch an IMAX film or just enjoy the current educational exhibits. Then, if you are up for a walk, head across the 3-mile-long Riverwalk, a scenic palm-lined walkway along the New River where you can enjoy your picnic lunch; or try one of the restaurants dotting the way to Las Olas Boulevard and the Las Olas Riverfront. When you are ready for some shopping or a sit-down meal, reboard and head to Beach Place at Las Olas Boulevard and Cortez Street in the heart of Fort Lauderdale's most famous "strip." Stop for refreshments at Casablanca Cafe and then hit the beach.

In the evening, the water taxi is ideal for barhopping—no worrying about parking or choosing a designated driver. Make your first stop at Shooters, where professionals, boaters, and tourists share the large lively patio for a popular happy hour from 5 to 7pm on weekdays. Right next door is Bootlegger's, featuring more than 70 beers at an outside bar. Later debark at O'Hara's, in the downtown section of Las Olas Boulevard (see "The Hollywood & Fort Lauderdale Area After Dark," later in this chapter), where you'll hear a great mix of live jazz and blues.

Starting daily from 10am, boats usually run until midnight, and until 2am on weekends, depending on the weather. The cost is $7.50 per person per trip, $14 round-trip, and $16 for a full day. Children under 12 ride for half-price and free on Sunday. Opt for the all-day pass; it's worth it.

Fla. A1A and U.S. 1 (© **954/920-1511** or 954/426-4330), is a great place to spend an afternoon or evening.

Wrapped around an artificial lake, **Gulfstream Park,** at U.S. 1 and Hallandale Beach Boulevard, Hallandale (© **305/931-7223**), is pretty and popular. Large purses and important races are commonplace at this recently refurbished suburban course, and the track is often crowded. It hosts the Florida Derby each year. Call for schedules. Admission is $3 to the grandstand, and $3 to the clubhouse. Parking is free. From January 3 to March 15, post times are Wednesday to Monday at 1pm, and the doors open at 11am. Many weekends feature live concerts by well-known musicians.

In the sport of ice hockey, the young Florida Panthers (© **954/835-7000**) have already made history. In the 1994–95 season, they played in the Stanley Cup finals, and the fans love them. They play in Sunrise at the National Car Rental Center at 2555 NW 137th Way. Tickets range from $14 to $100. Call for directions and ticket information.

TENNIS There are hundreds of courts in Broward County, and plenty are accessible to the public. Many are at resorts and hotels. If not at yours, try one of these.

Famous as the spot where Chris Evert got in her early serves, the **Jimmy Evert Tennis Center,** 701 NE 12th Ave. (off Sunrise Boulevard), Fort Lauderdale (© **954/761-5378**), has 18 clay and 3 hard courts (15 lighted). Her coach and father, James Evert, still teaches young players here, though he is very picky about whom he'll accept. Nonresidents of Fort Lauderdale pay $3.50 (singles) to $4.50 (doubles) per hour. Reservations are accepted after 2pm for the following day but cost an extra $3. Lights are also an extra $3 per hour and are available only for the clay courts.

At the **Marina Bay Resort,** 2175 S.R. 84, west of I-95 and just behind the Ramada Inn, Fort Lauderdale (© **954/791-7600**), visitors can play free on any one of nine hard courts on a first-come, first-served basis. Three are lighted at night.

SEEING THE SIGHTS

For an overview of Fort Lauderdale, you may want to take an informative spin around the downtown area with **South Florida Trolley Tours** (© **954/946-7320**). Drivers narrate the history of the area as they loop around the city's streets past all the major (and many minor) sights. The charge for the 90-minute tour is $12 for adults, free for children 11 and under. The trolleys pick up passengers from most major hotels for six tours daily, starting at 9am. Call for current schedule.

For a tour by water, see the box below.

Museum of Discovery & Science ★★ *Kids* This museum's high-tech, interactive approach to education proves unquestionably that science equals fun. Adults won't feel as if they're in a kiddie museum, either. During the week, school groups meander through the cavernous two-story modern building. Kids 7 and under enjoy navigating their way through the excellent explorations in the "Discovery Center." Florida Ecoscapes is particularly interesting, with a living coral reef, bees, bats, frogs, turtles, and alligators. However, most weekend nights you'll find a diverse crowd ranging from hip high-school kids to thirtysomethings enjoying a rock film in the IMAX 3-D theater, which also shows short, science-related, supersize films daily. Out front, see the 52-foot-tall "Great

Gravity Clock," located in the museum's atrium, the largest kinetic-energy sculpture in the state. Exhibits vary, so call for the latest details.

401 SW 2nd St., Fort Lauderdale. © 954/467-6637. Fax 954/467-0046 www.mods.org. Museum admission (includes admission to 1 IMAX film) $12.50 adults, $11.50 seniors, $10.50 children 3–12. Mon–Sat 10am–5pm; Sun noon–6pm. From I-95, exit on Broward Blvd. E. Continue to SW 5th Ave.; turn right, garage on right.

Billie Swamp Safari 🐊 Catch a glimpse of how Florida looked *before* developers went wild. Skimming across the shallow swamps in an airboat with Native American guides, you may spot alligators and rare birds. Swamp buggy rides are especially amusing, and if you're lucky you'll see what seems to be strategically placed deer, buffalo, wild pigs, and ornery ostriches. A stop at an alligator farm reeks of Disney, but the kids won't care. Swamp buggy rides leave every hour on the hour until 5pm. You can also stay overnight in a native tiki hut if you're really looking to immerse yourself in the culture.

Big Cypress Reservation, 1½-hr. drive west of Fort Lauderdale. © 800/949-6101. Free admission. Boat tours $10–$20. Daily 8am–8pm. Airboats depart every 30 min.; last ride at 4:30pm.

Bonnet House 🐊🐊🐊 This historic 35-acre plantation home and estate, accessible by guided tour only, will provide you with a fantastic glimpse of old South Florida. Built in 1921, the sprawling two-story waterfront home surrounded with formal tropical gardens is really the backdrop of a love story, which the very chatty volunteer guides will share with you if you ask. Some have actually lunched with the former resident of the house, the late Evelyn Bartlett, the wife of world-acclaimed artist Frederic Clay Bartlett. The worthwhile 1¼-hour tour brings you quirky people, whimsical artwork, lush grounds, and interesting design. Inquire about literary walks and science workshops offered regularly on the grounds.

900 N. Birch Rd. (1 block west of the ocean, south of Sunrise Blvd.), Fort Lauderdale. © 954/563-5393. Fax 954/561-4174. www.bonnethouse.com. Admission $9 adults, $8 seniors, $7 students under 18, free for children 6 and under. Tours Wed–Fri 10am–1:30pm; Sat–Sun 12:30pm–2:30pm.

Butterfly World One of the world's largest butterfly breeders, Butterfly World cultivates more than 150 species of these colorful and delicate insects. In the park's walk-through, screened-in laboratory, visitors can see thousands of caterpillars and watch newborn butterflies emerge from their cocoons and flutter around as they learn to fly. Depending on how interested you are in these winged beauties, you may want to allow from 1 to 2 hours to tour the gardens and the well-stocked gift shop. There's a new lorikeet aviary that offers visitors the opportunity to hand-feed the butterflies, too.

Tradewinds Park S., 3600 W. Sample Rd., Coconut Creek (west of the Florida Tpk.). © 954/977-4400. Fax 954/977-4501. www.butterflyworld.com. Admission $12.95 adults, $7.95 children 4–12, free for children 3 and under. Mon–Sat 9am–5pm; Sun 1–5pm; last admission at 4pm.

International Swimming Hall of Fame and Aquatic Complex 🐊 Olympic diver Greg Louganis dove here, and you will want to do the same when you see the two 10-lane, 50-meter pools. Fortunately you can, for just $3, so bring your bathing suit. For inspiration, take in a swim flick (featuring Esther Williams and other aquatic stars) at the complex's theater or visit the comprehensive exhibition of medals, photos, and other memorabilia of swimming contests past.

1 Hall of Fame Dr., Fort Lauderdale. © 954/462-6536 or 954/468-1580 for the pool. $3 for museum, $3 for pool. Family rate $5. Museum open daily from 9am–7pm. Pool weekdays from 8am–4pm; weekends from 8am–4pm; closed late December to mid-January.

Stranahan House ★★★   In a town whose history is younger than many of its residents, visitors may want to take a minute to see Fort Lauderdale's very oldest standing structure and a prime example of classic "Florida Frontier" architecture. Built in 1901 by the "father of Fort Lauderdale," Frank Stranahan, this house once served as a trading post for Seminole trappers who came here to sell pelts. It's been a post office, town hall, and general store and now is a worthwhile little museum of South Florida pioneer life, containing turn-of-the-last-century furnishings and historical photos of the area. It is also the site of occasional concerts and social functions. Call for details.

335 SE 6th Ave. (Las Olas Blvd. at the New River Tunnel), Fort Lauderdale. ℂ 954/524-4736. Fax 954/525-2838. www.stranahanhouse.com. Admission $5 adults, $2 students and children. Wed–Sat 10am–4pm; Sun 1–4pm. Tours are on the hour; last tour at 3pm. Also accessible by water taxi.

SHOPPING & BROWSING

It's all about malls in Broward County. And while most of the best shopping is located within Fort Lauderdale proper, there are other areas in the county worth browsing.

Dania is known as the **Antique Capital of the South** ★ because it is within 1 square mile of Federal Highway that the city has over a hundred dealers selling everything from small collectibles to the finest antiques. **R. Cook & Co.,** 44 N. Federal Hwy. (ℂ **954/922-1118**), for instance, deals in vintage Louis Vuitton, plus exotic skins from Ernest Hemingway and antique scientific instruments, among other things. **Louis Kleinman Collectibles,** 60 N. Federal Hwy. (ℂ **954/920-2801**), boasts a large collection of china, including Limoges porcelain pillboxes. **Iris Fields of Dania,** 60 N. Federal Hwy. (ℂ **954/926-5658**), features a fabulous collection of antique perfume bottles. **Daddy's Inc.,** 19 N. Federal Hwy. (ℂ **954/920-4001**) has a huge selection of Tiffany lamps, furniture, watercolors, silver, and gold.

For bargain mavens, there's a strip of "fashion" stores on **Hallandale Beach Boulevard's "Schmatta Row,"** east of Dixie Highway and the railroad tracks, where off-brand shoes, bags, and jewelry are sold at deep discounts. Hollywood Boulevard also offers some interesting shops with everything from Indonesian artifacts to used and rare books to leather bustiers to handmade hats. Dozens of shops line the pedestrian-friendly strip just west of Young Circle. The art galleries are clustered along Harrison Street just east of Dixie Highway.

The area's only beachfront mall, **Beach Place,** is in Fort Lauderdale on Fla. A1A just north of Las Olas Boulevard. Completed in 1997 at a cost of $23 million, this 100,000-square-foot giant sports the usual chains like Sunglass Hut, Limited Express, Banana Republic, and The Gap, as well as lots of popular bars and restaurants.

Other more traditional malls include the upscale **Galleria,** at Sunrise Boulevard near the Fort Lauderdale Beach, and Broward Mall, west of I-95 on Broward Boulevard, in Plantation.

If you are looking for unusual boutiques, especially art galleries, head to trendy **Las Olas Boulevard** ★, where there are hundreds of shops with alluring window decorations (like kitchen utensils posing as modern art sculptures) and intriguing merchandise such as mural-size oil paintings.

On the edge of the Arts and Science District is **Las Olas Riverfront,** a retail complex with 260,000 square feet of restaurants, clothing stores, arcades, and a multiplex movie theater.

Lord & Taylor department store has a little-known clearance center where discounts on new clothing for women, kids, and men can be as much as 75%

off. If you can handle open dressing rooms, overstuffed racks, and surly sales help, it's a great find at 6820 N. University Dr. in Tamarac. You may want to call © **954/720-1915** to find out about specials.

The Fort Lauderdale Swap Shop, 3291 W. Sunrise Blvd. (© **954/ 791-SWAP**), is one of the world's largest flea markets. I think it's rather schlocky, actually. In addition to endless acres of vendors, there's a miniature amusement park, a 13-screen drive-in movie theater, weekend concerts, and even a free circus complete with elephants, horse shows, high-wire acts, and clowns.

The monster of all outlet malls is **Sawgrass Mills,** 12801 W. Sunrise Blvd., Sunrise (© **800-FL-MILLS** or 954/846-2350; fax 954/846-2312). Since the most recent expansion completed in mid-1999, which added more than 30 new designer outlet stores, this behemoth (shaped like a Florida alligator) now holds more than 300 shops, kiosks, a 24-screen movie theater, and many restaurants and bars including a Hard Rock Cafe. Stores include Donna Karan Company Store, Levi's Outlet, Sunglass Hut, Ann Taylor Loft, and Barney's New York, all selling goods at between 20% and 80% below retail. You may want to invest in a coupon booklet ($5), which entitles you to even greater discounts at many of the mall's stores and restaurants as well as area attractions. A booklet is good for up to a year and can be turned in for an updated booklet at no charge. To get there, take I-95 to I-595 west to the Flamingo Road exit, turn right, and drive 2 miles to Sunrise Boulevard; you will see the large complex on the left. From the Florida Turnpike, exit Sunrise Boulevard west.

Fishing enthusiasts won't want to miss **Bass Pro Outdoor World** (© **954/ 929-7710**), a sprawling retail complex at Griffin Road and I-95 in Dania where you can buy anything from yachts to lures.

WHERE TO STAY

The Fort Lauderdale beach has a hotel or motel on nearly every block, and they range from the run-down to the luxurious. Both the **Howard Johnson** (© **800/ 327-8578** or 954/563-2451), at 700 N. Atlantic Blvd. (on Fla. A1A, south of Sunrise Boulevard), and the **Days Inn** (© **800/329-7466** or 954/462-0444), at 435 N. Atlantic Blvd. (Fla. A1A), offer clean ocean-side rooms starting at about $150.

In Hollywood, where prices are generally cheaper, the **Holiday Inn** at 101 N. Ocean Blvd. (© **954/921-0990**) operates a full-service hotel right on the ocean. With prices starting at around $110 in season and discounts for AAA members, it's a great deal. **Howard Johnson** (© **800/423-9867** or 954/925-1411) has a good location right on the beach at 2501 N. Ocean Dr. (I-95 to Sheridan Street east to Fla. A1A south).

Extended Stay America/Crossland Economy Studios (© **800/398-7829**) has four superclean properties in Fort Lauderdale and offers year-round rates as low as $49 a night and $159 per week. The studios are designed with business travelers in mind. Each includes free local calls, a dataport, a kitchenette, a recliner, and a well-lit desk.

Especially for rentals for a few weeks or months, call **Florida Sunbreak** (© **800-SUNBREAK**). Or call the **South Florida Hotel Network** (© **800/ 538-3616**) for help in finding small inns and lodges in any price range. Also, check out the annual list of small lodgings compiled by the **Fort Lauderdale Convention & Visitors Bureau** (© **954/765-4466**). It is especially helpful for those looking for privately owned, charming, and affordable lodgings.

VERY EXPENSIVE

The Diplomat Resort Country Club & Spa In its day, the Hollywood Diplomat was a swanky affair, an oceanfront playground attending to a host of celebs that included Sinatra and Co. The new Diplomat, scheduled to open in early 2002, is being built on the site of the original to the tune of $600 million and, at press time, was considered the largest and priciest beach resort project currently being developed in the U.S.

When complete, expect a 1,060-room full-service beach resort that's loaded with amenities. The hotel's main building is a 39-story oceanfront tower (with adjacent conference center) surrounded by 8 acres of man-made lakes. A gorgeous bridged, glass-bottomed swimming pool with cascading waterfalls, private cabanas, and a slew of water sports and activities adds a tropical touch.

The Diplomat's Country Club opened in March 2000 and is modeled after an Italian villa, with 60 luxurious guest rooms, yacht slips, a 155-acre golf course, and a world-class spa and tennis club. Rooms are spacious and comfortable, done up in Art Deco style; over 70% of them feature balconies with an ocean or Intracoastal view. Bathrooms are luxurious, too, with large tubs and bidets. In addition to the clubby Marty's restaurant, a 24-hour restaurant and airy cafe will ensure that you never go hungry. The Celebrity Lounge is a throwback to the hotel's glory days, with nightly '50s-style entertainment.

3555 S. Ocean Dr. (A1A), Hollywood, FL 33019 © **800/327-1212** or 954/457-2000. www.diplomatresort. com. 1,060 units. Winter $285–$370; off-season $195–$315. AE, DC, DISC, MC, V. Valet parking $16. **Amenities:** 8 restaurants; 3 lounges; golf course; 10 clay tennis courts; health club & spa; water-sports equipment/rental. *In room:* A/C, TV, fax, dataport, Web TV, minibar, coffeemaker, hair dryer.

Hyatt Regency Pier Sixty-Six 🏵🏵 Located on 22 tropical acres on the Intracoastal Waterway, this resort is best known for its world-class marina and its rooftop lounge that spins every 66 minutes. If you experience vertigo after sitting in the revolving lounge, a treatment at the hotel's exquisite Spa LXVI will help relocate your sense of balance. An intimate, private European spa features a host of invigorating body and skin care treatments. Equally invigorating are the hotel's recreational amenities, which include a sprawling three-pool complex with a 40-person hydrotherapy pool, tennis courts, and an aquatic center complete with every water sport imaginable. The hotel's California Cafe is a popular, eclectic eatery. After a recent renovation, the tropical-style rooms are spruced up with cherry-wood furnishings and bathrooms with marble floors and granite vanities. All rooms have balconies with views of the Intracoastal and the hotel's lushly landscaped gardens. Designer suites come with Jacuzzi, wet bar, living room, dining room, and exceptional views.

2301 SE 17th St. Causeway, Fort Lauderdale, FL 33316. © **800/233-1234** or 954/525-6666. Fax 954/728-3541. www.hyatt.com. 380 units. Winter $289 double; off-season $229 double. Year-round from $1,000 suite. AE, DC, DISC, MC, V. Valet parking $10; self-parking $8 a day. **Amenities:** 3 restaurants; 3 bars; 2 swimming pools; 2 lighted clay tennis courts; spa; water-sports equipment/rental; bike rental; children's center/programs; concierge; tour desk; courtesy car; business center; shopping arcade; salon; 24-hr. room service; baby-sitting; self-service laundry; laundry and dry-cleaning services. *In room:* A/C, TV, dataport, minibar, coffeemaker, hair dryer.

Marriott's Harbor Beach 🏵🏵🏵 This resort is loaded with the same amenities as Pier Sixty-Six but with a more secluded setting, located on 16 oceanfront acres just south of Fort Lauderdale's "strip." Everything in this place is huge—from the guest rooms and suites to the 8,000-square-foot swimming pool to the $8 million 24,000-square-foot European spa. A huge 1999 renovation added a bit more personality to the formerly stale guest rooms and suites. Accommodations now feature marble, deep crown molding, and all new bathrooms with granite vanities, Italian marble flooring, and wrap-around mirrors. A revamped lobby affords sweeping ocean views. All rooms open onto private balconies overlooking either the ocean or the Intracoastal Waterway. The hotel's 3030 Ocean is an excellent seafood restaurant and raw bar; Riva, a Mediterranean-style, oceanfront eatery is also top-notch. Return guests include many convention groups and families who enjoy the space and the great location off the beaten strip. Accessible rooms are available for travelers with disabilities.

3030 Holiday Dr., Fort Lauderdale, FL 33316. ℂ **800/222-6543** or 954/525-4000. Fax 954/766-6193. www. marriottharborbeach.com. 659 units. Winter $259–$429 double; off-season $99–$279 double. Year-round from $600 suite. AE, DC, DISC, MC, V. Valet parking $10. From I-95, exit on I-595 east to U.S. 1 N.; proceed to SE 17th St.; make a right and go over the Intracoastal bridge past 3 traffic lights to Holiday Dr.; turn right. **Amenities:** 4 restaurants; 2 bars; outdoor heated pool; 5 clay tennis courts; health club; European-style spa; extensive water-sports equipment; bike rental; children's center and programs; game room; concierge; tour desk; courtesy car; business center; salon; 24-hr. room service; in-room massage; baby-sitting; laundry services and self-service laundry. In room: A/C, TV, dataport, minibar, coffeemaker, hair dryer.

EXPENSIVE

Lago Mar Resort and Club ₡₡₡   A charming lobby with a rock fireplace and saltwater aquarium sets the tone of this utterly inviting resort, a casually elegant piece of Old Florida that occupies its own little island between Lake Mayan and the Atlantic. Lago Mar guests have access to the broadest and best strip of beach in the entire city, not to mention the wonderful bougainvillea-lined, 9,000-square-foot swimming lagoon. Lago Mar is very family oriented, with lots of facilities and supervised activities for children, especially during Spring Break and Christmas vacations. Service is spectacular. The rooms and suites have Mediterranean or Key West influences and are well appointed—but it's likely you won't be spending much time inside. The hotel's Northern Italian restaurant, Acquario, is worth a visit even if you don't stay here. Accessible rooms are available for travelers with disabilities.

1700 S. Ocean Lane, Fort Lauderdale, FL 33316. ℂ **800/524-6627** or 954/523-6511. Fax 954/524-6627. www.lagomar.com. 212 units. Winter $195 double, from $295 suite; off-season $100–$135 double, from $135 suite. AE, DC, MC, V. Free valet parking. From Federal Hwy. (U.S. 1), turn east onto SE 17th St. Causeway; turn right onto Mayan Dr.; turn right again onto S. Ocean Dr.; turn left onto Grace Dr.; then left again onto S. Ocean Lane to the hotel. **Amenities:** 4 restaurants; cocktail lounge; wine room; outdoor pool and lagoon; 4 tennis courts; exercise room; water-sports equipment rental; children's programs during holiday periods; game room; concierge; tour desk; business center; 24-hr. room service; laundry and dry-cleaning services. In room: A/C, TV, dataport, kitchenette, coffeemaker in some units; hair dryer.

Riverside Hotel ₡₡   A touch of New Orleans hits Fort Lauderdale's popular Las Olas Boulevard in the form of this six-story 1936 hotel. There's no beach here, but the hotel is located on the sleepy and scenic New River, capturing the essence of that ever-elusive Old Florida. On weekends, the hotel is often packed with wedding guests who attend poolside ceremonies at the hotel, but it's definitely manageable. Guest rooms are a bit nicer than the public areas (outfitted in Mexican tile and wicker furnishings) and are spacious and well maintained. Details like intricately tiled bathrooms and old-style furniture enhance the charm of the otherwise stark building. The best rooms face the New River, but it's hard to see the water past the parking lot and trees. Twelve rooms offer king-size beds with mirrored canopies and flowing drapes. There are also seven elegantly decorated suites with wet bars and French doors that lead to private balconies. As of press time, the hotel had plans to nearly double its capacity by February 2002. The hotel has two restaurants worth trying: Indigo, a fantastic

Asian/Indonesian restaurant in the hotel lobby (see "Where to Dine," below), and the Grill Room, for Old World elegance. Accessible rooms are available for travelers with disabilities.

620 E. Las Olas Blvd., Fort Lauderdale, FL 33301. ℂ 800/325-3280 or 954/467-0671. Fax 954/462-2148. www.riversidehotel.com. 116 units. Winter $179–$369 suite; off-season $124–$339 suite. Special packages are available; discount for online bookings. AE, DC, MC, V. Valet parking $8–$10. From I-95, exit onto Broward Blvd.; turn right onto Federal Hwy. (U.S. 1). Then left onto Las Olas Blvd. **Amenities:** 2 restaurants; outdoor pool; concierge; secretarial services; limited room service; baby-sitting; laundry and dry-cleaning services. *In room:* A/C, TV, dataport, minibar, fridge, coffeemaker, hair dryer.

MODERATE

Banyan Marina Apartments ★★ These fabulous waterfront apartments located on a beautifully landscaped residential island may have you vowing never to stay in a hotel again. They're intimate, charming, *and* reasonably priced. Built around a stunning 75-year-old banyan tree, the Banyan Marina Apartments are located directly on the active canals halfway between Fort Lauderdale's downtown and the beach. When available, you'll choose between one- and two-bedroom apartments. Apartments have been recently renovated and all are comfortable and spacious, with French doors, full kitchens, and living rooms. The best part of staying here, besides your gracious and knowledgeable hosts, Dagmar and Peter Neufeldt, is that the water taxi will find you here and take you anywhere you want to be day or night. There is also a small outdoor heated pool and a marina for those with boats in tow. In 1998, the Neufeldts were honored by a local campaign to enhance the area, Broward Beautiful, winning First Place in the category of small multifamily dwellings.

111 Isle of Venice, Fort Lauderdale, FL 33301. ℂ 954/524-4430. Fax 954/764-4870. www.banyanmarina. com. 10 units. Winter $95–$225 apt.; off-season $60–$160 apt. Weekly and monthly rates available. MC, V. Free parking. To get there from I-95, exit Broward Blvd. E.; cross U.S. 1 and turn right on SE 15th Ave. At the first traffic light (Las Olas Blvd.), turn left. Turn left at the third island (Isle of Venice). **Amenities:** Restaurant; pool; dock. *In room:* A/C, TV, dataport, kitchen, coffeemaker, hair dryer.

Blue Seas Courtyard ★ *Value* This 1940s motel will take you back to the days of Old Florida, thanks to a careful restoration and renovation. Rooms are large and bright, with full kitchens, huge bathrooms, terra-cotta tiles, Haitian and Peruvian art, and Southwest and Danish furnishings. Outside are a brick pool, flowing fountains, and lounges and tables facing the gardens or even the ocean, which is just a block away. Run by Cristie and Marc Furth, the Blue Seas is a wonderful discovery—like a unique shell you might find on the beach.

4525 El Mar Dr., Lauderdale-by-the-Sea, FL 33308 [tel **877/225-8373** or 954/772-6337. Fax 954/772-6337. www.blueseascourtyard.com. 12 units. Winter $64–$94; off-season $60–$69. Free parking. MC, V. **Amenities:** Heated pool; access to nearby tennis court; nearby children's playground; coin laundry. *In room:* A/C, TV.

La Casa Del Mar ★★ *Finds* The 10 rooms in this Spanish-Mediterranean B&B, situated right on the beach, are splendid, with private baths, each decorated in a motif inspired by an artist (such as Monet) or a regional style (such as

---

Fun Fact To Dive For

The tiny, oceanfront enclave of Lauderdale-by-the-Sea is known as the Shore Diving Capital of Florida, with its own living reef just a hundred yards offshore. Only 15 feet deep and right off the beach, the reef lets you experience the underwater world of manta rays, sea turtles, octopus, coral reefs, and other sea life.

Southwestern). Enjoy exquisite personal service by the English- and German-speaking co-owners. A delicious, home-cooked buffet-style breakfast is served in the main house but can be enjoyed outdoors under a mango tree in the resplendent garden. The swimming pool is large for such a small accommodation and is a great place to mingle at a late afternoon wine and cheese party with the other guests, who range from young couples to savvy European travelers. Best of all, it's a deal and a pretty well-kept secret.

3003 Granada St., Fort Lauderdale, FL 33304. ✆ **954/467-2037.** Fax 954/467-7439. www.lacasadelmar. com. 10 units. Winter $110–$145; off-season $80–$100. Rates include breakfast. AE, MC, V. **Amenities:** Outdoor pool. *In room:* A/C, TV/VCR, fridge.

Traders Ocean Resort 𝄐   Located directly on the beach, this recently renovated hotel is not luxurious; but its service is superb, amenities are plentiful, and its atmosphere is completely conducive to a most relaxing vacation. Rooms are large and comfortable, and many feature ocean views. An outdoor tiki bar, often with live entertainment, provides further encouragement to unwind. The hotel attracts a more mature crowd. However, if it's a tranquil vacation you're after, Traders may make a loyal customer out of you regardless of your age.

1600 S. Ocean Blvd., Pompano Beach, FL 33062. ✆ **800/325-5220** or 954/941-8400. Fax 954/941-1024. www.tradersresort.com. 93 units. Winter $95–$239; off-season $79–$139. AE, DC, DISC, MC, V. **Amenities:** Restaurant; lounge; tiki bar; freshwater heated outdoor pool; extensive water-sports equipment/rental; shuffleboard; volleyball; concierge; massage. *In room:* A/C, TV.

INEXPENSIVE

Ronny Dee Resort Motel 𝄐   The good news is that this family-owned motel is just 100 yards from the beach and extremely affordable. The bad news is that it's located on busy Fla. A1A. Popular with European guests, this two-story yellow motel is wrapped around a central swimming pool; its guest rooms are wood-paneled (suburban style) and filled with an eclectic mix of furniture. A new coat of paint and new flooring helped to spruce up the place recently. It's clean but not overflowing with all the creature comforts of other chain motels.

717 S. Ocean Blvd., Pompano Beach, FL 33062. ✆ **954/943-3020.** Fax 954/783-5112. 35 units. Winter $49–$72 double, from $390 efficiency; off-season $35–$41 double, from $249 efficiency. AE, MC, V. From I-95, exit Atlantic Blvd. E. to Fla. A1A N. **Amenities:** Outdoor heated pool; game room. *In room:* A/C, TV, dataport, fridge.

Sea Downs (and the Bougainvillea) 𝄐𝄐   This bargain accommodation is often booked months in advance by returning guests who want to be directly on the beach without paying a fortune. The hosts of this superclean 1950s motel, Claudia and Karl Herzog, live on the premises and keep things running smoothly. Renovations completed in 1997 have replaced bathroom fixtures, and many rooms have been redecorated here and at the Herzogs' other even less expensive property next door, the Bougainvillea. Guests at both hotels share the Sea Downs pool.

2900 N. Surf Rd., Hollywood, FL 33019. ✆ **954/923-4968.** Fax 954/923-8747. www.seadowns.com or www. bougainvilleahollywood.com. 14 units. Winter $75–$126 daily, $301–$595 weekly; off-season $46–$91 daily; $280–$574 weekly. No credit cards accepted. From I-95, exit Sheridan St. E. to Fla. A1A S.; drive ½ mile to Coolidge St.; turn left. **Amenities:** Freshwater outdoor pool; concierge; laundry facilities. *In room:* A/C, TV, dataport, kitchen, fridge, coffeemaker.

WHERE TO DINE

It took a while for a more sophisticated, varied Epicurean scene to reach these shores, but Fort Lauderdale, and to some extent Hollywood, finally have several fine restaurants. Increasingly, ethnic options are joining the legions of surf-and-turferies that have dominated the area for so long. **Las Olas Boulevard** has so many eateries that the city has put a moratorium on the opening of new restaurants on the 2-mile-long street.

VERY EXPENSIVE

Darrel & Oliver's Cafe Maxx ✮✮ FLORIDIAN/NEW WORLD   Despite its bleak location in an unassuming storefront, Darrel & Oliver's Cafe Maxx is one of the best restaurants in Broward County. When it opened in 1984, it was the first restaurant to have an open kitchen and what a stir that caused! Now, instead of focusing on the kitchen, it's what comes out of the kitchen that's a marvel. Consider duck and smoked mozzarella ravioli with brown butter, basil, and sun-dried tomatoes; sweet onion-crusted yellowtail snapper with Madeira sauce; or a macadamia-pesto–crusted veal chop.

2601 E. Atlantic Blvd., Pompano Beach. ✆ **954/782-0606.** Fax 954/782-0648. Reservations recommended. Main courses $18–$37. AE, DC, DISC, MC, V. Mon–Thurs 5:30–10:30pm, Fri–Sat 5:30–11pm, Sun 5:30–10pm. From I-95, exit at Atlantic Blvd. E. The restaurant is 3 lights east of Federal Hwy.

Left Bank ✮✮✮ FRENCH   Regulars complain that the usually brilliant provençal cuisine at the Left Bank has suffered now that Jean-Pierre Brehier has joined the celebrity-chef bandwagon. I think they just miss him. Brehier's sous-chefs handle his menu like pros. Compared with other chefs who flee the galley for the Food Network, Brehier is still very much devoted to his own kitchen. The Left Bank provides an elegant, romantic atmosphere that's bolstered by dark woods and large murals—perfect for Valentine's Day or an anniversary.

214 SE Sixth Ave. (north of Las Olas Blvd.), Fort Lauderdale. ✆ **954/462-5376.** Reservations strongly recommended. Main courses $22.95–$34.95. AE, DC, MC, V. Sun–Thurs 5:30–9:30pm, Fri–Sat 5:30–10pm.

EXPENSIVE

Armadillo Cafe ✮✮✮ SOUTHWESTERN   The city of Davie may be best known for farmland and rodeos, but it's also celebrated for this outstanding Southwestern restaurant, which attracts city slickers from all over South Florida. The Armadillo recently expanded its strip-mall digs to accommodate all the foodies who flock here in search of porcini-dusted sea bass and lobster quesadillas, among other things. At press time, a more casual offshoot, Armadillo Cafe 2.0, was slated to open, offering light meals, lunch, and dinner.

4630 SW 64th Ave. (Griffin Rd.), Davie. ✆ **954/791-5104.** Reservations essential. AE, MC, DC, DISC, V. $16.95–$28.95. Mon–Thurs 5–10pm; Fri–Sun 5–11pm.

Burt and Jack's ✮ SEAFOOD/STEAKS   Burt—as in Reynolds—may not know how to pick a good script, but he sure can scout a great location. Located at Port Everglades in plain view of the mammoth cruise ships pulling in and out, Burt and Jack's serves adequate, albeit overpriced, surf 'n' turf to expense-account types and couples celebrating special occasions.

Berth 23 (South Terminal), Port Everglades. ✆ **954/522-5225.** Reservations strongly recommended. Jacket required for men. Main courses $14.95–$37.95. AE, DC, DISC, MC, V. Sun–Thurs 4:30–9:30pm, Fri–Sat 4:30–10:30pm.

East City Grill ✮✮ AMERICAN/SEAFOOD   This happening spot on the beach, owned by the same folks who own the pricier Cafe Maxx (see above), offers an ocean-side location and a comprehensive and eclectic menu. For starters consider steamed crab and goat-cheese dumplings, innovative sushi dishes, or Jamaican beer-steamed prawns. A steamer bar allows you to create your own dinner with a choice of steaming broths, sauces, and sides. If you must, a printed menu also exists. Wait for your table at the elegant oak bar, from which you can observe the open kitchen. Try to score a seat on the covered patio overlooking the beach.

505 N. Fort Lauderdale Beach Blvd. (Fla. A1A between Las Olas Blvd. and Sunrise Blvd.), Fort Lauderdale. ✆ 954/565-5569. Fax 954/565-5582. Reservations recommended well in advance. Main courses $17–$28. AE, DC, DISC, MC, V. Mon–Thurs 6pm–midnight, Fri 11:30am–3pm and 6pm–midnight; Sat brunch 11:30am–3pm, Sun brunch 8am–3pm; Sat–Sun dinner 5:30–10:30pm.

Himmarshee Bar & Grille ✪ AMERICAN   Located on a popular street of bars frequented by Fort Lauderdale's young professionals, Himmarshee Bar & Grille is better known for its cool scene than its cuisine. A mezzanine bar upstairs is ideal for people-watching; outdoor tables, if you can score one, are tight but strategically situated in front of all the street's action. On Friday and Saturday nights, in particular, it's difficult to get a table here. However, if you can deal with cramming into the bar, it's worth a cocktail or two. The wine list is particularly impressive, and the grilled sirloin burger with creamy basil Gorgonzola is a delicious meal in itself for only $7.50.

210 SW Second St. (south of Broward Blvd., west of U.S. 1), Fort Lauderdale. ✆ 954/524-1818. Reservations recommended. Main courses $12–$24. AE, MC, V. Mon–Fri 11:30am–2:30pm, Sun–Thurs 6–10:30pm, Fri–Sat 6–11:30pm.

Hobo's Fish Joint ✪✪ SEAFOOD   Huge portions of extremely fresh fish are prepared in more than a dozen ways at this steakhouse-style restaurant with wood floors and white tablecloths. Despite the fact that it's located away from the ocean in the utterly suburban enclave of Coral Springs, this joint is worth the trip for little neck clams in garlic bouillon or Chilean sea bass oreganato on a bed of orzo.

10317 Royal Palm Blvd. (at Coral Springs Dr.), Coral Springs. ✆ 954/346-5484. Reservations for 6 or more. Main courses $17–$27. AE, MC, V. Mon–Thurs 5:30–9:30pm, Fri–Sat 5:30–10:30pm, Sun 5:30–9pm.

Mai Kai ✪✪✪ CHINESE/POLYNESIAN   Forget you're in the middle of a tacky stretch of Fort Lauderdale and immerse yourself in this fabulous vestige of Polynesian kitsch: hula dancers, fire-eaters, potent (and sickly sweet) drinks served in coconuts. The food, which draws an ambiguous line between Chinese, Polynesian, and other forms of Asian cuisine, is tasty enough but definitely over-priced. No matter, it's bound to get cold as you watch the hilarious show, which includes everything from Tahitian classics to Polynesian versions of American hits. Trippy and undeniably fun, a trip to Mai Kai is a must even if you just go for cocktails, which cost almost as much as a meal.

3599 N. Federal Hwy. (between Commercial Blvd. and Oakland Park Blvd.), Fort Lauderdale. ✆ 954/563-3272. www.maikai.com. Reservations required. Main courses $14.50–$34. Shows (2 nightly) are $9.95 for adults; children 12 and under free. AE, DC, DISC, MC, V. Daily 5pm–midnight.

MODERATE

Aruba Beach Café CARIBBEAN   A local favorite, Aruba Beach Café is quintessential South Florida, located directly on the beach with a spectacular view of the ocean. As for the food, it's good for the proverbial "quick bite" or some drinks after beaching it all day. Enjoy safe bets like salads, pastas, and ham-burgers; trying-too-hard-to-be-creative dishes such as Caribbean bamboo chicken and Pacific crab nachos may sound tasty, but they're better left on the menu. A lively, friendly atmosphere of singles, boaters, and assorted beach bums contributes to Aruba's enormous popularity. Although the restaurant stops serving food at 11pm, the bar scene is alive and well until at least 2am.

1 E. Commercial Blvd. (east of A1A), Lauderdale-by-the-Sea. ℂ 954/776-0001. Main courses $7.95–$15.95. AE, DC, DISC, MC, V. Mon–Fri 11am–11pm, Sat–Sun 8:30am–11pm. Bar until 2am.

Calypso ℱ CARIBBEAN   A small strip-mall restaurant, Calypso has its pulse on the beat of Caribbean cuisine, serving delicious, spicy Caribbean dishes such as Jamaican jerk wings, barbecued shrimp, and smoked pork.

460 S. Cypress Rd., Pompano Beach [tel]954/942-1633. Main courses $8–$15. AE, MC, V. Mon–Thurs 11am–10pm; Fri–Sat 11am–10:30pm; Sun noon–9:30pm.

Creolina's ℱℱ CREOLE   You'll find authentic Louisiana Creole cuisine at this small but very popular restaurant, situated along the River Walk in old town. Try the shrimp jambalaya with shrimp sausage and vegetables in a rich brown Cajun sauce served over rice, or the crayfish étouffée with crayfish tail simmered in a mellow Cajun sauce served over rice. The mashed potatoes are homemade, and the delicious fresh-squeezed lemonade is made daily. There is also a terrific New Orleans Sunday brunch. Ask to sit in sassy Rosie's section—she will have you endlessly amused with her pithy comments such as, "Thank you, I needed to mail a letter anyway," uttered upon receipt of an undeserved bad tip.

209 SW 2nd St., Fort Lauderdale. ℂ 954/524-2003. Appetizers $4–$9; main courses $13–$18. AE, MC, V. Mon–Fri 11am–2:30pm and 5–10pm; Fri–Sat 5–11pm; Sun brunch 11am–2:30pm.

Indigo ℱℱ SOUTHEAST ASIAN/ECLECTIC   It seems a little strange to chow down on southeast Asian food in an utterly New Orleans–style hotel, but this is South Florida—the wackier, the better. This not-so-traditional meal begins with a basket of pappadoms, puffy nan bread, and shrimp puff bread. Next might be a superrich grilled vegetable cassoulet au gratin and a fried rice dish with shallots, corn, and asparagus; or pizzas baked on top of nan covered with such toppings as onions, shiitake mushrooms, goat cheese, spinach, eggplant, garlic, curried tomato, and pine nuts. Particularly good is the meaty soy and portobello mushroom combination wrapped in fluffy puff pastry and served with a delicate broccoli sauce. Sounds like a lot of activity going on in one dish, but, like the restaurant itself, somehow it all works.

In the Riverside Hotel, 620 E. Las Olas Blvd., Fort Lauderdale. ℂ 954/467-0671. Reservations only for groups of 6 or more. Main courses $12–$22. AE, DC, DISC, MC, V. Daily 7am–9:45pm.

Sugar Reef ℱℱ FRENCH VIETNAMESE   I could go on about the restaurant's priceless, unobstructed ocean view, but the menu of Mediterranean, Caribbean, and French-Vietnamese dishes is just as outstanding. A pleasant tropical decor is bolstered by the fresh air wafting in from the Atlantic through the open windows. Seafood bouillabaisse in green curry and coconut broth and pork loin Benedict—layers of jerk-spiced pork and hollandaise sauce—are among the restaurant's most popular dishes. The restaurant puts a savory spin on duck, roasted and topped with sweet chile and papaya salsa. This is not a restaurant you'd expect to find on a beach boardwalk. And that's what makes it all the more delightful.

600 N. Surf Rd. (on the boardwalk just north of Hollywood Blvd.), Hollywood. ℂ 954/922-1119. Reservations for 6 or more. Main courses $10–$24; sandwiches and salads $4–$9. AE, DISC, MC, V. Mon 4–10:30pm; Tues–Thurs 11am–10:30pm; Fri–Sun 11am–11pm (sometimes later in winter).

INEXPENSIVE

Carlos & Pepe ⭐ MEXICAN   Tucked away in yet another strip mall, Carlos & Pepe is a restaurant that doesn't need fancy digs to convince you that its authentic homemade Mexican cuisine is worth eating. The salsa, in particular, is excellent, not the watery bottled version you find in many Mexican establishments. The food is extremely fresh and flavorful and typical of what you'd find on a Mexican menu: fajitas, burritos, quesadillas, and enchiladas. The margaritas are also quite good, but beware—they do not skimp on the tequila. A low-key local crowd tends to frequent this very casual restaurant.

1302 SE 17th St. (south of Broward Blvd.), Fort Lauderdale. ✆ **954/467-7192**. Main courses $8–$16. AE, DC, DISC, MC, V. Mon–Thurs 11:30am–11pm; Fri–Sat 11:30am–midnight; Sun noon–10pm.

The Floridian Restaurant ⭐ *Value* AMERICAN/DINER   The Floridian has been filling South Florida's diner void for over 63 years, serving breakfast, lunch, and dinner, 24/7. It's especially busy on weekend mornings when locals and tourists come in for huge omelets, fresh oatmeal, sausage, and biscuits.

1410 E. Las Olas Blvd., Fort Lauderdale. ✆ **954/463-4041**. Fax 954/761-3930. Sandwiches $3–$7; breakfast combos $3.50–$8; hot platters $7–$14. No credit cards. Open 24 hours.

Jaxon's ⭐ *Kids* ICE CREAM   South Florida's best and only authentic old-fashioned ice cream parlor and country store attracts sweet teeth from all over the area looking to satisfy their cravings with an unabridged assortment of homemade ice cream served any which way. Kids love the place because of the candy store in the front of the restaurant, and adults love it for its pre–Ben & Jerry's authenticity. For the calorie-conscious, the sugar-free and fat-free versions are pretty good. Jaxon's most famous everything-but-the-kitchen-sink sundae features countless scoops and endless toppings.

128 S. Federal Hwy., Dania Beach. ✆ **954/923-4445**. Sundaes $2.75–$7.95. AE, DISC, MC, V. Mon–Thurs 11:30am–11pm, Fri–Sat 11:30am–midnight; Sun noon–11pm.

Thai Spice ⭐⭐ THAI   This could be the best Thai in Fort Lauderdale, but you'd never guess it from the tacky decor. Regular menu items include a slightly sweet and almost buttery pad Thai with a generous serving of shrimp, chicken chunks, and scallions. Lunch specials are incredibly cheap and include all the favorites.

1514 E. Commercial Blvd. (east of I-95), Fort Lauderdale. ✆ **954/771-4535**. Fax 954/771-5678. Reservations recommended. Main courses $9.95–$26. AE, DC, DISC, MC, V. Lunch Mon–Fri 11am–3pm; dinner Sun–Thurs 5–10pm; Fri–Sat 5–11pm.

Taverna Opa ⭐⭐ *Value* GREEK   Don't get nervous if you hear plates breaking when you enter this raucous, authentic Greek taverna situated directly on the Intracoastal Waterway—it's just the restaurant's lively staff making sure your experience here is 100% Greek. Delicious *meze* (appetizers), including a large Greek salad with hunks of fresh feta cheese, moist and savory stuffed grape leaves, and grilled calamari, are offered at ridiculously cheap prices. If you've had enough ouzo, you may want to consider hopping up on one of the tables and dancing to the jacked-up Greek music. If not, don't worry; the waiters usually wind up on the tabletop, encouraging diners to shout the restaurant's name, "Opa!" making sure you don't forget it. You won't.

410 N. Ocean Dr., Hollywood. ✆ **954/929-4010**. Reservations accepted weekdays only. Meze (appetizers) $2.95–$10. AE, DC, DISC, MC, V. Open daily from 4pm "until the ouzo runs out."

HOLLYWOOD & FORT LAUDERDALE AFTER DARK

Fort Lauderdale no longer mimics the raucous antics of *Animal House* as far as nightlife and partying are concerned. It has gotten hip to the fact that an active nightlife is vital to the city's desires to distract sophisticated, savvy visitors from the magnetic lure of South Beach.

Hollywood's nightlife seems to be in the throes of an identity crisis, touting itself as the next South Beach, while at the same time hyping its image as an attitude-free nocturnal playground. Here's the real deal: At press time, Hollywood nightlife was barely awake, with the exception of a few bars and one struggling dance club. If you're looking for a somewhat civilized, quiet night out, it's probably your best bet. But don't come too late—after midnight, the city is absolutely deserted.

For information on clubs and events, pick up a free copy of Fort Lauderdale's weekly newspaper *City Link* or the Fort Lauderdale edition of the *New Times*.

O'Hara's   What used to be a mediocre jazz club has turned into a premier venue for excellent, live R&B, pop, and funk music. Two locations: 1905 Hollywood Blvd., Hollywood (*(C)* 954/925-2555 or the 24-hr. Jazz & Blues Hotline *(C)* 954/524-2801); and 722 E. Las Olas Blvd., Fort Lauderdale (*(C)* 954/524-1764).

Warehaus 57   This is the place that gives Hollywood the right to boast about its burgeoning arty and bohemian scene. A funky cafe, bookstore, and clothing store, Warehaus 57 is the city's best (and only) acoustic club, in which the storefront window doubles as a stage for poets, singers, and other creative types. Despite the place's popularity, it doesn't stay open as late as it should and closes at 6pm on weeknights, at midnight on weekends. 1904-B Hollywood Blvd., Hollywood. *(C)* 954/926-6633.

Nick's   With an idyllic location on Hollywood's broadwalk, Nick's is the best place to enjoy cocktails with an unobstructed view of the ocean. 1214 N. Broadwalk, Hollywood. *(C)* 954/920-2800. Open from 10am to 4am. No cover.

Deco Drive   While its name suggests South Beach, this 15,000-square-foot, three-story dance club tries too hard to be something it isn't. In fact, the only thing remotely South Beachy about Deco Drive is the number of silicone-enhanced women who seem to frequent the place. As for the men, can you say *Miami Vice* throwbacks? It's a decent place if you *must* dance, but remember: A 20-minute drive south to the real Deco Drive can make all the difference. 2031 Harrison St., Hollywood. *(C)* 954/925-3326. Friday and Saturday 10pm till closing. No cover before midnight, $5 after midnight.

Chili Pepper   David Bowie, who rarely gives concerts anymore, played here: not on South Beach, but right in the heart of downtown Fort Lauderdale. And what a coup that was. Since Bowie, there've been tons of Billboard-charting, mostly alternative musicians who have made Chili Pepper a requisite stop on their touring itineraries. 200 W. Broward Blvd., east of I-95. *(C)* 954/525-0094. Wednesday through Saturday 10pm to 3am. Cover varies from $0 to $20.

The Culture Room   If you consider rock and heavy metal to be culture, visit the Culture Room and bang your head to local bands. 3045 N. Federal Hwy. (at the corner of Oakland Park Blvd.), Fort Lauderdale. *(C)* 954/564-1074. Daily 8pm to 3am. Cover varies.

Elbo Room   Formerly Spring Break central, the Elbo Room has actually managed to maintain its rowdy and divey reputation by serving up frequent drink specials and live bands. 241 S. Atlantic Blvd. on the corner of Las Olas Boulevard and Fla. A1A. *(C)* 954/463-4615. Daily 10am to 2am. No cover.

Where the Boys Are: Gay Fort Lauderdale

While South Beach is a magnet for the so-called circuit boys—gay men who party on a continual, ritualistic basis—Fort Lauderdale has more of a low-key, small-town scene similar to, say, Provincetown. Here, local gay-owned and -operated bars, clubs, and restaurants are the places of choice for those who find South Beach's scene too pretentious, superficial, and drug infested. The Fort Lauderdale neighborhood of Wilton Manors is the hub of gay life, but there is a smattering of gay establishments throughout the city.

The Copa, located at 2800 S. Federal Hwy. (east on I-595, near the airport; ✆ **954/463-1507**) is the hottest gay spot north of South Beach—the granddaddy of Fort Lauderdale's gay club scene. Patrons of **Cathode Ray** call this bar their "Cheers." It's located at 1105 E. Las Olas Blvd. (✆ **954/462-8611**). **Georgie's Alibi** is Wilton Manors' most popular gay bar. Find it at 2266 Wilton Dr., Wilton Manors (✆ **954/ 565-2526**). Two great dance clubs are the **Coliseum** (2520 S. Miami Rd.; ✆ **954/832-0100**) and **The Saint** (1000 W. S.R. 84; (✆ **954/525-7883**).

The Parrot   Fort Lauderdale's most famous—and fun—dive bar, The Parrot is a local's and out-of-towner's choice for an evening of beer (16 kinds on tap), bonding, and browsing of the bar's virtual gallery of photos of almost everyone who's ever imbibed here since its opening in 1970. 911 Sunrise Lane, Fort Lauderdale. ✆ **954/563-1493.** Sun–Thurs 11am–2am, Fri–Sat 11am–3am. No cover.

The Poor House   Despite its unfortunate name, the Poor House is rich in live blues music and is a good spot for a couple of drinks and conversation. 110 SW 3rd Ave., Fort Lauderdale. ✆ **954/522-5145.** Daily 8pm–4am. No cover.

Rush Street   Known for its ice-cream flavors of martinis, from chocolate to Key lime, Rush Street is a sleek bar, with two dance floors, that attracts a young professional crowd. 220 SW 2nd St., Fort Lauderdale. ✆ **954/522-6900.** No cover.

Shooters   This waterfront bar is quintessential Fort Lauderdale. Inside, you'll find nautical types, families, and young professionals mixed in with a good dose of sunburned tourists enjoying the live reggae, jazz, or Jimmy Buffett–style tunes with the gorgeous backdrop of the bay and marinas all around. 3033 NE 32nd Ave., Fort Lauderdale. ✆ **954/566-2855.** Mon–Fri 11:30am–2am; Sat 11:30am–3am; Sun 10am–2am. No cover.

The Velvet Lounge   This lounge and dance club comes closest to the South Beach vibe with a (sometimes) chic crowd, pretty good DJs, and very little attitude. (The two times I was there, however, two people were arrested for fighting.) 2975 N. Federal Hwy. ✆ **954/563-4331.** Tues, Fri, and Sat 10pm–3am. Cover $0 to $10.

Beach Place   outdoor shopping and entertainment complex modeled after Coconut Grove's hugely successful CocoWalk Beach Place landed on the legendary "strip" with several franchised bars and restaurants popular with young, rowdy set. There amid the requisite Gap and Banana Republic, Sloppy Joe's (of Key West fame), Howl at the Moon, and Hooters. The view overlooking the ocean makes it worth a stop for a drink. 17 S. Atlantic Blvd., Fort Lauderdale. ✆ **954/ 760-9570.**

Riverwalk   You'll find this outdoor shopping and entertainment complex located in the heart of downtown Fort Lauderdale on the sleepy yet scenic New River—as a result of its river site, it's got more charm than most such complexes. In fact, if you've got a boat, you can sail here and anchor away until you're ready to move on. A host of bars, restaurants, and shops, not to mention a high-tech virtual reality arcade, The Escape, and a multiplex cinema, are enough to keep you occupied for at least a few hours. On weekends, this place is packed. 400 SW 2nd St. (along the New River from NE 6th Avenue to SW 6th Avenue), Fort Lauderdale.

2 Boca Raton ★★ & Delray Beach ★

26 miles S. of Palm Beach, 40 miles N. of Miami

Boca Raton is one of South Florida's most expensive, well-maintained cities— home to ladies who lunch and SUV-driving yuppies. The city's name literally translates as "rat's mouth," but you'd be hard-pressed to find rodents in this area's fancy digs. Instead, you might check out the International Museum of Cartoon Art (see below) for rodents of the Disney kind.

If you're looking for funky, wacky, and eclectic, look elsewhere. Boca is a luxurious resort community and, for some, the only place in South Florida worth staying in. Although Jerry Seinfeld's TV parents retired to the fictional Del Boca Vista, Boca's just too pricey to be a retirement community. With minimal nightlife, entertainment in Boca is restricted to leisure sports, excellent dining, and upscale shopping. The city's residents and vacationers happily comply.

Delray, named after a suburb of Detroit, grew up completely separate from its southern neighbor. This community was founded in 1894 by a Midwestern postmaster who sold off 5-acre lots through Michigan newspaper ads. Because of their close proximity, Boca and Delray can easily be explored together. Budget-conscious travelers would do well to eat and sleep in Delray and dip into Boca for sightseeing and beaching only.

ESSENTIALS

GETTING THERE   Like the rest of the cities on the Gold Coast, Boca Raton and Delray are easily reached from I-95 or the turnpike. Both the Fort Lauderdale/Hollywood International Airport and the Palm Beach International Airport (at Congress Avenue and Belvedere Road) are convenient. Amtrak (© 800/USA-RAIL; www.amtrak.com) trains make stops in Delray Beach at an unattended station at 345 S. Congress Ave.

VISITOR INFORMATION   Before your trip, call or write the **Palm Beach County Convention and Visitors Bureau,** 1555 Palm Beach Lakes Blvd., Suite 204, West Palm Beach, FL 33401 (© **800/554-PALM** or 561/233-3000; fax 561/471-3990; www.palmbeachfl.com). On weekdays from 8:30am until at least 4pm, stop by the **Boca Raton Chamber of Commerce** at 1800 N. Dixie Hwy., 4 blocks north of Glades Road (© **561/395-4433;** fax 561/392-3780; www.bocaratonchamber.com), Boca Raton, FL 33432, for information on attractions, accommodations, and events in the area. Also, try the **Delray Beach Chamber of Commerce** (© **561/278-0424;** fax 561/278-0555; www.delraybeach.com), at 64 SE 5th Ave., half a block south of Atlantic Avenue on U.S. 1, Delray Beach, FL 33483.

WHERE TO PLAY, ON & OFF THE BEACH

BEACHES   Thankfully, Florida had the foresight to set aside some of its most beautiful coastal areas for the public's enjoyment. Many of the area's best beaches are located in state parks and are free to pedestrians and bikers. Most do charge for parking.

The **Delray Beach Public Beach,** on Ocean Boulevard at the east end of Atlantic Avenue, is one of the area's most popular hangouts. Weekends especially attract a young and good-looking crowd of active locals and tourists. Regular volleyball, Frisbee, and paddleball games make for good entertainment. For refreshments, snack shops, bars, and restaurants are just across the street. Families enjoy the protection of lifeguards on the clean, wide beach. Gentle waters make it a good swimming beach, too. There's limited parking at meters along Ocean Boulevard.

Spanish River Park, on North Ocean Boulevard (Fla. A1A), 2 miles north of Palmetto Park Road in Boca Raton, is a huge oceanfront park with a large grassy area, making it one of the best choices for picnicking. Facilities include picnic tables, grills, restrooms, and a bilevel 40-foot observation tower. You can walk through tunnels under the highway to access nature trails that wind through fertile grasslands. Volleyball nets are ocean-side and always have at least one serious game going on. The park is open from 8am until 8pm. Also, read below about Red Reef Park.

GOLF   This area has plenty of good courses. The best ones that are not located in a gated community are found at the **Boca Raton Resort & Club** (see below) and the **Inn at Boca Teeca** (see below). Another great place to swing your clubs is at the **Deer Creek Golf Club** in Deerfield Beach (✆ **954/421-5550**), a 300-plus-yard driving range where a large bucket of balls costs $7, and a small one costs $4. However, from May to October or November, about a dozen private courses open their greens to visitors staying in Palm Beach County hotels. This "Golf-A-Round" program is free or severely discounted (carts are additional), and reservations can be made through most major hotels. Ask at your hotel, or contact the **Palm Beach County Convention and Visitors Bureau** (✆ **561/ 471-3995**) for information on which clubs are available for play.

The semiprivate, 18-hole, par-61 course at the **Boca Raton Executive Country Club,** 7601 E. Country Club Blvd. (✆ **561/997-9410**), is usually open to the public. A driving range is on the property as well as a pro shop, where you can rent clubs, and a restaurant. If you like, take lessons from a PGA pro. From Yamato Road East, turn left onto Old Dixie Highway; after about a mile, turn left onto Hidden Valley Boulevard and continue straight to the club. Greens fees are $11 to $27.

The **Boca Raton Municipal Golf Course,** 8111 Golf Course Rd. (✆ **561/ 483-6100**), is located just north of Glades Road, half a mile west of the Florida

The Man Who Built Boca

Self-taught architect Addison Mizner was so impressed with the Palm Beach lifestyle when he visited in 1918 that he set about designing the community's mansions, country clubs, and most of exclusive Worth Avenue. In 1925 he focused his talents on Boca Raton, joining with his brother in bringing his visions of a Mediterranean-style resort city to fruition. When the stock market plunged in 1926, Mizner's plans came to a halt. However, his legacy is visible throughout the city of Boca Raton, whose houses, strip malls, and various buildings maintain Spanish barrel-tile roofs, arches, and columns.

Turnpike. This public 18-hole, par-72 course covers approximately 6,200 yards. There's a snack bar and a pro shop where clubs can be rented. Greens fees are $11 to $14 for 9 holes and $19 to $25 for 18 holes. Ask for special summer discount fees.

SCUBA DIVING & SNORKELING   Moray Bend, a 58-foot dive spot located about ¾ mile off Boca Inlet, is the area's most popular. It's home to three moray eels that are used to being fed by scuba divers. The reef is accessible by boat from **Force E Dive Center,** 877 E. Palmetto Park Rd., Boca Raton (© **561/368-0555**). Phone for dive times. Dives cost $40 to $45 per person.

    Red Reef Park, 1400 N. Ocean Park Blvd. (© **561/393-7974**), a fully developed 67-acre oceanfront park in Boca Raton, has good swimming and year-round lifeguard protection. There's snorkeling for beginners around the rocks and reefs that lie just off the beach in 2 to 6 feet of water. The park also has restrooms and a small picnic area with grills and tables. Located a half-mile north of Palmetto Park Road, it is open daily from 8am to 10pm. You pay only if you drive in. It's $8 per car during the week or $10 on weekends.

TENNIS   The snazzy **Delray Beach Tennis Center,** 201 W. Atlantic Ave. (© **561/243-7360;** www.delraytennis.com), has 14 lighted clay courts and 5 hard courts available by the hour. Phone for rates and reservations.

    The 17 public lighted hard courts at **Patch Reef Park,** 2000 NW 51st St. (© **561/997-0881;** www.tennistwist.com/patchreefpark.htm), are available by reservation. The fee for nonresidents is $5.75 per person per hour. Courts are available Monday to Saturday from 7:30am to 10pm and Sunday from 7:30am to dusk; you can phone ahead to see if a court is available. To reach the park from I-95, exit at Yamato Road West and continue past Military Trail to the park.

SEEING THE SIGHTS

Dagger Wing Nature Center ★★★   Seen enough snowbirds? Head over to this 39-acre swampy splendor where birds of another feather reside, including herons, egrets, woodpeckers, and warblers. The park's trails come complete with a soundtrack provided by songbirds hovering above (watch your head).

South County Regional Park, 11200 Park Access Rd., Boca Raton. © 561/488-9953. Free admission. Tues–Fri 1–4:30pm, Sat 9am–4:30pm. Call for tour and activity schedule.

Boca Raton Museum of Art ★★   In addition to a relatively small but well-chosen permanent collection that's strongest in 19th-century European oils, the museum stages a wide variety of temporary exhibitions by local and international artists. Lectures and films are offered on a fairly regular basis, so call ahead for details. Additional fees may apply for special exhibits and performances.

Mizner Park, 501 Plaza Real, Boca Raton. © 561/392-2500. Admission $3 adults, $2 seniors, $1 students, children under 12 free. Free on Wed. Tues, Thurs, Sat 10am–5pm; Wed, Fri 10am–9pm; Sun noon–5pm.

Gumbo Limbo Environmental Complex ★★★   If manicured lawns and golf courses aren't your idea of communing with nature, then head to Gumbo Limbo. Named for an indigenous hardwood tree with continuously shedding bronze bark, the 20-acre complex protects one of the few surviving coastal hammocks, or forest islands, in South Florida. Visitors can walk through the hammock on a ½-mile-long elevated boardwalk that ends at a 40-foot observation tower, from which you can see the Atlantic Ocean, the Intracoastal Waterway, and much of Boca Raton. From mid-April to September, sea turtles come ashore here to lay their eggs. During this time, the center conducts turtle-watching tours and sea turtle lectures.

1801 N. Ocean Blvd. (on Fla. A1A between Spanish River Blvd. and Palmetto Park), Boca Raton. © 561/ 338-1473. Fax 561/338-1483. Free admission. Mon–Sat 9am–4pm, Sun noon–4pm.

International Museum of Cartoon Art ★★ *Kids*   This extensive collection of cartoon art spans the decades and styles in its glitzy home in Mizner Park. In a gorgeous 52,000-square-foot gallery space, cartoon fans can see prints, frames, moving pictures, and books by some of the world's greatest cartoonists, including many by the museum's late founder, Mort Walker (of *Beetle Bailey* fame). A fantastic gift shop offers posters, books, and lots of memorabilia.

201 Plaza Real at Mizner Park, Boca Raton. © 561/391-2200. www.cartoon.org. Admission $6 adults, $5 seniors, $4 students, $3 children 6–12 years old, members and ages 5 and under free. Tues–Sat 10am–6pm, Sun noon–6pm.

Morikami Museum and Japanese Gardens ★★★   Slip off your shoes and enter into a serene Japanese garden community that dates from 1905, when an entrepreneurial farmer, Jo Sakai, came to Boca Raton to build a tropical agricultural community. The Yamato Colony, as it was known, was short-lived; by the 1920s only one tenacious colonist remained: George Sukeji Morikami. But Morikami was quite successful, eventually holding one of the largest pineapple plantations in the area. The 200-acre Morikami Museum and Japanese Gardens (a stroll through the garden is actually ⅞ mile), which opened to the public in 1977, was Morikami's gift to Palm Beach County and the State of Florida. The park section, dedicated to the preservation of Japanese culture, is constructed to appeal to all the senses. An artificial waterfall that cascades into a koi- and carp-filled moat; a small rock garden for meditation; and a large bonsai collection that includes miniature maple, buttonwood, juniper, and Australian pine trees are all worth contemplation. The Gardens have been expanded, and there's also a cafe with a Japanese- and Asian-inspired menu if you want to stay for lunch.

4000 Morikami Park Rd., Delray Beach. © 561/495-0233. Museum $7 adults, $6 seniors, $4 children 6–18, free for members and children 5 and under. Museum Tues–Sun 10am–5pm; gardens Tues–Sat 10am–5pm. Closed major holidays.

SHOPPING & BROWSING

Even if you don't plan to buy anything, a trip to Boca Raton's **Mizner Park** ★ is essential for capturing the essence of the city. Like Main Street in a small town, Mizner is the place to see and be seen, where Rolls Royces and Ferraris are parked curbside, freshly coifed women sit amidst shopping bags at outdoor cafes, and young movers and shakers make evening plans on their constantly buzzing cell phones. Beyond the human scenery, however, Mizner Park is scenic in its own right with beautiful landscaping. It's really an outdoor mall, with 45 specialty shops, seven good restaurants, and a multiplex. Each shop front faces a grassy island with blue and green gazebos, potted plants, and garden benches. Mizner Park is located on Federal Highway (between Palmetto Park Road and Glades Road; © **561/362-0606**).

Boca's **Town Center Mall,** located on the south side of Glades Road, just west of I-95, has seven huge department stores, including the state's only Nordstrom as well as Bloomingdale's, Burdines, Lord & Taylor, and Saks Fifth Avenue. Add to that the hundreds of specialty shops, an extensive food court, and a range of other restaurants, and you have the area's most comprehensive shopping center.

Boca Raton & Delray Beach Accommodations & Dining

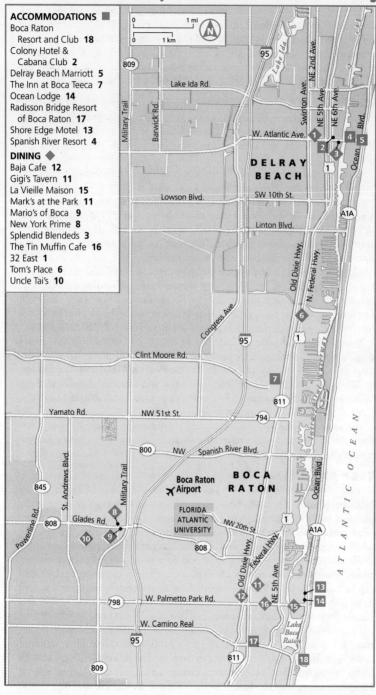

ACCOMMODATIONS ■

Boca Raton
  Resort and Club **18**
Colony Hotel &
  Cabana Club **2**
Delray Beach Marriott **5**
The Inn at Boca Teeca **7**
Ocean Lodge **14**
Radisson Bridge Resort
  of Boca Raton **17**
Shore Edge Motel **13**
Spanish River Resort **4**

DINING ◆

Baja Cafe **12**
Gigi's Tavern **11**
La Vieille Maison **15**
Mark's at the Park **11**
Mario's of Boca **9**
New York Prime **8**
Splendid Blendeds **3**
The Tin Muffin Cafe **16**
32 East **1**
Tom's Place **6**
Uncle Tai's **10**

A lifeless, overrated area, but good enough for a quick stroll, is the more artsy community of **Delray Beach,** known by many as Pineapple Grove. Here, along Atlantic Avenue, especially east of Swinton Avenue, you'll find a few antique shops, clothing stores, and art galleries shaded by palm trees and colorful awnings. Pick up the "Downtown Delray Beach" map and guide at almost any of the stores on this strip, or call ✆ **561/278-0424** for more information.

WHERE TO STAY

If you choose to stay in Boca Raton or the surrounding areas, you will find some very luxurious lodgings, epitomized by the famous and often photographed pink **Boca Raton Resort and Club,** where Boca's country-club lifestyle is alive and well.

A number of national chain hotels worth considering include a moderately priced **Holiday Inn Highland Beach Oceanside** at 2809 S. Ocean Blvd., on Fla. A1A southeast of Linton Boulevard (✆ **800/234-6835** or 561/278-6241). **The Radisson Bridge Resort** (see review below), at 999 E. Camino Real (✆ **800/333-3333** or 561/368-9500), operates a particularly popular and affordable resort on the Intracoastal Waterway just a few blocks from the Boca Raton Resort. Beware: It books up well in advance.

Although you won't find rows of cheap hotels as in Fort Lauderdale and Hollywood, a handful of mom-and-pop motels have survived along Fla. A1A between the towering condominiums of Delray Beach. Look along the beach just south of Atlantic Boulevard. Especially noteworthy is the pleasant little two-story, shingle-roofed **Bermuda Inn** at 64 S. Ocean Blvd. (✆ **561/276-5288**).

Even more economical options can be found in Deerfield Beach, Boca's neighbor, south of the county line. A number of beachfront efficiencies offer great deals, even in the winter months. Try the **Panther Motel and Apartments,** at 715 S. A1A (✆ **954/427-0700**). This clean and convenient motel has rates starting as low as $40, although in season you may have to book for a week at a time. Weekly rates in season start at $457.

If you are looking for something more private or for longer than just a few days, you may want to call a reservations service for help. **Palm Beach Accommodations** (✆ **800/543-SWIM**) handles rentals for a few weeks or months.

VERY EXPENSIVE

Boca Raton Resort and Club ★★   Built in 1926 as the Cloister Inn by Addison Mizner, the posh Boca Raton Resort now comprises three oddly matched buildings: the original, more traditional Cloister building; the somewhat drab, pink 27-story Tower; and the more modern, airier Beach Club, which is accessible by a water shuttle. Everything at this resort, which straddles the Intracoastal and encompasses over 350 acres of land, is fully at your fingertips but may sometimes require a little effort to reach it. The amenities here cannot be beat. The resort features two 18-hole championship golf courses as well as 60 golf villas located directly on the course, a $10 million Tennis and Fitness Center, indoor basketball and racquetball courts, a 25-slip marina with full fishing and boating facilities, and a private beach with various water-sports equipment for rent. With a choice of 10 places to dine, including Lucca, a grand waterfront Tuscan-style restaurant designed by David Rockwell and run by Drew Nieporent's Myriad Restaurant Group; and 27 Ocean Blue, an eclectic restaurant combining the flavors of the Pacific Rim, Caribbean, Deep South, Hawaii, and Florida's "New World" cuisine; plus five pools to swim in and an excellent children's program, the resort is ideal for families. Malone's Magic Bar features table-side magic tricks, while Bar Luna offers an elegant and inviting wine library. Upon check in, see if Harry the bellman is available to take you to your room—he's been at the resort for over 46 years and has a photographic memory of the hotel's previous guests, from Joseph Cotton and Charlton Heston to Bill Gates, who became a partner in the hotel after spending enough time there.

501 E. Camino Real (P.O. Box 5025), Boca Raton, FL 33431. ℂ 800/327-0101 or 561/395-3000. Fax 561/447-3183. www.bocaresort.com. 963 units, 120 golf villas. Winter $260–$625 double; off-season $160–$370. Reasonable seasonal packages available. AE, DC, DISC, MC, V. From I-95 N., exit onto Palmetto Park Rd. E. Turn right onto Federal Hwy. (U.S. 1), and then left onto Camino Real to the resort. **Amenities:** 10 restaurants; 6 bars; 5 pools; 2 18-hole championship golf courses; 34 tennis courts; 3 health clubs; indoor basketball court; 4 indoor racquetball courts; 25-slip marina with full fishing and boating; water-sports equipment/rental; extensive children's programs; concierge; business center; 24-hr. room service; laundry. *In room:* A/C, TV, minibar, hair dryer.

MODERATE

Colony Hotel & Cabana Club ✨✨   The Colony was recently added to the National Trust for Historic Preservation's prestigious list of 150 hotels, resorts, and inns that combine history and architectural significance. The hotel is definitely up to speed with modern amenities but remains steeped in the Old Florida tradition of the seasonal resort, and is open only from November 1 to May 1. This three-story hotel is 2 miles from the Cabana Club, its meticulously maintained private beach and club with 250 feet of beach and a heated pool. Shuttles are available, but the walk is a pleasant one if you're not in a hurry. The guest rooms are modest in size and style but comfortable and clean with wood floors and antique John Wanamaker furniture dating back to the hotel's inception. All rooms are nonsmoking. Service is friendly, not overbearing, contributing to the feeling that you're staying at someone's plush beach house in, say, Kennebunkport, Maine, where the hotel's sister property is located.

525 E. Atlantic Ave. (P.O. Box 970), Delray Beach, FL 33483. ℂ 800/552-2363 or 561/276-4123. Fax 561/276-0123. www.thecolonyhotel.com. 66 units. Winter $165–$205 double; off-season $75–$135 double. AE, MC, V. **Amenities:** Restaurant; bar; heated pool; music room; putting green; weight room; afternoon tea. *In room:* A/C, TV, dataport, hair dryer.

Delray Beach Marriott ✨   Delray Beach may be a sleepy beach town, but those looking for a bit more excitement will find it in this Marriott, which features a host of activities and amenities that may almost convince you that Delray is an exciting, lively place! The hotel, decked out in a typical, yet charming, Marriott-Florida decor, offers the best of both worlds: It's located directly across the street from the slumberous beach, but on premises it has an enormous, active outdoor pool and a lively lounge. Children under 18 stay free with an adult.

10 N. Ocean Blvd., Delray Beach, FL 33483. ℂ 800/228-9290 or 561/274-3200. Fax 561/274-3202. 268 units. Winter $245–$269; Off-season $119–$139. AE, DC, DISC, MC, V. **Amenities:** Restaurant; lounge; large outdoor pool; health club; concierge. *In room:* A/C, TV, dataport, coffeemaker, hair dryer.

The Inn at Boca Teeca ✨✨✨   For over three decades, this inn has been attracting golf fanatics who could care less about the small, but comfortable, rooms because they're too busy out on the superb 27-hole golf course at the Inn's Boca Teeca Country Club, open only to members and guests of the Inn. For the golf widow(er)s, however, most of the rooms in this three-story building have balconies or patios from which to watch or signal their significant others that it's time for dinner.

5800 NW 2nd Ave., Boca Raton, FL 33487. ℂ **561/994-0400.** Fax 561/998-8279. 46 units. Winter $140 and up; off-season $80–$120. AE, DC, MC, V. **Amenities:** Restaurant; small pool; golf course; 6 tennis courts; fitness center. *In room:* A/C, TV.

Radisson Bridge Resort of Boca Raton ★★ Not as pricey as the Boca Raton Resort, this resort nevertheless does feature priceless water views and is an excellent choice for the money. All guest rooms have balconies with views of the Intracoastal or the Atlantic, and some corner suites have both. Its popular outdoor waterfront restaurant, Watercolors, is the only place in the city to dine on the water. The restaurant and lounge at the top of the hotel behold gorgeous panoramic views. Just a 5-minute walk to the beach, this Radisson bridges the gap between ultra-pricey and ultra-schlocky area hotels.

999 E. Camino Real, Boca Raton, FL 33432. ℂ **800/333-3333** or 561/368-9500. Fax 561/362-0492. www.radisson.com. 121 units. Winter $209–$299; off-season $109–$189. Some rates include breakfast. AE, DC, MC, V. **Amenities:** 2 restaurants; outdoor heated pool; health club & spa; water-sports equipment/rental; bike rental; concierge. *In room:* A/C, TV, coffeemaker, hair dryer.

Spanish River Resort ★★★ An especially good value for those staying longer than a few days, this pleasant family-oriented property offers fully furnished condominiums half a block from a popular beach and within walking distance of Delray's best shops, restaurants, and galleries. The 11-story Mediterranean-style building has lighted tennis courts, a large outdoor pool, and lovely ocean-view balconies from the fourth floor and above. Apartments are spacious and outfitted with fully equipped kitchens. All units also have pullout queen-size sofa beds and, incredibly, there is no additional charge for extra guests. A one-bedroom unit can comfortably fit four or five people; a two-bedroom unit can easily accommodate six. Cots and rollaway beds are available at a minimum charge. Compared with many of the run-down 1950s motels in the area, this moderately priced, well-maintained tower is a real find.

1111 E. Atlantic Ave., Delray Beach, FL 33483. ℂ **800/543-SWIM** or 561/243-7946. Fax 561/276-9634. 75 units. Winter $150 studio; $350 2-bedroom. Off-season from $98 studio; $228 2-bedroom. Free 6th and 7th nights with weekly booking. AE, DISC, MC, V. **Amenities:** Restaurant; outdoor pool; lighted tennis courts. *In room:* A/C, TV.

INEXPENSIVE

Ocean Lodge ★ Situated around a small heated pool and sundeck, this two-story motel is a particularly well-kept accommodation in an area of run-down or overpriced options. The large rooms offer furnishings and decor that are clean but a bit impersonal. A recent renovation that added modern Formica and floral wallpaper lifts this a notch above a basic motel. Ask for a room in the back since the street noise can be a bit loud, especially in season. The bonus is that you are across the street from the ocean and in one of Florida's most upscale resort towns.

531 N. Ocean Blvd. (just north of Palmetto Park Rd. on Fla. A1A), Boca Raton, FL 33432. ℂ **800/STAY-BOCA** or 561/395-7772. Fax 561/395-0554. 18 units. Winter $99–$125 double; off-season $75–$99 double. AE, MC, V. **Amenities:** Pool. *In room:* A/C, TV.

Shore Edge Motel Another relic of the 1950s recently spiffed up with new landscaping and some redecorating, this motel is a good choice, especially because of its location—across the street from a public beach, just north of downtown Boca Raton. It's the quintessential South Florida motel: a small, pink, single-story structure surrounding a modest swimming pool and courtyard. Although the rooms are on the small side, they're very neat and clean. The higher-priced accommodations are larger and come with full kitchens.

425 N. Ocean Blvd. (on Fla. A1A, north of Palmetto Park Rd.), Boca Raton, FL 33432. ℂ 561/395-4491. Fax 561/347-8759. 16 units. Winter $85–$99 double; off-season $55–$65 double. AE, MC, V. **Amenities:** Pool. *In room:* A/C, TV.

WHERE TO DINE

Boca Raton, and its surrounding area, is the kind of place where you discuss dinner plans at the breakfast table. Nightlife in Boca means going out to a restaurant. But who cares? These are some of the best restaurants in South Florida.

VERY EXPENSIVE

La Vieille Maison ✸✸✸ FRENCH   The luxurious setting, a Mediterranean-inspired home filled with a variety of antique French furnishings and paintings, gives you the feeling of walking into a small chateau. Culinarily speaking, this place is a castle. Begin with lobster bisque, gratin of escargots with fennel and pistachio nuts, or pan-seared foie gras—each is equally delectable. It's difficult to choose from the many enticing entrees, which range from red snapper in black- and green-olive potato crust to medallions of beef, lamb, and venison over three sauces. You'll surely have to try at least a few of the gorgeous cheeses the server offers after your main course—the most extensive selection I've seen in this country. The lemon crepe soufflé with raspberry sauce is the dessert of choice—remember to order it early.

770 E. Palmetto Park Rd., Boca Raton. ℂ 561/391-6701 or 561/737-5677. Reservations recommended. Main courses $18–$50; fixed-price dinners $42 and $68. AE, DC, DISC, MC, V. Daily 6–9:30pm (call for seating times).

New York Prime ✸✸✸ STEAKHOUSE   Forget Morton's and Smith & Wollensky. This South Florida outpost of a South Carolina–based chain is the prime spot for carnivores looking to satisfy their cravings for big, succulent steaks. Fish dishes are also available, including lobsters ranging from 3 to 13 pounds. But the price of excess does not come cheap. In fact, the restaurant brazenly states its case on the menu: "We strive to be the Mercedes of steakhouses by offering the very best . . . but you can't drive a Mercedes for the same price as a Buick." To me, this is more like the DeLorean of steakhouses—a rare find.

2350 Executive Center Dr., Boca Raton. ℂ 561/998-3881. Reservations recommended. Main courses $22.50–$64. AE, MC, V. Daily 5–11pm.

EXPENSIVE

32 East ✸✸ NEW AMERICAN   The menu changes every day at this very popular people-watching outpost of tasty, contemporary American food that has finally added a little hip to the Delray Beach dining scene. Delicious items have included rigatoni with braised lamb shank and oregano; hanger steak on roasted-garlic polenta; and grilled salmon with arugula purée and olive tapenade.

32 E. Atlantic Ave., Delray Beach. ℂ 561/276-7868. Reservations recommended. Main courses $10–$16. AE, DC, MC, V. Sun–Thurs 5:30–10pm, Fri–Sat 5:30–11pm; bar until 2am.

Gigi's Tavern AMERICAN   Gigi's is a nightclub in the guise of a restaurant. Noisy and jampacked, especially on weekends, Gigi's makes it hard for diners to focus on their plates, nearly impossible to converse with their fellow diners. Not surprisingly, service is as rushed as the latest dance remix. Oysters and other appetizers are your best bets. Just make sure to let your food digest before you start spinning on the small dance floor.

346 Plaza Real, in Mizner Park, Boca Raton. ℂ 561/368-4488. Reservations suggested. Main courses $15–$20. AE, DC, MC, V. Mon–Thurs 11:30am–11pm, Fri–Sat 11:30am–midnight, Sun 11:30am–10:30pm.

Mark's at the Park ★★ MEDITERRANEAN   Star chef Mark Militello's contribution to Boca Raton's restaurant scene attracts a well-toned, sleek crowd that seems only to pick at the restaurant's excellent thin-crusted pizzas, grilled meats, and seafood. Indoor seating is loud and bustling, and outdoor tables are coveted for their views of Mizner Park pedestrian traffic. Sunday brunch here is a fabulous all-you-can-eat affair of pizzas, salads, pastas, and assorted gourmet breakfast foods.

In Mizner Park, 344 Plaza Real, Boca Raton. ✆ 561/395-0770. Reservations suggested. $11–$28. AE, DC, MC, V. Sun–Thurs 5:30–11pm, Fri–Sat 5:30pm–midnight.

Uncle Tai's ★★★ CHINESE   Not your average egg roll and lo-mein kind of place, Uncle Tai's, Boca's best upscale Chinese restaurant, offers a savory spin on classics such as garlic chicken and duck with plum sauce. A family-run restaurant, Uncle Tai's is the product of Wen Dah Tai, a man who studied with the master chefs in China, Japan, and the Philippines. Like your favorite uncle, Tai wants to make sure you will emerge from his restaurant fully satisfied and will even go the extra mile to discourage you from ordering a dish that's less suited to Western palates, having been created for the restaurant's many Chinese diners (always a good sign).

5250 Town Center Circle (between Glades Rd. and Palmetto Park Rd.), Boca Raton. ✆ **561/368-8806.** Reservations suggested. Main courses $12–$32. AE, DISC, MC, V. Daily 11:30am–2:30pm and 5–10pm.

MODERATE

Mario's of Boca ★ ITALIAN   This extremely popular, bustling Italian bistro keeps Boca's biggest mouths busy with massive portions of great homemade Italian food. The garlic rolls and the pizza are especially worth piping down for. If you're really hungry, there's an all-you-can-eat buffet 7 days a week.

2200 Glades Rd. (between 19th St. and Sheridan Way), Boca Raton. ✆ **561/392-5595.** Reservations not accepted. Main courses under $15. AE, MC, V. Mon–Thurs 11:30am–10pm, Fri–Sat 11:30am–11pm, Sun noon–9:30pm.

Splendid Blendeds ★★ *Finds* ECLECTIC   Loyal regulars would like to keep this storefront bistro a secret so that the lines won't get even longer on weekends. The draw here is fresh, uncomplicated seafood and pastas that are interesting without being overly ambitious. The Southwestern-inspired chicken Santa Cruz is tender and juicy, served with a black-bean sauce and tangy pico de gallo. Many seafood specialties, like tuna, snapper, and shrimp dishes, are slight departures from classic recipes and work most of the time. The only drawback of this otherwise superb spot, aside from the name, is the well-meaning but easily flustered staff.

432 E. Atlantic Ave., Delray. ✆ **561/265-1035.** Reservations recommended. Main courses $10.95–$21.95; sandwiches and salads $3.50–$8.95. AE, DC, MC, V. Mon–Fri 11:30am–2:30pm, Mon–Sat 5:30–10pm. Closed Aug.

INEXPENSIVE

Baja Cafe ★ MEXICAN   A jeans and T-shirt kind of place with wooden tables, Baja Cafe serves fantastic Mexican food at even better prices. It's located right by the Florida East Coast Railway tracks, so don't be surprised if you feel a little rattling. Live music and entertainment in the evening make this place a hot spot for an unpretentious crowd.

201 NW First Ave., Boca Raton. ✆ 561/ 394-5449. No reservations. Main courses $6–$10. No credit cards. Mon–Thurs 11:30am–10:30pm, Fri–Sat 11:30am–11pm, Sun 5–10pm.

The Tin Muffin Cafe 𝒢 BAKERY/SANDWICH SHOP   Popular with the downtown lunch crowd, this excellent storefront bakery keeps them lining up for big fresh sandwiches on fresh bread, plus muffins, quiches, and good home-made soups like split pea or lentil. The curried chicken sandwich is stuffed with oversized chunks of only white meat doused in a creamy curry dressing and fruit. There are a few cafe tables inside and even one outside on a tiny patio. Be warned, however, that service is forgivably slow and parking is a nightmare. Try parking a few blocks away at a meter on the street.

364 E. Palmetto Park Rd. (between Federal Hwy. and the Intracoastal Bridge), Boca Raton. ℭ 561/ 392-9446. Sandwiches and salads $6.50–$10.95. No credit cards. Mon–Fri 11am–5pm, Sat 11am–4pm.

Tom's Place 𝒢𝒢 *Finds* BARBECUE   There are two important factors in a suc-cessful barbecue: the cooking and the sauce. Tom and Helen Wright's no-non-sense shack wins on both counts, offering flawlessly grilled meats paired with well-spiced sauces. Beef, chicken, pork, and fish are served soul-food style, with your choice of two sides such as rice with gravy, collard greens, black-eyed peas, coleslaw, or mashed potatoes. Signed celebrity photographs decorate the walls.

7251 N. Federal Hwy., Boca Raton. ℭ 561/997-0920. Reservations not accepted. Main courses $8–$15; sandwiches $5–$6; early bird special $7.95. AE, MC, V. Tues–Thurs 11:30am–9:30pm, Fri 11:30am–10; Sat noon–10pm.

BOCA RATON & DELRAY AFTER DARK
THE BAR, CLUB & MUSIC SCENE
South Ocean Boulevard and Atlantic Avenue in Delray Beach are slowly but surely getting hip to nightlife—though still a far cry from the Fort Lauderdale "strip." In Boca Raton, Mizner Park is the nucleus of a makeshift nightlife, with restaurant-bars and restaurants disguising themselves as nightclubs (see Gigi's Tavern, above).

Boston's on the Beach is a family restaurant with a somewhat lively bar scene. It's a good choice for post-sunbathing, supercasual happy hours on Monday to Friday from 4 to 8pm, or for live reggae on Monday. With two decks overlook-ing the ocean, Boston's is an ideal place to mellow out and take in the scenery. 40 S. Ocean Blvd., Delray Beach. ℭ 561/278-3364. Daily 7am–2am. No cover.

Dakotah 624   Creative cocktails such as the Kissing Cousin (Southern Com-fort, Fris vodka, lime juice, and triple sec) and its own line of cigars attract a hip, young clientele to this vaguely Southwestern-style bar on the beach. 270 E. Atlantic Ave., Delray Beach. ℭ 561/274-6244. Mon–Wed 4pm–1am, Thurs–Sat 4pm–2am, Sun 4–11pm. No cover.

Gatsby's   This always-busy bar is singles central, featuring big-screen TVs, microbrews, and martinis. Thursday-night college nights are especially popular, as are Friday happy hours. 5970 SW 18th St., Boca Raton. ℭ 561/393-3900. Mon–Fri 4pm–2am, Sat–Sun 6pm–4am. No cover.

Mezzanotte   The Mezzanotte on South Beach's Washington Avenue used to be *the* place for a bacchanalian funfest. Then the place went from crazy to closed. The good times have traveled north to this Boca offshoot, where a well-tanned, glitzy crowd of young and old let their hair (or toupees) down, especially on weekends. 150 E. Palmetto Park Rd., Boca Raton. ℭ 561/361-0111. Sun–Thurs 5–10pm, Fri–Sat 5pm–2am. No cover.

Radius   This big, noisy techno-trance warehouse west of the highway attracts a range of big-haired girls and macho guys with gold chains. It's Boca's only attempt at a clubby nightlife and, if you don't mind dancing with a really young crowd, it can be amusing depending on your sense of humor. If you can, try to have your hotel concierge put you on the "list" so you won't have to shell out $20 or more for this nocturnal gamble. 7000 W. Palmetto Park Rd. (at the SW corner of Powerline Rd. in the Bank of America building). © 561/392-3747. Thurs–Sun 9pm–5am. Cover varies $5–$20.

THE PERFORMING ARTS

For details on upcoming events, check the *Boca News* or the *Sun-Sentinel,* or call the **Palm Beach County Cultural Council** information line at © **800/ 882-ARTS.** During business hours, a staffer can give details on current performances. After hours, a recorded message describes the week's events. The *Sun-Sentinel* also hosts a comprehensive "Source Line" for information on everything from weather to garage sales. Detailed arts information is included.

The **Florida Symphonic Pops,** a 70-piece professional orchestra, performs jazz, swing, rock, big band, and classical music throughout Boca Raton. For nearly 50 years, this ever-growing musical force has entertained audiences of every age. Call © **561/393-7677** for a schedule of concerts.

Boca's best theater company is the **Caldwell Theatre,** and it's worth checking out. Located in a strip shopping center at 7873 N. Federal Hwy., this equity showcase does well-known dramas, comedies, classics, off-Broadway hits, and new works throughout the year. Prices are reasonable (usually between $29 and $38). Full-time students will be especially interested in the little-advertised "Student Rush." When available, tickets are sold for $5 to those who arrive at least an hour in advance. Call © **561/241-7432** for details.

3 Palm Beach ★★ & West Palm Beach ★

65 miles N. of Miami, 193 miles E. of Tampa

Palm Beach County encompasses cities from Boca Raton in the south to Jupiter and Tequesta in the north. But it is Palm Beach, the small island town across the Intracoastal Waterway, that has been the traditional winter home of America's aristocracy—the Kennedys, the Rockefellers, the Pulitzers, the Trumps, titled socialites, and plenty of CEOs.

The island holds the distinction of being the only continental destination with three resorts that have earned the AAA five-diamonds rating. And beyond the upscale resorts and chic boutiques, it holds some surprises too, from a world-class art museum to one of the top bird-watching areas in the state.

Over the bridge from Palm Beach proper, or the "island" as locals call it, is downtown West Palm Beach, which is where everybody else lives. Clematis Street is the area's nightlife hub, with a great selection of bars, clubs, and restaurants. City Place is West Palm's version of Mizner Park; shops, restaurants, and other entertainment options liven up this once-dead area of West Palm. In addition to good beaching, boating, and diving, you'll find great golf and tennis throughout the county.

ESSENTIALS

GETTING THERE If you're driving up or down the Florida coast, you'll probably reach the Palm Beach area by way of I-95. Exit at Belvedere Road or Okeechobee Boulevard and head east to reach the most central part of Palm Beach.

> **Tips** **Winter Advisory**
>
> Palm Beach's population swells from 20,000 in the summer to 40,000 in the winter. Book early if you plan to visit during the winter months!

Visitors on their way to or from Orlando or Miami should take the Florida Turnpike, a toll road with a speed limit of 65 miles per hour. Tolls are pricey, though; you may pay upward of $9 from Orlando and $4 from Miami. If you're coming from Florida's west coast, you can take either State Route 70, which runs north of Lake Okeechobee to Fort Pierce, or State Route 80, which runs south of the lake to Palm Beach.

Among the airlines serving Palm Beach International Airport, at Congress Avenue and Belvedere Road (© **561/471-7400**), are **American** (© **800/433-7300**), **Continental** (© **800/525-0280**), **Delta** (© **800/221-1212**), **Kiwi** (© **800/538-5494**), **Northwest** (© **800/225-2525**), **TWA** (© **800/221-2000**), **United** (© **800/241-6522**), and **US Airways** (© **800/428-4322**).

Amtrak (© **800/USA-RAIL**; www.amtrak.com) has a terminal in West Palm Beach, at 201 S. Tamarind Ave. (© **561/832-6169**).

GETTING AROUND   Although a car is almost a necessity in this area, a recently revamped public transportation system is extremely convenient for getting to some attractions. Palm Tran underwent a major expansion in late 1996, increasing service to 32 routes and more than 140 buses. The fare is $1 for adults and 50¢ for children ages 3 to 18, seniors, and riders with disabilities. Free route maps are available by calling © **561/233-4-BUS.** Information operators are available from 6am to 7pm, except Sunday.

In downtown West Palm, free shuttles operate Monday through Friday from 9am until 4pm, with plans to expand operations to evenings and weekends too. Look for the bubble-gum–pink minibuses throughout downtown. Call © **561/833-8873** for more details.

For a more nostalgic route, consider the stately wicker chariots that run in the downtown area especially on weekends and during special events. Rates vary according to the time of day but average $1 to $2 per block, plus a per person charge of $1. Call © **561/835-8922** for pickup or information.

VISITOR INFORMATION   The **Palm Beach County Convention and Visitors Bureau,** 1555 Palm Beach Lakes Blvd., Suite 204, West Palm Beach, FL 33401 (© **800/554-PALM** or 561/471-3995; www.palmbeach.com), distributes an informative brochure and will answer questions about visiting the Palm Beaches. Ask for a map as well as a copy of its Arts and Attractions Calendar, a day-to-day guide to art, music, stage, and other events in the county.

FUN ON & OFF THE BEACH

BEACHES   Public beaches are a rare commodity here in Palm Beach. Most of the island's best beaches are fronted by private estates and inaccessible to the general public. However, there are a few notable exceptions, including **Midtown Beach** on Ocean Boulevard, between Royal Palm Way and Gulfstream Road, which boasts more than 100 feet of undeveloped beach. There are no restrooms or concessions here, although a lifeguard is on duty until sundown. This newly widened sandy coast is now a centerpiece and a natural oasis in a town dominated by commercial glitz. Also, about 1½ miles north **near Dunbar Street** is a popular hangout for locals, who enjoy the relaxed atmosphere. Parking is available at meters along Fla. A1A. To the south is a less popular but better-equipped beach at **Phipps Ocean Park.** On Ocean Boulevard, between the Southern Boulevard and Lake Avenue causeways, is a large and lively public beach encompassing more than 1,300 feet of groomed and guarded oceanfront. With picnic and recreation areas, as well as plenty of parking, the area is especially good for families.

BIKING   Rent anything from an English single-speed to a full-tilt mountain bike at the **Palm Beach Bicycle Trail Shop,** 223 Sunrise Ave. (© **561/ 659-4583**). The rates are $7 an hour, $18 a half day (9am to 5pm), or $24 for 24 hours and include a basket and lock (not that a lock is necessary in this fortress of a town). The most scenic route is called the Lake Trail, running the length of the island along the Intracoastal Waterway. On it you'll see some of the most magnificent mansions and grounds. Enjoy the views of downtown West Palm Beach and some great wildlife.

CRUISES   The *Palm Beach Princess* (© **800/841-7447** or 561/845-7447), is a small cruise ship (421 feet) offering reasonably priced casino gambling cruises out of the Port of Palm Beach (U.S. 1 between 45th Street and Blue Heron Boulevard) every day and evening. Choose from craps, roulette, poker, blackjack, and slots. Cruises include a large buffet with average food like spaghetti and meatballs, chicken, Greek salad, and vegetables; best is the prime rib at the carving board. Five-hour cruises sail daily at 12:30pm (returning at 5:30pm) and 7pm (returning at 12:30am). Friday and Saturday evening cruises leave at 7pm and return at 1am. Sunday cruises sail from 11am to 5pm and 6 to 11pm. Prices during the week are $40 per person; on weekends, it's $45 per person. If your birthday is in the month you plan to sail, pay $20. AAA discounts are available.

GOLF   There's good golfing here, but many of the private club courses are maintained exclusively for the use of their members. Ask at your hotel, or contact the **Palm Beach County Convention and Visitors Bureau** (© **561/ 471-3995**) for information on which clubs are currently available for play. In the off-season, some private courses open their greens to visitors staying in a Palm Beach County hotel. This "Golf-A-Round" program offers free greens fees (carts are additional); reservations can be made through most major hotels.

The best hotel for golf in the area is the **PGA National Resort and Spa** (see later in this chapter, © **800/633-9150**), which features a whopping 90 holes of golf.

One of the state's best courses that is open to the public is **Emerald Dunes Golf Course** ⛳, 2100 Emerald Dunes Dr. in West Palm Beach (© **561/ 687-1700**). Courses are also found in Delray Beach and Boynton Beach. Designed by Tom Fazio, this dramatic 7,006-yard, par-72 course was voted "One of the Best 10 You Can Play" by *Golf* magazine. It is located just off the Florida Turnpike at Okeechobee Boulevard. Bookings are taken up to 30 days ahead. Fees start at $125, including carts.

The **Palm Beach Public Golf Course,** 2345 S. Ocean Blvd. (© **561/ 547-0598**), a popular public 18-hole course, is a par-54. The course opens at 8am and runs on a first-come, first-served basis. Club rentals are available. Greens fees start at $20 per person.

POLO   What's Palm Beach without polo? See the "Sport of Kings" (below) for details.

SCUBA DIVING Year-round warm waters, barrier reefs, and plenty of wrecks make South Florida one of the world's most popular places for diving. One of the best-known artificial reefs in this area is a vintage Rolls-Royce Silver Shadow, which was sunk offshore in 1985. Mother Nature has taken her toll, however, and divers can no longer sit in the car, which has been ravaged by time and saltwater.

Call either of the following outfitters for gear and excursions: **Dixie Divers,** 1401 S. Military Trail, West Palm Beach (© **561/969-6688**); and **Ocean Sports Scuba Center,** 1736 S. Congress Ave., West Palm Beach (© **561/641-1144**).

TENNIS There are hundreds of tennis courts in Palm Beach County. Wherever you are staying, you are bound to be within walking distance of one. In addition to the many hotel tennis courts (see "Where to Stay," below), you can play at **Currie Park,** 2400 N. Flagler Dr., West Palm Beach (© **561/835-7025**), a public park with three lighted hard courts. They are free and available on a first-come, first-served basis.

 The Sport of Kings

The annual ritual of the ponies is played out each season at the posh Palm Beach Polo and Country Club. It is one of the world's premier polo grounds and hosts some of the sport's top-rated players.

Even if you're not a sports fan, you must attend a match. Although the field is actually on the mainland in an area called Wellington, rest assured that the spectators, and many of the players, are pure Palm Beach. After all, a day at the pony grounds is one of the only good reasons to leave Palm Beach proper.

Don't worry, though—you need not be a Vanderbilt or a Kennedy to attend. Matches are open to the public and are surprisingly affordable.

Even if you haven't a clue to how the game is played, you can spend your time people-watching. Stargazers have spotted Prince Charles, Sylvester Stallone, Tommy Lee Jones, Bo Derek, and Ivana Trump in recent years, among others. Dozens of lesser-known royalty, and just plain old characters, keep box seats or chalets right on the grounds.

Incidentally, the point of polo is to keep the other team from getting the ball through your goal. The fast-paced game is divided into six chukkers—like an inning in baseball—each 7 minutes long. There are 3-minute breaks between chukkers except at half time, which lasts 10 minutes. The whole thing is narrated by a British chap who sounds as though he walked off a Monty Python set.

Dress is casual; a navy or tweed blazer over jeans or khakis is a standard for men, while neat-looking jeans or a pantsuit is the norm for women. On warmer days, shorts and, of course, a polo shirt are fine, too.

General admission is $6 to $10; box seats cost $10 to $36. Matches are held throughout the week. Schedules vary, but the big names usually compete on Sunday at 3:30pm from January to April.

The fields are located at 11809 Polo Club Rd., Wellington, 10 miles west of the Forest Hill Boulevard exit of I-95. Call © **561/793-1440** for tickets and a detailed schedule of events.

WATER SPORTS   Call the **Seaside Activities Station** (✆ **561/835-8922**) to arrange sailboat, jet ski, bicycle, kayak, water ski, and parasail rentals.

SEEING THE SIGHTS

Flagler Museum ★★★   The Gilded Age is preserved in this luxurious mansion commissioned by Standard Oil tycoon Henry Flagler as a wedding present to his third wife. *Whitehall,* also known as the "Taj Mahal of North America," is a classically columned Edwardian-style mansion containing 55 rooms, including a Louis XIV music room and art gallery, a Louis XV ballroom, and 14 guest suites outfitted with original antique European furnishings. Out back, climb aboard "The Rambler," Mr. Flagler's private, restored railroad car. Allow at least 1½ hours to tour the stunning grounds and interior. School and group tours are available, but, for the most part, this is a self-guided museum.

1 Whitehall Way (at Cocoanut Row and Whitehall Way), Palm Beach. ✆ 561/655-2833. www.flagler.org. Admission $8 adults, $3 children ages 6–12. Tues–Sat 10am–5pm, Sun noon–5pm.

Norton Museum of Art ★★★   Since a 1997 expansion doubled the Norton's space, the museum has gained even more prominence in the art world. It is world famous for its prestigious permanent collection and top temporary exhibitions. The museum's major collections are divided geographically. The American galleries contain major works by Edward Hopper, Georgia O'Keeffe, and Jackson Pollock. The French collection contains Impressionist and post-Impressionist paintings by Cézanne, Degas, Gauguin, Matisse, Monet, Picasso, Pissarro, and Renoir. And the Chinese collection contains more then 200 bronzes, jades, and ceramics, as well as a collection of monumental Buddhist sculptures.

1451 S. Olive Ave., West Palm Beach. ✆ 561/832-5196. Fax 561/659-4689. www.norton.org. Admission $6 adults, $2 students, free for children 12 and under. Mon–Sat 10am–5pm, Sun noon–5pm. Free admission Wed from 1:30pm–5pm. From I-95, take Belvedere Rd. (Exit 51) east to the end; then turn left onto S. Olive Ave. to the museum.

Playmobil Fun Park ★★ *Kids*   In a child's mind, it doesn't get any better than this. The 17,000-square-foot Playmobil Fun Park is housed in a replica castle

Unreal Estate

No trip to Palm Beach is complete without at least a glimpse of Mar-A-Lago, the stately residence of Donald Trump, the 21st century's answer to Jay Gatsby. In 1985, Trump purchased Mar-A-Lago, the former estate of cereal heiress Marjorie Merriweather Post, for what was considered a meager $8 million (for a fully furnished beachfront property of this stature, it was a relative bargain, actually) to the great consternation of locals who feared that he would turn the place into a casino. Instead, Trump, who resides in a portion of the palace, opened the house to the public—for a price, of course—as a tony country club (membership fee: $100,000).

While there are currently no tours open to the public, you can glimpse the gorgeous manse as you cross the bridge from West Palm Beach into Palm Beach. Its website, at www.pbol.com/maralago/tour.html, offers photos, a calendar of events, and more details than you'd ever care to know. 1100 S. Ocean Blvd., Palm Beach. ✆561/833-2466.

and loaded with themed areas for imaginative play: a medieval village, a western town, a fantasy doll house, and more. Plus, there are two water-filled tables on which kids can play with the Playmobil boats. Tech-minded kids could get bored, but toddlers (and up to age 5 or so) will love this place. You *could* spend hours here and not spend a penny, but parents beware: Everything is available for purchase.

8031 N. Military Trail, Palm Beach Gardens. ℂ **800/351-8697** or 561/691-9880. Fax 561/691-9517. www. playmobil.com. Admission free. Daily 10am–6pm. From I-95, go north to Palm Beach Lakes Blvd.; then west to Military Trail. Turn left, and the park is about a mile down on the right .

NATURE PRESERVES & ATTRACTIONS

Lion Country Safari ✦ *Kids*   More than 1,300 animals on this 500-acre preserve are divided into their indigenous regions, from the East African preserve of the Serengeti to the American West. Elephants, wildebeest, ostriches, American bison, buffalo, watusi, pink flamingos, and many other more unusual species roam the preserve. When I visited, most of the lions were asleep; when they are awake, they travel freely throughout the cageless grassy landscape. In fact, you're the one who's confined in your own car without an escort (no convertibles allowed). You're given a detailed informational pamphlet with photos and descriptions and are instructed to obey the 15-mile-per-hour speed limit—unless you see the rhinos charge (a rare occasion), in which case you're encouraged to floor it. To drive the loop takes just over an hour, though you could make a day of just watching the chimpanzees play on their secluded islands. Included in the admission price is Safari World, an amusement park with paddleboats, a carousel, miniature golf, and a nursery for baby animals born in the preserve. Picnics are encouraged, and camping is available (call for reservations). The best time to go is late afternoon right before the park closes when they herd up all the animals; plus, it's much cooler then, so the lions are more active.

Southern Blvd. W. at S.R. 80, West Palm Beach. ℂ **561/793-1084,** or 561/793-9797 for camping reservations. Admission $15.50 adults, $10.50 seniors, $10.50 children 3–9, free for children under 3. Van rental is $6 per hr. Daily 9:30am–5:30pm (last vehicle admitted at 4:30pm). From I-95, exit on Southern Blvd. Go west for about 18 miles.

Palm Beach Zoo at Dreher Park ✦   If you want animals, go to Lion Country Safari. Unlike big-city zoos, this intimate 23-acre park is more like a stroll in the park than an all-day excursion. It features about 500 animals representing more than 100 different species. A special monkey exhibit and petting zoo are favorites with kids. Stroller and wagon rental available.

1301 Summit Blvd. (east of I-95 between Southern Blvd. and Forest Hill Blvd.). ℂ **561/547-WILD.** Fax 561/585-6085. www.palmbeachzoo.org. Admission $6, $5 senior citizens, $4 children 3–12, children under 3 free. Daily 9am–5pm.

Rapids Water Park ✦ *Kids*   It may not be on the same grand scale as the theme parks in Orlando, but Rapids is a great way to cool off on a hot day. There are 12 acres of water rides, including a children's area and miniature golf course.

6566 N. Military Trail, West Palm Beach (1 mile west of I-95 on Military between 45th St. (exit 54) and Blue Heron Blvd. (exit 55) in West Palm Beach. ℂ **561/842-8756.** www.rapidswaterpark.com. Admission $17–$24 per person; free ages 2 and under. Open mid-March through Sept. Hours vary.

SHOPPING & BROWSING

No matter what your budget is, be sure to take a stroll down Worth Avenue, "the Rodeo Drive of the South, " and a window-shopper's dream. Within the 4 blocks (between South Ocean Boulevard and Cocoanut Row on Worth) there are more than 200 boutiques, posh shops, art galleries, and upscale restaurants. Dress as if you were going to an elegant luncheon, and not to the mall down the street, if you want to fit in.

Despite the presence of the usual suspects (Gucci, Chanel, Armani, Hermes, Louis Vuitton, among others), Worth Avenue is not impervious to the mainstream. Victoria's Secret, Limited Express, and several other chains have sneaked in here too, but so have a good number of unique boutiques. **History Buff,** 32 Via Mizner (© 561/366-8255), is a virtual museum, selling every genre of original historical autograph, some dating back to the 1600s, as well as vintage signed photos, first-edition books, and memorabilia. A similar store is **Paper Treasures,** at 217 Worth Ave. (© 561/835-1891), an autograph gallery with a priceless collection of John Hancocks, including those of Joe DiMaggio, Mickey Mantle, Andrew Jackson, Abraham Lincoln, Howard Hughes, and hundreds more, all displayed in beautiful frames. For privileged feet, **Stubbs & Wooton,** 323 Worth Ave. (© 561/655-4105), sells velvet slippers that are a favorite of the loofah-ed locals. **The Purple Turtle,** 150 Worth Ave. (© 561/655-1625) in the Esplanade shopping promenade, sells designer clothes for infants, including Baby Dior and Baby Armani. For rare and estate jewelry, **Richter's of Palm Beach,** 224 Worth Ave. (© 561/655-0774), has been specializing in priceless gems since 1893. Just off Worth Avenue, at 374 S. County Rd., is the **Church Mouse** (© 561/659-2154), a great consignment/thrift shop with antique furnishings and tableware. Lots of good castaway clothing and shoes are reasonably priced. This shop usually closes for 2 months during the summer. Call to confirm.

City Place, 222 Lakeview Ave., West Palm Beach (© 561/835-0862), is a $550 million, Mediterranean-style shopping, dining, and entertainment complex that's responsible for revitalizing what was once a lifeless downtown West Palm Beach. Among the 78 mostly-chain stores are Macy's; FAO Schwarz; Benneton, which has an in-line skating track inside; Armani Exchange; and Pottery Barn. Restaurants include a Ghiradelli ice cream shop, Legal Sea Food, City Cellar Wine Bar and Grill, and Cheesecake Factory. Best of all is the Muvico Parisian, a 20-screen movie theater where you can wine and dine while watching a feature.

Elsewhere, Downtown West Palm Beach has a scant amount of interesting boutiques along Clematis Street. In addition to a large and well-organized bookstore, Clematis Street Books, at 206 Clematis (© 561/832-2302), there are a few used-record stores, clothing shops, and several art galleries.

The **Palm Beach Outlet Center,** at 5700 Okeechobee Blvd. (3 miles west of I-95), West Palm Beach, is the most elegant outlet mall I have ever seen. Upscale clothing, luggage, and shoes are offered at bargain prices in lushly decorated surroundings. The fully enclosed mall also sports a food court.

WHERE TO STAY

The island of Palm Beach is the epitome of *Lifestyles of the Rich and Famous,* oozing with glitz, glamour, and the occasional scandal. Royalty and celebrities come to winter here, and there are plenty of lavishly priced options to accommodate them. Happily, there exist a few special little inns that offer reasonably priced rooms in elegant settings. Surrounding the island are many more modest places to lay your straw hat.

A few of the larger hotel chains operating in Palm Beach include the **Howard Johnson Palm Beach,** at 2870 S. Ocean Blvd. (© 800/654-2000 or 561/582-2581), which is across the street from the beach. Also beachside is the pricey

Palm Beach & West Palm Beach Accommodations & Dining

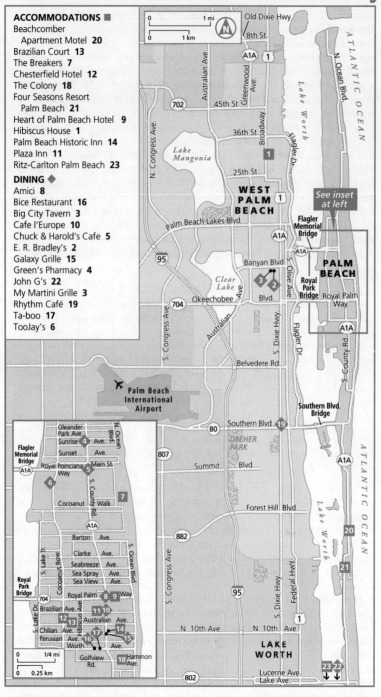

ACCOMMODATIONS ■
Beachcomber
  Apartment Motel **20**
Brazilian Court **13**
The Breakers **7**
Chesterfield Hotel **12**
The Colony **18**
Four Seasons Resort
  Palm Beach **21**
Heart of Palm Beach Hotel **9**
Hibiscus House **1**
Palm Beach Historic Inn **14**
Plaza Inn **11**
Ritz-Carlton Palm Beach **23**

DINING ◆
Amici **8**
Bice Restaurant **16**
Big City Tavern **3**
Cafe l'Europe **10**
Chuck & Harold's Cafe **5**
E. R. Bradley's **2**
Galaxy Grille **15**
Green's Pharmacy **4**
John G's **22**
My Martini Grille **3**
Rhythm Café **19**
Ta-boo **17**
TooJay's **6**

Palm Beach Hilton, at 2842 S. Ocean Blvd. (© **800/433-1718** or 561/ 586-6542).

An excellent and affordable alternative right in the middle of Palm Beach's commercial section is a condominium that operates as a hotel, too: the **Palm Beach Hotel,** at 235 Sunrise Ave. (between County Road and Bradley Place, across the street from the Publix supermarket; © **561/659-7794**). With winter prices starting at about $105, this clean and comfortable accommodation is a great option for those looking for the rare bargain in Palm Beach.

In West Palm Beach, the chain hotels are mostly located on the main arteries close to the highways and a short drive to the activities in downtown. They include a **Best Western,** 1800 Palm Beach Lakes Blvd. (© **800/331-9569** or 561/683-8810), and, just down the road, a **Comfort Inn,** 1901 Palm Lakes Blvd. (© **800/221-2222** or 561/689-6100). Further south is the **Parkview Motor Lodge,** 4710 S. Dixie Hwy., just south of Southern Boulevard (© **561/ 833-4644**). This 28-room, single-story motel is the best of the many motels along Dixie Highway (U.S. 1). With rates starting at $50 for a room with television, air-conditioning, and telephone, you can't ask for more.

For other options, try Palm Beach Accommodations (© **800/543-SWIM**).

VERY EXPENSIVE

Brazilian Court ★★★   This bright yellow, Mediterranean-style hotel dates back to the 1920s and exudes a glamour that has been lost through the decades. The rooms, renovated in 1997, are spacious, albeit a bit blasé, but the marble bathrooms are beautiful and modern. Service is doting, but a bit aloof—you won't always be received by smiling faces, but you will get whatever you want. There's even room service exclusively for pets (you know the type: held hostage in Mummy's Gucci bag). A large hotel by Palm Beach standards (The Breakers notwithstanding), Brazilian Court is sprawled over half a block and features fountains and private courtyards.

301 Australian Ave., Palm Beach, FL 33480 © 800/552-0335 or 561/655-7740. Fax 561/655-0801. www.braziliancourt.com. 103 units. Winter $335–$875; off-season $165–$525. Special packages available. AE, DC, DISC, MC, V. Amenities: Restaurant; private dining room (up to 12); bar; heated outdoor pool; exercise room; spa treatments; library; concierge; salon; 24-hr. room service. In room: A/C, TV, coffeemaker, hair dryer, iron.

The Breakers ★★★   This 140-acre beachfront hotel is what Palm Beach is all about. Elaborate, stately, and resplendent in all its Italian-Renaissance–style glory, it's where old money mixes with new money, and the old world gives way, albeit reluctantly, to a bit of modernity. In what was a complete juxtaposition of old and new, I spotted rocker Stevie Nicks and her fellow Fleetwood Mac members kicking back in the Breakers lobby. The place is also frequented by Internet moguls who, no doubt, are pleased by the hotel's recent elimination of the jackets-required rule.

Seemingly older and more elegant than the modernized Boca Raton Resort & Club, the Breakers consists of a seven-story building with a frescoed lobby and long, majestic hallways reminiscent of a palace more than a palatial estate. A $100 million renovation took parts of the hotel out of the 1930s and into the 21st century. The indulgent Oceanfront Spa and Beach Club features a spectacular ocean-view fitness center (makes workouts a lot less grueling), four ocean-front pools, cabanas, and saunas. Rooms were also modernized a bit, with Internet access and modem connections, but remain elegant, not sterile, with plush furnishings, huge bathrooms with telephones, and views of the ocean or the hotel's magnificently manicured grounds. A revamp of Florida's oldest existing golf course, led by Brian Silva, transformed The Breakers Ocean Course into a 6,200-yard, championship-level par 70.

1 S. County Rd., Palm Beach, FL 33480. © **800/833-3141,** 888/BREAKERS, or 561/655-6611. Fax 561/659-8403. www.thebreakers.com. 569 units. Winter $405–$1200; off-season $260–$690. Special packages available. AE, DC, DISC, MC, V. Valet parking $17. From I-95, exit Okeechobee Blvd. E., head east to S. County Rd., and turn left. **Amenities:** 5 restaurants; 3 bars; 4 outdoor pools; golf course; 14 tennis courts; health club & spa; water-sports equipment rental(including scuba and sailing); croquet; beach volleyball courts; bike rental; children's programs; game rooms; concierge; business center; shopping arcade; salon; 24-hr. room service; in-room massage; baby-sitting; laundry and dry-cleaning services. *In room*: A/C, TV, CD player, dataport, minibar, hair dryer.

Four Seasons Resort Palm Beach ✦✦ Built in 1989 at the edge of Palm Beach's downtown district, this elegant resort has quickly gained accolades from around the world. An incredibly hospitable staff works hard to be sure this beachfront gem lives up to its reputation. The elegant marble lobby is replete with hand-carved European furnishings, grand oil paintings, tapestries, and dramatic flower arrangements—though I did feel like I was in a museum, unable to touch anything. The rooms are spacious with private balconies and lavish bathrooms with color TVs. The main dining room for dinner serves one of the best meals in Palm Beach. An impeccable menu of Southeastern regional cuisine includes daily fish, meat, and pasta specials served in white-glove elegance. Two other less formal restaurants, including a pool bar and grill, round out the dining options. Accessible rooms are available for travelers with disabilities.

2800 S. Ocean Blvd., Palm Beach, FL 33480. © **800/432-2335** or 561/582-2800. Fax 561/547-1557. www.fourseasons.com. 210 units. Winter $395–$695 double; from $1,500 suite. Off-season $275–$595 double; from $850 suite. AE, DC, DISC, MC, V. Valet parking $17. Pets under 20 pounds accepted. From I-95, take 6th Ave. exit east and turn left onto Dixie Hwy. Turn east onto Lake Ave. and north onto S. Ocean Blvd., and the hotel is just ahead on your right. **Amenities:** 3 restaurants; lounge; outdoor heated pool; 3 tennis courts; spa; water-sports rentals; bike rental; cooking classes weekly; children's programs; concierge; business center; salon; 24-hr. room service; in-room massage; baby-sitting; laundry and dry-cleaning services. *In room:* A/C, TV/VCR, dataport, minibar, fridge, hair dryer.

Ritz-Carlton Palm Beach ✦✦✦ If the Breakers is too mammoth for your tastes, consider the Ritz-Carlton. A lot warmer than the Four Seasons, the Ritz, though hyperluxurious, manages to lack pretension. Located on a beautiful beach in a tiny town about 8 miles from Palm Beach's shopping and dining area, the Ritz-Carlton is a plus for those who seek privacy but may be a drawback for those interested in the activity of "town." The hotel's elegant and dramatic lobby is dominated by a huge, double-sided pink-marble fireplace, and French 18th- and 19th-century antique furnishings give no hint that the property is not yet 10 years old. Each room has a private balcony and at least a glimpse of the ocean below. All are spacious and decorated in lush contemporary design. Large marble bathrooms are extremely inviting and have telephones. The elegant dining room serves continental-style dinners in ornate surroundings. Other restaurants on the property include a grill, for dinner only; a casual restaurant, open all day; and a poolside cafe and bar. Cocktails are also served in the lobby lounge, where you can often find live entertainment. Afternoon tea is served daily but is best Wednesday to Saturday when a jazz trio entertains. The hotel is so discreet, in fact, that Palm Beach's luminaries often escape here for a rare weekend or night of anonymity.

100 S. Ocean Blvd., Manalpan, FL 33462. © **800/241-3333** or 561/533-6000. Fax 561/540-4999. www.ritzcarlton.com. 270 units. Winter $395–$820; $3,150 suite. Off-season $285–$725; $2,700 suite. AE, DISC, MC, V. Valet parking $15. From I-95, take Exit 45, heading east. After 1 mile, turn left onto Federal Hwy. (U.S.

1). Continue north for about a mile, and turn right onto Ocean Ave. Cross the Intracoastal Waterway; turn right onto Fla. A1A. **Amenities:** 4 restaurants; bar; outdoor pool; health club; Jacuzzi; sauna; water-sports equipment/rental; bike rental; children's center/programs; concierge; business center; salon; 24-hr. room service; in-room massage; laundry and dry-cleaning services. *In room:* A/C,TV, dataport, minibar, hair dryer.

EXPENSIVE

Chesterfield Hotel ★★★   Reminiscent of an English country manor, the Chesterfield Hotel in all its flowery, Laura Ashley–inspired glory is a magnificent, charming hotel with exceptional service to rival that of the Ritz. Warm and inviting, the Chesterfield is one of the only places in South Florida in which the idea of a fireplace (there's one in the hotel's library) doesn't seem ridiculous. Traditional English tea is served every afternoon, with fresh baked scones, petit fours, and sandwiches. Rooms are decorated with bright fabrics and wallpaper and antiques. The roomy marble bathrooms are stocked with an array of luxurious toiletries. A small heated pool and courtyard are nice, and the beach is only 3 blocks away, but the real action's inside. At night, the hotel's retro-elegant Leopard Lounge serves decent continental cuisine but is better as a later-night hangout for live music, schmoozing, and staring at the local cognoscenti.

363 Cocoanut Row, Palm Beach, FL 33480. (C) **800/243-7871** or 561/659-5800. Fax 561/659-6707. www. redcarnationhotels.com. 65 units. Winter $309–$350 single or double; off-season $99–$539. Rollaway bed $15 extra. Packages available. AE, DC, DISC, MC, V. Free valet parking. From I-95, exit onto Okeechobee Blvd. E., cross the Intracoastal Waterway, and turn right onto Cocoanut Row. **Amenities:** Restaurant; lounge; small heated swimming pool; access to nearby health club; Jacuzzi; bike rental; concierge; business center; 24-hr. room service; in-room massage; baby-sitting; dry-cleaning service. *In room:* A/C, TV, VCR on request, dataport, hair dryer.

Plaza Inn ★★   This three-story, family-run bed-and-breakfast–style inn located 1 block from the beach is as understated and luxurious as the guests it hosts. From the simple and elegant flower arrangements in the marble lobby to the well-worn period antiques haphazardly placed throughout, the Plaza Inn, whose exterior was renovated in 2001, has the look of studied nonchalance. The courtyard, with its waterfalls and pool, and the intimate piano bar are just two examples of the inn's infinite charms. A small staff is remarkably hospitable and knowledgeable about the island's inner workings. Each uniquely decorated room—Italian, French, or traditional style—is dressed with quality furnishings, several with carved four-poster beds, hand-crocheted spreads, and lace curtains. The bathrooms, renovated in 2000, are lovely if quite small, and the wall-mounted air conditioners can be noisy when they are needed in the warm months. Choose a corner room or one overlooking the small pool deck for the best light. The Stray Fox Pub, a comfortable little bar with mahogany tables, serves cocktails throughout the evening and sometimes has live piano music on the weekends. It's a tough call to decide which is better—the Plaza Inn or the Chesterfield, but the Plaza, unlike the Chesterfield, does include a full breakfast in the price of the room.

215 Brazilian Ave., Palm Beach, FL 33480. (C) **800/233-2632** or 561/832-8666. Fax 561/835-8776. www. plazainnpalmbeach.com. 48 units. Winter $225–$375; off-season $105–$195. Rates include breakfast. AE, MC, V. From I-95, exit onto Okeechobee Blvd. E. and cross the Intracoastal Waterway. Turn right onto Cocoanut Row; then left onto Brazilian Ave. Small pets permitted. **Amenities:** Restaurant; lounge; heated outdoor pool; exercise room; Jacuzzi; access to nearby health club ($15 per day); bike rental; concierge; secretarial services; limited room service; in-room massage; baby-sitting; laundry and dry-cleaning services. *In room:* A/C, TV, dataport, fridge, coffeemaker and hair dryer on request.

MODERATE

The Colony ★★   The sign outside of this Palm Beach mainstay should read: Roxanne Pulitzer slept here. She did, actually, for quite a while after her 7-week marriage went bust. For years, the colony has been a favorite hangout—hide-out, perhaps—for assorted old timers, socialites, and mysterious luminaries. Beyond that, the Colony is a Georgian-style hotel known for its attentive staff, floral-decorated rooms and, unfortunately, really small bathrooms. The 39 suites and apartments, not to mention the seven two-bedroom villas with Jacuzzis, are much more lavish—and lavishly priced.

155 Hammon Ave., Palm Beach, FL 33480. © **800/521-5525** or 561/655-5430. Fax 561/659-8104. www. thecolonypalmbeach.com. 63 units, 39 suites, 7 villas. Winter $285–$695; off-season $125–$495. AE, DC, MC, V. From I-95, exit onto Okeechobee Blvd. E. and cross the Intracoastal Waterway. Turn right on S. County Rd.; then left onto Hammon Ave. **Amenities:** Restaurant; bar; heated Florida-shaped pool; spa; concierge, limited, seasonal room service. *In room:* A/C, TV, dataport, hair dryer.

Heart of Palm Beach Hotel ✿
It's this hotel's location—in the heart of Palm Beach, within walking distance of Worth Avenue shopping, and just half a block from the beach—that is its greatest asset. Ongoing renovations since the 1990s have improved the patio space, as well as the rooms in the hotel's two buildings, but there's nothing particularly inspiring about this hotel's rather bland atmosphere and decor. A new exterior paint job and refurbished land-scaping have improved the hotel's appearance slightly, however. Most rooms are decorated with modest but new furnishings and fittings in a colorful contemporary style; all come with a balcony or a patio. The tiled bathrooms are small, clean, and functional. Additionally, the staff is particularly outgoing and will help guests plan outings and itineraries. There's also a heated swimming pool. A clubby restaurant serves a mediocre selection of salads, sandwiches, and pastas.

160 Royal Palm Way, Palm Beach, FL 33480. © **800/523-5377** or 561/655-5600. Fax 561/832-1201. 88 units. Winter $169–$325; off-season $79–$225 suite. AE, DC, MC, V. Free parking. From I-95, exit onto Okee-chobee Blvd. E. and continue over the Royal Palm Bridge onto Royal Palm Way. Pets are accepted. **Amenities:** Restaurant; heated pool; access to nearby health club; bike rental; concierge; room service; baby-sitting; laundry and dry-cleaning services. *In room:* A/C, TV, dataport, fridge, hair dryer.

Palm Beach Historic Inn ✿✿
Built in 1923, the Palm Beach Historic Inn is an area landmark located within walking distance of Worth Avenue, the beach, and several good restaurants. The small lobby is filled with antiques, books, magazines, and an old-fashioned umbrella stand, all of which add to the homey feel of this intimate bed-and-breakfast. In your room, wine, fruit, snacks, tea, and cookies ensure that you won't go hungry—never mind the excellent conti-nental breakfast that is brought to you daily. All the rooms are on the second floor, and each is uniquely decorated and full of frills. Floral prints, sheer cur-tains, and the plethora of lace can sometimes be overwhelming, masking rather than complementing beautiful antique writing desks and dressers. Happily, there are also fluffy bathrobes, an abundance of towels, and plenty of good-smelling toiletries. Be sure to save some dimes, as 10¢ will buy you an 8-ounce bottle of Coke dispensed by an original 1944 Coca Cola machine.

365 S. County Rd., Palm Beach, FL 33480. © **561/832-4009.** Fax 561/832-6255. www.palmbeachhis-toricinn.com. 13 units. Winter $150–$325; off-season $95–$175. Rates include continental breakfast. Chil-dren stay free in parents' room. Small pets accepted. No smoking. AE, MC, V. *In-room:* A/C, TV/VCR, fridge, hair dryer.

MODERATE/INEXPENSIVE

Beachcomber Apartment Motel ✿✿
It's not just the bright pink building that makes this two-story beachfront motel stand out. For more than 35 years, the Beachcomber has been bringing sanity to pricey Palm Beach by offering a good standard of accommodation at reasonable prices. Squeezed between beach-front high-rises, the motel is located on a 300-foot private beach, adjacent to

Lake Worth Beach and a short drive from Worth Avenue shops and local attractions. Every room has two double beds, large closets, and distinctive green-and-white tropical-style furnishings; some have kitchenettes. The most expensive have balconies overlooking the ocean. The bathrooms are basic, and amenities are limited to towels and soap.

3024 S. Ocean Blvd., Palm Beach, FL 33480. © 800/833-7122 or 561/585-4646. Fax 561/547-9438. 45 units. Winter $95–$250; off-season $55–$130. AE, DISC, MC, V. From I-95, exit 10th Ave. N. Head east to Federal Hwy. and turn right. Continue to Lake Ave. and turn left. Go over bridge and turn right at first traffic light. **Amenities:** Large pool; coin-operated laundry. *In room:* A/C, TV.

Hibiscus House ★★ *Finds*   Inexpensive bed-and-breakfasts are rare in Southeast Florida, making the Hibiscus House, one of the area's firsts, a true find. Located a few miles from the coast in a quiet residential neighborhood, this 1920s-era B&B is filled with handsome antiques and tapestries in luxurious fabrics. Every room has its own private terrace or balcony. The Red Room has a fabulous new bathroom with Jacuzzi. The backyard, a peaceful retreat, has been transformed into a tropical garden, complete with heated swimming pool and lounge chairs. Also, there are plenty of pretty areas for guests to enjoy inside; one little sitting room is wrapped in glass and is stocked with playing cards and board games. *Beware:* Breakfast portions are enormous. The gourmet creations are as filling as they are beautiful. Ask for any special requests in advance; owners Raleigh Hill and Colin Rayer will be happy to oblige.

501 30th St., West Palm Beach, FL 33407. © 800/203-4927 or 561/863-5633. Fax 561/863-5633. www. hibiscushouse.com. 8 units. Winter $95–$250 double; off-season $65–$170 double. Rates include breakfast. AE, MC, V. From I-95, exit onto Palm Beach Lakes Blvd. E. and continue 4 miles. Turn left onto Flagler Dr. and continue for about 20 blocks. Then turn left onto 30th St. Pets accepted. **Amenities:** Heated pool; concierge. *In room:* A/C, TV, hair dryer.

WHERE TO DINE

Palm Beach has some of the area's swankiest restaurants. Thanks to the development of downtown West Palm Beach, there is also a great selection of trendier, less expensive spots. Dress here is slightly more formal than in most other areas of Florida: Men wear blazers, and women generally put on modest dresses or chic suits when they dine out, even in the oppressively hot days of summer.

EXPENSIVE

Amici ★ *Overrated* ITALIAN   This is one of those restaurants in which the scene is tastier than the cuisine. An upper-crusty Palm Beach set tends to convene here and consistently rave about what can only be considered above-average, overpriced Italian food. The best item on the entire menu is gnocchi with white truffle oil, fontina cheese, and spinach. Everything else is fairly standard: grilled sandwiches, pastas with rustic sauces, pizzas, grilled shrimp, and fish. Despite its less than stellar food, it's always crowded and very noisy.

288 S. County Rd. (at Royal Palm Way), Palm Beach. © 561/832-0201. Reservations strongly recommended on weekends. Main courses $18–$27; pastas and pizzas $8–$19. AE, DC, MC, V. Mon–Thurs 11:30am–3pm and 5:30–10:30pm, Fri–Sat 11:30am–3pm and 5:30–11pm; Sun 5:30–10:30pm.

Cafe l'Europe ★★★ FRENCH/CONTINENTAL   One of Palm Beach's finest, this award-winning formal restaurant gives you good reason to get dressed up. The interior is made romantic and luxurious by the tapestried cafe chairs and linen-topped tables set with crystal and china. The enticing appetizers served by a superb staff might include Chinese spring rolls, baked goat-cheese salad with raspberry-walnut dressing, poached salmon, or chilled gazpacho with avocado.

Main courses run the gamut from sautéed potato-crusted Florida snapper to lamb chops to roast Cornish game hen. Seafood dishes and steaks in sumptuous but light sauces are always exceptional.

331 S. County Rd. (at the corner of Brazilian Ave.), Palm Beach. © 561/655-4020. Reservations recommended. Main courses $18–$34. AE, DC, DISC, MC, V. Tues–Thurs noon–2:30pm and 5:45–10:30pm, Fri–Sat noon–2:30pm and 5:45pm–1am, Sun 6–10:30pm.

Chuck & Harold's Cafe AMERICAN   This old standby delivers predictable American fare at somewhat inflated prices. But remember, you are paying for one of the area's best people-watching perches. Main dishes include fresh grilled or broiled fish, boiled lobster, and a small variety of straightforward homemade pasta and chicken dishes. If you happen to visit during the season for stone crabs, order them. The crab claws are steamed or chilled and served with a traditional honey-mustard sauce. Considering Chuck and Harold's status as a Waspy enclave, its surprise treat is excellent matzo ball soup!

207 Royal Poinciana Way (corner of S. County Rd.), Palm Beach. © 561/659-1440. Reservations recommended. Main courses $13–$28. AE, DC, DISC, MC, V. Mon–Thurs 7:30am–midnight; Fri–Sat 7:30am–1am, Sun 8am–11pm.

Galaxy Grille NEW AMERICAN   Stargazing is certainly at a premium at this Deco-inspired Palm Beach hot spot known for a stellar clientele and a menu to match it. Two favorites include a superb horseradish-encrusted yellowtail snapper and an even better grilled swordfish with fresh tomato, black olives, grilled polenta, garlic, and escarole.

350 S. County Rd., Palm Beach. © **561/833-9909.** Reservations recommended. Main courses $27–$38. AE, DC, MC, V. Daily 5–11pm.

MODERATE

Big City Tavern AMERICAN   If the Palm Beach proper dining scene is too stuffy for you, head over the bridge to Clematis Street, downtown West Palm's hub of urban chic, where you will find this setting of brick and pressed tin in which people-watching is at a premium and the cuisine is as varied as its clientele. Despite its all-American appearance, Big City Tavern offers a varied menu, including coconut shrimp tempura with a salmon inside-out sushi roll and a delicious bowl of littleneck clams in wine broth with roasted garlic and escarole. On weekends, the Tavern is mobbed, so be prepared for a long wait that's best spent at the action-packed bar.

224 Clematis St., West Palm Beach. © 561/659-1853. Reservations suggested. Main courses $7.95–$28. AE, MC, V. Mon–Fri 11am–11pm, Sat. 6pm–1am, Sun 6–10pm.

E. R. Bradley's AMERICAN   What used to be a swank saloon on the island of Palm Beach is now a very casual, friendly indoor/outdoor bar in downtown West Palm, attracting a mixed crowd. People don't really come here for the food, though it's quite busy with families during the early evening hours. It's the later-night bar scene that's the real draw. If you are hungry, try the "crab bomb," Maryland lump crabmeat baked in a light cream sauce with steamed vegetables. Sunday brunch is also pretty good.

104 Clematis St. (Datura St.), West Palm Beach. © 561/ 833-3520. Main courses $6–$16. AE, MC, V. Sun–Wed 8am–3am, Thurs–Sat 8am–4am.

My Martini Grille ECLECTIC AMERICAN   Reminiscent of a 1930s supper club, this dark wood–lined restaurant is hardly popular with those who lived through those times, but, rather, with retro-loving trendies who really

come for the martinis (over 32 flavors). An affordable three-tiered appetizer platter includes just about everything needed to absorb the trail of martinis; special
entrees include a rack of lamb with rosemary mint demi-glacé and Gorgonzola
potatoes.

225 Clematis St., West Palm Beach. ℭ **561/832-8333.** Reservations suggested. Main courses $15–$25.
AE, MC, V. Tues–Sat 6pm–midnight.

Rhythm Café ✩ ECLECTIC AMERICAN   This funky hole-in-the-wall is
where those in the know come to eat some of West Palm Beach's most laid-back
gourmet food. On the handwritten, photocopied menu (which changes daily),
you'll always find a fish specialty accompanied by a hefty dose of greens and gar-
nishes. Also reliably outstanding is the sautéed medallion of beef tenderloin,
served on a bed of arugula with a tangy rosemary vinaigrette. Salads and soups
are a great bargain, since portions are relatively large and the display usually
spectacular. The kitschy decor of this tiny cafe comes complete with vinyl tablecloths and a changing display of paintings by local amateurs. Young, handsome
waiters are attentive but not solicitous. The old drugstore where the restaurant
recently relocated features an original 1950s lunch counter and stools.

3800 S. Dixie Hwy., West Palm Beach. ℭ **561/833-3406.** Reservations recommended on weekends. Main
courses $10–$26. AE, DISC, MC, V. Tues–Sat 6–10pm. From I-95, exit east on Southern Blvd. Go 1 block north
of Southern Blvd.; restaurant on the right. Closed in early September.

Ta-boo ✩ AMERICAN BISTRO   Ta-boo is reminiscent of an upscale TGI
Fridays—one that caters to a well-heeled crowd—with lots of greenery, a fireplace, and a somewhat cheesy Southwestern decor. For lunch, the kitchen creates California-style individual pizzas with such toppings as barbecued chicken,
goat and mozzarella cheeses, and sweet roasted red peppers. The best dinner
starter is fresh tuna marinated in ginger and lime. Dinner choices change nightly
and may include grilled swordfish topped with olive-caper sauce or grilled veal
served on the bone.

221 Worth Ave., Palm Beach. ℭ **561/835-3500.** Reservations recommended. Main courses $10–$25.
AE, DC, MC, V. Sun–Thurs 11:30am–11pm, Fri–Sat 11:30am–1am.

INEXPENSIVE

Green's Pharmacy ✩ AMERICAN   This neighborhood corner pharmacy
offers one of the best meal deals in Palm Beach. Both breakfast and lunch are
served coffee-shop style either at a Formica bar or at plain tables placed on a
black-and-white checkerboard floor. Breakfast specials include eggs and omelets
served with home fries and bacon, sausage, or corned-beef hash. At lunch, the
grill serves burgers and sandwiches, as well as ice-cream sodas and milkshakes,
to a loyal crowd of pastel-clad Palm Beachers.

151 N. County Rd., Palm Beach. ℭ **561/832-0304.** Fax 561/832-6502. Breakfast $2–$5; burgers and sandwiches $3–$6; soups and salads $2–$7. AE, DISC, MC, V. Mon–Sat 7am–5pm, Sun 7am–3pm.

John G's ✩ AMERICAN   This coffee shop is the most popular in the county.
For decades, John G's has been attracting huge breakfast crowds; lines run out
the door (on weekends, all the way down the block). Stop in for some good,
greasy-spoon–style food served in heaping portions right on the beachfront.
This place is known for fresh and tasty fish and chips and its selection of creative
omelets and grill specials.

10 S. Ocean Blvd., Lake Worth. ℭ **561/585-9860.** Reservations not accepted. Breakfast $3–$8.50; lunch
$5–$14. No credit cards. Daily 7am–3pm. From the Florida Tpk., take the Lake Worth exit and head toward
the ocean.

TooJay's DELI   This simple and predictable restaurant and take-out spot is a favorite with locals and out-of-towners who want good old-fashioned deli. So popular, in fact, that TooJay's now has more than a dozen outlets. This is no Carnegie Deli, but by South Florida deli standards the food is excellent. All the classic sandwiches are available: hot pastrami, roast beef, turkey, chicken, chopped liver, egg salad, and more. Comfort food in the form of huge portions of stuffed cabbage, chicken pot pie, beef brisket, and sautéed onions and chicken livers is sure to satisfy.

313 Royal Poinciana Plaza (3 miles east of I-95 off Exit 52A), Palm Beach. ✆ 561/659-7232. Reservations not accepted. Main courses $8–$13. DC, MC, V. Daily 8am–9pm.

THE PALM BEACHES AFTER DARK
THE BAR, CAFE & MUSIC SCENE: DOWNTOWN WEST PALM BEACH

A decade-old project to revitalize downtown West Palm Beach has finally become a reality, with **Clematis Street** ✦ at its heart. Artist lofts, sidewalk cafes, bars, restaurants, consignment shops, and galleries dot the street from Flagler Drive to Rosemary Avenue, creating a hot spot for a night out, especially on weekends when yuppies mingle with stylish Euros and disheveled artists. Every Thursday night is a mob scene of twenty- and thirty-somethings who come out for "Clematis by Night." Each week features a different rock, blues, or reggae band plus an art show. Vendors sell food and drinks, and the street's bars and restaurants are packed. It is a bit raucous at times, but fun. Minors unaccompanied by their guardians are not permitted in the downtown area around Clematis Street after 10pm on weeknights and after 11pm on weekend nights.

Over the bridge, it's a completely different world. Palm Beach is much quieter and better known for its rather private society balls and estate parties. With the exception of some restaurants that are more of a scene—Ta-boo, Amici, and Galaxy Grille—Palm Beach nightlife is more likely to entail sipping port at one of the finer hotels like the Breakers, the Colony, the Ritz-Carlton, Four Seasons, or the Chesterfield.

West Palm Beach

Bliss   With its house music and VIP rooms, this West Palm club seems like it belongs in the velvet-roped world of South Beach clubs. 313 Clematis St. ✆ 561/833-1444. Thurs–Sat. $7 cover.

Liquid Room   Former South Beach hot spot Liquid may have evaporated from the scene, but this Clematis Street location is flowing with club kids who revel in the fact that they finally have a chic, celebrity-saturated dance club to call their own. 313 Clematis St. ✆ 561/655-2332. Thurs–Sat. $10 cover.

Lost Weekend   I'm not sure whether it's the local artist displays, the pool tables, or the more than 200 beers from around the world sold here, but for some reason, many of Palm Beach's hipsters love getting lost in this place, which is actually quite nice. 115 S. Olive Ave. ✆ 561/832-3452. Tues–Fri from 4:30pm. No cover.

Monkey Club   This tacky yet trendy Caribbean-inspired dance club is 7,500-square-feet of wall-to-wall, well-dressed revelers. Theme nights are popular here, from ladies nights to the classier version of the wet T-shirt contest—the Miss Hawaiian Tropic Model Search. 219 Clematis St. ✆ 561/833-6500. Cover up to $10.

Respectable Street Café   This is one of the premier live music venues in South Florida. In addition to the requisite DJs, this grungy bar features an impressive lineup of alternative music acts. The cafe's plain storefront exterior belies its funky high-ceilinged interior decorated with large black booths, psychedelic wall murals, and a large checkerboard-tile dance floor. 518 Clematis St. ℂ 561/832-9999. Wed–Sat 9pm–4am. Cover varies.

Palm Beach

Brazilian Court Bistro and Rio Bar   Despite its location in the ritzy Brazilian Court Hotel, the bar here is surprisingly laid-back and unpretentious, featuring a mostly older crowd of couples and, at times, swinging singles. 301 Australian Ave. ℂ 561/655-7740.

The Leopard Lounge *Finds*   *The Flintstones* meets *Dynasty* at the spotty lounge in the Chesterfield Hotel in which the carpeting, tablecloths, and waitstaff's waistcoats are all in leopard print. There's live music every night from Cole Porter to swing. The crowd's a bit older here, but younger couples and a celebrity or two often find their way here, which makes for an amusing scene. 363 Cocoanut Row. ℂ 561/659-5800.

THE PERFORMING ARTS

With a number of dedicated patrons and enthusiastic supporters of the arts, this area happily boasts many good venues for those craving culture. Check the *Palm Beach Post* or the *Palm Beach Daily News,* known as "the shiny sheet," for up-to-date listings and reviews.

The **Raymond F. Kravis Center for the Performing Arts,** 701 Okeechobee Blvd., West Palm Beach (ℂ **561/832-7469**), is the area's largest and most active performance space. With a huge curved-glass facade and more than 2,500 seats in two lushly decorated indoor spaces, plus a new outdoor amphitheater, The Kravis, as it is known, stages more than 300 performances each year. Phone for a current schedule of Palm Beach's best music, dance, and theater.

4 Jupiter ⊀ & Northern Palm Beach County ⊀

20 miles N. of Palm Beach, 81 miles N. of Miami

While Burt Reynolds is Jupiter's hometown hero (and Celine Dion just built a sprawling manse there, too), the true stars of quaint Jupiter are the beautiful beaches. In the springtime, you can also catch a glimpse of the St. Louis Cardinals and the Montreal Expos during their spring training seasons. North Palm Beach County's other towns—Tequesta, Juno Beach, North Palm Beach, Palm Beach Gardens, and Singer Island—are inviting for tourists who want to enjoy the many outdoor activities that make this area so popular with retirees, seasonal residents, and families.

ESSENTIALS

GETTING THERE   The quickest route from West Palm Beach to Jupiter is on the Florida Turnpike or the sometimes congested I-95. You can also take a slower but more scenic coastal route, U.S. 1 or Fla. A1A. Since Jupiter is so close to Palm Beach, it's easy to fly into the **Palm Beach International Airport** (ℂ **561/471-7420**) and rent a car there. The drive should take less than half an hour.

VISITOR INFORMATION   A **Visitor Information Center** is located between I-95 and the Florida Turnpike at 8020 Indiantown Rd. in Jupiter (ℂ **561/575-4636;** www.jupiterfloridausa.com) and is open from 9am to 6pm daily.

BEACHES & OUTDOOR PURSUITS

BASEBALL The **Roger Dean Stadium,** 4751 Main St. (© **561/775-1818**), hosts spring training for both the St. Louis Cardinals and the Montreal Expos, along with minor-league action from Florida's state league, the Hammerheads. Tickets range in price from $6 to $18. Call for schedules and specific ticket information.

BEACHES The farther north you head from populated Palm Beach, the more peaceful and pristine the coast becomes. Just a few miles north of the bustle, castles and condominiums give way to wide open space and public parkland. There are dozens of recommendable spots. Following are a few of the best.

John D. MacArthur Beach is a spectacular beach that preserves the natural heritage of subtropical coastal habitat that once covered Southeast Florida. This state park has a remarkable 4,000-square-foot Nature Center with exhibits, displays, and a video interpreting the barrier island's plant and animal communities. Dominating a large portion of Singer Island, the barrier island just north of Palm Beach, this beach has lengthy frontage on both the Atlantic Ocean and Lake Worth Cove. The beach is great for hiking, swimming, and sunning. To reach the park from the mainland, cross the Intracoastal Waterway on Blue Heron Boulevard and turn north on Ocean Boulevard.

Jupiter Inlet meets the ocean at **Dubois Park,** a 29-acre beach that is popular with families. The shallow waters and sandy shore are perfect for kids, while adults can play in the rougher swells of the lifeguarded inlet. A footbridge leads to **Ocean Beach,** an area popular with windsurfers and surfers. There's a short fishing pier and plenty of trees shading barbecue grills and picnic tables. Visitors can also explore the Dubois Pioneer Home, a small house situated atop a shell mound built by the Jaega Indians. The park entrance is on Dubois Road, about a mile south of the junction of U.S. 1 and Fla. A1A.

BIKING Rent a bike from **Raleigh Bicycles of Jupiter,** at 103 U.S. 1, Unit F1 (© **561/746-0585**) for $15.50 per day. Bike enthusiasts will enjoy exploring this flat and uncluttered area. North Palm Beach has hundreds of miles of smooth, paved roads. Loggerhead Park in Juno Beach or Fla. A1A along the ocean has great trails for starters. You'll find many more scenic routes over the bridges and west of the highway.

BOATING & CANOEING You can rent a boat at several outlets throughout northern Palm Beach County, including **Canoe Outfitters,** 8900 W. Indiantown Rd. (west of I-95), North Jupiter (© **561/746-7053**), which provides access to one of the area's most beautiful natural waterways. Canoers start at Riverbend Park along an 8-mile stretch of Intracoastal Waterway, where the lush foliage supports dozens of exotic birds and reptiles. Keep your eyes open for the gators who love to sunbathe on the shallow shores of the river. You'll end up exhausted at Jonathan Dickinson Park about 5 or 6 hours later. A pamphlet describing local flora and fauna is available for $1. Trips run Wednesday to Sunday and cost $25 for a single-person kayak, $35 for a double kayak or canoe.

CRUISES Several sightseeing cruises offer tours of the magnificent waterways that make up northern Palm Beach County. Water taxis conduct daily narrated tours through the scenic waters. One interesting excursion departs from **Panama Hatties** at PGA Boulevard and the Intracoastal Waterway. Prices are $17 for adults and $9 for children under 12 for the 1½-hour ride. Call © **561/775-2628.** The Manatee Queen, 1065 N. Ocean Blvd. (at the Crab House),

Jupiter (© **561/744-2191**), is a 40-foot catamaran with bench seating for up to 49 people. Two-hour tours of Jupiter Island depart daily at 2:30pm, passing Burt Reynolds' and Perry Como's mansions, among other historical and natural spots of interest. Reservations are highly recommended, especially in season. The cruise is wheelchair-accessible. Prices start at $15 for adults, $10 for children. Bring your own lunch or purchase chips and sodas at the minisnack bar.

FISHING Before you leave, send for an information-packed fishing kit with details on fish camps, charters, tournament, and tide schedules, distributed by the **West Palm Beach Fishing Club,** c/o Fish Finder, P.O. Box 468, West Palm Beach, FL 33402. The cost is $10 and well worth it. Allow at least 4 weeks for delivery.

Once in town, several outfitters along U.S. 1 and Fla. A1A have vessels and equipment for rent if your hotel doesn't. One of the most complete facilities is the **Sailfish Marina & Resort,** 98 Lake Dr. (off Blue Heron Boulevard), Palm Beach Shores (© **561/844-1724**). Call for equipment, bait, guided trips, or boat rentals.

GOLF Even if you're not lucky enough to be staying at the **PGA National Resort,** you may still be able to play on their award-winning courses. If you or someone in your group is a member of another golf or country club, have the head pro write a note on club letterhead to Jackie Rogers at PGA (see "Where to Stay," below) to request a play date. Be sure the pro includes his PGA number and contact information. Allow at least 2 weeks for a response. Also, ask about the Golf-A-Round program, where selected private clubs open to non-members for free or discounted rates. Contact the **Palm Beach County Convention and Visitors Bureau** (© **561/471-3995**) for details.

Plenty of other great courses dot the area, including the **Golf Club of Jupiter,** 1800 Central Blvd., Jupiter (© **561/747-6262**). A well-respected 18-hole, par-70 course is situated on more than 6,200 yards featuring narrow fairways and fast greens. Fees are $55 until noon, $45 after noon, and $25 after 3pm, and include a mandatory cart. The course borders I-95.

HIKING In an area that's not particularly known for extraordinary natural diversity, **Blowing Rocks Preserve** has a terrific hiking trail along a dramatic limestone outcropping. You won't find hills or scenic vistas, but you will see Florida's unique and varied tropical ecosystem. The well-marked mile-long trail passes oceanfront dunes, coastal strands, mangrove wetlands, and a coastal hammock. The preserve, owned and managed by the Nature Conservancy, also protects an important habitat for West Indian manatees and loggerhead turtles. The preserve is located along South Beach Drive (Fla. A1A), north of the Jupiter inlet, about a 10-minute drive northeast of Jupiter. Free guided tours are available Fridays and Sundays at 11 am, and no reservations are necessary. From U.S. 1, head east on S.R. 707 and cross the Intracoastal Waterway to the park. Admission is free, but a $3 per person donation is requested. For more information, contact the Preserve Manager, Blowing Rocks Preserve, P.O. Box 3795, Tequesta, FL 33469 (© **561/744-6668**).

SCUBA DIVING & SNORKELING Year-round warm, clear waters make northern Palm Beach County great for both diving and snorkeling. The closest coral reef is located a quarter-mile from shore and can easily be reached by boat. Three popular wrecks are clustered near each other, less than a mile offshore of the Lake Worth Inlet at about 90 feet. If your hotel doesn't offer dive trips, call

Discovering a Remarkable Natural World

North Palm Beach is well known for the giant sea turtles that lay their eggs on the county's beaches from May to August. These endangered marine animals return here annually, from as far away as South America, to lay their clutch of about 115 eggs each. Nurtured by the warm sand, but preyed upon by birds and other predators, only about one or two babies from each nest survive to maturity.

Many environmentalists recommend that visitors take part in an organized turtle-watching program (rather than going on their own) to minimize disturbance to the turtles. The Jupiter Beach Resort (see "Where to Stay," below) and the Marinelife Center of Juno Beach (see below) both sponsor free guided expeditions to the egg-laying sites from May to August. Phone for times and reservations.

Just south of Jupiter, in Juno Beach, is the **Marinelife Center of Juno Beach,** in Loggerhead Park, 14200 U.S. 1, Juno Beach (© **561/ 627-8280**). Combining a science museum and nature trail, the small Marinelife Center is dedicated to the coastal ecology of northern Palm Beach County. Hands-on exhibits teach visitors about wetlands and beach areas, as well as offshore coral reefs and the local sea life. This is one place in which you're guaranteed to see live sea turtles year-round, and during high breeding season (June and July) the center conducts narrative walks along a nearby beach. Reservations are a must. The booking list opens on May 1 and is usually full by midmonth. Admission to the center is free, though donations are accepted. Open Tuesday to Saturday from 10am to 4pm and Sunday from noon to 3pm.

the **South Florida Dive Headquarters,** 23141 Lyons Rd., Boca Raton (© **800/ 771-DIVE** or 561/627-9558); or **Seafari Dive and Surf,** 75 E. Indiantown Rd., Suite 603, Jupiter (© **561/747-6115**).

TENNIS   In addition to the many hotel tennis courts (see "Where to Stay," below), you can swing a racquet at a number of local clubs. The **Jupiter Bay Tennis Club,** 353 U.S. 1, Jupiter (© **561/744-9424**), has seven clay courts (three lighted) and charges $12 per person per day. Reservations are highly recommended.

More economical options are available at relatively well-maintained municipal courts. Call for locations and hours (© **561/966-6600**). Many are available free on a first-come, first-served basis.

A HISTORIC LIGHTHOUSE

Jupiter Inlet Lighthouse ✦   Completed in 1860, this redbrick structure is the oldest extant building in Palm Beach County. Still owned and maintained by the U.S. Coast Guard, the lighthouse is now home to a small historical museum, located at its base. The Florida History Museum sponsors tours of the lighthouse, enabling visitors to explore the cramped interior, which is filled with artifacts and photographs. First, a 15-minute video explains the shipwrecks, Indian wars, and other events that helped shape this region.

500 State Road 707, Jupiter. ℂ **561/747-8380.** Admission $5. Sun–Wed 10am–4pm (last tour departs at 3:15pm). Children must be 4 feet or taller to climb.

SHOPPING

Northern Palm Beach County may not have the glitzy boutiques of Worth Avenue, but it does have an impressive indoor mall, the **Gardens of the Palm Beaches,** at 3101 PGA Blvd., where you can find large department stores including Bloomingdale's, Burdines, Macy's, and Saks Fifth Avenue, as well as more than 100 specialty shops. A large and diverse food court and fine sit-down restaurants in this 1.3 million-square-foot facility make this shopping excursion an all-day affair. Call ℂ **561/775-7750** for store information.

WHERE TO STAY

The northern part of Palm Beach County is much more laid-back and less touristy than the rest of the Gold Coast. Here, there are relatively few fancy hotels or attractions. In addition to several Holiday Inns, there is a reasonably priced and recently renovated **Wellesley Inn,** at 34 Fisherman's Wharf (I-95, exit east on Indiantown Road; turn left before the bridge), in Jupiter (ℂ **800/444-8888**). Suites include sofa beds, refrigerators, and microwave ovens. Although not within walking distance of the beach, the inn is located near shops and restaurants and Fla. A1A.

VERY EXPENSIVE

Jupiter Beach Resort ★★　The only resort located directly on Jupiter's beach, this unpretentious retreat is popular with families and seems a world away from the more luxurious resorts just a few miles to the south. The lobby and public areas have a Caribbean motif, accented with green marble, arched doorways, and chandeliers. The simple and elegant guest rooms are furnished in a comfortable island style, and every room has a private balcony with ocean or sunset views looking out over the uncluttered beachfront. A thorough refurbishing in the mid-1990s is responsible for the resort's increasing popularity. In fact, it is so popular that it is being gradually converted into a time-share property. Excursions are available to top-rated golf courses in the area.

5 N. A1A, Jupiter, FL 33477. ℂ **800/228-8810** or 561/746-2511. Fax 561/747-3304. www.jupiterbeachresort. com. 153 units. Winter $170–$450; off-season $97–$205. AE, DC, DISC, MC, V. Valet parking $5. From I-95, take Exit 59A, going east to the end of Indiantown Rd. at A1A. Jupiter Beach Resort is at this intersection on the ocean. **Amenities:** Restaurant; 2 bars; pool; tennis court; exercise room; extensive water-sport equipment/rental; bike rental; children's programs; concierge; business center; room service; in-room massage; dry cleaning. *In room:* A/C, TV, minibar, coffeemaker, kitchenette and VCRs in suites.

PGA National Resort & Spa ★★★　This rambling resort, the national headquarters of the PGA, is a premier golf vacation spot—but its top-rated Mediterranean spa could be a destination in itself. With five 18-hole courses on more than 2,300 acres, golfers and other sports-minded travelers will find plenty to keep them occupied—croquet, tennis, sailing, a health and fitness center, and the sublime spa. Constant updating has kept the grounds and buildings in like-new condition. In 2000 the lobby and all rooms were completely renovated. The par-72 Champion Course, redesigned in 1990 by Jack Nicklaus, is the resort's most valuable asset. More than 100 sand bunkers and plenty of water on 6,400-square-foot greens keep golfers of all levels alert. Watch out for hole 16. Rooms are spacious and comfortable with immense bathrooms. This is not a beach resort, however. Six outdoor therapy pools known as "Waters of the World" are surrounded by mineral pools, which are so sublime, they make the ocean look like a kiddie pool. Don Shula's award-winning steakhouse and restaurant is the hotel's best and most popular restaurant. Accessible rooms are available for travelers with disabilities.

400 Avenue of the Champions, Palm Beach Gardens, FL 33418. *C* 800/633-9150 or 561/627-2000. Fax 561/622-0261. www.pga-resorts.com. 339 units. Winter $319–$389 double; from $489 suite. Off-season $129–$169 double; from $249 suite. Children 16 and under stay free in parents' room. Special packages available. AE, DC, DISC, MC, V. From I-95, take Exit 57B (PGA Blvd.) going west and continue for approximately 2 miles to the resort entrance on the left. **Amenities:** 6 restaurants and lounges; 9 swimming pools; 5 18-hole tournament courses, plus the PGA National's Academy of Golf; 19 clay tennis courts; 5 tournament croquet lawns; 5 indoor racquetball courts; Mediterranean spa; aerobics studio; water-sports equipment/rentals; concierge; car-rental desk; salon; room service; baby-sitting; laundry. *In room:* A/C, TV, dataport, kitchenette in suites, minibar, hair dryer.

MODERATE/INEXPENSIVE

Baron's Landing Motel & Apartments ★   This charming family-run inn is a perfect little beach getaway. It's not elegant, but it's cozy. The single-story motel fronting the Intracoastal Waterway is often full in winter with snowbirds, who dock their boats at the hotel's marina for weeks or months at a time. Nearly all rooms, which are situated around a small pool, have small kitchenettes. Each unit has a hodgepodge of used furniture, and some have pullout sofas. Bathrooms have been remodeled. Considering that you're a few blocks from some of the most expensive real estate in the country, this is a good deal. Dock rentals are available.

18125 Ocean Blvd. (Fla. A1A at the corner of Clemens St.), Jupiter, FL 33477. *C* 561/746-8757. 8 units. Winter $75–$125 double; $1,350–$1,700 monthly. Off-season $45–$75 double; $700–$900 monthly. No credit cards. **Amenities:** Small pool. *In room:* A/C, TV, kitchen, coffeemaker, hair dryer.

Cologne Motel   A modest roadside motel, the Cologne is a well-maintained one-story building with a pool but very little in the way of amenities. The small rooms were updated in 1999 with modest but bright bedspreads and curtains, and the retiled bathrooms are small but clean. The area is safe if not scenic and only about a 5-minute drive to the beach. A more direct route by foot gets you there in about 15 minutes. Accessible rooms are available for travelers with disabilities.

220 U.S. 1, Tequesta/Jupiter, FL 33469. *C* 561/746-0616. 9 units. Winter $70 double; off-season $36 double. Weekly rates available. AE, MC, V. **Amenities:** Pool. *In room:* A/C, TV, fridge. No phone.

WHERE TO DINE

In addition to all the national fast-food joints that line Indiantown Road and U.S. 1, you'll find a number of touristy fish restaurants serving battered and fried everything. There are only a few really exceptional eateries in North Palm Beach and Jupiter. Try those listed below for guaranteed good food at reasonable prices.

Athenian Cafe ★ GREEK   Peter Papadelis and his family have been running this pleasant storefront cafe for more than a decade. Tucked in the corner of a strip mall, this place is a favorite with businesspeople, who stop in for a heaping portion of rich and meaty moussaka or a flaky spinach pie made fresh by Peter himself. You could make a meal of the thick and lemony Greek soup and the large fresh antipasto. In a town replete with tourist-priced fish joints, this is a welcome alternative. Early bird specials, served until 7pm, include many Greek favorites and broiled local fish.

In the Chasewood Shopping Center, 6350 Indiantown Rd., Suite 7, Jupiter. ℂ **561/744-8327.** Main courses $5–$16. AE, MC, V. Mon–Sat 11am–9pm; Sun 4–9pm during season.

Capt. Charlie's Reef Grill 🐾🐾 SEAFOOD/CARIBBEAN   The trick here is to arrive early, ahead of the crowd of local foodies who come for the more than a dozen daily local-catch specials prepared in dozens of styles. Imaginative appetizers include Caribbean chili, a rich chunky stew filled with fresh seafood; and a tuna spring roll big enough for two. The enormous Cuban crab cake is moist and perfectly browned without tasting fried and is served with homemade mango chutney and black beans and rice. Sit at the bar to watch the hectic kitchen turn out perfect dishes on the 14-burner stove. Somehow, the pleasant waitresses keep their cool even when the place is packed.

12846 U.S. 1 (behind O'Brian's and French Connection), Juno Beach. ℂ **561/624-9924.** Reservations not accepted. Main courses $9.95–$18.95. MC, V. Sun–Thurs 11:30am–9:30pm; Fri–Sat 11:30am–10pm.

Nick's Tomato Pie 🐾 ITALIAN   A fun, family restaurant, Nick's is a popular attraction that's known to bring folks even from Miami for a piece of this Pie. With a huge menu of pastas, pizzas, fish, chicken, and beef, this cheery (and noisy) spot has something for everyone. On Saturday night, you'll see lots of couples on dates and some families leaving with take-out bags left over from the impossibly generous portions. The homemade sausage is a delicious treat, served with sautéed onions and peppers. The *pollo marsala,* too, is good and authentic.

1697 W. Indiantown Rd. (1 mile east of I-95, Exit 59A), Jupiter. ℂ **561/744-8935.** Reservations accepted only for parties of 6 or more. Main courses $12–$20; pastas $10–$15. AE, DC, DISC, MC, V. Mon–Thurs and Sun 5–10pm; Fri–Sat 5–11pm.

No Anchovies! 🐾 ITALIAN   This large and colorful restaurant is popular with families that appreciate the large portions and reasonably priced children's specials. An equally colorful menu offers a large variety of pastas, pizzas, salads, and meat and fish specials. Mix and match your pasta with half a dozen sauces. You may also want to try some of the delicious chicken or meats prepared on the oak-burning grill.

2650 PGA Blvd., Palm Beach Gardens. ℂ **561/622-7855.** Pizza and pasta $7–$13; main courses $9–$22; appetizers $6–$10. AE, DC, MC, V. Mon–Thurs 11:30am–10:30pm; Fri–Sat 11:30am–11pm; Sun 4:30–10pm.

Sinclair's Ocean Grill & Rotisserie 🐾🐾 CARIBBEAN   As close to upscale as Jupiter gets, Sinclair's is the Jupiter Beach Resort's excellent restaurant overlooking the pool and featuring fresh, locally caught fish as well as an excellent filet mignon. Especially popular are the Sunday brunches.

Jupiter Beach Resort, 5 N. Rte. A1A ℂ **561/745-7120.** Reservations recommended. Main courses $9.95–$18. AE, MC, V. Daily 6:30–11am, 11:30am–2:30pm, and 6–10pm.

JUPITER & NORTHERN PALM BEACH COUNTY AFTER DARK

With one notable exception, there just isn't much going on here after dark. **Club Safari,** 4000 PGA Blvd. (just east of I-95), in Palm Beach Garden's Marriott Hotel (ℂ **561/622-8888**), does a hilarious Vegas-style safari theme. The huge, sunken dance floor is surrounded by vines and lanky, potted trees. Nearby, a large Buddha statue blows steam and smoke while waving its burly arms in front of a young gyrating crowd. There is deejay music, a large video screen, and a modest cover charge on the weekends. Open nights, Wednesday through Sunday.

The Treasure Coast: Stuart to Sebastian

by Lesley Abravanel

While the area from Fort Lauderdale to Palm Beach is known as the Gold Coast because of the discovery of priceless treasures in the water, the area north of Palm Beach is known as the Treasure Coast for the same reason—it's been documented that the area was the site of a number of shipwrecks that date back to over 300 years ago. In fact, some historians believe that treasures from these sunken vessels still lie buried deep beneath the ocean floor. The difference, however, is that while the Gold Coast is a bit, er, tarnished as far as development is concerned, the Treasure Coast remains, for the most part, an unspoiled, quiet natural jewel. From the northern tip of Palm Beach County, the Treasure Coast extends through Martin, St. Lucie, and Indian River counties. Miles of uninterrupted beaches and aquamarine waters attract swimmers, boaters, divers, anglers, and sun worshippers who love to dip, dive, and surf. If you love the great outdoors and prefer a more understated environment, the Treasure Coast is a real find.

For hundreds of years, Florida's east coast was a popular stopover for European explorers, many of whom arrived from Spain to fill coffers with gold and silver. Rough weather and poor navigation often took a toll on their ships, but in 1715 a violent hurricane stunned the northeast coast and sank an entire fleet of Spanish ships laden with gold. Although Spanish salvagers worked for years to collect the lost treasure, much of it remained buried beneath the shifting sand. Workers hired to excavate the area in the 1950s and 1960s discovered centuries-old coins under their tractors. The McLarty Treasure Museum at Sebastian Inlet State Recreation Area in Melbourne Beach highlights the history of the 1715 Treasure Fleet. There are also incredible barrier reefs and shipwrecks in St. Lucie County that can be reached from the beaches of Fort Pierce and Hutchinson Island.

Today, on these same beaches you'll find an occasional treasure hunter trolling the sand with a metal detector, alongside swimmers and sunbathers who come to enjoy the stretches of beach that extend into the horizon. The sea, especially around Sebastian Inlet, is a mecca for surfers, who find some of the largest swells in the state.

Along with the pleasures of the talcum powder sands, the Treasure Coast also offers great shopping, entertainment, clubbing, sporting, and numerous other opportunities to take a reprieve from the hubbub of the rat race. The array of wildlife you'll find here is extensive. The endangered West Indian manatee can be spotted along the Treasure Coast's inland waterways. You can learn more about this mammal at The Manatee Observation and Education Center in Fort Pierce. St. Lucie Inlet State Preserve has a wonderful nesting area for log-gerhead and leatherback turtles. Take a boat tour through the Loxahatchee Everglades, home to tropical fish, alli-gators, deer, and exotic birds. Go trolling in Lake Okeechobee for the best freshwater fish around.

If you're a sports enthusiast, you'll enjoy the boundless sporting opportu-nities here—from golf and tennis to polo and motorcar racing. If you tire from your own activities, take time out to watch the pros play hard. Catch the New York Mets practicing at the St. Lucie City Stadium in Port St. Lucie during spring training.

The downtown areas of the Treasure Coast have been experiencing a rebirth in the past few years, along with the influx of unprecedented numbers of new residents. The area's growth has occurred at a reasonable pace so that the neighborhoods have been able to retain their small-town feel. The result

is a batch of freshly spruced-up accom-modations, shops, and restaurants from Stuart to Sebastian.

Southern Martin County's well-to-do Hobe Sound, in particular, is a Treasure Coast hot spot with its pris-tine beaches, Banyan tree–canopied streetscapes, one-of-a-kind antique shops and art galleries. Hobe Sound rests at the front door of the Gold Coast and the back door of the Trea-sure Coast, and it has immediate access to the Atlantic Ocean and the Intracoastal Waterway. Real estate here is at a premium, with million-dollar waterfront mansions lining the shores.

For the purposes of this chapter, the Treasure Coast runs roughly from Hobe Sound in the south to the Sebastian Inlet in the north, encom-passing some of Martin, St. Lucie, and Indian River counties and all of Hutchinson Island.

TREASURE COAST ESSENTIALS
GETTING THERE
Since virtually every town described in this chapter runs along a straight route, along the Atlantic Ocean, I've given all directions below.

BY PLANE   The **Palm Beach International Airport** (© **561/471-7420**), located about 35 miles south of Stuart, is the closest gateway to this region if you're flying. See the "Getting Around" section on Palm Beach in chapter 8 for complete information. If you are traveling to the northern part of the Treasure Coast, **Melbourne International Airport,** off U.S. 1 in Melbourne (© **407/ 723-6227**), is less than 25 miles north of Sebastian and about 35 miles north of Vero Beach.

BY CAR   If you're driving up or down the Florida coast, you'll probably reach the Treasure Coast via I-95. If you are heading to Stuart or Jensen Beach, take Exit 61 (Route 76/Tanner Highway) or 62 (Route 714); to Port St. Lucie or Fort Pierce, take Exit 63 or 64 (Okeechobee Road); to Vero Beach, take Exit 68 (State Route 60); to Sebastian, take Exit 69 (County Road).

You can also take the Florida Turnpike; this toll road is the fastest (but not the most scenic) route, especially if you're coming from Orlando. If you are heading to Stuart or Jensen Beach, take Exit 133; to Fort Pierce, take Exit 152 (Okee-chobee Road); to Port St. Lucie, take Exit 142 or 152; to Vero Beach, take Exit 193 (State Route 60); to Sebastian, take Exit 193 to State Route 60 east and con-nect to I-95 north.

If you are staying in Hutchinson Island, which runs almost the entire length of the Treasure Coast, you should check with your hotel or see the listings below to find the best route to take.

Coastal Science Center **12**
Dodgertown **5**
Elliott Museum **10**
Environmental Learning Center **4**
Gilbert's House of Refuge Museum **11**
Harbor Branch Oceanographic Institution **7**

Indian River Citrus Museum **6**
McKee Botanical Garden **1**
McLarty Treasure Museum **2**
Mel Fisher's Treasure Museum **3**
Savannahs Recreation Center **9**
UDT-SEAL Museum **8**

   Finally, if you're coming directly from the west coast, you'll probably take State Route 70, which runs north of Lake Okeechobee to Fort Pierce, located just up the road from Stuart.

BY RAIL   Amtrak (© **800/USA-RAIL;** www.amtrak.com) stops in West Palm Beach at 201 S. Tamarind Ave., and in Okeechobee at 801 N. Parrot Ave., off U.S. 441 north.

BY BUS   Greyhound buses (© **800/231-2222;** www.greyhound.com) service the area with terminals in Stuart, at 1308 S. Federal Hwy.; in Fort Pierce, at 7005 Okeechobee Rd. (© **561/461-3299**); and in Vero Beach, at U.S. 1 and State Route 60 (© **561/562-6588**).

GETTING AROUND
A car is a necessity in this large and rural region. Although heavy traffic is not usually a problem here, on the smaller coastal roads, like Fla. A1A, expect to travel at a slow pace, usually between 25 and 40 miles an hour.

1 Hobe Sound ✮✮✮, Stuart & Jensen Beach

130 miles SE of Orlando, 98 miles N. of Miami.

Once just a stretch of pineapple plantations, the towns of Martin County, which include Stuart, Jensen Beach, Port Salerno, and Hobe Sound, still retain much of their rural character. Dotted between citrus groves and mangroves are modest homes and an occasional high-rise condominium. Although the area is definitely still seasonal (with a distinct rise in street and pedestrian traffic beginning after the Christmas holidays), the atmosphere is pure small town. Even in historic downtown Stuart, the result of a successful, ongoing restoration, expect the storefronts to be dark and the streets abandoned after 10pm.

ESSENTIALS

The **Stuart/Martin County Chamber of Commerce,** 1650 S. Kanner Hwy., Stuart, FL 34994 (✆ **800/524-9704** in Florida, or 561/287-1088; fax 561/ 220-3437), is the region's main source for information. The **Jensen Beach Chamber of Commerce,** 1901 NE Jensen Beach Blvd., Jensen Beach, FL 34957 (✆ **561/334-3444;** fax 561/334-0817), also offers visitors information about its simple beachfront town.

BACK TO NATURE: THE BEACHES & BEYOND

BEACHES Beaches are easily accessible throughout Hutchinson Island, the long, thin barrier island that stretches north and south from Stuart. Look for "coastal access" signs pointing the way to the public beach areas.

The best of them is **Bathtub Beach,** on North Hutchinson Island. Here, the calm waters are protected by coral reefs, and visitors can explore the region on dune and river trails. Pick a secluded spot on the wide stretch of beach, or enjoy marked nature trails across the street. Facilities include showers and toilets open during the day. To reach the park, head east on Ocean Boulevard (Stuart Causeway) and turn right onto MacArthur Boulevard. The beach is about a mile ahead on your left, just north of the Indian River Plantation. Parking is plentiful.

CANOEING **Jonathan Dickinson State Park** (see "Wildlife Exploration," below) is the area's most popular for canoeing. The route winds through a variety of botanical habitats. You'll see lots of birds and, of course, the occasional manatee. Canoes cost $6 per hour. The concession is open Monday to Friday from 9am to 5pm and Saturday and Sunday from 8am to 5pm.

FISHING Several independent charter captains operate on Hutchinson Island and Jensen Beach. One of the largest operators is the **Sailfish Marina,** 3565 SE St. Lucie Blvd., in Stuart (✆ **561/221-9456**), which maintains half a dozen charter boats for fishing excursions year-round. Also on-site are a bait-and-tackle shop and a knowledgeable, helpful staff. Other reputable charter operators include **Hungry Bear Adventures, Inc.,** docked at Indian River Plantation Marriott Resort, 4730-1 SE Teri Place in Stuart (✆ **561/283-8034;** fishing@tci.net); and **Bone Shaker Sportfishing,** 3585 SE St. Lucie Blvd., in Stuart (✆ **561/286-5504;** veejay4842@aol.com).

GOLF The pricey **Indian River Plantation Beach Resort** ✦ is a terrific destination for golfers, but you must be a guest at the resort or a guest of a member in order to play. Instead, try the **Champions Club at Summerfield** ✦, on U.S. 1, south of Cove Road in Stuart (✆ **561/283-1500**), a somewhat challenging championship course designed by Tom Fazio. This rural course, the best

**Wildlife Exploration: From Gators
to Manatees to Turtles**

One of the most scenic areas on this stretch of the coast is **Jonathan
Dickinson State Park** 🐊, at 16450 S. Federal Hwy. (U.S. 1), Hobe Sound
(📞 561/ 546-2771). The park receives less maintenance intentionally so
that it will resemble the habitat of hundreds of years ago, before Europeans started chopping, dredging, and "improving" the area. Dozens
of species of Florida's unique wildlife, including alligators and manatees, live on more than 11,300 acres. Bird watchers should bring their
books and binoculars to spot the many ospreys, woodpeckers, ibises,
herons, anhingas, egrets, and even some bald eagles. Deer, reptiles,
tortoises, and snakes also call this area home. There are concession
areas for daytime snacks and four different scenic nature and bike
trails through the scrublands and flatwoods. You can also rent canoes
from the concession stand to explore the Loxahatchee River on your
own. Admission is $3.25 per car of up to eight adults. Day hikers, bik-
ers, and walkers pay $1 each. The park is open from 8am until sun-
down. See "Where to Stay," below for details on camping.

Nearby is **Hobe Sound Wildlife Refuge,** on North Beach Road off
State Route 708, at the north end of Jupiter Island (📞 **561/546-6141**).
This is one of the best places to see sea turtles that nest on the shore
in the summer months, especially in June and July. Because it's home
to a large variety of other plant and animal species, the park is worth
visiting at other times of year as well. Admission is $4 per car, and the
preserve is open daily from sunrise to sunset. Exact times are posted at
each entrance and change seasonally.

For turtle walks in Hutchinson Island, call 📞 **877/375-4386.** These
walks take place from May 22 through July 22 at 9pm, Friday and Saturdays. Reservations are necessary and should be made well in
advance, as walks are limited to 50 people. Reservations are accepted
as of May 1.

in the area, offers great glimpses of wildlife amid the wetlands. Winter greens
fees are around $60, and carts are mandatory. Reservations are a must and are
taken 4 days in advance.

SCUBA DIVING & SNORKELING Three popular artificial reefs off
Hutchinson Island provide excellent scenery for both novice and experienced
divers. The *USS Rankin,* sunk in 120 feet of water in 1988, lies 7 miles east-
northeast of the St. Lucie Inlet. The 58-foot-deep **Donaldson Reef** consists of
a cluster of plumbing fixtures sunk in 58 feet of water. It's located due east of the
Gilbert's House of Refuge Museum. The **Ernst Reef,** made from old tires, is a
60-foot dive located 4½ miles east-southeast of the St. Lucie inlet. Local dive
shops have "tips" on the best spots and rules and regulations for safe diving. The
Donald F. Welton Scuba Repair Shop (📞 **561/225-9717;** dfwelton@aol.com)
in Jensen Beach is a great place to check out.

The Power of Nature

In the middle of Hutchinson Island, approximately 6 miles south of Ft. Pierce Beach and 6 miles north of the Jensen Beach causeway, is the oddly placed St. Lucie Nuclear Power Plant. As you approach the cooling towers from either the north or the south, you'll also see emergency evacuation sirens that eerily attest to the possible dangers of this ill-sited facility. On the positive side, the construction of this power plant has helped preserve large stretches of isolated shoreline. The St. Lucie Nuclear Power Plant manages an 85-acre nature preserve ¼ mile north of its reactor and cooling towers. It features a public boardwalk through a swamp full of mangroves and bird life. The trailhead begins at the "Power Plant Road" beach parking lot and is worth a visit.

Blind Creek Beach, located ½ mile north of the plant, has become something of a nude beach—unofficially, that is. Since tanning in the altogether isn't sanctioned in Hutchinson Island, you might wish to cover up if you see motorized sheriff patrols or clothed people (who could be police in plain clothing) approaching. You won't be arrested, but you may be told to get dressed.

SEEING THE SIGHTS

Coastal Science Center ★★ This is a nature lover's Disney World. Opened by the South Florida Oceanographic Society in late 1994, this 44-acre site surrounded by coastal hammock and mangroves is its own little ecosystem and serves as an outdoor classroom, teaching visitors about the region's flora and fauna. The modest building houses saltwater tanks and wet and dry "discovery tables" with small indigenous animals. The incredibly eager staff of volunteers encourages visitors to wander the lush, well-marked nature trails.

890 NE Ocean Blvd. (across the street from the Elliott Museum), Hutchinson Island, Stuart. © 561/ 225-0505. www.fosusa.org. Admission $6 adults, $3 children 3–12, free for children under 3. Mon–Sat 10am–5pm. Sunday noon–4.

Balloons Over Florida ★★★ *Finds* For a lofty view of Martin County's wildlife, take a hot air balloon ride above the animals' natural habitat. Two fully licensed and insured balloons and pilots will take a maximum of four people up, up, and away for about an hour, depending on wind and weather conditions. After you've landed, drink in the sights over a glass of complimentary champagne and a continental breakfast. A certificate of flight is given to each passenger as a souvenir.

Tours begin at approximately 6:30am from a destination point to be determined. © 561/334-9393. $150 per person, including continental breakfast and champagne.

Elliott Museum ★★ A treasure trove of early Americana, the Elliott Museum is a rich tribute to inventors, sports heroes, and collectors. A series of life-size dioramas depicts an apothecary, a barbershop, a blacksmith forge, a clock and watch shop, and other old-fashioned commercial enterprises. Sports fans will appreciate the baseball memorabilia—a half-million dollars' worth—including an autographed item from every player in the Baseball Hall of Fame.

A gallery of patents and models of machines, invented by the museum's founder, Harmon Parker Elliott, and his son, provides an intriguing glimpse into the business of tinkering. Their collection of restored antique cars is also impressive. Expect to spend at least an hour seeing the highlights.

825 NE Ocean Blvd. (north of Indian River Plantation Resort), Hutchinson Island, Stuart. © 561/225-1961. Admission $6 adults, $2 children 6–13, free for children 5 and under. Daily 10am–4pm.

Gilbert's House of Refuge Museum ✦ Gilbert's, the oldest structure in Martin County, dates from 1875, when it functioned as one of 10 such rescue centers for shipwrecked sailors. After undergoing a thorough rehabilitation to its original condition along the rocky shores, the house now displays marine artifacts and turn-of-the-century lifesaving equipment and photographs and is worth a quick visit to get a feel for the area's early days.

301 SE MacArthur Blvd. (south of Indian River Plantation resort), Hutchinson Island, Stuart. © 561/225-1875. Admission $4 adults, $2 children 6–13, free for children 5 and under. Daily 10am–4pm.

A BOAT TOUR

The *Loxahatchee Queen* ✦✦✦, a 35-foot pontoon boat (© 561/746-1466) in Jonathan Dickinson State Park in Hobe Sound, makes daily tours of the area's otherwise inaccessible backwater, where curious alligators, manatees, eagles, and tortoises often peek out to see who's in their yard. Try to catch the 2-hour tour, given Wednesday to Sunday as the tide permits, when it includes a stop at Trapper Nelson's home. Known as the "Wildman of Loxahatchee," Nelson lived in primitive conditions on a remote stretch of the water in a log cabin he built himself, which is preserved for visitors to see. Tours leave four times daily at 9am, 11am, 1pm, and 3pm and cost $12 for adults, $7 for children 6 to 12, and free for children 5 and under. See the "Wildlife Exploration" box, above, for more information on the park.

SHOPPING

Downtown Stuart's historic district, along Flagler Avenue between Confusion Corner and St. Lucie Avenue, offers shoppers diversity and quality in a small old-town setting. Shops offer a range of goods: antique bric-a-brac, old lamps and fixtures, books, gourmet foods, furnishings, and souvenirs. For bargains, check out the **B & A Flea Market** (© 561/288-4915), the Treasure Coast's oldest and largest flea market.

WHERE TO STAY

Although the area boasts some beautiful beaches, the bulk of the hotel scene is downtown, where the nicer (and more reasonably priced) accommodations can be found among the shops and restaurants. There are, however, a few excellent beachfront hotels and inns. One of the bigger hotel chains in the area is the **Holiday Inn.** Its recently renovated, stunning beachfront property is at 3793 NE Ocean Blvd., on Hutchinson Island in Jensen Beach (© 800/992-4747 or 561/225-3000). Rates in season range from $130 to $180. Holiday Inn also has a downtown location at 1209 S. Federal Hwy. (© 561/287-6200). This simple two-story building on a busy main road is kept in very good shape and is convenient to Stuart's downtown historic district. Rates range from $99 to $140.

VERY EXPENSIVE

Hutchinson Island Marriott Beach Resort and Marina ✦✦✦ This sprawling 200-acre compound offers so many diversions for active (or not-so-active) vacationers, and families in particular, that you won't want to leave. After a $6 million renovation in 1998, this is definitely Hutchinson Island's best resort, occupying the lush grounds of a former pineapple plantation. Activities include tennis, golfing, and boating. Sportfishing (especially for sailfish) is a big draw here, as are scuba diving and other water sports.

Generously sized rooms, all with fully equipped kitchens, are decorated with colorful spreads and draperies. A complete room renovation occurred in 2000, and in 2001 the hotel's beach building was completely redone. Some rooms overlook the Intracoastal and the resort's marina, while others face the ocean or the gardens. Accommodations are available for travelers with disabilities.

In the summer months, be sure to sign up for a "turtle watch," during which you can watch the large turtles crawl onto the sand to lay their eggs. Another great activity offered at an extra cost is a sightseeing cruise along the St. Lucie and Indian rivers, which leaves from the hotel on a daily basis and costs $13.95 to $30.95 for adults and $10.50 to $23.50 for children.

555 NE Ocean Blvd., Hutchinson Island, Stuart, FL 34996. ℭ 800/775-5936 or 561/225-3700. Fax 561/225-0003. www.marriott.com/marriott/pbiir. 298 units. Winter $209–$399; off-season $99–$349. AE, MC, V. From downtown Stuart, take E. Ocean Blvd. over 2 bridges to NE Ocean Blvd.; turn right. Pets accepted with a $50 deposit. **Amenities:** Restaurant; coffee shop; lounge; 4 large pools; 18-hole golf course; 13 tennis courts; fitness center & spa; extensive water sports; bike rental; children's programs; game room; concierge; on-property transportation; limited room service; baby-sitting; laundry and dry-cleaning services. *In room:* A/C, TV, dataport, kitchenette, minibar, coffeemaker, hair dryer.

MODERATE

Harborfront Inn Bed & Breakfast 🖈🖈 *Finds*   A bona fide return to Old Florida, the Harborfront Inn has the advantage of being right on the river, where you can sail, kayak, and water-ski. It consists of a series of little blue-trimmed shingled cottages within walking distance of the restaurants of downtown Stuart. Each room in this highly recommended B&B, which dates back to 1908, has its own private entrance, making it more like a rambling inn. Also, every accommodation has a sitting area and private bathroom. The two best rooms are the bright Garden Suite, which has a queen-size bed, rattan furnishings, and a deck with river and garden views; and the Guest House, which has an extra-large bathroom with two sinks and can be rented with an adjoining full kitchen.

A must-do is the in-room candlelight dinner. The inn's cozy public areas are surrounded by an enclosed porch where breakfast is served. The morning meal usually includes fresh fruit from the trees that grow on the property. No children are allowed here, and smoking is not permitted.

310 Atlanta Ave., Stuart, FL 34994. ℭ 800/294-1703 or 561/288-7289. Fax 561/221-0474. www.harborfrontinn.com. 6 units. Winter $90–$183 double. Off-season discounts available. Rates include breakfast. DISC, MC, V. Free dockage. From I-95 take Exit 61 heading east to U.S. 1 N. Turn left on W. Ocean Blvd. and make the first right (Atlanta Ave.). **Amenities:** Jacuzzi; water-sports equipment/rentals. *In room:* A/C, TV/VCR, hair dryer.

Hutchinson Inn 🖈🖈   It doesn't look like much from the road—only the tennis court is visible—but you'll soon happen upon striking white gazebos dotting thick green lawns. Located directly on the beach, the Hutchinson Inn is a quiet and charming two-story hideaway. Unfortunately, so many people know about it that it's usually booked a year in advance in high season. The refurbished rooms have rattan furnishings; sofas convert into pull-out beds, and several rooms can be joined to accommodate large families. Some contain kitchens.

9750 S. Ocean Dr. (Fla. A1A), Jensen Beach, FL 34957. ℭ 561/229-2000. www.hutchinsoninn.com. 21 units. Winter from $125 double; $165–$235 efficiency or suite. Off-season from $95 double; $125–$195 efficiency or suite. Rates include continental breakfast. MC, V. From I-95 take Exit 61, heading east to Monterey; turn right and cross U.S. 1. Go to second light; turn right on E. Ocean Blvd. onto the island. Inn is about 8 miles ahead. **Amenities:** Large outdoor heated pool, lighted tennis court, water-sports equipment/rental, bike rental, coin-op washers and dryers. Freshly baked cookies before bedtime. *In room:* A/C, TV, kitchen in some rooms, fridge, hair dryer.

CAMPING

There are comfortable campsites in **Jonathan Dickinson State Park** in Hobe Sound (see the "Wildlife Exploration" box earlier in this chapter). You can stay overnight in rustic cabins or in your tent or camper in two different sections of the park. The River Camp area offers the benefit of the nearby Loxahatchee River, while the Pine Grove site has beautiful shade trees. There are concession areas for daytime snacks and 135 campsites with showers, clean restrooms, water, optional electricity, and an open-fire pit for cooking. Overnight rates in the winter are $18 without electricity, $20 with electricity. In the summer, rates are about $14 for four people.

For a more cushy camping experience, reserve a wood-sided cabin with a furnished kitchen, a bathroom with shower, heat and air-conditioning, and an outdoor grill. Bring your own linens. Cabins rent for $65 and up a night and sleep four people comfortably, six if your group is really into togetherness. Call © **561/546-2771** Monday to Friday from 9am to 5pm, well in advance to reserve a spot. A $50 key deposit is required.

WHERE TO DINE
EXPENSIVE

Eleven Maple Street ★★★ AMERICAN   The most highly rated restaurant in Jensen Beach, Eleven Maple Street occupies a lovely little house with a white picket fence, French doors, lace curtains, and pink-clothed tables. Dining is both indoors and out, in any one of a series of cozy dining rooms or on a covered patio surrounded by gardens. Straightforward meat and fish dishes run the gamut from local seafood to game and poultry such as venison and duck. Maine lobster, filet mignon, and pastas are also available, and most everything is spiced with fresh-picked herbs from the restaurant's own organic garden.

11 Maple St., Jensen Beach. © 561/334-7714. Reservations recommended. Main courses $16–$29. MC, V. Wed–Sun 6–10pm. Head east on Jensen Beach Blvd. and turn right after the railroad tracks.

Flagler Grill ★★ AMERICAN/FLORIDA REGIONAL   In the heart of historic downtown, this seemingly out-of-place Manhattan-style bistro serves up classics with a twist. The dishes are not so unusual as to alienate the conservative pink-shirted golfers who frequent the place, yet they're fresh and light enough to quench the appetites of the more adventurous—for example, the saffron and mushroom pasta with Cajun shrimp and roasted tomatoes. The menu changes every few weeks, so see what your server recommends. It's hard to go wrong with any of the many salads, pastas, fishes, or delectable beef choices. The desserts, too, are worth the calories. No smoking is allowed in the restaurant or bar.

47 SW Flagler Ave. (just before the Roosevelt Bridge), downtown Stuart. © 561/221-9517. Reservations strongly suggested in season. Main courses $17–$25. AE, MC, V. Winter daily 5–10pm. Off-season Thurs–Sat 5:30–9:30pm. Lounge and bar open to 11:30pm. Special sunset menu offered from 5–6pm.

MODERATE

Black Marlin ★ FLORIDA REGIONAL   Although it sports the look and feel of a dank English pub, the Black Marlin offers full Floridian flavor. The salmon BLT is typical of the dishes here—grilled salmon on a toasted bun topped with bacon, lettuce, tomato, and coleslaw. Designer pizzas are topped with shrimp, roasted red peppers, and the like; and main dishes, all of which are served with vegetables and potatoes, include a lobster tail with honey-mustard sauce, and a charcoal-grilled chicken breast served on radicchio with caramelized onions.

53 W. Osceola St., downtown Stuart. ☎ **561/286-3126.** Reservations not accepted. Salads and sandwiches $4–$8, full meals $9–$24. AE, MC, V. Mon–Thurs 5–10pm, Fri–Sat 5–11pm (the bar is open later).

Conchy Joe's Seafood 🦀🦀 *(Finds)* SEAFOOD   Known for fresh seafood and Old Florida hospitality, Conchy Joe's enjoys an excellent reputation that's far bigger than the restaurant itself. Dining is either indoors, at red-and-white cloth-covered tables, or on a covered patio overlooking the St. Lucie River. The restaurant features a wide variety of freshly shucked shellfish and daily-catch selections that are baked, broiled, or fried. Beer is the drink of choice here, though other beverages and a full bar are available. Conchy Joe's has been the most active place in Jensen Beach since it opened in 1983. The large bar is especially popular at night and during weekday happy hours.

3945 NE Indian River Dr. (½ mile from the Jensen Beach Causeway), Jensen Beach. ☎ **561/334-1130.** Reservations not accepted. Main courses $12–$20. AE, DISC, MC, V. Daily 11:30am–2:30pm and 5–10pm (happy hour daily 3–6pm).

INEXPENSIVE

Bubba's Fish Camp 🦀🦀 *(Finds)* SEAFOOD/SOUTHERN   As you would imagine from its name, Bubba's is an ultracasual spot designed to resemble an old-Florida fish camp. Don't miss the great crawfish gumbo, corn bread, catfish, creamy spinach, hush puppies, and fried green tomatoes, too. After 4pm, you'll find bargain deals on hearty Southern classics like meatloaf, baked Virginia ham with red-eye gravy, fried chicken, and pork chops. Each includes a choice of delicious side dishes. Fresh and crispy onion rings are actually served on tiny bathroom plunger handles. Locals and highway travelers line up outside the screened porch to get into this rustic eatery.

421 S. Federal Hwy. (at south side of Roosevelt Bridge), Stuart. ☎ **561/220-3747.** Full meals $8–$10. AE, MC, V. Daily 4–10pm and later on weekends. Call for details on weekend breakfasts.

Nature's Way Cafe 🦀 HEALTH FOOD   This lovely, clean, and green dining room has dozens of little tables, a few barstools, and some sidewalk seating, too. A sort of health-food deli, Nature's Way excels in serving quick and nutritious meals such as huge salads, vegetarian sandwiches, and frozen yogurts. Try some of the homemade baked goods. Sit outside on quaint Osceola Street or ask them to pack your lunch for you to take to the beach.

25 SW Osceola St., in the Post Office Arcade, Stuart. ☎ **561/220-7306.** Sandwiches and salads $4–$7, juices and shakes $1–$3. No credit cards. Mon–Fri 10am–4pm, Sat 11am–3pm.

STUART & JENSEN BEACH AFTER DARK

Local restaurants serve as the nightlife centers of Stuart and Jensen Beach. And "night" ends pretty early here, even on the weekends. The bar at the Black Marlin (see "Where to Dine," above) is popular with locals and out-of-towners alike.

No list of Jensen nightlife would be complete without mention of Conchy Joe's Seafood (see "Where to Dine," above), one of the region's most active spots. Inside, locals chug beer and watch a large-screen TV, while outside on the waterfront patio, live bands perform a few nights a week for a raucous crowd of dancers. Happy hours, weekdays from 3 to 6pm, draw large crowds with low-priced drinks and snacks. No cover.

In a strip mall just outside of downtown, you'll find pickup trucks as far as the eye can see parked outside the **Rock 'n' Horse,** 1580 S. Federal Hwy. (U.S. 1), Stuart (© **561/286-1281**). It's a real locals' country-and-western spot that rocks, especially on Tuesday night, when women drink all night for $5. Bring your hat and boots for line dancing, beer drinking, and a good time in one of the only real late-night spots in town. Cover varies.

The centerpiece of Stuart's slowly expanding cultural offerings is the newly restored **Lyric Theater,** at 59 SW Flagler Ave. (© **561/286-7827**). This beautiful 1920s-era, 600-seat theater hosts a variety of shows and films throughout the year. Programs run the gamut from amateur plays to top-name theatrical shows, poetry readings, and concerts.

2 Port St. Lucie, Fort Pierce & North Hutchinson Island (★(★

7 miles N. of Stuart

Port St. Lucie and Fort Pierce, two Old Florida towns, thrive on sportfishing. A seemingly endless row of piers juts out along the Intracoastal Waterway and the Fort Pierce Inlet for both river and ocean runs. Here visitors can also dive, snorkel, beachcomb, and sunbathe in an area that has been left untouched by the overdevelopment that has altered its neighbors to the south and north.

Most sightseeing takes place along the main beach road. Driving along Fla. A1A on Hutchinson Island, you'll discover several secluded beach clubs interspersed with 1950s-style homes, a few small inns, grungy raw bars, and a few high-rise condominiums. Much of this island is government owned and kept undeveloped for the public's enjoyment.

ESSENTIALS

The **St. Lucie County Chamber of Commerce,** 2200 Virginia Ave., Fort Pierce, FL 34982 (© **561/595-9999**), is the region's main source of information. There's another branch at 1626 SE Port St. Lucie Blvd., in Port St. Lucie. Both spots are open Monday through Friday from 9am to 5pm.

BEACHES & NATURE PRESERVES

North Hutchinson Island's beaches are the most pristine in this area. You won't find restaurants, hotels, or shopping; instead, spend your time swimming, surfing, fishing, and diving. Most of the beaches are private along this stretch of the Atlantic Ocean. Thankfully, the state has set aside some of the best areas for the public.

Fort Pierce Inlet State Recreation Area (© **561/468-3985**) is a stunning 340-acre park with almost 4,000 feet of sandy shores that were once the training ground for the original Navy frogmen. A short nature trail leads through a canopy of live oaks, cabbage palms, sea grapes, and strangler figs. The western side of the area has swamps of red mangroves that are home to fiddler crabs, osprey, and a multitude of wading birds. Jack Island State Preserve, in the State Recreation Area, is popular with bird watchers and offers hiking and nature trails. Jutting out into the Indian River, the mangrove-covered peninsula contains several marked trails, varying in distance from a half-mile to over 4 miles. The trails go through mangrove forests and lead to a short observation tower.

The best beach here, called Jetty Park, lies in the northern part of the State Recreation Area. Families enjoy the large picnic areas and barbecue grills. There are restrooms and outdoor showers, and lifeguards look after swimmers.

The park is located at 905 Shorewinds Dr., north of Fort Pierce Inlet. To get there from I-95, take Exit 66 east (Route 68) and turn left onto U.S. 1 north; in about 2 miles, you will see signs to Fla. A1A and the North Bridge Causeway. Turn right on A1A and cross over to North Hutchinson Island. Admission is $3.25 per vehicle, and the park is open daily from 8am to sunset.

SPECTATOR SPORTS & OUTDOOR PURSUITS

BASEBALL   The **New York Mets** hold spring training in Port St. Lucie from late February through March at the **Thomas J. White Stadium,** 525 NW Peacock Blvd. (© **561/871-2115**). Tickets cost $10 to $15. From April through August, their farm team, the Port St. Lucie Mets, plays home games in the stadium.

FISHING   The **Fort Pierce City Marina,** 1 Ave. A, Fort Pierce (© **561/ 464-1245**), has more than a dozen charter captains who keep their motors running for anglers anxious to catch a few. Brochures available at the marina list all the privately owned charter operators. The price usually starts at $150 per person for half-day tours, depending on the season. Charters are organized on an as-desired basis. In general, plan to arrive very early in the morning (by 6am) before all the other early birds.

GOLF   The most notable courses in Port St. Lucie are at the **PGA Golf Club at the Reserve** (© **561/467-1300**), at 1916 Perfect Dr. The club's first of three 18-hole public golf courses opened in January 1996 and was designed by Tom Fazio; another course was designed by Pete Dye. The PGA Learning Center offers lessons for amateurs. The South Course, a classic Old Florida–style course, is set on wetlands and offers views of native wildlife. It is the most popular. The club is open 7am to 6pm daily. Greens fees are usually under $45; after 2pm, $25. Reserve at least 9 days in advance.

SEEING THE SIGHTS

Harbor Branch Oceanographic Institution ☆☆   Harbor Branch is a working nonprofit scientific institute that studies oceanic resources and welcomes visitors on regularly scheduled tours. The first stop is the J. Seward Johnson Marine Education Center, which houses institute-built submersibles that are used to conduct marine research at depths of up to 3,000 feet. A video details current research projects, and several large aquariums simulate the environments of the Indian River Lagoon and a saltwater reef. Tourists are then shuttled by minibus to the Aqua-Culture Farming Center, a research facility containing shallow tanks growing seaweed and other oceanic plants. The 90-minute Lagoon Wildlife Tour on a pontoon boat, which examines the Indian River Lagoon, is fascinating and runs from Monday through Saturday at 10am, 1pm, and 3pm. The tour costs $15 for adults and $12 for children 3 to 13.

5600 U.S. 1 N., Fort Pierce. © 800/333-4264 or 561/465-2400. www.hboi.com. Admission $10 adults, $6 children 6–12, free for children 5 and under. Mon–Fri 8am–5pm; Visitor Center Gift Shop Mon–Sat 9am–5pm. Arrive at least 20 min. before tour.

UDT-SEAL Museum   Florida is full of unique museums, but none is more curious than the UDT-SEAL Museum, a most peculiar tribute to the secret forces of the U.S. Navy frogmen and their successors, the SEAL teams. Chronological displays trace the history of these clandestine divers and detail their most important achievements. The best exhibits are those of the intricately detailed equipment used by the navy's most elite members.

3300 North State Road A1A, Fort Pierce. © 561/595-5845. Admission $4 adults, $1.50 children, free for children 6 and under. Mon–Sat 10am–4pm, Sun noon–4pm. Closed Mon in off-season.

Savannahs Recreation Area ★★★ *Finds*   A 550-acre former reservoir, Savannahs is a veritable wilderness, with botanical gardens, nature trails, campsites, a petting zoo, and scenery reminiscent of the Florida Everglades, but in a much more contained environment.

1400 E. Midway Rd., Fort Pierce. © 561/464-7855. Admission $1 per car. Daily 8am–6pm.

WHERE TO STAY

The Port St. Lucie mainland is pretty run-down, but there are a number of inexpensive hotel options on scenic Hutchinson Island that are both charming and well priced. Probably the best option is the **Hampton Inn** (© 800/426-7866 or 561/460-9855), 2831 Reynolds Dr., which is relatively new and beautifully maintained. However, if you want to be closer to the water, try the **Days Inn Hutchinson Island,** 1920 Seaway Dr. (© 800/325-2525 or 561/461-8737), a small motel that sits along the Intracoastal inlet and is simple but very well kept.

Budget travelers will be glad to know about the **Edgewater Motel and Apartments,** 1160 Seaway Dr. (next door to and under the same ownership as the Harborlight Inn), Fort Pierce (© 800/286-1745 or 561/468-3555). Motel rooms start at less than $60 in high season, and efficiencies are also available from $80. Guests can enjoy a private pool, shuffleboard courts, and a nearby fishing pier.

EXPENSIVE

Club Med–Sandpiper ★★ *Kids*   A former Hilton Hotel, the 400-acre Sandpiper resort was purchased by Club Med in 1985 and marketed to Europeans looking for a Florida getaway. They come in droves (Americans, too) with all the kids and nannies for a sunny, active vacation with meals, for a reasonable prepaid price. The drawback is that guests are 20 minutes from the nearest beach. The buildings could use a major overhaul, but there are plenty of diversions on the grounds, such as golf and tennis, and water-skiing, sailing, and boating on the Indian River. There's even a circus school.

The atmosphere here is fairly sedate and very family-oriented. There's even a Parenting Skills Workshop. The rooms are sparse and small, but not uncomfortable. Because most of the activities here are outdoors, you probably won't spend much time inside anyway.

3500 SE Morningside Blvd., Port St. Lucie, FL 34952. © 800/CLUB-MED or 561/335-4400. Fax 561/398-5101. www.clubmed.com. 338 units. Winter $170–$280 per person, based on double occupancy. Off-season $150–$275 per person, based on double occupancy. Rates include 3 meals per day. AE, MC, V. From U.S. 1 S., turn left onto Westmoreland Blvd. Make another left onto Pine Valley Rd.; the resort entrance is straight ahead. **Amenities:** 2 restaurants; bar; 4 pools; 3 golf courses; 19 tennis courts (9 are lighted); fitness center; water-sports equipment; game rooms; coin-op washers and dryers. *In room:* A/C, TV, hair dryer.

MODERATE

Dockside–Harbor Light Resort ★   Fronting the Intracoastal Waterway, the Harbor Light is a great choice for boating and fishing enthusiasts, offering 15 boat slips and two private fishing piers. The hotel itself carries on the nautical theme with pierlike wooden stairs and rope railings. While not exactly captain's quarters, the rooms, which are simply decorated with pastel colors and small wall prints, are attractive, especially since a thorough renovation was completed in 1999. Higher-priced rooms have either waterfront balconies or small kitchenettes.

1160 Seaway Dr., South Hutchinson Island, FL 34949. © **800/286-1745** or 561/468-3555. Fax 561/489-9848. 64 units. www.docksideinn.com. Winter $55 standard rooms, $69–$115 efficiencies. Off-season $42–$89 standard rooms and efficiencies. AE, DC, DISC, MC, V. From I-95, exit at 66A east to U.S. 1 north to Seaway Dr. **Amenities:** Outdoor heated pool; self-service laundry. *In room:* A/C, TV, minibar, higher-priced rooms have kitchenettes with coffeemaker.

Mellon Patch Inn ★★ *Finds* Opened in mid-1994 by innkeepers Andrea and Arthur Mellon, the Mellon Patch offers just four bright rooms in what looks like a single-family house. Each room has a large bathroom and sturdy soundproof walls, making it very quiet. The public living room is nicer than any of the small guest rooms. It's designed with a two-story vaulted ceiling, a fireplace, and lots of windows that overlook the Indian River. A gourmet breakfast that might include waffles topped with strawberries and pecans, chocolate-chip pancakes, or spinach soufflé is served here each morning. The best part is that there are free tennis courts and a public beach across the street. The inn is nonsmoking, and children aren't allowed.

3601 N. Fla. A1A, North Hutchinson Island, FL 34949. © **561/461-5231.** Fax 561/464-6463. www.sunet.net/mlnptch. 4 units. $85–$150 double year-round. Rates include breakfast. AE, DISC, MC, V. *In-room:* A/C, TV.

Villa Nina Island Inn ★★ *Finds* A more private option just down the road from the Mellon Patch is Villa Nina, in another simple but new home on the river's edge. Although it's more private, the silence is not nearly as heavy here as it is at the Mellon Patch. In fact, the atmosphere is rather cheery. Innkeepers Nina and Glenn live in the main house and have built rooms along the back, each with a private entrance and either a fully equipped kitchen or a kitchenette. Riverfront rooms are very homey, with comfortable beds and private baths. Enjoy breakfast poolside or delivered to your room (you may also opt out of breakfast for a $10 nightly savings). Smoking is not permitted.

On this stunning 8-acre property, you can find canoes and rowboats for river rides. A nearby shipwreck site makes for an excellent diving excursion.

The nearby **Sterling Casino Lines Cruise ship** welcomes Inn guests with free shuttle service from Vero Beach (© **800/ROLL-7-11**).

3851 North State Road A1A, North Hutchinson Island 34949. © and fax **561/467-8673.** www.villanina.com. 4 units. Winter $125–$195; off-season $105–$165. DISC, MC, V. **Amenities:** Outdoor heated pool; canoe and snorkel rental; bike rental; free laundry facilities. *In room:* A/C, TV, kitchen or kitchenette, minibar (in most rooms), fridge, coffeemaker.

WHERE TO DINE

There are a number of good seafood restaurants in the Fort Pierce and St. Lucie area, but it's also easy to drive to Stuart for more diverse dining options. See section 1 of this chapter for recommendations in Stuart.

MODERATE

Mangrove Mattie's ★★ SEAFOOD A rustic restaurant on the Fort Pierce Inlet, Mangrove Mattie's is the best place for outdoor dining, with its priceless location—right on the inlet, affording panoramic views of the Atlantic—and excellent fresh seafood. Weekday happy hours (4 to 7pm) are especially popular, thanks to the view and the free buffet.

1640 Seaway Dr., Fort Pierce. © **561/466-1044.** Main courses $11–$18. AE, DISC, MC, V. Daily 11:30am–10pm.

P.V. Martin's ★★ SEAFOOD/AMERICAN This relatively elegant eatery with an eclectic American menu is as funky as it gets in Fort Pierce. The wood floors, beamed ceilings, tiled tabletops, and rattan chairs would be nice any-where, but here diners enjoy them as they look out through floor-to-ceiling win-dows onto sweeping ocean vistas. At night the room is warmed by a huge central stone fireplace, and on weekends there's live entertainment in the adjacent bar. Surf 'n' turf dinners run the gamut from crab-stuffed shrimp and grouper baked with bananas and almonds to Brie- and asparagus-stuffed chicken breast and barbecued baby back ribs. An excellent selection of appetizers includes escargots in mushroom caps and a succulent fried soft-shell crab (available in season). Be sure to try the lively Sunday champagne brunch.

5150 North State Road A1A, North Hutchinson Island. (© 561/569-0700. Reservations recommended. Main courses $9–$20. AE, MC, V. Mon–Sat 5–9pm, Sun 10:30am–2:30pm and 5–8:30pm.

Theo Thudpucker's Raw Bar and Seafood Restaurant 𝄪 SEAFOOD Located in a little building by the beach and wallpapered with maps and news-papers, Thudpucker's is a straightforward chowder bar. There's not much more to the dining room than one long bar and a few simple tables. Prominently placed signs attest to the food's purity: *Both clams and oysters are packed with ice and are not opened until you place your order. Please be patient.* Chowder and stews, often made with sherry and half-and-half, make excellent starters or light meals. The most recommendable (and filling) dinner dishes are sautéed scallops, deviled crabs, and deep-fried Okeechobee catfish.

2025 Seaway Dr., Fort Pierce. (© 561/465-1078. Reservations not accepted. Main courses $8–$24. MC, V. Mon–Thurs 11:30am–9:30pm, Fri–Sat 11:30am–11pm, Sun 1–9:30pm.

PORT ST. LUCIE & FORT PIERCE AFTER DARK

ArtWalk, a monthly event to showcase the downtown galleries, restaurants, and shops of Fort Pierce, takes place the second Wednesday of every month from 5 to 8pm and costs $5 per person, beginning in front of downtown's Sunrise Theater (© 561/466-3880). The **Friday Fest Street Festival** occurs on the first Friday of every month at the Historic Downtown Riverfront in Fort Pierce and is free of charge, featuring live music and refreshments for sale. The **St. Lucie Blues Club,** 338 Port St. Lucie Blvd. (© 561/873-1111), features live jazz, blues, and rock music Tuesday through Sunday nights. Reservations are recommended.

3 Vero Beach 𝄪 & Sebastian 𝄪𝄪

85 miles SE of Orlando, 130 miles N. of Miami

Old Florida is thriving in these remote and tranquil villages. Vero Beach, known for its exclusive and affluent winter population, and Sebastian, known as one of the last remaining fishing villages, are located at the northern tip of the Treasure Coast region in Indian River County. These two beach towns are populated with folks who knew Miami and Fort Lauderdale in the days before massive high-rises and overcrowding. They appreciate the area's small-town feel, and that's exactly the area's appeal for visitors: a laid-back, relaxed atmosphere, friendly people, and friendlier prices.

A crowd of well-tanned surfers from all over the state descends on the region, especially the Sebastian Inlet, to catch some of the state's biggest waves. Other water-sports enthusiasts enjoy the area's fine diving and windsurfing. Anglers are in heaven here. In spring, baseball buffs can catch some action from the L.A. Dodgers as they train in exhibition games.

ESSENTIALS

The **Indian River County Tourist Council,** 1216 21st St., Vero Beach, FL 32961 (© **561/567-3491;** fax 561/778-3181; www.vero-beach.fl.us/chamber), will send visitors an incredibly detailed information packet on the entire county, which includes Vero Beach and Sebastian and Fellsmere.

BEACHES & OUTDOOR ACTIVITIES

BEACHES You'll find plenty of free and open beachfront along the coast. Most beaches are uncrowded and are open from 7am until 10pm.

South Beach Park, on South Ocean Drive, at the end of Marigold Lane, is a busy, developed, lifeguarded beach with picnic tables, restrooms, and showers. It's known as one of the best swimming beaches and also attracts a young crowd that plays volleyball and Frisbee. A nicely laid-out nature walk takes you into beautiful secluded trails.

At the very north tip of the island, **Sebastian Inlet** ⋆ has flat sandy beaches with lots of facilities, including kayak, paddleboat, and canoe rentals; a well-stocked surf shop; picnic tables; and a snack shop. The winds seem to stir up the surf with no jetty to stop their swells, to the delight of surfers and boarders, who get here early to catch the big waves. Campers enjoy fully equipped sites in a woody area. Admission to the Sebastian Inlet State Recreation Area, 9700 S. Fla. A1A, Melbourne, is $3.25 per car and $1 for those who walk or bike in.

FISHING Captain Jack Jackson works 7 days a week out of **Vero's Tackle and Sport-Shop,** 57–59 Royal Palm Point (© **561/567-6550**), taking anglers out on his 25-foot boat for private river excursions. Captain Jackson provides all the equipment. Half-day jaunts on the Indian River cost $250 for two people (the minimum required for a charter), tackle, rigs, and everything included; $50 extra for a third person. You can either bring your own food and drinks or purchase food from the shop.

Many other charters, guides, party boats, and tackle shops operate in this area. Consult your hotel for suggestions, or call the chamber of commerce (© **561/ 567-3491**) for a list of local operators.

GOLF Hard-core golfers insist that of the dozens of courses in the area, only a handful are worth their plot of grass.

Set on rolling hills with uncluttered views of sand dunes and sky, the **Sandridge Golf Club** (© **561/770-5000**), at 5300 73rd St., Vero Beach, offers two par-72 18-holers. The Dunes is a long course with rolling fairways, and the newer Lakes course has lots of water. Both charge $38, including a cart. Weekends cost $32 after 12 noon. There is a small snack bar selling beer and sandwiches. Reservations are recommended and are taken 2 days in advance.

Although less challenging, the **Sebastian Municipal Golf Course** (© **561/ 589-6800**), at 1010 E. Airport Dr., is a good 18-hole par-72. It's scenic, well maintained, and a relative bargain. Greens fees are $35.31 per player with a cart and about half that if you want to play 9 holes after 1:30pm.

SURFING See Sebastian Inlet details under "Beaches," above. Also, consider the beach north of the Barber Bridge (State Route 70), where waves are slightly gentler and the scene less competitive; and Wabasso Beach, Fla. A1A and County Road 510, a secluded area near Disney's resort where lots of teenage locals congregate, especially when the weather gets rough.

TENNIS There are dozens of tennis courts around Vero Beach and Sebastian, many of which are at hotels and resorts. Check the local phone book, or try

Riverside Racket Complex, 350 Dahlia Lane, at Royal Palm Boulevard at the east end of Barber Bridge in Vero Beach (℮ **561/231-4787**). This popular park has 10 hard courts (6 lighted) that can be rented for $3.21 per person per hour, and two racquetball courts also with reasonable rates. Reservations are accepted up to 24 hours in advance. Nature trails are also on the premises.

SEEING THE SIGHTS

Environmental Learning Center ★★ *Kids*   The Indian River is not really a river at all, but a large brackish lagoon that's home to a greater variety of species than any other estuary in North America. The privately funded Environmental Learning Center was created to protect the local habitat and educate visitors about their environment. Situated on 51 island acres, the center features a 600-foot boardwalk through the mangroves and dozens of hands-on exhibits that are geared to both children and adults. There are live touch-tanks, exhibits, and microscopes for viewing the smallest sea life up close. Join one of the center's interpretive canoe trips, offered by reservation only ($10 for adults, $5 for children).

255 Live Oak Dr. (just off the 510 Causeway), Wabasso Island. ℮ **561/589-5050**. www.elcweb.org. Free admission. Tues–Fri 10am–4pm, Sat 9am–noon, Sun 1–4pm.

Indian River Citrus Museum   You may as well be in a supermarket, really. The tiny Indian River Citrus Museum exhibits artifacts relating to the history of the citrus industry, from its initial boom in the late 1800s to the present; a small grove displays several varieties. The gift shop sells clever citrus-themed gift items, along with, of course, ready-to-ship fruit.

2140 14th Ave., Vero Beach. ℮ **561/770-2263**. Admission $1 donation. Tues–Fri 10am–4pm.

McKee Botanical Garden ★★   This impressive attraction was originally opened in 1932 and featured a virtual jungle of orchids, exotic and native trees, monkeys, and birds. After years of neglect, it was placed on the National Register of Historic Places in 1998. It underwent a top-to-bottom overhaul that was completed in February 2000, and you can now again experience the full charms of this little Eden.

350 U.S. 1, Vero Beach. ℮ **561/794-0601**. Fax 561/794-0602. www.mckeegarden.org. Admission $6 adults, $5 seniors, $3.50 children 5–12. Tues–Sat 10am–5pm, Sun noon–5pm.

McLarty Treasure Museum ★   If you're unconvinced about why this area's called the Treasure Coast, then this is a must see, along with Mel Fisher's Treasure Museum (see below). Erected on the actual site of a salvaging camp from a wreck in 1715, this quaint little museum is full of interesting history. It may not have the vast treasures of the nearby Fisher museum, but it does offer a very engaging 45-minute video describing the many aspects of treasure hunting. You'll also see household items salvaged from the Spanish fleet and dioramas of life in the 18th century. For the price, you can't beat it.

13180 N. Fla. A1A, Sebastian Inlet State Recreation Area, Vero Beach. ℮ **561/589-2147**. Admission $1; children under 6 free. Daily 10am–4:30pm.

Mel Fisher's Treasure Museum ★★★ *Finds*   This museum is truly priceless. Here's where you can see millions of dollars of treasures from the doomed Spanish fleet that went down in 1715. Although not as extensive as the museum in Key West, this exhibit includes gold coins, bars, and Spanish artifacts that are worth a look. Also, the preservation lab shows how the goods are extricated, cleaned, and preserved.

1322 U.S. 1, Sebastian. ℂ **561/589-9874.** www.melfisher.com. Admission $5 adults, $4 seniors over 55, $1.50 children 6–12, free for children 5 and under. Mon–Sat 10am–5pm, Sun noon–5pm.

DODGERTOWN

Vero is the winter home of the **Los Angeles Dodgers** (at least for the time being; there's been talk of a move), and the town hosts the team in grand style. The 450-acre compound at 3901 26th St. (ℂ **561/569-4900**) encompasses two golf courses, a conference center, a country club, a movie theater, and a recreation room. You can watch afternoon exhibition games during the winter (usually between mid-February and the end of March) in the comfortable 6,500-seat outdoor stadium. Even if the game sells out, you can sprawl on the lawn for just $5. The stadium has never turned away an eager fan.

Even when spring training is over, you can still catch a game; the Dodgers' farm team, the Vero Beach Dodgers, has a full season of minor-league baseball in summer.

Admission to the complex is free; tickets to games are $12 for a reserved seat. The complex is open daily from 9am to 5pm; game time is usually 1pm. From I-95, take exit for State Route 60 east to 43rd Avenue and turn left; continue to 26th Street and turn right.

SHOPPING

Ocean Boulevard and Cardinal Drive are Vero's two main shopping streets. Both are near the beach and lined with specialty boutiques, including antique and home-decorating shops.

If you want to send fruit back home, the local source is **Hale Indian River Groves,** 615 Beachland Blvd. (ℂ **561/231-1752**), a shipper of local citrus and jams since 1947. Note that it is closed 2 to 3 months a year, usually from summer through early fall, depending on the year's crop; the season generally runs from November through Easter. There are four locations in Vero Beach.

The **Horizon Outlet Center,** at State Route 60 and I-95, Vero Beach (ℂ **877/GO-OUTLET** or 561/770-6171), contains more than 80 discount stores selling name-brand shoes, kitchenware, books, clothing, and more. The mall is open Monday to Saturday from 9am to 8pm and Sunday from 11am to 6pm.

The **Indian River Mall** (ℂ **561/770-6255**), 6200 20th St. (State Route 60 about 5 miles east of I-95), is a big deal in Vero Beach. This monster mall has all the big national chains, such as the Gap, Structure, and Victoria's Secret, as well as several large department stores, and is open Monday through Saturday from 10am to 9pm and Sunday from noon to 6pm.

WHERE TO STAY

You can choose from accommodations on the mainland or on the beach. Although the beaches in many areas have eroded, leaving only narrow strips of sand, most areas offer pristine beachfronts where turtles lay eggs and sand crabs scurry around. As you might expect, the beachfront accommodations are a bit more expensive—but, I think, worth it. There are deals to be had in the chain hotels and some lovely privately owned properties, especially on weekdays and during off-season. Both **The Palm Court Inn** (ℂ **800/245-3297** or 561/ 231-2800), at 3244 Ocean Dr., and the **Holiday Inn Oceanside** (ℂ **800/ 465-4329** or 561/231-2300), at 3384 Ocean Dr., offer oceanfront rooms and suites at comparable prices (from around $80 for a standard room off-season to $185 for an oceanfront suite). The Holiday Inn may be a better choice since it offers discounts to AAA members and its restaurant and lounge directly face the ocean. The Palm Court (formerly a Days Inn) was thoroughly renovated in 1998. Also, a great spot to know, especially if you are planning to fish, is **Captain Hiram's** (see "Fishing," above, and also "Vero Beach & Sebastian After Dark," below), where there are four clean and cozy rooms available adjacent to the restaurant and overlooking the water. Rates are between $80 and $110.

Comfortable and inexpensive chain options near the Vero Beach Outlet Center off State Route 60 include a **Holiday Inn Express** (*C* **800/465-4329** or 561/567-2500), which opened in June 1998, and a slightly older **Hampton Inn** (*C* **800/426-7866** or 561/770-4299). Rates for both run between $70 and $80 and include breakfast and free local phone calls.

EXPENSIVE

Disney's Vero Beach Resort ★★★ (*Kids*)   Situated on the tip of 71 acres of pristine beaches, this Disney time-share resort is reminiscent of a turn-of-the-last-century Florida beach community. The resort takes advantage of its setting by offering exciting children's programs, such as canoe adventures, campfire tales, and stargazing from a powerful telescope. The best part is a large pool designed like a lagoon with a two-story winding slide. And, for younger kids, a pirate ship that squirts water is a fun way to cool off. Rooms are bright and spacious, many with balconies. The resort offers reservation-only Disney character breakfasts on select days and is less than 2 hours away from Walt Disney World. And unlike most prefab resorts in the hyperdeveloped Orlando area, Disney's Vero Beach Resort manages to successfully convey a sense of serenity without compromising the entertainment value.

9250 Island Grove Terrace, Vero Beach, FL 32963. *C* **800/359-8000** or 561/234-2000. Fax 561/234-2030. 112 units, 60 cottages. Winter from $290 ocean-view double, from $355 and way up for villas, from $920 cottages (sleep up to 12); off-season from $170 ocean-view double, from $239 villas. AE, MC, V. From I-95 take Exit 69 (512 going east); turn right onto County Rd. 510 heading east. Turn right again onto S. Fla. A1A. **Amenities:** 2 restaurants; bar; large pool; miniature golf; 2 lighted tennis courts; health club; Jacuzzi; sauna; water-sports equipment/rental; extensive children's programs; game room and sports areas; tour desk; concierge; business center; room service, baby-sitting; laundry and dry-cleaning services. *In room:* A/C, TV.

Doubletree Guest Suites ★   This chain is conveniently located directly on the beach and is close to local restaurants and shops. First-class suites are located in a modern four-story building. The guest rooms are unremarkable, but clean and attractive. Bathrooms are spacious, and most suites overlook the pool or the ocean.

3500 Ocean Dr., Vero Beach, FL 32963. *C* **800/841-5666** or 561/231-5666. Fax 561/234-4866. 55 units. Winter $235–$265 1-bedroom suite; off-season $125–$185 1-bedroom suite. AE, DC, DISC, MC, V. **Amenities:** Restaurant; bar; outdoor heated pool; kids' pool; access to nearby health club; Jacuzzi; room service; laundry and dry-cleaning services or coin-op washers and dryers. *In room:* A/C, TV, fridge, coffeemaker, hair dryer.

MODERATE

Driftwood Resort ★★ (*Finds*)   Originally planned in the 1930s as a private estate by eccentric entrepreneur Waldo Sexton, the Driftwood was opened to the public after several travelers stopped by to inquire about renting a room here. Today the hotel's rooms and public areas are filled with the nautical knickknacks collected by Sexton on his travels all over the world. All of the guest rooms were renovated in 2000, and each is unique. Some feature terra-cotta–tiled floors and lighter furniture, while others have a more rustic feel with hardwoods and antiques. Some of the rooms contain Jacuzzis, and all are equipped with full kitchens. The resort is listed on the National Register of Historic Places and, to say the least, has lots of quirky charm.

3150 Ocean Dr., Vero Beach, FL 32963. ✆ **561/231-0550.** Fax 561/234-1981. www.thedriftwood.com. 100 units. Winter $110–$180 double; off-season $75–$130 double. AE, MC, V. **Amenities:** 2 outdoor heated pools; dry-cleaning service. *In room:* A/C, TV, coffeemaker, kitchen (in most 1- and 2-bedroom units), Jacuzzi in some rooms.

Islander Inn 🌟 Resident owner Tom Collins runs one of the most comfortable and welcoming inns in the area. Well located in downtown Vero Beach, this small Key West–style motel is just a short walk to the beach, restaurants, and shops. Every guest room has a small refrigerator and either a king-size bed or two double beds. The accommodations are designed in a Caribbean motif with bright fabrics and white rattan furniture.

3101 Ocean Dr., Vero Beach, FL 32963. ✆ **800/952-5886** or 561/231-4431. 16 units. Winter $105–$120 double; off-season $72–$99 double. Efficiencies cost $10 extra. AE, MC, V. **Amenities:** Cafe; pool. *In room:* A/C, TV.

INEXPENSIVE

Davis House Inn 🌟🌟 Each of the dozen rooms in this contemporary three-story, blue-and-white B&B has a private entrance. The rooms are large and clean, although somewhat plain, and each has a king-size bed, a pull-out sofa, and a small kitchenette, making the rooms popular with long-term guests. The bathrooms are equally ample and have plenty of counter space. Guests will find a large wooden deck for sunbathing and a sunny second-floor breakfast room. The inn is a bit out of the way but is within walking distance to some nearby restaurants; the beach is a 10-minute drive.

607 Davis St., Sebastian, FL 32958. ✆ **561/589-4114.** Fax 561/589-1722. 12 units. Winter $69–$79 double; off-season $59–$79 double. Rates include continental breakfast. Nightly rooms are unavailable in February. Weekly and monthly rates available. AE, DISC, MC, V. From I-95, take Exit 69, heading east to Indian River Dr. and turn left. Go 1¼ miles to Davis St.; turn left. **Amenities:** Coin-op washers and dryers. *In room:* A/C, TV.

Sea Turtle Inn & Azalea Lane Apartments 🌟 This two-part property offers the very best value on the beach (just 2 blocks from the ocean). The 1950s motel and an adjacent apartment building have been fully renovated and outfitted with understated but efficient furnishings. You won't find any fancy amenities (or even a phone for that matter, unless you request one), but its price and beachfront location make up for what it lacks in frills. The properties share a small pool and sundeck. Book early, especially in season.

835 Azalea Lane, Vero Beach, FL 32963. ✆ **561/234-0788.** Fax 561/234-0717. www.vero-beach.fl.us/ seaturtle. 21 units. Winter $69–$99 double; off-season $54–$79 double. Weekly and monthly rates available. MC, V. From I-95, go east on S.R. 60 (about 10 miles) to Cardinal Dr.; turn right. **Amenities:** Small pool. *In room:* A/C, TV, fridge, coffeemaker.

CAMPING

This area is popular with campers, who can choose from nearly a dozen sites throughout Vero and Sebastian. If you aren't camping at the scenic and very popular Sebastian Inlet (see "Beaches," earlier in this chapter), then try the **Vero Beach KOA RV Park,** 8850 U.S. 1, Wabasso (✆ **561/589-5665**). This 120-site campground is 2 miles from the ocean and the Intracoastal Waterway and a quarter-mile from the Indian River, a big draw for the crowd of regular fishing fanatics. There's access to running water and electricity, as well as showers, a shop, and hookups for RVs. Rates range from $20 to $24 per site, and $19 for tents. To get there, take I-95 to Exit 69 east; at U.S. 1 turn left.

WHERE TO DINE
EXPENSIVE

Chez Yannick ★★★ FRENCH/CONTINENTAL   Excellent cooking, a comprehensive wine list, and white-glove service complement the crystal and gilded decor at this French standout. Excellent starters include a succulent sliced duckling breast, cream of lobster soup, and hearts-of-palm salad with a slightly spicy vinaigrette. Some items, like lobster and shrimp in a cognac-dill sauce, are available as either an appetizer or an entree. Other main courses include beef tenderloin stuffed with Gorgonzola cheese and sautéed soft-shell crabs. Desserts might include profiteroles with ice cream and chocolate or raspberry sauce, crème caramel, chocolate-mousse pie, or raspberry sorbet.

1605 S. Ocean Dr., Vero Beach. © **561/234-4115.** Reservations recommended. Main courses $15–$30; fixed-price dinner $19–$21 is available in the off-season. AE, MC, V. Mon–Sat open at 6pm; closing time varies based on last reservation.

MODERATE

Black Pearl Brasserie and Grill ★★ CONTINENTAL   This sophisticated brasserie seems out of place in this beachy town, but it happens to be one of Vero Beach's trendiest spots. The restaurant's small list of appetizers includes salads, chilled sweet-potato vichyssoise, crispy fried chicken fingers with mango dipping sauce, and grilled oysters with tangy barbecue sauce. Equally creative main courses are uniformly good. Don't miss their signature dish, an onion-crusted mahimahi with caramel citrus glaze. Both this original, unassuming restaurant and its newer counterpart, The **Black Pearl Riverfront,** at 4445 N. Fla. A1A (© **561/234-4426**), serve fantastically fresh *and* inventive food. The riverfront location is more formal and serves only dinner from 5pm.

2855 Ocean Dr., Vero Beach. © **561/234-4426.** Fax 561/234-9074. Reservations recommended. Main courses $12–$21. AE, DC, DISC, MC, V. Mon–Sun 11:30am–10pm, Sun brunch 10:30am–2pm.

Ocean Grill ★★ *(Finds* AMERICAN   The Ocean Grill is an institution that attracts locals and faithful devotees with its simple but rich cooking and its stunning locale, right on the ocean's edge. For a dramatic experience, ask for a table along the wall of windows that open onto the sea. This huge and handsome old-timer specializes in steaks and seafood, and dinners are uniformly good. Try stone crab claws when they are in season or any of the big servings of pasta or meats. Try the house shrimp scampi baked in butter and herbs and served with a tangy mustard sauce. The only tacky element of this place is the gift shop.

1050 Sexton Plaza (by the ocean at the end of S.R. 60), Vero Beach. © **561/231-5409.** Reservations only for large parties. Main courses $17–$30. AE, DC, DISC, MC, V. Mon–Fri 11:30am–2:30pm and 5:30–10pm, Sat–Sun 5:30–10pm.

INEXPENSIVE

Beachside Restaurant at the Palm Court Resort ★ AMERICAN/DINER
For a great big, cheap American breakfast with an ocean view, this is the place to go. You can get omelets, home fries, cream chipped beef, corn beef hash, pancakes, Belgian waffles, and even grits. Friendly waitresses also serve lunch and dinner in the comfy wooden booths. The best dishes, like chili, fried chicken, and steaks, are hearty and delicious. No smoking.

3244 Ocean Dr., Vero Beach. © **561/234-4477.** Breakfast $2–$5; dinner $8.95 and up. AE, DC, DISC, MC, V. Mon–Sat 6am–2:30pm, happy hour 4–6pm, dinner 5–9pm, Sun 6am–1:30pm.

Nino's Cafe ★ ITALIAN   This little beachside cafe looks like a stereotypical pizza joint, complete with murals of the Italian countryside and red-and-white checked tablecloths. The atmosphere is pure cheese and so is much of the food. Pizza and parmigiana dishes are smothered in the stuff. Still, the thin crust and fresh toppings make the pizza here a cut above the rest. Entrees and pastas are also tasty, thanks to a tangy and rich homemade sauce.

1006 Easter Lily Lane (off Ocean Dr., next to Humiston Park), Vero Beach. ✆ 561/231-9311. Main courses $8.50–$11.95. No credit cards. Mon–Thurs 11am–9pm, Fri–Sat 11am–10pm, Sun 4–9pm.

VERO BEACH & SEBASTIAN AFTER DARK

More than half the residents in this area are retirees, so it shouldn't be a surprise that even on weekends, this town retires relatively early. Still, there are a few popular spots, in addition to the many hotel lounges, that have live music and a good bar scene, especially in high season. For beachside drinks, go to the Driftwood Resort. See "Where to Stay," above.

A mostly 30-something and younger crowd goes to **Bombay Louie's** in Vero Beach, at 398 21st St. (✆ **561/978-0209**), where a DJ spins dance music after 9pm from Wednesday to Saturday. Vero Beach is also known as an artsy enclave, hosting galleries such as **The Art Works,** 2855 Ocean Dr., Vero Beach (✆ **561/ 231-4688)** and the **Bottalico Gallery,** 3121 Ocean Dr., Vero Beach (✆ **561/ 231-0414). The Civic Arts Center** at Riverside Park is a hub of culture, including the Riverside Theatre (✆ **561/231-6990**), the Agnes Wahlstrom Youth Playhouse (✆ **561/234-8052**), and the Center for the Arts (✆ **561/231-0707**), known for films and an excellent lecture series.

In Sebastian, you'll find live music every weekend (and daily in season) at **Captain Hiram's,** 1606 N. Indian River Dr. (✆ **561/589-4345**), a salty outdoor restaurant and bar on the Intracoastal Waterway. The feel is tacky Key West, complete with a sand floor and thatched-roof bar that locals and tourists love at all hours of the day and night.

North of the inlet, head for the tried-and-true **Sebastian Beach Inn** (or SBI to locals), 7035 S. Fla. A1A (✆ **321/728-4311**), for live music on the weekends. Jazz, blues, or sometimes rock 'n' roll starts at 9pm on Friday and Saturday. On Sunday, it's old-style reggae after 2pm. The inn is open daily for drinks from 11am until anywhere from midnight to 2am.

4 A Side Trip Inland: Fishing at Lake Okeechobee ⟨★⟨★⟨★

60 miles SW of West Palm Beach

Many visitors to the Treasure Coast come to fish, and they certainly get their fill of it off the miles of Atlantic shore and on the inland rivers. But if you want to fish freshwater and nothing else, head for "The Lake"—**Lake Okeechobee,** that is. The state's largest, it's chock-full of good eating fish. Only about a 1½-hour drive from the coast, it makes a great day or weekend excursion.

Two things happen in the area surrounding Lake Okeechobee: sugar production and fishing. The area, which actually encompasses five counties, is known as the bass-fishing and winter-vegetable capital of the state.

Okeechobee comes from the Seminole Indian word for "big water"—and big it is. The lake covers more than 467,000 acres; that's more than 730 square miles. At one time, the lake supported an enormous commercial fishing industry. Due to a commercial fishing-net ban, much of that industry has died off, leaving to the sportfishers all the rich bounty of the lake.

As you approach the lake area, you'll notice a large levy surrounding its circumference. This was built after two major hurricanes, including one in 1947 that killed hundreds of area residents and cattle. In an effort to control future flooding, the Army Corps of Engineers, which had already built a cross-state waterway, constructed a series of locks and dams. The region is now safe from the threat of floods, but the ecological results of the flood control have not been as positive. The bird and wildlife population suffered dramatically, as did the southern portion of the Everglades, which relied on the down flow of water from the lake to replenish and clean the entire ecosystem. In early 2001, 30,000 acres of the lake's bottom caught fire due to a severe drought or, some say, arson. Drought had reduced the lake's depth to below 11 feet, provoking officials to impose water restrictions. Surprisingly, however, experts say the fire was beneficial for the lake. High water levels had previously prevented fire, which is a part of the natural cycle of the lake, and surrounding torpedo grass threatened to take over the marshes where native fish tend to swim. The fire brought with it the hope that now that the grass has been burned, the fish and the native plants will return to the lake.

Another threat to the region is posed by the area's largest employer, U.S. Sugar, which owns most of the land around Belle Glade and Clewiston, "America's Sweetest Town."

Still, the area retains its rural charm and boasts the best bass fishing in the state.

ESSENTIALS

GETTING THERE The best route is to take I-95 south to Southern Boulevard (U.S. 98 west) in West Palm Beach, which merges with State Route 80 and State Route 441. Follow signs for State Route 80 west through Belle Glade to South Bay. In South Bay, turn right onto U.S. 27 north, which leads directly to Clewiston.

VISITOR INFORMATION Contact the **Clewiston Chamber of Commerce,** 544 W. Sugarland Hwy., Clewiston, FL 33440 (© **863/983-7979;** www.clewiston.org), for maps, business directories, and the names of numerous fishing guides throughout the area. In addition, you might contact the **Pahokee Chamber of Commerce,** 115 E. Main St., Pahokee, FL 33476 (© **561/924-5579;** fax 561/924-8116; www.pelinet.net/pahokee); they'll send a complete package of magazines, guides, and accommodations listings.

For an excellent map and a brief history of the area, contact the **U.S. Army Corps of Engineers,** Natural Resources Office, 525 Ridgelawn Rd., Clewiston, FL 33440 (© **863/983-8101;** fax 863/983-8579). It is open weekdays from 8am to 4:30pm.

OUTDOOR PURSUITS

FISHING See the "Going After the Big One," box.

SKY DIVING Besides fishing, the biggest sport in Clewiston is jumping out of planes. Because of the limited air traffic and vast areas of flat undeveloped land, this area attracts novice and expert sky divers alike. **Air Adventures** (© **800/533-6151** or 863/983-6151) operates a year-round program from the Airglades Airport. If you've never jumped before, you can go on a tandem dive, which means, as the name implies, you'll be attached to a "jumpmaster." For the first 60 seconds, the two of you free-fall, from about 12,500 feet. Then, a quick pull of the chute turns your rapid descent into a gentle, balletic cruise to the ground, with time to see the whole majestic lake from a privileged perspective. Dive packages start at $165; group rates start at $150.

Going After the Big One

Fishing on Lake Okeechobee is a year-round affair, though the fish tend to bite a little better in the winter, perhaps for the benefit of the many snowbirds that flock here (especially in February and March). RV camps are mobbed with fish-frenzied anglers who come down for weeks at a time for a decent catch.

You'll need a fishing license to go out with a rod and reel. It's a simple matter to apply. The chamber of commerce and most fishing shops can sign you up on the spot. The cost for non-Florida residents for 7 days is $16.50 and $31.50 for the year.

You can rent, charter, or bring your own boat to Clewiston; just be sure to schedule your trip in advance. You don't want to show up during one of the frequent fishing tournaments only to find you can't get a room, campsite, or fishing boat.

There are, of course, more than a few marinas where you can rent or charter boats. If it's your first time on the lake, I suggest chartering a boat with a guide who can show you the lake's most fertile spots and handle your tackle while you drink a beer and get some sun. **Roland Martin,** 920 E. Del Monte (*©* 863/ 983-3151), is the one-stop spot where you can find a guide, boat, tackle, rods, bait, coolers, picnic supplies, and a choice of boats. Rates, including the boat, start at $175 for a half day. A full day costs $250 and includes all necessary equipment except bait. You'll need a license for this, too, which Roland Martin also sells. They also have boat rentals: A 16-foot johnboat is $40 for half a day and $60 for a full day with a $40 deposit. A 26-foot pontoon is $125 for a full day and $85 for half a day with a $50 deposit.

Another reputable boat-rental spot is **Angler's Marina,** 910 Okeechobee Blvd. (*©* 800/741-3141 or 863/983-BASS). Rentals for a 14-footer start at $40 for a half day, for a maximum of four people. A full day is $60. If you want a guide, rates start at $150 (for two people) for a half day, though in the summer (June to October), when it's slow, you can usually get a cheaper deal.

WHERE TO STAY

If you aren't camping, book a room at the **Clewiston Inn** ⭐⭐, 108 Royal Palm Ave., Clewiston (*©* **800/749-4466** or 863/983-8151). Built in 1938 by U.S. Sugar to house executives and visitors, this Southern plantation–inspired hotel is the oldest in the Lake Okeechobee region. It still hosts sugar executives and visiting sportfishers in its 52 simply decorated, nondescript, Holiday Inn–style rooms. The lounge area sports a 1945 mural depicting the animals of the region. Double rooms start at $99 a night; suites begin at $129. All have air-conditioning and TVs.

Another choice, especially if you're here to fish, is **Roland Martin,** 920 E. Del Monte (*©* **800/473-6766** or 863/983-3151), the "Disney of fishing." This RV park offers modest motel rooms, efficiencies, condominiums, apartments, or campsites, with two heated pools, gift and marina shops, and a restaurant. The modern complex, dotted with prefab buildings painted in white and gray, is clean and well manicured. Rooms rent for $68 and efficiencies cost $88. Condominiums are about $150 a night with a 3-night minimum. RV sites are about $25 with TV and cable hookup.

CAMPING

During the winter, campers own the Clewiston area. Campsites are jammed with regulars, who come year after year for the simple pleasures of the lake and, of course, the warm weather. Every manner of RV, from simple pop-top Volkswagens to Winnebagos to fully decked-out mobile homes, finds its way to the many campsites along the lake. Also, see Roland Martin, above.

Okeechobee Landings, U.S. 27 east (© **863/983-4144**), is one of the best; it has every conceivable amenity included in the price of a site. More than 250 sites are situated around a small lake, clubhouse, snack bar, pool, Jacuzzi, horseshoe pit, shuffleboard court, and tennis court. Full hookup includes a sewage connection, which is not the case throughout the county. RV spots are sold to regulars. But there are usually some spots available for rental to one-time visitors. Rates start at $24.50 a day or $150 weekly plus tax, including hookup. Year-round rates for trailer rentals, which sleep two people, start at $32 from Sunday to Thursday and from $37 on Friday and Saturday.

WHERE TO DINE

If you aren't frying up your own catch for dinner, you can find a number of good eating spots in town. At the **Clewiston Inn** (see "Where to Stay," above), you can get catfish, beef stroganoff, ham hocks, fried chicken, and liver and onions in a setting as Southern as the food. The dining room is open daily from 6am to 2pm and 5 to 9pm, and entrees cost $9 to $18.

10

Southwest Florida

by Bill Goodwin

Thanks to a citizenry that has fought to protect both its history and its present-day environment, the southwest corner of Florida is one of the best parts of the state in which to discover remnants of Old Florida and enjoy the great outdoors.

Bordered on the east by the wild, wonderful Everglades and on the west by an intriguing island-studded coast, Southwest Florida traces its nature-loving roots to inventor and amateur botanist Thomas A. Edison, who was so enamored of it that he spent his last 46 winters in Fort Myers. His friend Henry Ford liked it, too, and built his own winter home next door. The world's best tarpon fishing lured President Teddy Roosevelt and his buddies to the 10,000 or so islands dotting this coast. Some of the planet's best shelling helped entice the du Ponts of Delaware to Gasparilla Island, where they founded the Nantucket-like village of Boca Grande. The unspoiled beauty of Sanibel and Captiva so entranced Pulitzer Prize–winning political cartoonist J. N. "Ding" Darling that he campaigned to preserve many of those islands in their natural states. And the millionaires who built Naples enacted tough zoning laws that to this day make their town one of the most alluring in Florida.

Southwest Florida International Airport, on the eastern outskirts of Fort Myers, is this region's major airport (see "Essentials," in section 1, below). From here it's only 20 miles to Sanibel Island, 35 miles to Naples, or 46 miles to Marco Island. If you have a car, you can see the area's sights and participate in most of its activities easily from one base of operations.

EXCURSIONS TO THE EVERGLADES & KEY WEST You won't be in Southwest Florida for long before you see advertisements for excursions to the Everglades. Naples is only 36 miles from Everglades City, the "back door" to wild and wonderful Everglades National Park, so it's easy to combine a visit to the national park with your stay in Southwest Florida. See chapter 7 for full details about the Everglades.

You also can easily make a day trip to Key West from here by air or sea. **Cape Air** (© 800/352-0714; www.flycapeair.com) shuttles its small planes several times a day between Key West and both Southwest Florida International Airport and Naples Municipal Airport. The same-day round-trip is about $170.

The **Key West Shuttle** (© 888/539-2628 or 941/732-7744; www.keywestshuttle.com) runs boats to Key West from both Fort Myers Beach and Naples; the **Key West Express** (© 800/273-4496 or 941/765-0808; www.keywestshuttle.com) operates from Fort Myers Beach; and the **Key West Water Express** (© 800/650-5397 or 941/394-0014; www.keywestwaterexpress.com) departs from Marco Island. The boats run daily from November through May, departing in the morning, arriving in Key West about midday, and beginning

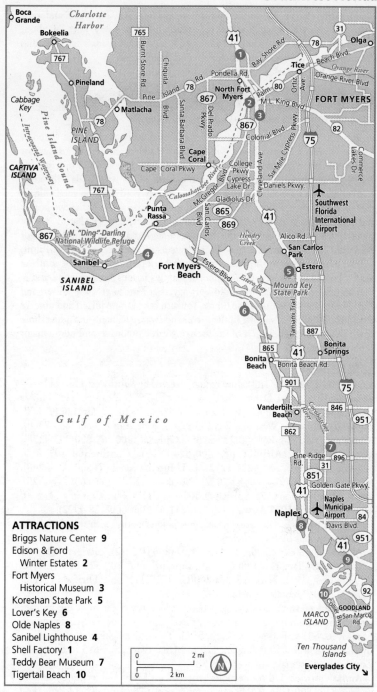

Southwest Florida

Boca Grande
Charlotte Harbor
Bokeelia
765
41
1
31
78
Olga
Beach Blvd.
Tice
80
Orange River
Orange River Blvd.
FORT MYERS
Pineland
Pine Island
78
Pondella Rd.
North Fort Myers
867
Palm
Ortiz Ave.
Cabbage Key
867
Matlacha
Del Prado Pkwy
2
M.L. King Blvd.
78
Burnt Store Rd.
Chiquita Blvd.
3
867
Santa Barbara Blvd
Colonial Blvd.
82
75
PINE ISLAND
Commerce Lakes Dr.
CAPTIVA ISLAND
767
Pine Island Sound
Intracoastal Waterway
Cape Coral
College Pkwy
Cypress Lake Dr.
Cleveland Ave.
Six Mile Cypress Pkwy.
Daniels Pkwy.
Southwest Florida International Airport
Cape Coral Pkwy.
Caloosahatchee River
McGregor Blvd.
Gladiolus Dr.
865
41
Punta Rassa
San Carlos Blvd.
869
Hendry Creek
Alico Rd.
San Carlos Park
867
J.N. "Ding" Darling National Wildlife Refuge
4
Sanibel
Fort Myers Beach
Estero Blvd.
Estero Bay
Estero
5
Mound Key State Park
SANIBEL ISLAND
6
Tamiami Trail
887
865
Bonita Springs
41
Bonita Beach
Bonita Beach Rd.
75
901
Imperial River
846
951
Vanderbilt Beach
862
7
896
Gulf of Mexico
Pine Ridge Rd.
31
851
Golden Gate Pkwy.
41
Naples Municipal Airport
84
Naples
8
Davis Blvd.
951
41
9
92
10
GOODLAND
MARCO ISLAND
San Marco Rd.
Collier Blvd.
Ten Thousand Islands
Everglades City

0   2 mi
0   2 km
N

their return voyages by about 5pm. That will give you about 5 hours in Key West, so you may want to stay there overnight in order to more thoroughly explore the town. Round-trip fare is about $120 for adults, and most places offer one-way fares of about $65. Contact the boats for schedules and reservations.

1 Fort Myers

148 miles NW of Miami, 142 miles S. of Tampa, 42 miles N. of Naples

It's difficult to picture this pleasant city of broad avenues along the Caloosahatchee River as a raucous cow town, but that's exactly what Fort Myers was just a few years before inventor Thomas Alva Edison came here in 1885 to regain his health after years of incessant toil and the death of his wife. Today, the city's prime attractions are the homes Edison and Henry Ford built on the banks of the Caloosahatchee. Edison planted lush tropical gardens around the two homes and royal palms in front of the properties along McGregor Boulevard, once a cow trail leading from town to the docks at Punta Rassa. Now lining McGregor Boulevard for miles, the trees give Fort Myers its nickname: The City of Palms.

Like most visitors to the area, you'll probably opt to stay near the sands at nearby Fort Myers Beach or on Sanibel or Captiva Islands (see sections 2 and 3, later in this chapter), but drive into Fort Myers at least to visit the Edison and Ford homes and have a riverside lunch. You also can venture inland and observe incredible numbers of wildlife in their river and swamp habitats, including those at the Babcock Ranch, largest of the surviving cattle producers and now a major game preserve.

ESSENTIALS

GETTING THERE   This entire region is served by **Southwest Florida International Airport,** on Daniels Parkway east of I-75. You can get here on **Air Canada** (© 800/776-3000), **Air Transat** (© 800/470-1011), **AirTran** (© 800/247-8726), **America West** (© 800/235-9292), **American** (© 800/433-7300), **American Trans Air** (© 800/225-2995), **Canada 3000** (© 800/993-4378), **Condor German Airlines** (© 800/524-6975), **Continental** (© 800/525-0280), **Delta** (© 800/221-1212), **LTU International** (© 800/888-0200), **Midwest Express** (© 800/452-2022), **Northwest/KLM** (© 800/225-2525), **Royal** (© 800/667-7692), **Spirit** (© 800/772-7117), **Sun Country** (© 800/359-5786), **United/US Airways** (© 800/241-6522 or 800/428-4322).

The two baggage-claim areas have information booths (with maps) and free phones to various hotels in the region.

Alamo (© 800/327-9633), **Avis** (© 800/331-1212), **Budget** (© 800/527-0700), **Dollar** (© 800/800-4000), **Enterprise** (© 800/325-8007), **Hertz** (© 800/654-3131), **National** (© 800/CAR-RENT), and **Thrifty** (© 800/367-2277) have rental cars here.

Vans and taxis are available at a booth across the street from the baggage claim. The maximum fares for one to three passengers are $24 to downtown Fort Myers, $35 to Fort Myers Beach, $37 to $44 to Sanibel Island, $56 to Captiva Island, $38 to $56 to Naples, $70 to Marco Island, and $85 to Everglades City. Each additional passenger pays $8.

Amtrak provides bus connections between Fort Myers and its nearest station, in Tampa (© **800/USA-RAIL;** www.amtrak.com). The Amtrak buses arrive and depart the **Greyhound/Trailways** bus station, 2275 Cleveland Ave. (© **800/231-2222;** www.greyhound.com).

VISITOR INFORMATION For advance information about Fort Myers, Fort Myers Beach, and Sanibel and Captiva Islands, contact the **Lee Island Coast Visitor and Convention Bureau,** 2180 W. First St., Suite 100, Fort Myers, FL 33901 (© **800/237-6444** or 941/338-3500; fax 941/334-1106; www.leeislandcoast.com).

Volunteers staff information booths in the baggage-claim areas at Southwest Florida International Airport.

The **Greater Fort Myers Chamber of Commerce** (© **800/366-3622** from outside Florida, or 941/332-3624; fax 941/332-7276; www.fortmyers.org) has walk-in visitor centers at the corner of Edwards Drive and Lee Street on the downtown waterfront and in the Daniels Crossing shopping center at the corner of Daniels Parkway and Six Mile Cypress Parkway. The chamber gives away brochures and other information and sells a detailed street map of the area. The centers are open Monday to Friday from 8am to 4:30pm.

There's also an information booth at the Edison and Ford Winter Estates (see "Exploring the Area," below).

The **North Fort Myers Chamber of Commerce** (© **941/997-9111**) has an information office at 2787 N. Tamiami Trail (U.S. 41) in the Shell Factory (see "Shopping," below).

GETTING AROUND LeeTran (© **941/275-8726**) operates public buses. System maps are available from the Greater Fort Myers Chamber of Commerce (see "Visitor Information," above). There's no public bus service to Sanibel and Captiva Islands.

For a taxi, call **Yellow Cab** (© **941/332-1055**), **Bluebird Taxi** (© **941/275-8294**), or **Admiralty Taxi** (© **941/275-7000**). Metered fares are $1.35 at flag fall, plus $1.35 for each mile.

EXPLORING THE AREA
TOURING THE ESTATES

Edison and Ford Winter Estates ✹✹ Thomas Edison and his second wife, Mina, brought their family to this Victorian retreat—they called it Seminole Lodge—in 1886 and wintered here until the inventor's death in 1931. Mrs. Edison gave the 14-acre estate to the city of Fort Myers in 1947, and today it's Southwest Florida's stop historic attraction. In fact, it looks exactly as it did during Edison's lifetime. Costumed actors portraying the Edisons, the Fords, and their friends such as Harvey Firestone give "living history" accounts of how the wealthy lived in those days.

An avid amateur botanist, Edison experimented with the exotic foliage he planted in the lush tropical gardens surrounding the mansion (he turned goldenrod into rubber and used bamboo for light-bulb filaments). Some of his light bulbs dating from the 1920s still burn in the laboratory where he and his staff worked on some of his 1,093 inventions. The monstrous banyan tree that shades the laboratory was 4 feet tall when Harvey S. Firestone presented it to Edison in 1925; today it's the largest banyan in Florida. A museum displays some of Edison's inventions, as well as his unique Model-T Ford, a gift from friend Henry Ford. In 1916 Ford and his wife, Clara, built **Mangoes,** their bungalow-style house next door, so they could winter with the Edisons. Like Seminole Lodge, Mangoes is furnished as it appeared in the 1920s.

Allow an extra hour here to take a scenic ride on the river in a replica of Edison's electric boat *Reliance.*

Fort Myers

2350 McGregor Blvd. ℭ **941/334-3614** for a recording, or 941/334-7419. www.edison-ford-estate.com. Winter admission $12 adults, $5.50 children 6–12, free for children 5 and under. Off-season $11 adults, $5.50 children 6–12, free for children 5 and under. Boat rides $4 per person. Homes open Mon–Sat 9am–4pm, Sun noon–4pm (1½-hr. tours of both homes depart continuously). Boat rides Mon–Fri 9am–3pm (weather permitting). Closed Thanksgiving, Christmas Eve, and Christmas Day.

OTHER DOWNTOWN ATTRACTIONS

A good way to explore downtown Fort Myers during the winter season is on a leisurely, 2-hour guided walking tour hosted by the **Fort Myers Historical Museum,** 2300 Peck St., at Jackson Street (ℭ **941/332-5955**). The tours are held on Wednesday from 10am to noon and cost $5 a head. Reservations are required.

The historical museum itself is housed in the restored Spanish-style depot served by the Atlantic Coast Line from 1924 to 1971. Inside you'll see exhibits depicting the city's history from the ancient Calusa peoples and the Spanish conquistadors to the first settlers, including the remains of a P-39 Aircobra, which helps explain the town's role in training fighter pilots in World War II. Outside stands a replica of an 1800s "cracker" home and the Esperanza, the longest and one of the last of the plush Pullman private cars. Admission is $6 for adults, $5.50 for seniors, $3 for children 3 to 12, free for kids under 3. Open Tuesday to Saturday from 9am to 4pm.

The Georgian Revival **Burroughs Home,** 2505 1st St., at Fowler Street (ℭ **941/332-6125**), was built on the banks of the Caloosahatchee River in 1901 by cattleman John Murphy and later sold to the Burroughs family. You must take a 30-minute tour; they usually are given from November to June, Tuesday to Friday, on the hour from 11am to 3pm and by appointment off-season, but call ahead any time of year. Admission is $6 for adults, $3 for children 3 to 12, free for children under 3. You can park free in the Ramada Inn & Suites at Amtel Marina garage across the street (see "Where to Stay," later in this chapter).

Rather than have the kids go stir-crazy on a rainy day, head for the **Imaginarium,** 2000 Cranford Ave., at Martin Luther King Jr. Boulevard (© **941/ 337-3332**), a hands-on museum in the old city water plant. A host of toylike exhibits explains such basic scientific principles as gravity and the weather. Admission is $6 for adults, $5.50 for seniors, $3 for children 3 to 12. Open Tuesday to Saturday from 10am to 5pm, Sunday noon to 5pm. Closed Thanksgiving and Christmas.

A NEARBY HISTORICAL ATTRACTION

Koreshan State Historic Site   Worth a 15-mile drive south of downtown Fort Myers if you're into canoeing or quirky gurus, these 300 acres on the narrow Estero River were home to the Koreshan Unity Movement (pronounced Ko-*RESH*-en), a sect led by Chicagoan Cyrus Reed Teed. The Koreshans, who believed that humans lived *inside* the earth and—ahead of their time—that women should have equal rights, established a self-sufficient settlement here in 1894. You can visit their garden and several of their buildings, plus view photos from their archives. Canoeists will find marked trails winding down the slow-flowing river to **Mound Key,** an islet made of the shells discarded by the Calusa Indians (see "Canoeing & Kayaking" under "Enjoying the Outdoors," below). There's also a picnic and camping area with 60 wooded sites for tents or RVs. For information, contact the park superintendent at P.O. Box 7, Estero, FL 33928.

U.S. 41 at Corkscrew Rd., Estero (15 miles south of downtown Fort Myers). © 941/992-0311. www8. myflorida.com/communities/learn/stateparks/district4/koreshan. Admission $3.25 per vehicle, $1 pedestrians or bikers; tours $1 adults, 50¢ children. Canoes $3 an hour, $15 per day. Camping, winter $16; off-season $10. Park daily 8am–sunset; settlement buildings daily 8am–5pm; 1-hr. tours Sat–Sun 1pm. From I-75, take Corkscrew Rd. (Exit 19), go 2 miles west, and cross U.S. 41 into site.

AN OLD-FASHIONED TRAIN RIDE

The **Seminole Gulf Railway** (© **941/275-8487;** www.semgulf.com), the original railroad that ran between Fort Myers and Naples, today chugs on dinner excursions and sightseeing trips south to Bonita Springs and north across the river, and there's an occasional twilight and murder-mystery run. Call for the seasonal schedule and for reservations, which are required for the dinner trip. The trains depart Fort Myers from the Amtel Fleamarket Mall Station, a small blue building on the western edge of the mall's parking lot on Colonial Boulevard at Metro Parkway. The Bonita Springs station is on Old U.S. 41 at Pennsylvania Avenue.

SHOPPING

A kitschy tourist attraction, **The Shell Factory,** 5 miles north of the Caloosahatchee River bridge on U.S. 41 (© **888/4-SHELLS** or 941/995-2141; www.shellfactory.com), not only carries one of the world's largest collections of shells, corals, sponges, and fossils, but also has bumper boat rides, a light show, a gallery of African art, a small zoo, and two restaurants. Inside the store, entire sections are devoted to shell jewelry and shell lamps, and many items here cost under $10, some under $1. Open daily from 10am to 6pm.

"Buggy" Rides Through a Mysterious Swamp

One of the easiest and most informative ways to see Southwest Florida's abundant wildlife is on a "swamp buggy" ride with **Babcock Wilderness Adventures** ⭐⭐, 8000 S.R. 31, Punta Gorda, about 11 miles northeast of Fort Myers (© 800/500-5583 or 941/338-6367; www. babcockwilderness.com). Experienced naturalists lead 90-minute tours through the Babcock Ranch, the largest contiguous cattle operation east of the Mississippi River and home to countless birds and wildlife as well as domesticated bison and quarter horses. Unlike most wildlife tours in the region, this one covers five different ecosystems, from open prairie to cypress swamp. Admission is $17.95 for adults, $9.95 for children 3 to 12. The tours usually leave on the hour between 9am and 3pm from November to April, from 9am to noon from May through October. Reservations are required, so call ahead. Three-hour off-road bicycle tours cost $35 for adults, $30 for children 10 to 14. Reservations are required at least 3 days in advance.

Bargain hunters can browse more than 800 booths carrying antiques, crafts, fashions, and produce at **Fleamasters,** 4135 Dr. Martin Luther King Jr. Blvd. (Fla. 82), 1½ miles west of I-75 (© 941/334-7001). Open Friday through Sunday from 8am to 4pm. Anchored by Saks Fifth Avenue and Jacobson's, the Spanish-style **Bell Tower Shops,** Tamiami Trail (U.S. 41) at Daniels Parkway (© 941/489-1221), is Fort Myers's upscale mall. You'll find most of the familiar national stores at **Edison Mall,** Cleveland Avenue (U.S. 41) at Winkler Avenue (© 941/939-5464).

Outlet shoppers will find a large Levi's store among other major-brand shops at the **Sanibel Tanger Factory Stores,** on the way to the beaches at the junction of Summerlin Road and McGregor Boulevard (© 888/SHOP-333 or 941/454-1616). Another Levi's store, plus Brooks Brothers, Donna Karan, Dockers, Fila, Nike, Reebok, Maidenform, Nautica, OshKosh B'Gosh, and many more stores are at the much larger **Miromar Outlets,** on Corkscrew Road at I-75 in Estero (© 941/948-3766), about halfway between Fort Myers and Naples. Both outlet malls are open Monday to Saturday from 10am to 9pm, Sunday from 11am to 6pm.

ENJOYING THE OUTDOORS

CANOEING & KAYAKING   The area's slow-moving rivers and quiet, island-speckled inland waters offer fine canoe and kayak ventures; you'll visit birds and manatees along the way. Two popular local venues are the winding waterways around Pine Island west of town and the Estero River south of Fort Myers. The Estero River route is an official Florida canoe trail and leads 3½ miles from U.S. 41 to Estero Bay, which is itself a state aquatic preserve (see the introduction to section 2). Near the mouth of the river lies **Mound Key State Archeological Site,** one of the largest Calusa shell middens. Scholars believe that this mostly artificial island dates back some 2,000 years and was the capital of the Calusa chief who ruled all of South Florida when the Spanish arrived. There's no park ranger on the key, but signs explain its history.

Koreshan State Historic Site, half a mile south of the bridge at the intersection of U.S. 41 and Corkscrew Road (© **941/992-0311**), rents canoes (see "A Nearby Historical Attraction," above). Less than a mile from the site, **Estero River Tackle & Canoe Outfitters,** 20991 S. Tamiami Trail (U.S. 41), Estero, at the Estero River bridge (© **941/992-4050;** www.all-florida.com/swestero.htm), has guided historic and nature tours (call for schedule and prices) and rents canoes and kayaks at prices ranging from $17.50 to $27.50 a day. Open daily 7am to 6pm.

In addition to its cruises mentioned below, the *Tropic Star,* based at Knight's Landing marina, 16499 Porto Bello in Bokeelia on Pine Island (© **941/283-0015**), rents kayaks and has guided tours over 18 miles of paddling trails. Rentals cost $35 a day for single seaters, $45 for doubles. Call for schedule and prices of guided tours. The company also has a ferry service to Cayo Costa State Park, where it rents kayaks (see "Nearby Island Hopping," in section 30).

CRUISES   J. C. Boat Cruises (© **941/334-7474**) presents a variety of year-round cruises on the Caloosahatchee River and its tributaries, including lunch and dinner voyages on the sternwheeler *Captain J. P.* The 3-hour Everglades Jungle Cruise is a good way to observe the area's wildlife, with lots of manatees to be seen from November to April. A full-day cruise goes all the way up the Caloosahatchee to Lake Okeechobee and back. The ticket office is at the downtown Fort Myers City Yacht Basin, Edwards Drive at Lee Street, opposite the chamber of commerce. Prices range from $12 to $75 for adults. Schedules change and advance reservations are required.

The *Tropic Star* (© **941/283-0015**) leaves Knight's Landing marina, 16499 Porto Bello in Bokeelia on Pine Island, daily at 9:30am on all-day nature cruises on Pine Island Sound. Cruises include a stop at Cayo Costa and Cabbage Key and cost $25 for adults, $15 for kids under 12. The company also runs a daily ferry from Pine Island to Cayo Costa State Park. Fares are $20 for adults, $15 for children 3 to 12. Call for departure times. See "Nearby Island Hopping," in section 3, on Sanibel and Captiva Islands, for information about Cabbage Key and Cayo Costa.

The sleek, 100-foot-long yacht *Sanibel Harbour Princess* (© **941/644-2128**) goes on sunset dinner cruises from its base at Sanibel Harbour Resort & Spa (see "Where to Stay," below). Dinner cruises range from about $40 for adults, $25 for children, depending on the season. A Sunday brunch cruise during winter costs $22 for adults, $15 for children. Call ahead for departure times and reservations.

GOLF & TENNIS   For an excellent rundown of Southwest Florida golf courses, pick up a free copy of *Golfer's Guide,* available at the visitor information centers and many hotel lobbies, or on the Internet at www.golfersguide.com. See "The Active Vacation Planner," in chapter 2, for information about subscribing or ordering the current edition. And don't forget that you can call **Tee Times USA** (© **800/374-8633** or 888/465-3356) and book starting times at Florida courses.

Although it looks like an exclusive private enclave, the **Fort Myers Country Club,** McGregor Boulevard at Hill Avenue (© **941/936-2457**), actually is a municipal course. Designed in 1917 by Donald Ross, it's flat and uninteresting by today's standards, but it's right in town. A steak-and-seafood restaurant now occupies the fine old clubhouse. The city's other municipal course is the more challenging **Eastwood Golf Club,** on Ortiz Avenue between Colonial

Boulevard and Dr. Martin Luther King Jr. Boulevard in the eastern suburbs (© 941/ 275-4848). Greens fees at both range from about $30 in summer to $55 during winter. Nonresidents must book tee times at least 24 hours in advance.

Other area courses open to the public include the Tom Fazio–designed **Gateway Golf & Country Club,** on Daniels Parkway east of the airport (© 941/ 561-1010); the two nationally acclaimed **Pelican's Nest** courses in Bonita Springs (© 941/947-4600); **Coral Oaks Golf Club** in Cape Coral (© 941/ 283-4800); **Alden Pines Country Club** on Pine Island (© 941/283-2179); **San Carlos Golf Club** in South Fort Myers (© 941/267-3131); **Bonita Springs Golf & Country Club** in Bonita Springs (© 941/992-2800); and **El Rio Golf Club** (© 941/995-2204) and **Riverbend Golf Club** (© 941/ 543-2200), both in North Fort Myers.

Tennis buffs can play at the **Fort Myers Racquet Club,** 4900 Deleon St. (© 941/278-7277), which has eight lighted courts. **Sanibel Harbour Resort & Spa** is well known for its excellent tennis programs for both juniors and adults (see "Where to Stay," below).

SPECTATOR SPORTS While many Major League baseball teams have jumped around Florida for their **spring training,** the Boston Red Sox and the Minnesota Twins have worked out in Fort Myers for years. The **Boston Red Sox** play at the 6,500-seat City of Palms Park, at Edison Avenue and Broadway (© 877/733-7699 or 941/334-4799; www.redsox.com). The **Minnesota Twins** work out at the 7,500-seat William Hammond Stadium in the Lee County Sports Complex on Six Mile Cypress Parkway between Daniels Parkway and Metro Parkway (© 800/338-9467 or 941/768-4200; www.twinsbaseball.com). The Twins minor league affiliate, the **Fort Myers Miracle** (© 941/768-4210; www.miraclebaseball.com), play in the stadium from April through August.

Fort Myers is about an hour's drive south of Charlotte County Stadium (© 941/625-9500), where the **Texas Rangers** hold their spring training. To get there, take I-75 north to Exit 31 and go south on Kings Highway (Fla. 769); then take an immediate right on Veterans Boulevard (Fla. 776) to the stadium on the left.

The **Florida Everblades** (© 941/948-7825) play minor league professional hockey at TECO Arena, at Exit 19 off I-75 in Estero.

WHERE TO STAY

As in the rest of Southern Florida, room rates here are highest, and reservations essential, during winter, from mid-December to April. Even the chain hotels and motels along U.S. 41 in Fort Myers—most brands are represented along this busy thoroughfare—charge premium rates then. During the off-season, they drop by as much as 50% or more.

If you can't get a room at the properties mentioned below, the **Lee Island Coast Visitor and Convention Bureau** operates a free reservation service (© 800/733-7935) covering many more accommodations in Fort Myers, Fort Myers Beach, and Sanibel and Captiva Islands.

A few blocks from the Edison and Ford homes, Jim Haas's **The Li-Inn Sleeps Bed & Breakfast,** 2135 McGregor Blvd., at Clifford Street (© 941/332-2651; fax 941/332-8922; www.cyberstreet.com/users/li-inn/li-inn.html), has five comfortable rooms, all with private bathroom, in a charming wooden house built a century ago in North Fort Myers. The building was later split in two, floated across the river, and nailed back together. Almost twice the size of the others,

"Therese" is the choice unit here. Rates range from $95 to $150 in winter, $65 to $85 off-season, including full breakfast.

The 25-story, 416-unit **Ramada Inn & Suites at Amtel Marina,** 2500 Edwards Dr., at Fowler Street (*©* **800/833-1620** or 941/337-0300; fax 941/ 337-1530), is downtown Fort Myers's only large hotel. It's adequate but needs renovation. Rates range from $90 to $130 double in winter, less off-season.

All hotel bills in Southwest Florida are subject to a 9% tax.

The only true campground near here is at **Koreshan State Historic Site** (see "Exploring the Area," earlier in this chapter).

VERY EXPENSIVE

Sanibel Harbour Resort & Spa 🦆🦆 This secluded, sports-oriented resort overlooks San Carlos Bay and Sanibel Island from Punta Rassa, next to the Sanibel Causeway (a complimentary shuttle takes guests to the island's beaches and to a bike-rental shop three times a day). A waterside cupola-topped pavilion evokes the turn-of-the-century resort that once stood on this point, but the 11-story main hotel (240 rooms) and the boutique-style **Inn at Sanibel Harbour** (107 rooms) nearby are both modern and luxurious throughout. All of the hotel rooms and most of the condominium apartments have wonderful water and island views from their balconies, including spectacular sunsets over Sanibel. A large attractive pool and sunning complex sits by the water, but don't be disappointed by the quality of the beach here-this is the bay and not the Gulf, after all, so stay over on the islands if a great beach is among your top priorities. But if tennis is your game, the resort has 13 lighted courts and a 5,000-seat stadium that has hosted Davis Cup matches.

17260 Harbour Pointe Rd., Fort Myers, FL 33908. *©* **800/767-7777** or 941/466-4000. Fax 941/466-2150. www.sanibel-resort.com. 417 units, including 70 condo apts. Winter $279–$369 double; $329–$419 suite; $449–$609 condo apt. Off-season $149–$279 double; $199–$329 suite; $229–$399 condo apt. $10 per unit per day resort benefits fee. Packages available. AE, DC, DISC, MC, V. Valet parking $10; free self-parking. Take the last exit off Summerlin Rd. before the Sanibel Causeway toll plaza. **Amenities:** 5 restaurants; 2 bars; 6 heated outdoor pools; 13 tennis courts; health club & spa; water-sports equipment/rentals; concierge; activities desk; business center; 24-hr. room service; laundry and dry cleaning service. *In room:* A/C, TV, kitchen (condos only), minibar (main building only), fridge, coffeemaker, hair dryer, iron.

MODERATE

Baymont Inn & Suites Like most members of this small chain, this modern, four-story establishment offers good value with relatively large rooms equipped with many extras, including easy chairs and large desks. It is centrally situated near the Courtyard by Marriott (see below). Rooms are entered from exterior walkways, so there are no balconies or patios. Your pet can stay with you here for an additional fee. The hotel's one suite has a full kitchen.

2717 Colonial Blvd., Fort Myers, FL 33907. *©* **800/301-0200** or 941/275-3500. Fax 941/275-5426. www. baymontinn.com. 123 units. Winter $116 double; off-season $76–$95 double. Rates include continental breakfast and local phone calls. AE, DC, DISC, MC, V. Pets accepted ($25 fee). **Amenities:** Outdoor pool. *In room:* A/C, TV, coffeemaker, hair dryer, iron.

Courtyard by Marriott 🦆 This member of the exceptionally comfortable hotel chain designed for business travelers is situated 4 miles south of downtown and 10 miles north of the beach. The hotel is surrounded by a landscaped courtyard with swimming pool. The marble lobby features a fireplace and dining area serving breakfast only. The sizable rooms all have patios or balconies, sofas or easy chairs, and rich mahogany writing tables and chests of drawers.

4455 Metro Pkwy. (at the corner of Colonial Blvd.), Fort Myers, FL 33901. ℂ **800/321-2211** or 941/
275-8600. Fax 941/275-7087. 149 units. Winter $119–$149 double; off-season $84 double. Weekend rates
available. AE, DC, DISC, MC, V. **Amenities:** Heated outdoor pool; exercise room with whirlpool; coin-op washers and dryers. *In room:* A/C, TV, dataport, coffeemaker, hair dryer, iron.

Holiday Inn Riverwalk & Marina   This islandlike riverside hotel is best
known locally for the adjacent Shooters Waterfront Cafe USA, a popular restaurant and bar (see "Where to Dine," below). Some of the suites are near the outdoor bar where Shooters' bands play-which can mean a bit too much
entertainment for some guests' ears (others love the constant nighttime action).
Rooms at the front of the property, however, are far enough removed to render
a quiet and convenient base from which to explore the nearby Edison and Ford
Winter Estates and other downtown attractions.

2220 W. 1st St. (at Euclid Ave.), Fort Myers, FL 33901. ℂ **800/HOLIDAY** or 941/334-3434. Fax 941/334-3844.
146 units. Winter $139–$189 double; off-season $69–$109 double. AE, DC, DISC, MC, V. **Amenities:** Restaurant, bar, outdoor adult and children's pools, activities desk, salon with massage, limited room service, reading room, guest laundry. *In room:* A/C, TV, coffeemaker, refrigerator, hair dryer, iron.

Quality Inn Historic District   Many business travelers stay at this art deco,
coral-and-aqua motel, whose location near the corner of Edison Avenue is a plus
for vacationers too; it's a 2-block walk to the Boston Red Sox training facility
and a short drive to the Edison and Ford homes. Minor league hopefuls stay here
during baseball spring training, so you could meet a future major-leaguer. The
property has been around since the 1970s, but renovations have brought it up
to modern standards. You'll have to do without a patio or balcony, but the rooms
are a bit larger than normal for a Quality Inn motel. Guests on the more expensive, restricted-entry top floor have microwave ovens and refrigerators in their
rooms, and they get complimentary breakfasts on weekdays.

2431 Cleveland Ave. (U.S. 41), Fort Myers, FL 33901. ℂ **800/998-0466** or 941/332-3232. Fax 941/332-0590.
126 units. Winter $129–$250 double; off-season $79–$99 double. AE, DC, DISC, MC, V. **Amenities:** Restaurant (American); bar; unheated outdoor pool; limited room service; coin-op washers and dryers; concierge-
level rooms. *In room:* A/C, TV, coffeemaker, hair dryer, iron.

INEXPENSIVE

Fairfield Inn By Marriott *(Value*   About halfway between downtown and the
beaches, this 1999-vintage Marriott property is one of the best budget choices
here. Although it's right in the middle of the U.S. 41 action—many chain
restaurants and stores are within an easy walk—it sits far enough from the highway to escape the noise. Although sparsely equipped, the rooms are spacious and
have writing desks and easy chairs.

7090 Cypress Terrace (off U.S. 41 a block south of Daniels Pkwy.), Fort Myers, FL 33907. ℂ **800/228-2800**
or 941/437-5600. Fax 941/437-5616. 104 units. Winter $79–$119 double; off-season $64 double. Rates
include continental breakfast and local phone calls. AE, DC, DISC, MC, V. **Amenities:** Heated outdoor pool;
whirlpool; exercise room. *In room:* A/C, TV.

WHERE TO DINE

Fort Myers' main commercial strip, Cleveland Avenue (U.S. 41), has most
national fast-food and family chain restaurants, especially near College Parkway.

EXPENSIVE

Peter's La Cuisine ⋆⋆ CREATIVE CONTINENTAL   Even other restaura-
teurs say Bavarian-born chef Peter Schmid's establishment, in downtown's sec-
ond-oldest building, is their favorite place for fine dining. Peter's seasonally

changing menus offer a creative spin to continental preparations of quail, veal, steaks, racks of lamb, salmon, and fresh local seafood, fruits, and vegetables. Tuxedoed waiters provide efficient and unobtrusive service in the refined first-floor dining room, where everything's strictly a la carte (be careful if you're on a budget). At the Upstairs Bar & Bistro, Peter's casual, lively, supper club, a few main courses such as the wonderful salmon with a light champagne sauce are half-price. There's nightly entertainment in the bistro, and you can wander up to the rooftop Sky Bar, whose view makes it one of the town's favorite watering holes.

2224 Bay St. (at Bayview Court). © **941/332-2228.** Reservations recommended. Main courses $28–$37; upstairs bistro $7–$20. AE, MC, V. Mon–Fri 11:30am–2pm and 5:30–9:30pm; Sat–Sun 5:30–9:30pm. Upstairs bistro Mon–Fri 4pm–2am; Sat–Sun 5:30pm–2am.

MODERATE

Sasse il Pizzaiuolo ★★ *Finds* CONTINENTAL/ITALIAN   In a small shopping strip north of the Edison Mall, Michael and Karen Gavala's popular spot offers one of the area's most unusual and reasonably priced dining experiences. Aromas waft from Michael's wood-fired oven in the open kitchen, from which come enormous slabs of pizzalike bread (served with seasoned olive oil for dipping). The selections change daily, although you can usually count on braised lamb shank served over polenta, and veal scaloppini stuffed with prosciutto, roasted peppers, and mozzarella. It's all of a quality rarely found at these prices, and the portions are so huge that most patrons carry home doggie bags.

3651 Evans Ave., in Carrell Corner shopping center (between Carrell Rd. and Winkler Ave.). © **941/278-5544.** Reservations not accepted. Main courses $8–$18. No credit cards. Tues–Fri 11:30am–1:15pm; Wed–Sat 5:30–8:15pm.

Shooters Waterfront Cafe USA ★ AMERICAN   Granted, this pub turns into one of Fort Myers' most popular drinking-and-meeting spots after dark on weekends. But its sliding-glass walls open to a riverside deck, making this the most attractive place in town for taking a relaxing, alfresco lunch break while seeing the sights or for watching the sun set over the Caloosahatchee. The cuisine is typically modern pub fare: a variety of pizzas, California-style pastas, grilled fish, seafood platters, steaks, and prime rib. The best bet for lunch is the reliable fried, blackened, or grilled grouper sandwich.

At Holiday Inn Riverwalk & Marina, 2220 W. First St. (at Euclid Ave.). © **941/334-2727.** Reservations accepted. Main courses $10–$19.50; salads and sandwiches $7–$10; Sun brunch $15 adults, $6 children under 11. AE, DC, DISC, MC, V. Daily 7am–10pm (bar open later); Sun brunch 10am–2pm.

INEXPENSIVE

Farmers Market Restaurant ★★ *Finds* SOUTHERN   Cabbage, okra, green beans, and tomatoes at the retail Farmers Market next door provide the fodder for some of the best country-style cooking in Florida at this plain and simple restaurant frequented by everyone from business executives to truck drivers. Specialties are beef and pork barbecue from the tin smokehouse out by Edison Avenue, plus other Southern favorites like country-fried steak, fried chicken livers and gizzards, and smoked ham hocks with a bowl of lima beans. Yankees can order fried chicken, roast beef, or pork chops, and they can have hash browns instead of grits with their big breakfast. No alcohol is served, nor is smoking permitted.

2736 Edison Ave. (at Cranford Ave.) © **941/334-1687.** Breakfast $3–$6; sandwiches $2.50–$6; meals $7.50. No credit cards. Mon–Sat 6am–8pm; Sun 6am–7pm.

Oasis Restaurant AMERICAN   A fine place for breakfast before touring the nearby Edison and Ford homes, Bonnie Grunberg and Tammie Shockey's narrow storefront spot also appeals to local professionals who don't mind sitting elbow to elbow while recovering from a night at Shooters Waterfront Cafe USA (just behind this shopping center) with a "hangover" omelet chock full of bacon, cheese, peppers, tomatoes, and onions.

In Edison-Ford Sq., 2222 McGregor Blvd. (at Euclid Ave.) © **941/334-1566**. Breakfast $3–$6; sandwiches, burgers, and salads $4–$6. No credit cards. Mon–Fri 7am–3pm; Sat–Sun 8am–2pm.

FORT MYERS AFTER DARK

For entertainment ideas and schedules, consult the daily *News-Press* (www.news-press.com), especially Friday's "Gulf Coasting" section. Also be on the lookout for *Happenings,* a tabloid-size entertainment guide distributed free at the visitor information offices and in some hotel lobbies. Tickets for most events are available from **Ticketmaster** (© **941/334-3309**).

The city's showcase performing-arts venue is the $7 million **Barbara B. Mann Performing Arts Hall** ✦, 8099 College Pkwy., at Summerlin Road (© **800/440-7469** or 941/481-4849 for tickets; www.bbmannpah.com), on the campus of Edison Community College. It features world-famous performers, Broadway plays, and wintertime concerts by the **Gulf Coast Symphony** (© **941/472-6197**; www.gulfcoastsymphony.net).

Originally a downtown vaudeville playhouse, the 1908-vintage **Arcade Theater,** 2267 1st St., between Bay and Hendry streets (© **941/332-6688**), presents a variety of performances.

Leading the bar scene, **Shooters Waterfront Cafe USA,** at the Holiday Inn Riverwalk & Marina, 2220 W. 1st St. (© **941/334-2727**), has live bands or a DJ spinning most nights at a riverside "chickee hut," a thatched-roof bar. Musicians occasionally perform in the casual **Upstairs Bar & Bistro** above Peter's La Cuisine, 2224 Bay St. (© **941/332-2228**). Peter's rooftop Sky Bar is another popular local place to meet, especially on weekends. See "Where to Dine," above, for more about these two establishments.

2 Fort Myers Beach ✦✦

13 miles S. of Fort Myers, 28 miles N. of Naples, 12 miles E. of Sanibel Island

Often overshadowed by trendy Sanibel and Captiva Islands to the north and ritzy Naples to the south, down-to-earth Fort Myers Beach, which occupies all of skinny Estero Island, offers just as much sun and sand as its affluent neighbors, both a half-hour drive away, but at more moderate prices.

Droves of families and young singles flock to the busy intersection of San Carlos Boulevard and Estero Boulevard, an area so packed with bars, beach-apparel shops, restaurants, and motels that the locals call it "Times Square." That Coney Island image certainly doesn't apply to the rest of Estero Island, where old-fashioned beach cottages, manicured condominiums, and quiet motels beckon couples and families in search of more sedate vacations. In fact, promoters of the southern end of the island say that they're not in Fort Myers Beach; they're on Estero Island. It's their way of distinguishing their part of town from congested Times Square.

Narrow Matanzas Pass leads into broad Estero Bay, which separates the island from the mainland. While the pass is the area's largest commercial fishing port (when they say "fresh off the boat" here, they aren't kidding), the bay

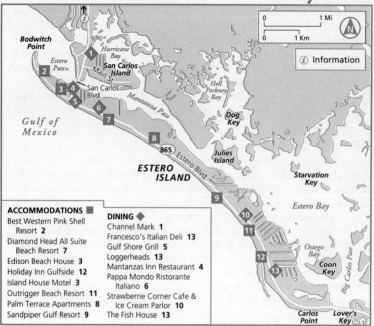

ACCOMMODATIONS ■

Best Western Pink Shell
    Resort **2**
Diamond Head All Suite
    Beach Resort **7**
Edison Beach House **3**
Holiday Inn Gulfside **12**
Island House Motel **3**
Outrigger Beach Resort **11**
Palm Terrace Apartments **8**
Sandpiper Gulf Resort **9**

DINING ◆

Channel Mark **1**
Francesco's Italian Deli **13**
Gulf Shore Grill **5**
Loggerheads **13**
Mantanzas Inn Restaurant **4**
Pappa Mondo Ristorante
    Italiano **6**
Strawberrie Corner Cafe &
    Ice Cream Parlor **10**
The Fish House **13**

is an official state aquatic preserve inhabited by a host of birds as well as manatees, dolphins, and other sea life. Nature cruises go forth onto this lovely protected bay, which is dotted with islands.

A few miles south of Fort Myers Beach, a chain of pristine barrier islands includes unspoiled **Lover's Key,** a state park where a tractor-pulled tram runs through a mangrove forest to one of Florida's best beaches.

ESSENTIALS

GETTING THERE   See section 1 on Fort Myers, earlier in this chapter, for information about Southwest Florida International Airport, car-rental firms, Amtrak's trains, and Greyhound/Trailways bus service to the area.

VISITOR INFORMATION   You can get advance information from the Lee Island Coast Visitor and Convention Bureau (see "Essentials," in section 1, earlier in this chapter) and from the **Fort Myers Beach Chamber of Commerce,** 17200 San Carlos Blvd., Fort Myers Beach, FL 33931 (© **800/782-9283** or 941/454-7500; fax 941/454-7910; www.fmbchamber.com), which provides free information, sells a detailed street map for $2, and operates a visitor welcome center on the mainland portion of San Carlos Boulevard just south of Summerlin Road. The chamber is open Monday to Friday from 8am to 5pm, Saturday from 10am to 5pm, Sunday from 11am to 5pm.

GETTING AROUND   An alternative to heavy wintertime traffic and limited parking is the **Beach Connection Trolley,** which during winter operates daily from 8am to 8pm between Summerlin Square Shopping Center, at Summerlin Road and San Carlos Boulevard on the mainland, and Bonita Beach. The route takes it along the full length of Estero Boulevard, including Lover's Key. During the off-season, it runs from Bowditch Regional Park at the north end of Estero

Boulevard south to Lover's Key. It costs 25¢ per ride. Ask your hotel staff or call **LeeTran** (© **941/275-8726**) for schedules.

For a cab, call **Local Motion Taxi** (© **941/463-4111**).

There are no bike paths per se here, although many folks ride along the paved shoulders of Estero Boulevard. A variety of rental bikes, scooters, and in-line skates are available at **Fun Rentals,** 1901 Estero Blvd. at Ohio Avenue (© **941/ 463-8844**), and **Scooters, Inc.,** 1698 Estero Blvd. at Avenue E (© **941/ 463-1007**). Charges start at $40 a day for one-passenger scooters, $14 a day for bikes.

HITTING THE BEACH

A prime attraction for both beachgoers and nature lovers is the gorgeous **Lover's Key State Park** ★★★, 8700 Estero Blvd. (© **941/463-4588;** www8.myflorida. com/communities/learn/stateparks/district4/loverskey), on the totally preserved Lover's Key, south of Estero Island. Although the highway runs down the center of the island, access to this unspoiled beach from the parking lot is restricted to footpaths or a tractor-pulled tram through a bird-filled forest of mangroves. The beach itself is known for its multitude of shells. There are bathhouses with outdoor showers, and a snack shop. The park is open daily from 8am to sunset. Admission is $4 per vehicle with two to eight occupants, $2 for vehicles with a single occupant, and $1 for pedestrians and bicyclists. No alcohol is allowed, nor are pets permitted on the beach or in the water (you must keep them on a leash elsewhere in the park). A branch of Tarpon Bay Recreation on Sanibel Island (see section 3, below), **Kayak Shack** (© **941/765-1880;** www.loverskey.net) provides kayak and canoe rentals for $20 a half day, $35 for a full day, and bicycles for $5 for a half day, $10 a day. Kayak Shack also offers 2- and 3-hour guided paddling tours to Mound Key and the back bays, starting at $25 (reservations are essential).

On Estero Island, **Lynn Hall Memorial Park** features a fishing pier and beach in the middle of Times Square. It has changing rooms, restrooms, and one of the few public parking lots in the area; the meter costs 75¢ per hour, but keep it fed—there's a $32 fine if your time runs out. At the island's north end, **Bowditch Regional Park** has picnic tables, cold-water showers, and changing rooms. It has parking only for drivers with disabilities permits, but it's the turn-around point for the Beach Connection Trolley.

Several beach locations are hotbeds of parasailing, jet skis, sailboats, and other beach activities. **Times Square,** at the intersection of San Carlos Boulevard and Estero Boulevard, and the **Best Western Beach Resort,** about ¼ mile north, are popular spots on Estero's busy north end. Other hotbeds are **Diamond Head All Suite Beach Resort** (see "Where to Stay," below), just south of Times Square, and the **Junkanoo Beach Bar** in the middle beach area (see "Where to Dine," later in this chapter). Down south, activities are centered at the **Holiday Inn** and the **Outrigger Beach Resort** (see "Where to Stay," below).

ENJOYING THE OUTDOORS

BOATING & BOAT RENTALS Powerboats are available from the **Mid Island Marina** (© 941/765-4371), the **Fort Myers Beach Marina** (© 941/ 463-9552), the **Fish Tale Marina** (© 941/463-3600), the **Palm Grove Marina** (© 941/463-7333), and the **Summer Winds Marina** (© 941/454-6333). **Dockside Boat Rentals** (© 941/765-4433) rents them at the Best Western Pink Shell Beach Resort on Estero Island's northern end. Boats cost about $125 for half a day, $200 for a full day.

CRUISES   Two of the most detailed nature tours in this area are conducted by **Calusa Coast Outfitters,** 7225 Estero Blvd., at the Fish Tale Marina behind Villa Santini shopping center (© 941/463-4448; www.calusacoast.com). Guests who go with Arden Arrington, a director of the Southwest Florida Historical Society, can listen through hydrophones as dolphins "speak" to each other, or they can go on a guided walk on historic Mound Key, the old Calusa Indian shell island at the mouth of the Estero River. The 3-hour dolphin tours cost $25 for adults, $20 for seniors, $14 for kids under 13. The Mound Key trips can be exhaustive, in both the amount of information and the physical exertion required, so they are not recommended for children, adults with health problems, or anyone without a reasonably serious interest in archaeology and history. They cost $25 for adults. Reservations are required for all trips, so call ahead.

Another way to see the dolphins up close is on a 1½-hour jet ski tour with **CRS Beach Service,** which operates on the beach at the foot of Avenue C (© 941/463-3509). The rides cost $75 for one person, $85 for two, and free for a third rider. Call for details and reservations.

Much easier nature excursions take place on the *Island Princess* (© 941/765-4433, ext. 246), a pontoon boat based at the Best Western Pink Shell Beach Resort marina on the north end of the island (see "Where to Stay," below). The boat usually goes on 1½-hour nature cruises Monday, Wednesday, and Friday afternoons. Prices are $12.50 for adults, $7 for children. The *Island Princess* also has bay fishing trips Monday, Wednesday, and Friday mornings ($25 adults, $22.50 children) and shelling trips on Thursday ($25 adults, $12 children). Reservations are recommended.

Docked at Snug Harbor under the Estero Island end of the Sky Bridge, the steel-hulled, 70-foot-long *Gulf Breeze* (© 941/572-3555 or 941/936-9300) goes on daytime and sunset nature cruises on the gulf and the backwaters. The trips depart at 10:30am and 1 hour before sunset, daily from December to April, Wednesday to Sunday off-season. Fare is $25 per person. There's a bar on board.

FISHING   You can surf-cast, throw your line off the pier at Times Square, or venture offshore on a number of charter fishing boats here. The staff at **Getaway Marina,** 18400 San Carlos Blvd., about half a mile north of the Sky Bridge (© 941/466-3600), is very adept at matching clients with skilled charter-boat skippers. Expect to spend about $600 a day for a full day's fishing for up to 6 persons.

No reservations are required on "party boats" that take groups out. Operating year-round, the *Great Getaway* and *Great Getaway II* (© 941/466-3600) sail from the Getaway Marina, about half a mile north of the bridge. The *Island Lady* (© 941/482-2005) is docked at Fisherman's Wharf, virtually under the San Carlos Island end of the Skyway Bridge. They all depart between 8 and 9:30am; charge between $30 and $50 per person, depending on the length of the voyage; and have air-conditioned lounges with bars. Call for details and reservations.

SCUBA DIVING & SNORKELING   Scuba diving is available at **Seahorse Scuba,** 17849 San Carlos Blvd. (© 941/454-3111; www.seahorsescuba.com). Two-tank dives start at $59. Groups of four snorkelers can go on their own excursions for $35 each, including equipment.

The live-aboard dive boat *Ultimate Getaway,* based at Getaway Marina, 18400 San Carlos Blvd. (© 941/466-3600; fax 941/644-7529; www. ultimategetaway.net), makes 4-day voyages to the Dry Tortugas (70 miles west of Key West). This 100-foot vessel carries a maximum of 20 divers and is equipped with a dive platform, chase boat, and TV/VCR. Trips cost $495 per person, including meals, beer, air, and weights, but bring your own regulator, mask, and fins.

WHERE TO STAY

The hostelries recommended below are removed from the crowds of Times Square, but three chain motels offer comfortable accommodations right in the center of the action: **Ramada Inn** (© 800/544-4592 or 941/463-6158), **Days Inn** (© 800/544-4592 or 941/463-9759), and **Howard Johnson's Motel** (© 800/544-4592 or 941/463-9231). The mid-rise **Best Western Beach Resort** (© 800/336-4045 or 941/463-6000) is ¼ mile north, just far enough to escape the noise but still have a lively beach.

Sunstream Resorts, 6640 Estero Blvd., Fort Myers Beach, FL 33931 (© 800/625-4111; fax 941/463-3060; www.sunstream.com), manages three "condominium hotels" here, including the plush **Casa Playa,** 510 Estero Blvd. (© 800/569-4876 or 941/765-0510; www.casaplayaresort.com), and the **Lover's Key Beach Club & Resort, 8771 Estero Blvd.** (© 877/798-4879 or 941/765-1040; www.loverskey.com), both of which opened in 2000. The latter and the **Grand View Resort,** 8701 Estero Blvd. (© 941/765-4422), are on the north end of Lover's Key. The 60 spacious apartments in the older, 16-story **Pointe Estero Island Resort,** 6640 Estero Blvd. (© 941/765-1155), all have whirlpool bathtubs and screened balconies with gorgeous gulf or bay views. The less expensive **Santa Maria,** 7317 Estero Blvd. (© 941/765-6700), is on the bay side of the island.

A number of agents offer weekly or monthly rentals, including **VIP Realtors** (© 888/765-5993 or 941/765-8686; www.viprealty.com) and **Bluebill Properties** (© 800/237-2010 or 941/463-1141; www.naplesvacation.com), which represents properties throughout Southwest Florida. The chamber of commerce (see "Essentials," above) publishes a complete list of accommodations and rental agents.

For information about rate seasons, see "Where to Stay," in section 1, earlier in this chapter.

For campers, the somewhat-cramped **Red Coconut RV Resort,** 3001 Estero Blvd. (© 941/463-7200; fax 941/463-2609; www.redcoconut.com), has sites for RVs and tents both on the gulf side of the road and right on the beach. They start at $39 a night during winter, $25 off-season.

EXPENSIVE

Best Western Pink Shell Beach Resort ★★ Not to be confused with the nearby Best Western Beach Resort, this popular, family-oriented establishment fronts both the gulf and the Matanzas Pass from its perch on Estero's quiet northern end. It has efficiencies, suites, and one- and two-bedroom fully equipped apartments in three mid-rise, gulf-front buildings with lovely views of Sanibel Island from screened balconies. The standard efficiencies are the least-expensive units here. Sailboats and nature and sightseeing cruises pick up guests at the bay-side marina, which rents boats and bikes. The scenic Hungry Pelican Cafe, on a covered deck overlooking the channel, is a great spot for breakfast or lunch.

275 Estero Blvd., Fort Myers Beach, FL 33931. © 800/554-5454 or 941/463-6181. Fax 941/481-4947. www.pinkshell.com. 208 units. Winter $175–$449 condo or cottage; off-season $135–$309 condo or cottage. Packages and weekly rates available. AE, DC, DISC, MC, V. **Amenities:** Restaurant (American); bar; 4 heated

outdoor pools; lighted tennis courts; water-sports equipment rental; bike rental; baby-sitting; laundry service; coin-op washers and dryers. *In room:* A/C, TV, kitchen, coffeemaker, hair dryer, iron.

Diamond Head All Suite Beach Resort ⚓

Opened in 1999, this luxurious, 12-story, beachside building sports large, comfortable one-bedroom apartments. Sliding-glass doors lead from both the living quarters and the bedroom to screened balconies. The beachfront apartments are the choice, but every unit has a view (spectacular from the upper floors). Cabana's Beach Bar provides libation and light lunches beside the pool, and an urbane lounge bar provides live music during the winter season.

2000 Estero Blvd. (at Palm Ave.), Fort Myers Beach, FL 33931. 𝄠 **888/765-5002** or 941/765-7654. Fax 941/765-1694. www.diamondheadfl.com. 124 units. Winter $195–$275 double; off-season $145–$165. AE, DC, DISC, MC, V. **Amenities:** Restaurant (American); 2 bars; heated outdoor pool; Jacuzzi; water-sports equipment rental; game room; limited room service; laundry service; coin-op washers and dryers. *In room:* A/C, TV, kitchen, coffeemaker, hair dryer, iron.

Edison Beach House ⚓⚓

No standardized list of amenities does justice to this intimate, 5-story beachside inn, for when owner Larry Yax built it in 1999, he equipped every unit as if he were going to live in it. In fact, Larry does live in one of the top-floor suites here. The light and airy units all have a balcony, a ceiling fan, a fully equipped kitchen (look for your complimentary bag of popcorn in the microwave oven), a writing desk stocked with office supplies, and a linen closet packed with extra towels. Most of the bathrooms have a combo washer-dryer. The freshly laundered bedspreads provided each new guest are but one example of the premium Larry puts on cleanliness. The beachfront units have the best view, but much more romantic are the "A" suites, whose queen-size beds are almost surrounded by windows formed by a turret on one corner of the building—as in, you fall asleep and wake up to a panoramic view spanning from gulf to bay.

830 Estero Blvd., Fort Myers Beach, FL 33931. 𝄠 **800/399-2511** or 941/463-1530. Fax 941/765-9430. www.edisonbeachhouse.com. 24 units. Winter $250–$350 double; off-season $95–$175. AE, DC, DISC, MC, V. **Amenities:** Heated outdoor pool. *In room:* A/C, TV, dataport, kitchen, coffeemaker, hair dryer, iron.

MODERATE

Holiday Inn Gulfside

Built by the shifting sands, the slowly emerging Little Estero Island (actually a peninsula) has left the surf a considerable distance from this conventional two-story motel, the center of beach activity on Estero's south end. Guests need not walk far, however, to a courtyard swimming pool, tiki bar, and a grill serving lunches and snacks. Beachfront suites are the choice accommodation here. Otherwise, you're better off paying a little more for a room facing the central courtyard rather than one looking out on the parking lots. They're all entered from common walkways running the length of the building, but you will get two plastic patio chairs to call your own out there. The shops and restaurants of Villa Santini Plaza are a short walk away.

6890 Estero Blvd., Fort Myers Beach, FL 33931. 𝄠 **800/465-4329** or 941/463-5711. Fax 941/463-7038. fmybesm@aol.com. 105 units. Winter $140–$230 double; $400 suite. Off-season $95–$145 double; $270–$300 suite. AE, DC, DISC, MC, V. **Amenities:** 2 restaurants (American); 2 bars; outdoor pool; 2 lighted tennis courts; water-sports equipment rental; game room; business center; shopping arcade; salon; limited room service; coin-op washers and dryers. *In room:* A/C, TV, dataport, kitchen (suites only), fridge (some rooms), coffeemaker, hair dryer, iron.

Outrigger Beach Resort

Well known for its beachside tiki bar (one of the best places for sunset-watching here), this clean, pleasant motel has been owned and operated by the same family since 1965. Their "garden efficiencies" in the original building have the feel of small cottages, with excellent ventilation through both front and rear windows and doors opening to backyard decks. Other buildings here are two-story blocks containing motel-style rooms and efficiencies, which have views of the large parking lot. The **beachside bar** is one of the best places here to watch the sun set.

6200 Estero Blvd. (P.O. Box 271), Fort Myers Beach, FL 33931. ℂ **800/749-3131** or 941/463-3131. Fax 941/ 463-6577. www.outriggerfmb.com. 144 units. Winter $130–$200 double; off-season $100–$185 double. AE, DISC, MC, V. **Amenities:** Restaurant (American); bar; heated outdoor pool; small exercise room; Jacuzzi; water-sports equipment rental; game room; coin-op washers and dryers; concierge-level rooms. *In room:* A/C, TV, kitchen, coffeemaker, hair dryer.

Sandpiper Gulf Resort   The units at this quiet, family-oriented gulf-side motel all have living and sleeping areas, full kitchens, convertible sofas, and overlook either the gulf or a courtyard. Steps lead from the pool directly to the beach. Some suites are in two- or three-story buildings arranged in a U, with the flattened ends right on the beach; others are in the Sandpiper II, a palm-fronted mid-rise with its own heated pool next door. All suites are identical, but those facing directly onto the beach are more expensive. Restaurants are nearby.

5550 Estero Blvd., Fort Myers Beach, FL 33931. ℂ **800/584-1449** or 941/463-5721. Fax 941/765-0039. www.sandpipergulfresort.com. 63 units. Winter $146–$199 double; off-season $85–$115 double. DISC, MC, V. **Amenities:** Heated outdoor pool; Jacuzzi; water-sports equipment rental; bike rental; coin-op washers and dryers. *In room:* A/C, TV, dataport, kitchen, coffeemaker, hair dryer, iron.

INEXPENSIVE

Island House Motel *Value*   Sitting on stilts in the Old Florida fashion, but with modern furnishings, Ken and Sylvia Lachapelle's clapboard-sided Island House Motel enjoys a quiet location along a bay-side channel, directly across the boulevard from the Best Western Beach Resort and within walking distance of busy Times Square. Four of their units have screened porches; all have kitchens and ceiling fans. Ken and Sylvia maintain an open-air lounge with a small library beneath one of the units. They also provide free beach chairs and bikes. Book as early as possible for February and March. The Lachapelles also operate the three-story **Edgewater Inn,** less than a block away at 781 Estero Blvd. (same phone, fax, website, and e-mail). The two one-bedroom and four two-bedroom apartments there all have screened lanais. They are available on a weekly basis during winter, for 3-day minimum stays off-season.

701 Estero Blvd., Fort Myers Beach, FL 33931. ℂ **800/951-9975** or 941/463-9282. Fax 941/463-2080. www.edgewaterfmb.com. 5 units. Winter $99–$119 double; off-season $49–$69 double. Rates include local phone calls. Weekly rates available. MC, V. **Amenities:** Heated outdoor pool; access to nearby health club; coin-op washers and dryers. *In room:* A/C, TV, kitchen, coffeemaker, hair dryer, iron.

Palm Terrace Apartments *Value*   Many European guests stay in these comfortable, well-maintained apartments about midway down the beach. In fact, between them, husband-and-wife owners Deborah Bowers and Peter Piazza speak fluent German and French and passable Italian. Their smaller, less-expensive units are on the ground level, with sliding-glass doors opening to a grassy yard, but even these units have cooking facilities including microwave ovens. Most units are upstairs, with screened porches or decks overlooking a courtyard with a heated swimming pool, a shuffleboard court, and a charcoal grill for barbecuing. There's no daily maid service, but you'll have an ample supply of clean linens.

3333 Estero Blvd., Fort Myers Beach, FL 33931. ℂ **800/320-5783** or 941/765-5783. Fax 941/765-5783. www.all-florida.com/travel/palmterr.htm. 9 units. Winter $85–$130 double; off-season $49–$81 double.

3-day minimum stay required in winter. Weekly rates available. AE, DISC, MC, V. **Amenities:** Heated outdoor pool; coin-op washers and dryers. *In room:* A/C, TV/VCR, dataport, kitchen, coffeemaker.

WHERE TO DINE

The busy area around Times Square has fast-food joints to augment several local restaurants catering to the beach crowds. The pick is the moderately priced **Beach Pierside Grill,** directly on the beach at the foot of Lynn Hall Memorial Pier (© **941/765-7800**), a lively pub with bright-blond wood trim and vivid fabric colors reminiscent of establishments in Miami's South Beach. It all opens onto a large beachside patio with dining at umbrella tables, outstanding sunsets, and live bands playing at night. The reasonably priced fare is a catchall of conch fritters, shrimp and fish baskets, burgers, and seafood main courses. They take reservations—a plus in this busy area. Food is served daily from 11am to 11pm.

For dessert, drop into the local branch of **Kilwin's Chocolates,** 50 Old San Carlos Blvd. (© **941/463-4500**), in Times Square near the pier. It's open daily 10am to 11pm in winter, daily 10am to 10pm off-season.

MODERATE

Channel Mark ✿✿ SEAFOOD   Maryland-style crab cakes, delicately seasoned with Old Bay spice in true Maryland fashion, are enough to make this the beach's best place for seafood. Nestled by the "Little Bridge" leading onto San Carlos Island's northern end, every table here looks out on a maze of channel markers on Hurricane Bay. A dock with palms growing through it makes this a relaxing place for a waterside lunch. At night, a relaxed tropical ambience is ideal for kindling romance. The adjacent lounge offers the same menu and has live entertainment on weekends.

19001 San Carlos Blvd. (at the north end of San Carlos Island) © **941/463-9127**. Reservations not accepted. Main courses $10–$21. AE, DISC, MC, V. Sun–Thurs 11am–10pm; Fri–Sat 11am–11pm.

Gulf Shore Grill SEAFOOD/AMERICAN   On the southern fringes of Times Square, this old clapboard building offers splendid views of the gulf and the beach. It began life in the 1920s as the Crescent Beach Casino and has seen various incarnations as a bathhouse, gambling casino, dance hall, and rooming house. These days, an extensive salad bar accompanies traditional Florida-style main courses such as baked grouper imperial, grilled mahi-mahi, and shrimp wrapped in bacon and coated with honey. This is one of the best breakfast spots on the beach, with choices ranging from biscuits under sausage gravy to eggs served on a muffin under Alaskan crabmeat and a charon sauce. The kitchen also provides the pub fare for **The Cottage,** an open-air drinking establishment next door (it's open daily from 11am to 2am), and for a walk-up hot dog and ice cream counter next to the beach downstairs.

1270 Estero Blvd. (on the beach at Ave. A) © **941/463-9951**. Reservations accepted for dinner. Main courses $14–$31; breakfast $4.50–$10; sandwiches and burgers $6–$9. AE, DISC, MC, V. Daily 8am–3pm and 5–10pm.

Loggerheads SEAFOOD/AMERICAN   The motto "The Local's Nest" accurately describes this friendly storefront restaurant, the best bet on the island's south end. Charter boat captains and other locals congregate around a big square bar on one side of the knotty-pine–accented dining room. The menu offers a wide range of appetizers, big salads, sandwiches, burgers, and main course options from both land and sea. Grouper prepared in a number of satisfying if not spectacular ways leads the main courses, but you can order traditionally fried, grilled, broiled, or blackened seafood plus pastas, steaks, ribs, and jerk chicken.

In Villa Santini Plaza, 7205 Estero Blvd. (at Lennel Rd.) ⓒ **941/463-4644**. Reservations recommended on weekends. Sandwiches and burgers $7–$8; main courses $12–$17. AE, DISC, MC, V. Mon–Thurs 11am–11pm, Fri–Sat 11am–midnight, Sun 10:30am–11pm.

Matanzas Inn Restaurant SEAFOOD   Although this casual, friendly, and consistent restaurant is located in the busy Times Square tourist district, it is popular with local residents who appreciate seafood fresh off the boats docking at Matanzas Marina. Dining is on a dock or an enclosed deck next to the marina or in a dark-paneled room hung with ceiling fans. Blackened or stuffed grouper are the house specialties, while the scampi-style shrimp and scallops are passable. A light-fare menu offers shrimp salad, fish sandwiches, and hamburgers. Up on the roof, the Upper Deck Lounge provides evening entertainment.

At Matanzas Marina, 416 Crescent St. (under the Skyway Bridge on Estero Island) ⓒ **941/463-3838**. Reservations not accepted. Main courses $13–$19; sandwiches and light fare $6.50–$11. AE, DC, DISC, MC, V. Daily 11am–10pm. Closed Thanksgiving and Christmas.

Pappa Mondo Ristorante Italiano ⭐⭐ *Value* NORTHERN ITALIAN Brothers-in-law Pasquale Riso (he's the chef) and Andrea Mazzonetto hail from Italy, and the fare they present in their attractive dining room-or out on their roadside patio—is authentic old-country cooking. They make everything from scratch—you can watch them producing pasta at a big machine behind a large picture window. Especially tasty is the ravioli, either ricotta-and-cheese topped with butter and sage sauce, or stuffed with veal and served with a light cream sauce tinged with balsamic vinegar.

1821 Estero Blvd. (at Ohio Ave.) ⓒ **941/765-9660**. Reservations recommended. Main courses $11–$16. AE, MC, V. Daily 3:30–10pm. Closed Christmas.

INEXPENSIVE

The Fish House SEAFOOD   You'll find the beach's least-expensive outdoor dining at the dockside tables of this no-frills friendly pub. You'll also see charter boat skippers slaking their thirst at a large wooden bar occupying about half the open-air but screened dining room. Go for the fried or grilled grouper and other fish the captains have just landed. Sandwiches are available all day, including a tasty grouper version.

7225 Estero Blvd. (at Fish Tale Marina, behind Villa Santini Plaza) ⓒ **941/765-6766**. Reservations not accepted. Sandwiches $6.50–$9; main courses $8–$15. AE, DISC, MC, V. Daily 11am–11pm. Closed Thanksgiving and Christmas.

Francesco's Italian Deli & Pizzeria ⭐ ITALIAN   Wonderful aromas of baking pizzas, cannoli, breads, cookies, and fabulous calzones waft from this New York–style Italian deli. Order at the counter over a chiller packed with fresh deli meats, Italian sausage, and cheeses; then devour your goodies at tables inside or out on the covered walkway, or take them to the beach for a picnic. You can also take "heat and eat" meals of spaghetti, lasagna, eggplant parmigiana, manicotti, and ravioli to your hotel or condominium oven. Shelves are loaded with Italian wines, pastas, butter cookies, and anisette toast.

In Villa Santini Plaza, 7205 Estero Blvd. (at Lennel Rd.) ⓒ **941/463-5634**. Subs and sandwiches $4.50–$6; pizzas $12–$14; ready-to-cook meals $8–$10. No credit cards. Mon–Sat 8am–8pm; Sun 9am–5pm.

FORT MYERS BEACH AFTER DARK

To find out what's going on while you're here, pick up copies of the daily *News-Press* (www.news-press.com) and of the *Beach Bulletin* and the *Fort Myers Beach Observer*, two local tabloid newspapers. They're available at the chamber of commerce (see "Essentials," earlier in this chapter).

The area around Times Square is always active, every day during winter and on weekends off-season. In the very heart of Times Square at the foot of Lynn Hall Memorial Pier, the **Beach Pierside Grill,** 1000 Estero Blvd. (© **941/ 765-7800**), has live entertainment on its beachside patio. Facing due west, **Jimmy's Beach Bar,** in the Days Inn at 1130 Estero Blvd. (© **941/463-9759**), has live music nightly for the "best sunsets on the island" (actually, you can say that of all the beachside establishments here). It's not directly on the beach, but locals in the know head for the rooftop bar at **The Beached Whale,** 1249 Estero Blvd. (© **941/463-5505**), which supplies free chicken wings during nightly happy hour. Rock and reggae music is played downstairs for nighttime dancing.

Away from the crowds in the "middle beach" area, the **Junkanoo Beach Bar,** under Anthony's on the Gulf, 3040 Estero Blvd. (© **941/463-2600**), attracts a more affluent crowd for its bohemian-style parties that run from 11:30am to 1:30am daily. Live bands here specialize in reggae and other island music. The menu offers inexpensive subs, sandwiches, burgers, and pizzas, and a concessionaire rents beach cabanas and water-sports toys, making it a good place for a lively day at the beach.

On Sunday afternoons, revelers jam the docks for the famous outdoor reggae parties at **The Bridge Waterfront Restaurant,** 708 Fisherman's Wharf (© **941/ 765-0050**), which is under the Sky Bridge on San Carlos Island.

3 Sanibel & Captiva Islands ✦✦✦

14 miles W. of Fort Myers, 40 miles N. of Naples

Sanibel and Captiva are unique in Florida. Here you will find none of the neon signs, amusement parks, and high-rise condominiums that clutter most beach resorts in the state. Indeed, Sanibel's main drag, Periwinkle Way, runs under a canopy of whispery pines and gnarled oaks so thick they almost obscure the small signs for chic shops and restaurants. This wooded ambience is the work of local voters, who have saved their trees and tropical foliage, limited the size and appearance of signs, and permitted no building higher than the tallest palm and no WaveRunner or other noisy beach toy within 300 yards of their gorgeous, shell-strewn beaches. I had been to Sanibel many times before I saw an aerial photo of the island and realized that its southern shore is lined with hotels and condominiums. The foliage disguises the buildings that well.

Furthermore, more than half of the two islands is preserved in its natural state as wildlife refuges. Here you can ride, walk, bike, canoe, or kayak through the J. N. (Ding) Darling National Wildlife Refuge, one of Florida's best.

Legend says that Ponce de León named the larger of these two barrier islands "San Ybel," after Queen Isabella of Spain. Another legend claims that Captiva's name comes from the captured women kept here by the infamous pirate Jose Gaspar. The modern era dates from 1892, when a few farmers settled on the islands. One of them, Clarence Chadwick, started an unsuccessful key lime and copra plantation on Captiva; many of his towering coconut palms still stand, adding to that skinny island's tropical luster.

ESSENTIALS

GETTING THERE   See "Getting There," in section 1 of this chapter, for information about air, train, bus, and rental-car services. The Amoco station at 1015 Periwinkle Way, at Causeway Road, is the Sanibel agent for **Enterprise Rent-a-Car** (© **800/325-8007** or 941/395-3880).

VISITOR INFORMATION The Sanibel–Captiva Islands Chamber of Commerce, 1159 Causeway Rd., Sanibel Island, FL 33957 (© **941/472-1080;** fax 941/472-1070; www.sanibel-captiva.org), maintains a visitor center on Causeway Road as you drive onto Sanibel from Fort Myers. The chamber gives away an island guide and sells a detailed street map for $3 ($4 by mail). Other books are for sale, including comprehensive shelling guides and a helpful collection of menus from the islands' restaurants. There are phones for making hotel and condominium reservations (check the brochure racks for discounts during summer and December). Open Monday to Saturday from 9am to 7pm, Sunday from 10am to 5pm.

GETTING AROUND Neither Sanibel nor Captiva has public transportation. **No parking** is permitted on any street or road on Sanibel. Free beach parking is available on the Sanibel Causeway. Other municipal lots either are reserved for local residents or have a 75¢ hourly fee. Accordingly, many residents and visitors get around by bicycle (see "More Ways to Enjoy the Outdoors," below).

If you need a cab, call **Sanibel Taxi** (© **941/472-4160**).

PARKS & NATURE PRESERVES

Named for the *Des Moines Register* cartoonist who was a frequent visitor here and who started the federal Duck Stamp program, the outstanding **J. N. (Ding) Darling National Wildlife Refuge** ★★★, on Sanibel-Captiva Road, is home to alligators, raccoons, otters, and hundreds of species of birds. Occupying more than half of Sanibel Island, this 6,000-plus–acre area of mangrove swamps, winding waterways, and uplands has a 2-mile boardwalk nature trail and a 5-mile, one-way **Wildlife Drive.** The visitor center shows brief videos about the refuge's inhabitants every half-hour and sells a map keyed to numbered stops along the Wildlife Drive. The best times for viewing the wildlife are early morning, late afternoon, and at low tide (tables are posted at the visitor center and are available at the chamber of commerce). Mosquitoes and "no-see-ums" (tiny, biting sand flies) are especially prevalent at dawn and dusk, so bring repellent.

Admission to the visitor center is free. The Wildlife Drive costs $5 per vehicle, $1 for hikers and bicyclists (free to holders of current federal Duck Stamps and National Park Service access passports). The visitor center is open from November to April, Saturday to Thursday from 9am to 5pm; off-season, Saturday to Thursday from 9am to 4pm. The center is open on federal holidays from January through May, closed on holidays the rest of the year. The Wildlife Drive is open all year, Saturday to Thursday from 1 hour after sunrise to 1 hour before sunset.

For more information, contact the refuge at 1 Wildlife Dr., Sanibel Island, FL 33957 (© **941/472-1100**).

You'll get a lot more from your visit by taking a naturalist-narrated tram tour given by **Tarpon Bay Recreation,** at the north end of Tarpon Bay Road (© **941/472-8900;** www.tarponbay.com). The tours last 2 hours and cost $10 for adults, $5 for children 12 and under. You can board at the wildlife refuge visitor center during winter, at Tarpon Bay off-season. Schedules are seasonal, so call ahead.

Tarpon Bay Recreation also offers a variety of guided **canoe and kayak tours,** with an emphasis on the historical, cultural, and environmental aspects of the refuge (call for the schedule and reservations, which are required). It also rents canoes, kayaks, and small boats with electric trolling motors (see "More Ways to Enjoy the Outdoors," below).

ACCOMMODATIONS ■
Beachview Cottages **34**
Best Western Sanibel
Island Beach Resort **33**
Buttonwood Cottages **22**
Captiva Island Inn
Bed and Breakfast **5**
Casa Ybel Resort **31**
Gulf Breeze Cottages **29**
Island Inn **32**
Jensen's On the Gulf **5**
Palm View Motel **28**

Sanibel Inn **27**
Sanibel's Seaside Inn **25**
Song of the Sea **26**
South Seas Resort **1**
Sundial Beach Resort **32**
Tarpon Tale Inn **24**
'Tween Waters Inn **6**

ATTRACTIONS ●
Bailey-Matthews
Shell Museum **10**
J.N. (Ding) Darling
National Wildlife
Refuge **8**
Sanibel Historical Village
& Museum **14**
Sanibel Lighthouse **23**
Sanibel/Captiva
Conservation
Foundation **9**
Tarpon Bay Recreation **11**

DINING ◆
The Bubble Room **2**
Captiva Sunshine Cafe **2**
Grandma Dot's
Seaside Saloon **20**
The Green Flash **4**
Hungry Heron **13**
Jacaranda **18**
Jerry's Family
Restaurant **16**
The Lazy Flamingo I **19**
Lighthouse Cafe **21**
Mad Hatter **7**
McT's Shrimp House
& Tavern **17**
Morgan's Forest **30**
Mucky Duck **3**
R.C. Otter's Island Eats **2**
Sanibel Cafe **15**
The Timbers Restaurant
& Fish Market **12**

A short drive from the visitor center, the nonprofit **Sanibel/Captiva Conservation Foundation,** 3333 Sanibel-Captiva Rd. (🕿 **941/472-2329**), maintains a nature center, a native plant nursery, and 4½ miles of nature trails on 1,100 acres of wetlands along the Sanibel River. You can learn more about the islands' unusual ecosystems through environmental workshops, guided 1½ -hour trail walks, beach walks, and a 2-hour natural-history boat cruise (call for seasonal schedules and reservations). Various items are for sale, including native plants and publications about the islands' birds and other wildlife. Admission is $3 for adults, free for children 16 and under. The nature center is open November 15 to April 14, Monday to Friday from 8:30am to 4pm, Saturday 10am to 3pm; off-season, Monday to Friday 8:30am to 3pm.

Also nearby, the **Clinic for the Rehabilitation of Wildlife (C.R.O.W.),** 3883 Sanibel-Captiva Rd. (🕿 **941/472-3644**), is dedicated to the care of sick, injured, or orphaned wildlife. Tours of the facility usually take place year-round Monday to Friday at 11, Sunday at 1pm, but call to make sure. Tours cost $3 per person.

HITTING THE BEACH: SHELLING & SEA LIFE

BEACHES   Sanibel has four public beach-access areas with metered parking: the eastern point around **Sanibel Lighthouse,** which has a fishing pier; **Gulfside City Park,** at the end of Algiers Lane, off Casa Ybel Road; **Tarpon Bay Road Beach,** at the south end of Tarpon Bay Road; and **Bowman's Beach,** off

Sanibel-Captiva Road. **Turner Beach,** at Blind Pass between Sanibel and Captiva, is highly popular at sunset since it faces due west; there's a small free parking lot on the Captiva side, but parking on the Sanibel side is limited to holders of local permits. All except Tarpon Bay Road Beach have restrooms. *Be fore-warned:* Although nude bathing is illegal, the end of Bowman's Beach near Blind Pass often sees more than its share of bare straight and gay bodies.

Another popular beach on Captiva is at the end of Andy Rosse Lane in front of the Mucky Duck Restaurant. It's the one place here where you can rent motorized water-sports equipment (see "More Ways to Enjoy the Outdoors," below). There's limited free parking just north of here, at the end of Captiva Drive (go past the entrance to South Seas Resort to the end of the road).

SHELLING   Sanibel and Captiva are famous for their seashells, and local residents and visitors alike can be seen in the "Sanibel stoop" or the "Captiva crouch" while searching for some 200 species.

Before you start scouring the beaches, visit the impressive **Bailey-Matthews Shell Museum** ★★, 3075 Sanibel-Captiva Rd. (© **941/395-2233;** www. shellmuseum.org), the only museum in the United States devoted solely to saltwater, freshwater, and land shells (yes, snails are included). Shells from as far away as South Africa surround a 6-foot globe in the middle of the main exhibit hall, thus showing their geographic origins. A spinning wheel-shaped case identifies shells likely to wash up on Sanibel. Other exhibits are devoted to shells in tribal art, fossil shells found in Florida, medicinal qualities of various mollusks, the endangered Florida tree snail, and "sailor's Valentines"-shell craft made by natives of Barbados for sailors to bring home to their loved ones. The upstairs library attracts serious malacologists—for the uninitiated, those who study mollusks—and a shop purveys clever shell-themed gifts. The museum is open Tuesday to Sunday from 10am to 4pm; admission is $5 adults, $3 children 8 to 16, free for children under 8.

The months from February to April, or after any storm, are the prime times of the year to look for whelks, olives, scallops, sand dollars, conch, and many other varieties. Low tide is the best time of day. The shells can be sharp, so wear Aqua Socks or old running shoes whenever you go walking on the beach.

With so many residents and visitors scouring Sanibel, you may have better luck finding that rare shell on the adjacent shoals and nearby islands, such as Upper Captiva and Cayo Costa (see "Nearby Island Hopping," later in this chapter). **Captiva Cruises** ★★ (© **941/472-5300;** www.captivacruises.com) has shelling trips from the South Seas Resort on Captiva daily at 9am and noon. They cost $35 for adults, $17.50 for children. Reservations are required. Captiva Cruises also has popular dolphin watching and wildlife cruises, with narration by a naturalist from the Sanibel-Captiva Conservation Foundation, daily from 4 to 5:30pm. These cost $20 for adults, $10 for kids. All of Captiva Cruises' boats are air conditioned and have restrooms and snack bars.

At least 15 charter-boat skippers also offer to take guests on shelling expeditions to these less-explored areas. Their half-day rates are about $200 for up to four people, so get up a group to go. Several operate from the **'Tween Waters Inn Marina** (© **941/472-5161**) on Captiva, including **Capt. Mike Fuery** (© **941/472-1015,** or 941/994-7195 on his boat). Others are based at **Jensen's Twin Palms Marina,** on Captiva (© **941/472-5800**), and at the **Sanibel Marina,** on North Yachtsman Drive, off Periwinkle Way east of Causeway Boulevard (© **941/472-2723**). They all distribute brochures at the chamber of commerce visitor center (see "Essentials," above) and are listed in the free tourist publications found there.

Caution: Florida law prohibits taking live shells from the beaches, and federal regulations prevent them from being removed from the J. N. (Ding) Darling National Wildlife Refuge.

MORE WAYS TO ENJOY THE OUTDOORS

BICYCLING, WALKING, JOGGING & IN-LINE SKATING   Paved bicycle paths follow alongside most major roads, including the entire length of Periwinkle Way and along Sanibel-Captiva Road to Blind Pass, making Sanibel a paradise for cyclists, walkers, joggers, and in-line skaters. And you can walk or bike the 5-mile, one-way nature trail through the J. N. (Ding) Darling National Wildlife Refuge.

The chamber of commerce visitor center has bike maps, as do Sanibel's rental firms: **Finnimore's Cycle Shop,** 2353 Periwinkle Way (© 941/472-5577); **The Bike Rental,** 2330 Palm Ridge Rd. (© 941/472-2241); **Billy's Rentals,** 1470 Periwinkle Way (© 941/472-5248); **Boats, Bikes & Beach Stuff,** 2427 Periwinkle Way (© 941/472-8717); and **Tarpon Bay Recreation,** at the north end of Tarpon Bay Road (© 941/472-8900). On Captiva, **Jim's Bike & Skate Rentals** on Andy Rosse Lane (© 941/472-1296) rents bikes and beach equipment. Bike rates range from $3 per hour to $15 a day for basic models. Both Finnimore's and Jim's rent in-line skates.

There are no bike paths on Captiva, where trees alongside the narrow roads can make for dangerous riding.

BOATING & FISHING   On Sanibel, rental boats and charter-fishing excursions are available from **The Boat House** at the Sanibel Marina, on North Yachtsman Drive (© 941/472-2531), off Periwinkle Way east of Causeway Road. **Tarpon Bay Recreation,** at the north end of Tarpon Bay Road (© 941/472-8900), rents boats with electric trolling motors and tackle for fishing.

On Captiva, check with **Sweet Water Rentals** at the 'Tween Waters Inn Marina (© 941/472-6376), **Jensen's Twin Palms Marina** (© 941/472-5800), and **McCarthy's Marina** (© 941/472-5200), all on Captiva Road. Rental boats cost about $125 for half a day, $200 for a full day.

Many **charter-fishing captains** are docked at these marinas. Half-day rates are about $300 for up to four people. The skippers leave free brochures at the chamber of commerce visitor center (see "Essentials," above), and they're listed in the free tourist publications found there.

CANOEING & KAYAKING   As noted under "Parks & Nature Preserves," above, **Tarpon Bay Recreation** (© 941/472-8900; www.tarponbay.com) has guided canoe and kayak trips in the J. N. (Ding) Darling National Wildlife Refuge. Do-it-yourselfers can rent canoes and kayaks here. They cost $20 for the first 2 hours, $5 for each additional hour. On Captiva, the **'Tween Waters Inn Marina** (© 941/472-5161) rents canoes and kayaks, as does **Captiva Kayak Co./WildSide Adventures,** based at McCarthy's Marina (© 941/935-2925) rents canoes and kayaks.

Naturalist, avid environmentalist, and former Sanibel mayor **Mark "Bird" Westall** (© 941/472-5218; fax 941/472-6833) takes visitors on guided canoe trips through the wildlife refuge and on the Sanibel River. His excursions are timed for low tide and cost $35 for adults, $15 for children under 18. He will tailor shorter trips to accommodate children or anyone else not up to 2½ to 3 hours in a canoe. Naturalist **Brian Houston** leads kayaking trips from 'Tween Waters Inn Marina on Captiva, but make your reservations at Tarpon Bay Recreation on Sanibel (© **941/472-8900**). Brian charges $35 per person. Richard Finkel of **Captiva Kayak Co./WildSide Adventures,** based at McCarthy's Marina on Captiva (© **877/395-2925** or 941/395-2925; www.captivakayak. com), leads both day and night back-bay ecology trips for $35 for adults, $25 for teenagers, $20 for children (add $10 to each price for night trips). Richard will customize tours, including camping on Cayo Costa (see "Nearby Island Hopping," later in this chapter) for advanced kayakers. Reservations are essential with all these operators.

GOLF & TENNIS   Golfers may view a gallery of wild animals while playing the 5,600-yard, par-70, 18-hole course at the **Dunes Golf and Tennis Club,** 949 Sandcastle Rd., Sanibel (© **941/472-2535**), whose back nine runs across a wildlife preserve. Call a day in advance for seasonal greens fees and a tee time. The Dunes also has seven tennis courts. You can also play 9 water-bordered holes at **Beachview Golf Club,** 1100 Par View Dr. (© **941/472-2626**). The **South Seas Resort** has tennis courts and a 9-hole golf course, but they're for guests only.

SAILING   If you want to learn how to sail, noted yachties Steve and Doris Colgate have a branch of their **Offshore Sailing School** at the South Seas Resort (© **888/454-9002** or 941/472-5111, ext. 7141; www.offshore-sailing.com). You can either learn to sail or polish your skills here. Clinics ranging from half a day to a full week are available. Also ask about their popular women-only, father/son, and mother/daughter programs.

Also based on Captiva, two sailboats take guests out on the waters of Pine Island Sound: The *Adventure* (© **941/472-6300** or 941/472-4386) and the *New Moon* (© **941/395-1782**). They cost $95 per hour with a 2-hour minimum. Reservations are required.

WATER SPORTS   Sanibel may prohibit motorized water-sports equipment on its beaches, but Captiva doesn't. **Yolo Watersports** (© **941/472-9656**) offers parasailing and WaveRunner rentals on the beach in front of the Mucky Duck Restaurant, at the gulf end of Andy Rosse Lane on Captiva.

MORE TO SEE & DO

Worth a brief stop after you've done everything else here, the **Sanibel Historical Village & Museum,** 950 Dunlop Rd. (© **941/472-4648**), includes the 1913-vintage Rutland home and the 1926 versions of Bailey's General Store (complete with Red Crown gasoline pumps), the post office, and Miss Charlotta's Tea Room. Displays highlight the islands' prehistoric Calusa tribal era, as well as old photos from pioneer days, turn-of-the-century clothing, and a variety of other memorabilia. Open from November to May, Wednesday to Saturday from 10am to 4pm; June to mid-August, Wednesday to Saturday from 10am to 1pm. Admission is by $3 donation.

At the east end of Periwinkle Way, the **Sanibel Lighthouse** has marked the entrance to San Carlos Bay since 1884. The lightkeepers used to live in the cottages at the base of the 94-foot tower. The now-automatic lighthouse isn't open to visitors, but the grounds and beach are.

The best way to get the lay of the land and learn all about the islands' history is on a 2-hour **Sanibel Island Eco-History Trolley Tour,** staged by Adventures in Paradise (© **941/472-3796** or 941/472-1080). They depart the chamber of commerce (see "Essentials," earlier in this chapter) Monday to Saturday at

10:30am and 1pm and cost $15 for adults, $12 for children, free for kids 3 and under. Call for reservations.

In addition to its other trips, **Captiva Cruises** (℃ 941/472-5300; www. captivacruises.com) goes out daily on sunset cruises from the South Seas Resort on Captiva. These cost $17.50 for adults, $10 for children. Reservations are required.

SHOPPING

If you have no luck at beach hunting for shells, several Sanibel shops sell thousands of them. **Sanibel Sea Shell Industries,** 905 Fitzhugh St. (℃ 941/472-1603), has one of the largest collections, with more than 10,000 shells in stock. **She Sells Sea Shells** has two locations: 1157 Periwinkle Way near Causeway Road (℃ 941/472-6991) and 2422 Periwinkle Way near the island's center (℃ 941/472-8080). Others include **Neptune's Treasures Shell Shop,** in the Tree Tops Center, 1101 Periwinkle Way opposite the Dairy Queen (℃ 941/472-3132), which also has a good collection of fossils.

You can burn up a rainy day and lots of credit at Sanibel's numerous upscale boutiques carrying expensive jewelry, apparel, and gifts. Many are in **Periwinkle Place** and **Tahitian Gardens,** the main shopping centers along Periwinkle Way. The larger Periwinkle Place sports mostly high-end men's and women's clothiers, while Tahitian Gardens has some excellent gift shops, including the **Audubon Nature Store** (℃ 941/395-2020), which carries gifts and books with a wildlife theme, and **The Cheshire Cat** (℃ 941/472-3545), offering nature toys and other unique items for kids.

More than a dozen Sanibel galleries feature original works of art; pick up a gallery guide at the chamber of commerce visitor center (see "Essentials," earlier in this chapter). On Captiva, the treehouselike **Jungle Drums,** on Andy Rosse Lane (℃ 941/395-2266), has the area's most unique collection of wildlife art.

Founded in 1899, **Bailey's General Store** is still going strong at the corner of Periwinkle Way and Tarpon Bay Road (℃ 941/472-1516), with a supermarket, deli, salad bar, hardware store, beach shop, shoe repair, and Western Union all under one roof.

WHERE TO STAY

Sanibel & Captiva Central Reservations, Inc. (℃ 800/325-1352 or 941/472-0457; www.sanibel-captivarents.com) and **1-800-SANIBEL** (℃ 800/726-4235 or 941/472-1800; fax 941/395-9690; www.1-800-sanibel.com) are reservations services that will book you into most condominiums and cottages here.

In general, Sanibel and Captiva room and condominium rates are highest during the shelling season, February to April. January is usually somewhat less expensive. But note that most rates fall drastically during the off-season. Don't hesitate to ask for a discount or special deal then. Since most properties on the islands are geared to 1-week vacations, you can also save by purchasing a package deal if you're staying for 7 nights or longer.

The islands' sole campground, the **Periwinkle Trailer Park,** 1119 Periwinkle Way, Sanibel Island (℃ 941/472-1433), is so popular it doesn't even advertise. No other camping is permitted on either Sanibel or Captiva.

SANIBEL ISLAND
Very Expensive

Best Western Sanibel Island Beach Resort ☆ One of only two chain properties here, this excellently managed motel boasts spacious rooms, efficiencies, and apartments whose screened balconies face either the beach or a lawn festooned with palms, pink hibiscus, orange trees, a swimming pool, tennis courts, and white Adirondack chairs for lounging.

3287 W. Gulf Dr. (at St. Kilda Rd.), Sanibel Island, FL 33957. ☎ **800/645-6559** or 941/472-1700. Fax 941/472-5032. www.bwsanibel.com. 45 units. Winter $235–$405 double; off-season $129–$285 double. AE, DC, DISC, MC, V. **Amenities:** Heated outdoor pool; tennis courts; coin-op washers and dryers; free use of bikes. *In room:* A/C, TV, kitchen, coffeemaker, hair dryer, iron.

Casa Ybel Resort 🏕🏕🏕   On the historic site of Sanibel's first beachfront resort, the Thistle Lodge, the present-day Casa Ybel's turn-of-the-century central building houses a restaurant of that name, where both guests and nonguests can enjoy wonderful cuisine and magnificent gulf views. Reflecting Thistle Lodge, the swimming pool in front of the restaurant is one of Florida's most picturesque. In four-story, gray buildings on the island's most beautifully landscaped grounds, the spacious one- and two-bedroom condominiums all have screened porches facing the gulf. With upstairs bedrooms, the townhouse-style units provide more privacy than most condominiums on Sanibel. Complimentary daily maid service is provided in the one-bedroom units, but it costs $35 a day in the two-bedroom condominiums.

2255 W. Gulf Dr., Sanibel Island, FL 33957. ☎ **800/276-4753** or 941/472-3145. Fax 941/472-2109. www.casaybelresort.com. 114 units. Winter $310–$475 condo; off-season $200–$375 condo. Packages and weekly rates available. AE, DISC, MC, V. **Amenities:** Restaurant (American); bar; heated outdoor pool; tennis courts; Jacuzzi; water-sports equipment rental; bike rental; children's programs; concierge; massage; baby-sitting; laundry service. *In room:* A/C, TV, kitchen, coffeemaker, hair dryer, iron.

Sanibel Inn 🏕🏕   A back-to-nature theme prevails at this beachside inn, in both the room decor and the grounds planted with native Florida foliage specifically designed to attract butterflies and hummingbirds. In fact, back-to-nature children's programs make this a great choice for eco-friendly families. The inn offers attractively furnished hotel rooms and fully equipped two-bedroom, two-bathroom condominium apartments (the latter are some of Sanibel's most luxurious). All units have screened porches.

937 E. Gulf Dr., Sanibel Island, FL 33957. ☎ **800/237-1491** or 941/472-3181. Fax 941/472-5234. www.sanibelinn.com. 96 units. Winter $285–$465 double; off-season $159–$239 double. Packages available. AE, DC, DISC, MC, V. **Amenities:** Restaurant (Italian); bar; heated outdoor pool; tennis courts; access to nearby health club; water-sports equipment rental; bike rental; children's programs; limited room service; baby-sitting; laundry service. *In room:* A/C, TV, dataport, kitchen, fridge, coffeemaker, hair dryer, iron.

Sanibel's Seaside Inn 🏕🏕   This comfortable and friendly Key West–style establishment enjoys a tranquil location near the island's southeastern tip. The duplex, 1960s-style cottages are spacious, brightly furnished one-bedroom apartments, but if you can do without a kitchen, the choice units here are the beachfront hotel rooms, whose screened porches face the gulf. All units have ceiling fans and open-air balconies or decks. No smoking indoors.

541 E. Gulf Dr., Sanibel Island, FL 33957. ☎ **800/831-7384** or 941/472-1400. Fax 941/472-6518. www.seasideinn.com. 32 units. Winter $205–$385 double; off-season $159–$209 double. Rates include continental breakfast. Packages available. AE, DC, DISC, MC, V. **Amenities:** Heated outdoor pool; tennis courts; health club; access to nearby health club; exercise room; spa; Jacuzzi; sauna; water-sports equipment rental; frees use of bikes; children's programs; game room; concierge; activities desk; car-rental desk; business center; shopping arcade; salon; limited room service; massage; baby-sitting; laundry service; coin-op washers and dryers; concierge-level rooms. *In room:* A/C, TV, fax, dataport, kitchen (some units), minibar, fridge, coffeemaker, hair dryer, iron.

Song of the Sea 🏕🏕   Popular with Europeans, this beachside inn offers motel-like efficiencies and one-bedroom suites with plantation-style shutters behind sliding-glass doors opening to screened porches. Don't expect a lot of extra space in the suites, whose bedrooms are barely large enough to hold their king-size beds. A pathway leads next door to the Sanibel Inn (see above), where guests can use the facilities. An extensive continental breakfast is served in the public building and eaten at umbrella tables on a brick patio. Guests get discounts on the facilities at the Sundial Beach Resort (see below).

863 E. Gulf Dr., Sanibel Island, FL 33957. (C) **800/231-1045** or 941/472-2220. Fax 941/472-8569. 30 units. www.songofthesea.com. Winter $315–$419 double; off-season $155–$239 double. Rates include continental breakfast. Packages available. AE, DC, DISC, MC, V. **Amenities:** Heated outdoor pool; Jacuzzi; coin-op washers and dryers. *In room:* A/C, TV, fax, dataport, kitchen, minibar, fridge, coffeemaker, hair dryer, iron.

Sundial Beach Resort 🐾🐾 *Kids*   The largest resort on Sanibel, this condominium complex lacks intimacy but has lots to keep families occupied, from a palm-studded, beachside pool area to a complimentary marine biology program and a small ecology center with a touch tank. The one-, two-, and three-bedroom condominiums are housed in two- and three-story buildings (as high as they get on Sanibel) and have screened balconies overlooking the beach or tropically landscaped gardens. Among several dining options here, the award-winning **Windows on the Water** dining room offers glorious gulf views at breakfast, lunch, and dinner; master chefs put on a show as they prepare delicious steak, chicken, and seafood dishes right by your table in **Noopie's Japanese Seafood & Steakhouse,** where dinner reservations are required ((C) **941/ 395-6014**). Overlooking the pool and the gulf, the relaxing Beaches Grill & Bar is popular at sunset and has entertainment nightly from 7 to 11pm.

1451 Middle Gulf Dr., Sanibel Island, FL 33957. (C) **800/237-4184** or 941/481-3636. Fax 941/481-4947. www. sundialresort.com. 275 units. Winter $209–$635 condo apt.; off-season $155–$350 condo apt. Packages available. AE, DC, DISC, MC, V. **Amenities:** 4 restaurants (American; Japanese); 2 bars; 5 heated outdoor pools; 12 tennis courts; exercise room; Jacuzzi; water-sports equipment rental; bike rental; children's programs; game room; concierge; activities desk; business center; limited room service; massage; baby-sitting; laundry service; coin-op washers and dryers. *In room:* A/C, TV/VCR, kitchen, coffeemaker, hair dryer, iron.

Moderate

Island Inn 🐾🐾   It's difficult to get accommodations here during the peak winter season, but it's worth trying because this classic beach resort has been in business for more than a century. Its original central building houses a bright, genteel dining room, a spacious lounge, and a library brightly furnished with old-style bentwood and wicker sofas and chairs. This is the kind of place where guests dress for dinner—jackets and collared shirts required, ties recommended for men at dinner—and seating is assigned (some guests have had the same table for years). This main building looks out over a sandy, South Pacific–like yard to the Gulf. Although neither charming in an Old Florida sense nor luxurious by today's standards, the cottages and motel rooms (with or without kitchens) are modern and comfortable. Most have screened porches or balconies.

3111 W. Gulf Dr., Sanibel Island, FL 33957. (C) **800/851-5088** or 941/472-1561. Fax 941/472-0051. www. islandinnsanibel.com. 57 units, including 9 cottages. Winter (including breakfast and dinner) $175–$345 double; off-season (no meals) $105–$205 double. AE, DISC, MC, V. **Amenities:** Restaurant (American); bar; small heated outdoor pool; tennis court; croquet area; coin-op washers and dryers. *In room:* A/C, TV, kitchen (some units), fridge, coffeemaker, hair dryer, iron.

Tarpon Tale Inn 🐾 *Finds*   Owners Dawn and Joe Ramsey preside over this low-slung gray building in the "Old Sanibel" neighborhood, the island's first settlement where the ferries from Fort Myers used to dock near the lighthouse. White walls and tile floors make their comfortable units bright; French doors lead to gardens dense with seagrape, palm, and ficus trees, which provide privacy for a large outdoor hot tub. Three of their five units have separate bedrooms, while two other "deluxe studios" actually are two-bedroom suites. All units have shower-only bathrooms. Continental breakfast makings are delivered the night before.

367 Periwinkle Way, Sanibel Island, FL 33957. *C* **941/472-0939.** Fax 941/472-6202. www.tarpontale.com. 5 units. Winter $119–$210 double; off-season $79–$159 double. Rates include continental breakfast. DISC, MC, V. Some pets accepted ($30 fee); call first. **Amenities:** Jacuzzi; coin-op washers and dryers. *In room:* A/C, TV/VCR, kitchen, coffeemaker, hair dryer and iron on request, no phone.

Inexpensive

Palm View Motel   In a quiet residential area less than a block from the Holiday Inn Beach Resort and Morgan's Forest restaurant, this little property is one of Sanibel's few inexpensive motels. The best choices here are the spacious, well-ventilated one- and two-bedroom apartments. Two motel rooms are the only units without kitchens, but they have microwave ovens and refrigerators. They also interconnect and are often rented together to make a two-bedroom unit. You'll have to do without a phone in your room, but you can bring your pet. There's a hot tub in the backyard.

706 Donax St., Sanibel Island, FL 33957. *C* **941/472-1606.** Fax 941/472-1606. www.palmviewmotel.com. 8 units. A/C TV. Winter $95 double; $120–$180 efficiency and apts. Off-season $65 double; $75–$110 efficiency and apts. MC, V. Pets accepted ($10 per day). **Amenities:** Jacuzzi; coin-op washers and dryers. *In room:* A/C, TV, kitchen (most units), fridge, no phone.

CAPTIVA ISLAND

Captiva Island Inn Bed & Breakfast ✦   This B&B complex sits virtually surrounded by restaurants, art galleries, and boutiques along Captiva's block-long commercial street. That can make it a bit too busy for some eyes and ears, but it has its charms. Two suites in the Key West–style main building open to porches overlooking the lane, while four Dutch clapboard cottages sit out back on the fringes of a gravel parking lot (you get just enough yard here for hammocks and a gas grill). The ceiling in one cottage that once housed aviator Charles Lindbergh has clouds painted against a blue sky. It and the rest of the units have ceiling fans, kitchens, large bathrooms, queen-size sofa beds in their living rooms, cool tile floors, and designer bed linens (including down comforters for the occasional chilly night). Some rooms have only showers in their bathrooms. Guests get free use of bicycles and towels and chairs for the beach (a block away) and get a complimentary full breakfast at R. C. Otter's Island Eats across the lane.

11509 Andy Rosse Lane (P.O. Box 848), Captiva Island, FL 33924. *C* **800/454-9898** or 941/395-0882. Fax 941/395-0862. www.captivaislandinn.com. 6 units. Winter $220–$260 double; off-season $130–$150 double. Rates include full breakfast. AE, DISC, MC, V. *In room:* A/C, TV, kitchen, fridge, coffeemaker.

South Seas Resort ✦✦✦ *Kids*   Formerly Clarence Chadwick's 330-acre copra plantation, this exclusive establishment is the premier property on these two islands. It's one of the best choices in southern Florida for serious tennis buffs, its gulf-side golf course is one of the most picturesque 9-holers anywhere, and its two marinas host scuba dive operators. The resort occupies all of Captiva's northern third, making it ideal if you want to step from your luxury house or condominium right onto 2½ miles of gorgeous beach. The resort is so spread out along the shore that a free trolley shuttles back and forth through the mangrove forests.

Most accommodations are so-called villas (actually condominium apartments), but there's a great variety of offerings, including luxury homes with private pools and their own tennis courts (many are occupied exclusively by their owners; watch for famous folks wandering about). With three bedrooms or more, some units are ideal for families or couples who want to share the cost of a vacation. The least-expensive (and least-inspired) units are the "Harbourside" hotel rooms at the yacht basin and marina near the island's northern tip, the jumping-off point for Captiva Cruises and Steve and Doris Colgate's Offshore Sailing School. Next up are the "Bayside Villas" and "Beachside Villas"—condominium apartments in three-story buildings near the main-gate area and its shops and restaurants. Whatever type of living space you choose, by all means inquire about package deals, which can result in significant savings for stays of 3 nights or more.

Outside the main gate, Chadwick's Shopping Center includes high-fashion boutiques, jewelry stores, and gift shops, all open to the public, but the resort's no-cash, charge-to-your-room policy prevents gate-crashers from the resort proper.

P.O. Box 194, Captiva Island, FL 33924. ℭ **800/554-5454** or 941/472-5111. Fax 941/481-4947. www.southseas-resort.com. 600 units. Winter $150–355 double; $335–$630 condo; $370–$975 house. Off-season $140–$290 double; $260–$410 condo; $260–$665 house. $8 per person per day added to room bills, 18% to 19% to food and bar bills, in lieu of tipping. Packages available. AE, DC, DISC, MC, V. **Amenities:** 3 restaurants (American); 2 bars; 18 heated outdoor pools; 9-hole golf course; 18 tennis courts; health club; Jacuzzis; water-sports equipment rental; bike rental; children's programs; game room; concierge; activities desk; business center; shopping arcade; salon; limited room service; massage; baby-sitting; laundry service; coin-op washers and dryers. *In room:* A/C, TV, dataport (some units), kitchen (larger units only), coffeemaker, hair dryer, iron.

'Tween Waters Inn ✦✦   Wedged between the gulf beach and the bay on the narrowest part of Captiva, this venerable establishment was the regular haunt of cartoonist J. N. (Ding) Darling. Anne Morrow Lindbergh also dined often here while writing *A Gift from the Sea.* Just as Darling preserved the islands' wildlife, the 'Tween Waters has saved the cottages he stayed in. Situated in a sandy palm grove, these pink shiplap buildings have been upgraded but still capture Old Florida. Some face the gulf; others, the bay. Themed to honor their famous guests, they range in size from the bay-side honeymoon cottage with barely enough room for its king-size bed and a tiny kitchen to a three-bedroom, two-bath house. The modern, spacious hotel rooms and apartments are in three modern buildings on stilts; they all have screened balconies facing the gulf or the bay.

The Old Captiva House restaurant appears very much as it did in Ding Darling's days (note his cartoons adorning the dining room walls), and The Canoe and The Kayak restaurant provides inexpensive lunches on its bay-side deck. The popular Crow's Nest Lounge has live entertainment and provides snacks and light evening meals from 9pm to 1am.

Charter captains dock at the full-service marina.

P.O. Box 249, Captiva Island, FL 33924. ℭ **800/223-5865** or 941/472-5161. Fax 941/472-0249. www.tweenwaters.com. 138 units. Winter $225–$280 double; $285–$580 suites; $140–$350 cottage. Off-season $185–$200 double; $200–$395 suites; $110–$255 cottage. Rates include continental breakfast. Packages available. AE, DC, MC, V. Pets accepted in cottages ($15 per day).

COTTAGES

The islands have several Old Florida–style cottages that offer charming and often less expensive alternatives to hotels and condominiums. Some of the best are members of the **Sanibel-Captiva Small Inns & Cottages Association.** You can contact the association (via its website only) at www.sanibelsmallinns.com for a complete listing of properties.

Sitting between two condominium complexes off Middle Gulf Drive, **Gulf Breeze Cottages** ★★, 1081 Shell Basket Lane, Sanibel Island, FL 33957 (© **800/388-2842** or 941/472-1626; www.gbreeze.com), is a collection of clapboard cottages separated from the beach by a lawn with covered picnic area and outdoor shower. One two-story building is divided into four efficiencies (the pick is no. 7, with a two-way view of the gulf from its big picture windows). Rates are $200 to $335 a day in winter, $100 to $215 a day off-season.

With only one monstrous mansion standing between them and a narrow bay beach near Sanibel Lighthouse, **Buttonwood Cottages** ★, 1234 Buttonwood Lane, Sanibel Island, FL 33957 (© **887/395-COTTAGE** or 941/395-9061; fax 941/395-2620; www.buttonwoodcottages.com), are less expensive options at $125 to $220 a day in winter, $75 to $160 off-season. Recently remodeled and equipped with many modern amenities, the five units occupy two long cottages built on stilts. Four of them have screened porches, with two overlooking a lushly tropical backyard sporting two hammocks and two hot tubs. The Lighthouse Cafe (see "Where to Dine," below) is around the corner.

Barely updated since the 1950s are the 32 pink clapboard structures at **Beachview Cottages,** 3325 W. Gulf Dr., Sanibel Island, FL 33957 (© **800/860-0532** or 941/472-1202; fax 941/472-4720; www.beachviewsanibel.com). None of the cottages has a phone, and some have shower-only bathrooms. There's a heated outdoor swimming pool here. Winter rates are $149 to $249 a day, off-season $109 to $179 a day.

On Captiva, **Jensen's On the Gulf,** P.O. Box 460, Captiva Island, FL 33924 (© **941/472-4684;** www.jensen-captiva.com), has cottages as well as homes, apartments, and studios ranging from $200 to $550 a day in winter, $135 to $375 a day off-season. **Jensen's Twin Palm Resort & Marina,** P.O. Box 191, Captiva Island, FL 33924 (© **941/472-5800;** same website), on the bay side near the Andy Rosse Lane dining district, has cottages ranging from $135 to $185 a day during winter, from $95 to $120 a day off-season.

WHERE TO DINE

No restaurant can survive on these affluent islands without serving good food, so you're assured of getting a fine meal wherever you go. Oddly, only a handful of restaurants offer dining with water views.

SANIBEL ISLAND

Much of the "help" on this affluent island dines at **Jerry's Family Restaurant,** 1700 Periwinkle Way at Casa Ybel Road (© **941/472-9300**), which offers wholesome and inexpensive diner fare (ingredients come fresh from the adjacent Jerry's Supermarket). Both the restaurant and the supermarket are open daily from 6am to 11pm. Breakfast is served from 6am to 4pm, and you can usually get a table quickly here (which can't be said of Sanibel's other popular breakfast spots).

You'll find very reasonably priced pub fare at Sanibel's sports bars, such as **The Lazy Flamingo I** (see below) and **Sanibel Grill,** 703 Tarpon Bay Rd., near Palm Ridge Road (© **941/472-3128**), which actually serves as the bar for Timbers, the fine seafood restaurant next door (see below). They all have reduced-price beer and munchies during televised football games.

There's no Starbucks coffee emporium here, so the local cure for caffeine withdrawal is **The Bean,** 2240 Periwinkle Way, in Sanibel Square shopping center west of Dunlop Road (© **941/395-1919**). This little open-air spot sits next to the J. Howard Wood Theatre, so it draws an after-show crowd.

For picnics at Sanibel's beaches or on a canoe, the deli and bakery in **Bailey's General Store,** at Periwinkle Way and Tarpon Bay Road (© **941/472-1516**), carries a gourmet selection of breads, cheeses, and meats. **Huxter's Deli and Market,** 1203 Periwinkle Way, east of Donax Street (© **941/472-6988**), has sandwich fixings and "beach box" lunches to go.

Very Expensive

Mad Hatter ✿✿ ECLECTIC   Sanibel's best choice for a romantic special dinner, this gulf-front restaurant has only 12 tables, but each has a view that's perfect at sunset. Chef Horst Roellkes' ever-changing eclectic menu features flavors from around the world, such as Thai-style peanut sauce over a seared, sesame-encrusted yellowfin tuna steak. His jumbo shrimp Wellington is a fascinating twist on the classic beef dish, and his stuffed crab served with a lobster volute is another winner.

6467 Sanibel-Captiva Rd., at Blind Pass. © 941/472-0033. Reservations suggested. Main courses $25–$35. AE, MC, V. Feb–Apr Sun–Mon 5–9:30pm; Tues–Sat 11:30am–2pm and 5–9:30pm. May–Jan Mon–Sat 5–9:30pm. Closed Sept after Labor Day.

Moderate

Jacaranda SEAFOOD/PASTA/STEAKS   With live music nightly, the Patio Lounge attracts an affluent over-40 crowd to this friendly and casual restaurant named for the purple-flowered jacaranda tree. Although the Jacaranda is best known as a local gathering spot, it has received several dining awards. Fresh fish is well prepared here, or you can choose certified Angus steaks or prime rib. The linguine with a dozen littleneck clams tossed in a piquant red or white clam sauce is consistently excellent. For dessert, the gooey turtle pie—ice cream, caramel, fudge sauce, chopped nuts, and whipped cream—will send you away stuffed.

1223 Periwinkle Way (east of Donax St.). © 941/472-1771. Reservations recommended. Main courses $15–$22. AE, MC, V. Daily 5–10pm. Lounge daily 4pm–12:30am. Closed Christmas.

McT's Shrimp House & Tavern SEAFOOD   Shrimp reigns at this casual Old Florida–style establishment, where you'll see a line outside at 4pm waiting for the early bird specials served to the first 100 persons in the door. Everyone else gets to view the daily catch displayed in a chiller case, including the night's shrimp ready for the chef to prepare in one of at least a dozen ways, from steamed to fried in a coconut-and-almond batter. There are also grouper and swordfish, plus steaks and chicken for the land-minded, but stick to the shrimp here (see below for the Timbers Restaurant & Fish Market, which does a much better job of cooking fish). McT's Tavern offers an extensive choice of appetizers and light dinners.

1523 Periwinkle Way (at Fitzhugh St.). © 941/472-3161. Reservations not accepted. Main courses $13–$20; early bird specials $10. AE, DC, DISC, MC, V. Shrimp House daily 4:45–10pm. McT's Tavern daily 4pm–midnight.

Morgan's Forest *Kids* SEAFOOD   The kids will love dining in this miniature jungle patterned after the Rainforest Cafes elsewhere. Almost hidden among all the foliage are mechanical but lifelike moving jaguars, monkeys, birds, and a huge python entangled in vines above the bar. Squawking bird sounds, strobe-lightning bolts followed by claps of thunder, and an occasional faux fog rolling across the floor add to the Amazonian ambience. The owner of Fort Myers Beach's excellent Channel Mark restaurant is in charge here, which means that your taste buds will be as entertained as your eyes and ears. The fine crab cakes

---

Tips **Deals on Meals**

Local restaurants often run advertisements containing discount coupons in the "Sanibel-Captiva Shopper's Guide," a free publication available at the chamber of commerce visitor center.

---

are the pick of a menu otherwise accented with South- and Central-American seasonings. Obviously, there's a children's menu.

1231 Middle Gulf Dr., at the Holiday Inn Beach Resort. ✆ 941/472-3351. Reservations not accepted. Main courses $14–$23. AE, DC, DISC, MC, V. Mon–Sat 7–11am and 5–10pm; Sun 7am–noon and 5–10pm.

The Timbers Restaurant & Fish Market ☆☆ SEAFOOD/STEAK   This casual upstairs restaurant, with bamboo railings, oversized canvas umbrellas, and paintings of tropical scenes through faux windows, consistently is Sanibel's best place for fresh fish and aged beef. In the fish market out front, you can view the catch and have the chef charcoal-grill or blacken it to order. The steaks, cut on the premises, are the island's best. You can order a drink from the adjoining Sanibel Grill sports bar and wait for a table outside on the shopping center's porch.

703 Tarpon Bay Rd. (at Palm Ridge Rd.). ✆ 941/472-3128. Reservations not accepted. Main courses $15–$19; early birds get $2.50 off regular price. AE, MC, V. Winter daily 4:30–9:30pm; Off-season daily 5–9:30pm.

Inexpensive

Grandma Dot's Seaside Saloon SEAFOOD   One of Sanibel's most popular lunch spots, this open-air but screened cafe on the docks of Sanibel Marina offers excellent salads (try the seafood Caesar) and fine sandwiches plus a few main courses led by broiled grouper in a sauce of lemon, dill, butter, and white wine.

At Sanibel Marina, 634 N. Yachtsman Dr. ✆ 941/472-8138. Reservations not accepted. Main courses $6–$23; salads and sandwiches $6–$12. MV, V. Daily 11:30am–7:30pm.

Hungry Heron ☆☆ *Kids* AMERICAN   This tropically decorated eatery is Sanibel's most popular family restaurant. There's something for everyone on the huge, tabloid-size menu—from hot and cold appetizers and overstuffed "sea-wiches" to pasta and steamed shellfish. And if the 250 regular items aren't enough, there's a list of nightly specials. Seafood, steaks, and stir-frys from a sizzling skillet are popular with local residents, who bring the kids here for fun and a children's menu. An all-you-can-eat breakfast buffet on Saturday and Sunday in winter is an excellent value.

In Palm Ridge Place, 2330 Palm Ridge Rd. (at Periwinkle Way). ✆ 941/395-2300. Reservations not accepted, but call for preferred seating. Main courses $9–$18; sandwiches, burgers, snacks $6–$11; weekend breakfast buffet $8 adults, $4 children under 10. AE, DISC, MC, V. Winter Mon–Fri 8am–9pm; Sat–Sun 7:30am–noon and 7:30–10pm. Off-season daily 11am–9pm.

The Lazy Flamingo I *Value* SEAFOOD/PUB FARE   T-shirts and shorts or jeans are the dress code at this friendly pub that always seems packed by the young and young-at-heart, who flock here for reasonably priced food, a wide choice of beers iced down in a huge box behind the bar, and sports TVs. Some of that beer is used to steam shrimp and a finger-stinging collection of oysters, clams, and spices known as "The Pot." Best pick, however, is grouper from the charcoals, as either a main course or a sandwich. The flamingo-pink menu also has an array of sandwiches, burgers, fish platters, and very spicy "Dead Parrot Wings." Fillet your own catch, and the chef will cook it to order for you. Happy-hour prices prevail whenever football games are on the TVs. A sister institution, the **Lazy Flamingo II,** 6520-C Pine Ave., at Sanibel-Captiva Road, ¼ mile south of Blind Pass ((C) **941/472-5353**), has the same menu and hours.

1036 Periwinkle Way, west of Causeway Blvd. (C) **941/472-6939**. Reservations not accepted. Main courses $11–$15; sandwiches and snacks $5–$9. Cook your catch $8. AE, DISC, MC, V. Daily 11:30am–1am.

Lighthouse Cafe (C) *Value* AMERICAN   Decorated with photos and draw-ings of lighthouses, this casual storefront establishment located appropriately near the Sanibel Lighthouse dishes up breakfast omelets that are meals in them-selves, especially the ocean frittata containing delicately seasoned scallops, crab-meat, shrimp, broccoli, and fresh mushrooms, and crowned with an artichoke heart and creamy Alfredo sauce. Seafood Benedict is another unusual offering. Interesting sandwiches are served after 11am. Reasonably priced cafe-style din-ners are served during winter only.

In Seahorse Shops, 362 Periwinkle Way (at Buttonwood Lane, east of Causeway Rd.). (C) **941/472-0303**. Reservations not accepted but call ahead to get on waiting list. Main courses $10–$15; breakfast $3.50–$7.50; sandwiches and salads $4.50–$8.50. MC, V. Daily 7am–3pm and 5–9pm. Closed for dinner Easter to mid-Dec.

Sanibel Cafe (C) *Value* AMERICAN   Seashells are the theme at Lynda and Ken Boyce's pleasant cafe, whose tables are museum-like glass cases containing deli-cate fossilized specimens from the Miocene and Pliocene epochs. Fresh-squeezed orange and grapefruit juice, Danish Havarti omelets, and homemade muffins and biscuits highlight the breakfast menu (eggs Benedict and fruit-filled waffles are served until closing). Lunch features specialty sandwiches; shrimp, Greek, and chicken-and-grape salads made with a very light, fat-free dressing; and a limited list of main courses such as grilled or blackened chicken breast. At din-ner they add homemade meatloaf, crunchy grouper, and certified Angus steaks. Fatten up on Lynda's homemade red raspberry jam, apple or cherry crisps, and terrific Key lime pie.

In the Tahitian Gardens Shops, 2007 Periwinkle Way. (C) **941/472-5323**. Call ahead for preferred seating. Main courses $5–$19; breakfast $3–$9; sandwiches and burgers $4.50–$8. MC, V. Daily 7am–9pm.

CAPTIVA ISLAND

Just outside South Seas Plantation & Yacht Harbour, **Chadwick's Restaurant & Lounge** ((C) **941/472-1511,** ext. 5181) is noted in these parts for its all-you-can-eat theme buffets at lunch Monday to Saturday ($11 per adult, $7 for kids 4 to 10, free for children under 4) and at dinner nightly ($20 to $27 adults, $11 to $14 for kids).

Big deli sandwiches and picnic fare are available at the **Captiva Island Store,** Captiva Road at Andy Rosse Lane ((C) **941/472-2374**), and the gourmet-ori-ented **C. W.'s Market and Deli,** at the entrance to the South Seas Resort ((C) **941/472-5111**). The beach is a block from these stores.

The Bubble Room (C)(C) *Kids* STEAK/SEAFOOD   The gaudy bubble-gum pink, yellow, purple, and green exterior of this amusing restaurant is only a prel-ude to the 1930s, 1940s, and 1950s Hollywood motif inside. The dining rooms are adorned with a collection of puppets, statues of great movie stars, toy trains, thousands of movie stills, and antique jukeboxes that play big band–era tunes. The menu carries on the cinematic theme: prime ribs Weissmuller, Eddie Fish-erman fillet of fresh grouper, and Henny Young-One boneless breast of young chicken. Both adults and children are attracted to this expensive but fun establishment, where the portions are huge. For lighter appetites, the "Tiny Bubble" sampler includes a salad, a choice of appetizer, and a dessert.

15001 Captiva Rd. (at Andy Rosse Lane). ℂ **941/472-5558**. Reservations not accepted, but call for preferred seating. Main courses $17–$30; lunch $7.50–$15. AE, DC, DISC, MC, V. Daily 11:30am–2:30pm and 5–10pm. Closed Christmas.

Captiva Sunshine Cafe ✯ ECLECTIC   This friendly, open-kitchen cafe has only 12 tables—5 of them inside, 7 on the shopping center's porch—but the food is worth the close quarters. Everything except the bread is prepared on the premises; all of it is available for take-out. Specialties are steak, fish, and shrimp from a wood-fired grill. The portions are as big as the prices are high here; in fact, appetizers such as black beans and rice can make a meal for lighter appetites. Various desserts are offered daily; the apple crisp is a winner.

In Captiva Village Sq., Captiva Rd. at Laika Lane. ℂ **941/472-6200**. Reservations recommended. Main courses $23–$33; burgers $10. AE, MC, V. Daily 11:30am–3:30pm and 5–9pm.

The Green Flash ✯ SEAFOOD   You can't miss this restaurant, which sits at the infamous "curve" where Captiva Road takes a sharp turn to the north. You won't see the real "green flash" as the sun sets here, because this modern building looks eastward across Pine Island Sound, but it does make for a nice view at lunch. And seeing the full moon turn the sound into glistening silver is worth having at least an evening drink here. The overall quality of the cuisine is very good, and the prices are very reasonable for Captiva. Start with oysters Rockefeller or shrimp bisque. Both are house specialties, as is the garlicky grouper "café de Paris" and salmon with a dill-accented béarnaise sauce.

15183 Captiva Rd. ℂ **941/472-3337**. Reservations recommended. Main courses $13–$20. AE, DC, DISC, MC, V. Daily 11:30am–3:30pm and 5:30–9:30pm (bar open 11:30am–9:30pm).

Mucky Duck ✯ SEAFOOD/PUB FARE   A Captiva institution since 1976, this lively, British-style pub is the only place on either island here where you can dine right by the beach. If you don't get a real seat with this great view, the humorous staff will gladly roll a fake window over to appease you. The menu offers a selection of fresh seafood items, plus English fish and chips, steak-and-sausage pie, and a ploughman's lunch. There's a vegetarian platter. No smoking is allowed inside. You can't make a reservation, but you can order drinks, listen to live music (Monday to Saturday), and bide your wait at beachside picnic tables out front (come early for sunset).

Andy Rosse Lane (on the gulf). ℂ **941/472-3434**. Reservations not accepted. Lunch $5.50–$11; dinner main courses $13–$18.50. AE, DC, DISC, MC, V. Mon–Sat 11:30am–2:30pm and 5–9:30pm.

R. C. Otter's Island Eats ✯✯ (Value) AMERICAN   Occupying an old clapboard-sided island cottage, this Key West–style cafe brings informality and good inexpensive food to Captiva. In contrast to the island's 15 or so formal haute-cuisine restaurants, you can dine in your bare feet and not spend a fortune for an excellent breakfast, snack, lunch, or full meal. The tables are covered with wrapping paper, and rolls of paper towels substitute for napkins. The choice seats are under ceiling fans on the front porch or beneath umbrellas on the brick patio. In hot weather you can opt for the air-conditioned dining room whose walls are adorned with the works of local artists. The wide-ranging menu includes salads, hot dogs, burgers, sandwiches, stir-fries, meatloaf, country-fried steak, broiled fish, and soft-shell crabs, plus delicious nightly specials. The island's best breakfasts are equally varied, from bacon and eggs to a seafood quesadilla. Musicians perform out in the yard every day, and you could find yourself dancing on the front porch.

11506 Andy Rosse Lane. (C) 941/395-1142. Reservations not accepted, but call for preferred seating. Main courses $10–$20; breakfast $6–$12; salads, sandwiches, burgers $6–$12. AE, DISC, MC, V. Daily 7:30am–10:30pm (breakfast to 11:30am).

SANIBEL & CAPTIVA ISLANDS AFTER DARK

You won't find glitzy nightclubs on these family-oriented islands, but night owls have some fun places to roost at the resorts and restaurants mentioned above. Here's a brief recap:

ON SANIBEL The Sundial Beach Resort's **Beaches Bar & Grill,** 1451 Middle Gulf Dr. ((C) 941/472-4151), features entertainers during dinner, then live bands for dancing from 9pm on. The **Patio Lounge,** in the Jacaranda, 1223 Periwinkle Way ((C) 941/472-1771), attracts an affluent crowd of middle-agers and seniors to its live music every evening. **McT's Tavern,** 1523 Periwinkle Way ((C) 941/472-3161), has darts, video games, and a large-screen TV for sports fans. The **Sanibel Grill,** 703 Tarpon Bay Rd. ((C) 941/472-4453), and the two **Lazy Flamingo** branches (see "Where to Dine," earlier in this chapter) are other popular sports bars.

The Pirate Players, a group of professional actors, perform Broadway dramas and comedies from November to April, in Sanibel's state-of-the-art, 150-seat **J. Howard Wood Theatre,** 2200 Periwinkle Way ((C) 941/472-0006). The **Old Schoolhouse Theater,** 1905 Periwinkle Way ((C) 941/472-6862), complements its neighbor by offering Broadway musicals and revues from December to April. Call for the current schedule and prices.

ON CAPTIVA Local songwriters perform their works nightly at **R. C. Otter's Island Eats,** 11500 Andy Rosse Lane ((C) 941/395-1142). The **Crow's Nest Lounge,** in the 'Tween Waters Inn, on Captiva Road ((C) 941/472-5161), is Captiva's top nightspot for dancing. **Chadwick's Lounge,** at the entrance to the South Seas Resort ((C) 941/472-5111), has a large dance floor and music from 9pm on.

NEARBY ISLAND HOPPING

Sanibel and Captiva are jumping-off points for island-hopping boat trips to barrier islands and keys teeming with ancient legends and Robinson Crusoe–style beaches. You don't have to get completely lost out there, however, because several islets have comfortable inns and restaurants. The trip across shallow Pine Island Sound is itself a sightseeing adventure, with playful dolphins surfing on the boats' wakes and a variety of cormorants, egrets, frigate birds, and (in winter) rare white pelicans flying above or lounging on sandbars between meals.

Captiva Cruises ((C) 941/472-5300; www.captivacruises.com) has daily trips from the South Seas Resort on Captiva. One vessel goes daily to Cabbage Key and Useppa Island, where passengers disembark for lunch. During the winter months, another goes to Boca Grande by way of Cayo Costa State Park. These day trips cost $27.50 per adult, $15 for children to Cabbage Key or Useppa; $35 for adults, $17.50 for children to Boca Grande or Cayo Costa. The Boca Grande/Cayo Costa cruises usually leave at 10am; those bound for Cabbage Key and Useppa, at 10:30am. Reservations are required.

From Pine Island off Fort Myers, you can take the *Tropic Star* ferry service ((C) 941/283-0015) to Cayo Costa (see "Cruises" in section 1).

CABBAGE KEY ★★

You never know who's going to get off a boat at 100-acre Cabbage Key and walk unannounced into the funky **Cabbage Key Inn** ★★, a rustic house built in 1938 by the son and daughter-in-law of mystery novelist Mary Roberts Rinehart. Ernest Hemingway liked to hang out here in the early days, and novelist John D. MacDonald was a frequent guest 30 years later. Today you could find yourself rubbing elbows at the bar with the likes of Walter Cronkite, Ted Koppel, Sean Connery, or Julia Roberts. Singer and avid yachtie Jimmy Buffett likes Cabbage Key so much that it inspired his hit song "Cheeseburger in Paradise."

A path leads from the tiny marina across a lawn dotted with coconut palms to this white clapboard house that sits atop an ancient Calusa shell mound. Guests dine in the comfort of two screened porches and seek libations in the Rineharts' library-turned-bar, its pine-paneled walls now plastered with dollar bills left by visitors. The straight-back chairs and painted wooden tables show their age, but that's part of Cabbage Key's laid-back, don't-give-a-hoot charm.

In addition to the famous thick, juicy cheeseburgers so loved by Jimmy Buffett, the house specialties are fresh broiled fish and shrimp steamed in beer. Lunches range from $5 to $10; main courses at dinner, $15 to $20.

Most visitors come out here for the day, but if you want to stay overnight, the Cabbage Key Inn has six rooms and six cottages. The more expensive cottages, four of which have kitchens, are preferable to the rooms. Although the units have private bathrooms and air conditioners, they are very basic by today's standards, and some of their original 1920s furnishings have seen better days. Service for overnight guests can leave a lot to be desired, and there's no place on the islet to buy snacks or sundries. If you do decide to rough it, room rates are $89 single or double for rooms, $145 to $239 for cottages. For information or reservations, contact Cabbage Key Inn, P.O. Box 200, Pineland, FL 33945 (© **941/ 283-2278;** fax 941/283-1384; www.cabbage-key.com).

Captiva Cruises (© **941/472-5300;** www.captivacruises.com) goes to Cabbage Key daily from Captiva Island, charging $27.50 per adult, $15 for children (reservations are required). You can get here from Pine Island near Fort Myers via the inn's own launch, which leaves daily from the Mattson Marine marina ($12.50 per person round-trip), or via the *Tropic Star* nature cruises (© **941/ 283-0015**), which depart Knight's Landing marina daily at 9:30am ($25 adults, $15 for children).

CAYO COSTA ★★★

You can't get any more deserted than at **Cayo Costa State Park** ★★★ (pronounced *Kay*-oh *Cos*-tah), which occupies a 2,132-acre, completely unspoiled barrier island with miles of white-sand beaches, pine forests, mangrove swamps, oak-palm hammocks, and grasslands. Other than natural wildlife, the only permanent residents here are park rangers.

Day-trippers can bring their own supplies and use a picnic area with pavilions. A free tram carries visitors from the sound-side dock to the gulf beach. The state maintains 12 very basic cabins and a primitive campground on the northern end of the island near Johnson Shoals, where the shelling is spectacular. Cabins cost $20 a day, and campsites are $13 a day all year. There's running water on the island but no electricity.

The park is open daily from 8am to sundown. There's a $1-per-person honor-system admission fee for day visitors. Overnight slips at the dock cost $13 a day.

Fishing with the Bushes

Former President George Bush, present President George W. Bush, Florida Governor Jeb Bush—indeed, the entire Bush clan—like to retreat to **Boca Grande** ⭑⭑ for a little rest and relaxation every now and then. And well they should, for this charming village on Gasparilla Island is a head-of-state's kind of place. The du Ponts, the Astors, the Morgans, the Vanderbilts, and other moneyed folk started coming here in the 1920s and still turn the island into a Florida version of Nantucket during their winter "social season." In addition to the warm weather, the lure was then, and still is, some of the world's best tarpon fishing. Descendants of the watermen who were here first still guide the rich and famous. They live in modest homes on streets named Dam-If-I-Know, Dam-If-I-Care, and Dam-If-I-Will. You can see their backyards full of boats and fishnets, but high hedges hide the manicured "beachfronter" mansions over by the gulf.

You can explore the little village in a few hours on foot or on a bike rented from **Island Bike 'n' Beach,** 333 Park Ave. (📞 941/964-0711). The pink-brick **Railroad Depot,** at the corner of Park Avenue and 4th Street, has been restored to its turn-of-the-century grandeur and now houses a cluster of upscale boutiques and the **Loose Caboose** restaurant and ice cream parlor (📞 941/964-0440), where Katherine Hepburn once satiated her sweet tooth. **Banyan Street** (actually 2nd Street) is canopied with tangled banyan trees and is one of the prettiest places for a stroll. The **Johann Fust Community Library,** at Gasparilla Road and 10th Street (📞 941/964-2488), contains the extraordinary **Du Pont Shell Collection,** gathered by Henry Francis du Pont during nearly 50 years of combing the island's beaches. At the island's south end, **Boca Grande Lighthouse Museum and Visitor's Center** (📞 941/964-0060) occupies the wood-frame lighthouse that began marking the pass into Charlotte Harbor in 1890. Exhibits explain the island's history, its tarpon fishing, and its wildlife and seashells. The white sand beaches of **Gasparilla Island State Recreation Area** (📞 941/964-0375; www8.myflorida.com/communities/learn/stateparks/district4/GasparillaIsland/index.htm) surround the lighthouse.

Captiva Cruises (📞 941/472-5300) has daily trips here during the winter season (see "Nearby Island Hopping"). The fare is $35 adults, $17.50 children, and reservations are required. For more information contact the **Boca Grande Chamber of Commerce,** 5800 Gasparilla Rd. (P.O. Box 704), Boca Grande, FL 33921 (📞 941/964-0568; fax 941/964-0620; www.charlotte-online.com/bocagrande).

You can rent single-seat kayaks for $35 a day, $45 a day for two-seaters; for reservations, call the *Tropic Star* on Pine Island (📞 941/283-0015).

For cabin reservations or more information about the park, contact **Cayo Costa State Park,** P.O. Box 1150, Boca Grande, FL 33921 (📞 941/964-0375; www8.myflorida.com/communities/learn/stateparks/district4/CayoCosta). Office hours are Monday to Friday from 8am to 5pm.

UPPER (NORTH) CAPTIVA

Cut off by a pass from Captiva, its northern barrier-island sibling is occupied by the upscale resort of **North Captiva Island Club,** P.O. Box 1000, Pineland, FL 33945 (© **800/576-7343** or 941/395-1001; fax 941/472-5836; www. northcaptiva.com). Despite the development, however, about 750 of the island's 1,000 acres are included in a state preserve. The club rents accommodations ranging from efficiencies to luxury homes. There's scheduled water-taxi service from **Jensen's Twin Palms Marina** on Captiva (© **941/472-5800**), or you can get here from Matson Marine on Pine Island with **Island Charters** (© **800/ 340-33321** or 941/283-1113). Both charge $25 per person round-trip.

USEPPA ISLAND

Useppa was a refuge of President Theodore Roosevelt and his tarpon-loving industrialist friends at the turn of the century. New York advertising magnate Barron G. Collier bought the island in 1906 and built a lovely wooden home overlooking Pine Island Sound. His mansion is now the **Collier Inn,** where day-trippers and overnight guests can partake of lunches and seafood dinners in a country-club ambience. They also can visit the **Useppa Museum,** which explains the island's history and displays 4,000-year-old Calusa artifacts. Admission is by $2 donation.

The Collier Inn is the centerpiece of the **Useppa Island Club,** an exclusive development with more than 100 luxury homes, all of the clapboard-sided, tin-roofed style of Old Florida. For information, rates (all on the modified American plan), and reservations, contact **Collier Inn & Cottages,** P.O. Box 640, Bokeelia, FL 33922 (© **941/283-5255;** fax 941/283-0290; www.useppa.com).

4 Naples ★★★

42 miles S. of Fort Myers, 106 miles W. of Miami, 185 miles S. of Tampa

Because its wealthy residents are accustomed to the very best, Naples is easily Southwest Florida's most sophisticated city. Indeed, its boutiques and galleries are at least on a par with those in Palm Beach or Beverly Hills. And yet Naples has an easygoing friendliness to all comers, who can find some surprisingly affordable places to stay within easy reach of its long, magnificent beach.

Naples was born in 1886, when a group of 12 Kentuckians and Ohioans bought 8,700 acres fronted by a gorgeous beach, laid out a town, and started selling lots. They built a pier and the 16-room Naples Hotel, whose first guest was President Grover Cleveland's sister Rose. She and other notables soon built a line of beach homes known as "Millionaires' Row." Today that area is known as Olde Naples and is carefully protected by its modern residents. Despite a recent building boom that has expanded the city to the north and east, the original settlement still retains the air of that time a century ago.

Although high-rise buildings now line the beaches north of the old town, the newer sections of Naples still have their charm, thanks to Ohio manufacturer Henry B. Watkins Sr. In 1946 Watkins and his partners bought the old hotel and all the town's undeveloped land and laid out the Naples Plan, which created the environmentally conscious city you see today.

About 4 miles north of Olde Naples, Vanderbilt Beach has a more traditional beach-resort character than the historic district. Lined with a mix of two-story, 1960s-style motels and high-rise hotels and condominiums, the main beach here sits like an island of development between two preserved areas: Delnor-Wiggins

Pass State Recreation to the north, and a county reserve fronting the expensive Pelican Bay golf-course community to the south.

ESSENTIALS

GETTING THERE   Most visitors arrive at the **Southwest Florida International Airport,** 35 miles north of Naples (see "Getting There," under "Essentials," in section 1). **Naples Municipal Airport,** on North Road off Airport-Pulling Road (© 941/643-6875), is served by the commuter arms of **American** (© 800/433-7300) and **United/US Airways** (© 800/428-4322), which means you'll have to change planes in Miami, Tampa, or Orlando. Taxis await all flights outside the small terminal building; **Avis** (© 800/331-1212), **Budget** (© 800/ 527-0700), **Hertz** (© 800/654-3131), and **National** (© 800/CAR-RENT) have booths at the airport. **Enterprise** (© 800/325-8007) is in town.

VISITOR INFORMATION   The most comprehensive source of information is the **Naples Area Chamber of Commerce,** which maintains a visitor center at 895 5th Ave. S. (at U.S. 41), Naples, FL 34102 (© **941/262-6141;** fax 941/ 435-9910; www.napleschamber.org). The center has a host of free information and phones for making hotel reservations, and it sells a detailed street map for $2. By mail, it will send you a free list of accommodations and other basic information, or you can order a complete Naples vacation packet for $8 ($12 to Canada and other countries) and the street map for $5. The visitor center is open Monday to Friday from 9am to 5pm, Saturday from 9am to 2pm.

GETTING AROUND   You can get to the beach and most establishments in Olde Naples on foot or by bicycle. Rent a bike from **The Bike Route,** 655 N. Tamiami Trail (© **941/262-8373**). For scooters, call **Good Times Rental,** 1947 Davis Blvd. (© **941/775-7529**).

For longer distances, the **Naples Trolley** (© **941/262-7300**) clangs around 25 stops between the Marketplace at Tin City in Olde Naples and Vanderbilt Beach on Monday to Saturday from 8:30am to 5:15pm and on Sunday from 10:15am to 5:15pm. Daily fares are $15 for adults, $6 for children 5 to 12, free for children under 5, with free reboarding. You can buy tickets from the driver or at the Naples Trolley General Store and Welcome Center, 1010 6th Ave. S. at 10th Street South (2 blocks west of Tin City). Schedules are available in brochure racks in the lobbies of most hotels and motels.

Call **Yellow Cab** (© 941/262-1312), **Checker Cab** (© 941/455-5555), **Maxi Taxi** (© 941/262-8977), or **Naples Taxi** (© 941/775-0505). Fares are $1.75 for the first $\frac{1}{10}$ mile, 30¢ for each $\frac{2}{10}$ mile thereafter.

HITTING THE BEACH

Unlike many Florida cities where you have to drive over to a barrier island to reach the beach, this city's beach is right in Olde Naples. And rather than being fronted by tall condominium buildings, here the mansions along Millionaires' Row form the backdrop. Access to the gorgeous white sand is at the gulf end of each avenue, although parking in the neighborhood can be precious. Try the metered lots on 12th Avenue South near the **Naples Pier,** the town's most popular beaching spot (see "Exploring the Town," below), where there's also a food concession. Families gather on the beach north of the pier, while local teens congregate on the south side.

Also popular with families, lovely **Lowdermilk Park,** on Millionaire's Row at Gulf Shore Boulevard and North Banyan Boulevard, has a pavilion, restrooms, showers, a refreshment counter, professional-quality volleyball courts (the area's best players practice here), a duck pond, and picnic tables. There's metered parking, so bring quarters. A few blocks farther north is another metered parking lot with beach access beside the Naples Beach Hotel & Golf Resort, 851 Gulf Shore Blvd. N., at Golf Drive.

Nature lovers head to the Pelican Bay development north of the historic district and the popular **Clam Pass County Park** 🐾🐾 (© **941/353-0404**). A free tram takes you along a 3,000-foot boardwalk winding through mangrove swamps and across a back bay to a beach of fine white sand. It's a strange sight, what with high-rise condominiums standing beyond the mangrove-bordered backwaters, but this actually is a miniature wilderness. Some 6 miles of canoe and kayak trails—with multitudes of birds and an occasional alligator—run from Clam Pass into the winding streams. The beach pavilion here has a bar, restrooms with foot showers only, picnic tables, and beach equipment rentals, including one- and two-person kayaks and 12-foot canoes. Entry is from a metered parking lot beside The Registry Resort at the end of Seagate Drive. There's a $3-per-vehicle parking fee. You can push, but not ride, bicycles on the boardwalk.

At Vanderbilt Beach, about 4 miles north of Olde Naples, the **Delnor-Wiggins Pass State Recreation Area** 🐾🐾🐾, at the west end of Bluebill Avenue–111th Avenue North (© **941/597-6196**; www8.myflorida.com/communities/learn/stateparks/district4/delnorwiggins), has been listed among America's top 10 stretches of sand. It has bathhouses, a boat ramp, and the area's best picnic facilities. A concessionaire sells hot dogs, sandwiches, and ice cream and rents beach chairs, umbrellas, kayaks, canoes, and snorkeling gear. Fish viewing is great over a small reef under 12 feet of water about 50 yards offshore. Fishing from the beach is excellent here, too.

The area is open daily from 8am to sunset. Admission is $2 per vehicle with one occupant, $4 for vehicles with two to eight occupants, $1 for pedestrians and bikers. To get here from Olde Naples, go north on U.S. 41 about 4 miles and take a left on 111th Avenue, which turns into Bluebill Avenue before reaching the beach. Note that 111th Avenue is known as Immokalee Road east of U.S. 41.

OTHER OUTDOOR ACTIVITIES

BOATING Powerboat and WaveRunner rentals are available from **Naples Watersports,** at the Old Naples Seaport, 10th Avenue South at 10th Street South in Olde Naples (© **941/435-9595**); from **Club Nautico,** at the Boat Haven Marina, 1484 E. Tamiami Trail (© **941/774-0100**), on the east bank of the Gordon River behind Kelly's Fish House; and from **Port-O-Call Marina,** also behind Kelly's Fish House (© **941/774-0479**).

Houseboat Rentals of Southwest Florida (© **941/775-2003**; www. ivacation.com/p6950.htm) offers live-aboard boats, which will sleep up to six persons. Prices start at $525 for a 2-night rental and go up to $1,000 for a week.

CRUISES The Gordon River and Naples Bay from the U.S. 41 bridge on 5th Avenue South to the gulf are prime territory for sightseeing, dolphin watching, and sunset cruises. The double-decked *Double Sunshine* (© **941/263-4949**) sallies forth onto the river and bay daily from Tin City, where it has a ticket office. The 1½ -hour cruises usually leave at 10am, noon, 2pm, and an hour before sunset. They cost $20 for adults, $10 for children under 12. A sister boat, the *Captain Paul,* goes on afternoon shelling and beachcombing excursions to

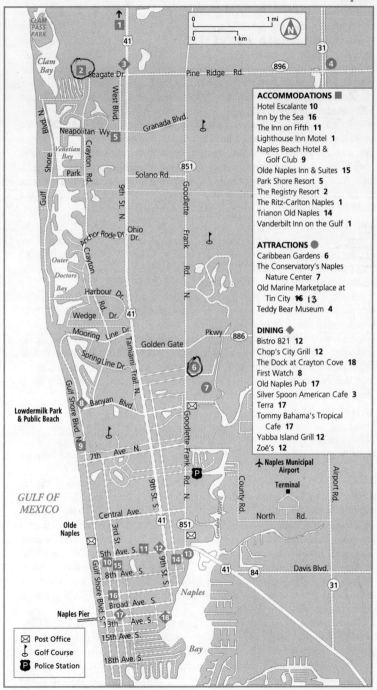

ACCOMMODATIONS ■
Hotel Escalante **10**
Inn by the Sea **16**
The Inn on Fifth **11**
Lighthouse Inn Motel **1**
Naples Beach Hotel &
   Golf Club **9**
Olde Naples Inn & Suites **15**
Park Shore Resort **5**
The Registry Resort **2**
The Ritz-Carlton Naples **1**
Trianon Old Naples **14**
Vanderbilt Inn on the Gulf **1**

ATTRACTIONS ●
Caribbean Gardens **6**
The Conservatory's Naples
   Nature Center **7**
Old Marine Marketplace at
   Tin City **16** **13**
Teddy Bear Museum **4**

DINING ◆
Bistro 821 **12**
Chop's City Grill **12**
The Dock at Crayton Cove **18**
First Watch **8**
Old Naples Pub **17**
Silver Spoon American Cafe **3**
Terra **17**
Tommy Bahama's Tropical
   Cafe **17**
Yabba Island Grill **12**
Zoë's **12**

⊠ Post Office
⚲ Golf Course
Ⓟ Police Station

387

Keewaydin Island, a private wildlife sanctuary south of Olde Naples. Its cruises cost $30 per adult, $20 for children under 12.

The *Sweet Liberty* (© 941/793-3525), a 53-foot sailing catamaran, makes morning shelling cruises to Keewaydin Island. The vessel then spends the afternoon sightseeing and the evening on sunset cruises on Naples Bay before docking at Boat Haven Marina on the east side of the Gordon River Bridge. Shelling cruises cost $25 for adults, $10 for children; sightseeing and sunset cruises cost $22 for adults, $15 for children.

For a good deal more luxury, the 83-foot *Naples Princess* (© 800/728-2970 or 941/649-2275) has narrated breakfast, lunch, and sunset dinner cruises from Port O'Call Marina, on the eastern shore of the Gordon River. With extensive buffets, the sightseeing, lunch, sunset, and dinner cruises are good values at $22, $27, $27.50, and $40 per person, respectively. Once a week there's a nature cruise sponsored and narrated by The Conservancy of Naples; it costs $24 and includes continental breakfast. Call for schedules and reservations.

FISHING   The locals like to fish from the **Naples Pier** (see "Exploring the Town," below). The pier has tables on which to clean your catch, but watch out for the ever-present pelicans, which are master thieves. You can buy tackle and bait from the local marinas (see "Boating," above). The pier is open around the clock, and admission is free. No fishing license is required.

The least-expensive way for singles, couples, and small families to fish without paying for an entire boat is on the 45-foot *Lady Brett* (© 941/263-4949), which makes two daily trips from Tin City for $45 for adults, $40 for kids under 12. Rod, reel, bait, and fishing license are included, but bring your own drinks and lunch. Its sister boat, the *Captain Paul,* goes on half-day backcountry fishing trips, departing daily at 9am. These cost $40 for adults, $35 for children.

A number of charter boats are based at the marinas mentioned under "Boating," above; call or visit them for booking information and prices.

GOLF   Naples has an extraordinary number of fine golf courses for a city its size. Most are out in the suburbs, but not the flat but challenging 18 holes at the **Naples Beach Hotel & Golf Club** ★★ (see "Where to Stay," below), which are right in the middle of town. Nonguests can play here, but call ahead for a tee time.

Two of the best-known courses are **Lely Flamingo Island Club** ★★ and the **Lely Mustang Golf Club,** both on U.S. 41 between Naples and Marco Island (© 800/388-GOLF or 941/793-2223). The Lely Flamingo course was designed by Robert Trent Jones Sr., and its hourglass fairways and fingerlike bunkers present many challenges. Designed by Lee Trevino, the Lely Mustang course is more forgiving but still fun. Former PGA Tour player Paul Trittler has his golf school at these courses. You'll pay a price here in winter, when 18-hole fees are about $135 at Lely Flamingo and $150 at Lely Mustang, including cart and range balls, but they drop progressively after Easter to about $40 and $50, respectively, in the muggy summer months.

Boyne South, on U.S. 41 between Fla. 931 and Fla. 92 (© 941/732-5108), is another winner, with lots of wildlife inhabiting its many lakes (a 16-foot alligator reportedly resides near the 17th hole). There are a driving range, practice facility, and restaurant; instruction is available. Wintertime fees are about $70, but in the off-season they drop to $45 or less. Tee times are taken up to 4 days in advance.

Another local favorite is the player-friendly **Hibiscus Golf Club,** a half-mile east of U.S. 41 off Rattlesnake Hammock Road in East Naples (© **941/774-0088**). A pro shop and teaching professional are available. Fees are about $70 in winter, cart included, dropping to about $30 in summer.

Greg Norman designed the 27 championship holes at the new **Tiburon Golf Club** ✿✿, 2620 Tiburon Dr. (© **877/WCI-PLAY** or 941/594-2040), to play like a British Open course—but without the thick-thatch rough. Fees reach $200 in winter but drop as low as $70 in summer. In Golden Gate, west of I-75, the **Quality Inn Golf & Country Club,** 4100 Golden Gate Pkwy. (© **800/228-5151** or 941/455-1010), has an 18-hole course and 153 rooms, suites, and efficiencies.

The area has several other courses worth playing, most described in the Naples–Fort Myers edition of the *Golfer's Guide* available at the chamber of commerce visitor center (or check the magazine's website at www.golfersguide.com).

SCUBA DIVING   The **Under Seas Dive Academy,** 998 6th Ave. S., in Olde Naples (© **941/262-0707**), takes divers into the gulf, teaches diver-certification courses, and rents water-sports equipment. So does Kevin Sweeney's **SCUBAdventures,** 971 Creech Rd., at Tamiami Trail (© **941/434-7477**), which also has a base on Marco Island (see section 5, later in this chapter).

TENNIS   In Olde Naples, the city's **Cambier Park Tennis Center** ✿✿, 755 8th Ave. S., at 9th Street South (© **941/434-4694**), is one of the country's finest municipal facilities. In fact, it matches those found at many luxury resorts. Play on its 12 lighted clay courts costs $10 for 90 minutes. Book at the pro shop upstairs in the modern building, which has restrooms but no showers. The courts are open daily from 8am to 9pm.

Nonguests can play at the **Naples Beach Hotel & Golf Club,** 851 Gulf Shore Blvd. N. (© **941/261-2222**), but call ahead to reserve court time.

Dedicated buffs can play to their hearts' content on the 11 clay and 5 hard courts at **World Tennis Center Resort & Club,** 4800 Airport-Pulling Rd., at Pine Ridge Road (© **800/292-6663** or 941/263-1900; fax 941/649-7855; www.worldtenniscenter.com), but you must stay in one of the 72 two-bedroom condominiums here to use them.

WATER SPORTS   **Good Times Rental,** 1947 Davis Blvd. (© **941/775-7529**), rents WaveRunners, Windsurfers, skim boards, snorkeling gear, and other beach equipment. Hobie Cats and Windsurfers can also be rented on the beach at the **Naples Beach Hotel & Golf Club,** 851 Gulf Shore Blvd. N. (© **941/261-2222**), and at **Clam Pass County Park,** at the end of Seagate Drive (© **941/353-0404**). See "Hitting the Beach," above, for more about Clam Pass.

EXPLORING THE TOWN
OLDE NAPLES ✿✿✿

Its history may go back only to 1886, but the beach skirting **Olde Naples** still has the charm of that Victorian era. The heart of the district lies below 5th Avenue South (that's where U.S. 41 takes a 45° turn). The town docks are on the bay side, the glorious **Naples Beach** along the gulf. Laid out on a grid, the tree-lined streets run between many houses, some dating from the town's beginning, and along Millionaires' Row between Gulf Shore Boulevard and the beach. With these gorgeous homes virtually hidden in the palms and casuarinas, the Naples Beach seems a century removed from the high-rise condominiums found farther north.

The **Naples Pier,** at the gulf end of 12th Avenue South, is a focal point of the neighborhood. Built in 1888 to let steamers land potential real-estate customers, the original 600-foot-long, T-shaped structure was destroyed by hurricanes and damaged by fire. Local residents have rebuilt it because they like strolling its length to catch fantastic gulf sunsets—and to get a glimpse of Millionaire's Row from the gulf side. The pier is now a state historic site. It's open 24 hours a day, but parking in the nearby lots is restricted between 11pm and 7am.

Nearby, **Palm Cottage,** 137 12th Ave. S., between 1st Street and Gordon Drive (© **941/261-8164**), was built in 1885 by one of Naples's founders, *Louisville Courier-Journal* publisher Walter Haldeman, as a winter retreat for his chief editorial writer. After World War II, its socialite owners hosted many galas attended by Hollywood stars such as Hedy Lamarr, Gary Cooper, and Robert Montgomery. One of the few remaining Southwest Florida houses built of tabby mortar (made by burning shells), Palm Cottage today is the home of the Naples Historical Society, which maintains it as a museum filled with authentic furniture, paintings, photographs, and other memorabilia. Tours are given during winter, Monday to Friday from 1 to 3:30pm; during the off-season Sunday and Friday from 1 to 3:30pm. Adult admission is by $5 donation, free for children.

Near the Gordon River Bridge on 5th Avenue South, the old corrugated waterfront warehouses are now a shopping-and-dining complex known as the **Marketplace at Tin City,** which tourists throng to and local residents assiduously avoid during the winter months.

MUSEUMS & ZOOS

Caribbean Gardens *Kids*   A family favorite once headed by the late Colonel Larry Tetzlaff, a noted animal collector and wildlife filmmaker, this 52-acre, environmentally conscious zoo features a variety of animals and birds, including a fascinating community of primates living free on their own island. You can see them on a boat safari through the spectacular tropical gardens. Three of the world's 40 golden tigers live here, too. Kids especially will be captivated by the "Scales and Tail Show," in which zookeepers handle reptiles and animals (show times vary, so call for the schedule). Also attractive to kids are a petting farm, elephant rides, and a playground. The Canyon Cafe serves snacks, and there are picnic facilities on the premises.

1590 Goodlette-Frank Rd. (at Fleischmann Blvd.). © **941/262-5409.** www.caribbeangardens.com. Admission $14.95 adults, $9.95 children 4–15, free for children 3 and under. Daily 9:30am–5:30pm (last admission at 4:30pm). Closed Easter, Thanksgiving, Christmas.

Teddy Bear Museum *Kids*   Another family favorite, this entertaining museum contains 3,000-plus examples of stuffed bears from around the world. They're displayed descending from the rafters in hot-air balloons, attending board meetings, sipping afternoon tea, and even doing bear things like hibernating.

2511 Pine Ridge Rd. (at Airport-Pulling Rd.). © **800/365-2327** or 941/598-2711. www.teddymuseum.com. Admission $6 adults, $4 seniors, $2 children 4–12, free for children under 4. Dec–Apr Mon and Wed–Sat 10am–5pm; Sun 1–5pm. May–Nov Wed–Sat 10am–5pm. Closed New Year's Day, July 4, Thanksgiving, Christmas.

PARKS & NATURE PRESERVES

You don't have to go far east of Naples to reach the magnificent Everglades, much of it protected by Everglades National Park and Big Cypress National Preserve. See chapter 7 for full details on activities in and near the national park. Other nearby nature preserves are described in section 5 of this chapter, on Marco Island.

You can experience Southwest Florida's abundant natural life without leaving town at **The Conservancy's Naples Nature Center** ⚡, 14th Avenue North, east of Goodlette-Frank Road (© 941/262-0304; www.conservancy.org), one of two preserves operated by The Conservancy of Southwest Florida (see the Briggs Nature Center in section 5, later in this chapter). There are nature trails and an aviary with bald eagles and other birds. You can take 45-minute guided boat rides beginning at 10am, 11am, noon, 2pm, and 3pm, weather permitting. The naturalist guides will explain the vegetation along the upper reaches of the Gordon River, and you may see some wildlife-including an occasional monkey escapee from Caribbean Gardens next door (see "Museums & Zoos," above). You can also rent canoes and kayaks and see it by yourself. An excellent nature store carries gift items. Admission fees of $7.50 for adults and $2 for children 3 to 12 (free for children under 3) include the boat rides. Canoes and kayaks cost $13 for 2 hours, $5 for each additional hour. The center is open year-round Monday to Saturday from 9am to 4:30pm. Closed July 5, Labor Day, Thanksgiving, Christmas Eve, and Christmas Day.

The National Audubon Society operates the **Corkscrew Swamp Sanctuary,** 375 Sanctuary Rd. (© **941/348-9151;** www.audubon.org/local/sanctuary/ corkscrew), 16 miles northeast of Naples off Immokalee Road (County Road 846). One of the state's largest private preserves, this 11,000-acre wilderness is home to countless wood storks that nest high in the cypress trees from November to April. Wading birds also are best seen in winter, when the swamp is likely to be dry (they don't nest when water levels are high). The birds congregate around pools near a boardwalk that leads 2 miles through the largest bald cypress forest, with some of the oldest trees in the country. Ferns and orchids also flourish. Admission is $8 for adults, $5.50 for full-time college students, $3.50 for children 6 to 18, and free for children 5 and under. The sanctuary is open December to April, daily from 7am to 5pm; May to November, daily from 8am to 5pm. To reach the sanctuary, take Exit 17 off I-75 and go 15 miles east on Immokalee Road (County Road 846).

About a 30-minute drive away, the **Crew Management Area,** on Corkscrew Road (County Road 850) south of Fla. 82, has a short boardwalk out to the edge of the marsh and 5 miles of trails through mostly pine forest. This 7,060-acre slice of the marsh is managed jointly by the CREW Land and Water Trust, 2301 McGregor Blvd., Fort Myers, FL 33901 (© **941/332-7771;** http://hawk.net/ lee/orgs/crew) and the South Florida Water Management District (www.sfwmd. gov). The trails are free but have no drinking water or restrooms. There are primitive campsites here, too, but you'll need advance permission from the CREW trust.

SHOPPING

Two blocks of **3rd Street South** ⚡⚡, at Broad Avenue, is the Rodeo Drive of Naples. This glitzy collection of jewelers, clothiers, and art galleries may be too rich for many wallets, but the window shopping here is unmatched. Be sure to pick up a free brochure from the chamber of commerce visitor center (see "Essentials," earlier in this chapter); it lists the merchants and has a map of the area,.

Nearby, the **5th Avenue South** ⚡ shopping area, between 3rd and 9th streets South, has seen a renaissance in recent years and is now Naples's hottest dining spot. The avenue is longer and a bit less chic than 3rd Street South, with stockbrokerages and real-estate offices thrown into the mix of boutiques and antique dealers. The most unusual stop here is **Prospero's Gallerie Eclectic,** 659 5th Ave. S. (© **941/435-4517**), featuring fanciful paintings and sculpture, plus fabulous, relatively inexpensive sunset shots taken by local photographer Allan Hoelzle and watercolors of Naples houses painted by artist Julie Carlson.

Also in Olde Naples, the **Old Marine Marketplace at Tin City,** 1200 5th Ave. S., at the Gordon River (© **941/262-4200**), has 50 boutiques selling everything from souvenirs to avant-garde resort wear and imported statuary. There are more boutiques in the **Dockside Boardwalk,** a half block west on 6th Avenue South.

Even the malls in Naples have their charms. The **Village at Venetian Bay,** 4200 Gulf Shore Blvd., at Park Shore Drive (© **941/261-0030**), evokes images of its Italian namesake, with 50 canal-side shops featuring high-fashion men's and women's clothiers and fine-art galleries. Ornate Mediterranean architecture and a tropical waterfall highlight the open-air **Waterside Shops at Pelican Bay,** Seagate Drive at North Tamiami Trail (U.S. 41; © **941/598-1605**), where the anchor stores are Saks Fifth Avenue and Jacobson's. There's a huge Barnes & Noble bookstore across Seagate Drive.

Discount shoppers can head to **Prime Outlets Naples,** on Fla. 951 about a mile south of U.S. 41 on the way to Marco Island (© **888/545-7196** or 941/775-8083). You'll find the usual clothiers here, including Liz Claiborne, Jones New York, and Anne Klein, plus Mikasa, Coach Leathers, and Dansk factory stores. Shops are open 10am to 8pm Monday to Saturday, 11am to 6pm Sunday.

WHERE TO STAY

While Naples has some of the most expensive resorts in the region, it also has some surprisingly reasonable properties, particularly several older but very well-maintained "apartment hotels" in the historic district within a few blocks of the beach. The **Olde Naples Inn & Suites** is the best (see below). Others include **The Glenwood,** 179 7th Ave. S. (© **941/404-0542**), with just three two-bedroom, two-bath units, and the **Neptune Apartment Hotel,** 651 3rd Ave. S. (© **941/262-6126;** fax 941/263-6126). They are very popular from mid-December to mid-April, when many guests stay a month or more, so book as early as possible.

Branches of most chain hotels sit along U.S. 41, but even these tend to be of higher quality and better value than their counterparts elsewhere in Southwest Florida. The new **Hilton Naples & Towers,** 5111 Tamiami Trail N. (© **800/HILTONS** or 941/430-4900; fax 941/430-4901; www.naples.hilton.com), north of Olde Naples near the Waterside Shops at Pelican Bay, is luxurious, but since it's not on the beach it attracts mainly business travelers and groups. It also contains a Don Shula's Steak House.

An inexpensive choice is the **Quality Inn Gulfcoast,** 2555 N. Tamiami Trail (© **800/330-0046** or 941/261-6040; fax 941/261-5742; www.qinaples.com), at North 26th Avenue. This 121-unit older but very well maintained motel sports a courtyard with resort-style swimming pool and a lively thatch-roof tiki bar, which makes it a fun place for singles and couples. Rates are $100 to $120 double in winter, $60 off-season.

One of the most reasonably priced of the town's many condominium complexes, **Park Shore Resort,** 600 Neapolitan Way, Naples, FL 34103 (© **800/548-2077** or 941/263-2222; fax 941/263-0946; www.parkshore.com), has 156 attractive one- and two-bedroom condominiums surrounding an artificial lagoon with waterfalls cascading on its own island. Guests can walk across a bridge to the artificial island, where they can swim in the heated pool, barbecue on gas grills, or order a meal from the restaurant or a drink from the bar. There's once-a-day complimentary transport to the beach. The condominiums range from $195 to $235 in winter but drop to $99 to $145 off-season.

One of the biggest condominium-rental agents here is **Bluebill Properties,** 26201 Hickory Blvd., Bonita Springs, FL 33923 (© **800/237-2010** or 941/597-1102; fax 941/597-7175; www.naplesvacation.com).

I have organized the accommodations below geographically: in Olde Naples and north of the historic district, including Vanderbilt Beach.

IN OLDE NAPLES
Very Expensive

Hotel Escalante ★★ On the western end of the 5th Avenue shopping district and two blocks from the beach, this new boutique hotel is perfect for singles or couples who want convenience, no crowds, and a bit of pampering. The Escalante seems smaller and more intimate than most properties with 65 units. The large rooms and spacious one-bedroom suites are in eight one- and two-story buildings spread out over most of a city block (this was the old Beachcomber apartment hotel until being gutted and rebuilt in 2000). The cottagelike suites have private patios opening to lush courtyards with walkways of old brick from Chicago, fountains from France, and 300 species of tropical plants from around the world. All units are luxuriously appointed, and the bathrooms have two hand basins, ample vanity space, and big shower heads (the majority have walk-in showers as opposed to tubs). Special services include lunch served on the beach, a day spa with facials and massage, an evening wine reception, and an honor bar and complimentary cookies in the library.

290 5th Ave. S., Naples, FL 34102. © **877/GULF-INN** or 941/659-3466. Fax 941/262-8748. www. hotelescalante.com. 65 units. Winter $250–$400; off-season $130–$280. Rates include continental breakfast and evening wine reception. AC, DC, DISC, MC, V. **Amenities:** Bar; heated outdoor pool; exercise room; day spa; Jacuzzi; sauna; 24-hour room service; massage; laundry service. *In room:* A/C, TV, dataport, minibar, fridge, coffeemaker, hair dryer, iron.

Naples Beach Hotel & Golf Club ★★★ (Kids) In contrast to The Ritz-Carlton Naples and The Registry Resort (see below), which could be anywhere, this charming resort definitely belongs in Olde Naples. In fact, the beachside setting on Millionaires' Row couldn't be better for carrying on the friendly and relaxed Old Florida ambience installed by Henry B. Watkins a half century ago and carried on by his family today. This is also Southwest Florida's only resort with its own 18-hole golf course, tennis center, and full-service spa right on the premises. The spa, golf club, and a restaurant are in a stunning new building across Gulf Shore Boulevard from reception. Since the hotel predates the city's strict historic-district zoning laws, it also has Olde Naples's only restaurants and bar directly on the beach. Of these, the **Sunset Beach Bar** is one of the region's most famous beachside open-air bars and is always crammed as the sun sets over the gulf and when live bands perform on Sunday afternoons during the winter season. Facing the gulf, the semicircular Everglades Dining Room emphasizes traditional Florida cuisine, offers a reasonably priced breakfast buffet to guests and nonguests alike, and has live entertainment and dancing Tuesday to Saturday night in winter. Complimentary afternoon tea is served in the lobby lounge, and guests can hang shopping lists on their doorknobs at night for the staff to deliver breakfast goodies from the Seminole Store, which sells inexpensive pastries, pizzas, salads, and sandwiches.

Rooms and suites are in several buildings spread over lush gardens hung with more than 5,000 orchids. The least-expensive are in the Florida Wing, a two-story relic from 1948 whose recently updated rooms and suites open to a long, railing-enclosed porch with views across a manicured lawn to the swimming pool by the gulf. Units in the Tower are over the main dining room and directly across the boulevard from the golf course, tennis center, and spa. The Watkins Wing houses the most spacious suites here. Rooms in the Penthouse Wing, removed from the action at the north end of the property, directly face the beach and are the best choice for couples, especially during holidays and the summer when many families stay here (the clientele is mostly couples at other times).

851 Gulf Shore Blvd., Naples, FL 33940. ✆ **800/237-7600** or 941/261-2222. Fax 941/261-7380. www.naplesbeachhotel.com. 318 units. Winter $225–$385 double; $315–$525 suite. Off-season $175–$225 double; $250–$310 suite. Packages available. AE, DC, DISC, MC, V. **Amenities:** 4 restaurants (all American); 2 bars; heated Olympic-size outdoor pool; 18-hole golf course; 6 tennis courts; full-service spa; water-sports equipment rental; bike rental; children's programs; game room; concierge; activities desk; limited room service; salon; massage; baby-sitting; laundry service. *In room:* A/C, TV, dataport, hair dryer, iron.

Expensive

The Inn on Fifth ✪   Built in 1998, this three-story boutique hotel sits in the center of the 5th Avenue South business district, with all its dining and shopping diversions just outside the door and McCabe Brothers' Steakhouse and the lively McCabe's Irish Pub downstairs. All the spacious guest quarters come equipped with writing tables, three phones (one in the bathroom), and sliding-glass doors opening to standing-room–only balconies. A brick patio on the parking-lot roof is equipped with a swimming pool, a gazebo, and chairs for sunning. A small spa here offers facials, massages, and other services at 15% to 20% less than at the big beachside resorts.

699 5th Ave. S., Naples, FL 34102. ✆ **888/403-8778** or 941/403-8777. Fax 941/403-8778. www.naplesinn.com. 87 units. Winter $210–$375 double; off-season $109–$250 double. AE, DC, DISC, MC, V. **Amenities:** 2 restaurants (Irish/American); 1 bar; heated outdoor pool; exercise room; spa; limited room service; massage; laundry service. *In room:* A/C, TV, dataport, coffeemaker, hair dryer, iron.

Trianon Old Naples ✪   Constructed in 1998 in a quiet residential neighborhood, this elegant Mediterranean-style building with a classical European interior offers convenience and comfort without a lot of frills. The spacious rooms are equipped with Ritz-Carlton–quality furniture, including mahogany armoires, chairs, and writing desks. All have seating areas and extra-large bathrooms. Some units have balconies large enough for chairs, but others are for standing only. There's no restaurant here, but continental breakfast is served on silver in a refined lounge, where coffee and tea are available all day, and the staff will arrange for meals to be delivered from local restaurants. Champagne and port are served at a wine bar in the evenings.

955 7th Ave. S., Naples, FL 34102. ✆ **877/482-5228** or 941/437-9600. Fax 941/261-0025. www.trianon.com. 58 units. Winter $140–$275 double; off-season $95–$190 double. Rates include continental breakfast. AE, DC, DISC, MC, V. **Amenities:** Heated outdoor pool; laundry service. *In room:* A/C, TV, dataport, fridge (in some units), coffeemaker, hair dryer, iron.

Moderate

Inn by the Sea ✪   Listed in the National Register of Historic Places, this bed-and-breakfast 2 blocks from the beach in the heart of Olde Naples was built in 1937 as a boardinghouse by Alice Bowling, one of Naples's first schoolteachers and a grocer and entrepreneur to boot. The Federal-style house still has much of its original pine floors and pine or cypress ceilings and woodwork. With windows on three sides, the Sanibel on the ground floor is the lightest and airiest unit here, while the Bokeelia suite is the most romantic, with its bed set at an angle in one corner. The upstairs suites have assigned bathrooms, but you'll have to cross the hallway to get to them. Bikes, beach chairs, and towels are provided; in season, guests are served oranges from the backyard tree. You'll have to do without a phone or TV in your room here.

287 11th Ave. S., Naples, FL 34102. © **800/584-1268** or 941/649-4124. www.innbythesea-bb.com. 5 units (3 with bathroom). Winter $149–$189 double; off-season $94–$114 double. Rates include continental breakfast. AE, DISC, MC, V. Children 13 and under not accepted. *In room:* A/C, hair dryer, no phone.

Inexpensive

Olde Naples Inn & Suites ★★ *(Value)* In the heart of Olde Naples, this extraordinarily well-maintained apartment hotel is just 2 blocks from the beach and 4 blocks from the 3rd Street South and 5th Avenue South shopping areas (a location that more than makes up for the lack of an on-site restaurant). Decorated by an interior designer, its eclectic combination of rooms, efficiencies, and one- and two-bedroom suites are in three buildings occupying about 60% of a city block, but the tropical landscaping makes the property seem smaller. Most units open to two courtyards with heated swimming pools. The units are comfortably furnished, immaculately maintained, and breezy. Small pets may stay with you here if you sign a waiver of responsibility for any damages.

801 3rd St. S., Naples, FL 34102. © **800/637-6036** or 941/262-5194. Fax 941/262-4876. www. oldenaplesinn.com. 60 units. Winter $119–$195 double; off-season $69–$138 double. Weekly rates available. Rates include continental breakfast. AE, DISC, MC, V. **Amenities:** Heated outdoor pools; bike rental; coin-op washers and dryers. *In room:* A/C, TV, kitchen, fridge.

NORTH OF OLDE NAPLES

The **Ritz-Carlton Naples Golf Resort** (© **800/241-3333;** www.ritz-carlton.com), to be Naples's second Ritz-Carlton, was slated to open in the area near Airport and Vanderbilt Beach roads northeast of Olde Naples in late 2001. Guests at this high-luxe hotel will have golf privileges at the Greg Norman–designed Tiburon Golf Club (see "Other Outdoor Activities," earlier in this chapter).

Very Expensive

The Registry Resort ★★ This sports-minded luxury high rise is not directly on the beach: guests must ride the free Clam Pass County Park shuttle along a 3,000-foot boardwalk through mangroves to the Gulf (see "Parks & Nature Preserves," earlier in this chapter). Once there, they can charge lounge chairs, cabanas, water-sports equipment rentals, and drinks to their rooms. To compensate for lack of beachside setting, the resort recently installed a big outdoor complex with two swimming pools with waterslide and waterfall. Plus, there is a 15-court tennis center, one of the main draws here. Inside its architecturally nondescript modern tower, the Registry radiates a more relaxed ambience than the traditional Ritz-Carlton, but none of the old-Florida charm of its other chief rival, the Naples Beach Hotel & Golf Club (see above). Dining here is at least on a par with the Ritz-Carlton, with the magnificent **Lafite** dining room offering some of the city's finest French cuisine (open nightly during winter, on Friday and Saturday evenings off-season). The multilevel Club Zanzibar nightclub has dancing to deejay music every night. There's a full-service spa here, too.

475 Seagate Dr., Naples, FL 34103. © **941/597-3232** or 800/247-9810. Fax 941/597-3147. www.registryresort. com. 424 units, including 29 suites. Winter $395–$475 double; $460–$715 suite. Off-season $160–$395 double; $205–$450 suite. $10 per day resort amenities fee. Packages available. AE, DC, DISC, MC, V. From Olde Naples, go about 1½ miles north on U.S. 41, and turn left on Seagate Dr. Hotel is on right. **Amenities:**

5 restaurants (French; American); 2 bars; 5 heated outdoor pools; access to golf course; 15 tennis courts; spa; Jacuzzi; sauna; water-sports equipment rental; bike rental; children's programs; game room; concierge; business center; salon; 24-hr. room service; massage; baby-sitting; laundry service. *In room:* A/C, TV, fax, dataport, minibar, coffeemaker, hair dryer, iron.

The Ritz-Carlton Naples ★★★   This opulent 14-story Mediterranean-style hotel is a favorite among affluent guests who like standard Ritz-Carlton amenities such as imported marble floors, antique art, Oriental rugs, Waterford crystal chandeliers, British-style afternoon tea, and a staff that starts fawning over you from the moment you arrive. Still, it lacks the wonderful Old Florida charm of the Naples Beach Hotel & Golf Club (see above). Nor is it as close to the beach, for guests must walk through a narrow mangrove forest to reach the sands. The beach here is part of a public park, but the hotel has staff out there to answer phones, deliver drinks and snacks, and rent cabanas, boats, and other toys (only towels, chairs, and ice water are complimentary). The plush, fully equipped guest rooms and suites overlook the gulf, but not all have balconies. The **Dining Room,** the hotel's signature restaurant, prepares seafood with an Asian flair, while the wood-paneled **Grill Room** is a beef emporium reminiscent of a British private club. Together, they serve some of Naples's finest and most expensive cuisine. The Club turns into a nightclub with dancing after 10pm. A $50 million, full-service spa opened in April 2001.

280 Vanderbilt Beach Rd., Naples, FL 34108. ⓒ **800/241-3333** or 941/598-3300. Fax 941/598-6690. www. ritzcarlton.com. 463 units, including 32 suites. Winter $449–$899 double; $769–$969 suite. Off-season $200–$439 double; $365–$625 suite. AE, DC, DISC, MC, V. Valet parking $18; free self-parking. From Olde Naples, go north 3½ miles on U.S. 41. Turn left on Vanderbilt Beach Rd. (C.R. 862), to hotel on left. **Amenities:** 5 restaurants (French; American); 2 bars; 5 heated outdoor pools; access to golf course; 15 tennis courts; spa; Jacuzzi; sauna; water-sports equipment rental; bike rental; children's programs; game room; concierge; business center; salon; 24-hr. room service; massage; baby-sitting; laundry service. *In room:* A/C, TV, fax, dataport, minibar, coffeemaker, hair dryer, iron.

Expensive

Vanderbilt Inn on the Gulf ★   Cheerful tropical decor in the accommodations and public areas sets the tempo for a casual, fun vacation at this two-story motel right on Vanderbilt Beach, where you can go parasailing and rent boats and water-sports equipment. Nature lovers can walk along the beach and into Delnor-Wiggins Pass State Recreation Area next door (see "Parks & Nature Preserves," earlier in this chapter). The 16 efficiencies (with kitchens) on the ends of the building open to the beach. About half the standard motel-style rooms face a magnificently landscaped courtyard with a kidney-shaped swimming pool surrounded by a brick terrace, while the other, least-expensive units open to parking lots. Although the rooms are entered from exterior walkways, their big windows are darkly tinted to provide privacy. A thatch-roof bar and full-service outdoor restaurant serve lunches and dinners by the beach and draw a crowd for sunset happy hour. Another restaurant turns lively when bands play on Friday and Saturday nights. Kids 13 and under dine free when accompanied by adults here.

11000 Gulf Shore Dr., Naples, FL 34108. ⓒ **800/643-8654** or 941/597-3151. Fax 941/597-3099. www. vanderbilt.com. 147 units. Winter $205–$335 double; off-season $110–$210 double. Weekly rates available. AE, DC, DISC, MC, V. From Olde Naples, go 4 miles north on U.S. 41; take a left on 111th Ave. (which becomes Bluebill Ave.) to hotel on left. **Amenities:** 5 restaurants (French; American); 2 bars; 5 heated outdoor pools; access to golf course; 15 tennis courts; spa; Jacuzzi; sauna; water-sports equipment rental; bike rental; children's programs; game room; concierge; business center; salon; 24-hr. room service; massage; baby-sitting; laundry service. *In room:* A/C, TV, fax, dataport, minibar, coffeemaker, hair dryer, iron.

Inexpensive

Lighthouse Inn Motel A relic from decades gone by, Judy and Buzz Dugan's no-frills but spotlessly clean motel sits across the street from other more expensive properties on Vanderbilt Beach and within walking distance of The Ritz-Carlton Naples. The efficiencies and apartments are simple, with freshly painted cinder-block walls and small kitchens. The one kitchenless room has a small fridge and coffeemaker, but note: No unit has a telephone, and four of them have shower-only bathrooms. Most guests take advantage of weekly and monthly rates in winter, when it's heavily booked. The Dugans also operate Buzz's Lighthouse Cafe next door, a pleasant place for an inexpensive dockside breakfast, lunch, or dinner.

9140 Gulf Shore Dr. N., Naples, FL 34108. *©* **941/597-3345.** Fax 941/597-5541. 15 units. Winter $100 double; $105 efficiency; $115 apt. Off-season $49 double; $59 efficiency; $69 apt. MC, V. From Olde Naples, go 3¹/₂ miles north on U.S. 41; take left on Vanderbilt Beach Rd. (C.R. 862). Turn right on Gulf Shore Dr. to hotel on right. **Amenities:** Restaurant (American); bar; heated outdoor pool. *In room:* A/C, TV, kitchen, fridge, coffeemaker.

WHERE TO DINE

If this is your first time here, you may opt to have a lunch or dinner at the touristy **Marketplace at Tin City,** on the Gordon River at 5th Avenue South, where the **Riverwalk Fish & Ale House** (*©* **941/262-2734**) specializes in moderately priced seafood and steaks. Like its sibling, The Dock at Crayton Cove (see below), it's a fun establishment with dockside seating.

You'll find budget-priced fast-food and family-style restaurants along U.S. 41, including a branch of the inexpensive **Mel's Diner,** 3650 Tamiami Trail N. (*©* **941/643-9898**).

Naples's beaches are ideal for picnics. In Olde Naples, you can get freshly baked breads and pastries, prepackaged gourmet sandwiches, and fruit plates at **Tony's Off Third,** 1300 3rd St. S. (*©* **941/262-7999**). **Wynn's on Fifth,** 745 5th Ave. S. (*©* **941/261-0901**), between 8th St. and Park St. S., has high-quality deli items, prepackaged sandwiches, salads, take-out meals, and gourmet pastries at very reasonable prices. Both have a few sidewalk tables and are fine places for coffee or a snack while window-shopping on 3rd and 5th avenues South.

Expensive

Chop's City Grill ★★ STEAKS/SEAFOOD Wonderful aromas waft from the open kitchen at the rear of this urbane bistro. Aged, top-quality steaks and lamb chops are the house specialties, either char-grilled to perfection and served with thick onion rings and mashed potatoes, or peppered and served with a blackberry and cabernet wine sauce. Fresh fish from the grill is another good choice. Asian influences appear here, too, such as sea scallops "shocked" in a wok with Thai curry sauce and served over noodles with wild mushrooms and stir-fried vegetables.

837 5th Ave. S. (between 8th and 9th Sts. S.). *©* **941/262-4677.** Reservations recommended. Main courses $17–$30. AE, DC, DISC, MC, V. Daily 5:30–10pm.

Terra ★ MEDITERRANEAN This elegant yet casual restaurant in the heart of the 3rd Street South shopping district has muted lighting, a few antiques and paintings, and green-and-black woven rattan chairs at oak tables inlaid with terra-cotta tiles. A pianist lends romance as you enjoy Mediterranean dishes such as lamb shank osso buco, tasty wild mushroom lasagna, or a pasta of the day. Hamburgers are served at both lunch and dinner, so you don't necessarily have to spend a fortune here.

1300 3rd St. S. (actually on 13th Ave. S., between 2nd and 3rd Sts. S.) ⓒ **941/262-5550.** Reservations recommended. Main courses $17–$24; burgers $10. AE, DC, DISC, MC, V. Daily 11:30am–2:30am and 5:30–10pm.

Zoë's ⭑⭑ ECLECTIC   This slightly Art Deco bistro draws a lively crowd of young professionals who preen at the big bar to one side or at a raised, English pub–style drinking table (you can dine at the table, too, which is handy if you're traveling alone since you're sure to get into conversations with your fellow guests). The eclectic menu changes every week or so to take advantage of fresh produce. Meatloaf, macaroni and cheese, and pot roast are regulars. They sound on the menu like those your mother made, but they're seasoned as lively as Zoë's patrons. If they're offered, opt for the pecan-crusted sea bass or the seared, sesame-coated yellowfin tuna served with a cucumber relish, a horseradish-tinged mayonnaise drizzle, and spicy soba noodles. Zoë's turns into a high-energy nightclub on Friday and Saturday nights.

720 5th Ave. S. (between 7th and 8th Sts. S.) ⓒ **941/261-1221.** Reservations recommended. Main courses $15–$34. AE, MC, V. Sun–Thurs 5–10pm; Fri–Sat 5–10:30pm (music and dancing Fri–Sat 11pm–1:30am).

Moderate

Bistro 821 ⭑ MEDITERRANEAN   Although this noisy bistro has lost some of its popularity lately to Chop's City Grill and Zoë's (see above), it launched the dining revitalization along 5th Avenue South and still is an excellent choice for Mediterranean-influenced cuisine. A bench covered in bright print fabric runs down one side of this storefront to a bar and open kitchen in the rear. Although the quarters are too close for private conversations, small spotlights hanging from the ceiling romantically illuminate each table. The house specialty is rotisserie chicken, and a daily risotto leads a menu featuring penne pasta in a vodka sauce, and a seasonal vegetable plate with herb couscous. There's sidewalk dining here, too.

821 5th Ave. S. (between 8th and 9th Sts. S.) ⓒ **941/261-5821.** Reservations recommended. Main courses $13–$26. AE, DC, MC, V. Mon–Thurs 11:30am–2:30pm and 5–10pm; Fri 11:30am–2:30pm and 5–10pm; Sat–Sun 5–10:30pm.

The Dock at Crayton Cove ⭑ *Value* SEAFOOD   Located right on the City Dock, this lively pub is the best place in town for an open-air meal or a cool drink while watching the boats go back and forth across Naples Bay. The chow ranges from hearty chowders by the mug to seafood with a Floribbean fare, with Jamaican-style jerk shrimp thrown in for spice; main courses are moderately priced. Grilled seafood Caesar salad and a good selection of sandwiches, hot dogs, and other pub-style fare also appear on the menu. "Margarita madness" happy hour and a half-price raw bar (don't miss the steamed mussels with French bread for dipping the garlic sauce) run daily from 9:30 to 11:30pm. The "Great Dock Canoe Race" draws thousands on the second Saturday in May.

12th Ave. S. (at the City Dock in Olde Naples). ⓒ **941/263-9940.** Reservations not accepted. Main courses $11–$22; sandwiches $8–$12. AE, DISC, MC, V. Daily 11am–midnight.

Tommy Bahama's Tropical Cafe ⭑⭑ CARIBBEAN   You walk through a thatch gateway into this lively, island-style pub-an incongruous sight in the middle of the staid 3rd Street South shopping enclave. Diners gather on a large front patio under shade trees, where a musician performs, or inside, where a large back-wall mural creates a Polynesian scene. An open kitchen and service bar are on one side of the dining room, a real bar dispensing drinks on the other. In between, round-backed cane chairs and classic ceiling fans add to the exotic mood. Although the Jamaican pork, salmon St. Croix, and other Caribbean-style cuisine don't quite live up to the ambience, you'll have too much fun here to care whether or not it's gourmet—and the huge portions will satisfy any appetite. They don't appear on the dinner menu, but sandwiches are served if you ask for them (the meal-size grouper sandwich is a bargain at $10).

1220 3rd St. S. (between 12th and 13th Aves. S.) © 941/643-6889. Reservations recommended. Main courses $17–$26; sandwiches $8–$10. AE, DC, MC, V. Winter daily 11am–11pm; off-season daily 11am–10pm.

Yabba Island Grill ★★ *Value* CARIBBEAN   Naples's most reasonably priced chic restaurant, this lively joint re-creates a raucous Caribbean beachside bar in the middle of the 5th Avenue South dining district. The chow is as lively as Yabba's pastel color scheme, with most items providing a riot of flavors from across the Caribbean. I'll come back here for the St. Croix Sizzler, a terrific combination of small lobster tail, a chunk of mahi-mahi, and mussels over a bed of peppers, onions, and a sweet mango curry sauce. Also worthy of a repeat: the Monsoon salad consisting of grilled chicken breast, hearts of palm, candied pecans, and mushrooms under a warm bacon-and-berry vinaigrette and topped with crispy onion rings.

711 5th Ave. S. (between 8th St. S. and Park Ave. S.). © 941/262-5787. Reservations not accepted. Main courses $13–$20; sandwiches $8–$9. AE, DISC, MC, V. Tues–Sat 11:30am–2:30pm and 5–10pm; Sun 5am–10pm (bar to 2am Fri–Sat).

Inexpensive

First Watch *Value* AMERICAN   Just like its siblings elsewhere in Florida, this corner shop has big louvered shutters to temper the morning sun and is one of Naples's favorite spots for breakfast, late brunch, or a midday meal. This is anything but a diner, however. Instead you get classical music and widely spaced tables topped with pitchers of lemon-tinged ice water. A young staff provides quick and friendly service. The menu leans heavily on healthy selections, but you can get your cholesterol from a sizzling skillet of fried eggs served over layers of potatoes, vegetables, and melted cheese. Lunch features large salads, sandwiches, and quesadillas. In addition to the dining room, there's additional seating at umbrella tables in the shopping center's courtyard.

In Gulf Shore Sq., 1400 Gulf Shore Blvd. (at Banyan Rd.). © 941/434-0005. Reservations not accepted. Most items $3.50–$6.50. AE, DISC, MC, V. Daily 7am–2:30pm. Closed Christmas.

Old Naples Pub ★ *Value* AMERICAN/PUB FARE   You would never guess that the person sitting next to you at the bar here is very, very rich, so relaxed is this small somewhat-cramped pub in the middle of the fabulous 3rd Street South shops. Diners fortunately find more room at tables on the shopping center's patio. Inside, the pine-paneled walls are hung with trophy fish, a dartboard, and old newspaper clippings about Naples. The menu features very good pub fare (and at extraordinarily inexpensive prices for Olde Naples), including homemade soups, nachos, burgers, and sandwiches ranging from charcoal-grilled bratwurst to fried grouper. Only five main courses are offered: platters with New York strip steak, grilled tuna, the catch of the day, fried grouper, and baby back ribs. Best bets are the chicken salad with grapes and walnuts, and the burgers, steaks, and fish from the charcoal grill. You can catch live entertainment here nightly during winter, Wednesday to Saturday off-season.

255 13th Ave. S. (between 3rd and 4th Sts. S., behind Thalheimer's Jewelers). ℭ **941/649-8200.** Main courses $11–$15; salads, sandwiches, and burgers $5–$9. AE, DISC, MC, V. Mon–Sat 11am–11pm; Sun noon–10pm.

Silver Spoon American Cafe *Value* AMERICAN/ITALIAN/SOUTHWEST
Even though this chic member of the American Cafe chain is in the swanky Waterside Shops complex, it is one of Naples's best dining bargains. It flaunts sophisticated black-and-white high-tech decor and has large window walls over-looking the mall action. Thick sandwiches are served with french fries, spicy pecan rice, or black beans. The tomato-basil soup is worth a try, and the bruschetta appetizer—served on toasted French bread—is nearly a full meal in itself. Gourmet pizzas and pasta dishes also are popular, especially with the after-theater crowds from the nearby Philharmonic Center for the Arts, and the less-expensive main courses such as Cajun or herb-grilled chicken are both tasty and an excellent value. Matron shoppers love to do lunch here, so come early or be prepared for a wait.

In the Waterside Shops at Pelican Bay, 5395 N. Tamiami Trail (at Seagate Dr.). ℭ **941/591-2123.** Reservations not accepted, but call ahead for preferred seating. Main courses $9.50–$14; pizza and pasta $8–$12; soups, salads, and sandwiches $7–$9. AE, DC, DISC, MC, V. Sun–Thurs 11am–10pm; Fri–Sat 11am–11pm. From Olde Naples, go north on U.S. 41 and left on Seagate Dr. right into shopping center. Go right at dead end to restaurant on left.

NAPLES AFTER DARK

For entertainment ideas, check the *Naples Daily News* (www.naplesnews.com), especially the "Neapolitan" section in Friday's edition.

PERFORMING ARTS   The impressive **Philharmonic Center for the Arts** 𝄢𝄢, 5833 Pelican Bay Blvd., at West Boulevard (ℭ **800/597-1900** or 941/ 597-1900; www.naplesphilcenter.org), is the home of the Naples Philharmonic, but its year-round schedule is filled with cultural events, concerts by celebrated artists and internationally known orchestras, and Broadway plays and shows aimed at children and families. Call "The Phil" for a copy of its seasonal calendar.

A fine local theater group, the **Naples Players,** holds their winter-season per-formances in the new Sugden Community Theatre, 701 5th Ave. S. (ℭ **941/ 263-7990;** www.naples.net/presents/theatre). Tickets can be hard to come by, so call well in advance.

THE CLUB & BAR SCENE   The restaurants and bistros along 5th Avenue South are popular watering holes, especially for young professional singles who make this their "meat market" on Friday nights. **Zoë's,** 720 5th Ave. S. (ℭ **941/ 261-1221;** see "Where to Dine," above), turns into a high-energy nightclub Fri-day and Saturday from 10:30pm to 2am. Nearby, **McCabe's Irish Pub,** in the Inn on Fifth, 699 5th Ave. S. (ℭ **941/403-7170**), features traditional Irish music nightly.

In the 3rd Street South shopping area, **Old Naples Pub,** 255 13th Ave. S. (ℭ **941/649-8200**), has live music nightly during winter, Wednesday to Satur-day nights off-season. See "Where to Dine," above.

The **Old Marine Marketplace at Tin City,** comprising the restored water-front warehouses on 5th Avenue South on the west side of the Gordon River, comes alive during the winter when visitors flock to its shops and the **Riverwalk Fish & Ale House** (ℭ **941/262-2734**), which has live entertainment during the season.

Some of the hotels mentioned above have entertainment throughout the year. The beachside "chickee hut" bar at the **Naples Beach Hotel & Golf Club** (© 941/261-2222) is always popular, has live entertainment many nights, and is *the* place to go on Sunday afternoon and early evening. So is the beachside bar at the **Vanderbilt Inn on the Gulf** (© 941/597-3151).

5 Marco Island

15 miles SE of Naples, 53 miles S. of Fort Myers, 100 miles W. of Miami

Captain William Collier would hardly recognize Marco Island if he were to come back from the grave today. No relation to Collier County founder Barron Collier, the captain settled his family on the north end of this largest of Florida's Ten Thousand Islands back in 1871. He traded pelts with the Native Americans, caught and smoked fish to sell to Key West and Cuba, and charged fishermen and other guests $2 a day for a room in his home. A few turn-of-the-century buildings still stand here, but Captain Collier would be shocked to come across the high-rise bridge to the island and see it now sliced by human-made canals and virtually covered by resorts, condominiums, shops, restaurants, and winter homes. These are the products of an extensive real-estate development begun in 1965, which means that Marco lacks any of the charm found in Naples and on Sanibel and Captiva Islands. Much of the sales effort here was aimed at the northeastern states, so the island smacks more of New York and Massachusetts than of the laid-back Midwestern style of its neighbors.

Marco's top attractions are its crescent-shaped beach and access to the nearby waterways running through a maze of small islands, its excellent boating and fishing, and the island's proximity to thousands of acres of wildlife preserves.

ESSENTIALS

GETTING THERE See sections 1 and 4, above, for information about the **Southwest Florida International Airport** and the **Naples Municipal Airport,** respectively, and about Amtrak's train service and Greyhound/Trailways buses to those cities.

VISITOR INFORMATION The **Marco Island Area Chamber of Commerce,** 1102 N. Collier Blvd., Marco Island, FL 34145 (© **800/788-6272** or 941/394-7549; fax 941/394-3061; www.marcoislandeverglades.com or www. marco-island-florida.com/chamber), provides free information about the island. A message board and a phone are located outside for making hotel reservations even when the office is closed. The chamber is open Monday to Friday from 9am to 5pm and Saturday from 10am to 3pm during winter.

GETTING AROUND **Marco Island Trolley Tours** (© **941/394-1600**) makes four complete loops around the island from 10am to 3:15pm Monday to Saturday. The conductors sell tickets and render an informative narration about the island's history. Daily fare is $12 for adults, $6 for children 11 and under, with free reboarding.

Enterprise Rent-a-Car (© 800/325-8007 or 941/642-4488) has an office here. For a cab, call **A-Action Taxi** (© 941/394-4400), **Classic Taxi** (© 941/394-1888), or **A-Okay Taxi** (© 941/394-1113).

Depending on the type, rental bicycles cost $5 an hour to $65 a week at **Scootertown,** 842 Bald Eagle Dr. (© **941/394-8400**), north of North Collier Boulevard near Olde Marco. Scooters cost about $50 a day.

HITTING THE BEACH & OTHER OUTDOOR ACTIVITIES

BEACHES The sugar-white Crescent Beach curves for 3½ miles down the entire western shore of Marco Island. Its southern 2 miles are fronted by an unending row of high-rise condominiums and hotels, but the northern 1½ miles are preserved in **Tigertail Public Beach** (© 941/642-8414). There are restrooms, cold-water outdoor showers, a children's playground, a water-sports rental concessionaire, and a snack bar. The park is at the end of Hernando Drive. It's open daily from dawn to dusk. There's no admission charge to the beach, but parking in the lot costs $3 per vehicle.

The beaches in front of the Marriott, Hilton, and Radisson resorts have parasailing, windsurfing, and other water-sports activities, all for a fee.

If you're not staying at the big resorts, Collier County maintains a $3-per-vehicle parking lot and access to the developed beach on the southern end of the island, on Swallow Avenue at South Collier Boulevard.

OUTDOOR ACTIVITIES **Marco River Marina,** 951 Bald Eagle Dr. (© 941/394-2502; www.marcoriver.com), is the center for boat rentals, fishing, and cruises. Operating from a booth on the marina's dock, **Sunshine Tours** (© 941/642-5415) will book offshore fishing charters and arrange back-bay fishing ($45 adults, $35 kids under 10), shelling excursions to the small islands ($35 adults, $25 children under 10), sunset cruises ($27.50 adults, $17.50 children), and dinner cruises ($45 per person). The back-bay fishing trips go at high tide, the shelling trips at low tide, so call for the schedule and reservations.

Experienced or beginning kayakers can reach remote areas of the Ten Thousands Islands on a guided tour with **Osprey Adventures** (© 941/642-6600; www.ospreyadventures.net). Owners Ky Adeduji and Ron Michaels take their guests out to the islands via powerboat and then lead the kayak tours. Three-hour trips to Rookery Bay (see the Briggs Nature Center under "Parks & Nature Preserves," below) cost $65 per person. Shorter coastal and sunset trips go for $40 per person. They also offer parasail rides out over the mangrove forests, as opposed to off the beachfront resorts. These cost $60 per person. Book through Sunshine Tours (see above) or call directly for reservations, which are required.

SCUBAdventures has a base at 845 Bald Eagle Dr. (© 941/389-7889) in Olde Marco. Two-tank dives range from $65 to $85 depending on distance offshore.

Naples's Lely and Boyne South golf courses are a short drive away (see "Other Outdoor Activities," in section 4, earlier in this chapter). The closest public courses are the **Marco Shores Golf Club,** 1450 Mainsail Dr. (© 941/394-2581), and **Marriott's Golf Club at Marco** (© 941/353-7061), both in the marshlands off Fla. 951 north of the island. A sign at the Marriott's course ominously warns: PLEASE DON'T DISTURB THE ALLIGATORS. Fees range from about $120 in winter down to $75 in summer.

PARKS & NATURE PRESERVES

Operated by The Conservancy and part of the Rookery Bay National Estuarine Research Reserve, the **Briggs Nature Center** ✷, on Shell Island Road, off Fla. 951 between U.S. 41 and Marco Island (© 941/775-8569), has a half-mile boardwalk through a pristine example of Florida's disappearing scrublands, home to the threatened scrub jays and gopher tortoises. Rangers lead a variety of nature excursions (call for the seasonal schedule), and there is a self-guided canoe trail, with canoes for rent from Tuesday to Saturday ($13 for the first

2 hours, $5 for each additional hour). The center is open Monday to Friday from 9am to 4:30pm year-round (call for Saturday and Sunday winter hours). The interpretive center and a butterfly garden (27 varieties) are free. Admission to the boardwalk is $7.50 for adults, $3 for children 3 to 12, free for children under 3. For more information, contact **The Conservancy of Southwest Florida,** 1450 Merrihue Dr., Naples, FL 34102 (© **941/262-0304;** fax 941/262-0672; www.conservancy.com).

Many species of birds inhabit **Collier Seminole State Park,** 20200 E. Tamiami Trail, Naples, FL 34114 (© **941/394-3397;** www8.myflorida.com/communities/ learn/stateparks/district4/collierseminole), an inviting 6,423-acre preserve on the edge of Big Cypress Swamp, 12 miles east of Marco Island on U.S. 41 (just east of Fla. 92). It offers fishing, boating, picnicking, canoeing over a 13-mile loop with a primitive campsite, observing nature along 6 miles of hiking trails (open during dry periods) and a 1-mile nature walk, and regular tent and RV camping (see "Where to Stay," below). A "walking" dredge used to build the Tamiami Trail in the 1920s sits just inside the park entrance. Housed in a replica of a Seminole Wars–era log fort, an interpretive center has information about the park, and there are ranger-led programs from December to April. One-hour narrated boat tours, well worth taking, wander through the winding waterways, daily from 9:30am to 3:30pm (© **941/642-8898**). The boat tours cost $10 for adults, $7.50 for children 6 to 12, free for children 5 and under. Canoes can be rented, but the park has only four camping sites along the canoe trails. Canoes rent for $3 per hour, $15 a day. The park has 130 tent and RV sites laid out in circles and shaded by palms and live oaks. The campground has hot showers and a screened, open-air lounge. Sites cost $15 with electricity, $13 without from December through April. Off-season rates are $10 with electricity, $8 without. Reservations are accepted up to 11 months in advance. Admission to the park is $3.25 per vehicle, $1 for pedestrians and bikers. The park is open daily from 8am to sundown. You can bring your pets but must keep them on a leash.

WHERE TO STAY

There are no chain hotels on Marco Island other than the large Marriott, Hilton, and Radisson properties listed below, which stand in a row along Crescent Beach on the island's southwestern corner. Rental agents representing house and condominium owners include **Century 21 First Southern Trust** (© **800/ 255-9487** or 941/394-7658; fax 941/394-0004; cent21sst@aol.com) and **Marco Beach Rentals** (© **800/423-7809** or 941/642-5400).

As elsewhere in South Florida, the high season here is from mid-December to mid-April. Rates drop precipitously in the off-season.

The nearest campground is in **Collier Seminole State Park,** 12 miles east via Fla. 92 (see "Parks & Nature Preserves," above).

Boat House Motel *Value*   One of the best bargains in these parts, this comfortable little motel sits beside the Marco River in Olde Marco, on the island's northern end. The rooms are in a two-story, lime green and white building that ends at a wooden dock with a small heated swimming pool, lounge furniture, picnic tables, and barbecue grills. Two rooms on the end have their own decks, and all open to tiny courtyards. Bright paint, ceiling fans, and louvered shutters add a tropical ambience throughout. The one-bedroom condominiums next door open to a riverside dock, upon which is built a two-bedroom cottage named "The Gazebo," whose peaked roof is supported by umbrella-like spokes from a central pole. Olde Marco restaurants are a short stroll away.

1180 Edington Place, Marco Island, FL 34148. ℂ **800/528-6345** or 941/642-2400. Fax 941/642-2435. www.theboathousemotel.com. 25 units. Winter $92.50–$147.50 double; $107.50–$240 apt. or cottage. Off-season $57.50–$77.50 double; $75–$135 apt. or cottage. MC, V. Pets accepted ($15 fee plus $5 per day). **Amenities:** Heated outdoor pool; bike rental; coin-op washers and dryers. *In room:* A/C, TV, fridge, iron.

Marco Island Hilton Beach Resort ★★

About half the size of the nearby Marco Island Marriott Resort & Golf Club (see below) but nevertheless a group-oriented hotel, this 11-story beachside tower overlooks the gulf and a courtyard with a multiangled swimming pool wrapped around four coconut palms. The spacious units have curved balconies angled to give water views. One-bedroom units have cooking facilities. One kitchen here serves two outlets: the elegant Sandcastles for dinner and the adjacent Paradise Cafe for casual breakfasts, lunches, and dinners. The Beach Club by the pool serves lunches, snacks, and drinks. Sandcastles Lounge has a piano bar with nightly entertainment.

560 S. Collier Blvd., Marco Island, FL 34145. ℂ **800/HILTONS** or 941/394-5000. Fax 941/394-8410. www. marcoisland.hilton.com. 298 units. Winter $299–$399 double; off-season $139–$219 double. $8 per unit per day resort amenities fee (includes local calls). Packages available. AE, DC, DISC, MC, V. **Amenities:** 2 restaurants (American); 2 bars; heated outdoor pool; 3 tennis courts; exercise room; Jacuzzi; sauna; water-sports equipment rental; children's programs; game room; concierge; activities desk; business center; salon; limited room service; massage; baby-sitting; laundry service; concierge-level rooms. *In room:* A/C, TV, dataport, kitchen (suites only), minibar, fridge, coffeemaker, hair dryer, iron.

Marco Island Marriott Resort & Golf Club ★★ *Kids*

One of the biggest resorts on Florida's Gulf Coast, this deluxe hotel attracts large conventions but is also popular with families (it's one of the few North American resorts to have won the National Parenting Center's seal of approval). The sprawling complex has two nine-story towers and two A-frame public wings forming two beach-front courtyards with swimming pools, bars, and water-sports centers. Luxuriously furnished and decorated, the spacious accommodations range from hotel rooms to two-bedroom suites. All have balconies or patios with indirect views of the gulf. Golfers can play the resort's 18-hole championship golf course, which is on the mainland.

400 S. Collier Blvd., Marco Island, FL 34145. ℂ **800/438-4373** or 941/394-2511. Fax 941/642-2672. www. marcoislandmarriott.com. 797 units. Winter $330–$375 double; from $520 suite. Off-season $150–$260 double; from $300 suite. Packages available. Valet parking $9; free self-parking. AE, DC, DISC, MC, V. **Amenities:** 5 restaurants (American; Italian); 4 bars; 3 heated outdoor pools; golf course; 1 tennis court; exercise room; Jacuzzi; water-sports equipment rental; children's programs; game room; concierge; activities desk; car-rental desk; business center; shopping arcade; salon; limited room service; massage; baby-sitting; laundry service; concierge-level rooms. *In room:* A/C, TV, dataport, minibar, fridge, coffeemaker, hair dryer, iron.

Radisson Suite Beach Resort ★ *Kids*

Although it lacks the extensive amenities of the Marriott and Hilton resorts, units at this 11-story beachside resort are perfect for families, with one- and two-bedroom apartments with fully equipped kitchens and dining areas (some have two bathrooms). The 55 hotel rooms have microwave ovens and coffeemakers. All units have screened balconies. A Pizza Hut Express is on the premises, and a small store provides limited groceries, wine, and beer. A recreation center keeps the kids busy.

600 S. Collier Blvd., Marco Island, FL 34145. ℂ **800/333-3333** or 941/394-4100. Fax 941/394-0419. www. marcobeachresort.com. 269 units. Winter $269 double; $309–$519 suite. Off-season $149–$159 double; $179–$289 suite. Packages available. Valet parking $6; free self-parking. AE, DC, DISC, MC, V. **Amenities:** 2 restaurants (American); 2 bars; heated outdoor pool; exercise room; Jacuzzi; water-sports equipment rental; children's programs; game room; concierge; limited room service; baby-sitting; laundry service. *In room:* A/C, TV, dataport, kitchen, fridge, coffeemaker, hair dryer, iron.

WHERE TO DINE

For inexpensive fare, head for the Town Center Mall, at the corner of North Collier Boulevard and Bald Eagle Drive, where you'll find two good choices. **Susie's Diner** (📞 941/642-6633) is popular with the locals for breakfasts and especially for Susie's inexpensive full-meal lunch specials. She's open Monday to Saturday from 6:30am to 2:30pm and Sunday from 6:30am to 1pm (for breakfast only). **Breakfast Plus** (📞 941/642-6900) has eye-openers ranging from bacon and eggs to kippers to latkes. It's open daily from 7am to 2:30pm.

The island's popular sports bars also offer inexpensive pub fare to go with their multitudinous TVs. Most popular are **Rookie's Bar & Grill,** in Mission de San Marco Plaza at the corner of South Collier Boulevard and Winterberry Drive (📞 941/394-6400), and the **Crazy Flamingo,** in the Town Center Mall, North Collier Boulevard at Bald Eagle Drive (📞 941/642-9600).

Cafe de Marco ⭐⭐ SEAFOOD   Purveyor of some of the island's finest cuisine, this homelike establishment at the Marco Village shops was originally constructed as housing for maids at Captain William Collier's Olde Marco Inn. The chef specializes in excellent treatments of fresh seafood, from your choice of shrimp or fresh baked fish with mushrooms, seasoned shallots, and garlic butter to his own luscious creation of seafood and vegetables combined in a lobster sauce and served over linguine. If your waistline can stand it, finish with a Cafe Puff, an almond praline ice-cream ball rolled in chocolate cookie crumbs, placed in a puff pastry shell, and served with whipped cream. Early bird specials here are a very good value. You can dine inside or on a screened patio.

244 Palm St., Olde Marco. 📞 941/394-6262. Reservations recommended. Main courses $17–$35; early bird specials $13. Minimum charge $13 per adult, $4.50 per child. AE, MC, V. Winter daily 5–10pm. Off-season Mon–Sat 5–10pm. Early bird specials 5–6pm.

Kahuna Restaurant AMERICAN   With fanciful Hawaiian themes highlighted by a small steaming volcano and a big mural of porpoises playing underwater on one wall, Kahuna is the least-expensive choice here. You can sit outside on the shopping center's parking lot or inside at colored booths and round tables under black ceiling fans. The burgers are some of Marco's best (there's a condiment bar with a variety of fixings). Main courses include several fried seafood selections, baked crab cakes, and charcoal-grilled tuna, but your best bet should be a nightly special such as salmon in a light dill sauce. Don't expect gourmet dining here, but the quality is good for the price.

1035 N. Collier Blvd., in Town Center Mall (at Bald Eagle Dr.). 📞 941/394-4300. Reservations not accepted. Main courses $8.50–$15; sandwiches and burgers $3.50–$7.50. MC, V. Daily 11am–9pm.

Kretch's ⭐⭐ (Value) SEAFOOD/CONTINENTAL   Noted pastry chef Bruce Kretschmer rules this shopping-center roost, Marco's best all-around restaurant. Bruce has created a sinfully rich seafood strudel by combining shrimp, crab, scallops, cheeses, cream, and broccoli in a flaky Bavarian pastry and serving it all under a lobster sauce. It's available in appetizer or main course–size portions. Cholesterol counters can choose from broiled or charcoal-grilled fish, shrimp, Florida lobster tail, steaks, or lamb chops. Bruce's popular "Mexican Friday" lunches feature delicious tacos and other inexpensive south-of-the-border selections. Sunday is home-cooking night during winter, with chicken and dumplings, Yankee pot roast, and braised lamb shanks.

527 Bald Eagle Dr. (south of N. Collier Blvd.). 📞 941/394-3433. Reservations recommended in winter. Main courses $13.50–$25. DC, DISC, MC, V. Mon–Fri 11am–3pm and 5–9pm; Sat–Sun 5–9pm. Closed Sun off-season and Easter, July 4, Thanksgiving, Christmas Eve, and Christmas Day.

Snook Inn SEAFOOD   The choice dinner seats at this Old Florida establishment are in an enclosed dock right beside the scenic Marco River, but for lunch or libation head to the dockside Chickee Bar, a fun place anytime but especially at sunset. Live entertainment is featured out there both day and night during the winter season, nightly the rest of the year. Although seafood is the specialty, tasty steaks, chicken, burgers, and sandwiches are among the choices. Even the sandwiches come with a trip to the salad bar at dinner, making them a fine bargain. Bring a fillet of that fish you caught today and the chef will cook it for you. Call A-Okay Taxi (see "Essentials," above) for a free ride from anywhere on Marco Island.

1215 Bald Eagle Dr. (at Palm St.), Olde Marco. ℂ 941/394-3313. Reservations not accepted. Main courses $11.50–$20.50; sandwiches $8–$10; cook-your-catch $11. AE, DC, DISC, MC, V. Daily 11am–10pm. Closed Thanksgiving, Christmas.

MARCO ISLAND AFTER DARK

To find out what's going on, check the *Naples Daily News* (www.naplesnews. com), especially the "Neapolitan" section in Friday's edition and its weekly "The Marco Islander" section, available at the chamber of commerce (see "Essentials," above).

It's not after dark, but one of the biggest parties in Florida takes place every Sunday afternoon at **Stan's Idle Hour Seafood Restaurant,** on County Road 892 in Goodland (ℂ **941/394-3041**), where owner Stan Gober-an Ernest Hemingway look-alike-plays host and fires up the barbecue grills; bands crank up country music for dancing the "Buzzard Lope"; and men compete to see who has the best legs. Stan's Goodland Mullet Festival, always the weekend before the Super Bowl, is the mother of all parties.

Marco Island's much tamer but nevertheless entertaining version is the **Snook Inn**, where bands play out in the dockside Chickee Bar.

Much more sedate are the lounges in the **Marriott and Hilton resorts** (see "Where to Stay," above), which provide pianists every evening.

Everyone turns out for free outdoor entertainment at the **Mission San Marco Plaza** shopping center, South Collier Boulevard at Winterberry Drive, every Tuesday night year-round, and at the **Town Center Mall,** at North Collier Boulevard and Bald Eagle Drive, every Thursday night.

One of the liveliest local spots is **La Casita Mexican Restaurant,** in the Shops of Marco, San Marco Road at Barfield Drive (ℂ **941/642-7600**), where owners Frankie Ray and Maryellen play a variety of Mexican, Irish, popular, and traditional music Monday to Saturday. On Sunday, 1950s and 1960s dance music is highlighted.

The Tampa Bay Area

by Bill Goodwin

Many families visiting Orlando's theme parks eventually drive an hour west on I-4 to another major kiddie attraction, Busch Gardens Tampa Bay. But this area shouldn't be a mere side trip from Disney World, for Florida's central west coast is an exciting destination unto itself.

At the head of the bay, the city of Tampa is the commercial center of Florida's west coast—a major seaport and a center of banking, high-tech manufacturing, and cigar making (half a billion drugstore stogies a year). Downtown Tampa may roll up its sidewalks after dark, but a short ride will take you to Ybor City, the historic Cuban enclave, which is now an exciting entertainment and dining venue. You can come here during the day to see the sea life at the Florida Aquarium and stroll through the Henry B. Plant Museum, housed in an ornate, Moorish-style hotel built a century ago to lure tourists to Tampa.

Two bridges and a causeway will whisk you westward across the bay to

the Pinellas Peninsula, one of Florida's most densely packed urban areas. Over here on the bay front, lovely downtown St. Petersburg is famous for wintering seniors, a shopping and dining complex built way out on a pier, and the world's largest collection of Salvador Dalí's surrealist paintings.

Keep driving west and you'll come to a line of barrier islands where St. Pete Beach, Clearwater Beach, and other gulf-side communities boast 28 miles of sunshine, surf, and white sand.

Heading south, the Sunshine Skyway will take you soaring 175 feet above the bay to Sarasota and to another 42 miles of barrier islands. One of Florida's cultural centers, affluent Sarasota is the gateway to St. Armands and Longboat Keys, two playgrounds of the rich and famous, and to Lido and Siesta Keys, both attractive to families of more modest means. Even more reasonably priced is Anna Maria Island, off the riverfront town of Bradenton.

1 Tampa

200 miles SW of Jacksonville, 254 miles NW of Miami, 63 miles N. of Sarasota

Even if you stay at the beaches 20 miles to the west, you should consider driving into Tampa to see its sights. If you have children in tow, they may *demand* that you go into the city so they can ride the rides and see the animals at Busch Gardens. While in the city, you can educate them at the Florida Aquarium and the city's fine museums. If you don't have kids, historic Ybor City has the bay area's liveliest nightlife.

Tampa was a sleepy little port when Cuban immigrants founded Ybor City's cigar industry in the 1880s. A few years later, Henry B. Plant put Tampa on the tourist map by building a railroad into town and constructing the bulbous

Tampa & St. Petersburg

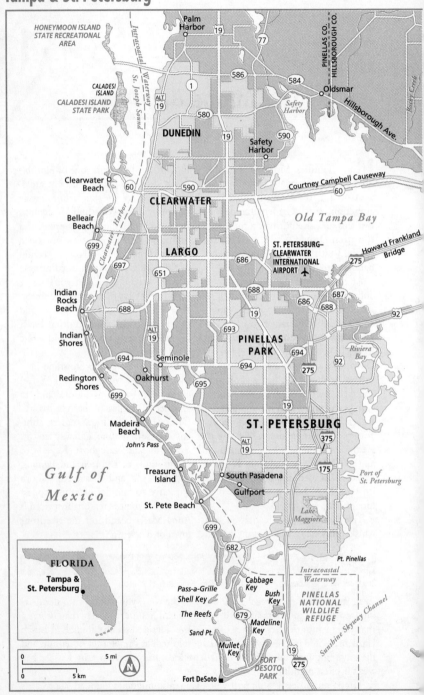

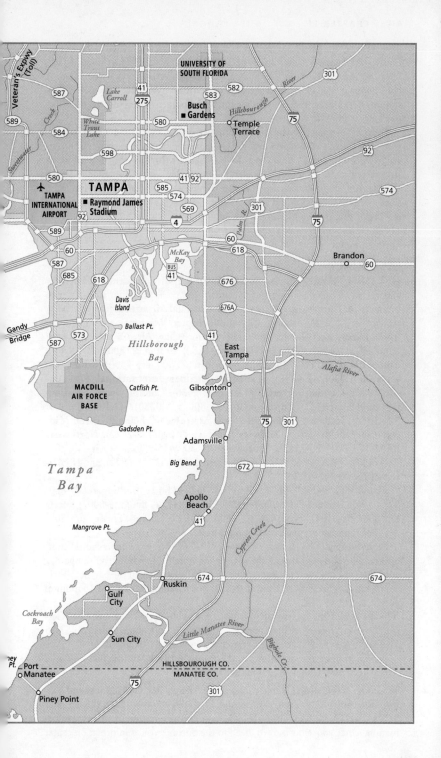

minarets over his garish Tampa Bay Hotel, now a museum named in his honor. During the Spanish American War, Teddy Roosevelt trained his Rough Riders here and walked the Ybor City streets with Cuban revolutionary José Marti. A land boom in the 1920s gave the city its charming, Victorian-style Hyde Park suburb, now a gentrified redoubt for the baby boomers just across the Hillsborough River from downtown.

Today's downtown skyline is the product of the 1980s and 1990s booms, when banks built skyscrapers and the city put up an expansive convention center, a performing-arts center, and the Ice Palace, a 20,000-seat bayfront arena that is home to professional hockey's Tampa Bay Lightning. Alongside the Florida Aquarium, the Garrison Seaport Center is a major home port for cruise ships bound for Mexico and the Caribbean, while the brand new Channelside is a major shopping-and-dining complex.

You won't want to spend your entire vacation here, but all this adds up to a fast-paced, modern city on the go.

ESSENTIALS

GETTING THERE   **Tampa International Airport,** off Memorial Highway and Fla. 60, 5 miles northwest of downtown Tampa, is the major air gateway to this area (**St. Petersburg–Clearwater International Airport** has limited service; see section 2, "St. Petersburg," later in this chapter). Most major and many no-frills airlines serve Tampa International, including **Air Canada** (© 800/268-7240 in Canada, 800/776-3000 in the U.S.), **AirTran** (© 800/AIR-TRAN), **America West** (© 800/235-9292), **American** (© 800/433-7300), **British Airways** (© 800/247-9297), **Canadian Airlines International** (© 800/426-7000), **Cayman Airways** (© 800/422-9626), **Condor German Airlines** (© 800/524-6975), **Continental** (© 800/525-0280), **Delta** (© 800/221-1212), **JetBlue** (© **800/538-2583**), **MetroJet** (© 800/428-4322), **Midway** (© 800/446-4392), **Midwest Express** (© 800/452-2022), **Northwest/KLM** (© 800/225-2525), **Southwest** (© 800/435-9792), **Spirit** (© 800/722-7117), **TWA** (© 800/221-2000), **United** (© 800/241-6522), and **US Airways** (© 800/428-4322).

Alamo (© 800/327-9633), **Avis** (© 800/331-1212), **Budget** (© 800/527-0700), **Dollar** (© 800/800-4000), **Enterprise** (© 800/325-8007), **Hertz** (© 800/654-3131), **National** (© 800/CAR-RENT), and **Thrifty** (© 800/367-2277) all have rental-car operations here.

SuperShuttle/The Limo (© **800/BLUE-VAN;** www.supershuttle.com) operates van services between the airport and hotels throughout the Tampa Bay area. Fares for one person range from $15 to $19 anywhere in the bay area. **Taxis** are plentiful at the airport; the ride to downtown Tampa takes about 15 minutes and costs $11 to $14.

Local **HARTline buses** stop in front of the red baggage-claim area (see "Getting Around," below). A sign is posted there with a route map. Rides cost $1.15 for local buses, $1.50 for express service. Exact change is required.

Amtrak trains arrive downtown at the **Tampa Amtrak Station,** 601 Nebraska Ave. N. (© **800/USA-RAIL;** www.amtrak.com).

VISITOR INFORMATION   Contact the **Tampa Bay Convention and Visitors Bureau,** 400 N. Tampa St., Tampa, FL 33602-4706 (© **800/826-8358** or 813/342-4077; fax 813/229-6616; www.visittampabay.com), for advance information. Once you're downtown, head to the bureau's visitor information center at the corner of Ashley and Madison streets. It's open Monday to Saturday from 9am to 5pm.

The **Ybor City Chamber of Commerce** has a visitor center in Centro Ybor, 1600 E. 8th Ave. (between 16th and 17th Sts. E.), Tampa, FL 33605 (© **877/ 934-3782** or 813/248-3712; fax 813/242-0398; www.ybor.org). The center is open Monday to Saturday from 9am to 6pm, Sunday from noon to 5pm.

GETTING AROUND   Like most other Florida destinations, it's virtually impossible to see Tampa's major sights and enjoy the best restaurants without a car.

In the works at press time, the **TECO Line Trolley** is destined to haul passengers between downtown and Ybor City via the Ice Palace, Channelside, Garrison Seaport, and the Florida Aquarium. Meanwhile, the free **Uptown- Downtown Connector Trolley** runs southbound on Tampa Street, northbound on Florida Street every 10 minutes Monday to Friday from 6am to 6pm. Check with the visitor center (see above), or call the Hillsborough Area Regional Transit/ HARTline (© **813/254-HART;** www.hartline.org).

If you're on a budget, HARTline also provides regularly scheduled **bus service** between downtown Tampa and the suburbs. Pick up a route map at the visitor information center (see above).

Taxis in Tampa don't normally cruise the streets for fares, but they do line up at public loading places, such as hotels, the performing-arts center, and bus and train depots. If you need a taxi, call **Tampa Bay Cab** (© **813/251-5555**), **Yellow Cab** (© **813/253-0121**), or **United Cab** (© **813/253-2424**). Fares are 95¢ at flag fall, plus $1.50 for each mile.

EXPLORING THE THEME & ANIMAL PARKS

Adventure Island   If the summer heat gets to you before one of Tampa's famous thunderstorms brings late-afternoon relief, you can take a waterlogged break at this 25-acre outdoor water theme park near Busch Gardens Tampa Bay (see below). In fact, you can frolic here even during the cooler days of spring and fall, when the water is heated. The Key West Rapids, Tampa Typhoon, Gulf Scream, and other exciting water rides will drench the teens, while other, calmer rides are geared for younger kids. There are places to picnic and sunbathe, a games arcade, a volleyball complex, and an outdoor cafe. If you forget to bring your own, a surf shop sells bathing suits, towels, and suntan lotion.

10001 McKinley Dr. (between Busch Blvd. and Bougainvillea Ave.). © 813/987-5600. www.4adventure. com. *Note:* Admission and hours vary from year to year so call ahead, check website, or get brochure at visitor centers. Admission at least $25.95 adults, $23.95 children 3–9, plus tax; free for children 2 and under. Combination tickets with Busch Gardens Tampa Bay (1 day each) $59.95 adults, $49.95 children 3–9, free for children under 3. Late Feb to Labor Day daily 10am–5pm; Sept–Oct Fri–Sun 10am–5pm (extended hours in summer and on holidays). Closed Nov to late Feb. Take Exit 33 off I-275 and go east on Busch Blvd. for 2 miles. Turn left onto McKinley Dr. (N. 40th St.) and entry is on right.

Busch Gardens Tampa Bay ★★ *Kids*   Although its heart-stopping thrill rides get much of the ink, this venerable theme park (it predates Disney World) ranks among the largest zoos in the country. It's a don't-miss attraction for children, who can see in person all those wild beasts they've watched on the *Animal Planet*—and they'll be closer to them here than at Disney's Animal Kingdom in Orlando (see chapter 12). Several thousand animals live in naturalistic environments and help carry out the park's overall African theme. Most authentic is the 80-acre plain, strongly reminiscent of the real Serengeti of Tanzania and Kenya, upon which zebras, giraffes, and other animals actually graze. Unlike the animals

Tampa Attractions

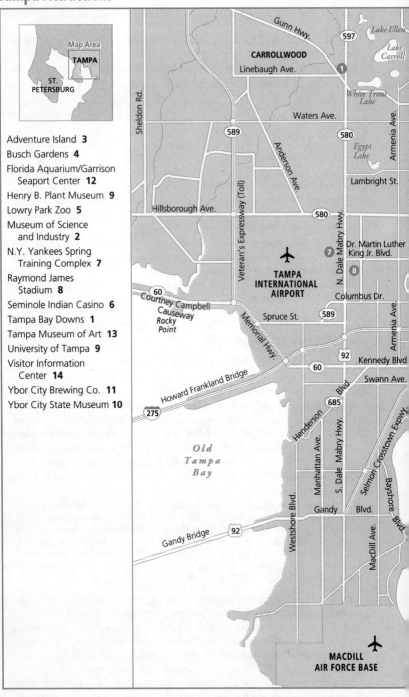

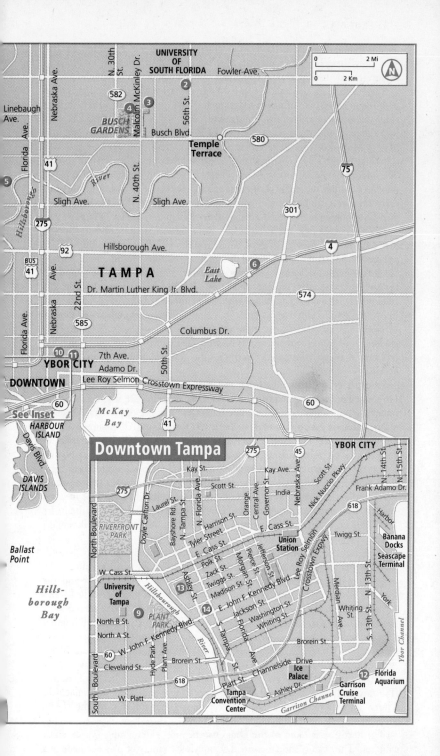

on the real Serengeti, however, the grazing animals have nothing to fear from lions, hyenas, crocodiles, and other predators, which here are confined to enclosures—as are hippos and elephants.

Most of the large animals live in the **Edge of Africa,** the most unique of the park's eight areas, each of which has its own theme, animals, live entertainment, thrill rides, kiddie attractions, dining, and shopping. A Skyride cable car soars over the park, offering a bird's-eye view of it. Turn left after the main gate and head to **Morocco,** a walled city with exotic architecture, craft demonstrations, a sultan's tent with snake charmers, and an exhibit featuring alligators and turtles. The Moorish-style Moroccan Palace Theater features an ice show, which many families consider to be the park's best entertainment for both adults and children. Here you can also attend a song-and-dance show in the Marrakech Theater. Overlooking it all is the Crown Colony Restaurant, the park's largest.

After watching the snake charmers, walk eastward past Anheuser-Busch's fabled Clydesdale horses to **Egypt,** where you can visit King Tut's tomb with its replicas of the real treasures and listen to comedian Martin Short narrate "Akbar's Adventure Tours," a wacky simulator that "transports" one and all across Egypt via camel, biplane, and mine car. The whole room moves on this ride, which lasts only 5 minutes—much less time than the usual wait to get inside. Adults and kids over 53 inches tall can ride Montu, the tallest and longest inverted roller coaster in the world with seven upside-down loops. Your feet dangle loose on Montu, so make sure your shoes are tied tightly and your lunch has had time to digest. Youngsters can dig for their own ancient treasures in a sand area.

From Egypt, walk onto the **Edge of Africa,** home of most of the big animals. Go immediately to the Expedition Africa Gift Shop and see if you can get on one of the park's zoologist-led wildlife tours (see "Upclose & Personal," below).

Next stop is **Nairobi,** where you can see gorillas and chimpanzees in the Myombe Reserve. The most beautiful part of the park, this lush area replicates their natural rainforest habitat. Nairobi also has a baby animal nursery, a petting zoo, turtle and reptile displays, an elephant exhibit (alas, the magnificent creatures seem to be bored to the point of madness), and Curiosity Caverns, where bats, reptiles, and small mammals that are active in the dark are kept in cages (it's the most traditional zoolike area here). The entry to Rhino Rally, the park's new safari adventure, is at the western end of Nairobi (see "Upclose & Personal," below).

Next, head to **The Congo,** highlighted by rare white Bengal tigers that live on Claw Island. The Congo also is home to two roller coasters: the Kumba, the largest and fastest roller coaster in the southeastern United States; and the Python, which twists and turns for 1,200 feet. You will get drenched—and refreshed on a hot day—by riding the Congo River Rapids (you're turned loose in round boats that float down the swiftly flowing "river"). There are bumper cars and kiddie rides here, too.

From The Congo, walk south into **Stanleyville,** a prototype African village, with a shopping bazaar, orangutans living on an island, and the Stanleyville Theater, usually featuring shows for children. Two more water rides are here: the Tanganyika Tidal Wave (you'll come to a very damp end) and the Stanley Falls Flume (an aqua version of a roller coaster). Serving ribs and chicken, the picnic-style Stanleyville Smokehouse has some of the best chow here.

The next stop is **Land of the Dragons,** the most entertaining area for small children. They can spend an entire day enjoying a variety of play elements in a

How to See Busch Gardens

You can save a few dollars and avoid waiting in long lines by buying your tickets to Busch Gardens Tampa Bay at the privately owned **Tampa Bay Visitor Information Center,** opposite the park at 3601 E. Busch Blvd., at North Ednam Place (✆ **813/985-3601;** fax 813/985-7642). Owner Jim Boggs worked for the park for 13 years and gives expert advice about how to get the most out of your visit. He sells discounted tickets to Busch Gardens, Adventure Island, and other attractions; and he will book hotel rooms and car rentals for you, often at a discount. The center is open Monday to Saturday from 10am to 5:30pm, Sunday from 10am to 2pm.

Allow at least a day to see the park. Arrive early—but try not to come when it's raining, since some rides may not operate. Bring comfortable shoes; and, remember, you will get wet on some of the rides, so wear appropriate clothing (shops near the rides sell inexpensive plastic ponchos).

As soon as you're through the turnstiles, pick up a copy of a park map and the day's activity schedule, which tells what's showing and when at 14 entertainment venues. Then take a few minutes to carefully plan your time—it's a big park with lots to see and do. Busch Gardens continues to grow, so be on the lookout for new attractions.

Although you'll get close to Busch Garden's predators, hippos, and elephants in their glass-walled enclosures, the only way to get out on the plain among the grazers is on a tour. The park's new **Rhino Rally** adventure ride will take you out there in four-wheel-drive Land Rovers like those used on photo safaris in Africa, but they have a thrill-ride aspect by plunging into a river (you'll probably get wet) and then racing each other across the plains. More like the real thing—and a much better bet for actually learning something—is an **Animal Adventure Tour** 🐾🐾, on which you'll roam the plains in the company of a zoologist. These 2-hour excursions cost an extra $75 per person and usually leave at 1:30pm daily. Go immediately to the Expedition Africa Gift Shop, opposite the Crown Colony Restaurant in the Edge of Africa, to reserve a spot. Also good are the 30-minute, zoologist-led **Serengeti Safari Special Tours** 🐾. These are well worth an extra $20 per person regardless of age. You can make reservations for the morning tour at the Expedition Africa Gift Shop, but the midday and afternoon tours are first-come, first-served. Note that children under 5 are not allowed on either tour.

fairy-tale setting, plus just-for-kids rides. The area is dominated by Dumphrey, a whimsical dragon who interacts with visitors and guides children around a three-story tree house with winding stairways, tall towers, stepping stones, illuminated water geysers, and an echo chamber.

The next stop is **Bird Gardens,** the park's original core, offering rich foliage, lagoons, and a free-flight aviary for hundreds of exotic birds, including golden and American bald eagles. Catch the Bird Show here, and be sure to see the Florida flamingos and Australian koalas.

Next take a break at the **Hospitality House,** which offers piano entertainment and free samples of Anheuser-Busch's famous beers. You must be 21 to imbibe (there's a limit of two free mugs per seating), but soft drinks also are available.

If your stomach can take another hair-raising ride, the last stop is at **Gwazi,** the park's pair of old-fashioned wooden roller coasters named the Lion and the Tiger, which start simultaneously and whiz within a few feet of each other six times as they roar along at 50 miles per hour. Since the coasters rise to "only" 90 feet (that's low compared to the park's other thrillers), most family members can give them a go. In Gwazi's "Water Wars," participants shoot water-filled balloons at each other with big slingshots. It's a soaking way to end your visit.

You can exchange foreign currency in the park, and interpreters are available.

Note: You can get here from Orlando via shuttle buses, which pick up between 8:00am and 10:15am for the 60-minute ride, with return trips starting at 5pm and continuing until the park closes. Round-trip fares are $5 per person. Call ℂ **800/511-2450** for schedules and reservations.

3000 E. Busch Blvd. (at McKinley Dr./N. 40th St.). ℂ 813/987-5283. www.buschgardens.com. *Note:* Admission and hours vary so call ahead, check website, or get brochure at visitor centers. Admission at least $43.70 adults, $37.70 children 3–9, plus tax; free for children 2 and under. Annual pass $84.95 adults, $74.95 children 3–9. Combination tickets with Adventure Island (1 day each) $59.95 adults, $49.95 children 3–9. Daily 10am–6pm (extended hours to 7 and 8pm in summer and holidays). Parking $6. Take I-275 north of downtown to Busch Blvd. (Exit 33), and go east 2 miles. From I-75, take Fowler Ave. (Exit 54) and follow the signs west.

The Florida Aquarium ★★ *Kids* See more than 5,000 aquatic animals and plants that call Florida home at this entertaining and informative aquarium. The exhibits follow a drop of water from the pristine springs of the Florida Wetlands Gallery, through a mangrove forest in the Bays and Beaches Gallery, and out onto the Coral Reefs, where an impressive 43-foot-wide, 14-foot-tall panoramic window lets you look out to schools of fish and lots of sharks and stingrays. Also worth visiting are the "Explore a Shore" playground to educate the kids, a deep-water exhibit, and a tank housing moray eels. A special exhibit features rare sea dragons (it's difficult to tell whether they're sea horses or seaweed) and other creatures from Australia. The Cafe Ray serves snacks and light meals.

701 Channelside Dr. ℂ 813/273-4000. www.flaquarium.net. Admission $12.95 adults, $11.95 seniors, $7.95 children 3–12, free for children under 3. Parking $4. Daily 9:30am–5pm. Closed Thanksgiving, Christmas.

Lowry Park Zoo *Kids* Watching 2,000-pound manatees, komodo dragons, and rare red pandas makes this a worthwhile excursion after the kids have seen the plains of Africa at Busch Gardens. With lots of greenery, bubbling brooks, and cascading waterfalls, this 24-acre zoo displays animals in settings similar to their natural habitats. Other major exhibits include a Florida wildlife display, an Asian Domain, a Primate World, an Aquatic Center, a free-flight aviary with a birds-of-prey show, a children's petting zoo and hands-on Discovery Center, and an endangered-species carousel ride.

1101 W. Sligh Ave. ℂ 813/935-8552 or 813/932-0245 for recorded information. www.lowryparkzoo.com. Admission $9.50 adults, $8.50 seniors, $5.95 children 3–11, free for children 2 and under. Daily 9:30am–5pm. Closed Thanksgiving, Christmas. Take I-275 to Sligh Ave. (Exit 31) and follow the signs.

VISITING THE MUSEUMS

Henry B. Plant Museum ★★ Originally built in 1891 by railroad tycoon Henry B. Plant as the 511-room Tampa Bay Hotel, this ornate building alone is worth a short trip across the river from downtown. Its 13 silver minarets and distinctive Moorish architecture, modeled after the Alhambra in Spain, make this National Historic Landmark a focal point of the Tampa skyline. Although the building itself is the highlight of a visit, don't skip the contents: art and furnishings from Europe and the Orient; and exhibits that explain the history of the original railroad resort, Florida's early tourist industry, and the hotel's role as a staging point for Teddy Roosevelt's Rough Riders during the Spanish–American War.

401 W. Kennedy Blvd. (between Hyde Park and Magnolia Aves.). (C) 813/254-1891. www.plantmuseum. com. Admission free; suggested donation $5 adults, $2 children 12 and under. Tues–Sat 10am–4pm; Sun noon–4pm. Closed Thanksgiving, Christmas Eve, and Christmas Day. Take Kennedy Blvd. (Fla. 60) across Hillsborough River.

Museum of Science and Industry (MOSI) ★ *Kids* A great place to take the kids on a rainy day, MOSI is the largest science center in the Southeast and has more than 450 interactive exhibits. You can step into the Gulf Hurricane and experience 74 mile-per-hour winds, defy the laws of gravity in the unique *Challenger* space experience, cruise the mysterious world of microbes in LifeLab, and explore the human body in The Amazing You. You can also watch stunning movies in Florida's first IMAX dome theater. Outside, trails wind through a 47-acre nature preserve with a butterfly garden.

4801 E. Fowler Ave. (at N. 50th St.). (C) 813/987-6300. www.mosi.org. Admission $13 adults; $11 seniors, college students with identification, and children 13–18; $9 children 2–12; free for children under 2. Admission includes IMAX movies. Daily 9am–5pm or later. From downtown, take I-275 north and then Fowler Ave. east for 2 miles to museum on right.

Tampa Museum of Art Located on the east bank of the Hillsborough River next to the round NationsBank building (locals facetiously call it the "Beer Can"), this fine-arts complex offers eight galleries with changing exhibits ranging from classical antiquities to contemporary Florida art. There's also a 7-acre riverfront park and sculpture garden.

600 N. Ashley Dr. (at Twiggs St.), downtown. (C) 813/274-8130. www.tampamuseum.com. Admission $5 adults, $4 seniors, $3 children 6–18, free for children under 6, by donation Thurs 5–8pm and Sat 10am–noon. Tues–Wed and Fri–Sat 10am–5pm, Thurs 10am–8pm, Sun 1–5pm. Parking 90¢ per hour. Take I-275 to Exit 25 (Ashley St.).

YBOR CITY

Northeast of downtown, the city's historic Latin district takes its present name from Don Vicente Martinez Ybor (*Ee*-bore), a Spanish cigar maker who arrived here in 1886 via Cuba and Key West. Soon his and other Tampa factories were producing more than 300,000 hand-rolled stogies a day.

It may not be the cigar capital of the world anymore, but Ybor is the happening part of Tampa and it's one of the best places in Florida to buy hand-rolled cigars. It's not on a par with New Orleans's Bourbon Street, Washington's Georgetown, or New York's SoHo, but good food and great music dominate the scene, especially on weekends when the streets bustle until 4am. Live-music offerings run the gamut from jazz and blues to indie rock.

At the heart of it all is **Centro Ybor,** a new dining-shopping-entertainment complex sprawling between 7th and 8th avenues and 16th and 17th streets ((C) 813/241-4545). Here you'll find a multiscreen cinema, a comedy club, several restaurants, a large open-air bar, and several mall regulars such as Victoria's Secret and American Eagle Outfitters. The Ybor City Chamber of Commerce has its visitors center here (see "Essentials," earlier in this chapter), as does the Ybor City State Museum its gift shop (see below).

Even if you're not a cigar smoker, you'll enjoy a stroll through the **Ybor City State Museum** 🖈, 1818 9th Ave., between 18th and 19th streets (© **813/ 247-6323;** www.ybormuseum.org), housed in the former Ferlita Bakery (1896 to 1973). You can take a self-guided tour around the museum to see a collection of cigar labels, cigar memorabilia, and works by local artisans. Admission is $2 per person. Depending on the availability of volunteer docents, admission includes a 15-minute guided tour of **La Casita,** a renovated cigar worker's cottage adjacent to the museum; it's furnished as it was at the turn of the last century. The museum is open daily from 9am to 5pm, but plan to be here when La Casita is open, Monday to Saturday from 10am to noon and 1 to 2:30pm.

Check with the museum about **walking tours** of the historic district. **Ybor City Ghost Walks** (© **813/242-4660**) will take you to the spookier parts of the area at night. Call for reservations, schedules, and prices.

Housed in a 100-year-old, three-story former cigar factory, **Ybor City Brewing Company,** 2205 N. 20th St., facing Palm Avenue (© **813/242-9222**), produces Ybor Gold and other brews, none with preservatives. Admission of $2 per person includes a tour of the brewery and a taste of the end result. Tours usually are given Monday to Friday at 11am to 1pm.

ORGANIZED TOURS

Swiss Chalet Tours, 3601 E. Busch Blvd. (© **813/985-3601**), opposite Busch Gardens in the privately run Tampa Bay Visitor Information Center (see "How to See Busch Gardens" box, above), operates guided bus tours of Tampa, Ybor City, and environs. The 4-hour tours of Tampa are given from 10am to 2pm daily, with a stop for lunch at the Columbia Restaurant in Ybor City. They cost $40 for adults and $35 for children. The 7-hour full-day tours of both Tampa and St. Petersburg cost $70 for adults and $65 for children. Reservations are required at least 24 hours in advance; passengers are picked up at major hotels and various other points in the Tampa/St. Petersburg area. You also can book bus tours to Orlando, Sarasota, Bradenton, and other regional destinations (call for schedules, prices, and reservations).

Gray Line (© **800/282-8020** or 727/526-9086; www.grayline.com) has full-day guided tours to Busch Gardens and Adventure Island ($59 and $42 per person, respectively) and has bus trips to Orlando.

OUTDOOR ACTIVITIES & SPECTATOR SPORTS

BIKING, IN-LINE SKATING & JOGGING   Bayshore Boulevard, a 7-mile-long promenade, is famous for its sidewalk right on the shores of Hillsborough Bay and is a favorite for runners, joggers, walkers, and in-line skaters. The route goes from the western edge of downtown in a southward direction, passing stately old homes in Hyde Park, a few high-rise condominiums, retirement communities, and houses of worship, ending at Ballast Point Park. The view from the promenade across the bay to the downtown skyline is unmatched here (Bayshore Boulevard also is great for a drive).

> **Walk This Way**
>
> Bayshore Boulevard's 7-mile-long promenade is reputed to be the world's longest continuous sidewalk.

FISHING   One of Florida's best guide services, **Light Tackle Fishing Expeditions,** 6105 Memorial Hwy., Suite 4 (© **800/972-1930** or 813/963-1930; www. leftcoastfishing.com), offers private sportfishing trips for tarpon, redfish, cobia, trout, and snook. Call for prices, schedule, and required reservations.

GOLF Tampa has three municipal golf courses where you can play for about $30, a relative pittance when compared with fees at the privately owned courses here and elsewhere in Florida. The **Babe Zaharias Municipal Golf Course,** 11412 Forest Hills Dr., north of Lowry Park (© **813/631-4374**), is an 18-hole, par-70 course with a pro shop, putting greens, and a driving range. It's the shortest of the municipal courses, but small greens and narrow fairways present ample challenges. Water provides obstacles on 12 of the 18 holes at **Rocky Point Municipal Golf Course,** 4151 Dana Shores Dr. (© **813/673-4316**), located between the airport and the bay. It's a par-71 course with a pro shop, a practice range, and putting greens. On the Hillsborough River in north Tampa, the **Rogers Park Municipal Golf Course,** 7910 N. 30th St. (© **813/673-4396**), is an 18-hole, par-72 championship course with a lighted driving and practice range. All the courses are open daily from 7am to dusk, and lessons and club rentals are available.

Another inexpensive place to play is the **University of South Florida Golf Course,** Fletcher Avenue and 46th Street (© **813/632-6893**), just north of the University of South Florida campus. This 18-hole, par-71 course is nicknamed "The Claw" because of its challenging layout. It offers lessons and club rentals. Greens fees range from about $19 to $25, or $25 to $35 with a cart, depending on the season and time of day. It's open daily from 7am to dusk.

Other public courses include the **Hall of Fame Golf Club,** just south of the airport at 2222 N. Westshore Blvd. (© **813/876-4913**), an 18-hole, par-72 course with a driving range; **Persimmon Hill Golf Club,** 5109 Hamey Rd. (© **813/623-6962**); **Silver Dollar Trap & Golf Club,** 17000 Patterson Rd., Odessa (© **813/920-3884**); and **Westchase Golf Club,** 1307 Radcliff Dr. (© **813/854-2331**).

You can book starting times and get information about these and the area's other courses by calling **Tee Times USA** (© **800/374-8633**).

If you want to do some serious work on your game, the **Arnold Palmer Golf Academy World Headquarters** is at Saddlebrook Resort, 5700 Saddlebrook Way, Wesley Chapel, 12 miles north of Tampa (© **800/729-8383** or 813/973-1111; www.saddlebrookresort.com). Half-day and hourly instruction is available, and 2-, 3-, and 5-day programs are available for adults and juniors. You have to stay at the resort or enroll in the golf program to play at Saddlebrook. See "Where to Stay," below, for more information about the resort.

SPECTATOR SPORTS National Football League fans can catch the defensive-minded **Tampa Bay Buccaneers** at the modern, 66,000-seat Raymond James Stadium, 4201 N. Dale Mabry Hwy., at Dr. Martin Luther King Jr. Boulevard (© **813/879-2827;** www.buccaneers.com). The Bucs' season runs from September through December.

The National Hockey League's **Tampa Bay Lightning** play in the Ice Palace, beginning in October (© **813/229-8800;** www.tampabaylightning.com).

New York Yankees fans can watch the Boys in Blue during baseball spring training from mid-February through March at Legends Field (© **813/879-2244** or 813/875-7753; www.yankees.com), opposite Raymond James Stadium. This scaled-down replica of Yankee Stadium is the largest spring-training facility in Florida, with a 10,000-seat capacity. The club's minor-league team, the **Tampa Yankees** (same phone and website), plays at Legends Field from April through August.

The only oval thoroughbred race course on Florida's west coast, **Tampa Bay Downs,** 11225 Racetrack Rd., Oldsmar (© **800/200-4434** in Florida, or

813/855-4401), is the home of the Tampa Bay Derby. Races are held from December to May, and the track presents simulcasts year-round. Call for post times.

TENNIS   Players at all levels can sharpen their games at the **Hopman Tennis Program,** at the Saddlebrook Resort (see "Where to Stay," below). You must be a member or a guest to play here.

SHOPPING

Hyde Park and Ybor City are two areas of Tampa worth some window shopping, perhaps sandwiched around lunch at one of their fine restaurants (see "Where to Dine," later in this chapter).

CIGARS   Ybor City no longer is a major producer of hand-rolled cigars, but you can watch artisans making stogies at the **Gonzales y Martinez Cigar Factory,** 2025 7th Ave., in the Columbia Restaurant building (© 813/247-2469). Gonzales and Martinez are recent arrivals from Cuba and don't speak English, but the staff does at the adjoining **Columbia Cigar Store** (it's best to enter here). Rollers are on duty Monday to Saturday from 10am to 6pm.

You can stock up on fine domestic and imported cigars at **El Sol,** 1728 E. 7th Ave. (© 813/247-5554), the city's oldest cigar store; **King Corona Cigar Factory,** 1523 E. 7th Ave. (© 813/241-9109); and **Metropolitan Cigars & Wine,** 2014 E. 7th Ave. (© 813/248-3304).

SHOPPING CENTERS   **Old Hyde Park Village,** 1507 W. Swann Ave., at South Dakota Avenue (© 813/251-3500), is a terrific alternative to cookie-cutter suburban malls. Walk around little shops in the sunshine and check out Hyde Park, one of the city's oldest and most historic neighborhoods at the same time. The cluster of 50 upscale shops and boutiques is set in a village layout. The selection includes Williams-Sonoma, Pottery Barn, Banana Republic, Brooks Brothers, Crabtree & Evelyn, Godiva, and Anthropologie, to name a few. There's a free parking garage on South Oregon Avenue behind Jacobson's department store. The shops are open Monday to Wednesday and Saturday from 10am to 6pm, Thursday and Friday from 10am to 9pm, and Sunday from noon to 5pm.

At press time, a multiscreen cinema and a few stores have opened in the huge new mall known as **Channelside at Garrison Seaport,** on Channelside Drive between the Garrison Seaport and the Florida Aquarium (© 813/274-8000). Many more shops and restaurants will be opening throughout 2001.

The regular suburban mall in the city is **West Shore Plaza,** on Kennedy Boulevard where it turns into Memorial Highway (Fla. 60). **University Mall** is nearest Busch Gardens, on Fowler Avenue just east of I-275. The area's largest complex is **Brandon TownCenter,** at I-4 and Fla. 60 in the eastern suburb of Brandon, where most stores have unusually large amounts of floor space and, hence, more merchandise from which to choose.

WHERE TO STAY

I've organized the accommodations listings below into three geographic areas: near Busch Gardens, downtown, and Ybor City. If you're going to Busch Gardens, Adventure Island, Lowry Park Zoo, and the Museum of Science and Industry (MOSI), the motels near Busch Gardens are much more convenient than those downtown, about 7 miles to the south. The downtown hotels are geared to business travelers, but staying there will put you near the Florida

Aquarium, the Tampa Museum of Art, the Henry B. Plant Museum, the Tampa Bay Performing Arts Center, scenic Bayshore Boulevard, and the dining and shopping opportunities in the Hyde Park historic district.

The Westshore area, near the bay west of downtown and south of Tampa International Airport, is another commercial center, with a wide range of national chain hotels catering to business travelers and conventioneers. It's convenient to Raymond James Stadium and the New York Yankees' spring-training complex. Check with your favorite chain for a Westshore-Airport location.

The high season in Tampa generally runs from January to April, but you won't find as large an increase here as at the beach resorts. Most hotels offer discounted package rates in the summer and weekend specials all year, dropping their rates by as much as 50%. Hotels often combine tickets to major attractions like Busch Gardens in their packages, so always ask about special deals.

Hillsborough County adds 12% tax to your hotel room bill.

NEAR BUSCH GARDENS

The nearest chain motel to the park is **Howard Johnson Hotel Near Busch Gardens Maingate,** 4139 E. Busch Blvd. (© **800/444-5656** or 813/ 988-9191), an older property which was extensively renovated and reopened in 1999. It's 1½ blocks east of the main entrance.

A bit farther away, the 500-room **Embassy Suites Hotel and Conference Center,** 3705 Spectrum Blvd., facing Fowler Avenue (© **800/EMBASSY** or 813/977-7066; fax 813/977-7933), is the plushest and most expensive establishment near the park. Almost across the avenue stands **LaQuinta Inn & Suites,** 3701 E. Fowler Ave. (© **800/NU-ROOMS** or 813/910-7500; fax 813/910-7600). Side-by-side just south of Fowler Avenue are editions of **AmeriSuites,** 11408 N. 30th St. (© **800/833-1516** or 813/979-1922; fax 813/ 979-1926), and **DoubleTree Guest Suites,** 11310 N. 30th St. (© **800/ 222-TREE** or 813/971-7690; fax 813/972-5525).

Baymont Inn & Suites *Value*   Fake banana trees and a parrot cage welcome guests to the terra-cotta–floored lobby of this comfortable and convenient member of the small chain of cost-conscious but amenity-rich motels. All rooms are spacious and have ceiling fans and desks. Rooms with king beds also have recliners, business rooms sport dataport phones and extra large desks, and the suites have refrigerators and microwave ovens. Outside, a courtyard with an unheated swimming pool has plenty of space for sunning. There's no restaurant on the premises, but plenty are within walking distance.

9202 N. 30th St. (at Busch Blvd.), Tampa, FL 33612. © 800/428-3438 or 813/930-6900. Fax 813/930-0563. www.baymontinns.com. 146 units. Winter $80–$109 double; off-season $65–$94 double. Rates include continental breakfast and local phone calls. AE, DC, DISC, MC, V. **Amenities:** Heated outdoor pool; game room; coin-op washers and dryers. *In room:* A/C, TV, dataport, fridge, coffeemaker, hair dryer, iron.

Best Western All Suites Hotel *★★ Value*   This three-story all-suites hotel is the most beachlike vacation venue you'll find close to the park. Whimsical signs lead you around a lush tropical courtyard with heated pool, hot tub, and a lively, sports-oriented tiki bar. The bar can get noisy before closing at 9pm, and ground-level units are musty, so ask for an upstairs suite away from the action. Suite living rooms are well equipped and separate bedrooms have narrow screened patios or balconies. Great for kids, 11 "family suites" have bunk beds in addition to a queen-size bed for parents. Another 28 suites especially equipped for business travelers (but are great for couples, too) with ergonomic chairs at big writing desks with speaker phones.

Tampa Accommodations & Dining

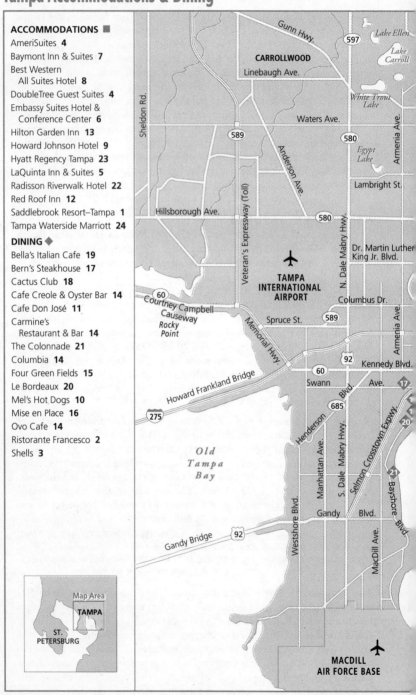

ACCOMMODATIONS ■

AmeriSuites **4**
Baymont Inn & Suites **7**
Best Western
  All Suites Hotel **8**
DoubleTree Guest Suites **4**
Embassy Suites Hotel &
  Conference Center **6**
Hilton Garden Inn **13**
Howard Johnson Hotel **9**
Hyatt Regency Tampa **23**
LaQuinta Inn & Suites **5**
Radisson Riverwalk Hotel **22**
Red Roof Inn **12**
Saddlebrook Resort–Tampa **1**
Tampa Waterside Marriott **24**

DINING ◆

Bella's Italian Cafe **19**
Bern's Steakhouse **17**
Cactus Club **18**
Cafe Creole & Oyster Bar **14**
Cafe Don José **11**
Carmine's
  Restaurant & Bar **14**
The Colonnade **21**
Columbia **14**
Four Green Fields **15**
Le Bordeaux **20**
Mel's Hot Dogs **10**
Mise en Place **16**
Ovo Cafe **14**
Ristorante Francesco **2**
Shells **3**

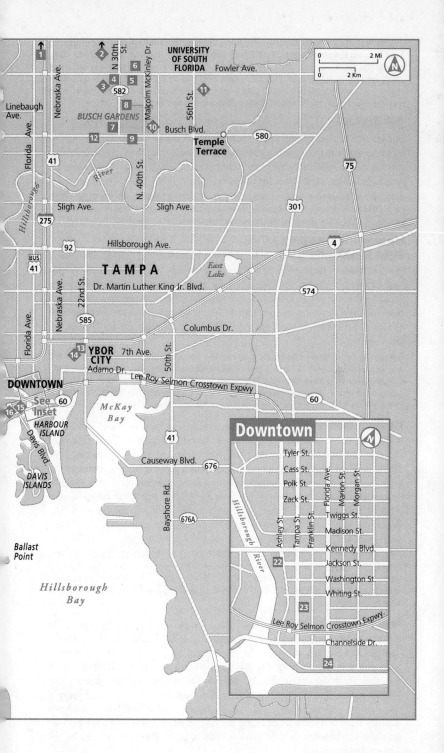

Near University of South Florida, behind Busch Gardens, 3001 University Center Dr. (faces N. 30th St. between Busch Blvd. and Fowler Ave.), Tampa, FL 33612. ✆ **800/786-7446** or 813/971-8930. Fax 813/971-8935. www.thatparrotplace.com. 150 units. Winter $99–$159 suite for 2; off-season $89–$139 suite for 2. Rates include full breakfast buffet. AE, DC, DISC, MC, V. **Amenities:** Restaurant (dinner only); bar; heated outdoor pool; access to nearby health club; Jacuzzi; game room; limited room service; laundry service; coin-op washers and dryers. *In room:* A/C, TV, dataport, fridge, coffeemaker, hair dryer, iron.

Red Roof Inn   Less than a mile west of Busch Gardens, this is the best low-budget choice close to the park. Most of the rooms in the pleasant two-story building are away from the busy boulevard, but make sure to request one toward the rear of the building to avoid the road noise. Although in-room amenities are scarce, the units are spacious for the price.

2307 E. Busch Blvd. (between 22nd and 26th Sts.), Tampa, FL 33612. ✆ **800/THE-ROOF** or 813/932-0073. Fax 813/933-5689. 108 units. Winter $60–$85 double; off-season $40–$76 double. Rates include local phone calls. AE, DC, DISC, MC, V. **Amenities:** Heated outdoor pool; Jacuzzi; sauna. *In room:* A/C, TV, dataport.

DOWNTOWN TAMPA

Hyatt Regency Tampa ✿   Although this Hyatt lost its place as downtown's premier hotel to the new Tampa Marriott Waterside, it still attracts the corporate crowd. It's just off the Franklin Street pedestrian mall. Thoroughly renovated to the tune of $11 million in 1998 and 1999, the spacious rooms lack balconies, and views are restricted by the higher office towers that now surround the hotel. Office workers congregate at the Avanzare restaurant for inexpensive light lunches.

2 Tampa City Center (corner of Tampa and E. Jackson Sts.), Tampa, FL 33602. ✆ **800/233-1234** or 813/225-1234. Fax 813/273-0234. 521 units. $199–$270 double. Weekend packages available in summer. AE, DC, DISC, MC, V. Valet parking $10. **Amenities:** 2 restaurants (American); bar; heated outdoor pool; exercise room; Jacuzzi; concierge; business center; shopping arcade; salon; 24-hr. room service; baby-sitting; laundry service; coin-op washers and dryers; concierge-level rooms. *In room:* A/C, TV, dataport, coffeemaker, hair dryer, iron.

Radisson Riverwalk Hotel ✿   Sitting on the east bank of the Hillsborough River, this six-story hotel was completely remodeled in 1998. Half the rooms face west and have views from their balconies of the Arabesque minarets atop the Henry B. Plant Museum across the river—quite a scene at sunset. They cost the same as units on the east, which face downtown's skyscrapers, so be sure to request a riverside room. Beside the river, the Ashley Street Grill serves indoor-outdoor breakfasts and lunches, then turns to fine dining in the evenings. The Boulanger baker and deli, open from 5am to midnight, purveys fresh pastries, soups, sandwiches, and snacks.

200 N. Ashley St. (at Jackson St.), Tampa, FL 33602. ✆ **800/333-3333** or 813/233-2222. Fax 813/221-5929. 282 units. $119–$219 double. AE, DC, DISC, MC, V. Valet parking $7. **Amenities:** Restaurant (American); bar; heated outdoor pool; golf course; tennis courts; exercise room; access to nearby health club; sauna; concierge; limited room service; laundry service; coin-op washers and dryers; concierge-level rooms. *In-room:* A/C, TV, dataport, coffeemaker, hair dryer, iron.

Tampa Marriott Waterside ✿✿   This luxurious 22-story hotel opened in 2000 in downtown's most strategic location—beside the river and between the Tampa Convention Center and the Ice Palace. Opening to a riverfront promenade, the towering, 3-story lobby is large enough to accommodate the many conventioneers drawn to the two neighboring venues and the hotel's own 50,000 square feet of meeting space. The third floor has a fully equipped spa, modern exercise facility, and outdoor heated pool. About half of the guest quarters have balconies overlooking the bay or city (choice views are high up on the south side). Although spacious, the regular rooms are dwarfed by the 720-square-foot suites.

400 N. Florida Ave. (at Ice Palace Dr.), Tampa, FL 33602. (C) **800/228-9290** or 813/221-4900. Fax 813/221-0923. 717 units. $159–$264 double. AE, DC, DISC, MC, V. Valet parking $12; no self-parking. **Amenities:** 3 restaurants (American); 3 bars; heated outdoor pool; health club; spa; Jacuzzi; concierge; activities desk; car rental desk; business center; salon; limited room service; massage; baby-sitting; laundry service; coin-op washers and dryers; concierge-level rooms. *In room:* A/C, TV, fax, dataport (with high-speed Internet), fridge, coffeemaker, hair dryer, iron.

YBOR CITY

Hilton Garden Inn   Built in 1999, this four-story hotel stands just 2 blocks north of the heart of Ybor City's dining and entertainment district. A one-story brick structure in front houses the bright lobby, a comfy relaxation area with fireplace, a restaurant providing cooked and continental breakfasts, and a small pantry selling beer, wine, soft drinks, and frozen dinners. You can heat up the dinners in your comfortable guest room's microwave oven or store them in your fridge. Since Hilton's "Garden" hotels are aimed primarily at business travelers (they compete with Marriott's Courtyards), your room also will have a large desk and two phones. If you opt for a suite, you'll have a separate living room and a larger bathroom than in the regular units.

1700 E. 9th Ave. (between 17th and 18th Sts.), Tampa, FL 33605. (C) **800/HILTONS** or 813/769-9267. Fax 813/769-3299. 95 units. $99–$199 double. AE, DC, DISC, MC, V. **Amenities:** Restaurant (breakfast only); heated outdoor pool; exercise room; Jacuzzi; business center; laundry service; coin-op washers and dryers. *In room:* A/C, TV, dataport (with high-speed Internet), fridge, coffeemaker, hair dryer, iron.

A NEARBY SPA & SPORTS RESORT

Saddlebrook Resort–Tampa   Set on 480 rolling acres, Saddlebrook is off the beaten path (30 minutes north of Tampa International Airport) but worth the trip if you're into spas, tennis, or golf. You can treat yourself to complete spa treatments, join the pros at the Hopman Tennis Program, or perfect your swing at the Arnold Palmer Golf Academy (see "Outdoor Activities & Spectator Sports," earlier in this chapter). This is a condominium development, so you'll stay in privately owned hotel rooms or one-, two-, or three-bedroom suites. Much more appealing than the rooms, the suites have kitchens and a patio or balcony overlooking lagoons, cypress and palm trees, and the resort's two 18-hole championship golf courses.

5700 Saddlebrook Way, Wesley Chapel, FL 33543. (C) **800/729-8383** or 813/973-1111. Fax 813/973-4504. www.saddlebrookresort.com. 800 units. Winter $185–$197 per person; off-season $120–$132 per person. Rates include breakfast and dinner. Packages available. AE, DC, DISC, MC, V. Valet parking $10; free self-parking. Take I-75 north to Fla. 54 (Exit 58); go 1 mile east to resort. **Amenities:** 3 restaurants (American); 2 bars; heated outdoor pool; 2 golf courses; 45 tennis courts; health club; spa; Jacuzzi; sauna; massage; bike rental; concierge; activities desk; car-rental desk; business center; limited room service; children's activities program; laundry service; coin-op washers and dryers. *In room:* A/C, TV, dataport, kitchen, minibar, fridge, coffeemaker, hair dryer, iron.

WHERE TO DINE

As with the hotels, I have organized the restaurants below by geographic area: near Busch Gardens, in or near Hyde Park (across the Hillsborough River from downtown), and in Ybor City. Although Ybor City is better known, Tampa's trendiest dining scene is along South Howard Avenue—"SoHo" to the locals—between West Kennedy Boulevard and the bay in affluent Hyde Park.

NEAR BUSCH GARDENS

You'll find the national fast-food and family restaurants east of I-275 on Busch Boulevard and along Fowler Avenue near University Mall.

Cafe Don José SPANISH/AMERICAN   It's not nearly on a par with Columbia in Ybor City (see below), but this Spanish-themed restaurant is among the best there is within a short drive of Busch Gardens. High-back chairs, dark wood floors, and Spanish posters and paintings set an appropriate scene for the house specialties of traditional paella (allow 30 min. for preparation) and Valencia-style rice dishes. Don José also offers non-Spanish fare such as chateaubriand and red snapper baked in parchment.

11009 N. 56th St. (in Sherwood Forest Shopping Center, ¼ mile south of Fowler Ave.). © **813/985-2392.** Main courses $13–$20. AE, DC, MC, V. Tues–Fri 11:30am–4:30pm and 5–9:30pm; Sat 5–9:30pm.

Mel's Hot Dogs *Kids* AMERICAN   Catering to everyone from businesspeople on a lunch break to hungry families craving inexpensive all-beef hot dogs, Mel Lohn's red-and-white cottage offers everything from "bagel-dogs" to bacon/cheddar Reuben-style hotdogs. All choices are served on a poppy-seed bun and can be ordered with french fries and a choice of coleslaw or baked beans. Even the decor is dedicated to wieners: The walls and windows are lined with hot-dog memorabilia. And just in case hot-dog mania hasn't won you over, there are a few alternative choices (chicken, beef and veggie burgers, and terrific onion rings).

4136 E. Busch Blvd., at 42nd St. © **813/985-8000.** Reservations not accepted. Most items under $6. No credit cards. Daily 11am–9pm.

Ristorante Francesco ★★ NORTHERN ITALIAN   Gregarious owner Francesco "Frankie" Murchesini patrols the tables in the hottest dining spot in North Tampa (as witnessed by the photos of famous patrons adorning the walls). When not playing his harmonica to celebrate someone's birthday, Frankie's making sure everyone is enjoying his delicious *cernia portofino* (grouper in a brandy sauce with shrimp) and other Northern Italian dishes. His sister makes the pasta, which shows up in more traditional fare such as seafood over linguini *pestatore* with a choice of marinara or white wine sauce. Be sure to start with half a Caesar salad.

In La Place Village Shopping Center, 1441 E. Fletcher Ave. (between 14th and 15th Sts.). © **813/971-3649.** Reservations recommended. Main courses $10–$27. AE, DC, DISC, MC. V. Mon–Fri 11:30am–2:30pm and 5:30–10pm, Sat 5:30–10pm, Sun 5–9pm.

Shells ★ *Value* SEAFOOD   You'll see Shells restaurants in many parts of Florida, and with good reason, for this casual, award-winning chain consistently provides excellent value. They all have virtually identical menus, prices, and hours. Particularly good are the spicy Jack Daniel's buffalo shrimp and scallop appetizers. Main courses range from the usual fried seafood platters to pastas and charcoal-grilled shrimp, fish, steaks, and chicken.

11010 N. 30th St. (between Busch Blvd. and Fowler Ave.). © **813/977-8456.** Reservations not accepted. Main courses $9–$20 (most $10–$12). AE, DISC, MC, V. Sun–Thurs 11:30am–10pm; Fri–Sat 11:30am–11pm.

HYDE PARK
Expensive

Bern's Steak House ★★ STEAKS   The exterior of this famous steak house looks like a factory. Inside, however, you'll find eight ornate dining rooms with themes like Rhône, Burgundy, and Irish Rebellion. Their dark atmospheres are perfect for meat lovers, for here you order and pay for expertly charcoal-grilled steaks of perfectly aged beef according to the thickness and weight (the 60-oz., 3-in.-thick Porterhouse can feed four adults). The phone book–size wine list offers more than 7,000 selections, with many available by the glass.

The big secret here, however, is the sandwiches available at the bar but not mentioned on the menu. Smaller versions of the char-grilled steaks and chicken served in the dining rooms, they come with a choice of french fries or crispy onion rings. Add a salad and you have a terrific meal for half the price of the least-expensive main course.

The surprise here is the dessert quarters upstairs, where 50 romantic booths paneled in aged California redwood can privately seat from 2 to 12 guests each. All of these little chambers are equipped with phones for placing your order and closed-circuit TVs for watching and listening to a resident pianist. The dessert menu offers almost 100 delicious selections, plus some 1,400 after-dinner drinks. It's possible to reserve a booth for dessert only, but preference is given to those who dine.

1208 S. Howard Ave. (at Marjory Ave.). 𝒞 **813/251-2421.** Reservations recommended. Main courses $17–$58.50; sandwiches $5–$8. AE, DC, DISC, MC, V. Daily 5–11pm. Closed Christmas. Valet parking $4.

Le Bordeaux ⭐⭐ COUNTRY FRENCH   Located in a converted home, this romantic bistro's authentic French fare is some of the region's best. French-born chef/owner Gordon Davis offers seating in the living room–style main dining room of this converted house, which was expanded to include a plant-filled conservatory. His predominately French country menu changes seasonally, but you can count on homemade patés and pastries, and specials such as *filet de snook a la pistache* (local snook encrusted with pistachio nuts). Part of the establishment is the lounge-style Left Bank Jazz Bistro, featuring live jazz Monday to Friday from 5:30 to 8pm.

1502 S. Howard Ave. (2 blocks north of Bayshore Blvd.). 𝒞 **813/254-4387.** Reservations recommended. Main courses $16–$27. AE, DC, MC, V. Mon–Sat 5:30–10pm; Sun 5–9pm.

Moderate

Mise en Place ⭐⭐ ECLECTIC   Look around at all those happy, stylish people soaking up the trendy ambience, and you'll know why chef Marty Blitz and his wife, Maryann, have been among the culinary darlings of Tampa since 1986. They present the freshest of ingredients, with a creative menu that changes daily. Main courses often include fascinating choices such as Creole-style mahimahi served with chili cheese grits and a ragout of black-eye peas, andouille sausage, and rock shrimp.

In Grand Central Place, 442 W. Kennedy Blvd. (at S. Magnolia Ave., opposite the University of Tampa). 𝒞 **813/254-5373.** Reservations recommended. Main courses $16–$27; tasting menu $35. AE, DC, DISC, MC, V. Tues–Thurs 5:30–10pm; Fri–Sat 5:30–11pm.

Inexpensive

Bella's Italian Cafe ⭐ 𝘝𝘢𝘭𝘶𝘦 ITALIAN   Creative dishes and very reasonable prices makes this sophisticated yet informal cafe one of SoHo's most popular neighborhood hangouts. Although you can order the homemade pasta under traditional Bolognese or Alfredo sauces, the stars here feature the tasty likes of blackened chicken in a creamy tomato sauce over fettuccine, or shrimp and scallops in a roasted tomato sauce over bow-tie pasta. Finish off with the house version of tiramisù. Local professionals flock to the friendly bar during two-for-one happy hours nightly from 4 to 7pm and from 11pm until closing. The open kitchen provides only appetizers after 11pm.

1413 S. Howard Ave. (at Mississippi Ave.). **850/254-3355.** Reservations not accepted. Main courses $7–$12; pizza $6.50–$8.50. AE, DISC, MC, V. Mon–Thurs 11am–midnight, Fri 11am–2am, Sat 4pm–2am, Sun 4pm–midnight.

Cactus Club _Value_ AMERICAN SOUTHWEST   You can definitely taste the freshness at this Texas roadhouse–style cantina in the middle of the Old Hyde Park shops, because all ingredients except the beans come straight from the market. My favorite dish is the "fundido"—a spicy casserole of marinated fajita-style chicken strips and sautéed vegetables topped with melted Jack cheese, with beans and rice on the side. Other offerings are more traditional: tacos, enchiladas, chili, sizzling fajitas, hickory-smoked baby back ribs, Jamaican jerk chicken, burgers, quesadillas, enchiladas (including vegetarian versions), sandwiches, and smoked chicken salad. The lively Cactus Cantina bar is another favorite neighborhood watering hole. Dine inside or outside, but get here early at lunchtime—it's usually packed.

In Old Hyde Park shopping complex, 1601 Snow Ave. (south of Swan St.). © 813/251-4089. Reservations not accepted. Main courses $6.50–14; burgers and sandwiches $7–$8. AE, DC, MC, V. Mon–Thurs 11am–10:30pm; Fri–Sat 11am–midnight; Sun 11am–10:30pm.

The Colonnade SEAFOOD   Local couples and families have been flocking to this rough-hewn, shiplap place since 1935, primarily for the great view of Hillsborough Bay across Bayshore Boulevard. The food is a bit on the Red Lobsterish side, but the vista from the window tables more than makes up for any shortcomings in the fresh seafood: grouper prepared seven ways, crab-stuffed flounder, Maryland-style crab cakes, even wild Florida alligator as an appetizer. Prime rib, steaks, and chicken are also available.

3401 Bayshore Blvd. (at W. Julia St.). © 813/839-7558. Reservations accepted only for large parties. Main courses $8–$20 (most $11–15). AE, DC, DISC, MC, V. Sun–Thurs 11am–10pm; Fri–Sat 11am–11pm.

Four Green Fields IRISH/AMERICAN   Just across the bridge from the downtown convention center, America's only thatched-roof Irish pub may be surrounded by palm trees instead of potato fields, but it still offers the ambience and tastes of Ireland. Staffed by genuine Irish immigrants, the large room with a square bar in the center smells of Bass and Harp ales. The Gaelic stew is predictably bland, but the salads and sandwiches are passable. The live Irish music on Thursday, Friday, and Saturday nights draws a crowd ranging from post-college to early retirees.

205 W. Platt St. (between Parker St. and Plant Ave.). © 813/254-4444. Reservations accepted. Main courses $9.50–$15; sandwiches $6–$7. AE, MC, V. Daily 11am–3am.

YBOR CITY
Moderate

Cafe Creole and Oyster Bar ★★ _Value_ CREOLE/CAJUN   Resembling a turn-of-the-century railway station, this brick building dates from 1896 and was originally known as El Pasaje, the home of the Cherokee Club, a gentlemen's hotel and private club with a casino and an opulent decor with stained-glass windows, wrought-iron balconies, Spanish murals, and marble bathrooms. Today it's home to Tampa's best Creole and Cajun restaurant. Specialties include exceptionally prepared Louisiana crab cakes, oysters, blackened grouper, and jambalaya. If you're new to bayou cuisine, try the Creole sampler. Dine inside or out.

1330 9th Ave. (at Avenida de Republica de Cuba/14th St.). © 813/247-6283. Reservations not accepted, but call for preferred seating. Main courses $10.50–$18. AE, DC, DISC, MC, V. Mon–Thurs 11:30am–10pm; Fri 11:30am–11:30pm; Sat 5–11:30pm.

Columbia ★★ SPANISH   Dating from 1905, this hand-painted tile building occupies an entire city block in the heart of Ybor City. Tourists flock here to soak up the ambience and so do the locals because it's so much fun to clap along during fire-belching Spanish flamenco floor shows Monday to Saturday at 7 and 9:30pm. You can't help coming back time after time for the famous Spanish bean soup and original "1905" salad. The paella à la valenciana is outstanding, with more than a dozen ingredients from gulf grouper and gulf pink shrimp to calamari, mussels, clams, chicken, and pork. The decor throughout is graced with hand-painted tiles, wrought-iron chandeliers, dark woods, rich red fabrics, and stained-glass windows. You can breathe your own fumes in the Cigar Bar.

2117 E. 7th Ave. (between 21st and 22nd Sts.). ℭ 813/248-4961. Reservations recommended. Main courses $12–$23. AE, DC, DISC, MC, V. Mon–Thurs 11am–10pm; Fri–Sat 11am–11pm; Sun noon–9pm.

Inexpensive

Carmine's Restaurant & Bar ⭑ *Value* CUBAN/ITALIAN/AMERICAN
Bright blue poles hold up an ancient pressed-tin ceiling above this noisy corner cafe, where a great variety of loyal local patrons gather for genuine Cuban sandwiches—smoked ham, roast pork, Genoa salami, swiss cheese, pickles, salad dressing, mustard, lettuce, and tomato on a crispy submarine roll. There's a vegetarian version too, and the combination half-sandwich and choice of black beans and rice or a bowl of Spanish soup made with sausages, potatoes, and garbanzo beans all make a hearty meal for just $6 at lunch, $7 at dinner. Main courses are led by Cuban-style roast pork, thin-cut pork chops with mushroom sauce, spaghetti with a blue-crab tomato sauce, and a few seafood and chicken platters.

1802 E. 7th Ave. (at 18th St.). ℭ **813/248-3834.** Reservations not accepted. Main courses $7–$17; sandwiches $4–$8. No credit cards. Mon–Tues 11am–10pm; Wed–Thurs 11am–midnight, Fri–Sat 11am–3am, Sun 11am–6pm.

Ovo Cafe ⭑ INTERNATIONAL This cafe, popular with the business set by day and the club crowd on weekend nights, features a melange of sophisticated offerings. Pierogies and pasta pillows come with taste-tempting sauces and fillings, and there are several creative salads and unusual individual-size pizzas. Strawberries or blackberries and a splash of liqueur cover the thick waffles. Portions are substantial, but be careful with your credit card here: Pricing is strictly a la carte. The big black bar dispenses a wide variety of martinis, plus some unusual liqueur drinks.

1901 E. 7th Ave. (at 19th St.). ℭ 813/248-6979. Reservations strongly recommended Fri–Sat. Main courses $10–$15; sandwiches $7–$8.50; pizza $8.50–$10. AE, DC, DISC, MC, V. Mon–Tues 11am–3pm, Wed–Thurs 11am–10pm, Fri–Sat 11am–1am, Sun noon–6pm.

TAMPA AFTER DARK

The Tampa/Hillsborough Arts Council maintains an **Artsline** (ℭ 813/229-ARTS), a 24-hour information service providing the latest on current and upcoming cultural events. Racks in many restaurants and bars have copies of *Weekly Planet* (www.weeklyplanet.com), *Focus,* and *Accent on Tampa Bay,* three free publications detailing what's going on in the entire bay area. And you can also check the "Baylife" and "Friday Extra" sections of the *Tampa Tribune* (www.tampatrib.com) and the Thursday "Weekend" section of the *St. Petersburg Times* (www.sptimes.com). The visitor center usually has copies of the week's newspaper sections (see "Essentials," earlier in this chapter).

THE CLUB & MUSIC SCENE Ybor City is Tampa's favorite nighttime venue by far. All you have to do is stroll along 7th Avenue East between 15th and 20th streets, and you'll hear music blaring out of the clubs. The avenue is packed with people, a majority of them high schoolers and early twentysome-things, on Friday and Saturday from 9pm to 3am, but you'll also find something going on from Tuesday to Thursday and even on Sunday. You don't need addresses or phone numbers; your ears will guide you along 7th Avenue East.

Parking can be scarce during nighttime here, and the area has seen an occa-sional robbery late at night; so play it safe and use the municipal parking lots behind the shops on 8th Avenue East.

Starting at 15th Street and heading east, you'll come first to **The Masquer-ade,** with retro and old wave bands on Friday to Sunday. The body-pierced 20-something crowd gets primed at **Club Hedo, Atomic Age Cafe & Lounge,** and **Cherry's** before dancing at **The Rubb** across the avenue.

At 16th Street you will come to the multiscreen cinema, comedy club, several restaurants, and large open-air bar of **Centro Ybor** (© **813/242-4660;** www.thecentroybor.com), the district's large new shopping-and-entertainment complex. The restaurants and pubs in this family-oriented center tend to be con-siderably tamer than many of those along 7th Avenue, at least on non-weekend nights.

Between 17th and 18th streets, you'll smell the cigar smoke coming from the sidewalk tables of the **Green Iguana Bar & Grill,** a refined establishment fre-quented by young professionals. The **Irish Pub** is just that, while **Fat Tuesday** has a large dance floor and long bar. Between 18th and 19th streets, you'll see **Harpo's,** which doesn't extract a cover charge. Keep going across 19th Street to one of Ybor's best clubs, **Blues Ship Café on Top,** which features live blues, jazz, and reggae. And last but not least is the warehouselike **Frankie's Patio Bar & Grill** ⭐, known for its reasonably priced food as well as its outstanding musical acts. Across the avenue, country meets city at **Spurs in Ybor,** a country-and-western joint.

Elsewhere in town, you can lose your life's savings playing bingo, poker, and the video slot machines at the **Seminole Indian Casino,** 5223 N. Orient Rd., at Hillsborough Road east of the city (© **800/282-7016** or 813/621-1302). It's open 24 hours every day of the year.

THE PERFORMING ARTS With a prime downtown location on 9 acres along the east bank of the Hillsborough River, the huge **Tampa Bay Perform-ing Arts Center** ⭐, 1010 N. MacInnes Place (© **800/955-1045** or 813/229-STAR; www.tampacenter.com), is the largest performing-arts venue south of the Kennedy Center in Washington, D.C. Accordingly, this four-theater com-plex is the focal point of Tampa's performing-arts scene, presenting a wide range of Broadway plays, classical and pop concerts, operas, cabarets, improv, and spe-cial events.

A sightseeing attraction in its own right, the restored **Tampa Theatre,** 711 Franklin St. (© **813/223-8981;** www.tampatheatre.org), between Zack and Polk streets, dates from 1926 and is on the National Register of Historic Places. It presents a varied program of classic, foreign, and alternative films, as well as concerts and special events.

The 66,321-seat **Raymond James Stadium,** 4201 N. Dale Mabry Hwy. (© **813/673-4300;** www.raymondjames.com/stadium), is frequently the site of headliner concerts. The **USF Sun Dome,** 4202 E. Fowler Ave. (© **813/974-3111**), on the University of South Florida campus, hosts major concerts by touring pop stars, rock bands, jazz groups, and other contemporary artists.

Ticketmaster (© **813/287-8844**) sells tickets to most events and shows.

2 St. Petersburg ⭐

20 miles SW of Tampa, 289 miles NW of Miami, 84 miles SW of Orlando

On the western shore of the bay, St. Petersburg stands in contrast to Tampa, much like San Francisco compares to Oakland in California. Whereas Tampa is the area's business, industrial, and shipping center, St. Petersburg was conceived and built almost a century ago primarily for tourists and wintering snowbirds. Here you'll find one of the most picturesque and pleasant downtowns of any city in Florida, with a waterfront promenade and the famous, pyramid-shaped Pier offering great views across the bay, plus quality museums, interesting shops, and a few good restaurants.

Away from downtown, the city pretty much consists of strip malls dividing residential neighborhoods, but plan at least to have a look around the charming bayfront area. If you don't do anything else, go out on The Pier and take a pleasant stroll along Bayshore Drive.

ESSENTIALS

GETTING THERE **Tampa International Airport,** approximately 16 miles northeast of St. Petersburg, is the prime gateway for the area (see "Essentials," in section 1, earlier in this chapter). **St. Petersburg–Clearwater International Airport,** on Roosevelt Boulevard (Fla. 686) about 10 miles north of downtown St. Petersburg (© 727/535-7600), primarily handles charter flights by the Canadian carriers **Air Transat** (© 800/470-1011) and **Canada 3000** (© 800/993-4378). **Amtrak** (© 800/USA-RAIL; www.amtrak.com) has rail service to Tampa with bus connections to downtown St. Petersburg (see "Getting There," in section 1).

VISITOR INFORMATION For advance information about both St. Petersburg and the beaches, contact the **St. Petersburg/Clearwater Area Convention & Visitors Bureau,** 14450 46th St. N., Clearwater, FL 34622 (© **800/345-6710,** or 727/464-7200 for advance hotel reservations; fax 727/464-7222; www.stpete-clearwater.com).

A wealth of information is available from the **St. Petersburg Area Chamber of Commerce,** 100 2nd Ave. N. (at 1st Street), St. Petersburg, FL 33701 (© **727/821-4069;** fax 727/895-6326; www.stpete.com). This downtown main office and visitor center is open Monday to Friday from 8am to 5pm, Saturday 9am to 4pm, Sunday noon to 3pm. Ask for a copy of the chamber's visitor guide, which lists hotels, motels, condominiums, and other accommodations.

Also downtown, there are **walk-in information centers** on the first level of The Pier and in the lobby of the Florida International Museum (see "Seeing the Top Attractions," below).

The chamber also operates the **Suncoast Welcome Center** (© **727/573-1449**), on Ulmerton Road at Exit 18 southbound off I-275 (there's no exit here for northbound traffic). The center is open daily from 9am to 5pm except New Year's Day, Easter, Thanksgiving, and Christmas.

GETTING AROUND You can see everything on the very pink **Downtown Trolleys** (© 727/571-3440), which run out to the end of The Pier and past all of the downtown attractions every 30 minutes from 11am to 5pm daily except Thanksgiving and Christmas. Rides cost 50¢ per person.

The **Pinellas Suncoast Transit Authority/PSTA** (© **727/530-9911**) operates regular bus service throughout Pinellas County.

If you need a cab, call **Yellow Cab** (© 727/821-7777) or **Independent Cab** (© 727/327-3444). Fares are $1.50 at flag fall, plus 20¢ for each ½ mile.

SEEING THE TOP ATTRACTIONS

Residents don't have to go inside to get mail out of their boxes at St. Petersburg's oft-photographed open-air **Post Office,** at the corner of 1st Avenue North and 4th Street North.

Florida Holocaust Museum ✪ This thought-provoking museum has exhibits about the Holocaust, including a boxcar used to transport human cargo to the Auschwitz death camp in Poland. Its main focus, however, is to promote tolerance and understanding in the present. It was founded by Walter P. Loebenberg, a local businessman who escaped Nazi Germany in 1939 and fought with the U.S. Army in World War II.

55 5th St. S. (between Central Ave. and 1st St. S.). © 727/820-0100. www.flholocaustmuseum.org. Admission $6 adults, $5 seniors and colleges students, $2 children under 18. Mon–Fri 10am–5pm, Sat–Sun noon–5pm. Closed Easter, Rosh Hashanah, Yom Kippur, Thanksgiving, and Christmas.

Florida International Museum ✪✪ Housed in the former Maas Brothers Department Store, long an area landmark, this excellent museum attracted 600,000 visitors from around the world when it opened its first exhibition in 1995, and the success has continued. Its outstanding exhibit on the Cuban Missile Crisis was such a smash hit that it's now permanent—and well worth seeing even if the two temporary exhibits don't catch your fancy. On the other hand, they very well could, since the museum is associated with—and gets some of its staff on loan from—the Smithsonian Institution in Washington, D.C. Call to see what's scheduled during your visit. Allow at least 3 hours to tour all three exhibitions. There's an excellent museum store here.

100 2nd St. N. (between 1st and 2nd Aves. N.). © 877/535-7469 or 727/822-3693. www.floridamuseum. org. Admission to all exhibits $11.95 adults, $10.95 seniors, $5.95 children 6–18, free for children under 6. Admission to Kennedy exhibit $8.95 adults, $7.95 seniors, $4.95 children 6–18, free for children under 6. Mon–Sat 9am–4:30pm, Sun noon–4:30pm.

Museum of Fine Arts ✪✪ Resembling a Mediterranean villa on the waterfront, this museum houses an excellent permanent collection of European, American, pre-Colombian, and Far Eastern art, with works by such artists as Fragonard, Monet, Renoir, Cézanne, and Gauguin. Other highlights include period rooms with antiques and historical furnishings, plus a gallery of Steuben crystal, a new decorative-arts gallery, and world-class rotating exhibits. The best way to see it all is on a free, guided tour, which takes about 1 hour. Ask about classical-music performances from October to April.

255 Beach Dr. NE (at 3rd Ave. N.). © 727/896-2667. www.fine-arts.org. Admission Mon–Sat $6 adults, $5 seniors, $2 students, free for children under 6. Admission free on Sun (donation suggested). Admission includes guided tour. Tues–Sat 10am–5pm; Sun 1–5pm. Winter, third Thurs of each month 10am–9pm. Guided tours Tues–Fri 10 and 11am, 1 and 2pm; Sun 1 and 2pm. Closed New Year's Day, Thanksgiving, Christmas.

The Pier Walk or ride out on The Pier and enjoy this festive waterfront dining-and-shopping complex overlooking Tampa Bay. Originally built as a railroad pier in 1889, today it's capped by a spaceshiplike inverted pyramid offering five l xevels of shops, three restaurants, a tourist information desk, an observation deck, catwalks for fishing, boat docks, miniature golf, boat and water-sports rentals, sightseeing boats, and a food court, plus an aquarium and **Great Explorations** (www.stpete-clearwater.com/explore), a hands-on children's museum

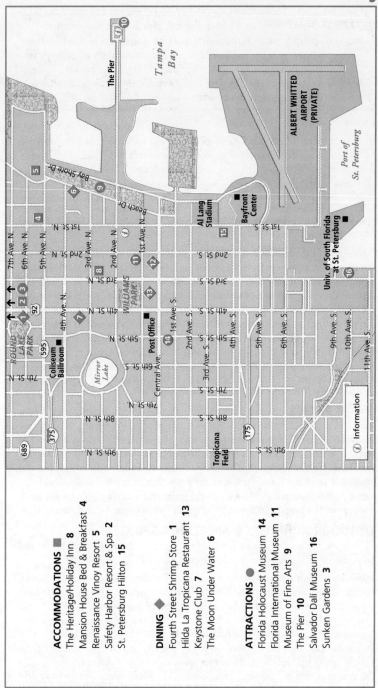

ACCOMMODATIONS ■
The Heritage/Holiday Inn **8**
Mansion House Bed & Breakfast **4**
Renaissance Vinoy Resort **5**
Safety Harbor Resort & Spa **2**
St. Petersburg Hilton **15**

DINING ◆
Fourth Street Shrimp Store **1**
Hilda La Tropicana Restaurant **13**
Keystone Club **7**
The Moon Under Water **6**

ATTRACTIONS ●
Florida Holocaust Museum **14**
Florida International Museum **11**
Museum of Fine Arts **9**
The Pier **10**
Salvador Dalí Museum **16**
Sunken Gardens **3**

> **Tips Car Smarts**
>
> You can spend a small fortune in a parking garage or in feeding the meters in St. Petersburg, but you can cut costs substantially by parking at The Pier ($3 all day) and taking The Looper, the city's free trolley service, which operates between The Pier and all major downtown attractions. See "Getting Around" in this section.

offering a variety of exhibits—great for a rainy day or for kids who've overdosed on the sun and need to cool off indoors. You can rent boats and go on cruises from here (see "Outdoor Activities & Spectator Sports," below).

800 2nd Ave. NE. (C) 727/821-6164. www.stpete-pier.com. Free admission to all the public areas and decks; donations welcome at the Pier Aquarium. Great Explorations $4, $2 seniors, free for children under 3. Valet parking $6; self-parking $3. Pier Mon–Thurs 10am–9pm Fri–Sat 10am–10pm, Sun 11am–7pm. Aquarium Mon–Sat 10am–8pm, Sun noon–6pm. Great Explorations Mon–Sat 10am–8pm, Sun 11am–6pm. Shops and restaurant hours vary.

Salvador Dali Museum ★★★   This starkly modern museum houses the world's most comprehensive collection of works by the renowned Spanish surrealist—and for art lovers is reason enough to visit downtown St. Petersburg. It includes oil paintings, watercolors and drawings, and more than 1,000 graphics, plus posters, photos, sculptures, objets d'art, and a 5,000-volume library on Dalí and surrealism. Reynolds Morse, an Ohio plastics engineer, and his wife, Eleanore, discovered the Catalonian artist and began collecting his works in 1943. They moved the collection here in 1980.

1000 3rd St. S. (near 11th Ave. S.). (C) 727/823-3767. www.salvadordalimuseum.org. Admission $10 adults, $7 seniors, $5 students, free for children 9 and under. Thurs 5–8pm 50% discount. Mon–Sat 9:30am–5:30pm, Thurs 9:30am–8pm, Sun noon–5:30pm. Closed Thanksgiving and Christmas.

Sunken Gardens   Dating back to 1935, this former tourist attraction is now operated as a 7-acre botanical garden by the City of St. Petersburg. It contains a vast array of 5,000 plants, flowers, and trees; plus a butterfly aviary; a display of snakes, spiders, and scorpions; and a rainforest information center. There's a whimsical Comedy Safari Bird Show Wednesday to Friday at 1 and 2:30pm and weekends at 11am, 1 and 2pm. Call for a schedule of exhibits and tours.

1825 4th St. N. (between 18th and 19th Aves. NE). (C) 813/896-3186. www.stpete.org/sunken.html. Admission $4 adults, $3 seniors, $1 children 3–12, free for children 2 and under. Wed–Sun 10am–4pm.

OUTDOOR ACTIVITIES & SPECTATOR SPORTS

You can get up-to-the-minute recorded information about the city's sports and recreational activities by calling the **Leisure Line** ((C) 727/893-7500).

BIKING   With miles of flat terrain, the St. Petersburg area is ideal for bikers, in-line skaters, and hikers. The **Pinellas Trail** is especially good, since it follows an abandoned railroad bed 47 miles from St. Petersburg north to Tarpon Springs and from there to Tampa. It crosses the bay via the old Gandy Bridge, now known as the **Friendship TrailBridge** ((C) 813/289-4400). The 2.6-mile-long bridge is open to hikers, bikers, bicyclists, fishers, and in-line skaters, but be careful going up and down the center span, especially if you're on skates. The St. Pete trailhead is on 34th Street South (U.S. 19) between 8th and Fairfield avenues south. It's packed on the weekends. Free strip maps of the trail are available at the St. Petersburg Area Chamber of Commerce (see "Visitor Information," above).

It's a long way from the trailhead, but **Teddy's Rentals,** on The Pier (© 727/ 822-8697), rents bicycles and in-line skates for $7.50 an hour, $20 a day. Open Monday to Saturday 10am to 5pm, Sunday 11am to 5pm; closed if the forecast temperature will not exceed 60°F (15.5°C).

BOAT RENTALS   On The Pier, **Teddy's Rentals** (© 727/822-8697) rents paddleboats and kayaks for $7.50 a hour, jet skis for $25 to $55 a hour, depending on the season. See "Biking," above, for Teddy's business hours. On the bay front at the mainland end of the pier, **VinoyBasinBoatRentals.com** (© 727/ 709-7393) also rents kayaks and pedal- and electric-powered boats. Rates range from $15 to $25 per hour. Open Wednesday to Sunday 10am to sunset.

CRUISES   The stern-wheeler *Caribbean Queen* (© 727/895-BOAT) offers 1-hour sightseeing and dolphin-watching cruises around Tampa Bay. Sailings are daily at 1, 3, and 5pm; they cost $12 for adults, $10 for seniors and juniors 12 to 17, $6 for children 3 to 11, and free for children 2 and under. More exciting are the sightseeing, sunset, and nighttime "boogie" cruises aboard the pirate-themed **Buccaneer Adventure Cruises** (© 877/274-4263 or 727/560-0689; www.royalconquest.com). Its 1-hour afternoon sightseeing cruises usually depart at 11am and at 12:30, 2, and 3:30pm, and cost $10 a person. Reservations are required for the 90-minute evening cruises, which depart at 5pm and cost $15 for adults, $13 for seniors and students 13 to 18, $12 for kids under 13. Children under 5 ride free on all voyages.

For a more personalized experience, contact Robert Ray of the Mansion House Bed & Breakfast (© 800/274-7520 or 727/821-9391), who takes up to six persons on half- or full-day cruises on his 23-foot speed boat, the *Aussie Spirit.* Rates are $75 per hour (for captain and boat), with a 2-hour minimum rental.

FISHING   You can try your luck for snook, tarpon, cobia, Spanish mackerel, gulf flounder, speckled sea trout, black drum, redfish, whiting, and mangrove snapper off The Pier, where **The Pier Baithouse** (© 727/821-3750) rents rod, reel, bait, bucket, hook, line, and sinker for $10 a day. It's open daily 6am to 10pm. Together, the north and south spans of the old **Sunshine Skyway** (the section of I-275 that soars across the entrance to Tampa Bay), form the "World's Longest & Luckiest Fishing Piers." You can drive out on the old spans for free and rent equipment at the bait shops (© 727/865-0668 for the north pier, © 941/729-0117 for the south span).

GOLF   One of the nation's top 50 municipal courses, the **Mangrove Bay Golf Course** ♣♣, 875 62nd Ave. NE (© 727/893-7797), hugs the inlets of Old Tampa Bay and offers 18-hole, par-72 play. Facilities include a driving range; lessons and golf-club rental are also available. Fees are about $22, $32 including a cart in winter, slightly lower off-season. The course is open daily from 6:30am to 6pm.

The city also operates the **Twin Brooks Golf Course,** 3800 22nd Ave. S. (© 727/893-7445).

In Largo, the **Bardmoor Golf Club,** 7919 Bardmoor Blvd. (© 727/ 397-0483), is often the venue for major tournaments. Lakes punctuate 17 of the 18 holes on this par-72 championship course. Lessons and rental clubs are available, as is a Tom Fazio–designed practice range. Call the clubhouse for seasonal greens fees. The course is open daily from 7am to dusk.

Adjacent to the St. Petersburg–Clearwater airport, the **Airco Flite Golf Course,** 3650 Roosevelt Blvd., Clearwater (℅ **727/573-4653**), is a championship 18-hole, par-72 course with a driving range. Golf-club rentals are also available. Greens fees, including cart, range from $25 to $35 in winter, about $20 off-season. The course is open daily from 7am to 6pm.

Call **Tee Times USA** (℅ **800/374-8633**) to reserve times at these and other area courses.

If you want to take up golf or sharpen your game, TV "Golf Doctor" Joe Quinzi hosts his **Quinzi Golf Academy** (℅ **727/725-1999**) at the Safety Harbor Resort and Spa (see "Where to Stay," below). His school offers personalized instruction and clinics.

SAILING Both Steve and Doris Colgate's **Offshore Sailing School** (℅ **800/221-4326** or 941/454-1700; www.offshore-sailing.com) and the **Annapolis Sailing School** (℅ **800/638-9192** or 727/867-8102; www.annapolissailing.com) have operations here. Various courses lasting from 2 days to a week are offered. Contact the schools for prices and schedules.

SPECTATOR SPORTS St. Petersburg has always been a baseball town, and **Tropicana Field,** a 45,000-seat domed stadium alongside I-175 between 9th and 16th streets (℅ **727/825-3100;** www.stpete.org/dome.htm), is the home of the American League **Tampa Bay Devil Rays** (℅ **727/898-RAYS;** www.devilrays.com). The baseball season runs from April through September. Call for schedule and ticket information. The Devil Rays move outdoors to Al Lang Stadium, on 2nd Avenue South at 1st Street South (℅ **727/825-3137** or 727/825-3242), for their spring-training games from mid-February through March.

The **Philadelphia Phillies** play their spring-training season at Jack Russell Stadium, 800 Phillies Dr., in nearby Clearwater (℅ **727/442-8496** or 215/436-1000; www.phillies.com). Their minor-league affiliate, the **Clearwater Phillies** (℅ **727/441-8638;** www.clearwaterphillies.com), plays in the stadium from April through August. The **Toronto Blue Jays** do their spring thing at Grant Field, 373 Douglas Ave. in Dunedin (℅ **800/707-8269** or 813/733-9302; www.bluejays.com), which also is home to their minor-league affiliate, the **Dunedin Blue Jays** (℅ **727/733-9302;** www.dunedinbluejays.com), from April through August.

TENNIS You can learn to play or hone your game at the **Phil Green Tennis Academy** at Safety Harbor Resort and Spa (see "Where to Stay," below).

SHOPPING

The Pier, at the end of 2nd Avenue Northeast (see "Seeing the Top Attractions," earlier in this chapter), houses more than a dozen boutiques and craft shops; but nearby Beach Drive, running along the waterfront, is one of the most fashionable downtown strolling and shopping venues. Here you'll find the **Glass Canvas Gallery,** at 4th Avenue Northeast (℅ **727/821-6767**), featuring a dazzling array of glass sculpture, tableware, art, and craft items by 250 local, national, and international artists. Also at 4th Avenue Northeast is **P. Buckley Moss** (℅ **727/894-2899**), a museum-grade store carrying the works of the individualistic artist best known for her portrayal of the Amish and the Mennonites. The works include paintings, graphics, figurines, and collector dolls. **Red Cloud,** between 1st and 2nd avenues (℅ **727/821-5824**), is an oasis for Native American crafts, including jewelry, headdresses, and art.

Downtown's new showplace is **BayWalk,** an open-air shopping, dining, and entertainment complex bordered by 1st and 2nd streets and 2nd and 3rd avenues North. Opened in late 2000, it has branches of Ann Taylor, Chico's, Sunglass Hut and a few other mall stores, plus some small boutiques.

Central Avenue is another shopping area, featuring the **Gas Plant Antique Arcade,** between 12th and 13th streets (℗ **727/895-0368**), the largest antique mall on Florida's west coast, with more than 100 dealers displaying their wares. (Downtown has several antiques-and-collectibles dealers; get a list and map from the chamber of commerce.) The **Florida Craftsmen Gallery,** at 5th Street (℗ **727/821-7391**), is a showcase for the works of more than 150 Florida artisans and craftspeople: jewelry, ceramics, woodwork, fiber works, glassware, paper creations, and metalwork.

In the suburbs, outlet shoppers can browse in air-conditioned comfort at **Bay Area Outlet Mall,** at the intersection of U.S. 19 and East Bay Drive (℗ **727/535-2337**), west of St. Petersburg–Clearwater International Airport. If you're heading south toward Sarasota and Bradenton, you'll have more choices at the huge Prime Outlets on I-75 in Ellenton (see "Shopping" in section 5, later in this chapter).

WHERE TO STAY

The **St. Petersburg/Clearwater Area Convention & Visitors Bureau** (see "Essentials," earlier in this chapter) publishes a brochure that lists members of its Superior Small Lodgings program; all establishments have fewer than 50 rooms and have been inspected and certified for cleanliness and value. In addition, the bureau has a free **reservations service** (℗ **800/345-6710**).

Other than the Renaissance Vinoy Resort and Golf Club (see below), the only chain hotel downtown is the **St. Petersburg Hilton,** 333 1st St. S., between 3rd and 4th avenues South (℗ **800/HILTONS** or 727/894-5000; fax 727/823-4797), a 15-story business and convention hotel within steps of the Salvador Dali Museum, Al Lang Field, and the Bayfront Center's theaters. Otherwise, views from the upper-floor rooms are its main draw for casual travelers.

VERY EXPENSIVE

Renaissance Vinoy Resort and Golf Club ★★   Built as the grand Vinoy Park in 1925, this elegant Spanish-style establishment reopened in 1992 after a total and meticulous $93 million restoration that made it once again the city's finest hotel. Dominating the northern part of downtown, it overlooks Tampa Bay and is within walking distance of The Pier, Central Avenue, museums, and other attractions. All the guest rooms, many of which enjoy lovely views of the bay front, offer the utmost in comfort and include three phones, an additional TV in the bathroom, and bath scales. Some rooms in the original building have standing-room-only balconies; so if you need enough room to sit outside, request a balconied unit in the new Tower wing (some of these have whirlpool tubs, too). Overlooking the bay, the Mediterranean-style **Marchand's Grille** is the city's most elegant dining room and serves some of the best steaks and chops in town.

501 5th Ave. NE (at Beach Dr.), St. Petersburg, FL 33701. ℗ **800/HOTELS-1** or 727/894-1000. Fax 727/822-2785. 360 units. Winter $320–$390 double; off-season $200–$360 double. Packages available. AE, DC, DISC, MC, V. Valet parking $12; self-parking $8. **Amenities:** 4 restaurants (Mediterranean; American); 2 bars; 2 heated outdoor pools (connected by a waterfall); Jacuzzi; golf course; 12 tennis courts; health club & spa; concierge; activities desk; business center; salon; 24-hr. room service; massage; laundry service; concierge-level rooms. *In room:* A/C, TV, dataport, minibar, coffeemaker, hair dryer, iron.

MODERATE

The Heritage Holiday Inn ⭐　No ordinary Holiday Inn, the Heritage dates from the early 1920s, and although significantly updated, it still retains the ambience of an old-fashioned hotel, with tall double-hung windows and hardwood floors that creak as you walk down the long central hallway. A sweeping verandah, French doors, and a tropical courtyard help attract an eclectic clientele, from business travelers to seniors. The furnishings include period antiques and brass beds. Some one-bedroom suites have sofa beds, two televisions, two phones, and two bathrooms.

234 3rd Ave. N. (between 2nd and 3rd Sts.), St. Petersburg, FL 33701. © 800/283-7829 or 727/822-4814. Fax 727/823-1644. www.holidayinnstpete.com. 71 units. $97–$139 double. AE, DC, DISC, MC, V. **Amenities:** Restaurant (American); bar; heated outdoor pool; Jacuzzi; limited room service; laundry service. *In room:* A/C, TV, dataport, coffeemaker, hair dryer, iron.

Mansion House Bed & Breakfast ⭐　Mirror images of each other, these two Arts-and-Crafts–style houses separated by a landscaped courtyard were built between 1901 and 1912. The comfortable living room in the main house, which has 6 of the 10 units here, opens to a sun room, off which a small screened porch provides mosquito-free lounging and the only place where guests can smoke. Both houses have upstairs front parlors with TVs, VCRs, and libraries. Tall, old-fashioned windows let lots of light into the attractive guest rooms. The pick of the litter is the "Pembroke" room, upstairs over the carriage house. It has a four-poster bed with mosquito netting, and its residents have their own whirlpool in an outdoor screened hut. The brick courtyard between the two houses (there's a heated swimming pool and Jacuzzi out there) is a popular spot for weddings, receptions, and other functions.

105 5th Ave. NE (at 1st St. N.), St. Petersburg, FL 33701. © 800/274-7520 or 727/821-9391. Fax 727/821-9391 (same as phone). www.mansionbandb.com. 10 units (all with bathroom). $125–$220 double. Rates include full breakfast. AE, MC, V. **Amenities:** Heated outdoor pool; Jacuzzi. *In room:* A/C, TV, dataport, hair dryer.

A NEARBY SPA

Safety Harbor Resort and Spa ⭐⭐ *Value*　Hernando de Soto thought he had found Ponce de León's fabled Fountain of Youth when he happened upon five mineral springs here on the shores of Old Tampa Bay in 1539. You may not recover your youth at this venerable spa, which has been in operation since 1926 and got a face lift in 1998, but you will be rejuvenated with such services as massage and hydrotherapy and a full menu of fitness classes from boxing to yoga. The mineral springs enable it to offer acclaimed water-fitness programs, and this a good place to work on your games at the Quinzi Golf Academy and the Phil Green Tennis Academy (see "Outdoor Activities & Spectator Sports," earlier in this chapter). The sprawling complex of beige stucco buildings with Spanish tile roofs sits on 22 waterfront acres in the sleepy town of Safety Harbor, north of St. Petersburg. Moss-draped Safety Harbor has a charming small-town ambience, with a number of shops and restaurants just outside the spa's entrance. Given the reasonable room rates and special packages available, this is one of Florida's better spa values.

105 N. Bayshore Dr., Safety Harbor, FL 34695. © 888/BEST-SPA or 727/726-1161. Fax 727/724-7749. www. safetyharborspa.com. 193 units. Winter $119–$209 double; off-season $89–$139 double. Packages available. AE, DC, DISC, MC, V. Valet parking $8; free self-parking. Pets accepted ($35-per-night charge). **Amenities:** 2 restaurants (American); bar; heated indoor and outdoor pools; golf course; tennis courts; full-service spa; concierge; activities desk; car-rental desk; business center; limited room service; laundry service; coin-op washers and dryers. *In room:* A/C, TV, dataport, coffeemaker, hair dryer, iron.

WHERE TO DINE

Don't overlook the food court at **The Pier,** where the inexpensive chow is accompanied by a very rich, but quite free, view of the bay. Among The Pier's restaurants is a branch of Tampa's famous **Columbia** (© **727/822-8000**). Downtown also has an offshoot of Ybor City's **Ovo Cafe,** at 515 Central Ave. (© **727/895-5515**). See "Where to Dine," in section 1, earlier in this chapter, for details about Columbia and Ovo Cafe.

EXPENSIVE

Chateau France ★★ TRADITIONAL FRENCH   Chef Antoine Louro provides St. Petersburg's finest cuisine and most romantic setting in this charming pink Victorian house built in 1910. He specializes in traditional French favorites such as homemade paté, Dover sole meunière, filet mignon au poivre, coq au vin, orange duck, and a rich seafood bouillabaisse. Fresh baby vegetables, Gruyère cheese potatoes, and Antoine's special Eiffel Tower salad accompany all main courses. The wine list is excellent, as are the bananas flambé and crêpes suzette.

136 4th Ave. N. (between Bay Shore Dr. and 1st St. N.). © 727/894-7163. Reservations recommended. Main courses $18–$29. AE, DC, DISC, MC, V. Daily 5–11pm.

MODERATE

Keystone Club ★ STEAKS/PRIME RIB   Resembling an exclusive men's club, this cozy restaurant's forest green walls accented by dark wood and etched glass create an atmosphere that's reminiscent of a Manhattan-style chophouse. But women are also welcome to partake of the beef, which is king here. Specialties include roast prime rib, New York strip steak, and filet mignon. Seafood also makes an appearance, with fresh lobster and grouper at market price. During winter, "sunset" early-bird specials include lunch-size portions, a beverage, and dessert.

320 4th St. N. (between 3rd and 4th Aves. N.). © 727/822-6600. Reservations recommended. Main courses $12–$24; early bird specials $10. AE, DC, DISC, MC, V. Sun–Thurs 4:30–9pm, Fri–Sat 4:30–10pm.

INEXPENSIVE

Fourth Street Shrimp Store ★★ *Value* SEAFOOD   If you're anywhere in the area, don't miss at least driving by to see the colorful, cartoonlike mural on the outside of this eclectic establishment just north of downtown. On first impression it looks like graffiti, but it's actually a gigantic drawing of people eating. Inside, it gets even better, with paraphernalia and murals on two walls making the main dining room seem like a warehouse with windows that look out on an early-19th-century seaport (one painted sailor permanently peers in to see what you're eating). You'll pass a seafood market counter when you enter, from which comes the fresh namesake shrimp, the star here. You can also pick from grouper, clam strips, catfish, or oysters fried, broiled, or steamed, all served in heaping portions. This is the best and certainly the most interesting bargain in town.

1006 4th St. N. (at 10th Ave. N.). © 727/822-0325. Reservations not accepted. Main courses $5–$14; sandwiches $2.50–$7. MC, V. Sun–Thurs 11am–8:30pm; Fri–Sat 11am–9pm.

Hilda La Tropicana Restaurant *Finds* CUBAN   You'll get authentic Cuban food at this colorful storefront cafe, a favorite office-worker lunch spot and a gathering place for local Latinos when it turns into a salsa nightclub after hours on Friday and Saturday. The house specialty is Cuban-style roast pork (pulled off the bone and served in its own juices with sliced raw onions), but a better bet is the baked chicken—half of a perfectly done bird served with vegetables. The crispy Cuban sandwich is another winner. Try the homemade sangria.

320 1st Ave. N. (opposite Williams Park, between 3rd and 4th Sts. N.). ℂ 727/898-9902. Reservations not accepted. Main courses $8.50–$12; sandwiches $4.50–$7. DISC, MC, V. Mon–Thurs 11am–9pm, Fri–Sat 11am–10pm.

The Moon Under Water ✦ ASIAN/MIDDLE EASTERN Tables on the verandah or sidewalk in front of this pub are a great place to take a break during your downtown stroll. The British Raj rules supreme inside the darkly paneled dining room with its slowly twirling ceiling fans and plethora of colonial artifacts, including obligatory pith helmets. Your taste buds are in for a treat here, because the bill of fare covers a number of former British outposts, including America (burgers and Philly cheese steaks), but the emphasis here is on mild, medium, or blazing-hot Indian curries—with a recommended Irish, British, or Australian beer to slake the resulting thirst. For lighter fare, consider Mideastern tabbouleh. There's entertainment Friday and Saturday evenings.

332 Beach Dr. (between 3rd and 4th Aves.). ℂ 727/896-6160. Reservations accepted only for groups. Main courses $7.50–$17; sandwiches and salads $6–$8. AE, DC, DISC, MC, V. Daily 11:30am–11pm. Closed New Year's Day, Thanksgiving, Christmas.

ST. PETERSBURG AFTER DARK

Good sources of nightlife information are the Thursday "Weekend" section of the *St. Petersburg Times* (www.sptimes.com), the "Baylife" and "Friday Extra" sections of the *Tampa Tribune* (www.tampatrib.com), and the *Weekly Planet* (www.weeklyplanet.com), a tabloid available at the visitor information offices and in many hotel and restaurant lobbies.

THE CLUB & MUSIC SCENE A historic attraction as well as an entertainment venue, the Moorish-style **Coliseum Ballroom,** 535 4th Ave. N. (ℂ 727/892-5202;** www.stpete.org/coliseum.htm), has been hosting dancing, big bands, boxing, and other events since 1924 (it even made an appearance in the 1985 movie *Cocoon*). Come out and watch the town's many seniors doing the jitterbug just like it was 1945 again! Call for the schedule and prices.

PERFORMING-ARTS VENUES The **Bayfront Center,** 400 1st St. S. (ℂ 727/892-5767,** or 727/892-5700 for recorded information), houses the 8,100-seat Bayfront Arena (www.stpete.org/bayfront.htm) and the 2,000-seat Mahaffey Theater (www.stpete.org/mahaffey.htm). The schedule includes a variety of concerts, Broadway shows, big bands, ice shows, and circus performances. **Ticketmaster** (ℂ 813/287-8844) sells tickets to most events and shows.

Tropicana Field, 1 Stadium Dr. (ℂ 727/825-3100; www.stpete.org/dome.htm), has a capacity of 50,000 for major concerts, but it also hosts a variety of smaller events when the Devil Rays aren't playing baseball.

3 St. Pete & Clearwater Beaches ✦✦

If you're looking for sun and sand, you'll find plenty of both on the 28 miles of slim barrier islands that skirt the gulf shore of the Pinellas Peninsula. With some one million visitors coming here every year, don't be surprised if you have lots of company. But you'll also discover quieter neighborhoods geared to families, and this area has some of the nation's finest beaches, which are protected from development by parks and nature preserves.

At the southern end of the strip, St. Pete Beach is the granddaddy of the area's resorts. In fact, visitors started coming here nearly a century ago, and they haven't quit. Today St. Pete Beach is heavily developed and often overcrowded during the winter season. If you like high rises and mile-a-minute action, St. Pete Beach is for you. But even here, Pass-a-Grille, on the island's southern end, is a quiet residential enclave with eclectic shops and a fine public beach.

A more gentle lifestyle begins just to the north on 3½-mile-long Treasure Island. From there, you cross famous John's Pass to Sand Key, a 12-mile-long island occupied by primarily residential Madeira Beach, Redington Beach, North Redington Beach, Redington Shores, Indian Shores, Indian Rocks Beach, and Belleair Beach. Finally the road crosses a soaring bridge to Clearwater Beach, whose silky sands attract active families and couples.

If you like your great outdoors unfettered by development, the jewels here are Fort Desoto Park, down below St. Pete Beach at the mouth of Tampa Bay, and Caladesi Island State Park, north of Clearwater Beach. They are consistently rated among America's top beaches. And Sand Key Park, looking at Clearwater Beach from the southern shores of Little Pass, is one of Florida's finest local beach parks.

ESSENTIALS

GETTING THERE   See "Getting There," in section 1 for information about getting to the beaches.

VISITOR INFORMATION   See "Visitor Information," in section 2 for the St. Petersburg/Clearwater Area Convention & Visitors Bureau and the St. Petersburg Area Chamber of Commerce. You can get information specific to the beaches from the **Gulf Beaches of Tampa Bay Chamber of Commerce,** 6990 Gulf Blvd. (at 70th Avenue), St. Pete Beach, FL 33706 (© **800/944-1847** or 727/360-6957; fax 727/360-2233; www.gulfbeaches-tampabay.com). The chamber's visitor center is open Monday to Friday from 9am to 5pm.

For advance information about Clearwater Beach, contact the **Greater Clearwater Chamber of Commerce,** 128 N. Osceola Ave. (P.O. Box 2457), Clearwater, FL 34615 (© **727/461-0011**). You can also walk into the **Clearwater Tourist Information Center,** on Causeway Boulevard in the lobby of the Clearwater Beach Marina Building (© **727/462-6531**). It's open Monday to Saturday from 9am to 5pm, Sunday from 1 to 5pm.

GETTING AROUND   The **Pinellas Suncoast Transit Authority/PSTA** (© **727/530-9911**) operates a motorized trolley service along Gulf Boulevard (Fla. 699) between the Hurricane Restaurant in St. Pete Beach and the Sheraton Sand Key Resort, where it connects with Clearwater Beach's Jolly Trolley (© 727/445-1200). The PSTA trolley costs $1 per ride, or you can buy a daily pass for $2.50. One-ride fares on the Jolly Trolley are 50¢ per person, 25¢ for seniors. Call the trolleys for schedules, or pick up printed copies at the Gulf Beaches of Tampa Bay Chamber of Commerce (see "Visitor Information," above).

Along the beach, the major cab company is **BATS Taxi** (© **727/367-3702**). Fares are $1.50 at flag fall, plus 20¢ for each ½ mile.

HITTING THE BEACH

This entire stretch of coast is one long beach, but since hotels, condominiums, and private homes occupy much of it, you may want to sun and swim at one of the area's public parks. The very best are described below, but there's also the fine

Pass-a-Grille Public Beach, on the southern end of St. Pete Beach, where you can watch the boats going in and out of Pass-a-Grille Channel and slake your thirst at Hurricane restaurant (see "Where to Dine," later in this chapter). This and all other Pinellas County public beaches have metered parking lots, so bring a supply of quarters.

The fine **Sand Key Park** ⊛, on the northern tip of Sand Key facing Clearwater Beach, sports a wide beach and gentle surf and is relatively off the beaten path in this commercial area. It's great to get out of the hotel for a morning walk or jog here. The park is open 8am to dark. Admission is free, but the parking lot has meters. For more information, call ✆ **727/464-3347.**

Clearwater Public Beach (also known as Pier 60) has beach volleyball, watersports rentals, lifeguards, rest rooms, showers, and concessions. The swimming is excellent, and there is a fishing pier with a bait and tackle shop, plus a children's playground. Gated municipal parking lots here cost $1 per hour or $7 a day. The lots are right across the street from Clearwater Beach Marina, a prime base for boating, cruises, and other waterborne activities (see "Outdoor Activities," below). A somewhat-less-crowded spot in Clearwater Beach is at the gulf end of Bay Esplanade; the metered parking lot here is flanked by two lively beach bars: the Palm Pavilion Inn's grill and bar (see "Where to Stay," below) and Frenchy's Rockaway Grill (see "Where to Dine," later in this chapter).

CALADESI ISLAND STATE PARK ⊛⊛⊛

Occupying a 3½-mile-long island north of Clearwater Beach, **Caladesi Island State Park** boasts one of Florida's top beaches—a lovely, relatively secluded stretch with fine soft sand edged in sea grass and palmettos. Dolphins often cavort in the waters offshore. In the park itself is a nature trail, and you might see one of the rattlesnakes, black racers, raccoons, armadillos, or rabbits that live here. A concession stand, a ranger station, and bathhouses (with rest rooms and showers) are available. Caladesi Island is accessible only by ferry from **Honeymoon Island State Recreation Area,** which is connected by Causeway Boulevard (Fla. 586) to Dunedin, north of Clearwater.

You'll first have to pay the admission to Honeymoon Island: $4 per vehicle with two to eight occupants, $2 per single-occupant vehicle, $1 for pedestrians and bicyclists. Beginning daily at 10am, the ferry departs Honeymoon Island every hour on winter weekdays, every 30 minutes on summer weekdays, and every 30 minutes on weekends year-round. Round-trip rides cost $7 for adults, $4 for kids.

Neither Caladesi nor Honeymoon allows camping, but pets are permitted in the inland parts of the island and on South Beach (bring a leash and use it at all times).

The two parks are open daily from 8am to sunset and are administered by Gulf Islands Geopark, 1 Causeway Blvd., Dunedin, FL 34698 (✆ **727/ 469-5942;** www8.myflorida.com/communities/learn/stateparks/district4/ caladesi and www8.myflorida.com/communities/learn/stateparks/district4/ honeymoonisland).

To really get to know the islands, go with Linda Taylor of **It's Our Nature, Inc.** (✆ **888/535-7448** or 727/441-2599; www.itsournature.com;), on one of her guided walks of Honeymoon (usually at 9:30am Wednesday) and Caladesi (10am on Thursday). They last about 2 hours and cost $15 for adults, $8 for children. Call for reservations, which are required.

St. Pete & Clearwater Beaches

ACCOMMODATIONS ■

Beach Haven **14**
Belleview Biltmore
  Resort & Spa **1**
Best Western Beach
  Front Resort **9**
Best Western Sea
  Stone Resort **24**
Clearwater Beach Hotel **18**
Don CeSar Beach
  Resort and Spa **15**
Great Heron Inn **4**
Island's End Resort **17**
Pelican—East & West **2**
Radisson Suite Resort
  on Sand Key **26**
Sheraton Sand Key
  Resort **25**
Sun West Beach Motel **23**
TradeWinds Island
  Grand Resort **11**
TradeWinds Sirata
  Beach Resort **12**
Travelodge St. Pete
  Beach **8**

DINING ◆

Beachside Grill **6**
Bob Heilman's
  Beachcomber **20**
Bobby's Bistro
  & Wine Bar **21**
Crabby Bill's **13**
Frenchy's Cafe **19**
Guppy's **3**
Hurricane **16**
Internet Outpost **7**
Lobster Pot **6**
Seafood & Sunsets
  at Julie's **22**
The Salt Rock Grill **5**
Skidder's **10**

FORT DESOTO PARK ★★

South of St. Pete Beach at the very mouth of Tampa Bay, **Fort Desoto Park** encompasses all of Mullet Key, set aside by Pinellas County as a 900-acre bird, animal, and plant sanctuary. Besides the stunning white-sugar sand, other diversions include a Spanish-American War–era fort, great fishing from piers, large playgrounds for kids, and 4 miles of trails winding through the park for in-line skaters, bicyclists, and joggers.

Sitting by itself on a heavily forested island, the park's **campground** is one of Florida's most picturesque (many sites are beside the bay). It's such great camping that the 233 sites usually are sold out, especially on weekends, so it's best to reserve well in advance. But, there's a catch: You must appear in person and pay for your site no more than 30 days in advance at the campground office, at 631 Chestnut St. in Clearwater, or at 150 5th St. N. in downtown St. Petersburg. You must reserve for at least 2 nights, but you can stay no more than 14 nights in any 30-day period. Sites cost $33.30 a night from August through December, $23.20 a night the rest of the year, and you must pay when you make your reservation in cash or by traveler's check (no credit cards). All sites have water and electricity hookups.

Admission to the park is free. It's open daily from 8am to dusk, although campers and persons fishing from the piers can stay later. To get here, take the Pinellas Byway (50¢ toll) east from St. Pete Beach and follow Fla. 679 (35¢ toll) and the signs south to the park. For more information, contact the park at 3500 Pinellas Byway, Tierra Verde, FL 33715 (② **727/582-2267;** www. fortdesoto.com).

OUTDOOR ACTIVITIES

BICYCLING & IN-LINE SKATING   With miles of flat terrain and paved roads, the beach area is ideal for bikers and in-line skaters, and the 47-mile-long Pinellas Trail runs close by on the mainland (see "Outdoor Pursuits & Spectator Sports," in section 2, earlier in this chapter). In St. Pete Beach, you can rent bicycles, skates, and scooters from **Beach Cyclist Sports Center,** 7517 Blind Pass Rd. (② **727/367-5001**). **East End Bike Rentals** (② **727/398-4811**) has them at John's Pass Village in Madeira Beach. In Clearwater Beach, contact **Transportation Station,** 652 Gulfview Blvd. (② **727/443-3188**).

BOATING, FISHING & OTHER WATER SPORTS   You can indulge in parasailing, boating, deep-sea fishing, wave running, sightseeing, dolphin watching, water-skiing, and just about any other waterborne diversion your heart could desire here. All you have to do is head to one of two beach locations: **Hubbard's Marina,** at John's Pass Village and Boardwalk (② **727/393-1947;** www.hubbardsmarina.com), in Madeira Beach on the southern tip of Sand Key; or **Clearwater Beach Marina,** at Coronado Drive and Causeway Boulevard (② **800/772-4479** or 727/461-3133), which is at the beach end of the causeway leading to downtown Clearwater. Agents in booths there will give you the schedules and prices (they are approximately the same at both locations), answer any questions you have, and make reservations if necessary. Go in the early morning to set up today's activities, or in the afternoon to book tomorrow's.

CRUISES   The top nature cruise here is the **Sea Life Safari** ★★ (② **727/462-2628**), operated by the Clearwater Marine Aquarium (see "Attractions on Land," below). These 2½-hour "sealife safaris" are more like field trips than pleasure cruises. Aquarium biologists go along to explain what they pull up in trawl nets (don't worry: they throw it all back). You'll see birds and other wildlife on a visit to a bird sanctuary islet. Dolphin sightings are likely, too. The cruises leave from the aquarium daily at 12:30 and 3:15pm, from Clearwater Beach Marina at 10am, 12:45pm, and 3:15pm. They cost $13.95 for adults, $9 for kids 3 to 12. You can combine the cruise with aquarium admission and save $3. Call to confirm the schedule and reserve. Also ask about sunset nature cruises from mid-April to mid-October.

Hubbard's Sea Adventures, based at John's Pass Village and Boardwalk in Madeira Beach (© 727/398-6577), offers a 2-hour dolphin-watching excursion, departing Monday to Saturday at 10am, 1pm, and 4pm (Sun at 1 and 4pm), at $12 for adults, $6 for kids under 12. Another cruise goes to **Egmont Key State Park,** on historic Egmont Key at the mouth of Tampa Bay (www8.myflorida.com/communities/learn/stateparks/district4/egmontkey). This uninhabited island is the site of a lighthouse, of now-crumbling Fort Dade (built in 1900 during the Spanish-American War but abandoned long ago), and of threatened gopher tortoises. Sea turtles come ashore here to nest. You can go snorkeling and shelling here, so bring your swimsuit (snorkeling gear is available for $5 per person). This cruise leaves at 10:30am Wednesday, Friday, and Sunday and costs $30 for adults, $20 for children. A barbecue lunch on either Shell or Egmont Keys costs $7 for adults, $5 for kids. A 6-hour trip goes to lovely **Shell Key,** one of Florida's last completely undeveloped barrier islands. Shell Key is great for bird watchers, who could spot a remarkable 88 different species, including some of North America's rarest shorebirds. These trips usually depart at 10:30am Monday, Tuesday, Thursday, and Saturday, for $25 adults, $13 kids. You can rent beach chairs, umbrellas, snorkeling gear, and other equipment once you get there. Call to confirm the schedule and make reservations, which are recommended.

The ride to Shell Key is shorter on the **Shell Key Shuttle,** Merry Pier, on Pass-a-Grille Way at the eastern end of 8th Avenue in southern St. Pete Beach (© 727/360-1348). Boats leave daily at 10am, noon, and 2pm. Prices are $12 for adults, $6 for children 12 and under. The ride takes 15 minutes, and you can return on any shuttle you wish.

The most unusual outings here are with **Captain Memo's Pirate Cruise,** at Clearwater Beach Marina (© 727/446-2587; www.pirateflorida.com), which sails the *Pirate's Ransom,* a reproduction of a pirate ship, on 2-hour daytime "pirate cruises," as well as sunset and evening champagne cruises. Cruises operate year-round, daily at 10am and at 2, 4:30, and 7pm. For adults, daytime or sunset cruises cost $28, and evening cruises are $30; both daytime and evening cruises cost $22 for seniors and for juniors 13 to 17, $17 for children 2 to 12, free for children under 2.

Two paddle-wheel riverboats operate here: The *Show Queen* has lunch, sunset dinner, and Sunday brunch cruises from Clearwater Beach Marina (© 727/461-3113; www.marinetours.com). The *Starlite Princess* does likewise from 3400 Pasadena Ave. S. (© 800/444-4814 or 727/462-2628; www.starlitecruises.com), at the eastern side of the Corey Causeway linking St. Pete Beach to the mainland. Call for prices, schedules, and reservations.

SCUBA DIVING   You can dive on reefs and wrecks with **Dive Clearwater,** P.O. Box 3594, Clearwater, FL 33767 (© 800/875-3483 or 727/443-6731), which also operates the live-aboard boat *Plunger V.* Call for schedule and prices.

ATTRACTIONS ON LAND

Clearwater Marine Aquarium ★★ *Kids*   This little jewel of an aquarium on Clearwater Harbor is very low-key and friendly; it's dedicated to the rescue and rehabilitation of marine mammals and sea turtles. Exhibits include otters, sea turtles, sharks, stingrays, mangroves, sea grass, and Sunset Sam, an Atlantic bottlenose dolphin who has lived here since he was stranded on the beach in 1984.

249 Windward Passage, Clearwater Beach. © **888/239-9414** or 727/441-1790. www.cmaquarium.org. Admission $7.75 adults, $5.25 children 3–11, free for children 2 and under. Mon–Fri 9am–5pm, Sat 9am–4pm, Sun 11am–4pm. The aquarium is off the causeway between Clearwater and Clearwater Beach; follow the signs.

John's Pass Village and Boardwalk   Casual and charming, this Old Florida fishing village on John's Pass consists of a string of simple wooden structures topped by tin roofs and connected by a 1,000-foot boardwalk. Most of the buildings have been converted into shops, art galleries, restaurants, and saloons. The focal point is the boardwalk and marina, where many water sports are available for visitors (see "Outdoor Activities," above). If you don't go out on the water, this is a great place to have an alfresco lunch—**Sculley's** (© **727/ 393-7749**) is the best restaurant here—and watch the boats go in and out of the pass.

12901 Gulf Blvd. (at John's Pass), Madeira Beach. © **800/944-1847** or 727/397-1511. Free admission. Shops and activities daily 9am–6pm or later.

Suncoast Seabird Sanctuary ★   At any one time there are usually more than 500 sea and land birds living at the sanctuary, from cormorants, white herons, and birds of prey to the ubiquitous brown pelican. The nation's largest wild-bird hospital, dedicated to the rescue, repair, recuperation, and release of sick and injured wild birds, is also here.

18328 Gulf Blvd., Indian Shores. © **727/391-6211**. Free admission, donations welcome. Daily 9am–dusk. Free tours Wed and Sun 2pm.

SHOPPING

John's Pass Village and Boardwalk, on John's Pass in Madeira Beach (see "Attractions on Land," above), has an unremarkable collection of beach souvenir shops, but the atmosphere makes it worth a stroll. The pick of the lot is the **Bronze Lady** (© 727/398-5994), featuring the world's largest collection of works by the late comedian-artist Red Skelton, best known for his numerous clown paintings. The shops are open daily from 9am to 6pm or later.

If you're in the market for one-of-a-kind hand-hammered jewelry, try **Evander Preston Contemporary Jewelry,** 106 8th Ave., Pass-a-Grille (© **727/ 367-7894**), a unique gallery/workshop housed in a 75-year-old building in Pass-a-Grille's 1-block-long 8th Avenue business district. Check out the golden miniature train with diamond headlight (it's not for sale). Open Monday to Saturday from 10am to 5:30pm. There's a branch in the TradeWinds Island Grand Resort (see "Where to Stay," below).

Among the shops in St. Pete Beach's Corey Landings Area, the town's original business strip along 75th Street east of Gulf Boulevard, **The Shell Store** (© 727/360-0586) specializes in corals and shells, with an on-premises minimuseum illustrating how they live and grow. There's a good selection of shell home decorations, shell hobbyist supplies, shell art, planters, and jewelry. The store is open Monday to Saturday from 9:30am to 5pm.

WHERE TO STAY

St. Pete Beach and Clearwater Beach have national chain hotels and motels of every name and description. For even more choices, the **St. Petersburg Area Chamber of Commerce** lists a wide range of hotels, motels, condominiums, and other accommodations in its annual visitor guide (see "Essentials," in section 2), and it publishes a brochure listing all members of its Superior Small Lodgings program. You can also use the St. Petersburg/Clearwater Convention & Visitors Bureau's free **reservations service** (© 800/345-6710).

As is the case throughout Florida, there are more rental condominiums here than there are hotel rooms. Many of them are in high-rise buildings right on the beach. Among several local rental agents, **Excell Vacation Condos,** 14955 Gulf Blvd., Madeira Beach, FL 33708 (© 800/733-4004 or 727/391-5512; fax 727/393-8885; www.islandtime.com/vacation), and **JC Resort Management,** 17200 Gulf Blvd., North Redington Beach, FL 33708 (© 800/535-7776 or 727/397-0441; fax 727/397-8894; www.jcresort.com), have many from which to choose. **Resort Rentals,** 9524 Blind Pass Rd., St. Pete Beach, FL 33707 (© 800/293-3979 or 727/363-3336; fax 727/360-5086; www.resort-realty.com), specializes in luxury rental homes.

I have organized accommodations geographically, starting with the congested St. Pete Beach area on the south end of the strip, then the mostly residential Indian Rocks Beach area, and finally the relatively quiet but still-busy Clearwater Beach at the north end.

ST. PETE BEACH
Very Expensive

Don CeSar Beach Resort & Spa ★★★   This Moorish-style "Pink Palace" was built to be a grand hotel (it's on the National Register of Historic Places), but its scheduled 1928 opening was derailed when Florida real estate went bust. The federal government used it as a rest-and-recreation center for soldiers during World War II and as an office building until 1967. Developer William Bowman Jr. bought it in 1972 and restored it to its intended glory. Today it appeals to a wide range of clientele, from groups to families, from honeymooning couples to local ladies taking treatments in the full-service spa. Sitting majestically on 7½ acres of beachfront, the landmark sports a lobby of classic high windows and archways, crystal chandeliers, marble floors, and original artwork. Extensively renovated in 2000, some of the 275 rooms under the minarets of the original building may seem rather small by today's standards, but they have high windows and offer views of the gulf or Boca Ciega Bay. Some but not all of them have balconies. If you want more room but less charm, the resort has 70 spacious luxury condominiums in The Don CeSar Beach House, a mid-rise building ¾ mile to the north (there's 24-hr. complimentary transportation between the two).

3400 Gulf Blvd. (at 34th Ave./Pinellas Byway), St. Pete Beach, FL 33706. © 800/282-1116, 800/637-7200, or 727/360-1881. Fax 727/367-6952. www.doncesar.com. 347 units. Winter $288–$389 double; $304–$699 suite. Off-season $209–$329 double; $251–$699 suite. $7.50 per person per day activities fee. Packages available. AE, DC, DISC, MC, V. Valet parking $10, free self-parking. **Amenities:** 4 restaurants (American); 3 bars; 2 heated outdoor pools; exercise room; spa; Jacuzzi; water-sports equipment rental; children's programs; game room; concierge; business center; shopping arcade; salon; 24-hr. room service; massage; babysitting; laundry service; coin-op washers and dryers. *In room:* A/C, TV, dataport, minibar, hair dryer, iron.

Expensive

TradeWinds Island Grand Resort ★★   Don't be dismayed by the outward appearance of this six- and seven-story, concrete-and-steel monstrosity, for underneath and beside it runs a maze of brick walkways, patios, and lily ponds connected by ¼ mile of streams. Many of the guest units, which look out on the gulf or the 18 acres of grounds, have up-to-date kitchens or kitchenettes, and most have private balconies. Choice units directly face the gulf, but note that like its sister property, the TradeWinds Sirata Resort, this hotel has a great variety of accommodations; so consult with the reservation clerk when booking. Although the resort draws large meetings and conventions, it's a big hit with families, too, especially Europeans, all of whom appreciate the children's program, ice cream parlor, Pizza Hut outlet, and summer packages. One of the four heated swimming pools is reserved for adults, and there's lots more to keep grownups busy, such as the libation offered by a unique Florida cracker-house–style beachside bar floating on one of the lily ponds and the live entertainment nightly in another pub.

5500 Gulf Blvd. (at 55th Ave.), St. Pete Beach, FL 33706. ✆ **800/237-0707** or 727/562-1212. Fax 727/562-1222. www.tradewindsresort.com. 577 units. Winter $209–$439 double; off-season $179–$359 double. Resort amenities fee of $12 per day per unit covers most activities. Packages available summer and fall. AE, DC, DISC, MC, V. Valet parking $6; free self-parking. **Amenities:** 4 restaurants (American); 4 bars; 4 heated outdoor pools; 4 tennis courts; health club; Jacuzzi; sauna; water-sports equipment rental; children's programs; game room; concierge; car-rental desk; business center; salon; limited room service; massage; baby-sitting; laundry service; coin-op washers and dryers. *In room:* A/C, TV, dataport, kitchen, fridge, coffeemaker, hair dryer, iron.

TradeWinds Sirata Beach Resort ★★   A ton of money was spent in 1999 to completely renovate this older property and bring it up to second-tier status here, almost on a par with its sister hotel, the TradeWinds Island Resort, but well below the Don Cesar Beach Resort and Spa. In fact, if you've been here before you may not recognize the Sirata from Gulf Boulevard, because a yellow-and-green Old Florida–style facade now disguises the eight-story main building, which houses hotel rooms and one-bedroom suites upstairs (upper-level units have nice views) and a convention center. Some guest rooms in this two-story building face the courtyard, but the choice quarters here are its gulf-side rooms, the only units with patios or balconies opening directly onto the beach. The most spacious units are efficiencies and one-bedroom suites in two long, two-story buildings; they all have kitchenettes, but they look out primarily on parking lots.

5300 Gulf Blvd. (53rd Ave.), St. Pete Beach, FL 33706. ✆ **800/237-0707** or 727/562-1212. Fax 727/562-1222. www.tradewindsresort.com. 380 units, including 170 suites. Winter $185–$327 double; $277–$409 suite. Off-season $155–$255 double; $208–$337 suite. AE, DC, DISC, MC, V. **Amenities:** 2 restaurants (American); 2 bars; 2 heated outdoor pools; exercise room; Jacuzzi; water-sports equipment rental; children's programs; game room; concierge; business center; limited room service; baby-sitting; laundry service; coin-op washers and dryers. *In room:* A/C, TV, dataport, kitchen, fridge, coffeemaker, hair dryer, iron.

Moderate

Best Western Beachfront Resort   Two long, gray buildings flank a courtyard with heated swimming pool at this beachside property popular with young families. Furnished in dark woods and rich tones, most of the guest rooms have picture-window views of the courtyard. They open to wide exterior walkways, but each room has its own plastic chairs and drink table out there. About half of the units are efficiencies with kitchenettes. Jimmy B.'s beach bar is a fine place for a sunset cocktail (happy hour runs from noon to 7:30pm) and for evening entertainment, including beachside bonfires on Saturdays in winter.

6200 Gulf Blvd. (at 62nd Ave.), St. Pete Beach, FL 33706. ✆ **800/544-4222** or 727/367-1902. Fax 727/367-4422. www.bestwesternstpetebeach.com. 102 units. Winter $168–$228 double; off-season $108–$168 double. Rates include continental breakfast. AE, DC, DISC, MC, V. **Amenities:** Restaurant (American); 2 bars; heated outdoor pool; game room. *In room:* A/C, TV, kitchen, fridge, coffeemaker, hair dryer, iron.

Island's End Resort ★★ *Value*   A wonderful respite from the maddening crowd, and a great bargain to boot, this little all-cottage hideaway sits right on the southern tip of St. Pete Beach, smack-dab on Pass-a-Grille, where the Gulf of Mexico meets Tampa Bay. You can step from the six contemporary cottages right onto the beach. And since the island curves sharply here, nothing blocks your view of the emerald bay. Strong currents run through the pass, but you can safely swim in the gulf or grab a brilliant sunset at the Pass-a-Grille public beach, just one door removed. Linked to each other by boardwalks, the comfortable one- or three-bedroom cottages have dining areas, living rooms, VCRs, and fully equipped kitchens. You will love the one monstrous unit with two living rooms (one can be converted to sleeping quarters), two bathrooms (one with a whirlpool tub and separate shower), and its own private bay-side swimming pool. Maid service on request.

1 Pass-a-Grille Way (at 1st Ave.), St. Pete Beach, FL 33706. ✆ **727/360-5023.** Fax 727/367-7890. www. islandsend.com. 6 units. Winter $100–$235 cottage; off-season $77–$107 cottage. Weekly rates available. Complimentary breakfast served Tues, Thurs, Sat. MC, V. **Amenities:** Coin-op washers and dryers. *In-room:* A/C, TV, kitchen, coffeemaker, hair dryer, iron.

Travelodge St. Pete Beach   This U-shaped beachfront complex of one- and two-story units is a favorite with cost-conscious families traveling on package tours from Canada and the United Kingdom. All units were completely renovated in 1999. Some open to the surrounding parking lots; much more preferable are those facing a landscaped central courtyard with pool and large sunning area. About half have refrigerators. On the premises is a branch of the inexpensive and very good Shells seafood restaurant (see "Where to Dine," in section 1). An indoor lounge and a lively beach bar offer light refreshments. The watersports shack here offers parasailing equipment rentals and also services the Best Western Beachfront Resort next door (see above).

6300 Gulf Blvd. (at 63rd Ave.), St. Pete Beach, FL 33706. ✆ **800/237-8918** or 727/367-2711. Fax 727/ 367-7068. 200 units. Winter $104–$144 double; off-season $80–$112 double. AE, DC, DISC, MC, V. **Amenities:** Restaurant (American); 2 bars; heated outdoor pool; water-sports equipment rental; game room; coin-op washers and dryers. *In room:* A/C, TV, fridge, coffeemaker, hair dryer, iron.

Inexpensive

Beach Haven ★ *Value*   Nestled on the beach between two high-rise condominiums, these low-slung, pink-with-white-trim structures look from the outside like the early 1950s motel they once were. But Jone and Millard Gamble, who used to own this motel and still have the charming Island's End Resort (above), replaced the innards and installed bright tile floors, vertical blinds, pastel tropical furniture, and many modern amenities, including VCRs and refrigerators. Five of the original quarters remain as motel rooms (with shower-only bathrooms), but the others are linked to make 12 one-bedroom units and 1 two-bedroom unit, all with kitchens. The top choice is the one-bedroom suite with sliding-glass doors opening to a tiled patio beside an outdoor heated pool. There's also a sunning deck with lounge furniture by the beach. You don't get maid service on Sunday or holidays, and the rooms and bathrooms are 1950s smallish; but every unit here is bright, airy, and comfortable.

4980 Gulf Blvd. (at 50th Ave.), St. Pete Beach, FL 33706. ✆ **727/367-8642.** Fax 727/360-8202. www. beachhavenvillas.com. 18 units. Winter $88–$144 double; off-season $55–$120 double. AE, DISC, MC, V. **Amenities:** Heated outdoor pool; coin-op washers and dryers; concierge-level rooms. *In room:* A/C, TV, dataport, kitchen, coffeemaker, hair dryer, iron.

INDIAN ROCKS BEACH AREA

Great Heron Inn *(Value)*   A real heron named Harry patrols the beach at this family-oriented motel owned and operated by transplanted Michiganders Ralph and Teena Hickerson. It sits at the narrowest section of Indian Rocks Beach, facing the gulf on one side and its own Intracoastal Waterway dock on the other. The buildings flank a central courtyard, with a heated pool, which opens to the beach. The airy one-bedroom apartments offer modern furnishings and Berber carpets, and each has a full kitchen and dining area. There are no king- or queen-size beds here, only doubles (plus pullout sleeper sofas in the living rooms).

68 Gulf Blvd. (south of 1st Ave.), Indian Rocks Beach, FL 33785. ℰ 727/595-2589. Fax 727/517-2705. www. heroninn.com. 16 units. Winter $85–$100 double; off-season $67–$75 double. Weekly and monthly rates available. DISC, MC, V. Hotel is 4 blocks south of Fla. 688. **Amenities:** Coin-op washers and dryers. *In-room:* A/C, TV, fax, kitchen, coffeemaker.

Pelican—East & West *(Value)*   Mike and Carol McGlaughlin's simple but friendly motel complex offers a choice of two settings. You'll pay more at Pelican West, but it's directly on the beachfront. Its four beachside apartments each have a living room, a bedroom, a kitchen, a patio, tub-shower combination bathrooms, and unbeatable views of the gulf. The lowest rates are at Pelican East, in a residential area 500 feet from the beach, where four apartments each have a bedroom, a separate kitchen, and shower-only bathrooms. Also over there, a motel room and one-bedroom apartment reside in a newer building sitting on stilts. You won't get any frills here, but this is a clean and comfortable choice.

108 21st Ave. (at Gulf Blvd.), Indian Rocks Beach, FL 33785. ℰ **727/595-9741.** Fax 727/596-4170. www. beachdirectory.com/pelican. 40 units. Winter $45–$75 double; off-season $45–$65 double. Weekly rates available. MC, V. *In room:* A/C, TV, kitchen, coffeemaker, iron.

CLEARWATER BEACH
Moderate

Best Western Sea Stone Resort   Located just across the street from the gulf in Clearwater Beach's busy south end, the Sea Stone is a six-story building of classic Key West–style architecture, containing 43 one-bedroom suites, each with a kitchenette and a living room. The living-room windows of the suites look across external walkways to the harbor. A few steps away, the older five-story Gulfview Wing offers 65 standard motel rooms, the least-expensive choices here.

445 Hamden Dr. (at Coronado Dr.), Clearwater Beach, FL 33767. ℰ **800/444-1919,** 800/528-1234, or 727/ 441-1722. Fax 727/441-1680. www.seawake.com. 106 units. Winter $89–$179 double; off-season $59–$115 double. AE, DC, DISC, MC, V. Pets accepted ($50 nonrefundable fee). **Amenities:** Restaurant (American); bar; heated outdoor pool; Jacuzzi; coin-op washers and dryers. *In room:* A/C, TV, kitchen, fridge, coffeemaker, hair dryer, iron.

Clearwater Beach Hotel *(★)*   Besides the great beach location, you'll enjoy easy access to many nearby shops and restaurants from this Old Florida–style structure, built in 1986 to replace an old wooden hotel. The resort has been owned and operated by the same family since the 1950s and attracts a mixed clientele including European families. Directly on the gulf, the complex consists of the six-story main building and two contemporary motel-style wings. Some rooms have balconies, and the efficiencies in the wings have kitchenettes. Offering French cuisine, the formal dining room is romantic at sunset and offers great views of the gulf, while the nautically themed lounge has entertainment nightly. A bar provides snacks and libations beside an outdoor heated swimming pool.

500 Mandalay Ave. (at Baymont St.), Clearwater Beach, FL 33767. ℭ 800/292-2295 or 727/441-2425. Fax 727/449-2083. www.clearwaterbeachhotel.com. 157 units. Winter $159–$269 double; off-season $115–$209 double. AE, DC, MC, V. Free valet parking. **Amenities:** Restaurant (French); bar; heated outdoor pool; limited room service; laundry service. *In room:* A/C, TV, kitchen (efficiencies only), fridge, coffeemaker (efficiencies only).

Radisson Suite Resort on Sand Key *(Kids)*   You'll see the beauty of Sand Key from the suites in this boomerang-shaped, 10-story, all-suites hotel located across the boulevard from the Sheraton Sand Key Resort (see below). Although the resort sits on the bay and not the gulf, it has a large swimming pool complex next to the water, and the beach and beautiful Sand Key Park are short walks or trolley rides away. The whole family will enjoy exploring the adjacent boardwalk with 25 shops and restaurants, including a branch of Tampa's excellent Columbia (see "Where to Dine" in section 1). Each suite has a bedroom with a balcony offering water views, as well as a complete living room with a sofa bed, a wet bar, an entertainment unit. Like the Sheraton Sand Key across the boulevard (see below), this Radisson gets many European guests during the summer months.

1201 Gulf Blvd., Clearwater Beach, FL 33767. ℭ 800/333-3333 or 727/596-1100. Fax 727/595-4292. www. radissonsandkey.com. 220 units. $149–$319 suite. Packages available. AE, DC, DISC, MC, V. **Amenities:** 2 restaurants (American); 2 bars; heated outdoor pool; golf course; exercise room; Jacuzzi; sauna; children's programs; game room; car-rental desk; shopping arcade; limited room service; baby-sitting; laundry service; coin-op washers and dryers. *In room:* A/C, TV, dataport, minibar, coffeemaker, hair dryer, iron.

Sheraton Sand Key Resort *(★)*   Away from the honky-tonk of Clearwater, this nine-story Spanish-look hotel on 10 acres next to Sand Key Park is a big favorite with water-sports enthusiasts and groups. It also gets lots of European guests year-round. You'll appreciate being next to the park, since it's a 150-yard walk across the broad beach in front of the hotel to the water's edge. The moderately spacious guest rooms here all have traditional dark wood furniture and balconies or patios with views of the gulf or the bay. The exercise room here is on the top floor, rendering great workout views.

1160 Gulf Blvd., Clearwater Beach, FL 33767. ℭ 800/325-3535 or 727/595-1611. Fax 727/596-8488. 390 units. $135–$240 double. AE, DC, DISC, MC, V. **Amenities:** 2 restaurants (American); 2 bars; 24-hr. convenience store; heated outdoor pool; 3 tennis courts; exercise room; Jacuzzi; sauna; water-sports equipment rental; children's programs (summer only); game room; concierge; business center; limited room service; baby-sitting; laundry service; concierge-level rooms. *In room:* A/C, TV, fax, dataport, kitchen, minibar, fridge, coffeemaker, hair dryer, iron.

Inexpensive

Sun West Beach Motel   Sitting among several small motels a 2-block walk from the beach, Scott and Judy Barrows's simple one-story establishment dates from 1954, but it's well maintained, overlooks the bay, and has a fishing/boating dock and a heated bay-side pool and sundeck. All units, which face the bay, the pool, or the sundeck, were recently upgraded and have tropical-style furnishings, which make the place seem more modern than it is. The four motel rooms have small refrigerators, the 10 efficiencies have kitchens, and a few suites have separate bedrooms. The biggest and best unit is the Bayside Suite, which has vaulted ceilings, a steam room in its bathroom, and a fully equipped kitchen.

409 Hamden Dr. (at Bayside Dr.), Clearwater Beach, FL 33767. ℭ 727/442-5008. Fax 727/461-1395. 15 units. $44–$62 double; $52–$89 efficiency; $70–$125 suite. MC, V. **Amenities:** Heated outdoor pool; golf course; access to nearby health club; coin-op washers and dryers. *In room:* A/C, TV, kitchen (some units), fridge, coffeemaker.

TWO NEARBY GOLF RESORTS

Belleview Biltmore Resort & Spa   The Gulf Coast's oldest operating tourist hotel, this gabled clapboard structure was built in 1896 by Henry B. Plant as the Hotel Belleview to attract customers to his Orange Belt Railroad. Sited on a bluff overlooking the bay, it's the largest occupied wooden structure in the world. Today it attracts mostly groups and serious golfers (guests can play at the adjoining Belleview Country Club, an 18-hole, par-72 champion—ship course), but there's no denying its Victorian charm and old-fashioned ambience—once you get past the out-of-place glass-and-steel foyer added by more recent owners. Historic tours are given daily (call for schedule and prices). The creaky hallways lead to several shops and a museum explaining the hotel's history. At press time, the high-ceilinged guest rooms were undergoing serious renovation, including a departure from the Victorian theme (although they will get to keep their ceiling fans). The hotel provides complimentary shuttle service to the country club and to Clearwater Beach.

25 Belleview Blvd., Clearwater, FL 33756. (℅ **800/237-8947** or 727/442-6171. Fax 727/441-4173 or 727/ 443-6361. www.belleviewbiltmore.com. 240 units. Winter $159 double; $230–$310 suite. Off-season $109 double; $159–$229 suite. AE, DC, DISC, MC, V. Valet parking $3; free self-parking. Resort is 1 mile south of downtown on Belleview Rd., off Alt. U.S. 19. **Amenities:** Restaurant (American); 21 bars; heated outdoor and outdoor pools; golf course; 4 tennis courts; health club; Jacuzzi; sauna; concierge; business center; shopping arcade; salon; limited room service; baby-sitting; laundry service. *In room:* A/C, TV, coffeemaker, hair dryer, iron.

The Westin Innisbrook Resort ★★   *Golf Digest, Golf,* and other magazines pick this as one of the country's best places to play (provided you stay here, of course). Situated off U.S. 19 between Palm Harbor and Tarpon Springs, this 1,000-acre, all-condominium resort has 90 holes on championship courses that are more like the rolling links of the Carolinas than the usually flat courses found in Florida. Some golf magazines think the **Copperhead course** ★★, for-mer home of the annual JCPenney Classic, is number one in Florida. If you want to learn, Innisbrook has the largest resort-owned and -operated golf school in North America, and it boasts a tennis center with instruction, too. It's simi-lar to the sports-oriented Saddlebrook Resort near Tampa (see "Where to Stay" in section 1, earlier in this chapter), except that the courses are more challeng-ing here and you're much closer to the beach. A free shuttle runs around the property, and another goes to the beach three times a day. The spacious quarters actually are privately owned apartments spread all over the premises. The focal points are the golf and tennis clubhouses, all of which have restaurants and bars.

36750 U.S. 19 N., Palm Harbor, FL 34684. (℅ **800/456-2000** or 727/942-2000. Fax 727/942-5577. www. westin-innisbrook.com. 700 units. Winter from $240 condo; off-season from $190 condo. Golf packages avail-able. AE, DC, DISC, MC, V. **Amenities:** 7 restaurants (American/Italian); 7 bars; heated outdoor pools; 4 golf courses; 15 tennis courts; health club; Jacuzzis; sauna; children's programs; concierge; activities desk; car rental desk; limited room service; massage; baby-sitting; laundry service; coin-op washers and dryers. *In room:* A/C, TV, dataport, minibar, kitchen, coffeemaker, hair dryer, iron.

WHERE TO DINE

St. Pete Beach and Clearwater Beach both have a wide selection of national chain fast-food and family restaurants along their main drags.

As with the accommodations above, I have grouped the restaurants by geo-graphic area: St. Pete Beach, including Pass-a-Grille; Indian Rocks Beach, including Madeira Beach, Redington Beach, North Redington Beach, Reding-ton Shores, and Indian Shores; and, finally, Clearwater Beach.

ST. PETE BEACH

Crabby Bill's *Kids* SEAFOOD   The least-expensive gulf-side dining here, this member of a small local chain sits right on the beach in the heart of the hotel district. There's an open-air rooftop bar, but big glass windows enclose the large dining room. They offer fine water views from picnic tables equipped with rolls of paper towels and buckets of saltine crackers, the better to eat the blue, Alaskan, snow, and stone crabs that are the big draws here. The crustaceans fall into the moderate price category or higher, depending on the market, but most other main courses, such as fried fish or shrimp, are inexpensive—and they aren't overcooked or overbreaded. The creamy smoked fish spread is a delicious appetizer, and you'll get enough to whet the appetites of at least two persons. This is a very good place to feed the entire family.

5100 Gulf Blvd. (at 51st Ave.), St. Pete Beach. ✆ **727/360-8858.** Reservations not accepted. Main courses $7.50–$20; sandwiches $4.50–$7. AE, MC, V. Mon–Thurs 11:30am–10pm; Fri–Sat 11:30am–11pm; Sun noon–10pm.

Hurricane SEAFOOD   A longtime institution across the street from Pass-a-Grille Public Beach, this three-level gray Victorian building with white gingerbread trim is a great place to toast the sunset, especially at the rooftop bar. It's more beach pub than restaurant; but the grouper sandwiches are excellent, and there's always fresh fish to be fried, broiled, or blackened, and shrimp and crab to be steamed. Downstairs you can dine inside the knotty-pine paneled dining room or on the sidewalk terrace, where bathers from across Gulf Way are welcome (there's a walk-up bar for beach libation). The second-floor dining area also has seating on a wraparound verandah. You must be at least 21 years old to go up to the Hurricane Watch rooftop bar or to join the revelry when the second level turns into Stormy's Nightclub at 10pm Wednesday to Saturday.

807 Gulf Way (at 9th Ave.), Pass-a-Grille. ✆ **727/360-9558.** Reservations not accepted. Main courses $10–$18; sandwiches $7. AE, MC, V. Daily 8am–1am (breakfast Mon–Fri 8–11am; Sat–Sun 8am–noon).

Internet Outpost Cafe *Finds* PASTRIES/SANDWICHES   If you left your laptop at home and can't stand not getting your e-mail or surfing the Net, head for this cozy coffee emporium with nine computer terminals, all with fast Internet connections ($2 for 15 min. of access time). You can also lounge on the sofas and wing chairs while sipping your latte, passing a rainy afternoon playing chess. In addition to coffees, teas, and pastries available at all hours, the lunch fare (11am to 2pm) includes freshly made chicken salad, Cuban, spicy turkey, vegetarian, and other sandwiches.

7400 Gulf Blvd. (at Corey Ave./75th Ave.), St. Pete Beach. ✆ **727/360-7806.** Reservations not accepted. Coffee and pastries $1–$3; sandwiches $5–$6. AE, MC, V. Mon–Thurs 9am–10pm; Fri–Sat 9am–11pm.

Skidder's Restaurant *Value* ITALIAN/GREEK/AMERICAN   A local favorite, this inexpensive family restaurant in the hotel district offers a full range of breakfast fare plus handmade pan pizzas (available to eat here or carry out), burgers and sandwiches, big salads, gyro and souvlaki platters, and Italian-style veal, fish, and chicken dishes (Italian-style grouper is a house specialty). A children's menu features burgers and spaghetti.

5799 Gulf Blvd. (at 60th Ave.), St. Pete Beach. ✆ **727/360-1029.** Reservations accepted. Main courses $8–$16; breakfast $3–$6; sandwiches and burgers $3.50–$8; pizza $6–$16. AE, DC, DISC, MC, V. Daily 7am–11pm.

INDIAN ROCKS BEACH AREA

You'll find a bayfront edition of **Shells,** the fine and inexpensive local seafood chain, opposite the Lobster Pot on Gulf Boulevard at 178th Avenue in Redington

Shores (© **813/393-8990**). See "Where to Dine," in section 1, for more information about Shells's menu and prices, which are the same at all branches.

Beachside Grille ★ *Finds* SEAFOOD/RIBS Locals don't mind waiting for the best seafood bargains on the beach at Lynne and Douglas Casey's tiny place (seven tables plus five seats at the bar) tucked into the rear of a two-story commercial building opposite the landmark Friendly Tavern. They are rewarded with a savory Louisiana seafood gumbo as a starter, then fresh off-the-boat grouper or mahimahi grilled or blackened, salmon under a dill sauce, or grilled shrimp with a zesty fruit salsa. The smoky, falling-off-the-bone barbecued ribs justifiably have been voted the best on the beach. Char-grilled steaks and steamed shrimp and crab legs also appear. Main courses come with rice, sautéed vegetables, and a salad with the Caseys' superb pesto salad dressing—it's so good they sell it by the bottle. Try a pitcher of the homemade white or red sangria, another local favorite. You can order lunch to take to the beach (there's public access next door).

35 182nd Ave. (at Gulf Blvd., opposite Friendly Tavern), Redington Shores. © 727/397-1865. Reservations not accepted. Main courses $10–$15; sandwiches and burgers $5–$7.50. AE, DISC, MC, V. Daily 11am–10pm. Closed Thanksgiving and Christmas.

Guppy's ★★ SEAFOOD Locals also love this small bar and grill across from Indian Rocks Public Beach because they know they'll always get terrific chow (it's associated with the excellent Lobster Pot, below). You won't soon forget the salmon coated with potatoes and lightly fried, then baked with a creamy leek and garlic sauce; it's fattening, yes, but also a bargain at $10. Another good choice is lightly cooked tuna finished with a peppercorn sauce. The atmosphere is casual beach friendly, with a fun bar in the middle of it all. Scotty's famous upside-down apple-walnut pie topped with ice cream will require a little extra work on the weights tomorrow. You can dine outside on a patio beside the main road.

1701 Gulf Blvd. (at 17th Ave.), Indian Rocks Beach. © 727/593-2032. Reservations not accepted. Main courses $10–$20; sandwiches $5–$9. AE, DC, DISC, MC, V. Sun–Thurs 11:30am–10:30pm; Fri–Sat 11:30am–11pm.

Lobster Pot ★★ SEAFOOD/STEAKS Step into this weathered-looking restaurant near the beach, and owner Eugen Fuhrmann will tell you to get ready to experience the finest seafood in the area. The prices are high, but the variety of Maine lobster dishes is amazing. The lobster américaine is flambéed in brandy with garlic, and the bouillabaisse is as authentic as any you'd find in the south of France. In addition to lobster, there's a wide selection of grouper, snapper, salmon, swordfish, shrimp, scallops, crab, Dover sole, and steaks, most prepared with elaborate sauces. The children's menu here is definitely out of the ordinary: It features half a Maine lobster and a petite filet mignon.

17814 Gulf Blvd. (at 178th Ave.), Redington Shores. © 727/391-8592. Reservations recommended. Main courses $15.50–$39.50. AE, DC, MC, V. Mon–Thurs 4:30–10pm; Fri–Sat 4:30–11pm; Sun 4–10pm.

The Salt Rock Grill ★★ SEAFOOOD/STEAKS Affluent professionals and other gorgeous folk always pack this waterfront restaurant, making it *the* place to see and be seen on the beaches. The big urbane dining room is built on three levels, thus affording every table a view over the creeklike waterway out back. And in warm, fair weather you can dine out by the dock or slake your thirst at the lively tiki bar (bands play out here on Saturday and Sunday during the summer). Anything from the wood-fired grill is excellent here. Thick, aged steaks are the house specialties, as are crusted rack of lamb and Havana-style pork tenderloin. You can get a good sampling with the mixed grill: small portions of filet mignon, pork tenderloin, a two-bone lamb chop, and dessert-sweet coconut shrimp. Pan-seared peppered tuna and salmon cooked on a cedar board lead the seafoods. You can avoid spending a fortune by showing up in time for the early bird specials or by ordering the meatloaf topped with mashed potatoes and onion straws ($9) or the ½-pound sirloin steak ($11).

19325 Gulf Blvd. (north of 193rd Ave.), Indian Shores. ② **727/593-7625.** Reservations strongly advised. Main courses $9–$36 (early bird specials $8–$10). AE, DC, DISC, MC, V. Sun–Thurs 4–10pm; Fri–Sat 4–11pm (early bird specials daily 4–5:30pm. Tiki bar opens Sat–Sun 2pm.

CLEARWATER BEACH

Bob Heilman's Beachcomber ✪ AMERICAN   In a row of restaurants, bars, and T-shirt shops, Bob and Sherri Heilman's establishment has been popular with the locals since 1948. Each dining room here is unique: large models of sailing crafts create a nautical theme in one, a pianist makes music in a second, works of art create a gallery in the third, and booths and a fireplace make for a cozy fourth. The menu presents a variety of well-prepared fresh seafood and beef, veal, and lamb selections. If you tire of fruits-of-the-sea, the "back to the farm" fried chicken—from an original 1910 Heilman family recipe—is incredible. The Beachcomber shares valet parking and an extensive wine collection with Bobby's Bistro & Wine Bar (see below).

447 Mandalay Ave. (at Papaya St.). ② **727/442-4144.** Reservations recommended. Main courses $13–$29. AE, DC, DISC, MC, V. Mon–Sat 11:30am–11pm; Sun noon–10pm.

Bobby's Bistro & Wine Bar ✪ AMERICAN   Son of Bob Heilman's Beachcomber, this chic bistro draws a more urbane crowd than its parent. A wine-cellar theme is amply justified by the real thing: a walk-in closet with several thousand bottles kept at a constant 55°F. Walk through and pick your vintage, then listen to jazz while you dine inside at tall, bar-height tables or outside on a covered patio. The chef specializes in gourmet pizzas on homemade focaccia crust (as a tasty appetizer), plus charcoal-grilled veal chops, filet mignon, fresh fish, and monstrous pork chops with caramelized Granny Smith apples and a Mount Vernon mustard sauce. Everything's served a la carte here, so watch your credit card. On the other hand, there's an affordable sandwich menu featuring the likes of bronzed grouper and chicken with a spicy Jack cheese.

447 Mandalay Ave. (at Papaya St., behind Bob Heilman's Beachcomber). ② **727/446-9463.** Reservations accepted only for parties of 6 or more. Main courses $8–$22; sandwiches and pizzas $6–$10. AE, DC, DISC, MC, V. Sun–Thurs 5–11pm; Fri–Sat 5pm–midnight, bar later.

Frenchy's Café SEAFOOD   Always popular with locals and visitors in the know, this casual pub makes the best grouper sandwiches in the area and has all the awards to prove it. The sandwiches are fresh, thick, juicy, and delicious. The atmosphere is pure Florida casual style. There can be a wait during winter and on weekends all year-round. For a similarly relaxed setting, directly on the beach, **Frenchy's Rockaway Grill,** at 7 Rockaway St. (② **727/446-4844**), has a wonderful outdoor setting.

41 Baymont St. ② **727/446-3607.** Reservations not accepted. Sandwiches and burgers $5–$7.50. AE, MC, V. Mon–Thurs 11:30am–11pm; Fri–Sat 11:30am–midnight; Sun noon–11pm.

Seafood & Sunsets at Julie's ✪ *Value* SEAFOOD   A Key West–style tradition takes over Julie Nichols's place at dusk as both locals and visitors gather at

Mermaids & Manatees

Drive north of Clearwater for an hour on congested U.S. 19, and you'll come to one of Florida's original tourist attractions, the famous **Weeki Wachee Spring Water Park** (© 800/678-9335 or 352/596-2062; www.weekiwachee.com). "Mermaids" have been putting on acrobatic swimming shows here every day since 1947. It's a sight to see them doing their dances in waters that come from one of America's most prolific freshwater springs, pouring some 170 million gallons of 72°F (22°C) water a day into the river. There's more than mermaids here; you can take a Wilderness River Cruise across the Weeki Wachee River and send the kids on the flume ride at **Buccaneer Bay,** the water-park part of the attraction. Admission is $15.95 for adults, $11.95 for children 3 to 10. Kids under 3 get in free. The spring is open daily from 10am to 3pm in winter, to 4 or 5pm in spring and fall, to 6pm in the hot summer months (call for precise times and special shows). The water park is open from March to mid-autumn, daily from 10am to 5pm. You can also rent canoes (© 352/597-0360) and go scuba diving in the springs with **Neptune Divers** (© 352-597-4300; www.neptune-divers.com).

From Weeki Wachee, travel 21 miles north to the **Homosassa Springs State Wildlife Park,** 4150 S. Suncoast Blvd. (U.S. 19) in Homosassa Springs (© 352/628-5343; www8.myflorida.com/communities/learn/stateparks/district2/HomosassaSprings). The highlight here is a floating observatory where visitors can "walk" underwater and watch manatees in a rehabilitation facility, as well as thousands of fresh- and saltwater fish. You'll also see deer, bear, bobcats, otters, egrets, and flamingos

sidewalk tables or in the rustic upstairs bar to toast the sunset over the beach across the street. The predominantly seafood menu features fine and very reasonably priced renditions of charcoal-broiled mahimahi with sour cream, Parmesan and herb sauce; bacon-wrapped barbecued shrimp on a skewer; broiled, fried, or blackened fresh Florida grouper; and flounder stuffed with crabmeat. Everything is cooked to order here, so come prepared to linger over a cold drink.

351 S. Gulfview Blvd. (at 5th St.). © 727/441-2548. Reservations not accepted. Main courses $10–$18; salads and sandwiches $5–$9. AE, MC, V. Daily 11am–10pm.

THE BEACHES AFTER DARK
If you haven't already found it during your sightseeing and shopping excursions, the restored fishing community of **John's Pass Village and Boardwalk,** on Gulf Boulevard at John's Pass in Madeira Beach, has plenty of restaurants, bars, and shops to keep you occupied after the sun sets. Elsewhere, the nightlife scene at the beach revolves around rocking bars that pump out the music until 2am.

Down south in Pass-a-Grille is the popular, always-lively lounge in **Hurricane,** on Gulf Way at 9th Avenue opposite the public beach (see "Where to Dine," earlier in this chapter).

along unspoiled nature trails. The park is open daily from 9am to 5:30pm. Admission is $7.95 for adults and $4.95 for children 3 to 12, plus tax, and includes a 20-minute narrated boat ride. Kids under 3 get in free.

About 7 miles north of Homosassa Springs, some 300 manatees spend the winter in Crystal River, and you can **swim or snorkel with the manatees** ✿ in the warm-water natural spring of Kings Bay. **American Pro Diving Center,** 821 SE Hwy. 19, Crystal River, FL 34429 (✆ **800/291-DIVE** or 352/563-0041; fax 352/563-5230; www.americanprodive.com), offers daily swimming and snorkel tours. Early mornings are the best time to see the manatees, so try to take the 6:30am departure. The trips range from about $30 to $50 per person. Call for the schedule and reservations. American Pro Diving also rents cottages on the Homosassa River.

Baseball fans won't want to miss the **Ted Williams Museum & Hitters Hall of Fame,** 2455 N. Citrus Hills Blvd., off C.R. 486 west of Hernando (✆ **352/527-6566**). Built in the shape of a baseball diamond, the museum holds the great hitter's personal memorabilia, including his two Triple Crown batting titles. It's open Tuesday to Sunday from 10am to 4pm. Admission is $5 adults, $1 for children.

For more information about the area, contact the **Nature Coast Chamber of Commerce,** 28 NW Hwy. 19, Crystal River, FL 34425 (✆ **352/795-3149;** fax 352/795-4260). The chamber's visitor center is open Monday to Thursday from 8:30am to 5pm, Friday from 8:30am to 4pm.

On Treasure Island, **Beach Nutts,** on West Gulf Boulevard at 96th Avenue (✆ 727/367-7427), is perched atop a stilt foundation, like a wooden beach cottage, on the Gulf of Mexico. The music ranges from Top 40 to reggae and rock. Up on the northern tip of Treasure Island, **Gators on the Pass** (✆ 727/367-8951) claims to have the world's longest waterfront bar, with a huge deck overlooking the waters of John's Pass. The complex also includes a no-smoking sports bar and a three-story tower with a top-level observation deck for panoramic views of the Gulf of Mexico. There's live music, from acoustic and blues to rock, most nights.

In Clearwater Beach, the **Palm Pavilion Grill & Bar,** on the beach at 18 Bay Esplanade (✆ 727/446-6777), has live music Tuesday through Sunday nights during winter, on weekends off-season. Nearby, **Frenchy's Rockaway Grill,** at 7 Rockaway St. (✆ 727/446-4844), is another popular hangout.

If you're into laughs, **Coconuts Comedy Club,** at the Howard Johnson motel, Gulf Boulevard at 61st Avenue in St. Pete Beach (✆ 727/360-5653), has an ever-changing program of live stand-up funny men and women. Call for the schedule, performers, and prices.

For a more highbrow evening, go to the Clearwater mainland and the 2,200-seat **Ruth Eckerd Hall,** 1111 McMullen-Booth Rd. (✆ 727/791-7400; www. rutheckerdhall.com), which hosts a varied program of Broadway shows, ballet, drama, symphonic works, popular music, jazz, and country music.

4 An Excursion to Tarpon Springs ★★

30 miles N. of St. Petersburg, 23 miles W. of Tampa, 13 miles N. of Clearwater

One of Florida's most fascinating small towns and a fine day trip from Tampa, St. Petersburg, or the beaches, **Tarpon Springs** calls itself the "Sponge Capital of the World." That's because Greek immigrants from the Dodecanese Islands settled here in the late 19th century to harvest sponges, which grew in abundance offshore. By the 1930s, Tarpon Springs was producing more sponges than any other place in the world. A blight ruined the business in the 1940s, but the descendants of those early immigrants stayed on. Today they compose about a third of the population, making Tarpon Springs a center of transplanted Greek culture.

Although sponges still arrive at the historic Sponge Docks on Dodecanese Boulevard, the town's mainstays today are commercial fishing and tourism. With a lively, carnival-like atmosphere, the docks are a great place to spend an afternoon or early evening, poking your head into shops selling sponges and other souvenirs while Greek music comes from the dozen or so family restaurants purveying authentic Aegean cuisine. You can also venture offshore from here, because booths on the docks hawk sightseeing and fishing cruises.

Just south of the docks, restored Victorian homes facing the winding creek known as Spring Bayou make this one of the most picturesque towns in the state.

ESSENTIALS
GETTING THERE   From Tampa or St. Petersburg, take U.S. 19 north and turn left on Tarpon Avenue (C.R. 582). From Clearwater Beach, take Alt. U.S. 19 north through Dunedin. The center of the historic downtown district is at the intersection of Pinellas Avenue (Alt. U.S. 19) and Tarpon Avenue. To reach the Sponge Docks, go 10 blocks north on Pinellas Avenue and turn left at Pappas' Restaurant onto Dodecanese Boulevard.

VISITOR INFORMATION   The **Tarpon Springs Chamber of Commerce,** 11 E. Orange St., Tarpon Springs, FL 34689 (© **727/937-6109;** fax 727/ 937-2879; www.tarponsprings.com), has an information office on Dodecanese Boulevard at the Sponge Docks, which is open Tuesday to Saturday from 10:30am to 4:30pm, Sunday from 11am to 5pm.

EXPLORING THE TOWN
Two areas are worth visiting here. You'll first come to the **Tarpon Springs Downtown Historic District,** with its turn-of-the-last-century commercial buildings along Tarpon Avenue and Pinellas Avenue (Alt. U.S. 19). The **Tarpon Springs Cultural Center,** on Pinellas Avenue a block south of Tarpon Avenue, explains the town's history and has visitor information. On Tarpon Avenue west of Pinellas Avenue, you'll come to the Victorian homes overlooking **Spring Bayou.** This creek-side area makes for a delightfully picturesque stroll.

The carnival-like **Sponge Docks** run alongside Dodecanese Boulevard, which is peppered with shops, restaurants, and fishing and sightseeing boats pulling at their mooring lines along the riverside boardwalk. Poke your head into the tin-roofed **Spongeorama** (no phone), a museum dedicated to sponges and sponge divers. You can buy a wide variety of sponges here (they'll ship your purchase home) and watch a 30-minute video several times a day about sponge diving.

Admission is free. The Spongeorama is open daily from 10am to 5pm. In the **Coral Sea Aquarium,** at the western end of the boulevard (© 727/938-5378), a scuba diver feeds sharks at 11:30am and at 1, 2:30, and 4pm. The aquarium is open daily from 10am to 5pm. Admission is $4.75 adults, $4 seniors, $2.75 for children 3 to 11, free for kids under 3.

You also can go on sightseeing, lunch, or sunset cruises down the Anclote River with **Island Wind Cruises** (© 727/934-6208); spend 30 minutes watching the sponge divers at work with **St. Nicolas Boat Line** (© 727/942-6425); or try your luck out in the gulf on a party boat operated by **Miss Milwaukee Boat Lines** (© 727/937-5678). Booths along the docks sell tickets for these and other excursions. Make your reservations as soon as you get here; then go sightseeing ashore while you wait for the next boat to shove off.

Bikers, in-line skaters, hikers, and joggers can come right through downtown on the **Pinellas Trail,** which runs along Safford Avenue and crosses Tarpon Avenue 2 blocks east of Pinellas Avenue (see "Outdoor Activities & Spectator Sports" in section 2, earlier in this chapter).

WHERE TO DINE

Your Tarpon Springs experience would be incomplete without taking a Greek meal here. In addition to Hellas Restaurant & Bakery listed below, you'll find about a dozen other family-owned restaurants along the lively Sponge Docks, all of them clean, inviting, and serving authentic, inexpensive Greek fare.

Weight watchers should studiously avoid the **Parthenon Bakery & Pastry Shop,** 751 Dodecanese Blvd. (© 727/938-7709), where huge cabinets are filled with Greek and other delights, including luscious chocolate-covered baklava. The shop is open daily 9am to 10pm.

Hellas Restaurant & Bakery *Value* GREEK The lovely hand-painted tile tables on the street-side patio here make fine spots from which to watch the action on the Sponge Docks while sampling authentic Aegean cuisine. If you like feta cheese, you'll enjoy the pungent Greek-style shrimp or scallops. If not, opt for the perfectly panfried grouper or any of the Aegean standbys: moussaka, pastisio, dolmades, or one of the largest gyro sandwiches in town (you can try a little of each on the sampler platter). The bakery supplies baklava, galactombouriko (egg custard), and other desserts from the old country. With Greek cuisine, Greek music, and a Greek-looking (if not Greek-accented) waiter, it's easy to imagine yourself quayside on Mykonos.

Sponge Docks, 785 Dodecanese Blvd. © 727/943-2400. Reservations accepted. Main courses $7.50–$14; sandwiches and salads $4–$6. AE, DC, DISC, MC, V. Daily 11am–10pm.

Louis Pappas' Restaurant and Riverside Cafe GREEK/SEAFOOD The most upscale restaurant here, Pappas is famous statewide for its fresh Greek- and American-style seafood—shrimp, grouper, red snapper, and even stone crab claws in season—most of it right off the boat. There are also Greek salads and other dishes with an Aegean flair. The family-run restaurant has been operating on the banks of the Anclote River since 1925, when it was founded by Louis Pappamichaelopoulus of Sparta, Greece. You get nice river views from the tall windows of this modern building.

Sponge Docks, 10 Dodecanese Blvd. (at Pinellas Ave./Alt. U.S. 19). © 727/937-5101. Reservations accepted. Main courses $10–$18; sandwiches $6–$8. AE, MC, V. Sun–Thurs 11:30am–10pm; Fri–Sat 11:30am–11pm (bar closes 1 hr. later).

5 Sarasota & Bradenton ★★★

52 miles S. of Tampa, 150 miles SW of Orlando, 225 miles NW of Miami

Far enough away from Tampa Bay to have an identity very much its own, Sarasota is one of Florida's cultural centers. In fact, many retirees spend their winters here because there's so much to keep them entertained and stimulated, including the very fine Asolo Center for the Performing Arts and the Van Wezel Performing Arts Hall. Like Naples down in Southwest Florida, Sarasota also has an extensive array of first-class resorts, restaurants, and upscale boutiques. Its neighbor, the riverside city of Bradenton, is much more down-to-earth, with many of its residents earning their livelihood at the city's huge Tropicana juice factory. You can drive up to Bradenton to visit its most famous resident, "Snooty" the manatee.

Offshore, more than 40 miles of gloriously white beaches fringe a chain of long, narrow barrier islands stretching from Tampa Bay to Sarasota. To the south, **Siesta Key** is a quiet residential enclave popular with artisans and writers and is home to Siesta Village, this area's funky, laid-back, and often-noisy beach hangout. Shielded from the gulf by **Lido Key,** which has a string of affordable hotels attractive to family vacationers, **St. Armands Key** sports one of Florida's ritziest shopping and dining districts, while adjacent **Longboat Key** is one of the country's swankiest islands. To the north off Bradenton, **Anna Maria Island** boasts no glitzy resorts, just casual island getaways popular with cost-conscious family vacationers.

Legend has it that Sarasota was named after the explorer Hernando de Soto's daughter, Sara (hence, Sara-sota). In more recent times, the town's most famous resident was circus legend John Ringling, who came here in the 1920s. Ringling built a palatial bayfront mansion known as Ca'd'Zan, acquired extensive real-estate holdings, erected a magnificent museum to house his world-class collection of baroque paintings, and built the causeway out to St. Armands and Lido Keys.

ESSENTIALS

GETTING THERE   You probably will get a less-expensive airfare by flying into **Tampa International Airport,** an hour's drive north of Sarasota (see "Essentials," in section 1, earlier in this chapter), and you could save even more since Tampa's rental-car agencies often offer some of the best deals in Florida. If you don't rent a car, **Sarasota-Tampa Express** (© **800/326-2800** or 941/727-1344) provides bus connections for $20 per person. Reservations are required.

If you decide to fly directly here, **Sarasota-Bradenton International Airport** (© **941/359-2770**), north of downtown off University Parkway between U.S. 41 and U.S. 301, is served by **America Trans Air** (© 800/225-2995), **American** (© 800/433-7300), **Canada 3000** (© 800/993-4378), **Continental** (© 800/525-0280), **Delta** (© 800/221-1212), **Northwest/KLM** (© 800/225-2525), **TWA** (© 800/221-2000), and **US Airways** (© 800/428-4322).

Alamo (© 800/327-9633), **Avis** (© 800/331-1212), **Budget** (© 800/527-0700), **Dollar** (© 800/800-4000), **Enterprise** (© 800/325-8007), **Hertz** (© 800/654-3131), and **National** (© 800/CAR-RENT) have car rentals here.

Diplomat Taxi (© **941/355-5155**) has a monopoly on service from the airport to hotels in Sarasota and Bradenton. Look for the cabs at the west end of the terminal outside baggage claim. The fare is about $9 to downtown Sarasota,

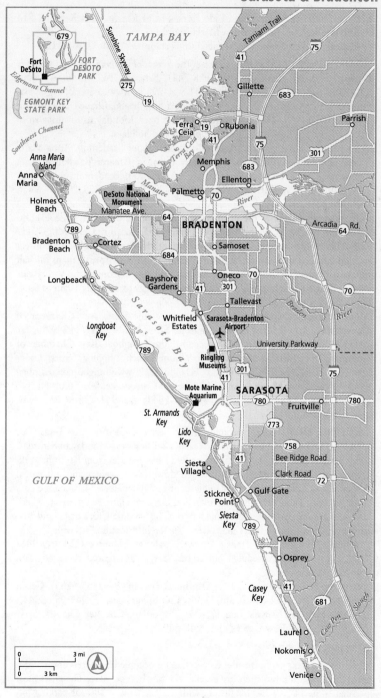

Sarasota & Bradenton

TAMPA BAY

Tamiami Trail

Sunshine Skyway

679
Fort
DeSoto
FORT
DESOTO
PARK

Edgemont Channel

275

EGMONT KEY
STATE PARK

Southwest Channel

19

Terra
Ceia
19
Rubonia

41

Gillette

683

Parrish

41

75

75

301

Anna Maria
Island
Anna
Maria

Memphis

683

Holmes
Beach

DeSoto National
Monument
Manatee Ave.

Ellenton

Palmetto

70

Manatee
River

Arcadia Rd.

789

64

BRADENTON

64

Bradenton
Beach

Cortez

684

Samoset

70

Longbeach

Bayshore
Gardens

Oneco

70

41

301

Tallevast

Longboat
Key

789

Sarasota Bay

Whitfield
Estates

Sarasota-Bradenton
Airport

Braden
River

University Parkway

Ringling
Museums

75

301

41

Mote Marine
Aquarium

SARASOTA

St. Armands
Key

780

Fruitville

780

Lido
Key

773

758

Bee Ridge Road

Siesta
Village

41

Clark Road

72

GULF OF MEXICO

Stickney
Point

Gulf Gate

Siesta
Key

789

Vamo

Osprey

Casey
Key

41

681

Cow Pen Slough

Laurel

Nokomis

N

0   3 mi
0   3 km

Venice

$10 to $15 to St. Armands and Lido Keys, $14 to $23 to Siesta Key, and $14 to $32 to Longboat Key or Anna Maria Island.

Amtrak has bus connections to its Tampa station (© **800/USA-RAIL**).

VISITOR INFORMATION   Contact the **Sarasota Convention and Visitors Bureau,** 655 N. Tamiami Trail (U.S. 41), Sarasota, FL 34236 (© **800/ 522-9799** or 941/957-1877; fax 941/951-2956; www.sarasotafl.org). The bureau and its helpful visitor center are in a blue pagoda-shaped building on Tamiami Trail (U.S. 41) at 6th Street. They're open Monday to Saturday from 9am to 5pm, Sunday from 11am to 3pm; closed holidays.

You can get a packet of advance information about Bradenton, Anna Maria Island, and surrounding Manatee County from the **Greater Bradenton Area Convention and Visitors Bureau,** P.O. Box 1000, Bradenton, FL 34206 (© **800/4-MANATEE** or 941/729-9177; fax 941/729-1820; www. floridaislandbeaches.org).

If you're driving from the north via I-75, get off at U.S. 301 (Exit 43) and head west to the **Manatee County Tourist Information Center** (© **941/ 729-7040**). Open daily except holidays from 8:30am to 5pm, it has a volunteer staff on hand to answer your questions, and it sells excellent road maps for half off the list price. The office has an information kiosk in front of the Vanity Fair store at **Prime Outlets,** across I-75. It's open Monday to Saturday 10am to 6pm, Sunday 11am to 6pm.

For information specific to the keys, contact the **Siesta Key Chamber of Commerce,** 5100-B Ocean Blvd., Sarasota, FL 34242 (© **941/349-3800;** fax 941/349-9699; www.siestakeychamber.com); the **Longboat Key Chamber of Commerce,** 6854 Gulf of Mexico Dr. (in Whitney Beach Shopping Center), Longboat Key, FL (© **941/383-2466;** fax 941/383-8217; www.longboatkeychamber. com); or the **Anna Maria Island Chamber of Commerce,** 5337 Gulf Dr. N., Holmes Beach, FL 34217 (© **941/778-1541;** fax 941/778-9679; www. amichamber.org).

GETTING AROUND   Operated by the Sarasota County Area Transit, or SCAT (© **941/316-1234**), the free **Sarasota Trolley** runs Monday to Saturday, every 20 minutes from 9am to 5pm. Its Red Line operates from Bayfront Park, Bayfront at Ringling Boulevard, through downtown Sarasota and out to St. Armands and Lido Keys (but not to Siesta or Longboat Keys). A Blue Line goes from Bayfront Park through downtown and eastward along Main Street. SCAT also operates regularly scheduled bus service. The Sarasota Convention and Visitors Bureau distributes route maps (see "Visitor Information," above).

Manatee County Area Transit, known locally as **Manatee CAT** (© **941/ 749-7116**), operates scheduled public bus service throughout the Bradenton and Anna Maria area.

Sarasota taxi companies include **Diplomat Taxi** (© 941/355-5155), **Green Cab Taxi** (© 941/922-6666), and **Yellow Cab of Sarasota** (© 941/955-3341). In Bradenton call **Bruce's Taxi** (© 941/755-6070), **Checker Cab** (© 941/ 751-3181), and **Yellow Cab** (© 941/748-4800).

HITTING THE BEACH

Many of the area's 40-plus miles of beaches are occupied by hotels and condominium complexes, but there are excellent public beaches here. The area's most popular is **Siesta Key Public Beach,** with a picnic area, a 700-car parking lot, crowds of families, and quartz sand reminiscent of the blazingly white beaches in Northwest Florida. There's also beach access at **Siesta Village,** which has a plethora of casual restaurants and pubs with outdoor seating (see "Where to Dine," later in this chapter). More secluded and quiet is **Turtle Beach,** at Siesta Key's south end. It has shelters, boat ramps, picnic tables, and volleyball nets.

After you've driven the length of Longboat Key and admired the luxurious homes and condominiums blocking access to the beach, take a right off St. Armands Circle onto Lido Key and **North Lido Beach.** The south end of the island is occupied by **South Lido Beach Park,** with plenty of shade making it a good spot for picnics and walks.

On Anna Maria Island the largest and best is **Coquina Beach,** which occupies the southern mile of the island below Bradenton Beach. It has both gulf and bay sides, is sheltered by whispering Australian pines, and has a nature trail and large parking lots. **Cortez Beach** is in Bradenton Beach, just north of Coquina Beach. In the island's center, **Manatee County Public Beach** is at Gulf Drive. **Holmes Beach** is at the west end of Manatee Avenue (Fla. 64). **Anna Maria Bayfront Park** is on Bay Boulevard at the northwest end of the island, fronting both the bay and the Gulf of Mexico.

OUTDOOR ACTIVITIES & SPECTATOR SPORTS

BICYCLING & IN-LINE SKATING   The flat terrain makes for good in-line skating and for fine if not challenging bike riding. You can bike and skate from downtown Sarasota to Lido and Longboat Keys, since paved walkways/bike paths run alongside the John Ringling Causeway and then up Longboat Key. **Siesta Sports Rentals,** 6551 Midnight Pass Rd., in the Southbridge Mall just south of Stickney Point Bridge on Siesta Key (© **941/346-1797**), rents bikes of various sizes, including stroller attachments for kids, plus motor scooters, in-line skates, kayaks, and beach chairs and umbrellas. Bike rentals range from about $14 a day to $50 a week. The shop is open daily 9am to 5pm.

On Anna Maria, **Island Rental Service,** 3214 E. Bay Dr. (© **800/248-8797** or 941/778-1472), next to Shells Restaurant in Holmes Beach; **Native Rentals,** in S&S Plaza, 5340 Marina Dr. in Holmes Beach (© **941/778-7757**); and **Neumann's Island Beach Store,** 427 Pine Ave., at Tarpon Street in Anna Maria (© **941/778-3316**), all rent bikes and various beach equipment. Island Rental Service will deliver.

BOAT RENTALS   **All Watersports,** in the Boatyard Shopping Village, on the mainland end of Stickney Point Bridge (© **941/921-2754**), rents personal watercraft such as jet skis, speedboats, runabouts, and bowriders. At the island end of the bridge, **C. B.'s Saltwater Outfitters,** 1249 Stickney Point Rd. (© **941/349-4400**), and **Siesta Key Boat Rentals,** 1265 Old Stickney Point Rd. (© **941/349-8880**), both rent runabouts, pontoon boats, and other craft. Bait and tackle are available at the marinas.

On Anna Maria Island, you can rent boats from **Bradenton Beach Marina,** 402 Church Ave. (© **941/778-2288**); **Captain's Marina,** 5501 Marina Dr., Holmes Beach (© **941/778-1977**); and **Five O'Clock Marina,** 412 Pine Ave., Anna Maria (© **941/778-5577**). On northern Longboat Key, **Cannons Marina,** 6040 Gulf of Mexico Dr. (© **941/383-1311**), also rents boats. Several deep-sea fishing charter boats are based at these marinas.

CRUISES   The area's best nature cruises go forth from Mote Marine Aquarium (see "Exploring the Area," below).

From October to May, you can head over to Marina Jack's Marina, U.S. 41 at Island Park Circle, for 2-hour dolphin-watching, sightseeing, and sunset cruises around Sarasota's waterways aboard the 65-foot, two-deck *Le Barge* (© **941/366-6116**). The cruises run Tuesday to Sunday, with the dolphin-watching excursion departing at 11am, the sightseeing cruise at 2pm. The sunset cruises with live music change with the time of sunset. The cruises cost $15 adults, $10 for kids under 13. Snacks and libations are available for an extra charge, but credit cards are not accepted. Call for reservations.

That paddle wheeler you see going up and down the bay is the *Seafood Shack Showboat*, operated by the Seafood Shack restaurant, 4110 127th St. W., in Cortez (© **800/299-5048** or 941/794-5048). It has afternoon and sunset cruises to Sarasota Bay, Tampa Bay, and as far away as the Sunshine Skyway. Prices range from $13 to $15 for adults, $11 to $13 for seniors, and $4.70 to $5.65 for children 4 to 11. The *Showboat* goes to a different destination each day and may be cancelled in inclement weather, so call for the schedule and reservations.

FISHING   Charter fishing boats dock at most marinas here. Check out www. sarasotaboating.com for a list. In downtown Sarasota, the **Flying Fish Fleet,** at Marina Jack's Marina, U.S. 41 at Island Park Circle (© **941/366-3373**), offers party-boat charter fishing excursions, with bait and tackle furnished. Prices for half-day trips are $30 adults, $25 seniors, $20 for kids 4 to 12. All-day voyages cost $45, $40, and $35, respectively. Call for the schedule. Charter boats also line up along the dock here.

In the old fishing village of Cortez, at the east end of the Cortez Bridge opposite Bradenton Beach, you can go deep-sea fishing with the **Cortez Fleet,** 4330 127th St. W. (© **941/794-1223**). Party-boat deep-sea fishing voyages range from 4 to 9 hours, with prices starting at $28 for adults, $25 for seniors, and $14 for children. Call for the schedules, which can change from day to day.

You also can fish for free from **Anna Maria City Pier,** on the north end of Anna Maria Island, and at the **Bradenton Beach City Pier,** at Cortez Road.

GOLF   The **Bobby Jones Golf Complex** ⚐, 1000 Circus Blvd. (© **941/ 365-GOLF**), is Sarasota's only municipal facility, but it has two 18-hole championship layouts—the American (par-71) and British (par-72) courses—and the 9-hole Gillespie executive course (par-30). Tee times are assigned 3 days in advance. Greens fees range from $25 to $31, including cart rental.

You can also tune your game at the public **Village Green Golf Club,** 3500 Pembroke Dr., near Bee Ridge and Beneva roads (© **941/925-2755**), whose executive-length 18 holes can be parred in 58.

The semiprivate **Rolling Green Golf Club,** 4501 Tuttle Ave. (© **941/ 355-6620**), is an 18-hole, par-72 course. Facilities include a driving range, rental clubs, and lessons. Tee times are assigned 2 days in advance. Prices, including cart, are about $40 in winter, $25 off-season. Also semiprivate, the **Sarasota Golf Club,** 7820 N. Leewynn Dr. (© **941/371-2431**), is an 18-hole, par-72 course. Facilities include a driving range, lessons, club rentals, a restaurant, a lounge, and a golf shop. Fees, including cart, are about $42 in winter, $25 off-season.

If you have reciprocal privileges, **University Park Country Club,** west of I-75 on University Parkway (© **941/359-9999**), is Sarasota's only nationally ranked course.

In Bradenton, locals say they prefer the county's 18-hole, par-72 **Buffalo Creek Golf Course,** on the north side of the river at 8100 Erie Rd. in Palmetto (© **941/776-2611**). At well over 7,000 yards, it's the longest in the area, and lots of water and alligators will keep you entertained. Wintertime greens fees are about $35 with cart, $25 without. They drop to about $18 and $16, respectively, during summer. You'll pay the same at **Manatee County Golf Course,** 5290 66th St. W. (✆ **941/792-6773**), an 18-hole, par-72 course on the southern rim of the city. Both county courses require that tee times be set up at least 2 days in advance. Also open to the public, the city's **River Run Golf Links,** 1801 27th St. E. (✆ **941/747-6331**), set beside the Braden River, is an 18-hole, par-70 course with lots of water in its layout. Winter fees here are about $26 with cart, $17 walking. They're about $16 riding, $8 walking in summer. A 2-day advance notice is required for tee times here too.

Other courses include the **Palma Sola Golf Club,** 3807 75th St. W. (✆ **941/792-7476**), just north of Fla. 684 and east of Palma Sola Bay, with an 18-hole, par-72 course and the same 2-day advance booking requirement.

Situated just off U.S. 41, the **Heather Hills Golf Club,** 101 Cortez Rd. W. (✆ **941/755-8888**), operates an 18-hole, par-61 executive course on a first-come, first-served basis. There's a driving range and clubs can be rented. It's open daily from 6:30am until dark.

Bradenton also is home to the well-known **David Leadbetter Golf Academy,** 1414 69th Ave., at U.S. 41 (✆ **800/424-3542** or 941/739-2483; www.leadbetter.com), a part of the Nick Bollettieri Sports Academy (see "Tennis," below). Presided over by one of golf's leading instructors, this facility offers practice tee instruction, video analysis, and scoring strategy, as well as general tuition.

KAYAKING Based at Mote Marine Aquarium (see "Exploring the Area," below), **Sarasota Bay Explorers** ★★ (✆ **941/388-4200**), uses a 38-foot pontoon boat to ferry both novice and experienced kayakers and their craft to a marine sanctuary, where everyone paddles through tunnels formed by mangroves to visit the creatures. The paddling is easy and the waters are shallow. Experienced naturalists serve as guides. Wear swimsuits and tennis shoes or rubber-soled booties, and bring a towel and lunch. The 3-hour trips cost $50 for adults, $40 for children 5 to 17, free for kids under 5 (seats are provided for the youngsters). Call for reservations.

On Anna Maria, **Native Rentals,** in S&S Plaza, 5340 Marina Dr., opposite the BP service station in Holmes Beach (✆ **941/778-7757**), rents one- and two-person kayaks and has guided tours around the mangrove islands dotting some of the bay near here. Rentals start at $29 for 4 hours, $39 a day. Guided tours cost $10 per person. Call for details about the tours.

SAILING The 41-foot, 12-passenger sailboat *Enterprise,* docked at Marina Jack's Marina, U.S. 41 at Island Park Circle (✆ **941/951-1833**), cruises the waters of both Sarasota Bay and the Gulf of Mexico. Half-day cruises cost $35; the sunset cruise, $20. Departure times vary, and reservations are required.

Siesta Key Sailing, 1219 Southport Dr. (✆ **941/346-7245;** www.siestakeysailing.com), has half-day, full-day, and 2-day cruises. Reservations are essential.

You can also get to historic Egmont Key, 3 miles off the northern end of Anna Maria Island at the mouth of Tampa Bay (see "Cruises," under "Outdoor Activities," in section 3, earlier in this chapter, for more information), on a 30-foot sloop-rigged sailboat with **Spice Sailing Charters** (✆ **941/778-3240**), based at the Galati Yacht Basin on Bay Boulevard on northern Anna Maria Island. The company also has sunset cruises. Call for schedule, prices, and reservations, which are required.

SPECTATOR SPORTS **Ed Smith Stadium,** 2700 12th St., at Tuttle Avenue, east of downtown (© **941/954-4464**), is the winter home of the **Cincinnati Reds** (© **941/955-6501;** www.cincinnatireds.com), who hold spring training here in February and March. From April to August, the stadium is home to the **Sarasota Red Sox** (© **941/365-4460,** ext. 2300; www.sarasox.com), a Class A minor-league affiliate of the Boston Red Sox.

The **Pittsburgh Pirates** (© **941/748-4610;** www.pirateball.com) do their February-through-March spring training at 6,562-seat McKechnie Field, 9th Street West and 17th Avenue West, south of downtown Bradenton.

The **Sarasota Polo Club,** 8201 Polo Club Lane, Sarasota (© **941/ 359-0000**), midway between Sarasota and Bradenton, is the site of weekly polo matches from November through March, on Sunday afternoons. Call for the schedule of matches and admission fees.

TENNIS The **Nick Bollettieri Sports Academy,** 5500 34th St. W. (© **800/ 872-6425** or 941/755-1000; www.bollettieri.com), is one of the world's largest tennis training facilities, with more than 70 championship courts and a pro shop. It's open year-round, and reservations are required for all activities. The academy also has training courses in soccer, baseball, and golf.

WATER SPORTS You'll find water-sports activities in front of the major hotels out on the keys (see "Where to Stay," later in this chapter). **Siesta Sports Rentals,** 6551 Midnight Pass Rd. on Siesta Key (© **813/346-1797**), rents kayaks and sailboats, plus beach chairs and umbrellas. You can soar above the bay with **Siesta Parasail,** based at C. B.'s Saltwater Outfitters at the western end of the Stickney Point Bridge (© **941/349-1900;** www.siestaparasail.com).

The downtown Sarasota center for jet skiing, wave running, sailing, and other water-sports activities is **O'Leary's,** in the Island Park Marina, U.S. 41 and Island Park Circle (© **941/953-7505**). It's open daily from 8am to 8pm.

EXPLORING THE AREA
IN SARASOTA

Art Center Sarasota Sarasota is home to more than 40 art galleries and exhibition spaces, all open to the public year-round. A convenient artistic starting point is this downtown community art center, next to the Sarasota Convention and Visitors Bureau. It contains three galleries and a small sculpture garden, presenting the area's largest display of art by national and local artists, from paintings and pottery to sculpture, cartoons, jewelry, and enamelware. There are also art demonstrations and special events.

707 N. Tamiami Trail (at 6th St.). © 941/365-2032. www.artsarasota.org. Admission free ($2 suggested donation). Tues–Sun 10am–4pm.

Marie Selby Botanical Gardens ★★ A must-see for serious plant lovers, this peaceful retreat on the bay just south of downtown is said to be the only botanical garden in the world specializing in the preservation, study, and research of epiphytes; that is, "air plants" such as orchids. It's home to more than 20,000 exotic plants, including more than 6,000 orchids, as well as a bamboo pavilion, a butterfly and hummingbird garden, a medicinal plant garden, a waterfall garden, a cactus and succulent garden, a fernery, a hibiscus garden, a palm grove, two tropical food gardens, and a native shore-plant community. Selby's home and the Payne Mansion (both on the National Registry) are also located here.

811 S. Palm Ave. (south of U.S. 41). © 941/366-5731. www.selby.org. Admission $8 adults, $4 children 6–11, free for children 5 and under accompanied by an adult. Daily 10am–5pm. Closed Christmas.

Ringling Museums ★★   By far the top attraction here, this 60-acre site is where showman John Ringling and his wife, Mable, collected art and built houses on a grand scale. Now under the aegis of Florida State University, **The John and Mable Ringling Museum of Art** is the state's official art museum. It's filled with more than 500 years of European and American art, including one of the world's most important collections of grand 17th-century baroque paintings. The old-master collection also includes five world-renowned tapestry cartoons by Peter Paul Rubens and his studio. The museum also contains collections of decorative arts and traveling exhibits. Built in 1925 and modeled after a Venetian palace, the Ringlings' 30-room winter residence **Ca'd'Zan** ("House of John" in the Venetian dialect) has been closed for a substantial restoration; it was scheduled to reopen in the fall of 2001. An 8,000-square-foot terrace leads down to the dock at which Mable Ringling moored her Venetian gondola. The **Ringling Museum of the Circus** is devoted to circus memorabilia including parade wagons, calliopes, costumes, and colorful posters. The grounds also include a classical courtyard, a rose garden, a museum shop, and the historic **Asolo Theater,** a 19th-century Italian court playhouse, which the Ringlings moved here in the 1950s. It's now the centerpiece of the Florida State University Center for the Performing Arts. You'll need most of a day to see it all. It's best to visit on a weekday when you can take a guided tour of the art museum. The Banyan Cafe serves lunch daily.

5401 Bay Shore Rd. at N. Tamiami Trail (U.S. 41). ✆ 941/359-5700 or 941/351-1660 for recorded information. www.ringling.org. Admission $9 adults, $8 seniors, free for children 12 and under. Admission free Sat to art museum. Daily 10am–5:30pm. Art museum tours Mon–Fri 10:15, 10:45, 11:15, and 11:45am, and 1:15, 1:45, 2:15, and 2:45pm. West Gallery tours Mon–Fri 11:00am. Closed New Year's Day, Thanksgiving, Christmas. From downtown, take U.S. 41 north to University Pkwy. and follow signs to museum.

Sarasota Classic Car Museum   There's more to this museum than its 90-plus classic and "muscle" autos, from Rolls-Royces and Pierce Arrows to the four cars used personally by circus czar John Ringling. Also here are more than 1,200 antique music boxes and several of Thomas Edison's early phonographs, including a 1909 diamond-tipped needle model. Check out the Penny Arcade with antique games, and grab a cone at the ice-cream and sandwich shop.

5500 N. Tamiami Trail (at University Pkwy.). ✆ 941/355-6228. www.sarasotacarmuseum.org. Admission $8.50 adults, $7.65 seniors, $5.75 children 13–17, $4 children 6–12, free for children under 6. Daily 9am–6pm. Take U.S. 41 north of downtown; museum is 2 blocks west of the airport.

Sarasota Jungle Gardens (Kids)   If you don't mind black Asian leopards, squirrel monkeys, and other animals going stir-crazy in cages, you and the kids should enjoy this commercial park's lush tropical vegetation, cool jungle trails, tropical plants, alligators and other reptiles, and exotic waterfowl including a resident flock of pink flamingoes. Among the reptiles is "Roscoe," a huge Aldabra tortoise similar to those found in the Galapagos Islands. Children like the petting zoo, pony rides, and bird and animal shows, too (call for a show schedule).

3701 Bayshore Rd. ✆ 941/355-5305. www.sarasotajunglegardens.com. Admission $10 adults, $9 seniors, $6 children 3–12, free for children 2 and under. Daily 9am–5pm. Closed Christmas. From downtown, take U.S. 41 north to Myrtle St., turn left, and go 2 blocks.

ON ST. ARMANDS KEY

Mote Marine Aquarium ★★ (Kids)   Kids get to touch cool stuff like a stingray (minus the stinger, of course) and watch sharks in the shark tank at this excellent aquarium. Part of the noted Mote Marine Laboratory complex, it is more broad-based than Tampa's Florida Aquarium, which concentrates primarily on local sea life. The kids won't believe all the seahorse babies that come from the dad's pouch (one of Mother Nature's strange-but-true surprises), and they surely will gawk at a 35-foot-long deceased giant squid (it was 45 feet long when alive). They can see manatees in the Marine Mammal Center, a block's walk from the aquarium. There are also many research-in-progress exhibits. Start by watching the aquarium's 12-minute film on the feeding habits of sharks; then allow at least 90 minutes to take in everything on land and another 90 minutes to take a narrated sea-life encounter cruise with **Sarasota Bay Explorers** (© **727/ 388-4200**). These fun and informative cruises visit a deserted island, and the guides throw out nets and bring up sea life for inspection. This company has unusual kayaking adventures too (see "Outdoor Activities & Spectator Sports," above).

1600 Ken Thompson Pkwy. (on City Island). © **800/691-MOTE** or 941/388-4441. www.mote.org. Admission $10 adults, $7 children 4–17, free for children 3 and under. Nature cruises $24 adults, $20 children 4–17, free for kids under 4. Combination aquarium-cruise tickets $29 adults, $23 children. Daily 10am–5pm. Nature cruises daily 11am, 1:30pm, and 4pm. From St. Armands Circle, go north toward Longboat Key; turn right just before the Lido-Longboat bridge.

Pelican Man's Bird Sanctuary   Next to the Mote Marine Aquarium (see above), this sanctuary and rehabilitation center treats more than 5,000 injured birds and other wildlife each year. It is home to about 30 species of birds. Allow about 30 minutes to see it all, a few more to check out the gift shop with many bird-oriented items for sale.

1708 Ken Thompson Pkwy. © **941/388-4444**. Admission by donation ($4 adults), free for children 18 and under. Daily 10am–5pm.

IN AND NEAR BRADENTON

On weekends, you can see the sights of rural Manatee County northwest of Bradenton on a 1¼-hour narrated sightseeing tour aboard a 1950s diesel-engine train operated by the **Florida Gulf Coast Railroad Museum,** 83rd Street East, off U.S. 301 in Parrish (© **877/869-0800** or 941/722-4272; www.fgcrrm.org). The schedule and fares are seasonal, so call before driving out here.

DeSoto National Memorial   Nestled on the Manatee River west of downtown, this park attracts history buffs by re-creating the look and atmosphere of the period when Spanish explorer Hernando de Soto landed here in 1539. It includes a restoration of de Soto's original campsite and a scenic half-mile nature trail that circles a mangrove jungle and leads to the ruins of one of the first settlements in the area. Start by watching a 21-minute film about de Soto in America. From December to March, park employees dress in 16th-century costumes and portray the way the early settlers lived, including demonstrations of cooking and the firing of an arquebus, one of the world's earliest firearms.

DeSoto Memorial Hwy. (north end of 75th St. W.). © **941/792-0458**. www.nps.gov/deso. Free admission. Daily 9am–5pm. Costumed presentations Dec–Mar daily 10:30am, 11:30am, 2:30pm, and 3:30pm. Take Manatee Ave. (Fla. 64) west to 75th St. W. and turn right; follow the road to its end and the entrance to the park.

Gamble Plantation   Situated northeast of downtown Bradenton, this is the oldest structure on the southwestern coast of Florida, and a fine example of an antebellum plantation home. Built over a 6-year period in the late 1840s by Major Robert Gamble, it was constructed primarily of "tabby mortar" (a mixture of oyster shells, sand, molasses, and water), with 10 rooms, verandahs on three sides, 18 exterior columns, and eight fireplaces. Maintained as a state historic site, it includes a fine collection of 19th-century furnishings. Entrance to the house is by tour only, although you can explore the grounds on your own. The Prime Outlets Ellenton is a 5-minute drive from here via U.S. 301, so you can combine a plantation visit with some bargain hunting (see "Shopping," below).

3708 Patten Ave. (U.S. 301), Ellenton. ℂ 941/723-4536. www8.myflorida.com/communities/learn/stateparks/district4/myakkariver. Free admission. Tours $3 adults, $1.50 children 6–12, free for children under 6. Thurs–Mon 9am–4:30pm; 30-min. guided house tour 9:30 and 10:30am, and 1, 2, 3, and 4pm. Take U.S. 301 north of downtown to Ellenton; the site is on the left just east of Ellenton-Gillette Rd. (Fla. 683).

South Florida Museum, Bishop Planetarium, and Parker Manatee Aquarium (Kids) If you haven't seen manatees in the wild, the star at this downtown complex is "Snooty," the oldest manatee born in captivity (1948) and Manatee County's official mascot. Snooty and his pal "Mo" live in the Parker Manatee Aquarium. The South Florida Museum tells the story of Florida's history, from prehistoric times to the present, including a Native American collection with life-size dioramas and a Spanish courtyard containing replicas of 16th-century buildings. The Bishop Planetarium features a 50-foot hemispherical dome that arcs above a seating area, where laser-light and educational star shows take place.

201 10th St. W. (on the riverfront, at Barcarrota Blvd.). ℂ 941/746-4131. www.sfmbp.org. Admission $7.50 adults, $6 seniors, $4 children 5–12, free for children 4 and under. Admission includes planetarium shows. Jan–Apr and July Mon–Sat 10am–5pm; Sun noon–5pm. Rest of year Tues–Sat 10am–5pm; Sun noon–5pm. Closed New Year's Day, Thanksgiving, and Christmas. From U.S. 41, take Manatee Ave. west to 10th St. W. and turn right.

A NEARBY STATE PARK & THE LIPIZZANER STALLIONS

About 20 miles southeast of Sarasota, the **Myakka River State Park** ⚘, on Fla. 72 about 9 miles east of I-75, is Florida's largest, covering more than 35,000 acres flanking 14 miles of the Myakka River, one of two official Wild and Scenic Rivers in the state. It's an outstanding wildlife sanctuary and breeding ground, home to hundreds of species of plants and animals, including alligators. There are 39 miles of backcountry trails and boardwalks, including one snaking high up in the treetops, giving great views over the surrounding wetlands, prairies, and dense woodlands. The park is open daily from 8am to sunset. Admission is $4 per car with two to eight occupants, $2 for car with driver, or $1 per pedestrian or bicyclist. You can stay out here in a campground or in five log cabins built by the Civilian Conservation Corps during the Great Depression (they now have air conditioners, electric stoves, refrigerators, and hot water showers). Campsites cost $11 a night from May to November, $15 from December to April (plus $2 for electricity all year-round). Cabins rent for $55 a night year-round. For more information, contact the headquarters at 13207 S.R. 72, Sarasota, FL 34241 (ℂ **941/361-6511;** www8.myflorida.com/communities/learn/stateparks/district4/myakkariver).

The best and certainly easiest way to see the park is on a 1-hour-long nature excursion by boat and tram with **Myakka Wildlife & Nature Tours** (ℂ **941/365-0100**). These informative excursions cost $7 for adults, $4 for children 6 to 12, free for kids 5 and under. Call for the schedules, which change seasonally.

Nearby, horse lovers are drawn to the famous **Lipizzaner Stallions,** who do their spectacular leaps at the Ottomar Herrmann training grounds, 32755 Singletary Rd., Myakka City (ℂ **941/322-1501**), from late December through March (they tour the country the rest of the year). Members of a now-rare breed, the parents of these milky white stallions were brought here from Austria in the

1960s by Colonel Ottomar Herrmann. Their *haute école* performances are straight from Vienna's famous Spanish Riding School. Call for schedule and directions. Admission is by donation.

SHOPPING

Visitors come from all over the world to shop at **St. Armands Circle** ★★, on St. Armands Key just inside Lido Key. Wander around this outdoor circle of more than 150 international boutiques, gift shops, galleries, restaurants, and nightspots, all surrounded by lush landscaping, patios, and antiques. Pick up a map at the Sarasota Convention and Visitors Bureau (see "Essentials," earlier in this chapter). Many shops here are comparable to those in Palm Beach and on Naples's Third Avenue South, so check your credit-card limits—or resort to some great window shopping. I love to browse through **Global Navigator** (© 813/388-4515), a travel-equipment and apparel shop that reminds me of Banana Republic when it carried really cool stuff (open daily 10am to 10pm).

Parking on or near St. Armands Circle can be scarce, and on-street parking is limited to 3 hours. Your best bets are the free, unrestricted lots on Adams Drive at Monroe and Madison drives.

Downtown, the **Burns Court** and **Herald Square** historic districts, centered on Pineapple Avenue south of Ringling Boulevard, have a trove of upscale boutiques and art galleries worth exploring. You can pick from the freshest of Florida's fruits and vegetables at the downtown **farmer's market,** from 7am to noon on Saturday on Lemon Avenue between Main and 1st streets.

For discount shopping, the focal point of this area is the **Prime Outlets Ellenton,** on U.S. 301 at exit 43 off I-75 in Ellenton (© 941/723-1150), about a 15-minute drive northeast of downtown Bradenton (turn left at the first stoplight east of I-75). This Spanish-style outdoor center has more than 100 factory and outlet stores, including a Saks Off Fifth Avenue, Coach Leather, Liz Claiborne, Bass Shoes, Corning Revere, Jockey, Levi's, Nike, Ann Taylor, Donna Karan, Jones New York, Paul Harris, DKNY, Tommy Hilfiger, Geoffrey Beene, Van Heusen, Maidenform, Royal Doulton, Mikasa, Seiko, Sony, and Bose. Shops are open Monday to Saturday from 10am to 9pm and Sunday from 11am to 6pm. A free trolley runs around this sprawling complex Tuesday to Sunday from noon to 6pm. Forget **Sarasota Outlet Mall,** on University Parkway just west of I-75 (© 941/359-2050), which is struggling.

Sarasota Square Mall, 8201 S. Tamiami Trail, at Beneva Road (© 941/922-9600) south of downtown, is the area's largest enclosed mall.

WHERE TO STAY

Most visitors stay out at the beaches, but if you want to be close to the fine evening entertainment here, a new 270-room **Ritz-Carlton Sarasota** (© 800/241-3333; www.ritz-carlton.com) was scheduled to open in mid-2001 on the downtown waterfront just north of the Ringling Causeway. The nearby **Hyatt Sarasota,** 1000 Blvd. of the Arts (© 800/233-1234 or 941/953-1234; fax 941/952-1987), is adjacent to the Civic Center and the Van Wezel Performing Arts Hall and within walking distance of downtown shops and restaurants.

For cost-conscious travelers, the older but well-maintained **Best Western Midtown,** 1425 S. Tamiami Trail (U.S. 41), at Prospect St. (© 800/722-8227 or 941/955-9841; fax 941/954-8948; www.bwmidtown.com), is 2 miles in either direction from the main causeways leading to the keys. Near the airport are a **Comfort Inn** (© 800/228-5150 or 941/355-7091), a **Days Inn** (© 800/329-7466 or 941/355-9271), and a **Hampton Inn** (© 800/336-9335 or

941/351-7734). All of recent vintage and thoroughly modern, they stand side-by-side on Tamiami Trail (U.S. 41) near the Ringling Museums and the Asolo Center for the Performing Arts.

With the beaches here virtually lined with condominiums, it's not surprising that the Resort at Longboat Key Club and the Colony Beach & Tennis Resort (see below) actually are all-condominium projects operated as hotels. The annual visitors guide published by the Sarasota Convention and Visitors Bureau (see "Essentials," earlier in this chapter) is a good starting point for finding other options. Among the rental agencies requiring stays of less than a month are **Argus Property Management,** 1200 Siesta Bayside, Sarasota, FL 34242 (© **800/237-2252** or 941/346-3499; fax 941/349-6156; www.argusmgmt. com); **Longboat Accommodations,** 4030 Gulf of Mexico Dr., Longboat Key, FL 34228 (© **800/237-9505** or 941/383-9505; fax 941/383-1830; www. longboatkey.com); and **Michael Saunders & Company,** 100 S. Washington Blvd., Sarasota, FL 34236 (© **800/881-2222** or 941/951-6668; www. michaelsaunders.com). **A Paradise Rental Management,** 5201 Gulf Dr., Holmes Beach, FL 34217 (© **800/237-2252** or 941/778-4800; fax 941/ 778-7090; www.aparadiserentals.com), represents a number of condominium complexes on Anna Maria Island.

The Bradenton Area Convention and Visitors Bureau (see "Essentials," earlier in this chapter) operates a free **reservation service** (© **800/4-MANATEE**), and its annual visitor guide lists all accommodations on Anna Maria Island. The bureau also publishes a list of Superior Small Lodgings, clean and comfortable properties with no more than 50 rooms (see "Tips on Accommodations," in chapter 2).

The hotels below are organized by geographic region: on Lido Key, on Longboat Key, on Siesta Key, and on Anna Maria Island. The high season here is from January to April. The hotel tax here is 9%.

ON LIDO KEY

Half Moon Beach Club ★   Near the south end of Lido, this two-story Art Deco–style hotel is right on the beach and less than half a block from South Lido Beach Park. The front of the building forms a circle around a small but very attractive courtyard with a heated pool and sunning area. From there, guests take a hallway through a motel-style block of spacious rooms to the beach, where they can rent cabanas and order drinks to be delivered from the bar inside. All units have balconies or patios, some have kitchenettes with microwave ovens, but only the four beachfront rooms have Gulf views.

2050 Ben Franklin Dr. (at Taft Dr.), Sarasota, FL 34236. © 800/358-3245 or 941/388-3694. Fax 941/ 388-1938. www.halfmoon-lidokey.com. 85 units. Winter $144–$274 double; off-season $124–$194 double. AE, DC, DISC, MC, V. **Amenities:** Restaurant (American); bar; heated outdoor pool; water-sports equipment rental; bike rental; limited room service; coin-op washers and dryers. *In room:* A/C, TV, dataport, kitchen, fridge, coffeemaker, hair dryer, iron.

Holiday Inn Lido Beach   Conveniently located at the north end of Lido, this modern seven-story hotel is within walking distance of St. Armands Circle. Unfortunately, the beach across the street (you'll have to dodge the traffic) isn't the best stretch of sand here. The motel-style bedrooms have balconies that face the gulf or the bay, and the rooftop restaurant and lounge offer panoramic views of the Gulf of Mexico.

233 Ben Franklin Dr. (at Thoreau Dr.), Sarasota, FL 34236. © 800/HOLIDAY or 941/388-5555. Fax 941/ 388-4321. 135 units. Winter $179–$319 double; off-season $125–$235 double. AE, DC, MC, V. **Amenities:**

Restaurant (American); 2 bars; heated outdoor pool; access to nearby health club; exercise room; water-sports equipment rental; bike rental; limited room service; baby-sitting; laundry service; coin-op washers and dryers; concierge-level rooms. *In room:* A/C, TV, dataport, coffeemaker, hair dryer, iron.

ON LONGBOAT KEY

Colony Beach & Tennis Resort Sitting 3 miles north of St. Armands Circle, this beachside facility is consistently rated one of the nation's finest tennis resorts. The beachside Colony Restaurant and swimming pool date from 1952 when this was a beach club, but today's accommodations are in modern, luxurious one- and two-bedroom condominium apartments complete with living rooms, dining areas, fully equipped kitchenettes, sun balconies, and whirlpool tubs and steam showers. The choice accommodations are three private cottages right on the superb beach (they also are the most expensive units). The condominiums are built around a 21-court tennis center, where a staff of professionals conducts highly acclaimed programs for both adults and children. The beachside Colony Restaurant offers fine continental cuisine for lunch and dinner (jackets requested for men at dinner).

1620 Gulf of Mexico Dr., Longboat Key, FL 34228. © 800/4-COLONY or 941/383-6464. Fax 941/383-7549. www.colonybeachresort.com. 235 units. Winter $270–$455 suite; off-season $195–$365 suite. Packages available. AE, DISC, MC, V. **Amenities:** 2 restaurants (continental/American); 2 bars; heated outdoor pool; 21 tennis courts; health club; Jacuzzi; sauna; water-sports equipment rental; bike rental; children's programs; game room; concierge; activities desk; car-rental desk; business center; salon; limited room service; massage; baby-sitting; laundry service; coin-op washers and dryers. *In room:* A/C, TV, kitchen, coffeemaker, hair dryer, iron.

Hilton Longboat Key Beach Resort About 7½ miles north of St. Armands Circle, this five-story concrete building is more geared to couples than the nearby Holiday Inn Hotel & Suites (see below). Lush foliage and gardens and a charming gray wooden structure holding all of the public facilities help make up for the blandness of the guest-room building. In fact, the bar and pool area are pleasant areas for relaxing lunches or sunset cocktails even if you aren't staying here. Last refurbished in 1998, most of the bedrooms have a patio or narrow balcony. A few gulf-front rooms have larger balconies. Guests can ride a free shuttle to St. Armands Key.

4711 Gulf of Mexico Dr., Longboat Key, FL 34228. © 800/282-3046 or 941/383-2451. Fax 941/383-7979. 102 units. Winter $215–$305 double; $289–$309 suite. Off-season $155–$245 double; $229–$329 suite. Packages available. AE, DC, MC, V. **Amenities:** Restaurant (American); bar; heated outdoor pool; exercise room; water-sports equipment rental; bike rental; concierge; limited room service; laundry service; concierge-level rooms. *In room:* A/C, TV, dataport, minibar, coffeemaker, hair dryer, iron.

Holiday Inn Hotel & Suites *Kids* Longboat Key's only family-oriented beachside motel is built around an indoor courtyard with a swimming pool, a whirlpool, a games area, and the island's only fast-food outlets (Pizza Hut, Nathan's Famous, Mrs. Field's Cookies, and Seattle's Best Coffee). In addition, there's a restaurant with adjacent clubby bar plus a beachside snack bar. The enclosed area makes this a good respite on rainy days, during a cool snap, or when it's stiflingly hot outside. No matter what the weather's doing, there's plenty here to keep the kids busy. Extensively refurbished in 1999, most of the contemporary rooms and suites open to walkways overlooking the inside pool area; accordingly, the more expensive units with patios or balconies facing the beach are preferable.

4949 Gulf of Mexico Dr., Longboat Key, FL 34228. © 800/HOLIDAY or 941/383-3771. Fax 941/383-7871. www.hilongboat.com. 146 units. Winter $209–$259 double; $229–$369 suite. Off-season $169–$279 double; $189–$299 suite. AE, DC, DISC, MC, V. **Amenities:** 2 restaurants (American); 2 bars; heated indoor and outdoor pools; tennis courts; exercise room; Jacuzzi; sauna; water-sports equipment rental; bike rental; children's programs; game room; concierge; limited room service; baby-sitting; laundry service; coin-op washers and dryers. *In room:* A/C, TV, dataport, fridge, coffeemaker, hair dryer, iron.

The Resort at Longboat Key Club ★★   Part of a real-estate development on 410 acres at the southern end of Longboat Key, this award-winning condominium resort pampers the country-club set with upscale restaurants and a variety of recreational activities in a lush tropical setting. The spacious and luxurious rooms and suites all have private balconies overlooking either the Gulf of Mexico, a lagoon, or golf-course fairways. All have custom-designed furnishings and neo-classical decor, and all but 20 have full kitchens. Among several dining options here, the gulf-side Orchid's Restaurant has the feel of an informal but elegant supper club, serving classical Italian cuisine in a romantic setting by the gulf, while the adjacent Orchid's Lounge offers casual dining and live entertainment. Other choices are in the clubhouses at the resort's two golf courses and two tennis centers (all with instruction).

301 Gulf of Mexico Dr. (P.O. Box 15000), Longboat Key, FL 34228. ☎ **800/237-8821** or 941/383-8821. Fax 941/383-0359. www.longboatkeyclub.com. 232 units. Winter $375–$410 double; $400–$1,075 suite. Off-season $160–$295 double; $195–$525 suite. Packages available. AE, DISC, MC, V. From St. Armands Key, take Gulf of Mexico Dr. north; take first left after bridge. **Amenities:** 5 restaurants (American/Italian); bars; heated outdoor pool; 2 golf courses (45 holes); 38 tennis courts; health club with spa treatments; Jacuzzi; sauna; water-sports equipment rental; bike rental; children's programs; concierge; activities desk; salon; limited room service; massage; baby-sitting; laundry service. *In room:* A/C, TV, dataport, kitchen, coffeemaker, hair dryer, iron.

ON SIESTA KEY

Captiva Beach Resort ★ *Value*   Owners Robert and Jane Ispaso have substantially upgraded and improved this older property in the Stickney Point business district, about half a block from the beach on a narrow, closely packed circle populated by other small motels. Every one of the comfortable, sparkling-clean units here has some form of cooking facility, and some have separate living rooms with sleeper sofas. These are older buildings, so you'll find window air conditioners mounted through the walls, and shower-only bathrooms in some units. It's very popular with longer-term guests during winter. You'll get fresh towels daily but maid service only once a week. This and the circle's other motels share a common pool area, and guests get complimentary use of beach towels, chairs, and umbrellas. Several restaurants are a short walk away.

6772 Sara Sea Circle, Siesta Key, FL 34242. ☎ **800/349-4131** or 941/349-4131. Fax 941/349-8141. www.captivabeachresort.com. 20 units. Winter $130–$250; off-season $80–$180. Weekly and monthly rates available. AE, DISC, MC, V. **Amenities:** Heated outdoor pool; coin-op washers and dryers. *In room:* A/C, TV, coffeemaker, hair dryer.

Turtle Beach Resort ★★★   On Siesta Key's south end, 2½ miles south of the Stickney Point Bridge, this intimate little bay-side charmer is one of Florida's most romantic retreats. It began life years ago as a traditional Old Florida fishing camp, but owners Gail and Dave Rubinfeld have renovated the five original clapboard cottages and added five more in a modern building. The complex is tightly packed; and although some units are very close to a small bay-side swimming pool, heavy tropical foliage provides a reasonable degree of privacy, and high wooden fences surround each unit's private outdoor hot tub. Sitting right on the bay, the two choice units also have one-way mirror walls, allowing guests to look out at the water in complete privacy, while passersby see only reflections of themselves. The cottages are done in various styles such as Caribbean and

Nantucket, and have at least one bedroom each. Although they can accommodate small families, they are better suited as a terrific escape for couples. There's no restaurant on the grounds, but Ophelia's on the Bay is a seafood restaurant next door, once the old fishing camp's dining room, and all units have kitchens. Guests can use fishing poles, rowboats, kayaks, canoes, and paddleboats. No smoking is allowed inside.

9049 Midnight Pass Rd., Sarasota, FL 34242. ℂ **941/349-4554.** Fax 941/312-9034. www.turtlebeachresort. com. 10 units. Winter $250–$370 double; off-season $170–$270 double. Weekly rates available. AE, DISC, MC, V. Pets accepted at extra charge. **Amenities:** Outdoor pool; Jacuzzi; water-sports equipment rental. *In room:* A/C, TV, kitchen, coffeemaker, hair dryer, iron.

ON ANNA MARIA ISLAND

Anna Maria's lone chain motel is the moderately priced **Econo Lodge Surfside,** 2502 Gulf Dr. N. (at 25th Street North), Bradenton Beach, FL 34217 (ℂ **800/ 55-ECONO** or 941/778-6671; fax 941/778-0360). This clean and well-maintained beachfront facility has 18 suites and 36 spacious rooms in its main three-story building, plus 18 rooms in another building on the beach and 5 more across the street (the latter are the least expensive).

The Beach Inn ⭐ Jo and Frank Davis, owners of the Harrington House (see below), have turned this two-story beachfront motel into a couples-oriented inn. The property has two buildings, one on the beach, the other to the rear facing a tropical courtyard. Beachfront rooms have fireplaces, raised Jacuzzi tubs, bar areas, small microwaves, king-size beds, shower-only bathrooms, and either upstairs balconies or downstairs spacious decks separated from the gulf by sea oats. The less-expensive units in the rear building are less well equipped; they have two double beds. Bungalows and apartments in other buildings are available, too. There's no restaurant here, but guests receive complimentary continental breakfast, and the excellent Beach Bistro (see below) is next door.

101 66th St., Holmes Beach, FL 34217. ℂ **800/823-2247** or 941/778-9597. Fax 941/778-8303. www. thebeachinn.com. 14 units. Winter $139–$209 double; off-season $99–$179 double. Rates include continental breakfast. MC, V. **Amenities:** Jacuzzi; coin-op washers and dryers. *In room:* A/C, TV, fridge, coffeemaker, hair dryer, iron.

Bungalow Beach Resort ⭐⭐ If you want an Old Florida–style bungalow by the beach, owners Bert and Gayle Luper have them at this romantic little complex. In fact, white-sand walkways join the beach to these bright and airy clapboard cottages, built in the 1930s and 1940s but considerably spiffed up in recent years with hardwood floors, bright tropical furniture, and ceiling fans. Ranging in size from efficiencies to three bedrooms, they all have cooking facilities and a deck or porch. A few have single-person whirlpool bathtubs, while some have shower-only bathrooms. The five choice cottages open directly to the beach; the largest has a whirlpool bathtub with a steam maker, a full gourmet kitchen, and a deck. Three others are grouped around an outdoor swimming pool. There is no restaurant on the grounds, but several are within walking distance. No smoking in the units here.

2000 Gulf Dr. N. (between 17th and 22nd Aves.), Bradenton Beach, FL 34217. ℂ **800/779-3601** or 941/ 778-3600. Fax 941/778-1764. www.bungalowbeach.com. 15 units. Winter $134–$314 double; off-season $84–$254 double. AE, MC, V. **Amenities:** Heated outdoor pool; Jacuzzi; coin-op washers and dryers; concierge-level rooms. *In room:* A/C, TV, kitchen, coffeemaker, hair dryer.

Harrington House ⭐⭐ Flowers will be awaiting when you arrive at Jo and Frank Davis's exceptional bed-and-breakfast. In a tree-shaded setting on the beach overlooking the gulf, this three-story coquina-and-rock house was built in

1925 and exudes an Old Florida ambience. The eight bedrooms are individually decorated with antique, wicker, or rattan furnishings. Some units have four-poster or brass beds, and the higher-priced rooms have French doors leading to balconies overlooking the gulf. In addition to the bedrooms in the main house, four rooms are available in the adjacent Spangler Beach House, a remodeled 1940s captain's home, and four more are in the nearby Huth House, a low-slung beachside residence (three units here open to an expansive covered lanai facing the beach through a row of Australian pines). All guests enjoy use of the high-ceilinged living room with fireplace, a beachside pool, a patio, and complimentary use of bicycles, kayaks, and other sports equipment. No smoking inside here.

5626 Gulf Dr. (at 58th St.), Holmes Beach, FL 34217. ℂ 888/828-5566 or 941/778-5444. Fax 941/778-0527. www.harringtonhouse.com. 14 units. Winter $179–$249 double; off-season $129–$199. Rates include full breakfast. MC, V. No children under 12 allowed. **Amenities:** Heated outdoor pool; complimentary use of sports equipment. *In room:* A/C, TV, hair dryer.

Rod & Reel Motel   Sitting beside the Rod & Reel Fishing Pier on Anna Maria Island's northeastern end, this basic but clean and well-maintained motel opens to a sandy beach with a great view of the Skyway Bridge across Tampa Bay. The one-story, L-shaped structure flanks a courtyard with barbecue grills and a large thatch-roof cabana for shady picnics. The two best rooms open directly to the beach, but four others have views across the courtyard to the bay. The units are smallish (as are their 1950s-vintage, shower-only bathrooms), but they are bright and airy, and sport kitchenettes. You can walk out on the pier and have breakfast, lunch, or dinner at the Rod & Reel Pier Restaurant & Snack Bar (see "Where to Dine," below).

877 N. Shore Dr. (P.O. Box 1939; at Allamanda St.), Anna Maria, FL 34216. ℂ 941/778-2780. www. rodandreelmotel.com. 10 units. Winter $84–$119; off-season $60–$89. Minimum 1-week rental Feb–Apr. AE, DISC, MC, V. *In-room:* A/C, TV, kitchen, coffeemaker, hair dryer.

Tropic Isle Inn ⭐ *Value*   Owners Bill and Heather Romberger have worked marvels in renovating and upgrading this older motel, across Gulf Drive from its own narrow strip of beach. They installed a high wall along the roadside, behind which you'll find a lushly landscaped courtyard surrounding a big tin-roof gazebo for lounging in the shade and a pool and brick patio for swimming and sunning. Most guest units open to the courtyard, and all have their own balconies or brick patios behind white fences. Three of the bright and airy units are standard motel rooms. The others are apartments with one or two bedrooms and living areas with kitchens. The top choice—and by far the most expensive—is an apartment with two upstairs bedrooms sporting balconies and a two-person whirlpool tub in the bathroom they share. The Tropic Isle Inn attracts more families than the other Anna Maria resorts mentioned here. Some rooms have shower-only bathrooms. Restaurants are within walking distance. No smoking in the rooms.

2103 Gulf Dr. N. (at 22nd St.), Bradenton Beach, FL 34217. ℂ 800/883-4092 or 941/778-1237. Fax 941/ 778-7821. www.annamariaisland.com. 15 units. Winter $110–$275; off-season $80–$235. Rates include conti-nental breakfast and evening reception. Weekly rates available. Minimum 3-night stay Feb–Apr. AE, DISC, MC, V. **Amenities:** Heated outdoor pool; free washers and dryers. *In room:* A/C, TV, dataport, kitchen, coffeemaker.

WHERE TO DINE

The restaurants below are organized geographically: in downtown Sarasota, in Southside Village, on St. Armands Key (next to Lido Key), on Longboat Key, on Siesta Key, and on Anna Maria Island.

IN DOWNTOWN SARASOTA

Downtown's best breakfast spot is the local branch of **First Watch,** 1395 Main St., at Central and Pineapple avenues (© **941/954-1395**). Like its siblings in Naples (see "Where to Dine," in section 4 of chapter 10) and elsewhere, First Watch offers a wide variety of inexpensive breakfast and lunch fare. It's open daily from 7:30am to 2:30pm. If the wait's too long, walk south along Central Avenue; this block has several coffeehouses and cafes with sidewalk seating.

The local **Shells** seafood restaurant is at 7253 S. Tamiami Trail (U.S. 41), south of downtown in the vicinity of Sarasota Square Mall (© **941/924-2568**). See "Where to Dine," in section 1, earlier in this chapter, for details about this inexpensive chain. You'll also find most of the national chain fast-food and family restaurants nearby along U.S. 41.

Bijou Cafe ★★ INTERNATIONAL   Chef Jean-Pierre Knaggs prepares award-winning cuisines from around the world in his charming cafe in the heart of the theater district. Although the more casual Michael's on East (see below) bistro draws a hefty after-theater crowd, this is the best place to dine within walking distance of the downtown entertainment venues. Jean-Pierre artfully presents the likes of prime veal Louisville (with crushed pecans and bourbon-pear sauce), pan-seared crab cakes served under a remoulade and over a bed of fresh greens, and gently simmered lamb shanks with rosemary and garlic. His outstanding wine list has won accolades from *Wine Spectator* magazine.

1287 1st St. (at Pineapple Ave.). © **941/366-8111.** Reservations recommended. Main courses $17–$26. AE, DC, MC, V. Mon–Thurs 11:30am–2pm and 5–9:30pm; Fri 11:30am–2pm and 5–10:30pm; Sat 5–10:30pm; Sun 5–9:30pm. Closed Sun June–Dec. Free valet parking nightly in winter, on weekends off-season.

Marina Jack SEAFOOD/CONTINENTAL   Overlooking the waterfront with a wraparound 270° view of Sarasota Bay and Siesta and Lido Keys, this two-restaurants-in-one establishment has spectacular water vistas and a carefree "on vacation" attitude, especially on the open-air raw bar deck, which often is packed all afternoon on weekends and at sunset every day. The food is good but not the best in town, so come here for a relaxing, fun time. You may have to wait for a table or barstool down on the deck, but be sure to make reservations if you want to have a meal in the upstairs dining room. Fresh local seafood is served upstairs—grilled grouper is your best bet. The downstairs lounge and raw bar also serves sandwiches and burgers.

In Island Park, Bayfront at Central Ave. © **941/365-4232.** Reservations accepted in dining room, not accepted on deck. Dining room main courses $15–$30. Deck main courses $14–$17; sandwiches and salads $8–$11. AE, MC, V. Dining room daily 11:30am–2:30pm and 5–10pm. Deck daily 11:30am–11pm.

Michael's on East ★★ CREATIVE INTERNATIONAL   At the rear of the Midtown Plaza shopping center on U.S. 41 south of downtown, Michael Klauber's chic bistro is one of the top places here for fine dining and is the locals' favorite after-theater haunt. Huge cut-glass walls create three intimate dining areas, one with a black marble bar for pre- or after-dinner drinks. Prepared with fresh ingredients and a creative flair, the offerings here will tempt your taste buds. The menu changes with the seasons. In autumn, you might start with yellowfin tuna sashimi with a vegetable sushi roll and caviar. From there, you could progress to slightly spicy Louisiana-style crab cakes, seared Chilean sea bass with couscous and artichoke hearts in a thyme-accented tomato coulis, or perhaps grilled duck breast with Napa cabbage, sweet potato, and smoked bacon in an apple-cider reduction. A light-fare menu goes until midnight, and there's dancing in the lounge starting at 9:30pm.

1212 East Ave. S. (between Bahia and Prospect Sts.). ℂ **941/366-0007.** Reservations recommended. Main courses $16.50–$36. AE, DC, MC, V. Winter Mon–Fri 11:30am–2pm; daily 5:30–10pm. Off-season Mon–Fri 11:30am–2pm; Mon–Sat 6–10pm. Complimentary valet parking.

Patrick's AMERICAN/PUB FARE   With a semicircular facade, this informal, polished-oak and brass-rail brasserie offers wide-windowed views of downtown's main intersection. The menu offers very good pub fare: steaks and chops, burgers, seafood, pastas, small pizzas, salads, sandwiches, and omelets. Other entrees include broiled salmon with dill-hollandaise sauce, sesame chicken, and veal done three ways—piccata, française, or marsala.

1400 Main St. (at Pineapple and Central Aves.). ℂ **941/952-1170.** Reservations not accepted. Main courses $11–$21; sandwiches and burgers $6–$8. AE, MC, V. Daily 11am–midnight; Sun brunch 11am–3pm. Closed Christmas.

Yoder's ⭐ *(Value)* AMISH/AMERICAN   Just 3 miles east of downtown is an award-winning, value eatery operated by an Amish family (Sarasota and Bradenton have sizable Amish communities and several other Amish restaurants). Evoking the Pennsylvania Dutch country, the simple dining room displays handcrafts, photos, and paintings celebrating the Amish way. The menu emphasizes plain, made-from-scratch cooking such as home-style meatloaf, baked and southern fried chicken, country-smoked ham, and fried filet of flounder. Burgers, salads, soups, and sandwiches are also available. Leave room for Mrs. Yoder's traditional shoo-fly and other homemade pies, one of the biggest draws here. There's neither alcohol nor smoking here.

3434 Bahia Vista St. (west of Beneva Rd.). ℂ **941/955-7771.** Reservations not accepted. Main courses $6–$12; breakfast $2–$6; sandwiches and burgers $3–$6. No credit cards (ATM machine on premises). Mon–Sat 6am–8pm.

IN SOUTHSIDE VILLAGE

Sarasota's hottest dining spot is **Southside Village,** centered on South Osprey Avenue between Hyde Park and Hillview streets, about 15 blocks south of downtown. Here you'll find several hip restaurants, including Fred's and Pacific Rim (see below). The village landmark is **Morton's Gourmet Market** ⭐, 1924 S. Osprey Ave. (ℂ **941/955-9856**), which offers a multitude of deli items, specialty sandwiches, a ton of fresh salads, freshly baked pastries and desserts, and cooked meals dispensed from a cafeteria-style steam table. You dine picnic-fashion on sidewalk tables outside. Most ready-to-go items cost less than $6. Open Monday to Saturday 8am to 8pm, Sunday 10am to 5pm.

Fred's ⭐ INTERNATIONAL   Directly across the avenue from Morton's Gourmet Market, Fred's is one of the city's biggest gathering places for single professionals, especially on Friday night. They have plenty of space to spread out in several dining rooms and bars, all accented with dark wood and etched glass. The fare, although often second on everyone's mind, consists of well-seasoned pizzas and main courses such as pan-seared tuna with Japanese noodles in a basil and lemongrass broth. There's even old-fashioned chicken pot pie and an open-face meatloaf sandwich with a wild mushroom ragout to clearly set it apart from your mother's. You can sample selections from the extensive wine list in a cigar-bar–style tasting room (it offers an appetizer menu); then buy a bottle at the adjoining liquor store.

1917 S. Osprey Ave. (between Hyde Park and Hillview Sts.). ℂ **941/364-5811.** Reservations not accepted. Main courses $10–$28; pizza $8–$10. AE, DC, DISC, MC, V. Mon–Thurs 11am–11pm, Fri–Sat 11am–midnight, Sun 10:30am–9pm.

Pacific Rim ☆ *Value* JAPANESE/THAI   Sarasotans love this chic and very casual restaurant for exceptional cuisine at economical prices. Japanese influence is felt at the authentic sushi bar along one side of the dining room, while Thai spices make a strong impact on the regular menu. I found the char-grilled shrimp with Thai curry and coconut milk sauce to be especially tasty, as was the combination of chicken and vegetables stir-fried in the wok. Here you can select your meat and vegetables separately from the sauce and the chefs will combine them on the grill, the wok, or the bowl (as in, rice dishes).

In Hillview Centre, 1859 Hillview St. (between Osprey Ave. and Laurent Place). ℂ **941/330-8071.** Reservations not accepted. Main courses $7.50–$14. AE, DISC, MC, V. Mon–Thurs 11:30am–2pm and 5–9pm, Fri 11:30am–2pm and 5–10pm, Sat 5–10pm.

ON ST. ARMANDS KEY

While the locals are hanging out in Southside Village, part-year residents and visitors flock to St. Armands Circle. Plan to spend at least one evening here, since the nighttime scene is like a fair, with everyone strolling around the circle, poking heads into a few stores that stay open after dark and window-shopping the others. It's fun and safe, so come early and plan to stay late. See "Shopping," earlier in this chapter, for parking tips.

A branch of Tampa's famous **Columbia** (see "Where to Dine," in section 1, earlier in this chapter) is found here on St. Armands Circle between John Ringling Boulevard and John Ringling Parkway (ℂ **941/388-3987**). The Spanish food is excellent, there's outdoor seating, and the Patio Lounge is one of the liveliest spots here for evening entertainment from Thursday to Sunday.

Like its sibling in Naples (see "Where to Dine," in section 4 of chapter 10), the local edition of **Tommy Bahama's Tropical Cafe,** 300 John Ringling Blvd., (ℂ **941/388-2888**), draws a lively crowd of young professionals to its moderately priced seafood. It's upstairs over Tommy Bahama's clothing store.

For dessert, you may wish to forgo an expensive dessert after your dinner on St. Armands Circle and wander over to the local branch of **Kilwin's,** 312 John Ringling Blvd. (ℂ **941/388-3200**), for some gourmet chocolate, Mackinac Island fudge, or ice cream or yogurt in a homemade waffle cone. Enjoy your sweets on one of the sidewalk park benches—everyone else does. Kilwin's is open Sunday to Thursday until 10:30pm, Friday and Saturday until 11pm.

Cafe l'Europe ☆☆ CONTINENTAL   As its name implies, a European atmosphere prevails at this consistently excellent restaurant, the best place on the circle for fine dining. You can ask for a table out on the sidewalk, but brick walls and arches, dark woods, brass fixtures, pink linens, and hanging plants all lend an elegant ambience indoors. The menu offers selections ranging from a bouillabaisse in a piquant pepper broth to a veal tenderloin glazed with balsamic vinegar and served with a rich blackberry and port wine sauce.

431 St. Armands Circle (at John Ringling Blvd.). ℂ **941/388-4415.** Reservations recommended. Main courses $15–$30. AE, DC, DISC, MC, V. Daily 11am–4pm and 5–10pm.

Charley's Crab ☆☆ SEAFOOD   A favorite for people-watching, Charley's is popular not just for crabs from Florida, Alaska, and Australia but for a full range of fresh seafood dishes (if the local fishers haven't caught any fish today, it's flown in via FedEx). Several varieties of excellent wine are available by the glass. Alfresco diners fill sidewalk tables early at lunch and dinner as shoppers stroll past. A pianist adds to the lively outdoor atmosphere. Large windows in the comfortable indoor dining room give a great view of the passing parade as well.

420 St. Armands Circle (between John Ringling Blvd. and Blvd. of the Presidents). ℭ **941/388-3964.** Reservations recommended. Main courses $16–$39; dinner sandwiches $9–$11. AE, DC, MC, V. Mon–Thurs 11:30am–4:30pm and 5–10pm; Fri–Sat 11:30am–4:30pm and 5–10:30pm; Sun noon–4pm and 5–10pm.

Hemingway's ⍟ FLORIDIAN/CARIBBEAN   For a casual spot with an eclectic Floribbean menu and a large bar with a friendly, laid-back Key West ambience, take the elevator or climb the winding stairs to this second-floor hideaway. Hemingway's is a charming and comfortable combination of good food and Old Florida tradition. You can dine inside or on one of two second-floor balconies.

325 John Ringling Blvd. (½ block off St. Armands Circle). ℭ **941/388-3948.** Reservations accepted. Main courses $16–$22. AE, DC, DISC, MC, V. Sun–Thurs 11:30am–10pm; Fri–Sat 11:30am–11pm.

Hungry Fox AMERICAN   This upstairs restaurant is the only place on St. Armands Circle offering three inexpensive meals a day. It's not much to look at inside, with marble-look tables and plastic lawn chairs, so wait for a table out on the verandah, especially next to the railing where you can oversee all the action down below. Breakfast, which is served until noon, offers everything from lox and bagels to Virginia ham and eggs. Sandwiches and salads are served for lunch, followed by steaks, chicken, pastas, and spicy jambalaya for dinner. Most items are good value for the price, but stay away from anything cooked in the deep fryer.

419 St. Armands Circle (above Cafe l'Europe). ℭ **941/388-2222.** Reservations not accepted. Main courses $8.50–$15; sandwiches, burgers, salads $6–$9; breakfast $4.50–$7. AE, DISC, MC, V. Mon–Sat 8am–9pm; Sun 8am–2:30pm.

ON LONGBOAT KEY

Euphemia Haye/The Haye Loft ⍟⍟⍟ INTERNATIONAL   This area's most extraordinary restaurant, the romantically lighted Euphemia Haye is best known for Chef Raymond Arpke's crispy roast duck filled with bread stuffing and accompanied by a tangy fruit sauce. His prime strip steak rolled in cracked peppercorns and served with an orange, brandy, and butter sauce is another winner, as are his shrimps in a delightful curry and coconut cream sauce. If all this sounds sweet, wait until you go upstairs to The Haye Loft, his casual dessert bar. Up here you can take your pick from fabulous pies topped with thick whipped cream or Ben & Jerry's ice cream. You also can sample the kitchen's offerings, for the loft has its own light fare menu, including soups, appetizers, small pizzas, and sandwiches. If you're lucky, the night's special sandwich will be steak topped with Raymond's peppercorn sauce. Served open-face and garnished with a field-greens salad, it's a meal for just $9. Add a glass of superb wine and a slice of pie a la mode, and you've had a wonderful dinner for under $20.

5540 Gulf of Mexico Dr. (at Gulfbay Rd.). ℭ **941/383-3633.** Reservations recommended downstairs, not accepted in The Haye Loft. Main courses $19.50–$37; sandwiches, pizzas, and salads $7–$9. DC, DISC, MC, V. Restaurant Sun–Thurs 5–10pm. Haye Loft daily 6pm–midnight.

Moore's Stone Crab SEAFOOD   Located in Longbeach, the old fishing village on the north end of Longboat Key, this popular bayfront restaurant began in 1967 as an offshoot of a family seafood business established 40 years earlier. From the outside, in fact, it still looks a little like a packing house, but the view of the bay dotted with mangrove islands makes a fine complement to stone crabs fresh from the family's own traps from October to March. Otherwise, the menu offers an incredibly large variety of seafood, most of it fried or broiled. Sandwiches and salads are served all day.

800 Broadway (at Bayside Dr.). ℂ **941/383-1748.** Reservations not accepted. Main courses $9–$23; sandwiches and salads $7–$13. AE, DISC, MC, V. Winter daily 11:30am–9:30pm. Off-season Mon–Fri 4:30–9:30pm; Sat–Sun 11:30am–9:30pm.

ON SIESTA KEY

Ocean Boulevard, which runs through **Siesta Village,** the area's funky, laid-back beach hangout, is virtually lined with restaurants and pubs, including Blasé Café (see below). Most have outdoor seating and bars, which attract the beach crowd during the day. At night, rock 'n' roll bands draw teenagers and college students to this lively scene.

Blasé Café ★★ *Finds* INTERNATIONAL   One of Florida's most unusual restaurants, Ralph and Cynthia Cole's supercasual establishment has tables indoors and a few under the cover of the Village Corner shopping center's walkway, but most are alfresco, on a wooden deck built around a palm tree in the center's asphalt parking lot. Never mind the cars pulling in and out virtually next to your chair: Ralph's food is so good that it draws droves of locals, who don't mind waiting for an umbrella table. This is the Siesta Key's best breakfast spot, offering Italian- and Louisiana-flavored frittatas as well as plain old bacon-and-eggs. Lunch sees burgers, big salads, and platters such as chicken Alfredo and Florentine crèpes with shrimp. At night, Ralph puts forth the likes of pan-seared sushi-quality yellowfin tuna with tangy wasabi and pickled ginger.

In Village Corner, 5263 Ocean Blvd. (at Calle Miramar), Siesta Village. ℂ **941/349-9822.** Reservations accepted. Main courses $11–$22; breakfast $5–$9; lunch $5–$9. MC, V. Mon–Thurs 8:30am–9:30pm, Fri–Sat 8:30am–10pm. Closed Mon June–Nov.

Turtles AMERICAN   With tropical overtones and breathtaking water vistas across from Turtle Beach, this informal restaurant on Little Sarasota Bay has tables both indoors and on an outside deck. Unique seafood offerings include snapper New Orleans and potato-encrustsed mahimahi. You can't go wrong ordering grouper grilled, broiled, blackened, or fried. There's also a selection of pastas on the menu. The early bird specials include a medium-sized fish portion.

8875 Midnight Pass Rd. (at Turtle Beach Rd.). ℂ **941/346-2207.** Reservations not accepted, but call for preferred seating. Main courses $11–$19; salads and sandwiches $6.50–$11; early bird specials $8–$10. AE, DC, DISC, MC, V. Winter daily 11:30am–10pm; off-season daily 11:30am–9:30pm. Early bird specials daily 4–6pm.

ON ANNA MARIA ISLAND

Anna Maria's **Shells** seafood restaurant is at 3200 East Bay Dr. in Holmes Beach (ℂ **941/778-5997**). See "Where to Dine," in section 1, earlier in this chapter.

Beach Bistro ★★★ INTERNATIONAL   Winner of a Golden Spoon award as one of Florida's 20 best restaurants, Sean Murphy's culinary oasis is Anna Maria Island's top pick for fine dining. It sits right beside the beach, offering wide-windowed views of the sparkling gulf waters. Crisp linens, cut crystal, and fresh flowers on every table enhance a romantic ambience and overall elegance. Bistro bouillabaisse made with premium fish, shrimp, scallops, and squid is the signature dish here. Other regular offerings include Floribbean-style grouper— sautéed in a coconut and cashew crust and finished with a red-pepper and papaya sauce. (Also excellent is Sean's less-expensive **Bistro at Island's End,** 10101 Gulf Dr. in Anna Maria (ℂ **941/779-2444**), which has live jazz and a late-night menu.)

6600 Gulf Dr. N. (at 66th St.), Holmes Beach. ℂ **941/778-6444.** Reservations recommended. Main courses $23–$37. Tasting menu $48–$62 per person. AE, DC, DISC, MC, V. Daily 5:30–10pm.

The Beachhouse ☆ AMERICAN   This large lively place sits right on Bradenton Beach with a huge open deck and a covered pavilion facing out to the gulf. Even inside, wide windows let in the view. Owned by Ed Chiles, son of the late U.S. senator and Florida governor Lawton Chiles, the Beachhouse offers daily fresh fish, including the signature beechnut grouper (with nutty crust in citrus-butter sauce). There's also a good variety of fare, including seafood salads and pastas, crab cakes, fish and chips, and broiled steaks. Local musicians play on the patio most evenings.

200 Gulf Dr. N. (at Cortez Rd.), Bradenton Beach. ℂ 941/779-2222. Reservations not accepted, but call for preferred seating. Main courses $11–$18; sandwiches $6–$10. AE, DC, DISC, MC, V. Daily 11:30am–10:30pm.

Duffy's Tavern PUB FARE   This little ramshackle pub, right off Manatee County Public Beach, serves icy cold beer and the island's hottest hamburgers. It looks like a dive from the outside, but you'll find everyone from state senators to construction workers at the bar and the tavern's few tables. License plates and baseball caps are nailed to every inch of the ceiling over the screened porch. Other than burgers, the menu is limited to sandwiches, navy bean soup, hot dogs, and chili. There's no table service, so order at the bar.

3901 Gulf Dr. (at Manatee Ave.), Holmes Beach. ℂ 941/778-2501. Reservations not accepted. Burgers and sandwiches $2–$4. No credit cards. Mon and Wed–Sat 11am–7pm; Sun noon–7pm.

Gulf Drive Café ☆☆ *Value* AMERICAN   Locals flock to this bright gulf-side cafe for one of the best bargains on any beach in Florida. With big windows, bentwood cafe chairs with colorful cushions, and lots of hanging plants and ceiling fans, the coral and green dining room opens to a beachside patio with tables shaded by a trellis (the wait is worth it). The breakfast fare is led by sweet Belgian waffles, which are available all day. You can also order salads, sandwiches, and burgers anytime here, with quiche du jour, Mediterranean seafood pasta, and regular seafood platters joining the show at 4pm.

900 Gulf Dr. N. (at 9th St.), Bradenton Beach. ℂ 941/778-1919. Reservations not accepted. Main courses $7–$12; breakfast $3–$6; sandwiches and burgers $4.50–$6. DISC, MC, V. Daily 7am–9:30pm.

Rod & Reel Pier Restaurant & Snack Bar SEAFOOD   Sitting out on the Rod & Reel Pier at the north end of the island, this little no-frills fish camp enjoys a million-dollar view of Tampa Bay, including Egmont Key and the Skyway Bridge on the horizon. The chow is mostly fried or grilled seafood—fish, shrimp, scallops, forgettable crab cakes, and a piled-high combination platter of all of the above. The lone exception, a tasty Mexican-style grouper (sautéed with peppers, onions, and salsa) is by far the best dish here. They will cook your catch, provided you snag it from the pier.

875 N. Shore Dr., Anna Maria. ℂ 941/778-1885. Reservations not accepted. Main courses $7–$10; breakfast $2.50–$6; sandwiches $3–$8. AE, DISC, MC, V. Daily 7am–10pm. Closed Thanksgiving and Christmas. From Gulf Dr., turn toward the bay on Pine Ave. and take left at dead-end onto Bay Blvd. Go right on N. Shore Dr. to pier.

Rotten Ralph's SEAFOOD/ENGLISH   On the north end of the island overlooking Bimini Bay, this casual pub has both indoor and outdoor seating right by the boats docked in the Anna Maria Yacht Basin. You can order pots of two dozen steamed oysters, clams, or crabs, or many other seafood choices from fried clam strips to sautéed scallops. Most fall in the moderate category, but you can opt for inexpensive British-style fish and chips (the house specialty) or linguini either plain or with chicken, vegetables, or shrimp under marinara or Alfredo sauce. Other choices include Danish baby back ribs and Anna Maria chicken (marinated and grilled with a honey-mustard sauce).

902 S. Bay Blvd., Anna Maria. 🕐 **941/778-3953.** Reservations not accepted. Main courses $6–$17; sandwiches and burgers $5.50–$8. DC, DISC, MC, V. Daily 11am–9pm. From Gulf Dr., turn toward the bay on Pine Ave.; take right at dead-end to the end of Bay Blvd.

Sandbar ✪ SEAFOOD Sitting on the site of the former Pavilion, built in 1913 when people from Tampa and St. Pete took the ferry here, this popular restaurant is perched right on the beach overlooking the Gulf. The air-conditioned, knotty-pine dining room offers several traditional as well as innovative preparations of seafood (crab cakes with a Creole mustard sauce, for example). The real action here is under the umbrellas on the lively beachside deck, where appetizers, sandwiches, salads, and platters are served all day and night. Live music makes a party on the deck Monday to Friday nights and on Saturday and Sunday beginning at 1pm. The inside bar is one of the few I've seen in Florida with no sports TVs.

100 Spring Ave. (east of Gulf Dr.), Anna Maria. 🕐 **941/778-0444.** Reservations not accepted; call ahead to get on waiting list. Main courses $13–$19; salads and sandwiches $6–$10. AE, DC, DISC, MC, V. Daily 11:30am–10pm.

SARASOTA & BRADENTON AFTER DARK

The cultural capital of Florida's west coast, Sarasota is home to a host of performing arts, especially during the winter season. To get the latest update on what's happening anytime of year, call the city's 24-hour **Artsline** (🕐 **941/ 365-ARTS**). Also check the "Ticket" section in Friday's *Herald-Tribune* (www. newscoast.com), the local daily newspaper; the Sarasota Convention and Visitors Bureau usually has copies (see "Essentials," earlier in this chapter).

THE PERFORMING ARTS Located at the Ringling Museums (see "Exploring the Area," earlier in this chapter), the **Florida State University Center for the Performing Arts** ✪✪✪, 5555 N. Tamiami Trail (U.S. 41; 🕐 **941/ 351-8000;** www.asolo.org), presents the winter-through-spring Asolo Theatre Festival, a program of ballet and Broadway-style musicals and drama. In addition to the **Asolo Theatre,** a 19th-century Italian court playhouse moved here from Asolo, Italy, in the 1950s by the Ringlings, the center uses the 487-seat **Harold E. and Ethel M. Mertz Theatre,** originally constructed in Scotland in 1900 and transferred piece by piece to Sarasota in 1987. The 161-seat Asolo Conservatory Theatre was later added as a smaller venue for experimental and alternative offerings. The complex is under the direction of Florida State University (FSU).

The city's other prime venue is the lavender, seashell-shaped **Van Wezel Performing Arts Hall** ✪✪✪, 777 N. Tamiami Trail (U.S. 41), at 9th Street (🕐 **800/826-9303** or 941/953-3366; www.vanwezel.org). Recently renovated, it offers excellent visual and acoustic conditions and a wide range of year-round programming, including touring Broadway shows and visiting orchestras and dance troupes. Both it and the FSU Center host performances by the **Florida West Coast Symphony** (🕐 **941/953-4252;** www.fwcs.org), the **Jazz Club of Sarasota** (🕐 **941/366-1552** or 941/316-9207; www.jazzclubsarasota.com), the **Sarasota Pops** (🕐 **941/795-7677**), and the **Sarasota Ballet** (🕐 **800/361-8388** or 941/351-8000; www.sarasotaballet.org).

Downtown Sarasota's theater district is home to the **Florida Studio Theatre,** 1241 N. Palm Ave., at Cocoanut Avenue (🕐 **941/366-9796;** www.fst2000.org), which has contemporary performances from December to August, including a New Play Festival in May. Built in 1926 as the Edwards Theater, **The Opera House,** 61 N. Pineapple Ave., between Main and 1st streets (© **941/953-7030;** www.sarasotaopera.org), presents classical operas (in their original languages) as well as high-brow concerts. Next door to The Opera House, the **Golden Apple Dinner Theatre,** 25 N. Pineapple Ave. (© **941/366-5454**), presents cocktails, dinner, and a professional Broadway-style show year-round. The professional, nonequity **Theatre Works,** 1247 1st St., at Cocoanut Avenue (© **941/952-9170**), presents musical revues and other works all year.

THE CLUB & MUSIC SCENE   You can find plenty of music to dance to on the mainland at **Sarasota Quay,** the downtown waterfront dining-shopping-entertainment complex on Tamiami Trail (U.S. 41) a block north of John Ringling Causeway. Just walk around this brick building and your ears will take you to the action. The laser sound-and-light crowd gathers at **In Extremis** (© **941/954-2008**), where a high-energy deejay spins Top 40 tunes for twenty-somethings. Michael's Mediterranean Grill turns into **Anthony's After Dark** rocking disco at 10:30pm. An older but still energetic crowd dances to contemporary jazz at the **Downunder Jazz Bar** (© **941/951-2467**).

Over on St. Armands Circle, the Patio Lounge in **Columbia** restaurant (© **941/388-3987**) is one of the liveliest spots along the beach strip, featuring live, high-energy dance music Tuesday to Sunday evenings. And on Siesta Key, the pubs and restaurants along Ocean Boulevard in Siesta Village have noisy rock 'n' roll bands entertaining a mostly young crowd (see "Where to Dine," above).

The action on Anna Maria is at beach restaurants and pubs. Live bands lend a party atmosphere to the gulf-side deck at the **Sandbar** restaurant every night and from 1pm on weekends (see "Where to Dine," above). **D. Coy Ducks Bar & Grille,** in the Island Shopping Center at Marina Drive and 54th Street in Holmes Beach (© **941/778-5888**), has a varied program of live Dixieland bands, jazz pianists, and guitarists.

12

Walt Disney World & Orlando

by Jim and Cynthia Tunstall

When Disney opened the Magic Kingdom in 1971, few could imagine what Central Florida was going to be like three decades later. Today, the region is bursting (and in some cases imploding) with newer, bigger, and better things for you to do.

Walt Disney World (WDW) alone has four theme parks, dozens of smaller attractions, tens of thousands of hotel rooms, scores of restaurants, dozens of bars and clubs, and a pair of cruise ships. When Universal Orlando, SeaWorld, and the marginal players add their share, well, it's pretty overwhelming.

Most of you don't have unlimited time and money, so it's our job to show you how to save both. Later in this chapter, you'll find the best deals on hotels, restaurants, attractions, and more. These tips will make your vacation easier to plan and more enjoyable and affordable.

1 Getting There

BY PLANE

THE MAJOR AIRLINES There are 40 scheduled airlines and nearly as many charter companies serving the more than 30 million Orlando passengers each year. **Delta** (© 800/221-1212; www.del-air.com) has more than 25% of the flights to and from Orlando International Airport. It offers service from 200 cities.

Other carriers include **Air Canada** (© 888/247-2262; www.aircanada.ca), **America West** (© 800/235-9292; www.americawest.com), **American** (© 800/433-7300; www.im.aa.com), **British Airways** (© 800/247-9297; www.britishairways.com), **Canadian Airlines** (© 800/426-7000; www.cdnair.com), **Continental** (© 800/525-0280; www.continental.com), **Midway** (© 800/446-4392; www.midwayair.com), **Northwest** (© 800/225-2525; www.nwa.com), **TWA** (© 800/221-2000; www.twa.com), and **US Airways** (© 800/428-4322; www.usairways.com).

Several so-called no-frills airlines—low fares but no meals or other amenities—fly to Florida. The biggest is **Southwest Airlines** (© 800/435-9792; www.iflyswa.com), which has flights from many U.S. cities to Orlando and Tampa.

The best fares into Orlando International Airport are during the months of November, December, and January. Orlando is a very user-friendly airport. It hosts all of the major airlines and is only 25 miles from Walt Disney World. **Mears Transportation** (© 407/423-5566) provides shuttle vans from the airport to all resorts. The vehicles run 24 hours a day, departing every 15 to 25 minutes. Round-trip fares are $21 to $25 for adults and $14 to $17 for children 4 to 11, depending on the destination.

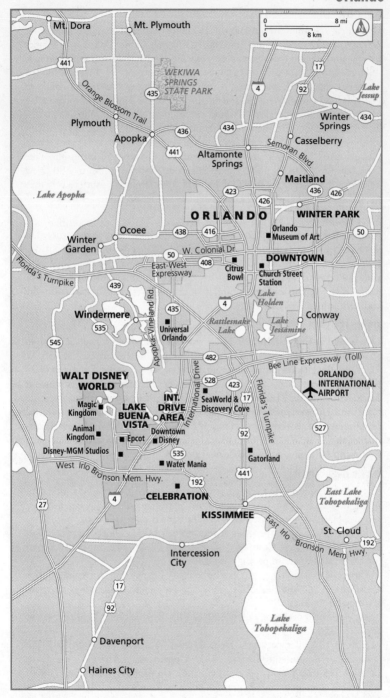

Orlando

Mt. Dora

Mt. Plymouth

441

WEKIWA SPRINGS STATE PARK

435

Orange Blossom Trail

17

4

92

Lake Jessup

Plymouth

Apopka

441

436

434

Winter Springs

434

Casselberry

Semoran Blvd.

Altamonte Springs

Maitland

436

426

Lake Apopka

423

O R L A N D O

426

WINTER PARK

Orlando Museum of Art

50

Ocoee

438

416

Winter Garden

50

W. Colonial Dr.

DOWNTOWN

Florida's Turnpike

East-West Expressway

408

Citrus Bowl

Church Street Station

4

Lake Holden

439

535

Windermere

435

Apopka-Vineland Rd.

Universal Orlando

Rattlesnake Lake

Lake Jessamine

Conway

545

482

Bee Line Expressway (Toll)

ORLANDO INTERNATIONAL AIRPORT

WALT DISNEY WORLD

528

423

17

SeaWorld & Discovery Cove

Florida's Turnpike

Magic Kingdom

LAKE BUENA VISTA

INT. DRIVE AREA

527

Animal Kingdom

Epcot

Downtown Disney

92

Disney-MGM Studios

535

Gatorland

West Irlo Bronson Mem. Hwy.

Water Mania

441

192

East Lake Tohopekaliga

27

4

CELEBRATION

KISSIMMEE

East Irlo Bronson Mem. Hwy.

St. Cloud

192

Intercession City

17

92

Lake Tohopekaliga

Davenport

Haines City

BY CAR

Orlando is 436 miles from Atlanta, 1,312 miles from Boston, 1,120 miles from Chicago, 1,009 miles from Cleveland, 1,170 miles from Dallas, 1,114 miles from Detroit, 1,088 miles from New York City, and 1,282 miles from Toronto.

From Atlanta, take I-75 south to the Florida Turnpike to I-4 west. From the Northeast, take I-95 south to I-4 west. From Chicago, take I-65 south to Nashville, I-24 south to I-75, and then south to the Florida Turnpike to I-4 west. From Cleveland, take I-77 south to Columbia, South Carolina, then I-26 east to I-95, and south to I-4 west. From Dallas, take I-20 east to I-49, then south to I-10, east to I-75, and south to the Florida Turnpike to I-4 west. From Detroit, take I-75 south to the Florida Turnpike to I-4 west. From Toronto, take Canadian Route 401 south to Queen Elizabeth Way, then south to I-90 (New York State Thruway), east to I-87 (New York State Thruway), south to I-95 over the George Washington Bridge, and continue south on I-95 to I-4 west.

BY TRAIN

Amtrak trains (© 800/872-7245; www.amtrak.com) pull into stations in downtown Orlando (about 23 miles from Walt Disney World) and in Kissimmee (about 15 miles from Walt Disney World). There are also stops in Winter Park (10 miles north of downtown) and Sanford (23 miles northeast of downtown Orlando). The Sanford Station, located at 600 Persimmon Ave., is also the end terminal for the Auto Train.

BY BUS

Greyhound buses (© 800/229-9424; www.greyhound.com) connect Orlando to just about anywhere in the country. They pull into a terminal at 555 N. Magruder Blvd. (John Young Parkway), between West Colonial Drive and Winter Garden Road, a few miles west of downtown Orlando; and in Kissimmee at 16 N. Orlando Ave., between Emmett and Mabbette streets, about 14 miles from Walt Disney World. There is van transport from the Kissimmee terminal to most area hotels and motels. From Orlando, you can call for **Mears Transportation** (© 407/423-5566), which offers a shuttle service that costs $25 round-trip for adults, $17 for children ages 4 to 11.

PACKAGE TOURS

The number of Orlando packages available is staggering. It can be a little confusing finding the one that's best for you, partly because most offer different services. Start by looking att he ads in your Sunday newspaper's tar.

If you're planning to spend all of your time in Mickeyville, contact the **Walt Disney World Travel Company** (© 800/828-0228; www.disneyworld.com) for a wide assortment of packages available.

Universal Orlando packages can be booked by contacting **Universal Studios Vacations** at © 888/322-5537. You can get online information at **www. universalorlando.com**.

For **SeaWorld** packages, call © 800/423-8368 or visit their website at **www. seaworld.com**.

Airlines also offer packages. **Delta Dream Vacations** (© 800/872-7786; www.deltavacations.com/disney.html.), **Continental Airlines Vacations** (© 800/525-0280; www.coolvacations.com), **US Airways Vacations** (© 800/ 455-0123; www.usairwaysvacations.com), and **American Airlines Vacations** (© 800/321-2121; www.im.aa.com) are a few options.

American Express Vacations (℃ 800/241-1700; http://travel.americanexpress. com/travel/personal) has special deals for cardholders.

Other tour options include **SunStyle** (℃ **888-786-7895**; www.sunstyle. com), a wholesale tour operator that offers packages targeting Disney, Universal Orlando, SeaWorld, and International Drive properties and **Touraine Travel** (℃ **800/967-5583**; www.tourainetravel.com), which offers a variety of packages to Disney and Disney properties, Universal Orlando, SeaWorld, and the Disney Cruise Line.

DISNEY ON THE HIGH SEAS

There's hardly a lucrative Florida tourist market that WDW hasn't tapped. Cruise ships are no exception. The Disney *Magic* and Disney *Wonder* were launched in 1998 and 1999, respectively.

Subtle differences aside, these two ships are nearly identical twins: 83,000 tons, 12 decks, 875 cabins, room for 2,400 guests, and some adults-only areas, but no casinos. Both have extensive kids and teen programs broken down into age groups, and both sport some state-of-the-art computer equipment. There are also nurseries for 3-month- to 3-year-olds. Restaurants, shows, and other onboard activities are very family oriented. A dine-around option lets you move among main restaurants (each ship has four). The *Magic* and *Wonder* depart from Port Canaveral on 3- to 7-day excursions, and 7-day land-sea packages are also available. Prices range from $439 to $4,299 per adult, $229 to $799 for children 3 to 17, and $99 to $119 for children under 3, depending on the cabin level and length of trip (℃ **800/951-3532**; www.disneycruise.com).

VISITOR INFORMATION

The best overall source is the **Orlando/Orange County Convention & Visitors Bureau,** 8723 International Dr., Suite 101, Orlando, FL 32819 (℃ **407/ 363-5872**; www.orlandoinfo.com). The bureau can answer your questions and send maps and brochures, such as the *Official Visitors Guide, African-American Visitors Guide, Area Guide* to restaurants, and *Official Accommodations Guide.* The packet should land in your mailbox in about 3 weeks and include the "Magicard," which is good for up to $500 in discounts on accommodations, car rentals, attractions, and more. If you don't require a human voice, you can order by calling ℃ **800/643-9492** or 800/551-0181.

For general information about **Walt Disney World**—including vacation brochures and videos—write or call Walt Disney World, Box 10000, Lake Buena Vista, FL 32830-1000 (℃ **407/934-7639** or 407/824-2222; www. disneyworld.com).

For information about **Universal Studios Florida, CityWalk,** and **Islands of Adventure,** call ℃ **800/837-2273** or 407/363-8000, surf over to **www. universalorlando.com,** or write to **Universal Orlando,** 1000 Universal Studios Plaza, Orlando, FL 32819.

You can obtain SeaWorld information online at **www.seaworld.com**.

You also can contact the **Kissimmee–St. Cloud Convention & Visitors Bureau,** 1925 E. Irlo Bronson Memorial Hwy. (U.S. 192), Kissimmee, FL 34744, or P.O. Box 422007, Kissimmee, FL 34742-2007 (℃ **800/327-9159**; www.floridakiss.com).

There's also information available online at **www.orlandosentinel.com** and **www.go2orlando.com**.

Tips   **Help for Guests with Disabilities**

Walt Disney World's services are outlined in the *Guidebook for Guests with Disabilities,* which you can pick up at Guest Services near the front entrance to the parks, or call © **407/824-4321** for answers to any questions regarding special needs. **Universal Orlando** distributes a *Disabled Guest Guidebook* at the Guest Services office just inside the main entrances (© **407/363-8000**). **SeaWorld** has a similar guide at Guest Services (© **407/351-3600**).

CITY LAYOUT

The major highway is I-4, which runs diagonally across the state from Tampa to Daytona Beach. Exits from I-4 take you to Disney, SeaWorld, International Drive, Universal Orlando, Kissimmee, Lake Buena Vista, Church Street Station, downtown Orlando, and Winter Park. *Note:* I-4 is woefully congested. It's best to use it during nonpeak hours, when the locals aren't rushing to and from work.

The Florida Turnpike crosses I-4 and links to I-75 to the north. U.S. 192, a major east-west highway, runs along Kissimmee's major motel area to U.S. 27, where it crosses I-4 near the Disney World entrance. The Bee Line Expressway goes east from I-4 past Orlando International Airport to Cape Canaveral.

NEIGHBORHOODS IN BRIEF

Walt Disney World   The empire, its big and little parks, resorts, restaurants, shops, and assorted trimmings are scattered across 30,500 acres. The surprising thing to some folks: WDW isn't in Orlando. It's southwest of the city, off I-4 on west U.S. 192.

Lake Buena Vista   Meet Disney's next-door neighbor. It's where you'll find "official" (though not Disney-owned or located) hotels. It's near Downtown Disney West Side and Pleasure Island. It has manicured lawns, tree-lined thoroughfares, and free transportation throughout the realm, though it may take a while to get where you're going.

Celebration   Imagine living in a Disney world 365 days a year. This 4,900-acre town eventually will have thousands of residents living in Disney-designed homes. Celebration's downtown area is designed for tourists, including shops, restaurants, and a hotel.

Downtown Disney   This is more a Disney *doo-wa-diddy* than an actual neighborhood; simply put, it's what WDW has taken to calling its two nighttime entertainment areas, Pleasure Island and West Side, as well as its shopping complex, Downtown Disney Marketplace.

Kissimmee   This once-sleepy city is closer to WDW than Orlando is. It's a short drive from Mickey and more of a bargain, but some find it a tad on the tacky side, with modest motels and every fast-food joint known to civilization.

International Drive Area (Hwy. 536)   Can you say tourist Mecca? Known as **I-Drive,** it extends 7 to 10 miles north of the Disney parks between Highway 535 and the Florida Turnpike. The northern end has everything from bungee jumping and ice skating to dozens of theme restaurants and T-shirt shacks. The central and southern ends have numerous hotels. I-Drive also provides easy access to Sea-World and Universal Orlando.

Downtown Orlando   The downtown is northeast of Walt Disney World on I-4. It includes Church Street Station, the Orlando Science Center, restaurants, hotels, and "Antique Row" on Orange Avenue.

Winter Park   Just north of downtown Orlando, Winter Park features a collection of upscale shops and restaurants along Park Avenue, but it's a bit too far north for hotels if you're spending much time at the Disney parks.

2 Getting Around

In a city that thrives on tourists, you won't find it difficult to get from point A to point B—especially if you have a car—but it can be slow. If you're traveling outside the tourist areas, avoid the weekday rush hour (7 to 9am and 4 to 6pm) like the plague, which they are. Rush hours are bad anywhere, but commuter traffic here compounds the tourist traffic.

ON INTERNATIONAL DRIVE

I-Drive has two alternative methods of transportation: Foot power (points of interest in many areas are reasonably close together and there are plenty of sidewalks) and the **I-Ride Trolley** (© 407/354-5656; www.iridetrolley.com), which stops about every 2 blocks. The trolley runs at 15-minute intervals, 7am to midnight (75¢ adults, 25¢ seniors, children under 12 free). This is a great way to get around if you're staying on this strip.

BY THE DISNEY TRANSPORTATION SYSTEM

If you plan to stay at a Disney resort and spend most of your time in Disney parks and attractions, there's a thorough, free transportation network that runs throughout the Disney complex.

WDW resorts and official hotels offer unlimited complimentary transportation via bus, monorail, ferry, or water taxi to all of the parks from 2 hours before opening until 2 hours after closing. There is also service to the water parks, Pleasure Island, and the shopping areas. You can get to other area attractions as well, but you'll have to pay extra.

The pluses: The system is free; you can save on a rental car, insurance, and gas; and you don't have to pay for theme-park parking. The minuses: You're at the mercy of the schedule, and often the system doesn't travel in a straight line from where you are to where you want to go.

BY SHUTTLE

Mears Transportation operates vans and buses that go to all of the theme parks, as well as Cypress Gardens, Kennedy Space Center, Busch Gardens (yes, in Tampa), and Church Street Station, among others. Call © 407/423-5566 for rates.

BY TAXI

Taxis gather at some major hotels, and smaller properties will call a cab for you. You can also call **Yellow Cab** (© 407/699-9999) and **Ace Metro** (© 407/855-0564) on your own. Rates usually are $2.50 for the first mile, $1.50 per mile thereafter. They're generally not an economical option unless you have a party of four or five.

FAST FACTS: **Walt Disney World & Orlando**

American Express There's a Travel Service Office at Epcot's main gate and in the lobby of the Disney's Contemporary Resort. The one closest to Universal is at **A Time to Travel,** 7512 Dr. Phillips Blvd. (✆ **407/345-1181**).

Baby-Sitters Some Orlando hotels offer baby-sitting services. Several Disney properties and other hotels have good child-care facilities with counselor-supervised activity programs on the premises. Disney properties have used **KinderCare** sitters since 1981 (✆ **407/827-5444**). If you're not staying at Disney, you can call them on your own. You can have them take your kids to the park or to any of the services at your resort, except swimming. Rates for in-room service are $12 per hour for one child, $13 per hour for two children, and $14 per hour for three. There's a 4-hour minimum, the first half-hour of which is travel time for the sitter.

Business Hours Theme park hours vary, depending on the time of year. Most open at 9am and close at 9pm or later during summer and holidays (6 to 8pm during the off-season). Businesses are generally open 9am to 5pm, Monday through Friday. Bars are usually open until 2am.

Doctors and Dentists There are basic first-aid centers in all of the theme parks. If you need to see a doctor while you're in Orlando, you can get a reputable referral from **Ask-A-Nurse** (in Kissimmee, call ✆ **407/870-1700**; in Orlando, call ✆ **407/897-1700**). They'll ask whether you have insurance, but that's for information purposes only so that they can track who uses the system. It's a free service open to everyone. There's also a 24-hour, toll-free number for the **Poison Control Center** (✆ **800/282-3171**). To find a dentist, call **Dental Referral Service** at ✆ **888/343-3440** or go online to **www.dentalreferral.com**.

Disney offers in-room medical service 24 hours a day by calling ✆ **407/238-2000**. **Doctors on Call Service** (✆ **407/399-3627**) is a group that makes house and room calls in most of the Orlando area. **Centra-Care** lists several walk-in clinics in the Yellow Pages, including ones on International Drive, ✆ **407/370-4881**, and at Lake Buena Vista near Disney, ✆ **407/934-2273**.

Emergencies Dial ✆ **911** for police, fire departments, and ambulance.

Hospitals **Sand Lake Hospital,** 9400 Turkey Lake Rd. (✆ **407/351-8550**), is about 2 miles south of Sand Lake Road. From the WDW area, take I-4 east to Exit 29, turn left at the exit onto Sand Lake Road, and make a left on Turkey Lake Road. The hospital is 2 miles up on your right. **Celebration Health** (✆ **407/303-4000**), located in the Disney-owned town of Celebration, is at 400 Celebration Place. From I-4, take Exit 25A. At the first traffic light, turn right onto Celebration Avenue. At the first stop sign, take another right.

Kennels All of the theme parks board pets for about $6 per day while you visit the parks. WDW resort guests can board their pets overnight for $11 at the Transportation and Ticket Center's kennel on Seven Seas Drive near the Polynesian Resort.

Lost Children Every theme park has a designated spot for parents to reunite with lost children (or spouses). Ask a park staffer or check at guest services as you enter the park.

Newspapers The Friday edition of the *Orlando Sentinel* includes extensive entertainment and dining listings as does the *Sentinel's* website, **www.orlandosentinel.com**, and *Orlando Weekly,* a free, alternative paper.

Pharmacies Walgreens, 1003 W. Vine St. (Hwy. 192), just east of Bermuda Avenue (© **407/847-5252**), operates a 24-hour pharmacy. There's an Eckerd Drugs at 7324 International Dr. (© **407/345-0491**) that's open 24 hours a day.

Post Office The main post office in Lake Buena Vista is at 12541 Hwy. 535, near T.G.I. Friday's in the Crossroads Shopping Center (© **800/275-8777**). It's open Monday through Friday from 9am to 4pm, Saturday from 9am to noon.

Taxes Florida's 6% sales tax is charged on all goods except most grocery store items and medicines. Additionally, hotels add another 5% or 6% to your bill for a total of 11% or 12%.

Telephone If you're making a local call in Orlando's 407 area code region, even to someone just across the street, *you must dial the 407 area code followed by the number you wish to call,* for a total of 10 digits.

Tourist Information See "Visitor Information," earlier in this chapter.

Weather Call © **407/851-7510** for the local weather forecast.

3 Accommodations

There are more than 111,000 rooms in the Orlando area, and thousands more will open in the coming year. Disney's rooms are in high demand, boasting a 90% occupancy rate, so if you're planning to stay in one of Mickey's resorts, book as far ahead as possible.

Orlando stays busy year-round, but the lowest rates are usually obtainable in the fall (Sept through Nov) and winter (Jan and Feb). High season occurs during holidays and the summer months.

WALT DISNEY WORLD CENTRAL RESERVATIONS OFFICE

To reserve a room or book packages at Disney's resorts, villas, campgrounds, and official hotels, call the **Walt Disney World Travel Company** at © **800/ 828-0228** or 407/828-4101. You can also contact **Central Reservation Operations** (CRO), P.O. Box 10000, Lake Buena Vista, FL 32830-1000 (© **407/ 934-7639;** www.disneyworld.com).

Both can recommend accommodations suited to your price range and specific needs, such as proximity to your favorite park, or facilities that offer supervised child-care centers, or a lap pool. The clerks who answer the telephones can be very helpful but usually won't volunteer information about a better deal or a special *unless you ask.*

DISNEY RESORTS
VERY EXPENSIVE

Disney's Beach Club Resort ⚐ This Cape Cod–style hotel is close enough to Epcot that health-and-fitness types can walk to the park. Stormalong Bay, one of its main draws, is a huge pool with a water park that sprawls over 3 acres.

Walt Disney World Accommodations & Dining

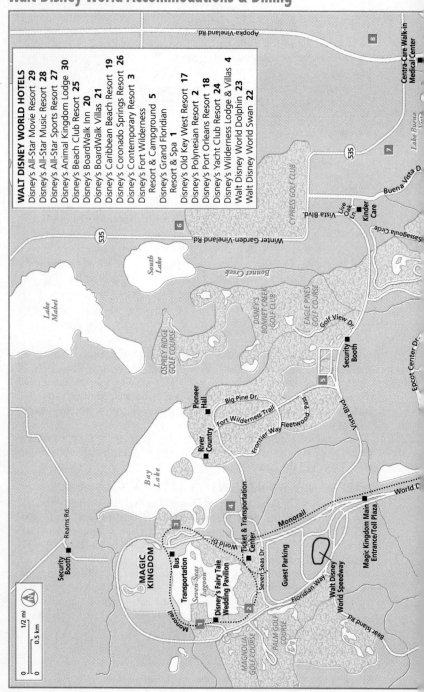

WALT DISNEY WORLD HOTELS
Disney's All-Star Movie Resort **29**
Disney's All-Star Music Resort **28**
Disney's All-Star Sports Resort **27**
Disney's Animal Kingdom Lodge **30**
Disney's Beach Club Resort **25**
Disney's BoardWalk Inn **20**
Disney's BoardWalk Villas **21**
Disney's Caribbean Beach Resort **19**
Disney's Coronado Springs Resort **26**
Disney's Contemporary Resort **3**
Disney's Fort Wilderness
  Resort & Campground **5**
Disney's Grand Floridian
  Resort & Spa **1**
Disney's Old Key West Resort **17**
Disney's Polynesian Resort **2**
Disney's Port Orleans Resort **18**
Disney's Yacht Club Resort **24**
Disney's Wilderness Lodge & Villas **4**
Walt Disney World Dolphin **23**
Walt Disney World Swan **22**

Exit 27 ↗ I-4 to Orlando

535

15

To Kissimmee

16 →

To Orlando Int'l Airport

536

Exit 26B
To: EPCOT, DOWNTOWN DISNEY MARKETPLACE

4

Bonnet Creek

LAKE BUENA VISTA HOTELS

Cypress Glen **6**
DoubleTree Club Hotel **14**
Hawthorn Suites Lake Buena Vista **8**
Hyatt Regency Grand Cypress **7**
Marriott's Orlando World Center **16**
The Villas of Grand Cypress **7**
Summerfield Suites Lake Buena Vista **15**

192

U.S. 192 to Kissimmee →

Celebration

Exit 25B

To:
MAGIC KINGDOM PARK, DISNEY-MGM STUDIOS, DISNEY'S ANIMAL KINGDOM, DISNEY'S FORT WILDERNESS RESORT & CAMPGROUND

I-4 to Tampa

192

U.S. 192 to U.S. 27

Reedy Creek

30

DISNEY'S ANIMAL KINGDOM

26

West Buena Vista Dr.

Blizzard Beach

27

28

29

World Dr.

Osceola Pkwy.

Disney's Wide World of Sports

Fantasia Gardens

Buena Vista Dr.

DISNEY-MGM STUDIOS

Guest Parking
Handicap Parking
Bus Transportation

Studios Main Entrance / Toll Plaza

OFFICIAL HOTELS

Best Western Lake Buena Vista Hotel **9**
Courtyard by Marriott **13**
DoubleTree Guest Suites **10**
Hotel Royal Plaza **11**
The Wyndham Palace Resort & Spa **12**

Epcot Parking
Bus Transportation

EPCOT

Epcot Resort Blvd

Epcot Main Entrance / Toll Plaza

25
24
23
22
21
20

Sea Breeze Dr.

Cayman Way

19

Toll Plaza

Bonnet Creek Pkwy

Orleans Dr.

18

Downtown Disney West Side

17

Typhoon Lagoon

Pleasure Island

DOWNTOWN DISNEY MARKETPLACE

Team Disney

Community Dr.

Villa Ave.

12

Black Lake

9

Hotel Plaza Blvd.

10

11

13

14

Buena Vista Dr.

Epcot Center Dr.

493

Some rooms have balconies and accommodate five people; a typical room here is 400 square feet, comparable to other WDW resorts in this price range, and the bathrooms won't induce claustrophobia.

1800 Epcot Resorts Blvd. (off Buena Vista Dr., P.O. Box 10000), Lake Buena Vista, FL 32830-0100. ✆ 407/ 934-7639 or 407/934-8000. Fax: 407/934-3850. www.disneyworld.com. 583 units. $279–$610 double; $465–$1,965 suites. Extra person $25. Children 17 and under stay free with parents. AE, DC, DISC, MC, V. Free parking. Pets $11 a night. Take I-4 east to Exit 26B. Follow signs to WDW, then to the resort. **Amenities:** Restaurant (Seafood); grill; 4 lounges; 2 heated outdoor pools; children's pool; 2 lighted tennis courts; Jacuzzi; water-sports equipment; children's club; video arcade; WDW Transportation System; transportation for a fee to non-Disney theme parks; business center; salon; 24-hr. room service; baby-sitting; guest laundry; non-smoking rooms. *In room:* A/C, TV, dataport, minibar, fridge ($10 a night), hair dryer, iron, safe.

Disney's BoardWalk Inn ★★★

Romantics like staying at this plush 1940s-style "seaside" resort (it's really on a lake). Those who come to life after dark will appreciate the clubs and restaurants on the quarter-mile boardwalk. The B&B–style rooms sleep 4, and some have balconies. Hang on to your swimsuit if you hit the pool's famous—or infamous, depending on how you look at it— 200-foot "keister coaster" waterslide. The Boardwalk's villas range from studios to units that can sleep up to 12 people.

2101 N. Epcot Resorts Blvd. (off Buena Vista Dr.; P.O. Box 10000), Lake Buena Vista, FL 32830-1000. ✆ 407/ 934-7639 or 407/939-5100. Fax 407/934-5150. www.disneyworld.com. 378 units. $279–$630 double; $535–$2,175 for suites; $375–$1,800 villas. Extra person $25. Children 17 and under free with parent. AE, DC, DISC, MC, V. Free parking. Pets $11 a night. Take I-4 east to Exit 26B. Follow signs to WDW, then to the resort. **Amenities:** 2 restaurants (Steak/Seafood, Mediterranean); groceries; grill; 2 lounges; 3 clubs; 2 outdoor heated pools; kids' pool; 2 lighted tennis courts; croquet; health club; Jacuzzi; children's activity center; arcade; concierge; WDW Transportation System; transportation to non-Disney parks for a fee; business center; shopping arcade; 24-hr. room service; baby-sitting; guest laundry; valet; nonsmoking rooms; concierge-level rooms. *In room:* A/C, TV, dataport, fridge ($10 a night), hair dryer, iron, safe.

Disney's Contemporary Resort ★

Location, Location, LOCATION. The Contemporary is one of three resorts on the monorail system, and it's near the WDW golf courses. Unfortunately, the 15-story, 30-year-old A-frame dates to WDW's infancy, and even a complete renovation in 1999 couldn't restore it to the same class as some of the top dogs in this price category. The best views are from the upper floors, which are a tad quieter than those on the lower floors, which are exposed to noisy public areas and the monorail. A standard room sleeps four.

4600 N. World Dr. (P.O. Box 10000), Lake Buena Vista, FL 32830-1000. ✆ 407/934-7639 or 407/824-1000. Fax 407/824-3535. www.disneyworld.com. 1,041 units. $224–$370 double; $280–$1,610 suites. Extra person $25. Children 17 and under stay free with parent. AE, DC, DISC, MC, V. Free parking. Pets $11 a night. Take I-4 east to Exit 26B. Follow signs to WDW, then to the resort. **Amenities:** 2 restaurants (Steak, New American); food court; 2 lounges; 2 heated outdoor pools; kids' pool; 6 lighted tennis courts; fitness center; Jacuzzi; water-sports equipment; kids' club; arcade; concierge; WDW Transportation System; transportation to non-Disney parks for a fee; business center; salon; 24-hr. room service; baby-sitting; guest laundry; valet; nonsmoking rooms; concierge-level rooms. *In room:* A/C, TV, dataport, fridge ($10 a night), hair dryer, iron, safe.

Disney's Grand Floridian Resort & Spa ★★★ (Finds)

From the moment you step into the opulent 5-story domed lobby, you'll feel as if you've slipped back to an era when a guy named Gatsby was at the top of his game. High tea is served in the afternoon; and as the sun sets, a small band plays music from the 1940s upstairs. The Grand Floridian is very popular among honeymooners and other romantic couples. It has a first-class spa and health club. The inviting, Victorian-style rooms are average size and sleep at least four; virtually all over-look a garden, pool, courtyard, or the Seven Seas Lagoon. This, too, is on the monorail system and close to the Magic Kingdom.

4401 Floridian Way (P.O. Box 10000), Lake Buena Vista, FL 32830-1000. ✆ 407/934-7639 or 407/824-3000. Fax 407/824-3186. www.disneyworld.com. 900 units. $314–$790 double; $810–$2,175 suites. Extra person $25. Children 17 and under free with parent. AE, DC, DISC, MC, V. Free parking. Pets $11 a night. Take I-4 east to Exit 25B. Follow signs to WDW, then to the resort. **Amenities:** 5 restaurants (American, Seafood); grill; 3 lounges; 1 heated outdoor pool; kids' pool; 2 lighted tennis courts; health club; spa; water-sports equipment; children's center; arcade; concierge; car-rental desk; WDW Transportation System; transportation to non-Disney parks for a fee; business center; shopping arcade; salon; 24-hr. room service; baby-sitting; guest laundry; valet; nonsmoking rooms; concierge-level rooms. *In room:* A/C, TV, dataport, minibar, fridge ($10 a night), hair dryer, iron, safe.

Disney's Old Key West Resort ⭐   This resort has tree-lined, brick walkways edged by white-picket fences reminiscent of Key West's Old Town district. The rooms come in three sizes (all with a balcony or patio): Standard rooms or studios have space for 4; one- and two-bedroom villas sleep 4 and 8 guests, respectively. The grand villas (over 2,000 square feet) have beds for 12. Villas have whirlpool tubs, and the grand villas are equipped with stereo systems. The resort is located between Epcot and Downtown Disney West Side.

1510 N. Cove Rd. (off Community Dr.; P.O. Box 10000), Lake Buena Vista, FL 32830-1000. ✆ 407/934-7639 or 407/827-7700. Fax 407/827-7710. www.disneyworld.com. 761 units. $244–$349 studios; $330–$730 1- and 2-bedroom villas; $955–$1,290 grand villas. Call for extra adult fees. Children 17 and under stay free with parent. AE, DC, DISC, MC, V. Free parking. Pets $11 a night. Take I-4 east to Exit 26B. Follow signs to WDW, then to the resort. **Amenities:** Restaurant (American); groceries; 4 heated outdoor pools; kids' pool; 2 lighted and 1 unlighted tennis courts; Jacuzzi; sauna; water-sports equipment; game room; WDW Transportation System; transportation to non-Disney parks for a fee; massage; baby-sitting; guest laundry; nonsmoking rooms. *In room:* A/C, TV, kitchenette or kitchen, fridge, coffeemaker, hair dryer.

Disney's Polynesian Resort ⭐   Just south of the Magic Kingdom, the 25-acre Polynesian is the third and last resort on the WDW monorail line. The resort's extensive play areas and themed swimming pools make this a good choice for those traveling with kids. Public areas have canvas cabanas, hammocks, and big swings overlooking a 200-acre lagoon. Rooms are average size, and all but a few accommodate five people. The main drawback is that there isn't much difference between the resort now and when it opened in the 1970s, making it overpriced for what's inside.

1600 Seven Seas Dr. (P.O. Box 10000), Lake Buena Vista, FL 32830-1000. ✆ 407/934-7639 or 407/824-2000. Fax 407/824-3174. www.disneyworld.com. 853 units. $289–$520 double; $365–$625 concierge-level; $465–$2,225 suites. Extra person $25. Children 17 and under free with parent. AE, DC, DISC, MC, V. Free parking. Pets $11 a night. Take I-4 east to Exit 25B. Follow signs to WDW, then to the resort. **Amenities:** Restaurant (Pacific Rim); cafe; 2 lounges; 2 heated outdoor pools; kids' pool; water-sports equipment; children's club; arcade; concierge; WDW Transportation System; transportation to non-Disney parks for a fee; shopping arcade; 24-hr. room service; baby-sitting; guest laundry; valet; nonsmoking rooms; concierge-level rooms. *In room:* A/C, TV, fridge ($10 a night), hair dryer, iron, safe.

Disney's Yacht Club Resort ⭐⭐   The Yacht Club is a cut above its sister, the Beach Club (see above), because the rooms, views, service, and atmosphere are a step or so better. It shares a 25-acre lake—Stormalong Bay—a first-class swimming pool, and magnificent landscaping with the Beach Club. The theme here is turn-of-the-20th-century New England. The rooms, like most others in this class, have space for up to five people. Most have balconies. Stay here and you can walk to Epcot.

1700 Epcot Resorts Blvd. (off Buena Vista Dr.; P.O. Box 10000), Lake Buena Vista, FL 32830-1000. ✆ 407/934-7639 or 407/934-7000. Fax 407/924-3450. www.disneyworld.com. 630 units. $279–$480 double; $405–$615 concierge-level; $490–$2,080 suites. Extra person $25. Children 17 and under free with paying parent. AE, DC, DISC, MC, V. Free parking. Pets $11 a night. Take I-4 east to Exit 26B. Follow signs to WDW, then to the resort. **Amenities:** 3 restaurants (Steaks, Seafood); grill; lounge; 2 heated outdoor pools; kids' pool; 2 lighted tennis courts; Jacuzzi; water-sports equipment; croquet; children's center; arcade; concierge; WDW Transportation System; transportation to non-Disney parks for a fee; business center; shopping arcade; salon; 24-hr. room service; baby-sitting; guest laundry; valet; nonsmoking rooms; concierge-level rooms. *In room:* A/C, TV, dataport, minibar, fridge ($10 a night), coffeemaker, iron, safe.

Walt Disney World Dolphin ★★ If Antoni Gaudí and Dr. Seuss had teamed up on an architectural design, they might have created something like this Westin resort and its sister, the Walt Disney World Swan (see below). This creation centers on a 27-story pyramid with two 11-story wings that are crowned by 56-foot twin dolphin sculptures that look more like the whale in *Pinnochio.* The 400-square-foot rooms can sleep up to four. The resort has a grotto pool with waterfalls, a water slide, and three whirlpools. The Swan and Dolphin share a Body by Jake health club. Epcot is the nearest park.

1500 Epcot Resorts Blvd. (off Buena Vista Dr.; P.O. Box 22653), Lake Buena Vista, FL 32830-2653. ✆ 800/248-7926, 800/227-1500, or 407/934-4000. Fax 407/934-4884. www.swandolphin.com. 1,509 units. $295–$425 double; $410–$3,100 suites. Extra person $25. Children 17 and under stay free with parent. AE, CB, DC, DISC, MC, V. Free parking; valet parking $8. Pets $11 a night. Take I-4 east to Exit 25B. Follow signs to WDW, then to the resort. **Amenities:** 4 restaurants (Steak, Mexican, American); grill; 2 lounges; 4 heated outdoor pools; 4 lighted tennis courts; health club; water-sports equipment; children's center; 2 game rooms; concierge; car-rental desk; WDW Transportation System; transportation to non-Disney parks for a fee; shopping arcade; salon; 24-hr. room service; massage; baby-sitting; guest laundry; valet; nonsmoking rooms; concierge-level rooms. *In room:* A/C, TV, Nintendo, dataport, minibar, hair dryer, iron, safe.

Walt Disney World Swan ★★ Not to be outdone by the huge dolphins at its sister resort next door, this high-rise Westin resort is topped with dual 45-foot swan statues and seashell fountains. It shares a beach, health club, some restaurants, and other trimmings with the Dolphin (see above). The Swan's rooms are a shade smaller, but they still have room for four. This resort, too, is near Epcot.

1200 Epcot Resorts Blvd. (off Buena Vista Dr.; P.O. Box 22786), Lake Buena Vista, FL 32830-2786. ✆ 800/248-7926, 800/228-3000, or 407/934-3000. Fax 407/934-4499. www.swandolphin.com. 758 units. $295–$425 double; $410–$3,100 suites. Extra person $25. Children 17 and under stay free with parent. AE, CB, DC, DISC, MC, V. Free parking; valet parking $8. Pets $11 a night. Take I-4 east to Exit 25B. Follow signs to WDW, then to the resort. **Amenities:** 4 restaurants (American, Italian, Pacific Rim); grill; lounge; 4 heated outdoor pools; 4 lighted tennis courts; health club; water-sports equipment; children's center; 2 game rooms; concierge; car-rental desk; WDW Transportation System; transportation to non-Disney parks for a fee; shopping arcade; salon; 24-hr. room service; massage; baby-sitting; guest laundry; valet; nonsmoking rooms; concierge-level rooms. *In room:* A/C, TV, Nintendo, dataport, minibar, hair dryer, iron, safe.

EXPENSIVE

Disney's Animal Kingdom Lodge ★★ Disney did a good job giving its newest resort the feel of an African game-reserve lodge. Well, with a little of your imagination. The rooms follow a *kraal* design, a semicircle that gives guests an occasional view of birds, giraffes, and animals on a 30-acre savanna. Typical rooms here are a bit smaller than those in Disney's Very Expensive category, making things slightly more crowded for four. The lodge is adjacent to Animal Kingdom, but most everything else on property is quite a distance away.

2901 Osceola Pkwy., Bay Lake, FL 32830. ✆ 407/934-7639 or 407/938-3000. Fax 407/352-2792. www.disneyworld.com. 1,293 units. $199–$510 double; $380–$565 concierge; $600–$2,350 suites. Extra person $25. Children 17 and under free with parent. AE, DC, DISC, MC, V. Free parking; valet parking $8. Pets $11 a night. Take I-4 east to Exit 25B. Follow signs to WDW, then to resort. **Amenities:** 3 restaurants (African, American); lounge; heated outdoor pool; kids' pool; health club; children's center; arcade; concierge; WDW Transportation System; transportation to non-Disney parks; shopping arcade; limited room service; baby-sitting; guest laundry; nonsmoking rooms; concierge-level rooms. *In room:* A/C, TV, dataport, fridge ($10 a night), hair dryer, iron, safe.

Disney's Wilderness Lodge ★★★   The geyser out back, a mammoth stone hearth in the lobby, and bunk beds for the kids give the Wilderness Lodge a rustic, national-park feel. The geyser "blows" periodically throughout the day, and nightly electric water pageants can be seen from the shore of Bay Lake. The standard rooms sleep four (on either two queen beds or one queen and bunk beds), and if a view is important to you, those with woods views are best. The nearest park is Magic Kingdom, but the resort is in a pretty remote area. The only drawback of staying at the lodge: It's more difficult to access other areas via the WDW Transportation System.

The 181 units of Villas at Disney's Wilderness Lodge were added in November 2000. Another Disney Vacation Club time-share property (the Boardwalk Villas and Old Key West are the others) that rents vacant rooms, the Villas offer a more upscale experience at the lodge, although you get less kitchen space here than in Old Key West. Studios are 356 square feet, and the one- and two-bedroom villas have 727 and 1,080 square feet, respectively.

901 W. Timberline Dr. (on the southwest shore of Bay Lake just east of the Magic Kingdom; P.O. Box 10000), Lake Buena Vista, FL 32830-1000. ✆ 407/934-7639 or 407/824-3200. Fax 407/824-3232. www. disneyworld.com. 909 units. Lodge $189–$475 double; $320–$445 concierge; $620–$990 suites. Villas $264–$400 studio; $360–$525 1-bedroom; $509–$895 2-bedroom. Extra person $25. Children 17 and under free with parent. AE, DC, DISC, MC, V. Free parking. Pets $11 a night. Take I-4 east to Exit 25B. Follow signs to WDW, then to the resort. **Amenities:** 2 restaurants (American); 2 lounges; heated outdoor pool; kids' pool; 2 Jacuzzis; water-sports equipment; children's center; arcade; WDW Transportation System; transportation to non-Disney parks for a fee; limited room service; baby-sitting; guest laundry; nonsmoking rooms; concierge-level rooms. *In room:* A/C, TV, fridge ($10 a night), hair dryer, iron, safe.

MODERATE

Disney's Caribbean Beach Resort ★   The Caribbean Beach isn't as bargain basement as the All-Star resorts that follow and offers good value for families who don't need a lot of frills or amenities. The units are grouped into five "villages" around a large duck-filled lake. The main pool replicates a Spanish-style fort complete with slide. The closest park is Disney–MGM Studios. Speaking of closeness, the bathrooms are pretty tight.

900 Cayman Way (off Buena Vista Dr.; P.O. Box 10000), Lake Buena Vista, FL 32830-1000. ✆ **407/934-7639** or 407/934-3400. Fax 407/934-3288. www.disneyworld.com. 2,112 units. $129–$209 double. Extra person $15. Children 17 and under stay free in parents' room. AE, DC, DISC, MC, V. Free parking. Pets $11 a night. Take I-4 east to Exit 26B. Follow signs to WDW, then to resort. **Amenities:** Restaurant (American); grill; lounge; large heated outdoor pool; 6 smaller ones in the villages; kids' pool; Jacuzzi; water-sports equipment; arcade; WDW Transportation System; transportation to non-Disney parks for a fee; limited room service; baby-sitting; guest laundry; nonsmoking rooms. *In room:* A/C, TV, fridge ($10 a night), hair dryer, iron, safe.

Disney's Coronado Springs Resort ★   Here's another clone of the Disney moderate-price class. Were it not for exterior gingerbread and inside-the-room decor (in this case, American Southwest), it would be hard to tell one from the other. Coronado's pool is inspired by a Mayan temple. Rooms are smallish, suitable for four people who get along; don't expect to fit more than one into the bathroom at a time. The nearest park is Animal Kingdom.

1000 Buena Vista Dr., near All-Star Resorts and Blizzard Beach, Lake Buena Vista, FL 32830. ✆ **407/ 934-7639** or 407/939-1000. Fax 407/939-1001. www.disneyworld.com. 1,967 units. $129–$209 double; $258–$1,010 suites. Extra person $15. Children 17 and under free with parent. AE, DC, DISC, MC, V. Free parking. Pets $11 a night. Take I-4 east to Exit 25B. Follow signs to WDW, then to the resort. **Amenities:** Restaurant (Mexican); grill/food court; 2 lounges; 4 heated outdoor pools; kids' pool; health club; Jacuzzi; sauna; water-sports equipment; 2 arcades; WDW Transportation System; transportation to non-Disney parks for a fee; business center; salon; limited room service; massage; baby-sitting; guest laundry; nonsmoking rooms. *In room:* A/C, TV, dataport, fridge ($10 a night), hair dryer, iron, safe.

Disney's Port Orleans Resort ★★ *Value*   This resort, resembling turn-of-the-20th-century New Orleans, grew substantially in late 2000 when Disney merged the neighboring **Dixie Landings Resort** into it. The resulting resort has two sides: The original Port Orleans area is called French Quarter, and the Dixie Landings area is known as Riverside. Other than the name consolidation and the loss of one restaurant, there's little difference. Port Orleans has the best location, landscaping, and, perhaps, the coziest atmosphere of the resorts in this class. The resort's huge Doubloon Lagoon pool has a waterslide that curves out of a dragon's mouth. Typical rooms are large enough to squeeze in four. Port Orleans is east of Epcot and Disney–MGM Studios.

2201 Orleans Dr. (off Bonnet Creek Pkwy.; P.O. Box 10000), Lake Buena Vista, FL 32830-1000. ℂ 407/934-7639 or 407/934-5000. Fax 407/934-5353. www.disneyworld.com. 3,056 units. $129–$209 double. Extra person $15. Children 17 and under stay free with parent. AE, DC, DISC, MC, V. Free parking. Pets $11 a night. Take I-4 east to Exit 26B. Follow signs to WDW, then to the individual resorts. **Amenities:** 2 restaurants (American); grill/food court; 2 lounges; 6 heated outdoor pools; 2 kids' pools; Jacuzzi; water-sports equipment; 2 arcades; WDW Transportation System; transportation to non-Disney parks for a fee; limited room service; baby-sitting; guest laundry; nonsmoking rooms. *In room:* A/C, TV, fridge ($10 a night), hair dryer, iron, safe.

INEXPENSIVE

Disney's All-Star Movie Resort   Kids love the larger-than-life themes at the All-Star resorts, but adults usually cringe at the visual overload. Giant cartoon characters such as Buzz Lightyear adorn this one and also serve to mask a 21st-century rendition of a 1950s Holiday Inn. The rooms are spartan and very small—the bathrooms are even worse. Like its two siblings, the All-Star Movie Resort is buried in WDW's southwest corner to avoid frightening the higher-paying guests.

1991 W. Buena Vista Dr., Lake Buena Vista, FL 32830-1000. ℂ 407/934-7639 or 407/939-7000. Fax 407/939-7111. www.disneyworld.com. 1,900 units. $77–$109 double. Extra person $10. Children 17 and under stay free with parent. AE, DC, DISC, MC, V. Free parking. Pets $11 a night. Take I-4 east to Exit 25B. Follow signs to WDW, then to resort. **Amenities:** Food court, lounge; 2 heated outdoor pools; kids' pool; arcade; WDW Transportation System; transportation to non-Disney parks for a fee; limited room service; baby-sitting; guest laundry; nonsmoking rooms. *In room:* A/C, TV, dataport, fridge ($10 a night), safe.

Disney's All-Star Music Resort *Value*   Giant trombones and musical themes from jazz to calypso can't hide the fact that this is a clone of the All-Star Movie Resort (see above). The small rooms are compounded by cramped bathrooms, where opening a door can injure a loved one. The perks? They're at least $50 a night (and in some cases hundreds of dollars) cheaper than Disney's other resorts. Location-wise, the closest off-site activities are the Winter Summerland Miniature Golf Course, Blizzard Beach, and Animal Kingdom.

1801 W. Buena Vista Dr. (at World Dr. and Osceola Pkwy.; P.O. Box 10000), Lake Buena Vista, FL 32830-1000. ℂ 407/934-7639 or 407/939-6000. Fax 407/939-7222. www.disneyworld.com. 1,920 units. $77–$109 double. Extra person $10. Children 17 and under stay free with parent. AE, DC, DISC, MC, V. Free parking. Pets $11 a night. Take I-4 east to Exit 25B. Follow signs to WDW, then to resort. **Amenities:** Food court, lounge; 2 heated outdoor pools; kids' pool; arcade; WDW Transportation System; transportation to non-Disney parks for a fee; limited room service; baby-sitting; guest laundry; nonsmoking rooms. *In room:* A/C, TV, dataport, fridge ($10 a night), safe.

Disney's All-Star Sports Resort *Value*   Yogi Berra said it best: "It's déjà vu all over again." It's a different theme, but the same routine. Rooms are the same size and equipped with the same minibathrooms as the All-Stars above. This resort's buildings sport football, baseball, basketball, tennis, and surfing motifs.

1701 W. Buena Vista Dr. (at World Dr. and Osceola Pkwy.; P.O. Box 10000), Lake Buena Vista, FL 32830-1000. ℂ 407/934-7639 or 407/939-5000. Fax 407/939-7333. www.disneyworld.com. 1,920 units. $77–$109 double. Extra person $10. Children 17 and under stay free with parent. AE, DC, DISC, MC, V. Free parking. Pets

Coming Soon

Scheduled to begin opening in early 2002, Disney's latest All-Star entry, the **Pop Century Resort,** will add 5,760 rooms—that's 20 more than the three existing All-Star resorts combined. It will fall into the same price and size category as those resorts. The themes are by-decade time capsules of the 20th century.

$11 a night. Take I-4 east to Exit 25B. Follow signs to WDW, then to resort. **Amenities:** Food court, lounge; 2 heated outdoor pools; kids' pool; arcade; WDW Transportation System; transportation to non-Disney parks for a fee; limited room service; baby-sitting; guest laundry; nonsmoking rooms. *In room:* A/C, TV, dataport, fridge ($10 a night), safe.

ROUGHING IT, DISNEY-STYLE

Disney's Fort Wilderness Resort & Campground ⭐   Pines, cypress trees, and fish-filled lakes and streams surround this woodsy 780-acre camping resort. The biggest knock against it is that it's situated quite a distance from Epcot, Disney–MGM Studios, and Animal Kingdom. But it's close to the Magic Kingdom, and if you're a true outdoors type, you'll enjoy the break from some of the Mickey madness. There are 784 campsites for RVs, pull-behind campers, and tents (110/220-volt outlets, grills, picnic tables, and comfort stations with showers and rest rooms).

Some sites are open to pets—at a cost of $3 per site, not per pet—which is cheaper than using the WDW overnight kennel, where you pay $11 per pet. The 408 wilderness cabins and homes (actually trailers) offer 504 square feet, enough for six people once you pull down the Murphy beds, and also have kitchens. If you have a choice, go for the newer cabins, which feature an outside deck.

3520 N. Fort Wilderness Trail (P.O. Box 10000), Lake Buena Vista, FL 32830-1000. ☎ **407/934-7639** or 407/824-2900. Fax 407/824-3508. www.disneyworld.com. 784 campsites, 408 wilderness cabins. Campsite $34–$77 double; wilderness home $184–$254 double; wilderness cabin $219–$299 double. Extra person $2 for campsite, $5 for wilderness home and cabin. Children 17 and under free with parent. AE, DC, DISC, MC, V. Free parking. Take I-4 east to Exit 26B. Follow signs to WDW, then to resort. **Amenities:** 2 restaurants (American); grill; lounge; 2 heated outdoor pools; kids' pool; 2 lighted tennis courts; water-sports equipment; outdoor activities (fishing, horseback and hay rides, campfires); 2 game rooms; WDW Transportation System; transportation to non-Disney parks for a fee; baby-sitting; guest laundry; nonsmoking homes. *In room:* A/C, TV, VCR (cabins only), kitchens, fridge, coffeemaker, outdoor grill, hair dryer (cabins only).

LAKE BUENA VISTA/OFFICIAL HOTELS

The "official" Disney hotels are located on or around Hotel Plaza Boulevard, which is on the northeast side of the main Disney property. Guests enjoy many of the "Perks of Staying with Mickey" (see earlier in this chapter), including free transportation to Disney parks. But keep in mind that they're not on the WDW Transportation System. You can reserve a room at these hotels through Central Reservations Operations ☎ **407/934-7639.** It wouldn't hurt, however, to call each hotel or the parent chain to check on special deals or packages.

EXPENSIVE

The Wyndham Palace Resort & Spa ⭐⭐   This attractive hotel is the most upscale of the Hotel Plaza Boulevard properties and is popular with both business and leisure travelers. Rooms are an average comfortable size and can sleep at least four. Many rooms have balconies or patios. The lobby has a clubby atmosphere; you can lounge in the overstuffed chairs and sip a brandy or enjoy a quiet conversation and the view. Arthur's 27, the signature restaurant here, offers a great panoramic view from the main building's 27th floor. The resort also has a full-service, European-style spa.

1900 Buena Vista Dr. (just north of Hotel Plaza Blvd.; P.O. Box 22206), Lake Buena Vista, FL 32830. ✆ 800/327-2990 or 407/827-2727. Fax 407/827-6034. www.downtowndisneyhotels.com or www.bvp-resort.com. 1,014 units. $209–$398 double; $289–$718 suites. Extra person $20. Children 17 and under stay free with parent. AE, DC, DISC, MC, V. Free parking; valet parking $9. From I-4, take Exit 27 (Hwy. 535/Apopka-Vineland Rd.) north to Hotel Plaza Blvd. and go left. At first stoplight, turn right onto Buena Vista Dr. It's the first hotel on the right. **Amenities:** 2 restaurants (Continental, Steaks); grill; 4 lounges; 3 heated outdoor pools; kids' pool; spa; Jacuzzi; children's center; arcade; concierge; complimentary bus service to WDW parks; transportation for a fee to non-Disney parks; salon; 24-hr. room service; massage; baby-sitting; guest laundry; valet; nonsmoking rooms; concierge-level rooms. *In room:* A/C, TV w/pay movies, dataport, minibar, coffeemaker, hair dryer, iron.

MODERATE

Best Western Lake Buena Vista Hotel *(Value)* This 12-acre lakefront hotel has been kept abreast of the times, with nicer rooms and public areas than you might find in others within the chain. The 340-square-foot rooms are located in an 18-story tower, and all of them come with balconies. The views improve from the eighth floor up, and those guests on the west side have a better chance of seeing something Disney. Accommodations in this category are usually a step above the "moderates" inside WDW. You can reserve an oversized room (20% larger) or one with a view of WDW fireworks for $10 more a night. You can also add a full American breakfast for up to four people for $20 more a night.

2000 Hotel Plaza Blvd. (between Buena Vista Dr. and Apopka-Vineland Rd./Hwy. 535), Lake Buena Vista, FL 32830. ✆ 800/348-3765 or 407/828-2424. Fax 407/828-8933. www.downtowndisneyhotels.com or www.orlandoresorthotel.com. 325 units. $89–$199 for 4 persons; $319 suites. Fifth person $10. AE, DC, DISC, MC, V. Free parking. From I-4, take Exit 27 (Hwy. 535/Apopka-Vineland Rd.) north to Hotel Plaza Blvd. and go left. It's first hotel on right. **Amenities:** Restaurant (American); grill; heated outdoor pool; kids' pool; guest-services desks; complimentary bus service to WDW parks; transportation for a fee to other parks; limited room service; guest laundry; nonsmoking rooms. *In room:* A/C, TV w/pay movies, Nintendo, coffeemaker, hair dryer, iron, safe.

Courtyard by Marriott *(Value)* This moderately priced member of the Marriott chain had a $4.5 million facelift in 1997 and is popular with families. The inner and outer glass elevators are almost as fun as a thrill ride, it's in a good location, and the price is, well, decent. The guest rooms are clean and can sleep four comfortably. Ask for a room on floors 8 to 14 on the hotel's west side for the best view of the Kingdom and fireworks. Standard rooms have about 340 square feet and beds for four.

1805 Hotel Plaza Blvd. (between Lake Buena Vista Dr. and Apopka-Vineland Rd./Hwy. 535), Lake Buena Vista, FL 32830. ✆ 800/223-9930 or 407/828-8888. Fax 407/827-4626. www.downtowndisneyhotels.com or www.courtyardorlando.com. 323 units. $89–$219 double. AE, DC, DISC, MC, V. Free parking. From I-4, take Exit 27 (Hwy. 535/Apopka-Vineland Rd.) north to Hotel Plaza Blvd. and go left. It's the third hotel on left. **Amenities:** Restaurant (American); 2 lounges; 2 heated outdoor pools; kids' pool; Jacuzzi; arcade; guest-services desk; complimentary bus service to WDW parks; transportation for a fee to non-Disney parks; car-rental desks; limited room service; guest laundry; nonsmoking rooms. *In room:* A/C, TV w/pay movies, Nintendo, coffeemaker, hair dryer, iron, safe.

DoubleTree Guest Suites *★* *(Kids)* Children have their own check-in desk and theater, and they get a gift upon arrival at this hotel, which is the best of the official hotels for families traveling with little ones. All of the accommodations in this seven-story hotel are two-room suites, large by most standards, and there's space for up to six to cut some *zz*'s. This is the easternmost of the "officials," meaning it's farthest from the other Disney action but closest to (even within walking distance) the cheaper free-world shops on Apopka-Vineland Road.

2305 Hotel Plaza Blvd. (just west of Apopka-Vineland Rd./Hwy. 535), Lake Buena Vista, FL 32830. ✆ **800/222-8733** or 407/934-1000. Fax 407/934-1011. www.downtowndisneyhotels.com or www. doubletreeguestsuites.com. 229 units. $129–$249 double. Extra person $20. Children 17 and under stay free with parent. AE, DC, DISC, MC, V. Free parking. From I-4, take Exit 27 (Hwy. 535/Apopka-Vineland Rd.) north to Hotel Plaza Blvd. and go left. It's first hotel on left. **Amenities:** Restaurant (American); 2 lounges; heated outdoor pool; kids' pool; 2 lighted tennis courts; arcade; concierge; car-rental desk; complimentary bus service to WDW parks; transportation for a fee to non-Disney parks; limited room service; guest laundry; nonsmoking rooms. *In room:* A/C, TV, dataport, fridge, microwave, coffeemaker, hair dryer, iron, safe.

Hotel Royal Plaza ⭐ The Plaza is one of the boulevard's originals, but renovations over its 25-year history (its most recent makeover was completed only a year ago) have kept it in good shape. A favorite with the budget-minded, its hallmark is a friendly staff who provides excellent service. The nicely decorated rooms are medium-sized and have enough space for five. Poolside rooms have balconies and patios; the tower rooms have separate sitting areas, and some offer whirlpool tubs in the bathrooms. If you want a view from up high, ask for a room facing west and WDW; the south and east sides keep a watchful eye on I-4 traffic.

1905 Hotel Plaza Blvd. (between Buena Vista Dr. and Apopka-Vineland Rd./Hwy. 535), Lake Buena Vista, FL 32830. ✆ **800/248-7890** or 407/828-2828. www.downtowndisneyhotels.com or www. orlandotravel.com/hotels/royal.htm. 394 units. $109–$215 double; $139–$660 suites. Extra person $15. Children 17 and under stay free with parent. AE, DC, DISC, MC, V. Free parking; valet parking $8 a day. From I-4, take Exit 27 (Hwy. 535/Apopka-Vineland Rd.) north to Hotel Plaza Blvd. and go left. It's second hotel on left. **Amenities:** Restaurant (American); lounge; heated outdoor pool; whirlpool; 4 lighted tennis courts; fitness center; guest-services desk; complimentary bus service to WDW parks; transportation for a fee to non-Disney parks; limited room service; guest laundry; nonsmoking rooms. *In room:* A/C, TV w/pay movies and VCR, dataport, minibar, coffeemaker, hair dryer, iron, safe.

OTHER LAKE BUENA VISTA–AREA HOTELS

The hotels in this section are within a few minutes' drive of WDW parks. They offer the location but not the privileges of staying at an "official" hotel.

VERY EXPENSIVE

Cypress Glen ⭐⭐⭐ *Finds* This delightful Art Deco surprise, built in 1992 by a Disney executive, isn't cheap, but you get what you pay for. Only a 10-minute drive from WDW, it's an exceptional retreat for couples seeking romance or adults looking for peace and quiet. This modern inn has just two rooms. One, dubbed the Josephine Baker Suite in honor of innkeeper Sandy Sarillo's passion for jazz, is a 350-square-foot getaway with a private entrance, small private bath, and a more traditional B&B atmosphere. The Sophia Suite—named for Sarillo's mother—is a 1,200-square-foot wonder whose standouts include a sitting room, a beautiful 430-square-foot bathroom highlighted by a two-person whirlpool tub, a small exercise room, a stocked mini fridge (the beer, wine, sodas, and snacks inside are free), and a magnificent four-poster bed. The rates include an excellent and bountiful breakfast of bagels, fresh English muffins, pecan cakes, pastries, at least three kinds of fresh juice, sorbets in cream, fresh fruit, and/or cereals

10336 Vista Oaks Court (P.O. Box 2202), Lake Buena Vista, FL 32830. ✆ **888/909-0338** or 407/909-0338. Fax 407/909-0345. www.cypressglen.com. 2 units. $250–$355 double. AE, DC, DISC, MC, V. Free parking. From I-4 take Exit 27/Lake Buena Vista; go north to the second light (Hwy. 535); turn left and go 2¹⁄₂ miles. Turn right on Vista Oaks and go to the pink building on the left. Children under 16 are not permitted. **Amenities:** Outdoor heated pool; Jacuzzi; nonsmoking rooms. *In room:* A/C, TV/VCR, fax, dataport, fridge (Sophia Suite only), coffeemaker, hair dryer, iron.

Hyatt Regency Grand Cypress ★★★ *Finds*　A favorite of honeymooners and those seeking a resort vacation without the Mickey Mouse extras, this romantic getaway's lobby has lush foliage in which several macaws wave to passersby and the 18-story atrium has inner and outer glass elevators (ride the outers to the roof for a panoramic rush). The rooms are beautifully decorated and sleep four. The Hyatt shares a golf club and academy, racquet club, and equestrian center with its sister property, The Villas of Grand Cypress (see below); both offer excellent packages aimed at the sports set. The Hyatt's half-acre, 800,000-gallon pool is one of the best in Orlando and features caves, grottoes, waterfalls, and a 45-foot waterslide.

1 N. Jacaranda (off Hwy. 535), Orlando, FL 32836. ✆ 800/835-7377 or 407/239-1234. Fax 407/239-3800. www.grandcypress.com. 750 units. $325–$400 double; $450–$1,500 suites. Extra person $20. Children 17 and under free with parent. AE, DC, DISC, MC, V. Free parking; valet $10. Take I-4 Exit 27 north; then turn left at 2nd light after ramp light onto Hwy. 535. It's on right. **Amenities:** 4 restaurants (American, Seafood, Steaks); deli/general store; 4 lounges; large heated outdoor pool; 45 holes of golf; 12 tennis courts (5 lighted); equestrian center; 2 racquetball courts; spa; health club; water-sports equipment; children's center; arcade; concierge; free Disney shuttle; transportation to non-Disney parks for a fee; car-rental desk; salon; 24-hr. room service; in-room massage; baby-sitting; guest laundry; valet; nonsmoking rooms; concierge-level. *In room:* A/C, TV, dataport, minibar, hair dryer, iron, safe.

The Villas of Grand Cypress. ★★★ *Finds*　As long as you're willing to splurge—and we mean *splurge*—this is an exceptional place to set up camp. At its "modest" end, this Mediterranean-inspired resort starts with 425-square-foot junior suites with sleep space for four, Roman tubs, and patios. Floor plans progress to elegant one- to four-bedroom villas that reach about 1,100 square feet on the top end. All include kitchens, dining rooms, and patios. The resort shares equestrian amenities and golf and racquet clubs with the Hyatt (see above).

1 N. Jacaranda (off Hwy. 535), Orlando, FL 32836. ✆ 800/835-7377 or 407/239-4700. Fax 407/239-7219. www.grandcypress.com. 146 villas. $215–$450 junior suites; $315–$1,800 villas. Extra person $20. Children 17 and under stay free with parent. AE, DC, MC, V. Free parking; valet $10. Take I-4 Exit 27 north; then go left at 2nd light (after ramp light) onto Hwy. 535. It's on right. **Amenities:** 2 restaurants (American, Continental); 2 lounges; heated outdoor pool; 45 holes of golf; 12 tennis courts (5 lighted); equestrian center; 2 racquetball courts; spa; health club; water-sports equipment; kids' center; arcade; concierge; free Disney shuttle; transportation to non-Disney parks for a fee; car-rental desk; salon; 24-hr. room service; in-room massage; baby-sitting; guest laundry; nonsmoking rooms; concierge-level. *In room:* A/C, TV, dataport, minibar, hair dryer, iron, safe.

EXPENSIVE

Marriott's Orlando World Center ★　Golf, tennis, and spa lovers will find plenty to do at this sprawling 230-acre resort, which is centered on a 28-story tower fronted by flowers and fountains. The resort's sports facilities are first-class and the largest of its five pools has waterslides and waterfalls. The location, only 2 miles from the Disney parks, is another plus. The large comfortable rooms sleep four, and the higher poolside floors offer views of Mickeyville.

8701 World Center Dr. (on Hwy. 536 between I-4 and Hwy. 535), Orlando, FL 32821. ✆ 800/621-0638 or 407/239-4200. Fax 407/238-8777. www.marriottHotels.com/MCOWC/. 2,111 units. $179–$309 for up to 5 persons; $425–$2,400 suites. Children 17 and under stay free with parent. AE, DC, DISC, MC, V. Free parking; valet $10. Take I-4 Exit 27/Hwy. 535 south 1.5 miles; then turn right on Hwy. 536. **Amenities:** 4 restaurants (Japanese, Steaks, Italian, American); 2 lounges; 3 heated outdoor pools; heated indoor pool; kids' pool; 18-hole golf course; 8 lighted tennis courts; spa; health club; whirlpool; sauna; concierge; car-rental desk; transportation to all theme parks for a fee; business center; salon; 24-hr. room service; massage; baby-sitting; guest laundry; nonsmoking rooms. *In room:* A/C, TV w/pay movies, dataport, minibar, coffeemaker, hair dryer, iron, safe.

Summerfield Suites Lake Buena Vista 𝄞 An excellent choice for families, this modern low-rise shares the near-Disney location of all Lake Buena Vista accommodations. Room size, price, and a friendly staff are three of this hotel's biggest pluses. It has nicely decorated one- and two-bedroom suites, which can accommodate four and eight guests, respectively.

8751 Suiteside Dr. (off Apopka-Vineland Rd./Hwy. 535), Lake Buena Vista, FL 32836. ℂ 800/833-4353 or 407/238-0777. Fax 407/238-2640. www.summerfield-orlando.com. 150 units. $129–$259 1-bedroom for up to 4 persons; $189–$329 2-bedroom for up to 8 persons. AE, DC, DISC, MC, V. Free parking. Take I-4 Exit 27/ Hwy. 535) right to 3rd light (Vinings Way Rd.); go right and hotel is on left. **Amenities:** Deli; heated outdoor pool; kids' pool; exercise room; Jacuzzi; arcade; guest-services desk; free Disney shuttle; transportation to non-Disney parks for a fee; guest laundry; valet; nonsmoking rooms. *In room:* A/C, TV/VCR, kitchen, fridge, coffeemaker, iron, safe.

MODERATE

DoubleTree Club Hotel This family favorite offers rates one-third less than its "official Disney hotel" cousin (see above). Marked by a 2½-story pineapple facing the highway, it's 2½ miles outside of the World, but the hotel provides free lifts to the parks. The 330-square-foot standard rooms have beds for four; Kid Club Suites are 400 square feet and have a separate sleeping area equipped with bunk beds and a second TV.

12490 Apopka-Vineland Rd. (Hwy. 535), Lake Buena Vista, FL 328363. ℂ 800/521-3297 or 407/239-4646. Fax 407/239-8469. www.doubletreeclublbv.com. 246 units. $99–$169 for up to 4 persons. AE, DC, DISC, MC, V. Free parking. From I-4, take Exit 27/Hwy. 535; go north and look for the DoubleTree pineapple ½ mile on left. **Amenities:** Cafe; heated outdoor pool; kids' pool; exercise room; arcade; guest-services desk; free Disney shuttle; transportation to non-Disney parks for a fee; guest laundry; valet; nonsmoking rooms. *In room:* A/C, TV/Nintendo, dataport, coffeemaker, hair dryer, iron.

Hawthorn Suites Lake Buena Vista 𝄞 *Value* One of the features that appeals to us most about this property, which opened in summer 2000, is its floor plan. Its sizable standard rooms have four areas: a living room with pullout sofa, chair and TV; full kitchen with dining-room table for four; bathroom with vanity; and bedroom with recliner and TV. Two-bedroom units are also available. The atmosphere is friendly, the service is good, and it's just 3 minutes from Hotel Plaza Boulevard.

8303 Palm Pkwy., Orlando, FL 32836. ℂ 800/269-8303, 800/527-1133, or 407/597-5000. Fax 407/ 597-6000. www.hawthorn.com. 120 units. $99–$159 for 4 to 6 persons. Rates include full American breakfast. AE, DC, DISC, MC, V. Free parking. From I-4, take Exit 27 (Hwy. 535) east to Palm Pkwy.; then go right ¼ mile to hotel. **Amenities:** Heated outdoor pool; whirlpool; basketball court; exercise room; free shuttle to Disney parks; transportation for a fee to other parks; guest laundry; nonsmoking rooms. *In room:* A/C, TV w/pay movies, dataport, kitchen, microwave, fridge, coffeemaker, hair dryer, iron.

ON U.S. 192/KISSIMMEE

This tin-glitz stretch of highway is dotted with fast-food eateries, burger barns, and T-shirt shops. It's not scenic, but it has fairly inexpensive motels 1 to 8 miles from the Disney parks. Almost all provide, or can arrange, shuttle service to Mickeyville for around $10 to $20 per person, round-trip.

EXPENSIVE

Celebration Hotel 𝄞𝄞 Living the yuppie life? Then you'll love this hotel inspired by the same-name Disney development that surrounds it. Its three-story, wood-frame design is straight out of 1920s Florida. Rooms are a good sized and have *very comfy* beds; to enjoy a soothing view, ask for a lakefront room. The hotel's biggest perk: A location near Disney. The downside: You or your driver must tackle U.S. 192's traffic and construction delays.

700 Bloom St. Orlando, FL 34747. ⓒ **888/499-3800** or 407/566-6000. Fax 407/566-6001. Fax 407/566-6001. www.srs-worldhotels.com/usa/orlando/hotel_mcocel.html. 115 units. $165–$255 for up to 4 persons; $205–$470 for studios and suites. AE, DC, DISC, MC, V. Free parking; valet $8. Take I-4 to Exit 25A (U.S. 192); go east to second light and then right on Celebration Ave. Follow the signs. **Amenities:** Restaurant (American/breakfast-lunch only); lounge; 4 restaurants nearby; heated outdoor pool; 18-hole golf course; state-of-the-art health-and-fitness center; spa; concierge; free shuttle to Disney parks; transportation to non-Disney parks for a fee; nearby shopping district. *In room:* A/C, TV/Nintendo, dataport, hair dryer, iron, safe.

MODERATE

Holiday Inn Nikki Bird Resort ⚡ *Kids*   Here's a family-friendly inn with a roaming mascot (Nikki Bird) and a dedication to kids. The hotel renovated all of its rooms in 1997 and is in excellent shape. Kids Suites are larger than the standard rooms and have a separate area for youngsters. Varying suite themes include a circus tent. Kids under 12 eat free at a breakfast buffet next door; they also get entertainment, including puppet shows, songs, and games.

7300 W. Irlo Bronson Memorial Hwy. (U.S. 192), Kissimmee, FL 34747. ⓒ **800/206-2747** or 407/396-7300. Fax 407/396-7555. www.holidayinnsofcentralflorida.com. 530 units. $89–$129 for up to 4 persons. AE, DC, DISC, MC, V. Free parking. Take I-4 to Exit 25B. The hotel is 1.5 miles past the Disney entrance on the left. **Amenities:** Restaurant (American); grill; lounge; heated outdoor pool; kids' pool; whirlpool; 3 lighted tennis courts; exercise room; kids' club; concierge; free shuttle to Disney parks; transportation to non-Disney parks for a fee; guest laundry; valet. *In room:* A/C, TV w/pay movies, dataport, fridge, coffeemaker, hair dryer, iron.

INEXPENSIVE

Econo Lodge Maingate Hawaiian Resort *Value*   Location and price are the perks here. The inn is just 1.2 miles from the WDW entrance and is a bargain for those who come on a budget. The rooms are clean, but the price means you're not getting any frills.

7514 W. Irlo Bronson Memorial Hwy. (U.S. 192), Kissimmee, FL 34747. ⓒ **800/356-6935**, 407/390-9063, or 407/396-2000. Fax 407/390-1226. www.enjoyfloridahotels.com. 445 units. $35–$119 double. Extra person $10. Children 18 and under stay free with parent. AE, DC, DISC, MC, V. Free parking. From I-4, take Exit 25B (U.S. 192) and go west 2.2 miles; hotel is on left, past Reedy Creek Blvd. **Amenities:** Restaurant (Steak); lounge; heated outdoor pool; Jacuzzi; arcade; guest-services desk; car-rental desk; free shuttle to Disney parks; transportation to non-Disney parks for a fee; guest laundry; nonsmoking rooms. *In room:* A/C, TV.

Ramada Disney Eastgate *Value*   If you're looking for a peer comparable in rates and quality to a Howard Johnson's, this Ramada is it. Remodeled in 1998, it's a cut cleaner that many of the chain's standard motels, but no fancier. Standard rooms average 300 square feet, sleep up to four persons, and sport balconies. One child eats free for each paying adult. The inn is 4 miles from Disney.

5150 W. Irlo Bronson Memorial Hwy. (U.S. 192), Kissimmee, FL 34746. ⓒ **888/298-2054** or 407/396-1111. Fax 407/396-1607. www.ramada.com. 402 units. $59–$99 double. Extra person $10. Children 17 and under stay free with parent. AE, DC, DISC, MC, V. Free parking. From I-4 take Exit 25A (U.S. 192) and go east 2½ miles to the motel. **Amenities:** Restaurant (American); lounge; heated outdoor pool; kids' pool; Jacuzzi; arcade; car-rental desk; free shuttles to WDW parks; transportation to non-Disney parks for a fee; limited room service; guest laundry; valet; nonsmoking rooms. *In room:* A/C, TV w/pay movies and Nintendo, dataport, coffeemaker, hair dryer, iron, safe.

INTERNATIONAL DRIVE AREA

The hotels and resorts listed here are 7 to 10 miles north of the Walt Disney World parks (via I-4) and 1 to 3 miles from Universal Orlando and SeaWorld, which makes this zone centrally located for those who want to sample more than one area. The disadvantages: The northern end of International Drive is badly congested. The shops, motels, eateries, and attractions along this stretch can be as tacky as those on U.S. 192, and many of the motels and hotels don't offer free transportation to any of the parks.

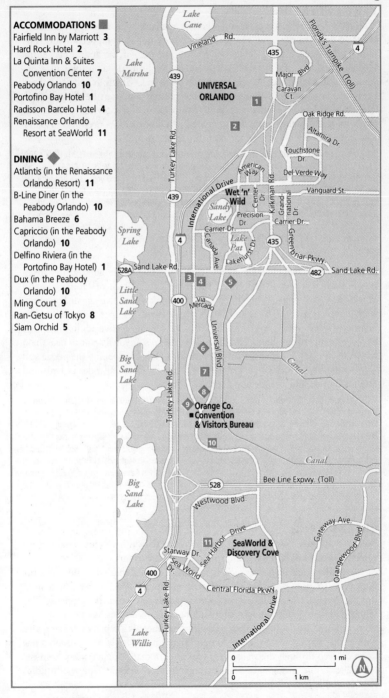

ACCOMMODATIONS ■

Fairfield Inn by Marriott **3**
Hard Rock Hotel **2**
La Quinta Inn & Suites
  Convention Center **7**
Peabody Orlando **10**
Portofino Bay Hotel **1**
Radisson Barcelo Hotel **4**
Renaissance Orlando
  Resort at SeaWorld **11**

DINING ◆

Atlantis (in the Renaissance
  Orlando Resort) **11**
B-Line Diner (in the
  Peabody Orlando) **10**
Bahama Breeze **6**
Capriccio (in the Peabody
  Orlando) **10**
Delfino Riviera (in the
  Portofino Bay Hotel) **1**
Dux (in the Peabody
  Orlando) **10**
Ming Court **9**
Ran-Getsu of Tokyo **8**
Siam Orchid **5**

VERY EXPENSIVE

Peabody Orlando *Finds* The five mallards who march into a lobby fountain every morning at 11am and then back out at 5pm, accompanied by John Philip Sousa's *King Cotton March,* are just part of the appeal at Central Florida's friendliest hotel. The Peabody Orlando is primarily a business and convention destination, but it's one of our top picks in O-Town. It's classy without being stuffy, and if your budget allows the splurge you won't be disappointed. The 400-square-foot rooms sleep up to five persons, and those on the west side (sixth floor and higher) offer a distant view of Disney and its fireworks displays. The hotel also offers some of the best dining in town.

9801 International Dr. (between the Bee Line Expressway and Sand Lake Rd.), Orlando, FL 32819. © 800/732-2639 or 407/352-4000. Fax 407/354-1424. www.peabody-orlando.com. 891 units. $330–$420 standard room for up to 3 persons; $520–$1,500 suites. Extra person $20. Children 17 and under stay free with parent. AE, DC, DISC, MC, V. Free parking; valet $8. From I-4 Exit 29/Sand Lake Rd., turn east to International Dr., then south. The hotel is on the left. **Amenities:** 3 restaurants (Continental, Northern Italian, American); 3 lounges; heated outdoor pool; kids' pool; whirlpool; 4 lighted tennis courts; fitness center; spa; concierge; guest-services desk; business center; shopping arcade; shuttle to WDW and other parks for a fee; 24-hr. room service; massage; valet; nonsmoking rooms; concierge-level rooms. *In room:* A/C, TV, dataport, minibar, hair dryer.

Portofino Bay Hotel *Finds* Universal entered the hotel game late in life, but when it did, it delivered a resort with the stature of Disney's Grand Floridian. The 2-year-old hotel is designed to look like the village of Portofino, Italy, complete with a harbor and canals that take you via boat to the parks. The luxurious rooms measure 450 square feet and sleep up to five adults. The beds have Egyptian-woven sheets, and the pillows are so soft you'll want to take them home. (You *won't,* but you'll want to.) Ask for a view overlooking the piazza and "bay" area. *Note:* Guests here get no-line access to almost all rides at Universal Studios Florida and Islands of Adventure.

5601 Universal Blvd., Orlando, FL 32819. © 888/322-5541 or 407/503-1000. Fax 407/224-7118. www.universalorlando.com. 750 rooms. $235–$395 double; $395–$495 butler concierge; $395–$2,320 suites. Extra person $25. Children 17 and under stay free with parent. AE, DISC, DC, MC, V. Free parking; valet $8. From I-4 take Exit 30 (Kirkman Rd./Hwy. 435) and follow the signs. **Amenities:** 3 restaurants (Northern Italian); deli; 3 lounges; 2 heated outdoor pools (1 for concierge and suite guests only); kids' pool; bocce courts (concierge and suite guests only); fitness center; spa; water-sports equipment; kids' club; arcade; concierge; tour desk; free water-taxi transportation to Universal Studios; Islands of Adventure; and CityWalk; free shuttle to SeaWorld; transportation for a fee to the WDW parks; business center; shopping arcade; 24-hr. room service; baby-sitting; guest laundry; valet; nonsmoking rooms; concierge-level rooms. *In room:* A/C, TV, hair dryer, iron, safe.

EXPENSIVE

Hard Rock Hotel You can't get any closer than this to CityWalk or Universal Studios Florida. This California mission–style resort sports a rock 'n' roll theme and opened in January 2001 with rack rates a shade cheaper than the Portofino (see above). Like all new hotels, this one has a few kinks that need ironing out, but we think it will develop into an excellent property. The 400-square-foot rooms come with a king bed or two queens. All the rooms are very comfortable; the bathrooms aren't big, but there is a separate dressing area with a sink. Unfortunately, even though the rooms are fairly soundproof, a few notes do seep through the walls, so ask for a room that's situated away from the lobby area. *Note:* Guests get no-line access to most rides at Universal Studios Florida and Islands of Adventure.

5000 Universal Blvd., Orlando, FL 32819. © 888/322-5541 or 407/363-8000. Fax 407/224-7118. www.universalorlando.com. $185–$315 double. Extra person $20. Children 17 and under stay free with parent.

AE, DISC, DC, MC, V. Free parking; valet $8. Take I-4 Exit 30 (Kirkman Rd./Hwy. 435) and follow the signs north. **Amenities:** 2 restaurants (American); grill; 2 lounges; heated outdoor pool; kids' pool; fitness center; kids' club; arcade; concierge; free water-taxi transportation to Universal Studios; Islands of Adventure; and CityWalk; free shuttle to SeaWorld; transportation for a fee to the WDW parks; shopping arcade; 24-hr. room service; baby-sitting; guest laundry; valet; nonsmoking rooms. *In room:* A/C, TV, hair dryer, iron, safe.

Renaissance Orlando Resort at SeaWorld ★★ This stylish hotel offers large rooms and a great location for theme-park nomads: It's across from Sea-World and about 10 to 15 minutes from Universal Orlando and Walt Disney World. The lobby charms guests with a 10-story atrium, a pond filled with koi (weighing up to 25 pounds, these fish are huge!), a free-flight aviary, and six glass elevators that overlook the atrium. The spacious and airy guest rooms measure 385 square feet. East-side rooms, especially from the sixth floor up, have a nice view of the Kraken roller coaster and SeaWorld, which is within walking distance (but watch the traffic).

6677 Sea Harbour Dr., Orlando, FL 32821. ℭ **800/327-6677** or 407/351-5555. Fax 407/351-4618. www.renaissancehotels.com. 778 units. $166–$289 double. Extra person $15. Children 17 and under stay free with parent. AE, DC, DISC, MC, V. Free parking; valet $9. Take I-4 Exit 27A and follow signs to SeaWorld. **Amenities:** 3 restaurants (Seafood, Northern Chinese, American); grill; 3 lounges; heated outdoor pool; kids' pool; 2 whirlpools; 4 lighted tennis courts; health club; spa; sauna; arcade; concierge; tour desk; car-rental desk; transportation for a fee to all the parks; business center; shopping arcade; 24-hr. room service; massage; baby-sitting; guest laundry; valet; nonsmoking rooms. *In room:* A/C, TV w/pay movies and PlayStation, dataport, safe.

MODERATE

La Quinta Inn & Suites Convention Center Opened in 1998, this is one of a handful of upscale, moderately priced motels on Universal Boulevard, which runs parallel to (but isn't as congested as) International Drive. Standard rooms here measure 300 square feet and have 2 double beds; the 375-square-foot king rooms are designed to accommodate extended stays and add in a fridge and microwave. A limited number of two-room suites offering separate living and sleeping areas are available.

8504 Universal Blvd., Orlando, FL 32819. ℭ **800/531-5900**, 800/687-6667, or 407/345-1365. Fax 407/345-5586. www.laquinta.com. 185 units. $79–$129 double. Rates include continental breakfast. Extra person $10. Children 18 and under stay free with parent. AE, DC, DISC, MC, V. Free parking. Take I-4 to Exit 29 (Sand Lake Rd./Hwy. 482), go east toward Universal, and then turn right. The hotel is on right. **Amenities:** Heated outdoor pool; whirlpool; transportation for a fee to all theme parks; exercise room; guest laundry; nonsmoking rooms. *In room:* A/C, TV w/pay movies and Nintendo, dataport, coffeemaker, hair dryer, iron.

Radisson Barcelo Hotel ★ Like many International Drive properties, the Radisson offers a good location for people whose vacations center on Universal Orlando or SeaWorld, as well as a central location for travelers who also plan to visit Disney and the downtown area. The bright guest rooms measure 384 square feet, a figure larger than the average in this price range, and are equipped with two queen beds. Views are pretty basic. The seventh floor (the highest) will give you a look at SeaWorld to the south.

8444 International Dr., Orlando, FL 32819. ℭ **800/333-3333** or 407/345-0505. Fax 407/352-5894. www.radisson.com/orlandofl_barcelo/. 520 units. $105–$199 double. Extra person $10. Children 17 and under stay free with parent. AE, DC, DISC, MC, V. Free parking. Take I-4 Exit 29/Sand Lake Rd., turn right on International Dr., and go ½ mile to hotel. **Amenities:** Restaurant (Florida/Regional); grill; lounge; heated outdoor pool; lighted tennis court; bocce court; guest-services desk; free shuttle to Universal Orlando and Sea-World; transportation for a fee to Disney parks; guest laundry; valet; nonsmoking rooms. *In room:* A/C, TV w/pay movies and Nintendo, dataport, fridge, coffeemaker, hair dryer, iron, safe.

So You Didn't Book a Room . . .

Coming to Orlando without a reservation isn't a good idea. But if you do, try one of these chains. They're moderate or inexpensive in price and located in the budget motel corridors of Kissimmee/U.S. 192 or International Drive. While we can't vouch for them personally, their brand names generally mean reliability:

In Kissimmee

Best Western Eastgate, 5565 W. Irlo Bronson Memorial Hwy., Kissimmee (© **407/396-0707**).

Best Western Maingate, 7571 W. Irlo Bronson Memorial Hwy., Kissimmee (© **407/396-7500**).

Budget Inn West, 4686 W. Vine St., Kissimmee (© **407/396-2322**).

Comfort Suites Maingate Hotel, 7888 W. Irlo Bronson Memorial Hwy., Kissimmee (© **407/390-9888**).

Comfort Suites Resort Maingate East, 2775 Florida Plaza Blvd., Kissimmee (© **407/397-7848**).

Days Inn East of the Magic Kingdom, 5840 W. Irlo Bronson Memorial Hwy., Kissimmee (© **407/396-7969**).

Days Inn West-Maingate, 7980 W. Irlo Bronson Memorial Hwy., Kissimmee (© **407/997-1000**).

DoubleTree Caste Hotel, 8629 International Dr., Orlando (© **407/345-1511**).

DoubleTree Guest Suites Resort, 4787 W. Irlo Bronson Memorial Hwy., Kissimmee (© **407/397-0555**).

Econo Lodge Maingate Resort, 7514 W. Irlo Bronson Memorial Hwy., Kissimmee (© **407/390-9124**).

INEXPENSIVE

Fairfield Inn by Marriott ★ *Value*   If you're looking for International Drive's best value, it's hard to beat the Fairfield. This Fairfield combines a quiet location off the main drag, down-to-earth rates, and a clean, modern motel in one package. The spacious guest rooms (375 sq. ft.) sleep four and are very comfortable.

8342 Jamaican Court (off International Dr. between the Bee Line Expressway and Sand Lake Rd.), Orlando, FL 32819. © 800/228-2800 or 407/363-1944. Fax 407/363-1944. www.fairfieldinn.com. 135 units. $69–$79 for up to 4 persons. Rates include continental breakfast. AE, DC, DISC, MC, V. Free parking. From I-4 take Exit 29 (Sand Lake Rd.) and go east 1 block. Turn right on International Dr. and then right on Jamaican Court. Hotel is on right. **Amenities:** Heated outdoor pool; guest-services desk; free shuttle to Universal Orlando and Sea-World; transportation for a fee to the Disney parks; guest laundry; valet; nonsmoking rooms. *In room:* A/C, TV w/pay movies, dataport, safe.

ORLANDO BED & BREAKFASTS

These properties offer a respite from the crowded, run-and-gun world of the resorts or chains, and they're ideal for couples looking for a little quiet time or romance. Note that most of the inns and B&Bs in Orlando do not accept children as guests—a major selling point in their favor for some visitors. If you choose to stay at one of these properties, you'll need a car or some other kind of transportation since none of these inns provides it.

Holiday Inn Main Gate West, 7601 Black Lake Rd., Kissimmee (© 407/390-9063).

Howard Johnson Maingate West, 8660 W. Irlo Bronson Memorial Hwy., Kissimmee (© 407/396-4500).

Quality Suites Maingate East, 5876 W. Irlo Bronson Memorial Hwy., Kissimmee (© 407/396-8040).

Ramada Eastgate Fountain Park, 5150 W. Irlo Bronson Memorial Hwy., Kissimmee (© 407/396-1111).

In the International Drive Area:

Days Inn East of Universal Studios, 5827 Caravan Court, Orlando (© 407/351-3800).

Days Inn International Drive, 7200 International Dr., Orlando (© 407/351-1200).

Holiday Inn International Drive Resort, 6515 International Dr., Orlando (© 407/351-3500).

Sheraton Studio City Hotel, 5905 International Dr., Orlando (© 407/351-2100).

Travel Lodge International Drive, 5859 American Way, Orlando (© 407/345-8880).

Also try **Disney's Central Reservation Service** (© 407/740-6442; www. reservation-services.com), or **Discount Hotels of America** (© 407/294-9600; www.discounthotelsamerica.com).

The Courtyard at Lake Lucerne ★ *Finds*   You might feel the sting of Cupid's arrows in this historic hideaway near Church Street Station. The inn has several historic buildings, such as the Art Deco Wellborn (one-bedroom apartments and a suite) and the I. W. Phillips House, built in 1919 and reminiscent of old Southern homes with large verandahs. Rooms range from 225 to 325 square feet.

211 N. Lucerne Circle E., Orlando, FL 32801. © 800/444-5289 or 407/648-5188. Fax 407/246-1368. www.orlandohistoricinn.com. 30 units. $89–$225 double. Rates include continental breakfast. AE, DC, MC, V. Free parking. Take Orange Ave. south immediately after City Hall (dome building with fountains and glass sculpture); turn left onto Anderson. After 2 lights, turn right at Delaney Ave. Take first right onto Lucerne Circle. Be aware of one-way streets. Follow the brown "historic inn" signs. Children are not permitted. **Amenities:** Restaurant (American/Southern); nonsmoking rooms. *In room:* A/C, TV, some with kitchens, fridges, microwaves, coffeemakers.

PLACES TO STAY ELSEWHERE IN ORLANDO

There are two good reasons to choose accommodations away from all of the hustle and hassle of the attractions: Crowds are thinner and, in some cases, prices are lower. On the flip side, if you're heading to the theme parks, your location off the beaten path means that you'll have to deal with a long drive and traffic.

Best Western Mount Vernon Inn *Value* The Colonial-style Mount Vernon is one of the best bargains in town. It's a place where guests get comfortable rooms and a shield from Mickeyville, which is 25 miles south. The Colonial-style Mount Vernon isn't fancy by resort standards, but its rooms are cozy and the staff is friendly. The standard rooms measure 325 square feet and sleep four; some overlook the pool, and a few have refrigerators. Deluxe rooms feature a small sitting area and offer a choice of one king or two queen beds.

110 S. Orlando Ave., Winter Park, FL 32789 **℃ 800/992-3379,** 800/780-7234, or 407/647-1166. Fax 407/647-8011. www.bestwestern.com. 147 units. $69–$109 double. Extra person $10. Children 17 and under stay free with parent. AE, DC, DISC, MC, V. Free parking. The inn is on U.S. 17–92, between Fairbanks Ave. and Lee Rd. **Amenities:** Restaurant (American); lounge; heated outdoor pool; guest laundry, valet; nonsmoking rooms. *In room:* A/C, TV, dataport.

4 Dining

Orlando has more than its share of fast fooderies and theme eateries. But it also has a growing number of upscale restaurants. Since most visitors spend much of their time at Disney, we're going to focus a lot of energy there. But we won't leave out worthwhile dining rooms that are out of this World. We'll also explore the better places to eat at Universal's CityWalk, along International Drive, and elsewhere in town.

HOW TO ARRANGE PRIORITY SEATING AT DISNEY RESTAURANTS

Priority seating *isn't* a reservation. It's a promise that you'll get the next available table once you arrive. There may be a wait, but if you don't use this system you may have an even longer wait. To get priority seating at any WDW restaurant, call ℃ **407/939-3463.** You can book as far as 60 days in advance of your arrival.

If you're staying on Disney property, you can arrange priority seating at your resort. At Epcot, you can do it at several locations: the WorldKey interactive terminals at Guest Relations near Innoventions East, the WorldKey Information Service on the main concourse to the World Showcase, and the restaurant of your choice.

TIPS ON WALT DISNEY WORLD RESTAURANTS

All park restaurants are **nonsmoking.**

Magic Kingdom restaurants don't serve alcohol, but those at Animal Kingdom, Epcot, and Disney–MGM Studios do.

Sit-down restaurants in WDW take American Express, Diners Club, Discover, MasterCard, Visa, and the Disney Card.

Unless otherwise noted, *restaurants in the theme parks require park admission.* Unless you're using Disney transportation, you're also going to face a $6 parking fee.

Nearly all WDW restaurants with sit-down or counter service offer children's menus with items ranging from $4 to $6.

INSIDE THE WDW THEME PARKS

With only a few exceptions, you won't find Disney's park restaurants winning accolades from *Food & Wine* or *Bon Appétit.* The food in most of them is on a par with the food at Universal Orlando—filling and palatable, but pretty overpriced for the quality received. The following list includes the Magic Kingdom, Epcot, Disney–MGM Studios, and Animal Kingdom. Information on all Disney restaurants can be obtained by calling ℃ **407/939-3463** or visiting **www.disneyworld.com.**

(*Tips* **Special Tastes**

Looking for kosher food? Worried WDW can't entertain your vegetarian taste buds? Disney usually can handle those diets and other special ones (people who need fat-free or sugar-free meals, folks who have allergies or a lactose intolerance, for instance) as long as guests give Disney advance notice—usually no more than 24 hours. You can do that when you make priority-seating arrangements (✆ **407/939-3463**) or, if you're staying at a Disney resort, at its guest-services desk. If you're not staying at WDW, call ✆ **407/824-2222**.

EPCOT
World Showcase

The World Showcase features the best dining options anywhere in WDW, thanks to the cultural cuisine of its 11 nation pavilions. Although many consider a meal here an essential part of the experience, we must point out that the victuals here (as in all theme parks) are priced higher than comparable fare on the outside world.

The restaurants below are arranged geographically, beginning at the Canada pavilion and proceeding counterclockwise around the World Showcase Lagoon.

CANADA   Located in the Victorian Hotel du Canada, **Le Cellier Steakhouse** has a castlelike ambience accentuated by vaulted stone arches. Red-meat main events (all Midwest, corn-fed) include the usual range of cuts—fillet, porterhouse, prime rib, sirloin, and so on. Wash down your meal with a Canadian wine or choose from a selection of Canadian beers. Lunch runs $12 to $23 per person; dinner is $16 to $25.

UNITED KINGDOM   The Tudor-beamed **Rose & Crown** ✿ is a cozy pub suggestive of Victorian England. Visitors from the U.K. flock to this spot, where English folk music and the occasionally saucy server entertain you as you feast your eyes and palate on a short but joyfully traditional menu. An outdoor dining area overlooks the lagoon and is a good place to see the IllumiNations fireworks display. The lunch entrees are $10 to $15; dinner is $14 to $21.

FRANCE   **Chefs de France** has an art nouveau interior agleam with mirrors and brass chandeliers. Three world-renowned French chefs—Paul Bocuse, Roger Verge, and Gaston LeNotre—designed the menu, which is respectable by theme-park standards but doesn't threaten better French restaurants in Orlando's free world. The dinner entrees include Mediterranean seafood casserole (grouper, scallops, and shrimp dusted with saffron, then allowed to swim in a mild garlic sauce) and short ribs of beef burgundy with pearl onions and mushrooms. There's an extensive wine list. Lunch is $15 to $19; dinner is $20 to $35.

MOROCCO   Of all the Epcot restaurants, **Restaurant Marrakesh** ✿✿ exemplifies the spirit of the park, yet a lot of guests don't know it's there or ignore it because they're worried that the menu is too exotic. Expect belly dancers to entertain while you feast on such options as marinated beef shish kebob, savory lamb roasted in its juices, and a medley of seafood, chicken, and lamb. Most entrees come with the national dish, couscous (steamed semolina with veggies and, sometimes, other embellishments). The palatial restaurant—with hand-set mosaic tiles, latticed shutters, and a ceiling painted in elaborate Moorish motifs—represents some 12 centuries of Arabic design. Lunch costs $14 to $17; dinner is $16 to $28.

JAPAN If you've been to any of the Japanese steakhouse chains (teppanyakis), you know the drill at **Teppanyaki:** Diners sit around communal grill tables while white-hatted chefs rapidly dice, slice, stir-fry, and sometimes launch the food onto your plate with amazing skill. Unfortunately, the culinary acrobatics here are better than the cuisine. Lunch is $10 to $20; dinner is $15 to $30. The adjoining **Yakitori House** is a bamboo-roofed cafeteria that serves casual fare for under $10.

ITALY Patterned after Alfredo De Lelio's celebrated ristorante in Rome, **L'Originale Alfredo di Roma** is Epcot's most popular restaurant. Nevertheless, we've heard critics say the overpriced pasta here is matched only by the carefree servers. It's hard to take issue with at least one meatless pasta dish topping the $20 mark—the celebrated fettuccine. On the meatier side of the menu, a small-ish though true veal chop is served with a chianti-and-truffle sauce, mushrooms, asparagus, and roasted potatoes. There's also a vegetarian menu and an extensive Italian wine list. If you want a quieter setting, ask for a seat on the verandah. Lunch entrees cost $10 to $20; at dinner they're $21 to $40.

GERMANY The **Biergarten** simulates a Bavarian village courtyard at Okto-berfest. Unfortunately, the festive atmosphere hardly makes up for the bland, food. Entertainment might be an oompah band or a strolling accordionist, and guests are encouraged to dance and sing along. The all-you-can-eat buffet is filled with traditional Bavarian fare (assorted sausages, chicken schnitzel, sauerbraten, spaetzle with gravy, sauerkraut, and a large assortment of trimmings). The lunch buffet is $12.95 for adults, $5.95 for children 3 to 11; dinner is $18.75 for adults, $7.95 for children. At **Sommerfest,** a cafeteria with indoor seating and courtyard tables overlooking a fountain, you can purchase bratwurst sandwiches with sauer-kraut, goulash soup, and apple strudel. All items are under $8.

CHINA When it comes to decor, **Nine Dragons** shines with carved rosewood furnishings and a dragon-motif ceiling. Some windows overlook the lagoon out-side. The food, alas, doesn't match its surroundings. Main courses feature four cuisines—Mandarin, Shanghai, Cantonese, and Szechuan—but portions tend to be smaller than you'd expect in an Oriental restaurant. You can order Chinese or California wines with your meal. Entrees cost from $10 to $25 for lunch; $15 to $30 at dinner. If you want something lighter, the open-air **Lotus Blossom Café** sells egg rolls, pork fried rice, and stir-fried chicken and vegetables served over noodles ($4 to $8).

NORWAY **Akershus** 𝕮 is a re-created 14th-century castle where you can sample a 40-item smorgasbord of *smavarmt* (hot) and *koldtbord* (cold) dishes, making it a bargain for big appetites. The reasonably good entrees usually include such dishes as venison stew, steamed whitefish, smoked pork with honey mustard, gravlax in mustard sauce, smoked mackerel, Norwegian herring, an array of Norwegian breads and cheeses, and more. Norwegian beer and aquavit complement a list of French and California wines. The lunch buffet costs $11.95 for adults, $5.25 for children 4 to 9; the dinner buffet is $18.50 for adults, $7.95 for kids. The **Kringla Bakeri og Kafe** offers covered outdoor seat-ing and inexpensive light fare—open-face sandwiches, cheese and fruit platters, waffles sprinkled with powdered sugar, and fresh-baked Norwegian pastries. All items cost under $10.

MEXICO It's always night at the **San Angel Inn** ✿, where you can feast on some of the best South-of-the-Border cuisine in all of the theme parks. Candlelit tables set the mood, and the menu delivers reasonably authentic food. One top seller is the *mole poblano* (chicken brought to life with more than 20 spices, carrots, and a hint of chocolate). Another favorite: *filete motuleno* (grilled beef tenderloin served over black beans, melted cheese, pepper strips, and fried plantains (a sweet, banana-like fruit). Lunch entrees run $9 to $17; dinners are $17 to $22. The **Cantina de San Angel,** a cafeteria with outdoor seating at umbrella tables overlooking the lagoon, offers tacos, burritos, and combination plates under $10.

Future World

At the Living Seas pavilion, the mood is half the fun at the **Coral Reef,** where the tables circle a 5.6-million-gallon aquarium that has 4,000 denizens of the not-so-deep. Tiered seating ensures everyone a good view. Menu standards include whole roasted snapper with vegetables and potatoes and sautéed rock shrimp in a tangy lemon cream sauce. Lunch entrees are $16 to $21; dinners are $18 to $29.

IN THE MAGIC KINGDOM

In addition to the restaurants already mentioned, there are plenty of fast-food outlets located throughout the park. But you may find that a quiet, sit-down meal is an essential though brief getaway from the forced-march madness. Don't forget to make priority-seating arrangements.

Fantasyland Romantics may find it hard to beat the ambience of eating at **Cinderella's Royal Table** ✿ in Cinderella's Castle, which happens to be the Magic Kingdom's icon. Servers treat you like a lord or lady while fetching you headliners such as spice-crusted salmon with arugula and corn mash, a tenderloin with smashed taters and shallot sauce, and (lunch only) prime-rib slices in a pastry crust with cabernet sauce and red potatoes. Lunch is $12 to $16; dinner sells for $20 to $29.

Liberty Square The **Liberty Tree Tavern's** colonial decor and mood music are fun, but the food (including the evening buffet) is basic. Expect roast turkey, marinated flank steak, and honey mustard ham. Lunch is $10 to $17; the buffet is $20 for adults, $10 for kids 3 to 11.

Main Street Breakfasts at **Tony's Town Square Restaurant** are traditional food; lunch and dinner are nondescript (and in some cases cardboard-quality) Italian. Evening fare includes pan-seared mahi-mahi over vegetables; shrimp sautéed with vine-ripened tomatoes, basil, and white wine over capellini pasta; and a grilled pork chop marsala with wild mushrooms. Breakfast is $6 to $8, lunch is $9 to $20, and dinner is $17 to $27.

The **Plaza Restaurant's** sundaes, banana splits, and other ice-cream creations—arguably the best in WDW—draw more folks than anything else, especially during the dog days of summer. The Plaza also has tasty if expensive sandwiches (turkey, Reuben, club, cheese steak, and chicken). You can eat inside in an art nouveau dining room or on a verandah overlooking Cinderella's Castle. Most items cost $9 to $11.

AT DISNEY–MGM STUDIOS

There are more than a dozen places to refuel in this Hollywood-style theme park. The ones listed below are the best of the bunch. Again, priority seating is a must.

Modeled after the famed Los Angeles celebrity haunt where Louella Parsons, Hedda Hopper, and others held court, the **Hollywood Brown Derby** offers a noisy, good-time meal, but one that's pretty pricey. The restaurant's signature Cobb salad ($12.75 for two) was invented by owner Bob Cobb in the 1930s. Dinner entrees at Disney's version include a savory skillet-seared grouper fillet (dusted with polenta and served with red onion, chick peas, and a lemon-tomato-butter sauce) and grilled salmon (with seafood minestrone and pasta). The Derby's signature dessert, grapefruit cake with cream-cheese icing, is a perfect meal capper. Main courses are $14 to $20 at lunch; $17 to $26 at dinner.

The concept behind the **50's Prime Time Cafe** is intriguing: Build a restaurant based on a 1950s time warp/sitcom psychodrama. The atmosphere delivers with black-and-white TV sets showing "My Little Margie" and servers threatening to withhold dessert if you don't eat all your food. But we won't blame you if you don't. Although the desserts are good, the meatloaf and chicken and biscuits don't deliver. Meals cost $10 to $17 at lunch; $11 to $19 at dinner.

The best (and safest) bet at **Mama Melrose's Ristorante Italiano** is the brick-oven baked pizza (tomato and vegetable, portobello mushroom, and grilled chicken). The menu is fleshed out with so-so Italian pretenders—chicken marsala, shrimp risotto, and lobster ravioli. Lunch is $11 to $19; dinner is $11 to $22.

If you read the above listing for the 50's Prime Time Cafe and then give it a science-fiction spin, well, welcome to the **Sci-Fi Dine-In Theater Restaurant.** Diners sit in chrome convertibles (with fins and whitewalls) under a starlit sky with the Hollywood hills as a backdrop and are treated to zany newsreels, cartoons, and "B" horror-movie clips, such as *Frankenstein Meets the Space Monster.* Forget food adjectives such as marinated, smoked, and pan-seared. It's still your basic beef, pork, poultry, tuna, and pasta. Lunches are $8 to $15; dinners are $11 to $20.

IN THE ANIMAL KINGDOM

You'll find few restaurants in Animal Kingdom, the newest Disney park, and most of those are grab-and-go places. Neverthelesss, there are three spots where you can park yourself.

Expect California fare with an island spin at the **Rainforest Café.** Menu offerings tend to be tasty and sometimes creative, but the cafe, like other Disney restaurants, charges more than the outside world. Dishes include a turkey pita with fried onions, romaine, tomatoes, and cranberry relish. The mixed grill has barbecued ribs, soy-ginger steak on skewers, barbecued chicken breast, and peppered shrimp. Lunch and dinner run $10 to $23.

Much like counter-service eateries in the other parks, the **Flame Tree Barbecue** offers grab-and-go food that includes sandwiches (smoked beef brisket, chicken, or pork shoulder), barbecued ribs, and a barbecued chicken-and-ribs platter. You can grab a beer here, too. Meals are $7 to $8.

Taste at the **Tusker House** is there, even if quantity and quality aren't. The options are grilled chicken salad in a sourdough-bread bowl; rotisserie or fried chicken; smoked turkey on focaccia bread; and a chicken, ham, and Swiss cheese sandwich. Beer and wine are served. Prices are $7 to $8.

IN THE WALT DISNEY WORLD RESORTS

Most of the following restaurants continue the Disney trend of being above market price, but the food in many of these is a notch or more higher than what you find in the theme parks.

VERY EXPENSIVE

Citricos ★★ NEW FRENCH   You can get a modified taste of the Victoria & Albert's treatment (see below) at Citricos, which isn't as posh or pricey as the Grand Floridian's premier dining room. The chef creates what the resort calls French, Alsatian, and Provençal cuisine with California and Florida touches. The menu changes on a regular basis, but you might see rack of lamb with black olives, pan-seared salmon in a mildly tart citrus beurre blanc, grilled Cornish hen with a mustard-oil drizzle, or pork tenderloin with pleasant goat-cheese polenta. The Chef's Domain offers an experience similar to the Chef's Table at Victoria & Albert's.

4401 Floridian Way, in Disney's Grand Floridian Resort & Spa. ✆ 407/939-3463 or 407/939-7707. Priority seating. Main courses $24–$38; Chef's Domain $650 for 2 to 12 people; $115 per person for wine pairing. AE, DC, DISC, MC, V. Daily 5:30–10pm; Chef's Domain seatings 6 and 8:30pm.

Victoria & Albert's ★★★ *Finds* HAUTE CUISINE   It's not often we can describe dinner as "an event," but Disney's most elegant restaurant earns that distinction. Dinner is next-to-perfect—if the portions seem small, we dare you to make it through all seven courses—and the setting is exceptionally romantic. The meal begins with a personalized menu and a rose for the lady in your party. The fare changes nightly, but you might find main events such as black bass with toasted couscous or beef tenderloin with onion risotto. Servers (always named Victoria and Albert) provide the kind of service that has most diners wishing they could take their servers home. There's an extensive wine list. We suggest a wine pairing, which provides an appropriate wine with most courses for an extra $35.

4401 Floridian Way, in Disney's Grand Floridian Resort & Spa. ✆ 407/939-7707 or 407/939-3463. Reservations required. Jackets required for men. Not recommended for children. Fixed-price meal $85 per person, $35 additional for wine pairing; $115 Chef's Table, $160 with wine. AE, DC, DISC, MC, V. 2 dinner seatings daily 5:45–6:30pm and 9–9:45pm. Chef's Table 6pm only. Free self- and validated valet parking.

Yachtsman Steakhouse ★ SEAFOOD/STEAKS   Even by outside-the-park standards, the Yachtsman is a solid steakhouse. You can see the prime cuts in a glass-enclosed beef-aging room, and the exhibition kitchen provides a tantalizing glimpse of steaks, chops, and seafood being grilled over oak and hickory. Beef options range from an 8-ounce fillet to a 16-ounce prime rib and a belly-expanding 28-ounce porterhouse. The seafood side features wood-grilled mahi-mahi, seared salmon, and lobster tail. Also on the menu is roasted pork or chicken. The Yachtsman has an extensive wine list, and its staff is exceptionally cordial.

⌒Moments   The Chef's Table: The Best Seat in the World

There's a special dining option at **Victoria & Albert's.** Reserve the **Chef's Table** (far, far in advance) and dine in a charming alcove hung with copper pots and dried flower wreaths at an elegantly appointed candlelit table in the heart of the kitchen! Begin by sipping bubbly with the chef while discussing your food preferences for a seven- to nine-course menu created especially for you. The Chef's Table can accommodate up to twelve people a night. It's a leisurely affair, lasting 3 or 4 hours. The price is $115 without wine, $160 per person including five wines. This is so popular that Disney takes reservations 180 days in advance, so reserve *early* by calling **407/939-3463.**

1700 Epcot Resorts Blvd., in Disney's Yacht Club Resort. (407/939-3463 or 407/824-4321. Priority seating. Main courses $20–$55. AE, DC, DISC, MC, V. Daily 5:30–10pm. Free parking.

EXPENSIVE

Artist Point *★★* *(Finds* SEAFOOD/STEAKS   Enjoy a grand view of Disney's
Wilderness Lodge while you select from a menu that changes seasonally. Seafood
is the specialty here, and you might discover a maple-glazed king salmon that
comes with roasted vegetables and apples. One of the better meat dishes is the
grilled buffalo rib-eye (bison, actually) served with glazed carrots. Artist's Point
isn't as "discovered" as most of the other restaurants in the Disney resorts (enjoy
that while it lasts), which makes for a more relaxed atmosphere.

901 W. Timberline Dr., in Disney's Wilderness Lodge. (407/939-3463 or 407/824-1081. Priority seating.
Main courses $14–$32. AE, DC, DISC, MC, V. Daily 5:30–10pm. Free parking.

California Grill *★★★* CALIFORNIA   Located on the 15th floor of the Contemporary Resort, views of the Magic Kingdom and Seven Seas Lagoon will
entertain you while your eyes and mouth feast on the menu. Headliners change
often but include seared grouper in a noodle bowl with a ginger-crab salad,
braised lamb shank with chanterelle risotto, and a respectable sushi menu (crab,
eel, tuna, and more). This is one of the most vegetarian-friendly restaurants in
the World and is also one of the few spots in WDW that isn't crawling with kids.
The list of California wines helps complement the meal and views.

It can be tough to get a table at the California Grill, especially on weekends and
during Disney fireworks hours, so make a reservation as far ahead as possible.

4600 N. World Dr., at Disney's Contemporary Resort. (407/939-3463 or 407/824-1576. Reservations
recommended. Main courses $20–$30; sushi $10–$30. AE, DC, DISC, MC, V. Daily 5:30–10pm. Free parking.

MODERATE

Boatwright's Dining Hall NEW ORLEANS   A family atmosphere (noisy),
good food (by Disney standards), and reasonable prices (ditto) make
Boatwright's a hit, especially with Port Orleans Resort guests. Most dinner
entrees have a Cajun/Creole spin. The jambalaya sadly lacks seafood but has
plenty of chicken and sausage. There really isn't anything French about the
"French Quarter" fillet, but the pasta and seafood dish (lightly blackened catfish,
scallops, and shrimp with vegetables, red beans, and rice) makes up for it.

2201 Orleans Dr. (off Bonnet Creek Pkwy.), in Disney's Port Orleans Resort. (407/939-3463 or
407/824-4321. Priority seating. Main courses $7–$9 at breakfast; $16–$23 at dinner. AE, DC, DISC, MC, V.
Daily 7:30–11:30am and 5–10pm. Free parking.

'Ohana *★* PACIFIC RIM   Its star is earned on the fun front, but the decibel
level will turn some diners off. As your luau is being prepared over an 18-foot-
wide fire pit, the staff keeps you busy with coconut races, hula lessons, and other
shenanigans. Salmon, pork sausage, turkey, shrimp, and steak fill out the menu.
You'll also find lots of trimmings and a full bar with a limited wine selection.

1600 Seven Seas Dr., at Disney's Polynesian Resort. (407/939-3463 or 407/824-2000. Priority seating.
Family-feast dinner $23 for adults, $10 for kids 3–11 Character meals. AE, DC, DISC, MC, V. Daily 7:30–11am
and 5–10pm. Free parking.

DOWNTOWN DISNEY
VERY EXPENSIVE

Fulton's Crab House *★* SEAFOOD   Oysters and stone crab claws are the
specialties of this fun and fashionable eatery, which is in a replica of a (permanently moored) 19th-century Mississippi riverboat. It's one of the area's best

seafood houses, but you might want to bring your banker along for the ride. One popular meal for two combines Alaskan king crab and lobster served over potatoes and creamed spinach. The grilled tuna mignon is delicious—it's served rare with lemongrass dipping sauce, steamed bok choy, and a jasmine rice cake. Fulton's has one of Lake Buena Vista's better wine lists.

1670 Buena Vista Dr., aboard the riverboat docked at Downtown Disney. ☎ 407/934-2628. Priority seating. Main courses $11–$37 at lunch; $17–$44 at dinner. AE, DC, DISC, MC, V. Daily 11:30am–11pm. Valet parking $6; free parking.

EXPENSIVE

Portobello Yacht Club ☀ SOUTHERN ITALIAN/MEDITERRANEAN The pizzas here go beyond the routine to *quattro formaggi* (four cheese, plus sundried tomatoes) and *abruzzese* (pepperoni, provolone, garlic, plum tomatoes, and parsley). But it's the less casual entrees that pack people into this joint. The menu changes from time to time, but you may find a nice *costoletta di mai'ale* (marinated roasted pork loin with fennel, carrots, and roasted garlic whipped potatoes) and *spaghettini alla portobello* with pieces of Alaskan king crab, scallops, shrimp, and clams in light olive oil, wine, and herbs. Situated in a gabled Bermuda-style house, Portobello's windows and its awning-covered patio overlook Lake Buena Vista. The cellar is small, but there's a nice selection of wine to match the meals.

1650 Buena Vista Dr., in Pleasure Island. ☎ 407/934-8888. Priority seating. Main courses $10–$18 at lunch; $15–$40 at dinner; pizzas $9. AE, DC, DISC, MC, V. Daily 11:30am–midnight (dinner served from 4pm). Free parking; valet parking $6.

MODERATE

House of Blues MISSISSIPPI DELTA Most folks come for the blues bands and Sunday's gospel brunch. The brunch's music is inspired, but the food is so-so. Dinner is a notch better with a heartier jambalaya (shrimp, chicken, ham, and andouille sausage), Louisiana crawfish and shrimp étouffée, and Cajun meatloaf.

1490 Buena Vista Dr., at Disney's West Side, beneath water tower. ☎ 407/934-2583. Reservations not accepted (except for the Gospel Brunch). Main courses $13–$24; pizza and sandwiches $9–$10; brunch $28 adults, $15 kids 4–12. AE, DISC, MC, V. Daily 11am–2am. Free parking.

Rainforest Cafe ☀ CALIFORNIA Don't arrive starving. Waits average 2 hours if you fail to call ahead for priority seating, although even then you'll wait longer than at Animal Kingdom's Rainforest Cafe (see earlier in this chapter). Fun dishes include Mojo Bones (pork ribs), Rumble in the Jungle Turkey Pita, and Mixed Grill (ribs, skewers of soy-ginger steak, chicken breast, and peppered shrimp).

Downtown Disney Marketplace; look for the smoking volcano. ☎ 407/827-8500. Priority seating. Main courses $10–$23 at lunch and dinner. AE, DISC, MC, V. Sun–Thu 10:30am–11pm; Fri–Sat 10:30am–midnight. Free parking.

Wolfgang Puck Café CALIFORNIA The wait can be distressing and the sticker prices depressing, but the chefs turn out a mean menu of pizza, sushi, and other Left Coast mainstays. Possibilities include barbecued duck quesadillas, tuna tartare bruschetta, vegetable spring rolls, and free-range chicken. The eclectic eatery is decked out with ceramic art, mosaic tiles, and vibrant lighting. It's often busy and noisy, making conversation difficult if not impossible.

1482 Buena Vista Dr., at Disney's West Side. ☎ 407/938-9653. Reservations not accepted. Main courses $15–$29 (many under $20). AE, DC, DISC, MC, V. Daily 11am–1am. Free parking.

ELSEWHERE IN LAKE BUENA VISTA
VERY EXPENSIVE

Arthur's 27 ★★ *Finds* CONTINENTAL   Insiders come for the 27th-floor views of Central Florida sunsets and the Wizard of Disney's fireworks. Those who can afford the high-altitude prices are rewarded with a romantic restaurant that has the feel of a 1930s supper club minus the billowing clouds of cigarette smoke. The menu has goodies such as pan-seared breast of squab with chestnut risotto, and steamed scallops with poached oysters in black cappellini pasta. The wine list is commendable.

1900 Lake Buena Vista Dr., in the Wyndham Palace Resort, just north of Hotel Plaza Blvd. ℂ 407/827-3450. Reservations stronly recommended. Main courses $31–$45; fixed-price menu $49–$60; *no kids' menu.* AE, DC, DISC, MC, V. Daily 6–10pm. Free parking. Take I-4 Exit 27/Hwy. 535 north to Hotel Plaza Blvd. and then left to the Wyndham.

Black Swan ★ *Finds* AMERICAN/CONTINENTAL   The lodgelike Black Swan is sometimes criticized as a glorified golf-course restaurant, but it has a tempting menu to go with its fireplace, knotty-pine ceiling, and, yes, golfer-heavy clientele. Featured attractions include a beefy veal chop with peppercorns and swimming in its own juices, a beef tenderloin with carmelized onions and Roquefort cheese, and banana-and-nut crusted prawns with pineapple salsa. The food is expertly prepared, and the service is professional. The Black Swan also has an extensive wine list.

1 N. Jacaranda (off Hwy. 535), in the Villas of Grand Cypress. ℂ 407/239-1999. Reservations recommended. Main courses $31–$43; *no kids' menu.* AE, DC, DISC, MC, V. Daily 6–10pm. Free parking. Take I-4 Exit 27/Hwy. 535 north to Winter Garden–Vineland Rd./Hwy. 535; then go left.

EXPENSIVE

White Horse Saloon & Steakhouse ★ STEAK   Beef rules in this country-and-western eatery. Three cuts of prime rib range from 10 to 20 ounces, the fillet is basted with garlic and herbs, and fish fans can dig into a slab of salmon grilled with red peppers and tomato salsa. Beer and margaritas are the main adult attractions. Western singers add to the fun.

1 Grand Cypress Blvd. (off Hwy. 535), in the Hyatt Regency Grand Cypress Resort. ℂ 407/239-1234. Reservations recommended. Main courses $20–$39. AE, DC, DISC, MC, V. Tue–Sat 6–11pm. Free parking. Take I-4 Exit 27/Hwy. 535 north to Winter Garden–Vineland Rd./Hwy. 535; then go left.

MODERATE

Pebbles ★★ *Finds* CALIFORNIA   If you want to dine like a gourmet without paying a heavy price, here's your meal ticket. Pebbles is a local four-restaurant chain that has earned a reputation for great food, a sexy-though-small wine list, and creative appetizers. The chèvre-coated lamb chops, when available, are worth fighting for. Like many entrees, they come with three-cheese mashed potatoes and zucchini wedges. Pebbles is popular with a crowd ranging from young yuppies to aging baby boomers and their kids or grandkids.

Pebbles has three other locations: downtown at 17 W. Church St. (ℂ **407/839-0892**); in Longwood, 2110 W. Hwy. 434 (ℂ **407/774-7111**); and in Winter Park, 2516 Aloma Ave. (ℂ **407/678-7001**).

12551 Hwy. 535, in the Crossroads Shopping Center. ℂ 407/827-1111. Reservations not accepted. Main courses $10–$23. AE, DC, DISC, MC, V. Sun–Thurs 11am–11pm; Fri–Sat 11am–midnight. Free parking. Take I-4 Exit 27/Hwy. 535 north to the Crossroads Shopping Center on the right.

PLACES TO DINE IN UNIVERSAL ORLANDO

Universal stormed the restaurant scene with the opening of its dining and entertainment venue, CityWalk, in 1999. Fortunately, the company's sudden entry into the food fray did not create a compromise in quality.

VERY EXPENSIVE

Delfino Riviera ✿ NORTHERN ITALIAN   Overlooking the Harbor Piazza at Universal's Portofino Bay Hotel, this romantic venue offers a slice of the Italian Riviera—complete with strolling musicians and crooners. It has indoor and terrace dining as well as a chef's table for eight. The pasta menu features a savory lobster-champagne risotto, black olive pasta with monkfish, and pesto-stuffed ravioli. Carnivores can dig into veal roasted with porcini mushrooms, while fish fans delight in sea bass with mushrooms and potatoes in chianti sauce. The service at Delfino's is efficient, and the dining areas are quiet enough to allow intimate conversation. Next to Emeril's, its wine list is one of the best in the International Drive/Universal Orlando area.

5601 Universal Studios Blvd., in the Portofino Bay Hotel. ℂ 407/503-3463. Reservations recommended. Main courses $25–$42. AE, MC, V. Tue–Sat 5–10pm. Free parking; valet $8. From I-4 take Exit 30A or 30B and follow signs to Universal Orlando.

Emeril's ✿✿ NEW ORLEANS   Those able to secure a reservation at this pricey restaurant say the dynamic, Creole-inspired cuisine is worth the struggle to get a table. One good bet is the andouille-crusted redfish (an extremely moist white fish with roasted pecan-vegetable relish and meunière sauce). Barbecued salmon and Southwestern-style seafood are two of the pizza offerings. Choose from one of the restaurant's 12,000 bottles of wine. If you want a show, we highly recommend you try for one of eight counter seats, where you can watch the chefs working their magic; but getting one of these coveted seats requires making reservations months in advance.

   Lunch costs about half what you'll spend on dinner, and the menu and portions are almost the same. It's also easier to get a reservation midday.

6000 Universal Studios Blvd., in CityWalk. ℂ 407/224-2424. www.universalorlando.com or Reservations recommended well in advance. Main courses $17–$26 lunch; $18–$38 dinner. Daily 11:30am–2:30pm and 5:30–10pm (11pm Fri–Sat). AE, DISC, MC, V. Parking $7 (free after 6pm). Take I-4 Exit 30A or 30B and follow the signs to Universal Orlando.

MODERATE

Jimmy Buffett's Margaritaville CARIBBEAN   As soon as the parrotheads have had enough to drink (no later than 4pm on weekends, 6pm the rest of the week), the noise here makes it futile to try to talk with your table mates, but most folks come to Margaritaville to sing and get stupid, not to gab. Despite the cheeseburgers in paradise (yes, they're on the menu at $7.95), Jimmy's victuals lean toward the Caribbean side, including jerk chicken and a Cuban meatloaf survival sandwich that's a cheeseburger of another kind.

1000 Universal Studios Plaza, in CityWalk. ℂ 407/224-2155. Reservations not accepted. Main courses $8–$17. AE, DISC, MC, V. Daily 11:30am–midnight. Parking $7 (free after 6pm). From I-4 take Exit 30A or 30B and follow signs to Universal.

Pastamore Ristorante SOUTHERN ITALIAN   This family-style restaurant greets you with display cases brimming with mozzarella and some of the other goodies from the menu. The antipasto primo is a meal unto itself. The mound includes bruschetta, eggplant Caponata, melon with prosciutto, grilled portobello mushrooms, olives, a medley of Italian cold cuts, olives, plum toma-toes, mozzarella, and more. The menu also has traditional features such as veal marsala, chicken piccata, shrimp scampi, fettuccine Alfredo, lasagna, and pizza. An open kitchen allows diners a view of the chefs at work.

1000 Universal Studios Plaza, in CityWalk. ℂ **407/363-8000.** Reservations accepted. Main courses $7–$20. AE, DISC, MC, V. Daily 5pm–midnight. Parking $7 (free after 6pm). From I-4 take Exit 30A or 30B and follow signs to Universal.

PLACES TO DINE IN THE INTERNATIONAL DRIVE AREA

International Drive has one of the area's larger collections of fast-food joints, but the midsection and southern third also have some of this region's better restau-rants. International Drive is 10 minutes by auto from the Walt Disney World parks.

VERY EXPENSIVE

Atlantis ⭐ SEAFOOD   Although a tad pricey for the quality, this is one of the better seafood restaurants in Orlando. The relatively small dining room of this hotel restaurant has a warm, woody feel, with intimate booths separated by etched-glass panels. Specials such as a Mediterranean seafood medley (Florida lobster, grouper, shrimp, and scallops) often complement menu standards that include grilled sea bass, pan-seared duck, and rock shrimp. Sunday's champagne brunch undertakes an enterprising fare. That often means quail, mandarin duck, lamb chops, Cornish hen, clams, snapper, sea bass, sushi, and much more.

6677 Sea Harbour Dr., in the Renaissance Orlando Resort. ℂ **407/351-5555.** Reservations recommended. Main courses $24–$34; Sunday brunch $30 adults, $20 kids. AE, DISC, DC, MC, V. Daily 6–10pm. Free parking; valet $9. From I-4 take Exit 27A and follow the signs to SeaWorld.

Dux ⭐⭐⭐ *Finds* INTERNATIONAL   The chefs at Dux (named for the Peabody Orlando's resident quacks) deliver a fabulous menu that changes quar-terly. Depending on when you visit, it might include oven-roasted grouper with bok choy, mushrooms, and ginger sauce or a veal chop roasted medium rare with an artichoke-basil fricassee and garlic au jus. The impeccable service that's a sig-nature of the hotel carries into the restaurant, and Dux has one of the best wine lists in Orlando.

Dux is best reserved for a special night out or a meal on an expense account. Since the convention trade slows in August, it's one of the best times to try Dux and avoid crowds. Early-birds sometimes have the dining room to themselves.

9801 International Dr., in the Peabody Orlando. ℂ **407/345-4550.** Reservations recommended. Main courses $26–$45. AE, DC, DISC, MC, V. Mon–Thur 6–10pm; Fri–Sat 6–11pm. Free self- and validated valet parking. From I-4 take Exit 29 (Sand Lake Rd./Hwy. 528) east to International Dr. and then south. The hotel is on the left across from the Convention Center.

EXPENSIVE

Ran-Getsu of Tokyo ⭐ JAPANESE   Wealthy Asian tourists have made Ran-Getsu a popular stop on their itineraries, both for the authentic cuisine and sushi bar. Westerners may find the atmosphere without warmth and the prices too high, but they're not out of line with many of the more upscale Orlando eateries. Top choices include *tekka-don* (tender slices of tuna mild enough for first-time sushi eaters) and *Yosenabe,* a bouillabaisse with an unconventional twist—duck and chicken have been added to the seafood mix. Fillets are grilled in kabayaki sauce. Less adventurous palates may prefer the shrimp tempura or a steak served in teriyaki sauce.

8400 International Dr., near Orlando Convention Center. ℂ **407/345-0044.** Reservations recommended. Main courses $14–$35 (most under $25); sushi entrees $14–$41 (most under $25). AE, DC, MC, V. Daily

5–11:30pm. From I-4 take Exit 29/Sand Lake Rd. east to International Dr., then south. Restaurant is on right, just north of Convention Center.

MODERATE

Bahama Breeze ⭐ *Value* CARIBBEAN   This chain with spunk uses traditional Caribbean food as a base for creative items, such as moist and tasty "fish in a bag" (strips of mahi-mahi in a parchment pillow flavored with carrots, sweet peppers, mushrooms, celery, and spices) and a B+ *paella* (rice brimming with shrimp, fish, mussels, chicken, and sausage). It's loud and always crowded, so arrive early and bring patience (the restaurant doesn't accept reservations and the wait can be up to 2 hours during prime time, 6 to 8pm).

8849 International Dr. ✆ **407/248-2499**. Reservations not accepted. Main courses: full orders $9–$18; half orders $7–$12; sandwiches and salads $8–$11. AE, MC, V. Sun–Thurs 4pm–1am; Fri–Sat 4pm–1:30am. Free parking. From I-4 take Exit 29 (Sand Lake Rd./Hwy. 528) east to International Dr., then south. It's on the left.

B-Line Diner ⭐ AMERICAN   Come to have fun in a chrome-plated, 1950s-style diner where you can sink into upholstered booths or belly up to the counter on a stool. The friendly service lasts round-the-clock, and the menu features comfort foods such as chicken pot pie that's up to what mom made; a ham-and-cheese sandwich on a baguette; and roast pork with grilled apples, sun-dried cherry stuffing, and brandy-honey sauce. The portions are hearty, but so are the prices for diner fare. There's a full bar.

9801 International Dr., in the Peabody Orlando. ✆ **407/345-4460**. Reservations not accepted. Main courses $4–$14 at breakfast; $7–$17 at lunch; $9–$26 (most under $17) at dinner. AE, DC, DISC, MC, V. Daily 24 hr. Free self- and validated valet parking. From I-4 take Exit 29 (Sand Lake Rd./Hwy. 528) east to International Dr., then south. The hotel is on the left across from the Convention Center.

Capriccio ⭐ NORTHERN ITALIAN   Like its upscale Peabody sister, Dux, Capriccio virtually ensures something different from visit to visit with a menu that not only has many options but changes seasonally. The entrees might include bucatini tossed with chunks of mesquite-grilled chicken and mushrooms in a slightly garlicky herbed white-wine/pesto sauce or pan-seared tuna with braised fennel and radicchio served with lentil flan and a buttery citrus sauce. Chefs in the exhibition kitchen also make pizzas and fresh breads in mesquite-burning ovens. There's an extensive wine list.

Capriccio's Sunday brunch is nice, but not quite up to the standards of the one at Atlantis (reviewed above).

9801 International Dr., in the Peabody Orlando. ✆ **407/345-4540**. Reservations recommended. Main courses $18–$36 (most pizza and pasta dishes priced below $15); Sunday champagne brunch buffet $31 adults, $15 for children 5–12. AE, DC, DISC, MC, V. Tue–Sun 6–11pm; Sun brunch 11am–2pm. Free self- and validated valet parking. From I-4 take Exit 29 (Sand Lake Rd./Hwy. 528) east to International Dr., then south. Hotel is on the left across from the Convention Center.

Ming Court ⭐ CHINESE   Local patronage and the diverse menu make this one of O-Town's most popular Chinese restaurants. The lightly battered, deep-fried chicken breast gets plenty of zip from a delicate lemon-tangerine sauce. If you're in the mood for beef, try the grilled filet mignon seasoned Szechuan-style (the topping has toasted onions, garlic, and chili). Portions are sufficient, there's a moderate wine list, and the service is excellent.

9188 International Dr., between Sand Lake Rd. & Bee Line Expressway. ✆ **407/351-9988**. Reservations recommended. Dim sum mostly $3–$4; main courses $6–$10 at lunch, $13–$33 at dinner. AE, DC, DISC, MC, V. Daily 11am–2:30pm and 4:30pm–midnight. Free parking. Take I-4 Exit 29 (Sand Lake Rd./Hwy. 528) east to International Dr., then south. It's on the right.

Siam Orchid ✸ *Finds* THAI Tim and Krissnee Martsching grow the mint, chilies, cilantro, lemongrass, and wild lime that go into their entrees. The star attractions include Pad Thai (rice noodles tossed with ground pork, garlic, shrimp, crab claws, crabmeat, and crushed peanuts in a tongue-twanging sweet sauce). Royal Thai (a curry with chicken chunks, potato, and onion in yellow curry sauce) is another crowd-pleaser. The split-level dining room seats diners in cushioned booths and banquettes and bamboo chairs; some tables overlook a lake. Siam Orchid serves sake, plum wine, and Thai beers from a full bar.

7575 Universal Dr. (between Sand Lake Rd. and Carrier Dr.). ✆ 407/351-0821. Reservations recommended. Main courses $11–$18. AE, DC, DISC, MC, V. Daily 5–11pm. Free parking. Take I-4 Exit 29/Sand Lake Rd. east to Universal Blvd., then south to the restaurant.

PLACES TO DINE ELSEWHERE IN ORLANDO

There's life beyond the main tourist areas, as a lot of locals and some enterprising visitors discover. Here's a look at the best spots outside of the theme park's ground zero.

MODERATE

Rolando's ✸ *Finds* CUBAN Big portions and authentic cuisine are the main draws at this mom-and-pop restaurant. Specials include *arroz con pollo* (chicken with yellow rice), *ropa vieja* (shredded beef), and, if you call a day in advance, *paella* (fish and shellfish served on a bed of rice). Entrees come with yucca or plantains. Soft lighting adds a smidgen of ambience, and there's a very limited beer and wine list.

870 E. Hwy. 436/Semoran Blvd. (between Red Bug Rd. and U.S. 17/92), in Casselberry. ✆ 407/767-9677. Reservations not accepted. Main courses $4–$6 at lunch; $8–$17 at dinner. AE, DC, MC, V. Sun noon–8pm; Tues–Thu 11am–9pm; Fri–Sat 11am–10pm. Free parking. Take I-4 east to the East-West Expressway, head east, and make a left on Hwy. 436.

INEXPENSIVE

Bubbaloo's Bodacious BBQ ✸ *Value* BARBECUE This is some of the best barbecue in Florida. You can smell the hickory smoke emerging from this restaurant for blocks. There are other things on the menu, such as fried clams, but go for the full pork platter that comes with a heaping helping of pork and all the fixin's. The uninitiated should stay away from the "Killer" sauce, which produces a tongue buzz that's likely to last for hours; you might even taste-test the mild sauce before moving up to the hot.

1471 Lee Rd., Winter Park (about 5 min. from downtown Orlando). ✆ 407/628-1212. Reservations not accepted. Main courses $5–$10. AE, MC, V. Mon–Thurs 10am–9pm, Fri–Sat 10am–10:30pm. Free parking. Take I-4 east to Lee Rd. (Exit 45). Follow your nose; Bubbaloo's is on the left next to a dry cleaner's.

Little Saigon ✸ *Finds* VIETNAMESE An influx of Asian immigrants created the demand for this great little eatery that's yet to be discovered by tourists. Be sure to try the summer rolls—a soft wrap filled with rice, shrimp, and pork served with a delicious peanut sauce. Head next for the grilled pork and egg over rice and noodles or barbecued beef with fried egg and rice. If your appetite is larger than average, try one of the traditional soups with noodles, rice, vegetables, and either chicken, beef, or seafood. The numbered menu isn't translated well, but your server or the manager can help. There are very limited wine and beer choices.

1106 E. Colonial Dr./Hwy. 50, near downtown Orlando. ✆ 407/423-8539. Reservations not accepted. Main courses under $5 at lunch; $5–$8 at dinner. AE, DISC, MC, V. Daily 10am–9pm. Free parking. Take the Colonial Dr./Hwy. 50 exit off I-4 and head east. Turn right onto Thornton Ave. Parking is on the left.

ONLY IN ORLANDO: DINING WITH DISNEY CHARACTERS

Dining with costumed characters is a treat for almost any Disney fan, but it's a special one for those under 10. Some of their favorite 'toons show up to greet them, sign autographs, pose for photos, and interact with the family. These meals aren't low-turnout events, so make priority-seating arrangements (© 407/939-3463) as early as possible, and call for schedules and prices. Character meals are offered at **Artist Point** (in Disney's Wilderness Lodge), **Cape May Café** (in Disney's Beach Club Resort), **Chef Mickey's** (at Disney's Contemporary Resort), **Cinderella's Royal Table** (in Cinderella's Castle, Magic Kingdom), **Crystal Palace Buffet** (at Crystal Palace, Magic Kingdom), **Donald's Prehistoric Breakfastosaurus** (in Dinoland U.S.A., Disney's Animal Kingdom), **Garden Grill** (in The Land Pavilion at Epcot), **Hollywood & Vine Character Dining** (at Hollywood & Vine, in Disney–MGM Studios), **Liberty Tree Tavern** (in Liberty Square, in the Magic Kingdom), **Minnie's Menehune** (in 'Ohana at Disney's Polynesian Resort), and **1900 Park Fare** (at Disney's Grand Floridian Resort & Spa).

5 Tips for Visiting Walt Disney World Attractions

Walt Disney World is the umbrella above four theme parks: the Magic Kingdom, Epcot, Disney–MGM Studios, and Animal Kingdom, which drew a combined 43.2 million guests in 2000, according to *Amusement Business* magazine. All four ranked in the top five in attendance nationally (the other was Disneyland, in California, ranking number two; with Universal Studios Florida and Islands of Adventure finishing numbers six and seven, respectively).

Besides its theme parks, Disney has an assortment of other venues, including Downtown Disney Marketplace, Downtown Disney West Side (Cirque du Soleil & DisneyQuest, a virtual arcade), Pleasure Island, River Country, Blizzard Beach, Typhoon Lagoon, and more.

TIPS FOR PLANNING YOUR TRIP

Information   Before leaving home, call or write the Walt Disney World Co., Box 10000, Lake Buena Vista, FL 32830-1000 (© **407/934-7639**), for a vacation video and the *Walt Disney World Vacations* brochure; both are valuable planning aids. When you call, also ask about any special events that will be going on during your visit. Don't forget to request park maps so you can get familiar with the layouts early. There are information booths in each park: In the Magic Kingdom at City Hall, in Epcot at Innoventions East near the World Key, and at Guest Services in Disney–MGM Studios and Animal Kingdom.

You can get information online at **www.disneyworld.com**, **www.orlandosentinel.com**, and **www.orlandoinfo.com**.

Arrive Early   If you want to be first on primo rides at the parks, we suggest you arrive up to 1 hour before opening.

Parking   Cars, light trucks, and vans currently pay $6 (though we expect Disney to follow Universal's lead and go up to $7). Visitors with mobility impairments can park in special areas near the entrances; ask the parking-lot attendants or call © **407/824-4321.** Don't forget to write down where you parked (area and row number), because it's easy to get lost after a long day.

When You Arrive   Grab an official guide map! It not only tells you where the fun stuff is but also lists the day's entertainment schedule. If you want to see certain shows or parades, arrive early to get a good seat. Use this guide and the map

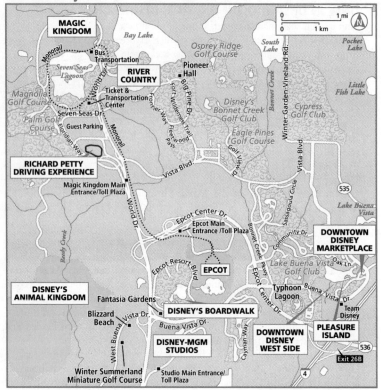

to come up with a game plan on where to eat, what to ride, and what to see during your stay.

Best Times to Visit There really isn't an "off"-season for Disney, but the crowds are usually thinner mid-January through March and mid-September until the week before Thanksgiving. The busiest days at all of the theme parks are generally Saturdays and Sundays, when the locals visit. Beyond that, Mondays and Thursdays are frantic in the Magic Kingdom, Tuesdays and Fridays are bad at Epcot, and Wednesdays spell insanity at Disney–MGM Studios and Animal Kingdom. The periods surrounding major holidays attract throngs to the parks: Christmas through New Year's is a frenzied time.

Note: In summer, when the masses throng to the parks, Central Florida's oppressive heat and humidity only add insult to injury.

Operating Hours Park hours vary throughout the year and can be influenced by special events, so it's a good idea to call before your visit or go to **www. disneyworld.com** to check opening/closing times. For example, Animal Kingdom opens as early as 7 or 8am during summer so that guests can get a look at the animals before the heat drives them into the brush. The other parks generally open at 9am and close from 7 to 9pm, although some are open later during summer and other peak periods.

Tickets There are several options, from 1-day to multiday tickets. The best values are the 4- and 5-day passes. The following don't include *6% sales tax* unless otherwise noted. All offer unlimited use of WDW's transportation. Call

Behind the Scenes: Special Disney Tours

Disney parks offer a number of walking tours and learning programs. The times, descriptions, and prices are subject to change. The program and tour details described here represent the most recent information available at press time. It's best to call ahead to Disney's tour line, ℭ **407/939-8687,** to make reservations or get additional information.

- The **Family Magic Tour** explores the nooks and crannies of the Magic Kingdom in the form of a 2-hour scavenger hunt. You meet and greet characters at the end. The cost for children ages 3 to 9 is $20; adults are $25. You must also buy admission tickets to the park, and you must book in advance. The tour begins each morning at 9:30 and 11:30am outside City Hall.

- The **Magic Behind Our Steam Trains** (ages 10 and up) is a fun tour for locomotive buffs. A pair of inveterate conductors give you insight that other guests don't get into the history and present tense of the little engines that could. Tours take place Monday, Thursday, and Saturday at 7:30am; cost is $30 per person, plus park admission.
  The following tours are for those 16 and older.

- The 3½-hour **Hidden Treasures of World Showcase** explores the architectural and entertainment offerings at Epcot (for ages 16 and older). The $49 tours (plus admission) begin at 9am on Tuesday, Thursday, and Saturday.

- **Gardens of the World,** a 3-hour tour of the extraordinary landscaping at Epcot is held Tuesday and Thursday at 9:30am and is led by a Disney horticulturist ($49 per person, plus admission).

- The 4½-hour **Keys to the Kingdom** tour provides an orientation to the Magic Kingdom and a glimpse into the high-tech systems behind the magic. The cost is $58 (lunch is included but mandatory park admission isn't), and the tour begins daily at 8:30, 9:30, and 10am and at 1pm.

- At the top of the price chain ($199 per person) is **Backstage Magic,** a 7-hour, combination self-propelled walk and bus tour through areas of Epcot, the Magic Kingdom, and Disney–MGM Studios that aren't seen by mainstream guests. The 9am weekday tour is limited to 20 adults, and you might have trouble getting a date unless you book early. Some will find that this tour isn't worth the price, but if you have a brain that must know how things work or if you simply want to know more than your family or friends, you might find the investment worthwhile. You'll see WDW mechanics and engineers repairing and building animatronic beings from "It's a Small World" and other attractions. You'll peek over the shoulders of cast members who watch close-circuit TVs to make sure other visitors are surviving the harrowing rides. And at the Magic Kingdom, you'll venture into tunnels used for work areas as well as corridors for the cast to get from one area to the other without fighting tourist crowds. Park admission isn't required.

ℭ **407/824-4321** for further information. *Note:* Almost all of these figures went up in January 2001. Price hikes are an annual occurrence at WDW, Universal, and SeaWorld.

FASTPASS

Don't want to stand in line as long as the other guests, yet not flush enough to hire a stand-in? Disney parks use a reservation system whereby you go to the primo rides, feed your theme-park ticket into a small ticket-taker machine, and get an assigned time to return. When you reappear at the appointed time, you get into a short line and climb aboard. Here's the drill:

Hang onto your ticket stub when you enter, and head to the hottest ride on your dance card. If it's a FASTPASS attraction (they're noted in the guide map you get when you enter), feed your stub into the waist-level ticket taker. Retrieve your stub and the FASTPASS stub that comes with it. Look at the two times stamped on the FASTPASS. Come back during that 1-hour window and you can enter the ride with almost no wait. In the interim, go to another attraction or show.

Note: Early in the day, your 1-hour window may begin 40 minutes after you feed the FASTPASS machine, but later in the day it may be hours. Initially, Disney allowed you to do this on only one ride at a time, but now you can get a pass for a second attraction 2 hours after your first assigned time.

1-day/1-park tickets, for admission to the Magic Kingdom, Epcot, Animal Kingdom, or Disney-MGM, are $48 for adults, $38 for children 3 to 9. (Ouch!)

4-Day Park Hopper Passes provide unlimited admission to the Magic Kingdom, Epcot, Animal Kingdom, and Disney–MGM Studios. Adults pay $192; children 3 to 9 pay $152.

5-Day Park Hopper Plus Passes also include your choice of two admissions to Typhoon Lagoon, River Country, Blizzard Beach, Pleasure Island, or Disney's Wide World of Sports. They sell for $247 for adults and $197 for children 3 to 9. Passes for 6 and 7 days are available, too.

1-day ticket to Typhoon Lagoon or Blizzard Beach is $29.95 for adults, $24 for children 3 to 11.

1-day ticket to River Country is $15.95 for adults, $12.50 for children 3 to 11.

1-day ticket to Pleasure Island is $21 including tax. Since this is primarily an 18 and over entertainment complex, there's no bargain price for children.

If you're staying at a WDW resort, you're eligible for a money-saving **Unlimited Magic Pass,** priced according to the length of your stay.

If you're planning an extended stay or going to visit Walt Disney World more than once during the year, annual passes ($349 for adults, $297 for children) are another option.

6 The Magic Kingdom

The Magic Kingdom offers 40 attractions, plus restaurants and shops, in a 107-acre package. Its symbol, Cinderella's Castle, forms the hub of a wheel whose spokes reach to **seven "lands."**

MAIN STREET, USA

The gateway to the Kingdom, Main Street is designed to resemble a turn-of-the-20th-century American street (okay, so it leads to a 13th-century European

---

Tips **A Note about Smoking**

Disney prohibits smoking in shops, attractions, restaurants, ride lines, and other areas. In 2000, a ruling allowed smokers to light up only in designated areas. Next: Well, we aren't predicting, but WDW may go smoke-free.

---

castle). Don't dawdle on Main Street when you enter the park; leave it for the end of the day when you're heading back to your hotel.

Walt Disney World Railroad & Other Main Street Vehicles   The WDW Railroad is an authentic 1928 steam-powered train that you board for a 15-minute tour of the park or you can use it to reach two other lands—Adventureland and Mickey's Toontown Fair. Other vehicles include horse-drawn trolleys and jitneys that travel along Main Street.

Main Street Cinema   This air-conditioned hexagonal theater features vintage black-and-white Disney cartoons, including 1928's *Steamboat Willie* in which Mickey and Minnie debuted. *Note:* This theater has no seats.

ADVENTURELAND

Cross a bridge and stroll through an exotic jungle of foliage, thatched roofs, and totems. Amid dense vines and stands of bamboo, drums are beating and swashbuckling adventures are taking place.

Jungle Cruise ✪   In the course of 10 minutes, you sail through an African veldt in the Congo, an Amazon rain forest, the Nile in Egypt, and several other sets. Dozens of animatronic birds, elephants, giraffes, crocodiles, tigers, and butterflies inhabit the lavish scenery that includes hanging vines, cascading waterfalls, and tropical foliage. On the shore, there's a temple guarded by snakes and a Buddha. If that's not bad enough, passengers find themselves threatened by angry elephants and warriors who attack with spears. Most boat captains keep up an amusing patter.

Pirates of the Caribbean ✪   The Disneyland version in California has become more politically correct, but the buccaneers here still chase "wenches." You board a fake log and enter a cave. Inside there are hundreds of audio-animatronic figures, from critters to "yo-ho-ho-ing" pirates who raid a Caribbean town. After a lot of looting and boozing, the pirates pass out. This ride might be scary for kids under 5.

Swiss Family Treehouse   This attraction, based on the movie *Swiss Family Robinson,* lets you walk a rope bridge to an adult-size house perched in a banyan tree built by Disney. The tree has 330,000 polyethylene leaves sprouting from a 90-foot span of branches. Travelers with disabilities should beware: This attraction requires lots of climbing.

FRONTIERLAND

From Adventureland, step into the wild and woolly past of the American frontier! The landscape is straight out of the Wild West, with log cabins and rustic saloons. Across the river is Tom Sawyer Island, reachable via log rafts.

Big Thunder Mountain Railroad ✪✪   This low-key roller coaster has tight turns and dark descents rather than sudden, steep drops. It's situated in a 200-foot-high, red-stone mountain with 2,780 feet of track winding through caves and canyons. Your runaway train careens through the ribs of a dinosaur, under a thundering waterfall, past geysers and bubbling mud pots, and over a bottomless volcanic pool. It's tailor-made for kids and grownups who want a thrill but aren't quite up to tackling the big coasters. *Note:* You must be 40 inches or taller to ride.

Splash Mountain ✺✺✺   Based on Walt Disney's 1946 film *Song of the South,* Splash Mountain takes you flume-style down a flooded mountain, past 26 colorful scenes that include backwoods swamps, bayous, spooky caves, and waterfalls. Riders are caught in the bumbling schemes of Brer Fox and Brer Bear as they chase the ever-wily Brer Rabbit. Your hollow-log vehicle twists, turns, and splashes, sometimes plummeting in darkness as the ride leads to a 45°, 52-foot-long, 40 mile-per-hour splashdown in a briar-filled pond. And that's not the end. The ride keeps going until it's a Zip-A-Dee-Doo-Dah kind of day. *Note:* You must be at least 40 inches tall to ride. *Warning:* Two people were injured, one fatally, on this ride in late 2000. *Stay seated until the ride stops.*

Tom Sawyer Island   Board Huck Finn's raft for a 1-minute float across the river to this densely forested island. Kids love exploring the narrow passages of Injun Joe's cave, a windmill, and an abandoned mine. There's also a rickety swing, barrel bridges, and sit-downs for weary parents. Aunt Polly's restaurant serves fried chicken and PB&J's on outdoor tables with views of the river.

Diamond Horseshoe Saloon Revue & Medicine Show   Enjoy Dr. Bill U. Later's turn-of-the-20th-century Wild West revue. Jingles plays honky-tonk, there's a magic act, and Miss Lucille L'Amour and her dance-hall girls do a spirited cancan—all with lots of humor and audience participation. There are several shows daily.

Frontierland Shootin' Arcade   Fog creeps across the graveyard, coyotes howl, bridges groan, and skeletons rise as state-of-the-art electronics combine with a traditional shooting gallery format. If you hit the tombstone, it spins and the epitaph changes. Fifty cents buys you 25 shots.

Country Bear Jamboree ✺✺   The Jamboree is a hoot. It's a 15-minute show featuring audio-animatronic bears belting out rollicking country tunes and crooning plaintive love songs. Trixie, decked out in a satiny skirt, laments lost love in "Tears Will Be the Chaser for Your Wine." Teddi Barra descends from the ceiling in a swing to perform "Heart We Did All That We Could." Big Al moans "Blood in the Saddle," which makes everyone laugh. Wisecracking commentary comes from a mounted buffalo, moose, and deer on the wall.

LIBERTY SQUARE

This zone between Frontierland and Fantasyland depicts an 18th-century America with Colonial architecture. Thirteen lanterns, symbolizing the colonies, hang from the Liberty Tree, an immense live oak. You might encounter a fife-and-drum corps on the cobblestone streets. The Liberty Tree Tavern (see earlier in this chapter) is one of the best Magic Kingdom restaurants.

Hall of Presidents ✺   Every American president is represented by a lifelike audio-animatronic figure. If you look closely, you'll see them fidget and whisper during the performance. The show begins with a film projected on a 180°, 70mm screen. Then the curtain rises on America's leaders and, as each comes into the spotlight, he nods or waves with presidential dignity. Lincoln rises and speaks, occasionally referring to his notes. Each president's costume reflects his period's fashion, fabrics, and tailoring techniques.

Haunted Mansion ✩✩ Cast members dressed as butlers and maids escort you past a graveyard and then turn you over to a ghostly host who encloses you in a windowless, doorless portrait gallery where the floor seems to descend. Darkness, spooky music, eerie howling, and mysterious screams and rappings enhance its ambience. The ride is replete with bizarre scenes and objects: a ghostly banquet and ball, a graveyard band, a suit of armor that comes alive, luminous spiders, a talking head in a crystal ball, and weird flying objects. At the end of the ride, a ghost joins you in your car. The experience is more amusing than terrifying, so you can take children, 6 and up, inside. This ride has changed little over the years and may be stale for Kingdom regulars, but it continues to draw long lines and a cult following.

Boat Rides A steam-powered sternwheeler, the *Liberty Belle,* and one or two Mike Fink keelboats depart Liberty Square for scenic cruises along the Rivers of America. Both ply the same route and make a restful interlude for foot-weary park-stompers.

FANTASYLAND

The attractions in this happy land are themed after classics such as *Snow White, Peter Pan,* and *Dumbo.* They're very popular with young visitors. If your kids are 8 and under, you may want to make this and Mickey's Toontown your primary stops in the Magic Kingdom.

Cinderella's Castle ✩ There's not a lot to do at the castle, but its status as the Magic Kingdom's icon makes it a must. Located at the end of Main Street, in the center of the park, this fairyland castle with Gothic spires is 185 feet high. The namesake character appears sometimes, and Cinderella's Royal Table restaurant is inside.

Cinderella's Golden Carousel ✩ This beauty was constructed by Italian carvers in 1917 and refurbished by Disney artists, who added 18 hand-painted scenes from Cinderella on a wooden canopy above the horses. The carousel organ plays Disney classics such as "When You Wish Upon a Star."

Dumbo, the Flying Elephant ✩ Here's a very tame kid's ride, in which the cars that are Dumbo clones go around in a circle, gently rising and dipping. If you can stand the lines, it's very exciting for wee ones and for those who are thrilled when the little ones are.

It's a Small World ✩ If you don't know the song, you will by the end of the ride. It'll crawl into your mind like a brain-eating mite, playing continually as you sail "around the world." All of the countries you meet are inhabited by appropriately costumed animatronic dolls incessantly singing "It's a small world after all," in tiny doll-like voices that are remarkably similar to how yours would sound if you sucked on a helium balloon. Every adult ought to pay his or her dues and ride it at least once.

Legend of the Lion King ✩ This stage show is based on Disney's motion-picture musical but shouldn't be confused with the much better "Festival of the Lion King" at Animal Kingdom (later in this chapter). This one combines animation, movie footage, sophisticated puppetry, and high-tech special effects. The show is enhanced by the music of Elton John and Tim Rice. Whoopi Goldberg and Cheech Marin are among the actors who provided their voices for the show.

Mad Tea Party *Overrated* This is a traditional amusement park ride à la Disney, with an Alice in Wonderland theme. Riders sit in big pastel-hued teacups on saucers that career around a circular platform while tilting and spinning. This can be a pretty active or nauseating ride.

The Many Adventures of Winnie the Pooh The Many Adventures of Winnie the Pooh features the cute-and-cuddly little fellow along with pals Eyeore, Piglet, and Tigger. You board a golden honey pot and ride through a storybook version of the Hundred-Acre Woods, keeping an eye out for Heffulumps, Woozles, and Blustery Days.

Peter Pan's Flight Riding in airborne versions of Captain Hook's ship, passengers experience the story of Peter Pan. The adventure begins in the Darlings' nursery and includes a flight over nighttime London—adults find the evening tableau *almost* worth the long waits—to Never-Never Land. There, riders encounter mermaids, Indians, a ticking crocodile, the Lost Boys, Princess Tiger Lilly, Tinker Bell, Hook, and Smee. It's fun the first time.

Snow White's Scary Adventures This once was a little too scary for its target audience. But Disney has toned things down and Snow White now appears in several pleasant scenes, such as at the wishing well and riding away with the prince to live happily ever after. There are new audio-animatronic dwarfs, and the colors have been brightened and made less threatening. Even so, this could be scary for kids under 5.

MICKEY'S TOONTOWN FAIR

Head off those cries of "Where's Mickey?" by taking young kids to this 2-acre site. Toontown provides a chance to meet their favorite Disney characters, including Mickey, Minnie, Donald, Goofy, and Pluto. The Kingdom's smallest land is set in a whimsical collection of cottages and candy-striped tents like those at long-gone county fairs.

The Barnstormer at Goofy's Wiseacre Farm 🎯🎯 This mini roller coaster may have been the inspiration for Woody Woodpecker's Nuthouse Coaster at Universal Studios Florida (see later in this chapter). It's designed to look and feel like a crop duster that flies slightly off-course and right through the Goofmeister's barn. The ride has very little in the dip-and-drop department but a little zip on the spin-and-spiral front. It even gets squeals of joy from some adults. The 60-second ride has a 35-inch height minimum.

Mickey's & Minnie's Country Houses 🎯 These separate cottages offer a lot of visual fun and some marginal interactive areas for youngsters. Mickey's place features garden and garage playgrounds. Minnie's lets kids play in her kitchen, where popcorn goes wild in a microwave and the utensils play melodies.

S.S. Miss Daisy 🎯 Daisy's ship offers a lot of interactive fun, and the "waters" around it feature fountains of water snakes and other wet fun things that earn squeals of joy (and relief on hot days).

TOMORROWLAND

In 1994, the WDW folks decided Tomorrowland (originally designed in the 1970s) was beginning to look a lot like "Yesteryear." So it was revamped to show the future as a galactic, science fiction–inspired community inhabited by humans, aliens, and robots.

The ExtraTERRORestrial Alien Encounter 🎯🎯 *Star Wars* director George Lucas earned a tidy payday when he added his space-age vision to this attraction, in which a corporation called X-S Tech sells transporter services to Earthlings

---

---

like you. But things go wrong when it tries to transport its CEO and instead an ugly extraterrestrial lands in your backyard. This sensory show carries a legitimate child warning: It's dark, scary, and confining (a shoulder plate locks you in). It delivers special effects such as the alien's breath on your neck and a mist of alien "slime." *Note:* Riders must be at least 48 inches tall.

Astro Orbiter *Overrated* This tame ride is like the ones in kiddie carnivals everywhere: Its "rockets" are on arms attached to "the center of the galaxy" and they move up and down. The line here tends to progress at the pace of a snail, so unless it's short, skip this one.

Buzz Lightyear's Space Ranger Spin ★ Join Buzz and try to save the universe while flying your cruiser through a world you'll recognize from the original *Toy Story* movie. Kids enjoy using the dashboard-mounted laser cannons as they spin through the sky (filled with gigantic toys instead of stars). If they're good shots, they can set off sight and sound gags with their lasers.

Space Mountain ★ This cosmic roller coaster usually has *long* lines (if you don't use FASTPASS), even though it's a few years past its prime. Once aboard a rocket, you'll climb and dive through the inky, starlit blackness of outer space. The hairpin turns and plunges make it seem as if you're going at breakneck speed, but your car doesn't go any faster than 28 miles per hour. If you like dark or semidark thrill rides, you'll be much happier with Rock 'n' Roller Coaster at Disney–MGM Studios. *Note:* Riders must be at least 44 inches tall.

The Timekeeper This multimedia presentation, inspired by Jules Verne and H. G. Wells, is hosted by a robot/mad-scientist (Robin Williams) and his assistant, 9-EYE, a flying, camera-headed 'droid that moonlights as a time-machine test pilot. In this jet-speed escapade, you hear Mozart as a prodigy, see medieval battlefields in Scotland, watch da Vinci work, and float in a hot-air balloon over Moscow's Red Square. *Note:* You have to stand in this one.

Tomorrowland Indy Speedway Younger kids love this ride, especially if their adult companion lets them drive (without a big person, there's a 52-inch height minimum for driving a lap), but teens and other fast starters hate it. The cars go only 7 miles per hour, and they run along steel rails that keep them from straying very far to the sides.

Tomorrowland Transit Authority These futuristic, five-car trains are engineless and provide an overhead look at Tomorrowland, including an interior look at Space Mountain. Its biggest virtue: a good place to rest your feet.

Walt Disney's Carousel of Progress *Overrated* Sorry, but this is a complete waste of 22 minutes unless (a) you need the break from the insanity rampant throughout the rest of the park or (b) you have no clue to what's happened, technology-wise, since the 1930s.

PARADES, FIREWORKS, & MORE

For up-to-the-moment information, see the entertainment schedule given in the park guidemap that you get when entering the park.

Fantasy in the Sky Fireworks ⊛   This is one of the most explosive displays in Orlando. Disney has pyrotechnics down to an art form, and this is clearly the best way to end your day in the Magic Kingdom. The fireworks go off nightly during summer and holidays, on selected nights the rest of the year.

Disney's Magical Moments Parade *Overrated*   With just a few floats and all of them showcasing Disney movies, this event has marginal interest. It's a good time to hit a primo ride while most other guests are watching the show.

SpectroMagic ⊛⊛ *Moments*   This after-dark display returned in 2001 for a second engagement at WDW, replacing the **Main Street Electrical Parade.** SpectroMagic is a 20-minute production that combines fiber optics, holographic images, clouds of liquid nitrogen, old-fashioned twinkling lights, and a soundtrack featuring classic Disney tunes. Mickey, dressed in an amber-and-purble grand magician's cape makes an appearance in a confetti of light. The parade is held every night during summer and other peak times, and Thursday through Saturday in the off-season.

7 Epcot

Epcot is an acronym for Experimental Prototype Community of Tomorrow, and it was Walt Disney's dream for a planned community rather than a theme park. But, after his death, it became Central Florida's second major tourist attraction when it opened in 1982.

The 260-acre theme park has two major sections, **Future World** and **World Showcase.** It's so large that hiking World Showcase from tip to tip (1.3 miles) can be exhausting. That's why some folks are certain that Epcot stands for "Every Person Comes Out Tired." Depending on how long you intend to linger at each country in World Showcase, this park can be tackled in 1 day (but it's better to enjoy it over at least 2). One way to conserve energy is to take the launches across the lagoon from the edge of Future World to Germany or to Morocco. You can also board double-decker buses circling the Promenade and making stops at Norway, Italy, France, and Canada.

FUTURE WORLD

Future World is centered on Epcot's icon, a giant geosphere known as Spaceship Earth. Major corporations sponsor Future World's 10 themed areas, and the focus is on discovery, scientific achievements, and tomorrow's technologies in areas running from energy to undersea exploration. Here are the headliners:

Innoventions ⊛   This attraction has dueling buildings. House of Innoventions in Innoventions East heralds a smart house equipped with a refrigerator that can make your grocery list, a picture frame that can store and send photos to other smart frames, and a commode that's outfitted with a seat warmer, automatic lid opener and closer, and a sprayer and blow dryer that eliminate the need for toilet paper. The exhibits in Innoventions West are led by Video Games of Tomorrow, in which Sega showcases games at nearly three dozen game stations.

Imagination ⊛   Even the fountains are magical at this pavilion—they fire "water snakes" that arch into the air and dare kids to avoid their "bite." The 3-D **Honey I Shrunk the Audience** ⊛⊛⊛ ride shrinks you first, then terrorizes you with larger-than-life mice, a cat, and a gigantic 5-year-old who gives you a sound shaking. **Journey into Your Imagination** ☆ takes a look at how gravity, sound, and other things affect your imagination.

The Land ☆ The largest of Future World's pavilions looks at our relationships to food and nature. **Living with the Land** ☆ is a 13-minute boat ride through a rain forest, an African desert, and the windswept American plains. **Circle of Life** ☆☆ blends spectacular live-action footage with animation in a 15-minute, 70mm motion picture based on *The Lion King* that delivers a cautionary environmental message. In **Food Rocks** ☆, audio-animatronic mock rock-performers deliver an entertaining message about nutrition.

The Living Seas This pavilion's 5.7-million-gallon saltwater aquarium has a coral reef and more than 4,000 sea creatures, such as sharks, barracudas, parrot fish, rays, and dolphins. A 2½-minute multimedia preshow about today's ocean technology is followed by a 7-minute film on the formation of the earth and seas as a means to support life. After the films, you enter "hydolators" for a rapid "descent" to the simulated ocean floor. Upon arrival, you board Seacabs that wind around a 400-foot-long tunnel as you enjoy stunning (but at about three minutes, all-too-brief) close-up views through acrylic windows of the denizens in a natural coral-reef habitat.

Spaceship Earth *Overrated* This large, silvery geosphere is Epcot's icon, but all that awaits inside is a 15-minute yawn of a show/ride that takes you through the history of communications—from an audio-animatronic Cro-Magnon shaman telling the story of a hunt, to the future, infinity, and beyond. *Tip:* If you must see this, you can avoid long lines by saving it until late in the day.

Test Track ☆☆ Test Track is a long-time-coming marvel that combines GM engineering and Disney imagineering. The line can be more than an hour long, so consider FASTPASS. The preride area (that's theme-park talk for the last part of the line) has a number of exhibits from GM's proving grounds. Once you're in your six-passenger convertible, the 5-minute ride follows what looks like a real highway and includes a brake test, climb, and tight S-curves. There's also a 12-second burst of speed that reaches 65 miles per hour on the straightaway. *Note:* Riders must be at least 40 inches tall. *Tip:* The left front seat has the most thrills through curves.

Universe of Energy ☆☆ Sponsored by Exxon, the main event here is a 32-minute ride, **Ellen's Energy Adventure,** that features comedian Ellen DeGeneres as an energy expert who is tutored by Bill Nye the Science Guy to be a "Jeopardy!" contestant. In the process, you learn about energy resources and demands from the dinosaurs to tomorrow, while Ellen beats the wicked Jamie Lee Curtis in the game show.

Wonders of Life ☆☆ Housed in a vast geodesic dome fronted by a 75-foot-tall replica of a DNA strand, this pavilion offers some of Future World's most engaging shows and attractions.

The *Making of Me* ☆☆ is a captivating 15-minute motion picture combining live action (starring Martin Short) with animation and spectacular in-utero pho-tography to create the sweetest introduction imaginable to the facts of life. But a word of warning: If your kids are under 10, this show may prompt certain questions about reproduction.

In **Body Wars** ☆, you're reduced to the size of a cell in order to effect a medical rescue inside the immune system of a human body. The motion simulator takes you on a wild ride through gale-force winds in the lungs and pounding heart chambers. This one isn't a smart choice for those prone to motion sickness or who generally prefer to be stirred rather than shaken. *Note:* Riders must be at least 40 inches tall.

In the hilarious, multimedia **Cranium Command** ✮✮✮, you tag along with Buzzy, an audio-animatronic brain-pilot-in-training charged with a seemingly impossible task—controlling the brain of a typical 12-year-old boy. The body parts are played by Charles Grodin, Jon Lovitz, Bobcat Goldthwaite, George Wendt, and Kevin Nealon and Dana Carvey (as Hans and Franz). You're theoretically seated in the boy's head as Buzzy guides him through such preadolescent traumas as running for the school bus, meeting a girl, and having a run-in with the school principal. It's another must-see attraction (recommended for ages 8 and up) and has a loyal following among Disney veterans.

WORLD SHOWCASE

This community of 11 miniaturized nations surrounds a 40-acre lagoon at the park's southern end. All of the World Showcase countries have authentically indigenous architecture, landscaping, background music, restaurants, and shops. The nations' cultural facets are explored in art exhibits, dance or other live performances, and innovative rides, films, and attractions. And all of the employees in each pavilion are natives of the country represented. The World Showcase opens at 11am daily, so there's time for Future World forays if you arrive earlier.

The American Adventure ✮   Housed in a Georgian-style structure, this 29-minute dramatization of U.S. history uses video, rousing music, and a large cast of lifelike audio-animatronic figures, including narrators Mark Twain and Ben Franklin. You'll see Jefferson writing the Declaration of Independence, Matthew Brady photographing a family about to be divided by the Civil War, the stock market crash of 1929, the attack on Pearl Harbor, and the *Eagle* heading toward the moon. While waiting for the show, you'll be entertained by the wonderful **Voices of Liberty** ✮✮ singers performing American folk songs in the Main Hall. Note the quotes from famous Americans on the walls here.

Canada ✮✮   The architecture ranges from a mansard-roofed replica of Ottawa's 19th-century, French-style Château Laurier (here called Hôtel du Canada) to a British-influenced stone building modeled after a famous landmark near Niagara Falls. But the highlight is **O Canada!** ✮✮, a dazzling, 18-minute, 360° CircleVision film that shows Canada's scenic splendor, from a dogsled race to the thundering flight of thousands of snow geese departing an autumn stopover near the St. Lawrence River.

China ✮   Bounded by a serpentine wall that wanders its perimeter, the China pavilion is entered via a triple-arched ceremonial gate inspired by the Temple of Heaven in Beijing, a summer retreat for Chinese emperors. Passing through the gate, you'll see a half-size replica of this ornately embellished red-and-gold circular temple, built in 1420 during the Ming dynasty. Gardens simulate those in Suzhou, with miniature waterfalls, fragrant lotus ponds, bamboo groves, corkscrew willows, and weeping mulberry trees. **Wonders of China** ✮✮ is a 20-minute, 360° CircleVision film that explores 6,000 years of dynastic and communist rule and the breathtaking diversity of the Chinese landscape. Narrated by the 8th-century Tang-dynasty poet Li Bai, it includes scenes of the Great Wall (begun 24 centuries ago!), a performance by the Beijing Opera, the

Forbidden City in Beijing, rice terraces of Hunan Province, the Gobi Desert, and tropical rain forests of Hainan Island.

France   This pavilion focuses on La Belle Époque, a period from 1870 to 1910 in which French art, literature, and architecture flourished. It's entered via a replica of the beautiful cast-iron Pont des Arts footbridge over the "Seine" and leads to a ¹/₁₀-scale model of the Eiffel Tower constructed from Gustave Eiffel's original blueprints. **Impressions de France** ✪✪ is an 18-minute film, shown in a palatial, sit-down theater à la Fontainebleau, which depicts diverse French landscapes enhanced by the music of French composers on a vast, 200-degree wraparound screen.

Germany   Enclosed by castle walls and towers, this festive pavilion is centered on a cobblestone square with pots of colorful flowers girding a fountain statue of St. George and the Dragon. The adjacent clock tower has glockenspiel figures that herald each hour with quaint melodies. The pavilion's **Biergarten** was inspired by medieval Rothenberg and features a year-round Oktoberfest and music by the **Alpine Trio.** Sixteenth-century facades replicate a merchant's hall in the Black Forest and the town hall in Römerberg Square.

Note: Model-train enthusiasts and kids enjoy the exquisitely detailed miniature version of a small **Bavarian town** ✪✪, complete with working train station. Many folks hurrying to get in and out miss this small marvel.

Italy   One of the prettiest World Showcase pavilions lures visitors over an arched stone footbridge to a replica of Venice's intricately ornamented pink-and-white Doge's Palace. Other highlights include an 83-foot-tall bell tower, Venetian bridges, and a central piazza enclosing a version of Bernini's Neptune Fountain. A troupe of street actors often performs a contemporary version of 16th-century *commedia dell'arte* in the piazza.

Japan ✪✪   A flaming red *torii* (gate of honor) leads the way to the graceful, blue-roofed Goju No To pagoda, inspired by a shrine built at Nara in A.D. 700. In a traditional Japanese garden, cedars, yews, bamboos, "cloud-pruned" evergreens, willows, and flowering shrubs frame pebbled footpaths, rustic bridges, waterfalls, exquisite rock landscaping, and a pond of golden koi. The Yakitori House is based on the 16th-century Katsura Imperial Villa in Kyoto, considered the crowning achievement of Japanese architecture. Another highlight is the moated **White Heron Castle,** a replica of the Shirasagi-Jo, a 17th-century fortress overlooking the city of Himeji. The drums of **Matsuriza**—one of the best performances in the World Showcase—entertain guests daily.

Mexico ✪   You'll hear marimbas and mariachi bands as you approach this festive showcase, fronted by a towering Mayan pyramid modeled on the Aztec temple of Quetzalcoatl (God of Life) and surrounded by dense Yucatán jungle landscaping. Upon entering the pavilion, you'll be in a museum of pre-Colombian art and artifacts. Down a ramp, a small lagoon is the setting for **El Rio del Tiempo** (River of Time) ✪, where visitors board boats for an 8-minute cruise through Mexico's past and present. Passengers get a close-up look at a Mayan pyramid.

Morocco ✪   Note the imperfections in the mosaic tile in the Koutoubia Minaret, the prayer tower of a 12th-century mosque in Marrakech. They were put there intentionally in accordance with the belief that only Allah is perfect. The **Medina** (old city), entered via a replica of an arched gateway in Fez, leads to Fez House (a traditional Moroccan home) and the narrow, winding streets of the *souk,* a bustling marketplace where all manner of authentic handcrafted merchandise is on display. The Medina's rectangular courtyard centers on a replica of the ornately tiled Najjarine Fountain in Fez, the setting for musical entertainment.

Treasures of Morocco is a daily, 35-minute guided tour (noon to 7pm) that highlights this country's culture, architecture, and history.

Norway   This pavilion is centered on a picturesque cobblestone courtyard. A *stavekirke* (stave church), styled after the 13th-century Gol Church of Hallingdal, features changing exhibits. A replica of Oslo's 14th-century **Akershus Castle,** next to a cascading woodland waterfall, is the setting for the pavilion's featured restaurant. Other buildings simulate the red-roofed cottages of Bergen and the timber-sided farm buildings of the Nordic woodlands.

Maelstrom 🌟🌟, a boat ride in a dragon-headed Viking vessel, traverses Norway's fjords before trolls cast a spell on you. The boat crashes through a narrow gorge and spins into the North Sea, where you're hit by a storm (don't worry—this is a relatively calm ride). The storm abates and passengers disembark safely at a 10th-century Viking village to view the 70mm film *Norway,* which documents a thousand years of Norwegian history.

United Kingdom   The U.K. pavilion takes you to Merry Olde England through **Britannia Square,** a formal London-style park complete with copper-roofed gazebo bandstand, a stereotypical red phone booth, and a statue of the Bard. Four centuries of architecture are represented along quaint cobblestone streets, complete with a traditional British pub. A formal garden with low box hedges in geometric patterns, flagstone paths, and a stone fountain replicates the landscaping of 16th- and 17th-century palaces.

Don't miss **The British Invasion** 🌟🌟, a group who impersonate the Beatles daily except Sundays, and pub pianist Pam Brody (Tuesdays, Thursdays, Fridays, and Sundays).

IllumiNations 🌟🌟 *Moments*   Disney has decided to hold over the Illuminations fireworks show and Tapestry of Nations parade from Epcot's 15-month millennium celebration. This is a grand nightcap, blending lasers, pyrotechnics, and fountains in a signature-Disney display. The show is worth tackling the crowds that flock to the parking lot at its conclusion. This is a very popular event and draws a lot of people, but there are tons of good viewing points around the lagoon. Still, it's best to stake your claim to a primo place at least a half-hour or so before show time, which is listed in your entertainment schedule.

8 Disney–MGM Studios

You'll probably spy the Tower of Terror and the Earrrful Tower, a water tower outfitted with gigantic mouse ears, well before you enter this park, which Disney bills as "the Hollywood that never was and always will be." Once inside, you'll find pulse-quickening rides such as the **Rock 'n' Roller Coaster,** movie- and TV-themed shows such as **Who Wants to Be a Millionaire—Play It,** and behind-the-scenes "reel-life" adventures. On Hollywood and Sunset boulevards, art deco movie sets remember the golden age of Hollywood. New York Street is lined with miniature renditions of Gotham's landmarks and typical characters, including peddlers hawking knock-off watches. This 110-acre park has some of the best street performing anywhere.

MAJOR ATTRACTIONS & SHOWS

Backstage Pass *Overrated*   The actual set from the ABC Television show "Home Improvement" is one of the areas you'll see on this lame, 25-minute walking tour of a working television production facility. Don't waste the time unless you have plenty of it to burn.

Disney–MGM Studios Backlot Tour ⚓ This 35-minute tram tour takes you behind the scenes for a close-up look at the vehicles, props, costumes, sets, and special effects used in movies and TV shows. But the real fun begins once the tram ventures into **Catastrophe Canyon** ⚓⚓⚓, where an earthquake in the heart of desert oil country causes canyon walls to rumble. A raging oil fire, massive explosions, torrents of rain, and flash floods threaten you and other riders before you're taken behind the scenes to see how filmmakers use special effects to make such disasters.

Bear in the Big Blue House—Live on Stage! Kids love this 15-minute show where they meet Bear, Ojo, Tutter, Treelo, Pip, Pop, and Luna as they perform some of the kids' favorite songs from the whimsical Disney Channel series. There are usually six shows scheduled per day.

Beauty and the Beast Live on Stage ⚓⚓ This 30-minute, live Broadway-style production has been adapted from the same-name movie. Musical highlights from the show include the rousing "Be Our Guest" opening number and the poignant title song featured in the romantic waltz-scene finale. The sets and costumes are lavish, and the production numbers are pretty spectacular. Arrive early to get a good seat.

Disney's Doug Live! ⚓ Live performances and animation gel in this 30-minute show, which tells the story of the 12-year-old, popular cartoon character. This is a must-see for the TV show's fans, who, during the audience participation parts, answer Doug trivia faster than you can say, "The Evil Dr. Rubber Suit." The show uses five members of the audience to play certain roles on stage.

Fantasmic! ⚓⚓⚓ *Moments* The show alone is wonderful, but the choreography, laser lights, and fireworks make it a spectacular, 25-minute, end-of-day experience. This visual feast lets Mickey come to life in an extravaganza featuring shooting stars, fireballs, and animated fountains that really charge the audience. The cast includes 50 performers, a giant dragon, a king cobra, and one million gallons of water, all of which are orchestrated by a sorcerer mouse that looks more than remotely familiar. Throughout, you'll be entertained by musical scores and characters from Disney classics.

Note: The amphitheater holds 9,000, but in busy periods (holidays and summers) there's often standing room only, so arrive early.

The Great Movie Ride Film footage and 50 audio-animatronic replicas of movie stars are used to re-create some of the most famous scenes in films on this 22-minute ride through movie history. Moments include the classic airport farewell scene by Bergman and Bogart in *Casablanca;* Brando bellowing "Stel-laaaaa"; and Gene Kelly singin' in the rain. There are some fun moments when the conductor warns, "Fasten your seat belts. It's going to be a bumpy night." Desperadoes hijack you along the way, but most of the ride is filmdom's version of a 1930s-to-1960s trip down memory lane.

Hunchback of Notre Dame: A Musical Adventure ⚓ This rollicking stage show brings the animated feature's main characters to life, mainly in costumes but sometimes in puppets. Dozens of performers tell the story of Quasimodo, an orphan banished to a church bell tower. Show up 30 minutes early to ensure a good seat during the summer and holiday seasons.

Indiana Jones Epic Stunt Spectacular ★★★   Peek into the world of movie stunts in this 30-minute show that re-creates major scenes from the Indiana Jones films. The show opens on an elaborate Mayan temple backdrop. Indy crashes the party on a rope and, as he searches with a torch for the golden idol, he encounters booby traps, fire, and steam, and spears popping up from the ground. Then a boulder chases him! The set is dismantled to reveal a colorful market where a sword fight ensues and the action includes bullwhip maneuvers, gunfire, and a truck bursting into flame. An explosive finale takes place in a desert scenario. Theme music and an entertaining narrative enhance the narrative, which helps explain how elaborate stunts are pulled off. Arrive early and sit near the stage for your shot at being an audience participant. Alas, this is a job for adults only.

Jim Henson's Muppet*Vision 3D ★★★   This must-see film stars Kermit and Miss Piggy in a delightful marriage of Jim Henson's puppets and Disney audio-animatronics, special-effects wizardry, 70mm film, and cutting-edge 3-D technology. Wow! The coming-right-at-you action includes flying Muppets, cream pies, cannonballs, high winds, fiber-optic fireworks, bubble showers, even an actual spray of water. Kermit is the host, Miss Piggy sings "Dream a Little Dream of Me," Statler and Waldorf critique the action (which includes numerous mishaps and disasters) from a balcony, and Nicki Napoleon and his Emperor Penguins (a full Muppet orchestra) provide music from the pit. The 25-minute show runs continuously.

The Magic of Disney Animation ★   Characters come alive at the stroke of a brush (or pen) as you tour glass-walled animation studios and sometimes see artists at work. Walter Cronkite and Robin Williams (guess who plays straight man?) explain what's going on via the video monitors, and they also star in a very funny 8-minute Peter Pan–themed film about the basics of animation. The 35-minute guided tour includes entertaining video talks by animators and a grand finale of magical moments from Disney classics such as *Pinocchio, Snow White, Bambi, Beauty and the Beast,* and *The Hunchback of Notre Dame.*

Rock 'n' Roller Coaster ★★★ *Finds*   Want the best thrill ride WDW has to offer? Then tackle this fast-and-furious coaster. You sit in a 24-passenger "stretch limo" customized with 120 speakers that blare Aerosmith at 32,000 watts as a light warns you to "prepare to merge as you've never merged before"; and faster than you can scream "Oh, no!" (around 2.8 seconds, actually), you shoot from 0 to 60 miles per hour and into the first gut-tightening inversion at 5Gs. It's a real launch (sometimes of lunch) followed by a wild ride through a make-believe California freeway system in the semidarkness. The ride lasts 3 minutes, 12 seconds, about the running time of Aerosmith's hit "Sweet Emotion." *Note:* Riders must be at least 48 inches tall.

Sounds Dangerous Starring Drew Carey ★   Drew Carey (is there an echo?) provides laughs while dual audio technology provides some hair-raising effects during this 12-minute show at ABC Sound Studios. You'll feel like you're right in the middle of the action of a TV pilot that features undercover police work and plenty of amusing mishaps. Even when the picture disappears and the theater is plunged into darkness, you continue on Detective Charlie Foster's chase via headphones that show off "3-D" sound effects.

Star Tours   Cutting-edge when it first opened, this galactic journey based on the original *Star Wars* trilogy (George Lucas collaborated on the ride) is now a

> **Tips   Is That Your Final Answer?**
>
> Disney–MGM Studios opened its newest attraction—based on the Disney-owned ABC hit TV show **"Who Wants to Be a Millionaire?"**—in April 2001. The Disney version is similar to the real show in that contestants try to answer up to 15 multiple-choice questions. They get three lifelines, including having two wrong answers removed, asking the audience for help, and an opportunity to call a stranger on phones set up along Mickey Avenue and the corridor to the Backlot Tour.
>
> The big difference: No millions. The contestants play for points and prizes. "Millionaires" get leather jackets and a trip to New York to meet Regis Philbin.

couple of rungs below the latest technology, but it's still fun. You board a 40-seat "spacecraft" for an other-worldly journey that greets you with sudden drops, crashes, and oncoming laser blasts as it careens out of control. This is another of those virtual rides where you go nowhere but it feels like you do. *Note:* Riders must be at least 40 inches tall.

The Twilight Zone Tower of Terror ★★★ *(Finds)*   Disney continues to fine-tune this ride into a true stomach-lifter. As legend has it, during a violent storm on Halloween night 1939, lightning struck the Hollywood Tower Hotel, causing an entire wing and an elevator full of people to disappear. And you're about to meet them as you become the star in a special episode of . . . "The Twilight Zone." After various spooky adventures, the ride ends in a dramatic climax: a 13-story free-fall. At 199-feet, it's surely the tallest ride in WDW, and it's a grade above Dr. Doom's Fearfall at Islands of Adventure (later in this chapter). *Note:* You must be at least 40 inches tall to ride.

Voyage of the Little Mermaid ★   Hazy lighting creates an underwater effect in a reef-walled theater and helps set the mood for a charming musical show that combines live performers with 100 puppets, film clips, and more. Sebastian sings the movie's theme, "Under the Sea"; Ariel shares her dream of becoming human in "Part of Your World"; and Ursula, the tentacled one, belts out "Poor Unfortunate Soul." This 17-minute show is a great place to rest, smile, and sing along on a day filled with walking.

9 Animal Kingdom

Disney's fourth major park combines animals, elaborate landscapes, and a handful of rides to create yet another reason that many guests don't venture outside this World. The bulk of the $800 million park opened in 1998; the most recent "land," Asia, was born in 1999.

Animal Kingdom ranks right up there with Tampa's Busch Gardens (see chapter 11) as one of the top two critter parks in Florida. Animal Kingdom is a 500-acre park for animals, a conservation venue as much as an attraction. It's easy for most of the animals to escape your eyes here. Busch (335 acres) has fewer places for hide-and-seek, so it's easier to see them there if you want to make the 2½-hour round-trip. Animal Kingdom wins the battle of the shows, however, with humdingers such as **Tarzan Rocks!** and **Festival of the Lion King,** but Busch wins hands-down the battle of thrill rides with five roller coasters.

THE OASIS

With its garden entrance and the sounds of birds chirping, this painstakingly landscaped point of entry has streams, grottoes, and waterfalls that set the tone for the rest of the park. It's a good place to see tiny deer, wallabies, anteaters, sloths, iguanas, tree kangaroos, otters, and macaws, if you get here early or stay late. But it's primarily a pass-through zone, so you won't spend much time here.

SAFARI VILLAGE

Like Cinderella's Castle in the Magic Kingdom and Spaceship Earth in Epcot, the 14-story **Tree of Life** ★★ is the park's central landmark. WDW artisans built the tree, which has 8,000 limbs, 103,000 leaves, and 325 mammals, reptiles, amphibians, bugs, birds, Mickeys, and dinosaurs in its trunk, limbs, and roots. Teams of artisans worked for a year creating its sculptures, and it's worth a walk around its roots, especially on the way to see *It's Tough to Be a Bug* (reviewed below).

It's Tough to Be a Bug! ★   Once you pass the Tree of Life, grab your 3-D specs and settle into a sometimes creepy-crawly seat. This show's special effects are pretty impressive. It's not a good one for very young kids (it's dark and loud) or bug haters, but for others it's a fun, sometimes poignant look at life from a smaller perspective. And near the conclusion, a stink bug truly awakens your senses.

Safari Village Trails   The trails offer a leisurely stroll through the root system of the Tree of Life and a chance to see real, not-so-rare critters, such as otters, flamingos, tamarinds, lemurs, tortoises, ducks, storks, and cockatoos.

DINOLAND U.S.A.

Enter by passing under "Olden Gate Bridge," a 40-foot Brachiosaurus reassembled from fossils. Speaking of which, until late summer 1999, this land had three paleontologists working on the very real skeleton of "Sue," a Tyrannosaurus Rex found in South Dakota. Her new home is at Chicago's Field Museum, but Dinoland has a replica cast from her 67 million-year-old bones.

The Boneyard ★   Kids love the chance to slip, slither, slide, and crawl through this giant playground and dig site where they can discover the real-looking remains of triceratops, T-rex, and other vanished giants. It's also a great place for parents to take a break from the pavement pounding that goes into a day in the park.

Dinosaur   Formerly called Countdown to Extinction, this ride hurls you through darkness in CTX Rover "time machines" that pass an array of snarling (though somewhat hokey) dinosaurs. Young children may find the large lizards and darkness a bit frightening. *Note:* You must be 40 inches or taller to climb aboard.

Tarzan Rocks! ★   Phil Collins's soundtrack and a cast of 27 very live performers (tumblers, dancers, and in-line skating daredevils) put on quite a show during this 28-minute production. The costumes and music are spectacular, second in Animal Kingdom only to Festival of the Lion King in Camp Minnie-Mickey (below).

CAMP MINNIE-MICKEY

Characters and one of the best theme-park shows in town are the main attractions in this small area of Animal Kingdom.

Character Greeting Trails ★ *Moments*   This is a must-do for people traveling with children. A variety of Disney characters, from Winnie the Pooh and

> ## Coming Soon
> Animal Kingdom is easing into the coaster craze. **Primeval Whirl** won't have inversions when it opens in a new area of Dinoland U.S.A. in spring 2002. But it will have a lot of spinning action in family-style, rider-controlled time machines that go through curves and short drops.
>
>   **Triceratops Spin** will be a kids' ride along the same lines; it opens about the time this book hits the stores.

Pocahontas to Timon and Baloo, have separate trails where you can meet and mingle. Mickey, Minnie, Goofy, and Pluto also make appearances.

Festival of the Lion King ⭐⭐ *Finds*   Almost everyone in the audience comes alive when the music starts in this rousing, 28-minute show in Lion King Theater. The eight-times-a-day extravaganza celebrates nature's diversity, with a talented troupe of singers, dancers, and life-size critters that lead the way to an inspiring sing-along that gets the crowd caught up in the fun. The action is onstage as well as moving around the audience. Even though the pavilion has 1,000 seats, it's best to arrive at least 20 minutes early.

Pocahontas and Her Forest Friends   The 15-minute show isn't close to the caliber of Festival of the Lion King and Tarzan Rocks! In this one, Pocahontas, Grandmother Willow, and some forest creatures hammer home the importance of treating nature with respect.

AFRICA
Enter through the town of Harambe, a run-down representation of an African coastal village on the edge of the 21st century. A central marketplace is surrounded by structures built of coral stone and thatched with reed by craftspeople brought over from Africa.

Kilimanjaro Safaris ⭐⭐   Animal Kingdom doesn't have many rides, so calling this the best may sound like a qualified endorsement. But the animals make it a winner as long as your timing is right. They're scarce at midday most times of year (in cooler months you may get lucky), so ride this one as close to the park's opening or closing as you can. Your vehicle is a very large truck that takes you through a simulated African landscape. These days, you might see black rhinos, hippos, antelopes, crocodiles, wildebeests, zebras, and a male lion that, if your timing is good, might offer a half-hearted roar toward some gazelles that are safely out of his reach.

Pangani Forest Exploration Trail ⭐ *Moments*   Hippos, tapirs, ever-active mole rats, and some other critters often are there on the trail for your viewing, but the real prize here is getting a look at the gorillas. The gorilla trail has two habitats: One houses a family of six, including a 500-pound silverback and his wives and children; the other has five bachelors. They're not always cooperative, especially in hot weather when they tend to spend most of the day in shady areas out of view. Those who come early, stay late, are patient, or make return visits can be rewarded with a close look at some special creatures.

Rafiki's Planet Watch *Overrated*   Board an open-sided train near the Pangani Trail for a trip to the back edge of the park and **Conservation Station,** which offers a behind-the-scenes look at how Disney cares for animals. You'll pass nurseries and veterinarian stations, but these facilities need to be staffed to be interesting and that's not always the case.

ASIA

Disney's Imagineers did a good job of creating the mythical kingdom of **Anadapour.** The intricately painted artwork out front helps make the lines seem to move a tad faster.

Flights of Wonder *Overrated*   This bird show is a low-key break from the madness and has a few laughs, but it's not much different from the other bird shows you'll find throughout Florida, except for some new faces.

Kali River Rapids 🉠   Here's a darn good raft ride—slightly better, we think, than Congo River Rapids at Busch Gardens in Tampa, but not quite as good as Popeye & Bluto's Bilge Rat Barges at Islands of Adventure (later in this chapter). Its churning water mimics real rapids, and some optical illusions will have you wondering if you're about to drop over the falls. You *will* get wet. *Note:* There's a 42-inch height minimum.

Maharajah Jungle Trek 🉠   With this exhibit, Disney keeps its promise to provide up-close views of animals. If you don't show up in the midday heat, you may see Bengal tigers through the thick glass, while nothing but air divides you from dozens of giant fruit bats (wing spans up to 6 feet) that are in what looks like a courtyard.

10 Other WDW Attractions

TYPHOON LAGOON 🉠🉠

A storm-stranded fishing boat—the *Miss Tilly*—sits atop 95-foot-high Mount Mayday and overlooks this Disney water park. Every few minutes the boat blows its stack, shooting a 50-foot geyser of water into the air. It has several other attractions.

Castaway Creek's rafts and inner tubes glide along a 2,100-foot-long river that circles most of the park and includes a misty rain forest, caves, and secluded grottoes. It has a theme area called **Water Works,** where jets of water spew from shipwrecked boats.

Ketchakiddie Creek is for 2- to 5-year-old guests. An innovative water playground, it has bubbling fountains to frolic in, mini–water slides, a pint-sized "white-water" tubing run, spouting whales and squirting seals, rubbery crocodiles to climb on, grottoes to explore, and waterfalls to loll under.

At **Shark Reef,** guests get free equipment and instructions for a 15-minute swim through this very small snorkeling area that includes a simulated reef populated by parrotfish, rays, and small sharks.

Typhoon Lagoon, the park's 2.75 million-gallon wave pool, launches **large breakers** every 90 seconds. A foghorn warns you when, in case you want to head for cover. Young children can wade in the lagoon's more peaceful tidal pools—**Blustery Bay** or **Whitecap Cove.**

Humunga Kowabunga consists of three 214-foot-high Mount Mayday slides that propel you down the mountain on a serpentine route through waterfalls and bat caves and past nautical wreckage before depositing you into a bubbling catch pool. *Note:* You must be 48 inches or taller to ride this. White-Water Rides at Mount Mayday is the setting for three white-water rafting adventures—**Keelhaul Falls, Mayday Falls,** and **Gangplank Falls**—all offering steep drops coursing through caves and passing lush scenery.

Typhoon Lagoon is open at least from 10am to 5pm, with extended hours during some holiday periods; 9am to 8pm in the summer (© **407/560-4141;**

www.disneyworld.com). A 1-day ticket is $29.95 for adults, $24 for children 3 to 9.

BLIZZARD BEACH 🏔🏔

Disney's newest water park is a 66-acre "ski resort" in the midst of a tropical lagoon centering on the 90-foot Mount Gushmore.

Its 2,900-foot-long **Cross Country Creek** is a lazy tube run, but watch out for the cave where you'll get splashed with melting ice. **Runoff Rapids** offers another tube job. This one lets you careen down one of three twisting, turning runs through semidarkness.

Ski-Patrol Training Camp, designed for preteens, features a rope swing, a T-bar hanging over the water, the wet and slippery **Mogul Mania** slide, and an ice-floe walk along slippery floating icebergs.

Snow Stormers has three flumes descending from the top of Mount Gushmore, following a switchback course through slalom-type gates.

Summit Plummet is one of the most breath-defying adventures in any water park. Read every speed, motion, vertical-dip, wedgie, and hold-onto-your-breast-plate warning before hopping on. This puppy starts slow, with a lift ride (even in Florida's 100° dog days) to the 120-foot summit. But it finishes as the world's fastest body slide—a test of your courage and swimsuit—that virtually goes straight down and has you moving sans vehicle at 60 miles per hour into the catch pool. *Note:* It has a 48-inch height minimum.

Teamboat Springs is this World's longest white-water raft ride, twisting down a 1,200-foot series of rushing waterfalls.

Tike's Peak is a kiddie version of Mount Gushmore. It has short water slides, animals to climb aboard, a snow castle, a squirting ice pond, and a fountain play area for young guests.

Blizzard Beach is open at least from 10am to 5pm, with extended hours during some holiday periods; 9am to 8pm in the summer (📞 **407/560-4141;** www. disneyworld.com). A 1-day ticket is $29.95 for adults, $24 for children 3 to 9.

RIVER COUNTRY 🏔

Yes, another (and we promise, the last) water park in Disney. This Fort Wilderness Resort mini park is themed after Tom Sawyer's swimming hole. Kids scramble over boulders that double as diving platforms for a 330,000-gallon pool. Two 16-foot slides provide access to the pool. Attractions on **Bay Lake,** equipped with ropes and ships' booms for climbing, include two flumes—one 260 feet long, the other 100 feet—that corkscrew through Whoop-N-Holler Hollow. **White Water Rapids** carries inner-tubers along a winding, 230-foot-long creek with a series of chutes and pools, while **The Ol' Wading Pool** is a smaller version of the swimming hole designed for younger children.

Note: River Country has fewer attractions and therefore is less crowded than the other Disney water parks, making it attractive to those looking for a less hectic place to swim.

River Country is open 10am to 5pm most of the year (with extended hours during holidays), 10am to 7pm during the summer. A 1-day admission to River Country is $15.95 for adults, $12.50 for children (📞 **407/824-2765;** www. disneyworld.com). *Note:* River Country usually is closed from just after Labor Day until early March.

Fantasia Gardens & Winter Summerland Miniature Golf 🏔🏔   Hippos, ostriches, and alligators decorate the **Fantasia Gardens** course, where the

Sorcerer's Apprentice presides over the final hole. This course is a good bet for beginners and kids. Seasoned mini-golfers probably will prefer the second 18-hole course, **Fantasia Fairways,** which is a scaled-down golf course complete with sand traps, water hazards, tricky putting greens, and holes ranging from 40 to 75 feet.

Santa Claus and his elves provide the theme for **Winter Summerland,** which offers two more 18-hole courses. The Winter course takes you from an ice castle to the North Pole. The Summer course is pure Florida, from sandcastles to surfboards to a visit with Santa on the "Winternet."

Tickets for both are $9.25 for adults and $7.50 for children 3 to 9. Winter Summerland also offers a combination ticket with Blizzard Beach ($35 for adults, a $1.75 saving; $28 for kids, a $1 saving). Both courses are open 10am to 11pm daily. For information about Fantasia Gardens, call ✆ **407/560-8760.** For information on Winter Summerland call ✆ **407/560-3000.** Find both on the Internet at www.disneyworld.com.

DISNEY'S WIDE WORLD OF SPORTS 🏈

This 200-acre complex has a 7,500-seat baseball stadium, 10 other baseball and softball fields, six basketball courts, a dozen lighted tennis courts, a track-and-field complex, golf driving range, and six sand volleyball courts.

Organized programs and events include:

- The **NFL Experience.** Ten drills test your running, punting, passing, and receiving skills. You can dodge cardboard defenders and run pass patterns while a machine shoots you passes. Depending on your stamina and size of the crowds, the experience lasts 45 minutes to several hours. It's open daily, 10am to 5pm; $9 for adults, $7 for kids 3 to 9.
- The **Atlanta Braves** play 18 spring-training games during a month-long season that begins in early March. Tickets cost $8.50 and $15.50. For information, call ✆ **407/828-3267;** you can get tickets through **Ticketmaster** (✆ **407/839-3900**).
- The **NFL, NBA, NCAA, PGA,** and **Harlem Globetrotters** also host events, sometimes annually and sometimes more frequently, at the complex. Admission varies by event.

Disney's Wide World of Sports is located on Victory Way, just north of U.S. 192 (west of I-4), ✆ **407/939-1500.**

RICHARD PETTY DRIVING EXPERIENCE 🏁

Epcot's Test Track is for sissies. Here's the real thing: The Petty team gives you a chance to drive a 600-horsepower, Winston-Cup car. How real is it? Expect to sign a two-page waiver that features words like *dangerous* and *calculated risk* before you climb in. At one end of the spectrum, you can ride shotgun for a couple of laps at 145 miles per hour ($90). At the other, spend from 3 hours to 2 days learning how to drive this machine yourself and race fellow daredevils in 8 to 30 laps of excitement ($350 to $1,200). *Note:* You must be 18 years old to do this. Hours and seasons vary. For reservations, call ✆ **800/237-3889.**

11 What to See & Do Beyond Disney: Universal Orlando, SeaWorld & Other Orlando Attractions

There are so many attractions in Orlando that it's impossible to see half of them unless you're here 10 to 14 days or longer. But the following should help you finish picking your A-Team.

DisneyQuest

The reaction to DisneyQuest's virtual video arcade ☆☆ is usually the same, whether it's from kids who are just reaching the video-game age, teens who are firmly hooked, or adults who never outgrew Pong. Almost everyone leaves saying, "Awesome!"

This five-level arcade has everything from nearly old-fashioned pinball to virtual games and rides. Here's a sampling:

- **Aladdin's Magic Carpet Ride** puts you astride a motorcycle-like seat while you fly through the 3-D Cave of Wonders.
- **Invasion: An Extraterrestrial Alien Encounter** finds you trying to save colonists from intergalactic bad guys. One member of your group flies the module as the other three fire an array of weapons at the uglies.
- **Pirates of the Caribbean: Battle for Buccaneer Gold** outfits you and three mates in 3-D helmets so you can battle pirate ships virtual reality–style. One of you plays captain, steering the ship, while the others use cannons to blast the black hearts into oblivion.
- **Songmaker** lets you step into a phone booth–size recording studio to make your own CD (for $10 extra).
- Try the **Mighty Ducks Pinball Slam** if you're a pinball fan. It's an interactive, life-size game in which you ride platforms and use body English to score points.
- If you have an inventive mind, stop in **The Create Zone,** where Bill Nye the Science-Turned-Roller-Coaster Guy helps you create the ultimate loop-and-dipster, which you then can ride in a lifelike simulator.
- Finally, if you need some quiet time, sign up at **Animation Academy** for a minicourse in Disney cartooning.

Snack and food areas round out the offerings, but keep in mind that heavy crowds after 1pm can cut into your fun time.

DisneyQuest (© **407/828-4600;** www.disneyworld.com) is located in Downtown Disney West Side on Buena Vista Drive. The admission ($29 for adults, $23 for children 3 to 9) gives you unlimited play from 10:30am to midnight.

UNIVERSAL STUDIOS FLORIDA

Even with fast-paced, grown-up rides such as Twister, Terminator, and Men in Black Alien Attack, Universal Studios Florida is fun for kids. And as a plus, it's a working motion-picture and TV-production studio, so occasionally there's live filming done at Nickelodeon's sound stages or elsewhere in the park. **Hanna-Barbera characters** such as Yogi Bear, Scooby Doo, and Fred Flintstone usually are on hand to greet visitors as is a talented group of actors portraying Universal stars ranging from Harpo Marx to the Blues Brothers.

Last year's big news: the opening of **Men in Black Alien Attack.** This interactive, other-worldly show lets you blast aliens with weapons called alienators.

TICKET PRICES   A **1-day ticket** costs $48 (plus 6% sales tax) for adults, $38 for children 3 to 9. A 2-day, two-park unlimited-access escape pass is

$89.95 for adults, $74.95 for children 3 to 9; a 3-day, two-park pass is $99.95 for adults, $79.95 for children 3 to 9.

THE FLEXTICKET The cheapest way to see Universal, SeaWorld, *and* Wet 'n Wild is with one of these **FlexTicket** passes. They are Universal's version of Disney's Park Hopper tickets. With FlexTicket, you pay one price to visit any of the participating parks during a 14-day period. A four-park pass to Universal Studios Florida, Islands of Adventure, Wet 'n Wild, and SeaWorld is $160 for adults and $128 for children 3 to 9. A five-park pass, which adds Busch Gardens in Tampa, is $197 for adults and $158 for kids. The **FlexTicket** can be ordered through Universal (© **407/363-8000;** www.universalorlando.com).

MAJOR ATTRACTIONS

Back to the Future: The Ride ✮ Blast through the space-time continuum in a flight simulator built to look like the movie's famous DeLorean car. You'll blaze a trail through volcanic tunnels, collide with glaciers, thunder through caves and canyons, and briefly get swallowed by a dinosaur in a spectacular multisensory adventure. You twist, turn, dip, and dive—all the while feeling like you're really flying. This is similar to but *more intense* than Body Wars at Epcot (earlier in this chapter). *Note:* It's bumpy and might not be a good idea if you're prone to dizziness or motion sickness. Riders must be at least 40 inches tall.

Beetlejuice's Rock 'n' Roll Graveyard Revue Dracula, Wolfman, Franken-stein, and Beetlejuice stage a rock musical with loud and lively pyrotechnic special effects and MTV-style choreography.

A Day in the Park with Barney ✮ Set in a parklike theater-in-the-round, this 25-minute musical stars the Purple One, Baby Bop, and BJ. It uses song, dance, and interactive play to deliver an environmental message. This could be the highlight of the day for preschoolers. However, for many adults, it has the same brain-eating effects as It's a Small World at WDW's Magic Kingdom (see earlier in this chapter).

Earthquake—The Big One ✮ Not long after you climb on a BART train in San Francisco, there's a big one—an earthquake that's 8.3 on the Richter scale! As you sit helplessly trapped, concrete slabs collapse around you, a propane truck bursts into flames, a runaway train hurtles your way, and the station floods (65,000 gallons of water cascade down the steps). *Note:* Riders must be at least 40 inches tall.

E.T. Adventure ✮ Soar with E.T. on a mission to save his ailing planet, through the forest and into space aboard a bicycle. You'll also meet some new characters that Steven Spielberg created for the ride, including Botanicus, Tickli Moot Moot, Horn Flowers, and Tympani Tremblies. This family favorite is def-initely a charmer. If there is a criticism, it's that there are two waiting areas—inside and outside. But most folks come away feeling the ride is worth it.

The Funtastic World of Hanna-Barbera ✮ This spaceship/motion-simula-tor offers a surprisingly wild ride as pilot Yogi Bear tries to save Elroy Jetson from Dick Dastardly. Its brain-scrambling motion is similar to Back to the Future (above), although this one's a lot tamer. If you were one of those children who got up early to watch the Saturday morning cartoons, it will definitely bring back fond memories. *Note:* There's a 40-inch height minimum.

Jaws ✮ As your boat heads into a 7-acre, 5 million-gallon lagoon, a familiar dorsal fin cuts across the surface. Then, what goes with the fin—a 3-ton, 32-foot-long, mechanical great white shark—attacks. The wall of flame 30 feet high that surrounds your boat truly causes you to feel the heat in this $45 million attraction. *Note:* The effects of this ride are more spectacular after dark.

Kongfrontation   It's the last thing the Big Apple needs: King Kong is back! Everyone must evacuate to Roosevelt Island, so it's all aboard a tram. Cars collide and hydrants explode below you. Police helicopters hover overhead, putting you directly in the line of fire; then the tram malfunctions; and, of course, you encounter Kong—40 feet tall and 12,000 pounds. He belches banana breath into your face and terrifies you and your fellow passengers by dangling the tram over the East River. The big ape executes 46 movements, including simulated noogies on top of your tram. *Note:* The big gorilla and dark waiting area may frighten kids under 6.

Men in Black Alien Attack 🎢🎢🎢   Once you board a six-passenger cruiser, you'll buzz the streets of New York, using your "zapper" to splatter up to 120 bug-eyed targets. You have to contend with return fire and distractions such as light, noise, and clouds of liquid nitrogen (aka fog), any of which can spin out of control. Your lasertag–style gun fires infrared bullets. The 4-minute ride relies on 360° spins rather than speed for its thrill factor. At the ride's conclusion, you're swallowed by a giant roach (it's 30 feet tall with 8-foot fangs and 20-foot claws). Fortunately for you, it explodes at the ride's conclusion. Unfortunately for you, the blast douses you with bug guts (okay, it's only warm water) as you blast your way out. *Note:* Guests must be at least 42 inches tall for this $70 million ride.

Nickelodeon Studios Tour 🎢   You'll tour the sound stages where Nick shows such as "Kenan & Kel" and "The Mystery Files of Shelby Woo" are produced. You'll also view concept pilots, visit the kitchen where Gak and green slime are made, play game shows such as Double Dare 2000, and try new Sega video games. This 45-minute behind-the-scenes walking tour is a fun escape from the hustle of the midway. A child volunteer gets slimed, but it's only green apple-sauce or a reasonable facsimile.

Terminator 2: 3-D Battle Across Time 🎢🎢🎢 *(Finds)*   James Cameron, who directed the movie, supervised this $60 million production, which features Arnie and other original cast members (on film). It combines three huge screens with technical effects and live stage action that includes a custom Harley David-son "Fat Boy" and six 8-foot-tall cyberbots. *Note:* The crisp 3-D effects are among the best in any Orlando park, but Universal has given this show a PG-13 rating, meaning violence and loud noise may be too intense for young children and preteens.

Twister . . . Ride It Out 🎢   Two million cubic feet of air per minute (that's enough to fill four full-size blimps) create an ominous funnel cloud, five-stories tall. And the roar of a freight train, at rock-concert level, fills the theater as cars, trucks, and a cow fly by while the audience watches just 20 feet away. Crowds sometimes applaud when it's all over. *Note:* This show, too, has a PG-13 rating.

The Wild, Wild, Wild West Stunt Show 🎢   Actors demonstrate falls from three-story balconies, gun and whip fights, dynamite explosions, and other Wild West staples in this 18-minute show that's a real hit with Far East visitors, who are intrigued by America's Wild West. *Warning:* Heed the splash zone or you will get very wet.

Woody Woodpecker's Nuthouse Coaster 🎢🎢   This kiddie coaster will thrill some moms and dads, too. Although only 30 feet at its peak, it offers quick, banked turns while you sit in a miniature steam train. The ride lasts only about

60 seconds and waits can be 30 minutes or more, but few kids will want to miss the experience. It's much like The Barnstormer at Goofy's Wiseacre Farm in the Magic Kingdom (reviewed earlier in this chapter). *Note:* The coaster has a 36-inch height minimum.

ADDITIONAL ATTRACTIONS

The Boneyard is an oft-changing area where you can see props used in a number of Universal movies. **Alfred Hitchcock: The Art of Making Movies** is a tribute to the "master of suspense." The PG-13 show includes Tony Perkins narrating a reenactment of the shower scene from *Psycho* as well as a 3-D version of another one of Hitchcock's masterpieces, *The Birds*. The **Gory, Gruesome & Grotesque Horror Make-up Show** offers behind-the-scenes looks at transformation scenes from such movies as *The Fly* and *The Exorcist* (shows from 11am). **Lucy, A Tribute** is a remembrance of America's queen of comedy, and the **Blues Brothers** launch their foot-stomping revue five times a day.

Back at Woody Woodpecker's KidZone, **Fievel's Playland** is a wet, western-themed playground with a house to climb and a water slide for small fry. **Curious George Goes to Town** has water- and ball-shooting cannons, while **Animal Actors Stage** presents a 20-minute show featuring live-animal actors portraying Mr. Ed, Beethoven, and Lassie.

ISLANDS OF ADVENTURE

Islands of Adventure, Universal's second theme park, opened in 1999. At 110-acres, it's the same size as its big brother, Universal Studios Florida, but it seems larger. Roller coasters roar above pedestrian walkways and water rides slice through the park. (The trade-off: The park has only two shows.)

> **Full-Speed Ahead**
>
> Islands of Adventure is *the* Orlando park for thrill-ride junkies.

A few words of caution: *Ten of the park's 14 major rides have height restrictions.* Dueling Dragons and the Incredible Hulk Coaster, for instance, deny access to anyone under 54 inches. And many of those 10 rides may not be suitable for those who are tall enough but have health problems, physical restrictions, or a tendency toward motion sickness.

TICKET PRICES   A **1-day ticket** costs $48 (plus 6% sales tax) for adults, $38 for children 3 to 9. A 2-day, two-park unlimited-access escape pass is $89.95 for adults, $74.95 for children 3 to 9; a 3-day, two-park pass is $99.95 for adults, $79.95 for children 3 to 9.

THE FLEXTICKET   The cheapest way to see Universal, SeaWorld, *and* Wet 'n Wild is with one of these **FlexTicket** passes. They are the Universal equivalent of Disney's Park Hopper tickets. With FlexTicket, you pay one price to visit any of the participating parks during a 14-day period. A four-park pass to Universal Studios Florida, Islands of Adventure, Wet 'n Wild, and SeaWorld is $160 for adults and $128 for children 3 to 9. A five-park pass, which adds Busch Gardens in Tampa, is $197 for adults and $158 for kids. The **FlexTicket** can be ordered through Universal (© **407/363-8000;** www.universalorlando.com).

MAJOR ATTRACTIONS
Port of Entry

This park gateway has five shops, four restaurants, and the **Island Skipper Tours,** which ferries passengers to **Jurassic Park.**

Seuss Landing

The main attractions here are aimed at youngsters. But anyone who loved the good Doctor as a child will enjoy the nostalgic fun.

The Cat in the Hat 🎠🎠   Seuss fans will recognize the giant candy-striped hat looming over the entrance to this ride, and probably the chaotic journey. Comparable to, but a bit spunkier than It's a Small World at WDW, The Cat in the Hat puts you in a spinning couch that travels through 18 scenes from the famous book, retelling the tale of a day gone very much awry.

One Fish, Two Fish, Red Fish, Blue Fish 🎠   This kiddie charmer is similar to the Dumbo ride at WDW (including the ridiculously long line), although this one has a few added features. Your controls allow you to move your funky fish up or down 15 feet as you spin around on an arm attached to a hub. Watch out for "squirt posts," which spray unsuspecting riders who don't follow the rhyme that plays as your fish goes round and round.

Caro-Seuss-El 🎠🎠🎠 *Moments*   Forget tradition. This not-so-normal carousel gives you a chance to ride seven whimsical characters from Dr. Seuss (a total of 54 mounts), including Cowfish, elephant birds, and Mulligatawnies. *Note:* A special platform lets guests in wheelchairs experience the up-and-down motion of the ride.

If I Ran the Zoo 🎠   This 19-station interactive play land features flying water snakes and a chance to tickle the toes of a Seussian animal. Kids can also spin wheels, explore caves, fire water cannons, climb, slide, and otherwise burn off excited energy that most adults can't remember ever having.

Marvel Super Hero Island

Thrill junkies love the twisting, turning, stomach-churning rides on this island filled with building-tall murals of Marvel Super Heroes.

The Amazing Adventures of Spider-Man 🎠🎠🎠 *Finds*   The original web master stars in this mobile ride with 3-D action and special effects. Passengers wearing 3-D glasses squeal as their 12-passenger cars twist and spin, plunge and soar through this comic-book universe. There's a simulated 400-foot drop that feels an awful lot like the real thing. *Note:* Expectant mothers or those with heart, neck, or back problems shouldn't get on. Those who ride must be at least 40 inches tall.

Doctor Doom's Fearfall 🎠   Look! Up in the sky! It's a bird, it's a plane . . . uh, it's you falling 150 feet, if you're courageous enough to climb aboard this towering metal skeleton. The screams that can be heard at the ride's entrance add to the anticipation of a straight plunge. You're fired to the top, with feet dangling, and dropped in intervals, leaving your stomach at several levels. The fall isn't quite up to the Tower of Terror's at Disney–MGM Studios, but it's still frightful. *Note:* Expectant mothers or those with heart, neck, or back problems shouldn't ride. Minimum height is 52 inches.

Incredible Hulk Coaster 🎠🎠🎠 *Finds*   This rocking ride launches from a dark tunnel and hurtles you into daylight while accelerating from 0 to 40 miles per hour in 2 seconds. While that's only two-thirds the speed of Rock 'n' Roller Coaster at Disney–MGM Studios, the Hulk has more action. You spin upside down 128 feet from the ground, feel weightless, and careen through the center of the park over the heads of other visitors. Coaster-lovers will be pleased to know that this ride, which lasts 2 minutes and 15 seconds, includes seven inversions and two deep drops. As a nice touch, the 32-passenger metal coaster glows green at night (riders who ignore all the warnings occasionally turn green as well). *Note:* Expectant mothers or those with heart, neck, or back problems shouldn't ride. Riders must be at least 54 inches tall.

Storm Force Accelatron Despite the exotic name, this ride is little more than a spin-off of the Magic Kingdom's Mad Tea Party—spinning teacups that, in this case, have a 22nd-century design.

Toon Lagoon

More than 150 life-size cartoon images let you know you've entered an island dedicated to your favorites from the Sunday funnies.

Dudley Do-Right's Ripsaw Falls ★★ The staid red hat of the heroic Dudley can be deceiving: The ride that lies under it has a lot more speed and drop than onlookers think. Six-passenger logs launch you into a 75-foot dip at 50 miles per hour. You *will* get wet on this ride. *Note:* Once again, expectant mothers or folks with heart, neck, or back problems should go elsewhere. Riders must be 44 inches or taller.

Me Ship, The Olive ★ This three-story boat is family-friendly from bow to stern. Kids can toot whistles, clang bells, or play the organ. Sweet Pea's Playpen is a favorite of younger guests. Kids 6 and up, as well as adults, will love Cargo Crane, where you can drench riders on Popeye & Bluto's Bilge-Rat Barges (see below).

Popeye & Bluto's Bilge-Rat Barges ★★ These rafts provide the same kind of ride as Kali River Rapids at WDW's Animal Kingdom, but this ride is faster and bouncier. And, to add to the fun, you'll be squirted by water cannons fired from Me Ship, The Olive. Rafts bump, churn, and dip 14 feet at one point, as you travel a *c-c-cold* white-water course. *You will get soaked! Note:* Again, expectant mothers or people with heart, neck, or back problems shouldn't get in line. Riders must be at least 48 inches tall.

Toon Trolley Character Meet and Greet Beetle Bailey, Hagar the Horrible, and Dagwood & Blondie are just a few of the characters that show up several times daily in this comic-strip neighborhood.

Jurassic Park

All of the basics and some of the high-tech wizardry from Stephen Spielberg's wildly successful films are incorporated in this lushly landscaped tropical locale that includes a replica of the visitor's center from the *Jurassic Park* movie.

Camp Jurassic ★ This play area has everything from lava pits with dinosaur bones to a rain forest. Watch out for the spitters that lurk in dark caves. The multilevel play area has plenty of places for kids to crawl, explore, and spend energy. But keep an eye on young ones: It's easy to get turned around inside the caverns.

Jurassic Park Discovery Center ★ Here's an amusing, educational pit stop that offers life-size dinosaur replicas and interactive games. The sequencer lets you combine your DNA with a dinosaur's. The "Beasaur" exhibit allows you to see and hear as "they" did. The highlight is watching a velociraptor "hatch" in the lab.

Jurassic Park River Adventure ★★ After you enjoy a leisurely raft tour along a faux river, some raptors escape and could hop aboard your raft at any moment. At one point, a T-Rex decides you look like a tasty morsel, and at another, spitters launch "venom" your way. The only way out: an 85-foot plunge in your log-style life raft. It's steep and quick enough to lift your fanny out of the seat. (Spielberg designed it, but on a test run insisted on getting out before the drop.) Expect to get wet. *Note:* Expectant mothers or those with heart, neck, or back problems shouldn't ride. Guests must be at least 42 inches tall.

Pteranodon Flyers ☆ *Kids*   The ride's 10-foot metal frames and simple seats look flimsy, the landing is bumpy, and you'll swing from side to side, which makes some riders queasy. Unlike the traditional gondolas in sky rides, on this one your feet hang free from the two-seat, skeletal flyer and there's little but a restraining belt between you and the ground. *Note:* That said, this is a child's ride—single passengers must be between 36 and 56 inches tall; adults can climb aboard *only* when accompanying someone that size.

Triceratops Encounter   Meet a "living" dinosaur and learn from its "trainers" about the care and feeding of a 24-foot-long, 10-foot-high Triceratops. It responds to touch, and its movements include realistic blinks, breathing, and flinches.

The Lost Continent

Although Universal has mixed up its millennia—combining ancient Greece with a medieval forest—it has done a good job creating a foreboding mood in this section of the park, whose entrance is marked by menacing stone griffins.

Dueling Dragons ☆☆☆ *Finds*   Maniacal designers created two roller coasters that roar at each other at high speeds. True coaster crazies love the intertwined set of leg-dangling racers that climb to 125 feet, invert five times, and then three times come within 12 inches of each other as the dragons battle and you prove your bravery by tagging along. For the best ride, try to get one of the two outside seats in each of the eight rows. If you want the front seat, there's a special (yes, longer!) line near the loading dock so daredevils can claim the first car. *Note:* Expectant moms or those with heart, neck, or back problems shouldn't ride. Riders must be at least 54 inches tall.

The 8th Voyage of Sindbad *Overrated*   The mythical sailor is the star of a stunt show that includes six water explosions and 50 pyrotechnic effects, including a 10-foot circle of flames. It's pretty corny and doesn't come close to the Indiana Jones stunt show at Disney–MGM Studios.

The Flying Unicorn ☆☆   The Unicorn is a small roller coaster that travels through a mythical forest on the Lost Continent, next to Dueling Dragons. It's very much like Woody Woodpecker's Nuthouse Coaster at Universal Studios Florida and The Barnstormer at Goofy's Wiseacre Farm in the Magic Kingdom (both reviewed earlier in this chapter). That means a fast, corkscrew run sure to earn squeals but probably not at the risk of losing the contents of your stomach.

The Mystic Fountain ☆ *Finds*   Just outside Sindbad's show, this interactive "smart" fountain delights youngsters. It can "see" and "hear," leading to a lot of kibitzing with those who stand before it and take the time to kibitz back.

Poseidon's Fury: Escape from the Lost City ☆   This is the park's best show, though given the lack of competition that's something of a back-handed compliment. The Keeper, a ghostly white character, leads you on a journey where you become trapped in a battle between the evil Poseidon, god of the sea, and Zeus, king of the gods. From a small room, you proceed to others, including a 42-foot-wide vortex where 17,500 gallons of water swirl around you, barrel-roll style. In the battle royale, the gods hurl 25-foot fireballs at each other.

SEAWORLD

This 200-acre marine-life park explores the mysteries of the deep by combining conservation awareness with entertainment. The stars of the park are **Shamu,** a killer whale, and his ever-expanding family, which includes baby Orcas.

TICKET PRICES A **1-day ticket** costs $47.95 for ages 10 and over, $38.95 for children 3 to 9, plus 6% sales tax.

THE FLEXTICKET The most economical way to see SeaWorld, the Universal parks, and Wet 'n Wild is with one of these **FlexTicket** passes. They let you pay one price to visit any of the parks in a 14-day period. A four-park pass to Universal Studios Florida, Islands of Adventure, Wet 'n Wild, and SeaWorld is $160 for adults and $128 for children 3 to 9. A five-park pass, which adds Busch Gardens in Tampa (see chapter 11), is $197 for adults and $158 for kids. You can order a **FlexTicket** through SeaWorld (© **407/351-3600;** www.seaworld. com).

MAJOR ATTRACTIONS

Clyde & Seamore Take Pirate Island ⚡ A lovable sea lion and otter, with a supporting cast of walruses and harbor seals, appear in this fish-breath comedy with a swashbuckling conservation theme. It's corny, but don't hold it against the animal stars.

Intensity Water-Ski Show ⚡⚡ *Moments* Arguably, this is an unrivaled ski show that has evolved over more than 15 years. It's a not-to-be-missed hyper-competition involving some of the most skilled and daring athletes on water. The 20-person team includes world-class skiers, wake-boarders, and stunt men and women from across the United States performing nonstop aquabatics. This show and Shamu's (see below) are nearly worth the admission by themselves.

Journey to Atlantis ⚡⚡ Taking a cue from Disney imagineers, SeaWorld has created a story line to go with this $30 million water coaster. It has to do with a Greek fisherman and ancient Sirens in a battle between good and evil. But what really matters is the drop—a wild plunge from an altitude of 60 feet with luge-like curves and a shorter drop added for good measure. *Note:* Riders must be at least 46 inches tall and pregnant women as well as folks with heart, neck, or back problems should find something else to do.

Key West at SeaWorld This Caribbean-style village has island food, entertainers, and street vendors. But the big attractions include the hands-on encounters with harmless Southern diamond and cownose rays; Sea Turtle Point, the home of threatened and endangered species; and Dolphin Cove, where you can feed smelt to the namesakes. *Warning:* You get a half dozen fish for $3 or two trays for $5, and it's real easy to spend $20 feeding them.

Key West Dolphin Fest At the partially covered, open-air Whale and Dolphin Stadium, Atlantic bottlenose dolphins perform flips and high jumps, twirl, swim on their backs, and give rides to trainers. The tricks are impressive, but it's like any other dolphin show. If you go, see this before Shamu. He puts these little mammals to shame. *Note:* This show closed in the fall of 2000 for renovations, but it's scheduled to reopen about the time this book is published.

Kraken ⚡⚡ SeaWorld's deepest venture onto the field of the thrill-ride battle starts slow, like many coasters, but it ends with pure speed. Kraken is named for a massive, mythological underwater beast kept caged by Poseidon. This 21st-century version offers floor-less and open-sided 32-passenger trains that plant you on a pedestal high above the track. When the monster breaks loose, you climb 151 feet, fall 144 feet, hit speeds of 65 miles per hour, go underground three times (spraying bystanders with water), and make seven loops during a 4,177-foot-long course. It may be the longest 3 minutes and 39 seconds of your life. *Note:* Kraken has a 54-inch height minimum.

Manatees: The Last Generation   Underwater viewing stations, innovative cinema techniques, and interactive displays combine for a tribute to these gentle marine mammals. While this isn't as good as seeing them in the wild, it's as close as most folks get, and it's a much roomier habitat than the tight quarters their kin have at The Living Seas in Epcot (reviewed earlier in this chapter).

Penguin Encounter ⭐ *Overrated*   Sadly, this is a very superficial encounter that transports you by moving sidewalk through Arctic and Antarctic displays. On the other side of the Plexiglas, you'll get a glimpse of penguins as they preen, socialize, and swim at bullet speed in their 22° habitat. You'll also see puffins and murres in a similar, separate area.

Shamu's Happy Harbor ⭐   This 3-acre play area has a four-story net tower with a 35-foot-high crow's-nest lookout, water cannons, remote-controlled vehicles, nine slides, a submarine, and a water maze. Most kids love it.

The Shamu Adventure ⭐⭐⭐ *Moments*   Everyone comes to SeaWorld to see the big guy. Very good trainers and very smart Orcas stage a well-choreographed show. The whales (up to 25 feet and 10,000 pounds) really dive into their work. When you hear the warning that Hurricane Shamu is approaching, it's time for those sitting in the first 14 rows to hightail it. Those who don't are drenched with *icy water* as the Orcas race around the pool, creating a huge wave that rolls over the edge and into the audience. Veteran animal handler Jack Hanna also makes an appearance on the big overhead monitors, compliments of ShamuVision.

Note: Arrive 30 minutes early for a good seat. The stadium is large, but it fills quickly.

Terrors of the Deep   Remember Shark Encounter? SeaWorld has added other species—about 220 specimens in all. Pools out front have small sharks and rays (feeding isn't allowed here). The interior aquariums have big eels, beautiful but poisonous lionfish, hauntingly still barracudas, and bug-eyed pufferfish. *Note:* This isn't a tour for the claustrophobic, since you have to walk through an acrylic tube, beneath millions of gallons of water.

Wild Arctic   Enveloping guests in the beauty, exhilaration, and danger of a polar expedition, Wild Arctic combines a high-definition adventure film with flight-simulator technology to display breathtaking Arctic panoramas. After a hazardous flight over the frozen north, visitors emerge at a remote research camp that's home to four polar bears (including star residents and twins Klondike and Snow), seals, walruses, and beluga whales. Kids may find the bumpy ride a little much. There's a separate line for those who want to skip it.

ADDITIONAL ATTRACTIONS

Other features at SeaWorld include **Pacific Point Preserve,** a 2½-acre natural setting that duplicates the rocky home of California sea lions and harbor seals. **Tropical Rain Forest,** a bamboo and banyan-tree habitat, is the home of cockatoos and other birds. At the 5½-acre **Anheuser-Busch Hospitality Center,** indulge in free samples of Anheuser-Busch beers and then stroll through the stables to watch the famous Budweiser Clydesdale horses being groomed.

DISCOVERY COVE: A DOLPHIN ENCOUNTER

Anheuser-Busch spent $100 million building this second park, which debuted in 2000. That's 10 times less than Islands of Adventure at Universal (above), but the admission is as much as four times higher. There are two options: Pay $199 plus 6% sales tax (ages 6 and up only) if you want to swim with a dolphin. Or, if you can skip that perk, the cost is $89.

The **dolphin encounter** ✦✦ stars an amazing group of 28 of these mammals. They perform tricks and take guests for brief but thrilling rides. The experience lasts 90 minutes, about 35 to 40 minutes of which is spent in the lagoon with your dolphin. Trainers use the rest of the time to teach you about these remarkable mammals.

Here's what you get, with or without the dolphin encounter, for your money:

- A limit of *no more than 1,000 other guests a day.* (The average daily attendance at Disney's Magic Kingdom is 41,000.)
- Lunch (fajitas, salmon, stir fry, pesto chicken pasta, salads, or sandwiches), a towel, locker, snorkeling gear (you get to take the snorkel home), and a souvenir photo of you as you enter the park.
- Other 9am to 5:30pm activities include a chance to swim near (but on the other side of Plexiglas from) **barracudas and black-tip sharks.** There are no barriers, however, between you and the gentle rays and brightly colored tropical fish in the 1.3 million-gallon coral reef. The 3,300-foot-long Tropical River is a great place to swim or float in a mild current—it goes through a cave, two waterfalls, and a 100-foot-long, 30-foot-high aviary where you can take a stroll, becoming a human perch for some of the 30 exotic bird species. There are also beaches for tanning.
- Seven days of **unlimited admission** to SeaWorld (park admission normally costs $47.95 a day for adults, $38.95 for children 3 to 9).

You can get more information on Discovery Cove by calling ☎ 877/434-7268 or go to **www.discoverycove.com**. If you decide to try this adventure, make a reservation as far in advance as possible. Despite the price, it reaches its capacity almost every day.

12 Other Area Attractions

Now that we've covered the monster parks, we're going to explore some of Central Florida's best smaller attractions. Many of these require less than a day (or a fortune) to see, so we'll note how much time and money to budget.

IN KISSIMMEE

Kissimmee's tourist strip is 10 to 15 minutes west of Disney. **Add 6% sales tax** to the prices below unless otherwise noted.

China Town & Florida Splendid China   Crowds are reasonably small at this 76-acre attraction, partly due to a lack of publicity but mainly because it doesn't deliver the same entertainment pizzazz that the bigger parks do. Highlights include miniature replicas of China's man-made and natural wonders, such as a half-mile-long copy of the 4,200-mile Great Wall, the Forbidden City's 9,999-room Imperial Palace, and the Mongolian mausoleum of Genghis Khan. The *Mysterious Kingdom of the Orient* is a 90-minute dance-and-acrobatic show held nightly except Monday in the Golden Peacock Theater. Allow 4 to 5 hours to tour the park.

3000 Splendid China Blvd. (off U.S. 192). © 800/244-6226 or 407/396-7111. www. floridasplendidchina.com. Admission $27.25 adults, $17.25 children 5–12. Daily from 9:30am; closing time varies. Free parking. From I-4 take Exit 25A, stay left and follow U.S. 192 west; turn left at the Florida Splendid China dragons.

Flying Tigers Warbird Restoration Museum

If you're a fan of vintage flying machines and their restoration, you'll like this working museum, which displays aircraft from the World War II through Vietnam eras. There are guided tours through the museum, and the showroom has restored birds such as a B-25 Mitchell, a P-51 Mustang, a B-17, and P-38 Lightnings. Plan on spending 2 to 4 hours to tour.

231 N. Hoagland Blvd. (south of U.S. 192). © 407/933-1942. www.warbirdmuseum.com. Admission $9 adults, $8 seniors 60 and over, $8 children 6–12. Daily 9am–5pm. Free parking. Take U.S. 192 east of Disney to Kissimmee; turn south on Hoagland.

Gatorland

Founded in 1949 with only a handful of alligators living in huts and pens, Gatorland now houses thousands of alligators and crocodiles on its 70-acre spread. There are three shows. **Gator Wrestlin'** uses the old "put-them-to-sleep" trick, but it's more of an environmental awareness program. **The Gator Jumparoo** is a crowd-pleaser in which one of these big reptiles lunges 4 or 5 feet out of the water to snatch a dead chicken from a trainer's hand. And **Snakes of Florida** showcases some of our deadly natives. Plan to spend 4 to 5 hours here.

14501 S. Orange Blossom Trail/U.S. 441 (between Osceola Pkwy. and Hunter's Creek Blvd.). © 800/393-5297 or 407/855-5496. www.gatorland.com. Admission $17.95 adults, $7.95 children 3–12 including tax. Daily 9am–6pm usually; closing varies. Free parking. From I-4 take Exit 26A to 417 N.; then take Exit 11 to U.S. 441 S. Gatorland is 1 mile on left.

Water Mania

You can boogie board or body surf in the continuous-wave pools, float lazily along an 850-foot-long river, enjoy a white-water tube run on **Riptide,** and spiral down the **Twin Tornadoes** water slide. If you dare, ride the **Abyss,** an enclosed tube slide that corkscrews through 380 feet of darkness, exiting into a splash pool. There's a water playground for kids, a miniature golf course, and a picnic area, too. Allow 4 to 5 hours here.

6073 W. Irlo Bronson Memorial Hwy./U.S. 192 (just east of I-4). © 800/527-3092 or 407/396-2626. www.watermania-florida.com. Admission $17 3–adult. Mar–Oct daily 10am–5pm. Parking $5. From I-4 take Exit 25A ½ mile east on U.S. 192.

ON INTERNATIONAL DRIVE

Like Kissimmee attractions, these are a 10- to 15-minute drive from the Disney area and 5 to 10 minutes from Universal Orlando.

The Holy Land Experience

Backers of this new $20 million attraction are counting on folks interested in Bible heritage and the ever-after to visit a park that represents Jerusalem between 1450 B.C. and A.D. 66. There are models of Noah's Ark, the limestone caves where the Dead Sea Scrolls were discovered, and Jesus' tomb. The park has attracted its fair share of controversy. Orlando-area rabbis, among others, protested its opening, saying they believe it's a ploy to convert Jews to Christianity. Plan to spend 4 hours here.

4655 Vineland Rd. © 866/872-4659 or 407/872-2272. Admission $17 adults, $12 children 4–12. Mon–Thu 10am–7pm, Fri–Sat 10am–10pm, Sun noon–7pm. From I-4 take Exit 31; it's on the corner of Vineland and Conroy roads.

Ripley's Believe It or Not! Odditorium

Overrated Do you crave weird science? The oddities here include a two-headed kitten, a five-legged cow, a three-quarter–scale model of a 1907 Rolls-Royce made of 1 million matchsticks, and a Tibetan flute created from human bones. Allow 2 hours.

8201 International Dr. (south of Sand Lake Rd.). © **800/998-4418** or 407/363-4418. www.ripleys. com/orlando2.htm. Admission $13 for adults, $12 seniors, $9 children 4–12. Daily 9–1am. Free parking. From I-4 west, take Exit 29A/Sand Lake Rd. Turn right on International Dr.

Titanic—Ship of Dreams *Overrated* If you didn't get enough of the *Titanic* with the movie, news clips, and expedition, you will get that *no mas* feeling at this attraction. The exhibit has some 200 artifacts (a deck chair, life jacket, etc.), movie memorabilia, actors, and a replica of the great ship's grand staircase. Allow 1 or 2 hours.

8445 International Dr. (3 blocks south of Sand Lake Rd.). © **407/248-1166.** www.titanicshipofdreams.com. In The Mercado. Admission $17 adults, $12 kids 6–12. Free parking. Daily 10am–9pm. From Disney, take I-4 E. and Exit 27A (SeaWorld); veer right and turn left on International Dr. Go 2 miles.

Wet 'n Wild ★★ Orlando's favorite non-Disney water park offers 25 acres of fun including: **Fuji Flyer,** a six-story, four-passenger toboggan run through 450 feet of banked curves; **The Surge,** which is one of the longest (580 feet of curves) and fastest multipassenger tube rides in the Southeast; and **Black Hole,** a two-person, spaceship-style raft that makes a 500-foot, twisting, turning voyage through darkness (all three rides require that children 36 to 48 inches tall be accompanied by an adult). You also can ride **Raging Rapids,** a simulated white-water run with a waterfall plunge; **Blue Niagra,** a 300-foot-long, six-story loop-and-dipster that also has a plunge (48-inch height minimum); **Knee Ski,** a cable-operated knee-boarding course that's open in warm-weather months only (56-inch height minimum); and **Mach 5,** a trio of twisting, turning flumes. The park also has a large kids' area with miniversions of the big rides. If you enjoy the water, plan on spending a full day here.

In addition to the admission prices below, Wet 'n Wild is part of the multi-day **FlexTicket package** that includes admission to Universal Orlando (which owns this attraction), SeaWorld, and Busch Gardens in Tampa. You pay one price to visit any of them during a 14-day period. A four-park pass to Universal Studios Florida, Islands of Adventure, Wet 'n Wild, and SeaWorld is $160 for adults and $128 for children 3 to 9. A five-park pass, which adds Busch Gardens in Tampa, is $197 for adults and $158 for kids. You can order the passes through Wet 'n Wild at © **407/351-9453** or at **www.wetnwild.com**.

6200 International Dr. (at Universal Blvd.). © **800/992-9453** or 407/351-9453. www.wetnwild.com. Admission $30 adults, $24 children 3–9. Daily hours vary seasonally (call before you go). You can rent tubes ($5), towels ($2), and lockers ($5); all include a $2 refundable deposit. Parking is $5 for cars, light trucks, and vans. Take I-4 Exit 30A and follow the signs.

ELSEWHERE IN ORLANDO

Orlando has several cultural attractions that are about 35 minutes north of the Disney parks, and while you're in the area, consider a visit to nearby Winter Park.

Harry P. Leu Gardens *Value* This 50-acre garden offers a respite from theme-park razzle-dazzle. Paths lead through camphors, oaks, palms, cicadas, and camellias—the latter represented by one of the world's largest collections, 50 species and 2,000 plants that bloom October through March. There's also an extensive rose garden. Orlando businessman Harry P. Leu, who donated his 49-acre estate to the city in the 1960s, created the gardens. There are free 20-minute tours of his house, built in 1888. It takes about 2 hours to see everything.

1920 N. Forest Ave. (between Nebraska St. and Corrine Dr.). © **407/246-2849.** www.ci.orlando.fl.us/ departments/leu_gardens/. Admission $4 adults, $1 children grades K–12. Daily 9am–5pm (later in summer and during holidays). Tours 10am–3:30pm. Free parking. Take I-4 to Exit 43/Princeton St., go east and then right on Mills Ave. Left on Virginia Dr. The gardens are on your left.

Orlando Museum of Art ☆ A multimillion-dollar makeover in 1997 made this museum, already a local heavyweight, ready to handle some of the most prestigious traveling exhibits in the nation. The museum hosts special exhibits throughout the year, but even if you miss one it's worth a stop to see the rotating permanent collection of 19th- and 20th-century American art, pre-Colombian art dating from 1200 B.C. to A.D. 1500, and African art. Allow 2 to 3 hours.

2416 N. Mills Ave. (in Loch Haven Park). © **407/896-4231.** www.omart.org. Admission $6 adults, $4 seniors and students, $2 children 4–11. Tue–Sat 10am–5pm; Sun noon–5pm. Free parking. Take I-4 east to Exit 43/Princeton St. and follow signs to Loch Haven Park.

Orlando Science Center ☆☆ *(Finds* The four-story center, renovated in 1997, has 10 exhibit halls that allow visitors to explore everything from Florida swamps to the arid plains of Mars to the human body. One of the big attractions is the **Dr. Phillips CineDome,** a 310-seat theater that presents large-format films, planetarium shows, and laser light extravaganzas. In **KidsTown,** there's a pint-size park, construction site, and wellness center. **Science City,** located nearby, includes a power plant, and **123 Math Avenue** uses puzzles and other things to make learning fun. Allow 3 to 4 hours.

777 E. Princeton St. (between Orange and Mills Aves.), in Loch Haven Park. © **407/514-2000** or 888/672-4386. www.osc.org. Admission (exhibits only) $9.50 adults, $6.75 children 3–11, $8.50 seniors 55 and older; additional prices for CineDome film or a planetarium show. Open Tue–Thurs 9am–5pm; Fri–Sat 9am–9pm; Sun noon–5pm. Parking is available in a garage across the street and costs $3.50. Take I-4 Exit 43/Princeton St. east and cross Orange Ave.

A SIDE TRIP TO CYPRESS GARDENS

Cypress Gardens ☆☆ FDR was in his first term when this foundation tourist attraction opened in 1936. Water-ski shows and flowers are still its bread and butter, but a lot has changed over the years.

At **Carousel Cove,** kids ride ponies and an ornate carousel dating to the turn of the 20th century. The adjoining **Cypress Junction** is outfitted with a model railroad that travels 1,100 feet of track with up to 20 trains, visiting miniature places such as New Orleans and Mount Rushmore. **Electric boats** navigate a maze of lushly landscaped canals in the original botanical gardens. You can ascend 153 feet to the **Island in the Sky** for a panoramic vista of the gardens and a beautiful chain of Central Florida lakes.

Cypress Roots, the park's museum, displays photographs of famous visitors (Elvis on water skis and Tiny Tim tiptoeing through the, uh, roses). **"Calling All Animals"** features a show-and-tell with a 6-foot-long savanna monitor lizard, an alligator, some blue and gold macaws, and a 15-foot albino python that answers to the name of "Banana Boy."

On the water, the **Greatest American Ski Team** keeps a legendary tradition going strong with standards such as ramp jumping, the aqua-maid ballet line, human pyramid, flag line, and slapstick comedy. Shows change, but they usually combine yesterday with modern magic acts.

On the frozen-water front, **"Fairy Tales on Ice"** visits a number of favorites, including *Sleeping Beauty, Snow White, The Hunchback of Notre Dame,* and *1,001 Arabian Nights.* **Variete Internationale** performs **"European Circus Magic,"** a stage show that features popular clowns Zaripov and Gratchik, who weave magic acts into their zany antics.

"**Wings of Wonder**" is a conservatory with more than 1,000 brilliant butter-flies (50 species) in a Victorian-style, climate-controlled, free-flight aviary. The **Birdwalk Aviary** has 40 to 50 hand-raised lories and lorikeets that welcome vis-itors by landing on their shoulders. The young Australian parrots are brilliantly colored and very inquisitive.

Allow a full day to see Cypress Gardens.

2641 S. Lake Summit Dr. (Hwy. 540 at Cypress Gardens Blvd., 40 miles southwest of Disney World), Winter Haven. ✆ 800/282-2123. www.cypressgardens.com. Admission $33 for adults, $17 children 6–12. Parking $6. Daily 9:30am–5pm, later during some periods. Take I-4 west to U.S. 27 S. and proceed west to Hwy. 540.

WINTER PARK

This lakeside town is a lovely place to spend a half day. In addition to the two attractions described below, you can browse through the posh boutiques that line Park Avenue.

Charles Hosmer Morse Museum of American Art ★ *Value* Louis Com-fort Tiffany left a fingerprint on this museum, which has 40 vibrantly colored windows and 21 paintings of his. There are also non-Tiffany windows by Frank Lloyd Wright, paintings by John Singer Sargent and Maxfield Parrish, and photographs by Tiffany and other 19th-century artists. Allow 2 hours.

445 Park Ave. N. (between Canton and Cole). ✆ 407/645-5311 or 407/645-5324 (recording). www.morsemuseum.org. Admission $3 adults, $1 kids 12–17. Tue–Sat 9:30am–4pm, Sun 1–4pm. Make a left onto Park Ave. N., passing 4 traffic lights to the museum.

Florida Audubon Birds of Prey Center ★★ *Finds* In addition to being a rehabilitation center—one of the biggest and most successful in the Southeast—this is a great place to get to know rehabilitated winged wonders that roost here and earn their keep by entertaining the few visitors who come. You can get a close look at hams like Elvis, the blue-suede-shoe–wearing American kestrel; Daisy the polka-dancing barn owl; and Trouble, an eagle born with a misaligned beak. *Note:* The center has been closed pending the opening of a state-of-the-art rehab center and permanent residence. It's scheduled to reopen by the end of summer 2001, but call ahead. Allow 2 hours.

1101 Audubon Way, Maitland. ✆ 407/644-0190. www.adoptabird.org/. Recommended donation $5 adults, $3 children 3–12. Tue–Sun 10am–5pm. From Orlando, go north on I-4 to Lee Rd./Exit 46 and turn right/east. At the first light (Wymore Rd.), go left; then take a right/east at the next light (Kennedy Blvd.). Continue ½ mile to East Ave.; turn left and go to the stop sign at Audubon Way. Turn left and the center is on the right.

13 Staying Active

Disney and the surrounding areas have plenty of recreational options. The fol-lowing are open to everyone, no matter where you're staying. For further infor-mation about WDW recreational facilities, call ✆ **407/939-7529** or visit **www.disneyworldsports.com**.

BICYCLING

Bike rentals (single- and multispeed bikes for adults, tandems, baby seats, and children's bikes including those equipped with training wheels) are available from the **Bike Barn** (✆ **407/824-2742**) at Fort Wilderness Resort and Camp-ground. Rates are $6.60 per hour, $18.87 per day plus tax. Fort Wilderness offers wooded bike trails.

BOATING

WDW owns a navy of pleasure boats. **Captain Jack's** at Downtown Disney rents Water Sprites, canopy boats, and 20-foot pontoon boats ($20 to $32 per half hour). For information call ✆ **407/828-2204**. The **Bike Barn** at Fort Wilderness (✆ **407/824-2742**) rents canoes and paddleboats ($6.13 per half-hour, $10.38 per hour).

FISHING

Disney offers a variety of fishing excursions, but true anglers probably won't find them a challenge. The excursions can be arranged 2 to 90 days in advance by calling ✆ **407/824-2621**. The fee is $160 to $185 for up to five people for 2 hours. Bait isn't included.

GOLF

Disney operates five 18-hole, par-72 golf courses and one 9-hole, par-36 walking course. The rates are $100 to $145 per 18-hole round for resort guests ($5 more if you're not staying at a WDW property). For tee times and information, call ✆ **407/824-2270** up to 7 days in advance (up to 30 days for guests of the Disney resort and official properties). Call ✆ **407/934-7639** for information about golf packages.

Beyond Mickey's shadow, **Golfpac** (✆ **800/327-0878** or 407/260-2288; www.golfpacinc.com) is an organization that packages golf with accommodations and arranges tee times at more than 40 Orlando-area courses. **Tee Times USA** (✆ **800/465-3356**; www.teetimesusa.com) and **Florida Golfing** (✆ **866/833-2663**; www.floridagolfing.com) are two others offering package information and course reservations.

HAYRIDES

The hay wagon departs **Pioneer Hall** at Disney's Fort Wilderness nightly at 7 and 9:30pm for 45-minute, old-fashioned hayrides with singing, jokes, and games. Cost is $6 for adults, $4 for children ages 3 to 10. It's first-come, first-served. Call ✆ **407/824-2832** for more information.

HORSEBACK RIDING

Disney's **Fort Wilderness Resort and Campground** has 45-minute scenic guided-tour trail rides six times a day. The cost is $23 per person. Children must be at least 9 years old. Maximum weight limit is 250 pounds. Call ✆ **407/824-2832** for details.

Villas of Grand Cypress offers 45-minute, walk-trot trail rides (four times daily) for $45. A 30-minute private lesson is $55; an hour lesson is $100. Call ✆ **407/239-4700** and ask for the equestrian center.

SWIMMING

The **YMCA Aquatic Center** has a fitness center, racquetball courts, and an indoor pool. Admission is $10 per person, $25 for families. It's at 8422 International Dr. (Take I-4 to Exit 29 and turn right at the end of the ramp. Turn right again on International Drive. At second light, take another right.) For information call ✆ **407/363-1911**.

TENNIS

There are 22 lighted tennis courts throughout the Disney properties. Most are free and available on a first-come, first-served basis. If you're willing to pay, courts can be reserved at two Disney resorts, the **Contemporary** and the **Grand Floridian,** by calling ✆ **407/824-2270**. Both charge $15 per hour. Lessons are also available.

SPECTATOR & PARTICIPATION SPORTS

In addition to Disney's Wide World of Sports (reviewed earlier in this chapter), Central Florida has a number of other venues for active and inactive sportsters.

ARENA FOOTBALL

The **Orlando Predators** play from April until August and have a loyal and rowdy following. Game tickets ($5 to $35) are often available the day of the game at the **TD Waterhouse Centre,** 600 W. Amelia St., between I-4 and Parramore Avenue (✆ **407/447-7337**).

BASEBALL

The **Atlanta Braves** play 18 spring-training games at Disney's Wide World of Sports beginning in early March. Tickets are $9 and $16, available through **Ticketmaster** (✆ **407/839-3900**). From April to September, the **Orlando Rays,** the Tampa Bay Devil Rays' Class AA Southern League affiliate, play their 70 home games at the same complex. Tickets through **Ticketmaster** (✆ **407/ 839-3900**) sell for $3 to $7.

BASKETBALL

The 17,500-seat **TD Waterhouse Centre,** 600 W. Amelia St., between I-4 and Parramore Avenue, is the home court of the **Orlando Magic,** which plays 41 of its games here from October to April. Call ✆ **407/896-2442** for information, **407/462-2849** to charge tickets; or check out **www.nba.com/magic/.** Single-game tickets ($25 to $155) can be hard to come by. On the women's side, the WNBA's **Orlando Miracle** has a 16-game home stand beginning in early June on the same court. Tickets are $8 to $34. Call ✆ **407/916-9622** for information, ✆ **407/839-3900** for tickets; or surf over to **www.wnba.com/miracle/.**

HOCKEY

The **Orlando Solar Bears,** an International Hockey League team, play an October to April season at the TD Waterhouse Centre. Tickets are $9 to $30 (✆ **407/ 872-7825;** www.theihl.com/orlando/).

14 Shopping

Some of us get as much pleasure from shopping as a good meal or show. But if you're going to ring registers in the theme parks, expect to pay top dollar. So plan a day out of the parks if shopping is in your game plan, and be as savvy here as you are back home—don't blow your souvenir fund in the tourist areas.

On International Drive, look for **Pointe Orlando,** a complex that has more than three dozen specialty stores including FAO Schwarz and Banana Republic, ✆ **407/248-2838.** Also on International Drive, **Festival Bay** (✆ **407/ 345-1311**) has a 20-screen theater and a Bass Pro Shop, and is planning to add a Ron Jon Surf Shop, a skateboard park, and several restaurants.

There are several factory outlets around, but their publicized discounts of 25% to 75% and more are sometimes a mirage. The best way to avoid being taken is to come already knowing suggested retail prices, so you can decide whether or not you're making a killing. **Belz Factory Outlet World,** 5401 W. Oak Ridge Rd. (at the north end of International Drive; ✆ **407/354-0126;** www.belz.com), and the **Orlando Premium Outlets,** 8200 Vineland Ave. (✆ **407/238-7787;** www.premiumoutlets.com), are two of the more notable discount meccas. The latter opened in fall 2000.

Value **A Disney Bargain?**

Little-known, surplus-property auctions are, as the president of the National Auctioneers Association calls them, "the best bargain anywhere in Disney."

In addition to castoffs from the theme parks and Disney resorts, more-routine items are available, from over-the-hill lawn maintenance gear to never-used, stainless-steel pots and pans (too many of which were purchased for the Disney Cruise Line). If you're looking for a unique piece of Disney, the auctions are held four to six times a year—always on a Thursday, when Disney workers get paid. Some of the more unusual items sold in the past? Furniture from Miss Piggy's dressing room and a motorized surfboard. Since the auction takes place on Disney's back lots, you'll need to call ℂ 407/824-6878 for information, dates, and directions.

The malls include **Florida Mall,** 8001 S. Orange Blossom Trail (ℂ 407/851-7234; www.shopsimon.com), which offers Saks, Dillards, and 200 more stores; and **Mall at Millennia,** which is scheduled to open in summer 2002 at Conroy Road and I-4, near Universal Orlando. It will house a Bloomingdale's, Macy's, Neiman Marcus, and 200 other specialty stores.

Old-stuff buffs love **Antique Row** on Orange Avenue in downtown Orlando. This collection of two dozen shops is about as far away as you can get from the manufactured fun of Disney. Headliners include **Flo's Attic** (ℂ 407/895-1800) and **Pieces of Eight Emporium** (ℂ 407/896-8700), which sell traditional antiques. Down the road, a handful of places sell upscale clothing, cigars, and traditional works of art. **Art's Cigars** (ℂ 407/895-9772) is a two-story leather-and-tweed kind of place where patrons are encouraged to light up and enjoy the view of Lake Ivanhoe across the street. **Wildlife Gallery** (ℂ 407/898-4544) sells pricey, original works of wildlife art, including sculptures. And the **Fly Fisherman** (ℂ 407/898-1989) sells—no surprise here—fly-fishing gear. Sometimes, you can spot people taking casting lessons in the park across the street.

Most of these downtown shops are open from 9am to 5pm, Monday to Saturday; the owners usually run them, so hours can vary. (A small number are open on Sunday, but it's probably not worth the trip from the resorts—stick to weekdays.)

All of the shops are spread over 3 miles along Orange Avenue. The heaviest concentration of shops lies between Princeton Street and New Hampshire Avenue, although a few are scattered between New Hampshire and Virginia avenues. The more upscale shops extend a few blocks beyond Virginia. Parking is limited, so stop wherever you find a space along the street.

15 Walt Disney World & Orlando After Dark

Central Florida has plenty for night owls to do. Parties last into the wee hours at **Church Street Station, Pleasure Island** and **Downtown Disney,** Universal's **CityWalk,** and up and down **International Drive.**

DISNEY DINNER SHOWS

Hoop-Dee-Doo Musical Revue *(Moments)* As WDW's most popular show, Hoop-Dee-Doo requires reservations as early as possible. The reward: You can feast on a down-home, all-you-can-eat barbecue (fried chicken, smoked ribs, salad, corn on the cob, baked beans, freshly baked bread, strawberry shortcake, and coffee, tea, beer, sangria, or soda). While you stuff yourself silly, performers in 1890s garb lead you in a foot-stomping, hand-clapping high-energy show that includes jokes you haven't heard since second grade.

If you catch one of the early shows, stick around for the **Electrical Water Pageant** at 9:45pm, which can be viewed from the Fort Wilderness Beach.

3520 N. Fort Wilderness Trail (at WDW's Fort Wilderness Resort and Campground). (C) **407/939-3463**. www.disneyworld.com. Reservations required. Adults $46.33, kids 3–11 $23.78, including tax and gratuity. Free parking. Show times 5pm, 7:15pm, and 9:30pm daily.

Polynesian Luau Dinner Show *Moments*　Almost as popular as the Hoop-Dee-Doo, The Polynesian Luau presents a delightful 2-hour show that's a favorite among kids. They're invited on stage as part of an evening that includes hyperactive entertainers from New Zealand, Hawaii, and Tahiti, who perform hula, warrior, ceremonial, love, and fire dances on a flower-filled stage. Arrive early for a preshow featuring crafts (lei making, hula lessons, and more).

The all-you-can-eat meal includes island fruits, roasted chicken and pork, fried rice, vegetables, red and sweet potatoes, cinnamon bread, tropical ice-cream sundaes, coffee, tea, beer, wine, and soda.

1600 Seven Seas Dr. (at Disney's Polynesian Resort). (C) **407/939-3463**. www.disneyworld.com. Reservations required. Adults $46.33, kids 3–11 $23.78, including tax and gratuity. Free parking. Show times 5:15 and 8pm daily.

MORE DINNER SHOWS

These shows won't win any cuisine awards (the food frequently is overcooked and the meat chewy), but the entertainment is tons of fun.

Arabian Nights　If you're a horse fancier, this show is a must. It stars Arabians, Lipizzans, and many other breeds. On most nights, it begins with a ground trainer working one-on-one with a black stallion and progresses to Wild-West trick riders, a dual dressage performance, cowgirl thrill show, Native American riding treats, and other fun things such as chariot races and a magical unicorn. Dinner includes prime rib, vegetables, potatoes, salad, and dessert.

6225 W. Irlo Bronson Memorial Hwy. (U.S. 192), Kissimmee. (C) **800/553-6116** or 407/239-9223. www. arabian-nights.com. Reservations recommended. Adults $36.95, childen 3–11 $23.95. Shows daily at 7:30pm. Free parking.

Medieval Times　Guests pig out on barbecued ribs, roast chicken, soup, appetizer, potatoes, dessert, and beverage. But since this is the 11th century, you eat with your fingers from metal plates while mounted knights run around the arena, jousting and clanging to please the fair ladies. Arrive 90 minutes early and see the Medieval Village, a re-created Middle Ages settlement.

4510 W. Irlo Bronson Memorial Hwy. (U.S. 192), Kissimmee. (C) **800/229-8300** or 407/396-1518. www.medievaltimes.com. Reservations recommended. Adults $42, children 3–11 $26. The shows usually are at 8 or 8:30pm, but sometimes there's an earlier one. Free parking.

Pirates Dinner Adventure　This special-effects show includes a full-size ship in a 300,000-gallon lagoon, circus-style aerial acts, a lot of music, and a little drama. Dinner includes an appetizer buffet with the preshow, then roast chicken and beef, rice, vegetables, dessert, and coffee. After the show, there's a dance party.

6400 Carrier Dr. Orlando ⓒ **800/866-2469** or 407/248-0590. www.orlandopirates.com. Reservations recommended. Adults $41.95, $25.50 children 3–to 11. Daily at 7:45pm, doors open at 6:30pm. Free parking.

ENTERTAINMENT MECCAS: PLEASURE ISLAND, CITYWALK, CHURCH STREET STATION, & MORE
AT DISNEY

PLEASURE ISLAND ☆   This Walt Disney World launch pad is a rollicking 6-acre complex of nightclubs, restaurants, shops, and movie theaters where during the day you can enjoy for free whatever's open. At night, for a single admission price ($21), you can go club hopping and celebrate New Year's Eve into the wee hours every night of the week.

Pleasure Island is made to appear like an abandoned waterfront industrial district with clubs in its lofts and warehouses, but the streets are decorated with colored lights and balloons. The mood is festive, especially at midnight, when the New Year's Eve party gets started. *Note:* At night, this is primarily an adult venue. Here's the lineup:

Adventurers Club   The most unique of Pleasure Island's clubs, Adventurers Club occupies a multistory building that's chock full of such artifacts as 1940s aviation photos, hunting trophies, shrunken heads, Buddhas, goddesses, and a mounted "yakoose"—a half yak, half moose that occasionally speaks, whether you've been drinking or not. In the eerie Mask Room, more strange sounds are heard and the 100 or so masks move their eyes, jeer, and make odd pronouncements. Also on hand is a zany band of globetrotting friends and servants, played by skilled actors who interact with guests while staying in character. Improvisational comedy shows take place throughout the evening in the main salon, and there are diverse 20-minute cabaret shows/events in the library (during which "volunteers" are dragooned from the audience).

BET Soundstage   This club grooves with traditional R&B and the rhyme of hip-hop. If you like the BET Cable Network you'll love it. Boogie on an expansive dance floor or kick back on the terrace. The club sometimes has concerts for a separate charge (ⓒ **407/934-7666**).

Comedy Warehouse   A troupe of comics (the Who, What, and Warehouse Players) performs 45-minute improvisational comedy shows based on audience suggestions. The shows will not make anyone's top-ten list, but the theater often gets packed tighter than a sardine can anyway. There are five shows a night and drinks are available. Arrive early.

8Trax   Disco still rules in this 1970s-style club, where shows and videos are aired by 50 TVs positioned over the dance floor. The DJ plays everything from "YMCA" to "The Hustle." All you need to bring is your polyester.

PI Jazz Company   This big, barnlike club features contemporary and traditional live jazz, with sit-down dining and funky coffees. The performers are mostly locals, but about once a month there's a big name, such as Kenny Rankin, Lionel Hampton, or Maynard Ferguson.

Mannequins Dance Palace   Housed in a vast dance hall with a small-town movie-house facade, Mannequins is supposed to be a converted mannequin warehouse (remember, you're still in Disney World). This high-energy club has a big, rotating dance floor, and its popularity makes it one of the toughest nightspots to get into. It offers three levels of bars and hangout space that are

Moments **Not Your Ordinary Circus**

Cirque du Soleil, the famed no-animals circus here in partnership with Disney, is located in Downtown Disney West Side. Cirque du Soleil, whose name translates as "circus of the sun" and flutters off the tongue as *"Sairk* doo So-*lay,"* is nonstop energy. At times it seems as if all 64 performers are onstage simultaneously, especially during the intricately choreographed trampoline routine. Trapeze artists, high-wire walkers, an airborne gymnast, a posing strongman, mimes, and two zany clowns cement a show called **La Nouba** (it means "live it up") into a five-star performance.

But, in a world of pricey attractions, this is one of the pricier. The 90-minute show costs $67 for adults and $39 for children 3 to 9 (plus 6% tax). Shows are at 6 and 9pm, Wednesday through Sunday, though the times rotate and there's sometimes a matinee. Call ✆ **407/939-7600** or check out **www.cirquedusoleil.com** for details.

---

festooned with elaborately costumed mannequins and moving scenery suspended from the overhead rigging. A DJ plays contemporary tunes filtered through speakers that could wake the dead, and there are high-tech lighting effects. You must be 21 to get in, and they're *very* serious about it.

Rock 'n' Roll Beach Club   Live bands play classic rock from the 1960s through the 1990s. There are bars on all three floors, including one serving international brews. The first level has a dance floor; the others offer arcade-style games, pizza, and more.

Wildhorse Saloon   Country rules in this boot-scootin' joint. If you have two left feet, the Wildhorse Dancers will show you the moves before you hit the floor. If you don't want to buy the full Pleasure Island ticket, the Wildhorse has a $5 cover charge Tuesday to Saturday. It also has separate tickets for occasional concerts (✆ **407/827-4947**). Downtown Disney West Side. ✆ **407/934-7781.** www.disneyworld.com. Free admission before 7pm; $21, tax included, after 7pm. Admission included in the 5- to 7-Day Park Hopper Plus passes. Clubs open daily 7pm–2am; shops 11am–2am. Free parking; valet parking $6.

DOWNTOWN DISNEY WEST SIDE

Bongo's Cuban Café. *Overrated*   Created by Cuban-American singer Gloria Estefan and her husband, Emilio, the cafe is Disney's version of old Havana. There are leopard-spotted chairs and mosaic barstools shaped like bongo drums. A Desi Arnaz look-alike might even show up to sing a few tunes. There's no dance floor to speak of, though you could cha-cha on the patio, an upstairs number that overlooks the rest of West Side. It's a great place to sit back and enjoy a good cigar (sorry, it's not a real Cuban) while basking in the Latin rhythms. However, the food is lacking. Downtown Disney West Side. ✆ **407/828-0999.** www.bongoscubancafe.com. No reservations. No cover charge. Daily 11am–2am. Free parking.

House of Blues   You can hear a variety of once-big names performing here, including Jethro Tull, Quiet Riot, Duran Duran, and others. The barnlike building, with three tiers, may be a little difficult for those with disabilities to maneuver in, but there really isn't a bad seat in the house. The atmosphere is dark and boozy, perfect for the oft-featured bluesy sounds that raise the rafters. The dance floor is big enough to boogie on without doing the bump with a stranger. You can dine in the adjoining restaurant ($9 to $24) on baby-back ribs, blackened chicken, jambalaya, Orleans-style shrimp, and Cajun meatloaf. There's also a Sunday gospel brunch. Downtown Disney West Side. ℂ **407/934-2583.** www.hob.com. Cover charges vary by event/artist. Free parking.

CITYWALK

Located between Islands of Adventure and Universal Studios Florida, this club-and-restaurant district had its coming out party in 1999. At 30 acres, **CityWalk** (ℂ **407/363-8000;** www.citywalk.com or www.universalorlando.com.) is five times larger than Pleasure Island. Alcohol is prominently featured here, so an adult should accompany all teens, young children, and free-flowing peers. The party can get pretty wild.

You can walk the district for free or visit individual clubs for the cover charges in the following listings. CityWalk also sells three **"party passes."** A pass to all clubs costs $8, plus tax. For $11, plus tax, you can add a movie at Universal Cineplex (ℂ **407/354-5998**) to the basic club access. Combine dinner at one of eight restaurants with a movie or all-club access for $17 (tax and gratuity are included in this option). Universal also offers free club access to those who buy 2- and 3-day theme-park tickets. *Note:* Daytime parking in the Universal Orlando garages costs $7, but parking is free after 6pm.

Bob Marley—A Tribute to Freedom   This hybrid bar/restaurant has a party atmosphere that will make the food more appealing as the night wears on. The clapboard building is said to be a replica of Marley's home in Kingston. Jamaican food—such as meat patties, jerk red snapper, and, of course, the brew of champions, Red Stripe—is served under patio umbrellas amid portraits of the original Rastamon. If you try an Extreme Measure, have a designated driver. Reggae bands, local and national, perform on a microdot-sized stage. ℂ **407/ 224-2262.** Cover charge $4.25 after 8pm, more on special nights. Sun–Fri 4pm–2am; Sat 2pm–2am.

CityJazz   The cover charge includes the **Downbeat Jazz Hall of Fame** (which has memorabilia from Louie Armstrong, Ella Fitzgerald, Buddy Rich, and other greats) as well as the **Thelonious Monk Institute of Jazz,** a performance venue that's also the site of jazz workshops. The two-story, 10,500-square-foot build-ing has more than 500 pieces of memorabilia representing Dixieland, swing, bebop, and modern jazz. It also has a state-of-the-art sound system and stage. On the food side of the equation, look for tapas, sushi, grilled lamb chops, and more. ℂ **407/224-2189.** Cover charge $3.25 (more for special events). Sun–Thu 8:30pm–1am; Fri–Sat 8:30pm–2am.

the groove   This club is Universal's answer to Mannequin's at Pleasure Island, though it's not as popular and, therefore, has less of a waiting list. There's a high-tech sound system that makes your hair blow back and a spacious dance floor in a room gleaming with chrome. A deejay plays tunes most nights, featuring the latest in hip-hop, jazz-fusion, techno, and alternative music. Bands occasionally play the house, too. The decor touches five entertainment eras in as many areas, ranging from vaudeville to the millennium. Each has a unique design, separate bar, and specialty drink to fit its ambience. ℂ **407/363-8000.** Cover charge $5.25. Must be 21 to get in. Sun–Wed 9pm–2am; Thu–Sat 9pm–3am.

Hard Rock Cafe/Hard Rock Live *Overrated*   The cafe part of this restaurant/ concert hall is the chain's standard—a theme restaurant with memorabilia and other tributes to rock's greats. The difference is that this one has the first concert hall with the Hard Rock name on the door. Call ahead to find out what acts will be featured during your visit. Tickets for big-name performers sell fast. © **407 /351-7625.** No cover in the cafe; concerts range from $6–$150. Cafe daily 11am–midnight.

Jimmy Buffett's Margaritaville   Music from the maestro drifts through the building, and live music is performed on a small stage inside later in the evening. A Buffett sound-alike strums on the back porch. Inside, there are three themed bars: The Volcano erupts margarita mix; the Land Shark has fins hanging from the ceiling; and the 12 Volt, is, well, a little electrifying—we'll leave it at that. If you opt for dinner among the palm trees, go for the true Key West experience. Early in the day that means a cheeseburger (in paradise, of course); later it's one of several kinds of fish (pompano, sea bass, dolphin). © **407/224-2155.** Cover $3.25 after 10pm. Daily 11:30am–2am.

Latin Quarter   This two-level restaurant/nightclub offers you a chance to absorb the salsa-and-samba culture and cuisine of 21 Latin nations. If you don't know how to move your hips, there's a dance instructor to lend you a hand. The club features acts ranging from Merengue to Latin rock. The sound system is loud enough to blow you into the next county, but before that happens you can leave on your own to see a Latin American art gallery. © **407/363-5922.** Cover charge $7 Thurs–Sat after 10pm. Open 11am–2am.

Motown Cafe Orlando   Try finger food and sandwiches ($6 to $13.50), or just kick back to the canned music of such Motown artists as Smokey Robinson, the Supremes, the Temptations, the Four Tops, and Stevie Wonder (look for their statues, too). Spend time in the indoor/outdoor Big Chill Lounge or, if you're brave enough, immortalize your own warblings on CD or disk in the recording studio. A live band frequently plays, giving patrons plenty of incentive to shake their groove. © **407/363-8000.** Cover charge $3.25 after 9pm Mon–Thu, $5 Fri–Sat. Open Mon–Thurs 11am–midnight, Fri–Sat 11am–2am.

Pat O'Brien's *Overrated*   Just like the French Quarter, which is home to the original Patty O's, drinking, drinking, and more drinking are the highlights here. Enjoy dueling Baby Grands and a flame-throwing fountain while you suck down the drink of the Big Easy, a Hurricane. Pat O'Brien's certainly promotes the hard stuff, and no one under 21 is permitted after 7pm. If your plans for the evening fall anything short of full intoxication, this isn't the place for you. There's a limited menu of sandwiches and treats like jambalaya and shrimp Creole ($6 to $10). © **407/224-2122.** Cover charge $2 after 9pm. Daily 4pm–2am.

HOT SPOTS IN DOWNTOWN ORLANDO

There are dozens of clubs and restaurants along Orange Avenue, the main street in downtown Orlando. A free bus called **Lymmo** runs in a designated lane that connects many of the nighttime spots, but Lymmo stops running about 11pm. Keep money on hand for a taxi if you plan on being out late.

CHURCH STREET STATION   This downtown club/dining/shopping district is a lot like Pleasure Island and CityWalk for a good reason: It started the idea. Occupying a cobblestone city block with real turn-of-the-20th-century buildings, Church Street provides a diverse evening of entertainment for a single admission price.

Entry to the restaurants, the Exchange Shopping Emporium, and the Midway game area is free. Check out these other highlights:

Rosie O'Grady's Good Time Emporium   This 1890s-style gambling hall–cum–saloon has beveled- and leaded-glass panels, etched mirrors, and vast globe chandeliers suspended from a high, pressed-tin ceiling. The Dixieland revue band, a group of seasoned professionals, really jams. Banjo players, singing waiters, and cancan girls round out the entertainment. Light fare (sandwiches, chili dogs, etc.) is available. The house specialty drink is a rum-and-fruit concoction called the Flaming Hurricane (served in a souvenir glass).

Apple Annie's Courtyard   Brick floors and arched trusses from a 19th-century New Orleans church turn back the clock to a Victorian garden. An 18th-century French communion rail serves as the front bar. Seating is in wicker peacock chairs at English pub tables. Patrons sip potent tropical fruit while listening to folk and bluegrass music.

Phineas Phogg's Balloon Works   Hot-air balloons and airplanes hover over the dance floor in this whimsical, high-energy bar that features loud, pulsating music. It doubles as a virtual ballooning museum, housing photographs and artifacts from historic flights, including one by Orlando native Joe Kittinger—the first man to cross the Atlantic in a gas balloon. No one under 21 is admitted.

Cheyenne Saloon and Opera House   This tri-level, balconied saloon is built of golden oak lumber from a century-old Ohio barn and crowned with a stained-glass skylight. Western art is displayed throughout, including oil paintings and 11 Remington sculptures. The Cheyenne offers the best show of the bunch. Its tight country band knows how to kick, and well-known artists sometimes join in. There's balcony seating in restored church pews overlooking the stage—the setting for entertainment ranging from bands to cloggers.

Orchid Garden Ballroom   The Gatsbyian feel comes compliments of the white wrought-iron arches and Victorian lighting fixtures suspended from an elaborate oak-paneled ceiling. It's the setting for a dance club where a DJ plays rock 'n' roll classics, such as "Great Balls of Fire" and "Let's Go to the Hop," interspersed occasionally with live bands. As the night progresses, so do the musical decades.

Terror on Church Street *(Overrated)*   Spine-chilling noises, near-misses, a torture chamber, a morgue, and a graveyard set the mood for this haunted house. It's not for young kids or the faint-hearted. Terror on Church Street has a separate admission ($13 adults, $10 children 12 and under), and it opens at 6pm daily, except Mondays. West Church St. (off I-4, between Garland and Orange Aves. in downtown Orlando). ✆ **407/422-2434.** www.churchstreetstation.com. Admission $17.95 adults, $11.95 children 4–12. Free admission prior to 5pm. Daily 11am–2am. Clubs open nightly 7:15pm–2am; shops 11am–11pm. There are several metered lots nearby (call for specifics) that run about $1 an hour. Valet parking at the front door is only $7 and much more convenient.

Cairo   One of the newer arrivals to the downtown, this large, popular dance club has bars on three levels. You'll find lots of 1970s retro clothes and kids trying to look older than their age. Reggae makes an appearance on the weekends. 22 S. Magnolia Ave. (1 block off Orange Ave.), Orlando. ✆ **407/422-3595.** www.cairo-nightclub. com. Fri–Sun 10pm–3am. Cover charge $6 and up. Free street parking.

Cricketers Arms Pub   Regardless of whether you're British or just a sympathizer, this pub is a fun place to party. As the name implies, cricket (as well as soccer) matches are shown on the telly. Live blues and soft-rock bands are featured, too, mainly on weekends. The revelry offers a good excuse to try a pint or two of any of 17 imports (such as Boddingtons and Fullers ESB). There's also a fun menu that offers steak-and-ale pie and bangers and mash, among others ($6 to $12). 8445 International Dr. ✆ **407/354-0686.** No cover for music; $10 for soccer. Daily 11am–2am. Free parking.

8 Seconds *Finds*   Sure, there's a bar and dance floor inside, but what really sets this place apart is what happens outside. A rodeo pen just next to the parking lot features "Buckin' Bull Nights" with live bull riding. And monster-truck pulls take place in the back lot. Rising country stars occasionally hold concerts here. Saturday is $2 long neck night. 100 W. Livingston Ave. ℂ **407/839-4800** or 407/843-5775. www.8-seconds.com. Cover charge $5 for persons 21 and older; $7 under 21. Open Fri–Sat 8pm–2am. Parking in city lot $3.

Howl at the Moon Saloon   Your best bet is to hit this joint on a full moon—even if you're too shy to cock your head back and howllll with the best of them when the club's dueling pianos march through classic rock tunes from the 1950s to the 1990s. 55 W. Church St. ℂ **407/841-9118**. www.howlatthemoon.com. Daily 6pm–2am. Cover charge Wed–Sat $2–$4. Metered-lot parking runs about $1 an hour.

Sak Comedy Lab   Locals get together and perform at this 200-seat club that has 8 to 10 performances weekly (usually Tuesday to Saturday). Favorites include the Duel of Fools, where two teams face off in improvised scenes based on suggestions from the audience, and Lab Rats, where students play in improv formats. 380 W. Amelia St. ℂ **407/648-0001**. www.sak.com. Admission $8–$12. Shows usually at 8 and 10pm, plus midnight on Sat. Metered-lot parking runs about $1 an hour.

Sapphire Supper Club *Finds*   Local and national acts perform at this laid-back martini bar with vintage brick walls. Jazz legend Sam Rivers is one of the regulars. This place is as cool and jazzy as the music it often features (occasionally soul, rock, blues, folk, and funk nights, as well as martini and cigar nights). It's popular with young professionals and music lovers of all ages. 54 N. Orange Ave. ℂ **407/246-1599**. www.sapphiresupperclub.com. Daily 8pm–2am. Cover charge varies, but usually $5–$10. Metered parking available.

Northeast Florida

by Bill Goodwin

Northeast Florida traces its history to 1513, when the Spaniard Juan Ponce de León, who later undertook a quixotic quest for the Fountain of Youth, sighted this coast and landed somewhere between present-day Jacksonville and Cape Canaveral. Observing that the land was "very pretty to behold with many refreshing trees," he named it La Florida, or "the flowery land." In 1565 the Spanish established a colony at St. Augustine, making it the country's oldest permanent settlement.

If those early colonists were to come back to life, they would feel right at home in St. Augustine, where the streets of the restored Old City look much as they did in Spanish times. For us modern mortals, St. Augustine offers a rich look back to a time when the settlers struggled to establish a life in a new, unfamiliar, and often-hostile world.

But they would surely be astonished at what they would see elsewhere in Northeast Florida.

To the south, their eyes would pop open with disbelief at today's "Space Coast," where rockets blast off from the Kennedy Space Center at Cape Canaveral. Nearby in Cocoa Beach, they would see another of our curiosities: surfers. And in Daytona Beach, they would hear the deafening roar of the stock cars and motorbikes that make this beach town the "World Center of Racing."

Heading north along the coast, they would come to the rich folks' haven of Ponte Vedra Beach, where golf definitely takes precedence over manual labor. And they would marvel at sprawling Jacksonville, Florida's largest metropolis and a thriving example of today's New South.

Up near the Georgia border, they'd cross a bridge to Amelia Island, where exclusive resorts take full advantage of 13 miles of beautiful beaches. Amelia's Victorian-era town, Fernandina Beach, would seem modern to them; to us, it's a quaint and historic retreat.

1 Cocoa Beach, Cape Canaveral & the Kennedy Space Center ⊛

46 miles SE of Orlando, 186 miles N. of Miami, 65 miles S. of Daytona

Today's "Space Coast" around Cape Canaveral was once a sleepy place where city dwellers escaped the crowds from the exploding urban centers of Miami and Jacksonville. But then came the NASA space program. Today the region accommodates its own crowds, especially hordes of tourists who come to visit the Kennedy Space Center and enjoy 72 miles of beaches, plus fishing, surfing, and golfing. This is, after all, the closest beach to Orlando's mega-attractions.

Thanks to NASA, this also is a prime destination for nature lovers. The space agency originally took over much more land than it has needed to launch rockets. Rather than sell off the unused portions, it turned them over to the Cape

Canaveral National Seashore and the Merritt Island National Wildlife Refuge, which have preserved them in their pristine natural states.

A handful of the major Caribbean-bound cruise ships depart from the man-made Port Canaveral. The south side of the port is lined with seafood restaurants and marinas, which serve as home base for gambling ships and the area's deep-sea charter and group fishing boats.

ESSENTIALS

GETTING THERE The nearest airport is **Melbourne International Airport,** 22 miles south of Cocoa Beach, which is served by **AirTran** (© **800/ AIR-TRAN**), **Continental** (© **800/525-0280**), **Delta** (© **800/221-1212**), and **Spirit** (© **800/772-7117**); but **Orlando International Airport,** about 35 miles to the west, is a much larger hub with many more flight options and generally less expensive fares (see "Getting There," in chapter 12). It's an easy 45-minute drive from the Orlando airport to the beaches via the Beeline Expressway (Fla. 528)—it can take almost that long from the Melbourne airport. **Comfort Travel** (© **800/567-6139** or 407/799-0442) or the **Cocoa Beach Shuttle** (© **407/ 784-3831**) will take you from the Orlando to the beaches for about $20 per person.

VISITOR INFORMATION For information about the area, contact the **Florida Space Coast Office of Tourism,** 8810 Astronaut Blvd., Suite 102, Cape Canaveral, FL 32920 (© **800/872-1969** or 321/868-1126; fax 321/868-1139; www.space-coast.com). The office is in the Sheldon Cove building, on Fla. A1A a block north of Central Boulevard and is open Monday to Friday from 8am to 5pm.

The office operates an information booth at the John F. Kennedy Space Center Visitor Complex (see below).

GETTING AROUND A car is essential in this area, so rent one at the airport. The **Space Coast Area Transit** (© **321/633-1878**) operates buses, but routes tend to be circuitous and therefore extremely time-consuming.

SEEING THE ASTRONAUT ATTRACTIONS

In addition to the two attractions below, the **Astronaut Memorial Planetarium and Observatory,** 1519 Clearlake Rd., Cocoa Beach (© **321/634-3732**), south of Fla. 528, has its own International Hall of Space Explorers, but its big attractions are sound and light shows in the planetarium. Call for a schedule of events and prices.

Astronaut Hall of Fame 🎢 *Kids*   Children will enjoy a playful visit to this hands-on museum at the mainland end of NASA Causeway (Fla. 405). In addition to honoring our space voyagers, the museum has artifacts from the space program and several interactive exhibits. A flight simulator and a G-Force Trainer will subject you to four times the pull of gravity, and the "3-D 360" will flip you around 360°. Most kids eat this stuff up; we adults need a relatively strong stomach! A tamer moon walk uses swings to let you experience a degree of weightlessness, and a Mars mission ride will take you on a simulated trip to the red planet. That full-size replica of a space shuttle you see by the highway actually holds a theater with a multimedia presentation. The rooftop observation deck is a grand place to watch a shuttle launch if you can't get into the Kennedy Space Center (see below).

You can park your kids here for a week in the museum's **Space Camp** (© **800/63-SPACE;** www.spacecamp.com). They will come home trained to be junior astronauts; you will have had a quiet stay at the beach.

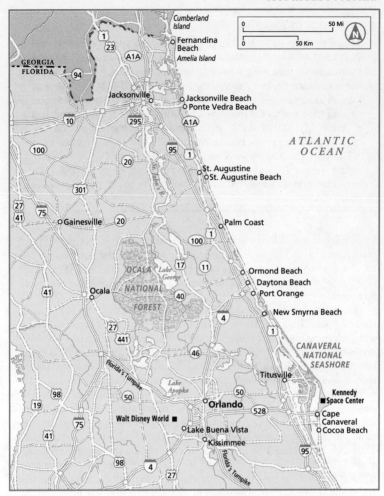

Cumberland
Island

Fernandina
Beach
Amelia Island

GEORGIA
FLORIDA

Jacksonville

Jacksonville Beach
Ponte Vedra Beach

ATLANTIC
OCEAN

St. Augustine
St. Augustine Beach

Gainesville

Palm Coast

OCALA   Lake
George

Ormond Beach
Daytona Beach
Port Orange

NATIONAL

Ocala

New Smyrna Beach

FOREST

CANAVERAL
NATIONAL
SEASHORE

Florida's Turnpike

Titusville

Lake
Apopka

Kennedy
Space Center

Orlando

Walt Disney World ■

Cape
Canaveral
Cocoa Beach

Lake Buena Vista
Kissimmee

Florida's Turnpike

6225 Vectorspace Blvd., Titusville. ℂ 321/269-6100. www.astronauthalloffame.com. Admission $13.95 adults, $9.95 children 6–12, free for kids under 6; family pass $39.95. Daily 9am–5pm.

John F. Kennedy Space Center ✪✪✪   Whether you're a space buff or not, you'll appreciate the sheer grandeur of the facilities and technological achievements displayed at NASA's primary space launch facility. Astronauts departed Earth at this site in 1969 en route to the most famous "small step" in history—humankind's first voyage to the moon—and today space shuttles regularly lift off on their missions in orbit.

Since all roads other than Fla. 405 and Fla. 3 are closed to the public in the space center, you must begin your visit at the **Kennedy Space Center Visitor Complex.** A bit like a themed amusement park, this privately operated complex recently completed a 5-year, $130 million expansion, which promises more tours, snazzier exhibitions, live shows, and more. Call beforehand to see what's happening on the day you plan to be here, and arrive early to plan your visit.

Tips Out to Launch

If you'd like to see a shuttle launch at the **Kennedy Space Center,** first call ☏ **321/867-4636** or check NASA's official website (www.ksc.nasa.gov) for a schedule of upcoming take-offs. You can buy launch tickets at the Kennedy Space Center Visitor Complex (☏ **321/449-4444**) or online at www.ksctickets.com. If you can't get into the space center, other good viewing spots are on the rooftop observation deck of the **Astronaut Hall of Fame** (☏ **321/269-6100;** www.astronauthalloffame.com), on the causeways leading to the islands, and on U.S. 1 as it skirts the waterfront in Titusville. The **Holiday Inn Riverside–Kennedy Space Center,** on Washington Avenue (U.S. 1) in Titusville (☏ **800/HOLIDAY** or 321/269-2121; www.holidayinnksc.com), has a clear view of the launch pads across the Indian River.

You'll need at least 2 hours to see the highlights on the bus tour through the space center, up to 5 hours if you linger at the stops along the way, a full day to see and do everything here. Buy a copy of the Official Tour Book ($5.95); it's easier to use than the rental cassette tapes, and you can take it home as a colorful souvenir.

The visitor complex has real NASA rockets and the actual Mercury Mission Control Room from the 1960s. Exhibits look at early space exploration and where it's going in the new millennium. There are space-related hands-on activities aimed at kids, a daily "Encounter" with a real astronaut, several dining venues, and a shop selling a variety of space memorabilia and souvenirs. IMAX movies shown on 5½-story-high screens are informative and entertaining.

While you could spend your entire day at the visitor complex, you must take one of the shuttle buses to see the actual space center where rockets and shuttles are prepared and launched. Plan to take the bus tour early in your visit. Be sure to hit the rest rooms before boarding the bus—there's only one out on the tour. The buses depart every 10 minutes, and you can reboard as you wish. They stop at the LC-39 Observation Gantry, with a dramatic 360° view over launch pads where space shuttles blast off; the International Space Station Center, where scientists and engineers prepare additions to the space station now in orbit; and the impressive Apollo/Saturn V Center, which includes artifacts, photos, interactive exhibits, and the 363-foot-tall Saturn V, the most powerful rocket ever launched by the United States.

It's worth the extra cost to take the **NASA Up Close** tour. These 90-minute excursions are better than the regular bus tours since they are narrated by program experts and go to the space shuttle launch pads, the shuttle landing facility, the massive Vehicle Assembly Building (where shuttles are prepared for launch), and other places normally restricted to NASA personnel. They generally take you along the same route the astronauts follow on launch days.

The 2-hour **Cape Canaveral Then and Now** guided tours concentrate on the history of the space program and also stop at sites where the shuttle buses don't. You get out of the bus and explore Hangar S, where the Mercury astronauts lived and worked; the launch pads where the Mercury, Gemini, and Apollo missions blasted off; the U.S. Air Force Space and Missile Museum; and historic Cape Canaveral Lighthouse.

Only 25 persons are allowed on board the two guided tours, and the last bus leaves 4 hours before closing, so call ahead for departure times and reservations.

For more information you can write to the Kennedy Space Center Visitor Complex, Mail Code DNPS, Kennedy Space Center, FL 32899.

NASA Pkwy. (Fla. 405), 6 miles east of Titusville, ½ mile west of Fla. 3. (✆ **321/452-2121** for general information, 321/449-4444 for guided bus tours and launch reservations. www.kennedyspacecenter.com. Admission $24 adults, $15 children 3–11. Annual passes $59.95 adults, $39.95 children 3–11. Add $20 per person for NASA Up Close and Cape Canaveral Then and Now guided tours. Audio tours $5 per person. All tours and movies free for children under 3. Daily 9am–dusk. Shuttle bus tours daily 9:45am–3pm (later in summer). Closed Christmas and some launch days.

BEACHES & WILDLIFE REFUGES

To the north of the Kennedy Space Center, **Canaveral National Seashore** ★★★ is a protected 13-mile stretch of barrier-island beach backed by cabbage palms, sea grapes, palmettos, marshes, and Mosquito Lagoon. This is a great area for watching herons, egrets, ibis, willets, sanderlings, turnstones, terns, and other birds. You might also glimpse dolphins and manatees in Mosquito Lagoon. Canoeists can paddle along a marked trail through the marshes of Shipyard Island, and you can go backcountry camping from November through April (permits required).

The main **visitor center** is at 7611 S. Atlantic Ave., New Smyrna Beach, FL 32169 (✆ **321/867-4077** or 321/867-0677 for recorded information). The center actually is on Apollo Beach at the north end of the island. The southern access gate is 8 miles east of Titusville on Fla. 402, just east of Fla. 3. A paved road leads from there to undeveloped **Playalinda Beach** ★★★, one of Florida's most beautiful. It's now officially illegal, but nude sunbathing has long been a tradition here (at least for those willing to walk a few miles to the more deserted areas). The beach has toilets but no running water or other amenities, so bring everything you will need. The seashore is open daily from 6am to 8pm during daylight saving time, daily 6am to 6pm during standard time. Admission fees are $5 per motor vehicle, $1 for pedestrians or bicyclists. National Park Service passports are accepted. Backcountry camping permits cost $10 for up to 6 persons and must be obtained from the New Smyrna Beach visitor center (see above). For advance information, contact the seashore headquarters at 308 Julia St., Titusville, FL 32796 (✆ **321/267-1110**; www.nps.gov/cana).

Its neighbor to the south and west is the 140,000-acre **Merritt Island National Wildlife Refuge** ★★, home to hundreds of species of shorebirds, waterfowl, reptiles, alligators, and mammals, many of them endangered. Stop and pick up a map and other information at the visitor center, on Fla. 402 about 4 miles east of Titusville (it's on the way to Playalinda Beach). The center has a ¼-mile-long boardwalk along the edge of the marsh and has displays showing the animals you may see here. You can see them from the 6-mile-long Black Point Wildlife Drive or one of the nature trails through the hammocks and marshes. The visitor center is open Monday to Friday from 8:30am to 4:30pm, Saturday and Sunday from 9am to 5pm (closed Sunday from April through October). Admission is free. For more information and a schedule of interpretive programs, contact the refuge at P.O. Box 6504, Titusville, FL 32782 (✆ **321/861-0667**; http://merrittisland.fws.gov).

Note: Those parts of the national seashore and the wildlife refuge near the Kennedy Space Center close three days before a shuttle launch and usually reopen the day after a launch.

The coast here is the second largest sea-turtle nesting site in the world, with some 8,000 turtle mothers crawling ashore to lay their eggs between May and August. Call the **Sea Turtle Preservation Society** (© 321/676-1701) for information about guided beach tours during the nesting season.

Other beach areas here include **Lori Wilson Park,** on Atlantic Avenue at Antigua Drive in Cocoa Beach (© **321/868-1123**), a fine municipal facility that preserves a stretch of beach backed by a forest of live oaks. It's home to a small but interesting nature center, and it has rest rooms by the beach. The park is open daily from sunrise to sunset; the nature center, Monday to Friday from 1 to 4pm.

The beach at **Cocoa Beach Pier,** on Meade Avenue east of Fla. A1A (© **321/783-7549**), is a popular spot, especially with surfers, who consider this the East Coast's surfing capital. The rustic pier was built in 1962 and has 842 feet of fishing, shopping, and food and drinks overlooking a wide, sandy beach (see "Where to Dine," below).

The privately owned **Jetty Park,** 400 E. Jetty Rd. (© **321/783-7111;** fax 321/783-5005), at the south entry to Port Canaveral, has lifeguards, a fishing pier with bait shop, a children's playground, a volleyball court, a horseshoe pitch, picnic tables, a snack bar, a grocery store, and the area's only campground. From here you can watch the big cruise ships as they enter and leave the port's narrow passage. The park is open daily from 7am to 10pm, and the pier is open 24 hours for fishing. Admission is $3 per car, $7 for RVs. The 150 tent and RV campsites (some of them shady, most with hookups) cost $19 to $26 a night, depending on location. No pets are allowed.

OUTDOOR ACTIVITIES

ECOTOURS **Funday Discovery Tours** (© 321/725-0796; www.fundaytours. com) offers a variety of day trips, including backcountry kayaking, airboat and swamp buggy rides, dolphin-watching cruises, bird-watching expeditions, and personalized tours of the Kennedy Space Center and Merritt Island National Wildlife Refuge. Reservations are required, so call, check the website, or pick up a copy of their list of trips from the visitor center (see "Essentials," above).

FISHING Whether you choose freshwater, shore, or deep-sea fishing, the Space Coast has endless opportunities to cast a line. **Mosquito Lagoon** and **Eddy Creek** to the north are where you'll find trout and redfish. The **Indian River** and **Banana River** also yield trout and redfish, as well as snook, ladyfish, and black drum. Bass fishers enjoy a region in the west called **Farm 13/Stick Marsh** with more than 20,000 acres of freshwater angling. For private outings, call **Dominics Guide Service** (© **800/BASS-909** or 321/242-892), one of the oldest licensed guides in the area.

Head to Port Canaveral for catches like snapper and grouper. **Jetty Park** (© **321/783-7111**), at the south entry to the port, has a fishing pier equipped with a bait shop (see "Beaches & Wildlife Refuges," above). The south bank of the port is lined with charter boats, and you can go deep-sea fishing on two party-vessels based here. The *Orlando Princess* (© **800/481-FISH** or 321/784-FISH; www.orlandoprincess.com) runs 6-hour trips, departing daily at 10:30am. These cost $40 for adults, $35 for children 11 to 17, and $30 for kids 6 to 10, and include lunch, soft drinks, gear, and bait. The *Miss Cape Canaveral* (© **321/783-5274** or 321/648-2211 in Orlando; www.misscape. com) has 9-hour voyages departing daily at 8am, for $60 per person, including breakfast, lunch, soft drinks, gear, and bait.

GOLF   You can read about Northeast Florida's best courses in the free *Golfer's Guide,* available at the tourist information offices and in many hotel lobbies. See "The Active Vacation Planner," in chapter 2, for information about ordering copies.

In Cocoa Beach, the municipal **Cocoa Beach Country Club,** 500 Tom Warringer Blvd. (℃ **321/868-3351**), has 27 holes of championship golf and 10 lighted tennis courts set on acres of natural woodland, rivers, and lakes. Greens fees are about $38 in winter, dropping to about $32 in summer, including cart.

On Merritt Island south of the Kennedy Space Center, **The Savannahs at Sykes Creek,** 3915 Savannahs Trail (℃ **321/455-1377**), has 18 holes over 6,636 yards bordered by hardwood forests, lakes, and savannahs inhabited by a host of wildlife. You'll have to hit over a lake to reach the seventh hole. Fees with cart are $35 in winter, less in summer.

The best nearby course is the Gary Player–designed **Baytree National Golf Club,** 8010 N. Wickham Rd., a half-mile east of I-95 in Melbourne (℃ **321/259-9060**), where challenging marshy holes are flanked by towering palms. This par-72 course has 7,043 yards with a unique red-shale waste area. Fees are $85 in winter, dropping to about $50 in summer, including cart.

In Melbourne Beach, the expanded executive course at **Spessard Holland Golf Club,** 2374 Oak St. (℃ **321/952-4530**), lies between the Atlantic and the bays, making it one of the area's most scenic. The par-67 course covers 5,130 yards, with six holes of no more than 191 yards presenting opportunities for holes-in-one. Winter fees here are $32 with cart, less in summer.

SPECTATOR SPORTS   Catch Miami's **Florida Marlins** play their spring-training baseball games from mid-February through March at the Space Coast Stadium, 5800 Stadium Pkwy., off I-95 Exit 73 in Melbourne (℃ **321/633-4487** or 321/633-9200; www.flamarlins.com).

SURFING   Rip through some occasionally awesome waves at the **Cocoa Beach Pier** area or down south at **Sebastian Inlet.** Get outfitted at Ron Jon Surf Shop (see below) and learn how with the store's **Cocoa Beach Surfing School** (⋆, 150 E. Columbia Lane (℃ **321/452-0854;** www.ronjons.com/surfschool). They offer equipment and lessons for beginners or pros at area beaches. Be sure to bring along a towel, flip-flops, sunscreen, and a lot of nerve.

WHERE TO STAY

The hotels listed below are all in Cocoa Beach, the closest resort to the Kennedy Space Center, about a 30-minute drive to the north. Closest to the space center and Port Canaveral is the **Radisson Resort at the Port,** 8701 Astronaut Blvd. (Fla. A1A) in Cape Canaveral (℃ **800/333-3333** or 321/784-0000; fax 321/784-3737). It isn't on the beach, but you can relax in a lushly landscaped courtyard with a waterfall cascading over fake rocks into an outdoor heated pool. This comfortable, well-equipped hotel caters to business travelers and passengers waiting to board cruise ships departing nearby Port Canaveral.

The newest chain motels in Cocoa Beach are the **Hampton Inn Cocoa Beach,** 3425 Atlantic Blvd. (℃ **877/492-3224** or 321/799-4099; www.hamptoninncocoabeach.com), and **Courtyard by Marriott,** 3435 Atlantic Blvd. (℃ **800/321-2211** or 321/784-4800). Opened in 2000 and 2001, respectively, they stand side-by-side and have access to the beach via a pathway through a condominium complex.

The **Florida Space Coast Office of Tourism** (see "Essentials," earlier in this chapter) publishes a booklet of the area's Superior Small Lodgings. See "Tips on Accommodations," in chapter 2 for information about this excellent program.

The area has a plethora of rental condominiums and cottages. **King Rentals Inc.,** 102 W. Central Blvd., Cape Canaveral, FL 32920 (© **888/295-0934** or 321/784-5046; www.kingrentals.com), has a wide selection in its inventory.

Given the proximity of Orlando, the generally warm weather all year, and business travelers visiting the space complex, there is little if any seasonal fluctuation in room rates here. They are highest weekends, holidays, and during special events, such as space-shuttle launches.

Tent and RV camping is available at **Jetty Park** in Port Canaveral (see "Beaches & Wildlife Refuges," above).

You'll pay a 4% hotel tax on top of the Florida sales tax here.

Cocoa Beach Hilton   Instead of balconies or patios from which you can enjoy the fresh air and view down the shore, the rooms at this seven-story Hilton have smallish, sealed-shut windows, and only 16 of them actually face the beach. That and other architectural features make it seem more like a downtown commercial hotel transplanted to a beachside location. Nevertheless, it's one of the few upscale beachfront properties here. No doubt you will run into a crew of name-tagged conventioneers, since it's especially popular with groups. Despite their lack of fresh air, the rooms are spacious and comfortable.

1550 N. Atlantic Ave., Cocoa Beach, FL 32931. © **800/526-2609** or 321/799-0003. Fax 321/799-0344. 296 units. $79–$179 double. AE, DC, DISC, MC, V. **Amenities:** Restaurant (American); 2 bars; heated outdoor pool; exercise room; game room; water-sports equipment rentals; business center; limited room service; laundry service; coin-op washers and dryers; concierge-level rooms. In room: A/C, TV, dataport, coffeemaker, hair dryer, iron.

DoubleTree Hotel Cocoa Beach Oceanfront ★   This six-story hotel was extensively remodeled and upgraded in 1998, and although not as upscale as the Cocoa Beach Hilton (see above), it's the pick of the full-service beachside hotels here. All rooms have balconies with ocean views. Oceanfront units also have easy chairs, and 10 suites have living rooms with sleeper sofas and separate bedrooms. A charming dining room facing the beach serves decent Mediterranean fare and opens to a bilevel brick patio with water cascading between two heated swimming pools. Conference facilities draw groups.

2080 N. Atlantic Ave., Cocoa Beach, FL 32931. © **800/552-3224** or 321/783-9222. Fax 321/799-3234. www.cocoabeachdoubletree.com. 148 units. $125–$179 double; $185–$275 suite. AE, DC, DISC, MC, V. **Amenities:** Restaurant (Mediterranean); bar; 2 heated outdoor pools; exercise room; game room; limited room service; laundry service; coin-op washers and dryers; concierge-level rooms. In room: A/C, TV, dataport, coffeemaker, hair dryer, iron.

Econo Lodge of Cocoa Beach (Value   About half of the spacious rooms at this Econo Lodge—more charming than most members of this budget-priced chain—face a tropical courtyard with a V-shaped swimming pool by which stands a sign bearing the names of the seven original astronauts, who once owned this motel. A variety of comfortable and clean units here include standard motel rooms and four suites with living rooms and kitchenettes. Amenities vary greatly, so tell the reservation clerk which features you require. Regardless of amenities, rooms facing the courtyard are preferable to those fronting the surrounding parking lots. For drinks, try the indoor sports bar or the poolside tiki hut.

1275 N. Atlantic Ave. (Fla. A1A, at Holiday Lane), Cocoa Beach, FL 32931. © **800/553-2666** or 321/783-2252. Fax 321/783-4485. 128 units. $45–$105 double. AE, DC, DISC, MC, V. Pets accepted, no fee. **Amenities:** Restaurant (Chinese); 2 bars; heated outdoor pool; coin-op washers and dryers. In room: A/C, TV, kitchen (suites only), fridge, coffeemaker.

Holiday Inn Cocoa Beach Oceanfront Resort (Kids   Set on 30 beachside acres, this sprawling family-oriented complex offers a wide variety of spacious hotel rooms, efficiencies, and apartments. A few suites even come equipped with bunk beds and Nintendo games for the kids. Most are in 1960s-style motel buildings flanking a long central courtyard with tropical foliage surrounding tennis courts. Only those rooms directly facing the beach or pool have patios or balconies; the rest are entered from exterior corridors. A convention center draws groups here.

1300 N. Atlantic Ave. (Fla. A1A, at Holiday Lane), Cocoa Beach, FL 32931. ℂ 800/206-2747 or 321/783-2271. www.holidayinnsofcentralflorida.com. Fax 321/783-8878. 500 units. $69–$159 double. AE, DC, DISC, MC, V. **Amenities:** 2 restaurants (American); 2 bars; heated outdoor pool; 8 tennis courts; access to nearby health club; exercise room; Jacuzzi; water-sports equipment rentals; children's programs; game room; concierge; limited room service; baby-sitting; laundry service; coin-op washers and dryers. *In room:* A/C, TV, dataport, coffeemaker, hair dryer, iron.

The Inn at Cocoa Beach 👍👍   Despite having 50 units, an intimate bed-and-breakfast ambience prevails at this seaside inn, far and away the most romantic place to stay here (the reason why it draws so many couples). The inn began as a beachfront motel but underwent a transformation under current owner Karen Simpler, a skilled interior decorator. She has furnished each unit with an elegant mix of pine, tropical, and French country pieces. Rooms in the three- and four-story buildings are much more spacious and have better sea views from their balconies than the "standard" units in the original two-story motel wing (all but six units here have balconies or patios). The older units open to a court-yard with a swimming pool tucked behind the dunes. Highest on the romance scale are two rooms with Jacuzzi tubs, double showers, and easy chairs facing gas fireplaces. Guests are served a deluxe continental breakfast in a room opening to a beachside lawn, are treated to evening wine-and-cheese social.

4300 Ocean Blvd., Cocoa Beach, FL 32932. ℂ 800/343-5307 or 321/799-3460. Fax 321/784-8632. www.theinnatcocoabeach.com. 50 units. $135–$250 double. Rates include continental breakfast. AE, DISC, MC, V. No childen under 12 accepted. **Amenities:** Bar; heated outdoor pool; sauna; massage; laundry service. *In room:* A/C, TV, dataport.

WHERE TO DINE

On the **Cocoa Beach Pier,** at the beach end of Meade Avenue, you'll get a fine view down the coast to accompany the seafood offerings at **Atlantic Ocean Grill** (ℂ 321/783-7549) and the mediocre pub fare at adjacent **Marlins Good Times Bar & Grill** (same phone). The restaurants may not justify spending an entire evening on the pier, but the outdoor, tin-roofed **Boardwalk Tiki Bar** 👍, where live music plays most nights, is a prime spot to have a cold one while watching the surfers or a sunset.

Bernard's Surf/Fischer's Seafood Bar & Grill 👍 SEAFOOD/STEAKS Photos on the walls testify that many astronauts—and Russian cosmonauts too—come to these adjoining establishments to celebrate their landings. It all started as Bernard's Surf, which has been serving standard steak-and-seafood fare in a nautically dressed setting since 1948. Bernard's offers house specials such as filet mignon served with sauteéd mushrooms and béarnaise sauce, but your best bets are char-grilled fish supplied by the Fischer family's own boats. The fresh seafood also finds its way into Fischer's Seafood Bar & Grill, a friendly, *Cheers*-like lounge popular with the locals. Fischer's menu features fried combo platters, shrimp and crab claw meat sautéed in herb butter, and mussels with a wine sauce over pasta, to mention a few worthy selections. Fischer's also provides sand-wiches, burgers, and other pub fare, and it has the same 25¢ happy-hour oysters and spicy wings as a branch of **Rusty's Seafood & Oyster Bar** (see below), also part of this complex.

2 S. Atlantic Ave. (at Minuteman Causeway Rd.), Cocoa Beach. ℂ 321/783-2401. Reservations recommended in Bernard's, not accepted in Fischer's. Bernard's main courses $14–$35. Fischer's main courses $9–$16; sandwiches and salads $4–$8. AE, DC, DISC, MC, V. Bernard's daily 4–11pm. Fischer's daily 11am–11pm. Closed Christmas.

The Mango Tree ⍟⍟ CONTINENTAL Gourmet seafood, pastas, and chicken are served in a plantation-home atmosphere with elegant furnishings in this stucco house, the finest dining venue here. Goldfish ponds inside and a waterfall splashing into a Japanese koi pond out in the lush tropical gardens provide pleasing backdrops. Start with finely seasoned Indian River crab cakes, then go on the chef's expert spin on fresh tuna fillets, roast Long Island duckling, tournedos with peppercorn mushroom sauce, and other excellent dishes drawing their inspiration from the continent.

118 N. Atlantic Ave. (Fla. A1A, between N. 1st and N. 2nd Sts.), Cocoa Beach. ℂ 321/799-0513. Reservations recommended. Main courses $13–$29. AE, MC, V. Tues–Sun 6–10pm.

Rusty's Seafood & Oyster Bar *Value* SEAFOOD/PUB FARE This lively sports bar beside Port Canaveral's man-made harbor offers inexpensive chow ranging from very spicy seafood gumbo to a pot of seafood that will give two people their fill of steamed oysters, clams, shrimp, crab legs, potatoes, and corn on the cob. Raw or steamed fresh oysters and clams from the raw bar are first-rate and a very good value, as is a lunch buffet on weekdays. Seating is available indoors or out, but the inside tables have the best view of fishing boats and cruise liners going in and out of the port. Daily happy hours from 3 to 6pm see beers drafted at 59¢ a mug, and tons of raw or steamed oysters and spicy Buffalo wings go for 25¢ each. It's a busy and sometimes noisy joint, especially on weekend afternoons, but the clientele tends to be somewhat older and better behaved than at some other pubs along the banks of Port Canaveral. There's another **Rusty's** in the Bernard's Surf/Fischer's Seafood Bar & Grill restaurant complex in Cocoa Beach (see above). It has the same menu but stays open daily until 2am.

628 Glen Cheek Dr. (south side of the harbor), Port Canaveral. ℂ 321/783-2033. Reservations not accepted. Main courses $7–$18; sandwiches and salads $4–$6; lunch buffet $6. AE, DC, DISC, MC, V. Sun–Thurs 11am–11:30pm; Fri–Sat 11am–12:30am (lunch buffet Mon–Fri 11am–2pm).

THE SPACE COAST AFTER DARK

For a rundown of current performances and exhibits, call the **Brevard Cultural Alliance's Arts Line** (ℂ 321/690-6819). For live music, walk out on the **Cocoa Beach Pier,** on Meade Avenue at the beach, where **Oh Shuck's Seafood Bar & Grill** (ℂ 321/783-7549), **Marlins Good Times Bar & Grill** (ℂ 321/783-7549), and the al fresco **Boardwalk Tiki Bar** ⍟ have bands on weekends, more often during the summer season. The tiki bar is a great place to hang out over a cold beer all afternoon and evening.

Down south, **Heidi's Lounge** in the Heidelberg Restaurant, on Minute Causeway at Fla. A1A southbound (ℂ 321/783-4559), has live jazz on weekend evenings.

2 Daytona Beach ⍟⍟

54 miles NE of Orlando, 251 miles N. of Miami, 78 miles S. of Jacksonville

Daytona Beach is a town with many personalities. It is at once the "World's Most Famous Beach," the "World Center of Racing," a mecca for tattooed motorcyclists and pierced spring-breakers, *and* the home of a surprisingly good art museum. The city also is spending millions of dollars to improve its image by turning the somewhat seedy beachfront area around the famous Main Street Pier into Ocean Walk Village, a redevelopment area of shops, entertainment, and resort facilities.

Daytona Beach has been a destination for racing enthusiasts since the early 1900s when "horseless carriages" raced on the hard-packed sand beach. One thing is for sure: Daytonans still love their cars. Recent debate over the environmental impact of unrestricted driving on the beach caused an uproar from citizens who couldn't imagine it any other way. As it worked out, they can still drive on the sand, but not everywhere, and especially not in areas where sea turtles are nesting.

Today, hundreds of thousands of race enthusiasts come to the home of the National Association for Stock Car Auto Racing (NASCAR) for the Daytona 500, the Pepsi 400, and other races throughout the year. The Speedway is home to DAYTONA USA, a state-of-the-art motor-sports entertainment attraction worth a visit even by nonracing fans.

Be sure to check the "Florida Calendar of Events," in chapter 2, to know when the town belongs to college students during Spring Break, hundreds of thousands of leather-clad motorcycle buffs during Bike Week, or racing enthusiasts for big competitions. You can't find a hotel room, drive the highways, or enjoy a peaceful vacation when they're in town.

ESSENTIALS

GETTING THERE **Continental** (© 800/525-0280; www.continental.com) and **Delta** (© **800/221-1212;** www.delta.com) fly into **Daytona Beach International Airport,** 4 miles inland from the beach on International Speedway Boulevard (U.S. 92), but you usually can find less expensive fares to **Orlando International Airport,** about a hour's drive away (see "Getting There," in chapter 12). **Daytona-Orlando Transit Service** (**DOTS**) (© **800/231-1965** or 386/257-5411) provides van transportation to or from Orlando International Airport. Fares are about $26 for adults one-way, $46 round-trip; children 11 and under are charged half. The service brings passengers to the company's terminal at 1034 N. Nova Rd., between 3rd and 4th streets, or to beach hotels for an additional fee.

There are no airport shuttles here. The ride from the airport to most beach hotels via **Yellow Cab Co.** (© **386/255-5555**) costs between $7 and $15.

Alamo (© 800/327-9633), **Avis** (© 800/331-1212), **Budget** (© 800/ 527-0700), **Dollar** (© 800/800-4000), **Hertz** (© 800/654-3131), and **National** (© 800/CAR-RENT) have booths at the Daytona airport. **Enterprise** (© 800/325-8007) is in town. If it suits you, why not rent a Harley? This is Daytona, after all. Contact **Daytona Harley-Davidson** (© 386/253-2453; www.daytonahd.com).

Amtrak (© **800/USA-RAIL;** www.amtrak.com) is planning rail service directly to Daytona Beach; meantime, the nearest train station is at Deland, about 15 southwest of here. Local companies provide connecting taxi service to the beach.

VISITOR INFORMATION The **Daytona Beach Area Convention & Visitors Bureau,** 126 E. Orange Ave. (P.O. Box 910), Daytona Beach, FL 32115 (© **800/854-1234** or 386/255-0415; fax 386/255-5478; www.daytonabeach. com), can help you with information on attractions, accommodations, dining, and events. The office is on the mainland just west of the Memorial Bridge. The information area of the lobby is open daily from 9am to 5pm. The bureau also maintains a branch at DAYTONA USA, 1801 W. International Speedway Blvd. (open daily 9am to 7pm), and a kiosk at the airport.

Web browsers can also visit the advertiser-supported **www.visitdaytona.com**.

GETTING AROUND   Although Daytona is primarily a driver's town, VOTRAN, Volusia County's public transit system (© **386/761-7700**), runs a **free shuttle** around the Main Street Pier/Ocean Walk Village area and a pay **trolley** along Atlantic Avenue on the beach, Monday to Saturday from noon to midnight during summer. Trolley fares are $1 for adults, 50¢ for seniors and children 6–17, free for kids under 6 riding with an adult. VOTRAN also runs **buses** throughout downtown and the beaches.

For a taxi, call **Yellow Cab** (© 386/255-5555) or **Southern Komfort Cab** (© 386/252-2222).

Over at the beach, **Scooters & Cycles,** 2020 S. Atlantic Ave. (Fla. A1A; © **386/253-4131**), rents both.

A VISIT TO THE WORLD CENTER OF RACING

Daytona International Speedway/DAYTONA USA 🏁🏁   You don't have to be a racing fan to enjoy a visit to the **Daytona International Speedway,** 4 miles west of the beach. Opened in 1959 with the first Daytona 500, this 480-acre complex is the keynote of the city's fame. The track presents about nine weekends of major racing events annually, featuring stock cars, sports cars, motorcycles, and go-karts, and is used for automobile and motorbike testing nearly every other day of the year. Its grandstands can accommodate more than 150,000 fans. Big events sell out months in advance (tickets to the Daytona 500 in February can be gone a year ahead of time), so get your tickets and hotel reservations as early as possible.

Start your visit at the **World Center of Racing Visitors Center,** in the NASCAR office complex at the east end of the speedway. Admission to the center is free, and you can walk out and see the track during nonrace days (there's a small admission to the track during qualifying races leading up to the main events). Entertaining 25-minute guided tram tours of the facility depart from the visitor center and are well worth taking.

The visitor center houses a large souvenir shop, a snack bar, and the phenomenally popular **DAYTONA USA,** a 60,000-square-foot, state-of-the-art interactive motor-sports entertainment attraction. Here you can learn about the history, color, and excitement of stock car, go-kart, and motorcycle racing in Daytona. You can participate in a pit stop on a NASCAR Winston Cup stock car, see the actual winning Daytona 500 car still covered in track dust, talk via video with favorite competitors, and play radio or television announcer by calling the finish of a race. An action-packed IMAX film will put you in the winner's seat of a Daytona 500 race, and a new NASCAR Thunder motion simulator goes even farther by letting you feel what it's like (well, sort of) to roar around the track.

To really experience what it's like, you can actually make three laps around the track in a stock car from May to October with the **Richard Petty Driving Experience Ride-Along Program** (© **800/BE-PETTY;** www.1800bepetty. com). Neither you nor racing legend Petty does the driving—other professionals will be at the wheel—but you'll see just how fast an average 115 miles per hour (185km per hour) speed really is.

Allow at least 3½ hours and definitely bring your video camera.

Write to the Daytona International Speedway at P.O. Box 2801, Daytona Beach, FL 32120-2801, for more information.

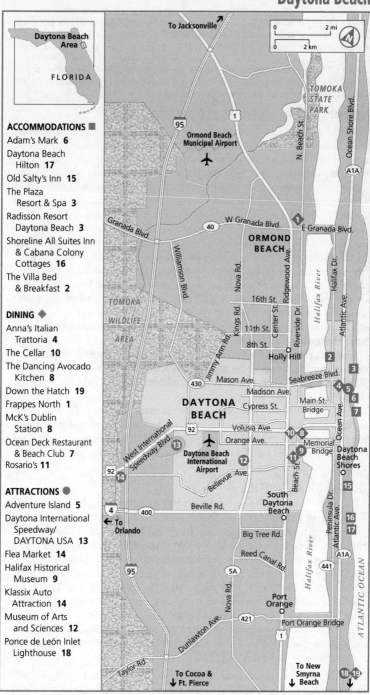

Daytona Beach

ACCOMMODATIONS ■

Adam's Mark **6**

Daytona Beach
Hilton **17**

Old Salty's Inn **15**

The Plaza
Resort & Spa **3**

Radisson Resort
Daytona Beach **3**

Shoreline All Suites Inn
& Cabana Colony
Cottages **16**

The Villa Bed
& Breakfast **2**

DINING ◆

Anna's Italian
Trattoria **4**

The Cellar **10**

The Dancing Avocado
Kitchen **8**

Down the Hatch **19**

Frappes North **1**

McK's Dublin
Station **8**

Ocean Deck Restaurant
& Beach Club **7**

Rosario's **11**

ATTRACTIONS ●

Adventure Island **5**

Daytona International
Speedway/
DAYTONA USA **13**

Flea Market **14**

Halifax Historical
Museum **9**

Klassix Auto
Attraction **14**

Museum of Arts
and Sciences **12**

Ponce de León Inlet
Lighthouse **18**

1801 W. International Speedway Blvd. (U.S. 92, at Bill France Blvd.). © **386/253-RACE** for race tickets, 386/253-7223 for information, 386/947-6800 for DAYTONA USA. www.daytonaintlspeedway.com and www.daytonausa.com. Speedway admission free except on race days; tram rides $6. DAYTONA USA admission $12 adults, $10 seniors, $6 children 6–12. Combination DAYTONA USA–tram tour $16 adults, $14 seniors, $11 children 6–12. Tram rides and DAYTONA USA admission free for children under 6. Speedway daily 9am–7pm; trams depart every 30 min. 9:30am–5pm except during races and special events. DAYTONA USA daily 9am to 7pm (later during race events). Closed Christmas.

HITTING THE WORLD'S MOST FAMOUS BEACH

The hard-packed beach here runs for 24 miles along a skinny peninsula separated from the mainland by the Halifax River. The bustling hub of activity is at the end of Main Street, near the Adam's Mark Daytona Beach Resort. Here you'll find the **Main Street Pier,** which was the longest wooden pier on the East Coast until Hurricane Floyd washed away about a third of its 1,006 feet in 1999. Out here you'll find a restaurant, a bar, a bait shop, beach-toy concessions, a chair lift running its entire length, and views from the 180-foot-tall Space Needle. Admission as far out as the restaurant and bar is free (at about a third of the way, this is far enough for a good view down the beach), but you'll have to pay $1 to walk out beyond there, more if you fish (see "Outdoor Activities," below). Beginning at the pier, the city's famous oceanside **Boardwalk** is lined with restaurants, bars, and T-shirt shops, as are the four blocks of Main Street nearest the beach. The city's Ocean Walk Village redevelopment project begins here and runs several blocks north.

There's another busy beach area at the end of **Seabreeze Boulevard,** which has a multitude of restaurants, bars, and shops.

Couples seeking greater privacy usually prefer the northern or southern extremities of the beach. Especially peaceful is **Ponce Inlet** at the very southern tip of the peninsula, where there is precious little commerce or traffic to disturb the silence.

You can drive and park directly on sections of the sand along 18 miles of the beach during daylight hours and at low tide (Hurricane Floyd and other recent storms have greatly reduced the beach's width). Watch for signs warning of sea turtles nesting. There's a $5 access fee, although in some areas like Ponce Inlet, the fee is waived in winter.

OUTDOOR ACTIVITIES

CRUISES   Take a leisurely cruise on the Halifax River aboard the 14-passenger, 25-foot *Fancy,* a replica of the old fantail launches used at the turn of the century. It's operated by **A tiny Cruise Line River Excursions,** 425 S. Beach St., at Halifax Harbor Marina (© **386/226-2343**). Captain Jim regales passengers with river lore and points out dolphins, manatees, herons, diving cormorants, pelicans, egrets, osprey, oyster beds, and other natural phenomena during the morning cruise. Cruises are $9 to $15 for adults, $6 to $8 for children 4 to 12, free for children 3 and under. Weather permitting, the cruises depart year-round (with a brief hiatus during the holidays), Monday through Saturday at 11:30am. A 1-hour tour of riverfront homes is at 2pm and of historic downtown at 3:30pm; there are no Monday cruises in winter months. Call for reservations. Romantic sunset cruises are also available.

FISHING   The easiest and least-expensive way to fish offshore for marlin, sailfish, king mackerel, grouper, red snapper, and more is with the **Critter Fleet,** 4950 S. Peninsula Dr., just past the lighthouse in Ponce Inlet (© **800/338-0850** or 386/767-7676; www.critterfleet.com), which operates two party boats. One goes on all-day trips (about $55 adults, $35 kids under 12), while the other makes morning and afternoon voyages (about $35 adults, $25 kids under 12). The fares include rod, reel, and bait. Call for schedules, prices, and reservations.

Deep-sea charter fishing boats are available from the Critter Fleet and from **Sea Love Marina,** 4884 Front St., Ponce Inlet (ⓒ **386/767-3406** or 407/293-2050 in Orlando).

Save the cost of a boat and fish with the locals from the **Main Street Pier,** at the ocean end of Main Street near the Adam's Mark (ⓒ **386/253-1212**). Admission for fishers is $3.50 for adults, $2 for kids under 12. Bait and fishing gear are available, and no license is required.

GOLF More than 25 courses await you within 30 minutes of the beach, and most hotels can arrange starting times for you. **Golf Daytona Beach,** 126 E. Orange Ave., Daytona Beach, FL 32114 (ⓒ **800/881-7065** or 386/239-7065; fax 386/239-0064; www.golf-daytona.com), publishes an annual brochure describing the major courses. It's available at the tourist information offices (see "Essentials," above).

Two of the nation's top-rated links for women golfers are at the **International** (★★, 300 Championship Dr. (ⓒ **386/274-5742**): Those are the Champions course designed by Rees Jones, and the Legends at LPGA course designed by Arthur Hills. Both boast 18 outstanding holes. LPGA International is a center for professional and amateur women golfers (workshops and teaching programs), and the pro shop carries a great selection of ladies' equipment and clothing. Greens fees with a cart are usually about $75, less in summer. You do not have to be female to play here.

A Lloyd Clifton–designed course, the centrally located 18-hole, par-72 **Indigo Lakes Golf Course,** 2620 W. International Speedway Blvd. (ⓒ **386/254-3607**), has flat fairways and large bunkered Bermuda greens. Fees here are about $55 in winter, including a cart, less in summer.

The semiprivate South Course at **Pelican Bay Country Club,** 550 Sea Duck Dr. (ⓒ **386/788-6494**), is one of the area's favorites, with fast greens to test your putting skills. Fees are $40 with cart in winter, less in summer (no walking allowed). The North Course here is for members only.

The city's prime municipal course is the **Daytona Beach Country Club,** 600 Wilder Blvd. (ⓒ **386/258-3119**), which has 36 holes. Winter fees here are $18 to walk, $26.50 to share a cart. They drop $3 in summer.

HORSEBACK RIDING **Shenandoah Stables,** 1759 Tomoka Farms Rd., off U.S. 92 (ⓒ **386/257-1444**), offers daily trail rides and lessons. Call for prices and schedules.

SPECTATOR SPORTS The **Daytona Cubs** (ⓒ **386/257-3172;** www.daytonacubs.com), a Class A minor-league affiliate of the Chicago Cubs, play baseball from April through August at Jackie Robinson Ballpark, on City Island downtown. A game here is a treat, since the park recently was restored to its classic 1914 style by the designers of Baltimore's Camden Yards and Cleveland's Jacobs Field.

WATER SPORTS Water-sports equipment, as well as bicycles, beach buggies, and mopeds, can be rented along the Boardwalk, at the ocean end of Main Street (see "Hitting the World's Most Famous Beach," above), and in front of major beachfront hotels. For jet-ski rentals, contact **Daytona High Performance—MBI,** 925 Sickler Dr., at the Seabreeze Bridge (ⓒ **386/257-5276**).

AMUSEMENT PARKS

Part of the Ocean Walk Village redevelopment project, **Adventure Landing,** 601 Earl St., west of Atlantic Avenue (© **386/258-0071;** www.adventurelanding. com), is a multifaceted amusement center offering indoor and outdoor activities to keep you and especially the kids entertained—and during the summer months, thoroughly wet. You enter into a cacophony of deafening noise and music in a huge electronic games arcade. Outside there are pools, slides, and waterfalls, plus go-kart rides and a 27-hole minigolf course. Vending machines dispense tokens for the electronic games. Admission is free to the games area, but water-park entry costs $20 for anyone over 48 inches tall, $17 for anyone shorter, and free for kids under 3. A "night splasher" (4 to 8pm) pass costs $13. Adventure Landing is open during summer daily 10am to midnight (water activities to 8pm). Off-season hours are Sunday to Thursday 11am to 10pm, Friday and Saturday 11am to 10pm (water activities closed).

MUSEUMS

Halifax Historical Museum   Located on Beach Street, Daytona's original riverfront commercial district on the mainland side of the Halifax River (see "Shopping," below), this local history museum is worth a brief peek just for the 1912 neoclassical architectural details of its home, a former bank. A mural of Old Florida wildlife graces one wall, the stained-glass ceiling reflects the sunlight, and across the room an old gold-metal teller's window still stands. The Halifax's eclectic collection includes Native American artifacts, more than 10,000 historic photographs, possessions of past residents (such as a ball gown worn at Lincoln's inauguration), and, of course, model cars. An interesting race exhibit opens annually in mid-January as a stage-setter for Race Week.

252 S. Beach St. (just north of Orange Ave.). © **386/255-6976.** www.halifaxhistorical.org. Admission $3 adults; $1 children 11 and under; free Sat for children. Tues–Sat 10am–4pm.

Klassix Auto Attraction   True aficionados of the car will enjoy a visit to this attraction, which showcases Corvettes—a model from every year since 1953—and historic vehicles from every motor sport. The rest of us will head to the original "Batmobile" from the 1960s *Batman* TV series, the car from *The Flintstones* series, the "Dragula" owned by the Munsters, and the "Greased Lightning" from the movie *Grease.* A 1950s-style soda shop and gift shop are on the premises.

2909 W. International Speedway Blvd., at Tomoka Farms Rd., just west of I-95. © **386/252-3800.** www. klassixauto.com. Admission $8.50 adults, $4.25 children 7–12, free for children under 7. Daily 9am–6pm.

Museum of Arts and Sciences ⟨★★⟩   An exceptional institution for a town Daytona's size, this museum is best known for its Cuban Museum, with paintings acquired in 1956, when Cuban dictator Fulgencio Batista donated his private collection to the city. Among them is a portrait of Eva ("Evita") Perón, said to be the only existing painting completed while she was alive (it hangs in the lobby, not in the Cuban Museum). The Dow Gallery displays Smithsonian-quality examples of American decorative arts, and the Bouchelle Study Center for the Decorative Arts contains both American and European masterpieces. Other rooms worth visiting include the Schulte Gallery of Chinese Art; Africa: Life and Ritual, with the largest collection of Ashante gold ornaments in the United States; and the Prehistory of Florida gallery, with the skeleton of a 13-foot-tall, 130,000-year-old giant ground sloth. The planetarium presents 30-minute shows of what the night sky will look like on the date of your visit. Except for the skeleton and the model railroads, children are apt to be bored here.

1040 Museum Blvd. (off Nova Rd./Fla. 5A between International Speedway Blvd. and Bellevue Ave.). (C) 386/255-0285. www.moas.org. Museum $5 adults, $1 children and students with ID, free for children 5 and under. Planetarium shows $3 adults, $2 children and students. Tues–Fri 9am–4pm; Sat–Sun noon–5pm. Planetarium shows Tues–Fri 2pm; Sat–Sun 1 and 3pm. Closed Thanksgiving, Christmas Eve, Christmas Day. Take International Speedway Blvd. west, make a left on Nova Rd. (Fla. 5A), and look for a sign on your right.

Ponce de León Inlet Lighthouse & Museum ★★   This National Historic Landmark is well worth a stop even if you're not a lighthouse enthusiast. The 175-foot brick-and-granite structure is the second-tallest lighthouse in the United States, second only to the beacon at Cape Hatteras, North Carolina. Built in the 1880s, the lighthouse and the graceful Victorian brick buildings surrounding it have been restored in recent years. There are no guided tours, but you can walk through the buildings and around the tugboat *F. D. Russell,* now sitting high-and-dry in the sand. Use common sense if you climb the 203 steps to the top of the lighthouse; it's a grinding ascent, but the view from up there is spectacular. Also on the grounds is a **Marine Science Center,** with guided nature walks along trails and a boardwalk.

4931 S. Peninsula Dr., Ponce Inlet. (C) 386/761-1821. www.ponceinlet.org. Admission $4 adults, $1 children under 12. Memorial Day–Labor Day daily 10am–8pm; rest of year daily 10am–4pm. Follow Atlantic Ave. south, make a right on Beach St., and follow the signs.

SHOPPING

On the mainland, Daytona Beach's main riverside drag, **Beach Street,** is one of the few areas in town where people actually stroll. The street is wide and inviting, with palms down its median and decorative wrought-iron archways and fancy brickwork overlooking a branch of the Halifax River that separates downtown from City Island, home of municipal offices and the lovingly restored Jackie Robinson Ballpark (see "Spectator Sports," above). Today, Beach Street between Bay Street and Orange Avenue offers antiques and collectibles shops, art galleries, clothiers, a magic shop, the local historical museum (see "Museums," above) and several good cafes.

You "Hog" riders will find several shops to your liking along Beach Street north of International Speedway Boulevard, including the **Harley Davidson Store,** 290 Beach St., at Dr. Mary McLeod Bethune Boulevard ((C) **386/ 253-2453**), a 20,000-square-foot retail outlet and diner serving breakfast and lunch. It's one of the nation's largest dealerships. In addition to hundreds of gleaming new and used Hogs, you'll find as much fringed leather as you've ever seen in one place.

The **Daytona Farmer's and Flea Market,** on Tomoka Farms Road at the junction of I-95 and U.S. 92, a mile west of the Speedway ((C) **386/252-1999;** www.daytonafleamarket.com), is huge, with 1,000 covered outdoor booths plus 100 antiques and collectibles vendors in an air-conditioned building. It's open year-round Friday through Sunday from 8am to 5pm. Admission and parking are free.

Anchored by Burdine's, Dillard's, Sears, and JCPenney, **Volusia Mall,** 1700 International Speedway Blvd. (U.S. 92), opposite the speedway ((C) **386/ 253-6783**), is the town's major retail complex. Stores are open Monday to Saturday 10am to 9pm, Sunday noon to 5pm.

WHERE TO STAY

Room rates here are among the most affordable in Florida. Some properties have as many as 20 rate periods during the year, but generally they are somewhat higher from the beginning of the races in February all the way to Labor Day.

They skyrocket during major events at the Speedway, during bikers' gatherings, and during college Spring Break (see "Florida Calendar of Events," in chapter 2), when local hotels fill to the bursting point. Even if you can find a room then, there's often a minimum-stay requirement.

Hundreds of hotels and motels line Atlantic Avenue along the beach, many of them family owned and operated. The Daytona Beach Area Convention & Visitors Bureau (see "Essentials," earlier in this chapter) distributes a list of **Superior Small Lodgings** for Daytona Beach and New Smyrna Beach (see the "Welcome to the Jungle" box, later in this chapter). See "Tips On Accommodations," in chapter 2 for information about this excellent program. All of the small motels listed below are members.

If you're going to the races and don't care about staying on the beach, some upper-floor rooms at the new **Hilton Garden Inn Daytona Beach Airport,** 189 Midway Ave. (© 877/944-4001 or 386/944-4000), actually overlook the international speedway track. Unlike most members of Hilton's Garden Inn chain, this one has a restaurant.

Thousands of rental condominiumss line the beaches here. One of the largest rental agents is **Peck Realty,** 2340 S. Atlantic Ave., Daytona Beach Shores, FL 32118 (© 800/44-PECK or 386/257-5000; www.peckrealty.com).

In addition to the 6% state sales tax, Volusia County levies a 4% tax on hotel bills.

Adam's Mark Daytona Beach Resort 𝔸

Already Daytona's largest beachfront hotel, the Adam's Mark is adding another 350 units as part of the city's Ocean Walk Village development plans. With extensive on-site meeting facilities and the city's Ocean Center convention complex across the street, that means lots of big groups staying here. It's also in the middle of the beach action, right on the city's Boardwalk and a block north of the busy Main Street Pier (see "Hitting the World's Most Famous Beach," earlier in this chapter). One of Daytona's best-equipped properties, it's designed so that every room has an ocean view.

100 N. Atlantic Ave. (Fla. A1A, between Earl St. and Auditorium Blvd.), Daytona Beach, FL 32118. © 800/872-9269 or 386/254-8200. Fax 386/253-0275. www.adamsmark.com. 436 units. $105–$195 double; $165–$260 suite. AE, DC, DISC, MC, V. Valet parking $8; free self-parking. **Amenities:** 3 restaurants (American); 3 bars; heated outdoor pool; exercise room; Jacuzzis; sauna; water-sports equipment rentals; bike rental; game room; concierge; limited room service; massage; baby-sitting; laundry service; coin-op washers and dryers; concierge-level rooms. *In room:* A/C, TV, dataport, coffeemaker, hair dryer, iron.

Daytona Beach Hilton Oceanfront Resort 𝔸𝔸

Far enough south to escape the maddening crowds at Main Street, the Hilton is among the best choices here. It welcomes you in an elegant terra-cotta–tiled lobby with comfortable seating areas, a fountain, and potted palms. The large guest rooms are grouped in pairs and can be joined to form a suite; only one of each pair has a balcony. All have ocean and/or river views and small refrigerators. A few also have kitchenettes. The surprisingly good Blue Water lobby restaurant is one of Daytona's most beautiful; patio dining is an option.

2637 S. Atlantic Ave. (Fla. A1A, between Florida Shores Blvd. and Richard's Lane), Daytona Beach, FL 32118. © 800/525-7350 or 386/767-7350. Fax 386/760-3651. 214 units. $89–$198 double; from $250 suite. AE, DC, DISC, MC, V. **Amenities:** Restaurant (American); bar; heated outdoor pool; Jacuzzi; exercise room; water-sports equipment rentals; game room; salon; limited room service; baby-sitting; laundry service; coin-op washers and dryers; concierge-level rooms. *In room:* A/C, TV, dataport, kitchen, coffeemaker, hair dryer, iron.

Old Salty's Inn

The most unusual of the many mom-and-pop beachside motels here, Old Salty's is a lush tropical enclave carrying out a "Gilligan's Island" theme, with old motors, rotting boats, lifesavers, and a Jeep lying about, and the

TV series' main characters depicted in big murals painted on the buildings. The two-story wings flank a courtyard festooned with palms and banana trees (you can pick one for breakfast). Facing this vista, the bright rooms have microwaves, refrigerators, and front-and-back windows to let in good ventilation. The choice units have picture windows overlooking the beach. There are gas grills and rocking chairs under a gazebo out by a heated beachside swimming pool.

1921 S. Atlantic Ave. (Fla. A1A, at Flamingo Ave.), Daytona Beach Shores, FL 32118. ✆ **800/417-1466** or 386/252-8090. Fax 386/947-9980. www.visitdaytona.com/oldsaltys. 19 units. $51–$119. AE, DISC, MC, V. **Amenities:** Heated outdoor pool; free use of bikes; coin-op washers and dryers. *In room:* A/C, TV, kitchen, fridge, coffeemaker, hair dryer, iron.

The Plaza Resort & Spa ★★   Remodeled to the tune of $26 million in 2000, these adjoining 7- and 13-story buildings now hold some of Daytona Beach's best rooms—provided you don't need a large bathroom. The choice units are the corner suites, which have sitting areas and two balconies overlooking the Atlantic; some even have a Jacuzzi for two. All units have balconies and microwave ovens (an on-premises convenience store sells frozen dinners). The renovations also saw the opening of the full-service **Ocean Waters Spa** ★★ (✆ **386/267-1660;** www.oceanwatersspa.com), the only such facility here. There are 16 treatment rooms and a soothing menu of facials, massages, and wraps.

600 N. Atlantic Ave. (at Seabreeze Ave.), Daytona Beach, FL 32118. ✆ **800/767-4471** or 386/255-4471. Fax 386/253-7543. www.plazaresortandspa.com. 323 units. $69–$329. AE, DC, DISC, MC, V. **Amenities:** Restaurant (seafood/sushi); bar; heated outdoor pool; exercise room; spa; Jacuzzi; water-sports equipment rentals; game room; business center; limited room service; massage; baby-sitting; laundry service; coin-op washers and dryers; concierge-level rooms. *In room:* A/C, TV, dataport, fridge, coffeemaker, hair dryer, iron.

Radisson Resort Daytona Beach ★   This 11-story, all-modern Radisson sits beachside a half-mile north of the Main Street Pier and around the corner from restaurants and bars on Seabreeze Boulevard. The rooms here are among the most spacious on the beach and have angled balconies facing the beach (your neighbor's air conditioner exhausts onto your balcony, however, which can create noise and heat when you're sitting out there). About a third have small additional rooms with wet bars with microwaves and refrigerators.

640 N. Atlantic Ave. (Fla. A1A, between Seabreeze and Glenview boulevards), Daytona Beach, FL 32118. ✆ **800/333-3333** or 386/239-9800. Fax 386/253-0735. 206 units. $89–$129 double. AE, DC, DISC, MC, V. **Amenities:** Restaurant (American); bar; heated outdoor pool; exercise room; water-sports equipment rentals; limited room service; baby-sitting; coin-op washers and dryers; concierge-level rooms. *In room:* A/C, TV, dataport, fridge, coffeemaker, hair dryer, iron.

Shoreline All Suites Inn & Cabana Colony Cottages *Value*   The Shoreline All Suites Inn, built in 1954 but substantially modernized, features one- and two-bedroom suites that occupy two buildings separated by a walkway leading to the beach. Most have small bathrooms with scant vanity space and—shall we say—intimate shower stalls. Every unit has a full kitchen, plus there are barbecue grills on premise. For a change of scenery, consider the fine little cottage complex at the Shoreline's sister property, the **Cabana Colony Cottages** ★. All 12 of the cottages were built in 1927 but were upgraded by owner-managers Frank and Barbara Molnar. They aren't much bigger than a motel room with a kitchen, but they're light and airy, are attractively furnished with white wicker pieces. The cottages share a heated beachside swimming pool with the Shoreline.

2435 S. Atlantic Ave. (Fla. A1A, at Dundee Rd.), Daytona Beach Shores, FL 32118. ✆ **800/293-0653** or 386/252-1692. Fax 386/239-7068. www.daytonashoreline.com. 32 units, including 12 cottages. $49–$249. Rates include continental breakfast. Golf packages available. AE, DISC, MC, V. **Amenities:** Heated outdoor pool; coin-op washers and dryers; concierge-level rooms. *In room:* A/C, TV/VCR, kitchen, coffeemaker.

The Villa Bed & Breakfast ⭐ You'll think you're in Iberia upon entering this Spanish mansion's great room with its fireplace, baby grand piano, terra-cotta floors, and walls hung with Mediterranean paintings. Also downstairs are a sun room equipped with a TV and VCR, a formal dining room, and a breakfast nook where guests gather at their leisure to start the day. The lush backyard surrounds a swimming pool and a covered, four-person Jacuzzi. Upstairs, the nautically themed Christopher Columbus room has a vaulted ceiling and a small balcony overlooking the pool. The largest quarters here are the King Carlos suite, the original master bedroom with a four-poster bed, entertainment system, refrigerator, rooftop deck, dressing area, and bathroom equipped with a four-head shower. The Queen Isabella room has a portrait of the queen over a queen-size bed, and the Marco Polo room has Chinese black-lacquer furniture and Oriental rugs evoking the great explorer's adventures.

801 N. Peninsula Dr. (at Riverview Blvd.), Daytona Beach, FL 32118. ℂ and fax **386/248-2020.** www. thevillabb.com. 4 units (all with bathroom). $85–$190 double. Rates include continental breakfast. AE, MC, V. No children or pets accepted. **Amenities:** Heated outdoor pool; Jacuzzi. *In room:* A/C, TV, hair dryer, no telephone.

WHERE TO DINE

Daytona Beach has a few interesting dining venues, but none is likely to leave an indelible memory. A profusion of fast-food joints line the major thoroughfares, especially along Atlantic Avenue on the beach and along International Speedway Boulevard (U.S. 92) near the racetrack. Restaurants come and go in the Beach Street district on the mainland, and along Main Street and Seabreeze Boulevard on the beach. A casual restaurant serves burgers and chicken wings and lots of suds out on the Main Street Pier.

The local **Shells** seafood restaurant is on the beach at 200 S. Atlantic Ave. (ℂ **386/258-0007**), a block north of International Raceway Boulevard. See "Where to Dine," in section 1 of chapter 11, for details about this inexpensive chain.

AT THE BEACHES

Anna's Italian Trattoria ⭐ SOUTHERN ITALIAN Originally from Sicily, the Triani family makes all the pastas at their simple yet comfortable trattoria, which offers more-formal dining than Rosario's equally good *ristorante* on the mainland (see below). The star here isn't the pasta, however; it's risotto alla Anna, an Italian version of Spanish paella. Portions are hearty; main courses come with soup or salad and a side dish of angel-hair pasta or a vegetable, and a bit of between-courses sorbet will cleanse the palate. There's a good selection of Italian wines to complement your meal. Everything is cooked to order, so be patient.

304 Seabreeze Blvd. (at Peninsula Dr.). ℂ **386/239-9624.** Reservations recommended. Main courses $10–$17. AE, DISC, MC, V. Tues–Sun 5–10pm. Closed 2 weeks in June.

Down the Hatch ⭐ *(Value)* SEAFOOD Occupying a 1940s fish camp on the Halifax River, Down the Hatch serves up big portions of fresh fish and seafood (note its shrimp boat docked outside). Inexpensive burgers and sandwiches are available, too, and you can start your day here with a Belgian waffle, French toast, or a country-style breakfast while taking in the scenic views of boats and shorebirds through the big picture windows—you might even see dolphins frolicking. At night, arrive early to catch the sunset over the river, and also to beat the crowd at this very popular place. In summer, light fare is served outside on an awninged wooden deck.

4894 Front St., Ponce Inlet. ℂ **386/761-4831.** Reservations not accepted; call ahead for priority seating. Main courses $9–$25 (most $10–$16); breakfast $2–$5; burgers and sandwiches $3–$6.50; early bird menu (served 11am–5pm) $6–$8. AE, MC, V. Daily 7am–10pm. Closed 1st week in Dec. Take Atlantic Ave. south, make a right on Beach St., and follow the signs.

Ocean Deck Restaurant & Beach Club *Value* SEAFOOD/PUB FARE Known by spring-breakers, bikers, and other beachgoers as Daytona's best "beach pub" since 1940, the Ocean Deck also is the best restaurant in the busy area around the Main Street Pier. Opening to the sand and surf, the downstairs reggae bar is as sweaty, noisy, and packed as ever. The upstairs dining room can be noisy, too, but both you and the kids can come here for some good food, reasonable prices, and great ocean views. You can choose from a wide range of seafood, chicken, sandwiches, and the best burgers on the beach, but don't pass up the mahimahi, first broiled with peppery Jamaican spices and then finished off on a grill, a bargain at $9. There's valet parking after dark ($5 per car), or you can park free at the lot behind the Ocean Deck's Reggae Republic surf shop, a block away on Atlantic Avenue.

127 S. Ocean Ave. (at Kemp St.). ℂ 386/253-5224. Reservations not accepted. Main courses $8–$16; salads and sandwiches $5–$8. DISC, MC, V. Daily 11am–2am (bar to 3am).

ON THE MAINLAND

The Cellar AMERICAN An excellent place for a ladies' lunch, this tea room occupies the basement of a Victorian home built in 1907 as President Warren G. Harding's winter home (he spent election eve here in 1920) and now is listed in the National Register of Historic Places. It couldn't be more charming, with low ceilings, back-lit reproduction Tiffany windows, fresh flowers everywhere, linen tablecloths and napkins, and china teacups. If you can play the piano, help yourself to the baby grand. A wide-ranging lunch menu offers the likes of walnut chicken salad as a platter or croissant sandwich, a quiche du jour, crab cakes with a Louis sauce, vegetarian lasagna, chicken pot pie, and hot chicken cordon bleu served on a croissant. In the warm months, there's outdoor seating at umbrella tables on a covered garden patio.

220 Magnolia Ave. (between Palmetto and Ridgewood Aves.). ℂ 386/258-0011. Soups, salads, sandwiches $6–$9. AE, MC, V. Mon–Fri 11am–3pm.

The Dancing Avocado Kitchen ★ VEGETARIAN A healthy place to start your day, or have lunch while touring downtown, this storefront establishment purveys a number of vegetarian omelets, burritos, salads, personal-size pizzas, and hot and cold sandwiches such as an avocado Reuben. A few chicken and turkey items are on the menu, but the only red-meat selection is a hamburger. You can dine outside or inside the store with vegetable drawings on its brick walls and ceiling fans suspended from black rafters. No smoking.

110 S. Beach St. (between Magnolia St. and International Raceway Blvd.). ℂ 386/947-2022. Reservations not accepted. Breakfast $2–$4.50; sandwiches, salads, pizzas $4–$6. MC, V. Mon–Sat 8am–4pm.

Frappes North ★★ CREATIVE AMERICAN/FUSION It's worth the 6-mile drive north to Bobby and Meryl Frappier's sophisticated, hip establishment, at which they provide this area's most entertaining cuisine. Several chic dining rooms—one has beams extending like spokes from a central pole—set the stage for an inventive, ever-changing "Menu of the Moment" fusing a multitude of styles. Ingredients are always fresh, and the herbs come from the restaurant's garden. Outstandingly presented with wonton strips and a multi-hued rice cake, my Southeast Asian–style pompano in a piquant peanut sauce was a memorable dish. Bobby and Meryl always have at least one vegetarian (though not necessarily nondairy) main course. Lunch is a steal here, with dinner-size main courses at a fraction of the dinnertime price. The restaurant is in a storefront on the mainland stretch of Granada Boulevard, Ormond Beach's main drag.

123 W. Granada Blvd. (Fla. 40; between Ridgewood Ave. and Washington St.), Ormond Beach. (℃ **386/ 615-4888.** Reservations recommended. Main courses $15–$24. AE, MC, V. Mon–Thurs 11:30am–2:30pm and 5–9pm; Fri 11:30am–2:30pm and 5–10pm; Sat 5–10pm. From the beaches, drive 4 miles north on Fla. A1A to left on Granada Blvd. (Fla. 40); cross Halifax River to restaurant on right.

McK's Dublin Station AMERICAN/IRISH   Worth knowing about because it serves food after midnight, this upscale Irish tavern has a highly eclectic menu. The pub fare includes club sandwiches, burgers, burritos, a tasty wrap of grilled vegetables and a peanut sauce, and a few main courses of steaks, chicken, and "Mumzy's" meatloaf. The food isn't exceptional, but it's perfectly acceptable after a few Bass ales. The service is sometimes rushed, but usually pleasant.

218 S. Beach St. (between Magnolia St. and Ivy Lane). (℃ **386/238-3321.** Reservations not accepted. Main courses $6–$13; salads and sandwiches $5–$7. AE, MC, V. Mon–Sat 11am–3am; Sun 11am–midnight.

Rosario's ★★ SOUTHERN ITALIAN/TUSCAN   A Victorian boarding house with lace curtains on high windows makes an incongruous setting for Chef Rosario Vinci's lively Italian restaurant. Originally from Florence, Italy, gregarious Rosario offers pastas with the familiar Bolognese and marinara sauces, but his nightly specials are much more intriguing, drawing inspiration from ancient Tuscan recipes. If the mixed grill of squirrel, pheasant, and quail in a hunter's sauce doesn't appeal, you can always opt for grouper Livornese. There's music in the cozy bar Thursday through Saturday nights.

In Live Oak Inn, 448 S. Beach St. (at Loomis Ave.). (℃ **386/258-6066.** Reservations recommended. Main courses $10–$19. MC, V. Tues–Sat 5–10pm.

DAYTONA BEACH AFTER DARK

Check the Daytona Beach *News-Journal* (www.njcenter.com) Friday edition for its weekly "Go-Do" and the Sunday paper for the "Master Calendar" section, both listing present and upcoming events. Other good sources are *Happenings Magazine* and *Backstage Pass Magazine,* two tabloids available at the visitor center (see "Essentials," earlier in this chapter) and in many hotel lobbies.

THE PERFORMING ARTS   The **Peabody Auditorium,** 600 Auditorium Blvd., between Noble Street and Wild Olive Avenue (℃ **386/255-1314**), is the city's major venue for serious performance, including concerts by the local Symphony Society (℃ **386/253-2901**). Professional actors perform Broadway musicals during winter and summer at the **Seaside Musical Theater,** 176 N. Beach St. downtown (℃ **800/854-5592** or 386/252-6200).

Under the city auspices, the **Oceanfront Bandshell** (℃ **386/258-3169**), on the boardwalk next to the Adam's Mark Hotel, hosts a series of free big-name concerts at the band shell every Sunday night from early June to Labor Day. It's also the scene of raucous Spring-Break concerts.

THE CLUB & BAR SCENE   In addition to the following, the sophisticated **Clocktower Lounge** at the Adam's Mark (see "Where to Stay," earlier in this chapter) is worth a visit.

Main Street and **Seabreeze Boulevard** on the beach are happening areas where dozens of bars (and a few topless shows) cater to leather-clad bikers.

A popular beachfront bar for more than 40 years, the **Ocean Deck Restaurant & Beach Club,** 127 S. Ocean Ave. (℃ **386/253-5224;** see "Where to

Dine," above), is packed with a mix of locals and tourists, young and old, who come for live music and cheap drinks. Reggae or ska bands play after 9:30pm. There's valet parking after dark, or leave your vehicle at Ocean Deck's Reggae Republic surf shop on Atlantic Avenue.

3 St. Augustine: America's First City (★(★

105 miles NE of Orlando, 302 miles N. of Miami, 39 miles S. of Jacksonville

With its 17th-century fort, old city gates, horse-drawn carriages clip-clopping along narrow streets, and reconstructed 18th-century Spanish Quarter, St. Augustine seems more like a picturesque European village than a modern American city. This is, after all, the oldest permanent European settlement in the United States (no, it wasn't Jamestown in 1607 or the Pilgrims at Plymouth Rock in 1620). A group of French Huguenots settled in 1562 near the mouth of the St. Johns River, in present-day Jacksonville. Three years later, a Spanish force under Pedro Menéndez de Avilés arrived on the scene, wiped out the Huguenot men (de Avilés spared their women and children), and established a settlement on the harbor he named "St. Augustín."

The colony survived attacks by pirates, Indians, and the British over the next 2 centuries. The Treaty of Paris ending the French and Indian War ceded the town to Britain in 1763, but the British gave it back 20 years later. The United States took control when it acquired Florida from Spain in 1821.

Tourism is St. Augustine's main industry these days; but despite the daily invasion, it's an exceptionally charming town, with good restaurants, an active nightlife, and shopping bargains. Give yourself 2 days here just to see the highlights, longer to savor this historic gem.

ESSENTIALS

GETTING THERE   St. Augustine is about an hour's drive south of Jacksonville's international airport and Amtrak train station. The Daytona Beach airport is about the same distance south, but services are more frequent, and fares usually lower, at Jacksonville. See "Essentials," in sections 2 and 4 of this chapter, for details.

VISITOR INFORMATION   Before you go, contact the **St. Johns County Visitors and Convention Bureau,** 88 Riberia St., Suite 400, St. Augustine, FL 32084 (© **800/OLD-CITY** or 904/829-1711; fax 904/829-6149; www. visitoldcity.com), and request the *Visitor's Guide,* detailing attractions, events, restaurants, accommodations, shopping, and more.

Web surfers can click on the advertiser-supported site at **www.oldcity.com**.

In the historic district, there's an information desk in Government House, King Street at St. George Street. It's open daily from 9am to 6pm except Christmas.

Over on St. Augustine Beach, there's a walk-in **visitors information center** at the St. Johns County Fishing Pier (350 A1A Beach Blvd.; © **904/471-1596**). It's open daily from 8:30am to 5pm.

THE VISITOR CENTER   Your first stop upon arrival should be the **St. Augustine Visitor Information Center,** 10 Castillo Dr., at San Marco Avenue, opposite the Castillo de San Marcos National Monument (© **904/825-1000**). There are numerous ways to see the city, depending on your interest and time, and this is the best place to make your plans. The Old City Gates are virtually across the street, so park your vehicle here (the $3 fee is good for 2 consecutive days, so you may leave and return). On-street parking is nonexistent in the historic district, and a number of metered parking lots here are difficult to find and often full. Before setting out, adults can pay $3, children $2 to watch "Dream of Empire," a 52-minute video about the town's first 14 years (history buffs will enjoy it; otherwise, it's a good way to kill an hour on a rainy day). A free 12-minute orientation video is more helpful in planning your visit. Once you've made a plan, you can buy tickets for sightseeing trains and trolleys, which include discount admissions to the attractions (see "Getting Around," below).

The center is open daily, from 8:30am to 6:30pm between March and Memorial Day and between Labor Day and October; from 8am to 7:30pm between Memorial Day and Labor Day; and from 8:30am to 5:30pm between November and February. It and most area attractions are closed on Christmas.

GETTING AROUND   Once you've parked at the visitor center, you can walk or take one of the sightseeing trolleys, trains, and horse-drawn carriages around the historic district. The trolleys and trains follow 7-mile routes, stopping at the visitor center and at or near most attractions between 8:30am and 5pm daily. You can get off at any stop, visit the attractions, and step aboard the next vehicle that comes along. Several vehicles make continuous circuits along the route throughout the day; you won't ever have to wait more than 15 or 20 minutes. If you don't get off at any attractions, it takes about 1 hour and 10 minutes to complete the tour. They don't all go to the same sights, so speak with their agents at the visitor center in order to pick the right one for you. You can buy tickets there or from the drivers. The companies also sell **discounted tickets** to some attractions.

St. Augustine Historical Tours (© **800/397-4071** or 904/829-3800) operates the green-and-white, open-air buses (and enclosed buses when it rains, a definite advantage). You can park your car at the headquarters (the Old Jail and Florida Heritage Museum, which are also stops on the tour). There are 25 stops, including Sebastian Winery, one of the few vintners in Florida.

St. Augustine Sightseeing Trains (© **800/226-6545** or 904/829-6545; www.redtrains.com) covers all the main sites except the Old Jail and Florida Heritage Museum, but its red open-air trains are small enough to go down more of the narrow historic-district streets.

You may also want to see the sights from the back of a horse-drawn carriage. **Colee's Carriage Tours** (© **904/829-2818**) has been showing people around town since 1877. The carriages line up at the bay front, just south of the fort. Slow-paced, entertainingly narrated 1-hour rides past major landmarks and attractions are offered from 8am to midnight. Private tours and hotel and restaurant pickups are available.

All three companies charge $12 for adults, $5 for children 6 to 12, free for children 5 and under. The carriages cost $15 per person after dark or if you board at the bay front.

For more-personalized tours, call **Tour St. Augustine** (© **800/797-3778** or 904/471-9010), which offers guided walking tours around the historical area and nightly ghost walks. You can also search for the old spirits with the nightly **Ghost Tours of St. Augustine** (© **904-461-1009;** www.aghostlyexperience. com), in which guides in period dress lead you through the northern historic district; tickets are $8 per person, children under 6 free. Also available are **Stroll Back in Time Nightly Walking Tours** (© **800/597-7177** or 904/797-5604), whose walks cost $5 per person. Call for schedule and reservations.

The Sunshine Bus Company (© **904/823-4816**) runs two public bus routes Monday to Saturday from 6am to 5pm. The north-south line runs between the St. Augustine Airport on U.S. 1 and the historic district via San Marco Avenue and the Greyhound bus terminal on Malaga Street. Rides cost $1 per person. Call for exact schedule.

For a taxi, call **Yellow Cab** (© **904/824-6888**).

Solano Cycle, 61 San Marco Ave., at Locust Avenue (© **904/825-6766**), 2 blocks north of the visitor center, rents bicycles, mopeds, and scooters. Bikes cost $12 a day; scooters and mopeds, $30 to $40 a day. Open daily 10am to 6pm.

SEEING THE TOP HISTORIC ATTRACTIONS

St. George Street from King Street north to the Old City Gate (at Orange Street) is the heart of the historic district. Lined with a plethora of restaurants and boutiques selling everything from T-shirts to antiques, these 4 blocks get the lion's share of the town's tourists. You'll have much less company as you poke around the narrow streets of the primarily residential neighborhood south of King Street.

Most of the town's attractions do not have guided tours, but most do have docents on hand to answer questions.

Castillo de San Marcos National Monument ★★

One of the two best attractions here, America's oldest and best-preserved masonry fortification took 23 years (1672 to 1695) to build. It is stellar in design, with a double drawbridge entrance over a 40-foot dry moat. Diamond-shaped bastions in each corner, which enabled cannons to set up a deadly crossfire, contained domed sentry towers. The seemingly indestructible Castillo was never captured in battle, and its coquina walls did not crumble when pounded by enemy artillery or violent storms throughout more than 300 years. Today the old storerooms house exhibits documenting the history of the fort, a national monument since 1924. Also, you can tour the vaulted powder magazine, a dank prison cell, the chapel, and guard rooms. A self-guided tour map and brochure are provided at the ticket booth. If available, the 20- to 30-minute ranger talks are well worth attending. There are popular torchlight tours of the fort in winter (call for schedule). At press time, a restoration project had begun at the fort, and access was limited; call for hours and information.

1 E. Castillo Dr. (at San Marco Ave.). © **904/829-6506.** www.nps.gov/casa. Admission $4 adults, free for children 16 and under with an adult. Fort daily 8:45am–4:45pm; grounds daily 5:30am–midnight. Closed Christmas.

Government House Museum

This museum is neither as informative nor as entertaining as the Old St. Augustine Village Museum or the Spanish Quarter Village (see below), but a walk through it will give you a quick overview of the Old City's history. Spanish coins, pottery, and other items unearthed during archaeological digs are the most fascinating exhibits.

48 King St. (at St. George St.). © **904/825-5079.** Admission $2.50 adults, $2 seniors, $1 children. Daily 9am–5pm.

Lightner Museum ★★

Henry Flagler's opulent Spanish Renaissance–style Alcazar Hotel, built in 1889, closed during the Depression and stayed vacant until Chicago publishing magnate Otto C. Lightner bought the building in 1948 to house his vast collection of Victoriana. The building is an attraction in itself and makes a gorgeous museum, centering on an open palm courtyard with an arched stone bridge spanning a fish pond. The first floor houses a Victorian village, with shop fronts representing emporia selling period wares. A Victorian Science and Industry Room displays shells, rocks, minerals, and Native American artifacts in beautiful turn-of-the-century cases. Other exhibits include stuffed birds, an Egyptian mummy, steam-engine models, and amazing examples of Victorian glassblowing. Plan to spend about 90 minutes exploring it all, and be sure to be here at 11am or 2pm, when a room of automated musical instruments erupts in concerts of period music. The imposing building across King Street was Henry Flagler's opulent rival resort, the Ponce de León Hotel. It now houses **Flagler College.** Across Cordova Street stands another competitor of the day, the 1888-vintage Casa Monica Hotel (see "Where to Stay," later in this chapter).

75 King St. (at Granada St.). ☎ **904/824-2874.** www.lightnermuseum.org. Admission $6 adults, $2 college students with ID and children 12–18, free for children 11 and under. Daily 9am–5pm (last tour 4pm).

Old St. Augustine Village Museum ☆☆

Along with the Castillo de San Marcos National Monument (see above), this living-history museum is head-and-shoulders above other local attractions. Operated by Daytona Beach's excellent Museum of Arts and Sciences, it brings to life each period of the city's history, from Spanish colonial times to the late 19th century. Costumed interpreters play real people from each period, including a pirate, a soldier, a quilt maker, a gardener, a cook, and a snake oil salesman. Even if you miss the performances, each house in the complex has exhibits and interactive displays that explain a historical period. The buildings here are original, the oldest of which was built in the 1790s and was owned by Achille Murat, Napoleon's exiled nephew (original letters from the French emperor are among the many fascinating exhibits). A snack bar specializes in Minorcan-style fare (preferred by the town's earliest settlers), and the reconstructed Star General Store sells preserves and other Victorian-era goods. You'll need 2 hours to see it all, but admission is good all day, so you can leave and come back for a presentation you would especially like to see.

250 St. George St. (entry on Bridge St. between St. George and Cordova Sts.). ☎ **904/823-9722.** www.old-staug-village.com. Admission $7 adults, $6 seniors, $5 children 5–12, children under 5 free. 2-day pass $10 per person. Daily 9am–5pm (last presentation 2:30pm).

The Oldest House ☆☆

Archaeological surveys indicate that a dwelling stood on this site as early as the beginning of the 17th century. What you see today, called the Gonzáles-Alvarez House (named for two of its prominent owners), evolved from a two-room coquina dwelling built between 1702 and 1727. The rooms are furnished to evoke various historical eras. Admission also entitles you to explore the adjacent **Manucy Museum of St. Augustine History,** where artifacts, maps, and photographs document the town's history from its origins through the Flagler era a century ago. Both are owned and operated by the St. Augustine Historical Society. Allow about 30 minutes.

14 St. Francis St. (at Charlotte St.). ☎ **904/824-2872.** Admission $5 adults, $4.50 seniors 55 and over, $3 students, free for children 6 and under; or $12 families. Daily 9am–5pm; tours depart every half-hour (last tour at 4:30pm).

The Oldest Store Museum ☆☆

The C&F Hamblen General Store was St. Augustine's one-stop shopping center from 1835 to 1960, and the museum on its premises today replicates the emporium at the turn of the century. On display are more than 100,000 items sold here in that era, many of them gleaned from the store's attic. They include high-button shoes, butter churns, spinning

St. Augustine

Genoply St.
Milton St.
Douglas Ave.
A1A
Dismure St.
Matanzas Ave.
May St.
Dufferin Ave.
Williams St.
Magnolia Ave.
BUS 1
Ballard Ave.
Myrtle Ave.
Ocean Ave.
Macaris Creek
San Sebastian River
Ponce de Leon Blvd.
San Marco Ave.
Old Mission Rd.
Pine St.
Locust St.
Rhode Ave.
Water St.
Mulberry St.
Castillo Dr.
5A
Orange St.
Malaga St.
Saragossa St.
Spanish St.
Cuna St.
Carrera St.
Cordova St.
Sevilla St.
Hypolita St.
Valencia St.
Treasury St.
Cathedral Pl.
King St.
BUS 1
214
Artillery Lane
Aviles St.
Cadiz St.
Bridge St.
Weedon St.
Granada St.
Riberia St.
DeHaven St.
St. Francis St.
Menendez
Bay St.
Marine St.
Charlotte St.
St. George St.
Maria Sanchez Lake
Washington St.
Lovett St.
Central Ave.
South St.
Bridge of Lions
To the Beach →
Matanzas River
St. Augustine Blvd.
Anastasia Blvd.
Arredondo Dr.
207

St. Augustine

FLORIDA

0   1/2 mi
0   0.5 km

wheels, 1890s bathing suits, barrels of dill pickles (you can purchase one), and medicines that were 90% alcohol. Some 19th-century brand-name products shown here are still available today, among them Hershey's chocolate, Coca-Cola, Ivory soap, and Campbell's soups. It all makes for about 30 minutes of fascinating browsing.

4 Artillery Lane (between St. George and Aviles Sts. behind Trinity Episcopal Church). ☎ **904/829-9729.** Admission $5 adults, $1.50 children 6–12, free for children 5 and under. Mon–Sat 9am–5pm; Sun noon–5pm (in summer Sun 10am–5pm).

The Oldest Wooden Schoolhouse in the U.S.A. ☆ (Kids) One of three structures here dating from the Spanish colonial period of more than 2 centuries ago, this red-cedar and cypress structure is held together by wooden pegs and handmade nails, its hand-wrought beams still intact. The last class was held here in 1864. Today the classroom is re-created using animated pupils and teacher, complete with a dunce and a below-stairs "dungeon" for unruly children. Today's kids may not approve of those stern disciplinary methods, but they will count their lucky stars they weren't in school back then.

14 St. George St. (between Orange and Cuna Sts.). ☎ **800/428-0222** or 904/824-0192. Admission $2.75 adults, $2.25 seniors 55 and over, $1.75 children 6–12, free for children 5 and under. Daily 9am–5pm (later during summer).

Spanish Military Hospital This clapboard building is a reconstruction of part of a hospital that stood here during the second Spanish colonial period from 1784 to 1821. A 20-minute guided tour will show you what the apothecary, the administrative offices, the patients' ward, and the herbarium probably looked like in 1791. The ward and a collection of actual surgical instruments of the period will enhance your appreciation of modern medicine.

3 Aviles St. (south of King St.). ☎ **904/825-6830.** Admission $2.50 adults, $2 seniors, $1.50 children. Mon–Sat 10am–5pm; Sun noon–5pm.

Spanish Quarter Village ☆☆ The city's colonial architecture and landscape have been re-created in this 2-square-block history park, which interprets St. Augustine's history circa 1750. Once inside, you can take a 20-minute guided tour of the **DeMesa-Sanchez House** (ca. 1740 to 1760), the only authentic colonial-era structure in the compound (the others are reproductions). Elsewhere, interpreters in 18th-century attire are on hand to help you envision the life of early inhabitants. If you have to make a choice of one or the other, the Old St. Augustine Village Museum (see above) covers more history.

33 St. George St. (between Cuna and Orange Sts.). ☎ **904/825-6830.** Admission $6.50 adults, $5.50 seniors, $4 students 6–18, free for children 5 and under; or $13 per family. Daily 9am–6pm.

MORE HISTORIC ATTRACTIONS

Authentic Old Jail This compact Victorian prison, a mile north of the visitor center, was built in 1890 and served as the county jail until 1953. The sheriff and his wife raised their children upstairs and used the same kitchen facilities to prepare the inmates' meals and their own. Downstairs are three cells: a maximum-security cell where murderers and horse thieves were confined; a cell housing prisoners condemned to hang (they could see the gallows being constructed from their window); and a grim solitary-confinement cell—with no windows or mattress. A restaurant serves inexpensive lunch fare.

167 San Marco Ave. (at Williams St.). ☎ **904/829-3800.** Admission $4.25 adults, $3.25 children 6–12, free for children 5 and under. Daily 8:30am–5pm.

Florida Heritage Museum at the Authentic Old Jail   After you've seen the Authentic Old Jail, you can spend another 30 minutes wandering through this commercial museum documenting 400 years of Florida's past, focusing on the colorful life of Henry Flagler, the Civil War, and the Seminole Wars. Highlights are an extraordinary collection of toys and dolls, mostly from the 1870s to the 1920s; and a replica of a Spanish galleon filled with weapons, pottery, and treasures complementing display cases filled with actual gold, silver, and jewelry recovered by treasure hunters. A typical wattle-and-daub hut of a Timucuan Indian in a forest setting illustrates the lifestyle of St. Augustine's first residents.

167 San Marco Ave. (at Williams St.). © 904/829-3800. Admission $4.25 adults, $3.25 children 6–12, free for children 5 and under. Daily 8:30am–5pm.

Fountain of Youth Archaeological Park *Overrated*   Never mind that Juan Ponce de León never did find the Fountain of Youth, this 25-acre archaeological park bills itself as North America's first historic site. Smithsonian Institution archaeological digs have established that a Timucuan Indian village existed on this site some 1,000 years ago, but there's no evidence that Ponce de León visited here during his 1513 voyage of discovery. You can wander around the grounds yourself, but you'll learn more on a 45-minute guided tour or a planetarium show about 16th-century celestial navigation.

11 Magnolia Ave. (at Williams St.). © 800/356-8222 or 904/829-3168. Admission $5.50 adults, $4.50 seniors, $2.50 children 6–12, free for children 5 and under. Daily 9am–5pm.

Mission of Nombre de Dios   This serene setting overlooking the Intracoastal Waterway is believed to be the site of the first permanent mission in the United States, founded in 1565. The mission is a popular destination of religious pilgrimages. Whatever your beliefs, it's a beautiful tree-shaded spot, ideal for quiet meditation.

27 Ocean Ave. (at San Marco Ave.). © 904/824-2809. Free admission; donations appreciated. Daily 8am–5:30pm.

St. Augustine Lighthouse and Museum ⭐   This 165-foot-tall structure was built in 1875 to replace the old Spanish lighthouse that had stood at the inlet since 1565. Sitting in a shady grove of live oaks, the lightkeeper's Victorian cottage was destroyed by fire in 1970 but meticulously reconstructed by the local Junior League. Also new is a Victorian-style visitor center that houses a museum explaining the history of both the lighthouse and the area. You should be in good physical condition and not pregnant to climb the 219 steps to the top of the lighthouse, where you can see 19 nautical miles on a clear day. Children must be at least 7 years old and 4 feet tall to make the ascent.

81 Lighthouse Ave. (off Fla. A1A east of the Bridge of Lions). © 904/829-0745. www.stauglight.com. Admission to museum and tower $6.50 adults, $5.50 seniors, $4 children 7–11, free for kids under 7. Museum and grounds only $4 adults, $3 seniors, $2 children 7–11, free for children under 7. Daily 9am–6pm. Closed Easter, Thanksgiving, Christmas Eve, and Christmas Day. Follow Fla. A1A south across Bridge of Lions; take last left before turnoff to Anastasia State Park.

OTHER ENTERTAINING ATTRACTIONS

Ripley's Believe It or Not! Museum *Kids*   This is the original Ripley's museum, housed in a converted 1887 Moorish Revival residence—complete with battlements, massive chimneys, and rose windows. Like the Ripley's in a dozen other U.S. cities, the exhibits run the gamut, from a Haitian voodoo doll owned by Papa Doc Duvalier to letters carved on a pencil with a chain saw by Ray "Wild Mountain Man" Murphy.

19 San Marco Ave. (at Castillo Dr.). ⓒ **904/824-1606.** Admission $9.95 adults, $7.95 seniors, $5.95 children 5–12, free for children 4 and under. June–Aug daily 9am–9pm; Sept–May 9am–7pm.

St. Augustine Alligator Farm and Zoological Park ⭐⭐ *Kids*   You can't leave Florida without seeing at least one real live gator, and there are more than 1,000 of them—including some rare white gators—on display at this century-old attraction. In fact, it houses the world's most complete collection of croco-dilians, a category that includes alligators, crocodiles, caimans, and gavials. Other creatures living here include geckos, prehensile-tailed skinks, lizards, snakes, tortoises, spider monkeys, and exotic birds. There are ponds filled with a variety of ducks, geese, and swans, as well as a petting zoo with pygmy goats, potbellied pigs, miniature horses, mouflon sheep, and deer. Entertaining (and educational) 20-minute alligator and reptile shows take place hourly throughout the day, and spring through fall you can often see narrated feedings. If you're into this kind of thing, allow at least 2 hours to tour the extensive and well-maintained facilities.

999 Anastasia Blvd. (Fla. A1A), east of Bridge of Lions at Old Quarry Rd. ⓒ **904/824-3337.** www.alligatorfarm.com. Admission $14.25 adults, $12.85 seniors 65 and over, $8.50 children 3–10, free for children under 3. June–Labor Day daily 9am–6pm; Labor Day–May daily 9am–5pm.

HITTING THE BEACH

There are several places to find sand and sea: in **Vilano Beach,** on the north side of St. Augustine Inlet; and in **St. Augustine Beach,** on the south side (the inlet dumps the Matanzas and North Rivers into the Atlantic). Be aware, however, that erosion has almost swallowed the beach from the inlet as far south as Old Beach Road in St. Augustine Beach. The U.S. Army Corps of Engineers is reclaiming the sand, but in the meantime hotels and homes here have rock sea-walls instead of sand bordering the sea.

Erosion has made a less noticeable impact on the beautiful **Anastasia State Park** ⭐⭐, on Anastasia Boulevard (Fla. A1A) across the Bridge of Lions and just past the Alligator Farm, where the 4 miles of beach are still backed by pictur-esque dunes. On its river side, the area faces a lagoon flanked by tidal marshes. Available here are shaded picnic areas with grills, rest rooms, windsurfing, sail-ing and canoeing (on a saltwater lagoon), a nature trail, and saltwater fishing (for bluefish, pompano, and whiting from the surf; sea trout, redfish, and flounder—a license is required for out-of-state residents). In summer, you can rent chairs, beach umbrellas, and surfboards. There's good bird watching here, too, especially in spring and fall; pick up a brochure at the entrance. The 139 wooded campsites are in high demand all year. They have picnic tables, grills, and electricity. Admission to the park is $3.25 per vehicle and $1 for bicyclists and pedestrians. Campsites cost $16 per night plus $2 for electricity. The day-use area is open daily from 8am to sunset. You can bring your pets. For more information and to make required campground reservations (up to 11 months in advance), contact Anastasia State Park, 1340A Fla. A1A S., St. Augustine, FL 32084 (ⓒ **904/461-2033;** www8.myflorida.com/communities/learn/stateparks/district3/anastasia).

All St. Augustine beaches charge a fee of $3 per car at official access points from Memorial Day to Labor Day; the rest of the year you can park free, but there are no lifeguards on duty and no toilet facilities on the beach.

Another Good Walk Spoiled

Passionate golf fans can easily spend a day at the **World Golf Hall of Fame** (© 904/940-4123), a state-of-the-art museum honoring professional golf, its great players, and the sport's famous supporters (including comedian Bob Hope and singer Dinah Shore). It's the centerpiece of **World Golf Village**, a complex of hotels, shops, offices, 18-hole golf courses (see "Fishing, Cruises & Other Outdoor Activities," below).There's an IMAX screen next door.

Museum admission is $10 adults, $9 seniors, $6 children 3 to 12. IMAX movie tickets range from $7 to $9 adults, $6 to $9 seniors, $5 to $7 children 3 to 12. Combination tickets $15 adults, $13 seniors, $10 children 3 to 12. Admission and movies free for children under 3. The museum is open daily from 10am to 6pm (IMAX movies to 8pm on Friday and Saturday).

You don't have to play the real courses, because the village is built around a lake with a "challenge hole" sitting out in the middle, 132 feet from the shoreline. You can hit balls at it or play a round on the nearby putting course. The Walkway of Champions (whose signatures appear in pavement stones) circles the lake and passes a shopping complex whose main tenant is the two-story **Tour Stop** (© 904/940-0422), a purveyor of pricey apparel and equipment. You can also stop for a meal or refreshment at **Sam Sneed's Tavern** (© 904/940-0220) and raise your energy level at a branch of **Kilwin's Chocolates** (© 904/940-0909).

You can stay at the luxurious **World Golf Village Renaissance Resort**, 500 S. Legacy Trail, St. Augustine, FL 32092 (© 800/228-9290 or 904/8000).

The village is at Exit 95A off I-95. For more information, contact World Golf Village, 21 World Golf Place, St. Augustine, FL 32092 (© 904/940-4000; www.wgv.com).

FISHING, CRUISES & OTHER OUTDOOR ACTIVITIES

For additional outdoor options, contact the St. Johns County Visitors and Convention Bureau (see "Essentials," earlier in this chapter) and ask them to send you a copy of their *Outdoor Recreation Guide.*

CRUISES   The Usina family has been running **St. Augustine Scenic Cruises** (© 800/542-8316 or 904/824-1806; www.scenic-cruise.com) on Matanzas Bay since the turn of the century. They offer 75-minute narrated tours aboard the double-decker *Victory III,* departing from the Municipal Marina just south of the Bridge of Lions. You can sometimes spot dolphins, brown pelicans, cormorants, and kingfishers. Snacks, soft drinks, beer, and wine are sold on board. Departures normally are at 11am and at 1, 2:45, and 4:30pm daily except Christmas, with an additional tour at 6:15pm from April 1 to May 21 and Labor Day to October 15; May 22 to Labor Day there are two additional tours, at 6:45 and 8:30pm. Call ahead—schedules can change during inclement weather. Fares are $9.50 adults, $8 seniors, $7 juniors ages 13 to 18, $5 children 4 to 12, free for children under 4. If you're driving, allow extra time to find a parking space on the street.

FISHING You can fish to your heart's content at **Anastasia State Park** (see "Hitting the Beach," above). You can also cast your line off **St. Johns County Fishing Pier,** on the north end of St. Augustine Beach (© **904/461-0119**). The pier is open 24 hours daily and has a bait shop with rental equipment that is open from 6am to 10pm. Admission is $2 ($1 children under 2) for fishing, 50¢ per person for sightseeing.

For full-day, half-day, and overnight **deep-sea fishing** excursions (for snapper, grouper, porgy, amberjack, sea bass, and other species), contact the **Sea Love Marina,** 250 Vilano Rd. (Fla. A1A north), at the eastern end of the Vilano Beach Bridge (© **904/824-3328;** www.sealovefishing.com). Full-day trips on the party boat *Sea Love II* cost about $50; half-day trips, $35. No license is required, and rod, reel, bait, and tackle are supplied. Bring your own food and drink.

GOLF The area's best golf resorts are in Ponte Vedra Beach about a half-hour's drive north on Fla. A1A, closer to Jacksonville than St. Augustine (see "Where to Stay," in section 4, later in this chapter, for details).

At World Golf Village, 12 miles north of St. Augustine at Exit 98B off I-95 (see the box, above), **The Slammer & The Squire** and **The King & The Bear** (© **904/940-6088;** www.wgv.com) together offer 36 holes amid a wildlife preserve. Locals say they're not as challenging as their greens fees, about $90 in summer, $165 in winter, including cart. For those not schooled in golf history, the "Slammer" is in honor of Sam Snead; the "Squire" is for Gene Sarazen; the "King" is Arnold Palmer, and the "Bear" is Jack Nicklaus. Palmer and Nicklaus actually collaborated in designing their course.

Nicklaus also had a hand in the stunning course at the **Ocean Hammock Golf Club** ☆☆ (© **904/477-4653;** www.oceanhammock.com), on Fla. A1A in Palm Coast, about halfway between St. Augustine and Daytona Beach. Opened in late 2000 with six of its holes actually skirting the beach, it is the first truly oceanside course built in Florida since the 1920s.

There are only a few courses in St. Augustine, including a rather-flat 18 at the **Radisson Ponce de León Golf & Conference Resort** (see "Where to Stay," below) and the **St. Augustine Shores Golf Club,** 707 Shores Blvd., off U.S. 1 (© **904/794-4653**). The latter is a par-70 course featuring 18 holes, lots of water, a lighted driving range and putting green, and a restaurant and lounge. Greens fees are about $26 to $30, including cart, less in the summer months.

SAILING You can spend 3- to 4 hours under sail with Captain Paul Kulik on board his *Voyager* (© **904/347-7183;** www.villavoyager.com), a 22-foot-wide trimaran, which departs the Municipal Marina next to the Bridge of Lions. The cruises cost $35 per person, including lunch, soft drinks, and beer. The boat can carry a maximum of six guests, so call for reservations and schedule.

WATER SPORTS Jet skis and surfing and windsurfing equipment can be rented at **Surf Station,** 1020 Anastasia Blvd. (Fla. A1A), a block south of the Alligator Farm (© **904/471-9463**); at **Raging Water Sports,** at the Conch House Marina Resort, 57 Comares Ave. (© **904/829-5001**), which is off Anastasia Avenue (Fla. A1A) halfway between the Bridge of Lions and the Alligator Farm; and at **Watersports of St. Augustine,** at Sea Love Marina, 250 Vilano Rd. (Fla. A1A north), at the eastern end of the Vilano Beach Bridge (© **904/ 823-8963**).

SHOPPING

The winding streets of the historic district are home to dozens of **antiques stores** and **art galleries** stocked full of original paintings, sculptures, bric-a-brac, fine furnishings, china, and other treasures. Brick-lined **Aviles Street,** 1 block from the river, has an especially good mix of shops for browsing, as does **St. George Street** south of the visitor center and the Uptown area on **San Marco Avenue** a few blocks north of the center. The **Alcazar Courtyard Shops** at the Lightner Museum (© **904/824-2874**) has a good selection of antiques shops (see "Seeing the Top Historic Attractions," earlier in this chapter). The visitor center has complete lists of art galleries and antiques shops; or you can contact the **Antique Dealers Association of St. Augustine,** 60 Cuna St., St. Augustine, FL 32084 (no phone), and **Art Galleries of Saint Augustine** (© **904/ 829-0065** or 904/825-4577).

Experience chocolate heaven at **Whetstone Chocolates,** 2 Coke Rd. (Fla. 312), between U.S. 1 and the Mickler O'Connell Bridge (© **904/825-1700**). Free tours of the store and factory usually take place Monday to Saturday from 10am to 5:30pm, but call to make sure of the factory's schedule. Whetstone has a retail outlet at 42 St. George St. in the historic district.

Outlet shoppers will find plenty of good hunting 7 miles northwest of downtown on Fla. 16 at I-95. Among the 95-plus stores in **St. Augustine Outlet Mall** (© **904/825-1555**), on the west side of I-95, are outlets by Levi's, Adolfo II, Mikasa, Brooks Brothers, Coach, Jones New York, Ann Taylor, Maidenform, Calvin Klein, The Gap, Bose, and OshKosh B'Gosh. A free trolley will take you along this half-mile strip of stores. On the east side of I-95, the enclosed, air-conditioned **Belz Factory Outlet World** (© **904/826-1311;** www.belz.com) has 65 shops headlined by Lenox, Pfaltzgraff, Royal Doulton, Waterford Wedgewood, Guess, Tommy Hilfiger, Liz Claiborne, Polo Ralph Lauren, Paul Harris, Black & Decker, Reebok, Adidas, Remington, and Timberland. Stores in both malls are open Monday to Saturday 9am to 9pm, Sunday 10am to 6pm.

WHERE TO STAY

There are plenty of moderate and inexpensive motels and hotels here. Most convenient to the historic district is the 40-room **Best Western Spanish Quarter Inn,** 6 Castillo Dr. (© **800/528-1234** or 904/824-4457; fax 904/829-8330), directly across the street from the visitor center. It's completely surrounded by an asphalt parking lot but does have a swimming pool and hot tub. Also close to the historic district, the two-story stucco **Comfort Inn,** 1111 Ponce de León Blvd., at Old Mission Road (© **800/575-5288** or 904/824-5554; fax 904/829-2948), has large suites with double-sink dressing rooms and parlor areas with extra TVs and pullout sofas.

St. Augustine Beach has several chain motels, all on A1A Beach Boulevard (Fla. A1A). Three are on the beach side of the highway: the **Hampton Inn St. Augustine Beach** (© **800/426-7866** or 904/471-4000; fax 904/471-4888), the **Holiday Inn Beachside** (© **800/626-7263** or 904/471-2555; fax 904/461-8450), and the **Howard Johnson Resort Hotel** (© **800/752-4037** or 904/471-2575; fax 904/471-1247). But note that erosion has removed the beach at the Hampton Inn and Howard Johnson (see "Hitting the Beach," above). On the western side of A1A, the **Hilton Garden Inn** (© **800/ HILTONS** or 904/471-5559; fax 904/471-7146) is the newest motel here. Nearby is an inexpensive **Econo Lodge** (© **800/446-6900** or 904/471-2330).

Almost all accommodations increase their prices on weekends when the town is most crowded with visitors. St. Johns County charges a 9% tax on hotel bills.

Hotels & Motels

Casa Monica Hotel ★★   Built in 1888 as a luxury hotel by Bostonian Franklin W. Smith, who founded the YMCA, this Spanish-style building was used as the St. Johns County Courthouse from the 1960s until 1997. Now totally restored, it's easily the top hotel here. Most of the guest quarters are spacious and fully modern hotel rooms, with Iberian-style armoires, wrought-iron headboards, and tapestry drapes. "Premier" rooms have sitting areas with sofas and easy chairs. All units have big bathrooms equipped with high-end toiletries and either a huge walk-in shower or a combination tub-shower. Much more interesting are the "signature suites" installed in the building's two tile-topped towers and fortresslike central turret. Each of these one- to four-bedroom units is unique. One in the turret has a half-round living room with gun-port windows overlooking the historic district, while a three-story townhouse model in one of the towers has a huge whirlpool bathroom on its top floor. The 95 Cordova restaurant serves excellent regional fare in a relaxed bistro setting. A player piano provides music in the adjoining bar.

95 Cordova St. (at King St.), St. Augustine, FL 32084. ℂ **800/648-1888** or 904/827-1888. Fax 904/819-6065. www.casamonica.com. 138 units, including 14 suites. $159–$239 double; $249–$529 suite. Packages available. AE, DC, DISC, MC, V. Valet parking $8; limited free self-parking 2 blocks from hotel. **Amenities:** Restaurant (American); bar; heated outdoor pool; access to nearby health club; exercise room; Jacuzzi; bike rental; children's programs; concierge; business center; limited room service; baby-sitting; coin-op washers and dryers. *In room:* A/C, TV, dataport, fridge, coffeemaker, hair dryer, iron.

Monterey Inn *Value*   For the price, you can't find a better choice than this modest, wrought iron–trimmed motel overlooking the Matanzas Bay and close to the attractions and nightlife of the Old City. Three generations of the Six family have run this simple two-story motel, and they keep the 1960s building and grounds always clean and functional. Rooms are not especially spacious but they are comfortable.

16 Avenida Menendez (between Cuna and Hypolita Sts.), St. Augustine, FL 32084. ℂ **904/824-4482.** Fax 904/829-8854. www.themontereyinn.com. 59 units. $39–$99 double. AE, DC, DISC, MC, V. **Amenities:** Heated outdoor pool. *In room:* A/C, TV, dataport, hair dryer.

Radisson Ponce de León Golf & Conference Resort   Located 2½ miles north of the historic district, this 400-acre complex is a good choice for golfers, who can play a round on its Donald Ross–designed par-72 course before heading off to see the sights. Although it's been in business since Henry Flagler built a resort here in 1916, today's establishment is a modern motel. Rooms are in one- and two-story buildings spread out in a virtual forest of palms, magnolias, centuries-old live oaks, and clumps of sawgrass, with a large swimming pool in the center. The units all have balconies or patios. Minisuites are ideal for families, with trellises separating small sitting rooms from sleeping areas. The Fairway Grill, with its big window walls overlooking the golf course and the marshes beyond, offers breakfast, lunch, and dinner. On weekend evenings you can join conferences unwinding in the lounge for live entertainment in a cozy bar overlooking the greens. Other activities include a putting green; volleyball, shuffleboard, croquet, bocce ball, and basketball courts; and a horseshoe pitch.

4000 U.S. Hwy. 1 N., St. Augustine, FL 32095. ℂ **800/333-3333** or 904/824-2821. Fax 904/824-8254. 193 units. $99–$179 double. Golf, family, and other packages available. AE, DC, DISC, MC, V. **Amenities:** Restaurant (American); bar; heated outdoor pool; golf course; 6 lighted tennis courts; varied sports facilities; limited room service. *In room:* A/C, TV, dataport, coffeemaker, hair dryer, iron.

Bed & Breakfasts

St. Augustine has more than two dozen bed-and-breakfasts in restored historic homes. They all provide free parking, complimentary breakfast, and 24-hour refreshments, but most accept neither young children nor guests who smoke (check before booking). Those listed below are in the historic district. For more choices, contact **Historic Inns of St. Augustine,** P.O. Box 5268, St. Augustine, FL 33085-5268 (no phone; www.staugustineinns.com), for descriptions of its member properties.

Bayfront Westcott House on the Bay ★   Overlooking Matanzas Bay, this two-story, wood-frame house offers rare opportunities for an uncluttered view from the porch, the second-story verandah, and a shady courtyard. The rooms—some with bay windows, two-person whirlpool tubs, and working fireplaces—are exquisitely furnished and immaculate. Yours might have authentic Victorian furnishings and a brass bed made up with a white quilt and lace dust ruffle.

146 Avenida Menendez (between Bridge and Francis Sts.), St. Augustine, FL 32084. ☎ **904/824-4301.** Fax 904/824-4301. www.westcotthouse.com. 9 units (all with bathroom). $95–$235 double. Rates include full breakfast. AE, DISC, MC, V. *In room:* A/C, TV, hair dryer.

Carriage Way Bed and Breakfast *Value*   Primarily occupying an 1883 Victorian wood-frame house fronted by roses and hibiscus, Bill and Diane Johnson's bed-and-breakfast isn't fancy or formal, but it is comfortable and relaxed. Rooms are furnished with simple antique reproductions, including many four-poster beds. One room even retains its original fireplace. A console TV, books, magazines, and games are provided in a homey parlor. For more privacy, two more rooms are down the street in "The Cottage," a one-story clapboard house built in 1885. It has its own living room and kitchen, and both the Miranda and the Ashton rooms have clawfoot bathtubs. Miranda also sports a two-person Jacuzzi, and Ashton has its own small back porch.

70 Cuna St. (between Cordova and Spanish Sts.), St. Augustine, FL 32084. ☎ **800/908-9832** or 904/829-2467. Fax 904/826-1461. www.carriageway.com. 11 units (all with bathroom). $69–$175 double. Rates include full breakfast. AE, DISC, MC, V. **Amenities:** free use of bikes. *In room:* A/C, TV, dataport, hair dryer.

Casablanca Inn on the Bay   This 1914 Mediterranean-style white stucco house faces the bay, although only a few of the rooms actually offer views. The most stunning are the two second-floor suites whose bayfront balconies have generously sized hammocks and private porches. The furnishings—a mix of turn-of-the-century American oak, European, and Victorian pieces—are of a higher quality than those at many other inns. One modern convenience is a cassette player with a small selection of classical tapes. This may be appreciated, especially if you are on a ground-floor room that unfortunately suffers from the noise of the street and the next-door bar and grill. Breakfast can be enjoyed alfresco on the porch or in a glass-enclosed conservatory. Six units have neither TVs nor telephones.

24 Avenida Menendez (between Hypolita and Treasury Sts.), St. Augustine, FL 32084. ☎ **800/826-2626** or 904/829-0928. Fax 904/826-1892. www.casablancainn.com. 20 units (all with bathroom). $89–$225 double. Rates include full breakfast. AE, DISC, MC, V. **Amenities:** free use of bikes. *In room:* A/C, TV, dataport.

Kenwood Inn   Mark and Kerianne Constant's inn is unusual because of its relatively large outdoor space, which includes a swimming pool, a lushly landscaped sundeck, and a secluded garden courtyard (complete with a fish pond and neat flower bed under a sprawling pecan tree). Their Victorian wood-frame house with graceful verandahs has served as a boardinghouse or inn since the late 19th century. Everything from the carpeting to the linens to the china is first-class. Rooms are larger and more private than most other accommodations in converted single-family homes. Some rooms have neither televisions nor telephones.

38 Marine St. (at Bridge St.), St. Augustine, FL 32084. ℂ 800/824-8151 or 904/824-2116. Fax 904/824-1689. www.oldcity.com/kenwood. 14 units (all with bathroom). $85–$160 double; bridal suite $200. Rates include continental breakfast. DISC, MC, V. **Amenities:** Outdoor pool; free use of bikes. *In room:* A/C, TV, fax, dataport, kitchen, minibar, fridge, coffeemaker, hair dryer, iron.

Victorian House *(Kids* Ken and Marcia Cerotzke's bed-and-breakfast is unusual in that it occupies an 1897-vintage Victorian residence, complete with wraparound porch, and an adjoining old store, now dubbed the "Carriage House." The latter is divided into four suites, one of which has a kitchenette. It's also unusual in that children are welcome to stay in the Carriage House units, all of which have TVs and private entrances. Kids are not welcome to stay in the main house, whose rooms lack TVs. Country Victorian antiques adorn all units here, but none of the units has a telephone.

11 Cadiz St. (between Aviles and Charlotte Sts.), St. Augustine, FL 32084. ℂ 877/703-0432 or 904/824-5214. Fax 904/824-7990. www.victorianhouse-inn.com. 8 units (all with bathroom). $85–$160 double. Rates include full breakfast. AE, DISC, MC, V. *In room:* A/C, TV (4 units).

WHERE TO DINE

In a town with as much tourist traffic as St. Augustine, there are, of course, a fair number of "tourist trap" restaurants. But on the whole, the food in St. Augustine, even at the popular eateries, is fairly priced and of good quality.

The historic district has a branch of Tampa's famous **Columbia** restaurant, at 98 St. George St., at Hypolita Street (ℂ **904/824-3341**). Like the original (see "Where to Dine," in section 1 of chapter 11), this one sports Spanish architecture, including intricate tile work and courtyards with fountains.

A1A Ale Works ✹ SEAFOOD   You can't miss this two-story Victorian-style building on the waterfront opposite the Bridge of Lions. One of the city's most popular watering holes, the noisy downstairs bar offers nightly entertainment, which sometimes filters up into the restaurant. Despite the noise potential, the kitchen turns out a surpisingly good blend of Floribbean, Cuban, Caribbean, and Latino styles, in a nice setting with big windows and outside balcony seating overlooking the river. Most of the seafood is very fresh, and the sauces are made to order. Especially good is the seared, sushi-quality yellowfin tuna either sesame-coated or rubbed with herbs. Don't overlook the nightly specials, especially fresh fish. The house brew ranges from a very light lager to a nonalcoholic root beer.

1 King St. (at Avenida Menedez) ℂ **904/829-2977.** Reservations not accepted, but call for preferred seating. Main courses $11.50–$20; sandwiches $7–$8.50. AE, DC, DISC, MC, V. Sun–Thur 11am–10:30pm; Fri–Sat 11am–11pm. Late-night menu served downstairs.

The Bunnery Bakery & Café ✹*Value* BAKERY/DELI   Alluring aromas waft from this bakery and cafe in the heart of the historic district. It's lovely to come here for breakfast before you start your rounds, or for a fresh pastry and hot cup of latte, cappuccino, or espresso anytime you need a break from sightseeing. At lunch, plop yourself into one of the colorful booths and indulge in soup, salads, burgers, panini, or a croissant stuffed with walnut-and-pineapple chicken salad. Order at the counter; the staff will call your number when it's ready.

121 St. George St. (between Treasury and Hypolita Sts.). ℂ **904/829-6166.** Reservations not accepted. Breakfast $3–$6; sandwiches and salads $3.50–$6.50. No credit cards. Daily 8am–6pm.

Gypsy Cab Co. *(Value)* NEW AMERICAN   Billing itself as a temple of "urban cuisine," owner-chef Ned Pollack's high-energy establishment, with gaudy purple neon stripes outside and bright, art-filled dining rooms inside, offers the town's most interesting culinary experience. Ned's creative menu changes daily, although a hearty black-bean soup is a constant winner. I had expertly cooked shrimp with artichokes sautéed with scallions, mushrooms, and julienned carrots and served with a pleasantly peppered white wine and butter sauce—a delightful combination of flavors. Grouper in a tomato basil sauce, strip steak under a peppercorn sauce, and Cayman Island–style pork were among the other offerings. The house salad dressing is so good they sell it by the bottle. Also worshipped here during autumn: Beaujolais nouveau, by the glass or bottle. Lunch is served in the Gypsy Bar & Grill next door, where you can also find live entertainment from Wednesday to Saturday evenings.

828 Anastasia Blvd. (Fla. A1A, at Ingram St., east of Bridge of Lions). ✆ 904/824-8244. Reservations not accepted. Main courses $10–$17; earlybird specials $9. AE, DC, DISC, MC, V. Mon–Thurs 11am–4pm and 4:30–10pm; Fri 11am–4pm and 4:30–11pm; Sat 11am–3pm and 4:30–11pm; Sun 10:30am–3pm and 4:30–10pm. Early bird specials daily 4:30–7pm.

La Parisienne *(★★)* CONTEMPORARY FRENCH   Evoking the French countryside, the lovely dining room has a rough-hewn beamed pine ceiling, lace-curtained windows, and ladder-back chairs. Changing seasonally, the menu always features fresh local seafood, and in fall you'll see venison and quail. If it's offered, begin with escargot in puff pastry with a garlic cream sauce; then go on to steak au poivre with a Cognac cream sauce, roast rack of lamb Provençal, or the day's treatment of fresh local fish. The lunch menu offers bistro fare, such as quiche Lorraine, croque monsieur, and salad niçoise.

60 Hypolita St. (between Spanish and Cordova Sts.). ✆ 904/829-0055. Reservations recommended. Main courses $24–$33. AE, DISC, MC, V. Thurs–Tues 11am–3pm; Thurs–Sun 5–9pm.

Raintree *(★)* INTERNATIONAL   Even if you don't have a full meal at this romantic 1879 Victorian house (about half a mile north of the historic district), the tempting variety of hot crêpes and an exemplary crème brûlée is worth a visit. Sweetness works its way onto the main menu, too, starting with fruit salsa with the blue-crab cake appetizer and progressing to the likes of cashew-encrusted pork tenderloin mignonettes with a champagne and frothed blackberry butter sauce. More-traditional main courses include beef Wellington and rack of New Zealand lamb. It's all very good, though not as exciting as at Gypsy Cab Co. or as expertly prepared as at La Parisienne (see above). The list of more than 300 vintages has won *Wine Spectator* awards.

102 San Marco Ave. (at Bernard St.). ✆ 904/824-7211. Reservations recommended. Main courses $12–$23; dessert bar $5.50. AE, MC, V. June–Sept Sun–Thurs 6–9:30pm; Fri–Sat 6–10pm. Rest of year Sun–Thurs 5–9:30pm; Fri–Sat 5–10pm. Courtesy car provides transportation from/to downtown hotels.

The Spanish Bakery COLONIAL   Occupying a reconstructed 17th-century kitchen building, this little family-operated establishment bakes almond, lemon, and cinnamon cookies, using recipes from the Spanish colonial period, when a lack of refrigeration limited the use of milk and eggs. A couple of these crunchy morsels, eaten at the picnic tables outside, make a fine snack while you're touring the historic district. Or you can have lunch here, choosing from daily specials such as spicy Spanish-style chili over rice.

Rear of 42½ St. George St. (between Cuna and Orange Sts.). ✆ 904/471-3046. Reservations not accepted. Lunch specials $4; cookies and rolls 40¢–50¢ each. No credit cards. Daily 9:30am–3pm. Closed Thanksgiving and Christmas.

ST. AUGUSTINE AFTER DARK

Especially on weekends, the Old Town is full of strollers and partyers making the rounds to the dozens of active bars, clubs, and restaurants. For up-to-date details on what's happening in town, check the local daily, the *St. Augustine Record* (www.staugustine.com), or the irreverent *Folio Weekly* (www.folioweekly.com).

Ann O'Malley's, 23 Orange St., near the Old City Gate (© **904/825-4040**), is the quintessential Irish pub open day and night until 1am. Besides the selection of ales, stouts, and drafts, this is one of the only spots in town where you can grab a late-night bite.

The best-looking crowd in town can be found at the **A1A Ale Works** (see "Where to Dine," above), which has live music in the downstairs bar. Twenty-something hipsters and middle-age partyers mingle at this handsome New Orleans–style microbrewery and restaurant. Thursday through Saturday nights downstairs on a crowded window-front stage, you'll find live music, often light rock and R & B tunes.

Popular with locals, **Mill Top Tavern,** 19½ St. George St., at the Fort (© **904/829-2329**), is a warm and rustic tavern housed in a 19th-century mill building (the waterwheel is still outside). Weather permitting, it's an open-air space. There's music every day from 1pm until 1am.

One of St. Augustine's most famous nighttime hangouts is **Scarlett O'Hara's** at 70 Hypolita St., at Cordova Street (© **904/824-6535**). A catacomb of cozy rooms with working fireplaces in a rambling, 19th-century wood-frame house is the setting for live rock, jazz, and R & B bands nightly from 9:30pm. Sporting events are aired on a large-screen TV in a tropically themed oyster bar. Park in a lot across Cordova Street.

4 Jacksonville

36 miles S. of Georgia, 134 miles NE of Orlando, 340 miles N. of Miami

Once infamous for its smelly paper mills, the sprawling metropolis of Jacksonville—residents call it "Jax," from its airport abbreviation—is now one of the South's insurance and banking capitals. Development is rampant throughout Duval County, with hotels, restaurants, attractions, and clubs rapidly springing up, especially in suburban areas near the interstate highways. Nevertheless, there are shady older neighborhoods to explore, 20 miles of Atlantic Ocean beaches upon which to sun and swim, many championship golf courses to play, and an abundance of beautiful and historic national and state parks to roam.

Spanning the broad, curving St. Johns River, downtown Jacksonville is a vibrant center of activity during weekdays and on weekend afternoons and evenings, when many locals return to the restaurants and bars of the Jacksonville Landing and Southbank Riverwalk, two dining-and-entertainment complexes facing each other across the river. Like Baltimore's Inner Harbor, the two centers have helped to revitalize downtown.

Although Jacksonville claims to be the capital of Florida's historic "First Coast," the city dates its beginnings from an early-1800s settlement named Cowford, because cattle crossed the St. Johns River here. Cowford changed its name to Jacksonville in 1822 to honor General Andrew Jackson, the provisional governor who forced Spain to cede Florida to the United States 2 years earlier.

ESSENTIALS

GETTING THERE   Jacksonville International Airport, on the city's north side about 12 miles from downtown, is served by **Air South** (© 800/247-7688),

AirTran (© 800/AIR-TRAN), **Air Transat** (© 800/470-1011), **American** (© 800/433-7300), **Continental** (© 800/525-0280), **Delta** (© 800/ 221-1212), **Midway** (© 800/446-4392), **Northwest** (© 800/225-2525), **Southwest** (© 800/435-9792), **TWA** (© 800/221-2000), **United** (© 800/ 241-6522), and **Metro Jet** and **US Airways** (© 800/428-4322).

You can get visitor information about Jacksonville, St. Augustine, and Amelia Island at the **First Coast Welcome Center,** on the lower level by the baggage area (© **904/741-4902**). Open daily from 9am to 10pm.

Alamo (© 800/327-9633), **Avis** (© 800/331-1212), **Budget** (© 800/ 527-0700), **Dollar** (© 800/800-4000), **Enterprise** (© 800/325-8007), **Hertz** (© 800/654-3131), and **National** (© 800/CAR-RENT) have rental-car booths at the airport.

Gator City Taxi (© **904/741-0008** at the airport or 904/355-TAXI elsewhere) provides cab service. Fares for up to four persons are about $20 to downtown, $38 to $45 to beach hotels, $55 to $65 to St. Augustine, and $40 to Amelia Island. **Express Shuttle** (© **904/353-8880**) provides van service to and from hotels and resorts throughout the area. Per-person fares are $16.50 to downtown Jacksonville, $21.50 to $26.50 to the beaches, $56.50 to $66.50 to St. Augustine, and $31.50 to Amelia Island.

There's an **Amtrak** station in Jacksonville at 3570 Clifford Lane, off U.S. 1, just north of 45th Street (© **800/USA-RAIL**).

VISITOR INFORMATION Contact the **Jacksonville and the Beaches Convention & Visitors Bureau,** 201 E. Adams St., Jacksonville, FL 32202 (© **800/733-2668** or 904/798-9111; fax 904/789-9103; www.jaxcvb.com), for maps, brochures, calendars, and advice. The bureau is open Monday to Friday from 8am to 5pm. There are information booths at the airport (see above) and in the upstairs food court of **Jacksonville Landing** (see "Exploring the Area," below). The latter is open Monday to Saturday from 10am to 8pm, Sunday 12:30 to 5:30pm.

GETTING AROUND You can get around downtown Jacksonville via the **Skyway,** an elevated and completely automated train that runs down Hogan Street from the Florida Community College Jacksonville campus through downtown and across the river via the Acosta/Fla. 13 bridge to the Southbank Riverwalk. The Skyway operates Monday to Friday from 6am to 11pm, Saturday from 10am to 1pm, Sunday only for special events. Skyway rides cost 35¢. **The Trolley** connects with the Skyway and runs east-west through downtown. It's free and operates Monday to Friday from 6:30 am to 7pm. Get maps and schedules from the convention and visitors bureau or at the visitor information booth at Jacksonville Landing (see above). Both are operated by the **Jacksonville Transportation Authority** (© **904/630-3100;** www.ridejta.net), which also provides local bus service.

Otherwise, you're better off having a car if you want to explore this vast area. You can hail a **taxi** downtown if you spot one, although it is usually best to call **Gator City Taxi** (© **904/355-8294**) or **Yellow Cab** (© **904/260-1111**) for a pickup. Fares are $1.25 when the flag drops, and 25¢ for each ⅕ mile thereafter.

Out at the beaches, the **St. Johns River Ferry** (© **904/241-9969**) shuttles vehicles across the river between Mayport, an Old Florida fishing village on the south side, and Fort George on the north shore. The boats depart Mayport on the hour and the half-hour Monday to Friday from 6am to 10pm, weekends from 6:20am to 10pm. One-way fare is $2.75 per vehicle. Even if you have to wait 30 minutes for the next ferry, the 5-minute ride greatly shortens the trip between the Jacksonville beaches and Amelia Island. I always stop for lunch at Singleton's Seafood Shack in Mayport (see "Where to Dine," later in this chapter).

EXPLORING THE AREA

Cummer Museum of Art & Gardens ★★ Built on the grounds of a private Tudor mansion, this modestly sized but outstanding museum is worth a visit for anyone who appreciates the visual arts. The permanent collection encompasses works from 2000 B.C. to the present. It's especially rich in American impressionist paintings and includes an impressive collection of 18th-century porcelain and 18th-century and early-19th-century Japanese Netsuke ivory carvings. Don't miss the stunning Italian and English gardens set on the scenic St. Johns River. Call to see what special exhibits are on tap.

829 Riverside Ave. (between Post and Fisk Sts.). ✆ 904/356-6857. www.cummer.org. Admission $6 adults, $4 seniors over 65 and military, $3 students, $1 children under 5; free Tues after 4pm. Tues and Thurs 10am–9pm; Wed and Fri–Sat 10am–5pm; Sun noon–5pm.

The Jacksonville Landing Resembling New York City's South Street Seaport, Boston's Faneuil Hall, and Baltimore's Inner Harbor, this glass-and-steel complex on the north bank of the river serves as the focus of downtown activity. There are more than 65 stores here, but shopping is secondary to dining and entertainment. You can choose from about half a dozen full-service restaurants, plus an inexpensive food court with indoor and outdoor seating overlooking the river. The Landing is the scene of numerous special events, ranging from arts festivals to baseball-card shows, and outdoor rock, blues, country, and jazz concerts. Call to find out what's going on during your stay.

2 Independent Dr. (between Main and Pearl Sts.), on the St. Johns River. ✆ 904/353-1188. www. jacksonvillelanding.com. Free admission. Mon–Thurs 10am–8pm; Fri–Sat 10am–9pm; Sun noon–5:30pm; bars and restaurants open later. Parking $4.80 maximum daily charge. From I-95, take Exit 107 downtown to Main St., go over the Blue Bridge, and turn left at Bay St. Then go 2 blocks and make a left on Laura St., which dead ends at the Landing. Park on east side of complex.

Jacksonville Zoo ★ *Kids* Between downtown and the airport, this environmentally sensitive zoo is well on its way to becoming one of the country's best. Mostly natural-habitat, the main exhibits feature an extensive and growing collection of African wildlife including lions, impalas, ostriches, rhinos, elephants, antelopes, Nile crocodiles, cheetahs, Kirk's dik-diks, monkeys, and western lowland gorillas. You'll enter the 73-acre park through the authentic thatched roof built in 1995 by 24 Zulu craftsmen. Whether you go on foot or by tram, allow at least 2 hours to tour this vast and lush zoo. When you arrive, ask about current animal shows and special events. Strollers and wheelchairs are available for rent.

8605 Zoo Pkwy. ✆ 904/757-4462 or 904/757-4463. www.jaxzoo.org. Admission $8 adults, $6.50 seniors, $5 children 3–12, free for children under 3. Daily 9am–5pm. Closed Thanksgiving and Christmas. Take I-95 north to Hecksher Dr. (Exit 124A) and follow the signs.

Ritz Theatre & LaVilla Museum From 1921 to 1971, the Ritz Theatre was the center of cultural life in LaVilla, an African-American neighborhood so vibrant that it was known as the Harlem of the South. Many entertainers played the Ritz before moving on to the Apollo Theater in the real Harlem. Most of LaVilla's small, clapboard "shotgun" houses (so called because you could fire a shotgun through the central hallway and not hit anything) have been torn down in anticipation of urban renewal, but the Ritz has been rebuilt and is once again a center of the city's cultural life. Only the northwest corner of the building, including the Ritz sign, is original, but the new 426-seat theater captures the spirit of vaudevillian times. Off the lobby, LaVilla Museum recounts local African-American history and exhibits the works of black artists. Plans call for three nearby shotgun houses to be part of the museum. There's a cafe across the street.

829 N. Davis St. (between State and Union Sts.). © 904/632-5555. Admission $4 adults, $2 seniors and children 18 and under. Tues–Fri 10am–6pm; Sat 10am–2pm; Sun 2–5pm.

Southbank Riverwalk Bordering the St. Johns River directly opposite the Jacksonville Landing (see above), this 1.2-mile wooden zigzag boardwalk is usually filled with joggers, tourists, folks sitting on benches, and lovers walking hand-in-hand, all of them watching the riverboats, the shorebirds, and downtown's skyline reflected on the water. At 200 feet in diameter, the **Friendship Fountain** near the west end is the nation's largest self-contained fountain; it's especially beautiful at night when illuminated by 265 colored lights. Farther along, you'll pass military memorials, a small museum dedicated to the city's history, and the **Museum of Science & History of Jacksonville,** at Museum Circle and San Marco Boulevard (© **904/396-7062**). The latter is an interactive children's museum focusing on science and the history of Northeast Florida. Admission is $6 adults, $4.50 seniors, $4 children 3 to 12, free for children under 3. Open Monday to Friday 10am to 5pm, Saturday 10am to 6pm, Sunday 1 to 6pm. The Riverwalk is the scene of seafood fests, parties, parades, and arts-and-crafts festivals.

On the south bank of the St. Johns River, flanking Main St. Bridge between San Marco Blvd. and Ferry St. © 904/396-4900. Take I-95 north to Prudential Dr. exit, make a right, and follow signs.

AN UNUSUAL BREED OF NATIONAL PARK
Named after the American Indians who inhabited Central and North Florida some 1,000 years before European settlers arrived, the **Timucuan Ecological and Historic Preserve** offers visitors an opportunity to explore untouched wilderness, historical buildings, and informative exhibits on the area's natural history. Unusual for a national park, this 46,000-acre preserve hasn't been hacked off from the rest of the community and drawn within arbitrary boundaries. The result is a vast, intriguing system of sites joined by rural roads alongside tumble-down fish camps, trailer parks, strip malls, condominiums, and stately old homes.

Admission to all park facilities is free (donations accepted). For more information, contact **The Timucuan Ecological & Historic Preserve,** 13165 Mt. Pleasant Rd., Jacksonville, FL 32225 (© **904/221-5568;** www.nps.gov/timu).

SOUTH OF THE RIVER
The preserve's prime attractions are 14 miles northeast of downtown on the south bank of the St. Johns River. Your starting point is the **Fort Caroline National Memorial** , 12713 Ft. Caroline Rd. (© **904/641-7155**), which serves as the preserve's visitor center. This was the site of the 16th-century French Huguenot settlement that was wiped out by the Spanish who landed at St. Augustine. This two-thirds–size replica shows you what the original was like. You can see archaeological artifacts and two very well produced half-hour videos highlighting the area.

The fort sits at the northwestern edge of the 600-acre **Theodore Roosevelt Area,** a beautiful woodland and marshland rich in history and undisturbed since the Civil War. On a 2-mile hike along a centuries-old park trail, you'll see a wide variety of birds, wildflowers, and maritime hammock forest. Bring binoculars if you have them, since such birds as the endangered wood stork, great and snowy egrets, ospreys, hawks, and painted buntings make their home here in spring and summer. On the ground, you might catch sight of a gray fox or raccoon. You may also want to bring a blanket and picnic basket to spread out under the ancient oak trees that shade the banks of the wide and winding St. Johns River. After the trail crosses Hammock Creek, you're in ancient Timucuan country, where their ancestors lived as far back as 500 B.C. Farther along is the site of a cabin in the wilderness that belonged to the reclusive brothers Willie and Saxon Browne, who lived without the modern conveniences of indoor plumbing or electricity until the last brother's death in 1960.

If you're here on a weekend, take the fascinating 1½-hour guided tours of the fort and Theodore Roosevelt Area, offered every Saturday and Sunday at 1pm (when weather and staffing permit). Call the fort for details and schedules.

The fort is open daily from 9am to 5pm except Christmas. The Roosevelt Area is open daily from 7am to 5pm during eastern standard time, daily from 7am to 8pm during daylight savings time. Closed Christmas.

The **Ribault Monument,** on St. Johns Bluff about a half-mile east of the fort, was erected in 1924 to commemorate the arrival in 1562 of French Huguenot Jean Ribault, who died defending Fort Caroline from the Spanish. It's worth a stop for the dramatic view of the area.

To get here from downtown, take Atlantic Boulevard (Fla. 10) east, make a left on Monument Road, and turn right on Fort Caroline Road; the Theodore Roosevelt Area is entered from Mt. Pleasant Road, about 1 mile southeast of the fort; look for the trailhead parking sign, and follow the narrow dirt road to the parking lot.

NORTH OF THE RIVER

On the north side of the river, history buffs also will appreciate the **Zephaniah Kingsley Plantation** (★, at 11676 Palmetto Ave. on Fort George Island (© **904/ 251-3537**). A winding 2½-mile dirt road runs under a canopy of dense foliage to the remains of this 19th-century plantation owned from 1817 to 1829 by Zephaniah Kingsley, a white man who held some seemingly contradictory views on race. Although he owned more than 200 slaves, he believed that "the coloured race were superior to us, physically and morally." He married a Senegalese woman—one of his former slaves—and in 1837 moved his family to what is now the Dominican Republic to escape what he called the "spirit of intolerant injustice" at home. The National Park Service maintains the well-preserved two-story clapboard residence, kitchen house, barn/carriage house, and remnants of 23 slave cabins built of "tabby mortar"—oyster shell and sand. Exhibits in the main house and kitchen focus on slavery as it existed in the rice-growing areas of Northern Florida, Georgia, and South Carolina. You can see it all on your own, but 40-minute ranger-guided tours are the best way. They usually are given at 1pm Monday to Friday, 1 and 3pm on weekends, but call to confirm. Allot some extra time to explore the grounds. A well-stocked book and gift shop will keep you even longer. The plantation is open daily from 9am to 5pm except Christmas.

To get here from I-95, take Heckscher Drive (Fla. 105) east and follow the signs. From Fort Caroline, take Fla. 9A north over the St. Johns River to Heckscher Drive east. The plantation is about 12 miles east of Fla. 9A, on the left. From the beaches, take Fla. A1A to the St. Johns River Ferry, ride it from Mayport to Fort George; the road is half a mile east of the ferry landing.

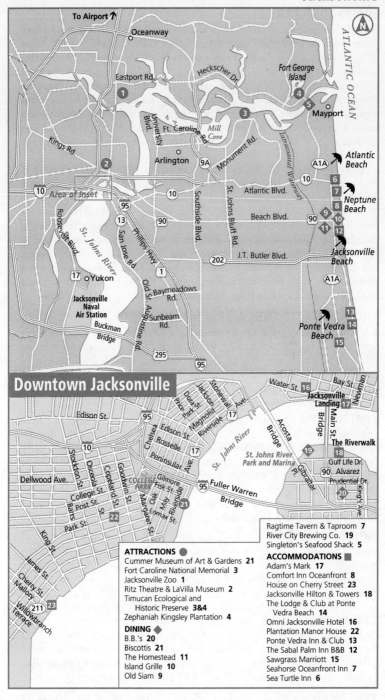

Jacksonville

To Airport ↑

Oceanway

Eastport Rd.

Heckscher Dr.

Fort George
Island

4

Mayport **5**

University Blvd.

Ft. Caroline Rd.

Mill Cove

3

ATLANTIC OCEAN

Kings Rd.

2

Arlington

9A

Monument Rd.

A1A

Atlantic
Beach

10 Area of Inset

10

10

6

7

Atlantic Blvd.

St. Johns Bluff Rd.

Neptune
Beach

8

9

10

Beach Blvd.

90

11

12

95

13

San Jose Rd.

Southside Blvd.

90

J.T. Butler Blvd.

202

Jacksonville
Beach

St. Johns River

Roosevelt Blvd.

Phillips Hwy.

17 Yukon

Old St. Augustine Rd.

Baymeadows Rd.

A1A

Jacksonville
Naval
Air Station

Buckman
Bridge

Sunbeam Rd.

13

14

Ponte Vedra
Beach

295

95

15

Downtown Jacksonville

Edison St.

95

Stonewall
Ave.

Water St. **16**

Bay St.

Newman

Jacksonville
Landing **17**

Dora St.

Jackson

Brick
Park

Magnolia

Riverside

17

Acosta
Bridge

Main St.

Chelsea

Edison St.

St. Johns River

10

Rosselle

17

Peninsular

St. Johns River
Park and Marina

19

Gibraltar
Pl.

The Riverwalk
18

Gulf Life Dr.

Dellwood Ave.

Osceola

Stockton St.

Goodwin St.

Copeland St.

Gilmore

Fisk St.

Mill

Oak

Riverside

95

Fuller Warren
Bridge

90 Alvarez

Prudential Dr.

20

College St.

Barrs St.

Post St.

Margaret St.

Comax St.

21

King's Ave.

Park St.

22

King St.

James St.

Cherry St.

Mallory

211

23

Willowbranch
Terrace

ATTRACTIONS ●
Cummer Museum of Art & Gardens **21**
Fort Caroline National Memorial **3**
Jacksonville Zoo **1**
Ritz Theatre & LaVilla Museum **2**
Timucan Ecological and
      Historic Preserve **3&4**
Zephaniah Kingsley Plantation **4**

DINING ◆
B.B.'s **20**
Biscottis **21**
The Homestead **11**
Island Grille **10**
Old Siam **9**

Ragtime Tavern & Taproom **7**
River City Brewing Co. **19**
Singleton's Seafood Shack **5**

ACCOMMODATIONS ■
Adam's Mark **17**
Comfort Inn Oceanfront **8**
House on Cherry Street **23**
Jacksonville Hilton & Towers **18**
The Lodge & Club at Ponte
      Vedra Beach **14**
Omni Jacksonville Hotel **16**
Plantation Manor House **22**
Ponte Vedra Inn & Club **13**
The Sabal Palm Inn B&B **12**
Sawgrass Marriott **15**
Seahorse Oceanfront Inn **7**
Sea Turtle Inn **6**

HITTING THE BEACH

You can fish, swim, snorkel, sail, sunbathe, or stroll on the sand dunes (at least from March to November, since winter can get downright chilly here). All of these activities are just a 20- to 30-minute drive east of downtown at Jacksonville's four beach communities.

Atlantic Boulevard (Fla. 10) will take you to **Atlantic Beach** and **Neptune Beach.** The boulevard divides the two towns, and where it meets the ocean you'll come to **Town Center,** a quaint community with a number of shops, restaurants, pubs, the Sea Horse Oceanfront Inn, and the Sea Turtle Inn (see "Where to Stay," below). You won't need your car to hit the beach, shop, dine, or imbibe here.

Beach Boulevard (U.S. 90) dead-ends at **Jacksonville Beach,** where'll you find beach concessions, rental shops, and a fishing pier. This is also the most popular local surfing beach.

To the south, the freeway-grade J. Turner Butler Boulevard (Fla. 202) leads from I-95 to the boundary between Jacksonville Beach and Ponte Verde Beach. A right turn there will take you to **Ponte Vedra Beach** (pronounced here as Ponti *Vee*-dra). This ritzy, golf-oriented enclave actually is in St. Johns County (St. Augustine), but it's so much closer to Jacksonville that I've included it in this chapter. Here you'll find the Sawgrass Marriott, the Ponte Vedra Inn & Club, and The Lodge & Club at Ponte Vedra Beach (see "Where to Stay," below).

OUTDOOR ACTIVITIES & SPECTATOR SPORTS

CRUISES   Jacksonville River Cruises (© 800/711-3470 or 904/396-2333; www.rivercruise.com) operates sightseeing, dinner, and dancing cruises on the stern-wheel paddleboats *The Lady St. Johns* and *The Annabelle Lee.* They usually dock at East Coast Line Drive at the foot of Liberty Street, on the north shore of the river. Prices range from $20 to $40, and schedules vary greatly by season, so call or check the website.

FISHING   The least-expensive way to fish for red snapper, grouper, sea bass, small sharks, amberjack, and more, 15 to 30 miles offshore in the Atlantic Ocean, is aboard the *King Neptune,* a 65-foot air-conditioned deep-sea party boat. The full-day trips depart at 8am daily from Monty's Marina, 4378 Ocean St. (Fla. A1A), half a mile south of the Mayport Ferry landing (© **904/ 246-7575**), and return at 5pm. The Monday-to-Thursday price is $40 for adults, $35 for seniors, $30 for children 6 to 12, including all bait and tackle. Add $10 on weekends. You don't need a license, but reservations are required.

GOLF   The Jacksonville area offers a great variety of golf courses, some of which are ranked among the top in the country. In Ponte Vedra Beach, the Sawgrass Marriott Resort sits on the most famous course, the **TPC at Sawgrass** ★★★, home of The Players championship in March. Ranked among the nation's top courses, its island hole is one of the most photographed in the world. Nearby are the Ocean and Lagoon courses at the Ponte Vedra Inn & Club. See "Where to Stay," below, for information about the resorts.

Top courses open to the public include the semiprivate **Cimarrone,** at 2690 Cimarrone Blvd. (© **904/287-2000**), a fast and watery course with affordable greens fees ranging from $30 to $50; and the public **Golf Club of Jacksonville,** at 10440 Tournament Lane (© **904/779-0800**), which is managed by the PGA Tour. It's a great bargain, with rates ranging from $30 to $40.

On your way out to the beach, the semiprivate **Windsor Parke Golf Club,** at 4747 Hodges Blvd., at Turner Butler Boulevard (© **904/223-GOLF**), is one of the most challenging and scenic courses in Jacksonville. Designed by Arthur Hill, the 6,740 yards of green are surrounded by towering pines and lots of water. Fees are usually less than $45 and include a cart, even on the weekends. Nonmembers should call 4 or 5 days in advance for tee times.

Be on the lookout for the free *Golfer's Guide* in visitor centers and hotel lobbies (see "The Active Vacation Planner," in chapter 2, for information about ordering copies).

HORSEBACK RIDING   For a scenic ride along the sand and dunes, call **Sawgrass Stables,** 23900 Marsh Landing Pkwy., off Fla. A1A in Ponte Vedra Beach (✆ **904/285-3791**). Call for rates and reservations. Lessons are also available.

SPECTATOR SPORTS   The 73,000-seat **Alltel Municipal Stadium,** 1 Stadium Place, at East Duval and Haines streets (✆ **904/630-3901** for information, or 904/353-3309 to charge tickets), hosts the annual Florida-Georgia football game every October, and other college football games September to December; it also hosts motor-sports events and the National Football League's **Jacksonville Jaguars** (✆ **800/618-8005** or 904/633-2000 for ticket information; www.jaguars.com). One of the stadium's biggest draws is the **Toyota Gator Bowl,** usually on New Year's Day (see "Florida Calendar of Events," in chapter 2).

Adjacent to the stadium, and under the same auspices, is the 10,600-seat **Jacksonville Veterans Memorial Coliseum,** 1145 E. Adams St. (✆ **904/630-3900** for information, or 904/353-3309 to charge tickets), home of the **Jacksonville Lizard Kings** East Coast Hockey team (✆ **904/358-7825;** www.lizardkings.com), and a venue for NHL exhibition games, college basketball games, ice-skating exhibitions, wrestling matches, and various family shows.

Jax has yet to get a big-league baseball team, but you can see the **Jacksonville Suns,** a Detroit Tigers affiliate, play their Class AA minor-league games from April through August at Wolfson Park, 1201 E. Duval St. (✆ **904/358-2842;** www.jaxsuns.com).

TENNIS   Adults and juniors can sign up for tennis camps at **ATP Tour International Headquarters,** 200 ATP Tour Blvd., Ponte Vedra Beach, FL 23082 (✆ **800/963-2444** or 904/285-6400; fax 904/285-2284; www.atptour.com), where top professional tennis players come to hone their games. The center has 19 courts, including hard, clay, and grass surfaces. Call or write for information about the camps and special tennis packages.

SHOPPING & BROWSING

Jacksonville has plenty of shopping opportunities, including an upscale mall, **The Avenues Mall,** south of town at 10300 Southside Blvd., as well as a number of flea markets, including the **Beach Boulevard Flea and Farmer's Market,** on Beach Boulevard (Fla. 90; ✆ **904/645-5961**). More than 600 vendors show up daily from 9am to 5pm to sell their wares in a partially covered facility.

San Marco Square, at San Marco and Atlantic boulevards, south of the river, is a quaint shopping district in the middle of a stunning residential area. Shops in meticulously refashioned Mediterranean-revival buildings sell antiques and home furnishings, as well as clothing, books, and records.

Another worthwhile neighborhood to explore is the **Avondale/Riverside** historic district southwest of downtown on St. Johns Avenue between Talbot Avenue and Boone Park, on the north bank of the river. More than 60 boutiques, antiques stores, art galleries, and cafes line the wide, tree-lined avenue.

Nearby, the younger set hangs out at **Five Points,** on Park Street, where used-record stores, vintage clothiers, coffee shops, and funky art galleries stay open late.

Like St. Augustine, Jacksonville is a mecca for chocoholics, particularly **Peterbrooke Chocolatier Production Center,** 1470 San Marco Blvd., on San Marco Square (© **904/398-4812**). If you've never tried chocolate-covered popcorn or pretzels, this is the place. Open Monday to Friday from 10am to 5pm. Peterbrooke also has a retail shop on St. Johns Avenue in Avondale.

WHERE TO STAY

I've arranged the accommodations listed below geographically, in and around downtown first, followed by the beach scene. The suburbs have dozens more to choose from, especially along I-95. Many are clustered south of downtown in the **Southpoint** (Exit 101, Turner Butler Boulevard/Fla. 202) and **Baymeadows** (Exit 101, Baymeadows Road/Fla. 152) areas. These locales have a multitude of chain restaurants, and you can hop on the highways and zoom to the beach or downtown—although you aren't really at either one if you stay out here. Tops is the **Jacksonville Marriott at Southpoint,** 4670 Salisbury Rd. (© **800/228-9290** or 904/296-2222), among the area's best all-around hotels.

Note that rates in the downtown hotels are higher midweek when rooms are in demand by business travelers. Beach accommodations are somewhat less expensive in the cold months from December through March.

IN JACKSONVILLE

Prudential Drive in the Southbank Riverwalk area is home to the **Radisson Riverwalk Hotel** (© **800/333-3333** or 904/396-5100), the **Hampton Inn Central** (© **800/HAMPTON** or 904/396-7770), and the all-suites **Extended Stay American Downtown** (© **800/EXT-STAY** or 904/396-1777; www.extendedstay.com).

Adam's Mark Jacksonville ★★ This 18-story hotel opened its doors in 2001 on a choice location a block east of Jacksonville Landing. This definitely is a convention hotel, with a whopping 110,000 square feet of meeting space, a showy lobby, two big restaurants, and a sports bar, all opening to a riverside promenade. Most of the guest rooms are rather small; in fact, those with two double beds have room for little else, so opt for a king-bed room or a suite. Although none has a balcony, about half have sliding glass doors (be careful!). The swimming pool is on the rooftop, where a tiki bar serves refreshments in summertime.

225 Coastline Dr., Jacksonville, FL 32202. © 800/444-ADAM or 904/633-9095. Fax 904/633-9988. www.adamsmark.com. 966 units. $189–$264. AE, DC, DISC, MC, V. **Amenities:** 2 restaurants (Italian/American); 4 bars; heated outdoor pool; exercise room; Jacuzzi; sauna; concierge; activities desk; business center; limited room service; laundry service; concierge-level rooms. *In room:* A/C, TV, dataport, coffeemaker, hair dryer, iron.

Hilton Jacksonville Riverfront ★ On the Southbank Riverwalk, this 10-story tower is famous for its Elvis Presley Suite, where "the King" purportedly stayed half a dozen times between 1955 and 1976 when this establishment was known as the Jacksonville Hotel. If you can afford its $300-a-night price tag, you will see some of Elvis's million-seller gold records mounted on the walls and can watch some of his movies on the suite's two VCRs. It and the other units have dark wood furniture and smallish marble-tiled bathrooms. Riverfront rooms have balconies (those on the west end catch traffic noise from the Main Street Bridge below). A branch of Ruth's Chris Steakhouse offers extraordinarily tender beef.

1201 Riverplace Blvd. (at Main St. on Southbank Riverwalk), Jacksonville, FL 32207. © 800/HILTONS or 904/398-8800. Fax 904/398-9170. www.jacksonvillehilton.com. 292 units. $99–$180 double. AE, DC, DISC, MC, V. Valet parking $8 Sun–Thurs, $3 Fri–Sat; self-parking $6. **Amenities:** 2 restaurants (American); 2 bars;

heated outdoor pool; exercise room; Jacuzzi; concierge; business center; limited room service; laundry service; concierge-level rooms. *In room:* A/C, TV, dataport, coffeemaker, hair dryer, iron.

The House on Cherry Street ☆   This colonial-style, wood-frame house, on the St. Johns River in the Riverside neighborhood, is ideal for a romantic B&B vacation. French doors open to a delightful screened-in back porch furnished with rocking chairs; it overlooks an expanse of tree-shaded lawn (where guests play croquet) leading to the river (where they play with kayaks and canoes). You might select the Rose or the Duck room, both with canopied four-poster beds and river views. Ducks are rather a theme here, with hundreds of antique decoys on display. All accommodations offer adjacent sitting rooms and ceiling fans and are supplied with fresh flowers, books, and magazines. Genial owners/hosts Carol and Merrill Anderson provide complimentary wine and hors d'oeuvres daily at 6pm on the patio or in the dining room. An upstairs refrigerator is stocked with free soft drinks and beer. No smoking is permitted inside.

1844 Cherry St. (on the St. Johns River), Jacksonville, FL 32205. © **904/384-1999.** Fax 904/384-5013. houseoncherry@compuserve.com. 4 units (all with bathroom). $85–$115 double. Rates include full breakfast. AE, MC, V. No small children accepted. **Amenities:** Free use of bikes. *In room:* A/C, TV, hair dryer; no phone.

Omni Jacksonville Hotel ☆   Located directly across the street from the Times Union Center for the Performing Arts (see "Jacksonville After Dark," later in this chapter) and a block west of Jacksonville Landing, the Omni enjoys a more convenient location than the Hilton across the river. It caters primarily to a corporate clientele who fill the meeting facilities during the week. Most rooms are of moderate size, with the pick being the Florida suites, which have sitting areas with river or city views. The reasonably priced Juliette's Restaurant & Bistro provides a locally famous pasta bar.

245 Water St. (between Pearl and Hogan Sts.), Jacksonville, FL 32202. © **800/THE-OMNI** or 904/355-OMNI. Fax 904/791-4809. www.omnihotels.com. 354 units. $149–$189 double. Weekend rates available. AE, DC, DISC, MC, V. Valet parking $10; self-parking $12. **Amenities:** Restaurant (American); bar; heated outdoor pool; small exercise room; Jacuzzi; concierge; business center; limited room service; laundry service; concierge-level rooms. *In room:* A/C, TV, dataport, minibar, coffeemaker, hair dryer, iron.

Plantation Manor Inn ☆   The setting for many weddings and special events, this three-story plantation-style bed-and-breakfast in the historic Riverside district is just 10 minutes from downtown and a short drive to Avondale's shopping and dining. Its homey interior, outfitted with a mix of thrift-store antiques, features glossy pine floors and gorgeous cypress paneling, wainscoting, and carved moldings. Breakfast, including freshly baked muffins and breads, is served in a lovely dining room with a working fireplace. When the sun is shining, take the morning meal on a brick patio, a delightful setting with ivy-covered walls, flower beds, and garden furnishings under the shade of a massive oak tree. The patio also contains a lap pool and whirlpool spa. On the second floor you can enjoy a big wraparound porch with seating amid potted geraniums, hibiscus, and bougainvillea. All but one of the rooms here have shower-only bathrooms.

1630 Copeland St. (between Oak and Park Sts.), Jacksonville, FL 32204. © **904/384-4630.** Fax 904/387-0960. www.plantationmanorinn.com. 9 units (all with bathroom). $145–$175 double. Rates include full breakfast. AE, DC, MC, V. **Amenities:** Outdoor pool; Jacuzzi. *In room:* A/C, TV, hair dryer.

AT THE BEACHES

A dozen modest hotels line Jacksonville Beach's 1st Street, along the Atlantic Ocean. Completely renovated in 1998, the **Comfort Inn Oceanfront,** 1515 N. 1st St., 2 blocks east of Fla. A1A (© **800/654-8776** or 904/241-2311; fax 904/249-3830; www.comfortinnjaxbeach.com), is one of the better values. Its rooms all have balconies or screened patios, and guests can enjoy a large pool with four rock waterfalls and a palm-fringed sundeck, a secluded grotto whirlpool, an exercise room, a gift/sundries shop, and a multicourt sand volleyball park.

Others hotels on this strip include the **Holiday Inn Sunspree** (✆ **800/HOLIDAY** or 904/249-9071), where all rooms come with refrigerators and microwaves; **Days Inn Oceanfront Resort** (✆ **800/321-2037** or 904/249-7924); and **Ramada Resort** (✆ **800/2-RAMADA** or 904/241-5333).

The Sabal Palm Inn B&B   Bed-and-breakfast lovers will find a comfortable and charming home in this Victorian-era house set on a residential street just half a block from the beach. Owner Todd Kemp has completely restored the yellow clapboard structure, including bringing all of its original pine woodwork back to natural. Todd grew up in New York State, and the decor here is a blend of tropical wicker, antiques, and Adirondack hunting trophies. Bay windows shed plenty of light in the first-floor formal parlor and dining room and in two of the three guest rooms upstairs. Those two units are at the top of a central stairway, from which a door leads to a porch with white wicker lounge furniture and a fine view of what's left of the Jacksonville Fishing Pier (Hurricane Floyd swept most of it away in 1999). A small lounge on the stairway landing is stocked with wine, beer, juices, and soft drinks. The other guest room, a suite at the rear of the house, has a sitting parlor, a monstrous bathroom with both shower stall and clawfoot tub, and its own stairway to the backyard. Beside the house is a small swimming pool with a sundeck. All rooms have telephones.

115 5th Ave. S. (between 1st and 2nd Sts.), Jacksonville Beach, FL 32250. ✆ **904/241-4545.** Fax 904/241-2407. http://hometown.aol.com/sabalpalmin. 3 units (all with bathroom). $85–$150 double. Rates include full breakfast. MC, V. **Amenities:** Outdoor pool. *In room:* A/C, TV, fax, dataport, kitchen, minibar, fridge, coffeemaker, hair dryer, iron.

Sea Horse Oceanfront Inn *Value*   One of the anchors of quaint Town Center, this well-run beachfront motel offers clean, spacious rooms with ocean views from balconies or patios. Families will appreciate the six units here with kitchenettes, not to mention a big beachfront lawn with pool, shuffleboard, picnic tables, and a barbecue grill. And young couples will enjoy proximity to some of Jacksonville's top night spots. If you have a large family or group, consider the vast and lovely third-floor penthouse—it has a big living room and dining area, a full kitchen, a separate bedroom as well as sofa beds, and a huge balcony furnished with a dining table and chaise lounges. A coffee shop adjoins the motel, and Town Center's restaurants and bars are across the street.

120 Atlantic Blvd. (at beach end of Atlantic Blvd.), Neptune Beach, FL 32266. ✆ **800/881-2330** or 904/246-2175. Fax 904/246-4256. www.seahorseresort.com. 38 units. $89–$109 double; $200–$225 penthouse suite for up to 6. AE, DC, DISC, MC, V. **Amenities:** Heated outdoor pool. *In room:* A/C, TV, dataport.

Sea Turtle Inn ✦✦   Completely gutted and restored in 1999 and 2000, this elegant, eight-story beachfront hotel is much more upscale than the Seahorse Oceanfront Inn, which it faces across Atlantic Boulevard. Everything in the spacious guest rooms is new, including faux-marble—but somewhat cramped—bathrooms. Choice units on the beachfront have balconies, but the majority of rooms don't face the beach nor do they have balconies. Plantains Restaurant is a fine spot for an alfresco beachside meal, and it has live music on weekends. There's a lounge in the restaurant and a summertime tiki bar beside the swimming pool by the beach.

1 Ocean Blvd. (at beach end of Atlantic Blvd.), Atlantic Beach, FL 32233. ℂ **800/874-6000** or 904/249-7402. Fax 904/247-1517. www.seaturtle.com. 193 units. $119–$209 double. AE, DC, DISC, MC, V. **Amenities:** Restaurant (American); 2 bars; outdoor pool; access to nearby health club; water-sports equipment rentals; limited room service; baby-sitting; laundry service, coin-op washers and dryers. *In room:* A/C, TV, fax, data-port, kitchen, minibar, fridge, coffeemaker, hair dryer, iron.

AT PONTE VEDRA BEACH

If you'd like to rent an old-fashioned cottage or a luxurious condominium in this affluent enclave, contact **Ponte Vedra Club Realty,** 280 Ponte Vedra Blvd., Ponte Vedra Beach, FL 32082 (ℂ **800/278-8171** or 904/285-6927; fax 904/285-5218; www.pvclubrealty.com). The company has more than 100 properties in its rental inventory, about 75% of them on the ocean. Its renters get a discount on use of facilities at The Lodge & Club and at the Ponte Vedra Inn & Club (see below).

The Lodge & Club at Ponte Vedra Beach ★★
One of Florida's more romantic hotels, this long, two-story Mediterranean-style building sits right along the beach, affording every unit an ocean view from its own private balcony or patio. The guest quarters have considerable charm, with gorgeous artwork on their walls, two-person settees recessed in front of windows looking out to the beach, and huge bathrooms with two-person tubs and separate showers. The "preferred" rooms and all of the suites also have gas fireplaces, and ceiling fans hang from vaulted ceilings in the upstairs units. The suites also come with sleeper sofas and kitchenettes, making them suitable for small families. Down by the beach, one swimming pool with a hot tub is reserved for couples, while families can use two other pool areas. Guests here also have access to all the facilities of the Ponte Vedra Inn & Club (see below), including the spa, tennis center, and two golf courses. Restricted to guests of the two properties, the bright Innlet Dining Room serves fine continental cuisine with an ocean view, and afternoon tea daily in the adjoining lounge, where a pianist performs by the fireplace at night. The poolside Oasis Bar & Grill is open daily during summer, weekends the rest of the year.

607 Ponte Vedra Blvd. (at Corona Rd.), Ponte Vedra Beach, FL 32082. ℂ **800/243-4304** or 904/273-9500. Fax 904/273-0210. www.pvresorts.com. 66 units. $185–$320 double; $255–$390 suite. Packages available. AE, DC, DISC, MC, V. **Amenities:** 2 restaurants (Continental/American); 2 bars; 3 heated outdoor pools; health club (with lap pool); access to nearby spa; Jacuzzi; sauna; water-sports equipment rentals; bike rental; concierge; business center; 24-hr. room service; baby-sitting; laundry service. *In room:* A/C, TV, fax, dataport, minibar, kitchen (suites only), coffeemaker, hair dryer, iron.

Ponte Vedra Inn & Club ★★
This luxurious 300-acre private country club and spa is a great place to pamper yourself between rounds of golf or games of tennis. The inn is ultraelegant from the moment you drive up to its manicured front lawn, which doubles as a putting green. Inside, a charming lobby adjoins the lodgelike Great Lounge, with overstuffed sofas and armchairs and massive fireplaces at either end. A gorgeous on-premises spa offers ocean-view massage, a salon, herbal and seaweed wraps, facials, hydrotherapy, fitness training, and much more. Across the road, the spacious condominiums are in two-story buildings along the beach. They all have furnished patios or balconies and are individually decorated; some have four-poster or sleigh beds. Ceiling fans are among the numerous in-room amenities. The larger units have full kitchens, and microwave ovens and small refrigerators are available upon request. In addition to the inn's two 18-hole golf courses, its excellent tennis center, and fully equipped gym with six-lane Olympic pool, guests can use the three beachside

swimming pools and other facilities at the nearby Lodge & Club at Ponte Vedra Beach (see above).

200 Ponte Vedra Blvd. (off Fla. A1A), Ponte Vedra Beach, FL 32082. ✆ 800/234-7842 or 904/285-1111. Fax 904/285-2111. www.pvresorts.com. 202 units. $180–$500 suite. Packages available. AE, DC, DISC, MC, V. **Amenities:** 3 restaurants (American); 3 bars; indoor pool; golf courses; tennis courts; health club & spa; water-sports equipment rentals; bike rental; children's programs (summer only); concierge; business center; 24-hr. room service; massage; baby-sitting; laundry service, coin-op washers and dryers. *In room:* A/C, TV, dataport, kitchen (some units), minibar, coffeemaker, hair dryer, iron.

Sawgrass Marriott Resort ★★   One of the nation's largest golf resorts, this duffer's paradise is virtually surrounded by 99 holes, including the Pete Dye–designed **TPC at Sawgrass** ★★★, home of the annual Players Championship in March. In fact, this course has appeared on every critic's "best of" list since it opened in 1980. Overlooking the TPC's picturesque 13th hole, the seven-story hotel sits beside one of the lakes that make the course so challenging. The view augments the gourmet fusion cuisine served in the Augustine Grille, the hotel's signature restaurant. The guest rooms are comfortable but of modest size. Best for families are the fully equipped one- and two-bedroom condominium apartments on or near a golf course, which offer large furnished patios or balconies. Especially luxurious are the one- to three-bedroom beachfront units, which sport huge kitchens, living rooms with working fireplaces, full dining rooms, and large screened wooden decks. A complimentary shuttle takes guests to the oceanside Cabana Beach Club for snacks and meals. The children's program here is overseen by Jacksonville's branch of the renowned Mayo Clinic.

1000 PGA Tour Blvd. (off Fla. A1A between U.S. 210 and J. Turner Butler Blvd.), Ponte Vedra Beach, FL 32082. ✆ 800/457-GOLF, 800/228-9290, or 904/285-7777. Fax 904/285-0906. www.sawgrassmarriott.com. 303 units, 186 condos. $109–$149 double; $159–$350 suites and condos. Golf packages available. AE, DC, DISC, MC, V. Valet parking $12; free self-parking. **Amenities:** 6 restaurants (Fusion/American); 4 bars; 3 outdoor pools (2 heated); 5 golf courses; 17 tennis courts; 2 health clubs; Jacuzzi; water-sports equipment rentals; bike rental; children's programs; game room; concierge; activities desk; business center; limited room service; baby-sitting; laundry service; coin-op washers and dryers; concierge-level rooms. *In room:* A/C, TV, dataport, kitchen (condos only), minibar, coffeemaker, hair dryer, iron.

WHERE TO DINE

The convention and visitors bureau's annual guide (see "Essentials," earlier in this chapter) contains a complete list of restaurants. For more choices, check listings in the "Shorelines" and "Go" sections of Friday's *Florida-Times Union* (www.jacksonville.com) and in *FolioWeekly* (www.folioweekly.com), the free local alternative paper available at restaurants, hotels, and nightspots all over town. I have concentrated here on restaurants in downtown Jacksonville and at the beaches.

IN DOWNTOWN JACKSONVILLE

Southbank Riverwalk is the city's up-and-coming mecca for eating out. In addition to B.B.'s and the River City Brewing Company, both reviewed below, the area has river-front branches of **Ruth's Chris Steakhouse,** in the Hilton Jacksonville Riverfront, 1201 Riverplace Blvd. (✆ **904/396-6200**); **Morton's of Chicago,** 1510 Riverplace Blvd. (✆ **904/399-3933**); and **The Chart House,** in the Radisson Riverwalk Hotel, 1515 Prudential Dr. (✆ **904/398-3353**). Also expensive, the **Wine Cellar,** 1314 Prudential Dr. (✆ **904/398-8989**) offers very good continental fare and has a wine list to justify its name.

You will find a plethora of good cafes and restaurants in which to break your shopping excursions to the San Marco Square and Avondale neighborhoods.

Don't forget that on the north side of the river, the **Jacksonville Landing** has several full-service restaurants and an inexpensive food court with outdoor seating (see "Exploring the Area," earlier in this chapter).

B.B.'s ★★ ECLECTIC   A block south of the Southbank Riverwalk, this bistro son of Biscottis (see below) is one of the city's hottest restaurants. You'll find local yuppies congregating at the big marble-top bar on one side of the sometimes noisy art-deco dining room, especially during weekday "wine-downs" featuring beer and wine specials and discounted appetizers (the mozzarella bruschetta is a big hit both here and at Biscottis), from 4 to 7pm. There's a small but inventive selection of sandwiches, salads, and individual-size pizzas available all day. Featuring local seafood, the nightly main-course specials run the gamut from roasted sea bass with citrus couscous to seared scallops with lemongrass-scented rice, sun-dried tomatoes, and lobster butter. Save room for the famous desserts, available for inspection in the chiller case located near the open kitchen. Saturday brunch sees the likes of yummy Benedict-style crab cakes and flaming bananas Foster.

1019 Hendricks Ave. (between Prudential Dr. and Home St.). ✆ **904/306-0100.** Reservations not accepted, but call for priority seating. Main courses $10–$19; sandwiches and salads $5–$8; pizzas $6–$8. AE, DC, DISC, MC, V. Mon–Thurs 11am–10:30pm; Fri 11am–midnight; Sat 10am–midnight (Sat brunch 10am–2pm).

Biscottis ★★ *Value* ECLECTIC   This brick-walled little gem in the trendy Avondale neighborhood might have come out of New York's East Village. A young and hip waitstaff is pleasant and well informed. You can start your day here with a pastry and cup of joe. For lunch and dinner, daily specials like pan-seared tuna or pork loin are always fresh and beautifully presented. The huge and inventive salads are especially good: Try the Oriental version with chicken breast, orange slices, roasted peppers, and creamy sesame dressing. Pizzas, too, are served with wonderfully exotic and delicious toppings—ever try guacamole and black beans on your slice? And by all means don't leave without sampling the wonderful desserts. On warm days choose a tiny sidewalk table for great people-watching. If the wait's too long here, several other choices ranging from a neighborhood diner to expensive haute cuisine line these 2 blocks of St. Johns Avenue in Avondale.

3556 St. Johns Ave. (between Talbot and Ingleside Aves. in Avondale). ✆ **904/387-2060.** Reservations not accepted. Main courses $9–$17; sandwiches and salads $5–$8; pizzas $7–$8.50. AE, DC, DISC, MC, V. Tues–Thurs 7am–10pm; Fri 7am–midnight; Sat 8am–midnight; Sun 8am–3pm.

River City Brewing Company ★★ NEW AMERICAN/LOUISIANA   Occupying a prime location on the Southbank Riverwalk, this gorgeous restaurant and microbrewery is a good choice for lunch or dinner with dramatic waterfront and skyline views. For an even better vantage point, sit outside on the enormous covered deck. The quality of the cuisine very nearly lives up to the vista, especially the "hanging" coconut shrimp served with a sweet Mandarin orange sauce. For a main course, try the Cajun chicken linguine with mushrooms and ham in a spicy cream sauce, or pretzel-encrusted mahimahi with a mustard cream sauce. While you can easily drop a bundle in the main dining room, you can devise an inexpensive, simpler meal in the Brew Haus, a large sports bar that opens to the big covered deck and the riverbank. Bands play on the deck weekend evenings. Sunday brunch brings incredible buffets with decadent desserts.

835 Museum Circle (on Southbank Riverwalk). ✆ **904/398-2299.** Reservations for groups only. Main courses $15–$26; sandwiches and salads $5–$11; Sun brunch buffet $18 adults, $16 seniors, $10 children 3–12. AE, DC, DISC, MC, V. Dining room Sun–Thurs 11am–3pm and 5–10pm; Fri–Sat 11am–3pm and 5–11pm; Sun 10:30am–2:30pm. Pub and deck (light fare) Sun–Thurs 3–10pm (bar to midnight); Fri–Sat 3–11pm (bar to 2am). Closed Christmas. Valet parking $3 (weekends only).

AT THE BEACHES

In addition to the Ragtime Tavern (see below), you'll have several dining (and drinking) choices in the brick storefronts of Town Center, the old-time beach village at the end of Atlantic Boulevard. Among the best is the oceanfront **Plantains,** in the Sea Turtle Inn (see "Where to Stay," earlier in this chapter).

The Homestead (Kids) SOUTHERN Occupying a log cabin built as a residence in the 1930s, this Jacksonville institution is usually packed with regulars waiting for crispy Southern fried chicken served in a skillet with homemade buttermilk biscuits and fresh honey and a choice of coleslaw, creamed green peas, rice and gravy, or daily vegetables. Fried gator tails are among the appetizers, along with chicken wings, gizzards, and livers. Not a cholesterol junkie? Skinless chicken breast, broiled or grilled, is also available. Other down-home favorites are meatloaf and chicken or beef pot pies, with all the fixings. There's fried fish and shrimp, too, but Singleton's Seafood Shack (see below) does a better job.

1712 Beach Blvd. (between 15th and 19th Sts.), Jacksonville Beach. ② 904/249-5240. Reservations only for large parties. Main courses $9–$17. AE, DISC, MC, V. Mon–Thurs 5–10pm; Fri 5–11pm; Sat 6–11pm; Sun noon–10pm.

Island Grille ✹✹ INTERNATIONAL Positioned on the beach but away from the crowds, this is one of the area's best oceanside dining venues, serving a varied menu of innovative, always fresh seafood, as well as basic offerings like shrimp scampi, New York strip steak, and pasta primavera. Nightly specials such as an excellent Szechwan-style tuna or Jamaican-style pork strips with creamy roasted pepper sauce are always good bets here. The many salads, including one topped with spicy shrimp, are delicious and large, and the house special dinner salad—dressed with a raspberry vinaigrette and topped with fresh berries, peanuts, and feta cheese—is extraordinary. The appetizers here are so good you might just graze; they range from Polynesian spring rolls to Bahamian conch fritters served with spicy pink rémoulade. Happy hour lasts from 4 to 7pm Monday to Friday and live piano music is played in the bar Wednesday through Saturday evenings.

981 N. 1st St. (at 9th Ave.), Jacksonville Beach. ② 904/241-1881. Reservations recommended. Main courses $15–$18. AE, DC, DISC, MC, V. Mon–Fri 4:30–10:30pm; Sat–Sun 11:30am–10:30pm. Bar open later.

Old Siam ✹✹ THAI The best of several Thai restaurants here, Pam Souvannasoth's sophisticated little cafe serves fine cuisine from his homeland and a good selection of wines to match the fare's spicy yet subtle flavors. Pam's signature dish is his seafood special: shrimp, sea scallops, mussels, squid, and crab claws in a red chili sauce accented with sweet basil. His "number 3" spice level (out of 6) touched my tongue but did not overwhelm the other seasonings. Standard favorites like Pad Thai are light and perfectly balanced with sweet and slightly sour fish sauce.

1716 N. 3rd St. (Fla. A1A, in Holiday Plaza shopping center, between 16th and 17th Aves. N.), Jacksonville Beach. ② 904/247-7763. Reservations only for parties of 6 or more. Main courses $10.50–$19. AE, DISC, MC, V. Mon–Thurs 5–10pm; Fri–Sat 5–11pm; Sun 5–9:30pm.

Panera Bread (Value) BAKERY/DELI Part of a small local chain, this chic bakery and cafe is the best place at the beaches for a breakfast of fresh-from-the-oven bagels, croissants, or Danish pastries washed down by an espresso, cappuccino, or latte. Baguettes and focaccia also accompany big salads and appear in both standard and creative sandwiches such as Tuscan chicken on rosemary- and onion-flavored focaccia.

In Pablo Plaza Shopping Center, 2104 S. 3rd St. (at S. 23rd Ave.), Jacksonville Beach. **904/246-6688.** Reservations not accepted. Sandwiches and salads $4.50–$6. AE, MC, V. Mon–Sat 6:30am–8pm; Sun 7:30am–7pm.

Ragtime Tavern & Taproom ★★ SEAFOOD/PASTA   In the heart of Town Center, this lively sister of St. Augustine's A1A Ale Works offers six handcrafted brews, including a refreshing pilsner known as Dolphin's Breath. You can imbibe at one of two bars on either end of the building. In between, a rabbit warren of dining rooms provides fine enough fare to keep it filled with local professionals right through the cool winter months. A variety of appetizers includes conch fritters and coconut shrimp, as well as more-entertaining items such as fried artichoke hearts served with a horseradish dipping sauce or the appetizer- or dinner-size curried spinach salad (go easy with the piquant dressing to avoid overwhelming the subtle curry flavor). For a main course, you can select from seared sesame-coated yellowfin tuna (the best dish here if you like rare fish) or several other treatments of fish, shrimp, chicken, and pastas. Save room for some New Orleans–style beignets for dessert. Also from the Big Easy, po'boy sandwiches are served at all hours. Good local bands make music here Thursday through Sunday evenings.

207 Atlantic Blvd. (at 1st Ave.), Atlantic Beach. © **904/241-6406.** Reservations not accepted, but call to get on waiting list. Main courses $11.50–$22; sandwiches and salads $6–$8. AE, DC, DISC, MC, V. Sun–Thurs 11am–10:30pm; Fri–Sat 11am–11pm (bar open later).

Singleton's Seafood Shack ★★ *Value* SEAFOOD   This rustic fish camp has been serving every imaginable kind of fresh-off-the-boat seafood since 1969. And rustic it is, constructed primarily of unpainted, well-weathered plywood nailed to two-by-fours. Unlike most other fish camps that tend to overwork the deep fryer, the fried standbys like conch fritters, shrimp, clam strips, oysters, and squid actually retain their seafood taste! In fact, the fried shrimp are among the best I've had anywhere. Singleton's also offers other preparations such as blackened mahimahi and Cajun shrimp. Best bets at lunch are the fried shrimp or oyster po-boy sandwiches covered in crispy onion rings. At dinner your Styrofoam plate will come stacked with a choice of side items like black beans and rice, marvelous horseradishy coleslaw, fries, and hush puppies. You can also choose from a selection of chicken, but for that, go to The Homestead (see above).

4728 Ocean St. (Fla. A1A, at St. Johns River Ferry landing), Mayport. © **904/246-4442.** Main courses $11–$18; sandwiches $2–$7. AE, DISC, MC, V. Sun–Thurs 10am–9pm; Fri–Sat 10am–10pm.

JACKSONVILLE AFTER DARK

In addition to the spots recommended below, check the listings in the "Shorelines" and "Go" sections of Friday's *Florida Times-Union* (www.jacksonville.com) and *FolioWeekly* (www.folioweekly.com), the free local alternative paper, available at restaurants, at hotels, and all over town. Another source is **www.jaxevents.com**.

THE PERFORMING ARTS   With the 73,000-seat **Alltell Stadium,** at East Duval and Haines streets (© **904/630-3900**); the 10,600-seat **Jacksonville Veterans Memorial Coliseum,** 1145 E. Adams St. (© **904/630-3900** for information or 904/353-3309 to charge tickets); the 3,200-seat **Florida Times Union Center for the Performing Arts,** 300 Water St., between Hogan and Pearl streets (© **904/630-3900**); and the revitalized **Ritz Theatre** (© **904/632-5555;** see "Exploring the Area," earlier in this chapter), Jacksonville has plenty of seats for concerts, touring Broadway shows, dance companies, and big-name performers. Call or check the sources above for what's playing.

THE BAR SCENE   You will find several libation options downtown at **Jacksonville Landing** (see "Exploring the Area," above), including a lively waterfront **Hooters** (℃ **904/356-5400**), plus free outdoor rock, blues, country, and jazz concerts every Friday and Saturday night except during winter. There's also live music on weekends across the river at the **River City Brewing Company** (see "Where to Dine," earlier in this chapter).

Out at Town Center, at the ocean end of Atlantic Boulevard, one of several popular spots is **Ragtime Tavern & Taproom** (see "Where to Dine," earlier in this chapter), where local groups play live jazz and blues Wednesday to Sunday nights. Weekends, especially, the place is really jumping and the crowd is young, but it's lively rather than rowdy. Across the street is the **Sun Dog Diner,** at 207 Atlantic Blvd. (℃ **904/241-8221**), with nightly acoustic music and decent diner food. If these don't fit your mood, there are more nightspots in Town Center.

5 Amelia Island ★★

32 miles NE of Jacksonville, 192 miles NE of Orlando, 372 miles N. of Miami

With 13 beautiful miles of beach and a quaint Victorian town, Amelia Island is a charming getaway about a 45-minute drive northeast of downtown Jacksonville. Overall, this skinny barrier island, 18 miles long by 3 miles wide, has more in common with the Low Country of Georgia (across Cumberland Sound from here) and South Carolina than with its compatriots in Florida. It's more like St. Simons Island in Georgia or Hilton Head Island in South Carolina.

Amelia itself has five distinct personalities. First is its southern end, an exclusive real-estate development built in a forest of twisted, moss-laden live oaks. Here you will find world-class tennis and golfing at two of Florida's most luxurious resorts. Second is modest **American Beach,** founded in the 1930s so that African Americans would have access to the ocean. Today it's a modest, predominately black community tucked away among all that south-end wealth. Third is the island's middle, a traditional beach community with a mix of affordable motels, cottages, condominiums, and a seaside inn. Fourth is the historic bay-side town of **Fernandina Beach** ★★★, which boasts a 50-square-block area of gorgeous Victorian, Queen Anne, and Italianate homes listed in the National Register of Historic Places. And fifth is lovely **Fort Clinch State Park,** which keeps developers from turning the island's northern end into more ritzy resorts.

The town of Fernandina Beach dates from the post–Civil War period, when Union soldiers who had occupied Fort Clinch began returning to the island. In the late 19th century Amelia's timber, phosphate, and naval-stores industries boomed. Back then, the town was an active seaport, with 14 foreign consuls in residence. Even earlier, a railroad went from here 155 miles across Florida to Cedar Key; it was part of a planned worldwide trade network cut short by the Civil War. You'll see (and occasionally smell) the paper mills that still stand near the small seaport here. The island experienced another economic explosion in the 1970s and 1980s, when real-estate developers built the condominiums, the cottages, and the two big resorts on the island's southern end. In recent years, Fernandina Beach has seen another big boom, this time in bed-and-breakfast establishments.

ESSENTIALS
GETTING THERE   The island is served by **Jacksonville International Airport** (see "Essentials," in section 4, earlier in this chapter). Skirting the Atlantic in places, the scenic drive here from downtown Jacksonville is via Fla. A1A and the St. Johns River Ferry. The fast, four-lane way is via I-95 north and the Buccaneer Trail (Fla. A1A) east.

VISITOR INFORMATION   For advance information, contact the **Amelia Island–Fernandina Beach–Yulee Chamber of Commerce,** 102 Centre St. (P.O. Box 472), Fernandina Beach, FL 32035 (© **800/2-AMELIA** or 904/277-0717; fax 904/261-6997; www.ameliaisland.org). The chamber's visitor information center, in the old train station at the bay end of Centre Street, is open Monday to Friday from 9am to 5pm, Saturday from 10am to 2pm.

GETTING AROUND   There's no public transportation on this 13-mile-long island, so you'll need a vehicle. The **Old Towne Carriage Company** (© **904/ 277-1555**) offers narrated, horse-drawn carriage tours of Fernandina Beach's historic district, leaving from the waterfront on Centre Street. The 30- to 40-minute rides cost $15 for adults, $7.50 for kids under 13. The carriage company closes for 2 months during the winter when the horses are put out to pasture.

An excellent way to see the town is on a walking tour sponsored by the Amelia Island Museum of History (see "An Old Jail Turned Historic Museum," below).

HITTING THE BEACH

Thanks to a reclamation project, the widest beaches here are at the exclusive enclave on the island's southern third. Even if you aren't staying at one of the swanky resorts, you can enjoy this section at **Peters Point Beach Front Park,** on Fla. A1A north of the Ritz-Carlton. The park has picnic shelters and rest rooms.

North of the resort, the beach has public access points with free parking every quarter mile or so. The center of activity is **Main Beach,** at the end of Atlantic Avenue (Fla. A1A), with good swimming, rest rooms, picnic shelters, showers, a food concession, and a playground. There's lots of free parking, and this area is popular with families.

The **beach at Fort Clinch State Park** 🐾🐾, which wraps around the island's heavily forested northern end, is backed by rolling dunes and is filled with shells and driftwood. A jetty and a pier jutting into Cumberland South are popular with anglers. You might see an alligator—and certainly some of the 170 species of birds who live here—by hiking the Willow Pond nature trail. Rangers lead nature tours on the trail, usually beginning at 10:30am on Saturday. There also are 6 miles of off-road bike trails here. You also can visit the remarkably well-preserved **Fort Clinch.** Construction began in 1847 on the northern tip of the island and was still underway when Union troops occupied it in 1862. The fort was abandoned shortly after the Civil War, except for a brief reactivation in 1898 during the Spanish-American War. Reenactors gather the first full weekend of each month to re-create how the Union soldiers lived in the fort in 1864. Rangers are on duty at the fort year-round, and they lead candlelight tours on Friday and Saturday evenings during summer, beginning about an hour after sunset. The candlelight tours cost $3 per person. You can arrange guided tours at other times for an extra fee. The park entrance is on Atlantic Avenue near the beach. Entrance fees are $3.25 per vehicle with up to eight occupants, $1 for pedestrians and bicyclists. Admission to the fort costs $2, free for children under 5. The park is open daily 8am to sunset; the fort, daily 9am to 5pm. For a current schedule of tours and events, contact the park at 2601 Atlantic Ave., Fernandina Beach, FL 32034 (© **904/277-7274;** www8.myflorida.com/ communities/learn/stateparks/district2/fortclinch).

The park has 62 **campsites,** some behind the dunes at the beach (no shade out there), most in a forest along the sound side. They cost $20.67 per night with electricity, $18.53 without, including tax. Pets cost an extra $2 a night. You can reserve a site up to 11 months in advance (a very good idea in summer).

Lying south of Amelia, both Big Talbot and Little Talbot barrier islands are preserved in their natural states. The highlight is **Little Talbot Island State Park,** whose entrance is on Fla. A1A, 8 miles south of Amelia Island Plantation. The 5 miles of beach here gently slope into the sea, making for good swimming. Boardwalks lead across the dunes from picnic shelters and bathhouses with cold-water showers. There are nature trails, a campground, excellent fishing (bring your own gear and bait), and bicycles and canoes for rent. The park is open from 8am to sunset. Entrance fees are $3.25 per vehicle with up to eight occupants, $1 for pedestrians and bicyclists. Campsites cost $14 a night from March through September, $10 off-season. For more information, or to reserve a campsite, contact the park at 12157 Heckscher Dr., Fort George, FL 32226 (© **904/251-2320;** www8.myflorida.com/communities/learn/stateparks/district2/littletalbot).

Pets on leashes are allowed on all the island's public beaches and in Fort Clinch and Little Talbot Island parks.

BOATING, GOLF & OTHER OUTDOOR ACTIVITIES

BOATING, FISHING, SAILING & KAYAKING   The **Amelia Island Charter Boat Association,** at Tiger Point Marina on 14th Street north of the historic district (© **800/229-1682** or 904/261-2870), can help arrange deep-sea fishing charters, party-boat excursions, and dolphin-watching and sightseeing cruises. Other charter boats dock at Fernandina Harbor Marina, downtown at the foot of Centre Street.

Voyager Adventures, based at Fernandina Harbor Marina, 3977 1st Ave. (© **904/321-1244;** fax 904/321-2505; schoonervoyager@net-magic.net), has several cruises aboard the *Voyager,* a 100-foot replica of a 19th-century gaff-rigged packet schooner. A prime destination is Cumberland Island, across the sound in Georgia (the late John F. Kennedy Jr. was married over there without a single member of the paparazzi being present). The trips cost $35 per person. Also based at the marina, **Windward Sailing School** (© **904/261-9125**) will teach you to skipper your boat. Call these companies for details and reservations.

You have to be careful in the currents, but the backwaters here are great for kayaking, whether you're a beginner or a pro. Ray and Jody Hetchka of **Kayak Amelia** ✿✿ (© **888/30-KAYAK** or 904/321-0697; www.kayakamelia.com) have beginner- and advanced-level trips on the back bays, creeks, and marshes. Half-day trips go for about $50 per person, all-day $85. Sunset paddles on Friday cost $25 per person. Reservations are required.

GOLF   If you're not staying in a resort with a golf course (see "Where to Stay," below), try the new 18-hole **Royal Amelia Golf Links** (© **904/491-8500;** www.royalamelia.com), or the older and less expensive 27-hole **Fernandina Municipal Golf Course** (© **904/277-7370**).

HORSEBACK RIDING   You can go riding on the beach with **Kelly Seahorse Ranch** (© **904/491-5166**), near Little Talbot Island State Park. Rides cost $35 per person, and reservations are required. There are pony rides for kids, too. The ranch is open daily from 10am to dark.

SCUBA DIVING   **Aqua Explorers Dive Center,** 2856 Sadler Rd. (© **904/ 261-5989**), open Monday to Saturday from 10am to 6pm, teaches certification courses, arranges charters, and sells and rents equipment.

AN OLD JAIL TURNED HISTORIC MUSEUM

Amelia Island Museum of History ✿   Housed in the Nassau County jail built of brick in 1878, this award-winning local museum explains Amelia

Island's fascinating history, from Timucuan Indian times through its possession by France, Spain, Great Britain, the United States, and the Confederacy (the island changed flags eight times). Only an upstairs photo gallery is open for casual inspection, so plan to take the 1-hour, 15-minute docent-led tour.

The museum also offers excellent **walking tours** of historic Centre Street on Thursday and Friday from September through June. These depart at 3pm from the chamber of commerce (see "Essentials," above) and cost $8 per person. Longer tours of the entire 50-square-block historic district can be arranged with 24-hour notice; these cost $10 per person, with a minimum of four persons required.

233 S. 3rd St. (between Beech and Cedar Sts.). (C) **904/261-7378.** Admission by donation. Tours $4 adults, $2 students. Mon–Fri 10am–5pm; Sat 10am–4pm. Tours Mon–Sat 11am and 2pm.

SHOPPING

Stroll down **Centre Street** in downtown Fernandina Beach, with its vintage storefronts and charming boutiques. Quality antiques shops, consignment shops, and bookstores line the wide boulevard ending at the marina. Be sure to poke your head into the **Island Art Association Gallery,** 205 Centre St. ((C) **904/261-7020**), a co-op exhibiting works by local artists.

On the south end of the island on Fla. A1A, **Palmetto Walk,** under a canopy of live oaks, and the **Village Shops,** at the entrance to Amelia Plantation, are other good shopping bets.

WHERE TO STAY

More than two dozen of the town's charming Victorian and Queen Anne houses have been restored and turned into B&Bs, and apparently they all stay busy, at least on weekends. Industry veteran David Caples, who holds seminars nationwide for wanna-be innkeepers, is based here at the Elizabeth Pointe Lodge (see below). For a complete list, contact the chamber of commerce (see "Essentials," above) or contact the **Amelia Island Bed & Breakfast Association** ((C) **888/ 277-0218;** www.ameliaislandinns.com). You can tour all the B&Bs during an island-wide open house the first weekend in December.

A number of agencies will book vacation properties ranging from affordable cottages to magnificent mansions. Contact **Amelia Island Lodging Systems,** 584 S. Fletcher Ave., Fernandina Beach, FL 32034 ((C) **800/872-8531** or 904/ 261-4148; fax 904/261-9200; www.amelialodgings.com), which even has two lighthouse replicas for rent. Or try **Lodging Resources, Inc.,** at the Elizabeth Pointe Lodge, 98 S. Fletcher Ave., Fernandina Beach, FL 32034 ((C) **904/ 277-4851;** fax 904/277-4851; www.lodgingresources.com), which also has a lighthouse in its inventory.

There's a **Hampton Inn** ((C) **800/HAMPTON** or 904/321-1111) on Sadler Road a block from the beach.

Your best **camping** option here is **Fort Clinch State Park** (see "Hitting the Beach," above).

VERY EXPENSIVE

The Ritz-Carlton Amelia Island ★★★   Sprawling over 13 acres of stunning beachfront, this member of the world-renowned chain offers glitzier and grander accommodations than its neighbor, the Amelia Island Plantation. Millions of dollars' worth of museum-quality art and furnishings decorate the public areas, and the staff provides prompt and flawless service. But this Ritz-Carlton is downright relaxed compared with some of its siblings. Well-heeled families will feel just as much at home as the conventioneers who flock here to meet and make use of the extensive recreational facilities, including a beautiful and challenging 18-hole championship golf course. The spacious guest rooms—all with oceanfront or ocean-view balconies or patios—have many extra amenities such as scales, cosmetic mirrors, and phones in their magnificent marble bathrooms. Concierge-level guests enjoy a stunning lounge with a working fireplace. Offering fine American cuisine with an ocean view, **The Grill** is one of Florida's best hotel restaurants. A gourmet take-out shop sells the oft-requested Ritz dressings, condiments, and sauces, in addition to salads, sandwiches, and decadent desserts.

4750 Amelia Island Pkwy., Fernandina Beach, FL 32034. Ⓒ **800/241-3333** or 904/277-1100. Fax 904/261-9064. 449 units. $239–$525 double; $339–$625 suite. Golf and tennis packages available. AE, DC, DISC, MC, V. Valet parking $13; no self-parking. **Amenities:** 3 restaurants (American); 3 bars; heated outdoor pool; golf course; 9 tennis courts; health club & spa; water-sports equipment rentals; bike rental; children's programs; game room; concierge; business center; salon; 24-hr. room service; massage; baby-sitting; laundry service; concierge-level rooms. In room: A/C, TV, dataport, minibar, coffeemaker, hair dryer, iron.

EXPENSIVE

Amelia Island Plantation 👫👫   This huge real-estate development occupies 1,250 lush beachfront acres that encompass manicured, emerald golf greens as well as a breathtaking coastal wilderness of marshes and lagoons. The resort is so spread out that a free tram runs around the grounds every 15 minutes. Unless you're here to attend a convention, choose this rustically elegant resort for its natural beauty and its outstanding sports offerings. Most notable are the three consistently top-rated championship golf courses open to resort guests; they comprise 54 holes bordering the ocean, swamps, marshes, and woodlands. The **Long Point** 👫👫 course, a breathtakingly beautiful 18-holer, has two par-3s in a row bordering the ocean. Ranked among the nation's top 50 by *Tennis* magazine, the plantation's 27 tennis courts host many professional tournaments, including the annual Bausch & Lomb Championships. At press time, the Spa at Amelia Island was slated to open in summer 2001. The 13,200-square foot spa will have 25 treatment rooms and will offer a rejuvenating array of massages, facials, peels, herbal wraps, and hydrotherapies. Along with the adjoining convention center, the six-story, Mediterranean-style **Amelia Inn & Beach Club** serves as the resort's focal point here and holds its 249 spacious, upscale hotel rooms. Traditionally furnished, the rooms boast patios or balconies facing the sea across a row of dunes. All of the inn's rooms are nonsmoking. The other accommodations here are one- to three-bedroom privately owned condominium apartments (or "villas" in Florida-speak). All but a few have balconies or patios. Each is uniquely decorated with an eclectic mix of high-end furnishings, and all offer living and dining areas (VCRs can be rented) and fully equipped kitchens. The inn's dining room, though not on a par with The Grill at the nearby Ritz-Carlton, offers exceptional and expensive new American cuisine, with stunning ocean views. An adjoining lounge offers dancing and entertainment.

3000 First Coast Hwy., Amelia Island, FL 32035-3000. Ⓒ **800/874-6878** or 904/261-6161. Fax 904/277-5945. www.aipfl.com. 249 units, 400 condo apts. $141–$305 double; $161–$705 condo. Packages available. AE, DC, DISC, MC, V. Free valet and self-parking. **Amenities:** 4 restaurants (American); 4 bars; 21 heated outdoor pools; 3 golf courses; 27 tennis courts; health club, spa; Jacuzzi; sauna; water-sports equipment rentals; bike rental; children's programs; game room; concierge; business center; shopping arcade; salon; limited room service; massage; baby-sitting; laundry service. In room: A/C, TV, dataport, kitchen (condos only), minibar (Amelia Inn only), coffeemaker, hair dryer, iron.

MODERATE

Elizabeth Pointe Lodge 👫👫   You'd swear that this three-story, Nantucket-style shingled beauty, sitting right on the beach, was a lovingly maintained Victorian home—but you'd be wrong. Built in 1991 by B&B gurus David and Susan Caples, it's has big-paned windows that look out from the comfy library

Amelia Island

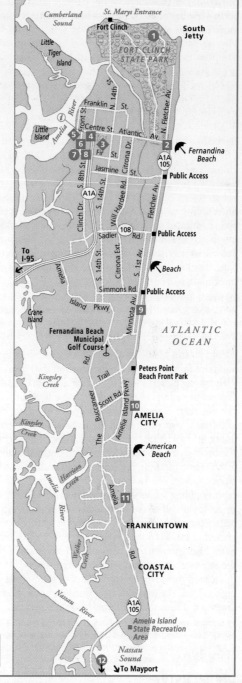

ACCOMMODATIONS ■
Amelia Island Plantation **11**
Beachside Motel Inn **9**
Elizabeth Pointe Lodge **2**
Fairbanks House **8**
Florida House Inn **4**
Hampton Inn & Suites **6**
The Ritz-Carlton
    Amelia Island **10**

ATTRACTIONS ●
Amelia Island Museum of
    History **7**
Fort Clinch State Park **1**
Little Talbot Island
    State Park **12**

DINING ◆
Beach Street Grill **3**
Brett's Waterfront Cafe **5**
The Main Squeeze Cafe &
    Juice Bar **5**
Marina Restaurant **5**

(with stone fireplace) and dining room to an expansive front porch and the surf beyond. Antiques and reproductions, handmade quilts, and other touches lend the 20 rooms in the main building a turn-of-the-century cottage ambience. They all have oversize bathtubs. Four other rooms are in the Harris Lodge next door, and the two-bedroom, two-bathroom Miller Cottage is also available.

98 S. Fletcher Ave. (just south of Atlantic Ave.), Fernandina Beach, FL 32034. © **800/772-3359** or 904/277-4851. Fax 904/277-6500. www.elizabethpointelodge.com. 24 units, 1 cottage. $160–$235 double; $255 cottage. Rates include buffet breakfast and evening social hour. Packages available. AE, DISC, MC, V. **Amenities:** Restaurant (American); bar; access to nearby health club; Jacuzzi; bike rental; 24-hr. room service; laundry service. *In room:* A/C, TV, dataport, hair dryer, iron.

Fairbanks House ⚛ Having all the amenities and almost as much privacy as a first-class hotel in a superbly refurbished 1885 Italianate home, the Fairbanks House is a top B&B choice in the historic district. Many rooms and all the cottages offer private entrances for guests who prefer not to walk through the main house. Room no. 3, in the back of the house on the main floor, is one of the finest rooms, with a private entrance, a large sitting room, a plush king-size bed, period antiques, porcelain, oil paintings, and fresh flowers. Occupying the entire top floor, the two-bedroom Tower Suite has plenty of room to spread out, plus 360° views and its own whirlpool tub. Five other units here have whirlpool tubs. Note that Fairbanks is the only B&B on the island with a swimming pool. No smoking indoors or out.

227 S. 7th St. (between Beech and Cedar Sts.), Fernandina Beach, Amelia Island, FL 32034. © **800/261-4838** or 904/277-0500. Fax 904/277-3103. www.fairbankshouse.com. 9 units, 3 detached cottages (all with bathroom). $150–$250 double; $195 cottage. Rates include full breakfast. Packages available. AE, DISC, MC, V. **Amenities:** Heated outdoor pool. *In room:* A/C, TV, fax, dataport, kitchen, minibar, fridge, coffeemaker, hair dryer, iron.

Hampton Inn & Suites ⚛⚛ When plans were announced a few years ago to build this four-story hotel in the center of the historic district, they created quite a stir among preservationists. But the all-woman hotel firm of Miriam Taylor & Co. put those fears to rest by designing one of the most unusual Hampton Inns I've ever seen. Although there's only one building, the exterior looks like a row of different structures, all in the styles and sherbet hues of the Victorian storefronts lining Centre Street. Above a curving staircase rising in the two-story Victorian-style lobby, quadrants of an unusual ceiling clock have been painted to represent the four centuries of Fernandina Beach's history. Wooden floors taken from an old Jacksonville church, slatted door panels evocative of 19th-century sailing schooners, and many other touches add to the Victorian ambience. About half of the guest rooms are near the top of the romance scale: king beds, gas-burning fireplaces, two-person whirlpool tubs. (If honeymooning in a Hampton Inn has never crossed your mind, you haven't seen the luxurious, two-room bridal suite here.) The standard suites are large enough for families, and the other standard rooms are adequately equipped for business travelers, making this a good choice for everyone. About a third of the units have balconies. Those higher up on the west side have fine views over the river and marshes. The only drawback: Trains slowly rumble by on the west side a few times a day.

19 S. 2nd St. (between Centre and Ash Sts.), Fernandina Beach, FL 32034. © **800/HAMPTON** or 904/491-4911. Fax 904/491-4910. $114–$179 double. Rates include extensive breakfast buffet. AE, DC, DISC, MC, V. **Amenities:** Outdoor pool; exercise room; Jacuzzi; business center; baby-sitting; laundry service; coin-op washers and dryers. *In room:* A/C, TV, dataport, fridge, coffeemaker, hair dryer, iron.

INEXPENSIVE

Beachside Motel Inn *Value* This family-run property—the only motel beside the beach here—is clean and well maintained. The white-and-blue, two-story,

1970s stucco building sits on a beautiful stretch of public but uncluttered beach. The rooms, many with ocean views, are spacious and furnished with standard motel furnishings. Many long-term visitors return each season to stay in the efficiencies, which have fully equipped kitchens. An outdoor pool is surrounded by lounge chairs and a spacious deck that overlooks the ocean. The hotel is convenient to lots of sports activities and restaurants.

3172 S. Fletcher Ave. (Fla. A1A, south of Simmons Rd.), Fernandina Beach, FL 32034. ℭ 904/261-4236. www. beachsidemotel.com. 20 units. $76–$139 double; $86–$199 efficiency. Rates include continental breakfast. Weekly discounts available. AE, DISC, MC, V. **Amenities:** Outdoor pool. *In room:* A/C, TV, kitchen (efficiencies only).

Florida House Inn ⋆ *Value* Built near a railroad in 1857, this clapboard Victorian building is Florida's oldest operating hotel. Ulysses S. Grant stayed here, as did Cuban revolutionary José Marti; and the Rockefellers and Carnegies broke bread at the boardinghouse-style dining room that still provides family-style, all-you-can-eat traditional Southern fare. You can rock away on the two gingerbread-trimmed front verandahs (Grant made a speech from the upstairs porch) or on a back porch overlooking a brick courtyard shaded by a huge oak tree. The 11 rooms in the original building, all up to modern standards, are loaded with antiques. Most have working fireplaces, and some have clawfoot tubs. Four rooms are in a wing added in 1998; one of these has log-cabin walls, and the others are done country-style. All have fireplaces and whirlpool tubs.

20 S. 3rd St. (between Centre and Ash Sts.), Fernandina Beach, FL 32034. ℭ 800/258-3301 or 904/261-3300. Fax 904/277-3831. www.floridahouse.com. 15 units. $79–$179. Rates include full breakfast. AE, DISC, MC, V. Pet dogs accepted ($10 nightly fee). **Amenities:** Restaurant (Southern); bar; coin-op washers and dryers. *In room:* A/C, TV, coffeemaker, hair dryer, iron.

WHERE TO DINE

You'll find several restaurants, pubs, and snack shops along Centre Street, between the bay and 8th Street (Fla. A1A), in Fernandina Beach's old town. Two fine dining options stand opposite the Hampton Inn & Suites on South 2nd Street, between Centre and Ash streets: the hip **Joe's 2nd Street Bistro** (ℭ 904/321-2558) and the more formal but still relaxed **Le Clos** (ℭ 904/261-8100). Joe's serves fine international fare in an old store, while Le Clos provides provincial French fare in a charming old house. Both are open for dinner only, and reservations are recommended. Drop by during the day for a look at the menus posted outside each.

And don't forget the **The Grill** at the Ritz-Carlton Amelia Island, where great food and impeccable service come at a high price. Also, the **Florida House Inn** (see "Where to Stay," above) serves boardinghouse-style, all-you-can-eat lunches and dinners Tuesday to Saturday from 11:30am to 2:30pm ($7 per person) and from 5:30 to 9pm ($12 per person).

Beech Street Grill ⋆⋆ REGIONAL NEW AMERICAN Almost on a par with The Grill in the Ritz-Carlton, the Beech Street Grill pleases all palates with a rich menu of fish, chicken, and meat choices, including seasonal game dishes like roasted venison loin in a black currant sauce with sweet potato and onion hash. Nightly fish specialties are always exceptional (some can be pricier than printed menu options). A Parmesan-encrusted red snapper with a mustard basil sauce is superb. Seared tuna is always perfect, too. The dense and tasty crab cakes and the chewy steamed dumplings are great choices for starters, as is the huge mixed-green salad with mustard-basil vinaigrette, toasted pecans, and blue cheese. Housed in a century-old landmark home and in a newer wing to one side, five dining rooms offer large tables in a lively atmosphere. Attentive and knowledgeable waiters serve the showy plates with efficiency and grace. The upstairs features a pianist.

801 Beech St. (at 8th St./Fla. A1A), Fernandina Beach. © **904/277-3662.** Reservations strongly suggested. Main courses $17–$25; pastas $13–$19. AE, DC, DISC, MC, V. Daily 5:30–10pm.

Brett's Waterway Cafe SEAFOOD/STEAKS You'll pay for the view, but this friendly waterfront cafe at the foot of Centre Street is the only place in town to dine while watching the boats coming and going on the river—and to sip a drink while watching the sun setting over the marshes between here and the mainland. In fine weather you can grab a table outside by the docks. One of the best dishes is shrimp broiled with a sun-dried tomato cream sauce. The nightly fresh fish specials are well prepared, and there are steaks and chops, some of them tossed with fresh oysters. At lunch, try the bacon, lettuce, and fried-green-tomato sandwich.

1 S. Front St. (at Centre St., on the water), Fernandina Beach. © **904/261-2660.** Reservations accepted only for parties of 6 or more. Main courses $15–$25. AE, MC, V. Mon–Sat 11:30am–2pm and 5:30–9:30pm; Sun 5:30–9:30pm.

The Main Squeeze Cafe and Juice Bar ⭐ *Finds* AMERICAN This little outdoor juice bar is the town's most unusual spot for an alfresco breakfast or lunch. The juicing and coffee brewing are done in a booth at the rear of the courtyard, while the cooking is done inside a clapboard building. You can dine outside at a wrought-iron patio table or inside. Breakfast is mostly of the pastry variety: bagels, cinnamon toast, waffles, fruit plates, coffee, cappuccino, latte, and the trademark squeezed-to-order orange, grapefruit, and carrot juice. Lunch features salads (the Fernandina is terrific), sandwiches (don't miss the crispy Cuban), and creative (as opposed to traditional) Mexican fare like nachos, burritos, and quesadillas. Dinners feature a few main courses.

105 S. 3rd St. (between Ash and Beech Sts.), Fernandina Beach. © **904/277-3003.** Reservations not accepted. Main courses $5–$10 (Fri–Sat only); breakfast $2–$4; sandwiches and salads $4–$6. AE, MC, V. Mon–Sat 7:30am–8pm; Sun 10am–2pm.

The Marina Restaurant *Value* AMERICAN Occupying a brick store built in the 1880s, this quintessential small-town restaurant has been feeding Low Country fare to the locals since 1965. Granted, a lot of the seafood here is fried and broiled, but you can order crab-stuffed shrimp or flounder as well as grouper topped with scallops and a garlicky wine sauce. Budgeteers love the $10-and-under list of Southern favorites such as country-fried steak, breaded veal cutlet, grilled pork chops, and fried chicken. Meatloaf with a tomato and basil gravy, stuffed bell peppers with a Greek-style tomato sauce, and other lunchtime specials come with three fresh country-style vegetables, which are themselves worth the price of the meal. Hearty breakfasts feature eggs, omelets, French toast, and hotcakes.

101 Centre St. (at Front St.), Fernandina Beach. © **904/261-5310.** Main courses $8–$19; breakfast $2–$6; sandwiches $5–$9. DC, MC, V. Daily 7–10am and 11:30am–9pm.

AMELIA ISLAND AFTER DARK

This romantic island goes to bed early. If you tire of the lounges in the island's resorts, check out the **Palace Saloon,** 117 Centre St., at 2nd Street (© **904/261-6320**). It claims to be Florida's oldest watering hole (open since 1878). Complete with a pressed-tin ceiling and a 40-foot-long mahogany bar, it once hosted the Carnegies and the du Ponts. Some nights you'll find live local blues or rock.

Another popular local watering hole, **O'Kane's Irish Pub & Eatery,** 318 Centre St., at 4th Street (© **904/261-1000**), has live music until midnight Monday to Thursday, until 1:30am on weekends.

Northwest Florida: The Panhandle

by Bill Goodwin

If you like beaches, you'll love Florida's northwestern Panhandle. Thanks to quartz washed down from the Appalachian Mountains, the beaches here along the Gulf of Mexico consist of dazzlingly white sand that is so talcumlike it actually squeaks when you walk across it. And walk across it you can, for some 100 miles of these incomparable sands are protected in state parks and the gorgeous Gulf Islands National Seashore.

Pensacola, Destin, Fort Walton Beach, and Panama City Beach have long been summertime beach meccas for families, couples, and singles from the adjoining states of Georgia and Alabama—a geographic proximity that lends this area the languid charm of the Deep South. Indeed, Southern specialties like turnip greens and cheese grits appear frequently on menus here.

But there's more to the northwestern Panhandle than beaches and Southern charm. Championship catches of grouper, amberjack, snapper, mackerel, cobia, sailfish, wahoo, tuna, and blue marlin have made Destin one of the world's fishing capitals. In the interior near Pensacola, the Blackwater, Shoal, and Yellow Rivers teem with bass, bream, catfish, and largemouth bass, and also offer some of Florida's best canoeing and kayaking adventures.

The area is steeped in history. Rivaling St. Augustine as Florida's oldest town, picturesque Pensacola carefully preserves a heritage derived from Spanish, French, English, and American conquests. Famous for its oysters, Apalachicola saw the invention of the air conditioner, a moment of great historical note in Florida. And Tallahassee, seat of state government since 1824, has a host of 19th-century buildings and homes, including the Old State Capitol.

EXPLORING NORTHWEST FLORIDA BY CAR

Both I-10 and U.S. 98 link Tallahassee and Pensacola, some 200 miles apart. The fastest route is I-10, but all you'll see is a huge pine forest divided by two strips of concrete. Plan to take U.S. 98, a scenic excursion in itself. Although it can be traffic-clogged in the beach towns during summer, U.S. 98 has some beautiful stretches out in the country, particularly as it literally skirts the bay east of Apalachicola and the Gulf west of Port St. Joe. It's also lovely along skinny Okaloosa Island and across the high-rise bridge between Fort Walton Beach and Destin. From the bridge you'll see the brilliant color of the Gulf and immediately understand why they call this the Emerald Coast.

1 Pensacola ★★

191 miles W. of Tallahassee, 354 miles W. of Jacksonville

Native Americans left pottery shards and artifacts in the coastal dunes here centuries before Tristan de Luna arrived with a band of Spanish colonists in 1559. Although his settlement lasted only 2 years, modern Pensacolans claim that de Luna made their town the oldest in North America. Pensacola actually dates its permanence from a Spanish colony established here in 1698, however, so St. Augustine wins this friendly feud, having been permanently settled in 1565.

France, Great Britain, the United States, and the Confederacy subsequently captured (and in one case recaptured) this strategically important deep-water port. They left Pensacola with a charming blend of Old Spanish brickwork, colonial French balconies reminiscent of New Orleans, magnificent Victorian mansions built by British and American lumber barons, and its motto, "City of Five Flags."

West of town, the excellent National Museum of Naval Aviation at the U.S. Naval Air Station celebrates the storied past of navy and marine corps pilots who trained at Pensacola. The Blue Angels, who are based here, demonstrate the high-tech present with thrilling exhibitions of precision flying in the navy's fastest fighters.

Also on the Naval Station, historic Fort Barrancas looks across the bay to Perdido Key and Santa Rosa Island, which reach out like narrow pinchers to form the harbor. Out there, powdery white-sand beaches beckon sun-and-surf lovers to their spectacular Gulf shores, which include Pensacola Beach, a small family-oriented resort, and most of Florida's share of Gulf Islands National Seashore, home of historic Fort Pickens.

ESSENTIALS

GETTING THERE **Pensacola Regional Airport,** on 12th Avenue at Airport Road, is served by **Continental** (© 800/525-0280), **Delta** (© 800/221-1212), **Northwest** (© 800/225-2525), and **US Airways** (© 800/428-4322).

Alamo (© 800/327-9633), **Avis** (© 800/331-1212), **Budget** (© 800/527-0700), **Dollar** (© 800/800-4000), **Enterprise** (© 800/325-8007), **Hertz** (© 800/654-3131), and **National** (© 800/CAR-RENT) have rental-car operations here.

Taxis wait outside the modern terminal. Fares are approximately $11 to downtown, $15 to Gulf Breeze, and $20 to Pensacola Beach.

The **Amtrak** transcontinental *Sunset Limited* stops in Pensacola at 980 E. Heinberg St. (© **800/USA-RAIL;** www.amtrak.com).

VISITOR INFORMATION The **Pensacola Visitor Information Center,** 1401 E. Gregory St., Pensacola, FL 32501 (© **800/874-1234** or 850/ 434-1234; fax 850/432-8211; www.visitpensacola.com), gives away helpful information about the Greater Pensacola area, including maps of self-guided tours of the historic districts, and sells a detailed street map of the area. The office is at the mainland end of the Pensacola Bay Bridge and is open daily from 8am to 5pm (until 4pm Saturday and Sunday from October through March).

For information specific to the beach, contact the **Pensacola Beach Chamber of Commerce,** 735 Pensacola Beach Blvd. (P.O. Box 1174), Pensacola Beach, FL 32561 (© **800/635-4803** or 850/932-1500; fax 850/932-1551; www.visitpensacolabeach.com). The chamber's offices and visitor center are on the right as you drive onto Santa Rosa Island across the Bob Sikes Bridge. They're open daily from 9am to 5pm.

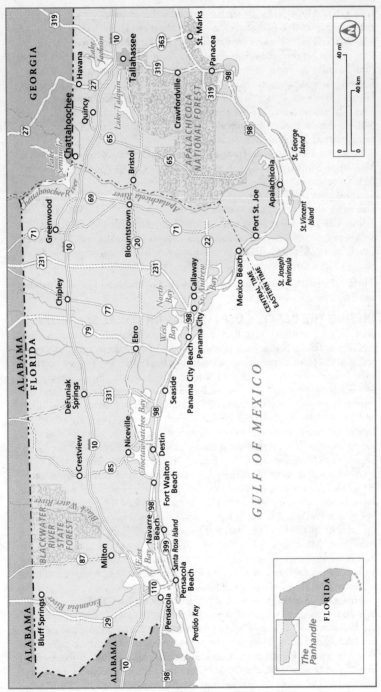

The Panhandle

633

GETTING AROUND To see the historic sights in town, park at the Pensacola visitor center (see above) and take the **Five Flags Trolley** (© 850/436-9383). The one-way East Bay (Blue) Line runs Monday to Friday from 9am to 4pm between the visitor center and downtown. The Palafox (Red) Line runs Monday to Friday from 7am to 6pm north-south along Palafox Street between the waterfront and North Hill Preservation District. Both pass through Historic Pensacola Village. The 25¢ fare includes a transfer between the two lines. The visitor center has free route maps.

A free **Island Trolley** operates along the full length of Pensacola Beach daily from 10am to 3am from May to September.

Escambia County Area Transit System (ECAT) runs buses around town Monday to Saturday but doesn't go to the beach. Call © **850/463-9383,** ext. 611, for schedules.

If you need a cab, call **Airport Express Taxi** (© 850/572-5555), **Crosstown Cab** (© 850/456-TAXI), **Pensacola Red & Gold Taxi** (© 850/505-0025), or **Yellow Cab** (© 850/433-3333). Fares are $1.50 at flag fall, plus $1.40 a mile.

You can rent bicycles and scooters from **Floats-N-Spokes,** 500 Quietwater Beach Rd. (© **850/934-RIDE**), in Pensacola Beach. Bike fees range from $5 an hour to $15 a day. Scooters go for $30 a hour to $90 a day.

TIME Pensacola is in the **central time zone,** 1 hour behind Miami, Orlando, and Tallahassee.

HITTING THE BEACH: GULF ISLANDS NATIONAL SEASHORE

Stretching eastward 47 miles, from the entrance to Pensacola Bay to Fort Walton Beach, skinny **Santa Rosa Island** is home to the resorts, condominiums, cottages, restaurants, and shops of **Pensacola Beach,** the area's prime vacation spot. This relatively small and low-key resort began life a century ago as the site of a beach pavilion, or "casino" as such facilities were called back then; and the heart of town—at the intersection of Pensacola Beach Boulevard, Via de Luna, and Fort Pickens Road—is still known as **Casino Beach.** This lively area at the base of the town's water tank sports restaurants, snack bars, a games arcade for kids, a minigolf course, public rest rooms, walk-up beach bars with live bands blaring away, an indoor sports bar, and an outdoor concert pavilion with summertime entertainment. And the shops, restaurants, and bars of **Quietwater Boardwalk** are just across the road on the bay side of the island. If you want an active beach vacation, it's all here in one compact zone.

One reason Pensacola Beach is so small is that most of Santa Rosa Island is included in the **Gulf Islands National Seashore** ✦✦✦. Jumping from island to island from Mississippi to Florida, this magnificent preserve includes mile after mile of undeveloped white-sand beach and rolling dunes covered with sea grass and sea oats. Established in 1971, the national seashore is a protected environment for more than 280 species of birds.

The most interesting part of the seashore is at **Fort Pickens** (© 850/934-2635), on the western end of Santa Rosa Island, about 7 miles west of Pensacola Beach. Built in the 1830s to team with Fort Barrancas in guarding Pensacola's harbor entrance, this huge brick structure saw combat during the Civil War, but it's best known as the prison home of Apache medicine man Geronimo from 1886 to 1888. The visitor center has a small museum featuring displays about Geronimo, coastal defenses, and the seashore's ecology. Plan to be here at 2pm, when rangers lead 1-hour guided tours of the fort (the schedule can change, so call the fort to make sure). Seven-day admission permits to the Fort

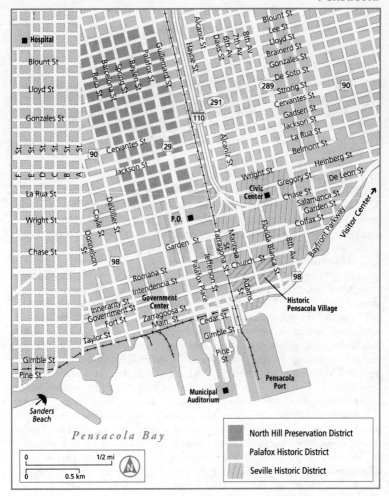

Pickens area are $6 per vehicle, $3 per pedestrian or bicyclist, free for holders of National Park Service passports. The fort and museum are open April to October daily from 9:30am to 5pm, November to March daily from 8:30am to 4pm. Both are closed on Christmas.

The Fort Pickens area has 200 **campsites** (135 with electricity) in a pine forest on the bay side of Santa Rosa Island. Nature trails lead from the camp through Blackbird Marsh and to the beach. A small store sells provisions. Sites cost $15 a night without power, $20 a night with it, and you have to pay the admission fee to the Fort Pickens area. Golden Age and Golden Access cardholders get a 50% discount. Call ☎ **800/365-2267** for reservations (enter code GUL), or 850/934-2621 for recorded information. You can make reservations up to 5 months in advance.

The national seashore's headquarters are in the 1,378-acre **Naval Live Oaks Area,** on U.S. 98, a mile east of Gulf Breeze (☎ **850/934-2600**). This former federal tree plantation is a place of primitive beauty, with nature trails leading through the oaks and pines to picnic areas and a beach. Pick up a map at the headquarters building, which has a small museum and a gorgeous view through the pines to Santa Rosa Sound. Picnic areas and trails are open from 8am to sunset all year except Christmas. Admission is free. The visitor center is open daily from 8am to 5:30pm.

The national seashore also maintains historic **Fort Barrancas** on the U.S. Naval Air Station west of town. See the listing for the National Museum of Naval Aviation under "Exploring Historic Pensacola," below, for details.

For more information, contact the **Gulf Islands National Seashore,** 1801 Gulf Breeze Pkwy., Gulf Breeze, FL 32561 (© **850/934-2600;** www.nps.gov/parks/guis).

OUTDOOR ACTIVITIES

CANOEING & KAYAKING   Less than 20 miles northeast of Pensacola via U.S. 90 is the little town of Milton, the official "Canoe Capital of Florida" (by an act of the state legislature, no less). It's a well-earned title, because the nearby Blackwater River, Coldwater River, Sweetwater Creek, and Juniper Creek are all perfect for canoeing, kayaking, tubing, rafting, and paddleboating.

The Blackwater is considered one of the world's purest sand-bottom rivers. It has remained a primordial, backwoods beauty, thanks chiefly to Florida's largest state forest (183,000 acres of oak, pine, and juniper) and **Blackwater River State Park** ★★, 7720 Deaton Bridge Rd., Holt, FL 32564 (© **850/983-5363;** www8.myflorida.com/communities/learn/stateparks/district1/blackwaterriver), where you can closely observe plant life and wildlife along nature trails. The park has facilities for fishing, picnicking, and camping. Admission is $3.25 per day per vehicle with up to eight occupants, $1 for pedestrians or bicyclists. Campsites cost $8 per night per person ($10 with electricity), plus $2 per pet with tags and vaccination papers. The park does not accept advance campsite reservations.

Adventures Unlimited, Route 6, Box 283, Milton, FL 32570 (© **800/239-6864** or 850/623-6197; fax 850/626-3124; www.adventuresunlimited.com), is a year-round resort with day and overnight canoeing, kayaking, and rafting expeditions. Special arrangements are made for novices. Canoe trips start at $16 per person, kayaking adventures from $22. Inner tubes start at $6. Campsites cost $15 a night, $20 with electricity. The resort also has 14 cottages on the Coldwater River ($39 to $109 a night), and bed-and-breakfast accommodations at the Wolfe Creek Old School House Inn (eight rooms, all with bathrooms, $79 to $109 double). Two-night minimum stays are required, 3 nights on holidays.

Blackwater Canoe Rental, 10274 Pond Rd., Milton, FL 32570 (© **800/967-6789** or 850/623-0235; www.blackwatercanoe.com), also rents canoes, kayaks, floats, tubes, and camping equipment. It has day and camping trips by canoe or kayak, or inner tubes ranging from $9 to $19 per person and overnight excursions ranging from $19 to $28 per person. Tents, sleeping bags, and coolers are available for rent.

FISHING   Red snapper, grouper, mackerel, tuna, and billfish are abundant offshore all along the Panhandle. Anglers congregate along the **Pensacola Bay Bridge Fishing Pier** (© **850/444-9811**), which has a bait shop next to the Pensacola Visitor Information Center (see "Essentials," above), and the **Bob Sikes Bridge Fishing Pier** between Gulf Breeze and Pensacola Beach. Both are on the old bridges.

Fishing-charter services are offered by **Scuba Shack/Charter Boat** *Wet Dream,* 711 S. Palafox St., in Pensacola (© 850/433-4319); *Hooligan* **Charters** (© 850/968-1898) and *Rocky Top* **Charters** (© 850/432-7536), both at Pitt Slip Marina off East Main Street in Pensacola; and *Lo-Baby* **Charters,** 38 Highpoint Dr., in Gulf Breeze (© 850/934-5285). At Pensacola Beach, choose from *Chulamar* (© 850/434-6977), *Lively One* (© 850/932-5071), *Boss Lady* (© 850/932-0305 or 850/477-4033), *Entertainer* (© 850/932-0305), *Exodus* (© 850/626-2545 or 850/932-0305), and *Lady Kady* (© 850/932-2065 or 850/932-0305). Expect to pay between $350 and $750 for one to four passengers, depending on length of trip. You may be able to save by driving to Destin, where party boats charge less per person (see "Outdoor Activities," in section 2, below). Sightseeing and evening cruises here go for about $50 per person.

GOLF The Pensacola area has its share of Northwest Florida's numerous championship golf courses. Look for free copies of *Gulf Coast Tee Time* (www.teetime.web.com), an annual directory describing all of them, at the visitor information offices and in many hotel lobbies (see "The Active Vacation Planner," in chapter 2, for information about ordering copies). Reasonably priced golf packages can be arranged through many local hotels and motels.

Among this region's best courses is **Marcus Pointe,** on Marcus Pointe Boulevard off North W Street (© **800/362-7287** or 850/484-9770), which has hosted the Nike Tour, the American Amateur Classic, and the Pensacola Open. *Golf Digest* magazine has described this wide-ranging, 18-hole course as a "great value," and it is: Greens fees with cart are about $40 to $50, depending on the season.

The Moors, on Avalon Boulevard north of I-10 (© **800/727-1010** or 850/995-4653), also has greeted the Nike Tour and is home to the Emerald Coast Classic, a PGA Seniors event. Pot bunkers here make you think you're playing in Scotland. Greens fees are about $30 without cart. The Moors also has a lodge with eight luxury rooms.

Others worth considering are **Lost Key Golf Club,** on Perdido Key (© **850/492-1300**), one of the area's more difficult courses; **Scenic Hills,** on U.S. 90 northwest of town (© **850/476-9611**), whose rolling fairways are unique for this mostly flat area; the 36-hole **Tiger Point,** 1255 Country Club Rd. east of Gulf Breeze by Santa Rosa Sound (© **850/932-1330**), overlooking the water (the 5th-hole green of the East Course actually sits all by itself on an island); **Hidden Creek,** 3070 PGA Blvd., in Navarre between Gulf Breeze and Fort Walton Beach (© **850/939-4604**); **Creekside Golf Course,** 2355 W. Michigan Ave. (© **850/944-7969**); and **Osceola Municipal Golf Course,** 300 Tonawanda, off Mobile Highway (© **850/456-2761**).

In addition, **The Sportsman Golf Resort,** 1 Doug Ford Dr. (© **850/492-1223;** www.sportsmanresort.com), on the mainland north of Perdido Key, has accommodations available for visiting golfers. It was the home of the PGA Pensacola Open from 1978 to 1987, when it was known as the Perdido Bay Golf Resort.

WATER SPORTS Visibility in the waters around Pensacola can range from 30 to 50 feet deep inshore to 100 feet deep 25 miles offshore. Although the bottom is sandy and it's too far north for coral, the battleship USS *Massachusetts,* submerged in 30 feet of water 3 miles offshore, is one of some 35 artificial reefs where you can spot loggerhead turtles and other creatures. There are also good snorkeling sites just off the beach; get a map from the Gulf Islands National Seashore (see "Hitting the Beach," above).

Scuba Shack, 711 S. Palafox St. (© **850/433-4319**), is Pensacola's oldest dive shop, offering sales, rentals, classes, and diving and fishing charters on the *Wet Dream,* moored behind the office. **Divers Den,** 512 N. 9th Ave. (© **850/ 438-0650;** www.diversden.com), also offers trips, equipment rental, and PADI instruction. **Gulf Breeze Dive Pros,** 297B Gulf Breeze Pkwy. (U.S. 98), in Gulf Breeze (© **850/934-8845**), offers rentals, all levels of instruction, and diving excursions on the 30-foot *Easy Dive.* The *Chulamar,* at Pensacola Beach (© **850/434-6977**), and the *Lo-Baby,* in Gulf Breeze (© **850/934-5285**), both make arrangements for diving excursions.

Key Sailing Center, 500 Quietwater Beach Rd., on the Quietwater Beach Boardwalk (© **850/932-5550**), and **Radical Rides,** 444 Pensacola Beach Blvd., near the Bob Sikes Bridge (© **850/934-9743**), rent Hobie Cats, pontoon boats, WaveRunners, jet skis, and windsurfing boards.

EXPLORING HISTORIC PENSACOLA

Adjacent to the Historic Pensacola Village, the city's **Vietnam Memorial,** on Bayfront Parkway at 9th Avenue, is known as the "Wall South," since it is a three-quarters–size replica of the national Vietnam Veterans Memorial in Washington, D.C. Look for the "Huey" helicopter atop the wall.

Civil War Soldiers Museum ⚔ Founded by Dr. Norman Haines Jr., a local physician who grew up discovering Civil War relics in Sharpsburg, Maryland, this storefront museum in the heart of the Palafox Street business district emphasizes how ordinary soldiers lived during that bloody conflict. The doctor's collection of military medical equipment and treatment methods is especially informative. A 23-minute video tells of Pensacola's role during the Civil War. The museum's bookstore carries more than 600 titles about the war.

108 S. Palafox St. (south of Romana St.). © 850/469-1900. www.cwmuseum.org. Admission $5 adults, $2.50 children 6–12, free for children 5 and under. Tues–Sat 10am–4:30pm. Closed New Year's Day, Thanksgiving, Christmas Eve, Christmas.

Historic Pensacola Village ⚔⚔ Bounded by Government, Taragona, Adams, and Alcanz streets, this original part of Pensacola resembles a shady English colonial town—albeit with Spanish street names—complete with town green and **Christ Church,** built in 1832 and resembling Bruton Parish in Williamsburg, Virginia. Some of Florida's oldest homes, now owned and preserved by the state, are here, and the village has charming boutiques and interesting restaurants. During summer, costumed characters go about their daily chores and demonstrate old crafts, and University of Florida archaeologists unearth the old Spanish commanding officer's compound at Zaragossa and Tarragona streets. Among the landmarks you'll visit are the **Museum of Industry,** the **Museum of Commerce,** the French Creole–style **Charles Lavalle House,** the elegant **Victorian Dorr House,** the French Colonial–Creole **Quina House,** and **St. Michael's Cemetery** (land was deeded by the king of Spain). Another fascinating site is the **Julee Cottage Black History Museum,** 204 Zaragossa St. Built around 1790, this small house was owned by Julee Panton, a freed slave who ran her own business, invested in real estate, and loaned money to slaves so they could buy their freedom. Today the museum recalls her life and deeds. Start your tour by buying tickets at **Tivoli House,** 205 E. Zaragossa St., just east of Tarragona Street, where you can get free maps and brochures. Try to take one of the 90-minute guided walking tours of the village, which will take you through Christ Church and other buildings not otherwise open to the public.

Admission to the village includes the **T. T. Wentworth Jr. Florida State Museum,** 330 S. Jefferson St. (© **850/595-5989**) at Church Street downtown, a classic yellow brick building housing exhibits of Western Florida's history and a special hands-on Discovery Museum for children.

205 E. Zaragossa St. (east of Tarragona St.). © 850/595-5985. www.historicpensacola.org. Admission $6 adults, $5 seniors, $2.50 children 4–16, free for children 3 and under. Mon–Sat 10am–4:30pm; 90-min. guided tours 11am and 1pm. Closed Mon in winter, New Year's Day, Thanksgiving, Christmas Eve, and Christmas.

National Museum of Naval Aviation ★★ The U.S. Navy and Marine Corps have trained at the sprawling U.S. Naval Air Station since they began flying airplanes early in this century. Celebrating their heroics, this truly remarkable museum has more than 100 aircraft dating from the 1920s to the space age. There's even a torpedo bomber flown by former President George Bush during World War II. Both children and adults can sit at the controls of a jet trainer. You can almost feel the tug of gravity while watching the Blue Angels and other naval aviators soaring about the skies in the stunning *Magic of Flight,* one of two IMAX films shown at the museum. All guides are retired naval and marine corps aviators, which adds a personal touch to the hour-long museum tours. There's also a free 20-minute Flight Line bus tour of more than 40 aircraft parked outside the museum's restoration hangar.

Radford Blvd., U.S. Naval Air Station. © 850/452-3604. www.naval-air.org. Free admission. IMAX movies $5.50 adults; $5.25 seniors, military, and children under 13. Daily 9am–5pm. Guided tours daily at 9:30am, 11am, 1pm, and 2:30pm; Flight Line bus tours daily every 30 min. 10am–12:30pm and 1–4pm. IMAX films daily 10am–4pm. Closed New Year's Day, Thanksgiving, Christmas. Enter naval station either at the Main Gate at the south end of Navy Blvd. (Fla. 295) or at the Back Gate on Blue Angel Pkwy. (Fla. 173) and follow the signs. No passes are required.

Pensacola Historical Museum To learn more about Pensacola's diverse, five-flag history, spend a few minutes at this local museum in the Arbona Building, a commercial structure built about 1882. An archaeological dig of the Spanish commanding officer's compound across Zaragossa Street has a boardwalk with explanatory signposts. The museum is operated by the Pensacola Historical Society, which has a resource center and library at 117 E. Government St. (© **850/434-5455**).

115 E. Zaragossa St. (between Tarragona and Jefferson Sts.). © 850/433-1559. www.pensacolahistory.org. Admission $1. Mon–Sat 10am–4:30pm.

Pensacola Museum of Art Housed in what was the city jail from 1906 to 1954, this museum showcases a fine collection of European and American decorative glass, some African tribal art, and minor works by Salvador Dali, John Marin, Thomas Hart Benton, Lynda Benglis, Milton Avery, and Alexander Calder, among others.

407 S. Jefferson St. (at Main St.). © 850/432-6247. www.pensacolamuseumofart.org. Admission free on Tues; other days $2 adults, $1 students and active-duty military, free for children under 6. Tues–Fri 10am–5pm; Sat 10am–4pm.

HISTORIC DISTRICTS

In addition to Historic Pensacola Village in the Seville Historic District (see below), the city has two other preservation areas worth a stroll. The Pensacola Visitor Information Center provides free walking-tour maps (see "Essentials," earlier in this chapter).

Pensacola's Other Fort

Standing on Taylor Road near the National Museum of Naval Aviation, **Fort Barrancas** ✦✦ (✆ **850/455-5167**) is definitely worth a visit while you're at the naval station. This imposing brick structure sits on a bluff overlooking the deep-water pass into Pensacola Bay. The Spanish built the water battery in 1797. Linked to it by a tunnel, the incredibly intricate brickwork of the fort's upper section was constructed by American troops between 1839 and 1844. Entry is by means of a drawbridge across a dry moat, and an interior scarp gallery goes all the way around the inside of the fort. Meticulously restored and operated by the National Park Service as part of Gulf Islands National Seashore, the fort is open from April to October, daily from 9:30am to 5pm; November through March, Wednesday to Sunday from 10:30am to 4pm. Ranger-led, 1-hour guided tours are well worth taking. The schedule changes seasonally, so call for the latest information. Admission and the tours are free.

The **Pensacola Lighthouse** (✆ **850/455-2354**), opposite the museum entrance on Radford Boulevard, has guided ships to the harbor entrance since 1825. Except for occasional guided tours (call the lighthouse or the Pensacola visitor centers for a schedule), the lighthouse is not open to the public, but you can drive right up to it. The nearby **Lighthouse Point Restaurant** (✆ **850/452-3251**) offers bountiful, all-you-can-eat luncheon buffets and magnificent bay views for about $6 per person; it's open Monday to Friday from 10:30am to 2pm, and reservations are not required.

PALAFOX HISTORIC DISTRICT   Running up Palafox Street from the water to Wright Street, the Palafox Historic District is also the downtown business district. Beautiful Spanish Renaissance- and Mediterranean-style buildings stand from the early days, including the ornate Saenger Theatre. In 1821 General Andrew Jackson formally accepted Florida into the United States during a ceremony in Plaza Ferdinand VII, now a National Historic Landmark. His statue commemorates the event.

The Palafox district is home to the **Pensacola Historical Museum;** the **Pensacola Museum of Art,** in the old city jail; and the **T. T. Wentworth Jr. Florida State Museum** (see "Exploring Historic Pensacola," above).

NORTH HILL PRESERVATION DISTRICT   Another entry in the National Register of Historic Places, the North Hill Preservation District covers the 50 square blocks north of the Palafox Historic District bounded by Wright, Blount, Palafox, and Reus streets. Descendants of Spanish nobility, timber barons, British merchants, French Creoles, buccaneers, and Civil War soldiers still live in some of the more than 500 homes. They are not open to the public but are a bonanza for anyone interested in architecture. In 1863 Union troops erected a fort in Lee Square, at Palafox and Gadsden streets. It later was dedicated to the Confederacy, complete with a 50-foot-high obelisk and sculpture based on John Elder's painting *After Appomattox.*

A NEARBY ZOO WITH WHITE TIGERS

The Zoo *Kids*   Situated in a 50-acre forest 15 miles east of Pensacola, this environmentally sensitive zoo has more than 700 exotic animals—including white tigers, rhinos, and gorillas—living in landscaped habitats. Japanese gardens, a giraffe-feeding tower, and a petting farm make for a fun visit. A Safari Line train chugs through a 30-acre wildlife preserve with free-ranging herds, and youngsters also will love riding the wild animals instead of horses on a merry-go-round. The Zoo is open evenings from the day after Thanksgiving until January 4 for a holiday lights festival, when proceeds go to charity.

5701 Gulf Breeze Pkwy., Gulf Breeze (U.S. 98). © 850/932-2229. www.pcola.gulf.net/about/thezoo. Admission $9.75 adults, $8.75 seniors, $5.75 children 3–11, children 2 and under free. Train and carousel rides $1.75 per person. Summer daily 9am–5pm; Sept–Nov and Jan–May daily 9am–4pm; day after Thanksgiving–Jan 4 daily 9am–3pm and 6–9pm. Closed day before Thanksgiving, Thanksgiving, Christmas Eve, and Christmas.

SHOPPING

Sightseeing and shopping can be combined in Pensacola's Palafox and Seville Historic Districts, where many shops are housed in renovated centuries-old buildings. The **Quayside Art Gallery,** on Plaza Ferdinand at the corner of Zaragossa and Jefferson streets (© **850/438-2363**), is the largest cooperative gallery in the Southeast. More than 100 artists display their works here, and the friendly staff will direct you to other nearby galleries.

North T Street between West Cervantes Street and West Fairfield Drive has so many antiques dealers and small flea markets that it's known as Antique Alley. Other dealers have booths in the **Ninth Avenue Antique Mall,** 380 N. 9th Ave. between Gregory and Strong streets (© **850/438-3961**). Get a complete list of local antiques dealers from the Pensacola Visitor Information Center (see "Essentials," earlier in this chapter).

Browsers will enjoy poking through the 400 dealer spaces covering 45 acres at the **Flea Market,** on U.S. 98, opposite The Zoo, 15 miles east of Pensacola (© **850/934-1971**). It's open on Saturday and Sunday 9am to 5pm. Admission is free.

WHERE TO STAY

Room rates at all Panhandle beaches are highest from mid-May to mid-August, and premiums are charged at Easter, Memorial Day, July 4, and Labor Day. Hotel or motel reservations are essential during these periods. There's another high-priced peak in March, when thousands of raucous college students invade during Spring Break. Economical times to visit are April (except Easter) and September—the weather is warm, most establishments are open, and room rates are significantly lower than during summer. The least-expensive rates occur during winter, but many attractions and some restaurants may be closed then.

The Pensacola Visitor Information Center (see "Essentials," earlier in this chapter) publishes a complete list of rental condominiums and cottages. Among the leading rental agents are **Gulf Coast Accommodations,** 400 Quietwater Beach Rd., Box 12, Pensacola Beach, FL 32561 (© **800/239-4334** or 850/932-9788; fax 850/932-3449; www.innisfree.com/gca); and **Tristan Realty,** P.O. Box 1611, Gulf Breeze, FL 32562 (© **800/445-9931** or 850/932-7363; fax 850/932-8361; www.tristanrealty.com).

The **Fort Pickens Area** of Gulf Islands National Seashore is your best bet here for camping (see "Hitting the Beach," earlier in this chapter).

Escambia County adds 11.5% tax to all hotel and campground bills.

The accommodations listed below are arranged by geographic area: downtown Pensacola and Pensacola Beach.

DOWNTOWN PENSACOLA

The University Mall complex at I-10 and Davis Highway, about 5 miles north of downtown, has a host of chain motels, and there's an ample supply of inexpensive restaurants on Plantation Road and in the adjacent mall. Another good bet is the 1998-vintage **Hampton Inn Airport,** 2187 Airport Blvd. (© **800/ HAMPTON** or 850/478-1123; fax 850/478-8519). This area is not as congested as that around University Mall. The inn runs a free shuttle to nearby Cordova Mall and its adjacent chain restaurants.

Several of the town's Victorian homes have been turned into luxurious bed-and-breakfasts. Among the best is **Springhill Guesthouse,** 903 N. Spring St. (© **800/475-1956** or 850/438-6887; www.bbonline.com/fl/springhill), whose wraparound porch faces the extraordinary Hopkins Boarding House across the street (see "Where to Dine," below).

Crowne Pensacola Grand Hotel   Opposite the Civic Center in the Seville Historic District near the southern end of I-110, this unique hotel has turned the historic L&N Railroad Depot into a grand lobby with bar, restaurants, lounges, meeting rooms, and a cozy library. You'll see such turn-of-the-century accoutrements as an ornate railroad clock, original oak stair rails, imported marble, ceramic mosaic tile floors, and old-fashioned carved furniture. An unimpressive 15-story glass-and-steel tower behind the depot holds the rooms and suites, which are popular primarily with business travelers and groups.

200 E. Gregory St. (at Alcanz St.), Pensacola, FL 32501. © **800/348-3336** or 850/433-3336. Fax 850/432-7572. www.pensacolagrandhotel.com. 212 units. $110–$135 double; $250–$408 suite. AE, DC, DISC, MC, V. **Amenities:** Restaurant (American); bar; outdoor pool; exercise room; business center; limited room service; laundry service; concierge-level rooms. *In room:* A/C, TV, dataport, fridge (suites only), coffeemaker, hair dryer, iron.

New World Inn   Near the scenic bay and in the historic district, this urban version of a comfortable country inn is part of a meeting facility known as New World Landing. From the colonial-style lobby, a grand staircase leads to high-ceilinged and spacious rooms and suites artistically decorated with antiques. The rooms depict aspects of Pensacola's rich history: four of them flaunt Spanish decor, four are très chic French style, four portray Early Americana, and four focus on Olde England.

600 S. Palafox St. (at Pine St.), Pensacola, FL 32501. © **850/432-4111.** Fax 850/432-6836. www.newworldlanding.com. 15 units. $75 double; $120 suite. Rates include continental breakfast. AE, MC, V. **Amenities:** Access to nearby health club; laundry service. *In room:* A/C, TV, dataport.

PENSACOLA BEACH
Moderate

Best Western Resort Pensacola Beach   This casual motel on the Gulf front is notable for bright, clean, and extraspacious accommodations, complete with refrigerators, coffeemakers, microwaves, and wet bars. Outside corridors lead to all rooms. Although none has its own balcony or patio, units facing the beach have great views; the less expensive "inland" rooms don't. Two swimming pools and a children's playground are on the beach. Chan's Market Cafe (see "Where to Dine," below) sits in the parking lot.

16 Via de Luna Dr., Pensacola Beach, FL 32561. © **800/934-3301** or 850/934-3300. Fax 850/934-4366. bestwesternpnsbch@worldnet.att.net. 123 units. Summer $149–$189 double; off-season $75–$129 double. Rates include continental breakfast. Golf packages available. AE, DC, DISC, MC, V. **Amenities:** 2 outdoor pools; water-sports equipment rentals; game room. *In room:* A/C, TV, dataport, fridge, coffeemaker, hair dryer, iron.

Clarion Suites Resort & Convention Center ⚜ This most charming of Pensacola Beach's resorts resembles a village of tin-roofed, pastel-sided cottages. The attractively decorated accommodations are one-bedroom suites that can accommodate four people. Only those directly facing the beach have balconies or patios.

20 Via de Luna Dr., Pensacola Beach, FL 32561. ℂ **800/874-5303** or 850/932-4300. Fax 850/934-9112. www.clarionsuitesresort.com. 86 units. Summer $122–$173 up to 4 persons. Off-season $79–$129 up to 4 persons. Rates include continental breakfast. AE, DC, DISC, MC, V. **Amenities:** Heated outdoor pool; watersports equipment rentals; coin-op washers and dryers. *In room:* A/C, TV, dataport, kitchen, coffeemaker, hair dryer, iron.

The Dunes ⚜ Totally renovated after hurricane damage in 1998, this eight-story beachfront tower has spacious rooms, all with gorgeous gulf or bay vistas. All rooms have a gulf-facing balcony, and the penthouse suites have their own whirlpool tubs. The extra-large suites can accommodate small families. The Dunes has a restaurant and bar (both with lovely views of the gulf), so you don't have to go out for lunch or dinner unless you want to. There's a jogging trail, bike path, and an undeveloped dune preserve next door.

333 Fort Pickens Rd., Pensacola Beach, FL 32561. ℂ **800/83-DUNES** or 850/932-3536. Fax 850/932-7088. www.theduneshotel.com. 76 units. Summer $115–$175 double; $295–$345 suite. Off-season $85–$115 double; $255–$305 suite. Packages available. AE, DISC, MC, V. **Amenities:** Restaurant (American); bar; heated outdoor pool; access to nearby health club; water-sports equipment rentals; limited room service; laundry service. *In room:* A/C, TV, dataport, coffeemaker, hair dryer, iron.

Hampton Inn Pensacola Beach ⚜ This pastel, four-story hotel sits right by the Gulf next to the action on Casino Beach. The bright lobby opens to a wooden sundeck with beachside swimming pools on either side (one is heated). Half the oversize rooms have balconies overlooking the Gulf; these are more expensive than rooms on the bay side, which have nice views but no outside sitting areas.

2 Via de Luna, Pensacola Beach, FL 32561. ℂ **800/320-8108** or 850/932-6800. Fax 850/932-6833. www.hamptonbeachresort.com. 181 units. Summer $125–$179 double; off-season $75–$139 double. Rates include continental breakfast and local phone calls. AE, DC, DISC, MC, V. **Amenities:** Bar; 2 outdoor pools; access to nearby health club; exercise room; water-sports equipment rentals; laundry service, coin-op washers and dryers. *In room:* A/C, TV, dataport, fridge, coffeemaker, hair dryer, iron.

Holiday Inn Express Pensacola Beach Another property that received a face-lift following a 1998 hurricane, this nine-story hotel boasts terrific views from its brightly furnished upper-floor rooms. It's one of the oldest hotels in the area, which means the rooms aren't as large as those at other new properties such as the Hampton Inn; there's adequate space for a king-size bed, but rooms with two double beds are relatively cramped. They all have private balconies, however, with the most expensive rooms facing directly onto the Gulf.

165 Fort Pickens Rd., Pensacola Beach, FL 32561. ℂ **800/465-4329** or 850/932-5361. Fax 850/932-7121. www.pensacolabeach.com/holiday. 150 units. Summer $110–$140 double; off-season $65–$110 double. Rates include continental breakfast. AE, DC, DISC, MC, V. **Amenities:** Heated outdoor pool; coin-op washers and dryers. *In room:* A/C, TV, dataport, coffeemaker, hair dryer, iron.

Inexpensive

Five Flags Inn *Value* Sitting between the Holiday Inn Express and The Dunes, this basic but friendly motel looks like a jail from the road, but don't be fooled. Big picture windows look from the rooms out to the swimming pool (heated from March through October) and to the gorgeous white-sand beach, which comes right up to the property. Although the accommodations are small, the rates are a bargain for clean, gulf-front rooms.

299 Fort Pickens Rd., Pensacola Beach, FL 32561. ℂ **850/932-3586.** Fax 850/934-0257. www.fiveflags.com. 49 units. Summer $95 double; off-season $55–$75 double. AE, DC, MC, V. **Amenities:** Heated outdoor pool. *In room:* A/C, TV, fax, dataport, kitchen, minibar, coffeemaker, hair dryer, iron.

WHERE TO DINE
PENSACOLA

Hopkins' Boarding House ★★★ *Value* SOUTHERN There's a delicious peek into the past when you dine at this extraordinary Victorian boardinghouse in the heart of the North Hill Preservation District. Outside, ancient trees shade a wraparound porch with old-fashioned rocking chairs in which to await the next available place at the large dining tables inside. It's all-you-can-eat family-style, so you could be seated next to the mayor or a mechanic, since everyone in town dines here. Platters are piled high with staples of down-home Southern cooking: black-eyed peas, collard greens, and other seasonal vegetables from nearby farms. Tuesday is famous as Fried Chicken Day, and you're likely to be served fried fish on Friday. You Yankees should sample the piping-hot grits accompanying each bountiful breakfast (slop on some butter to give them taste). In true boardinghouse fashion, you'll bus your own dishes and pay on the way out. No alcoholic beverages are served, but the "already-sweet" ice tea is great.

900 N. Spring St. (at Strong St.). ℂ 850/438-3979. Reservations not accepted. Breakfast $3.50–$7; full meals $7. No credit cards. Year-round Tues–Sat 7–9:30am and 11:15am–2pm; Sun 11am–2pm. Mar–Dec Tues–Sat 5:15–7:30pm. Jan–Feb Tues, Fri–Sat 5:15–7:30pm.

Jamie's ★★ TRADITIONAL FRENCH Occupying a restored Victorian home in Historic Pensacola Village, the town's classiest and most romantic restaurant enhances the dining experience with an Art Deco ambience augmented by glowing fireplaces, gleaming antiques, and subdued background music. The excellent fare is traditional French. Roast leg of lamb and tournedos of beef are good choices from the regular menu, but don't overlook the seafood specials.

424 E. Zaragossa St. (between Alcanz and Florida Blanca). ℂ 850/434-2911. Reservations recommended at both lunch and dinner. Main courses $19–$28. AE, DISC, MC, V. Tues–Thurs 5:30–9pm; Fri–Sat 5:30–10pm; Sun 5:30–9pm.

Marina Oyster Barn ★ *Value* SEAFOOD Exuding the ambience of the quickly vanishing Old Florida fish camps, this plain but clean restaurant at the Johnson-Rooks Marina is to seafood what the Hopkins Boarding House is to grits. It has been a local favorite since 1969, for both its view and its down-home–style seafood. Freshly shucked oysters, served raw, steamed, fried, or Rockefeller, are the main feature; but the seafood salad here is also first-rate, and the fish, shrimp, and oysters are breaded with cornmeal in true Southern fashion. The daily luncheon specials give you a light meal at a bargain price. No smoking.

505 Bayou Blvd. (on Bayou Texar). ℂ 850/433-0511. Reservations not accepted. Main courses $4–$12; sandwiches $2.50–$5.50; lunch specials $3.75–$6.50. AE, DISC, MC, V. Tues–Sat 11am–9pm (lunch specials 11am–2pm). Go east on Cervantes St. (U.S. 90) across the Bayou Texar Bridge, then take first left on Stanley Ave., and left again to the end of Strong St.

McGuire's Irish Pub ★ AMERICAN/IRISH Every day is St. Patrick's Day at this lively and popular Irish pub, complete with corned beef and cabbage, Irish stew, and other such Dublin delicacies. Super-size steaks are the best offerings here, however, as are hickory-smoked ribs and chicken. You can also order seafood, including a hearty bouillabaisse with shrimp, red snapper, clams, mussels, and oysters. Big burgers come with a choice of more than 20 toppings, from smoked Gouda cheese to sautéed Vidalia onions. You can watch your ale being brewed in copper kettles and dine in a cellarlike room with 8,000 bottles of wine on display. More than 125,000 dollar bills line the bar's walls and ceilings. Live music is offered most nights.

600 E. Gregory St. (between 11th and 12th Aves.). ✆ 850/433-6789. Reservations not accepted. Main courses $16–$25; snacks, burgers, and sandwiches $8–$10. AE, DC, DISC, MC, V. Sun–Thurs 11am–midnight; Fri–Sat 11am–2am; Sun brunch 11am–3pm.

Skopelos on the Bay ★ SEAFOOD/STEAKS/GREEK   Perched on a bluff overlooking the bay, this family-owned restaurant has been famous hereabouts since 1959 for its great views and creative seafood dishes, such as the scamp Cervantes (scamp is a deepwater fish with white, flaky meat). Other seafood selections range from broiled scallops to Mediterranean-style grouper prepared with a sauce of tomato and roasted eggplant. The menu also features charcoal-grilled steaks and chicken and roast leg of lamb. Befitting the owner's Greek heritage, roast lamb is served with moussaka, dolmades, titopita, and spanakopita. In warm weather opt for an outside table with bay view.

670 Scenic Hwy. (U.S. 90 east, at E. Cervantes St.). ✆ **850/432-6565.** Reservations recommended. Main courses $13–$19. AE, DISC, MC, V. Tues–Thurs and Sat 5–10:30pm; Fri 11:30am–2:30pm and 5–10:30pm.

PENSACOLA BEACH

Chan's Market Cafe *Value* AMERICAN   The aroma of pastries in the oven permeates this pleasant little cafe and bakery, which shares quarters with a liquor store in the parking lot of the Best Western Pensacola Beach. It's the best place on the beach for a breakfast of freshly baked croissants or bagels. Lunches and dinners feature economical specials such as meatloaf, barbecued chicken, pot roast, and grilled fish, all served with a choice of Southern-style veggies. Or you can order a heaping sandwich on one of Chan's large flaky croissants.

16 Via de Luna. ✆ **850/932-8454.** Breakfast/lunch/snacks $3–$7; meals $5–$10. AE, DISC, MC, V. Daily 7am–9pm.

Flounder's Chowder House ★ SEAFOOD   Inside, this restaurant radiates piousness, with decor featuring stained-glass windows from an old New York convent and confessional-booth walls from a New Orleans church. Outside on the sandy beach by the bay is a totally different story, however, for in summer this is one of the most popular reggae bars here (see "Pensacola After Dark," below). The food is pretty good, with chargrilled tuna, grouper, and mahi-mahi leading the list. If you're lucky, a big smoker grill outside will be producing more fish and some exceptional ribs. Burgers, salads, and sandwiches are offered all day. A glass of champagne accompanies a sumptuous bay-side Sunday brunch.

800 Quietwater Beach Rd. (at Via de Luna and Fort Pickens Rd.). ✆ **850/932-2003.** Reservations not accepted. Main courses $17–$20; burgers and sandwiches $8–$10. AE, DC, DISC, MC, V. Sun–Thurs 11am–midnight (to 11pm in winter); Fri–Sat 11am–2am (to 11pm in winter).

PENSACOLA AFTER DARK

For what's going on, pick up the daily *Pensacola News Journal* (www. pensacolanewsjournal.com), especially its Friday entertainment section. Other good sources are the *Independent*, the *Pensacola Downtown Crowd* (www. burchellpublishing.com/downtown.asp), and *The Insider Magazine* (www. insidermagazine.com), all free publications available at the Pensacola Visitor Information Center (see "Essentials," earlier in this chapter).

THE PERFORMING ARTS   Pensacola has a surprisingly sophisticated array of entertainment choices for such a relatively small city. For a schedule of upcoming events, get a copy of Vision, a bimonthly newsletter published by the Arts Council of Northwest Florida (✆ **850/432-9906;** www.atsnwfl.org). Also pick up **Sneak Preview,** a calendar of events at the Pensacola Civic Center and the Saenger Theater. Both publications are available at the Pensacola Visitor

Information Center (see "Essentials," earlier in this chapter). Tickets for all major performances can be purchased from **Ticketmaster** (© **800/488-5252** or 850/433-6311; www.ticketmaster.com).

The highlight venue here is the ornate **Saenger Theatre** ⭐, 118 S. Palafox St., near Romano Street (© **850/444-7686;** www.saengertheatre.com), a painstakingly restored masterpiece of Spanish baroque architecture that the locals call the Grande Dame of Palafox. The variety of presentations includes the local opera company and symphony orchestra, Broadway musicals, and touring performers. The 10,000-seat **Pensacola Civic Center,** 201 E. Gregory St., at Alcanz Street (© 850/433-6311), hosts a variety of concerts, exhibitions, and conventions. Call ahead for the current schedule.

THE CLUB & BAR SCENE   Pensacola's downtown nighttime entertainment center is **Seville Quarter,** 130 E. Government St., at Jefferson Street (© **850/ 434-6211**), in the Seville Historic District. This restored antique brick complex with New Orleans–style wrought-iron balconies is actually a collection of pubs and restaurants whose names capture the ambience: Rosie O'Grady's Goodtime Emporium, Lili Marlene's Aviator's Pub, Apple Annie's Courtyard, End o' the Alley Bar, Phineas Phogg's Balloon Works (a dance hall, not a balloon shop), and Fast Eddie's Billiard Parlor (which has electronic games, too). The pubs all serve up libations, food, and live entertainment from Dixieland jazz to country and western. Get a monthly calendar at the information booth next to Rosie O'Grady's. Open daily from 11am to 2am.

Every night is party time at **McGuire's Irish Pub & Brewery,** the city's popular Irish pub, brewery, and eatery (see "Where to Dine," above). Irish bands appear nightly during summer, on Saturday and Sunday the rest of the year.

Nightlife at the beach centers around **Quietwater Boardwalk,** Via de Luna at Fort Pickens Road (no phone), a shopping/dining complex on Santa Rosa Sound. With the lively **Flounder's Beach and Reggae Bar** just a few steps away, it's easy to barhop until you find a band and crowd to your liking. Across Via de Luna at Casino Beach is **The Dock,** (© 850/934-3316), which has beachside live bands nightly during summer, on weekends off-season. You can catch all the games here at **Sidelines Sports Bar & Restaurant** (© 850/934-3660). See "Where to Dine," above, for details about Chan's and Flounder's.

Over on Perdido Key, about 15 miles west of downtown Pensacola, the **Flora-Bama Lounge,** on Fla. 292 at the Florida-Alabama line (© **850/ 492-0611**), is almost a shrine to country music. This slapped-together gulf-side pub is famous for its special jam sessions from noon until way past midnight on Saturday and Sunday. Flora-Bama is the prime sponsor and a key venue for the Frank Brown International Songwriters' Festival during the first week of November. If you've never attended an Interstate Mullet Toss, catch the fun here during the last weekend of April. The raw oyster bar is popular all the time. Take in the great gulf views from the Deck Bar. It's open daily from 8:30am to 2:30am.

2 Destin & Fort Walton Beach

40 miles E. of Pensacola, 160 miles W. of Tallahassee

Sitting on a round harbor off East Pass, which lets broad and beautiful Choctowhatchee Bay flow into the Gulf of Mexico, Destin is justly famous for its fishing fleet, the largest in the state. It's also Northwest Florida's fastest-growing and most upscale vacation destination, with a multitude of high-rise condominiums, the huge Sandestin luxury resort, several excellent golf courses, and some of Northwest Florida's best restaurants and lively nightspots. By and large, Destin attracts a more affluent crowd than does Fort Walton Beach, its more down-to-earth neighbor.

Although Fort Walton Beach has its own gorgeous strip of white sand over on Okaloosa Island, it is a "real" city whose economy is supported less by tourism than by sprawling Eglin Air Force Base. Covering more than 700 square miles, Eglin is the world's largest air base and is home to the U.S. Air Force's Armament Museum and the 33rd Tactical Fighter Wing, the "Top Guns" of Operation Desert Storm in 1991.

To the east of Destin, development is picking up steam along the beaches of southern Walton County. Still, this picturesque area has mostly cottages nestled among rolling sand dunes covered with sea oats. Here you'll find Grayton Beach State Park, which sports one of America's finest beaches, and the quaint village of **Seaside** ✿✿, which served as the set for Jim Carrey's movie *The Truman Show*. Seaside was built on a lovely stretch of beach in the 1980s—but with Victorian architecture that makes it look a century older. The village's gulf-side honeymoon cottages make for one of Florida's most romantic retreats; and the village has interesting shops and art galleries, a stamp-sized post office, and a resident population of artists, writers, and other creative folks, who permit only their own cars in their relatively expensive little enclave.

ESSENTIALS

GETTING THERE   Flights arriving at and departing from **Okaloosa Regional Airport** actually use the enormous strips at Eglin Air Force Base. The terminal is on Fla. 85 north of Fort Walton Beach and is served by **AirTran** (© 800/AIR-TRAN), **Delta** (© 800/221-1212), **Northwest/KLM** (© 800/225-2525), and **US Airways** (© 800/428-4322).

Avis (© 800/331-1212), **Budget** (© 800/527-0700), **Hertz** (© 800/654-3131), and **National** (© 800/CAR-RENT) have rental cars at the airport, and **Enterprise** (© 800/325-8007) is in town.

Top Class Shuttle Service (© 888/SHUTTLE or 850/830-7229) and **Airport Shuttle Service** (© 850/897-5238) provide van transportation to and from the airport. Fares are based on a zone system: $12 to $15 to Fort Walton Beach, $25 to Destin, and $32 to $35 to Sandestin and southern Walton County.

The Sunset Limited transcontinental service on **Amtrak** (© **800/USA-RAIL**) stops at Crestview, 26 miles north of Fort Walton Beach.

VISITOR INFORMATION   For advance information about both Fort Walton Beach and Destin, contact the **Emerald Coast Convention and Visitors Bureau,** P.O. Box 609, Fort Walton Beach, FL 32549 (© **800/322-3319** or 850/651-7131; fax 850/651-7149; www.destin-fwb.com). The bureau shares quarters with the **Okaloosa County Visitors Welcome Center** in a tin-roofed, beachside building on Miracle Strip Parkway (U.S. 98) on Okaloosa Island at the eastern edge of Fort Walton Beach. Stop there for brochures, maps, and other information. The welcome center is open Monday to Friday from 8am to 5pm, Saturday and Sunday from 10am to 4pm.

The **Destin Area Chamber of Commerce,** P.O. Box 8, Destin, FL 32541 (© **850/837-6241;** fax 850/654-5612; www.destinchamber.com), gives away brochures and sells maps of the area. The chamber resides in the Gulf View Plaza, on U.S. 98 opposite the Holiday Inn of Destin, and is open Monday to Friday from 9am to 5pm all year.

For information about the beaches of South Walton, contact the **South Walton Tourist Development Council,** P.O. Box 1248, Santa Rosa Beach, FL 32459 (© **800/822-6877** or 850/267-1216; fax 850/267-3943; www. beachesofsouthwalton.com). Its **visitor center** is at the intersection of U.S. 98 and U.S. 331 in Santa Rosa Beach (© **850/267-3511**). Open daily 8:30am to 5:30pm.

GETTING AROUND   For a cab in Fort Walton Beach, call **Charter Taxis** (© 850/863-5466), **Checker Cab** (© 850/244-4491), **Crosstown Taxi** (© 850/244-7303), **JC's Cab** (© 850/865-0578), **Veterans Cab Co.** (© 850/ 243-1403), or **Yellow Cab** (© 850/244-3600). In Destin, call **Destin Taxi** (© 850/654-5700). Fares are based on a zone system rather than meters, with a $4 minimum. Trips within Fort Walton Beach or Destin should range from $4 to $8.

FINDING A STREET ADDRESS   Don't worry about getting lost, since most of what you'll want to see and do is either on, or no more than a few blocks from, U.S. 98, the area's main east-west drag. Finding a street address is another matter, however, for even many local residents don't fully comprehend the post office's bizarre naming and numbering system along U.S. 98.

In Fort Walton Beach, U.S. 98 is known as the "Miracle Strip Parkway," with "southwest" and "southeast" addresses on the mainland and "east" addresses on Okaloosa Island.

In Destin, U.S. 98 is officially known as "Highway 98 East" between the Destin Bridge and Airport Road, and street numbers get progressively higher as you head east from the bridge. East of Airport Road, however, the post office calls U.S. 98 the "Emerald Coast Parkway"—although locals still say a place is on "98 East." The highway also is known as the Emerald Coast Parkway in Walton County, but the street-numbering system changes completely once you pass the county line.

Adding to the confusion in Destin, "Old Highway 98 East" is a short spur from Airport Road to the western side of Henderson Beach State Recreation Area, and "Scenic Highway 98 East" parallels the real U.S. 98 along the beach from the eastern side of Henderson Beach to Sandestin.

In other words, call and ask for directions if you're not sure how to find an establishment here.

TIME   The area is in the central time zone, an hour behind Miami, Orlando, and Tallahassee.

HITTING THE BEACH

DESTIN   Like an oasis in the middle of Destin's rapid development, the 208-acre **Henderson Beach State Recreation Area** ✦✦, east of Destin Harbor on U.S. 98, allows easy access to swimming, sunning, surf fishing, picnicking, and seabird watching along its 1½ miles of beach. There are rest rooms, outdoor showers, and surf chairs for persons with disabilities. The area is open daily from 8am to sunset. Admission is $2 per vehicle, $1 for pedestrians and cyclists. Several good restaurants are just outside the park's western boundary. The park has 30 campsites in a wooded setting. They cost $16 per night, plus $2 for electricity, and can be reserved up to 11 months in advance. Pets on leashes are allowed in the park, including the beach and campground. To book a campsite, or for more information, contact the area at 1700 Emerald Coast Pkwy., Destin, FL 32541 (© **850/837-7550;** www8.myflorida.com/communities/ learn/stateparks/district1/hendersonbeach).

The **James W. Lee Park,** between Destin and Sandestin on Scenic Highway 98, has a long white-sand beach overlooked by covered picnic tables, an ice-cream parlor, and **The Crab Trap Restaurant** (© 850/654-2822), whose moderately priced snacks and seafood make it a fine spot for lunch with a view or dinner with a sunset.

FORT WALTON BEACH   Do your loafing on the white sands of **Okaloosa Island,** joined to the mainland by the high-rise Brooks Bridge over Santa Rosa Sound. Most resort hotels and amusement parks are grouped around the Gulfarium marine park on U.S. 98 east of the bridge. Here you'll find **The Boardwalk,** a collection of tin-roofed beachside buildings that have a games arcade for the kids, the Soggy Dollar Saloon for adults, covered picnic areas, a summertime snack bar, and another branch of the Crab Trap restaurant. Just to the east, you can use the free facilities at **Beasley Park,** home of the Okaloosa County Visitor Welcome Center.

Across U.S. 98, the **Okaloosa Area, Gulf Islands National Seashore** has picnic areas and sailboats for rent on Choctawhatchee Bay, plus access to the Gulf. Admission to this part of the national seashore is free.

SOUTHERN WALTON COUNTY   Sporting the finest stretch of white sand on the Gulf, **Grayton Beach State Park** ★★★, on County Road 30A, also has 356 acres of pine forests surrounding scenic Western Lake. There's a boat ramp and a campground with electric hookups on the lake. Get a leaflet at the main gate for a self-guided tour of the nature trail. Pets are not allowed anywhere in the recreation area. The area is open daily from 8am to sunset. Admission is $3.25 per vehicle with up to eight occupants, $1 per pedestrian or bicyclist. Campsites cost $14 from March to September, $8 from October to February. Add $2 for electricity. You can reserve sites up to 11 months in advance by contacting the area at 357 Main Park Rd., Santa Rosa Beach, FL 32459 (© 850/231-4210; www8.myflorida.com/communities/learn/stateparks/district1/graytonbeach).

Seaside has free public parking along County Road 30A and is a good spot for a day at the beach, a stroll or bike ride around the quaint village, and a tasty meal at one of its restaurants.

OUTDOOR ACTIVITIES

BOATING & BOAT RENTALS   Pontoon boats are highly popular for use on the back bays and on Sunday-afternoon floating parties in East Pass. Several companies rent them, including **Best Boat Rentals** (© 850/664-7872) on Okaloosa Island in Fort Walton Beach and **Adventure Pontoon Rentals** (© 850/837-3041), **B&J Boat Rentals** (© 850/243-4488), **East Pass Watersports** (© 850/654-4253), and **Premier Powerboat Rentals** (© 850/837-7755), all on Destin Harbor. Expect to pay about $70 for a half day, $120 for all day. Premier Powerboat Rentals also has speedboats for rent.

CRUISES   The *Emerald Magic* (© 888/654-1685 or 850/837-1293; www.moodysinc.com) and the *Southern Star* (© 888/424-7217 or 850/837-7741; www.dolphin-sstar.com) have daily dolphin and sunset cruises from June through August, by arrangement the rest of the year. The *Emerald Magic* is operated by Moody's, on U.S. 98 at Destin Harbor (see "Fishing," below), while the *Southern Star* docks in Destin at the Harbor Walk Marina, behind the Lucky Snapper Restaurant. Expect to pay $15 for adults, $7.50 for kids 3 to 12.

FISHING   Billing itself as the "World's Luckiest Fishing Village," Destin has Florida's largest charter-boat fleet, with more than 140 vessels based at the marinas lining the north shore of Destin Harbor, on U.S. 98 east of the Destin Bridge. Arranging a trip is as easy as walking along the Destin Harbor waterfront, where you will find the booking booths of several agents, such as **Boardwalk Fishing Charters** (© 800/242-2824 or 850/837-2343; www. harborwalkfishing.com), **Pelican Charters** (© 850/837-2343), **Harbor Cove Charters** (© 850/837-2222), and **Fishermen's Charter Service** (© 850/654-4665). Rates for private charters range from about $400 to $900 per boat, depending on length of voyage.

A less-expensive way to try your luck is on a larger group-oriented party boat such as those operated by **Moody's,** at 194 U.S. 98 east on Destin Harbor (© 888/654-1685 or 850/837-1293; www.moodysinc.com). Moody's charges $35 per person ($30 off-season) for its half-day runs (morning is the best time to fish). Children 8 to 12 and nonfishing sightseers are charged half price. Other party boats are the *Destin Princess* (© 888/837-5088 or 850/5088), *Emmanuel* (© 850/837-6313), the *Lady Eventhia* (© 850/837-6212), and three craft operated by **Olin Marler's Deep Sea Fishing Fleet** (© 850/837-7095), all based at Destin Harbor.

You don't have to go to sea to fish from the catwalk of the 3,000-foot **Destin Bridge** over East Pass. The marinas and bait shops at Destin Harbor can provide gear, bait, information, and a fishing license. In Fort Walton Beach, you can cast a line off **Okaloosa Island Fishing Pier,** 1030 Miracle Strip Pkwy. E. (U.S. 98; © 850/244-1023). The pier is open 24 hours a day. Adults pay $6.50 to fish, children $3.50. Observers pay $1.

GOLF The area takes great pride in having more than 250 holes of golf. For advance information on all area courses, contact the **Emerald Coast Golf Association,** P.O. Box 304, Destin, FL 32540 (© 850/654-7086). Also look for *Gulf Coast Tee Time,* the free annual directory published in Pensacola (see "Outdoor Activities," in section 1, earlier in this chapter). And be sure to inquire whether your choice of accommodations here offers golf packages, which can represent significant savings.

On the mainland, nonresidents are welcome to play at the city-owned **Fort Walton Beach Golf Club,** on Lewis Turner Boulevard (County Road 189) north of town (© 850/862-3314 or 850/862-0933). The club has two 18-hole courses—the **Pines** (© 850/833-9529) and the **Oaks** (© 850/833-9530)—plus a pro shop. Greens fees at both courses are about $27 year-round, including a cart.

In Destin, scenic **Indian Bayou Golf and Country Club,** off Airport Road (© 850/837-6191), has three 9-hole courses with large greens and wide fairways. They look easy, but watch out for water hazards and strategically placed hidden bunkers! Greens fees, including cart, are about $60.

In southern Walton County, **The Resort at Sandestin** on U.S. 98 East (© 850/267-8211 for tee times) is the largest facility here (see "Where to Stay," below). Its 63 holes are spread over three outstanding championship courses. The Baytowne and Links courses overlook Choctawhatchee Bay. Fees for 18 holes are about $70 for resort guests, $90 for nonguests.

Some of the 27 championship holes at **Emerald Bay Golf Club,** 2 miles east of the Mid-Bay Bridge on U.S. 98 (© 850/837-5197), run along Choctawhatchee Bay; the water adds both beauty and challenges to the otherwise wide and forgiving fairways. Greens fees are about $75 with cart.

In southern Walton County, the semiprivate **Santa Rosa Golf & Beach Club,** off County Road 30A in Dune Allen Beach (© 850/267-2229), offers a challenging 18-hole course through tall pines looking out to vistas of the Gulf. The club has a pro shop, a beachside restaurant, a lounge, and tennis courts. Fees are about $65 in summer, $50 off-season. The **Seascape Resort & Conference Center,** 100 Seascape Dr. (℃ 850/837-9181), off County Road 30A, features a Joe Lee–designed 18-hole course winding through woods and around lakes, with a premium placed on accuracy rather than power. The center also has tennis courts, accommodations, restaurant, bar, and pro shop.

In Niceville, a 20-minute drive north via the Mid-Bay Bridge, nonguests may play golf (four 9-hole courses) or tennis (21 courts) at the **Bluewater Bay Resort** (℃ 850/897-3613), which also has condominiums for rent.

Call ahead for reservations and current fees at all these clubs, and ask about afternoon and early-evening specials.

SAILING   Sailing South (℃ 850/837-7245), on U.S. 98 at Destin Harbor, has half-day cruises aboard the 72-foot schooner *Daniel Webster Clements* for $25 per person. It offers 3-day cruises at about $450 per person. You also can go out on the 54-foot schooners *Nathaniel Bowditch* (℃ 850/650-8787), *Flying Eagle* (℃ 850/837-4986 or 850/837-3700), or *Blackbeard* (℃ 850/837-2793), all of which have afternoon and sunset trips for about $25 per person.

On Okaloosa Island, **Leeside Bareboat Sailing,** at the Leeside Motel, 1352 U.S. 98 east (℃ 850/244-5454), rents 25- and 30-foot Catalina sloops bareboat (you do the skippering) for about $100 per half day to $450 for 3 days.

SCUBA DIVING & SNORKELING   At least a dozen dive shops are located along the beaches. Considered one of the best, **Scuba Tech Diving Charters** has two locations in Destin: at 301 U.S. 98 E. (℃ 850/837-2822; www.scubatechnwfl.com) and at 10004 U.S. 98 E. (℃ 850/837-1933), about a half-mile west of the Sandestin Beach Resort. **Fantasea,** at the foot of the Destin Bridge, 1 U.S. 98 E. (℃ 800/326-2732 or 850/837-6943; www.fantasea-destin.com), and the **Aquanaut Scuba Center,** 24 U.S. 98 E. (℃ 850/837-0359), are other local operators.

The three diving operators and *Kokomo* **Snorkeling Adventures,** 500 U.S. 98 E. in Destin (℃ 850/837-9029), all take snorkelers on excursions into the Gulf of Mexico and Choctawhatchee Bay for $25 per person, including gear.

TENNIS   The Resort at Sandestin, U.S. 98 East (℃ 850/837-2121), has 16 courts open to the public, including hard, clay, and grass. *Tennis* magazine rated it one of the nation's top 50 tennis resorts.

Also highly ranked, **Tops'l Beach and Racquet Resort,** 9011 Hwy. 98 W. (℃ 888/867-7535 or 850/837-4853; www.tennisresortsonline.com/trofiles/TopslBeach.cfm), about a half-mile east of The Resort at Sandestin, has 14 lighted courts plus a teaching professional available to guests staying in its luxury condominiums.

WATER SPORTS   Hobie Cats, WaveRunners, jet boats, jet skis, and parasailing are available all along the beach. The largest selection of operators, including **Boogies** (℃ 850/654-4497), is at the marinas just east of the Destin Bridge, behind Hooter's and Fat Tuesday's pubs. **Paradise Water Sports** (℃ 850/664-7872) rents equipment and offers parasailing rides at seven locations along U.S. 98 in both Destin and Fort Walton Beach.

EXPLORING THE AREA

Eden State Gardens   Evoking images from *Gone With the Wind,* the garden's magnificent 1895 Greek Revival–style Wesley Mansion has been lovingly restored and richly furnished. It stands overlooking scenic Choctawhatchee Bay and is surrounded by immense moss-draped oak trees and the Eden Gardens, resplendent with camellias, azaleas, and other typical Southern flowers. Your visit won't be complete without a guided tour of the house, so avoid coming here on a Tuesday or Wednesday. Picnicking is allowed on the plantation grounds.

181 Eden Gardens Rd. (off County Rd. 395), Point Washington. © 850/231-4214. www8.myflorida.com/communities/learn/stateparks/district1/edengardens. Grounds and gardens $2 per vehicle; mansion tours $1.50 adults, 50¢ children 12 and under. Gardens and grounds daily 8am–sunset; 45-min. mansion tours on the hour Thurs–Mon 9am–4pm.

Gulfarium *Kids* One of the nation's original marine parks features ongoing 25-minute shows with dolphins, California sea lions, Peruvian penguins, loggerhead turtles, sharks, sting rays, moray eels, and alligators. There are fascinating exhibits, including the Living Sea, with special windows for viewing undersea life. During one of the shows, a scuba diver explains the sea life while swimming amongst the various creatures.

1010 Miracle Strip Pkwy. (U.S. 98) on Okaloosa Island. © 850/244-5169. www.gulfarium.com. Admission $16 adults, $14 seniors, $10 children 4–11, free for children 3 and under. Daily 9am through last show; shows daily at 10am, noon, 2pm, and 4pm; additional shows at 6 and 8pm in summer.

Indian Temple Mound and Museum This ceremonial mound, one of the largest ever discovered, dates from A.D. 1200. The museum showcases part of its collection of more than 6,000 ceramic artifacts from southeastern American Indian tribes, the nation's largest such collection. Exhibits depict the lifestyles of the four tribes that lived in the Choctawhatchee Bay region for 12,000 years.

139 Miracle Strip Pkwy. SE, on the mainland. © 850/833-9595. Park free; museum $2 adults, $1 children 6–17, free for children 5 and under. Park daily dawn–dusk. Museum Sept–May Mon–Fri 11am–4pm, Sat 9am–4pm; June–Aug Mon–Sat 9am–4:30pm, Sun 12:30–4:30pm.

U.S. Air Force Armament Museum ★★ Although this fascinating museum is not on a par with Pensacola's National Museum of Naval Aviation, you'll love it if you're into war planes. Located on the world's largest air force base, it traces military developments from World War II through the Korean and Vietnam Wars to Operation Desert Storm. On display are reconnaissance, fighter, and bomber planes, including the SR-71 Blackbird spy plane.

100 Museum Dr., off Eglin Pkwy. (Fla. 85) at Eglin Air Force Base, 5 miles north of downtown. © 850/882-4062. Free admission. Daily 9:30am–4:30pm. Closed federal holidays.

SHOPPING

The third-largest "designer" outlet mall in the United States, **Silver Sands Factory Stores** ★★, on U.S. 98 between Destin and Sandestin (© 800/510-6255 or 850/864-9780), has the upscale likes of Anne Klein, Donna Karan, J. Crew, Brooks Brothers, Hartmann luggage, Coach leather, Bose electronics, and so on. Shops are open Monday to Saturday from 10am to 9pm (to 7pm in January and February), Sunday from 10am to 6pm (noon to 6pm in January and February). The fine food court here, **Morgan's Market** (© 850/654-3320), serves a varied menu. There are electronic games for kids and a sports bar for adults.

Over at the Sandestin Beach Resort on U.S. 98, you can window-shop in **The Market at Sandestin,** where boutiques purvey expensive clothing, gifts, and Godiva chocolates.

WHERE TO STAY

The area has a vast supply of condominiums and cottages for rent. One good-value example is Venus Condos, listed below. The tourist information offices (see "Essentials," earlier in this chapter) will provide lists of others for rent. The largest rental agent is **Abbott Realty Services,** 3500 Emerald Coast Pkwy., Destin, FL 32541 (© **800/336-4853** or 850/837-4853; fax 850/654-2937; www.abbott-resorts.com). It publishes a magazine-sized annual brochure picturing and describing its many properties throughout the area.

There are several commercial campgrounds here, but the best camping is at **Henderson Beach State Recreation Area** in Destin and at **Grayton Beach State Park** in south Walton County (see "Hitting the Beach," earlier in this chapter). State and local governments add 9% to all hotel and campground bills.

DESTIN

A former Comfort Inn, the local **Motel 6,** 405 U.S. 98 E. (© **800/466-8356** or 850/837-0007; fax 850/837-5325), sitting across the highway from the harbor, has rooms that are generally larger than those at many other members of this cut-rate chain. There's an outdoor swimming pool on the premises.

Expensive

Henderson Park Inn ✿✿   At the end of Old U.S. 98 on the undeveloped eastern edge of the Henderson Beach State Recreation Area, this shingle-sided, Cape Hatteras–style bed-and-breakfast is the area's most romantic get-away-from-it-all escape without screaming kids (no children are accepted, nor pets). Individually decorated in a Victorian theme, the rooms have high ceilings, fireplaces, Queen Anne furniture, and gulf views from private balconies. Most have Jacuzzis, and some have canopy beds. The main building (16 rooms are in a separate shingle-sided structure next door) sports a beachside verandah complete with old-fashioned rocking chairs in which to sit and admire the glorious sunsets. Guests are treated to a Southern-style buffet breakfast and to beer and wine at the nightly before-dinner social hour in the wonderful Veranda Restaurant (reservations recommended), which opens to the wraparound porch of the main building. Guests are provided with complimentary beach umbrellas and chairs.

2700 Scenic Hwy. 98 E. (P.O. Box 30), Destin, FL 32541. © 800/336-4853 or 850/837-4853. Fax 850/ 654-0405. www.hendersonparkinn.com. 35 units. Summer $189–$303 double; off-season $95–$181 double. Rates include full breakfast and evening cocktails. Packages and weekly rates available. AE, DISC, MC, V. No children or pets accepted. **Amenities:** Restaurant (American); bar; heated outdoor pool; Jacuzzi; limited room service; laundry service. *In room:* A/C, TV, dataport, fridge, coffeemaker, hair dryer, iron.

Moderate

Best Western SummerPlace Inn   Located across U.S. 98 from the Hampton Inn Destin (see below), this four-story, Spanish-motif building offers innlike rooms and suites decorated with wildlife prints. A few suites have hot tubs in their living rooms (you won't get those at the Hampton Inn). The more expensive gulf-side units have balconies (those facing the bay do not). Larger units have microwave ovens and refrigerators. Doors open from an indoor pool, a whirlpool, and an exercise room to an outdoor pool. You'll have to negotiate your way across busy U.S. 98 to reach the Gulf.

14047 Emerald Coast Pkwy. (U.S. 98, at Airport Rd.), Destin, FL 32541. © 888/BEACH-99 or 850/650-8003. Fax 850/650-8004. 72 units. Summer $115–$175; off-season $50–$100. Rates include continental breakfast and local telephone calls. AE, DISC, MC, V. **Amenities:** Indoor and outdoor pools; exercise room; Jacuzzi; business center; coin-op washers and dryers. *In room:* A/C, TV, fax, dataport, kitchen, minibar, fridge, coffeemaker, hair dryer, iron.

Hampton Inn Destin   This pink, two-story building sits at the junction of the new and old U.S. 98s, about 200 yards west of Henderson Beach State Recreation Area and near a covey of restaurants just outside the recreation area and another bunch of them across U.S. 98. There's beach a short walk away on the old highway, which means you don't have to fight the traffic on U.S. 98 to reach the Gulf. External corridors lead to the standard motel-style rooms and the suites with two rooms and kitchenettes. A gazebo-like sitting area offers shade next to a heated outdoor pool and hot tub.

1625 Hwy. 98 E. (at Old Hwy. 98 and Airport Rd.), Destin, FL 32541. Ⓒ 800/HAMPTON or 850/654-2677. Fax 850/654-0745. www.hamptoninndestin.com. 104 units. Summer $129–$149 double; $160–$180 suite. Off-season $69–$89 double; $99 suite. Rates include continental breakfast. AE, DC, DISC, MC, V. **Amenities:** Heated outdoor pool; Jacuzzi; coin-op washers and dryers. *In room:* A/C, TV, dataport, kitchen (suites only), fridge, coffeemaker, hair dryer, iron.

Holiday Inn of Destin ⟨*Kids*⟩   Many guest rooms in this family-friendly gulf-front resort are in a round high-rise building, but get one facing south or east because a tall condominium next door blocks southwest-facing units from enjoying the spectacular gulf views from their balconies. Better yet, request a room in the older, four-story building, where the rooms are more spacious and many open directly onto the beach. Others open to walkways in an enclosed "Holidome" sporting a comfortable mezzanine lounge with indoor pool and billiard and Foosball tables (plenty here to keep the kids occupied).

1020 Hwy. 98 E. (P.O. Box 577), Destin, FL 32541. Ⓒ 800/HOLIDAY or 850/837-6181. Fax 850/837-1523. www.holidayinndestin.com. 233 units. Summer $140–$208 double; off-season $100–$160 double. AE, DC, DISC, MC, V. **Amenities:** Restaurant (American); bar; 3 heated pools (1 indoor, 1 children's); exercise room; sauna; children's programs; game room; baby-sitting; laundry service; coin-op washers and dryers. *In room:* A/C, TV, dataport, kitchen, minibar, fridge, coffeemaker, hair dryer, iron.

FORT WALTON BEACH

The managers of Venus Condos (see below) also run the new **Sea Crest Condominiums,** located next door at 895 Santa Rosa Blvd. (Ⓒ **800/476-1885** or 850/301-9600; fax 850/301-9205; www.seacrestcondos.com). Units in this 7-story building aren't as spacious as those in Venus, but they're considerably more luxurious, and those on the higher floors have great views toward the west. The complex has indoor and outdoor pools (actually one pool; you can swim under a glass partition between them), and it sits next to a county park with a boardwalk leading over the dunes to the beach.

Among other chain motels here is the new **Hampton Inn Ft. Walton Beach,** 1112 Santa Rosa Blvd. (Ⓒ **800/HAMPTON** or 850/301-0906; www. hamptoninnfwb.com). It's adjacent to the Radisson Beach Resort and shares its facilities (see below).

Four Points By Sheraton ⟨*Kids*⟩   This beachfront resort sports spacious rooms decorated with vivid, tropical colors. The older, motel-style wings here surround a lush tropical courtyard with a whirlpool, heated swimming pool, and bar. With their balconies overlooking the beach, the choice units are in a newer, seven-story gulf-side building with a second swimming pool and bar. Some rooms have kitchenettes. A summertime children's program helps make this a good if not perfect family choice.

1325 E. Miracle Strip Pkwy. (U.S. 98), Fort Walton Beach, FL 32548. Ⓒ 800/874-8104 or 850/243-8116. Fax 850/244-3064. www.sheraton4pts.com. 217 units. Summer $115–$275 double; off-season $76–$175 double. Rates include full breakfast. AE, DC, DISC, MC, V. **Amenities:** 2 restaurants (American); bar; 2 heated outdoor pools; exercise room; Jacuzzi; water-sports equipment rentals; children's programs; game room; limited room service; baby-sitting; laundry service; coin-op washers and dryers. *In room:* A/C, TV, dataport, kitchenette (in some units), fridge, coffeemaker, hair dryer, iron.

Marina Motel   This family-operated, self-described "fisherman's motel" may be pedestrian-looking, but it has clean, comfortable rooms and apartments directly across U.S. 98 from the magnificent public beach at Beasley Park. A low-slung, brick-fronted motel block holds most of the rooms. Other units are in two-story stucco structures near a marina whose 560-foot pier is home to charter-fishing boats. Two one-bedroom apartments at the end of the complex overlook the marina and bay. All units here have refrigerators and microwaves; 16 have full kitchens. If traffic is too busy to cross U.S. 98 to the beach (there are no nearby overpasses or traffic lights), you can sun at the motel's little bayside beach or take a dip in its roadside pool.

1345 E. Miracle Strip Pkwy. (U.S. 98), Fort Walton Beach, FL 32548. ℭ **800/237-7021** or 850/244-1129. Fax 850/243-6063. www.marinamot.com. 38 units. Summer $65–$105 double; $115–$135 apt. Off-season $39–$61 double; $65–$80 apt. AE, DC, DISC, MC, V. **Amenities:** Outdoor pool; coin-op washers and dryers. *In room:* A/C, TV, kitchen, fridge, coffeemaker, iron.

Radisson Beach Resort   A glass-enclosed elevator climbs up through a soaring, six-story lean-to atrium lobby to rooms having spectacular gulf views from their standing-room-only balconies at this resort. Beach lovers are more likely to appreciate the units in an older two-story motel building that have sitting-room patios or balconies facing the gulf. Other units in the older building open to a lush courtyard surrounding a pool. In the atrium, a tropically adorned cafe serves breakfast, lunch, and dinner, and a bar has nightly entertainment during summer.

1110 Santa Rosa Blvd. (at U.S. 98), Fort Walton Beach, FL 32548. ℭ **800/333-3333** or 850/243-9181. Fax 850/664-7652. www.radissonresort.com. 287 units. Summer $129–$189 double; off-season $89–$129 double. Packages available. AE, DC, DISC, MC, V. **Amenities:** Restaurant (American); 2 bars; 3 outdoor pools (1 children's); 2 lighted tennis courts; exercise room; water-sports equipment rentals; limited room service; baby-sitting; laundry service. *In room:* A/C, TV, dataport, coffeemaker, hair dryer, iron.

Ramada Plaza Beach Resort ✿   This big resort boasts the prettiest outdoor areas in northwest Florida, with waterfalls cascading over lofty rocks and a romantic grotto bar, all surrounded by thick tropical foliage. Although there is another swimming pool, a large sundeck, and a bar out by the beach, this gorgeous courtyard would have even more charm if it weren't cut off from the gulf by a six-story block of hotel rooms. The guest rooms and the one-bedroom suites in this beachfront building are the best here, with gulf or courtyard views from balconies or patios. The least-expensive units, in the adjacent building, overlook a parking lot. On-site dining options include a barbecue shack out in the tropical forest. The Boardwalk beach pavilion and restaurants are next door. There's also a cozy lobby lounge with sports TVs.

1500 E. Miracle Strip Pkwy. (U.S. 98), Fort Walton Beach, FL 32548. ℭ **800/874-8962** or 850/243-9161. Fax 850/243-2391. www.ramadafwb.com. 335 units. Summer $120–$175 double; $280–$350 suite. Off-season $70–$135 double; $150–$270 suite. AE, DC, DISC, MC, V. **Amenities:** 3 restaurants (American); 3 bars; 2 outdoor pools (1 heated); Jacuzzi; water-sports equipment rentals; children's programs; game room; limited room service; coin-op washers and dryers. *In room:* A/C, TV, dataport, fridge, coffeemaker, hair dryer, iron.

Venus Condos ✿ *Value*   Offering considerably more space than a hotel would at these rates, this pleasant, three-story enclave on western Okaloosa Island was built in the 1970s and has been immaculately maintained ever since. Each of the one-, two-, and three-bedroom units has a long living/dining/kitchen room, with a rear door leading to a balcony or to a patio opening to a grassy courtyard. The beach is a short walk across the dunes, and you can stroll along the undeveloped beach at an Eglin Air Force Base auxiliary facility about 200 yards away. The same management also operates the new and much more luxurious **Sea**

Crest Condominiums next door (see above), and guests here can use the indoor-outdoor pool there.

885 Santa Rosa Blvd., Fort Walton Beach, FL 32548. ℂ **800/476-1885** or 850/301-9600. Fax 850/301-9205. 45 units. Summer $110–$180 apt.; off-season $50–$135 apt. Weekly and monthly rates available. Ask for off-season specials. MC, V. **Amenities:** Large outdoor pool, tennis courts, coin-op laundry. *In room:* A/C, TV/VCR, fax, kitchen, coffeemaker, iron.

SOUTHERN WALTON COUNTY

If you want to stay near The Resort at Sandestin (see below) without paying its prices, there's a modern **Sleep Inn** a mile west at 5000 Emerald Coast Pkwy. (U.S. 98; ℂ **800/627-5337** or 850/654-7022).

Hilton Sandestin Beach & Golf Resort ★★ *(Kids)* This all-suites beachside resort, housed in two adjacent towers, is the top full-service hotel here. It's nicely situated on the grounds of The Resort at Sandestin (see below) and shares its golf and tennis facilities. The elegant Elephant Walk restaurant is next door. "Executive suites" in one wing are equipped primarily for business travelers and conventioneers (lots of meeting space here), while the spacious "junior suites" in the old wing are geared to families, with a special area for children's bunk beds. Mom can send the kids off to a supervised summertime program (including movies) while pampering herself at the full-service spa.

4000 Sandestin Blvd. S., Destin, FL 32541. ℂ **800/445-8667** or 850/267-9500. Fax 850/267-3076. www. sandestinresort.hilton.com. 598 suites. Summer $245–$375 suite; off-season $150–$335 suite. Golf and tennis packages available. AE, DC, DISC, MC, V. **Amenities:** 2 restaurants (American); 2 bars; heated outdoor pool; golf course; tennis courts; health club, spa; Jacuzzi; water-sports equipment rentals; children's programs; game room; concierge; activities desk; car-rental desk; business center; shopping arcade; salon; 24-hr. room service; massage; baby-sitting; laundry service; coin-op washers and dryers; concierge-level rooms. *In room:* A/C, TV, dataport, minibar, coffeemaker, hair dryer, iron.

The Resort at Sandestin ★★ One of Florida's biggest sports-oriented resorts, this luxurious real-estate development sprawls over 2,300 acres complete with a spectacular beach 5 miles west of Destin, plus a marina. It's notable for its 81 holes of championship golf and its tennis clinic (both with instruction available), plus a fully equipped sports spa and health center. An array of handsomely decorated accommodations overlooks the Gulf or Choctawhatchee Bay, the golf fairways, lagoons, or a nature preserve. The hotel rooms and suites are in the Bayside Inn. They all have kitchenettes and balconies, but you'd be wise to opt for one of the much more spacious junior suites or one-, two-, and three-bedroom condominium apartments, which are in high- and mid-rise buildings either on the gulf or along the manicured fairways. The privately owned condominiums are individually decorated and come with full kitchen and patio or balcony, and many have washers and dryers. Most amenities are a short walk or bike or free tram ride away, and a tunnel runs under U.S. 98 to connect Sandestin's gulf and bay areas. Among the relatively limited on-site dining options is the romantic **Elephant Walk** (ℂ **850/267-4800**), located on the Gulf; it serves up different, gourmet-quality choices for dinner every evening.

9300 Hwy. 98 W., Destin, FL 32541. ℂ **800/277-0800** or 850/267-8000 in the U.S., or 800/933-7846 in Canada. Fax 850/267-8222. www.sandestin.com. 175 units, 700 condo apts. Summer $155–$210 double; $210–$560 condo apt. Off-season $75–$190 double; $105–$395 condo apt. Packages and weekly/monthly rates available. Rates include health club, bicycle, boogie board, canoe, and kayak use; 1-hr. tennis daily; discounts on other amenities. AE, DC, DISC, MC, V. **Amenities:** 3 restaurants (American); 3 bars; 9 heated outdoor pools; 4 golf courses; 18 tennis courts; spa; Jacuzzi; water-sports equipment rentals; children's programs; game room; concierge; shopping arcade; salon; limited room service (hotel only); massage; baby-sitting; laundry service; coin-op washers and dryers. *In room:* A/C, TV, dataports, kitchen, coffeemaker, hair dryer, iron.

SEASIDE

If you decide to rent a home or a **romantic honeymoon cottage** ★★ in this quaint village, contact the **Seaside Cottage Rental Agency,** P.O. Box 4730, Seaside, FL 32459 (© **800/277-8696** or 850/231-1320; fax 850/231-2293; www.seasidefl.com). The agency has some 275 cottages in its rental inventory, from one to six bedrooms, plus six rooms in a replica of a 1940s-style motel, starting at $150 double. The beachside honeymoon cottages are one of Florida's best getaways for newlyweds or anyone else looking for a romantic escape.

Josephine's French Country Inn at Seaside ★★   With its six large Tuscan columns reminiscent of an elegant Virginia mansion, Josephine's is an elegant country inn, with mahogany four-poster beds, lace comforters, rich furnishings, and marble bathtubs. Most guest rooms also have fireplaces. Conveniences like wet bars, microwaves, and small refrigerators are neatly incorporated into the design so that they don't conflict with the nostalgic charm. Sumptuous breakfasts are served either in-room (beside the fireplace or on your private verandah) or in the gracious dining room. The Guest House offers four suites, two with gulf views. Each has a fireplace, kitchen, and full bathroom. No smoking is allowed inside, nor are pets. With rich mahogany furniture and a wealth of period accoutrements, the dining room here is one of the region's finest places for a gourmet romantic dinner. Glowing with candlelight, this intimate room seats only 22 people (by reservation only). Josephine's Maryland-style crab cakes are consistently delicious.

County Rd. 30A (P.O. Box 4767), Seaside, FL 32459. © **800/848-1840** or 850/231-1940. Fax 850/231-2446. www.josephinesfl.com. 9 units (all with bathroom). $200 double; $240 suite. Rates include gourmet breakfast. Weekly rates available. AE, MC, V. **Amenities:** Restaurant (American); bar; free use of bikes. *In room:* A/C, TV, dataport, kitchen (in some suites) fridge, coffeemaker, hair dryer, iron.

WHERE TO DINE

Except for the strip on Okaloosa Island, a plethora of national fast-food and family chain restaurants line U.S. 98.

DESTIN

If you didn't catch a fish to be grilled at Fisherman's Wharf (see below), you can buy one to brag about from **Sexton's Seafood,** 602 Hwy. 98 E. opposite Destin Harbor (© **805/837-3040**). It's the best market here.

Moderate

AJ's Seafood & Oyster Bar SEAFOOD   Jimmy Buffett tunes set the tone at this fun, tiki-topped establishment on the picturesque Destin Harbor docks, where fishing boats unload their daily catches right into the kitchen. Obviously, the best items here are grilled or fried fish, but raw or steamed Apalachicola oysters also lead the bill of fare. You can sample a bit of everything with a "run of the kitchen" seafood patter. AJ's is most famous for its topside Club Bimini, a "meet bar" featuring reggae music and limbo contests every summer evening (you may want to have dinner elsewhere if you're not in the partying mood). At lunch, picnic tables on the covered dock make a fine venue with a view across the harbor.

116 Hwy. 98 E., Destin Harbor. © **850/837-1913.** Reservations not accepted. Main courses $12–$19; sandwiches and salads $6–$8. AE, DISC, MC, V. Summer daily 11am–midnight (bar until 4am). Off-season daily 11am–9:30pm.

Back Porch ★ SEAFOOD   This cedar-shingled seafood shack offers glorious beach and gulf views from its long porch. The popular, casual restaurant originated charcoal-grilled amberjack, which you'll now see on menus throughout Florida. Other fish and seafood, as well as chicken and juicy hamburgers, also come from the coals. Monthly specials feature crab, lobster, and seasonal fish. Come early, order a rum-laden Key Lime Freeze, and enjoy the sunset. The Back Porch sits with a number of other restaurants near the western boundary of the Henderson Beach State Recreation Area.

1740 Old Hwy. 98 E. © 850/837-2022. Reservations not accepted. Main courses $12–$20; sandwiches, burgers, and pastas $6.50–$8.50. AE, DC, DISC, MC, V. Sun–Thurs 11am–10pm; Fri–Sat 11am–11pm. From U.S. 98, turn toward the beach at the Hampton Inn.

Fisherman's Wharf Seafood House SEAFOOD   Have that fish you caught filleted, bring it here, and the chef will chargrill it at this atmospheric restaurant next to a charter fleet marina (the restaurant hosts most of Destin's fishing competitions). If you had no luck, and didn't stop by Sexton's Seafood on the way here to buy a few filets (see above), you can select from the restaurant's fresh-off-the-boat catch for grilling, broiling, frying, or blackening. Charcoal grilling is the house specialty—my triggerfish filet was white and flaky but still moist. All main courses include a trip to the salad bar, rice pilaf, baked potato, or roasted vegetables. Although this building dates from 1996, it evokes an Old Florida fish camp, with rough-hewn wood walls and double-hung windows looking out to a large harborside deck, a venue during the warmer months for two bars, an oyster bar, live music, and great sunsets.

210D Hwy. 98 E., Destin Harbor. © 850/654-4766. Reservations not accepted. Main courses $11–$18; sandwiches and burgers $7–$9; cook-your-catch $6 lunch, $8 dinner. AE, DC, DISC, MC, V. Summer daily 11am–11pm (deck bar open later). Off-season daily 11am–9pm.

Harbor Docks SEAFOOD/JAPANESE   The harbor views are spectacular from indoors or outdoors at this casual, somewhat-rustic establishment. You can order your fill of fried fish, but specialties such as the daily catch sautéed with artichoke hearts are far more enjoyable. Appetizers on the dinner menu might feature smoked yellowfin tuna with mustard sauce. Asian influences include a sushi bar and hibachi table, and Thai specialties, especially on the lunch menu. Except during winter, hearty fishermen's breakfasts are cooked by the owners of the Silver Sands, a popular local haunt that burned down several years ago. The bar here is popular with charter-boat skippers, and frequent live entertainment keeps the action going on the outdoor deck at night.

538 U.S. 98 E., Destin Harbor. © 850/837-2506. Reservations not accepted. Main courses $15–$22. AE, DC, DISC, MC, V. Feb–Oct daily 5:30am–10:30am and 11am–11pm. Nov–Jan daily 11am–11pm. Sushi bar daily 5–10pm.

Harry T's Boat House *Kids* AMERICAN   To honor the memory of trapeze artist "Flying Harry T" Baben, his family opened this lively spot on the ground floor of Destin Harbor's tallest building. Standing guard is the stuffed Stretch, Harry's beloved giraffe. Other decor includes circus memorabilia and relics from the luxury cruise ship *Thracia,* which sank off the Emerald Coast in 1927; Harry T was presented with the ship's salvaged furnishings and fixtures for personally leading the heroic rescue of its 2,000 passengers. The tabloid-style menu offers traditional seafood, steaks, chicken, and pasta dishes. Kids eat for 99¢ until 7pm and at Sunday brunch. Watch for clowns and other children's entertainment at least 1 night a week. Both the dining room and the downstairs lounge (with live entertainment Friday and Saturday nights) enjoy harbor views.

320 U.S. 98 E., Destin Harbor. © 850/654-4800. Reservations not accepted. Main courses $10.50–$20; sandwiches and salads $10–$12. AE, DISC, MC, V. Summer Mon–Sat 11am–2am; Sun 10am–2am. Off-season Mon–Sat 11am–11pm; Sun 10am–11pm. Bar open later. Sun brunch year-round 10am–3pm.

Marina Cafe ✰✰ NEW AMERICAN   Destin's finest restaurant provides a classy atmosphere with soft candlelight, subdued music, and walls of glass overlooking the harbor. The changing menu always offers nouveau preparations of seafood. Pizzas are topped with the likes of spicy cayenne rock shrimp, roasted corn, and onion marmalade, and pastas might feature fusilli with roast chicken, sun-dried tomatoes, goat cheese, broccoli, pine nuts, and an herb and balsamic vinegar broth. Any main course will be an exciting combination of flavors, too. If it's offered, try the grouper coated with crab and horseradish and served with herb-roasted potatoes and wild-mushroom parsnip and asparagus ragout. Enjoy the outdoor deck for drinks and appetizers.

404 Hwy. 98 E., Destin Harbor. © 850/837-7960. Reservations recommended. Main courses $17–$29; pizza and pasta $10–$17. AE, DC, DISC, MC, V. Daily 5–10pm. Closed first 2 weeks in Jan.

McGuire's Irish Pub & Brewery AMERICAN/IRISH   Like Pensacola's original McGuire's (listed above), this younger sibling sports thousands of dollar bills stuck on the ceilings and walls, plus Notre Dame football schedules, a prominent logo of the Boston Celtics, and other memorabilia recalling Irish American lore. This is Destin's most popular hangout, and local professionals congregate at the big oak bar in the center of the dining room, especially when live entertainment starts at 9pm Tuesday to Sunday. You can opt for a table on either side of the bar or up on a rooftop deck. Dining here is almost secondary to the see-and-be-seen scene, although the tender chargrilled steaks and giant hamburgers are worthy antidotes to a big appetite.

33 Hwy. 98 E., Destin Harbor (in Harborwalk Center near Destin Bridge). © 850/650-0000. Reservations not accepted. Main courses $16–$25; snacks, burgers, and sandwiches $8–$12. AE, DC, DISC, MC, V. Mon–Sat 11am–2am; Sun 11am–1am.

Inexpensive

Callahan's Island Restaurant & Deli ✰ *Value* AMERICAN/DELI   The best place in the area for picnic fare, this family-operated deli offers burgers, excellent Rubens, and other made-to-order sandwiches, pastas, and nightly specials such as charcoal-grilled chicken and grilled pork chops. A long refrigerator case across the rear holds a variety of top-grade cheeses, deli meats, steaks, and chops (choose your own cut, and the chef will chargrill it to order). Tables and booths are set up garden fashion, adding an outdoorsy ambience to this pleasant storefront establishment. Locals like to do lunch here. Breakfast is served only on Saturday morning.

950 Gulf Shore Dr. (2 blocks south of U.S. 98). © 850/837-6328. Main courses $8–$16; sandwiches, burgers, and salads $3.50–$6.50. DISC, MC, V. Mon–Fri 10am–9pm; Sat 8am–9pm.

Ciao Bella Pizza *Finds* PIZZA/SOUTHERN ITALIAN   This urbane little parlor offers more than just very good 12-inch pizzas; chef Gugliemo Ianni also whips up excellent salads and pastas, which he displays on a cafeteria-style steam table, just like they do in his native Italy. Afterwards enjoy some creamy gelato.

29 Hwy. 98 (in Harborwalk Center near Destin Bridge). © 850/654-9815. Reservations not accepted. Main courses $8–$11; pizza $8–$17. AE, DISC, MC, V. Summer daily 11am–11pm; off-season Mon–Sat 11am–10pm.

Donut Hole SOUTHERN   Available around the clock, breakfasts at this popular spot highlight eggs Benedict, hot fluffy biscuits under sausage gravy, Belgian waffles, and freshly baked doughnuts. Lunch sees fresh deli sandwiches, half-pound burgers, and big salads. The rough-hewn building has booths and counter seating. Be prepared to wait on the deck, especially on weekends. Daily specials such as half a Southern fried chicken with three country-style vegetables and dessert are a bargain. There's another Donut Hole on U.S. 98 East in southern Walton County 2½ miles east of the Sandestin Beach Resort (© **850/ 267-3239**). The restaurant is open daily from 6am to 10pm.

635 U.S. 98 E., Destin. © **850/837-8824.** Reservations not accepted. Entrees $4–$8. No credit cards. Daily 24 hr. Closed 2 weeks before Christmas.

FORT WALTON BEACH

Big City Coffeehouse and Cafe COFFEE/PASTRIES/DELI   For a caffeine fix, an inexpensive breakfast or lunch, or afternoon tea, head to Tina and Jim Ivanchukov's bright yellow-and-purple cafe on the mainland near the Brooks Bridge. In addition to offering gourmet coffees, the owners make great salads such as herb-roasted chicken with apples, walnuts, and tarragon dressing (sold by the pound), and sandwiches served on homemade focaccia bread.

201 Miracle Strip Pkwy. SE (U.S. 98). © **850/664-0664.** Reservations not accepted. Sandwiches and salads $5.50–$8.50. MC, V. Mon–Fri 7am–7pm; Sat–Sun 8am–5pm.

Caffè Italia ★★ NORTHERN ITALIAN   Nada Eckhardt is from Croatia, but she met her American husband, Jim, while working at a restaurant named Caffè Italia in northern Italy. The Eckhardts duplicated that establishment in this 1925 Sears & Roebuck mail-order house tucked away on the waterfront. You can dine on the patio with a view of the Sound through sprawling live oak trees (one table is set romantically under its own gazebo) or dine inside, where Nada has installed floral tablecloths and photos from the old country. A limited but fine menu includes excellent pizzas; pasta dishes such as tortellini with tomatoes, chicken, and peas in Alfredo sauce; northern Italian risotto with either asparagus or smoked salmon; and meat and seafood dishes to fit the season. Don't expect to make a full meal by ordering only a pasta here, because meals are served in the authentic Italian fashion, with a small portion of pasta preceding the seafood or meat course. On the other hand, you can quickly fill up on the seasoned, pizza-dough breadsticks served with olive oil for dipping. The cappuccino here is absolutely first-rate, as are the genuine Italian desserts.

189 Brooks St., on the mainland in the block west of Brooks Bridge. © **850/664-0035.** Reservations recommended. Main courses $15–$18; pizza and pasta $8–$13. AE, DC, DISC, MC, V. Tues–Sun 11am–10pm. Closed Thanksgiving and Christmas.

Pandora's Restaurant & Lounge ★ STEAKS/PRIME RIB/SEAFOOD   The front part of this unusual restaurant is a beached yacht now housing the main-deck lounge. Below is a beam-ceilinged dining room aglow with lights from copper chandeliers. Try for the private Bob Hope booth, where you can dine below two of the great comedian's golf clubs (he used to come here to raise money for a local Air Force widow's home). Anything from the charcoal grill is excellent, including the wonderful bacon-wrapped scallops offered as an appetizer. Several varieties of freshly caught fish are among the main-course choices, but steaks and prime rib keep the locals coming back for more. The tender beef is cut on the premises and grilled to perfection. The delicious breads and pies are homemade. Live entertainment and dancing are an added attraction in the lounge Wednesday to Saturday, as are free snacks during happy hour from 5 to 7pm weekdays. There's another Pandora's in Grayton Beach at the corner of Fla. 283 and County Road 30A (© **850/231-4102**).

1120B Santa Rosa Blvd. © **850/244-8669.** Reservations recommended. Main courses $13–$22. AE, DC, DISC, MC, V. Sun–Thurs 5–10pm; Fri–Sat 5–10:30pm.

Staff's Seafood Restaurant SEAFOOD/STEAKS Considered the first Emerald Coast restaurant, Staff's started as a hotel in 1913 and moved to this barnlike building in 1931. Among the display of memorabilia are an old-fashioned phonograph lamp and a 1914 cash register. Staff's tangy seafood gumbo has gained fame for this casual, historic restaurant. One of the most popular main dishes is the "seafood skillet," sizzling with broiled grouper, shrimp, scallops, and crabmeat drenched in butter and sprinkled with cheese. All main courses are served with heaping baskets of hot, home-baked wheat bread from a secret 70-year-old recipe, a salad, and dessert. A pianist plays at dinner year-round.

24 SW Miracle Strip Pkwy. (U.S. 98), on the mainland. ℂ 850/243-3526. Reservations not accepted. Main courses $13–$30. AE, DISC, MC, V. Summer daily 5–11pm. Off-season Mon–Thurs 5–9pm; Fri–Sat 5–10pm.

SOUTHERN WALTON COUNTY

A good budget choice here is **Morgan's Market** (ℂ **850/654-3320**), the food court at Silver Sands Factory Stores (see "Shopping," earlier in this chapter).

Cafe New Orleans ★ Value CAJUN Transplanted here from New Orleans, Ernie and Dawn Danjean bring a terrific taste of the Big Easy to their little fast-food–style restaurant (you place your order at the counter), tucked in a small shopping center about a mile west of the Silver Sands Factory Stores. Their breakfast beignets are made from dough blended back home by the company that supplies the French Quarter's famous Café du Monde. Or you can start your day with a po'boy of eggs, ham, and cheese. For lunch, their spicy gumbo comes in a whopping 16-ounce cup, large enough for a meal in itself. A platter of lightly breaded, highly seasoned fried seafood will also fill you up. Consider a mouth-watering daily special, such as lightly battered catfish under a spicy shrimp étouffée sauce.

12273 Emerald Coast Pkwy. (U.S. 98), in Holiday Plaza, 3 miles east of Mid-Bay Bridge. ℂ 850/650-4545. Reservations not accepted. Main courses $7–$10; beignets and sandwiches $2–$6. AE, MC, V. Mon–Sat 8am–8pm. Closed Easter weekend, Thanksgiving, 2 weeks at Christmas.

Criolla's ★★★ Value INTERNATIONAL One of Florida's finest restaurants, Johnny Earles's charming establishment derives its name from the archaic word *criollo*, signifying persons of pure Spanish descent born in the New World. The attractive decor, combining New Orleans with the Caribbean, features potted palms, whirling ceiling fans, and tropical island paintings. The menus change seasonally, but many fish dishes carry the wonderful aroma of smoke from a wood-fired grill (the bacon-wrapped swordfish is always a winner). Be sure to ask about a special four-course, fixed-price dinner, which draws inspiration from such warm spots as the Caribbean, Central America, and Tahiti. It's also worth asking in advance about special events featuring visiting chefs and spotlighting excellent vineyards (the wine cellar here has won awards).

170 E. Scenic Hwy. 30A, ¼ mile east of County Rd. 283, Grayton Beach. ℂ 850/267-1267. Reservations recommended. Main courses $19–$29. AE, DISC, MC, V. Mar–Aug daily 5:30–10pm. Sept–Feb Tues–Sat 5:30–10pm.

SEASIDE

Several cafes and sandwich shops in Seaside's gulf-side shopping complex offer inexpensive snacks to beachgoers.

Bud and Alley's ★★ SEAFOOD/STEAKS/MEDITERRANEAN Set among the gulf-side dunes, Seaside's first restaurant is still number one. The freshest seafood can be selected from seasonal menus featuring an innovative selection of Basque, Italian, Louisianan, and Floridian dishes prepared by owners and accomplished chefs Scott Witcoski and Dave Raushkolb. You can dine indoors or out, on the screened porch, or under an open-air gazebo where you'll hear the waves splashing against the white sands. The roof deck, open in season, serves appetizers and light meals and is a fabulous spot to watch the sun set on the Gulf of Mexico. Jazz is usually in the spotlight on weekends. On New Year's Eve, everyone in town and from miles around celebrates at Bud and Alley's. Call ahead to see whether a noted guest chef is cooking or a special wine-tasting dinner is scheduled. No smoking.

County Rd. 30A, in the beachside shops. ℂ 850/231-5900. Reservations recommended. Main courses $19–$27; lunch $7.50–$14. MC, V. Feb–Sept Sun–Thurs 11:30am–3pm and 6–9:30pm; Fri–Sat 11:30am–3pm and 6–10pm. Oct–Dec Sun–Thurs 5:30–9pm; Fri–Sat 5:30–9:30pm.

DESTIN & FORT WALTON BEACH AFTER DARK

Most resorts spotlight live entertainment during the summer season, including the Radisson Beach Resort and the Ramada Plaza Beach Resort in Fort Walton Beach, and the Sandestin Hilton Beach & Golf Resort and The Resort at Sandestin in southern Walton County (see "Where to Stay," earlier in this chapter). It's a good idea to inquire ahead to make sure what's scheduled, especially during the slow season from October through February.

For other ideas and listings of what's happening, pick up a copy of the weekly *Walton Sun* newspaper.

DESTIN Several Destin restaurants offer entertainment nightly during summer, on weekends off-season. The dockside **AJ's Club Bimini,** 116 U.S. 98 E. (ℂ 850/837-1913), has live reggae under a big thatch-roofed deck. A somewhat older, if not more sober, crowd gathers for entertainment at the big harborside deck at **Fisherman's Wharf,** on U.S. 98 East (ℂ 850/654-4766); at **The Deck,** on U.S. 98 East at the Harbor Docks restaurant, overlooking the harbor (ℂ 850/837-2506); at **Harry T's Boat House** (ℂ 850/654-6555), also on the harbor; and for Irish tunes nightly year-round at **McGuire's Irish Pub & Brewery** (ℂ 850/650-0000), in the Harborwalk Shops on U.S. 98 just east of the Destin Bridge. See "Where to Dine," earlier in this chapter, for details about the restaurants. The **Grande Isle Sky Bar,** above Grazti Italian Restaurant, 1771 Old Hwy. 98 (ℂ 850/837-7475), draws the after-dinner crowd from the Back Porch and other adjacent restaurants.

Twenty-somethings are attracted to the dance club, rowdy saloon, Jimmy Buffett–style reggae bar, and sports TV and billiards parlor all under one roof at the acclaimed **Nightown,** 140 Palmetto St. (ℂ 850/837-6448), near the harbor on the inland side of U.S. 98 East. One admission of $3 to $7 covers it all. Nearby, **Hogs Breath Destin,** 541 Hwy. 98 E. (ℂ 850/837-5991), is another lively pub with bands playing beach music.

Out toward Sandestin, **Fudrucker's Beachside Bar & Grill,** 20001 Hwy. 98 E. (ℂ 850/654-4200), opposite the Henderson Beach State Recreation Area, offers double the fun with two summertime stages. There's another Fudrucker's at 108 Santa Rosa Blvd. on Okaloosa Island in Fort Walton Beach (ℂ 850/243-3833).

FORT WALTON BEACH Country music and dancing fans will find a home at the **Seagull,** on Miracle Strip Parkway (U.S. 98) opposite the Gulfarium (ℂ 850/243-3413). The generations of air force pilots who have hung out here call it the "Dirty Gull." Its main rival for the country set is the **High Tide Oyster Bar,** at Okaloosa Island off the Brooks Bridge (ℂ 850/244-2624). Over at the Boardwalk on U.S. 98 East, **Howl at the Moon** (© **850/301-0111**) has an entertaining "dueling piano" rock 'n' roll show starting at 8pm.

3 Panama City Beach

100 miles E. of Pensacola, 100 miles SW of Tallahassee

Panama City Beach has long been known as the "Redneck Riviera," since it's a summertime mecca for millions of low- and moderate-income vacationers from nearby southern states. It still has a seemingly unending strip of bars, amusement parks, and old-fashioned motels. But this lively and crowded destination now also has luxury resorts and condominiums to go along with its 20-plus miles of white-sand beach, golf courses, fishing, boating, and fresh seafood.

Panama City Beach is the most seasonal resort in Northwest Florida, since many restaurants, attractions, and even some hotels close between October and Spring Break in March. Spring Break is a big deal here; MTV even sets up shop in Panama City Beach for annual beach-party broadcasts.

ESSENTIALS

GETTING THERE   The commuter arms of **Delta** (© 800/221-1212), **Northwest/KLM** (© 800/225-2525), and **US Airways** (© 800/428-4322) fly into **Panama City/Bay County International Airport,** on Lisenby Avenue, north of St. Andrews Boulevard, in Panama City.

Alamo (© 800/327-9633), **Avis** (© 800/331-1212), **Budget** (© 800/527-0700), **Enterprise** (© 800/325-8007), **Hertz** (© 800/654-3131), and **National** (© 800/CAR-RENT) have rental-cars here.

Taxi fares to the beach range from about $12 to $25.

The Sunset Limited transcontinental service on **Amtrak** (© **800/USA-RAIL;** www.amtrak.com) stops at Chipley, 45 miles north of Panama City.

VISITOR INFORMATION   For advance information, contact the **Panama City Beach Convention & Visitors Bureau,** P.O. Box 9473, Panama City Beach, FL 32417 (© **800/PC-BEACH** in the U.S., 800/553-1330 in Canada, or 850/233-6503; fax 850/233-5072; www.800pcbeach.com). It operates a visitor information center in the city hall complex, 17001 Panama City Beach Pkwy. (U.S. 98), at Fla. 79. The center is open daily from 8am to 5pm; closed New Year's Day, Thanksgiving, and Christmas.

GETTING AROUND   A **trolley** (© **850/769-0557**) runs four times a day Monday to Friday year-round along Thomas Drive and on Front Beach Road as far west as Fla. 79. Rides cost $1. Call for the schedule. Call **Yellow Cab** (© **800/763-0211** or 850/763-4691) or **AAA Taxi** (© **850/785-0533**). Fares at the beach are $2.50 for the first ⅖ mile plus 25¢ a mile thereafter, or $5 to $10 for rides within Panama City Beach. **Classic Rentals,** 13226 Front Beach Rd. (© **850/235-1519**), rents bicycles, scooters, and motorcycles. Call for prices and reservations.

TIME   The Panama City area is in the central time zone, 1 hour behind Miami, Orlando, and Tallahassee.

HITTING THE BEACH: ST. ANDREWS STATE PARK

A nearly unbroken strand of fine white sand fronts all 22 miles of Panama City Beach, but the highlight for many here is **St. Andrews State Park** ★★★, at the east end of the beach. With more than 1,000 acres of dazzling white sand and dunes, this preserved wilderness demonstrates what the area looked like before motels and condominiums lined the beach. Lacy, golden sea oats sway in the refreshing gulf breezes, and fragrant rosemary grows wild. Picnic areas are on both the gulf beach and the Grand Lagoon. Rest rooms and open-air showers are available for beachgoers. For anglers, there are jetties and a boat ramp. A nature trail reveals wading birds and perhaps an alligator or two. And drive carefully here, for the area is home to foxes, coyotes, and a herd of deer. Overnight camping is permitted (see "Where to Stay," below). On display is a historic turpentine still that was formerly used by lumbermen to make turpentine and rosin, both important for caulking the old wooden ships.

The park's 170 RV and tent **campsites** are among the state's most beautiful, especially the 40 situated in a pine forest right on the shores of Grand Lagoon. They are very popular, so reservations are highly recommended—and absolutely essential in summer. You can make them up to 11 months in advance. Sites cost $17 to $23 from March through September. They drop to $10 to $14 from October to February.

Park admission is $4 per car with two to eight occupants, $2 for single-occupant vehicles, and $1 for pedestrians and cyclists. The area is open daily from 8am to sunset. Pets are not allowed in the park. For more information or for camping reservations, contact the park at 4607 State Park Lane, Panama City, FL 32408 (© **850/233-5140**).

A few hundred yards across an inlet from St. Andrews State Park sits pristine **Shell Island** ★★, a 7½-mile-long, 1-mile-wide barrier island that's accessible only by boat. This uninhabited natural preserve is great for shelling and also fun for swimming, suntanning, or just relaxing. Visitors can bring chairs, beach gear, coolers, food, and beverages. The best way to get there is on the park's Shell Island Shuttle (© **850/233-5140**), which runs from April to October every 30 minutes: daily from 9am to 5pm in summer, weekends from 10am to 3pm in spring and fall. Fares are $7.50 for adults, $5.50 for children 11 and under, plus admission fees to the state recreation area (see above). A special snorkel package costs $16.95, including shuttle ride and equipment, and a 3-hour "ecosnorkel" tour for $24.95 departs twice daily. Kayak rentals cost $35 a day for a single-seat boat, $45 for a double seater.

Several cruise boats go to Shell Island, including the glass-bottomed **Captain Anderson III,** which cruises there from Captain Anderson's Marina, 5500 N. Lagoon Dr., at Thomas Drive (© **850/234-3435**). It charges $10 for anyone over age 12, $8 for kids. The **Glass Bottom Boat** (© **850/234-8944**) stops at Shell Island as part of its "sea school" trips from Treasure Island Marina, 3605 Thomas Dr. at Grand Lagoon (see "Cruises," under "Outdoor Activities," below).

OUTDOOR ACTIVITIES

BOATING A variety of rental boats are available at the marinas near the Thomas Drive bridge over Grand Lagoon. These include the **Captain Davis Queen Fleet,** based at Captain Anderson's Marina, 5500 N. Lagoon Dr. (© **800/874-2415,** or 850/234-3435 from nearby states); **the Panama City Boat Yard,** 5323 N. Lagoon Dr. (© **850/234-3386**); the **Passport Marina,** 5325 N. Lagoon Dr. (© **850/234-5609**); the **Port Lagoon Yacht Basin,** 5201 N. Lagoon Dr. (© **850/234-0142**); the **Pirates Cove Marina,** 3901 Thomas Dr. (© **850/234-3839**); and the **Treasure Island Marina,** 3605 Thomas Dr. (© **850/234-6533**).

Many resorts and hotels provide beach toys for their guests' use. WaveRunners, jet boats, inflatables, and other equipment can be rented from **Panama**

City Beach Sports (📞 850/234-0067), **Raging Rentals** (📞 850/234-6775), and **Lagoon Rentals** (📞 850/234-7245).

CRUISES You'll have your choice of numerous cruises here, from sailing to visiting the dolphins aboard noisy jet skis. The visitor information center (see "Essentials," above) has information about them all—and discount coupons for many.

One of the most comprehensive outings here is aboard the ***Glass Bottom Boat,*** based at Treasure Island Marina, 3605 Thomas Dr., at Grand Lagoon (📞 **850/234-8944**). Its 3-hour, narrated "sea school" cruise includes underwater viewing, dolphin watching, bird feeding, and a 1-hour stop for swimming at Shell Island. Along the way, the crew picks up and rebaits a crab trap and explains the creatures brought up in a shrimp net. The boat has a snack bar and an air-conditioned cabin. The trips cost about $14 for adults and $8 for children. This same company operates a **Super Shelling Safari,** on which guests are taken to the eastern end of Shell Island to scavenge in the shallow water for shells (wear your bathing suit). Call for cruise times, prices, and reservations.

The venerable **Captain Davis Queen Fleet,** based at Captain Anderson's Marina, 5500 N. Lagoon Dr. (📞 **800/874-2415,** or 850/234-3435 in Florida), has daily sightseeing trips, nature cruises, dolphin-watching and bird-feeding excursions, and dinner-dance cruises during the summer season.

Children get a kick out of the make-believe swashbucklers on the ***Sea Dragon*** (📞 **850/234-7400**), an 80-foot-long replica of a pirate ship that goes on 2-hour cruises from its dock next to the Treasure Ship on Thomas Drive at Grand Lagoon. The trips cost $15, $13 for seniors, $10 for children 3 to 12, and free for children under 3. Call for seasonal schedules and reservations.

FISHING The least-expensive way to try your luck fishing is with **Captain Anderson's Deep Sea Fishing,** at Captain Anderson's Marina on Thomas Drive at Grand Lagoon (📞 **800/874-2415** or 850/234-5940). The captain's party-boat trips last from 5 to 12 hours, with prices ranging from about $30 to $50 per person, including bait and tackle. Observers can go along for half-price.

More expensive are the charter-fishing boats that depart daily from March to November from the marinas mentioned in "Boating," above.

You won't get seasick casting your line from the **M. B. Miller County Pier,** 12213 Front Beach Rd. (📞 **850/233-3039**), or the **Dan Russell Municipal Pier,** 16101 Front Beach Rd. (📞 **850/233-5080**).

GOLF Marriott's **Bay Point Resort Village,** 4200 Marriott Dr., off Jan Cooley Road (📞 **850/234-3307**), offers 36 holes of championship play, including the Bruce Devlin–designed **Lagoon Legends** ★★ course, rated as one of the country's most difficult. Both it and the Club Meadows course have club-houses, putting greens, driving ranges, clinics, and private instruction. Greens fees with cart range from about $50 in summer to $80 in winter, depending on the day of the week. See "Where to Stay," below.

The **Edgewater Beach Resort,** 11212 U.S. 98A (📞 **850/235-4044**), also has a 9-hole resort course, and its guests have access to **The Hombre,** 120 Coyote Pass, 3 miles west of the Hathaway Bridge off Panama City Beach Parkway/U.S. 98 (📞 **850/234-3573**), a par-72 championship course that is home to the Nike Panama City Beach Classic. Fifteen of its 18 holes have water hazards (the unforgiving 7th hole sits on an island). Greens fees are about $65 in summer, $60 in winter, including cart.

The course at the semiprivate **Holiday Golf Club,** 100 Fairway Blvd. (📞 **850/234-1800**), sports lake-line fairways and elevated greens. Greens fees with cart are about $45 in summer, $35 in winter. You can play at night on a lighted 9-hole, par-29 executive course.

The least-expensive place to play here is the flat and forgiving **Signal Hill,** 9516 N. Thomas Dr. (© 850/234-3218), where you'll pay about $20 to walk 18 holes in summer, $15 in winter. Add about $10 per person for a cart.

SCUBA DIVING & SNORKELING Although the area is too far north for extensive coral formations, more than 50 artificial reefs and shipwrecks in the Gulf waters off Panama City attract a wide variety of sea life. The largest local operator is **Hydrospace Dive Shop,** 6422 W. Hwy. 98 (© **850/234-3036;** www.hydrospace.com). Others include **Panama City Dive Center,** 4823 Thomas Dr. (© **850/235-3390;** www.pcdivecenter.com); **Emerald Coast Divers,** 5121 Thomas Dr. (© **800/945-DIVE** or 850/233-3355); **West End Dive Center,** 17320 Panama City Beach Pkwy. (© **850/235-7873**); and **Pete's Scuba Center,** 9007 Front Beach Rd. (© **800/401-DIVE** or 850/230-8006). These companies lead dives, teach courses, and take snorkelers to the grass flats off Shell Island.

EXPLORING THE AREA

Gulf World Marine Park *Kids* This landscaped tropical garden and marine showcase features shows with talented dolphins, sea lions, penguins, and more. Not to be upstaged, parrots perform daily, too. Sea turtles, alligators, and other critters also call Gulf World home. Scuba demonstrations, shark feedings, and underwater shows keep the crowds entertained. Allow about 3½ hours to see it all, including the shows.

15412 Front Beach Rd. (at Hill Ave.), Panama City Beach. © 850/234-5271. ww.gulfworldmarinepark.com. Admission $19 adults, $12.50 children 5–11, free for children under 5. Summer daily 9am–4pm. Off-season daily 9am–2pm.

Museum of Man in the Sea Owned by the Institute of Diving, this small museum exhibits relics from the first days of scuba diving, historical displays of the underwater world dating from 1500, and treasures recovered from sunken ships, including Spanish treasure galleons. Hands-on exhibits explain water and air pressure, light refraction, and why diving bells work. Both kids and adults can climb through a submarine and see live sea animals in a pool. Videos and aquariums explain the sea life found in St. Andrew Bay.

17314 Panama City Beach Pkwy. (at Heather Dr., west of Fla. 79), Panama City Beach. © 850/235-4101. Admission $5 adults, $2.50 children 6–16, free for children 5 and under. Daily 9am–5pm. Closed New Year's Day, Thanksgiving, and Christmas.

ZooWorld Zoological & Botanical Park ★ *Kids* Sitting in a pine forest, this educational and entertaining zoo is an active participant in the Species Survival Plan, which helps protect endangered species by employing specific breeding and housing programs. Among the 350 guests here are orangutans and other primates, lions, tigers, leopards, and alligators and other reptiles. Also included are a walk-through aviary, a bat exhibit, and a petting zoo.

9008 Front Beach Rd. (near Moylan Dr.), Panama City Beach. © 850/230-1243. Admission $10.95 adults, $9.95 seniors, $7.50 children 3–11, free for children under 3. $2 discount in winter. Daily 9am–1 hr. before sunset.

AMUSEMENT PARKS

An exciting, 105-foot-high roller coaster is just one of the 30 rides at the **Miracle Strip Amusement Park,** 12000 Front Beach Rd., at Alf Coleman Road (© **850/234-5810;** www.miraclestrippark.com). Little ones will love the traditional carousel. Nine acres of fun include nonstop live entertainment and tons of junk food. Hours and prices change from year to year, so call for the latest. It's closed from Labor Day to mid-March.

Adjoining the Miracle Strip, the **Shipwreck Island Water Park** (© 850/ 234-0368; www.shipwreckisland.com) offers a variety of water amusements, including the 1,600-foot-long winding Lazy River for tubing and a daring 35-mile-per-hour Speed Slide. The Tad Pole Hole is exclusively for young kids. Lounge chairs, umbrellas, and inner tubes are free, and lifeguards are on duty. Admission is less than $20. The park is open June to mid-August; call for hours. Combination tickets for Miracle Strip and Shipwreck Island are available.

SHOPPING

An attraction in itself is the main branch of **Alvin's Island Tropical Department Store,** 12010 Front Beach Rd. (© 850/234-3048), opposite the James I. Lark Sr. Visitors Information Center. It not only sells a wide range of beach gear and apparel, but also has cages containing colorful parrots, tanks with small sharks, and an enclosure with alligators. The sharks are fed at 11am daily; the gators get theirs at 4pm (the older ones are too lethargic to eat during the cool winter months).

WHERE TO STAY

There are scores of motels along the beach here, ranging from small mom-and-pop operations to sizable members of national chains. The annual guide distributed by the Panama City Beach Convention & Visitors Bureau has a complete list (see "Essentials," above).

The most modern of the chain motels are the recently renovated **Howard Johnson Resort Hotel,** 9400 S. Thomas Dr. (© 800/654-2000 or 850-234-6521) and the **Four Points by Sheraton,** 9600 S. Thomas Dr. (© 888/625-5144 or 850) 234-6511), both part of the redeveloped Boardwalk Beach Resort area, a center of beach action.

Panama City Beach also abounds with condominium complexes, such as the Edgewater Beach Resort listed below. Among the many rental agents are **St. Andrew Bay Resort Management,** 726 Thomas Dr., Panama City Beach, FL 32408 (© 800/621-2462 or 850/235-4075; fax 850/233-2833; www. sabre1.net); and **Condo World,** 8815A Thomas Dr. (P.O. Box 9456), Panama City Beach, FL 32408 (© 800/232-6636 or 850/234-5564; fax 850/233-6725; www.condoworld.net).

The best camping is at the lovely sites in **St. Andrews State Park,** one of this area's major attractions (see "Hitting the Beach," above).

Rates at even the most expensive properties here drop precipitously during winter, when the town rolls up the sidewalks. Bay County adds 3.5% tax to all hotel and campground bills, bringing the total add-on tax to 9.5%.

EXPENSIVE

Edgewater Beach Resort ★★ One of the Panhandle's largest condominium resorts, this sports-oriented facility enjoys a beautiful beachfront location and 110 tropically landscaped acres. Units in five gulf-side towers enjoy commanding views of the emerald Gulf and gorgeous sunsets from their private balconies. A pedestrian overpass leads across Front Beach Road to low-rise apartments and townhomes fringing ponds and the fairways of the resort's own 9-hole golf course. A daytime shuttle runs around the resort to swimming pools, whirlpools, tennis center, and golf course (guests also get privileges at the 18-hole Hombre Golf Club, ¼ mile north). The Shoppes at Edgewater restaurants are across the road.

11212 Front Beach Rd. (P.O. Box 9850), Panama City Beach, FL 32407. © **800/874-8686** or 850/235-4044. Fax 850/235-6899. www.edgewaterbeachresort.com. 500 units. Summer $188–$414 condo; off-season $67–$167 condo. $5 per day per unit amenities fee. Weekly rates and maid service available. AE, DC, DISC, MC, V. **Amenities:** 2 restaurants (American); 2 bars; 11 heated outdoor pools; 9-hole golf course; 11 tennis courts; health club; Jacuzzi; water-sports equipment rentals; children's programs; concierge; car-rental desk; limited room service; baby-sitting; coin-op washers and dryers. *In room:* A/C, TV, dataport, kitchen, coffeemaker, hair dryer, iron.

MODERATE

Beachcomber by the Sea ✦

Watercolors by local artist Paul Brent grace every unit in this eight-story all-suites resort, built and opened in 1998 at the junction of Front Beach Road and Fla. 79. They also have balconies overlooking a Gulf-side swimming pool and hot tub bordered by a concrete deck accented by areas of palm trees. The well-equipped suites come in two sizes. The larger editions have living rooms with sleeper sofas, bedrooms with either king-size or two double beds, and their own phones and TVs. Bathrooms and kitchenettes separate the living rooms and bedrooms. The suites are similar to those at the Flamingo Motel & Tower (see below), except that here they have air conditioners in both living rooms and bedrooms. The smaller units are more like motel rooms, but they have microwaves. Two of the smaller units also have whirlpool tubs. There's no restaurant here but several are nearby, and complimentary continental breakfast is available in the lobby each morning. Spring-breakers are not welcome.

17101 Front Beach Rd., Panama City Beach, FL 32413. © **888/886-8916** or 850/233-3600. Fax 850/233-3622. www.beachcomberbythesea.com. 96 units. Summer $99–$189; off-season $49–$99. Rates include continental breakfast. Packages available. AE, DISC, MC, V. **Amenities:** Heated outdoor pool; access to nearby health club; Jacuzzi; game room; coin-op washers and dryers. *In room:* A/C, TV, dataport, kitchen, fridge, coffeemaker, hair dryer, iron.

Holiday Inn SunSpree Resort ✦

One building removed from the Edgewater Beach Resort and across the road from the Shoppes at Edgewater, this 15-story establishment is the top full-service gulf-front hotel here. It's designed in an arch, with all rooms having balconies looking directly down on the beach, where a heated, foot-shaped swimming pool and wooden sundeck are separated from the beach by a row of palms and Polynesian torches, which are lighted at night. The hotel has won architectural awards for its dramatic lobby with a waterfall and the Fountain of Wishes (coins go to charity). The attractive, spacious guest rooms feature full-size ice-making refrigerators, microwave ovens, and two spacious vanity areas with their own lavatory sinks.

11127 Front Beach Rd., Panama City Beach, FL 32407. © **800/633-0266** or 850/234-1111. Fax 850/235-1907. 342 units. Summer $185–$225 double; off-season $75–$129 double. AE, DC, DISC, MC, V. **Amenities:** 2 restaurants (American); 2 bars; heated outdoor pool; exercise room; Jacuzzi; water-sports equipment rentals; game room; concierge; limited room service; baby-sitting; laundry service; concierge-level rooms. *In room:* A/C, TV, dataport, fridge, coffeemaker, hair dryer, iron.

Marriott's Bay Point Resort Village ★★ (Value)

Not only is this luxurious vacation miniworld ranked among the nation's top golf and tennis resorts, but it's an extraordinarily good value for Florida, as well. Although guests pay extra for most activities, its room rates are among the top steals in the state. They would be higher if the property were beside the gulf; instead, it's the centerpiece of a manicured real-estate development sprawling over 1,100 acres on a peninsula bordered by St. Andrew Bay and the Grand Lagoon. Situated beside the lagoon, the luxurious, vivid-coral stucco hotel is surrounded by gardens, palm trees, oaks, and magnolias. From the glamorous three-story lobby, window walls look out to scenic water views and two swimming pools (one in its own glass-enclosed building). Furnished in dark woods, the Marriottesque rooms are spacious and luxurious, and all have balconies or patios. The highlights for duffers are the Lagoon Legends and the Club Meadows golf courses (see "Outdoor Activities," earlier in this chapter). Water sports here are at Grand Lagoon beach, reached by the hotel's long pier. There's a free shuttle to the Gulf beaches.

4200 Marriott Dr., Panama City Beach, FL 32408. © **800/874-7105** or 850/236-6000. Fax 850/236-6158. 355 units. Summer $119–$209 double; off-season $109–$169 double. Packages available. AE, DC, DISC, MC, V. From Thomas Dr., take Magnolia Beach Rd. and bear right on Dellwood Rd. to resort complex. **Amenities:** 2 restaurants (American); 2 bars; 3 heated outdoor pools; 1 indoor pool; 2 golf courses; 12 tennis courts; 2 health clubs; Jacuzzi; water-sports equipment rental; bike rental; concierge; business center; limited room service; baby-sitting; laundry service; coin-op washers and dryers; concierge-level rooms. *In room:* A/C, TV, dataport, fridge, coffeemaker, hair dryer, iron.

INEXPENSIVE

Flamingo Motel & Tower ★ *Value* Reggie, Rebecca, and Dana Lancaster take great pride in the gorgeous tropical garden surrounding a heated swimming pool and a large sundeck overlooking the Gulf at their well-maintained motel. The brightly decorated rooms have either full kitchens or refrigerators and microwave ovens. They can sleep two to six people, some in separate bedrooms. Kitchenette rooms in a two-story motel block across the road are less appealing but will accommodate six to eight. Budget-conscious families can opt for lower-priced rooms, accommodating two to four. Next door, the seven-story Flamingo Tower contains 49 suites, all sporting living rooms with sofa beds and dining tables; bedrooms with ceiling fans and their own TVs; kitchens; and balconies overlooking the Gulf and a beachside swimming pool and hot tub. These suites have air-conditioning units in their living rooms but not in their bedrooms (the ceiling fans will come in handy during the hot, humid summer months). Some older units here have shower-only bathrooms. The Dan Russell fishing pier is only half a mile away, and Gulf World Marine Park and Shuckums Oyster Pub & Seafood Grill are virtually across the road (see "Exploring the Area," above, and "Where to Dine," below). College spring-breakers not welcome.

15525 Front Beach Rd., Panama City Beach, FL 32413. © **800/828-0400** or 850/234-2232. Fax 850/234-1292. www.flamingomotel.com. 117 units. Summer $84–$139; off-season $32–$99. AE, DISC, MC, V. **Amenities:** 2 heated outdoor pools; access to nearby health club; Jacuzzi; water-sports equipment rental; coin-op washers and dryers. *In room:* A/C, TV, kitchen, fridge, coffeemaker.

Georgian Terrace Located right on the beach, this two-level motel offers clean, cozy apartments with knotty-pine paneling. Opening to the beach, all units have full kitchens and private, enclosed sun porches. Some units have desktop computers with high-speed Internet connections, and the "home theater" suite comes equipped with a 54-inch TV and a surround-sound system. A greenhouse-enclosed heated pool area with lush tropical plantings and attractive lounge chairs makes this place a good pick off-season. There's a rare stretch of undeveloped beach almost next door. The mother-son team of Karen and Wes Grant make sure that everyone feels at home here.

14415 Front Beach Rd., Panama City Beach, FL 32413. © **888/882-2144** or 850/234-2144. Fax 850/234-8413. www.georgianterrace.com. 28 units. Summer $89–$149 double off-season $39–$89 double. MC, V. **Amenities:** Heated indoor pool. *In room:* A/C, TV, kitchen, coffeemaker.

Sunset Inn This very well maintained establishment, off Thomas Drive between Chicksaw and Snapper streets near the east end of the beach, is right on the Gulf but away from the crowds. The spacious beachside motel rooms accommodate families in one- and two-bedroom apartments with kitchens, while across the street stands a block of refurbished efficiencies and a new building with tropically furnished one- and two-bedroom condominiums. The condominiums are the most expensive units here, but the units with patios or balconies right on the beach will better suit sun-and-sand lovers. Some of the older units have shower-only bathrooms.

8109 Surf Dr., Panama City Beach, FL 32408. © 850/234-7370. Fax 850/234-7370, ext. 303. http://poteau. com/sunset/suninn/htm. 62 units. Summer $65–$155 double; off-season $50–$125 double. Weekly and monthly rates available. AE, DISC, MC, V. **Amenities:** Heated outdoor pool; coin-op washers and dryers. *In room:* A/C, TV, kitchen, fridge, coffeemaker.

WHERE TO DINE

Except for fast-food joints, there aren't many national-chain family restaurants in Panama City Beach (you'll find those along 15th and 23rd streets over in Panama City). One local chain worth a meal is the **Montego Bay Seafood House,** which offer a wide range of fairly inexpensive munchies, sandwiches, burgers, and seafood main courses. Branches are at the "curve" on Thomas Drive (© **850/234-8687**); at the intersection of Thomas Drive and Middle and Front Beach roads (© **850/236-3585**); and in the Shoppes at Edgewater, Front Beach Drive at Beckrich Road (© **850/233-6033**).

Pay attention to the restaurant hours here, because some places are closed during the winter months. Even if they're open, many will close early when business is slow.

MODERATE

Boar's Head Restaurant ✩ STEAKS/SEAFOOD An institution since 1978, this shingle-roofed establishment appears from the road to be a South Seas resort. Inside, its impressive beamed ceiling, stone walls, and fireplaces create a warm, almost-English tavern atmosphere suited to the house specialties: tender, marbled prime rib of beef and perfectly cooked steaks. Beef eaters don't have the Boar's Head to themselves, however, because the coals are also used to give a charred flavor to salmon, grouper, and yellowfin tuna. Other cooking styles are offered, too, including a combination of lobster, shrimp, and scallops in a cream sauce over angel-hair pasta. And venison, quail, and other game dishes find their way here during winter. An extensive wine list has won awards, and a cozy tavern to one side has live music, usually Wednesday to Saturday evenings.

17290 Front Beach Rd. (just west of Fla. 79). © **850/234-6628.** Main courses $14–$22. AE, DC, DISC, MC, V. Summer daily 4:30–10pm. Off-season Sun–Thurs 4:30–9pm; Fri–Sat 4:30–10pm.

Canopies ✩✩ SEAFOOD/STEAKS This area's most elegant restaurant and purveyor of its finest cuisine occupies a 1910-vintage gray clapboard house with a magnificent view of St. Andrew Bay. Dining is on an enclosed verandah, but the dark, cozy bar in the old living room invites before- or after-dinner drinks. The menu changes monthly but always offers the consistently excellent creamy she-crab soup under a flaky croissant dome. Other selections could include sushi-quality yellowfin tuna in a sherry-soy sauce served over a haystack of leeks; a "trio" of tuna, salmon, and grouper with a citrus butter sauce served with a mandarin orange salsa and Vidalia-onion mashed potatoes; and sautéed grouper with lump crabmeat in a sherry-butter sauce. Forget the crab cakes. Landlubbers can partake of award-winning beef, veal, lamb, pork, and game dishes. White chocolate mousse is among several wonderful sweet endings.

4423 W. Hwy. 98, Panama City (1 mile east of Hathaway Bridge on U.S. 98). ✆ 850/872-8444. Reservations recommended. Main courses $16–$26. AE, DC, DISC, MC, V. Daily 5–10pm. Closed Thanksgiving and Christmas.

Captain Anderson's Restaurant & Waterfront Seafood Market

SEAFOOD   Since 1953 this famous restaurant has been attracting early diners who come to watch the fishing fleet unload the catch of the day at the busy marina on Grand Lagoon. It's so popular, in fact, that you may have to wait 2 hours for a table during the peak summer months; three bars are there to help you pass the time. The Captain's menu is noted for grilled local fish, crabmeat-stuffed jumbo shrimp, and a heaped-high seafood platter. The food isn't as interesting as at Hamilton's Seafood Restaurant & Lounge across the road (see below), but the local atmosphere makes it worth a visit while you're here.

5551 N. Lagoon Dr. (at Thomas Dr.). ✆ 850/234-2225. Reservations not accepted. Main courses $11–$35. AE, DC, DISC, MC, V. Summer Mon–Sat 4–10pm. Off-season Mon–Sat 4:30–10pm. Closed Nov–Jan.

Hamilton's Seafood Restaurant & Lounge ✪ SEAFOOD   Proprietor

Steve Stevens continues in the tradition of his noted Mississippi-born, restaurateur father. The attractive blond-wood and knotty-pine restaurant lies on Grand Lagoon. The baked oysters Hamilton appetizer—a rich combination of oysters, shrimp, and crabmeat—almost left me too full for a main course. Several other dishes are unique to Hamilton's, such as spicy snapper étouffée and a Greek-accented shrimp Cristo. Mesquite-grilled fish and steaks are also house specialties, and vegetarians can order a coal-fired vegetable kebab served over angel-hair pasta. The Lagoon Saloon makes the wait for a table go by quickly, and you can select from an extensive selection of well-chosen California and French wines.

5711 N. Lagoon Dr. (at Thomas Dr.). ✆ 850/234-1255. Reservations not accepted. Main courses $13–$22. AE, DISC, MC, V. Summer daily 4–10pm. Off-season Mon–Thurs 5–9pm; Fri–Sat 5–9:30pm. Closed 1 week in Jan.

INEXPENSIVE

Billy's Steamed Seafood Restaurant *Value* SEAFOOD   More a lively raw

bar than a restaurant, Billy and Eloise Poole's casual spot has been serving the best crabs in town since 1982. These are hard-shell blue crabs prepared Maryland style: steamed with spicy Old Bay Seasoning. Unlike crab houses in Baltimore, however, Billy and Eloise remove the crab's top shell, clean out the "mustard" (intestines), and cut the crabs in two for you; all you have to do is "pick" the meat. Don't worry, they'll show you. Other steamed morsels include shrimp (also with spicy seasoning), oysters, crabs, and lobster served with corn on the cob and garlic bread. Order anything from the briny deep here, but pass over other items.

3000 Thomas Dr. (between Grand Lagoon and Magnolia Beach Rd.). ✆ 850/235-2349. Reservations not accepted. Main courses $5.50–$16; sandwiches $2.50–$5.50. AE, DISC, MC, V. Feb–Oct Mon–Thurs 11am–9:30pm; Fri–Sat 11am–10pm. Nov–Dec Thurs–Sun 11am–9pm.

Cajun Inn LOUISIANA CAJUN   This lively, family-owned restaurant with

high-backed wooden booths brings the Big Easy to the Gulf. Offerings include jambalaya, seafood étouffée, peppered shrimp or crayfish, and Cajun-style blackened fish. Po' boy sandwiches stuffed with fried oysters or shrimp are a specialty. You won't get gourmet New Orleans cuisine at these prices, but your tongue will have plenty of spice to savor. Dine inside or outside. There's live music on weekends.

817 Azalea Ave. (near Front Beach Rd./Middle Beach Rd. intersection). ℂ **850/233-0403**. Reservations not accepted. Main courses $12–$17; sandwiches $6–$11. AE, DC, DISC, MC, V. Daily 11am–10pm.

Shuckums Oyster Pub & Seafood Grill SEAFOOD "We shuck 'em, you suck 'em" is the motto of this noisy, lively, and smoky pub, which became famous when comedian Martin Short tried unsuccessfully to shuck oysters here during the making of an MTV Spring-Break special. The original bar is virtually papered over with dollar bills signed by old and young patrons who have been flocking here since 1967. The obvious specialty is fresh Apalachicola oysters, served raw, steamed, or baked with a variety of toppings. Otherwise, the menu consists of pub fare and mediocre seafood main courses.

15614 Front Beach Rd. (at Powell Adams Dr.). ℂ **850/235-3214**. Reservations not accepted. Main courses $11–$17; burgers and sandwiches $6–$10. AE, DISC, MC, V. Summer daily 11am–2am. Off-season Sun–Thurs 11am–9pm; Fri–Sat 11am–midnight.

SPECIAL DINING EXPERIENCES

You've got to see the **Treasure Ship,** at Treasure Island Marina, 3605 S. Thomas Dr. at Grand Lagoon (ℂ **850/234-8881**), to believe it. This amazing 2 acres of ship space claims to be the world's largest land-based Spanish galleon and a reputed replica of the three-masted sailing ships that carried loot from the New World to Spain in the 16th and 17th centuries. You can get anything from an ice-cream cone to peel-it-yourself shrimp to a sophisticated dinner in the restaurant and bar here, which are open daily at 4:30pm; closed from October through December.

Lady Anderson **dinner-dance cruises** are a romantic evening escape; they're available from March through October. This modern, three-deck ship boards at Captain Anderson's Marina, 5550 N. Lagoon Dr. (ℂ **850/234-5940**), at 6:30pm Monday to Saturday, with the cruises lasting from 7 to 10pm. Buffet dinners are featured, followed by live music for dancing Monday, Wednesday, Friday, and Saturday nights; gospel music on Tuesday and Thursday. Dinner-dance tickets cost $37.50 for adults, $22.50 for children 6 to 11, $14.50 for children 2 to 5. Gospel music cruises go for $32.50 for adults, $22.50 for children 6 to 11, $14.50 for children 2 to 5. Tips are included. Summertime reservations should be made well in advance.

PANAMA CITY & PANAMA CITY BEACH AFTER DARK

THE PERFORMING ARTS The Rader family and a cast of 20 perform year-round in the **Ocean Opry Show,** 8400 Front Beach Rd., Panama City Beach (ℂ **850/234-5464**), the area's answer to the Grand Ole Opry. There's a show every night at 8pm during the summer, less frequently off-season. Popcorn, hot dogs, and soft drinks are available. Admission is about $20 for adults, half-price for children. Prices jump to $30 or more when stars like Kitty Welles, B. J. Thomas, and the Wilkensons are in town, usually during winter. The box office opens at 9am Monday to Saturday, and reservations are recommended but not required.

THE CLUB & BAR SCENE The **Breakers,** 12627 Front Beach Rd. (ℂ**850/ 234-6060**), is the area's premier supper club, with unsurpassed gulf views and music for dining and dancing. Open daily at 4pm during summer, Monday to Saturday during the off-season. The beachfront **Harpoon Harry's Waterfront Cafe** is part of the same complex.

You'll swear The King has risen from the grave as "Elvis Presley" and other impersonators perform at the **Rock 'n' Roll/Clutch Cafe,** in the Howard

Johnson Resort Hotel, 9400 S. Thomas Drive (© **850/230-4665**). A buffet dinner is served from 6 to 8pm, with shows starting at 9pm during summer, 8pm off-season (it closes after Christmas for the winter). Show tickets cost $15 for adults, $10 for children. Buffet and show together cost $29 adults, $15 for children.

Romantic lounges with live entertainment are at the **Treasure Ship,** 3605 S. Thomas Dr. (© **850/234-8881**), where comedian-hypnotist Mike Harvey performs during summer in the top-floor Captain's Quarters; and at the **Boar's Head,** 17290 Front Beach Rd. (© **850/234-6628**). See "Where to Dine" and "Special Dining Experiences," above, for more information.

The 20-something crowd likes to boogie all night at beach clubs such as **Schooners,** 5121 Gulf Dr. (© **850/235-9074**), where every table has a gulf view; **Spinnaker's,** on the beach at 8795 Thomas Dr. (© **850/234-7882**); **Club La Vella,** a bikini-contest kind of place and one of Florida's largest nightclubs, also on the beach at 8813 Thomas Dr. (© **850/234-3866**); and **Sharkey's on the Gulf,** 15201 Front Beach Rd. (© **850/235-2420**). The clubs often stay open until 4am in summer while their bands play on. **Pineapple Willie's Lounge,** beachside at 9900 S. Thomas Dr. (© **850/235-0928**), is open from 11am until 2am, serving ribs basted with Jack Daniels and spotlighting live entertainment during summer and a host of sports-TVs all year.

4 Apalachicola ★★

65 miles E. of Panama City, 80 miles W. of Tallahassee

Sometimes called Florida's Last Frontier, **Apalachicola** makes a fascinating day trip from Panama City Beach or Tallahassee, as well as a destination in its own right. The long, gorgeous beaches on **St. George Island,** 7 miles from town, are among the nation's best. Justifiably famous for Apalachicola oysters, the bays and estuaries are great for fishing and boating. And if you love nature, the area also is rich in wildlife preserves.

The charming little town of Apalachicola (pop. 2,600) was a major seaport during autumns from 1827 to 1861, when plantations in Alabama and Georgia shipped tons of cotton down the Apalachicola River to the Gulf. The town had a racetrack, an opera house, and a civic center that hosted balls, socials, and gambling. The population shrank during the mosquito-infested summer months, however, when yellow fever and malaria epidemics struck. It was during one of these outbreaks that Dr. John Gorrie of Apalachicola tried to develop a method of cooling his patients' rooms. In doing so, he invented the forerunner of the air conditioner, a device that made Florida tourism possible and life a whole lot more bearable for locals.

Apalachicola has traditionally made its living primarily from the Gulf and the lagoonlike bay protected by a chain of offshore barrier islands. Today this area produces the bulk of Florida's oyster crop, and shrimping and fishing are major industries. The town also has been discovered by a number of urban expatriates, who have moved here, restored old homes, and opened interesting antique and gift shops (there aren't many towns this size where you can buy Crabtree & Evelyn products).

ESSENTIALS

GETTING THERE   The nearest airport is 65 miles to the west at Panama City Beach (see "Essentials," in section 3, earlier in this chapter). From there you'll have to rent a car or take an expensive taxi ride. The Tallahassee airport is about 85 miles to the northeast (see "Essentials," in section 5, later in this chapter). **Croom's Transportation** (© **888/653-8132**) has airport shuttle service between Tallahassee and Apalachicola. Call for fares and schedule.

The scenic way to drive here is via the gulf-hugging U.S. 98 from Panama City Beach, or via U.S. 319 and U.S. 98 from Tallahassee. From I-10, take Exit 21 at Marianna, then follow Fla. 71 south to Port St. Joe, and take U.S. 98 east to Apalachicola.

VISITOR INFORMATION The **Apalachicola Bay Chamber of Commerce,** 99 Market St., Apalachicola, FL 32320 (© **850/653-9419;** fax 850/ 653-8219; www.baynavigator.com), supplies information about the area from its office on Market Street (U.S. 98) between Avenue D and Avenue E. The chamber is open Monday to Friday from 9:30am to 5pm.

TIME The town is in the eastern time zone, like Orlando, Miami, and Tallahassee (it's 1 hr. ahead of Panama City Beach and the rest of the Panhandle). Many shops are closed on Wednesday afternoon, when Apalachicolans go fishing.

BEACHES, PARKS & WILDLIFE REFUGES

Some experts consider the 9 miles of beaches in **St. George Island State Park** ★★★ to be among America's best. This pristine nature preserve occupies the eastern end of St. George Island, about 15 miles east of Apalachicola. A 4-mile-long paved road leads through the dunes to picnic areas, rest rooms, showers, and a boat launch. An unpaved trail leads another 5 miles to the island's eastern end, but be careful: It's easy to get stuck in the soft sand even in a four-wheel-drive sports utility vehicle. From a hiking trail leading from the campground out a narrow peninsula on the bay side, you can see countless terns, snowy plovers, black skimmers, and other birds. Entry costs $2 for a vehicle with one occupant, $4 for vehicles with up to eight occupants, and $1 for pedestrians and bicyclists. Campsites cost $15 from February through August, $8 from September through January. Add $2 for electricity. Primitive camping (take everything with you, including water) costs $3 a night per adult, $2 for children. The park is open daily from 8am to sunset. Pets are allowed. For more information, contact the park at 1900 E. Gulf Beach Dr., St. George Island, FL 32328 (© **850/927-2111;** www8.myflorida.com/communities/learn/stateparks).

There are no facilities whatsoever at the **St. Vincent National Wildlife Refuge,** southwest of Apalachicola. This 12,358-acre barrier island has been left in its natural state by the U.S. Fish and Wildlife Service, but visitors are welcome to walk through its pine forests, marshlands, ponds, dunes, and beaches. In addition to native species like bald eagles and alligators, the island is home to a small herd of sambar deer from Southeast Asia. Red wolves are bred here for reestablishment in other wildlife areas. Access is by boat only, usually from Indian Pass, 21 miles west of Apalachicola via U.S. 98 and County Roads 30A and 30B. The chamber of commerce (see "Essentials," above) has the names of boat captains who will take you over, and some cruise operators go there (see "Cruises," below). The refuge headquarters, at the north end of Market Street in town, has exhibits of wetland flora and fauna. It's open Monday to Friday from 8am to 4:30pm. Admission is free. For more information, contact the refuge at P.O. Box 447, Apalachicola, FL 32329 (© **850/653-8808**).

The huge **Apalachicola National Forest** begins a few miles northeast of town. It has a host of facilities, including canoeing and mountain-bike trails. See section 5, later in this chapter, for details.

OUTDOOR ACTIVITIES

CRUISES   Jeanni McMillan of **Jeanni's Journeys** ★ (© 850/927-3259) takes guests on narrated nature cruises to the barrier islands and on canoe and kayak trips in the creeks and streams of the Apalachicola River basin. She also has night hikes with blue-crab netting, shelling excursions, and fishing and scalloping trips, plus excursions tailored exclusively for children. Prices range from $25 to $75 per person. Reservations are required, so call her to find out what she's offering when you'll be in town. Jeannie also rents canoes, kayaks, sailboats, and sailboards.

An easier way to see the marshes, swamps, and shallow-water rivers is via a nature cruise with **EcoVentures, Inc.** (© 850/653-2593; www. apalachicolatours. com). It uses the *Osprey,* a 40-foot, all-weather boat that can carry up to 32 passengers. Fares are $20 adults, $10 for children under 16. Call for schedule and reservations.

The ***Governor Stone,*** an 1877-vintage Gulf Coast schooner, makes cruises on Apalachicola Bay each day during the summer months, less frequently off-season. This fine old craft has seen duty as a cargo freighter, an oyster buyer, a sponge boat, and a U.S. Merchant Marine training vessel. It departs from the Apalachicola River Inn dock on Water Street. Reservations are highly recommended, so book in advance at the Maritime Museum, 71 Market St. (© 850/653-8700). The cruises cost $20 for adults, $10 for children 12 and under.

A scaled-down version of an 1890s stern-wheeler, Captain Daniel Blake's ***Jubilee!*** (© 850/653-9502) makes 1½-hour voyages on the river, creeks, swamps, and marshes. This modern but old-looking vessel can accommodate up to six passengers. The trips usually depart the dock at 329 Water St., but reservations are required. Fare is $15 per person.

You can go afternoon or sunset sailing on the bay for hours on Captain Jerry Weber's 40-foot sloop ***Wind Catcher*** (© 850/653-3881). The 2½-hour voyages cost $35 for adults, $20 for children under 16, including snacks and soft drinks. Reservations are essential.

You can do it yourself on a houseboat rented from **Benign Boat Works, Inc.,** 317 Water St. (© 850/653-8214; fax 850/653-3579; www.benignboatrentals. com). Rates range from $175 for 1 day to $350 for 3 days and 2 nights. Benign is open Tuesday to Sunday from 8:30am to 5pm.

FISHING   You can't go oystering, but fishing is excellent in these waters, where trout, redfish, flounder, tarpon, shark, drum, and other fish abound. **Bay King Charters** (© 850/653-2048; www.bayking.com) has all-day fishing aboard a party boat for $50 per person plus $5 for tackle. At least 15 persons are necessary, so reservations are required. The chamber of commerce (see "Essentials," above) can help arrange charters on the local boats, many of which dock at the Rainbow Inn on Water Street. For guides, contact **Robinson Brothers Guide Service** (© 850/670-8896; fax 850/653-3118; www.flaredfish.com) or **Boss Guide Services** (© 850/653-8139).

EXPLORING THE TOWN

Start your visit by picking up a map and a self-guided tour brochure from the chamber of commerce (see "Essentials," above), and then stroll around Apalachicola's waterfront, business district, and Victorian-era homes. It's a great town for wandering, but you may also choose **Apalachicola Tours** (© 850/653-**TOUR**) for 90-minute guided tours in a van that holds up to eight. The tours usually depart Monday to Friday at 10am, noon, 2pm, and 4pm, but call for reservations. They cost $12.65 for adults, $11.40 seniors, $7.65 for children under 9.

Along Water Street, several tin warehouses evoke the town's seafaring days of the late 1800s, as does the 1840s-era **Sponge Exchange** at Commerce Street and Avenue E. A highlight of the residential area, centered around Gorrie Square at Avenue D and 6th Street, is the Greek Revival–style **Trinity Episcopal Church,** built in New York and shipped here in 1837. At the water end of 6th Street, Battery Park has a children's playground. A number of excellent art galleries and gift shops are grouped on Market Street, Avenue D, and Commerce Street.

The showpiece at the **John Gorrie Museum State Park** ☆, Avenue D at 6th Street (© 850/653-9347; www8.myflorida.com/communities/learn/stateparks), is a display replica of Doctor Gorrie's cooling machine, a prototype of today's air conditioner. It really does work. The park is open Thursday to Monday from 9am to 5pm; closed New Year's Day, Thanksgiving, and Christmas. Admission is $1, free for children 6 and under.

The small **Apalachicola Maritime Museum,** 71 Market St. (© 850/653-8700), is worth a brief stop. It's open Tuesday to Saturday from noon to 4:30pm during summer. Winter hours are Monday, Tuesday, Friday, and Saturday from noon to 4:30pm. Admission is free.

The **Estuarine Walk,** at the north end of Market Street on the grounds of the Apalachicola National Estuarine Research Reserve (© 850/653-8063), contains aquariums full of fish and turtles and displays of various other estuarine life. It's open Monday to Friday from 8am to 5pm. Admission is free.

WHERE TO STAY
IN APALACHICOLA

Built in 1997, the 42-room **Best Western Apalach Inn,** 249 Hwy. 98 W. (© 800/528-1234 or 850/658-9131; fax 850/653-9136), a mile west of downtown, is the only national chain hotel here. Rates range from $60 to $65 for a double, including continental breakfast and your first four local phone calls.

Apalachicola River Inn   The town's only waterfront accommodation, this two-story motel's rough-hewn exterior timbers make it look like one of the neighboring warehouses. Recently spiffed up, units in the main building all have views across a marina to Apalachicola Bay. Those on the second floor are larger and have their own balconies, making them preferable to the smaller downstairs units, whose doors open directly onto the marina's boardwalk. Most of the upstairs rooms have shower-only bathrooms. Two rooms and a two-bedroom apartment in a building next door have whirlpool tubs. Facing the river, Caroline's Restaurant serves breakfast, lunch, and seafood dinners (it's a bit pricey at dinner but a fine spot for an alfresco, dockside lunch). The Roseate Spoonbill Lounge, over the restaurant, is *the* local watering hole, with a grand view and music on an outdoor deck on weekends.

123 Water St., Apalachicola, FL 32320. © 850/653-8139. Fax 850/653-2018. www.apalachicolariverinn. com. 26 units. $70–$90 double; $150 suite. AE, DC, DISC, MC, V. Pets accepted in smoking rooms ($10 nightly fee). **Amenities:** Restaurant (American); bar. *In room:* A/C, TV.

Coombs House Inn ☆☆   The most luxurious accommodation here, this large bed-and-breakfast occupies two Victorian homes. The main house was built in 1905 by a lumber baron, and it shows: Polished black cypress paneling lines the entire central hallway and grand parlor. Each of the 10 guest rooms in the main house is tastefully decorated, with lots of Victorian reproductions. Outstanding is the Coombs Suite, with bay windows, sofa, four-poster bed, and its own whirlpool. The "Love Bungalow" has its own private entrance. Less grand but still impressive are eight rooms in another restored Victorian, known as the "Coombs House East," half a block away. One of these rooms has a whirlpool tub and bidet, and there's an apartment in the carriage house over there. One room in each house is equipped for guests with disabilities. A major truck route, U.S. 98, runs along the north side of both houses; request a south room to escape the periodic road noise. Guests are treated to complimentary wine receptions on weekends.

80 6th St., Apalachicola, FL 32320. ⒸⒻ 850/653-9199. Fax 850/653-2785. www.coombshouseinn.com. 18 units (all with bathroom). $79–$199 double. Rates include full breakfast. DISC, MC, V. **Amenities:** Access to nearby health club, free use of bikes. *In room:* A/C, TV, dataport, fridge (3 units), hair dryer.

Gibson Inn ⒶⒶ   Built in 1907 as a seaman's hotel and gorgeously restored in 1985, this cupola-topped inn is such a brilliant example of Victorian architecture that it's listed on the National Register of Historic Inns. No two guest rooms are alike (some still have the original sinks in the sleeping areas), but all are richly furnished with period reproductions. Nonguests are welcome to wander upstairs and peek into unoccupied rooms (whose doors are left open). Reservations are advised during summer and spring and fall weekends, and as much as 5 years ahead for the seafood festival in November. Grab a drink from the bar and relax in one of the high-back rockers on the old-fashioned verandah. The dining room serves excellent seafood and is open to all comers, so don't expect this to be private like a bed-and-breakfast; instead, you'll find yourself in a reborn, absolutely charming turn-of-the-century hotel.

51 Ave. C, Apalachicola, FL 32320. ⒸⒻ 850/653-2191. Fax 850/653-3521. www.gibsoninn.com. 30 units (all with bathroom). $85–$100 double; $100–$130 suite. AE, MC, V. **Amenities:** Restaurant (American); bar. *In room:* A/C, TV.

Rancho Inn   On the western edge of the historic district, this older, Spanish-look motel has been spiffed up by owners Mark and Mary Lynn Rodgers, who keep it clean and well maintained. Although the rooms are basically furnished and with minimal amenities (a few have microwave ovens and fridges), they are spacious and comfortable. Restaurants are within walking distance.

240 Hwy. 98 W., Apalachicola, FL 32320. ⒸⒻ 850/653-9435. Fax 850/653-9180. www.ranchoinn.com. 32 units. $45–$150 double. AE, DISC, MC, V. Pets accepted ($6 fee). **Amenities:** Outdoor pool; bicycle rental. *In room:* A/C, TV, dataport, fridge (10 rooms), coffeemaker.

WHERE TO DINE

Townsfolk still plop down on the round stools at the marble-topped counter to order Coca-Colas and milkshakes at the **Old Time Soda Fountain & Luncheonette,** 93 Market St. (ⒸⒻ **850/653-2006**). This 1950s relic was once the town drugstore. It's open Monday to Saturday from 10am to 5pm.

Local sweet-tooths also find satisfaction at **Delores Sweet Shoppe,** 29 Ave. E, at Commerce St. (ⒸⒻ **850/653-9081**), where Delores Roux's cookies, brownies, cakes, and Key lime pies are famous hereabouts. She also serves sandwiches and chili for lunch. Her shop is open Monday to Friday from 9am to 5pm.

The Boss Oyster ⒶⒶ SEAFOOD   You've heard about the aphrodisiac properties of Apalachicola oysters. Well, you can see if those properties are real at this rustic, dockside eatery, whose motto is "Shut Up and Shuck." In fact, this is one of the best places in Florida to try the bivalves raw, steamed, or under a dozen toppings ranging from capers to crabmeat. They'll even steam three dozen of them and let you do the shucking. Steamed shrimp also are offered, as are delicious po' boy sandwiches. Most main courses come from the fryer, so consider this joint a great local experience, not fine dining. Sit at picnic tables inside, on a screened porch, or out on the dock.

125 Water St. (between Aves. C and D). ✆ 850/653-9364. Reservations not accepted. Main courses $17–$22; oysters $4.50–$13.50; sandwiches and baskets $7–$10. AE, DC, DISC, MC, V. Sun–Thurs 11:30am–9pm; Fri–Sat 11:30am–10pm.

Chef Eddie's Magnolia Grill ★★★ CONTINENTAL/CAJUN One of the top places to dine in Northwest Florida, Boston-bred chef-owner Eddie Cass's pleasant restaurant offers nightly specials ranging from classic French rack of lamb and beef Wellington to fresh local seafood with New Orleans–style sauces. You will long remember Eddie's mahi-mahi Pontchartrain, with cream and artichoke hearts. The dry-aged, oak-grilled New York sirloin steak stuffed with roasted oysters, peppers, and artichoke hearts and served with a merlot bordelaise sauce is another memorable feast. Start with a bowl of spicy seafood gumbo, a consistent hit during the Florida Seafood Festival. No smoking inside.

99 11th St. (between Aves. E and F). ✆ 850/653-8000. Reservations advised. Main courses $12–$24. MC, V. Mon–Sat 6–9pm. Closed 2½ weeks starting the weekend after Thanksgiving.

The Owl Cafe ★★ SEAFOOD Ensconced on the first floor of a two-story clapboard commercial building in the heart of downtown, this sophisticated restaurant ranks only behind Chef Eddie's Magnolia Grill as having the best cuisine in town. Go for the nightly fresh seafood specials or opt for the terrific grouper with garlic, capers, and artichokes. Now paneled in rich wood, the walls are adorned with the works of noted local photographer Richard Bickel.

15 Ave. D (at Commerce St.). ✆ 904/653-9888. Reservations recommended. Main courses $12–$21. MC, V. Mon–Sat 11:30am–3pm and 5:30–10pm. Off-season Mon–Thurs 11:30am–8pm; Fri–Sat 11:30am–9pm.

Tamara's Cafe Floridita ★ FLORIBBEAN/LATIN AMERICAN Tamara Saurez's storefront cafe offers a change of pace. Before settling in Apalachicola, Tamara was a TV producer in Venezuela, and her black bean soup comes directly from the old country. Otherwise, you'll find Latino spices accentuating Floribbean fare, such as a creamy jalapeño sauce putting a little fire into pecan-encrusted grouper, and homemade mango chutney sweetening grouper stuffed with crabmeat. Her paella is a winner, too.

17 Ave. E (at Commerce St.). ✆ 904/653-4111. Reservations recommended. Main courses $12–$22. MC, V. Sun and Tues–Thurs 6–10pm; Fri–Sat 6–11pm.

APALACHICOLA AFTER DARK

Nocturnal diversions are scarce in this small town, but you can catch summerstock performances of plays like "Same Time Next Year" in the lovingly restored, 1912-vintage **Dixie Theatre,** 21 Ave. D (✆ **850/653-3200**). Tickets range from $2 to $12.

Locals like to have their after-work drinks in the fine old bar at the **Gibson Inn** and then hit the **Roseate Spoonbill Lounge,** in the Apalachicola River Inn (see "Where to Stay," above), where bands play on weekend evenings.

5 Tallahassee

163 miles W. of Jacksonville, 191 miles E. of Pensacola, 250 miles NW of Orlando

Tallahassee was selected as Florida's capital in 1823 because it was halfway between St. Augustine and Pensacola, then the state's major cities. That location puts it almost in Georgia; in fact, Tallahassee has more in common with Macon than with Miami. There's as much Old South ambience here as anywhere else you're likely to visit in Florida. You'll find lovingly restored 19th-century homes and buildings, including the 1845 Old Capitol. They all sit among so many towering pines and sprawling live oaks that you'll think you're in an enormous forest. The trees form virtual tunnels along Tallahassee's five official Canopy Roads, which are lined with historic plantations, ancient Native American settlement sites and mounds, gorgeous gardens, quiet parks with picnic areas, and beautiful lakes and streams. And the nearby Apalachicola National Forest is a virtual gold mine of outdoor pursuits.

While tradition and history are important here, you'll also find the modern era, beginning with the New Capitol Building towering 22 stories over downtown. Usually sleepy Tallahassee takes on a very lively persona when the legislature is in session and when the powerful football teams of Florida State University and Florida A&M University take to the gridiron.

If you're inclined to give your credit cards a workout, the nearby town of Havana is Florida's antiquing capital.

ESSENTIALS

GETTING THERE **Tallahassee Regional Airport,** 10 miles southwest of downtown on Southeast Capital Circle, is served by **Continental** (© 800/525-0280), **Delta** (© 800/221-1212), **Northwest/KLM** (© 800/225-2525), and **US Airways** (© 800/428-4322).

Alamo (© 800/327-9633), **Avis** (© 800/331-1212), **Budget** (© 800/527-0700), **Dollar** (© 800/800-4000), **Enterprise** (© 800/325-8007), **Hertz** (© 800/654-3131), **National** (© 800/CAR-RENT), and **Thrifty** (© 800/367-2277) have rental cars here.

You can take a taxi to downtown for about $12.50.

Amtrak's transcontinental train the Sunset Limited stops in Tallahassee at 918½ Railroad Ave. (© **800/USA-RAIL**).

VISITOR INFORMATION For information in advance, contact the **Tallahassee Area Convention and Visitors Bureau,** 200 W. College Ave. (P.O. Box 1369), Tallahassee, FL 32302 (© **800/628-2866** or 850/413-9200; fax 850/487-4621; www.seetallahassee.com). The bureau's excellent quarterly visitor's guide has descriptions (including hours and admission fees) of just about everything going on here.

Your first stop in town should be the **Tallahassee Area Visitor Information Center,** 106 E. Jefferson St. across from the capitol (same phone numbers as the bureau). Come here for free street and public-transportation maps, brochures, and pamphlets outlining tours of the historic districts and the Canopy Roads. The center is open Monday to Friday 8am to 5pm, Saturday 9am to 1pm.

For statewide information, a **Florida Welcome Center** is in the west foyer of the New Capitol Building.

GETTING AROUND Built like an old-time streetcar, the free **Old Town Trolley** (© **850/891-5200**) is the best way to see the sights of historic downtown Tallahassee. You can get on or off at any point between Adams Street Commons, at the corner of Jefferson and Adams streets, and the Governor's Mansion. The trolley runs Monday to Friday every 10 minutes between 7am and 6pm.

TALTRAN provides city bus service from its downtown terminal at Tennessee and Adams streets (© 850/891-5200). Both the ticket booth there and the Tallahassee Area Visitor Information Center in the New Capitol Building have route maps and schedules for the Old Town Trolley and TALTRAN buses.

For taxi service, call **Yellow Cab** (© 850/580-8080) or **City Taxi** (© 850/562-4222). Fares are $1.60 at flag fall, plus $1.50 per mile.

TIME   Tallahassee is in the eastern time zone, like Orlando, Miami, and Apalachicola. It's 1 hour ahead of the rest of the Panhandle.

EXPLORING THE CITY
THE CAPITOL COMPLEX

Florida's capitol complex, on South Monroe Street at Apalachee Parkway, dominates the downtown area and should be your first stop after the Tallahassee Area Visitor Center, just across Jefferson Street.

The **New Capitol Building** (© 850/488-6167), a $43 million skyscraper, was built in 1977 to replace the 1845-vintage Old Capitol. State legislators meet here from March to May. The chambers of the house and the senate have public viewing galleries. For a spectacular view, take the elevators to the 22nd-floor **observatory,** where on a clear day you can see all the way to the Gulf of Mexico. You can also view works by Florida artists while up here. The New Capitol is open Monday to Friday from 8am to 5pm, Saturday and Sunday from 9am to 3pm (closed major holidays). Free **guided tours** (© 850/413-9200) are scheduled on the hour, Monday to Friday from 9 to 11am and 1 to 3pm, and on Saturday, Sunday, and holidays from 9am to 3pm.

Directly in front of the skyscraper is the strikingly white **Old Capitol** ⭐ (© 850/487-1902). With its majestic dome, this "Pearl of Capitol Hill" has been restored to its original beauty. An eight-room exhibit portrays Florida's political history. Turn-of-the-century furnishings, cotton gins, and other artifacts are also of interest. The Old Capitol is open Monday to Friday from 9am to 4:30pm, Saturday from 10am to 4:30pm, and Sunday and holidays from noon to 4:30pm. Admission is free to both the old and the new capitols.

Across Monroe Street from the Old Capitol are the twin granite towers of the **Vietnam Veterans Memorial,** honoring Florida's Vietnam vets. Next to it, facing Apalachee Parkway, the **Union Bank Museum** (© 850/487-3803) is housed in Florida's oldest-surviving bank building. For a while, it was the Freedman's Savings and Trust Company, which served emancipated slaves. It's worth a brief visit. Admission is free. It's open Monday to Friday 9am to 4pm.

The Old Town Trolley will take you to the lovely Georgian-style **Governor's Mansion,** north of the capitol at Adams and Brevard streets (© 850/488-4661). Enhanced by a portico patterned after Andrew Jackson's columned antebellum home, the Hermitage, and surrounded by giant magnolia trees and landscaped lawns, the mansion is furnished with 18th- and 19th-century antiques and collectibles. Tours are given when the legislature is in session from March to May. Call for schedules and reservations.

Located adjacent to the Governor's Mansion, **The Grove** was home to Ellen Call Long, known as "The Tallahassee Girl," the first child born after Tallahassee was settled.

HISTORIC DISTRICTS

Although modern buildings have made inroads in the downtown area, Tallahassee makes an ongoing effort to preserve many of its historic homes and buildings.

Many of them are concentrated in three historic districts within an easy walk north of the capitol complex. The information center in the New Capitol (see "Essentials," above) distributes free brochures of walking tours that cover the three areas. Taken together, the tours are about 4 miles long and should take half a day. Most interesting is the Park Avenue District, 3 blocks north of the capitol, which you can see in about 1 hour.

Tours With A Southern Accent (© **850/513-1000**) offers 2-hour walking and van tours of downtown for $20 per person, free for children under 5. **Historic Tallahassee Tours** (© **850/222-4143**) has 90-minute walking tours of the historic districts for $6 adults, $4 students. Call the companies for schedules and reservations.

ADAMS STREET COMMONS   This 1-block-long winding brick and land-scaped area along Adams Street begins on the north side of the capitol complex. It retains an old-fashioned town-square atmosphere. Restored buildings include the Governor's Club, a 1900s Masonic lodge, and Gallie's Hall, where Florida's first five African-American college students received their Florida A&M University diplomas in 1892. Restaurants, shops, and Gallie Alley are also here. Adams Street crosses Park Avenue 3 blocks north of the capitol. This is a good place for lunch at one of several cafes that cater to downtown office workers.

PARK AVENUE HISTORIC DISTRICT   The 7 blocks of Park Avenue between Martin Luther King Jr. Boulevard and North Meridien Street are a lovely promenade of beautiful trees, gardens, and outstanding old mansions. This broad avenue with a shady median strip lined with moss-bearded live oaks was originally named 200 Foot Street and then McCarty Street, but was later renamed Park Avenue to satisfy a snobbish Anglophile society matron who didn't want an Irish name imprinted on her son's wedding invitations.

Several Park Avenue historic homes are open to the public, including the **Knott House Museum,** at Calhoun Street (see "Museums, Art Galleries & Archaeological Sites," below). **The Columns,** at Duval Street, was built in the 1830s and is the city's oldest-surviving building (it's the home of the Tallahassee Chamber of Commerce). **The First Presbyterian Church,** at Adams Street, built in 1838, is the city's oldest church and has been an important African-American historic site since slaves were welcome to worship here without their masters' consent. **The Walker Library,** between Monroe and Calhoun streets, was one of Florida's first libraries, dating from 1903 (it's home to Springtime Tallahassee, which sponsors the city's top special event). Just north of Park Avenue on Gadsden Street, the **Meginnis-Monroe House** contains the Lemoyne Art Gallery (see "Museums, Art Galleries & Archaeological Sites," below).

At Martin Luther King Jr. Boulevard, the **adjacent Old City Cemetery** and **Episcopal Cemetery** contain the graves of Prince Achille Murat, Napoleon's nephew, and Princess Catherine Murat, his wife and George Washington's grand-niece. Also buried here are two governors and numerous Confederate and Union soldiers who died at the Battle of Natural Bridge during the Civil War. The cemeteries are important to African-American history since a number of slaves and the first black Florida A&M graduates are interred here. The visitor information center in the New Capitol has a cemetery walking-tour brochure.

CALHOUN STREET HISTORIC DISTRICT   Affectionately called "Gold Dust Street" in the old days, the 3 blocks of Calhoun Street between Tennessee and Georgia streets, and running east on Virginia Street to Leon High School, sport elaborate homes built by prominent citizens between 1830 and 1880. A highlight here is the **Brokaw-McDougall House,** in front of Leon High School at the eastern end of Virginia Street, which was built in 1856.

MUSEUMS, GALLERIES & ARCHAEOLOGICAL SITES

Black Archives Research Center and Museum   Housed in the columned library built by Andrew Carnegie in 1908, and located on the grounds of the Florida Agricultural and Mechanical University (FAMU), this fascinating research center and museum displays one of the nation's most extensive collections of African-American artifacts, as well as such treasures as a 500-piece Ethiopian cross collection. The archives contain one of the world's largest collections on African-American history. Visitors here can listen to tapes of gospel music and of elderly people reminiscing about the past. FAMU was founded in 1887, primarily as a black institution. Today it's acclaimed for its business, engineering, and pharmacy schools.

Martin Luther King Jr. Blvd. and Gamble St., on the Florida A&M University campus. ℂ 850/599-3020. www.famu.edu. Free admission. Mon–Fri 9am–4pm. Closed major holidays. Parking lot next to building.

Florida State University Museum of Fine Arts   A permanent, 3,000-piece collection here features 16th-century Dutch paintings, 20th-century American paintings, Japanese prints, pre-Colombian artifacts, and much more. Touring exhibits are displayed every few weeks.

250 Fine Arts Building, Copeland and Call Sts. (on the FSU campus). ℂ 850/644-6836. www.fsu.edu. Free admission. Sept–Apr Mon–Fri 9am–4pm, Sat–Sun 1–4pm; May–July Mon–Fri 10am–4pm. Closed Aug.

Foster Tanner Art Center   The focus in this gallery is on works by local, national, and international African-American artists, with a wide variety of paintings, sculptures, and more.

Florida A&M University (between Osceola and Gamble Sts., off Martin Luther King Jr. Blvd.). ℂ 850/599-3161. www.famu.edu. Free admission. Mon–Sat 9am–6pm.

Knott House Museum ("The House That Rhymes") ⭐   Adorned by a columned portico, this stately mansion was constructed in 1843, probably by a free black builder named George Proctor. Florida's first reading of the Emancipation Proclamation took place here in 1865. In 1928 it was purchased by politician William Knott, whose wife Louella wrote eccentric rhymes about the house and its elegant Victorian furnishings, including the nation's largest collection of 19th-century gilt-framed mirrors, and about social, economic, and political events of the era. Attached by satin ribbons to tables, chairs, and lamps, her poems are the museum's most unusual feature. The house is in the Park Avenue Historic District and is listed in the National Register of Historic Places. It's preserved as it looked in 1928, when the Knott family left it and all of its contents to the city (it's now administered by the Florida Museum of History). The museum gift shop carries Victorian greeting cards, paper dolls, tin toy replicas, reprints of historic newspapers, and other nostalgic items.

301 E. Park Ave. (at Calhoun St.). ℂ 850/922-2459. dhr.dos.state.fl.us/museum/m_sites.html. Free admission. Wed–Fri 1–4pm; Sat 10am–4pm. 1-hr. tours depart on the hour.

Lemoyne Art Gallery ⭐   This restored 1852 antebellum home is listed on the National Register of Historic Places and is a lovely setting for fine art. Known as the **Meginnis-Monroe House,** the gallery itself is named in honor of Jacques LeMoyne, a member of a French expedition to Florida in 1564. Commissioned to depict the natives' dwellings and map the sea coast, LeMoyne was the first European artist known to have visited North America. Exhibits here include permanent displays by local artists, traveling exhibits, sculpture, pottery, and photography—everything from the traditional to the avant-garde. The gardens, with an old-fashioned gazebo, are spectacular during the Christmas holiday season. Programs of classical music are combined with visual arts during the year; check in advance for the current schedule.

125 N. Gadsden St. (between Park Ave. and Call St.). ℂ 850/222-8800. www.lemoyne.org. Admission $1, free for children 12 and under. Tues–Sat 10am–5pm; Sun 1–5pm. Closed holidays.

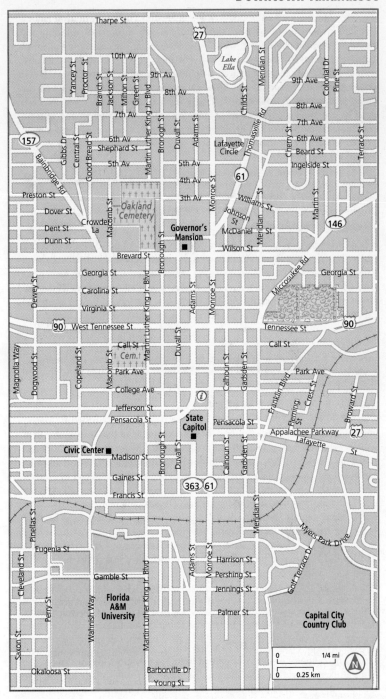

Mission San Luís de Apalachee ✦✦ A Spanish Franciscan mission named San Luís was set up in 1656 on this hilltop, already a principal village of the Apalachee Indians. From then until 1704, it served as the capital of a chain of Spanish missions in Northwest Florida. The mission complex included a tribal council house, a Franciscan church, a Spanish fort, and residential areas. Based on extensive archaeological and historical research, the council house and the 10-by-50-foot thatch-roofed church have been reconstructed. They are both open to the public. Work is in progress on a reconstruction of the mission church. Interpretive markers are located across the 60-acre site, and self-guided tour brochures are available at the visitor center. Call for a schedule of ranger-led guided tours on weekends.

2020 Mission Rd. (between W. Tennessee and Tharpe Sts.). ✆ **850/487-3711.** dhr.dos.state.fl.us/museum/m_sites.html. Suggested donation $3 adults, $1 children. Mon–Fri 9am–4:30pm; Sat 10am–4:30pm; Sun noon–4:30pm. Closed Thanksgiving, Christmas. From downtown, take Tennessee St. (U.S. 90) west, turn right on White Dr., and then right on Mission Rd. to the entrance.

Museum of Florida History ✦ An 11-foot-tall mastodon greets you at the official state history museum, where you look back 12,000 years to the first Native Americans to live in Florida (mastodons were very much alive back then). Ancient artifacts from Native American tribes are exhibited, plus such relics from Florida's past as a reconstructed steamboat and treasures from 16th- and 17th-century sunken Spanish galleons. Inquire about guided tours and special exhibits. There's an interesting museum gift shop. Visitor parking is available in the garage around the corner on St. Augustine Street between Bronough and Duvall streets.

Lower level of R. A. Gray Building, 500 S. Bronough St. (at Pensacola St.). ✆ **850/488-1484.** dhr.dos.state.fl.us/museum. Admission free (suggested donation $3 adults, $1 children). Mon–Fri 9am–4:30pm; Sat 10am–4:30pm; Sun and holidays noon–4:30pm. Closed Thanksgiving and Christmas.

PARKS & NATURE PRESERVES

Maclay State Gardens ✦✦ In 1923 New York financier Alfred B. Maclay and his wife, Louise, began planting the floral wonderland that surrounded their winter home on Lake Hall, on Tallahassee's northeastern outskirts. After her husband's death in 1944, Louise continued his dream of an ornamental garden to delight the public. In 1953 the land was bequeathed to the state of Florida. The more than 300 acres of flowers feature at least 200 varieties; 28 acres are devoted exclusively to azaleas and camellias. The surrounding park offers nature trails, canoe rentals, boating, picnicking, swimming, and fishing. The high blooming season is January to April, with the peak about mid-March. Beyond the house and gardens, the state park also includes Lake Overstreet, around which wind 5½ miles of hiking, biking, and horseback-riding trails, making this a major venue for those outdoor activities.

3540 Thomasville Rd. (U.S. 319, north of I-10). ✆ **850/487-4556;** www8.myflorida.com/communities/learn/stateparks/district1/maclaygardens. Admission to park $3.25 per vehicle with up to 8 passengers, $1 for pedestrians and cyclists. May–Dec admission to gardens free; Jan–Apr $3 adults, $1.50 children under 12. Gardens daily 8am–sunset. Maclay House daily 9am–5pm Jan–April; closed May–Dec.

TRAVELING THE CANOPY ROADS

Graced by canopies of live oaks draped with Spanish moss, the St. Augustine, Miccousukee, Meridian, Old Bainbridge, and Centerville roads are the five official Canopy Roads leading out of Tallahassee. Driving is slow on these winding, two-lane country roads (the locals only reluctantly are turning some limited sections of them into four-lane highways); some of them are canopied for as much as 20 miles. Take along a picnic lunch, since there are few places to buy a meal along these tranquil byways.

The visitor information center in the New Capitol provides a useful driving guide map of the Canopy Roads and Leon County's country lanes (see "Essentials," earlier in this chapter).

If you have time for only one, take **Old Bainbridge Road,** which leads to the Lake Jackson Mounds State Archaeological Site in the northwest suburbs and then on to Havana, Florida's antiquing capital (see "Shopping," below).

SHOPPING

Antique hounds flock to the little village of **Havana** 🐾🐾, 12 miles northwest of I-10 on U.S. 27. Havana used to make its living from shade-grown tobacco, and when that industry went into decline in the 1960s, the town went with it. Things turned around 20 years later, however, when Havana began opening art galleries and antiques, handcrafts, and collectibles shops. Today these are housed in lovingly restored, turn-of-the-century brick buildings along Havana's commercial streets. Just drive into town on Main Street (U.S. 27), turn left on 7th Avenue, find a parking place, and start browsing. You'll have plenty of company on weekends.

Bradley's Country Store, about 8 miles north of I-10 on Centerville Road (© 850/893-1647), sells more than 80,000 pounds a year of homemade sausage, both over the counter and from mail orders. You can also buy coarse-ground grits, country-milled cornmeal, hogshead cheese, liver pudding, cracklings, and specially cured hams. This friendly store, which is on the National Register of Historic Places, is also a sightseeing attraction with self-guided tours. It's open Monday to Friday from 9am to 6pm, Saturday from 9am to 5pm.

OUTDOOR ACTIVITIES & SPECTATOR SPORTS

BIKING & IN-LINE SKATING The 16-mile **Tallahassee–St. Marks Historic Railroad State Trail** is the city's most popular bike route. Constructed with the financial assistance of wealthy Panhandle cotton-plantation owners and merchants, this was Florida's oldest railroad, functioning from 1837 to 1984. Cotton and other products were transported to St. Marks for shipment to other cities. In recent years the tracks were removed and 16 miles of the historic trail were improved for joggers, hikers, bicyclists, and horseback riders. A paved parking lot is at the north entrance, on Woodville Highway (Fla. 363) just south of Southeast Capital Circle. See "Side Trips from Tallahassee," later in this chapter, for more about what you can see in the St. Marks area.

Rental bikes and in-line skates are available at the north entrance from **About Bikes** (© 850/656-0001; www.aboutbikes.com). Bikes rent for $4.50 per hour, $35 for 24 hours. In-line skates cost $7 per hour, $16 for 4 hours, $25 for 24 hours. Guide maps and refreshments are also on hand. The shop is open April through October, Monday to Friday from 2pm to dark, Saturday and Sunday from 9am to 5pm. November through March hours are Monday to Friday from noon to 6pm, Saturday and Sunday from 8am to 5pm.

The **Apalachicola National Forest** also has extensive mountain biking trails (see "Side Trips from Tallahassee," later in this chapter), and there are 5½ miles of trails at **Maclay State Gardens** (see "Parks & Nature Preserves," above).

GOLF Play golf at outstanding Hilaman Park, 2737 Blair Stone Rd., where the **Hilaman Park Municipal Golf Course** features 18 holes (par-72), a driving range, racquetball and squash courts, and a swimming pool. Rental equipment

---

Fun Fact *Semi-Tough:* The Prequel

Burt Reynolds played defensive back for Florida State University's football team in 1957 and is still an avid 'Noles booster.

---

is available at the club, and there's a restaurant too (℃ **850/891-3935** for information and fees). Compared with most courses in Florida, greens fees are a steal: about $25 on weekdays, $30 on weekends, including cart (they're about $13 and $17, respectively, if you walk). The park also includes the recently renovated **Jake Gaither Municipal Golf Course,** at Bragg and Pasco streets (℃ **850/891-3942**), with a 9-hole, par-35 fairway and a pro shop. Call for fees.

The leading golf course is at the **Killearn Country Club and Inn** (℃ **800/ 476-4101** or 850/893-2186), which once hosted the Sprint Classic. Moss-draped oaks enhance the beautiful 27-hole championship course, which is for members and hotel guests only (see "Where to Stay," below).

SPECTATOR SPORTS   Tallahassee succumbs to football frenzy whenever the perennially powerful Seminoles of **Florida State University** (FSU) take to the gridiron. Call ℃ **850/644-1830** (www.seminoles.com) well in advance for tickets. Even when the Seminoles play on the road, everything except Tallahassee's many sports bars comes to a stop while fans watch the games on TV.

The **Florida A&M University** (FAMU) Rattlers are cheered on by the school's high-stepping, world-famous Marching 100 Band. Call ℃ **850/599-3230** for FAMU schedules and tickets.

Both FSU and FAMU have seasonal basketball, baseball, tennis, and track schedules. Call the numbers above for information.

Hockey fans can watch the minor-league **Tallahassee Tiger Sharks** (℃ **850/ 224-GOAL**), who play their games in the Tallahassee–Leon County Civic Center, 505 W. Pensacola St.

WHERE TO STAY

There is no high or low season here, but every hotel and motel for miles around is completely booked during FSU and FAMU football weekends from September to November, and again at graduation in May. Reserve well in advance or you may have to stay 60 miles or more from the city. For the schedules, call FSU or FAMU (see "Spectator Sports," above).

Most hotels are concentrated in three areas: downtown Tallahassee, north of downtown along North Monroe Street at Exit 29 off I-10 (where you'll find most chains), and along Apalachee Parkway east of downtown.

Tax on all hotel and campground bills is 10% in Leon County.

MODERATE

Courtyard by Marriott   Just a mile east of the Old Capitol, this comfortable member of the business-traveler–oriented chain encloses a landscaped courtyard with a swimming pool and gazebo. About half of the rooms face the courtyard; the others face parking lots. They are a bit cramped for families but ideal for singles and couples. The marble-floored lobby features a lounge with fireplace, honor bar, and a dining area open for a breakfast buffet only. Several chain restaurants are within walking distance or a short drive away. The Parkway Shopping Center is also across the road.

1018 Apalachee Pkwy., Tallahassee, FL 32301. (C) **800/321-2211** or 850/222-8822. Fax 850/561-0354. 154 units. Sun–Thurs $119 double; Fri–Sat $79 double. AE, DC, DISC, MC, V. **Amenities:** Restaurant (breakfast only); bar; heated outdoor pool; exercise room; Jacuzzi; laundry service, coin-op washers and dryers. *In room:* A/C, TV, dataport, coffeemaker, hair dryer, iron.

DoubleTree Hotel Most of the media covering the Bush-Gore election contest stayed at this 16-story hotel, one of the tallest buildings in town. The best thing about it is the location, just 2 blocks north of the Capitol Building at Park Avenue, and the views from the spacious rooms, especially those on the upper floors. It's usually booked solid by politicians and lobbyists during legislative sessions from March through May.

101 S. Adams St., Tallahassee, FL 32301. (C) **800/222-TREE** or 850/224-5000. Fax 850/513-9516. 243 units. $89–$129 double. AE, DC, DISC, MC, V. **Amenities:** Restaurant (American); bar; outdoor pool; exercise room; limited room service; laundry service; concierge-level rooms. *In room:* A/C, TV, dataport, coffeemaker, hair dryer, iron.

Governors Inn ★★ Vice President Gore's lawyers stayed at this elegant, richly furnished inn just half a block north of the Old Capitol in the Adams Street Commons historic district. The building was once a livery stable, and part of its original architecture has been preserved, including the impressive beams. The guest rooms are distinctive, with four-poster beds, black-oak writing desks, rock-maple armoires, and antique accoutrements. Of the suites, each one named for a Florida governor, one has a whirlpool bathtub; another has a loft bedroom with wood-burning fireplace. Complimentary continental breakfast and afternoon cocktails are presented in the pine-paneled Florida Room, and a restaurant across the street provides limited room service.

209 S. Adams St., Tallahassee, FL 32301. (C) **800/342-7717** in Florida, or 850/681-6855. Fax 850/222-3105. 40 units. $119–$149 double; $149–$229 suite. Rates include continental breakfast and evening cocktails. AE, DC, DISC, MC, V. **Amenities:** Access to nearby health club; limited room service; laundry service. *In room:* A/C, TV, dataport.

Radisson Hotel President George W. Bush's legal team stayed at this seven-story hotel about a half-mile north of the Capitol. The innlike lobby with reproduction antiques strikes an elegant ambience, but the regular guest rooms are rather small (this hotel was built in the 1950s as a college dormitory), and air-conditioning units eat up about a third of each unit's window. The spacious suites are much better choices; they are equipped with four-poster beds, whirlpool bathtubs, and wet bars. The pleasant Plantation Dining Room is open daily for breakfast, lunch, and dinner, and the lobby lounge provides libation.

415 N. Monroe St. (at Virginia St.), Tallahassee, FL 32301. (C) **800/333-3333** or 850/224-6000. Fax 850/222-0335. 119 units. $111 double; $150–$197 suite. Weekend rates available. AE, DC, DISC, MC, V. **Amenities:** Restaurant (American); bar; exercise room; sauna; limited room service; laundry service; concierge-level rooms. *In room:* A/C, TV, dataport (high-speed Internet access), coffeemaker, hair dryer, iron.

Fun Fact **Count Them Out**

Demand for hotel rooms during Florida State University football weekends is so great that the high-powered lawyers representing Vice President Gore and Texas Governor George W. Bush had to vacate their rooms when the University of Florida Gators came to play the 'Noles during the 2000 election dispute.

INEXPENSIVE

Cabot Lodge North *Value* A clapboard plantation-style house with a tin roof and a partially screened wraparound porch provides Southern country charm to distinguish this friendly motel from its nearby competitors. Guests can relax in straight-back rockers on the porch or on comfy sofas and easy chairs by a fireplace in the living room. Although the guest rooms in the two-story motel buildings out back don't hold up their end of the atmosphere factor, they're still quite satisfactory at these rates, and they give quick access to the outdoor swimming pool. Guests can enjoy complimentary continental breakfast buffet and evening cocktails.

2735 N. Monroe St., Tallahassee, FL 32303. © **800/223-1964** or 850/386-8880. Fax 850/386-4254. www.cabotlodge.com. 160 units. $72–$80 double. Rates include continental breakfast and evening reception. AE, DC, DISC, MC, V. **Amenities:** Outdoor pool; golf course; access to nearby health club; laundry service. *In room:* A/C, TV, dataport, hair dryer (king-size bedrooms only).

Killearn Country Club and Inn Located in upscale Killearn Estates between Thomasville and Centerville roads north of I-10, about a 20-minute drive north of downtown, this country club is home to Tallahassee's leading 18-hole golf course, which only members and house guests can play. Each of the regular motel rooms has a balcony overlooking the woodland-bordered golf course. Across a parking lot from the motel rooms are cottages with guest rooms that open to central living rooms, allowing these rooms to be rented as suites (lobbyists turn them into hospitality areas to influence legislators from March to May). The swimming pool is Olympic size, and there are miles of surrounding roads for jogging. Guests enjoy all privileges at the country club.

100 Tyron Circle, Tallahassee, FL 32308. © **800/476-4101** or 850/893-2186. Fax 850/893-8267. 30 units. $72 double; $140–$320 suite. Golf packages available. AE, DISC, MC, V. **Amenities:** Restaurant (American); bar; outdoor pool; golf course; 8 tennis courts; exercise room; limited room service. *In room:* A/C, TV, dataport, fridge (some units), coffeemaker, hair dryer, iron.

Quality Inn & Suites *Value* In contrast to most Quality Inns, there's real charm here. In fact, an almost English country-inn atmosphere prevails in the classy, marble-lined lobby and spacious guest rooms, which are furnished with sofas and reclining wing chairs. A complimentary continental breakfast is served in a lounge with views of the inn's swimming pool, and guests can partake of a free wine bar Monday to Thursday evenings. A nearby restaurant will deliver food, and several fast-food and family-style restaurants are within a short walk.

2020 Apalachee Pkwy., Tallahassee, FL 32301. © **800/228-5151** or 850/877-4437. Fax 850/878-9964. www.qualityinn.com. 100 units. $79 double; $99 suite. Rates include continental breakfast and local phone calls. AE, DC, DISC, MC, V. **Amenities:** Outdoor pool; access to nearby health club; Jacuzzi; business center; limited room service; laundry service. *In room:* A/C, TV, dataport, fridge, coffeemaker, hair dryer, iron.

WHERE TO DINE

Numerous budget-priced fast-food and family chain restaurants lie along Apalachee Parkway and North Monroe Street. For inexpensive seafood, the local **Shells** is at 2136 N. Monroe St., at Universal Drive (© **850/385-2774**). See "Where to Dine," in section 1 of chapter 11, for details about the Shells chain.

MODERATE

Anthony's ✦ SOUTHERN ITALIAN Locals come to see and be seen at Dick Anthony's elegantly relaxed trattoria, which supplies them with the city's best Italian cuisine. Among his specialties is *pesce Venezia,* spinach fettuccine tossed in a cream sauce with scallops, crabmeat, and fish. Chicken piccata and chicken San Marino are also favorites, and Dick's thick, juicy steaks are always popular with beef eaters. A wall-size wine cupboard features choices from Italy and the United States by the bottle or glass. Espresso pie leads the dessert menu.

1950 Thomasville Rd., at Bradford Rd. in the Betton Place Shops. ℂ 850/224-1447. Reservations recommended. Main courses $12–$18. AE, DC, DISC, MC, V. Daily 5:30–9pm.

Chez Pierre ☆☆ TRADITIONAL FRENCH You become an instant Francophile in Florida at this chic restaurant in a beautifully restored 1920s brick home. French-born chef Eric Favier and his American wife and partner, Karen Cooley, offer traditional French cuisine either inside the house—where the walls are adorned with changing, for-sale works by local artists—or outside on a large deck nearly shaded by live oaks draped with Spanish moss. Opening to the deck, a bistro-style bar provides a light-fare menu between lunch and dinner. Eric offers daily specials to take advantage of fresh produce. Among his winners are rack of lamb, a version of Provençal-style ratatouille, and crab cakes with a luscious mustard and thyme demi-glacé. French table wines are moderately priced, and California house wines are also served. Live music regularly accompanies dining. No smoking except on the front porch, where stogies and brandy can be enjoyed while lounging in wicker chairs. Book as early as possible for Bastille Day (July 14), which sees a grand fete here.

1215 Thomasville Rd. (at 6th Ave.). ℂ 850/222-0936. Reservations recommended. Main courses $14–$23; lunch $6–$13. AE, DC, DISC, MC, V. Mon–Sat 11am–10pm.

Kool Beanz Cafe ☆☆ ECLECTIC The coolest cafe in town, this noisy emporium of trendy cooking draws lots of patrons in their late 20s and early 30s who appreciate exciting blends of flavors. The joint is dimly lit but painted in bright pastels from the Caribbean. You'll find many island-style items on the constantly changing menu, including Jamaican jerk grouper served with black beans, rice, and a sweet tropical fruit relish. You may want to get here early because more-inventive items like the seared but rare tuna crusted with spice and served with a terrific roasted peanut sauce will sell out early, as will the curried lamb shank and the pork tenderloin marinated with orange molasses.

921 Thomasville Rd. (at Williams St.). ℂ 850/224-2466. Reservations not accepted. Main courses $12–$16. AE, DISC, MC, V. Mon–Fri 11am–2pm and 5:30–10pm; Sat 5:30–10pm.

INEXPENSIVE

Bahn Thai THAI/CANTONESE Lamoi (Sue) Snyder and progeny have been serving the spicy cuisine of her native Thailand at this storefront since 1979. In deference to local Southerners, who may never have sampled anything spicier than cheese grits, much of her menu is devoted to mild Cantonese-style Chinese dishes. More adventurous diners, however, flock here to order such authentic tongue-burners as *yon voon-sen,* a combination of shrimp, chicken, bean threads, onions, lemongrass, ground peanuts, and the obligatory chili peppers. Sue's specialty is her deliciously sweet, slightly gingered version of Penang curry. You can ask her to turn down the heat in her other Thai dishes. Come at lunch and sample it all from the all-you-can-eat buffet, a real bargain.

1319 S. Monroe St. (between Oakland Ave. and Harrison St.). ℂ 850/224-4765. Main courses $6–$15. Lunch buffet $6. DISC, MC, V. Mon–Thurs 11am–2:30pm and 5–10pm; Fri 11am–2:30pm and 5–10:30pm; Sat 5–10:30pm.

Barnacle Bill's Seafood Restaurant SEAFOOD There's always plenty of action at this noisy, very casual spot, a favorite of the journalists and talking-heads who covered the Gore-Bush election contest. Freshly shucked Apalachicola oysters are the stars at the enormous tile-topped raw bar in the middle of the room, but the menu offers a mélange of seafood to please the palates of the singles, couples, and families who flock here. The cooking is simple and usually done by Florida State University students working part-time jobs. Best bets are charcoal-grilled mahi-mahi, tuna, amberjack, and grouper. For a smoked sensation, try the mahi-mahi and amberjack cured on the premises. During summer, guests can sit at outdoor tables under a lean-to tent. A downstairs bar serves the regular seafood items plus sushi, deli sandwiches, and salads.

1830 N. Monroe St. (north of Tharpe St.). (C) 850/385-8734. Reservations not accepted. Main courses $8–$17 (most $9); sandwiches and salads $5–$8. AE, MC, V. Sun–Thurs 11am–11pm; Fri–Sat 11am–midnight.

Food Glorious Food ★★ *Value* AMERICAN/INTERNATIONAL Very unusual and very healthy sandwiches, salads, and pastas make Susan Turner's deli/cafe one of the town's favorite lunch and early-dinner spots. Items displayed in a cold case change daily but always include gazpacho, a variety of gourmet salads, inventive sandwiches, a daily quiche, and plenty of tempting pastries and cookies. Main courses feature the likes of pineapple jerk chicken, Cuban chicken, and several pastas. You can get your selection to go or dine at a few tables inside or, in good weather, on the outside courtyard.

In Betton Place Shops, 1950 Thomasville Rd. at Bradford Rd. (C) 850/224-9974. Reservations not accepted. Main courses $9–$15; sandwiches and salads $5.50–$11. AE, DC, MC, V. Mon–Thurs 11am–8pm; Fri–Sat 11am–9pm (table service 11am–3pm).

TALLAHASSEE AFTER DARK

Check the "Limelight" section of Friday's *Tallahassee Democrat* (www.tallahasseedemocrat.com) for weekend entertainment listings.

As a college town, Tallahassee has numerous pubs and nightclubs with live dance music, not to mention a multitude of sports bars. Pick up a copy of *Break* (www.tdo.com/break) and other entertainment tabloids at **Barnacle Bill's Seafood Emporium** or other entertainment venues.

The major performing-arts venue is the **Tallahassee–Leon County Civic Center,** 505 W. Pensacola St. ((C) **800/322-3602** or 850/222-0400; www.tlccc.org), which features a Broadway series, concerts, and sporting events including Florida State University (FSU) collegiate basketball and Tiger Sharks pro hockey. Special concerts are presented by the **Tallahassee Symphony Orchestra** (www.tsolive.org) at FSU Ruby Diamond Auditorium, College Avenue and Copeland Street ((C) 850/224-0462). **The FSU Mainstage/School of Theatre,** Fine Arts Building, Call and Copeland streets ((C) 850/644-6500; www.fsu.org), presents excellent productions from classic dramas to comedies.

SIDE TRIPS FROM TALLAHASSEE

The following excursions generally are on the way to Apalachicola, so if you're headed that way, plan to make a detour or two.

WAKULLA SPRINGS ★★

The world's largest and deepest freshwater spring is 15 miles south of Tallahassee in the 2,860-acre **Wakulla Springs State Park** ★★, on Fla. 267 just east of its junction with Fla. 61. Edward Ball, a financier who administered the du Pont estate, turned the springs and the moss-draped surrounding forest into a preservation area. Divers have mapped an underwater cave system extending more than 6,000 feet back from the spring's mouth. Wakulla has been known to dispense an amazing 14,325 gallons of water per second at certain times. Mastodon bones, including those of Herman, now in Tallahassee's Museum of Florida History, were found in the caves. The 1930s *Tarzan* movies starring Johnny Weissmuller were filmed here.

A free 10-minute orientation movie is offered at the park's theater at the waterfront. You can hike or bike along the nature trails, and swimming is allowed, but only in designated areas. It's important to observe swimming rules since alligators are present.

If the spring water is clear enough, 30-minute glass-bottom–boat sightseeing trips depart daily, from 9:45am to 5pm during daylight saving time, 9:15am to 4:30pm the rest of the year. Even if the water is murky, you're likely to see alligators, birds, and other wildlife on 30-minute riverboat cruises, which operate during these same hours. Either boat ride costs $4.50 for adults, half-price for children under 13.

Entrance fees to the park are $3.25 per vehicle with up to eight passengers, $1 for pedestrians and bicyclists. The park is open daily from 8am to dusk.

For more information, contact the park at 550 Wakulla Springs Dr., Wakulla Springs, FL 32305 (© **850/224-5950;** fax 850/561-7251; www8.myflorida. com/communities/learn/stateparks/district1/wakulla).

Where to Stay & Dine

Wakulla Springs Lodge   On the shore of Wakulla Springs, this dated but charming lodge is distinctive for its magnificent Spanish architecture and ornate old-world furnishings, such as rare Spanish tiles, black-granite tables, marble floors, and ceiling beams painted with Florida scenes by a German artist (supposedly Kaiser Wilhelm's court painter). The guest rooms are simple by today's standards (you'll get a marble bathroom and phone but no TV). By all means ask for a room on the front so you'll have a lake view. You don't have to be a lodge guest to enjoy the warm, smoky ambience of the great lobby with its huge stone fireplace and arched windows looking onto the springs, or to enjoy reasonably priced meals featuring Southern cuisine in the lovely Ball Room (reservations recommended). The fountain provides snacks and sandwiches (there's a 60-ft.-long marble drugstore-style counter for old-fashioned ice-cream sodas).

550 Wakulla Park Dr., Wakulla Springs, FL 32305. © **850/224-5950.** Fax 850/561-7251. 27 units. $69–$90 double. AE, DISC, MC, V. **Amenities:** Restaurant (Southern). *In room:* A/C.

THE ST. MARKS AREA

Rich history lives in the area around the little village of **St. Marks,** 18 miles south of the capital at the end of both Fla. 363 and the Tallahassee–St. Marks Historic Railroad State Trail (see "Outdoor Activities & Spectator Sports," above).

After marching overland from Tampa Bay in 1528, the Spanish conquistador Panfilo de Narvaez and 300 men arrived at this strategic point at the confluence of the St. Marks and Wakulla rivers near the Gulf of Mexico. Since their only avenue back to Spain was by sea, they built and launched the first ships made by Europeans in the New World. Some 11 years later, Hernando de Soto and his 600 men arrived here after following Narvaez's route from Tampa. They marked the harbor entrance by hanging banners in the trees, then moved inland. Two wooden forts were built here, one in 1679 and one in 1718, and a stone version was begun in 1739. The fort shifted among Spanish, British, and Native American hands until General Andrew Jackson took it away from the Spanish in 1819.

Parts of the old Spanish bastion wall and Confederate earthworks built during the Civil War are in the **San Marcos de Apalache State Historic Site,** reached by turning right at the end of Fla. 363 in St. Marks and following the paved road. A museum built on the foundation of the old marine hospital holds exhibits and artifacts covering the area's history. The site is open Thursday to Monday from 9am to 5pm; closed New Year's Day, Thanksgiving, and Christmas. Admission to the site is free; admission to the museum costs $1, free for children 6 and under. For more information, contact the site at 1022 DeSoto Park Dr., Tallahassee, FL 32301 (© **850/925-6216** or 850/922-6007; www8.myflorida.com/communities/learn/stateparks/district1/sanmarcos).

De Soto's men marked the harbor entrance in what is now the **St. Marks Lighthouse and National Wildlife Refuge** ✮, P.O. Box 68, St. Marks, FL 32355 (© **850/925-6121**). Operated by the U.S. Fish and Wildlife Service, this 65,000-acre preserve occupies much of the coast from the Aucilla River east of St. Marks to the Ochlockonee River west of Panacea and is home to more species of birds than anyplace else in Florida except the Everglades. The visitor center is 3½ miles south of U.S. 98 on Lighthouse Road (Fla. 59); turn south off U.S. 98 at Newport, about 2 miles east of St. Marks. Stop at the center for self-guided-tour maps of the roads and extensive hiking trails, some of them built atop levees running through the marshland.

The 80-foot-tall **St. Marks Lighthouse,** 8 miles south of the visitor center, was built in 1842 of limestone blocks 4 feet thick at the base. The nearby beach is a popular crabbing spot.

Admission to the refuge is $4 per vehicle, $1 for pedestrians and bicyclists (federal Duck Stamps and National Park Service passports accepted). The refuge is open daily from sunrise to sunset; the visitor center, Monday to Friday from 8am to 4:15pm and Saturday and Sunday from 10am to 5pm (closed all federal holidays). Contact the refuge for information about seasonal tours and hunting.

In 1865, during the final weeks of the Civil War, Federal troops landed at the lighthouse and launched a surprise attack on Tallahassee. The Confederates quickly assembled an impromptu army of wounded soldiers, old men, and boys as young as 14. This ragtag bunch fought the Federal regulars for 5 days at what is now the **Natural Bridge State Historic Site.** Surprisingly, the old men and boys won. As a result, Tallahassee remained the only Confederate state capital east of the Mississippi never to fall into Yankee hands. The historic site is on County Road 2192, 6 miles east of Woodville on the St. Marks River, halfway between Tallahassee and St. Marks. Follow the signs from Fla. 363 and go to the end of the pavement. It's open daily from 8am to sunset and admission is free. For more information, contact the San Marcos de Apalache State Historic Site (see above) or check www8.myflorida.com/communities/learn/stateparks/district1/naturalbridge.

WHERE TO DINE Tallahasseeans love to drive or bike down to St. Marks and have a waterside lunch at **Posey's Oyster Bar,** at the end of Fla. 363 (© **850/925-6177**). Some nighttime patrons at this ramshackle wooden restaurant and bar can get rowdy, especially when country-and-western bands are playing on weekends, but it's a fine place for freshly shucked oysters or smoked mullet during the day. Be sure to walk all the way through the dining rooms to the bar beside the St. Marks River. Posey's opens daily at 11am.

APALACHICOLA NATIONAL FOREST

The largest of Florida's three national forests, this huge preserve encompasses 600,000 acres stretching from Tallahassee's outskirts southward to the Gulf

Coast and westward some 70 miles to the Apalachicola River. Included are a variety of woodlands, rivers, streams, lakes, and caves populated by a host of wildlife. There are picnic facilities with sheltered tables and grills, canoe and mountain-bike trails, campgrounds with tent and RV sites, and a number of other facilities, some of them especially designed for visitors with disabilities.

The **Leon Sinks Area** is closest to Tallahassee, 5½ miles south of Southeast Capital Circle on U.S. 319 near the Leon–Wakulla County line. Nature trails and boardwalks lead from one sinkhole (a lake formed when water erodes the underlying limestone) to another. The trails are open daily from 8am to 8pm.

A necessary stop before heading into this wilderness is the **Wakulla Area Ranger District,** 57 Taft Dr., Crawfordville, FL 32327 (© **850/926-3561;** fax 850/926-1904), which provides information about the forest and its facilities and sells topographical and canoe trail maps. The station is off U.S. 319 about 20 miles south of Tallahassee and 2 miles north of Crawfordville. It's open Monday to Thursday from 8am to 4:30pm, Friday from 8am to 4pm.

Index

FROMMER'S® COMPLETE TRAVEL GUIDES

Alaska
Amsterdam
Argentina & Chile
Arizona
Atlanta
Australia
Austria
Bahamas
Barcelona, Madrid & Seville
Beijing
Belgium, Holland &
   Luxembourg
Bermuda
Boston
British Columbia & the
   Canadian Rockies
Budapest & the Best of Hungary
California
Canada
Cancún, Cozumel & the
   Yucatán
Cape Cod, Nantucket &
   Martha's Vineyard
Caribbean
Caribbean Cruises & Ports
   of Call
Caribbean Ports of Call
Carolinas & Georgia
Chicago
China
Colorado
Costa Rica
Denmark
Denver, Boulder & Colorado
   Springs
England
Europe

European Cruises & Ports of Call
Florida
France
Germany
Greece
Greek Islands
Hawaii
Hong Kong
Honolulu, Waikiki & Oahu
Ireland
Israel
Italy
Jamaica
Japan
Las Vegas
London
Los Angeles
Maryland & Delaware
Maui
Mexico
Montana & Wyoming
Montréal & Québec City
Munich & the Bavarian Alps
Nashville & Memphis
Nepal
New England
New Mexico
New Orleans
New York City
New Zealand
Nova Scotia, New Brunswick &
   Prince Edward Island
Oregon
Paris
Philadelphia & the Amish
   Country
Portugal

Prague & the Best of the Czech
   Republic
Provence & the Riviera
Puerto Rico
Rome
San Antonio & Austin
San Diego
San Francisco
Santa Fe, Taos & Albuquerque
Scandinavia
Scotland
Seattle & Portland
Shanghai
Singapore & Malaysia
South Africa
Southeast Asia
South Florida
South Pacific
Spain
Sweden
Switzerland
Texas
Thailand
Tokyo
Toronto
Tuscany & Umbria
USA
Utah
Vancouver & Victoria
Vermont, New Hampshire
   & Maine
Vienna & the Danube Valley
Virgin Islands
Virginia
Walt Disney World & Orlando
Washington, D.C.
Washington State

FROMMER'S® DOLLAR-A-DAY GUIDES

Australia from $50 a Day
California from $70 a Day
Caribbean from $70 a Day
England from $70 a Day
Europe from $70 a Day

Florida from $70 a Day
Hawaii from $70 a Day
Ireland from $70 a Day
Italy from $70 a Day
London from $85 a Day

New York from $80 a Day
Paris from $80 a Day
San Francisco from $60 a Day
Washington, D.C.,
   from $70 a Day

FROMMER'S® PORTABLE GUIDES

Acapulco, Ixtapa &
   Zihuatanejo
Alaska Cruises & Ports
   of Call
Amsterdam
Australia's Great Barrier Reef
Bahamas
Baja & Los Cabos
Berlin
Boston
California Wine Country
Charleston & Savannah
Chicago

Dublin
Hawaii: The Big Island
Hong Kong
Houston
Las Vegas
London
Los Angeles
Maine Coast
Maui
Miami
New Orleans
New York City
Paris

Phoenix & Scottsdale
Portland
Puerto Rico
Puerto Vallarta, Manzanillo &
   Guadalajara
San Diego
San Francisco
Seattle
Sydney
Tampa & St. Petersburg
Vancouver
Venice
Washington, D.C.

FROMMER'S® NATIONAL PARK GUIDES

Family Vacations in the
   National Parks
Grand Canyon

National Parks of the American
   West
Rocky Mountain
Yellowstone & Grand Teton

Yosemite & Sequoia/
   Kings Canyon
Zion & Bryce Canyon

FROMMER'S® MEMORABLE WALKS

Chicago
London

New York
Paris

San Francisco
Washington, D.C.

FROMMER'S® GREAT OUTDOOR GUIDES

Arizona & New Mexico
New England

Northern California
Southern California & Baja

Southern New England
Vermont & New Hampshire

FROMMER'S® BORN TO SHOP GUIDES

Born to Shop: France
Born to Shop: Hong Kong,
  Shanghai & Beijing

Born to Shop: Italy
Born to Shop: London

Born to Shop: New York
Born to Shop: Paris

FROMMER'S® IRREVERENT GUIDES

Amsterdam
Boston
Chicago
Las Vegas
London

Los Angeles
Manhattan
New Orleans
Paris
San Francisco

Seattle & Portland
Vancouver
Walt Disney World
Washington, D.C.

FROMMER'S® BEST-LOVED DRIVING TOURS

America
Britain
California
Florida

France
Germany
Ireland
Italy

New England
Scotland
Spain
Western Europe

THE UNOFFICIAL GUIDES®

Bed & Breakfasts in California
Bed & Breakfasts in
  New England
Bed & Breakfasts in the
  Northwest
Bed & Breakfasts in Southeast
Beyond Disney
Branson, Missouri
California with Kids
Chicago
Cruises
Disneyland
Florida with Kids

Golf Vacations in the
  Eastern U.S.
The Great Smoky &
  Blue Ridge Mountains
Inside Disney
Hawaii
Las Vegas
London
Mid-Atlantic with Kids
Mini Las Vegas
Mini-Mickey
New England with Kids

New Orleans
New York City
Paris
San Francisco
Skiing in the West
Southeast with Kids
Walt Disney World
Walt Disney World for
  Grown-ups
Walt Disney World for Kids
Washington, D.C.
World's Best Diving Vacations

SPECIAL-INTEREST TITLES

Frommer's Britain's Best Bed & Breakfasts and
  Country Inns
Frommer's France's Best Bed & Breakfasts and
  Country Inns
Frommer's Italy's Best Bed & Breakfasts and
  Country Inns
Frommer's Caribbean Hideaways
Frommer's Adventure Guide to Australia &
  New Zealand
Frommer's Adventure Guide to Central America
Frommer's Adventure Guide to India & Pakistan
Frommer's Adventure Guide to South America
Frommer's Adventure Guide to Southeast Asia
Frommer's Adventure Guide to Southern Africa
Frommer's Gay & Lesbian Europe
Frommer's Exploring America by RV
Hanging Out in England

Hanging Out in Europe
Hanging Out in France
Hanging Out in Ireland
Hanging Out in Italy
Hanging Out in Spain
Israel Past & Present
Frommer's The Moon
Frommer's New York City with Kids
The New York Times' Guide to Unforgettable
  Weekends
Places Rated Almanac
Retirement Places Rated
Frommer's Road Atlas Britain
Frommer's Road Atlas Europe
Frommer's Washington, D.C., with Kids
Frommer's What the Airlines Never Tell You

Let Us Hear From You!

Dear Frommer's Reader,

You are our greatest resource in keeping our guides relevant, timely, and lively. We'd love to hear from you about your travel experiences—good or bad. Want to recommend a great restaurant or a hotel off the beaten path—or register a complaint? Any thoughts on how to improve the guide itself?

Please use this page to share your thoughts with me and mail it to the address below. Or if you like, send a FAX or e-mail me at frommersfeedback@hungryminds.com. And so that we can thank you—and keep you up on the latest developments in travel—we invite you to sign up for a free daily Frommer's e-mail travel update. Just write your e-mail address on the back of this page. Also, if you'd like to take a moment to answer a few questions about yourself to help us improve our guides, please complete the following quick survey. (We'll keep that information confidential.)

Thanks for your insights.

Yours sincerely,

Michael Spring

Michael Spring, *Publisher*

Name (Optional) ⸻

Address ⸻

City ⸻ State ⸻ ZIP ⸻

Name of Frommer's Travel Guide ⸻

Comments ⸻

Please tell us a little about yourself so that we can serve you and the Frommer's community better. We will keep this information confidential.

Age: ( )18-24; ( )25-39; ( )40-49; ( )50-55; ( )Over 55

Income: ( )Under $25,000; ( )$25,000-$50,000; ( )$50,000-$100,000; ( )Over $100,000

I am: ( )Single, never married; ( )Married, with children; ( )Married, without children; ( )Divorced; ( )Widowed

Number of people in my household: ( )1; ( )2; ( )3; ( )4; ( )5 or more

Number of people in my household under 18: ( )1; ( )2; ( )3; ( )4; ( )5 or more

I am ( )a student; ( )employed full-time; ( )employed part-time; ( )not employed at this time; ( )retired; ( )other

I took ( )0; ( )1; ( )2; ( )3; ( )4 or more leisure trips in the past 12 months

My last vacation was ( )a weekend; ( )1 week; ( )2 weeks; ( )3 or more weeks

My last vacation was to ( )the U.S.; ( )Canada; ( )Mexico; ( )Europe; ( )Asia; ( )South America; ( )Central America; ( )The Caribbean; ( )Africa; ( )Middle East; ( )Australia/New Zealand

( )I would; ( )would not buy a Frommer's Travel Guide for business travel

I access the Internet ( )at home; ( )at work; ( )both; ( )I do not use the Internet

I used the Internet to do research for my last trip. ( )Yes; ( )No

I used the Internet to book accommodations or air travel on my last trip. ( )Yes; ( )No

My favorite travel site is ( )frommers.com; ( )travelocity.com; ( )expedia.com;

other _____

I use Frommer's Travel Guides ( )always; ( )sometimes; ( )seldom

I usually buy ( )1; ( )2; ( )more than 2 guides when I travel

Other guides I use include _____

What's the most important thing we could do to improve Frommer's Travel Guides?

_____

_____

_____

_____

d me a daily e-mail travel update. My e-mail address is

_____

Michael Spring, Publisher and Vice President, Frommer's Travel Guides
09 Third Ave., New York, NY 10022   FAX: 212.884.5432